Praise for How Rude!

A "Book for the Teen Age"
—New York Public Library

A "Quick Pick" selection
—American Library Association

A "Read, America!" Classic selection

"This is one fast-paced, fun-to-read book that covers the basics of good behavior for teens. But before you dismiss it with a roll of your eyes and a huge yawn (now that's rude!), just one look at the table of contents will convince you that this isn't your grandma's guidebook. This is a wonderfully hip and humorous, easy read!"
—*College Bound* Magazine

"Covers everything from table manners to hygiene, handling friendship problems politely, thank-you notes, flaming online, and manners around the house."—*KLIATT*

"From its intriguing title to the tongue-in-cheek ideas for dealing with many kinds of situations, readers will find this manual humorous, nonthreatening, entertaining, and educational. You will return to it again and again."—*School Library Journal*

"*How Rude!* offers surprisingly simple ways for teens to respond to and interact with people to get the best results in today's world. It shows that if we'd all follow a few simple, common-sense rules, the world would be a far better place."—*Youthworker*

How Rude!

The Teenagers' Guide to Good Manners, Proper Behavior, and Not Grossing People Out

by Alex J. Packer, Ph.D.

Edited by Pamela Espeland
Illustrated by Jeff Tolbert

free spirit
PUBLiSHiNG®

Works
for kids®

Library of Congress Cataloging-in-Publication Data
 Packer, Alex J.
   How rude! : the teenagers' guide to good manners, proper behavior, and not grossing people out / by Alex J. Packer.
     p.   cm.
   Includes bibliographical references and index.
   Summary: A humorous but practical guide to good manners and social skills, discussing such areas as family life, behavior in public, manners in school, eating, and clothes.
     ISBN 1-57542-024-4
     1. Etiquette for children and teenagers. [1. Etiquette.]
 I. Title.
 BJ1857.C5P33   1997
 395.1'23—dc21

                                                              97-13015
                                                              CIP
                                                              AC

At the time of this book's publication, all facts and figures cited are the most current available; all telephone numbers, addresses, and Web site URLs are accurate and active; all publications, organizations, Web sites, and other resources exist as described in this book; and all have been verified as of November 2003. The author and Free Spirit Publishing make no warranty or guarantee concerning the information and materials given out by organizations or content found at Web sites, and we are not responsible for any changes that occur after this book's publication. If you find an error or believe that a resource listed here is not as described, please contact Free Spirit Publishing. Parents, teachers, and other adults: We strongly urge you to monitor children's use of the Internet.

The goal-setting steps on pages 435–436 are adapted from *The Gifted Kids' Survival Guide: A Teen Handbook* by Judy Galbraith, M.A., and Jim Delisle, Ph.D. (Free Spirit Publishing, 1996), pages 85–86. Used with permission.

Cover design by Circus Design
Interior design by Julie Odland Smith
Illustrations by Jeff Tolbert
Index prepared by Eileen Quam
    and Theresa Wolner

15 14 13 12 11
Printed in the United States of America

Free Spirit Publishing Inc.
217 Fifth Avenue North, Suite 200
Minneapolis, MN 55401-1299
(612) 338-2068
help4kids@freespirit.com
www.freespirit.com

The following are registered trademarks of Free Spirit Publishing Inc.:

FREE SPIRIT®
FREE SPIRIT PUBLISHING®
THE FREE SPIRITED CLASSROOM®
SELF-HELP FOR KIDS®
SELF-HELP FOR TEENS®
WORKS FOR KIDS®
HOW RUDE!™
LEARNING TO GET ALONG™
LAUGH & LEARN™

Learning to Get Along™   free spirit PUBLISHING® Works for kids®

For my sister Janet. . .

. . . who, except for call waiting, is impeccably polite.

Acknowledgments

Even if it weren't the polite thing to do, I would still want to thank the following individuals whose advice, support, and expertise were essential to the creation of this book.

Joel Anderson, Ida Del Vecchio, Launa Ellison, Richard V. Goodwin, Stephen Gustin, Jan Hassan, Ross Herbertson, Norman Jenkins, Janet Packer, and Charles L. Terry III for their help in distributing surveys;

The hundreds of teenagers, parents, and teachers who participated in our surveys;

Mindy Anderson, Jonah Klevesahl, Monica Longe, Jill Thunborg, and Jessica Wilber for reading and commenting on the manuscript;

Naomi and Max Rotenberg for generously providing me with a work-conducive tropical environment during the cold New England winter (see Chapter 5 for tips on vacation home house-sitting);

Kim Armstrong at the Killington Ski Resort in Killington, Vermont, for her help with slopeside courtesies;

The dudes at Maximus Skatepark in Cambridge, Massachusetts, for their thoughts on and demonstrations of skateboard etiquette;

Eddie Shaw of City Video, Porter Square, Cambridge, Massachusetts, for pointers on proper video store behavior;

The Inline Club of Boston for tips on skating etiquette;

Arthur Kinsman, Manager of Government and Community Relations, American Automobile Association, Massachusetts, for AAA safety advice and rules of the road;

Daniel Vest and The Gay and Lesbian Alliance Against Defamation (GLAAD) for suggestions and research data relating to bigotry and homophobia;

Debbie Fiore at the Federation for Children with Special Needs; Brad Pearson, Advocate, Massachusetts Office on Disability; Jody Williams, Abuse Prevention Project Coordinator, Commonwealth of Massachusetts Disabled

Persons Protection Commission; and The Massachusetts Association for the Blind for providing information on interacting with people with disabilities;

The Authors Guild for their tireless efforts on behalf of writers;

My agents Gail Ross and Howard Yoon of Lichtman, Trister, Singer & Ross for their advice, support, and generosity;

Lisa Leonard, Julie Smith, Elizabeth Verdick, and the staff of Free Spirit Publishing for their enthusiasm, openness, and unswerving professionalism;

Judy Galbraith, President of Free Spirit Publishing, for her courage and imagination as a publisher, and her encouragement and good humor as a friend;

Pamela Espeland for her brilliance and creativity as an editor; for putting up with my authorial moods and bad jokes; for keeping me within the bounds of good taste (or at least trying to); and for the respect and repartee which made the process of creating this book so stimulating and enjoyable;

And finally, I wish to thank the countless individuals whose ill-mannered, disgusting, boorish, vulgar, selfish, and arrogant behaviors kept me inspired and motivated throughout the course of this project.

Contents

List of Reproducible Pages

1

Minding Manners

Nobody's Polite Anymore, Why Should I Be?

This is a book about manners. If that makes you feel like throwing up, at least say "Excuse me" before rushing to the bathroom.*

You have every reason to feel queasy upon hearing the word *manners*. For it is under the guise of teaching manners that young people are subjected to a blizzard of rudely imparted criticisms. When adults do it, they call it "correcting." When you do it, they call it "being fresh."

"Use your fork."
"Don't talk with your mouth full."

---

* See "Ralphing" for more on the etiquette of upchucking.

How Rude!

"Sit up straight."
"Look at me when I'm talking."
"Don't interrupt."

If the idea of learning good manners makes you feel like a dog being trotted off to obedience school, this is understandable. But if you turn your back on manners, you end up hurting yourself. This is because having good manners involves a lot more than knowing not to drink from the toilet bowl. It means knowing how to handle yourself in your life and relationships. And people who know how to handle themselves come out on top. They get what they want, feel good about themselves, and enjoy life to the fullest.

This book will show you how to become a master of the art—and game—of proper social behavior. It will answer real questions from teenagers across America—such as:

"Is Miss Manners dead yet?"
Good gracious, no. She lives in Passaic with two cats and a doily.

"Do you have to extend your pinkie when drinking from a teacup?"
This practice is no longer necessary. But under NO circumstances should you extend your middle finger!

You'll find out things you've always wanted to know:

- Why do you put a napkin in your LAP when food falls on your SHIRT?
- How do you tell people they have spinach in their teeth?
- How much should you tip the pizza guy?
- Why should you be nice to people you don't like?
- Who came up with these ridiculous rules, and why are we expected to follow them?

You'll learn how to:

- deal with idiots
- react to bigoted remarks
- respond to adults who make rude comments
- tell someone his fly is open
- be the perfect host so your parents will beg you to have more friends over.

You'll know just what to do when:

- people spread nasty rumors about you
- a dog nuzzles at your crotch in public
- two of your friends aren't talking to each other
- your aunt gives you handkerchiefs for the sixth birthday in a row
- a friend pressures you to take drugs.

You'll discover:

- the Fourteen Commandments of Toiletiquette
- the best way to ask someone out
- surefire strategies for getting invited back wherever you want
- secrets of dressing for tactical advantage
- the most effective ways to put rude people in their place
- proper techniques for spitting, scratching, sneezing, yawning, coughing, hiccuping, nose-picking, and zit-popping.

Minding
Manners

You'll be cool, calm, and collected when a friend:

- asks you if she's ugly
- goes out with your ex-boyfriend
- comes to you with a serious problem
- wins the prize you were supposed to get
- tells you he's gay.

You'll find out how to:

- ace a job interview
- impress admissions officers when applying to schools
- broach the subject of condoms in a relationship
- respond to teachers who pick on you in class.

By now, you may be thinking *Holy Napkin Ring! I never knew manners could be such a source of power, pleasure, and self-confidence.* Or you may still find it heretical to embrace the etiquettical. You're thinking *Manners, shmanners. Nobody's polite anymore, why should I be?*

Thank you for asking.

Why Good Manners Are Good for You

Here are ten reasons why it's to your advantage to have good manners:

1. **Good manners put people at ease.** People at ease are more likely to agree to your requests.

2. **Good manners impress people.** People who are impressed by your behavior are more likely to treat you with respect.

3. **Good manners build self-esteem.** Teenagers with self-esteem are more likely to get what they want out of life.

How Rude!

4. **Good manners are attractive.** Kids with *savoir-faire** are more likely to have the friends and relationships they want.

5. **Good manners allow people to live and work together without unnecessary friction.** This makes your everyday world more pleasant.

6. **Good manners can save your life.** Teenagers who know what to do if they accidentally dis the wrong person are less likely to be shot.

7. **Good manners are rare.** Young people who have them sparkle like diamonds and immediately get elevated status in the eyes of adults.

8. **Good manners make you feel good.** You can hold your head high, knowing that you're doing your part to stop humanity's slide into the cesspool of incivility.

9. **Good manners make others feel good.** You can help to create a world in which people treat one another with care, respect, and compassion.

10. **Good manners don't cost anything.** You can have the BEST for free.

Most kids want to learn proper etiquette and behavior. In fact, 93 percent of the teenagers we asked in a survey on manners agree with the statement "It's important to have good manners." Why do they think so?

"It's a way of respecting yourself."
"People will like you better."
"I want to make good first impressions with people."
"The way you act is the way you get treated."
"If nobody was polite, the world would fall apart."
"Being polite feels better than being rude."

Some of our survey respondents agreed that good manners were important, but advised moderation:

"There is a time and a place for everything."
"I don't think you should become a perfectionist."
"Over the top can be too much."

True, we wouldn't want to have *too much* of a good thing. But having the *right amount* of manners can work to your advantage. How? Here are the Top Five ways in which being polite has paid off for the teenagers who responded to our survey:

---

* A fancy French term for "know-how"—the ability to say or do the right or graceful thing in social situations.

1. Got a job.
2. Got something I wanted from my parents.
3. Got compliments and respect.
4. Got in good with the opposite sex.
5. Got help from teachers.

Teenagers everywhere are discovering the bountiful blessings good manners bring:

"By letting someone go ahead of me, they got the bird doo-doo on their head instead of me."

"I was really polite so my mom saw how responsible I could be so she let me have a dog."

"I got to have a sleepover."

"I got my allowance raised."

"My family compliments me."

"Teachers respect me more."

"Good manners do a lot to ensure prompt service in restaurants."

"When I was meeting a distant aunt at a family reunion, I was very polite and she was so impressed she gave me a $100 bill."

"I gained the respect of my friends' parents through my good manners at the dinner table."

"I have been hired for different jobs because adults are looking for kids with good manners and don't think they exist."

"Because I am always polite and respectful, I avoid some of the misfortunes of adolescents, such as getting into fights."

"After you."

If this doesn't convince you of the advantages that come to those with good manners, listen to what teenagers said when we asked them to describe a time when NOT using good manners hurt them:

"I got shot."

"I got suspended."

How Rude!

"I got a bad reputation."

"I got grounded."

"I was rude to my foster mom, and that made her want me to leave. At the time I didn't care, but now I wish I had cared."

"I offended a good friend."

"I was talking with my mouth full and later my friend told his other friends behind my back."

"I lost respect from my teachers by insulting them."

"Once I wanted my parents to do something and I started yelling and then they said 'We would have let you, but not anymore because you are yelling.'"

"I got into a fight in eighth grade. I was beaten to a pulp."

"We used to spend every Christmas with my aunt. I was always a nasty, bored, annoying brat. When she died, I lost out in her $1,000,000 will."

You can see how important it is to have good manners. This book is going to show you how to get them and use them. Now that you've begun to read it, you won't want to put it down. You'll hole up in your room for the next four days until you've read it from cover to cover. But don't feel you have to. The book is designed so you can dip in and out of it—a question here, a question there. You can use the Contents to find chapters, and the Index to find topics, that are of most immediate interest to you. Meanwhile, a little background will help to set the stage.

What, Exactly, Are Manners?

Manners are the customs and traditions of a society that govern how people treat one another and behave in social situations. Manners are meant to smooth the rough edges of human nature. They maintain order, promote societal values, and foster positive human interactions. Imagine the chaos and hurt we would experience if everybody did whatever they wanted, whenever they wanted, without any regard for the feelings or interests of others.

Etiquette—the sets of rules that give expression to manners—can vary from culture to culture. In Japan, you would remove your shoes before entering someone's house. If you did this in America, people would give you strange looks and hold their noses. In some Asian and Middle Eastern countries, belching and smacking your lips is a way to compliment the chef. In the United States, it's a way to get sent to your room. It's important to know the manners of the culture in which you're operating. Otherwise, an innocent, friendly gesture could cause offense or embarrassment.*

---

* See "Body Language Around the World," page 33.

Here are some interesting things about etiquette:

Minding Manners

- It's alive. It changes as societies change. For example, children in Western countries no longer bow or curtsy when presented to adults. Women today do things—drive, pick up the tab, wear bikinis—that would have been scandalous 100 years ago. Sometimes, changing attitudes, styles, and technologies render some forms of etiquette extinct (such as how a lady should enter a horse-drawn carriage) while new ones emerge (such as how to send email).

- Etiquette is context-sensitive. For example, within every culture are many subcultures—surfers, bikers, teenagers, business executives, senators, musicians, women, men, adults, children, minorities, etc. These sub-cultures usually have their own rules that dictate, for example, who has the right-of-way when catching a wave, where to sit at a board meeting, what to bring to a sleepover, how to treat the opposing team at a home game. The manners men and women use in same-sex groups may differ from those they use in mixed settings. Similarly, teenagers have forms of greeting, address, and speech that are perfectly appropriate amongst themselves but not with adults, or are acceptable in a locker room but not in an assembly. People with good manners are sensitive to context and know how to adapt their behavior accordingly.

- Etiquette, like steering a car, requires constant adjustment. For example, it might be considered good manners to pick up the tab in a restaurant. Your dinner guest may protest. You insist. Your guest continues to protest. At a certain point, it might be more polite for you to relinquish the check and let your guest pay.

One thing you'll hear frequently is that the purpose of manners is to make people feel comfortable. That's very true. But sometimes—and here's where being polite can be so much fun—the purpose of manners is to make people *uncomfortable*! For example, when somebody makes a racial slur. Or allows their children to run wild in your living room. Or invades your private life. Being courteous doesn't mean letting people walk all over you. Sometimes, those who are unkind and inconsiderate need to be put in their place—politely, of course.

A Brief History of Manners

Manners go back thousands of years. For a long time, humans were hunter-gatherers. They had to forage for food to keep from starving. This took a lot of energy and kept them on the road quite a bit, so they'd just grab a quick bite

How Rude!

whenever they could. Around 9000 B.C., a new age of agriculture dawned in the Near East. People learned how to plant crops and farm. This led to a more stable existence, since food could be stored. As people began to eat communally, rituals evolved for the preparation and sharing of meals. These were then passed from one generation to the next.

The first known "etiquette scroll" was written around 2500 B.C. It was called *The Instructions of Ptahhotep* (after its Egyptian author), and it contained all sorts of advice for getting along with others and moving up in the world. This book was so widely read that many religious scholars believe its influence can be found in the Bible.

Over the centuries, manners continued to evolve. For example, prior to the 11th century, people in Europe ate with their fingers. A well-bred person used only three fingers—the thumb, the index, and the middle finger. You can imagine parents of that era saying "Ethelred, how many times do I have to tell you?!? Don't stick your whole hand into your food!"

The evolution of table manners can be quite fascinating. For example, when forks were first used for eating in Tuscany in the 11th century, they were condemned by the clergy. This was because food was seen as a gift from God. Only the human hand, another of God's creations, was fit to touch it. ("Ethelred, use your fingers, not your fork!")

Stone knives were first made 1,500,000 years ago by *Homo erectus* for slaughtering animals. By the Middle Ages, most men never left home without their knives, which were hung at the waist so they could be quickly drawn to kill an enemy or slice a steak. One of the biggest etiquette problems of the 17th century was that men would use the pointed ends of their knives to pick their teeth at the table. According to legend, this so disgusted the Duc de Richelieu that he had all the points filed off the table knives in his chateau, thus creating the blunt-tipped table knife we use today.

Modern etiquette books came into full flower in 13th-century Europe. They were written to instruct the upper classes on how to behave when invited to the royal court. These books contained such gems as:

> **When you blow your nose or cough,
> turn round so that nothing falls on the table.**

> **Refrain from falling upon the dish like a swine while eating,
> snorting disgustingly, and smacking the lips.**

Possibly the most influential etiquette book of all time was written in A.D. 1530 by Erasmus, a classical scholar who lived in Rotterdam. He believed that good manners were most easily acquired in childhood. His book, *On Civility in*

Children, became a huge bestseller and was required reading for kids throughout Europe for over two centuries. Here are some of the things he advised:

> 𝕿urn away when spitting lest your saliva fall on someone.
>
> 𝕯o not move back and forth in your chair. 𝖂hoever does that gives the impression of constantly breaking or trying to break wind.
>
> 𝖄ou should not offer your handkerchief to anyone unless it has been freshly washed. 𝕹or is it seemly, after wiping your nose, to spread out your handkerchief and peer into it as if pearls and rubies might have fallen out of your head.

If you look at old etiquette books, you can see that some manners have remained constant over the centuries ("Don't spit on anyone"), while others continue to evolve in response to changing technologies, economic forces, and societal attitudes.

Aren't Manners Sexist?

They certainly are. Why should men have to remove their hats indoors while women get to keep theirs on? It's not fair!

Manners reflect the values, beliefs, and traditions of a society. These include attitudes towards social caste, age, sexuality, and the proper place of women, men, and children. Over the centuries, many cultures have viewed women as weaker and in greater need of protection than men. This doesn't mean that all the men sat around a campfire toasting marshmallows one afternoon 15,000 years ago and said "How can we discriminate against women?" Sex roles developed out of necessity; it made more sense for men to go out to slaughter wild boars while women stayed home and had babies.

Soon, though, humans evolved. They discovered farming. Men no longer had to roam the forests, hunting and shouting "Ugh!" But instead of staying home, they went in search of new worlds to conquer. Armies of men crossed whole continents to wage war. Meanwhile, the women stayed home.

As history marched on, rules of chivalry developed. These rules governed the behavior of men towards women. The rules were based on principles of medieval knighthood, such as honor, bravery, protecting the weak, and not standing outside in your armor during a lightning storm. Thus, a gallant gentleman always treated the fairer (that is, weaker) sex with deference and respect. He would stand when a lady entered or left a room, defend her honor, hold doors, tip his hat, and offer his cloak.

How Rude!

Gradually, these rules of etiquette gave birth to many of the gender-based manners that ushered in the twentieth century. For example, a gentleman would offer his seat to a lady, carry the luggage, pay the tab, drive the car, earn the money, and run the roost. Women were forbidden by custom and law from doing all sorts of things. In fact, women in the United States couldn't even vote until 1920.

Happily, times have changed, and the role of women in America (and many other countries) has been transformed over the past several decades. Women now hold office, run corporations, drive buses, preach sermons, remove organs, fly planes, and drop bombs. Girls can ask boys for dates. Enlightened people no longer believe that women are "weak" and "inferior."

Society is often resistant to change, and women's rights have been won only after years of struggle, protest, and legal challenge. Manners are even slower to change because they are passed from older to younger generations. We are now in a period of great flux in terms of defining proper behavior between men and women. Attitudes and actions that were once considered polite are now considered rude or anachronistic.

By today's standards, certain rules of etiquette are sexist in that they are based on untrue and discriminatory presumptions about the nature and role of women. But manners, by definition, should not, and need not, be sexist. Kindness knows no gender.

Now that you know a bit about where manners come from, let's turn to our very first questions, sent in by genuine American teenagers.

"Aren't manners just for snobs and rich people?"

Not at all. Snobs, by definition, have bad manners. This is because snobs, in their attitudes and behavior, make people feel inferior and unschooled. This is the height of rudeness! If others put you down for using the wrong fork, *they're* the ones with terrible manners.

As far as rich people go, good manners are the one thing money can't buy. All you have to do is take one look around you to realize that rudeness is an equal opportunity annoyer. Thus, manners are a great equalizing force in society.

It's true that some rules of etiquette are more likely to be practiced by the affluent (for example, tipping the wine steward or setting a formal dinner table). And that the rich, because they have money, can get away with bad manners in ways that others can't. But a nose being picked at the dinner table is disgusting—whether its owner is rich or poor. ◆

"Why are manners so important? Isn't it what's inside a person that counts?"

Certainly, but nobody's going to stick around long enough to know the "real you" if being in your presence grosses them out. ◆

Minding Manners

The Survey Says . . .

When we asked teenagers "What's the rudest thing anyone's ever done to you?" here's what they said:

"Someone . . .

lifted me completely into the air by my underwear.
ignored me when I was talking to them.
farted in my face while we wrestled.
judged me before they met me.
spread rumors about me."

"My sister chewed up her food and spit it on the table."
"My brother always makes me feel stupid in front of other people."
"A kid with purple hair flicked me off."

"Someone . . .

stabbed me in the back.
slammed my arm in my locker.
smacked me in the face in front of a big crowd.
threw coffee in my face because I was taking too long on a pay phone.
told me that I will never amount to anything."

"My little sister picks up the phone while I'm on it and burps really loud right into it."
"A friend told a secret about me when I told him not to."
"My brother chews with his mouth open all the time to bug me (he's 16). He walks into my bedroom without knocking, and he defends my mom while she talks down to me."

"Someone . . .

pulled my pants down.
hung up on me.
accused me of stealing a videotape.
put down my thoughts because they are different.
made believe they were my friend."

continued

How Rude!

"My brother took something of mine, hid it, and wouldn't give it back when I needed it."

"I was spit on and cursed at."

"This boy kept coming up to me and saying 'Chinese, Japanese.' Finally I just told him I was Korean and he left me alone."

"Someone . . .

went through my personal things.
embarrassed me in front of my friends.
made me wait.
tried to trip me as I walked by them.
excluded me from a party for no reason other than seeing me suffer."

"My friend said a few times 'I have a dad and you don't' because my parents don't live together."

"My boyfriend dumped me because I wouldn't have sex with him."

"My mom went through my journal."

"My best friend lied to me and said she was grounded when we had plans. Later I discovered she was out with her boyfriend."

"For the sake of looking cool in public, a person has pretended not to know me."

"I bought concert tickets for a girl who was meeting me at the show. She never thanked me for the tickets, so that made me a little upset because I went through a lot of trouble to get them. Then she showed up an hour and a half late. I couldn't go in because then she wouldn't have been able to get in. Afterwards, she didn't meet me at the car until an hour after the concert was over, so we were stuck in the parking lot for two hours."

Which Manners Are Most Important?

Here, according to our survey, are the Top 20 Good Manners parents* would like you, their children, to practice:

1. Say "Please," "Thank you," "You're welcome," "May I . . . ?" and "Excuse me."
2. Write thank-you notes.
3. Look people in the eye.
4. Clean up after yourself.
5. Respect adults.
6. Don't interrupt. Wait for your turn to speak.
7. Treat people as you would like to be treated.

---

* We also surveyed parents.

8. Use good table manners (wait to begin; chew with your mouth closed; stay at the table until the last person is finished eating; etc.)

9. Give people a firm handshake.

10. Have compassion towards others.

11. Be thoughtful about opening doors and offering your seat.

12. Respond when spoken to.

13. Listen when others speak.

14. Show special consideration to guests.

15. Say "yes" rather than "yeah."

16. Don't say hurtful things.

17. Think before you speak.

18. Respect the property of others.

19. Respect the privacy of others.

20. Use good telephone manners.

Minding
Manners

Here's what teachers* said when we asked them "What manners-related behaviors most impress you in a student?"

1. Saying "Please" and "Thank you."

2. Thoughtful listening and questioning.

3. Asking for help in a polite manner.

4. Kindness and understanding towards peers and adults.

5. Free yet thoughtful expression of their views.

6. Saying they're sorry and meaning it.

7. Thanking me for teaching or helping them understand.

"Why should kids respect adults?"

So adults will learn how to respect kids. ◆

Having Manners vs. Being Fake

Some people equate "having manners" with "being fake." But why think of it this way when you could perceive it as "being tactful," "being kind," or "being clever"? "Being real" can hurt people's feelings, provoke fights, and work against your best interests. "Being fake" can preserve relationships, engender respect, and help others to feel good about you and themselves.

---

* And we surveyed teachers.

How Rude!

Here are some examples of "being real" and "being fake." Which would you rather hear?*

Being "Real"	Being "Fake"
"I wouldn't go out with you if you were the last person on earth."	"I'm sorry, but I already have plans for that night."
"This is so ugly I'm going to use it as a rag."	"Aunt Jane, thank you so much for the shirt."
"You are the most boring drone I've ever met. I'm outta here!"	"Excuse me, but I'd better be going. I've got a lot of homework to do."
"We wiped the floor with you, you bunch of losers."	"You had some bad luck, but you played a good game."
"You're a good-for-nothing idiot who's never going to amount to anything."	"I know that you have the potential to do anything you want if you work hard and use your talents."

Real　　　　　Fake

---

* Also see pages 370–372 for a discussion of when and whether honesty is the best policy.

"Manners restrict our emotions and make us act differently than we would without them. Why not just act natural?"

Human beings are a complex species. They can be selfish, violent, and aggressive; they can be generous, compassionate, and nurturing. These traits are all natural. If people just did what they felt like doing, if they acted solely according to their own desires and self-interest, life would be violent and chaotic. This is because any "society"—be it a family, a football team, a business, or a nation—must operate according to certain shared "rules" if its members are to live and work in harmony and get anything done. These rules go by many names: laws, values, expectations, goals, corporate policies, game plans—and manners.

At first glance, these rules may seem confining because they inhibit "natural" tendencies. But, on closer examination, you'll find that these rules, rather than restrict personal freedom, create it! Think about it. If there were no rules, how could anyone play baseball? If there were no traffic regulations, how could anyone drive? If there were no laws, how could people be secure in their own homes? And, if there were no manners, how could we get along without constantly fighting or hurting each other's feelings? Would you really want to live in a world in which there were no constraints on what people could do and say?

There's a certain romanticism associated with the "natural" human animal. But given a choice between a society that values grabbing and harassing, and one that values asking and respecting; given a choice between living with people who are greedy, insensitive, and unkind, and those who are generous, empathetic, and supportive; given a choice between neighbors who are noisy, destructive, and antisocial, and those who are peaceful, creative, and friendly; given a choice between an evening of bickering and belching, and one of fine food and conversation—which would you prefer? ◆

"Why do you have to be nice to ignorant jerks?"

Because you never know when one of them might be a Hollywood talent agent. ◆

How Rude!

"How can you have manners without people thinking you're weird?"

The only people who think manners are weird are those without any. Who cares what they think? ◆

The Survey Says . . .

When we asked teenagers "What's the rudest thing you ever did to anyone?" here's what they said:

"Borrowed a formal dress for a dance and forgot to return it for five months."
"Walked past a person I knew because I couldn't remember his name."
"Told a friend I was sick and went to another friend's house."

"Canceled a date to a dance a couple days before."
"Kicked some kids because I was mad at them."
"Made this girl fall while she was running down the hall."
"Bumped someone and told them to apologize."

"Talked about someone behind their back."
"Called someone 'four-eyes.'"
"Wrote a nasty note to my best friend because she was totally ignoring me."
"I once put a stinky sock in someone's mouth."

"Slammed a door in a girl's face."
"Stared at a handicapped person."
"Called someone a fag."
"Made fun of someone only to be part of the group."

"On my birthday, my grandparents asked us to go out to dinner at the last minute. All my friends were over so we brought them. My friends and I were really wild in the restaurant and my relatives thought we were crazy."
"I told someone she might be really pretty if she lost a lot of weight and you could see her features."

"Laughed when someone got hurt."
"Flipped the bird to a teacher."
"Told on someone."
"Repeated a secret."
"Chewed up my food and opened my mouth to show everyone."

"I invited someone to meet me somewhere and didn't show up on purpose."
"I snubbed a couple of childhood friends for a different group of newer friends."
"I told my mother that I hated her, told her I wished I was someone else's kid, and slammed the door in her face."

Is It Ever Okay Not to Have Manners?

Yes. Manners waivers are granted to:

1. those who are too young to know better
2. those with physical or mental illnesses that prevent them from having the necessary self-awareness or control
3. those who are responding to an emergency (firefighters need not say "Excuse me" as they brush past bystanders blocking their path)
4. those who are victims of crime (introductions are not necessary when being mugged)
5. those who are alone and unobserved and whose actions have no adverse consequences for others (it's okay to eat whipped cream from the can in the privacy of your bedroom)
6. those who are in the company of others, but who agree amongst themselves to suspend certain manners—as long as doing so does not have adverse consequences for anyone (it's okay to burp loudly while watching football and eating junk food with your friends).

"If someone's rude to you, is it okay to be rude back?"

Here's what the teenagers we surveyed said:

Yes	42%
No	41%
Depends	17%

And here are some reasons they gave:

"Yes, it's okay to be rude back because . . ."

"It gives them a taste of their own medicine."

"Everyone will think you're weak if you don't."

"It's good to stand up for yourself."

"There's no other choice but to be rude."

In fact, there *is* another choice. But before we get into it, let's hear from some teenagers who said:

"It depends."

"If the person is another student or peer, I feel that being rude back is justified. However, one should never be rude to a teacher, parent, or other adult in charge."

How Rude!

"I almost always let an occasional rudeness go. But if a person is rude all the time, telling them off or embarrassing them will sometimes make them stop and respect me."

"It all depends on who's being rude."

"We learned in religion class that there are four ways to deal with anti-Semitism, and you can use these same four options if someone is being rude: 1) fight back (physically); 2) fight back (legally, verbally); 3) educate; 4) ignore."

Finally, let's hear from teenagers who said:

"No, it's not okay to be rude back because . . ."

"Then they'll be rude again and then you'll be rude and it'll just go in a circle."

"Why lower yourself to their childish standards?"

"You should set a good example. People will feel weird if they're the only ones being rude."

"You might regret it later."

"It can feel as good as a comeback when you deliberately say something positive in response to a rude comment."

"Two wrongs don't make a right. But three rights make a left."

What's your opinion? Do two rudes make a right? Before you decide, read on.

If you respond to rudeness with more rudeness . . .

- you may offend someone who had no intention of being rude
- you may get into a fight
- you may end up in trouble yourself
- you add to the general level of rudeness in the world
- you miss the opportunity to educate or enlighten
- you let others control you. You let them set the agenda and the tone of the interaction.

When you use good manners to respond to rudeness . . .

- you stand the best chance of stopping the behavior
- you stand the best chance of getting what you want
- you stand the best chance of winning others over to your cause
- you serve notice that people can't walk all over you
- you maintain your own dignity
- you set an example that may change the behavior of others. ◆

"What's the best way to respond to rudeness?"

Actually, there are *two* ways.

1. Ignore it. Let's say you're standing in a long checkout line that extends into the aisle. Someone barges through with his cart and runs over your foot. He doesn't say "Excuse me." He doesn't apologize. He just keeps going.

You could yell "You stupid idiot! Why don't you watch where you're going?" Or you could ignore it. Which is better?

If you yell, you'll be letting some ill-mannered stranger pull your strings. You'll probably be seen as rude and foul-mouthed yourself. And you could easily get into an ugly argument or a fight.

If you ignore the barbaric buffoon, your toe will still hurt. But you'll have the satisfaction of knowing that you possess good manners and self-control. And your restraint will likely arouse the sympathy of spectators.

2. Be polite. Some people equate politeness with weakness. They think it's cool to be rude. Nothing could be further from the truth.

Politeness isn't a sign of weakness. It's a sign of *strength*. It's an incredibly powerful tool that can gain you respect, protect your rights, stop rude people in their tracks, and even make adults apologize. It can turn almost any situation to your advantage.

If politeness is so effective, you may wonder why more people don't practice it. The reason is, it's an acquired skill. It takes thoughtfulness, patience, empathy, and even a bit of cleverness. And, as you may have noticed, these commodities are in short supply these days. But that's to your advantage. Your politeness will stand out all the more.

You'll discover throughout this book how to use politeness to put others at ease and to stand up for yourself in virtually any situation. In general, though, the best way to respond politely to rudeness is with one of the following two tactics:

TACTIC #1
Assume that the Rude One is well-intentioned and would never knowingly cause offense.

This is the secret for getting rude people to stop their behavior and/or apologize. "Accusatory phrasing" puts them on the defensive. "Benefit-of-the-doubt" phrasing gives them a face-saving way out. Examples:

How
Rude!

Accusatory Phrasing and Likely Response	Benefit-of-the-Doubt Phrasing and Likely Response
A. _You say:_ "No cuts. End of the line, buttface!" **_He says:_** "@%!#&!" **_Analysis:_** This response accuses the Rude One of trying to cut into line. He probably is. But the remark, rather than sending him packing, turns the incident into a battle of egos.	**A. _You say:_** "Excuse me, it's a little confusing, but the line actually begins back there." **_He says:_** "Oh, sorry. I didn't see it." **_Analysis:_** If the Rude One truly didn't notice the line, your polite response is a pleasant way of steering him in the right direction. If he did try to pull a fast one, giving him the benefit of the doubt provides a face-saving way for him to slink off.
B. _You say:_ "What d'ya think you're doing? That's only for handicapped people. You can't park there." **_She says:_** "@%!#&!" **_Analysis:_** Once again, an "in-your-face" attack is likely to result in a "you-can't-tell-me-what-to-do" response.	**B. _You say:_** "I beg your pardon, the paint is so dull that you may not have noticed that's a handicapped space." **_She says:_** "Actually, I did notice. My handicap isn't visible. But thank you for caring about these parking spots." **_Analysis:_** Another good reason to give people the benefit of the doubt is that sometimes they deserve it. Maybe it's _your_ assumption rather than _their_ behavior that needs correcting.

TACTIC #2
Ask the Rude One to indulge your sensitivity
rather than stop being a boor.

This strategy is based on human nature. People don't like to be scolded or told what to do. But most people are willing to _modify_ their behavior in response to a _reasonable_ request.

Stop-Your-Boorishness Phrasing and Likely Response	Please-Indulge-Me Phrasing and Likely Response
A. *You say:* "Shut up! How do you expect anyone to hear what's going on? If you want to talk during the movie, go outside!"	**A. *You say:*** "Excuse me, but it's hard for me to hear in movie theaters. Would you mind not talking?"
They say: "@%!#&!"	***They say:*** "Sorry."
Analysis: When chastised, a lot of people lash out. Even if they know you're right, their hurt pride puts them on the defensive.	***Analysis:*** Talkers are more likely to quiet down if they feel they're doing a favor rather than "giving in."
B. *You say:* "Grandma, mind your own business! What makes you think you can tell me I can't go skiing with my friends?"	**B. *You say:*** "Grandma, I'd feel terrible if I thought your visit was going to be spoiled worrying about me. Mom and Dad wouldn't have gone to Greece if they didn't trust me. They let me go skiing all the time."
She says: "What a way to talk to your grandmother! I just don't want you to injure yourself."	***She says:*** "I just worry so. You know how grandmas are."
Analysis: Your grandma is hurt and upset. Your relationship has been damaged.	***Analysis:*** You're far more likely to retain your freedom if you empathize with your grandma's concern rather than reject it.

Minding Manners

The Survey Says . . .

Here are two questions we asked parents—and the results:

1. Do you think *adults* today are more polite, less polite, or the same as when you were growing up?

More polite	0%
Less polite	80%
The same	20%

2. Do you think *children* today are more polite, less polite, or the same as when you were growing up?

More polite	0%
Less polite	70%
The same	30%

Ask your parents what *they* think!

How Rude!

Why Don't People Have Manners Anymore?

There are a lot of different ideas as to why this is. Here's what the parents in our survey said when we asked them why they think *adults* today are less polite than those of a generation ago:

> *"Unfortunately, people seem to think that politeness is a sign of weakness."*
>
> *"Talk shows present bad manners as entertainment."*
>
> *"Confusion has developed about gender roles and polite behavior between the sexes."*
>
> *"Beginning in the 1960s, psychologists and others popularized the idea that openness (expressing your feelings) and individuality ('doing your own thing') were more important than politeness."*
>
> *"There's a lot more stress today. I think we're all in the fast lane and just don't take the time to help or acknowledge each other."*
>
> *"America is a melting-pot of cultures with varying ideas of manners. Rudeness is accepted under the name of 'diversity.'"*
>
> *"There has been a general relaxation of social mores."*
>
> *"Society has less respect for authority. The traditions that upheld manners and respect are crumbling."*

And here's why the parents in our survey think *children* today are less polite than those of a generation ago:

> *"Television."*
>
> *"Exposure to vulgarity in mass media."*
>
> *"Manners are not stressed in the home or reinforced in school."*
>
> *"Children today see so many public figures, such as sports stars and sitcom heroes, behaving rudely that they think bad manners are fashionable."*
>
> *"Adults treat children with less respect, and the result is that children are doing this to each other as well as to adults."*
>
> *"Peer pressure."*
>
> *"Children are given more freedom and less supervision."*
>
> *"Less is expected of kids by parents and society."*
>
> *"Parents involve children in too many decisions, forgetting who is the adult."*
>
> *"Too many activities, not enough family time."*

In other words, adults seem to think that rudeness in kids is the result of changing societal conditions, bad influences in the media, and the failure of adults to teach proper etiquette and behavior. So now we know that it's not necessarily your fault if you have bad manners. But if you grow up and pass them on to *your* children, then whose fault are *their* bad manners?

Minding
Manners

CHAPTER QUIZ

1. *You're excused from having to have good manners as long as:*
   a) you can't stand the person
   b) you just ate a gallon of baked beans
   c) you're in a bad mood
   d) you're dead.

2. *If kids are rude, it's because:*
   a) they weren't taught good manners at home
   b) they're imitating ill-mannered movie stars and sports heroes
   c) they think politeness is uncool
   d) they're having a bad hair day.

3. *Parents can best teach their children good manners by:*
   a) hitting them when they misbehave
   b) responding to rudeness with "Can't you do anything right, you moron?"
   c) coming to the dinner table in their underwear
   d) setting a good example.

4. *It's okay to be rude back if:*
   a) you're bigger than the other person
   b) your girlfriend or boyfriend is watching
   c) you enjoy being pummeled into dogmeat
   d) you don't know any better.

2
Social
Interactions 101

The Rituals of Relating

Unless you're a hermit, a castaway, or a monk who has taken a vow of silence, you experience many social interactions each day. Some are brief and anonymous, such as holding a door for a stranger or giving money to a sales clerk. Others are intimate and meaningful, such as consoling a friend or confiding in a parent. Yet they all have one thing in common: They are acted out according to certain unspoken rules and expectations for behavior. These rules and expectations govern everything from gift giving to eating, job hunting to baby-sitting, greeting people to meeting people. Your ability to "play the game" will help you to feel confident, and others to feel comfortable, in virtually any situation.

An Introduction to Introductions

Like it or not, first impressions count. You can make a lifetime of good first impressions by learning how to give and receive introductions.

INTRODUCING YOURSELF

This is the simplest introduction. All you have to do is remember your own name. At school or parties, or when others have neglected to introduce you, look the person you want to meet in the eye, smile, extend your right hand, and say "Hi, I'm _____." If the person doesn't respond with his or her name, you can continue with "And you're . . . ?"

INTRODUCING OTHERS

Let's start with the adult world, where things tend to be a bit more formal. If you're making the introduction, simply say "Mother, I'd like to present my friend, Sticky Fingers." It's not necessary to add "Sticky, this is my mother." Life is too short for such double-talk.

You may also use such phrases as "Mother, I'd like to introduce Sticky," or, if you're in a hurry, "Mom, this is Sticky."

If you think that the people might know each other but you're not sure, you can turn your introduction into a question: "Mother, have you met Sticky?"

Sometimes kids and parents have different last names. In which case you would say, after presenting Sticky to your mom, "Sticky, this is my mother, Mrs. Her-Last-Name." That way, he'll know not to call her Mrs. Your-Last-Name.

Piece of cake.

But how do you know *who* to present to *whom?* Here's the rule: You present the person of "lesser" status to the person of "greater" status. You address the person of "greater" status by saying his or her name first:

"Your Highness, I'd like to present Simon the Stableboy."
"Warden, I'd like to introduce my cellmate, Lucky."
"Professor Glockenspiel, this is my poodle, Puddles."

Since *who* outranks *whom* can be as confusing as knowing *when* to say *which*, the chart on the following page will help you to keep things straight.

How Rude!

"Greater" Status	"Lesser" Status
Adults	Children
Teachers	Students
Longtime friends	New friends
Females	Males
Relatives	Non-relatives
Bosses	Employees
The Queen of England	The town dogcatcher

Please don't have a fit about this status thing. It doesn't mean that royals are better than commoners, women are better than men, or adults are better than children. It's just the way things are done. And don't worry about making a mistake. If you present whoever to whomever when whomever should have been presented to whoever, few people will notice, since they'll be delighted that you made any introduction at all. And your own status will be tops in everyone's eyes.

When you make an introduction, try to include a little information about the person you're introducing. Otherwise, the people you've just introduced may stare at their feet with nothing to say.

You can try things like:

"Grandma, this is my friend Harry Houdini. He does magic tricks."
"Ms. Grier, I'd like to present my sister Charlotte. She designs Web sites."
"Dad, this is Ron Gomez. He's on the swim team with me."

You can see how these introductory add-ons provide openings for further conversation. Be discreet, though. The idea is to offer an enticing tidbit of information, not to reveal any secrets.

"How do you introduce people if you've forgotten their names?"

With difficulty. "Dr. Femur, I'd like you to meet . . . er, ah, um, uh . . . " is inadequate as an introduction. But we all forget names sometimes. Since it's worse to make *no* introduction, you have three choices when memory fails you:

1. be up-front
2. bluff, or
3. cheat.

Being up-front means coming clean about your mental lapse. You begin the introduction ("Dad, this is a friend from math class"), then turn to your friend and say "I'm so sorry, I've forgotten your name." At this point, your friend will supply her name.

If you're introducing yourself, you can say "Hi, we've met before, but I'm afraid I've forgotten your name. I'm _____."

What if you're introducing two people to each other and you've forgotten *both* of their names? The up-front approach would be "I'm sorry. I'm so terrible with names I'd forget my own if it wasn't sewn into my underwear. Do you think you could introduce yourselves?"

With the bluffing method, you hope to avoid detection by getting those people whose names you've forgotten to introduce themselves. Begin by looking warmly at both people. Then say "Do you two know each other?" If the bluff works, they reply "No" and introduce themselves. If it doesn't, they say "No" and turn to you with expectant looks on their faces. Uh-oh!

If you've forgotten just one person's name, turn to him and say "Have you met Mrs. Dickens? She was my eighth-grade English teacher." With any luck, he'll reply "No, I haven't had the pleasure. Hi, I'm Nicholas Nickleby."

You can even use the bluff technique when introducing yourself to someone whose name you've forgotten. Smile, stick out your hand, and say "Hi. It's good to see you again. I'm _____." Then hope that person will respond with her name.

Cheating isn't nice, but sometimes it's necessary. Assume a frantic air and invent an emergency: "Oh, dear, I think the dog just ate my gerbil." Then say "Could you please introduce yourselves?" as you rush from the room. ◆

GROUP INTRODUCTIONS

Situations may arise that call for group introductions. For example, let's say your cousin joins you and some friends for a movie. If the group is small (five people or fewer), you can introduce him to everyone. If the group is large, individual introductions will take forever and you'll miss the movie. At times like these, it's perfectly acceptable to make an efficient group presentation: "Hey, everybody, this is my cousin Alfredo Fettucine. He's visiting from Rome."

Alfredo can smile and say "Hi." The rest of you can smile and say "Hey" or "How's it goin'?" Physical gestures are also acceptable—a wave, a friendly salute, a tip of the baseball cap—anything that makes Alfredo feel welcome.

Handshakes and standing up (if you are sitting down) are unnecessary in such informal situations. Individual members of the group should introduce themselves to Alfredo as they talk with him.

How Rude!

"Why do people shake hands?"

The earliest hieroglyphic record of a handshake (in Egypt in 2800 B.C.) suggests that this was how a god transferred power to a king. A similar image appears on Michelangelo's Sistine Chapel ceiling, which shows God reaching for Adam's hand. And it reappears in the movie *E.T.*, when Elliott and E.T. touch fingertips.

Another possible reason for the handshake goes back to the days when strangers approached each other with suspicion. Men would brandish their daggers in their right hands until determining that no threat existed. At that point, they would sheath their daggers and hold out their right hands as a gesture of friendship and goodwill. (This helps to explain why women didn't shake hands until fairly recently.)

Today, people shake hands because it's a custom. Many sports teams, peer groups, and fraternal organizations use secret or special handshakes. Such greetings originated during the Middle Ages as a way to confirm the identities of messengers and spies. Special handshakes are perfectly appropriate within peer groups, as long as they're not used to make others feel excluded. ◆

The Secret Handshake of Those Who Survived Third Period Biology

BEING INTRODUCED

What should you do when you're being introduced? Follow these five steps:

1. **Assume the position.** If you're not already standing, stand up. Use good posture. Don't fidget or pace.

2. **Make eye contact.** Give people a friendly, welcoming look. Don't stare into space or study your shoes.

3. **Shake hands.** Exert enough pressure so they know they're shaking a hand, not an overcooked piece of linguine. A confident, steady grip sends the message that you're a confident, steady person.

4. **Express a greeting.** You can't go wrong with "How do you do?" A warm "Hello" or "Pleased to meet you" are suitable substitutes. Save "Yo," "Hey," and "What's up?" for people around your age. For extra credit, spice up your greeting with "I've really been looking forward to meeting you" or "My sister has told me so much about you."

5. **Converse.** If the introducer did his job, he gave you a clue about the person to whom you were introduced. Follow up with related questions and/or comments. For example, if a friend introduced you to one of his teammates, you might say "What position do you play?" or "What are practices like?" or "How do you think the team will do this season?" Try to avoid questions that can be answered with a simple yes or no.

You could ask a student who's new to your school "How do you like our town so far?" or "What courses are you taking?" or "What was your last school like?" or "What clubs are you thinking of joining?"

This isn't exactly the Oxford Debating Union. But it is a warm, friendly, well-intentioned way to put people at ease. If you keep at it, you'll soon discover interests and experiences you have in common. And if the person turns out to be a bore, there are ways to exit the conversation without being rude.*

Starting a conversation may feel awkward at first. Just remember that most people like to talk about themselves. They will be grateful for your attention and efforts to keep things going smoothly.

BONUS TIP: When you're being introduced, be alert to the possibility that the introducer may have forgotten your name. If she hesitates or asks if you know the other person, don't call her bluff. Help her out the way you'd want to be helped. Leap in with "Hi, I'm _____."

And that's about it for introductions. Any questions?

"What do you say if you're introduced to someone who's gay?"
"How do you do?"

---

* See pages 358–359.

How Rude!

"What do you say if you're introduced to someone you can't stand?"
"How do you do?"

"What do you say if you're introduced to triplets?"
"How do you do?" "How do you do?" "How do you do?"

"Is it okay to call adults by their first names?"

Only if they ask you to. Otherwise it's "Doctor," "Mister," "Mrs.," "Miss," or "Ms." Followed by their last names, of course. ◆

"What do you do when you shake a person's hand and he won't let go?"

Give the person's hand one final, authoritative squeeze. Then withdraw your hand while warmly intensifying eye and verbal contact. This shows that it's his hand, not his company, from which you wish to remove yourself. ◆

"I'm going to a new school, so I don't know a lot of people. I have this one friend and every time we walk down the hall people come up to talk to her. I don't know what to do. Do I say hello to these people if I don't know them? Do I say good-bye? Can I say good-bye if I haven't said hello? Help! I HATE standing around feeling stupid."

If your friend's hallway hailings are conducted in passing (i.e., at full, reduced, or momentarily suspended pace), no introductions are required. The speed of the exchange should spare you from feeling stupid.

If, however, bodies stop and information is exchanged, you have three choices:

1. **Meditate yourself** into a state of distant yet friendly contentment (daydream, hum, stare peacefully into the distance) so your friend won't feel uncomfortable and you won't feel stupid.

2. **Excuse yourself**, as in "I'm going to my locker for a sec. Be right back."

3. **Introduce yourself**, as in "I don't think we've met. I'm _____." Others should respond in kind, and before you know it, you'll be having a conversation. At the end, say "Good-bye" or "Later." From this point on, you can greet them and chat with them in the hall, just like your friend.

It's really your friend's obligation to introduce you, but she may not be aware of that. Help her out with a gentle suggestion: "Since I'm new and all, I'd really appreciate it if you could introduce me to people you know whenever you get the chance." ◆

The Social Kiss

The use of one's lips as an act of greeting is known as a *social kiss*. The use of one's lips as an act of intimacy is known as *making out*. Our concern here is with the former.

It's important to master the intricacies of social kissing, because the consequences of not doing so include locked braces, banged foreheads, and the silly feeling you get when the cheek you thought you were about to kiss turns out to be a nose.

The social kiss is body language for "It's so wonderful to see you again." You use it with people you've already met, never with those you're meeting for the first time. There are only two targets for the properly delivered social kiss:

1. the lips, or
2. the cheek.

Kisses to other destinations are either misdeliveries or indications that something else is going on. What makes social kisses tricky is the fact that sometimes the participants make different assumptions about the destination. If you head for the lips and the recipient turns her cheek, you'll end up with an ear. Thus, the art of social kissing involves paying attention to nonverbal cues—good practice for more intimate relationships later in life.

In America, social kissing has traditionally occurred between males and females (lips or cheeks) or between females (cheeks), but not between males. Sometimes American males hug each other in greeting. These aren't really hugs, though. They're more like extended hearty backslaps intended to show how macho they are. Males who are comfortable with their masculinity and sexual orientation have no problem giving other males real hugs. In fact, there's no reason why American men shouldn't be able to give each other social kisses. In Europe, the Middle East, Latin America, and many other cultures, men and teenage boys do this all the time.

The person of "greater" status* is the one who signals what kind of kiss it will be. Between men and women, this is always the woman. If she presents her face straight on, she is saying "Lip Kiss, please." Your gentle peck should follow. If she turns her head to the left, it's "Cheek Kiss." Permission is granted for you to enter her cheek zone and await further nonverbal instructions. These will come in the form of:

1. a peck on your cheek (signaling a full-fledged Cheek Kiss)
2. a nuzzle on your cheek (a Cheek-Bump Non-Kiss), or
3. a smacking sound near your ear (an Air Kiss).

You must be so alert that your response (made a mere microsecond later) seems simultaneous. If you can do this, you will have accomplished a perfect social kiss.

But wait . . . there's more! At this point, the person of "greater" status selects one of the following options:

1. breaking contact after one kiss (the Basic Social Kiss)
2. repeating the procedure with the other cheek (the Basic European Social Kiss), or
3. continuing with another right-cheek/left-cheek kiss, nuzzle, or air kiss for a total of four (the Advanced European Social Kiss).

Social kisses are sometimes accompanied by a hug-lite. These minimalist embraces are perfect for those times when you want to express affection without crushing your clothes.

Lip Kiss with Hug-Lite

Basic Social Air Kiss

Basic European Cheek-Bump Non-Kiss

Misdelivered Social Kiss

* For a reminder of who has "greater" and "lesser" status and why, see page 26.

"If two boys hug, does it mean they're gay?"

If a boy and a girl hug, does it mean they're straight? ◆

Body Language Around the World

Gestures considered friendly in one land might be offensive in another. For example, in Australia, an enthusiastic thumbs-up sign doesn't mean "All right!" It means "Up yours!" It's wise to learn a little about other countries before you visit them—or when you're making friends with people from other cultures—so you don't end up flat on your back for giving someone a "compliment."

Here are more ways in which rituals of greeting and friendship vary:

- Latinos, Asians, and people in Middle Eastern and Mediterranean countries consider same-sex hand-holding or arm-linking a sign of friendship. They would be amazed to learn that these gestures are interpreted in America as signs of homosexuality.

- Japanese people bow as a form of greeting. They disapprove of public displays of affection—even between husbands and wives.

- People in Sri Lanka, India, Bangladesh, and Thailand greet each other by placing their hands in a prayerlike position in front of their chins and nodding their heads.

- Most Middle Easterners refrain from body contact when greeting members of the opposite sex. But men and women often kiss and embrace when meeting those of the same sex.

- Most people in France, Italy, Spain, and other Mediterranean countries kiss each other on both cheeks in greeting.

- Because many Asians believe that a person's soul resides in the head, the American custom of patting a child's head is seen as threatening.

- Americans are taught to look each other in the eye when speaking. Children in many Asian, Latin American, and Caribbean countries are taught that it's respectful to avoid eye contact. In America's culturally diverse schools, teachers may misinterpret a child's avoidance of eye contact as a mark of disrespect when, in fact, it's the opposite. In some urban schools, direct eye contact between teenagers is considered a form of dissing and has led to fights.

How Rude!

Giving and Receiving Gifts

You'd think it would be easy to give people gifts, and even easier to receive them. Wrong! Here's how to avoid the most common mistakes:

GRACIOUS GIVING

Choose the gift carefully. Everyone says it's the thought that counts, but some thoughts count more than others. If you give a ten-pound box of Godiva chocolate truffles to a friend who's dieting, or a CD to someone who doesn't have a CD player, you haven't been paying attention. When your choice reflects careful consideration, you give a little something in addition to the gift.

Remove the price tag. But if the price is on the gift and can't be removed without damaging the gift or the packaging (for example, the price of a book is often printed on the inside of the dust jacket), leave it. Otherwise it might be hard for the receiver to return the gift. And if he thinks the book you paid a dollar for at Buck-a-Book cost $45, that's not *your* fault.

Wrap the gift. Tradition calls for beautiful paper, ribbons, and bows. Creativity allows for aluminum foil, cloth, yarn, dried macaroni, collages, rubber stamps, etc. Your handmade giftwrap becomes part of the gift.

Include a card. How else will the person know who the gift is from, especially if it arrives in the mail along with a dozen more? Or ends up in a pile upstairs while the Big Birthday Blow-Out Bash is happening downstairs? Your card can be short and simple. You don't even have to use complete sentences.

> *For Aunt Dotty, with hugs on your birthday*
>
> *Your loving nephew, Caspar*

If your gift is meant as a thank-you for someone's hospitality or thoughtfulness, that doesn't excuse you from having to write a thank-you note.* In fact, your gift will be much more impressive if it isn't seen as "payment" for services rendered, but rather as something that happened to tag along with your written thanks.

---

* For more on thank-you notes, see pages 40–42.

Give with confidence. Don't undercut your generosity by saying:

"I know you won't like this."
"This is a dumb present."
"I couldn't spend very much."
"I didn't know what to get you."
"You probably already have one of these."

Instead, adopt a modest smile, hand the gift to its recipient, and say:

"Happy Birthday!"
"Congratulations!"
"This is for you."
"I hope you like it."

With gifts of clothing, if the box or label indicates where the item was purchased, the recipient will know where to exchange it if need be. If it's not obvious where you bought it, it's fine to say "I hope I got the right size. If it doesn't fit, let me know, and I can tell you where I got it."

"My boyfriend (actually he's my ex-boyfriend now) gave me a necklace for my birthday. It cost over $300. My parents made me give it back. They said boys his age (15) shouldn't give girls my age (15) such expensive presents. I don't see why not. It was his money."

Your boyfriend's gift was thoughtful and generous. But it was also inappropriate, which is why your parents made you return it. Appropriateness is determined by a combination of four criteria: *selection, timing, proportion,* and *taste.*

1. Selection refers to the *relationship* between the gift and the receiver. The following gifts would *not* be appropriate:

- a case of expensive champagne for a recovering alcoholic
- a videocassette of a silent movie for a person who is blind
- the complete works of Shakespeare in a leather-bound edition for someone who really, really hates Shakespeare.

These are all fine things to give—just not to everyone. Since a necklace is a lovely gift for a young man to bestow upon a young woman, your boyfriend's *selection* was entirely appropriate.

How Rude!

2. Timing refers to the *when* of a gift. A beautiful tie presented to your favorite teacher *after* he writes 28 college recommendations for you is a gift. The same tie presented *before* he writes them is a bribe. Since a birthday is a wonderful occasion for gift-giving, your boyfriend's *timing* was excellent.

3. Proportion refers to the *magnitude* of the gift. This is a delicate way of saying how much it cost—in effort, money, or both. Did it cost too much or not enough? Determining the answer isn't easy, but luckily there's a formula you can use for this purpose:

$$P = \frac{V}{NR} \times \frac{AG}{AR} \times \frac{FRG}{FRR} \times \frac{3xy}{\pi}$$

In this equation, *proportional appropriateness* (P) is a function of the *value* (V) of the gift divided by the *nature of the relationship* (NR) times the *age of the giver* (AG) over the *age of the receiver* (AR) multiplied by the *financial resources of the giver* (FRG) divided by the *financial resources of the receiver* (FRR) times 3xy, where x equals *service or kindness previously rendered* and y equals *unspoken or unintended messages,* divided by pi.*

According to the formula, the following gifts would *not* be appropriate in terms of proportion:

* a bag of Doritos as a graduation present from your parents
* a Lear jet as a graduation present from your parents
* a $300 necklace from a 15-year-old boyfriend.

Your boyfriend goofed in the area of *proportion.* Expensive presents can cause embarrassment, resentment, discomfort, and/or confusion in relationships. They may be intended (or felt) as attempts to control or manipulate; they may place unspoken demands on the receiver, or require too much sacrifice from the giver.

Proportion is also related to context—the circumstances in which the gift-giving occurs. Your parents might have let you keep the necklace if your boyfriend had just won $13 million in the lottery, or if you were both 18 and had dated all through high school. But teenagers can go through relationships very quickly, and expensive gifts can complicate things. It's hard to be dumped; it's devastating to be dumped the day after giving someone a brand-new CD player for his car.

4. Taste is the final measure of appropriateness. That silk tie you gave your teacher? An excellent choice, but not if it was printed all over with the words "SCHOOL IS FOR FOOLS." Since taste is highly personal, mistakes are easy to

---

* Lemon meringue.

36

make. Be sure you know the receiver well before giving a gift with question-able humor value.

Even though your parents made you return your now ex-boyfriend's gift, I hope they will think kindly of him. After all, he only made a simple error of proportion. And your ex-boyfriend should think kindly of your parents. He may have lost you, but at least he has the necklace back. ◆

RIGHTEOUS RECEIVING

There are only two ways to receive a present:

1. with great pleasure, or
2. with greater pleasure.

Response #1 is for gifts you *don't* particularly like. It involves a warm smile, a look of delight and surprise, and expressions of gratitude such as:

"Thank you so much."

"I'm going to enjoy reading it."

"This will look so nice in my room."

"I'll sure stay warm in these."

For gifts you *do* like, use response #2. Wear an ear-to-ear grin. Let your jaw fall open and your eyes bug out. Remain speechless for a second or two as words fail you. Run around the room a few times. Do cartwheels. Say "I can't believe it" and "Oh, wow!" over and over while you try to regain control of your conscious mind. Then let loose a torrent of thanks:

"This is S-O-O-O-O fabulous!"

"I've wanted one of these forever and ever!"

"This is the greatest present!"

"I've never seen one this beautiful in my whole life!"

"Thank you! Thank you! Thank you!"

For the grand finale, shower the giver with hugs and kisses.

You'll notice that these responses do more than just convey gratitude. *They make the person who gave you the present feel like giving you another one.* This is a lovely by-product of the proper expression of thanks.

Now that you know what to do, here's what *not* to do:

Don't ask how much something cost. This is always a serious breach of etiquette.

Don't complain about gifts you receive. As in:

"Not another stupid wallet."

"Nobody wears these."

How Rude!

"Why'd you get me this?"

"I already have one."

This may be difficult, particularly if you were expecting a car and ended up with an Etch-A-Sketch. But sometimes, for the sake of the greater good, you have to pretend. (Think of the last time you faked being sick in order to stay home from school.) So, even if you're disappointed, act pleased and grateful because:

1. it's bad manners to deliberately hurt someone else's feelings, and

2. your behavior encourages the person to give you another present, thus giving her a chance to get it right the next time.

Don't ask for presents. Parents and other gift-givers don't like to hear:

"Can I have one of those?"

"Buy me that!"

"What are you going to get me?"

So, how do you let them know what you want?

Nobody said you couldn't share your hopes and dreams. If you're passing a bike store, it's okay to point and say wistfully to your dad "Someday, when I've saved up enough money, I'm going to buy one just like that." Or to confide to your mom "Isn't that sweater gorgeous? I wish I had one like it." This isn't begging. This is parent-child communication.

It's also okay if your parents happen to overhear you telling a friend that you'd give anything to have a pair of X-90 Kryptonite Glow-in-the-Dark Inline Skates. And you're certainly entitled to circle items in catalogs, or cut out ads, and keep them in your bedroom for handy reference where they might be discovered by parents who wander by.

For those of you who are interested in parent psychology, here's why this indirect approach works: When grownups give a gift, they like to feel that they're surprising you rather than filling an order. By subtle hints instead of outright asking, you can give them the opportunity to show how attentive and sensitive they are. You put icing on the cake of this method when you respond to the gift with:

"How did you ever know I wanted one of these?"

Your parents will smile, feel clever, and say "Oh, we have our ways." And you can smile inside and feel clever, too.

"Is it okay to return or give away a present you don't like?"

Social Interactions 101

It depends on what it is, who gave it to you, the particulars of the gift, the likelihood that the giver will ever find out, and your reason for returning it.

It's fine to exchange things that you already have, such as books, tapes, or CDs. No one would consider it rude to return clothing that doesn't fit or things you're allergic to. If you get tons of gifts all at once (for example, for a Bat Mitzvah or graduation) and end up with 11 sweaters and 43 bottles of perfume, it's okay to pare things down a bit.

The main thing you want to do is avoid hurting anyone's feelings. If one of those sweaters was handmade, you shouldn't give it away, even if you'll never wear it. The same goes for art people create especially for you, or items they consider very special or sentimental. You may just have to hang Aunt Fanny's hideous (er, lovely) paint-by-numbers portrait of Elvis when she comes for her annual visit, and then stick it back in the basement for the rest of the year.

Don't tell people you returned their gifts unless they ask. And then phrase your reply as gently as possible:

"I absolutely adored your going-away present, but since I'm moving to Hawaii I just don't know how often I'll get a chance to use a snowblower, so I exchanged it for a surfboard and now I'll think of you and your kindness every time I catch a wave." ◆

TRUE STORIES FROM THE MANNERS FRONTIER

Writer's Cramp

Sometimes it's safe to recycle gifts on to other victims (er, recipients) after a number of years have passed. But be careful!

I was browsing through a used bookstore one day and discovered a book that I had written. I picked it up to see if anyone had highlighted passages or otherwise mutilated it. And there, on the title page, was an inscription, in my handwriting, to the person to whom I had given it years earlier!

How Rude!

THANK-YOU NOTES

The reason teenagers have such a hard time writing thank-you notes is because they start off with the wrong attitude. They think of it as a *chore* instead of an *opportunity* to make the gift-giver feel wonderful. People who feel wonderful are more likely to keep giving you gifts than those who don't. Here's how to write terrific thank-you notes:

If you're not sure whether to write a thank-you note, write one. It's better to overthank than underthank. Notes are obligatory for all gifts received by mail, UPS, or Pony Express, whether for a birthday, graduation, Bar or Bat Mitzvah, confirmation, Christmas, Hanukkah, Kwanzaa, etc. You should also write notes for services rendered, hospitality provided, and thoughtfulnesses extended. Generally, it's not necessary to write notes for presents given in person and for which you have already thanked the person verbally. But think of the mileage you could get out of a follow-up note!

Written thanks aren't required every time a courtesy is extended, but might be in order after a period of time has passed. For example, let's say a friend's mother drives your team to sports practice twice a week for an entire school year. She never fails to have some munchies in the car for everybody's enjoyment. Your verbal thanks each time are sufficient. But if you send her a note in June to recognize the cumulative value of her chauffeur service, she'll think you're the greatest. The same goes for a teacher who has meant a lot to you over the year.

Write immediately. Thank-you notes get exponentially more difficult to write with each day that passes. By the second day, they are *four* times harder to write. By the third day, they are *nine* times harder, and if you wait 12 days, they are *144* times harder to write!

Write by hand. Thank-you notes should not be typed or word-processed. Use personal note stationery or attractive cards (the ones that are blank inside). However, if your handwriting is absolutely atrocious, it's better to send a laser-printed, personally signed letter than none at all.

Never begin with "Thank you for . . . ." Start with some news, a recollection of the event or visit, a reaffirmation of your friendship, or other charming chitchat.

For example, you've just spent a wonderful two weeks with the Gump family (distant cousins on your mother's side) at their California seaside condo. You might write:

> *Dear Mr. and Mrs. Gump,*
>
> *I'm back here in Iowa, safe and sound. School started three days ago, and it already seems as if I've been back for three months. I can't believe it was just last week that I left the sunny shores of the Pacific for the long flight back home.*
>
> *I can't tell you how much I enjoyed my visit . . .*

Continue by mentioning the places they took you to, the memories you'll always cherish, the delicious dinners, etc. Then, and only then, thank them for their thoughtfulness and generosity to you. Express the hope that you and your parents can one day host their kid for a stay in America's heartland. You'll bring smiles to the faces of the Gumps, make a fine impression, and guarantee that you'll have a standing invitation to return for more surf, sun, and fun.

Always mention the gift by name. If I give somebody a wedding present and I get a letter back that simply thanks me for my "wonderful and generous gift," I know it's a form letter they cranked out. Even if it's handwritten. Make the effort to refer to the gift in some way:

> *"All my friends are jealous of my new radio."*
> *"You must have read my mind to know I wanted a garlic press."*
> *"I'm absolutely thrilled with my Chia pet."*

Always mention special moments. If the gift was one of hospitality, you must send a note, even if you thanked your hosts during the visit. When you write, don't just say "Thanks for letting me stay with you." Let your hosts know the things that made the visit so special: falling into the river, being eaten alive by mosquitoes, having your picture taken with Mickey Mouse.

Tell how you're going to spend the money. If someone gives you the big green, mention what you plan to do with it. If you have no idea, make something up:

> *"I'm planning to buy a CD that I've been wanting for ages."*
> *"I've started saving for a car, and this gives me a real start towards that goal."*

Don't spoil your thanks with a bummer. Not every gift will be to your liking. Sometimes this is nobody's fault. Avoid saying things that let gift-givers know their efforts were unappreciated or pointless:

How Rude!

"I lost it the first time I took it to school."

"It hit a tree and broke."

"I got hives so my mom made me throw it out."

COMPLIMENTS

A compliment is a gift. The fact that it's verbal rather than material doesn't change a thing. If someone gives you a compliment, the proper way to receive it is by saying "Thank you." If you're really bowled over, you can add "You're very kind to say so."

Many people, however, deny, deflect, or deflate the compliments they are handed:

If someone says . . .	They reply . . .
"What a beautiful dress!"	"Oh, it's just a little nothing I picked up on sale" OR "I look terrible in it."
"You played beautifully!"	"I was totally out of tune" OR "Yo-Yo was so much better."

People do this because they have low self-esteem and can't imagine why anyone would compliment them. This comes from not receiving enough compliments.

Negating a compliment implies that the person giving it doesn't know what he's talking about. That's a rude way to respond to someone who's just said something nice about you.

Occasionally, you'll receive a compliment from someone you've just beaten at something. If your win was a squeaker or the result of subjective judging, accept the compliment with modest grace:

"I feel really lucky they picked me. Any of us could have won."

If the compliment comes from someone you wiped the floor with, try to say something nice:

"You put up a stiff fight."

"You had a bad day, but I saw you last week against Brewster High and you played great."

Won't people know you're just trying to make them feel better? Probably. And won't they still feel lousy that they lost? Probably. But at least they will have the comfort of your empathy. You will have been a nice human being. That counts for a lot.

Giving compliments can be just as hard as receiving them, especially if you're disappointed or upset. It's not easy to congratulate the classmate whose experiment just won first prize over yours at the Science Fair, or the teammate who beat you out for a starting position. But these compliments are the most valuable, precisely because they are hard to give. They will mean a lot to the other person, who may (believe it or not) be feeling guilty and uncomfortable about having won. And they will also mean a lot to *you*, because you'll know that you can behave nobly even though you feel like smooshing a banana cream pie in the person's face.

There are a few pitfalls to watch for when handing out accolades:

Don't compliment one person by putting another person down.

Wrong	Right
"You kiss so much better than Sean."	"I love the way you kiss."
"It's wonderful having someone on the team who doesn't drop the ball the way Chris does."	"It's great having you on the team."

Don't tarnish your applause with envy or bitterness.

Wrong	Right
"Congratulations on winning the scholarship. At least *you'll* be able to go to college.""	"Congratulations! You worked so hard!"
"You were great at the audition. But I don't see why I didn't get the part."	"Congratulations on getting the part. You'll make a great cat!"

Don't pollute your praise with criticism.

Wrong	Right
"You look so nice I didn't recognize you."	"You look really nice."
"You were great today. It's about time you scored."	"Great goal. You were terrific out there."

Don't undercut your compliment with nosiness.

How Rude!

Wrong	Right
"That's a gorgeous jacket. How on earth could you afford it?"	"Nice jacket!"
"Congratulations on your job. Who'd you have to bribe to get it?"	"Your new job sounds terrific!"

Applying for a Job

Sooner or later, most teenagers are motivated to get a job. This is due to a basic human drive called *wanting more money*. In order to get work, you'll need a social security number, which you probably already have. Depending on the job and your age, you may need to show a work permit, immigration papers if you're not a U.S. citizen, or even a statement from your doctor saying you're in good health. You can find out about this sort of stuff from your school, your state Labor Department, or potential employers.

It's nice to earn money. It's even nicer to earn it for doing something you like. So, before you go out looking for any old job, think of what you really enjoy. What fires you up? What do you want to learn? What are you good at? Fixing cars? Gardening? Music? Surfing? Baby-sitting? Biomolecular chromosome splitting?

Once you've identified your skills and interests, it's time to start looking. Finding a job can be difficult, particularly for younger teenagers. You may have more success creating your own job. Start a business. Provide a service. Depending on where you live, there may be a real demand for lawn and garden care, snow shoveling, dog walking, window washing, gutter cleaning, or baby-sitting. You might establish a grocery buying and delivery service, or run errands for people who are very busy or very lazy. You could go to people's homes or places of business and wash and wax their cars. A lot of people take vacations during the summer and could use someone responsible to water plants, care for pets, and look after the house while they're away. You could run a repair or sewing service for people like me who'll lose a button on a shirt and never wear it again. You could organize parties, a summer camp, or play groups for kids; do cooking and catering; do laundry and ironing. You could run a computer and Internet consulting service.

Have business cards printed. Put up flyers. Place an ad. Get letters of recommendation from people you've worked for to show to prospective customers. If you provide a necessary service, price it fairly, and don't fall asleep on the job, you'll build an income and a client base. Those clients will tell their friends and, before you know it, you'll have work coming out your ears. You might even have to hire someone to help you!

If you want to work for someone else instead of yourself, brainstorm people and places you could approach. Look in the classified ads in the newspaper. Network. Ask your parents and siblings; ask your friends and their parents; ask your teachers, coaches, and school counselors. Don't be afraid to contact people who are doing what you want to do and ask them for advice. Most adults enjoy helping polite and appreciative young people who are interested in exploring or entering their field of work. Call businesses and shops to see if they have positions available. Keep your eyes peeled for signs in storefronts. Check out bulletin boards at the supermarket, the laundromat, the public library. See if your school has a job placement service. Place your own ad. Use online discussion groups and email pals to get the word out.

Many positions are seasonal (such as camp counselors, lifeguards, and ski lift operators). Find out when these types of places do their hiring. Show your interest early. Get a jump on everybody else. Don't be a pest, but if you stay in touch and let it be known that you're really serious about a job, your perseverance may work to your advantage.

You might need to put together a *résumé*—a written summary of your skills and experience that you can send to places where you'd like a job. You can also leave copies of your résumé with people who interview you. Your résumé should include:

- your name, address, and phone number
- the schools you've attended and degrees you've attained (for example, a Ph.D. in classroom chair tilting)
- descriptions of any jobs you've held, and what your responsibilities and accomplishments were
- any honors or prizes you've received, and especially
- any activities, interests, and courses you've taken that relate to the type of work you hope to find.

You may want to include the names and phone numbers of people who have agreed to tell potential employers how great you are. These are called *references*. They should not be confused with parents or other relatives whose opinions might be biased. Be sure to get permission before you list someone as a reference.

Your résumé should be flawless. As in perfect. That is to say, no misteaks. It should represent the quality, care, exactitude, and smart appearance you would bring to the job. It is your stand-in. If you don't type, have someone else word-process it for you. In the computer age, there is no excuse for a sloppy résumé. And believe me, when employers are looking through hundreds of résumés, they want an excuse to throw out as many as they can. You

How Rude!

can find more information about preparing a résumé from your school guidance or career office, or the public library.

Once you've got a résumé and have identified where you'd like to work, you're ready to seek an interview. Some places, like fast-food joints and convenience stores, usually don't require you to make an appointment. You can just walk in, ask to see the manager, and say that you'd like to apply for a job. You'll be handed an application and asked if you want fries with that. The manager may interview you then and there, or ask you to come back at another time. Be sure you look nice when you make these preliminary rounds. If you make a crummy first impression, the manager may just tell you that there aren't any openings.

Other places require you to schedule an appointment for an interview. Call them up. Tell the person who answers the phone that you'd like to apply for a job. You'll either be told what to do or transferred to the personnel office.

You can also send a query letter. This is what I did when I was a lad of 14. I wanted a summer job working for an architect. I drafted a letter in which I spoke of my love of architecture, my desire to become an architect, drawings I'd done, places I'd traveled to, courses I'd taken, and what a hardworking, responsible, all-around great kid I was. I concluded by saying that I would call to schedule an interview.

Once I completed the draft of my letter, I made a list of 20 architectural firms to send it to. I then had to type 20 perfect letters—and this was before the era of word processing. I finished the letters, sent them off, and didn't get a job; there were too many college and graduate students applying. But most of the architects complimented me on my letter and invited me to visit their offices. I took some great tours, met some fascinating people, and ate some yummy donuts. Several architects said that I could come back anytime to hang out, use their libraries, and pick up tips on drawing and lettering from the people who worked there. Soon, some of the architects were giving me little projects to do, like drawing bricks and leaves.

This brings to mind one of the major challenges in job-hunting: A lot of places say "Sorry. We only hire people with experience." *But how do you get experience if nobody will hire you without it?* One way is to volunteer where you want to work. A place that can't hire you might still be willing to take you on as an unpaid intern or apprentice. That way, you get experience and on-the-job training. If you make a good impression, you could be first in line for a paying job at some later date.

In fact, that's what happened to me. When I was 15, I wrote another 20 letters. Only this time, I was able to truthfully* say that I had worked for

---

* See "Be honest but not stupid" on page 50.

architects. (The fact that I didn't get paid for my work was none of their business.) I was able to name-drop local architects I knew, and to use them as references. And, sure enough, the next summer I got a job. And the summer after that, I got a job with the same firm in their Tokyo, Japan, office! The rest, as they say, is history. One thing led to another, and before I could say Frank Lloyd Wright, I became . . . a developmental psychologist and writer of books for teenagers?!?

AT THE INTERVIEW

Let's say you've set up an interview. This is your chance to show in word and deed that YOU are the person for the job. Here are some pointers to keep in mind:

Be punctual. Coming late does not a good impression make. Leave enough time to get where you're going. Allow for the possibility of a traffic jam, or trouble finding the right building. If you see that you're going to be late, try to call the interviewer. This shows consideration and responsibility. When you get to your appointment, be sure to apologize. If it was your fault, admit it:

> *"I'm terribly sorry about being late. I got lost. I should have allowed more time."*

This shows that you're mature enough to accept responsibility rather than make excuses. On the other hand, if being late wasn't your fault, apologize and explain what happened:

> *"A barge hit the bridge, and traffic had to detour thirty miles around Lake Looney. I'm sorry, I hope this hasn't upset your schedule too much."*

A reasonable person will understand and won't hold your lateness against you.

Once you get where you're going, let the receptionist know who you are, who you're seeing, and the time of your appointment. He or she will probably tell you to have a seat. Try not to fidget, tap, or pace while waiting. You never know who might be watching. If other people are waiting, it's fine to engage in small talk:

> *"Have you worked for a landscaping company before? I think the opening here is because the last person fell into the wood chipper. I hear they force you to work fourteen hours a day. Chain saws make you go deaf, did you know that?"*

At worst, you'll have a pleasant conversation. And if you're lucky, the person will say "Excuse me" and head for the door. One less competitor for the job!

How Rude!

Dress appropriately. Wear clothes that are neat, clean, pressed, and non-odoriferous. A good rule of thumb is to put on something a little snazzier than what you'd normally wear on the job. Interviewing for a lifeguard position? Don't go in your Speedo. Wear nice shorts and a T-shirt or polo shirt. A job in construction, lawn care, or manual labor? A *good* pair of jeans, a work shirt, and boots or sneakers (laced and tied). If you're applying to work in a store or an office, boys should wear khakis or dress slacks (no jeans), a nice shirt (no T-shirts or tank tops), and presentable footgear (loafers, Top-Siders, dress shoes). If it's a fancy store or a very "establishment" business (such as a bank or a law firm), boys should wear a tie and jacket or even a suit. Girls would dress correspondingly: nice shorts, slacks, or skirts and tops for informal positions such as camp counseling, baby-sitting, or manual labor; a nice skirt or dress pants and blouse for office and service jobs; a businessy dress or suit for the pinstripe and Perrier establishment crowd.

Whatever position you're applying for, you should be well-groomed and well-coifed. That means no dirty fingernails, no milk mustaches, no green food particles between your teeth. Hair should be combed, brushed, and under a semblance of control. Boys should be clean shaven. If you happen to be a 14-year-old with a beard, keep it neat and trimmed. Avoid the five-day shadow look. Girls should use makeup in moderation. Both boys and girls should use scent in moderation and avoid wearing clothes that are too tight or sexually provocative: No bare midriffs or pants worn halfway to your knees.

"But that's the style!"
"I'm not going to be some phony."
"Why can't I wear sneakers?"
"I don't have a suit."
"I want them to know the real me."

TIP: Let them hire you first. Then they can get to know the *real* you. What we're really talking about here is avoiding extremes. You want your appearance to say "I have a sense of what's appropriate; I care about how I look; I care about the impression I make." When you work for someone else, you represent that person or business. You are their link to customers or clients, and the quality of *your* work reflects *their* competence. Employers need to know that you can be trusted with their image and reputation. They need to know that you'll behave appropriately and responsibly on their behalf. The way you present yourself at a job interview shows whether you know how to do so on *your* behalf.

Of course, there are exceptions to every rule. If you're auditioning for a role as a skinhead punk in a movie, you might come looking like a skinhead punk. If you're hoping to get a job playing drums in a band, you might help your chances by looking the part. It's probably a fair statement to say that people in the art, music, entertainment, fashion, and computer software fields tend to be more casual, individualistic, and diverse in how they dress than people in service industries or the worlds of business and finance.

The main idea is to use your good judgment—that thing your parents are always telling you to have more of. If you think it's okay to wear a T-shirt to an interview, just don't wear one with a picture or phrase that's going to offend anyone. If you don't own or can't borrow any dress clothes, dress casually, but show that you have a sense of style and appropriateness.

"Yeah, I applied for a job here, but they won't hire me. I don't get it."

Come prepared. Bring any documents or information you might need to show. This could include your résumé, proof of age or citizenship, social security number, certifications, etc. If you have examples of your own work that relate to the position, bring them along, too. For example, if you're applying for a job in a photography store, you could show the interviewer some photographs you've taken.

Mind your manners. An interview is one occasion where the sorry state of the world today works to your advantage. Use your best manners, and you'll set yourself apart from the unkempt competition who will grunt, mumble, and fidget their way through the meeting.

When the interviewer comes to greet you, stand up straight. Smile. Shake hands (firm grip). Look the interviewer in the eye. Be confident, even if your stomach's churning and your legs feel like jelly. Use your acting skills. Take deep breaths. Say "How do you do." Follow the interviewer to wherever your meeting is going to take place. Once you get there, she will tell you to take a seat. (Don't ask "Where should I take it?") If the interviewer doesn't cue you to sit but just sits down herself, take the seat opposite her. Sit up straight in the chair. Don't slump or stretch out. Try not to tap, bounce, drum, bite your nails, pick your skin, or crack your knuckles. Use "Sir" and "Ma'am." Don't chew gum, blow bubbles, spit tobacco, or smoke.

You may be asked if you'd like some coffee, water, or soda. It's fine to accept, but before doing so, think whether you want to risk spilling it all over yourself.

Be poised. Some interviewers may try to provoke you or throw you a curveball. They want to see how you react to stress. I can remember an interview during my teen years. The interviewer was asking all these rapid-fire questions about where I went to school and my courses and grades and extracurricular activities and what I had done previous summers and what I wanted to do with my life and all of a sudden he asked "What's 19 times 15?" Without missing a beat, I said "Seventy-eight" (I was always very good at math), and continued to talk about my hopes and dreams for the future. From this experience, I learned to expect the unexpected at interviews and to carry a pocket calculator.

Be honest but not stupid. Don't lie about your qualifications or experience. Prospective employers can easily check these things by contacting your references or previous employers. At the same time, don't be honest to a fault.

Let's say an interviewer asks "Why do you want to work here?" If you say "Because my stupid parents are forcing me to get a job," you're not going to help your cause. Tell a different truth. Say "Because I like children and being outdoors, and I've heard good things about your camp."

Getting a job can be an uphill battle. You need to persuade an employer to hire *you* over everyone else. Telling him what he wants to hear is part of the game. And what he wants to hear is that you're gung ho, responsible, and interested in the work.

Be enthusiastic. An interviewer is going to ask you questions. Give more than one-word answers. Without being hyper, show that you're excited about the opportunity. This suggests you might be energetic on the job, which is something employers like.

Suppose the interviewer says "So you want to work in a ski store?"

Say "Yeah" and she'll show you to the door.

Say "You bet!" and she might sit up and take notice.

Say "Boy, would I ever! I got my first pair of skis when I was three and I've been schussing down the double diamonds ever since" and she may offer you the job.

Have questions ready. Many interviewers will ask if you have any questions. Even if most of your questions have already been answered, try to come up with a few more. This shows that you're a thoughtful person who wants to evaluate the fit of the position. You could ask about the nature of your duties, the future plans of the company, the type of customer or client you'd be working with, the pay and benefits of the job, opportunities for training and growth, etc.

Send a thank-you note. When the interview is over, thank the interviewer for her time and willingness to see you. If the interview was very quick and impersonal—say, for a job in a fast-food restaurant—your verbal appreciation is ample. If, however, the interviewer spent a considerable amount of time with you, or the position was with an office or store that really appeals to you, send a thank-you note. Let her know how much you appreciated the opportunity to meet. Repeat how eager you are to work there. Even if you don't get the job, your letter will make a positive impression. And it just might improve your chances for the next job that opens up there.

"I've had my eyebrow, lip, and nose pierced. Is it all right to wear my rings to a job interview?"

Not unless you're applying for a job in a piercing parlor. Numerous metal objects poked through your flesh will not make the interviewer think how great you'd be in the job. It will make him think *eee-youch!!!* ◆

"I'm a 14-year-old girl and I baby-sit a lot for this one family. I like the kids, but every time I come over the mom always asks me to do the laundry or clean up from their dinner or something like that. I don't think housework should be part of my job, but I don't know how to tell her."

Housework should not be part of a baby-sitter's job unless:

1. the baby-sitter agrees to it and is paid extra, or

2. the work is directly related to child-care activities (for example, cleaning up the kitchen after giving the kids or yourself a snack, vacuuming the family room after a popcorn fight, etc.).

It's always tricky for employees to set limits for what they will and won't do, and even more so when the employee is a kid and the employer is an adult. But, since a good baby-sitter is worth her weight in gold, you're at a definite advantage. Simply say to the mother "I really enjoy baby-sitting for your family, but I don't feel housework should be part of my responsibilities. Of course, I'll clean up any messes we make while I'm baby-sitting." If you're willing to do extra work for extra pay, you can mention this and see what the mother says.

Since healthy relationships between parents and baby-sitters are crucial to the functioning of society, here's a summary of each party's responsibilities:

The parents should:

- drive you to and from the job as needed
- maintain adequate snacking supplies
- keep the television and VCR in working order
- leave emergency telephone numbers and information as to their where-abouts
- return at the agreed-upon hour
- provide instructions for feeding, medicating, and/or handling the children ("Johnny won't go to sleep unless Mr. Penguin faces north")
- inform their children that they must be good
- pay at the time services are rendered, and
- if they want to stay on your A-list, round off to the next highest hour or half-hour (as in three hours and forty minutes of baby-sitting = four hours of pay).

You should:

- approach your job as if it were one of the most awesome responsibilities a person could be entrusted with (because it is)
- give your full time and attention to the children you're sitting for
- make sure you ask for any information the parents may have forgotten to provide
- keep the phone line free (unless it has call waiting and you answer all incoming calls)
- admit no one into the house unless this has been cleared beforehand
- report significant problems or milestones ("Junior swallowed your wedding ring"), and

- if you want to stay on your employer's A-list, always do a little something extra that shows initiative and thoughtfulness—bake some cookies with the kids, wash the last few dishes that the parents left in the sink, help a child clean up her room or write a thank-you note. ◆

People with Disabilities

One of the greatest challenges that people with disabilities face is dealing with the manners-impaired. These "well-intentioned" folks will talk about a disabled person as if she weren't there:

"Can she walk?"
"Will she grow?"

They'll pry into areas that are none of their business:

"Were you born that way?"
"Can you have sex?"

They'll treat the person as an object of pity or praise, not as a human being with needs and feelings no different than their own.

Many people feel uncomfortable around people with disabilities because they don't know how to act—or react. Or they may not know how or whether to help. Or they may view the person's disability through their own perspective. A sighted person meets a person who is blind, imagines not being able to see, and feels a sense of loss, tragedy, and fear. Or a person who can walk sees a wheelchair user and feels immobile and claustrophobic. These feelings color the interaction, even though the person with the disability probably doesn't feel anything like that. The essence of good manners is the ability to put others at ease *regardless of one's own discomfort.*

In the sincere hope that you'll never be manners-impaired when relating to people with disabilities, here are some do's and taboos:

- Don't assume that one disability implies another. There's no need to shout at a person who is blind or speak slowly to someone in a wheelchair.
- Always address people with disabilities directly. Look them in the eye. Just because they may have a parent, friend, or nurse with them doesn't mean they can't speak for themselves. Never refer to them in the third person in their presence ("Would he mind if I took him for a walk?" "Can she swim?").
- When talking to a person who is deaf, face him so he can read your lips. Don't speak unusually slowly or overpronounce words. If an interpreter is present, face the person who is hearing impaired, not the interpreter.

How Rude!

- Never take a person's cane or crutches. If you're going to be seated for a while, you can ask "Would you like me to set these over here while we eat?"

- Always ask before helping. If you saw someone struggling to carry a lot of luggage, you wouldn't just grab the bags out of her hands. You'd ask if she could use some assistance. The same thing applies when you encounter people with disabilities. Don't start steering them across the street as if they were grocery carts. Say "Would you like to take my arm?" or "May I help in any way?"

- Don't pry. People with disabilities don't owe anyone a medical report. It's rude to ask about the source, duration, symptoms, prognosis, or limitations of their condition.

- If you're in the company of a friend with a disability, third parties (such as waiters, sales clerks, or acquaintances of yours) might address you rather than your friend. If this happens, don't respond or make eye contact. This will encourage them to speak directly to your friend.

- Be patient when interacting with people who have a speech disorder. Don't finish their sentences for them. Don't pretend that you understand what they're saying if you really don't. Say "I'm sorry, I didn't get that" or "You went where?" or "What was that number again?"

- Never touch a person with a disability without permission. This is an invasion of his or her personal space. (So is leaning on a wheelchair.) Similarly, never pet or call to a service animal such as a guide dog without the owner's permission. This could distract the animal and/or interfere with its training.

- Don't use euphemisms to describe disabilities. Disability groups object to terms such as "handicapable," "mentally different," "physically inconvenienced," and "physically challenged." These terms reinforce the idea that disabilities can't be dealt with up front.

- Use respectful terminology. Don't define people by their disabilities. And always put the person first, not the disability. For example, say "My friend who is deaf," not "My deaf friend."

Unacceptable	Preferred
generic labels like "the blind," "the deaf," "the retarded"	people who are blind; people who are deaf; people who are mentally retarded
a cripple	a person who is physically disabled
a retard	a person with mental retardation

continued

an epileptic	a person with epilepsy; a person with a seizure disorder
a spastic	a person with a motor disorder
a vegetable	a person with a brain injury
an HIV victim; an AIDS victim	a person with HIV; a person with AIDS
a mongoloid	a person with Down syndrome
a cerebral palsy victim; a person afflicted by multiple sclerosis; a person who suffers from muscular dystrophy	a person who has cerebral palsy; a person who has multiple sclerosis; a person who has muscular dystrophy
a person who is confined to a wheelchair	a person who uses a wheelchair
a "normal" person	a person without disabilities

"What should you do if you see some-one in a wheelchair? I know it's polite to help, but I've heard that handi-capped people don't want to be helped and might get mad if you try."

Start by thinking of a person in a wheelchair simply as a *person*. Then, if you think she might like or need some help, offer your assistance. It will either be accepted or declined. End of story. Never push or move people in wheelchairs without permission. In most cases, they are fully capable of getting where they want on their own.

When speaking to wheelchair users, try to position yourself at their eye level. Sit down and face them, or, if you're standing, bend at the waist. But don't squat or kneel. This might come across as condescending. ◆

"I use a wheelchair. You won't believe how many times total strangers just start pushing me. How do I tell them I don't need their help?"

It's a wonder that people who would never dream of swooping strangers into their arms and carrying them across the street feel at liberty to propel people

How Rude!

in wheelchairs into motion. Tell the eager beaver "Thank you, but I don't need any assistance." And then, if you feel like it, do a few 360s, pop a wheelie or two, and scorch on outta there. ◆

"There's this blind girl who started coming to a youth center in my neighborhood. I want to be friendly, but I'm scared I'll do something dumb or not know what to say."

Say "Hi. Welcome to the center. My name is _____. What's yours?" And then start a conversation, just as you would with any new acquaintance. You're approaching her not because she's blind, but because it's polite to welcome and get to know any new person. Ask about her interests and activities, where she lives, where she goes to school, etc. She's probably just like any other teenager—eager to have friends, talk, go places, and do things. The fact that she can't see presents her with challenges most kids don't face. But it doesn't *define* her. So don't focus on it as an initial topic of conversation unless she brings it up. As you build a friendship and begin to do things together, the subject may come up naturally.

If she uses a guide dog, don't pet it without her permission. If you go walking together, don't pull her by the hand or steer her by the shoulders. Offer her your elbow. If she chooses to take it, let her set the pace. If you approach an obstacle or hazard, don't just shout "Look out!" Instead, give her specific information: "There's a big mound of dog doo-doo and four really steep steps."

Identify yourself each time you see your new friend until you're positive that she recognizes your voice. If you're ever in a group conversation with her and somebody leaves, let her know. That way, she won't talk to a person who's no longer there. It's also fine to tell her things you see that she might find helpful or amusing:

"They're all laughing because Mrs. Finderstock just made a face."
"Larry shaved his head."
"Mr. Dripps looks so mad I think he's going to explode."
"That new guy is S-O-O-O cute!"

Don't worry about using words like "see," "watch," and "look." A blind person won't be offended if you say "See what I mean?" or "I hear the math sub is tough. You better watch out for her." But do avoid expressions that use disabilities as insults. For example, don't say "Whatsa matter, are you blind?!?" to a person who steps on your toe. Or "You retard!" to someone who makes a mistake. ◆

56

"The other day, I was introduced to someone who was missing his right hand. I went to shake hands, and I felt pretty embarrassed when I realized there was nothing to shake. What should I have done?"

The next time you meet him, let him take the lead. Anyone whose hand is unavailable, whether temporarily or permanently, is likely to have encountered this situation before. He may extend his left hand (which you may shake with either your left or right hand); he may extend a prosthetic hand for you to shake (not *too* vigorously, though); or he may extend no hand at all, in which case your interaction will be verbal. Take your cue from his behavior. ◆

"I was badly burned in a car accident. Wherever I go, people either stare at my face or avoid looking at it entirely. If I walk into a room, the conversation sometimes stops, or kids start whispering. It's bad enough what happened without having to be reminded of it every minute of the day. I don't want to be rude, but I think those people are being rude to me. What should I do?"

First, recognize that you don't owe anybody an explanation. Even though some people are likely to be curious, uncomfortable, and/or insensitive in your presence, you're not responsible for their social disabilities. But you can choose to respond in any of several ways:

1. **Ignore rude reactions.** Simply go about your business. In time, conversation will resume. Whispering will stop. And people will look beyond your skin to see the fine person inside.

2. **Intensify your social correctness.** Introduce yourself. Get the conversation going again. Your naturalness may make others feel self-conscious about their lapse in manners, and they will get with the program.

3. **Break the ice.** When you enter a room, *you* know that people are wondering what happened to you. And *they* know that you know. It becomes one of those situations in which everybody's *thinking* about the same thing but nobody wants to *say* anything about it.

How Rude!

It's not your obligation to satisfy people's curiosity or to compensate for their poor social skills. But there may be certain occasions when you feel comfortable about speaking out. You can do this in one of two ways, depending on which feels right to you. For example, you might simply say "I was burned in a car accident." Or you might take a light, humorous tone and say "Don't worry, it's not contagious." Either way, you're alleviating the awkwardness by bringing what's on people's minds out into the open. And either way, you're being *very* generous.

People will probably respond with embarrassed expressions of apology ("Sorry, I didn't mean—" or "It's none of my—"). In which case, you can say "Oh, that's okay." Then change the subject to something you want to talk about. ◆

"I have a birth defect that affects my coordination. People, even strangers, ask things like 'What's wrong with you?' or 'How did you get that way?' Is it okay to be rude back?"

No. But it *is* okay to make them squirm. Strangers merit no reply. You may, however, slowly turn your head towards your interrogator, give him a hard look a nanosecond short of a stare, and slowly look away. He'll get the message.

If someone asks "What's wrong with you?" you can smile and say "There's nothing *wrong* with me. Why? Is there something wrong with you?"

You can also ignore the question. Respond to any prying inquiry by saying "Do you think the Orioles will win the pennant?"

Another way to answer intrusive questions is by saying "I'm sorry, but I don't discuss such things with people I don't know."

Some people may ask about your disability because they want to get to know you better. (As opposed to those who simply want to satisfy their own curiosity.) You'll probably sense when a question indicates sincere interest, and you'll feel more comfortable answering it. ◆

CHAPTER QUIZ

1. *You're hosting a party when you notice that two of the guests, whose names you've forgotten, are standing awkwardly next to each other. Do you:*

a) yell across the room "If you're going to look so glum, you're going to have to leave"

b) introduce them using any old names you can think up, or

c) approach them and say "It's great to see you. Do you know each other? I've got to check the food, but why don't you two introduce yourselves"?

Social Interactions 101

2. *The proper social kiss is designed to:*

a) wipe a milk mustache off on someone's cheek

b) help you get to first base

c) express affection between friends.

3. *It's your birthday. Your aunt has just given you the most hideous shirt you've ever seen in your life. Do you:*

a) blow your nose in it

b) ask "How much did this horror set you back?" or

c) beam, give your auntie a kiss, and say "Thank you so much! I can't wait to show this to all my friends"?

4. *You've just finished a job interview for a position in a pet store. The owner rises, signaling that the interview is over. Do you:*

a) put your feet up on the desk and say "What's the rush, bossman?"

b) ask if the parrot knows any swear words, or

c) get up, shake hands, and thank the owner for his time?

5. *You're blading to school when you see a woman who is blind waiting to cross a busy street. The proper thing to do is:*

a) push her into the traffic

b) slam into her and yell "Why doncha watch where you're going?"

c) stop and say "Excuse me, can I give you a hand?"

3
Uncommon Courtesies

Saving the Earth from a Manners Meltdown

In your mind's eye, step back from your daily world of family, school, and friends; forget about homework, chores, and MTV; let go of all the little worries and hassles that crowd your consciousness. Zoom away from the planet. See Earth as a tiny dot, people as grains of sand. Travel through space to the edge of the universe, climb up on the wall, and have yourself a think about the state of the world.

War. Starvation. Poverty. Disease. Drugs. Murder. Terrorism. Barney.

Think about the rudeness you encounter every day. From classmates. Teachers. Parents. Store clerks. Brothers and sisters. People on the bus. Strangers in the subway. Think about the rude things *you* do every day.*

---

* Okay, every *other* day.

Think about talk shows that present cruelty as entertainment.

Think about kids being shot for a pair of sneakers.

Think about bumper stickers that beg people to be kind to one another.

Uncommon Courtesies

Now that you're in a cheery mood, think about this: Is it possible that human beings, at this very moment, are headed for extinction? Will greed, selfishness, and ignorance turn our species into an evolutionary laughing-stock? Or will generosity, kindness, and respect prevail? Will we do ourselves proud? Or will we die out, leaving nothing behind but golden arches and toxic waste?

The answer can be summed up in one word: *Beats me.* But I can tell you what the deciding factor will be: *Manners.*

The survival of the human race depends on everyone minding their manners. Manners allow people to live and work together in harmony, to go about the daily business of life without constant friction or fighting.

It is in the anonymous, everyday interactions of modern life that manners have most broken down. On sidewalks. In stores. At movie theaters. On the highways. Anonymity breeds rudeness. It's easier to give the finger to a stranger than to someone you know.

America is not the only country experiencing a manners meltdown. Many cultures around the globe are facing similar epidemics of impoliteness. French drivers tell pedestrians who refuse to get out of their way what they can do with their baguettes. In Singapore, you can be flogged for chewing gum or spitting in public. In China, according to a Reuters news report, rudeness by employees who serve the public has gotten so bad that 50 phrases are now banned in such places as post offices, airports, train stations, hospitals, and stores. Among them are:

"Ask someone else."

"If you're not buying, what are you looking at?"

"Don't you see I'm busy?"

"What do you have ears for?"

Of course, here in America, we would never deal with rudeness by banning it. We'd set up a congressional committee to study it. And it would become the discussion flavor-of-the-week on all the talk shows ("I Threw a Pie at My Sister's Boyfriend," "Men Who Pick Their Noses in Public and the Women Who Love Them").

Unfortunately, nothing is going to change if we leave the sorry state of manners in the hands of adults. If adults were behaving themselves and teaching manners to their offspring as they should, we wouldn't be in this mess. So it's up to you. Do you want to inherit a rude, ugly world? Or do you want to do your part to restore kindness, consideration, and proper behavior to our society?

The place to start is in that anonymous public sphere. If every teenager does his or her part—if we can all use good manners *with people we don't even know*—we can all attend concerts, get from A to B, and step out into the Real World without being jostled and sworn at. Remember, the future of the human race depends on it.

How Rude!

The Survey Says . . .

Here, according to our survey of adults, are the 25 Rudest Things Teenagers Do in Public:

1. Use obscene language in loud voices.
2. Spit, burp, and belch.
3. Display too much affection in public.
4. Smoke where it's prohibited.
5. Pick their noses.
6. Not say "Please" or "Thank you" to sales people.
7. Talk back to their parents.
8. Make fun of older adults.
9. Fill all the seating in a public place and not offer it to senior citizens.
10. Litter.
11. Behave inconsiderately towards people with disabilities or elderly people on public transportation.
12. Tease small children.
13. Swear or yell at people passing by.
14. Flip the bird.
15. Walk five abreast on a sidewalk or in a narrow corridor.
16. Play loud music in crowded places.
17. Act rowdy in movies.
18. Push and shove in lines.
19. Let doors close in other people's faces (on purpose or accidentally).
20. Not observe boundaries regarding personal space.
21. Not respect people's differences.
22. Engage in conversation while serving the public (for example, cashier chatting with bagger during rush-hour shopping).
23. Write on other people's property.
24. Embarrass and insult one another.
25. Ridicule people with disabilities.

Bodies in Motion

Have you noticed that bodies in motion tend to collide? Or that doors were not designed to admit 15 people simultaneously? Of course you have, as you've gotten shoved, knocked, and gouged while walking down a school corridor or bus aisle. Take heart! Here's what you need to know to travel through life without getting your toes stepped on.

THE UPS AND DOWNS OF ELEVATOR BEHAVIOR

The *ifs, ands,* and *butts* of elevator etiquette are:

Uncommon Courtesies

- *If* you're entering an elevator, allow those exiting to get off first.
- *If* the elevator is crowded, people closest to the door should exit first.
- *If* you're in front of the door but it's not your floor, stand aside as best you can. Or take a walk on the wild side: Step out for a moment to let people off, then dart back in before the door closes again.
- *If* you need to get off and people are blocking the way, say "Excuse me" and gently move towards the front. This should not be confused with pushing, shoving, or elbowing.
- *If* you're standing by the control panel, press the "Door Open" and "Door Close" buttons to assist the efficient flow of traffic.
- *If* the elevator isn't crowded, it's considered polite for males to let women and girls leave first (and enter first).
- *And* whatever you do, don't stare, fart, push all the buttons, or pinch anyone's *butt*.

SANDWICHED ON THE SUBWAY

The protocol for subways is similar to that for elevators, and the same rules apply with regard to entering and exiting: Don't block the doors, stand aside, and let people get off before you get on.

While five-course formal subway dining is to be discouraged, a soda or snack may be consumed discreetly. Just be sure you don't smack your lips, leave crumbs, or spill anything.

Reading is a long-established tradition on subways. Looking over someone's shoulder is acceptable; breathing down the person's neck is not.

Trash must be carried off the train and deposited in a receptacle. Leaving a newspaper neatly on the seat, however, is not littering. It is sharing.

ESCALATORS AND SLIDEWALKS

The etiquette for escalators is simple:

- Don't crowd or push. Some people are understandably nervous on stairs that move by themselves. You wouldn't want to cause anyone to lose his balance and get sucked into that little crack at the top or bottom.
- Stand right. Pass left. Escalators are essentially divided highways, with two lanes in each direction. Standers should occupy the right lane so sprinters can get by on the left. If someone is blocking the passing lane, it's not

polite to tailgate or go "BEEEP! BEEEP! Outta the way!" A brief "Excuse me" is sufficient.

- Tie your shoes, pull up your pants, return your tongue to your mouth, and gather together your waist-length hair. Escalators love to eat anything loose and flowing.

The same rules apply to slidewalks.

"Is it bad manners to go up the down escalator?"

If people are on it, yes. If nobody's on it, it isn't bad manners. It's bad judgment. But if your sneakers are tied and there's no one in sight, go ahead and do it—just this once. ◆

PUBLIC BUSES

Bus riding is fraught with tension and danger: crowded aisles, not enough seats, traffic jams, fumes, people with packages, people with children, people who are late, people who are lost, people who forgot to put on their deodorant, people who are two seconds away from a megaspew. These are the building blocks of bad manners. To maintain some level of civilization, everybody's cooperation is required. Here's all you need to know to bus with the best:

- Let people off before you get on.
- Have your money or pass ready so you don't hold up the line.
- If you have to stand, move to the rear. If everybody crowds into two square feet at the front because one person is blocking the aisle, a cattle prod works wonders. If you don't have one handy, a simple "Excuse me, could I get by?" or "Could you please move down?" should suffice.
- If the bus is crowded, don't take up more than your fair share of space by spreading your belongings and/or body parts over several seats. Check that you're not in a seat reserved for the elderly or people with disabilities.
- When it's time to get off, there's no need to ring the bell more than once. You're not a clock striking twelve. And when you do alight, it's nice to thank the driver. Especially if you see him or her every day.
- According to tradition, ladies get on first so men can catch them if they fall backwards. Similarly, men get off first so they can turn and offer assistance to disembarking females. (Why it was once assumed that women were prone to falling on and off of buses is a mystery.)
- Finally, don't misspell the plural of bus. It's *buses,* not *busses,* no matter what the signs say. And, as you'll soon discover (if you haven't already), the two are very different.

"Sometimes I'm on a bus and the person next to me will try to start a conversation. I don't want to be rude, but my parents have told me to never talk to strangers. What should I do?"

This is a bit of a dilemma. If all people are strangers until you get to know them, and if you can't talk to people you don't know, then how will you ever get to know anyone? Bus drivers could start making introductions, but that's not likely to happen. So here's what I suggest: Talk to your parents about their prohibition. It may be in need of updating. It certainly makes sense not to talk to strangers if you're a seven-year-old kid taking the bus by yourself and some weird guy offers you candy. But if you're a teenager in a nice, safe place with lots of people around—like a public bus, a waiting room, or an airplane—it would be a shame to slam the door on the many interesting souls whose paths you will cross. I mean, just think of the friendships, marriages, and business deals that all began with one stranger saying to another "Excuse me, but I couldn't help noticing the book you're reading."

If someone persists in having a conversation against your wishes, you can move to another seat (ideally, one close to the driver or another adult). Or say "I'm sorry, I don't mean to be rude, but I have a test tomorrow and I need to use this time to think about my answers."

By the same token, if you're the initiator of the conversation, be alert to signs that your overtures are unwanted. If they are, pipe down. ◆

OFFERING SOMEONE YOUR SEAT

This doesn't mean *giving up* your behind. It means *getting off* your behind. Few gestures are so easy, so appreciated, and so underutilized as this one. If you're in a crowded waiting room, or you're traveling on a bus, subway, or train, offer your seat to someone who could use it more than you. This could be a person who's elderly, injured, disabled, pregnant, loaded down with tons of packages, or carrying a baby. It could be a little kid who has a hard time standing, or a running back with a broken leg. It doesn't matter whether they're old or young, big or small, male or female. All that matters is that you notice the need and offer to help.

If they're adults, you might simply say "Ma'am, would you care to sit down?" or "Sir, would you like a seat?" For people your age or younger, you can dispense with "Sir" and "Ma'am," but avoid "Hey, you!"

People may thank you and decline your kind offer, in which case you'll feel great because you asked (*and* got to keep your seat), and they'll feel great because of your thoughtfulness.

How Rude!

Giving up your seat can be tough. There will be days when you'll be the one who's exhausted, sore from practice, or lugging a bag of books. At those times, you'll just have to make a judgment call as to whose need is greater, yours or the other person's. But here's a situation where having the right attitude can help. When you find yourself thinking:

Why do I have to give up my seat? Why doesn't someone else do it for a change? It's not fair. I'm tired and I got here first!

try thinking:

I sure am glad I don't have a hard time walking, or a broken collarbone, or a thousand things to carry, or a screaming kid in a stroller.

"Do I really have to call adults 'Sir' and 'Ma'am'?"

You don't *have* to, but there are reasons why you may *want* to. Addressing adults with "Sir" and "Ma'am" is a near-extinct custom in the United States. While this is bad news for society as a whole, it's good news for you: Simply by using these little words, you can reap fabulous rewards with virtually no effort! Any teenager who says "Yes, Ma'am" or "No, Sir" or "Excuse me, Ma'am" is automatically given a halo and a badge of honor by the adult so addressed. These are redeemable for many wonderful things: respect, trust, privileges, jobs, unsought-for gifts, and, best of all, the sense of confidence and self-worth you get when you know your behavior is appreciated and admired by others. Try it and see for yourself. ◆

CARPOOLING PROTOCOLS

Unless you're a city kid who gets around by public transportation, or a country kid who travels by mule, chances are you're a frequent carpooler. The idea behind carpools is that parents trade off misery. Actually, many parents like to drive carpool. It's how they learn all the neighborhood gossip and check out their children's friends. Since your mobility depends on staying in the good graces of these saints who moonlight as chauffeurs, here are some tips for being a tip-top traveler. Follow them, and adults will beg for the opportunity to drive you around.

Watch for your ride. This not only spares someone from having to come to your door, it spares the neighbors from being honked at daily at 7:00 A.M.

Be on time. Don't make everyone else late just because you are. Rather than keep anyone waiting, finish your muffin, your homework, and your toilette* in the car.

Don't be a no-show. If you won't be gracing the carpool with your presence, send advance word. This ensures that the carpool will neither wait for you in vain nor show up at your door for naught.

Swap favorite seats. There's no need to argue over who gets to ride shotgun. This is the computer age. Input days of the week, routes, vehicles, seat preferences, and nonnegotiables such as driver rules and babies in car seats. Then let the computer figure out a seating chart and rotation schedule.

Don't stick your head out the sunroof. In the event of a sudden stop, the sunroof could fly forward and decapitate you. This would not only cause your head to go on without you, but could also lead to a nasty lawsuit that would make things quite tense in the carpool.

Wear your seatbelt. Seatbelts save lives, and yours is worth saving.

Uncommon
Courtesies

  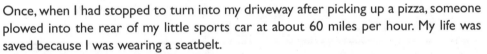

TRUE STORIES FROM THE MANNERS FRONTIER
Re: A Pizza

Once, when I had stopped to turn into my driveway after picking up a pizza, someone plowed into the rear of my little sports car at about 60 miles per hour. My life was saved because I was wearing a seatbelt.

The pizza was not so fortunate. All the toppings flew off, and when I opened the box I found a soggy mess of mushed cheese and mutilated pepperonis. To add insult to injury, my insurance company would not reimburse me for the cost of the pizza.

The moral of this story is: *Always check to see if your automobile policy includes pizza coverage.*

Don't make a mess in the car. While the discreet watercress sandwich is permissible, anything that drips, stains, or drops crumbs upon seats or seatmates is not.

No fighting. Physical or verbal fighting can result in the driver pulling to the side of the road to wait. This is one of life's most awkward moments. The

---

* This most certainly does not mean that you should go to the bathroom in someone else's Bronco. One's *toilette* is "the act or process of dressing or grooming oneself."

How Rude!

passengers sit in sheepish silence, or worse, say things like "She started it!" To avoid such embarrassment, squelch your squabbles.

Take your belongings. Most carpools have two phases. Phase One is the dropping off of children. Phase Two is the dropping off of everything they left behind. Try to remember your possessions. Abandoned backpacks, homework, volcano models, and tuna sandwiches have been known to disappear forever into the great beyond beneath the back seat.

Avoid making startling noises. If you suddenly scream "LOOK OUT!" the driver will assume you're speaking to her rather than to Ginny Taylor, whose jar of nail polish is about to spill. Sudden movements should also be avoided.

TRUE STORIES FROM THE
MANNERS FRONTIER
What's for Lunch?

I was once driving a station wagon full of six-year-olds (what possessed me to do so remains a mystery) when a lunchbox came flying into the front seat. It turned out that one of the boys in the way back, unable to "hold it" any longer, had relieved himself. The owner of said lunchbox, upon discovering that it contained an unwanted beverage, had flung it away, Jurassic Park and all. Only my nerves of steel saved us from a potentially dangerous situation.

The moral of this story belongs on our list of carpooling protocols: *Be sure to go to the bathroom before leaving home.*

Always thank the driver. Adults who drive children around a lot are at high risk of developing a medical condition known as Carpool Tunnel Syndrome. Its symptoms include a sore butt, fatigue, feeling unappreciated, and nightmares in which the rest of one's life is spent behind the wheel of a car full of noisy teenagers. Sufferers typically report that they have hallucinations of school parking lots, shopping malls, skating rinks, soccer fields, and freeways at rush hour.

There's no known treatment for this affliction. But it can be prevented if carpool passengers offer the driver their sincere thanks each and every time they alight from the car. Do this even if the driver happens to be your parent. Also, the child who brings the driver an occasional flower or cupcake will never lack for a ride.

"I'm in a lot of different carpools. There's one mother who's always late picking us up from hockey practice. I wouldn't mind, except I have to get to a job and this makes me late, which gets me in trouble with my boss. What can I do?"

Uncommon
Courtesies

You might say something like this:

"Mrs. Murphy, I want to thank you for driving me all these times, but I'm afraid I'm going to have to drop out of the carpool. You see, I have a job, and I'm just not getting there on time, and this is causing problems for me at work."

Notice that you're not blaming her for being late. You're simply presenting a set of facts. If she's perceptive, she'll put two and two together and come up with something like this:

"Oh, dear, I'd hate to lose your company. Let me see if I can pick you all up earlier."

If she isn't perceptive and doesn't put two and two together, you'll have to make alternate arrangements or try to change your hours at work.

Lack of punctuality is one of the most common and offensive forms of rudeness. People who are perpetually late always have explanations:

"Traffic was so bad." (Then you should have left earlier.)
"I had to stop at the cleaners." (You could have done that afterwards.)
"The phone rang." (You didn't have to answer it.)
"I just lost track of the time." (Then pay better attention.)

What they fail to realize is that an explanation isn't the same as an excuse. Lateness is rude because it implies that "my time is more valuable than your time," and it often sets up a chain of lateness that can affect others for hours or days to come. Lateness is excusable only when it results from events beyond one's control or unforeseen circumstances that are truly worthy of being given a higher priority. The fact that one person is doing another a favor doesn't absolve him of the responsibility for being on time.

It's very difficult for a child or teenager to call an adult on being late. The best way to do it is indirectly. If your piano teacher always runs behind schedule, you could say:

"Mr. Liszt, would it be easier for you if I came at 4:30 instead of 4:00? I noticed that you always give people extra time, and this way you wouldn't have to worry about keeping me waiting."

Notice how skillfully you cloak your message. You credit your teacher for being generous with his time and for feeling bad about keeping people waiting. But what you're really saying is "I hate having to sit around twiddling my thumbs every time I come for a lesson."

Another way to deal with the lateness of adults is by asking your parents to intervene on your behalf. Finally, always have a book, a sketchpad, some homework, a video game, or a personal stereo with you. That way, you can at least make use of the time you spend waiting.

If it's peers who are always late, you can be more assertive. Warn repeat offenders that a new policy is in effect by saying:

"Please be sure you get here on time. We're going to leave at 8:30 sharp, and I'd feel terrible if we had to go without you."

If they don't arrive by the appointed hour, give them a tiny grace period and then leave. Let them experience the consequences of their tardiness. If you're consistent, they'll shape up. ◆

BANNING BACKPACK ATTACKS

With all the focus on keeping guns and knives out of children's hands, it's amazing how little attention has been paid to the most dangerous weapon of all—backpacks. The Health Information Clearinghouse for Children Using Packs (HICCUP) estimates that more people are injured each year in backpack attacks than from biking, 'boarding, and 'blading combined. Most of those assaulted were minding their own business when someone turned or pushed past them and BAM!

Most perpetrators are unaware of the destruction they cause, which is scant comfort to the victims of this violence. But satchel savagery has got to stop! And it can—with a little help from you and your friends.

There are several things you can do to keep your canvas out of someone's kisser. If you're running, recognize that your purse, pack, or bag will be bouncing wildly to and fro. Allow extra clearance around objects, human or otherwise, that you pass.

If you're in a crowded setting like a bus or sidewalk, pretend that you're driving a car. Good drivers know exactly how much space their car occupies. This is useful information if you don't want to make a habit of clobbering pedestrians and clipping parked cars. Get to know how much space you occupy. A small backpack or shoulder bag may add as much as a foot to your upper body depth. A large backpack with a sleeping bag, bed roll, pick ax, and satellite dish may add several feet to your girth. Calculate your clearance before you pass fellow travelers on the road of life. If it's going to be tight, say "Excuse me, I don't want to hit you with my pack" as you squeeze by. And then, as your pack L. L. Beans them, which it inevitably will, they will at least be comforted by your good manners.

FEAR OF FLYING

Flying can be stressful. Bouncing through bad weather has a way of making people think they're going to miss their connection, hurl their lunch, or die. Throw in jet lag, airline food, a few screaming babies, and smokers having to go *two whole hours* (or longer) without a cigarette, and you've got a recipe for frayed nerves and bad manners.

Air travel used to be an elegant, civilized mode of transportation, but not anymore. In recent years, alleged adults have been arrested for having temper tantrums when told to put out cigarettes on nonsmoking flights. A food fight broke out on a Northwest Airlines plane when travelers were denied drinks. A Saudi princess attacked a flight attendant (and vowed to have her and the captain assassinated) for what she perceived as poor service on a Paris-to-Boston TWA flight. And an inebriated banker flying from Buenos Aires to New York— let's see, how shall we put this—defecated on a food trolley.

TRUE STORIES FROM THE
MANNERS FRONTIER
The Brothers Slobola

I was waiting for a flight to Paris in the international lounge of a major U.S. airport when my attention was drawn to a family of slobs. There was Mama Slob, Papa Slob,

How Rude!

and two grown-up, twentysomething Baby Slobs. They were sprawled over eighteen seats so nobody else could sit down. They were eating enough food to feed a frat house for a year, dripping juice and condiments all over the floor. And they were talking in loud, vulgar voices.

It was just my luck that the brothers Slobola claimed the middle section of five seats in the same row in which I was sitting (row 11, for you aviation buffs). Shortly after the flight took off, my attention was drawn to the brothers S. by a loud snorting sound. One of them, to the great amusement of his sibling, was blowing his nose into the barf bag. This was followed by a game of who could flip his reading light on and off faster.

We are not talking five-year-olds here. We are talking twenty-five-year-olds. My nausea was complete when, right after dinner, one of the brothers removed his shirt (allowing me to count the 38 layers of his stomach) and lay down across five seats to go to sleep. Yes, all night I could listen to him snoring and watch his hairy belly rise and fall. My only comfort was the thought that the French, who are a bit more fastidious about these things, might deny him and his family entry into their country based on aesthetic grounds.

Alas, they didn't, and my faith in the French was severely shaken as I watched the brothers Slobola pass through customs, giggling, snorting, and saying "Bone-jure, bone-jure" to each other.

How can you do your part to restore some civility to the once friendly skies?

- Before boarding, anticipate what you'll want to keep at your seat. This way, you can stow your carry-on bags quickly and efficiently, and 300 people won't have to wait while you stand in the aisle deciding which tapes to listen to during the flight.

- Don't throw up on your neighbor. Use the airsickness (a.k.a. barf) bag. If you're feeling queasy, take deep breaths. Aim the little fresh-air nozzle at your face. Pretend that you're lying on a calm, sunny beach.

- If you recline your seat back, do it slowly so the person behind you doesn't suddenly get a tray table in the jaw.

- Try not to tap, kick, or knee gouge the seat in front of you. (**TIP:** If you sit in an emergency exit row, the backs of the seats in front of you won't recline all the way for reasons of safety. This gives you a bit more room.)

- If you're sitting at an inside seat and want to get out, say "Excuse me, may I please get by?" Your neighbor will then either get up and stand in the aisle or remain seated. People who do the latter usually make a futile effort to occupy less space. This is a signal that means *Okay, you can step over me, but please don't crush my toes or land in my lap.* Restrain yourself from getting up 11 times an hour or when meals have just been served.

- If it's rush hour in the cabin bathrooms, this is not the time to count your freckles or braid your hair. Schedule major grooming tasks for off-peak periods.

- NEVER flush an airplane toilet if you're sitting on it. The suction is so great that you could easily be drawn into the toilet and expelled over Kansas.

- Flight attendants have demanding jobs. Try not to keep asking "Are we there yet?" "How much longer?" "What time is it?" "Did you hear that noise?" "Are the wings going to fall off?"

- Avoid pushing the call button every two minutes to ask for 1) a soda, 2) peanuts, 3) another soda, 4) a towelette, 5) aspirin, 6) a deck of cards, 7) a magazine, 8) another soda, and/or 9) a pair of Junior Captain's Wings. Issue your requests when the attendant comes to serve you, or during quiet times when meals aren't being served.

- If you place something in an overhead compartment, stow it securely so it doesn't topple onto the next person who opens the door. Try not to squash other packages; items carried into the cabin are often fragile, and you may inadvertently crush an ancient Etruscan vase destined for the Metropolitan Museum of Art.

- Disputes over reading lights and window shades have led to countless airborne etiquette atrocities. Here are some suggestions for nonviolent compromise when interests conflict:
  - If a movie is being shown, lower your window shade. Even if you've seen the movie and want to look at the pretty clouds, one unshaded window can make it difficult for others to watch the film (which is already difficult on those tiny screens). If the flight is long enough for a movie, there'll be time to look out the window after it's finished.
  - If you want to read, it's fine to turn your reading lamp on during a movie or at night when others are trying to sleep. Once you're through, remember to turn it off so it doesn't needlessly shine in someone else's eyes.

- Some people are sensitive to the clickity-clack of laptop computers. If you'd like to sleep and your seatmate will be up all night writing the annual report, move to a different seat. If none are available, ask the flight attendant if he or she can find someone who won't mind switching seats with you.

Finally, this is *really* serious, so PAY CLOSE ATTENTION: Never, *ever* joke about bombs or hijacking at or near airports or aboard airplanes. First, such jokes are usually rude and unfunny. Second, they can get you arrested.

Uncommon
Courtesies

How Rude!

THE INS AND OUTS OF DOORWAY DECORUM

As you enter and leave bus terminals, subway stations, airports, and various other public buildings, you may notice obstacles that have been placed in your path. These are called *doors*. They needn't pose a problem to you or others if you adhere to the following basic guidelines:

- When you approach a pull door, look to see if there are any people about to enter or leave who might have difficulty opening it on their own. If you see someone in a wheelchair, or pushing a stroller, or on crutches, or laden with packages or babies, it's very gracious to step aside and hold the door open for him or her.

- If there's someone on your heels who appears nondisabled and unburdened, you needn't hold the door. But do keep it open so he or she can grab it after you've passed through. (Otherwise, it's like being in the woods and letting a branch swing back and smack somebody in the face.)

- Where automatic electric-eye doors are concerned, it isn't necessary to leap in front of others, place yourself in the sensor beam, and say "Please, allow me."

Revolving doors were invented for people who are never quite sure whether they're coming or going. These dizzifying doorways are fraught with danger. So stay alert, or you could emerge from the spin cycle with your foot on the sidewalk and your head in the lobby.

- Revolving doors should never be rotated at more than a moderate walking speed. The object is to enter or leave a building, not to launch someone into space. If you happen to be going around with an elderly person or a three-year-old on a sit-down strike, the polite thing to do is reduce speed to the slowest common denominator. Use your cellular phone to cancel the afternoon's appointments.

- In the olden days, this was the traditional male-female protocol: If the door was already in motion, the woman entered first. The male followed and, with a light touch of his powerful hand, kept it spinning. If the door was not moving, the man got in first. He used his fabulous muscle power to get it going while the lady stepped into the compartment behind. Today it's considered proper for the pusher to be either male or female, depending on who's in possession of more strength and/or gallantry on a given day.

- Except for parents with small children and couples in perfect harmony, it's one person per compartment. Two tend to tangle, and woe to anyone who falls down.

- Otherwise well-behaved children are permitted, twice a year, to spin round and round and miss their exit, provided they establish a lookout who will warn them at the first sign of an approaching passenger.

Self-Propelled

Having looked at protocols for public transportation, let us now turn our attention to personal transportation systems—skates, bicycles, skateboards, skis, snowboards, and feet.

Uncommon Courtesies

The main courtesy you can offer as a self-propelled person is to *not run into anybody.* This means watching where you're going. And yielding to those with the right-of-way. On a sidewalk, the right-of-way belongs to those who are walking. (Note that it's called a side*walk*, not a side*blade, -bike,* or *-board.*) If you're jogging or cruising along a sidewalk on anything that rolls, it's your job to control your speed and course so you don't knock anybody down or scare them to death.*

Following are more courtesy pointers for the self-propelled:

INLINE SKATING

Faster than a speeding bullet. Able to leap tall buildings in a single bound. Superman? Nah. You—on your inline skates.

'Blading has swept the world. In 1995 alone, an estimated 105,000 skaters were stitched, set, realigned, patched, and put back together again in hospital emergency rooms—and 42 percent of the injuries were sustained by youths between the ages of 10 and 14.** Nothing can spoil an outing more than two broken wrists, a snapped femur, and eight crushed ribs. Here are some inline skating tips that will keep you in the pink:

- Take some lessons. Practice before you set out in search of crowded or tricky skating venues. Learn how to start, turn, cruise, and stop. *Especially* learn how to stop. It's rude to barrel into innocent bystanders.

- Don't be caught dead without a helmet. (Nearly all of the 42 reported inline skating fatalities since 1992 involved skaters who weren't wearing helmets.) Always wear guards on your wrists, elbows, knees, and other body parts you'd like to keep intact. For night skating, wear reflective gear, safety lamps, twinkling Christmas lights, etc.

- Yield the right-of-way. If you must skate on a sidewalk, it's your responsibility to maintain control at all times so as not to knock pedestrians into next week.

- Keep to the right. Don't sway from side to side and hog the entire path. If you want to pass someone, look behind you before pulling into the passing lane. Then check to make sure there's no oncoming traffic. Don't suddenly zoom past the skater you're overtaking. Say "On your left" as you approach.

---

* Similarly, someone on foot should yield the right-of-way to skiers on a slope or skateboarders in a skatepark.

** The statistics in this section come from the U.S. Consumer Products Safety Commission.

- Adjust your speed to path conditions. Slow down if it's crowded. Slow down for small children clogging your artery. Slow down for gravel, oil, tar, grass clippings, leaf piles, water, and large objects blocking your way. Otherwise you're liable to go sprawling, and it's rude to obstruct the trail with your splayed body.

- If you see a dog to the far *right* of the path and a human to the far *left* of the path (or vice versa), it's likely that the two are connected by a leash. Prepare to leap, limbo, or leave the path.

- Watch out for hazards. History has shown that inline skaters were not meant to roll over steel grates, bumpy manhole covers, roadkill, tree limbs, or human limbs.

- If you need to stop or rest, pull off the path. (Would you stop your car in the middle of a superhighway to check your map?)

- If you wear headphones, keep the volume very low. You need to be able to hear people say "On your left" or "Look out! A truck is heading your way!"

- Refrain from carrying objects that will interfere with your balance or the safe passage of others.

- Try to avoid skating in the street. If this is impossible, skate in the direction of the traffic. Unless you enjoy getting whomped in the stomach, be on the lookout for car doors that open into your path.

- Use your turn signals.

BICYCLING

Bicyclists should follow the same rules as inline skaters: wear a helmet, use safety lights at night, yield to pedestrians, ride with the traffic, watch out for car doors, dogs, and other hazards of the road, be alert to dangerous pavement conditions, check for oncoming or overtaking traffic when riding on bike paths, etc. In addition:

- Don't park your bike where others will trip over it. It's natural to want to lock your bike where you can keep an eye on it or where you think it will be safest. But don't block steps, stoops, sidewalks, entrances, or railings.

SKATEBOARDING

If there was ever a sport that belongs to the young, it's skateboarding. (Have you ever seen a 70-year-old stick a nollie five-O heelflip? Me neither.) So it was with great excitement that I plunged into the culture of youth to inquire into the protocols of skateboarding.

TRUE STORIES FROM THE
MANNERS FRONTIER
Totally Rad

I spied a pleasant-looking lad skating fast and gnarly down the street.

"Excuse me, young sir," I said. "May I interrupt your switchstance frontside kickflip long enough to ask you a question?"

"Sure, dude."

"Could you please enlighten me as to the rules of skateboarding?"

"Rooooools?" he replied.

"Quite. Do's and don'ts. Common courtesies. Codes of behavior. No-no's. That is to say—rules."

"Rooooools?"

Perhaps I needed to approach a skater with a more extensive vocabulary. Out of the corner of my eye, I detected a fast-moving, knee-padded youth.

"Excuse me," I said.

"Dude?"

"Yes, young sir, and might I congratulate you on that totally rad nollie noseblunt slide?"

"Dude?"

"Could you be so kind as to tell me, what might a skateboarder have to do to be considered rude?"

"Dude?"

"Rude?"

"Rude? Dude?"

Oh, dear. I wasn't making much headway with this concept. I decided on a new plan of attack. I would talk to the manager of my neighborhood skatepark. Surely a commercial establishment for skateboard enthusiasts would post a proper code of conduct.

I entered a warehouse in which was housed a mountain range of ramps, funboxes, and railings, as well as a regiment of whirling, airborne youth. As I watched these healthy striplings execute feats of physical prowess and derring-do, I was consumed with one thought: *How do their pants stay on?*

I located the service counter. A shaved-headed personage in his late teens approached me.

"Hey, dude," he said.

"Dude," I replied.

We then proceeded to have a lengthy conversation in which the bald dude elucidated the protocols of the skateboarding subculture. I will summarize them here: *Don't run into anybody.*

How Rude!

The basic principle skateboarders follow is this: *Chill.* Central to chilling is the avoidance of collisions. Towards that end, these remarkable young men on their flying machines exhibit extraordinary vigilance and courtesy. They give the right-of-way to those who are airborne. They wait patiently while their compatriots execute frontside 50-50 fakie heelflips. They don't step into the path of those in motion. And if a fellow enthusiast should monopolize the ramps, they don't get angry. They lay down some mellow vibes and say "Hey, dude."

I take off my helmet to these wholesome youths. I believe that every community in America should provide skateboard parks for its young citizens. But until they do, kids on skateboards will have to use public sidewalks and plazas. And they will want to observe the following rules:

- Yield the right-of-way to pedestrians.
- Don't ollie up a park bench if someone is sitting on it.
- Don't grind or backside lipslide on a handrail if someone is holding on to it.

The skateboarding community was so well-chilled in their receptivity to my queries that I can't wait to do further research in this domain. I already know what my first question will be: *Why don't more girls skateboard?*

SKIING AND SNOWBOARDING

Skiing is my favorite sport. I love the feeling of snot icicles hanging from my nose. And the thrill of careening down a 78-degree incline with my shades so fogged I can't see the forest for the tree I just ran into. And the sheer joy of standing on a mountaintop with the windchill at minus 166 degrees. It does wonders for my confidence to swoop down a slope as three-year-olds ski circles around me. And then it's on to the lodge, where the rich aromas of mulled cider, crackling logs, and sweat-drenched socks waft through the air.

To make sure that we all have a pleasant time on the slopes, here are a dozen ski tips:

1. Remember that skiing and snowboarding are dangerous sports that require your full attention if you don't want somebody's pole up your nose. The trail map for the Killington Ski Resort in Vermont lists several of the hazards that are part of the sport's challenge: "Snow, ice, moguls, spines, rolls, jumps, snowmaking mounds, shear drop-offs, bare ground, rocks, roots, stumps, trees, lift towers, ruts, bumps, snowmaking equipment, grooming vehicles, snowmobiles, [and] power poles." To this I would add "grizzly bears and out-of-control teenagers on snowboards." Stay alert for changing weather and terrain conditions.

2. Ski or snowboard only on designated trails, slopes, glades, and zones. In Vermont, if you ski off of designated areas, you're liable for all search and rescue expenses. A bill of $278,549 could put a crimp in your ski budget for next season.

Uncommon Courtesies

3. Never ski or snowboard alone. This is a no-brainer. Should you make an unscheduled departure from the trail, or injure yourself in a fall, you want to have a friend who knows where you are and can go for help. While woodpeckers are good company, they can't summon the ski patrol.

4. Know how to read the trail markings. Those double black diamonds don't mean "This Way to a Poker Game." They mean you're about to descend an advanced expert trail. A rope across a trail means the trail is closed, which means don't go down it.

5. Learn how to ride the lift before trying to get on. Ask a friend or the lift operator for instructions. Most lift operators would rather slow the lift to help you than stop it to untangle you from the bars.

6. Don't drop anything from the lift. Many trails go under or alongside ski lifts. It's rude to drop a soda can or boot on the people below. On a related note: Stow your trash properly. The pristine beauty of nature is part of the joy of skiing. Look for a slopeside trash receptacle.

7. Maintain control. Quite a few fearless teenagers begin their skiing or snowboarding careers by pointing themselves downhill and shoving off. Quite a few end up in ski resort hospitals. Don't ski beyond your ability to stop, turn, and avoid people and objects.

8. Yield the right-of-way to people ahead of you. If you pass other skiers, give them a wide berth. If the trail is narrow, or the skiers you're overtaking are schussing from side to side, say "On your left" or "On your right" prior to passing. Don't say "Through your legs."

9. Never stop on a trail and obstruct it. Skiers don't like to catch air over a crest and find another skier in the way. Be sure you're visible from above. Move to the edge for extended pit stops.

10. When you enter a trail or start downhill, look uphill. Those skiers already comin' 'round the mountain have the right-of-way.

11. Don't forget to use straps or other devices to prevent your skis or snowboard from continuing downhill without you. Unless you enjoy taking long and slippery hikes back to the lodge.

12. Stop when you're tired. Accidents are more likely to happen when skiers are weary and muscles are exhausted. Head for the lodge. Between

How Rude!

food, beverages, video games, more food, movies, saunas, blazing hearths, hot tubs, and ski bums and bummettes, you should find all sorts of things to keep you occupied.

And finally: Always wear your jammies to pipe jams.

ON FOOT

You wouldn't believe what a perilous place a sidewalk can be. So you don't get arrested for reckless reconnoitering, here are some protocols for polite promenading:

Sidewalk conventions. You wouldn't park your car in the middle of the street. By the same reasoning, don't park yourself in the middle of the sidewalk to have a conversation. Step to the edge. Don't force others to detour off the walk or pass between you.

Sidewalk snowplows. Sidewalks, like stairways, are two-way. That means each direction is entitled to no more than one-half its width. If there's no one coming the other way, then five of you can walk abreast. But if people *are* coming the other way, don't run them off the road. (Not only is this rude, it's intimidating.) Retreat to your lanes and let other walkers by.

Sidewalk shuffles. These are the mortifying maneuvers that occur when you're on a collision course with somebody and, to avoid them at the last minute, you go to your right just as they go to their left, and you counter-correct but so do they, and the two of you spend most of the afternoon shuffling back and forth unable to get by each other. Not only is this a total waste of time; it also makes you feel like an idiot.

The way to avoid sidewalk shuffles is to pretend you're a jet aircraft. Two planes speeding towards each other don't wait until the last moment to take evasive action. If there's even a chance that they might collide, one of them immediately changes course. So, if you and another person are walking towards each other with even the slightest possibility of intersection, make a sharp correction by changing lanes early on. Usually, this means moving to your right.

Sidewalk chicken. In sidewalk shuffles, you end up in somebody's face because of inattention, or a failure to walk defensively and anticipate the moves of other pedestrians. No ill will was intended, and both parties feel equally moronic. In sidewalk chicken, you walk down the sidewalk as if you own it. This means YOU DON'T MOVE FOR NOBODY! Not one inch. But that's okay. Because everyone else will be chicken and get out of your way.

You can always tell when you've passed one of these sidewalk marauders, because they're the ones who bang their shoulders or jackets or bags or purses into you. They're the ones who make you step off the curb, scrunch against a building, or turn sideways to avoid getting crunched. They're the ones with the look that says *What do you think you're doing on my sidewalk, you little warthog?* Unfortunately, there's not much you can do about them. But you can silently thank them as they run you off the road. For it's people like this who remind us how unattractive bad manners really are.

Pushing buttons. By all means, push the button that stops traffic at an intersection so you may cross the street safely. But if you do push it, WAIT FOR THE "WALK" SIGNAL! Don't push the button as insurance in case you can't jaywalk, and then waltz across the street at the first opportunity. It's not fair to make traffic come to a standstill while you're already halfway down the block.

"Aren't men supposed to walk on the outside of women?"

No. Walking on women is never proper. There is, however, a tradition of men walking on the outside of the *sidewalk* when escorting women down the street. In olden days, this offered the woman some protection against slop from above and slush from below.* Today, however, we have dry cleaning. And we recognize that the greatest sources of muck are no longer windows and roadways but politicians and talk shows. Young men who aspire to be gentlemen can do no wrong by walking on the street side of a lady. I mean, you gotta walk someplace. But true gentlemen have the sensitivity to accept the reciprocation of such thoughtful protection from the women of their acquaintance. ◆

Baby carriages. Sidewalks usually have strollers on them. And strollers usually have babies in them. And people with babies are usually stressed out. Why? Try diapers, crying, being up all night, teething, screaming, wiping up spills, more diapers, and other joys of parenting.

You can do two things to help harried parents with babies in strollers: First, hold doors open for them. Second, offer to help carry the stroller up and down steps and stairs. Just make sure you have a firm grip, or the stroller could tip upside down. While this would be a good lesson in gravity for the baby, it wouldn't go over well with the parent.

---

* In the days before indoor plumbing, people relieved themselves during the night in chamber pots, which they then dumped out their windows in the morning. (I'm not making this up!)

Behind the Wheel

If someone made a graph of parental worry, it would look something like this.

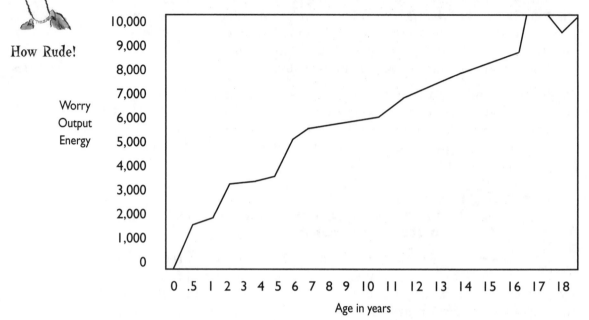

Worry Output Energy

Age in years

You can see that although parental worrying increases with the child's age, it does not do so in a straight line. Rather, it rises in fits (as in "Mom's having a hissy") and starts ("You can start by showing some responsibility"). Worrywartologists (scientists who study the protective instincts of parents) have determined that each jump in WOE (Worry Output Energy) can be traced to an increase in the child's mobility.

Thus, the surge around four months occurs when the infant is able to turn over and move around in her crib. Up to this point, parents only had to worry about their child being attacked by her teddy bear in the middle of the night. Soon the child will be able to crawl. This triggers worries such as:

What if she crawls under the sofa and won't come out?
What if I step on her?

Once the child learns to walk, new worries surface:

What if she climbs the stairs?
What if she goes into the street?
What if she tracks mud across the kitchen floor?

Worry increases in quantum leaps as the child becomes skateboard mobile:

What if she smashes her kneecap?

inline-skate mobile:

What if she breaks her wrists?

bike mobile:

What if she cracks her head open?

and auto-mobile:

What if she DENTS THE CAR?

The minute you get your driver's license, parental anxiety goes off the charts. Your parents will worry that their insurance premiums will skyrocket; that you'll get stopped for speeding, run someone over, or have an accident; that you'll drink and drive, that your friends will drink and drive, or that other drivers will drink and drive; that you'll be hurt, maimed, disabled, or killed. Most of all, they'll worry that you'll spend too much time in the backseat, and you won't be looking for quarters.

Their worries are not groundless. Forty-four percent of all teenagers are involved in a crash before their 17th birthday, and motor vehicle accidents are the #1 killer of 16- to 19-year-olds, accounting for nearly 40 percent of all deaths in that age group.

What you must remember is that your driving puts your parents' two most precious possessions—you and their car—together in the same place at the same time. Your parents' love for you, combined with your love for vehicular independence, makes teenage driving an emotionally charged arena for disputes. These can be minimized if you follow certain rules of the etiquette road:

Negotiate up-front. Before you get your license, impress your parents with your maturity (always a good thing to do when the issue is your driving). Ask them how they'd like to handle such issues as insurance, gas, maintenance, reserving the car, whether you can take the car when they aren't around, etc.

Don't litter. Clean up all candy wrappers, food, paper bags, and soda cans that you and your friends bring into the car.

Take good care of the car. Maybe a Taurus wagon isn't your dream car, but it's better than no car. Without being asked, give it a wash and a vacuum from time to time. Check the tires and fluid levels. Wax it twice a year.

Turn your driving into a family asset. Help your parents to realize the benefits that accrue from your new mobility. Offer to do errands in the car that your parents would normally have to do—and make good on your offer.

Give your parents gas. When people hop into a car, they are often in a hurry. They need to get to work, pick someone up, catch a plane. It's very annoying to get into a car (especially if it's your own) and discover that the previous driver left a thimbleful of fuel in the tank. Never return the car empty. Fill 'er up. Make an agreement with your parents about who pays. For example, if you use most of a tank for your personal driving, you should pay to fill it. If you use most of a tank for a combination of personal driving and errands for your parents, you can split the costs. If your folks do most of the driving, tell them you'll happily keep the tank topped if they'll keep your funds from running on empty.

Turn off the radio. Parents are fragile creatures with sensitive ears. They don't like to turn the key and get blasted out of their seat by a thousand decibels of hard rock when they were expecting the sweet purr of the engine.

Return the dial to your parents' radio station. A lot of parents listen to just one favorite station when driving. For some reason, they find it annoying to have to bump those digitals all the way from 106.3 back to 89.7. You can avoid this rude shock to their system, which could result in a rude shock to *your* system, by restoring the dial to the station to which it was tuned.

Return the seat to your parents' position. Tiny moms dislike getting into the driver's seat after their 6'4" sons have pushed it all the way back. And 6'4" moms dislike smashing their knees on the steering wheel after their tiny teens have pushed the seat all the way up. If your car has memory buttons for different seat positions, then each time you leave it, reset the seat to the preferred position of the person likely to drive the car next. If your car doesn't have presets, return the seat to the approximate position you found it in.

Finally: When your parents agree to let you drive—and especially when they agree to let you drive the family car—they are assuming that you are mature enough to handle it. Don't disappoint them. In fact, you should probably make a special effort to act *more* mature at home. This will help to reassure them that you won't drive like all those rude, impatient, and dangerous so-called ADULTS on the highway.

ON THE ROAD

Once you get behind the wheel, new rules come into effect. The rules of the road. Or, in other words, the rules of the jungle. For that's what it's like out there.

You should see what goes on in Boston, home of baked beans and steamed motorists. This city boasts the rudest drivers on the face of the planet. To the typical Boston driver, green means "Twice the speed limit." Yellow means

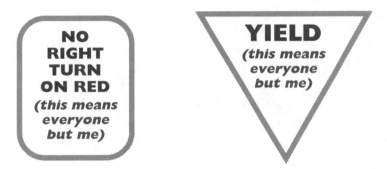
Uncommon
Courtesies

"What do you MEAN I'm too immature to use the car?!?!?!?"

"Pedal to the metal!" And red means "Outta my way, you moron!" Boston motorists are trained from birth to add the words *This Means Everyone But Me* to road signs. Thus, we have:

> **NO RIGHT TURN ON RED**
> *(this means everyone but me)*

> **YIELD**
> *(this means everyone but me)*

If a Boston driver runs you over in a crosswalk, he (or she) will get out of the car, rush back, and give you the finger. One motorist was shot dead for having the effrontery to beep at the inattentive driver in front of him. Naturally, the police are very concerned about the lawless barbarism on the Beantown byways. This is why they spend all their time handing out parking tickets.

Some of the rudest behavior *Homo sapiens* is capable of occurs behind the wheel of a car. There's no stopping the "ME FIRST!" mentality when it's reinforced by 4,000 pounds of steel. People feel anonymous and protected when

How Rude!

driving. They do things they wouldn't dare to do if they were in a face-to-face encounter with another human being.

Take tailgating, for example. Motorists think nothing of roaring down the highway at 60 miles per hour two inches behind the car in front of them. But they wouldn't dream of walking down the sidewalk two inches behind another pedestrian.

Or how about honking. If some poor guy doesn't burn rubber within .000001 seconds of the light turning green, the Very Important Person behind him blasts him out of his seat with a

HONK!!!!

Can you imagine being in line to buy concert tickets and having the person behind you scream in your ear:

"GET GOING, FUNGUS BRAIN!!! CAN'T YOU SEE THE LINE'S MOVED?!!"

There are three reasons why it's essential for you to master the finer points of proper driving etiquette:

1. so your parents will trust you with the car

2. so you'll be a safe driver, and

3. so you won't get shot by a motorist you've ticked off.

Here are some common (and commonsense) courtesies to abide by when behind the wheel:

- Don't run anyone over. This is very bad manners.
- Stop for pedestrians in crosswalks. Never aim for them.
- Refrain from tailgating. This is dangerous as well as discourteous. And, in the event of an accident, the person tailgating is almost always deemed to be at fault.
- On multilane freeways, use the right-hand lane for cruising, the left-hand lane for passing. Don't hog the passing lane. This is one of the rudest, most dangerous and egocentric things a driver can do. In Europe, nobody would dream of doing this. A car going slowly in the passing lane would be eaten for lunch and spit out by a Ferrari doing 150 m.p.h. But here in America, people dawdle along at 40 and refuse to pull over, causing accidents, strokes, anxiety attacks, arguments, traffic jams, acid rain, and just about everything else bad you can imagine.
- Yield the right-of-way when you don't have it.

- Yield the right-of-way when you *do* have it but that truck bearing down looks awfully serious.
- When honking to prevent an accident, lay on the horn as if your life depended on it.
- When honking to tell an inattentive driver that the light has changed, use a gentle, friendly chirp.
- Don't take up two spots in a parking lot. If your car is that new or fancy, park in a far corner.
- Avoid opening your car door into the vehicle parked next to you. Nobody likes to come back to their car and find a new gouge in it.
- If you hit a parked car, leave a note with your name and phone number. This is one of the most noble things a human can do. Imagine how you would feel if you returned to your car and found a dent. Now imagine how you'd feel if you also found a note assuming responsibility.
- Keep the radio volume low enough to hear other cars, emergency vehicles, etc. When you pull up to a light, the people in the car next to yours should not experience sonic booms within their chest cavities.
- Learn everything you can about defensive driving techniques and driving in snow or wet weather. These safety tips will keep you alive so you can continue to be a courteous driver.
- In heavy traffic, wave someone in who'd otherwise be stuck forever. You'll get where you're going .002 seconds later than you otherwise would have, but the look of amazement on the person's face, as well as the warm glow in your heart, will more than make up for it.
- Always wear your seat belt. Insist that your passengers do, too.
- Use your turn signals.
- Never, ever drink and drive.

Uncommon Courtesies

Public Events

As a teen about town, you no doubt frequent the opera, the theater, the symphony, the sports stadium, the movie house, and the concert hall or arena. Proper conduct varies with the entertainment. For example, at certain rock concerts it's appropriate to dive from the stage or pass one member of the audience over the heads of others. This would not be acceptable behavior at a slide lecture on Greek mythology. Conversely, many of these cultural offerings have a lot more in common than you would think. For example, both hockey and opera feature violent acts committed by well-padded individuals wearing strange headgear. Of course, hockey players use sticks instead of swords to draw blood.

How Rude!

You need to be on your toes when you go out to catch some culture. It just wouldn't do to heckle the harpsichordist or tell the conductor he or she needs glasses. Following are some more public performance protocol guidelines:

AT THE SYMPHONY, THEATER, AND OPERA

People attending the opera or theater tend to take these events quite seriously. You would, too, if you had paid $70 a ticket. Thus, the standards of conduct are somewhat more rigorous than those for a mud-wrestling match.

First, arrive on time. A stream of latecomers is distracting to those who are already seated, as well as to the performers themselves. In fact, many places refuse to seat latecomers until a natural break in the program—so you may miss even more of the show just waiting to be let in.

At the end of the event, people often have to hurry to catch a train, get to the garage before it closes, relieve the baby-sitter, or finish their homework. Thus, contrary to what some people think, it is not rude to leave as soon as the show is over. This is defined as the moment the curtain falls, or the final piece on the program has concluded. The event may continue for quite some time with curtain calls, standing ovations, rhythmic clapping, and/or encores. If you wish to leave right away, say "Excuse me" as you pass.

If, for some reason, you must leave before the conclusion of the performance, try to do so at intermission, between acts, when the music has stopped, or, as a last resort, during a moment of particularly frenzied stage activity or spontaneous applause, when the audience and performers are likely to be distracted. If you're about to be sick, these rules are suspended. You are permitted to quietly race for the exit. Throwing up off the balcony interferes with the enjoyment of more concertgoers than does leaving early.

Spontaneous laughter, applause, and gasps of surprise are welcome at the theater and opera. Talking is not. Neither is the kicking of seats, nor the blocking of anyone's view. If you are two years old and feel a good cry coming on, excuse yourself and go to the lobby.

APPLAUSE

One of the joys of live concerts and plays is the rapport that develops between audience and performer. Protocols have developed for how audiences communicate their delight and esteem. Although these vary with the event, in general a balance is sought between allowing the audience to express its appreciation as these moments occur and allowing the performers to carry on.* Of course, audiences may want to convey something other than approval. We'll get to that in a moment.

---

* For a good example of how obnoxious incessant applause can be, watch the President's State of the Union address sometime.

The most strict rules of applause apply to performances of classical music: orchestral and chamber works; concerti, sonati, rotini—you know, all those pieces that were written by men in wigs. The main rule when attending these concerts is *never applaud between movements.*

This doesn't refer to anyone's digestive schedule. Rather, it refers to those divisions within a piece of music that are noted on the program: e.g., allegro, largo, adagio, pesto. Each time the playing stops, another movement has passed, so to speak. The tempo, and often the key, will change.

Between movements, the conductor should keep the baton raised. At the end of the piece, he or she will lower it. Sometimes, composers make one movement sound like several to try to trick concertgoers into applauding at the wrong spot. Sometimes, you may zombie out and lose count. If you're in doubt as to when to applaud, wait for others. They may be wrong, but at least you won't be the one who started it.

It is also appropriate to clap when a guest soloist walks out onto the stage. It is never appropriate to clap if she falls off the stage.

At the end of the concert, assuming you're still there, you have numerous options for showing your appreciation. You can clap—mildly or enthusiastically. (In Europe, people usually clap in unison.) You can stand as you applaud. This is known as a *standing ovation.** You can shout "Encore!" This is concert-speak for "More, more!" You can also shout "Bravo!" This is Italian for "well done," unless you're referring to a steak.

If you want to get technical, you can shout "Bravo" for male artists and "Brava" for female artists. People in the audience may look at you like you're nuts, but at least you'll have the satisfaction of knowing you're correct.

At jazz concerts, individual musicians usually rotate solos. You can applaud after each improvisation—even if the piece is still being played by the others. It is also acceptable to applaud when jazz and pop artists begin playing songs they have made famous.

Standards for audience behavior at rock concerts vary with the group and the venue. Many bands bring their own culture, and audiences go to these events knowing that dancing in the aisles, swooning at the stage, or crashing into each other is acceptable and expected. At some concerts, audience members light candles or lighters and sway as if they were tipsy waves of grain holding a wake on some Nebraska wheat field.

Now you know what to do if a performance was terrific. But what if it was terrible? At the opera, or at the premiere of a composer's new work, tradition allows robust booing when it's over. (Of course, if it was *that* terrible, why are you still there?) Booing should be used with great discretion; this centuries-old custom should not be devalued by overuse.

---

* Duh.

How Rude!

The more typical response to a lackluster show is lukewarm applause. Unless the performance was so hideous that you're sitting in stunned silence, immobilized by disgust, it's only polite to acknowledge the performers' efforts. And, in fact, responsibility for the failure may reside with the composer or director, not with the performers. So dole out your applause as you would a tip in a restaurant:*

- none if you feel angry and/or insulted
- a little if you're displeased
- a standard amount if you're satisfied, or
- an extravagant measure if you're thrilled.

AT THE MOVIES

A lot of folks don't go to movies anymore. They're fed up with people who crinkle wrappers, crunch food, leave trash, kick and tap, block the view, put their feet up on seats, and talk through the whole picture.**

It's a shame that so many people have been chased away from theaters by the rudeness of others. Seeing a film on the Big Screen (which nowadays means anything over two inches square) is one of life's great pleasures. At the cinema, good manners mean good viewing. Here's how to maximize everyone's enjoyment, including your own:

Try not to sit in front of others. It's much better if everyone is spread out. If you need to go in or out and people are blocking the way, say "Excuse me" and scoot sideways past them, keeping the front of your body parallel to the screen. You'll need one "Excuse me" for each person you pass. If someone wants to get by you, you can either stand (this is what men are expected to do when women wish to get by) or turn both your knees in the direction in which they are traveling.

Don't dance in the aisles or squirt water at your fellow moviegoers (unless you're watching *The Rocky Horror Picture Show*).

And especially:

DON'T TALK!!!!!!!!!!!!

Few things are more annoying than people who keep up a running commentary during the whole show. Especially if they've already seen the picture. It really enhances your moviegoing pleasure to hear such gems as "In a minute

---

* For more on the topic of tipping, see pages 302–304.
** Not to mention high ticket prices and walls so flimsy you hear the sound from ten other movies.

he's gonna get shot" and "That's not really the detective" and "They won't fall in love because she's going to die"—like, thank you very much why don't you just tell me how the whole thing ends and I'll leave now.

If someone's talking disturbs you, you have several choices. A sharp, no-nonsense "Sssssshhh!" delivered at the first sign of trouble often nips it in the bud. This approach is especially useful when the perpetrators are unknown or sitting far away from you. Plus, it serves notice to those who haven't talked yet—but were going to—that this is a serious showing.

If the offenders are seated to your rear, a determined steady gaze in their direction can be effective in lighting the lamp of self-awareness that leads people to shut their traps. (Some might call this staring—but it's not, since we all know that it's rude to stare.)

You can also say something like "Could you please be quiet? I can't hear the movie when people are talking." A lot of people, though, if they are rude enough to talk in the first place, will ignore your request. (Which—and how sad that we must be grateful for such things—is at least better than dumping a tub of popcorn over your head.) If you get no satisfaction (or you'd rather not confront the person in the first place), you can either change your seat or go tell the manager. It's his or her job to ensure that people in the theater don't disturb others.

TRUE STORIES FROM THE MANNERS FRONTIER
Shut Up!

Make sure that your efforts to quiet somebody don't create an even greater disturbance. I was at a theater recently where this couple up front kept talking loudly.

"Shut up!" yelled someone in the back.

"You shut up!" the guy in the front replied.

"&#%@!" yelled the fellow in the back. (This was a very high-level conversation.)

Then the woman up front started shouting to her boyfriend about the guy who told them to shut up. "If he doesn't like it, he can just leave. Who the &#%!@ does he think he is?"

"He's just some %@#!& who's gonna get the &!$@! beat outta him."

"All of you shut the &#%!@ up!" Just what we needed. Another voice of calm and reason.

Pretty soon, half the audience was screaming "Shut up!" as well as suggesting anatomical acts individuals could commit upon themselves. It was quite an uproar. I hadn't seen such rowdiness since the French Revolution. Fortunately, it was a terrible movie, so this rare glimpse into how far we've come as a species was actually more entertaining that what was on the screen.

Still, it ruined the moviegoing experience for me. My only consolation was the free pass to another showing I received after my polite request to the manager.

If anything interferes with your enjoyment of the show, most theater managers will give you a complimentary pass so you can come back at another time. If your request is reasonable and refused, ask the manager for his or her name and explain that you'll be writing to the owner of the theater. If the manager refuses to give you his or her name, mention this fact when you write and note the time and day of the showing you attended. Corporations, too, must sometimes be reminded of their manners.

Requests for free passes should not be made while the final credits are rolling. Unless a disturbance or equipment failure occurs late in the show, asking at such a time makes it appear as if you're pulling a con. And while I know you'd never do such a thing, the manager doesn't.

Take your trash with you when you leave. If the person before you had done this, the bottoms of your sneakers wouldn't be glued to the floor with orange soda.

Try not to tap or kick the seat in front of you. Even if the nearest people are six seats away, they'll still feel your fidgeting.

Eat quietly. If God had intended people to have picnics at the movies, He would have installed tables and ants in the theater. Nothing is more annoying than someone chomping and smacking their way through a seven-course dinner during a movie. If you must unwrap something, at least do it quickly. People think that if they take five minutes to s-l-o-w-l-y unwrap foil, it's less annoying than if they do one quick, loud jerk. Well, they're WRONG!! It's MORE annoying!! It's a THOUSAND TIMES more annoying!!

And finally:

When you leave the theater, don't give away the ending to people waiting in line.

SPORTING EVENTS

It may seem ludicrous to be concerned with your own manners while the people you came to see are gouging each other's eyes out and spitting at umpires. Nonetheless, there are standards for sporting events. At least for the spectators. Here are some do's and don'ts:

- DO stand while the National Anthem is being played. But DON'T feel you have to sing. (Indeed, this may be an act of courtesy to your neighbors.)

- DO yell, stomp, and whistle. But DON'T do it in anybody's ear.

- DO insult the players and referees. But DON'T use personal slurs.
- DO come late, leave early, and get up to go buy a hotdog. But DON'T pass in front of anyone without excusing yourself.
- DO bring a glove to baseball games. But DON'T catch fly balls that have not been hit into the stands.
- DON'T spill refreshments on others.
- DON'T pat anyone on the fanny. Only football, baseball, and basketball players can do this to each other.
- DON'T block anyone's view.
- DON'T make waves. Unless everybody's doing the wave.
- DON'T throw snowballs at the opposing team.

Uncommon Courtesies

Some sporting events have a tradition of expecting spectators to remain quiet. These tend to be competitions where a great deal of concentration is required, or where the stands or galleries are close to the action. If you attend one of these, don't talk or move about in such a way as to distract the athletes.

For some sports, special rules apply.

- *Tennis:* Don't race onto the court to get a souvenir ball.
- *Golf:* Don't yell "Miss!" just as the golfer begins his swing.
- *Diving:* When the diver does her run-up, don't say in a stage whisper "She's going to do a belly flop."
- *Swimming:* Don't snicker at how tiny the men's swimsuits are.
- *Auto racing:* If your candy wrapper blows onto the track, don't chase after it.
- *Steeplechases:* Don't string wires across the course.
- *Baseball:* Don't use a mirror to flash the sun into the eyes of an outfielder who's about to catch a fly ball.

WAITING IN LINE

Nobody likes to wait in line. But lines are a fair system for giving people access to events or services in the order of their arrival. And waiting politely and patiently is better than a free-for-all slugfest.

Cutting in line is no fair, yet people try to do it all the time. You've probably seen some of the techniques they use—or attempted a few yourself:

The Unconscious Merge. As the line moves, you nonchalantly walk alongside it. When it halts, you continue for a few steps and then stop. You repeat this process until you have moved way ahead. You then start looking for a nonassertive individual who is unlikely to challenge you when the actual butt-in occurs.

The Puzzled Where-Am-I Merge. This approach is similar to the unconscious merge, except you affect a perplexed attitude, as if you can't quite

How Rude!

imagine what you're doing here and why you're lined up with all of these strangers. You scour your surroundings for clues. You search your pockets. You squinch up your face in bewilderment. And, finally, you sigh, give up, and cut in.

The Entitled Intrusion. At least this approach is honest. You just go to the head of the line and aggressively cut in. You're home free unless someone challenges you.

The Find-a-Friend Ploy. You scope out the line for people you know. As soon as you see a good friend, like that kid you once sat next to at lunch five years ago and haven't seen since, you say "Hey, how's it goin'?" and launch into an extended conversation. And since it would be rude to break it off, you continue to accompany this person right up to the ticket window.

The Don't-I-Know-You Gambit. This is what you do when the Find-a-Friend Ploy fizzles. Pick out a stranger. Act as if you know her. Start a conversation. Continue as above.

Those who cut in line succeed because most people would rather not confront them. But you're not going to confront them. You're going to *help* them. Because, obviously, they are lost. They can't find the end of the line!

"Excuse me," you'll say. "The end of the line is around the corner." Amateurs may be sufficiently humbled to slink to the end of the line. More brazen buttinskis may ignore you or say "I was here." In that case, there's safety in numbers. Engage the interest of those around you. "Excuse me," you can say to them. "I was trying to show this person [at this point you can address the person, as in 'I'm sorry, I don't know your name'] where the end of the line is. Is that it back there? I wouldn't want to point him in the wrong direction."

If you can get at least half a dozen people behind you interested in this question, the intruder will usually give up. He may try out his wares further along the line, but you'll have done your duty in trying to uphold the inherent fairness of the system. (You could also report the person to the manager, bouncer, guard, or anyone else in a position of authority.)

The gray area in queuing up has to do with holding places. If five people hold a spot for one who's off parking the car, that's fair. But if one person lets five in, and then one of those five admits a few more friends, and then one of *them* . . . . You get the picture. Suddenly, you're 30th in line instead of 10th.

In the hope of eliminating future in-line debates and debacles, here are the proper ratios for placeholding:

Number of Persons Already in Line	Maximum Number of Persons Who Can Be Let In
1	2
2	2
3	2
4	2
5	3
6	3
7	3
8	3
9 or more	No more than ⅓ the number already in line

Uncommon
Courtesies

Pollution Prevention

LITTER

Littering is a trashy thing to do. It messes up our environment and makes things ugly and unsanitary. It's dangerous—like when you step on broken glass at the beach or slip on a banana peel.* And it's ecologically unsound. Trash should be recycled; otherwise we'll run out of precious natural resources. Your grandchildren will never see a tree or know the joy of holding an aluminum can in their hands. Animals will choke on Styrofoam, since they don't know the Heimlich Maneuver.

TRUE STORIES FROM THE
MANNERS FRONTIER
The Brothers Slobola, Part Two

Speaking of animals, let's return briefly to the Slobolas, that loathsome family introduced earlier in this chapter.

While waiting for our flight to Paris, they all spread out on the floor of the lounge at the gate and stuffed themselves, having bought one of everything at the airport food court. When it came time to board the plane, they wiped their sticky hands across

---

* Which a friend of mine actually did, and he broke his arm in a zillion places and had to have surgery and be in a cast for about six years.

their meat-juice-covered faces and got up. And then Slobola junior, with a self-conscious little smirk, jauntily KICKED the trash under the seats. He acted as if he thought he was the coolest *Homo erectus* ever to stand on two legs. Meanwhile, there were forty-eight trash receptacles within three feet of him.

How Rude!

In addition to obvious things like candy wrappers, fast-food containers, cans, bottles, paper bags, and the entire Slobola family, litter includes such items as gum, peach pits, and cigarette butts. Even biodegradables such as toilet paper and watermelon rinds are considered litter if you leave them in somebody else's yard.

Littering is a perfect example of how one person's abdication of responsibility can affect others. The good news is, it could end tomorrow—if we all cleaned up after ourselves.

VISUAL POLLUTION

There are those who insist that graffiti is a form of urban art, and that people have the right to express themselves. It's true that graffiti can be artistically significant, and it's also true that self-expression is a good thing. But what if one person's "art" defaces another person's property? How would you feel if you came back to your room one day and found graffiti all over your walls, posters, and furniture? Spray painting someone's building, bridge, or car without permission is vandalism, even if you're the Michelangelo of the aerosol can.

NOISE POLLUTION

Few inventions have done more than headphones to preserve peaceful relations between teenagers and adults. Parents no longer have to yell "Turn that noise down!" a hundred times a day. On the other hand, their kids rarely come when called.

The rules for polite personal stereo listening are few but essential:

- Remove your headphones when speaking to someone. Show that you're giving your full attention to the conversation. This also eliminates the need to shout so you can hear yourself.

- If someone wearing headphones addresses you, mouth your response silently. He'll think the problem is on his end and will remove the headphones, which is what he should have done in the first place.

- In public places, keep the volume low enough so only you can hear it. If you're nuking your brain, it probably means that people at the other end of the bus can also hear your music. Only instead of the pleasant sounds you're enjoying, they're hearing a scratchy metallic noise comparable to fingernails scraping across a chalkboard.

- If you listen to music when walking downtown, riding a bike, jogging, skating, or strolling along train tracks, keep the volume very, very low. Make sure you can hear approaching traffic or someone shouting a warning. If you get run over by a truck or hit by a train, you'll make a mess that others will have to clean up, and that's bad manners.

- Don't wear your headphones while driving a car.

AIR POLLUTION

You've heard all about the health effects of smoking. You know that smoking is an addictive habit that will turn your teeth brown, stain your fingers, foul your breath, stink up your clothes, consume your allowance, sicken those around you, and ultimately kill you. You're aware that smoking causes lung cancer, throat cancer, esophageal cancer, and emphysema. You realize that most people who smoke wish they could stop, and that the recruitment of fresh, young teenage smokers by cigarette manufacturers is cynically and dishonestly nurtured by executives who care more about your money than your life. So there's no need to discuss any of these issues here. Besides, this is a book about etiquette, not health.

It used to be that only men smoked, and unwritten laws governed when and where they could light up. For example, in Northern Europe of the 19th century, it was never proper to smoke in the company of ladies, including one's wife. No gentleman would smoke a pipe in the street, or a cigarette in the street during daylight hours. Smoking was not permitted in any public place where ladies might be present, such as a racecourse, restaurant, church, flower show, or theater.

In the words of Thomas Tegg, who lived during the 19th century:

The tobacco smoker in public is the most selfish
animal imaginable; he perseveres in contaminating
the pure and fragrant air, careless whom he annoys,
and is but the fitting inmate of a tavern.
Smoking in the streets, or in a theater is only practiced
by shop-boys, pseudo-fashionables, and the "swell-mob."

Prior to meeting a lady, a gentleman who had been smoking was expected to change his clothes to avoid offending her with the smell of stale tobacco. (This is why men wore "smoking jackets.") At dinner parties, men would retire after the meal to the library to smoke, while women had coffee in the parlor.

Thus, there was a natural segregation of smokers and nonsmokers. Over time, it became acceptable for men to smoke in the presence of women, provided they asked permission first. In the 20th century, as the status of women in society began to change, more women began to smoke, thus achieving equal access to cancer. Once smoking became a mixed-company activity, smokers were in the majority, and the tradition of asking before lighting up began to die out. If nonsmokers didn't like it, too bad.

How Rude!

Today, we know much more about the harmful effects of smoking. The newly recognized dangers of secondhand smoke have led nonsmokers to demand smoke-free environments. Some smokers claim that this is an assault on their right to smoke. Nonsense. Virtually all rights are limited at the point at which exercising them harms others. Because smoking is still a legal activity, adults have the right to smoke—but not if it irritates other people's eyes, nose, or lungs. The law increasingly recognizes these limitations on smokers' rights, and this has led to new regulations that prohibit smoking in many buildings and require separate sections for smokers and nonsmokers.

The etiquette of smoking is based on mutual respect. Smokers have the right to smoke. They don't have the right to inflict their smoke on others. Nonsmokers have the right to smoke-free environments. They don't have the right to behave rudely towards smokers.

"What's the best way to ask someone whose smoke is bothering you to stop smoking?"

Simply say "Excuse me, but your smoke is bothering me. Would you mind putting out your cigarette?" Note that this wording embodies the principles for responding to rudeness:

- convey the assumption that the person would never knowingly wish to cause offense
- own the problem as your sensitivity, and
- allow the offender to see compliance as doing you a favor, as opposed to knuckling under. ◆

"I was having lunch at an outdoor café and the woman next to me was smoking. It was blowing straight into my face. I asked if she could please put out her cigarette, but she refused, saying she was outdoors and could smoke if she wanted. Was she right?"

Yes and no. If the outdoor seating area was divided into smoking and non-smoking areas, she was within her rights to smoke as long as she was seated in the smoking section. A polite response to your request would have been "I'm sorry my smoke is bothering you, but this is the smoking section. I think those tables over there are nonsmoking." If, however, there was no nonsmoking section, the courteous response would have been for her to put out her cigarette.

When smokers and nonsmokers both claim their rights on neutral turf, the decision must go in the favor of the nonsmoker. After all, nobody likes it when smoke gets in your fries. ◆

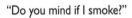

"Do you mind if I smoke?"   "Not at all. Do you mind if I spray?"

"My friend and her parents came to dinner at my house. My friend's father asked if he could smoke, and my mother said no. I was so embarrassed I could have died. Isn't it rude to tell a guest he can't smoke?"

Not if you do it politely. Let's assume that your mom said something like "I'm terribly sorry, but we maintain a nonsmoking home," not "Don't you dare light that filthy thing in here." She might have added "Please feel free to step out onto the patio." Guests are usually allowed to break a few minor house rules. But that immunity ends at the point where the behavior is abusive, illegal, or dangerous. ◆

"Sometimes I go over to a friend's house and his parents smoke. I have asthma, and the smoke really bothers me. Would it be polite to ask them not to smoke?"

This is a very complicated question. It involves the rights of smokers vs. those of nonsmokers; the prerogatives of hosts vs. the privileges of guests; and the

How Rude!

perks of age vs. the example that adults should set for youth. It even involves the issue of whether exceptions to etiquette can be made on the grounds of health.

In general, it's not proper for a young person visiting the home of a friend to ask the friend's parents to change their behavior. After all, it's *their* home. But smoke is smoke, and the fact that you have asthma grants you a certain latitude. You have four choices, ranging from worst to best:

1. Don't go to the house of that particular friend.

2. Go there, but stay out of rooms where the parents are smoking.

3. Say to the parents "Please forgive me for even mentioning this, it's so rude of me, but I have asthma and smoke makes it very hard for me to breathe. Do you think you could please put out your cigarettes?" They might be so impressed with your manners and courage that they will comply.

4. Tell your friend about your asthma and how smoke bothers you. Maybe he'll volunteer to ask his parents not to smoke around you. If he doesn't volunteer, ask him. If he makes the request in private, nobody loses face, and his parents may decide to adjust their behavior when you come to visit. ◆

"How do you know if other people mind your smoking?"

You know if they ask you to stop. Other clues include coughing loudly, holding their noses, and keeling over. In any case, the polite thing to do is to put out your cigarette without groaning, making faces, or muttering. ◆

"I was in a public place where smoking was prohibited and someone was smoking. I pointed to the 'No Smoking' sign and asked politely if they would stop. They refused and were very rude to me. What can I do the next time that happens?"

If smokers extinguished their smoking materials when asked to do so, we wouldn't need laws, signs, fines, and separate sections in public places. But they don't, so we do. Now that popular support has shifted in favor of non-smokers, it's they who often forget the basic principles of etiquette, treating smokers like moral delinquents. It's time for everybody to take a deep breath of pure, fresh air, relax, and recognize that the world is large enough to accommodate smokers and nonsmokers alike.

If your polite request to put out a cigarette is ignored, you can:

1. Move away from the smoker. The rudeness may escalate into something uglier if you persist in challenging him or her.

2. Call the situation to the attention of someone in authority—a manager, police officer, flight attendant, usher, maitre d', etc. Make it that person's responsibility to enforce the law. ◆

Uncommon
Courtesies

The Well-Mannered Mall Rat

AT THE VIDEO STORE

Here's a good example of how manners change as society changes. Twenty years ago, if you had asked someone how people should behave in a video store, they would have said "Huh?" Today, there are common courtesies that all videophiles should know and abide by:

Try to pass behind people who are looking at the display shelves. If you must walk in front of them, say "Excuse me." It's amazing how often somebody in a video store will pass in front of you and stop smack dab in the middle of where you're looking. How ruuuude! This would be like blocking the view of someone who's trying to watch a movie. (Just because the movie's still in the box doesn't make any difference.) Should this ever happen to you, you have two choices: You can make an internal comment to yourself along the lines of *What is the world coming to?* and slide over to the next section until the person moves on. Or you can say "Excuse me, I'm looking here. I'll be done in just a minute." Most people will vacate your viewing range.

If you're trying to decide what film to rent, don't scoop up twelve Hot New Releases only to put eleven back a half hour later. This isn't fair to others who may have hoped to see one of those films. It's okay to hang on to two or three possibilities, but try to put the rejects back as soon as possible.

Don't reshelve rejected videos in any old place. Believe it or not, some people will pick up a film in the drama section, decide not to rent it, and set it back on a shelf in comedy. When this happens, the film is lost—just as a misshelved book would be. Unless you're 100 percent sure you're returning a film to the right spot, give it to one of the clerks to restock. They'll be happy to do so.

Be courteous of others who are looking at films. Don't block their view by draping coats, sweaters, or gym bags over the displays. If you're reading the description on a video box, step back from the shelves so others may continue to browse.

Have your card and money ready before you go to the counter. As one video store clerk told me, "Taking receipts, keys, tissues, other cards, change, lint, candy, cough drops, hairpins, cigarettes, and lottery tickets out at the counter does not impress anyone, especially the people behind you. The contents of someone's purse or wallet need not be revealed when checking out a movie."

Curb thy tongue. Don't comment out loud if someone is holding the last available copy of a film you want. Similarly, there's no need to remark upon the viewing tastes of others as evidenced by the films in their hands. This doesn't mean you can't get into spirited discussions with fellow film critics over the relative merits of various movies. Just try not to be insulting.

AT THE SUPERMARKET

Many people seem unaware of the major distinction between restaurants and grocery stores. In the former, one dines and then pays; in the latter, one pays and then dines. It's bad behavior to help oneself to grapes, nuts, cookies, and salad bar ingredients while strolling the aisles, unless the store is handing out free samples. Here are a few more market manner musts:

Don't stand with the freezer doors open. The reason freezer doors are made out of glass (as opposed to brick) is so people can see through them. There's no need to stand for ten minutes with the doors wide open while you decide whether you want fudge ripple or marble fudge.

Drive carefully. The second most dangerous place in the world to drive is a supermarket parking lot. What's the first most dangerous place? The supermarket itself. You've got little kids running wild with carts. You've got some senior citizens poking along at .00001 miles per hour. You've got teenagers careening around corners, and people leaving their carts in the aisles. Follow these rules of the road for market maneuvering:

- Don't tailgate. Always leave at least a watermelon's length between you and the cart in front. This will prevent those horrible rear-end collisions.
- Pull to the side of the aisle when stopping. There's no need to cause a traffic jam while you squeeze a cantaloupe.
- Keep to the right except when passing. If everyone followed traditional highway protocol, there would be fewer bruised bananas (and shins) in the world.
- Know your cart. Things can get very confusing if you pull away from the pickles with someone else's shopping list.

- Keep personal belongings with you. Never leave your purse, backpack, or baby unattended in a cart. They might not be there when you get back.

Uncommon Courtesies

Have your money ready. Many shoppers seem totally surprised when the clerk says "That'll be forty-three dollars and twelve cents." How else to explain the fact that they wait until that moment to burrow in their bag for their purse, their purse for their wallet, their wallet for their checkbook, and back in their bag for a pen? At this point they s-l-o-w-l-y write a check, s-l-o-w-l-y enter the amount into their checkbook ledger, s-l-o-w-l-y fold the check along the perforation, and s-l-o-w-l-y tear it off. Naturally, this all takes place in the express lane. Do your part to avoid traffic jams and frayed tempers: Have your Saver's Card, coupons, credit card, and/or money ready. If you're writing a check, fill out everything except the amount while your groceries are being rung up.

AT THE FAST-FOOD RESTAURANT

If you frequent fast-food emporia, the last thing you need to do is commit a burger blunder. So let's ketchup with the latest in mall-meal manners:

- Know what you want before you get to the head of the line.
- If you're ordering as a group, get your act together so everyone can order quickly.
- Have your money ready.
- Remember that children are likely to be present, and they will be watching and idolizing cool teenagers such as yourself. Adjust your language and behavior accordingly.
- Clear your table when you're through.
- Never try to move a chair that's bolted to the floor.
- Smile when you eat a happy meal.

"What do you do when you're in a store and the clerk serves everyone else before you? This happens because I'm a kid, I think."

Customers should be served in the order of their arrival. If the clerk simply ignores you, say "Could you please help me?" If the clerk serves others in your stead, say "Excuse me, I believe I was next." If the clerk continues to overlook you, find the manager and report the incident. Politely describe what happened and explain that you won't continue to patronize the store if this reflects their policy towards younger customers.

How Rude!

If the situation is a free-for-all with everybody clamoring for service, the clerk may not know whose turn it is. You'll need to be assertive. To the next customer who tries to jump ahead, say "I'm sorry. You must not have noticed me waiting here in all the confusion. But I believe I'm next." ◆

AT THE LIBRARY

Here are two things to keep in mind when you visit Bookland:

1. *Sssssshhhh!* This doesn't mean that as long as you whisper you can talk to your heart's content. It means that if you absolutely *must* talk, do it as quietly as you can. Even whispers are distracting to people who are trying to read or study. Most libraries have lobbies, lounges, or reference areas where it's okay to talk in a regular voice. But if you really want to talk, go someplace else.

2. Don't reshelve books yourself. If you take a book down and put it back in the wrong place, it could be lost forever. This happens quite often in libraries. You misshelve a book, the next person goes to look for it, the book is missing, the librarian says "According to the computer, it's in," but nobody can find it since it's three shelves up and two shelves over from where it's supposed to be. Use the to-be-reshelved carts.

ASKING FOR THE TIME

From time to time, you'll find yourself in need of the time. It's perfectly fine to ask a stranger what time it is; just don't grab his wrist and look for yourself. Simply say "Excuse me, Sir (or Ma'am), do you have the time?" Most people under the age of six will say "Yes" and stand there with a stupid grin on their face. Those over the age of six will give you the time. Those over the age of sixty will be so impressed that a teenager actually addressed them as "Sir" or "Ma'am" that they'll probably hand over their Rolex.

CHAPTER QUIZ

Uncommon Courtesies

1. *An elderly woman wearing Air Jordans hobbles onto a crowded bus and stands in front of where you're sitting. As the bus lurches along its route, she struggles to keep from falling. Do you:*
   a) stretch out your feet and try to trip her
   b) say in a loud voice "Boy, it sure is great to be sitting down," or
   c) offer her your seat?

2. *One of the parents who drives your carpool insists that everyone wear seat belts. Do you:*
   a) let the air out of her tires
   b) spill a carton of sour milk on the carpet, or
   c) thank her for caring enough to protect you?

3. *You're skateboarding in a public square. You can stay within the bounds of propriety as long as you:*
   a) frontside bluntslide American cars only
   b) yell "On your fingers!" before grinding a handrail
   c) add "Is Not" to the "Skateboarding Prohibited" sign.

4. *You're at the symphony when you suddenly feel like throwing up. Do you:*
   a) heave to the beat
   b) ask the lady next to you if you can borrow her purse, or
   c) exit as quickly and quietly as you can?

5. *You and your best friend are doing the food shopping for your family. It's fine to play basketball with the produce as long as:*
   a) your hands are clean
   b) oranges are four for a dollar or less
   c) you don't dribble the tomatoes.

4
Family Life and Strife

Creating the Civilized Home

Belonging to a family means that you have a place where you can be yourself—even your worst self. You can brag, cry, and complain. You can be silly and moody, dreamy and weird. You can break a promise, tell a fib, slam a door, and shout "I wish I was never born!"—secure in the knowledge that your parents will still love you. This is because, in the context of family, we don't call such behavior "rudeness." We call it "growing up." And as long as you make progress along the road to maturity, your mistakes, tantrums, and occasional hurtfulness will be forgiven.

Somehow, though, this greater leeway for error and expression has spawned the strange notion that people don't have to be polite to each other at home. So we hear:

"I hate you."
"I wish you were dead."
"You can't make me."
"Yeah, right."
"Whatever."

And:

"You look like a tramp."
"Why did I ever have kids?"
"You're a selfish, spoiled brat."

Why do people behave so rudely to those they care about most? Probably because they can. If you're rude to an employer, you'll get fired. If you're rude to a boyfriend or girlfriend, you'll get dumped. If you're rude to your parents, they'll still be your parents in the morning.

Part of the problem has to do with the concept of "company manners." This implies that there are two sets of behaviors: one for show, and one for family. The one for show is the "phony" you—because it's polite and refined. The one for family is the "real" you—because it's sloppy and gross. But where did we get the idea that if we scrape away the surface to discover our "real" selves, we find disgusting slobs?

It's okay to relax our standards a bit when company isn't around. But we should strive for increased *informality* rather than increased *inconsideration*. In other words, it's okay to bring the ketchup bottle to the table, but it's not okay to ask for it without saying "please." It's okay to tell jokes and be silly, but it's not okay to belch, burp, and stick straws up your nose.

You spend more time with your parents and siblings than just about anyone else. Home should be the place where you feel safe and loved, relaxed and accepted. It should be the place where you know you'll be treated with kindness and understanding. It should be the place where you practice your best, rather than worst, manners.

The Survey Says . . .

Here, according to our survey of adults, are the 25 Rudest Things Teenagers Do at Home:

1. Interrupt conversations.
2. Not say "Please" or "Thank you."
3. Wear hats at the table.

continued

4. Throw backpacks and jackets on the floor when they come home.
5. Talk back.
6. Use vulgar language.
7. Behave unkindly to siblings; annoy each other on purpose.
8. Are discourteous on the telephone.
9. Say "Yeah" or "Uh-huh" instead of "Yes."
10. Whine.
11. Leave a mess for others to clean up.
12. Ignore their parents' requests.
13. Not respond when spoken to.
14. Watch TV with so much absorption that they ignore everything else.
15. Not appreciate the value of money.
16. Not appreciate the value of their belongings.
17. Not use silverware or napkins.
18. Chew with their mouth open.
19. Wipe their hands on their clothes.
20. Call people names.
21. Say "I hate . . . ."
22. Want to talk when parents are on the phone.
23. Insist that parents take care of their problems, even when parents have said they're too busy at the moment.
24. Treat adults as peers.
25. Not blow their noses.

Family Manners

Most families have domestic personnel who provide children with services such as cooking, cleaning, laundry, security, recreation, transportation, tutoring, and moral instruction. These staff persons are generally referred to as "Mom" and "Dad." Here's how to be on good terms with yours, along with other family members:

Acknowledge their presence. This doesn't mean you have to say "Hi, how are you? Lovely day! What's new?" each time you run into a room where a family member is present. And it doesn't mean you should interrupt someone in deep concentration. But it's nice, particularly in the morning when you're overjoyed to see that your parents and siblings didn't disappear during the night, to say "Good morning." Similarly, "Good night" is a pleasant way to end the day. And if, in between, your paths should cross, it's fine to engage family members in conversations that show you care about them and their lives.

Notice their moods. If your own moods go up and down faster than a speeding yo-yo, then you understand that sometimes people need to be left alone.

And that sometimes they need to be kept company, or given a hand. Be alert to your parents' and siblings' moods. If they seem upset, say "You seem kind of sad/upset/stressed-out today" and ask if there's anything you can do to help. If they want to talk, they will. And if they don't, they will still appreciate your kind sensitivity.

Watch your timing. If your brother just broke up with his girlfriend, it's not a good time to tease him. If your father just got a raise, it's an excellent time to mention that 16 MB RAM upgrade you've been wanting for your computer. Adjust your requests and behavior to the emotions and needs of others. This is not only a cornerstone of politeness, but also a way to increase the chances that your requests will be granted.

Talk to them. Just because they brought you into this world, nursed you, fed you, wiped you, clothed you, consoled you, and devoted umpteen thousands of hours and dollars towards your upbringing, your parents have this bizarre notion that they're entitled to know what's going on in your life. This is why the following typical parent-child conversation annoys them:

> Parent: *"What did you do in school today?"*
> Child: *"Nothin'."*
> Parent: *"Who was that you were talking with?"*
> Child: *"Nobody."*
> Parent: *"What are your plans for this evening?"*
> Child: *"I dunno."*
> Parent: *"Are you thinking of going to the rink again?*
> Child: *"Whatever."*

One of the most polite things you can do for your parents is *talk to them.* This may already happen in your family. Your parents may be the first people you think of when you have news to share and problems to sort out. If so, keep it up. You're probably enjoying the rewards of a loving, supportive relationship. If, however, you're muter than a sulking clam, it's likely that your parents feel hurt and ignored.

You shouldn't have to divulge your innermost secrets or provide résumés of your boyfriends or girlfriends. Simply engage in the kind of chitchat that says "Hello. I know you're here. Since we live in the same house, let's at least make our time together as positive as we can, even if we're not sharing much of our inner lives." You can do this in two ways:

1. Volunteer information about what went on at school, what you're thinking, how you're feeling. It doesn't have to be deeply personal—just stuff about classes, teachers, other kids, plans, reactions to current events, etc.

2. Ask questions of your parents. Remember, this is the secret to being a good conversationalist. Ask them about their work and friends. Ask them about their childhood. Where did they grow up? What kind of schools did they go to? What kind of students were they? How did they spend their time as kids? What did they worry about? How did they get along with their own parents? How did your mom and dad meet? The list is endless. In fact, one well-chosen question such as "Dad, what was it like growing up on military bases and moving all the time?" can keep your father talking for half an hour. And when he's through, he won't notice that he was doing all the talking. He'll appreciate your interest and feel a warm glow from having spent some time with you.

Bring things up before they become problems. Many of the petty irritations of family life can be avoided by thinking ahead. Don't wait until the last minute to ask to borrow the car, or to tell your mom you volunteered her to bake 400 brownies for the cast party. In fact, don't *ever* volunteer a parent to do *anything* without checking first.

Let your parents know where you are. The #1 qualification for being a parent is the ability to worry. If your parents expect you home from school at 3:00 every day, they will be in full worry mode by 3:30 if you haven't shown up. And then, when you appear at 5:00, instead of acting grateful that you weren't mugged, abducted, or run over, they'll bite your head off.

Establish a reasonable framework with your parents for the boundaries of your freedom. Depending on your age, your trustworthiness, and where you live, this may mean that within certain limits you can come and go as you please. Or it may mean that you must leave a note or a phone message so your parents know where you are. Taking these minimal steps to reduce parental anxiety doesn't mean you're a baby or untrustworthy. It means that you're courteous.

Smile on occasion. There's nothing like a scowling teenager to cast a pall over the home front. Granted, adolescence has its dark and gloomy days, but if you're fed, clothed, housed, and generally treated fairly well, why not show your appreciation by wearing a pleasant expression? This doesn't mean you have to grin like a monkey 12 hours a day, or that you should walk around with a fake smile plastered across your face. But your parents will notice (and appreciate in return) a happy, friendly demeanor.

TIP: If you've been in a permanent pout for the past few years, start slowly. Too obvious a show of cheerfulness will only raise your parents' suspicions and make them wonder what you're up to.

"Have you seen Chris?"

"Try the kitchen."

Pick up after yourself. Parents HATE IT when kids drop their belongings all over the house. If you're ever kidnapped, by all means try to leave a trail. Otherwise, close doors, shut drawers, wipe off, pick up, put away, take back, and clear off as required.

Do things without being asked. Your election to the Courteous Kids Hall of Fame will be guaranteed if you notice a need and fill it.

Say "Mom, let me hold that for you." Or "Dad, do you want me to get the blade sharpened?" If a faucet is running, turn it off. If car windows are open in the rain, close them. If the trash is overflowing, tie up and remove the bag and replace it with a new one. These thoughtful gestures will do wonders to enhance your standing at home.

TRUE STORIES FROM THE
MANNERS FRONTIER

Arrrgh!

I was once backing a very large school bus out of a very small parking lot. A student of mine found this very amusing as he perched on a nearby brick wall. He found it even more amusing when I crumpled the door of a teacher's brand-new car.

While I didn't wish to displace my anger and embarrassment onto this innocent observer, I was curious enough to inquire of him, "Why didn't you tell me I was about to hit her car?"

"Because you didn't ask," he replied.

"Should parents barge into their kids' rooms without knocking?"

Not unless flames and cries of "Help!" are coming from within. Respecting the privacy of others is one of the most basic concepts of polite behavior. Once children reach the age when they want privacy, parents should knock and wait for a "Come in" before entering their rooms. After all, your parents wouldn't want *you* barging into *their* room without being invited. As in: ◆

"The other day, I walked into my parents' bedroom and they were having sex. I left right away, but I know they saw me. Nobody's said anything about it since. I don't know what to do."

It can be quite a shock to witness parents' lovemaking. To think that they're still doing it at their age! Fortunately, the rule of etiquette in cases like this is simple: If you see something you weren't meant to see, act as if you didn't see it. However, if you notice a chill in the air, you might say something like this:

"I'm really sorry I barged in on you the other day. I was in such a rush to find a pencil that I forgot to knock. I had no idea you were, uh, sleeping. I promise I'll knock from now on." ◆

"Yesterday I walked in on
my parents having sex."

"Sex?!? But they're in their forties!"

"My father won't let anyone look at the newspaper until he's read it. Isn't he being selfish and rude?"

Why did your father establish this policy? Did he just announce it one day out of the blue? If so, it does seem a bit greedy. Or did he announce it after months of saying "Who cut this article out?" "Where's the sports section?" and "Why is there chili all over the stock quotes?"

For many adults, reading the newspaper is a cherished daily ritual. Your father probably likes to read his paper without having to hunt for missing sections or scrape oatmeal off of the comics. This is not unreasonable. People in England used to have their servants iron the newspaper so the pages would be crisp and wrinkle-free.*

There are two ways to solve your problem. One costs money, the other is free:

1. Have a second paper delivered to your home. While this would eliminate the conflict, you may want to save up for a second telephone line instead.

2. Propose a trial period during which you and other family members promise to restore the paper to its original condition after reading it. If you succeed, your father agrees to let people read the paper ahead of

---

* Nowadays, news is permanent press.

him. If you don't succeed, and the paper continues to look like kitty litter, you agree to keep your paws off it and stop hassling your dad about his policy. ◆

How Rude!

"My parents say I have to be nice to their friends. Why? They're not my friends. I don't see why I have to greet them and stay around while they talk about boring things."

Which would you rather encounter when you go over to your friends' homes—parents who express interest in you as a person and are glad to see you, or parents who are grouchy and give you the cold shoulder? Everybody feels more comfortable in a courteous and respectful environment, whether it's somebody's home, a restaurant, or a store.

Kids shouldn't have to be present the entire time their parents are entertaining, nor would most parents want them to. It should be enough to greet your parents' guests, engage in some conversation, pass the hors d'oeuvres a few times, and then excuse yourself. If the conversation is dull, do something about it. Ask questions about current events or topics that you find interesting.

TIP: Your parents' friends can be good resources for jobs, references, career and college advice, travel tips, etc. Many of my parents' friends have become my friends—especially those with nice vacation homes. ◆

"My mother gave me this big lecture about not being rude to people who do work in our house. All I did was tell this guy who was cleaning the carpets to come back to my room later, since I was in the middle of something. What was so wrong with that?"

There's nothing wrong with making a polite request:

"Do you think it might be possible for you to clean my rug last? I'm just finishing up here, and I can be out of your way in ten minutes."

But only employers—in this case, your mom—have the right to *tell* an employee what to do. And even then, politeness is required. You got hauled on the carpet because it wasn't your place to give instructions to someone your parents had hired.

Most households entertain a steady stream of service people: newspaper carriers, meter readers, caterers, landscapers, electricians, painters, house cleaners, Roto-Rooter routers, cockroach poisoners. Just because these people are paid for their efforts doesn't mean you can dispense with good manners.

Think of yourself as a fringe benefit for those who work at your house. Be polite and helpful to everyone—even if you're unlikely to see the person again. And if some people come regularly, try to build warm, respectful relationships with them. (One can never be on *too* good terms with the cook.) Without being intrusive, show interest in their lives and skills. Offer them a beverage. Compliment their work. Everyone likes to have their efforts and expertise appreciated. You do this because:

1. these people are human beings who deserve your friendliness and respect, and

2. good help really is hard to find.

Besides, imagine what might happen if parents had to choose between a rude child and a reliable plumber. ◆

"Do parents have the right to kiss their kids?"

Yes. But teenagers who wish to head off this behavior when peers are present can do so by politely asking their parents to please not kiss them in front of their friends. This request is most likely to be honored by parents whose kids spontaneously go up to them in private, say "I love you," and give them a hug. ◆

Fighting Fair

No family is an island of perfect peace and harmony. All families argue at times. In general, there's nothing wrong with arguing—as long as it occurs in a context of love and mutual respect. Arguing is okay if people listen to what others say, and work towards a resolution that respects everyone's needs and feelings. This is called *fighting fair.* Unfair fighting is when people break or throw things, commit acts of violence, reveal confidences, issue threats, call names, and/or say things they know will hurt. This kind of fighting rarely leads to solving a conflict. It only escalates it.

All families (especially large ones, in which it's easy for individual voices to be lost) should have a family meeting once a week. This is a regularly

How Rude!

scheduled time when everybody gathers to share news, set goals, air grievances, and solve problems. You can propose this to your family. Explain that people who share common interests and objectives—be they basketball players, management teams, faculty members, or parents and kids—need to get together regularly to discuss their plans and concerns.

Here's how to make family meetings work:

Establish a regular time to meet. If someone can't come because of an unavoidable conflict, try to reschedule. If one or more family members just decide not to show up, don't reschedule. It's their loss, and they have to abide by decisions made without their input.

Post an agenda in a conspicuous place. Encourage your parents and siblings to write down items they'd like to discuss. While late-breaking issues can always be brought up, the agenda lets people do some thinking ahead of time.

Appoint a "chair" for each meeting. This is the person who brings the agenda and runs the meeting. The position should be rotated among all family members so no one person dominates.

Don't meet for too long. When people get restless, tempers flare and thinking gets sloppy. Better to schedule another meeting than to run overtime.

Take notes. Appoint a scribe for each meeting. The scribe's job is to write down ideas, decisions, plans, etc. He or she can also remind people between meetings of actions they need to take.

Use the structured problem-solving method.* Virtually any conflict can be resolved if you:

1. define it in terms that don't accuse people of wrongdoing
2. brainstorm solutions together
3. discuss the options available to you
4. pick the best one and make a plan of action, and
5. monitor and adjust the solution.

Keep the mood positive. While family meetings are the place to bring problems and complaints, they shouldn't degenerate into gripe sessions. This can be avoided if you all agree to stick to the following rules:

- Listen when others speak.
- Think constructively. Focus on solving the problem rather than placing blame.

---

* See pages 128–129.

- Don't label people's ideas as lame, clueless, or silly.
- Don't accuse. Say how you feel.
- Make sure there's a fun item on every agenda (for example, taking a trip, getting a dog, deciding what to do for Grandma's birthday).
- End each meeting on an upbeat note. Rent a video, make ice cream sundaes, play a game. Try not to end a meeting when people are angry or upset.

"What do you do when your parents are rude, mean, and unfair? I've tried yelling, throwing things, threats, and giving them the silent treatment, but I just get in more trouble."

Rudeness in response to rudeness just causes more rudeness. You need to break the cycle—to set an example of politeness which, in time, your parents will probably adopt.

Talk to them. Don't try to win arguments; try to solve problems instead. Approach your parents at a calm moment and proceed as follows:

1. If needed, start with an apology:
   "I'm sorry about breaking the window. It was very careless of me."

2. Follow up by offering to make amends:
   "I'll pay for it."

3. Then define the issue of unfairness in a neutral way:
   "But I'd feel terrible if it means I can never use my boomerang again."

4. And propose a problem-solving session:
   "Do you think we could talk about this and try to come up with a way that I can have it back and you can feel safe?"

See if this helps. Most parents respond well to reasonableness, respect, and empathy . . . in other words, to good manners. Meanwhile, ask your parents if they would be willing to start having family meetings. ◆

How Rude!

"Whenever I do something my parents don't like, they dock my allowance or stop it totally. I think this is rude. If they make a mistake at work, they still get their salary."

But if they make *enough* mistakes, they could get fired. Because parents don't have the option of giving kids the pink slip, they use other methods—like withholding or stopping their allowance.

I don't agree with this approach to discipline. I believe that children should get an allowance with no strings attached. Simply because they're family members, they're entitled to a small share of the family income. They shouldn't have to beg their parents for money every time they want to buy a comic book or a pack of gum.

Before you run to your parents and show them this page, there's something else you should know: I also believe that children should do more around the house than collect an allowance. Because they're family members, they should act like it. This means doing chores and meeting certain standards of behavior. If you forget or refuse to do your chores, if you're rude and uncooperative, if you're a pain in the butt, you're not keeping your part of the bargain.

If you don't like having your allowance docked, here are two things you can do:

1. Consider stopping the behaviors your parents don't like, and/or
2. Propose alternative consequences for your actions. For example, maybe you can't go out with your friends until you do your chores. Or, if you leave tools out in the rain, you either have to replace them or you can't borrow them anymore.

Docking or withholding your allowance won't change your behavior. What *will* are consequences that relate directly to that behavior.

Now you can run to your parents and show them this page. ◆

"If I do something wrong at home, I say I'm sorry. But my parents keep harping on it over and over. Surely this isn't polite."

It *is* rude not to accept a *sincere* apology. Maybe your problem has to do with the *way* you apologize. Sometimes, when kids are embarrassed, angry, or defensive, they just mutter a quick "Sorry." Even if they are genuinely sorry, this doesn't get communicated. Instead, parents hear "What are you making such a big deal about this for?"

An even worse form of apology is "Well, I SAID I'm sorry!" This comes across as "Get off my back!" It implies that mere words of regret should be sufficient.

If you want your apologies to be accepted, show that you're sorry in word *and* deed. Saying you're sorry is only half an apology; doing something about it is the other half. The real test of a person's regret is whether they try to set things straight. The next time you get scolded for something you did wrong, try saying something like this:

"Oh, no, I can't believe I did such a thing. How could I have been such a mush mind? I'll never be able to look myself in the mirror again. You must think I'm the worst child that ever lived. I wouldn't blame you if you grounded me for life. I promise I'll be much more careful in the future."

Then offer to make amends for your actions by repairing, replacing, rebuilding, or reflecting. Your parents may take you up on your offer, which is only fair. Or they may be so impressed by the sincerity of your words that they'll be satisfied. ◆

Around the House

TV or not TV? That is the question—along with a thousand others that come up when families share the same living space:

"Who erased my video?"
"Who used my razor?"
"Who left these crumbs here?"
"Why can't I go barefoot?"
"Meatloaf AGAIN?!

If you want to witness manners mayhem, all you have to do is step into the family room, kitchen, or bathroom of the typical household. The way family members quibble, nibble, or dribble can be a recipe for disaster. Read on to learn how to do your part to keep pleasant family rituals from turning into free-for-alls.

The Fifty Commandments
of Family Etiquette

THOU SHALT . . .

. . . respect each other

. . . do thy part to keep the house neat

. . . say "Please" and "Thank you"

. . . be courteous when answering the phone and door

. . . use proper table manners

. . . disagree without being disagreeable

. . . ask without yelling

. . . listen attentively

. . . clean up after thyself

. . . keep thy room tidy

. . . turn down the volume on the TV and stereo when asked

. . . be willing to compromise

. . . treat others as thou would like to be treated

. . . share willingly

. . . clean up the house after thy friends leave

. . . treat each other's property with care and respect

. . . apologize sincerely when apologies are called for

. . . rejoice in each other's successes

. . . empathize with each other's pain

. . . put thy dirty clothes in the hamper

. . . recognize thine own contributions to family squabbles

. . . be thoughtful of each other—especially if thou knowest a family member is having a difficult day

. . . turn off the TV when company is over

. . . take responsibility for thine own actions and words

. . . smile.

THOU SHALT NOT . . .

. . . lie

. . . hit

. . . snoop

. . . whine

. . . interrupt

. . . use crude language

. . . accept phone calls during family meal times

. . . open a closed door without first knocking—and waiting to be invited in

. . . take each other's belongings without first asking

. . . tell each other's secrets

. . . leave thy sports and exercise equipment in the hall

. . . ignore each other's requests

. . . be afraid to speak up when thou feelest something is wrong

. . . pass each other first thing in the day without saying good morning, nor last thing at night without saying good night

. . . throw thy jackets, hats, and shoes all over the house

. . . spend all day or night on the telephone

. . . forget to take out the trash

. . . embarrass thy parents or siblings or children in front of their friends

. . . take money from each other's wallets without asking

. . . schedule commitments for each other without clearing them in advance

. . . drop thy clothes on the floor

. . . leave dirty dishes all over the house

. . . forget to do thy chores

. . . read each other's mail

. . . treat each other discourteously.

"I'm a 15-year-old boy with two older brothers. My mother makes us wear shirts inside the house, even when it's 95 degrees out. It's not like this is a McDonald's. Shouldn't you be able to be comfortable in your own home?"

All people have quirky little habits and preferences that make no sense to anyone else. For a three-year-old, maybe Mr. Moose has to be next to Thomas the Tank Engine or she can't go to sleep. For your father, maybe all lights in a room must be turned off when you leave, even if you're coming back in 30 seconds. For your mom, maybe young men must wear shirts in the house.

Problems arise when quirks conflict. For example, you like to leave projects you're working on in the living room ("I'll be coming back to it tomorrow"), but your mother wants the living room kept tidy ("You never know when company will drop by"). When these conflicts involve public areas of the house, the "higher" standard of behavior (neatness, cleanliness, modesty, serenity) usually wins. But the "loser" retains the right to indulge himself in private.

Here's what this means for you and your brothers: Wear shirts in the public areas of the house—with the understanding that you can take them off in the privacy of your bedrooms. If your mother will agree to knock before entering, this will give you time to indulge her by throwing on a T-shirt. ◆

"Whenever I do something wrong at the table, my mother says, 'Where were you brought up, in a barn?' It's so annoying! What can I say back?"

"Moo." ◆

TV CIVILITY

The invention of the remote-controlled television brought about a new era in TV watching. No longer did viewers have to leave their chairs and walk across the room to change channels; no longer were they forced to sit passively through commercials. The remote also led to a new variety of vegetable: the couch potato. And it gave rise to a new subject for family fights and arguments: who controls the remote.

"Whenever we watch television as a family, my brother grabs the remote. Every time there's a commercial, he starts flipping through the channels.

How Rude!

Then he'll see something that appeals to his intellectual level, like mud wrestling, and everyone has to start yelling 'Change back, change back,' and by the time he does, we've missed some of the program we were watching and everyone's in a bad mood."

In every family, one person usually emerges as the Keeper of the Remote. Ideally, he or she won't be a dictator or a hog. Instead, that person will hold the remote in trust for the rest of the family, and honor the responsibilities of such guardianship. These include:

- adjusting the volume to an acceptable level
- changing (or not changing) channels, based on the wishes of the majority, and
- leaving the remote in a convenient location so the next person to watch TV won't have to spend three hours looking for it.

Being the Keeper is like carrying the basket on a picnic. This is a position of honor, but it doesn't give the carrier the right to eat all the deviled eggs or decide who gets tuna and who gets liverwurst. Brothers who abuse their power should be sat on by the rest of the family until they surrender the remote or agree to operate it according to the wishes of the majority. Parents who turn into TV tyrants should be invited to a family meeting for the purpose of discussing this issue.

There are other protocols of polite TV watching. They include:

Choosing what to watch. This is done either by vote (all those in favor of "Wall Street Week" raise their hand), alternation ("I decide tonight, you decide tomorrow"), or fiat ("Because I'm the parent, that's why"). Multi-TV households can cut down on these conflicts, as can those with VCRs—simply tape one show while you're watching another.

Talking. Unfortunately for those who wish to concentrate on the screen, talking during family TV viewing is allowed. Sparkling commentary followed by a chorus of "Shut ups!" is what makes the experience so warm and delightful.

The typical family includes many different personality types. They are easily identified by the remarks they make while watching:

- *The Disdainful One:* "The whole space station is nothing but a bunch of cheesy miniatures."
- *The Literalist:* "That's so lame. He just fired eight shots and that gun only holds six."
- *The Distracted One:* "Are we going to the lake again this summer?"
- *The Clueless One:* "Is that the same woman? Where are they now? Why did he let her go?"

- *The Critic:* "'Mr. Rogers' was so much better when I was a child."
- *The Beans-Spiller:* "I already saw this movie. The kindergarten teacher did it."
- *The Cheerleader:* "Yeah! Kill 'em! Blast 'em in the kneecaps!"
- *The Heckler:* "Where did she learn to act? Who wrote this terrible script? And why did we just see a microphone dangling over their heads?"
- *The Shusher:* "Sssshhhh!"

"My parents don't let us watch TV at all. Doesn't this violate some rule of etiquette?"

I don't know why so many parents are so opposed to television. We should consider ourselves fortunate that a medium exists for the purpose of providing children with countless examples of people behaving badly. How else are kids supposed to learn what *not* to do?

As long as your parents are polite about laying down the law, their position lies outside the bounds of etiquette. Doubtless you've tried all the arguments about the educational value of watching PBS, the History Channel, and the Learning Channel. And you've probably thrown a few TV-related tantrums, only to be told "Someday you'll thank us for this." Meanwhile, you're limited to whatever watching you can do at your friends' houses.

It's tough when parents forbid television in the home. But the worst that can happen is you'll grow up to be a fascinating, creative, self-sufficient person with a million goals—and the intelligence and motivation to reach them. ◆

"Whenever we have company, my parents make us turn off the TV and socialize. It's always in the middle of a good show. What can I do?"

This policy is based on two assumptions: First, that people are more fascinating than television (this, of course, is not always the case). And second, that it's rude to give the guests the impression that they are less captivating than a TV show.

Try a compromise. When your parents' friends come to visit, go to greet them. Say hello, ask a few questions, submit to their inane remarks ("My, how you've grown!"), and then say "Please excuse me, I have a lot of homework tonight." You've fulfilled your social obligations . . . but you'll have to keep the volume low. (This assumes that the TV is in a different room from the one they're in.)

If the company can't be shaken that easily (such as relatives, or parents' friends with kids your age), you may be stuck. But you live in the VCR age. So pop in a tape, press "Record," and you won't miss a thing.

Sometimes it's okay to watch TV with company—for example, when guests drop by unannounced ("We're all watching the debate, come on in and join us"), or when TV watching is the main event (as on Super Bowl Sunday). ◆

IN THE KITCHEN

Kitchens are a prime source of calories, cholesterol, and conflict, as in:

> *"Don't drink out of the milk carton."*
> *"Don't stand there with the refrigerator door hanging open."*
> *"Wipe up your crumbs."*
> *"Why is there a four-foot stack of dirty dishes in the sink?"*
> *"Who do you think I am, the maid?"*

Here are the basics of proper kitchen protocol:

Clean up after yourself. This means putting away food, sweeping up crumbs, wiping the counter, and rinsing out your dishes (or putting them in the dishwasher).

Be a good inventory clerk. If you eat the last piece of bread, drink the last gulp of milk, or scarf the last pineapple popsicle, tell someone—preferably the person who does the food shopping for your household. Many families keep a shopping list on the refrigerator door just for this purpose. (There's no rule against trying to sneak your favorite foods onto the list.)

Check before you chomp. If something looks rare, special, and appetizing, chances are it's not for you. It may be hors d'oeuvres for company, or a cake for a bake sale. Ask.

Pretend you're a waiter. Let's say your family is watching TV together. If you get up to go to the kitchen for a soda or to make a sandwich, ask if anyone else wants anything. Why? Because it's rude to help yourself to food without offering some to others.

It's possible that your courtesy will be abused. This occurs when family members come to rely on your treks to the kitchen and stop getting up themselves. It's not fair if every time you say "May I bring anyone anything from the kitchen?" the responses are:

Dad: *"I'd love a ginger ale."*
Mom: *"A cup of tea would be nice."*
Sister: *"Could you get me a grapefruit with the sections cut out?"*

Brother: *"Yeah, bring me a ham-and-Swiss on whole wheat toast with lettuce, tomatoes, and mustard, tortilla chips with medium salsa, lemonade, and three pickles. Don't let the pickle juice get on the bread."*

One hopes that with your good example, other members of your family will offer to make their fair share of service runs to the kitchen. If they don't, you can always suggest that a different person be "on duty" each evening.

IN THE BATHROOM

Bathrooms rank way up there on the list of family squabble generators:

"Mom, Christine's hogging the bathroom!"

"Who used up all the hot water?"

"Someone stole my shampoo!"

"Whose slimy hairball is that in the drain?!?"

"How many times do I have to tell you, DON'T LEAVE WET TOWELS ON THE FLOOR!"

Want to avoid these conflicts? All you have to do is install a 3,000-gallon water heater and provide each family member with a personal lavatory attendant.

Or you can establish a Fair Use Policy.

If six people all need to use the same bathroom within the space of 20 minutes, family members will stack up like planes at LaGuardia. When needs conflict, try not to fight. Instead, work to solve the problem. Sit down with your family at a calm moment. Identify the issues. Phrase them in non-accusatory ways ("The water is always cold when I take my shower," not "Jeffrey uses up all the hot water"). Then brainstorm solutions. Maybe some people can shift to evening showers. Or get up earlier. Or use the laundry room sink for shaving. The solution may not be perfect, but it will be a lot better than starting every day with an argument.

"Why do parents make such a big deal about how you squeeze the toothpaste tube? What difference does it make? You wouldn't believe the fights we get into over this."

The "proper way" to squeeze a toothpaste tube is usually defined by parents as "my way." While parents would be smart to ignore little issues (such as missqueezed toothpaste) and conserve their energy for big issues (like drinking from the milk carton), this is unlikely to happen. Therefore, you'll need to take some action. On page 127, you'll find three proposals for solving the problem.

The Fourteen Commandments
of Toiletiquette

THOU SHALT . . .

. . . hang thy towel on the rack

. . . raise or lower the toilet seat, as the case may be (either way, make sure the seat is down and the lid is closed when thou leavest the bathroom)

. . . willingly give way to those whose need is greater than thine

. . . rinse out the tub after using it

. . . remove thy shed hairs from the soap and sink

. . . clean the mirror after brushing and flossing

. . . flush when thou art done.

THOU SHALT NOT . . .

. . . pee on the toilet seat

. . . finish a roll of toilet paper without replacing it

. . . use more than thy fair share of hot water

. . . appropriate the towels or toilet articles of others without permission

. . . enter without knocking and being invited in

. . . comment on the sounds or scents generated by others

. . . hang thine unmentionables where they will smite others in the face.

1. Accommodate your parents' neurosis (er, preference). Train yourself to squeeze and roll from the bottom up.
2. Buy your own tube. Squeeze it anyway you like and keep it out of sight.
3. Have your family switch to toothpaste in a pump. No-squeeze is bound to pleeze. ◆

Sharing a Room

In the adult world, one generally gets to choose one's roommates. And if things don't work out, one can unchoose. With kids, it's different. You're forced to share a room with your sister or brother—or maybe several sisters or brothers. If you're lucky, such cohabitation can lead to closeness and camaraderie. If you're unlucky, it can ruin your life.

Meanwhile, parents aren't very sympathetic. They tell you that "sharing a room is a learning experience." And that "you need to learn how to live with people you don't always get along with." You say "Isn't that what marriage is for?" But it doesn't do any good. You're stuck.

Siblings can be a joy to live with—IF you know the secrets of proper roommate etiquette. The key to getting along with roommates is to lock them in the closet until they behave. If that's not an option, try using *consideration* and *negotiation.*

- **Consideration** means anticipating the consequences of your actions on others.

It's not enough to just consider the effect *(Hmmm, if I throw a water balloon, he'll probably get wet)* and then go ahead and throw it anyway. The idea is to refrain from those behaviors that infringe upon the rights, property, and serenity of others. If you're not sure, you can always ask:

> *"Is it okay if I throw this water balloon at you?"*
>
> *"Do you mind if I get rid of this, or are you doing a science project on the regenerative properties of three-month-old bologna sandwiches?"*
>
> *"Would it be all right with you if I rearranged the furniture and put your bed in the garage?"*

- **Negotiation** enters the picture when roommates have conflicting wants, needs, tastes, and metabolisms.

For example, you need to throw a water balloon, and your roommate needs to remain dry. Or you prefer to see the floor, and your roommate prefers to hang her clothes on it. This doesn't mean that all siblings who share space are destined to fight. Yours may be as tolerant, considerate, generous, and cool as yourself. If that's the case, here's my advice for you:

```
┌─────────────────────────────────────────┐
│                                         │
│                                         │
│                                         │
│                                         │
│                                         │
│                                         │
└─────────────────────────────────────────┘
```

As you can see, when things are going swimmingly, there's not much to say. It's when things *aren't* going well that you need help.

You can be sure that conflicts will arise. Conflict is natural, and sometimes it's even healthy. Conflict *per se* is not what harms relationships. Rather, *unresolved conflict* and *unfairly resolved* conflict do the damage. While kindness, empathy, and consideration go a long way towards minimizing conflict, don't expect to eliminate discord from your relationships. Rather, strive to recognize conflict early and address it in ways that respect people's needs and feelings.

People who share space are bound to come into conflict because they have different definitions of noise and neatness, different aesthetic tastes, different daily rhythms, different priorities and attitudes. To nip potential problems in the bud (and solve those that do sprout), try this simple five-step problem-solving strategy:

1. Identify the problem. Gather the parties to the conflict. Ideally, this should be done when you're not screaming at each another. State the problem in terms of your needs and feelings rather than your roommate's transgressions. Examples:

Right	Wrong
"I can't study with music on."	"Your music is driving me crazy."
"I went to play tennis, and my racquet was gone."	"You're always taking my things without asking."

This approach creates the type of nonaccusatory climate that leads to thoughtful discussion and creative problem solving.

2. Brainstorm solutions. Come up with as many ideas as you can for addressing the issue. The more the merrier; the sillier the better. Don't censor your thoughts or anyone else's. Sometimes it's the wild ideas that lead to the best solutions. No criticism or analysis is allowed at this stage.

3. Discuss the possibilities. This is where you evaluate the options generated by your brainstorming. Some will strike you as impractical or unrealistic. But don't label them "stupid" or "lame." State your reasons for rejecting a suggestion without dumping on anyone. Be wary of "solutions" that sound great but are, in fact, wishful thinking unlikely to work.

Family Life and Strife

4. Choose the best solution. Decide which option seems to resolve the conflict most fairly and effectively. Identify the actions that must be taken to carry it out (such as buying a partition, seeking permission from a parent, or writing out a schedule). Then determine who will do what and when you will do it.

5. Monitor your progress. Check to see how things are going. Sometimes solutions get snagged and have to be retooled. If an unexpected glitch turns up, make any necessary midcourse corrections. If things are going well, acknowledge that fact. It will give you and your roommate pleasure to know that you can handle any problems that might come up.

This problem-solving method can be applied to virtually any conflict between roommates as long as *fairness* rather than *winning* is your goal. This assumes that the conflicting desires are equally legitimate—a question of *different* rather than right or wrong.

Sometimes it's very difficult to determine who's "right" and who's "wrong." In the meantime, the following Roomietisms will help you to figure out when the position of one roommate should be granted priority over that of another:

- Illegal behavior must yield to legal behavior.
- Rule-breaking behavior must yield to rule-following behavior. (Although, if both roommates agree to break the rules, this is no longer an issue of etiquette and they may do so at their own risk.)
- Health comes first. (Allergies to animal hair outrank the desire to keep a pet llama in the room.)
- Virtuous behavior takes precedence over nonvirtuous behavior. Virtuous behavior is defined as that which is creative, productive, charitable, compassionate, beneficial to humankind, and/or morally and spiritually uplifting. Nonvirtuous behavior is defined as that which is selfish, disgusting, manipulative, destructive, distracting, dishonest, impositional, and/or likely to cause itching in others. But let's not get carried away. The minute virtuousness turns into self-righteousness, it goes to the end of the line.

How Rude!

What do you do when *both* roommates' positions are reasonable? Look for the most sensible and easy-to-implement solution. If your roommate wants to play music and you need to study, it's easier for your roommate (the noise aggressor) to use headphones than it is for you to screen out the sound or leave the room. Or, let's say you like to sleep with the window wide open during winter (room temperature a nippy 50 degrees), and your roommate likes to sleep with it closed (room temperature a toasty 90 degrees). You can't say that either preference is "better" than the other. Since it's easier to make yourself warm in a cool environment (load on the blankets and flannel p.j.'s) than it is to keep cool in a warm environment (sleep naked and remove several layers of skin?), the simplest solution would be to crack the window open a bit (room temperature 63 degrees) and lend your down sleeping bag to your roommate.

As a last resort, roommates can petition the authorities for a divorce. Maybe you can swap with someone else who's unhappy with his or her living situation. Or scour the house for a corner that might be turned into a space for yourself. *

"My brother taps. He uses pencils, fingernails, feet, knuckles—you name it, he's tapped with it. He's the one who's nervous, but I'm becoming a nervous wreck. What's a polite way to ask him to stop his %$#@!* tapping?"

The issue here is unwanted noise. Unwanted noise comes in many varieties. The most common is music you don't like. Others are tapping, drumming, excessive volume, talking in one's sleep, and banging into objects that jump in front of you when you return late at night to a dark room and your roommate is sleeping (er, *was* sleeping).

In this case, a tap-free environment takes precedence over a tappy one. In other words, it's more reasonable to focus on cessation of tapping as the goal than to expect you to leave the room whenever your brother experiences a tap-attack. Decency, however, still requires you to take a sympathetic attitude towards your roommate's excess nervous energy.

Use the problem-solving method outlined on pages 128–129. Approach your brother when he's tapped out. Introduce the problem in a nonaccusatory way. Say:

---

* To learn more about living with roommates, see pages 239–241.

"I'm sure you don't realize it, but sometimes you tap, old chap. And when I nap or work on my laptop, my concentration goes snap. Let's not scrap or cause a flap, but have a rap. So put on your thinking cap."

If your roomie doesn't call the poetry police, you can then brainstorm possible solutions. Examples:

- Your brother agrees to get counseling.
- You buy him a nervous energy ball to squeeze whenever he gets the urge to tap.
- You work together to build an isolation chamber.
- You tie his hands and feet to the chair.
- One of you jumps off the Tappan Zee Bridge.
- You'll say "Tapping" whenever he starts. He'll try to stop.
- Your brother agrees to increase the frequency of activities known to dissipate excess energy.

When your list is done, weed out the wild suggestions. Then choose the one or ones that solve the problem most fairly. If things improve, congratulate yourselves. If they don't, go back to the drawing board.

Here are some other solutions that work for noise problems:

- Be quieter.
- Use earplugs.
- Use headphones.
- Schedule "quiet times" and "high decibel times."
- Build sound barriers with carpeting, blankets, foam, etc. ◆

"Is neatness automatically better than messiness?"

No. Messiness in the absence of an offended beholder is a victimless crime. This raises two questions: What grants a beholder the right to legitimacy as an interested party? And what constitutes an "offense"?

Generally speaking, the beholder must be affected by the mess in some tangible way. This raises another question: Is injury to one's aesthetic sense a tangible affront? YES—if the mess intrudes (visually or olfactorily) on the public areas of the house. NO—if the mess is contained within the child's domain. In fact, wise parents grant their underage roommates the right to keep their rooms anyway they like, as long as the following conditions are met:

How Rude!

- The door to the room remains shut.
- Children maintain parental standards in the rest of the house.
- Mutant life forms growing on leftover food and overripe clothing are not permitted.
- Housing and safety codes are not compromised.
- Possessions damaged by disarray are the inhabitant's responsibility to repair, replace, or do without.

Some parents will argue that the mere knowledge that a mess exists, even if it's hidden from view and doesn't stink, is more than their sensitive selves can handle. These parents should get a life. Parents should ensure that their children have adequate storage space, they should instruct their children on methods for ordering one's material world, and then they should butt out. Neatness is an acquired skill. It comes with age as children decide they don't want to spend half their days looking for things, or half their allowances replacing things they step on. It comes when a friend visits and says "How can you live in this pigsty?"

But what if it's not a case of a child's own bedroom? What if two siblings share a room, one a neatnik and the other a messnik? Then you've got a conflictnik. So dust off the problem-solving strategy described on pages 128–129. Identify the issues. Brainstorm solutions. As in:

- Hang blankets or build a partition to divide the space. (This way, you won't have to look at the neatness.)
- Define acceptable and unacceptable messes. (Examples: Cluttered desk—okay; food on floor—not okay.) You might establish a kitty so that any roommate who forgets and violates the agreed-upon standards has to deposit a quarter. When enough money accumulates, the kitty treats you to a movie or snack.
- Schedule a time twice a week when you turn the music up loud and blitz the room with a thorough cleanup.
- Hire a sibling to clean for you.
- Get a trunk or a big box. Throw the things you used to throw on the floor in there instead. ◆

Sibling Survivalry

"Permission to enter your side of the room?"   "Are you shedding?"

"What's so important about making your bed? I think it's a total waste of time because you're only going to unmake it again."

I've spent many years trying to discover an unimpeachable argument for why one should make one's bed—some scientific finding that would settle the dispute once and for all, like: *Children who don't make their beds are eighteen times more likely to have tapeworms than are those who do.* But the evidence just isn't there. The closest I can come to a justification for making your bed is this: If you ever turn up missing, a detective could come into your room, lay his hand on the mattress, and say "Hmmm, this bed hasn't been slept in."

So, where does this leave us? With bedmaking as an issue of *aesthetics* and *ritual*.

To many people, a made-up bed is more visually pleasing than an unmade bed. I belong to this camp. My interior life is so disordered that I need all the external help I can get, and a neat bed means one less thing cluttering up my mind. I'm not a fanatic about it—not anymore. When I was a lad, I had a thin blue bedspread with a busy plaid pattern on it. It took me so long to get the lines properly parallel and perpendicular that by the time I finished, I was ready to hop back into bed. Nowadays, I use a big, fluffy comforter. I can fling it over my bed in three seconds, and if the sheets are still bunched up at the foot of the bed, no one is the wiser. (**TIP:** If you get a thick comforter, you, too, can make your bed in three seconds.)

How Rude!

To other people, making one's bed is a ritual that signals the start of a new day. The phrase "make the bed" meant something entirely different during the Dark and Middle Ages. In those days, it was a luxury just to sleep indoors. Sometimes, people would take straw or leaves and stuff them into cloth sacks to "make a bed," which they would lay out on the floor or on a bench or table. There was just one problem: Because the stuffing was organic, it would attract rats, mice, bugs, and mold. (This is probably where the expression "Don't let the bedbugs bite" originated.) Thus, people would literally make and unmake their bed each day to dry out the stuffing, squash fleeing bugs, and hit rats and mice over the head with frying pans.*

Now that our history lesson is over, let's get straight to the bediquette:

- Parents should not harangue their children to make their beds. Bedmaking has taken on mythological proportions as one of those things children *should* do. But there's no reason a bed must be made other than to honor the parents' aesthetic sensibilities. And aesthetic tastes are subjective. Therefore, parents should lighten up and recognize that *it's not that big a deal.*

- Because *it's not that big a deal,* children whose parents refuse to follow the above advice should make their beds. Why? Because *it's not that big a deal.* Take three seconds, throw a comforter over your bed, and preserve the peace. Save your energy for the really big issues (like curfews).

- Children who are overnight guests in somebody's home must always make their beds. If it turns out that nobody in the host family makes their bed, and you have violated household standards of sloppiness, you may never get invited back. But you will be a martyr to the cause of good manners. ◆

The Blended, Shaken, Stirred, or Mixed Family

Families come in so many configurations these days that there's no longer a single definition of what "family" means. A mom, dad, two siblings, and a dog? Sometimes. A mom, dad, stepdad, stepmom, two siblings, four stepsiblings, a dog, and a stepdog? Two moms, four siblings, and an ocelot? A dad, a grandmother, six cousins, and a hundred hamsters? These are all possibilities, along with lots of others. You might be born into a particular type of family, then

---

* Fascinating as this tale is, you probably don't want share it with your parents. For if you do, the next time you have a dispute over making your bed, they'll say "You should consider yourself lucky that you *have* a bed to make!"

watch it change before your eyes. The most common type of change these days is divorce.

When parents get divorced, it's not only your home life that's affected. Friends and acquaintances at school ask questions like:

"Why are your parents splitting?"
"Who are you going to live with?"
"Whose fault was it?"

But it's none of their business, and you don't feel like talking about it. What's the polite way to respond?

It's easy. Just say:

"I'd rather not talk about it."

Some of the kids (and adults) who ask you these questions are simply insensitive boors who are sniffing for juicy gossip. Others, however, are well-intentioned. While their questions may be nosy and clumsy, what they're really saying is "I'm here if you'd like to talk about it."

You have every right to keep your personal life private. But I hope you'll talk about your feelings with someone you trust—a parent, teacher, close friend, counselor, or relative. This doesn't mean you have to spill the beans on private family matters. Teenagers whose parents are going through a breakup can feel scared, angry, ashamed, and guilty. They sometimes blame themselves for the divorce, or think their parents won't love them anymore, or take it upon themselves to try to get their parents back together. These feelings, if they're kept bottled up inside, can make it hard for kids to concentrate, enjoy life, trust people, and build new family relationships.

The following Codes of Etiquette give everybody a fair chance to get along and act like civilized, caring human beings during this difficult time. The "Code of Etiquette for Divorced or Divorcing Parents" on pages 136–137 may be copied and left lying about by children and teenagers. Similarly, the "Code of Etiquette for Children of Divorce" on page 138 may be copied and left lying about by parents.

Code of Etiquette for Divorced or Divorcing Parents

- Answer fully your children's questions about your divorce, especially those that relate to how it will affect their lives.
- Don't share intimate details about your marriage or the reasons for your breakup.
- Encourage your children to continue the rewarding relationships they have with your ex's relatives, such as grandparents, cousins, aunts, and uncles.
- Don't ask your kids to carry messages to your ex unless the message is purely logistical.

Okay	Not Okay
"Tell your mother I'll pick you up at eight."	"Tell your mother she'll get her money when they pry it from my cold, dead fingers."
"Tell your dad that your sister loves anything having to do with Curious George."	"Tell your dad that if he ever brings that hussy here again, I'll see him in court."

- Never badmouth or blame the other parent in front of your children. If the divorce truly was somebody's fault, older children already know it and younger children aren't ready to.
- Never ask your children to take sides.
- Don't say "We did it for the children's sake." Kids hear this as "It's our fault."
- Be sure your children have all the necessary gear for shuttling between abodes.
- Don't use material objects to buy your children's love or assuage your guilt. Use love, interest, and time spent together.
- Ascribe only the best motives to your children's other parent and or stepparent.

Okay	Not Okay
"I'm sure your mother didn't mean to ignore you. She must have been worried about something."	"Well, what did you expect? Your mother's never been able to think of anybody except herself."
"Felicia didn't mean to embarrass you. It's hard being a brand-new stepmother. I bet if you give her a chance, you'll like her."	"Of course little Miss Pom-Pom flirted with your boyfriend. She's barely out of high school herself."

- Be unfailingly polite to your ex in the presence of your children. What better way to show your children proper behavior for dealing with people who drive you bananas?

- Don't ask your children for the scoop on your ex. ("So, is your mom seeing anyone these days?")

- If you're an every-other-weekend parent, be a parent, not a party host. Share your life, interests, and routines with your child. This is more meaningful than 26 visits a year to the aquarium.

- Minimize the disruptive aspects of your children's shuttle between two dwellings. In fact, have you considered having the children stay put in one house while you and your ex make the switch? ("What! Live in two places?!? Me? I'd never know where anything is! How would people reach me? I'd go crazy without a permanent home." My point exactly.)

- Don't conceal new romantic interests from your children. While your children should treat these guests with the courtesy they extend towards all guests, don't expect them to necessarily welcome such rivals for your affection into the bosom of your family.

- Take things slowly with stepchildren. Older kids, who are used to their independence, may resent the appearance of a new authority figure. If you focus on building a caring, respectful relationship, your authority will evolve. If a problem develops, work out a strategy for dealing with it with the child's birth parent.

Code of Etiquette for Children of Divorce

- Don't play one parent off against the other. ("Daddy doesn't mind if I stay out 'til two in the morning, so I don't know why you do.")
- Treat your parents' new romantic interests with the same courtesy you extend towards all guests.
- Don't assume that your parents' dates wish to steal your mom or dad's affections from you.
- Don't ask your parents for details of what they do on or with dates.
- Never brag about one parent's "new friend" to the other parent. ("He's so cool, Dad. He drives a Ferrari and he said he'd teach me to fly his helicopter!")
- Put yourself in your parents' shoes. They, too, may feel angry, confused, scared, lonely, and betrayed. Try to help each other rather than hurt each other.
- Give stepparents a break. It's as hard for them as it is for you.
- Don't get caught in the middle of your parents' arguments. As you leave the room, say "I love you both, and I'm not going to take sides."

"My parents are divorced, but they both live nearby. Even though I live with my mom, I'm very close to my dad. The problem is, every time they get within fifty yards of each other, they start sending out these vibes, and the atmosphere gets spoiled even if they don't have an actual fight, which they sometimes do. Both my parents want to be active in my life, and I appreciate that, but do I have to invite both of them to things like plays or games or even graduation if it's going to spoil it for me?"

Family Life
and Strife

You have a tricky situation, but with some thought and advance planning, you can handle it. The answer to your question is yes . . . and no. Yes, you have to invite both your parents to certain once-in-a-lifetime events, such as graduation. No, you don't have to invite both of them to less significant or repeated events.

For example, if you're in a school play, you can ask your dad to opening night and your mom to closing night. They can alternate football games. If there's an open house at school, invite your mom for 7:00 P.M. and your dad for 8:00 P.M. If it's your birthday, have the party at your mom's, and ask your dad if you could have a special birthday dinner for just the two of you (double celebrations are one of the benefits of divorce). The secret is to make each parent feel as if they're getting the best deal.

Should your parents suspect that you're purposely keeping them apart, all the better. It may cause them to reflect on their immature behavior. If, however, they confront you with their suspicions, don't say "It's because you and Dad fight so much." Instead, say "I just wanted to be able to spend time with you without worrying that Dad was feeling left out." If they believe you, great. If they don't believe you, maybe they'll get the message. Equally great. ◆

"I call my stepfather 'Larry.' What should my friends call him?"

Anything he asks them to. If he doesn't ask for anything specific, they should call him Mr. Whatever-His-Last-Name-Is. ◆

How Rude!

"I live with my dad, and he's divorced. He's 37 and goes out a lot with different women, and sometimes they stay over for days, weeks, or months. My problem isn't really with my dad, it's with those women. They act like they own the place. They're always telling ME what to do. I refuse, but this leads to some nasty scenes. I couldn't care less what they think, but I don't want to be a drag on my dad. How can I politely tell these women to go to hell without upsetting my dad?"

That's a bit like asking "How can I politely throw a bucket of sludge at one Siamese twin without splattering the other?" It can't be done. When two adults are in a relationship, things that affect one affect the other. And your behavior is one of those things.

The situation you describe is a lapse of etiquette all around—his, hers, and yours. Let's start with your dad. Many people would disapprove of a parent bringing a string of overnight female guests into a house where impressionable minors live. Your disapproval won't necessarily change things, however, and might make them worse. In an ideal world, your dad (and ditto, Dad's dates) would be sensitive to the disruptive effect rotating "authority figures" can have on you. Thus, your father would invite each guest to enjoy your company and get to know you—but to leave the disciplining to him. He would make his expectations clear to them and to you. Each guest, recognizing that a "temp" has no claim to a parenting role, would happily agree. And you, absent provocation, would extend not rudeness but courtesy and social grace. Right? Right! But because he did and didn't, and she didn't and did, and you did and didn't, something's wrong.

The main problem here is that the situation is ambiguous. A guest, by convention, is allowed to be a total pain without suffering repercussions other than not being invited back again. (This appears to be what eventually happens with your father's lady friends.) Also by convention, a guest is not permitted to correct or chastise her host's children. At some point, however, if a "temp" stays long enough, she turns into a "long-hauler." When this occurs, she is no longer a guest, but a new adult member of the family. The change in job title vests her with the authority and responsibility to discipline, although even this may be limited by various factors (for example, if she's 22 and you're 17, this won't work).

How do you know when this change takes place? The easy answer is: when Dad marries her. The next easiest answer is: when Dad announces that she'll be living with you permanently as part of the family and he expects you to honor and obey and blah, blah, blah. Since Dad isn't announcing, the expectations for everyone's behavior are unclear.

Therefore, it's up to you to seek clarity. Go up to your dad at a calm moment when it's just the two of you. Say something like this:

"Pops, could we talk about what you expect of me when you have guests over? 'Cause I get upset when they act like a parent and tell me what to do. I know that's no excuse for my being rude, and I'm sorry for the times I've made a scene. But maybe if I try to be more polite, you could say something to them so that they won't try to be my mom, and that way everybody will get along better."

If you're reasonable and respectful in bringing up the subject, your dad should be responsive to your feelings. Have a problem-solving session (see pages 128–129). Brainstorm ways to improve the situation. Then put the best ideas into action. Since you can't control what other people do or say, there's always a chance the problem will continue. The best way to minimize the possibility of your father's friends disciplining you is to be as courteous and well-behaved as you can. If they still butt into your business, don't take the bait and get all riled up. Instead, respond as you would to any unauthorized comment from an insensitive adult.* ◆

"People always tell me how much I look like my mother. The thing is, she's not my *biological* mother. What should I say?"

Try "Thank you" or "Yes, we do look alike, don't we?" The people who say this are likely to be people you're never going to see again or with whom you have a superficial relationship. You're not required to correct them with a lengthy explanation:

"Oh, it's just a coincidence because, you see, even though she's raised me for the past ten years, she's not actually my birth mother, who moved to Iowa with the owner of a stud farm when I was in first grade."

Keep in mind that introductions are simply a social shorthand. They are designed to paint relationships in broad brush strokes, to suggest people's roles and functions. There's no need to issue DNA samples or a genealogical chart every time an introduction is made. Nor is there any need to correct

---

* For tips on how to do this, see pages 361–364.

people who make an erroneous assumption—unless allowing the assumption to stand would cause harm or embarrassment.

For example, if the conductor of your school orchestra says "I really enjoyed meeting your parents at the concert," you can just say "Thank you." There's usually no purpose served in saying "Oh, that wasn't my father, that was my mother's steady boyfriend who lives with us." If, however, your father is coming to the next concert, you might want to say "Actually, that was a friend of my mother's. My father will be attending next week, and I hope you can meet him."

As long as everyone's comfortable, it's perfectly fine to refer to your half brothers as "brothers," your stepmother as "Mom," and the parents of your father's second wife as "Grandma" and "Grandpa." And, if you're really stuck, you can just introduce someone as a "family friend," "one of my relatives," or simply by their name and leave it at that. That's a lot better than "I'd like you to meet the fiancée of my once-the-divorce-is-final ex-stepmother's soon-to-be husband's sister-in-law's son." ◆

 **"I never knew my father. About five years ago, my mother married this guy, Ed, who has two kids. I really love him and, as far as I'm concerned, he IS my father. But whenever he introduces the family, he always says 'These are my boys, Sean and Ed junior, and this is Sharon's daughter, Cindy.' It really hurts my feelings, but I don't know what to do."**

Of course it hurts your feelings. But it doesn't mean that Mister Ed feels any less love for you than he does for his biological children. Maybe he's just a methodical man who likes everything in its proper category. (He probably has one of those Dynamo labelers so he can make signs to show where all of his tools go.)

When families reconfigure themselves, it's not always easy to come up with names that make everyone comfortable. Kids may not be sure whether to call Dad's third wife (with whom they are now living) "Kathy," "Mom," "Stepmother," "Mrs. Remington," or "Female Parental Unit Number Three." And she may not be sure whether to refer to you kids as "my kids," "my step-kids," or "Bill's kids."

The best thing to do in situations like these is get it out in the open. Tell Big Ed how you feel. Say "I love you as my real father, and I would like it if you would introduce me as your daughter." Chances are he'll be glad you told him, and he'll follow your wishes. ◆

"I'm twelve and an only child. I've been living with my father, and everything's been fine. But now he's getting remarried, and I just learned that he and my stepmother are going to have a new baby. I don't see why they need another kid. I'm thinking of running away."

Family Life and Strife

It can be very upsetting when suddenly there's a big change in your life. You've been living happily with your father and BOOM, along comes the double whammy of a new stepmother and sibling. No wonder you're thinking about running away. But is that who you want to be? Someone who "runs away" from life? Nah. You can handle the rough spots.

One thing that can help is some "attitude work." It's natural to feel hurt that your father "needs" another kid when he already has you. Or to worry that he won't love you as much or have as much time to spend with you. Thoughts like these lead to the sort of anger and pain you're feeling. If you can question these assumptions and change your thoughts, you can change the way you feel.

For example, one of your assumptions seems to be that love is like a pie. The more pieces it gets divided into, the less there is for each person. Love doesn't work like that. Love is infinite. In fact, the more love someone gives, the better they get at it. A new child in the family may make your father love you all the more! He'll appreciate your maturity, your accomplishments, the help you are to the household; he'll remember with affection your infancy and early childhood; he'll thank his lucky stars that he doesn't have to change *your* diapers anymore.

Instead of thinking of the new baby as "taking something away," think of it as "giving something." Like what? Like the chance for you to be the best sibling any kid ever had. Or the chance to have someone who will adore and idolize you. Or the chance to learn exactly what babies are like and how they develop. Or the chance to feel good by helping out your father and step-mother.

In fact, this baby may come in quite handy. It could be a great tourist attraction for all your friends. Plus, a lot of people your age want more privacy and independence from their parents. If you stayed an only child, think of all the scrutiny you'd get. With a new baby, you can have a bit more breathing room. Yes, this kid-to-be sounds like good news. In fact, you may end up asking your dad and stepmom for six more. ◆

How Rude!

Relatives

We can choose our friends, but not our families. And especially not our extended families. This is a shame, because relatives as a category seem to include a higher-than-average proportion of people who put one to sleep.

You might be tempted to avoid your relations. This would be a mistake. It's very important to go and see them. Why? Because this gives you the chance to stay in the good graces of rich aunts, to lord your successes over the less fortunate branches of the family tree, and to keep family feuds alive. Also, family is a precious thing. This is what people mean when they say "Blood is thicker than soy sauce." When push comes to shove, when you're down on your luck, your relatives will be there to offer love, support, and loans. So here's the kinetiquette you need to know.

 **"Whenever relatives or friends of my parents come to visit, my mother tells embarrassing stories about me—like the one about the time I got splinters in my behind from sliding down a banister. And sometimes I'm right there in the room with them! Isn't this bad manners?"**

Yes. But the road to rudeness is often paved with good intentions. These stories are probably nothing more than the by-product of your mother's boundless affection for you. Still, parents shouldn't talk about their children in front of them, as if they were statues. The only exception to this rule would be sharing news of your accomplishments:

"I know Shannon is too modest to tell you, but she just won a blue ribbon at the county fair for her woodworking project."

The thing to do is to let your mother know how you feel when she does this. For best results, take the nonblaming approach.

Okay	Not Okay
"Mom, I get very embarrassed when you tell people stories about me, especially when I'm right there. I'd really appreciate it if you didn't do that."	"You ALWAYS talk about me in front of people and you have NO right to do that and I HATE it!"

Chances are good that your mother will respect your wishes, although you might have to repeat your request a few times to break her of the habit. If this doesn't work, the next time your mother embarrasses you, say to the audience "If you think that story was funny, wait 'til you hear the one about my mother going to the bathroom in the woods and—." At that point, your mother will remind you of something you have to go do RIGHT AWAY. But she probably won't tell any more questionable stories about you in your presence. ◆

The Survey Says . . .

When we asked parents "Have your children ever embarrassed you in front of your friends?" here's what they said:

Yes	66%
No	34%

"What was it they did?"

"Interrupted an adult conversation."

"Kicked in a school window in an emotional display."

"Talked back."

"Spoke disrespectfully to me and my friend."

"Used inappropriate language."

"Had a temper tantrum."

"Demanded attention when I was in conversation with another adult."

"Revealed family secrets."

"Hit me."

*"Took off his clothes in public."**

When we asked parents "Have you ever embarrassed your children in front of their friends?" they said:

Yes	73%
No	27%

* The child who did this was only three years old, but let it serve as a reminder to all you teenagers to keep your clothes on when you are out with your parents.

continued

How Rude!

"What was it you did?"

"Reprimanded them in front of their friends."

"Things they tell me only kids should do."

"Told a story of an embarrassing moment from their childhood."

"Scolded their friends and sent them home."

"Dressed too formally."

"Said 'Why can't you be like so-and-so?'"

"Corrected their friends' poor use of grammar."

"My parents are always making me do things I don't want to do. Just this past week, I had to go to my cousin's for a barbecue, to church, and to this stupid art gallery opening of this artist friend of my parents. I don't see why I should have to do these things."

Much of childhood consists of doing things one doesn't want to do. But take heart. Once you grow up, much of adulthood consists of doing things one doesn't want to do. So, in many ways, you're getting excellent practice for later in life.

There are three reasons why you should do things your parents ask, even if you don't want to:

1. **It's only fair.** Your parents do many things for you that they would rather not do.

2. **It's satisfying.** The route to happiness is not found in giving to oneself, but in giving to others. When you fulfill your parents' requests, think of the pleasure it brings them rather than the pain it brings you. If you do this right, their happiness can become yours. (This is how parents endure doing things for their kids that *they* don't want to do.)

3. **It's in your own best interests.** Showing that you're willing to share in the boring, dreary, unfair, unpleasant tasks of life indicates to your parents that you're mature enough to share in the fun, exciting, adult privileges of life. ◆

146

"We have a very big family with lots of relatives. Practically every week we go to my aunts' or uncles' or grandparents' house for some boring meal or picnic. I don't even think my parents like doing it. But whenever I ask why I have to go, they just say 'Because.' That doesn't answer my question. Why do I have to go?"

Family Life and Strife

Because.

This falls into the category of Doing Things One Doesn't Want to Do. For three reasons why one does these things, see the answer to the preceding question.

It's understandable that being smothered in the bosom of a tedious, nosy, gossipy relative isn't your first choice for a sunny Sunday afternoon. When duty calls, the thing to do is change your *attitude* so you can change your *experience*.

Instead of thinking of a visit to relatives as a dreary chore, think of it as an opportunity. Instead of being passive, be active. What about the visit bothers you the most? The food? Sitting around indoors talking? Doing the same thing every week? No other kids around? No matter what it is, you can do something about it. Volunteer to take charge of the cooking next time. Propose that people play a game, go for a hike, or visit a local attraction. Bring your bike and explore the neighborhood. If you see any kids, stop and talk to them. With your relatives' permission, ask a friend to come along. (You may have to promise that you'll accompany her to her relatives' at some future date.)

Another thing you can do is take charge of the conversation. Instead of being bored, think of things to talk about that interest you. This is a *great* opportunity to find out all about your parents. Go off with your aunts and uncles and grandparents and ask them for the scoop on your folks as kids.

What are your relatives into? Maybe one of them flies a plane or knows a lot about horses, computers, or photography. Use the visit as a chance to learn new skills and knowledge. Or incorporate one of *your* interests into the visit. Bring your guitar and play. Make a video. Offer to do some gardening. Whatever. ◆

How Rude!

"Whenever I go to my grandparents' house, they make a big point about dressing nice for dinner and using proper table manners. What should I do?"

Thank them. ◆

"I'm a 17-year-old girl. My grandparents live nearby, and I used to visit them a lot. But my grandfather always wants me to sit on his lap or give him a hug, and it just feels weird. I don't like it, and I've started making excuses about going there, but now my mother is mad at me and says my grandparents are very hurt that I don't see them anymore. I don't know what to do."

You've already done the best thing you could possibly do: You've removed yourself from a situation in which another person's physical contact makes you feel "weird." From this "safe" distance, let's look at your options.

In the most innocent scenario, it may be that your grandfather is an affectionate gentleman who has simply not recognized that his granddaughter has grown up. If that's the case, you could say to him:

"Grandpa, I really liked it when I was little and I sat on your lap, but now that I'm older I would prefer it if you treated me like a young lady."

Note that you haven't accused him of anything. You have "owned" the situation as a personal preference of yours, which is the essence of good manners.

A less innocent scenario would be that your grandfather is knowingly taking inappropriate liberties with you. The same request as above, delivered more pointedly, might work equally well in this case. By all means, tell your mother why you've stopped going to your grandparents'. In fact, she could be the one to say something if you would rather not:

"Dad, Jill is a young lady now and feels uncomfortable when you cuddle with her as if she were a little girl. You're going to have to start treating her as a young woman and not a child."

These responses give your grandfather the benefit of the doubt. They assume that his behavior is unintentionally discomforting to you; hence, the polite tone of your reaction. It's important to note, however, that children

148

don't always have to be polite or to respect their elders. Good manners may be suspended in the face of abuse. So, if your grandfather were to touch you in a private place under the dinner table, you have every right to jump up, interrupt the conversation, and shout "Grandpa, don't you ever touch me there again!"

If for some reason you can't talk to your mother, and if your grandfather (or any other relative) persists in behavior that feels "weird" to you, tell another adult you trust. This might be a teacher, counselor, pastor, rabbi, or friend. Don't give up. Keep looking until you find someone who will listen to you and help you. ◆

"I hate family reunions! All these relatives slobber all over me, and I end up with lipstick on every square inch of my face. What can I do to keep from getting kissed without being rude?"

Short of wearing a sign around your neck saying "Bubonic Plague Carrier," probably nothing. Overaffectionate relatives present a ticklish situation. It's hard to reject a kiss without insulting or hurting the person offering it. If you can, try to grin and bear it. Or grimace and bear it. Since your expression is hidden from the kisser, no one will be the wiser.

You can also try sticking out your hand. This creates a barrier that would have to be breached if someone were to plant a juicy one on your face. Another strategy is to go for an air kiss by turning your cheek. You might also try saying "Better not kiss me. I've got a cold. I'd feel terrible if you came down with what I have." This, accompanied by a handshake and repeated every time you see the person, often gets the message across. Your final recourse is to be explicit about your feelings:

"Auntie Jane, how lovely to see you. No, no kisses, I'm getting too old for that. But let me give you a hug." ◆

How Rude!

The Survey Says . . .

And now, for some good news—just what you need after reading all about family life and strife.

When we asked parents "Which best describes how you feel about your children's manners and social behaviors?" here's what they said:

Very disappointed	0%
Disappointed	18%
Satisfied	42%
Very satisfied	40%

Just look at how satisfied most parents are. You know what this means? All of those rude kids belong to other parents!

What some parents said:

"My children are generally thoughtful and considerate of others."

"Their everyday behavior at home and in public is fine. We're proud of them."

"While there is room for improvement, I believe that my daughter genuinely cares that she not hurt people."

"My son is totally lacking in social awareness, but is inherently good-natured (except when he gets upset)."

"My children very seldom engage in behaviors that offend people in public. However, they have a lot to learn about good manners, such as expressing appreciation and praise."

"We have spent lots of energy teaching and role modeling, but they just don't get it. I sometimes question whether or not I expect too much when I see how other families deal with the same situations."

"I feel my children are respectful and considerate of others. I know they are well-liked, and I can rest easy knowing that when they are with others they will do the 'right' thing, such as pick up after themselves, offer to help with dishes or clean up, etc."

"Once in a while, they have to be reminded, but I guess we all do at times."

"Most of the time, my kids are great!"

CHAPTER QUIZ

Family Life and Strife

1. *You walk in on your parents making love. Do you:*
   a) laugh
   b) say "You guys still do that?!?" or
   c) leave quietly and immediately?

2. *You and your brother are at each other's throats. The best way to settle your differences is to:*
   a) run his underwear up the flagpole at school
   b) remove the hard drive from his computer
   c) have a problem-solving session.

3. *Your divorced dad just remarried, and you have a new stepmom. Since things may feel strange for a while, the best thing to do is:*
   a) check into a hotel
   b) treat her like dirt and hope she'll leave
   c) be kind, respectful, and friendly.

4. *Your parents have several of your aunts, uncles, and cousins over for the afternoon. You go to use the bathroom and discover that someone has really stunk it up. When you return to the company, do you:*
   a) stick out your tongue, clutch your throat, and pretend to choke
   b) ask "Who let off the butt bomb in the bathroom?" or
   c) say and do nothing?

5
Artful Lodgers
Taking the Guesswork Out of Guestwork

If you gain just one piece of wisdom from reading *How Rude!*, let it be this:

Get to know as many people as you can who own beautiful vacation homes.

Live according to these words, and you will find much happiness and free lodging. Success in this area depends on knowing how to be a considerate, responsive guest—the type whose departure will cause hosts to exclaim "Good guest!" and not "Good riddance!"

Good guests get invited back. *Great* guests get invited to stay when the hosts are away! This, of course, is your ultimate goal, for nothing can ruin a week at the beach more surely than hosts running around the house as if they owned the place. On the occasion of your first house-sitting assignment (this term is preferable to "mooching"), follow another guiding principle:

Artful Lodgers

**When you stay in people's homes,
always leave them cleaner than you found them.**

This way, when your hosts next use their place, their jaws will drop at the sparkling kitchen, the freshly dusted furniture, the polished faucets, the vacuumed carpet, the shiny floors, and the scrubbed bathtubs. They will think *When can we ask him (or her) to house-sit again?* They may even experience a moment of embarrassment when they realize how dirty the place must have been upon your arrival. But this will quickly pass. They will whip out their calendar, flip through the months, and come up with all sorts of possible dates when they would love to have you clean, er, stay again.

Right now, you may be thinking *Won't all that cleaning cut into my sunbathing? Doesn't it take a lot of time?*

Of course it takes time. Which is why you need to invite a friend or two as *your* guests while you have the run of the place. (With your hosts' permission, of course.) Just be sure they're around at the end of your stay when the work has to be done.

This conscientious approach to guestwork has rewarded me with repeated stays in many beautiful homes over the years: a beach house in Delaware, a condo in Florida, a flat in London, townhouses in San Francisco and Washington, an estate in Connecticut, a ski chalet in Vermont, an apartment in Paris, a chateau in the Dordogne, a farm on Martha's Vineyard—to name but a few. My presence is so coveted by absent hosts that the demand far exceeds my supply. Thus, I sometimes find myself having to say "Hmmm, your villa in Tuscany for the month of May? I just don't know if I can squeeze you in this year. Does it come with a car?"

Your career as a guest began the first time you went to a friend's house to play. Now you get invited to dinners, parties, celebrations, and sleepovers. And one day, if you have shown yourself to be a guest above the rest, you, too, may be asked to house-sit.

Being a Guest with the Best

RESPONDING TO INVITATIONS

Being a great guest starts with responding appropriately to invitations. Hosts find this helpful. It's rather difficult to prepare a reception for 100 people when you're not sure whether 9 or 99 are showing up. How you reply to an invitation is determined by how it's given.

How Rude!

Example #1: Informal Passing-in-the-Hall Invitation

"Hey, fish face. How 'bout coming over after the game?"

This rather breezy verbal invitation may be answered in kind:

"Okay. And don't call me fish face."

Example #2: Informal Telephone Invitation

"Oh, hi, Deb. Say, look, uh, my parents, see, like, um, they're letting me have a party this Saturday night, 'cept they don't know 'cause they'll be out of town, but anyway, it starts at eight, can you come?"

Since we're talking here about invitations rather than honesty, we'll overlook the subterfuge. This slightly more formal verbal invitation may also be responded to verbally:

"I think so. I'll have to check with my dad, but I think I can. I'll call you back tomorrow.

If Deb follows through on her promise to call, she will have done the right thing.

Example #3: Informal Written Invitation

Look what came in the mail!

> **To:** Buffy
> **From:** The Kissimees
>
> ## It's a party!!!
>
> **What:** Beach and Barbeque
> **When:** 3:00 - 7:00 p.m.,
> Saturday, August 11
> **Where:** Jellyfish Beach State Park
>
> **Why:** Why not !!!
> **Bring:** Beach towel
> **RSVP:** 626-6377 (by August 5)

This is an informal multipurpose invitation that probably has tacky little pictures (balloons, confetti, party hats) printed all over it. Nonetheless, it's very kind of them to invite you.

Note the "RSVP" at the bottom. This is French for *Répondez, s'il vous plaît,* which means *Veuillez me donner une réponse,* which means "Respond, if you please." But it doesn't *really* mean that. OF COURSE YOU HAVE TO RESPOND! Whether it pleases you to do so or not. The phrasing is just a social nicety not to be taken literally.*

Because the Kissimees included their phone number, you would call with your response. If they had given their address, you would send a short, friendly note:

Thanks so much for the invitation to your beach party. Count me in! I'll be there with bells on my toes and sunscreen on my nose!

Or:

*Thanks for your kind invite! I regret that I must decline.
I'm grounded until the year 2029!*

You don't *owe* people an explanation for declining an invitation. In fact, it's rude for anyone to ask. This is because it either exposes the ugly truth ("You bore me to tears and I'd rather floss my teeth than waste an evening at your house"), or it forces you to concoct an excuse:

You: *"Because, uh, um, er, I have to baby-sit my little brother."*
The inviter: *"But you don't have a little brother."*

See what happens when people violate the etiquette of invitations?

Sometimes you'll want to give an explanation so the person will know that you really, truly wish you could have accepted. This is especially important if you hope the invitation will be reissued on another occasion.

Some hosts put "Regrets only" instead of RSVP on an invitation, the idea being that people should respond only if they *can't* attend. But what usually happens is something like this: You invite 200 friends, relatives, and acquaintances to your Bar Mitzvah Dinner Dance. Twelve call with their regrets. Does this mean you can safely assume that 188 will show up? Not on your yarmulke! It means that you can't distinguish those who haven't called because they have no regrets to extend from those who haven't called because they can't be bothered. So you're in the dark. And if you start phoning people you haven't heard from (so you can tell the caterer how many guests there'll

---

* Similarly, when someone says "Would you be so kind as to pass the sugar?" you don't have the option of saying "No."

be), those who are coming and didn't call because you said "Regrets only" will think you're daft for calling them.

So you're much better off using RSVP. You'll still have to check up on some people, but at least you'll know who. Give them a call and say "I hadn't heard whether you'll be able to come to my party, so I'm calling to make sure you got my invitation." They'll probably squirm and apologize (as well they should), but you'll get the information you need.

Example #4: Formal Engraved, Calligraphed, or Handwritten Invitation
My, you're popular! Let's see what you're invited to:

Mr. and Mrs. Ralphie Malone
request the honor of your presence
as their son,
Bugsy Albert,
performs his first tumbling routine
on Friday, the thirteenth of March
at half after one o'clock
Nadia Comaneci High School
The Gymnasium
Lakeville, New Jersey
Luncheon following the cartwheels

RSVP
112 Lottery Lane
Atlantic City, New Jersey 98765

If the envelope contains nothing else, you must send a handwritten reply by mail to Mr. and Mrs. Malone at the given address. It's not enough to catch Bugsy at school and accept (or decline) verbally. He is not the host. Use good quality note-sized paper (frayed edges okay). Then get yourself centered (because that's what your reply to a formal invitation needs to be) and write:

> Miss Moll Flanders
> accepts with pleasure
> the kind invitation of
> Mr. and Mrs. Malone
> for Friday, the thirteenth of March
> at half after one o'clock.

You may wonder why formal replies have to be centered and handwritten, and why, instead of just saying March 13 at 1:30 P.M., you have to spell everything out. BECAUSE IT TAKES MORE TIME, THAT'S WHY! It's assumed that people who issue and receive formal invitations either have a lot of leisure time or have other people who do their dirty work for them.

"But why do I have to tell the Malones when their stupid party is? If they don't know, who does?"

The Malones may be such social lions that they send out waves of invitations to all sorts of different events. This way, you let them know which particular party you plan to attend.

If the Malones are extra-smart, they'll make it extra-easy for you to RSVP. They'll include a response card and a stamped, self-addressed envelope along with the invitation. A response card is a bit like a miniature true-false exam:

Just fill in "iss," "s.," "rs.," or "r." after the multipurpose "M," followed

M_____

☐ *accepts*
☐ *declines*

Friday, March thirteenth
Nadia Comaneci High School

by your name. Check the appropriate box. Stick the response card in the envelope and don't forget to mail it.

You *really* have to be lazy, inconsiderate, and/or disorganized to fail to reply to an invitation that includes a response card.

How Rude!

GUESTLY BEHAVIOR

Now that you've responded properly to the invitation, here are 12 protocols of proper behavior that will establish your reputation as a guest with the best.

1. Show up. You've made a commitment. People are counting on your scintillating presence and smiling visage. If it turns out that you are *not* able to attend after all, let your host know ASAP.

2. Be on time. Invitations to some events, such as open houses or skating parties, usually list hours of operation (for example, 4:00–7:00 P.M.). This typically means that guests are free to arrive and depart at any time within the stated range. Other events, such as sit-down dinners, graduations, and religious services, are time-sensitive and must occur on schedule. Don't be late. You'll either miss the main event or cause others to. What's worse, you might have to spend the rest of your life with some host's dried-out chicken on your conscience.

3. Don't arrive early. The air of relaxation hosts affect when they answer the door is an act. Five seconds earlier, they were running around in a state of total panic—cooking, polishing, setting, cleaning, counting, checking, supervising, and yelling at their kids. The last thing any host needs is some guest coming early and interrupting all this anxiety. So, if you've arrived ahead of schedule, sit in the car. Go for a walk. Feed the squirrels. Do anything—but don't ring that doorbell.

4. Never bring people who weren't invited. It's the host's job to make up the guest list. Guest lists reflect interpersonal likes, dislikes, obligations, and aspirations; the number of plates in the pie pantry; the number of Cornish game hens that can fit in the oven. Bringing one uninvited guest can poison the chemistry of an evening, disrupt the seating plan, and precipitate a shocking scandal. Despite these attractions, it's something you must never do.

For large events where an additional guest is unlikely to cause undue expense or problems for the host, you can ask for permission to bring someone. Another way to ask is to decline the invitation with an explanation:

"I'd love to come. But a friend from my old school will be staying with me that weekend."

This gives the issuer of the invitation the opportunity to say either:

"Oh, well, let's do it another time then."

Or:

"Bring your friend. I'd love to meet her."

5. Dress appropriately. Chances are you'll know just what to wear. When in doubt, ask your host or someone who's been to these types of affairs before. It's better to err on the side of being too dressy rather than not dressy enough; this shows respect for your host and the occasion. It's a lot easier to remove a jacket you brought than to put one on that you didn't.

6. Introduce yourself. The first thing a host wonders after all the guests have left is *Did they have a good time?* A good host creates a setting and supplies raw material for an enjoyable event. After that, it's up to the guests to liven things up with spirited conversation and positive energy. If there are people you don't know, introduce yourself. You may meet the person who will become your best friend for the next five years. If you see people just standing around, talk to them or ease them into your group. If you help to make a party work, everybody will want you at theirs.

"I hope you don't mind, but I brought a few friends."

7. Don't hog the food. A fellow came (early!) to one of my parties and, while I scurried around with last-minute preparations, ate the entire beautiful oozy wedge of Brie cheese I had set out. Remember that the food is there for everybody's enjoyment.

8. Don't bring anything illegal. Underage drinking and the use of illegal drugs by guests puts hosts in legal and financial jeopardy. This is an abuse of their hospitality and is, therefore, rude, rude, rude.

159

9. Don't snoop. Even people with impeccable manners are tempted to know more about the private lives of friends and acquaintances than is wise or healthy. You must resist the temptation to peek into the closets and bureaus of your friends, parents, and the people for whom you baby-sit. Once you discover those amazing photos in the bottom drawer, you'll never be able to think of those people in the same way again.

10. Do your best to be cheerful. True, it's a bad idea to bottle up your feelings. But it's an even worse idea to come to somebody's party and let your woes dominate the mood.

You've probably seen this happen. Everybody's looking forward to having a great time. The party starts . . . and then Alice arrives. She looks tearful and washed out, and word quickly spreads that she was just dumped by Scott. Before you can say "What?!?" the party has turned into a group therapy and crisis-management session. Six girls in the bathroom plan the demise of Scott; four guys in the basement talk about how Alice had it coming; Andy practices shuttle diplomacy between the basement and the bathroom; a group in the den tries to figure out where love went wrong; Sally gets on the phone to Scott; and the poor host wonders what happened to her party.

Of course, Alice has every right to be upset. But she doesn't have the right to turn her misfortune into the theme of somebody else's long-planned event. She could have stayed home, or used the party to get her mind off of Scott, or talked privately to one or two close friends.

If one of your personal problems ever threatens to intrude on a public event, keep a stiff upper lip and remember that the show must go on. This will only add to the drama, for the next day people will say "Can you believe it?!? Alice didn't breathe one word last night!"

11. Don't linger. Watch for clues that the hosts wish to wrap things up. Such clues include yawning, turning off the music, turning up the lights, bringing things to the kitchen, and saying "I had no idea it was so late." Many hosts, however, are too polite to hint people out the door. So it's your responsibility to leave at a reasonable time. If an end time for the event was mentioned in the invitation, be prepared to honor it. Otherwise, look for signs that people are beginning to leave, and go with the flow. Sometimes a party will really click and continue waaaay past everyone's bedtimes. You'll know when this happens, because any efforts on your part to leave will be genuinely resisted ("Don't go. The party's just getting started!"). In such cases, it's perfectly fine to let your arm be twisted.

12. Thank the host. For informal teenagers' parties, it's usually enough to thank your host when you leave. It's nice to repeat your thanks the next day. If your host's parents helped to sponsor the event, be sure to thank them profusely as well. For smaller or more formal events, a written thank you is never out of order and will identify you as an especially well-mannered individual.*

Artful
Lodgers

The Survey Says . . .

Here, according to our survey of adults, are the 20 Rudest Things Their Children's Friends Do When They Visit:

1. Enter the house without saying "Hello" and/or leave without saying "Good-bye."
2. Not say "Please" or "Thank you."
3. Throw their shoes, jackets, and backpacks all over.
4. Are loud and disrespectful.
5. Not thank parents for preparing snacks, picking them up, etc.
6. Damage or break items without apologizing or offering to replace them.
7. Hint broadly for things they can't have, or ask for them outright.
8. Not look parents in the eye.
9. Not talk to them.
10. Wander into every room of the house without asking.
11. Use bad language.
12. Raid the refrigerator.
13. Not help to pick up before leaving.
14. Whisper behind parents' backs.
15. Look in cabinets and drawers; touch things that are considered private (read mail on counter, flip through calendars, etc.).
16. Question house rules.
17. Wear hats at the table.
18. Sit slumped in the living room watching TV and not move when someone enters the room.
19. Not call home for a ride, but wait for parents to suggest a departure time and/or to drive them home.
20. Not ask permission to use the TV or computer.

* For a refresher on writing thank-you notes, see pages 40–42.

How Rude!

THE POLITE OVERNIGHTER

There are many advantages to spending the night at a friend's house:

- You get a vacation from your parents.
- Your parents get a vacation from you.
- You learn all sorts of things that Jimmy's mother lets him do, which you can use as ammo at a later date.
- You learn all sorts of things that Jimmy's parents *don't* let him do, which you can keep to yourself.
- Jimmy's parents observe how polite and well-behaved you are and compliment your parents on it. Your parents wonder *Are we talking about the same kid?*
- You see how other families operate. You can go home to your parents and say "You know, you guys aren't that bad after all!"

Everyone benefits from swapping parents and kids on occasion. Here are the basics of the polite overnight:

Bring what you need. Arrive prepared. Bring your toothbrush, comb, pajamas, sleeping bag, lounging jacket, blankie, teddy bear, etc. If you wear orthodontic headgear or take medications, be sure to bring those, too. If you're in great demand as a guest, you may wish to keep a small overnight kit in your school locker or knapsack. That way, you can accept spontaneous invitations without having to make a pit stop at your house.

"Hi, Mrs. Canoli. It's real nice of you to let me stay over tonight."

Take what you bring. The ideal sleepover guest leaves behind only two things: profuse thanks and fond memories. Everything else you bring should leave the premises when you do.

Do what your friend does. She'll give you valuable tips on family rules and routines. Follow them. For example, if she gets up to clear plates, you do, too. If she says "I have to be quiet after 10:00 P.M.," you do, too.

Artful Lodgers

Don't do what your friend does. If your friend's behavior is at odds with that of being a good guest, don't go along. Instead, do what your friend's parents *wish* she would do. In this way, you become what's known as "A Good Influence." Good influences are welcome in any home. If you get caught in the middle and your friend asks "What are you being so perfect for?" you can say "Because I want to make sure your parents will let me stay over again."

Be nice to everybody. Your friend may ignore her parents or bully her brother. You, however, must exhibit courtesy to all living things in your host's household. This means being friendly to siblings, respectful to parents, and kind to animals.

Make the bed. Your friend may have an ongoing battle with her parents about neatness. You, however, should keep the immediate zone you occupy orderly and clean. Hang up the towels you use. Stow your gear someplace other than the middle of the living room floor. Take your dishes to the sink. Brush up your crumbs. And make the bed.

Ssshhh! Everybody knows that the whole point of a sleepover is to *not* sleep. (Whoever heard of a slumber party where people actually slumbered?) The successful nocturnal get-together requires:

- resisting parental suggestions of bedtime until the last possible moment, then
- taking ages to settle down, then
- having to rearrange where people are going to sleep, then
- getting up because you a) forgot to brush your teeth, b) have to go to the bathroom, and/or c) need a drink of water, then
- having a pillow fight, which brings Dad in for Warning #1, then
- talking about girls, boys, ghosts, and what's on the other side of the wall at the edge of the universe, then
- having an outbreak of giggling, which brings Dad in for Warning #2, then
- doing something not very nice to the first person who actually fell asleep, then
- drifting into slumberland one by one until everyone wakes up and denies that they fell asleep.

However, if this fun-filled event is ever to be repeated, it's essential that you not interfere with the host family's sleep. The party mood can fade awfully fast after Warning #2 if things don't quiet down. Therefore, thoughtful sleep-over guests will do their part to keep a lid on the after-hours noise.

Give advance warning. You may have allergies, phobias, and/or non-negotiable habits or eccentricities that require adjustments or extra effort on the part of your host. If so, advise your host ahead of time:

> *"I'd love to come, but I'm allergic to feathers and wool. Should I bring my own pillow and blanket?"*
>
> *"It sounds terrific, but I'd have to sleep with my head facing west."*
>
> *"I sleepwalk, so is it okay if we don't bed down in the hayloft?"*

Get permission to use the phone. Don't use your host's phone for personal calls without asking first. If the calls are long distance, call collect or use a calling card. An innocent query as to the proper procedure for making such calls will set your hosts' minds at ease, and they won't be wondering who's footing the bill while you talk to Australia for 48 minutes.

Don't overstay your welcome. You want to leave with your hosts wishing you could stay longer, rather than wishing you had left sooner. Don't hang around. Let people get on with their errands and other plans.

FIVE WAYS TO BE A GOOD FRIEND

As a guest in a friend's home—for a special event, an overnight, or longer—you have at least two hosts: your friend and your friend's parent(s). Your obligations towards each host differ. When you're alone with your friend, you can fight and make up, share secrets, insult each other, argue about what to do, and engage in all the other activities that make your relationship so special. When you and your friend are in her parents' presence, however, you must:

1. **Be discreet.** No spilling secrets!
2. **Be supportive.** ("Mrs. Huffy, did Kate tell you how she got the highest mark in Algebra?")
3. **Be courteous.** Your behavior is a reflection of your friend's judgment. If you're a jerk, she's the one who'll be in the hot seat after you leave.
4. **Be loyal.** Don't let your presence interfere with your friend's responsibilities towards her family. ("Come on, Kate. I'll help you with your chores and then we can go skating.")
5. **Like everything.** Particularly when you're staying longer than just one night, conscientious adult hosts will ask all sorts of questions, such as:

"How would you like to spend your time here?"
"Are you hungry?"
"What kinds of things do you like to eat?"

Sometimes these questions will be sneakily disguised as statements:

"I imagine you want to sleep late." (Translation: "When do you get up?")
"There's an exhibit on pre-Sumerian hieroglyphics at the museum." (Translation: "Do you want to go see it?")

Artful Lodgers

With friends, you can negotiate these things directly:

"I want to sleep until 3:00 P.M. and I'd sooner visit the sewers than go to that exhibit."

With adult hosts, however, you must play a different sort of game. The reason for this is simple: Behind every question, they already have a decided preference, attitude, or agenda in mind. As hosts, they want to accede to their guest's wishes. As human beings, they want to do what they want to do when they want to do it. Any guest who gets in the way of this does so at his own risk. For example, that innocent question "Are you hungry?" may mean:

"I hope you're not, because I don't want to eat until much later."
"We're all starving and want to eat, so I hope you didn't stuff yourself on the train."
"I don't have the faintest idea when I feel like eating, and it would be great if I could use you to make the decision for me."

Without knowing which of these subtexts is at work, you risk stepping into a trap. You don't want to come across as demanding and spoiled, nor do you want to appear wishy-washy and indifferent. So what do you do? *Like everything.* Present yourself as an open-minded individual of limitless flexibility and curiosity. This doesn't mean you can't express preferences and guide your host towards the choices you favor. You just have to do it in ways that escape detection.

Let's say you're visiting a friend for a weekend who lives in another city.

Your friend's parents ask: *"What would you like to see while you're here?"*
You say: *"I dunno."* (You sound lifeless, unimaginative, and bored. Your hosts start to worry that they're going to have to entertain you every second of the weekend. Not good.)
Or you say: *"I want to go waterskiing."* (You may be proposing something that's impossible to do or very undesirable to your hosts. Also not good.)
Or you say: *"I don't care."* (So why did you bother to visit?)

165

How Rude!

Three strikes! Try again.

They ask: *"What would you like to see while you're here?"*

You say: *"Oh, I've been so excited about the trip, I haven't even thought about it yet. What are some of your favorite things?"* (You show interest but pass the ball back to your hosts.)

They say: *"Well, there's the Museum of Nineteenth Century Vacuum Cleaners, the Institute of Ancient Greek Calendars, the financial district, and, of course, Disney World."*

You say: *"It all sounds so wonderful. It might be fun to see Disney World, since we've been studying it in school. And it's such a nice day out. But really, I'm just so thrilled to be here, whatever you decide would be terrific."*

Of course, they'll decide on Disney World. After all, it was one of their choices. And they can't very well go back on it. But there's no way they can accuse you of being inflexible or selfish.

If you couch your desires in accommodation, you'll usually get what you want while maintaining your status as an ideal guest. The following remarks can be infinitely reworked to respond to almost any question:

Desire	Flexibility	Parry
"I've heard wonderful things about the seafood . . .	. . . but it all sounds so delicious . . .	. . . what did you have in mind?"
"It's so quiet here I could sleep forever . . .	. . . but there's so much I want to do . . .	. . . when do you usually get up?"
"I've always wanted to try hang gliding . . .	. . . but I'll have many opportunities . . .	. . . what do you feel like doing?"

"Is it bad manners to play tricks on people while they're sleeping?"

You mean, like moving their bed into the middle of the freeway? Strictly speaking, it's quite rude to take advantage of a human being at his or her most vulnerable state. How would you like to be tucked away in slumberland, drooling onto your pillow, a sweet smile on your face, while your friends see how creative they can be with bowls of warm water, shaving cream, scissors, magic markers—and you?

You could, as a group, agree to suspend the manners prohibition against such subversive deeds. This often occurs among friends who have regular sleepovers. They know that this sort of activity is likely to happen—indeed, they consider it one of the high points of the evening. As long as the humiliation is evenly rotated, nobody should object. ◆

Artful Lodgers

Being a Host with the Most

Let's look at things from the other side of the doorbell—when you're the host rather than the guest.

HOSTING THE AFTER-SCHOOL GUEST

This is hosting at its most informal. Strays brought home from school may enter and exit so quickly that their presence goes unnoticed—except for the unwashed dishes on the kitchen counter. Sometimes after-school visitors travel in packs, roaming from house to house in search of the perfect snack.

In time, these frequent fliers may come in for so many landings at your home that their status changes from guest to quasi-family member. This confers special privileges and responsibilities. The privileges include increased access to your family's trust, affection, and refrigerator. Your parents will drop the host facade, and "adopted" offspring will get to hear genuine family squabbles and see your mother without makeup. But this comes at a cost. Honorary family members lose the untouchability of guests. Without this protection, they are prey to the same obligations and expectations as their "siblings." This means kitchen cleanup, trash duty, and "don't slam the door."

Your responsibilities as a host for after-school guests are simple:

Communicate with your parents. Is it okay to bring friends home from school without asking? What if your parents aren't there? Can you invite friends to stay for dinner? Avoid misunderstandings by negotiating and knowing your parents' expectations ahead of time.

Introduce your friends to your family. In general, parents like to know the names of those who are eating their food, watching their television, sprawling on their furniture, and leaving their smelly shoes by the door. You can keep introductions simple:

> *"Mom, this is Ken Tuckey. He's just moved here from Topeka. And you already know Biff, Bill, Bob, Ben, Bart, Brett—and Sticky."*

Explain house rules. If you don't want to be embarrassed by cameo parental appearances, you'll need to assume the role of disciplinarian. This puts you in that delicate spot between the maxim that "guests can do no wrong" and the reality that "guests can be total pains in the butt." The way to resolve the conflict is with tact. Phrase your admonitions so they come across as concern for your guests' comfort and/or safety:

> *"It would be best if you didn't go into my sister's room. She's a terror when intruded upon, and I wouldn't be able to guarantee your safety."*
>
> *"Hey, could you please not stand on the coffee table? I'd feel awful if it broke and you got glass shards up your nose."*

Alternately, you can state house rules as parental pronouncements that you're required to enforce. This is one of the handiest uses to which parents can be put. For example:

> *"I'm afraid my parents don't let us play croquet with the crystal."*
>
> *"If you want to smoke, you'll have to go outside. My parents don't allow smoking in the house."*
>
> *"My folks get very upset when people paint the dog."*

Help with extra burdens. Your parents may truly enjoy your friends and welcome the fact that their house doubles as a community recreation center. Still, running a home for wayward teens involves extra work and expense. Do your part to lessen the load. After you've finished eating, put away the food (if there's any left). Stack plates, glasses, and silverware in the dishwasher. Straighten the furniture. Your parents may not begrudge the extra 73 gallons of milk, 144 loaves of bread, and 35 quarts of peanut butter your friends consume each week if you do your part.

Assume the role of activity director. Few things annoy parents more than bored kids hanging around the house. If being bored is one of your favorite things, do it outside your parents' vision. Otherwise you're going to hear "If you guys have nothing to do, the garage needs cleaning." To avoid this scenario, be prepared. Suggest to your friends that you could shoot some hoops, surf the Net, watch a video, play a game, redecorate your bedroom, etc. Bothering siblings doesn't count as a legitimate activity.

Don't use guests to get away with murder. Some teenagers use the presence of visitors to violate household regulations. They're banking that their parents aren't going to scold them in front of their guests. This doesn't accomplish much. For one thing, the scolding will just come later. For another, it takes unfair advantage of parents who respect their kids' feelings enough to refrain from public reprimands.

HOSTING GROUPS

Your first responsibility is to issue a clear invitation. Maybe some friends who have been to your house 17,892 times know that "Ya wanna come over Friday?" means "Do you want to take the bus home from school with me, stay for dinner, go to a movie, spend the night, and sleep until 1:00 P.M. the next day?" Individuals less well-acquainted with your routines and verbal short-hands might be confused by such an economical invitation.

Artful
Lodgers

Before your guests even arrive, they should know what it is they're arriving for. Otherwise they'll worry about what to wear, what to bring, how to pack, when to tell their parents to pick them up—and you will have made them uncomfortable before they even set foot on your premises. Therefore, every invitation, be it written or verbal, should contain the following information:

The Event: Is it a birthday party? A swim party? A Super Bowl party?

The Time: When does it begin and end?

The Place: Is it at your house? The skating rink? The park?

The Hosts: Who should one blame, er, thank for this delightful occasion?

The Attire: Snowsuits? Bathing costumes? Formal wear?

The Response: Just show up? Regrets only? RSVP?

In addition, the invitation should contain any special instructions or reminders essential to the event's success and the guests' comfort, such as:

Please bring rope, shaving cream, and sleeping bags.

Sunblock and insect repellent recommended!

As the host of an event, your primary responsibility is to make your guests feel welcome and at ease. Your secondary responsibility is to see that this doesn't occur at the expense of the furniture. Accordingly:

- **Answer the door.** Guests feel dumb if they ring the bell and nobody comes to the door. They don't know whether to ring again and risk feeling dumber, or to walk in and risk being mistaken for a burglar.

- **Greet your guests**. Say "Hello. I'm glad you could come." Every arrivee should be made to feel that now the party can begin.

- **Take coats.** Visitors often arrive with coats, bags, and, one hopes, gifts. Relieve your guests of these burdens or point out where they can put them.

- **Say "Thank you" if you are handed a gift.** But don't dump your guest to go open it. You wouldn't want to give the impression that you're more interested in her presents than her presence.

- **Offer nourishment.** Take beverage orders or, if it's self-serve, point your guests towards the food and drink.

- **Make introductions.** Smooth your guests' entry. Introduce them to people they don't know. Provide conversation cues, as in "Beefy's been my trainer for the past year at Club Cholesterol."

- **Circulate.** Spend time with all your guests. Don't invite people just to ignore them for the evening.

- **See that everyone has a good time.** Make sure that no one is excluded from group activities. Similarly, make sure that no one feels pressured into group activities they wish to avoid.

- **Thank your guests for coming.** When the party or event is over, tell your guests how much you enjoyed having them. Walk them to the door. Their departure should not be something that goes unnoticed. Rather, portray it as a sad event that, with sufficient fortitude and time, you hope to get over.

"I get invited to a lot of parties, and I want to have one of my own. But my parents won't let me. Aren't you supposed to invite people who have invited you?"

Certainly. This is known as *reciprocation*. It's how we thank people for their hospitality—and ensure that invitations continue to flow in our direction.

In my experience, parents who forbid their children to entertain usually have their reasons. These range from the practical to the fantastical, the sound to the silly. If you don't know the source of your parents' objections, find out. Approach your folks when they're in a good mood. Pose your question as intellectual curiosity rather than angry accusation ("Could you please tell me your reasons for not wanting me to have a party?" as opposed to "Why can't I have a party? That's no fair! Everybody else's parents let them!"). Once your parents have told you their reasons, thank them and drop the subject for now.

Meanwhile, come up with a plan that addresses their concerns. Too expensive? You'll share the cost. House too small? You'll have your party at the rink. Fear of crashers? You'll have your friends from the football team as bouncers. If it's still no go, maybe you could cohost a party at a friend's house.

You can also reciprocate with kind gestures. Buy or make a gift. Bake a pie. Your friends will know you appreciate their invitations, even if you're not able to respond in kind. ◆

"My parents said I can have a party, but there's no way they'll let me invite all the people I want to. How do I invite some without offending others?"

First, don't issue the invitations at school. Mail them or call people at home. Word will still get out that you're having a party, and people will still know they weren't invited. But at least the process will be a little less public. Since you're going to work so hard to make the party a success and show your parents how responsible you and your friends are, chances are you'll be able to have a second party. This means you can tell those friends you were unable to invite:

> *"I really wanted to invite you to my party, except my parents said I could only have a few people. But I'm going to have another party, and you have to promise me that you'll come."* ◆

"There's a girl I'm friends with. I've invited her to sleepovers and parties at my house, but she's never invited me to her house. Isn't this rude?"

One of the hardest lessons in life is that we can't control other people, no matter how much in need of our guidance they may be. Does your friend invite other friends over? If so, they may be students from her dance class, or people she doesn't think you'd mix with, or friends she wouldn't be able to see otherwise—guest list categories to which you don't belong.

If your friend doesn't invite anyone over, it may be that she has never been taught the principle of reciprocation. Or perhaps her parents don't allow her to have guests. Or it could be that she's ashamed of her house or some family secret. Since you don't know the reasons, you shouldn't take offense or be hurt.

Your friend has the right to invite whomever she wishes to her house. Even the best of friends have social engagements that don't include each other. Since it would be rude of you to ask "How come you never invite me over?" your choices are as follows:

1. Maintain the status quo. If you enjoy her company and she seems happy to have you as a friend, the issue of where you see each other shouldn't really matter. It's just part of the package deal.

How Rude!

2. Stop inviting her to your house. The lack of reciprocation may mean that she wants to cool the friendship. If this *isn't* the case, she may eventually say something like "Hey, when can I sleep over again?" You could reply "I don't know, how about doing it at your house sometime?" Since you're not exactly inviting yourself over, this would pass manners muster. Her response may give you a better idea as to why she's never invited you over. ◆

Staying in Hotels

From time to time, you may be the guest of the Hiltons, Marriotts, or Super 8's. On these occasions, you're likely to be accompanied by your parents. Hotels are often the settings for parent-child rudeness. This is because the two generations have different and conflicting agendas. Parents want to unpack when they get to the room. Kids want to go to the pool. Parents think beds are for sleeping in. Kids think they're for roughhousing on.

So we can all get a good night's sleep, here are some guidelines for proper hotel behavior:

Walk, don't run. You know those long passages with all those doors? They're not tracks for running a 100-yard dash. They're corridors for getting to your room. Even if you've been cooped up in the car all day, even if you have so much energy you feel like you're going to explode, try not to run in the hallways, bang on the doors, jump on the bed, or play tennis against the wall. Instead, go for a walk. Find the pool. Use the health club.

Watch the volume. Keep conversation, roughhousing, and radio or television volumes at a level where they won't disturb your neighbors. During sleeping hours (no, that's not 3:00 A.M. to noon, that's 11:00 P.M. to 8:00 A.M.), be extra sure that you're not committing decibel mayhem.

Don't push all the buttons. If you're in a hotel with those neat glass elevators, just enjoy the ride. Go where others need to go. Don't make someone traveling from the 40th floor to the lobby stop at 39, 38, 37, 36, 35, 34, 33, 32, 31, 30, 29, 28, 27, 26, 25, 24, 23, 22, 21, 20, 19, 18, 17, 16, 15, 14, 13, 12, 11, 10, 9, 8, 7, 6, 5, 4, 3, and 2 before getting to 1.

Leave some ice for the other guests. If it's 98 degrees and you use the ice machine to fill your cooler chest, there may not be any ice left for anyone else. Ice machines are meant for beverages, not igloo construction. If you need a lot of ice, buy a bag at a nearby convenience store.

Resist temptation, Part One. Many hotel rooms now come with small refrigerators called mini-bars. They are so named because the portions of candy, chips, cookies, and beverages are microscopic. The prices, however, are not. Don't take anything without your parents' permission. Otherwise you could end up with a $48 bill for M&M's and a soda.

Resist temptation, Part Two. In crummy hotels, about the only things you can take with you for free are fleas. In finer hostelries, the innkeepers provide an array of little items guests are welcome to take. These include soap, shampoo, conditioner, hand cream, shower caps, postcards, three-inch-long pencils with no erasers, travel literature, chocolates, and fruit. (Do not confuse food set in the room with food set in the maxi-price bar.) Hotel rooms also contain many other items you might wish to have as souvenirs. These include towels, bathrobes, remote controls, radios, blankets, pillows, pretty paintings, and air conditioning units. If you take any of these items, the management does not think of it as availing yourself of the establishment's hospitality. They think of it as stealing.

Artful
Lodgers

Souvenirs

Not souvenirs

How Rude!

Don't be a total slob. If you're with your parents, they'll probably help you with this.* A lot of people have the same attitude towards hotel rooms that they do towards rental cars—namely, that they can trash 'em to pieces. Of course, there's the other extreme: Some people actually *clean up* their hotel room and *make the bed* because they're embarrassed to have the maid see a mess. Needless to say, this approach is a bit excessive. But there is a middle ground. When you leave, bed linens should be on the bed, not on the floor. Toilets should be flushed. Towels should be on racks or counters. Messy trash such as food and wrappers should be in the wastebaskets. The room should look as if somebody slept in it and used the bathing and toilet facilities, not as if the Mardi Gras passed through on its way to New Orleans.

Petiquette

You're sitting on a sofa as a guest in somebody's home. Their dog comes up to you and nuzzles at your crotch. Do you:

a) pretend it isn't happening
b) punch the dog and ask your host "What kind of a pervert animal is this?"
c) firmly steer the dog's snout away, allowing the owner the opportunity to make apologies and say "Down, Casanova! Bad dog!"

Sooner or later, you're bound to be the target of an overly inquisitive animal sticking its nose where it doesn't belong. You have the right to "just say no" to unwanted advances from four-legged suitors.

Of course, such overtures would never happen in the first place if pet owners exercised proper authority over the nonhuman members of their family. Call me unfriendly, but I have never developed a fondness for creatures that place muddy pawprints on my clothes or shake their wet, smelly, flea-infested hair in my face. The same parents who send their child to his room for the tiniest infraction are offended if you suggest that they send Romeo the Rottweiler to his kennel for assaulting the guests.

I am all for animal rights, so long as said animals keep their paws, snouts, and slobber to themselves. If they don't, it's the owner, not the animal, who is guilty of being rude.

---

* Not with being a slob. With being neat.

TRUE STORIES FROM THE
MANNERS FRONTIER
Quelle Horreur!

I was dining at my favorite restaurant in Paris *(Paree)* when a large dog *(chien)* came in (no, it was not a French Poodle) accompanied by its owner and her companions. While the owner affected indifference *(indifférence)*, the dog proceeded to wander all about the place, nuzzling customers and begging at tables.

Now, I, for one, do not appreciate having a dog sniffing at my sweetbreads while I'm eating. So I summoned the waiter and requested that the dog be restrained so I could eat in peace *(manger en paix)*.

The dog's owner, having nothing to tie it with, "borrowed" from the coat rack *(porte manteau)* a long, knit scarf that belonged to someone else and used it to tie up the dog. *Vraiment!*

So that you are never the agent of such a *faux pas,* here's all the petiquette you need to know to keep a well-mannered menagerie:

Control your pet. Guests should not be assaulted or smothered with affection by any member of your household unless you have established that said guests enjoy such attention.

Respect the allergies and/or phobias of your visitors. Some people are allergic to feathers and dog and cat hairs. Others are terrified of animals. If you discover this to be the case with any of your guests (often the ones covered in hives or cowering behind the credenza), take appropriate steps to rectify the situation. Let Fido romp in the backyard. Put Felix in the family room and Polly on the porch. Tell Boris the Boa to go stretch out in the sun and leave your visitor alone.

If you belong to the category of pet owners who refuse to restrict their animals' freedom, you must let guests know this in advance. You can say:

> *"I can't wait 'til Friday, when you're coming over after school. I just wanted to let you know that I have a very friendly ferret who is as dear to me as Mumsie and Popsie. I'm sure you'll all get on famously, but . . . ."*

Most people will respond by telling you how much they're looking forward to meeting your family—bi-, quadri-, and octapeds alike. If, however, your friends are ferret-averse, you must be prepared to forgo them in favor of your animal's freedom.

Never bring a pet with you unless you have received permission. In this regard, pets are just like people. You would never bring an uninvited friend to a party without first asking the host. By the same token, you would never bring an uninvited animal. Ask first.

Assume responsibility for your pet's behavior. If your pet bites someone, soils her clothes, or damages her property, it's fair and proper for you to assume the costs of this misbehavior. Whether you take it out of your dog's allowance later is for you to decide. At the time of the incident, however, there's only one thing to do: Apologize profusely and make things right. Don't attempt to shift or minimize your responsibility.

Wrong	Right
"I'm sure it will brush right off when it dries."	"I absolutely insist on having it dry cleaned for you."
"It didn't even break the skin."	"We must get a doctor to look at that right away."
"Dogs will be dogs."	"I should have been watching. Fifi and I will come over tomorrow afternoon and plant some new ones."

"Don't worry. Rex just LOVES children."

If you've been effective in assuming your rightful responsibility, the victims of your pet's misconduct will often minimize the occurrence, as in:

"It's only a small slobber. No big deal."

"It's just a little bruise."

"I meant to transplant those tulips anyway."

You can then defer to their protests. But you will have fulfilled your duties as a polite pet owner.

If you're neither the pet nor the owner, you're the *pettee*—someone who comes into contact with other people's pets. Here are some protocols for being a polite pettee:

Be kind to animals. It's rude to cut worms in half or throw cats from a moving train. Treat animals you dislike as you would humans you dislike—with courtesy. Don't tease or torture them.

Ask the pet's owner for guidance. With some animals you meet, it will be love at first sight. An instantaneous bond will spring into force. This is called *animal magnetism.* You'll know without words that it's fine for the two of you to nuzzle and snuzzle all over the ground in an ecstasy of furry friendship. At other times, you, or the pet, may be unsure of the bounds of your relationship. In such cases, ask the owner if it's all right to pet the dog, feed the horse, stroke the bird, or tap the turtle.

Be firm but polite about your limits. Animals have an unerring instinct for identifying those who don't like them. Therefore, in a room of 12 people, the animal will invariably bestow its attentions on the one person who doesn't want them. If this person should be you, you're well within the rules of petiquette to say so. You may first address yourself to the offending animal. Remove its body or head from where you don't wish it to be. In a firm yet respectful voice, say "Down" or "No. Don't lick me there." Many animals are sensitive to the language of rejection and will go off in search of greener pastures. If, however, the animal doesn't take the hint, turn to its master and say:

"Reginald, could you please keep Reggie, Jr. away from me? He's the cutest little Koala I've ever seen, but I'm just not comfortable around animals."

If your host doesn't control the little beast, you might innocently remark:

"Have you noticed the price of dry cleaning these days?"

Or:

"I can't believe what they're charging at the emergency room lately to treat an animal bite."

Artful
Lodgers

How Rude!

"My neighbor's dog goes to the bathroom in our backyard. This is a real pain because my friends and I like to play baseball there. What can I do?"

This certainly gives new meaning to the term "sliding into home." Your first recourse is to provide the dog's owner with the scoop on the poop. You do this in a polite tone of voice that suggests you're certain he's unaware of the problem (since otherwise it wouldn't be happening). Ask him if he could please mind his own dog's business—especially as it has been done in your backyard up to now.

If no positive results are forthcoming, then the caca is going to hit the fan (or, as the case may be, the rotary blade). At this point, you'd be doing your neighbor a kindness if you and your friends shoveled up the offending offal and placed it in a prominent location on his lawn, perhaps near the front door of his home. It's always polite to return things guests have left at your house. You might include a courteous note for your neighbor:

> Dear Mr. Smith,
>
> Your dog left this at our house. I just wanted to see that you got it back.
>
> Signed,
> A Friend

CHAPTER QUIZ

Artful
Lodgers

1. *The reason you must strive to be a perfect guest is:*
   a) you get more food that way
   b) a happy host is more likely to pay for everything
   c) you never know when Santa is watching.

2. *You're invited to a party you don't want to attend. The proper response is to:*
   a) picket
   b) tell the host you're coming but not show up
   c) toss a stink bomb through the window.

3. *You're entertaining two friends from school for the afternoon. One of them is getting quite rowdy, and you're afraid he's going to break your mother's favorite lamp. You should immediately:*
   a) bean him with a frozen burrito
   b) break the lamp yourself so he won't get blamed, or
   c) say "Chill, dude! That lamp's lookin' mighty peeved and I'd feel terrible if it electrocuted you."

4. *It's fine to bring a pet with you to someone's house as long as:*
   a) it's not in heat
   b) it matches their decor
   c) your dog can beat their dog.

5. *You're looking down from the 16th floor balcony in one of those fancy atrium hotels. A kid comes up to you and asks if you want to have a spitting contest. The best response is to:*
   a) yell "Ptooey!"
   b) prepare a loogie
   c) say "Sure, but you have to aim for the bald guys."

6. *Every written invitation should include:*
   a) the entire guest list, showing who's going with whom
   b) a detailed breakdown of how much the party is costing
   c) chocolate mints.

6
School Rules

Civility in the Land of Tater Tots

Schools, by their very nature, are breeding grounds for rudeness. You've got stressed-out kids competing for grades, popularity, and college admissions.

You've got homework, dissections, tests, and report cards.

You've got wedgies, squeaky chalk, dumped books, and metal detectors.

You've got prepositions, expositions, prohibitions, inquisitions
Computations, conjugations, confiscations, condemnations
Allegations, altercations, instigations, indignations
Derivations, deprivations, degradations, defamations
Preparations, palpitations, protestations, on-probations
ARRRRRGGGGGGGHHHHHHH!!!!

People wonder why there isn't more politeness in schools. How much politeness can there be in a place where toilet stalls have no doors? Where, every 43 minutes, you get bowled over by a million stampeding Doc Martens? It's hard to keep etiquette uppermost in mind when your entire future depends on knowing that in 1492, Marco Polo launched a line of men's sportswear.

School
Rules

It's a miracle there's as much politeness in schools as there is. But there needs to be *more*. Why? Because teenagers spend more of their waking day in school than anyplace else. And they deserve a school climate that's safe, respectful, and friendly.

The *climate* of a school is essentially what it feels like to be there. Research shows* that the better a school's climate is, the more likely its students are to enjoy school, do well academically, behave morally, and stay out of trouble with the law. Schools with outstanding social climates share a number of characteristics including:

- a prideful sense of community
- explicitly stated values
- high expectations for student behavior and achievement
- respect for the needs and feelings of others
- close student-teacher relationships, and
- creamed corn for lunch every Tuesday.

Translated into English, this means that in the best schools—schools that students enjoy attending and do well in—people are polite to one another. To come up with a code of school etiquette, we need to know more about what makes a school climate polite or rude. If only we could find out what students and teachers think about the climate in their school. Guess what—we can! Why? Because in our survey, we asked students and teachers all about . . .

Rudeness in the Learning Environment

The first thing we did was get a general idea of whether rudeness is a problem. Hold on to your baseball caps, because when we asked teachers "Do you think students today are more polite, less polite, or the same as when you were growing up?" 75 percent said "less polite."

And when we asked those same teachers how they felt about the manners and social behaviors of the students they teach, 56 percent said "very disappointed" or "disappointed," vs. 44 percent who said "satisfied" or "very satisfied."

---

* Only etiquette advisors with a Ph.D. can use this expression.

How Rude!

Before you conclude that these teachers were just dumping on kids, you should know that the same proportion of teachers (75 percent—a miracle of statistical coincidence) also said that *adults* are less polite today than they were a generation ago. In fact, they blamed grownups, TV, and society for the sorry state of kids' manners. As one teacher put it:

"I don't think ANY of us spend enough time teaching manners and politeness."

Another teacher said:

"Schools and students today are but a reflection of society's tolerance for lower standards of behavior."

Before you say "You see, it's not our fault," keep in mind that soon *you'll* be the adults. So it's up to *you* to raise the standards. To do this, you'll need to identify what those standards should be. So let's look at rudeness in schools from the teachers' perspective. Then let's look at it from the students' perspective. Then let's break for lunch. When we return, let's come up with a code of etiquette that will make the school climate warm, enriching, supportive, respectful, and joyful.*

The Survey Says . . .

When we asked *teachers* to describe The Rude Things Students Do to Teachers—things that cause them to go home at night, tear out their hair, and sob "Why do I do this?!? I can't go on. I'm going to find a nice, stress-free job clearing minefields!"—we came up with this Top Ten list:

1. Talk while the teacher is trying to teach.
2. Not raise their hand.
3. Not say "Please," "Thank you," and "Excuse me."
4. Talk back.
5. Make no attempt to hide their boredom, irritation, or anger.
6. Not pay attention.
7. Use physical or verbal aggression to get their way.
8. Swear.
9. Continue a behavior after being asked to stop.
10. Use disrespectful body language (rolling their eyes, slouching, etc.).

---

* Would you settle for bearable?

The Survey Says . . .

When we asked *teenagers* to describe The Rude Things Students Do to Teachers, here's what they said:

"Disobey them."　　　*"Humiliate them."*
"Mimic them."　　　*"Swear at them."*
"Ignore them."　　　*"Threaten them."*
"Contradict them."

"Talk back."
"Talk during class."
"Make weird noises."
"Make stupid jokes."

"Keep doing something after they tell you to stop."
"Tell them you hate their class."
"Interrupt them for something trivial."
"Reveal knowledge about their personal lives to other students."
"Insult their looks and/or sexual orientation."
"Make obscene gestures behind their back."

"Skip class."
"Come late."
"Come unprepared."
"Get up and leave."
"Fall asleep."

"Copy."　　　*"Take advantage of a sub."*
"Cheat."　　　*"Complain about the work."*
"Mess up books."　　　*"Not show up for appointments."*

"Hit them."
"Flick them off."
"Lie to them."
"Burp in their face."
"Call them names."
"Give them mean looks."
"Be a total nuisance."

"Not do the work. Teachers go to great lengths and really do their best to teach. Students who don't do schoolwork make their teachers' lives meaningless. Making a life meaningless is rude."

How Rude!

The Survey Says . . .

When we asked *teachers* to describe The Rude Things Students Do to Other Students—things that cause teachers to go home at night, tear out their hair, and sob "I can't stand it when students are so mean to each other!"—we came up with this Top Fifteen list:

1. Say unkind things to each other.
2. Call each other names.
3. Taunt each other.
4. Single out a scapegoat.
5. Make fun of each other.
6. Whisper about someone behind his or her back.
7. Trip each other in the hallways.
8. Dump their books.
9. Fight with each other.
10. Exclude each other.
11. Fail to apologize to each other.
12. Invade each other's space.
13. Interfere with each other's education.
14. Refuse to tolerate anything that isn't the status quo.
15. Pass gas.

The Survey Says . . .

When we asked *teenagers* to describe The Rude Things Students Do to Other Students, here's what they said:*

THE TOP TEN

1. Call you names.
2. Taunt you for no reason.
3. Deliberately pass gas near you.
4. Dis you.
5. Talk about you behind your back.
6. Exclude you.
7. Spread rumors about you.
8. Put you down if you're different.
9. Play with your feelings.
10. Embarrass you to make themselves look good.

MORE RUDE THINGS STUDENTS DO

"Ignore you."
"Have an attitude with everyone who isn't their friend."
"Borrow things without returning them."
"Tell inside jokes in front of you."
"Tell someone's secrets."

"Run into you without saying 'Excuse me.' "
"Step on your shoes or sneakers."
"Sexually harass you."
"Beat you up."
"Flick you off."
"Shoot at you."

"Curse."
"Brag."
"Lie."
"Tattle."

"Bully."
"Shove."
"Spit."
"Kick."

"Make prank calls."
"Blow smoke at you."
"Put gum in your pants."
"Close your locker on purpose when you just opened it."

"Burp the ABCs in your face."
"Steal your boyfriend or girlfriend."
"Trick you into doing things."

"Dis your family."
"Ditch you intentionally."
"Not give you a chance."

"Send you fake letters or breath savers."
"Call you degrading ethnic names."
"Insult your body size and looks."

---

* WARNING! The lists you're about to read make the teachers' list sound like it's describing the behavior of choir boys having an audience with the Pope.

How Rude!

You're probably sitting there with plumes of smoke rising from your ears, thinking: *Hmmm . . . rude things students do to teachers; rude things students do to each other. Isn't something missing? Like all the rude things TEACHERS do?*

Well, blackboard breath, you're absolutely right. School climate is just as much a function of how teachers behave as it is of how students behave. So let's turn the spotlight on *les professeurs.* *

The Survey Says . . .

When we asked *teenagers* to describe The Rude Things Teachers Do to Students, here's what they said:

THE TOP TEN

1. Make fun of us in front of the whole class.
2. Deliberately ignore us.
3. Give us too much work.
4. Punish the whole class for something one person did.
5. Call on us when they know we don't have the answer.
6. Say sarcastic things.
7. Talk down to us.
8. Accuse us of doing things based on suspicion, not facts.
9. Not listen to our side of the story.
10. Play favorites.

MORE RUDE THINGS TEACHERS DO

"Yell at us."
"Snap at us."
"Call us names."
"Make us feel stupid."
"Say that we're good for nothing."

"Underestimate our intelligence."
"Overestimate our intelligence."
"Call on certain people more than others."
"Call on boys more than girls."
"Not call on us when we raise our hand."
"Act impatient."
"Act like they know everything."
"Assume that all teenagers act the same."

continued

---

* WARNING: Teachers reading this are advised to sit down and take a deep breath. You'll be shocked to learn how rude other teachers can be!

"Accuse us of cheating."
"Lose our work and blame it on us."
"Grade according to their frame of mind."
"Let the rest of the class know a student's grade."
"Not return our papers or tests."
"Fail us because they don't like us."

"Take their crabbiness out on us."
"Breathe on us with their bad breath."
"Expect students to be on time and then saunter in 20 minutes late."

"Treat us like we're still in grade school."
"Say that we can't use the bathroom."
"Judge us by our clothes or speech."
"Take points off for talking in class."
"Act nosy about our personal lives."
"Think of us as 'teenagers,' not as human beings."

"Make boring lesson plans."
"Assign busywork."
"Not take the time to explain things."
"Act like they don't want to help us."
"Break up good discussions."
"Refuse to negotiate."
"Assume the worst without letting us explain."
"Not listen to our special circumstances or concerns."
"Put down our ideas."
"Condescend. Condescend. Condescend."

How Rude!

There you have it. Enough rudeness at school to last a lifetime. The point of reporting these rude behaviors is not to start an argument. Students and teachers can have different opinions about what's boring, or how much work is too much, or whether a given remark is disrespectful. The point is to make everyone aware of the types of attitudes and actions that injure feelings and interfere with every student's right to learn—and every teacher's right to teach—in a safe, respectful school climate.

"Is not doing your homework rude?"

It depends on whether this is a pattern or a singular event. If something makes it impossible for you to finish an assignment, that's not rude at all. These things happen. Even teachers aren't always able to grade papers or prepare lessons on time because something unexpected comes up. The best thing to do is to offer an honest explanation:

> *"I'm sorry, Mrs. Rousseau, but I wasn't able to do my assignment last night. There was a gas leak in our neighborhood and we had to evacuate our house. But I'll bring my paper in tomorrow."*

If you're usually responsible about doing your homework, your teacher should accept your explanation and appreciate your forthrightness.

But what if you've really fallen behind? This, too, is not necessarily rude—if you have a legitimate reason. For example, you may be feeling depressed, or your parents may have just split up, or other students may be bullying you. Being sad, upset, or scared doesn't mean you can ignore your schoolwork. But sometimes circuits get overloaded, and no matter how hard you try, you just can't cope. Most teachers are very understanding and supportive of students who show initiative and take responsibility for their actions and education. You don't have to tell a teacher personal details about your life if this makes you uncomfortable. You could say something like this:

> *"I'm sorry I've gotten so far behind in my work. I'm having some problems at home, and I haven't been able to concentrate lately. I want you to know that I really like your class, and I'm trying to get caught up again."*

When *is* it rude to not do your homework? When you're just goofing off. This behavior affects others. When some students don't live up to their part of the teacher-student bargain, the pace of learning slows for everyone. Class discussion is hindered when students are unprepared. Teachers often feel hurt, frustrated, and dispirited. But the person who suffers most when you don't do your homework is *you*. Why? Because you restrict your options for the future.

You miss out on the pleasures and benefits of learning. You create a reputation that is unlikely to garner much respect. Why be so rude to yourself? ◆

"What's so bad about getting good grades? In my school, kids act as if it's cool to flunk everything. They tease me all the time and treat me like a traitor because I do well."

You have my sympathies. But you'll also have the last laugh.

Why do some students badmouth others who get good grades? Because they're jealous, resentful, and hurting; because their own insecurity makes them think you look down on them; because your grades remind them of how poorly they're doing; because they know, deep down, that you're going to be able to do things and go places in life that they, most likely, will not. Dissing you is a defense mechanism.

What can you do? First, be sure you're not flaunting your grades or projecting a sense of superiority. Then approach the people who tease you. Ask about their interests and activities; congratulate them on their accomplishments. They may stop bothering you once they see that you're a regular person who doesn't put on airs.

Finally, hold your head high. Don't feel you have to apologize to anyone for your intelligence, motivation, or success. If people ask you how you did on a test, say "I did fine." If they press you, say "I've decided to keep my grades private from now on." Your astute friends will figure out why. ◆

"There's this teacher who really likes me, and people keep calling me his 'pet.' I don't think this is very polite of them. It's not my fault."

Ideally, teachers shouldn't let their personal likes and dislikes influence the way they relate to students. Good teachers make an effort to treat all students fairly. But it's only natural that they will like some students more than others, just as you like some teachers (and friends) more than others.

In most cases, students who are labeled "teachers' pets" are simply those who are interested in the subject and treat the teacher with respect. (Most teachers are turned off by students who butter them up.) If people bug you about being a teacher's pet, you might say:

How Rude!

"It's not my fault if Mr. Lime finds my winning personality, alert mind, and cheery demeanor so appealing. I'm no different in his class than I am in Miss Lemon's, and you know she can't stand me."

If, however, you're being phony with the bologna, your classmates have a genuine beef and the right to rib you. So, if you don't want to get lamb-basted for being a bratwurst, hold your tongue and go cold turkey with the sucking up. After all, your reputation is at steak. ◆

"My school does random drug testing. It's already happened to me. I don't use drugs, and I don't think I should have to take the tests. Isn't there some etiquette rule against this?"

There certainly is. Good manners are based on extending the benefit of the doubt. They reflect the assumption that one's fellow citizens are trustworthy people of goodwill who, if treated with respect and fairness, will respond in kind. Random drug testing violates these principles. It says to children "We don't trust you. You must, on demand, prove that you're not behaving improperly—even if, from all outward appearances, you're a model student."

You've probably heard the standard argument for drug testing: "If you're not using drugs, you have nothing to fear." But would politicians and school board members submit to random hidden cameras in their bedrooms to prove that they're not doing anything illegal?

People in favor of drug testing in schools insist that the tests are no different in principle than sobriety roadblocks, metal detectors, or screenings given to employees such as nuclear plant operators. But they are. Driving, flying, and working in certain fields are voluntary privileges which, if practiced irresponsibly, may put the lives of others at risk. If people object to the "test," they don't have to drive, fly, or apply. Schoolchildren, however, are required by law to attend school. They can't avoid being tested by choosing to stay home.

Students aren't yet driving school buses or piloting DC-10s. Until they are, politeness demands that school administrators show more interest in the process of education and less in the process of elimination. ◆

Classroom Decorum

This doesn't refer to the color of the drapes in Room 201. Rather, it refers to those behaviors that have proven over time to be most conducive to teaching and learning, such as shooting spitballs, playing radios—oops, wrong list. I meant behaviors such as paying attention, coming prepared, and respecting the rights and opinions of others.

Why is etiquette important in school? Because etiquette is the first line of defense against unpleasant and illegal behavior. When people refuse to control themselves voluntarily, all sorts of disagreeable things happen. In school, students find themselves harassed, bullied, suspended, afraid, and unable to learn. In the "real world," the collapse of etiquette leads to anarchy, lawsuits, and violence. Wouldn't you rather say "Oh, excuse me, I'm terribly sorry" than be slapped with a summons?

Everyone benefits (except lawyers) when people behave civilly to one another. If you don't want etiquette to play hooky from your school, look at the codes of conduct on the next two pages. They're guaranteed to create a warm, productive climate for students and teachers alike.

School Rules

"Teachers in my school act like they don't want to help you. Isn't that their job?"

It certainly is. The fact that something is somebody's job, however, doesn't relieve others from the duty of requesting services politely and acknowledging them gratefully. This may be a problem in your school. A teacher's willingness to help is not encouraged by students who whine "I don't get this stupid stuff. Why do we have to learn it anyway?" Nor do teachers feel warmly towards students who slack off all term and then appear the day before the final demanding private instruction.

You may be suffering the fallout from a school climate where these attitudes and actions prevail. If you need help, approach your teacher politely and respectfully. You might say:

"Excuse me, Miss Pinchley, I'm having trouble understanding why Attila the Hunk nailed Luther Vandross to a door with 97 species during the Spanish Imposition. Is there some time when you could please help me?"

With this well-mannered query, you'll awaken all the reasons Miss Pinchley went into teaching in the first place. You'll be a ray of sunshine and a breath of fresh air in the otherwise dank swamp of her classroom. (**TIP:** If your teacher has turned into a human storm cloud, unmoved by the courteous supplications of an eager young mind, you'll need to turn elsewhere for help—to a classmate, another teacher, or, if the problem persists, to your parents, guidance counselor, or principal.) ◆

The Thirty Commandments
of Classroom Etiquette for Teachers

THOU SHALT . . .

. . . treat all students with patience and respect

. . . listen to thy students

. . . avoid sarcasm

. . . encourage students to ask questions when they don't understand

. . . take the time to explain things

. . . keep thy personal likes and dislikes from affecting student-teacher relationships

. . . empathize with the pains and pressures of adolescence

. . . treat students as individuals

. . . expect the best, not the worst, from students

. . . model tolerance and compassion

. . . allow students to go to the bathroom

. . . reward responsibility with extra privileges

. . . treat boys and girls equally

. . . make corny jokes at thine own risk

. . . use breath mints.

THOU SHALT NOT . . .

. . . ignore students

. . . talk down to students

. . . accuse students based only on suspicions

. . . punish the whole class because of one person

. . . call on students just to embarrass them

. . . make fun of students in front of the whole class

. . . prejudice other teachers' opinions of a student

. . . invade a student's privacy

. . . play favorites

. . . keep students after class just to inconvenience them

. . . take thine own personal problems out on students

. . . assume the worst without letting a student offer an explanation

. . . judge students before getting to know them

. . . assume that all students who pass gas are doing it on purpose

. . . condescend.

The Thirty Commandments
of Classroom Etiquette for Students

THOU SHALT . . .

. . . listen to thy teacher

. . . think before speaking

. . . clean up after thyself

. . . come to class prepared

. . . raise thy hand to be called upon

. . . be respectful of other people's ideas

. . . compliment each other

. . . remove thy hat in class

. . . address thy classmates and teachers with kindness and respect

. . . keep thy hands and feet to thyself

. . . say "Please," "Thank you," "Excuse me," and "I'm sorry"

. . . find another response for displeasure besides anger

. . . work diligently in class, even if thou must pretend to be interested in a subject or assignment

. . . talk directly to the person with whom thou hast a conflict, rather than to everyone else

. . . remember that teachers have feelings, too.

THOU SHALT NOT . . .

. . . bully others

. . . be physically or verbally aggressive

. . . sexually harass others

. . . ignore a reasonable request

. . . talk when a teacher or classmate is talking

. . . take another's property without permission

. . . backbite or spread rumors

. . . put people down to look cool

. . . interfere with each other's learning

. . . act bored or fall asleep in class

. . . make hurtful comments about another person's looks, abilities, background, family, ethnic heritage, or sexual orientation

. . . pressure others into doing things that are mean, harmful, or illegal

. . . have an attitude

. . . belch or pass gas on purpose

. . . cause the chalk to squeak.

How Rude!

Dear Alex

"Sometimes I don't understand what's going on in class. But I'm afraid I'll look stupid if I ask a question."

Don't worry about appearing stupid. In fact, asking questions is a sign of intelligence. It means that you're listening and you care about learning. Teachers know that when one student doesn't understand something, chances are neither do others. Therefore, a good teacher appreciates questions. And you'll be a hero to your classmates for having the guts to ask the very question that was going through their minds. ◆

Dear Alex

"What do you do when you're so confused you don't even know what question to ask?"

Raise your hand and politely say:

"Excuse me, Mr. Plato, I'm so confused I'm not even sure what question to ask. Could you please explain that again?"

Mr. Plato will probably ask the class if others are confused, too. When all hands go up, he'll take another stab at the lesson. ◆

Dear Alex

"Some kids in my school suck up to all the teachers. They're such brown-nosers that nobody likes them. Is it okay to be rude to them?"

Rudeness can never be justified by the color of anybody's nose. We had brown-nosers in my day, too. (Let's take the high road and call them "apple-polishers.") Those were the kids who, if the teacher said "You don't have to take notes on this," would write that down in their color-coded notebooks.

Someone who does well in school, turns in her homework, acts responsibly, raises her hand, participates in class, and treats her teachers and classmates with courtesy and respect is not an apple-polisher. She is a lovely human being whose friendship you should seek.

So what, then, *is* an apple-polisher? It's someone who does all of the above—while giving off fumes of superiority. In other words, it's someone whose considerate behavior is transparently self-serving. Why don't we like these people? Because they give etiquette a bad name! They appropriate its tools for their own advancement. The benefits of good manners should be a by-product of such behavior, not its cause. Etiquette becomes apple-polishing when insincerity ceases to be invisible. ◆

Dear Alex

"I keep having these dreams that I'm naked in class. Is this normal?"

Absolutely. This is nothing to worry about, and it doesn't mean you're an exhibitionist. In fact, one out of every three teenagers has that very same dream. How do I know? From another survey I gave to hundreds of kids and teens. In case you're curious, here are some school-related dreams that many teenagers have:

Dream	Percent of girls who have this dream	Percent of boys who have this dream
I'm the only person in school without clothes on	32%	33%
I had to take a test I didn't know about or study for	44%	40%
I forgot the combination to my locker	23%	22%

To Cheat or Not to Cheat?

Over the years, many students have wondered *Is cheating bad manners?* Although that question ignores the more important issues involved in cheating, politeness demands a response.

What's *right* and what's *polite* are not always the same. A well-dressed gentleman could walk into a bank, remove his hat, allow a woman with two small children to go ahead of him in line, and then, when he reaches the teller, say "Excuse me, I'm terribly sorry, but this is a robbery. Could you be so kind as to hand over the money?" His manners are flawless, but his morals leave something to be desired.

Cheating is similar. If you use a crib sheet *and* no one notices *and* the teacher doesn't grade on a curve, cheating is not bad manners because it doesn't affect anyone but you. That does not, however, make it right. And if your cheating causes your classmates any discomfort, or places them in

How Rude!

disciplinary jeopardy, or alters their class standing, then it definitely *is* bad manners and wrong besides.

The main defense you hear for cheating is that "everybody does it." Everybody dies, too, but that doesn't mean we should all rush out and croak. Cheating deprives you of self-respect and self-confidence. If you cheat, chances are your friends and teachers will know and think less of you for it. How can you feel good about a grade you don't deserve? How can you believe in your abilities if you don't put them to a fair test? How can you be mellow if you live in constant fear of being caught?

If you're honest, hardworking, and passionate about something, there are a lot of routes to success besides good grades. Do the best you can *without* cheating. Your sense of pride and self-worth will carry you a lot further than fake A's.

 **"There's a kid in my class who always tries to copy off my paper during tests. I don't like it, but I don't know what to do."**

There's a range of responses available to you:

Change your seat. This may not be possible in classes with assigned or ritualized seating (seating by cliques).

Rat on the cheater. Most schools have such a strong student code against ratting and tattling that *you'd* end up in the doghouse. So you may want to rule this out.

Semi-rat on the cheater. You could inform your teacher in general terms that "some people" aren't doing their own work on tests. This would probably lead to increased vigilance on the teacher's part. But better solutions lie ahead.

Cover your paper. This is probably the best initial action to take. Shielding your answers sends a strong message to the cheater that you're not willing to let her copy from you. It also sends a message to the observant teacher.

Speak to the cheater. Some students cheat because they're lazy or not interested in doing their schoolwork. Other students cheat because they're under great pressure to achieve. These students often feel confused, anxious, guilty, and ashamed. If you confront someone copying your answers, etiquette requires nothing more than polite limit setting:

"I'm sorry, but I don't let people copy my papers."

It's not your job to lecture anyone on her morals. You could, however, reach out to the person by adding:

"But I would be happy to help you or explain how to do the problems later, if you're having trouble."

She may tell you to take a flying leap off a quadratic equation. Or she may be touched and heartened by your kind offer. What do you have to lose? ◆

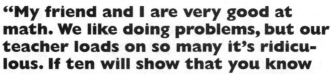

"My friend and I are very good at math. We like doing problems, but our teacher loads on so many it's ridiculous. If ten will show that you know how to do them, she assigns a hundred. So what my friend and I do is this: She comes over to my house, I do half, she does half, and we swap answers. We almost always get them all right. Would you call that cheating?"

I would call that efficiency. ◆

Getting Along with Teachers

If you follow the "Thirty Commandments of Classroom Etiquette for Students" on page 193, and if your teachers are sane and reasonable people, then getting along with them should be a breeze. However, you may encounter difficult teachers or special circumstances as you wend your way through school. Because it pays to be prepared, here's some advice to keep in mind for those challenging times.

"I have one of those names that people always mispronounce. What should I do when a teacher says it wrong?"

Sensitive teachers make a point on the first day of school of asking any student whose name is not Pat, Chris, Bob, Kate, or Lulu if they are pronouncing it right. If your teacher doesn't do this, your best bet is to go up to him after class. This is because people bristle at being corrected in public. Don't say "You pronounced my name wrong," as this implies that your teacher made a mistake. Instead, say "Excuse me, Mr. Baggypants," and then tell Mr. B. how you like to pronounce your name. Be good-humored about it. There's no way

How Rude!

a teacher will know that your parents, in their infinite wisdom, decided to name you "Karen" but pronounce it "Cahr-in." Or that you're French and therefore your name, Guy, rhymes with "key" and not with "sky."

Your teacher will be impressed with your good manners, and you'll be off to a great start for the year. ◆

DEALING WITH THE PROBLEM TEACHER

The global pool of teachers, like any group of people, includes many kinds. There are the saints, the nurturers, the lovable eccentrics, the quirky comedians, the inspiring orators, the dedicated mentors. But, by the law of averages, there are also bullies, crabapples, weirdos, and pontificators with superiority complexes and delusions of grandeur. And they will, on occasion, do things that are hurtful or unfair.

Outside of school, you can usually ignore or stay away from people you don't like. This isn't possible in the classroom. So what do you do? You follow the Five Golden Rules for Protesting the Bad Behavior of People in Authority:

1. Choose your moment well. Let timing work to your advantage. If you can possibly avoid it, don't approach a teacher who's in a rush or a foul mood. Wait until she has more time, patience, and warmth in her heart. Then say:

> *"Mrs. Moonshine, I wondered if I could please talk to you about something. Is this a good time?"*

2. Talk in private. Nobody likes to be challenged publicly. Audiences cause people to care more about scoring points and saving face than solving problems. If the injustice must be dealt with immediately and publicly, it's all the more important that you adhere to rules 3–5.

3. Empathize. Teachers are human, too. A few words of understanding from a student can go a long way towards laying the groundwork for a fruitful discussion. Try these for openers:

> *"It must be really frustrating when nobody pays attention."*
> *"I bet it's hard to teach when no one's done the homework."*

4. Explain, don't complain. Accusations—"That's not fair!" "You never listen to anything anybody says!"—put teachers on the defensive. If you're upset at something a teacher did, explain the situation from your point of view. Try not to mention the teacher's actions at all. For example, instead of saying "You had no right to make me take the test," say:

> *"I know I should have studied while I was out sick, but my headaches were so bad I couldn't read. My grade in this class is very important to me, because the only way I can go to college is if I get a scholarship."*

5. Offer alternatives. When teachers are unjust, it's often because they're angry, hurt, frustrated, or at their wits' end. Help them. Maybe the class could hold a problem-solving brainstorming session for what to do about stealing or bullying. Tender your own suggestions for dealing with a situation:

> *"Now that my headaches have gone away, I wondered if I could write an extra-credit paper on the material the test covered and try to bring up my grade."*

Most teachers admire initiative. If you're not just trying to evade responsibility or get out of work, you'll be surprised by how many teachers are willing to give you a fair shake.

"There's a teacher who keeps the whole class after if one person does something wrong. I don't think this is fair. What can I do?"

First, let's acknowledge that you're learning a valuable lesson from her: Life isn't fair. Sometimes you can do something about it, sometimes not. But it's worth a try.

Go up to her at a calm, private moment. Without accusations, empathize, explain, and offer an alternative:

> *"I'm really sorry that someone broke your plaster bust of Beethoven. I know it meant a lot to you. But keeping the whole class after doesn't solve the problem, and it punishes a lot of innocent people. I missed half of history and got a detention. One of my uncles runs an antique shop. If you want, I can ask him to keep an eye out for Beethoven busts."*

This approach focuses on solving the problem rather than blaming the teacher. She just may go along with it. ◆

"Every time I get called to the board, I get nervous and embarrassed and make these stupid mistakes, and then the teacher makes fun of me in front of the whole class. I hate it!"

Go up to your teacher in private. Explain that you get nervous at the board. Tell him how you feel when he makes fun of you. Suggest alternatives. Perhaps, instead of making you do the problem yourself, he'd be willing to let you lead the class in doing it. Or maybe you could complete a couple of extra problems for homework. If he insists that you continue to work at the board, he may at least be more sensitive to your feelings.

The good news is: Even though you may feel humiliated and upset for days after the event, your classmates will forget about it the moment you return to your seat. They're much too worried about being called on next to focus on your errors.

If the problem persists, talk to your guidance counselor or parents. ◆

"And we're going to STAY here until the person who did it confesses."

50 YEARS LATER . . .

TRUE STORIES FROM THE
MANNERS FRONTIER
School Can Be Cruel

Few situations in life afford greater opportunity to show how much you don't know than being called to the blackboard.

I still remember my tenth grade math class. I tried to cultivate an aura of invisibility so I wouldn't get called on, but it didn't always work. One day I was assigned a problem at the board. I struggled through it and stood there like a flagpole. Dead silence.

Then a fusillade of chalk ricocheted around the room. (Throwing chalk was this teacher's trademark.) The teacher launched into a tirade against stupidity—mine for the mistake I had made, and the class's for not detecting it.

Making fun of a student is inexcusably rude. Teachers who shame kids for their mistakes should be ashamed themselves. Some students may contribute to the problem by being class clowns or troublemakers, but that doesn't excuse the teacher. For, as we all know, Two Wrongs Don't Make Polite.

"A teacher accused me of stealing in front of the whole class. I didn't take anything. Later, they found out who did it, and I didn't even get an apology. I'm so mad!"

You have every right to be. It was rude of your teacher to accuse you. Since the accusation was public, the apology should be public. If your teacher doesn't offer one voluntarily, go up to him in private and say:

"Mr. Meaney, a lot of people in the class still think I stole those CDs and don't believe me when I say I didn't. I'd appreciate it if you could tell the class that it was someone else and I had nothing to do with it." ◆

GIVING TEACHERS GIFTS

The only "present" allowed in the classroom should be that which follows the calling of one's name during roll. The giving of gifts to teachers places burdens on the parents (who have to pay for them), the students (who have to choose them), and the teachers (who have to pretend they're thrilled to get them).

I speak from experience, having spent many glorious years inspiring young minds in the school environment. I witnessed the giving and receiving of truckloads worth of perfume, scarves, and calorie-laden candy. It's true that teachers deserve a bounty of appreciation. But gratitude should reflect heartfelt thoughtfulness rather than robotic ritual. If you *really* want to give a teacher a present, here are the best that money can't buy:

- *Your attention and enthusiasm throughout the year.* This is the greatest gift of all. Trust me.

- *A warm letter of appreciation.* Tell the teacher how much her teaching, example, and support have meant to you. Follow-up notes may initiate a lifelong friendship.

How Rude!

- *Support for better schools and teaching conditions.* Many schools are falling apart for want of money. Windows are broken, walls are peeling, and there aren't enough books to go around. While teachers make pennies, people who dribble make millions. If you want to give something back to your teachers, be an activist for higher salaries and increased funding for education. You can circulate petitions, speak at school board meetings, and encourage people to vote.
- *Something you make.* Take a photograph of the class and get everyone to sign it. Write a poem. Record a song you wrote. Create a work of art or craft. These are the gifts a teacher will want to keep forever.

In lieu of the above, a store-bought gift is fine—*if* it shows you made the effort to observe your teacher's interests. During the year, you can learn a lot about a teacher from what he shares with you, the way he dresses, and the physical environment of the classroom. If you discover that your teacher loves begonias, wild ties, and Tuscany, a floral print cravat from Italy may be just the ticket.

COPING WITH CRUSHES ON TEACHERS

It's wonderful to have a teacher you really like. In fact, most kids have crushes on one or more teachers before they finish school. These crushes can be based on feelings of attraction and romance, or feelings of respect and admiration. Either is normal and natural.

It's fine to "worship" someone or to have fantasies about the person—as long as this doesn't get in the way of your schoolwork or social life. If all you can do is dream about a particular teacher, if your grades are dropping, if you're cutting yourself off from your friends, then it's not a healthy situation. Perhaps you feel the need to be close to an adult and are projecting this onto your teacher. Are you having problems that you yearn to tell someone about? Are you and your parents having conflicts? Your desires to be loved and listened to may fuel a crush when what you really need is someone to confide in. Talk to a school counselor, a relative, your parents, or an older sibling about your feelings. This may take some of the pressure off.

What if it seems obvious that your teacher likes you, too? He (or she) probably does . . . but not in *that* way. Your attentiveness, enthusiasm, and friendliness are pleasurable and rewarding to him as a teacher. But it would be a mistake to interpret his fondness as romantic interest. Because he's a teacher and you're a much, much younger student, he can't have a relationship with you—no matter how much you (or he) might wish it. This would be unprofessional and illegal.

Don't tell the teacher how you feel about him. This would force him to "reject" you—which would be painful and awkward for both of you. At the end of the year, write him a thank-you note. Tell him how much you enjoyed his class and appreciated his help and interest. But don't tell him about those daydreams of you and him alone on a tropical island.

 **"There's a teacher I can't stop thinking about. I think he likes me, too. Is it okay to give him a Valentine's Day card?"**

If students in your school have traditionally given cards to teachers, then yes, it's okay. If not, it's not.

If you do give a card to a favorite teacher, make sure it's not mushy or romantic. Better yet, if you give a card to *one* teacher, give cards to *all* of your teachers. ◆

SUFFERING SUBSTITUTES

What is it about the presence of a substitute teacher that brings out the very worst in students? Why does a normally well-behaved class turn into a pack of spitball-lobbing rowdies when the "real teacher" is away? For what reason do otherwise polite students delight in tormenting temps?

"But our regular teacher lets us do this."

Let's not bother with rationales. Our focus here is on etiquette. And it's bad manners to make subs squirm (or, as has happened on more than one occasion, burst into tears and flee the room).

Substitute teachers enter the classroom at a disadvantage. They come on short notice, don't know the students, are unfamiliar with the teacher's rituals, and may never see the class again. They lack the teaching tools and clout

How Rude!

that come from having historical knowledge of, personal relationships with, and future report cards for the students. To take advantage of this is the height of rudeness. It is like (and I mean no disrespect to the legions of wonderful substitute teachers) torturing a turtle on its back.

While it may be common practice in your school to give subs a hard time, that hardly makes it proper. The presence of a substitute presents you with a rare opportunity to reap the rewards of good manners. This is because the behavior of the class reflects upon the absent teacher. Being helpful and polite not only makes the sub feel welcome and respected, but also makes her think highly of your teacher. So when the sub leaves her report (which all subs do), it will be full of accolades for those students who made her stay so pleasant.

Bullies, Bigotry, and Bad Behavior

A parent of my acquaintance told me the following story. During a visit to her son's school, she was walking down the hall towards his classroom when two students emerged from the media center. One bumped into the other, and the following verbal exchange occurred:

"Watch it, @#$%&!"*
"YOU watch it, @#$%&!"*
"Make me, @#$%&!"*
"I'll make you, @#$%&*! Get over here and I'll kick your @#$%&!"*
"Yeah, I'll kick your mother's @#$%&!"*
"@#$%& you!"*
"@#$%&* you, you @#$%&!"*

Did this happen at a high school? Or even a junior high? Had my friend overheard two teenagers showing off? No. She was visiting an elementary school, and the offenders were first graders.

They were bullies. They were bigots (as evidenced by the racial slurs in among the @#$%&*s). They were models of bad behavior. And you probably know students just like them in your school. Read on to learn what to do.

BULLY FOR YOU

You've seen students at your school getting picked on, and you're sick of it. Bullying sullies your school climate. Not only is it rude, it's harmful and potentially lethal. Some victims of bullying have dropped out of school; some have committed suicide; some have killed their tormentors (and others wish they could).

If you witness an act of bullying, don't just stand there. Try one or more of these suggestions:

Support and counsel the victim. Say:

> *"Don't let what Fowler says get to you. Everybody knows he's a jerk."*
> *"He's just doing it because you get so angry. Stay calm, hang out with us for a while, and try not to show that it bothers you."*

Confront the bully privately. Take him aside and voice your concern:

> *"I say, Fowler, old chap, I'm sure you don't realize it, but young Chumpley isn't frightfully keen on being teased. I thought I'd mention it since I know you're a sportsman and not the sort of cad who'd rag a young scamp, there's a good fellow."*

Of course, this is a total crock. And that's what makes using good manners so much fun—the total perversity of it all. Fowler may be so stunned by your appeal to his "sporting" nature that he'll actually lighten up on poor Chumpley.

Confront the bully publicly. Many bullies count on the silent complicity of others to get away with their bullying. If you see someone being hassled in the hall or bullied on the bus, speak up. Say:

> *"Cut it out. Nobody finds what you're doing amusing."*
> *"Leave him alone. How'd you like to be treated that way?"*

Enlist the support of bystanders. In the face of an act of bullying, turn to those present and say:

> *"Does anyone else here find it objectionable when Fowler picks on people?"*

Chances are good that others feel the same way you do and will lend their voices in protest.

Appeal to higher authorities. In the "good old days," the worst thing a bully might do would be to shake you down for your sasparilla soda under the threat of a bloody nose. Today's bullies may be packing AK-47s. This is no joke. "Normal" school-yard hazing has escalated to extortion, emotional terrorizing, physical torture, and drive-by shootings. The conventional wisdom used to be that bullies were lonely, insecure, and lacking in social skills—hurt, friendless children using fear and aggression to gain attention and status. Recent research, however, suggests that many bullies have tons of friends and self-confidence. They're not hurting at all. They've simply learned (from movies, TV, friends, and family) that violence and intimidation can get them what they want. If these are the bullies in your school, it may be dangerous for you to confront them directly. Instead, talk to your parents, guidance counselor, school authorities, or the police. You shouldn't have to attend a war zone to get an education.

How Rude!

Bullying is an awful breach of etiquette. The sad reality (boo-hoo) is that you'll encounter bullies your whole life. Some will go by other names: parents, professors, judges, police officers, bosses, bureaucrats. Etiquette depends on everyone agreeing to play by the same rules. If bullies adhere even minimally to the standards of society, you can use your good manners to address and rectify the situation. If, however, the bullies refuse to acknowledge the conventions of society, there isn't much you can do. You'll just have to put up with it, remove yourself from the situation, and/or look for a legal remedy.

STOPPING SEXUAL HARASSMENT

Sexual harassment is R-U-D-E. It's also illegal. Sexual harassment is neither loving nor complimentary. At its least offensive, it's an act of insensitivity or miscommunication. At its most offensive, it's an act of hostility, domination, or violence.

While most victims of sexual harassment are girls, it happens to boys as well. Here are some examples of sexually harassing behaviors that have been reported in U.S. high schools:*

- unwanted touching (of the arm, breasts, buttocks, genitals)
- verbal comments about looks, parts of the body, what type of sex the person would be "good at," etc.
- name-calling ("babe," "honey," "bitch," and worse)
- spreading sexual rumors
- leers and stares
- telling sexual or dirty jokes
- displaying pornography or sexually oriented cartoons or pictures
- pressuring someone for sexual activity
- cornering, blocking, or standing too close to someone
- publicly "rating" an individual (i.e., on a scale from 1–10)
- giving snuggies or wedgies
- sexual assault or attempted sexual assault
- rape
- touching or exhibiting oneself sexually in front of others
- sexual graffiti
- making kissing, smacking, or sucking sounds
- catcalls, whistles

---

* This list is adapted from *Sexual Harassment and Teens: A Program for Positive Change* by Susan Strauss with Pamela Espeland (Free Spirit Publishing, 1992), page 8. Used with permission of the publisher.

- repeatedly asking someone out when she or he isn't interested
- pulling down someone's pants or skirt
- facial expressions (winking, kissing, tongueing)
- creating "slam books" (lists of students with derogatory sexual comments written about them by other students).

You might be feeling skeptical about some of the items on this list. In fact, you might be asking yourself *What's wrong with a friendly touch, comment, or whistle? Is flirting a crime?* And even *Can't a person have fun anymore?*

Of course you can have fun—just not at the expense of others. Maybe you don't intend to harass a lass (or lad) with your interest and/or affections. But sexual harassment is defined by the person on the *receiving* end, not the *giving* end. If your actions or words cause someone to feel embarrassed, humiliated, fearful, powerless, invaded, or degraded, it's sexual harassment, not flirting. If the object of your attentions asks or signals you to stop and you don't, it's sexual harassment, not flirting.

Flirting makes people feel valued, flattered, attractive, and respected. Sexual harassment makes them feel confused, angry, intimidated, and demeaned. Flirting boosts self-esteem. Harassment undermines it. Flirting is reciprocal. Harassment is one-sided. Flirting is wanted. Harassment is unwanted.

Here's where things get tricky. During adolescence, you experience a lot of new sexual feelings and start to want deeper relationships with people. As you explore these new relationships, you may feel awkward or confused. You may not be sure if someone likes you or how they like you. You may wonder *Is it okay to put my arm around her? Is it okay to give him a good-night kiss? Is it okay to compliment an outfit she's wearing? Is it okay to tell him he turns me on?*

The answers to these questions aren't always clear. Human love and sexual desire are among the most powerful, mysterious, and profound feelings we experience. There's no way to regulate flirting or dating to guarantee that no one will get hurt or be misunderstood. And it would be a tragedy if schools, in their efforts to eliminate harassment, also eliminated warmth, trust, and affection between students.

You need not worry about overstepping the bounds of flirting as long as you practice courtesy in your relationships. This means being alert to verbal and physical cues. Taking things slowly. Asking permission. Saying "May I?" "Do you mind if . . . ?" "Is this all right with you?"

Another way to monitor your behavior and remarks is to ask yourself these questions:

Would I mind if somebody else did or said this to my sister, mother, or girlfriend (or brother, father, or boyfriend)?

How Rude!

Would I mind if a videotape of my behavior were shown to my parents, friends, teachers, and/or classmates?

Obviously, you might be doing something perfectly acceptable and mutually desired which, for reasons of privacy, you'd rather not see at your neighborhood multiplex. What we're talking about here is stuff that you'd be ashamed of—stuff that would reflect poorly on your character or reputation.

If you make a genuine effort to show sensitivity to the needs and feelings of others, you won't be considered a sexual harasser. But you might be considered very sexy.

BESTING BIGOTS

You've heard the comments, the sneers, and the slurs, and you've decided that enough is enough. Time for action! The key to besting bigots lies in refusing to tolerate their offensive remarks.

Precisely how you respond will depend on the circumstances. Start by considering the motive behind the insult. Some bigoted or inappropriate comments result not from prejudice but from a lack of awareness. While this doesn't lessen their ugliness, the speaker's lack of harmful intent allows you to assume the role of an educator.

For example: Your five-year-old brother calls someone a "fag." Since little kids often repeat words they hear, ask your brother if he knows what the word means. If he doesn't, tell him. Because he's so young, you'll have to gear your words to his level of understanding. You could say something like this:

"You know how Mom and Dad live and sleep together? Well, some grownups prefer to live and sleep with people of the same sex. Men who do this are called 'gay' or 'homosexual.' 'Fag' is a nasty word for a gay man. We don't use that word in our family because it's mean and hurtful."

Or: An exchange student struggling to learn English makes a comment about some "colored" students in your school. Explain to her that the word "colored" is offensive to many people because of its historical associations. Suggest that she use "black" or "African American" instead.

Or: Your grandfather, who lives with you, addresses your female classmates as "honey" when they come to visit. Since he means to be gracious rather than sexist, your job is to fill him in on the social changes of the past few decades. Inform him that young ladies of today don't appreciate being called "honey," no matter how sweet their disposition. Suggest that he refer to your friends by their given names.

Unfortunately, most bigoted comments can't be chalked up to innocence or cluelessness. They are the result of fear, ignorance, and/or prejudice. Silence in the face of such bigotry suggests approval, and silence doesn't stop hatred. As the 18th-century English statesman Edmund Burke once said, "The only thing necessary for the triumph of evil is for good men to do nothing."*

It's easy to "do nothing" in school or work environments. There's a lot of pressure to fit in that can make it difficult to challenge injustice, racism, and homophobia. Deep down, you know it's wrong, but no one else is doing anything, so why should *you* be the one to stick your neck out?

Because if you're not part of the solution, you're part of the problem. If you take a stand, the bigots may respond "You say we should be tolerant. Well, where's *your* tolerance for *our* beliefs?" Don't be taken in by this devious "defense." Tolerate intolerance the same way you do air pollution: Accept that it exists, recognize it as bad, and do everything in your power to eliminate it.

If you speak out against bigotry, the worst that can happen is you'll be disliked, scorned, or ostracized by people whose behavior is cruel, ignorant, offensive, hateful, and/or illegal. Like, big loss. The best that can happen is you'll discover that most of your classmates feel the same way you do. Once you break the ice, they'll cheer your courage and support your cause. You'll be a leader in creating a friendly, respectful, and inclusive climate for your school.

Following are five ways to respond to bigoted jokes and comments. Remember that bigotry is not an excuse for being rude back. In fact, politeness is the most powerful sword you can wield.

1. Walk out. You may attend a lecture or performance in which the speaker (or comedian, or musician) makes bigoted remarks. It may be impolite or impractical to speak out at the time. There may not be a forum for questions or discussion in which you'd have a chance to challenge the remarks. Therefore, get up and leave. Do it quietly. Don't disturb others. Your statement will be seen and "heard." It may cause others to follow your example. You will have taken a stand. Quite literally.

2. Stare. We all know that it's impolite to stare. So let's call this an "intense visual focus." Laser looks aimed at the perpetrator of an offensive remark can be an effective way of signaling disapproval. This is especially so if everyone present follows your lead. The target of 12 pairs of humorless eyes is likely to squirm, sweat, and wonder if he said something wrong. If however, your stare is lost in a general hubbub, you'll need to take more noticeable action.

3. Question the speaker. Many bigots assume that everyone present shares their view. Therefore, it can be quite unsettling to them if you draw attention to their remark by inquiring about it. Let's say a racist comment is made. With a pleasant expression and tone, you could say:

---

* Had Burke been a cool 20th-century statespersondude, he would, of course, have amended this to "good men and women."

209

How Rude!

"Excuse me?"

"I beg your pardon?"

"I'm sorry, I must have misheard you."

If the person repeats the offensive remark, you can repeat yours:

"I'm sorry, I still think I've misheard you."

This is a bit like the parent who says "I can't hear you" over and over until a child says "Please."

4. Ask for an explanation. In the face of a racist or homophobic comment or joke, say:

"I'm sorry, I don't get it. Could you please explain the joke to me?"

A perfectly civilized question—but the spotlight it shines on the speaker and the remark is stunning. You could also ask:

"Do you consider that funny?"

5. Reveal a connection. Another way to respond to bigotry is by informing the speaker of your personal stake in the matter:

"You may not realize that my mother is Polish."

"I'm sure you're unaware that my father is gay."

The speaker may fall all over herself with an apology and say that she didn't mean anything disrespectful and some of her best friends are gay and Polish if not both. Or she may escalate her abuse or accuse you of not being able to "take a joke."

You challenge discrimination, intolerance, and hatred because it's the right thing to do. Don't expect to change a bigot's mind. If that happens, great. If it doesn't, you may succeed in at least getting the person to keep his ideas to himself. But no matter what happens, you'll feel proud of yourself. Plus your actions will have a powerful effect on those who witness them and may lead to their speaking out in the future.

"What's so bad about ethnic jokes? They're funny."

Which are the funny ones? Those about your ethnicity or someone else's?

Ethnic jokes are comparable to getting your pants pulled down in school. If it happens to someone else, it's humorous. If it happens to you, it's hurtful. It all depends who's the butt (so to speak) of the joke.

Don't get me wrong; some ethnic jokes are very funny. And we all need to lighten up before political correctness turns humor into an endangered species. Poking fun at a group of people doesn't automatically imply disrespect. Many jokes that do this are good-natured; they tease, but without maliciousness. Other jokes, however, are rooted in prejudice. They are mean-spirited and reinforce the stereotypes that feed bigotry.

In order to tell ethnic jokes (and "fat" jokes and "lawyer" jokes and "dumb blonde" jokes) and stay within the bounds of proper etiquette, you need to consider their *content* and *context*.

School Rules

- **Content** means "What is the basis for, and character of, the humor?"

For example, a "Jewish" joke that makes fun of rabbis, yarmulkes, or gefilte fish is probably pretty safe to tell in the proper context. A "Jewish" joke about the Holocaust is likely to offend listeners no matter what the context may be.

- **Context** means "Where, when, and to whom are you telling the joke?"

Death jokes would be out of place at a funeral. Jokes about contortionists and Crisco would be out of place at your grandmother's dinner table (unless you have a very unusual granny). It's generally okay to tell a joke that skewers a group, a nationality, or a category of people if it falls into one of the following contexts:

1. The joke is at the expense of the person telling it. (An amputee tells a joke about a prosthetic limb.)

2. Everyone present belongs to the target group. (The speaker at a convention of amputees tells a joke about a prosthetic limb.)

3. The target of the joke is not present. (A joke about a prosthetic limb is told but no amputees are present.)

The third context is by far the trickiest. You may look around and see that all limbs are present and accounted for, but how do you know that the mother or sister of somebody listening didn't just have a terrible accident and lose a leg? Similarly, you may tell a "gay" joke without knowing that someone present is gay. Or a "moron" joke without knowing that someone present is a moron. Once you tell a joke, you can't control where it travels. So you may want to avoid third-context jokes altogether.

For example, let's say you tell sexist dirty jokes in the locker room. Just because your teammates are all guys doesn't mean some of them won't be offended. They might tell their girlfriends. Word could get out that you have some pretty sick attitudes towards women. Maybe you do, maybe you don't. But people will make judgments based on the things you say.

I'm not suggesting that you stick to knock-knock jokes for the rest of your life. But before you tell a joke, consider its content and context. Ask yourself *Would I be comfortable if people associated this joke with me?* ◆

How Rude!

"There's a teacher in my school who's gay. He's the best teacher I've ever had, and I really like him. But now people are starting to say that I'm gay (I'm not) and he's after me (he isn't). I don't want to stop being friendly, but I don't like what people are saying."

It would be a shame if you gave up a wonderful relationship just because of the rude gossip of bigoted people. Taking a stand always involves consequences. Sometimes fitting in and not making waves is the best course of action. But this is rarely the case when confronted with prejudice. As Martin Luther King Jr. once said, "Noncooperation with evil is as much a moral obligation as is cooperation with good."

Homophobia is a form of prejudice that breeds not only discrimination, violence, and hate, but also the depression and isolation that leads gay and lesbian teens to drug abuse and suicide in disproportionately high numbers. The people you risk alienating when you refuse to tolerate intolerance are probably not people you'd want to associate with anyway. This doesn't make it any easier, but it helps you to know you're doing the right thing.

Adolescence is a time of experimentation and discovery. Many teenagers are preoccupied with the feelings and fears that surround their emerging sexuality. They're trying to figure out what it means to "be a man" or "be a woman." People who question your sexuality are revealing concerns about their own. It's their insecurity that's showing. And because they're insecure, they need to put others—namely gays—down.

Your sexuality isn't anyone's business. If people call you gay, don't respond "I am not!" Defensiveness plays into their hands. It also suggests that there's something wrong with being gay. Instead, ignore them or calmly say:

"You seem very interested in other people's sexuality. Did you have some questions or concerns about your own that you'd like to share with me?"

More and more schools today are establishing support groups for gay, lesbian, and bisexual teens. Many straight kids join as a way of expressing their solidarity. No school should tolerate taunting or gaybashing, and you may want to approach school authorities about establishing such a group or having someone speak to the school about these issues.

It's important for schools to counter the homophobic messages kids may receive from peers, politicians, and popular culture. Some teens have gay relatives or family friends already serving as positive role models. Other teens are prey to misinformation spread by intolerant and ill-informed groups. Since prejudice is based on ignorance, it's important to debunk some of the myths that fuel discrimination against homosexuals.

School
Rules

Myths	Facts
AIDS is spread by gay people.	AIDS is spread by the exchange of bodily fluids, not by sexual orientation. New cases of AIDS are occurring at a far greater rate among heterosexuals than homosexuals.
Gay people are only interested in sex.	Gay people are just as desirous of finding and giving love and entering into a committed relationship as are heterosexuals.
People choose to be homosexual.	Sexual orientation isn't something people choose, it's something they discover about themselves.
Most child molesters are gay.	The vast majority of child molesters are heterosexual.
Homosexuality is an illness or perversion.	Neither the medical nor psychiatric professions view homosexuality as an illness or perversion.
You can tell if people are gay or not by the way they act.	There's no way to determine a person's sexual orientation from the way he or she looks or behaves.
Having a crush on, fantasy about, or sexual experience with someone of the same sex means you're gay.	Most heterosexual adults have had one or all of these experiences while growing up.
Gay parents and teachers recruit kids into being gay.	No one can be "recruited" to be gay or straight. Children with gay parents or teachers are no more likely to be gay than are children of straight parents or teachers.
Gay and lesbian people are unfit to be parents.	Gay and lesbian parents are just as capable of raising healthy, happy, emotionally sound children as are heterosexual parents.

Civility at School Sporting Events

SPECTATOR ETIQUETTE

Proper spectator behavior at interscholastic games differs markedly from that at other school events. For example, at a concert by the school orchestra, it is considered bad form to yell "Kill the bassoonist!" Audience members at school plays may not chant "We want an actor, not a weed whacker!"

"Go trombones!"

The standards are more relaxed at school sporting events. It's considered acceptable to hurl insults at (and cast spells upon) game officials and opposing team members. To be considered appropriate, however, these aspersions must have a direct bearing on the target's athletic role, performance, and/or relevant body parts. Thus, the eyes of an umpire, the arms of a pitcher, and the I.Q. of a coach are all fair game. The umpire's mother, the pitcher's religion, and the coach's race are not.

That tradition allows invective from the stands isn't the same as saying that it's a good thing. After all, we allow brussels sprouts. Don't get me wrong; I'm very sympathetic to those who pepper the playing field with such creative taunts as "Swing!" How else can they survive the tedium of interminable time-outs? But if the idea is to get one's mind off how boring the game is, couldn't this goal be achieved equally well by vigorously supporting one's own team, rather than casting asparagus on the character and performance of the opposing team?

In an era when fewer and fewer people practice even the basics of politeness, do we really need to institutionalize rudeness? This only encourages those who would spit on umpires or throw iceballs from the stands. Look at World Cup soccer. It has been overrun by hooliganistic yobs out to hit someone over the head with a bottle of beer. And the fans are even worse!

It's time to reassess spectator behavior at sporting events. A bit more of "Well played, sir!" and a bit less of "Throw the bum out!" can do no harm. After all, teams should be uplifted by their athletic supporters.

School Rules

"I play baseball for my school team. I used to really like it, but I'm thinking of quitting because it's no fun anymore. Parents are always yelling rude things at the players from the stands. Two fathers got into a real ugly fight at our last game. I want to win, too, but it's just a game. Is there any way to stop parents from being so rude?"

Parents who do this should have to sit in the corner and then go to bed without supper. There's no excuse for such behavior. If they want to spend an afternoon hurling insults and assisting in public humiliations, let them attend a talk show taping.

It's likely that many of your teammates feel the same way you do. Why not get together with them and talk to your coach? He can speak to particular parents or send a letter home to all parents reminding them of the importance of good sportsmanship. During a game, he can also approach offending parents and tell them that he won't tolerate any mean-spirited remarks addressed to his players.

Unfortunately, parental misbehavior is a common problem. Coaches as a group need to band together so that all teams, at the beginning of the season, inform parents that they must abide by certain rules of conduct if they plan to attend any games. ◆

PLAYER ETIQUETTE

Sports etiquette is the ultimate test of good manners. This is because good sportsmanship sometimes requires you to act in opposition to your feelings.

For example, when you've had your face wiped in the mud all afternoon only to lose by one fluky goal in the last two seconds of play and be knocked out of the finals, it's difficult to extend your hand to the winners and say "Great game!" What you really feel like saying is "You lucky shmucks!"

The reason you must put your feelings aside is because "it's not whether you win or lose, it's how you play the game." Yeah, right. If you believe that,

How Rude!

I've got another one for you: "Sticks and stones may break your bones, but names will never hurt you." OF COURSE IT MATTERS WHETHER YOU WIN OR LOSE! Self-confidence, scholarships, career paths, and endorsements can all be affected by your win-lose stats. But it's your behavior before, during, and after every match that determines whether, as a human being, you're a winner or a loser. You can be a winning athlete but a loser in life. And you can be a losing athlete but a winning person.

Here's how to be a winner no matter how the game turns out:

Have fun. What's the point of being out there if you're not enjoying yourself? Good vibes are contagious. Your teammates will catch your enthusiasm and the game will be that much more enjoyable for all.

Avoid temper tantrums. Nobody, with the exception of tabloid reporters, wants to witness an immature outburst. Resist the impulse to throw your tennis racquet, hit ball boys or ball girls, curse at umpires, or storm off the court. Only professional players making millions of dollars are allowed to do these things.

Don't make excuses. If you mess up, say you're sorry and let it go. You only draw more attention to yourself if you blame the sun, the wind, the ref, the racquet, or the gopher hole. If it truly wasn't your fault, that will be obvious to everyone.

Don't blame others. If your team members mess up, give them encouragement, not criticism. Saying "Good try" or "Don't worry about it" will do a lot more to help than "Smooth move, Ex-Lax."

TRUE STORIES FROM THE MANNERS FRONTIER
Yer Out!

Once, when I was in fifth grade, I struck out in a softball game. One of my teammates called me a boner. So, naturally, I picked up a banana peel I saw on the ground and threw it at him. He charged me, and we began to roll around in the dirt. The gym teacher intervened and made us both run around the backstops ten times.

The moral of this story is: *Don't go to a school where the backstops are far apart.*

Congratulate the winners. This is how character is built. Extend your hand and tell the victors they played a great game.

Compliment the losers. But be sincere. Don't tell them they played well when it's obvious they didn't. Instead, you might say:

"Thanks for the game."
"Thanks for playing us."
"You guys had an off day today, but you were great against Lincoln last week."

Choose up sides with tact. It feels terrible, time after time, to be the last person chosen for a team. You stand there, staring at your sneakers, hoping that the next pick will put you out of your misery. Finally, everyone's been chosen except you and somebody says "Ha, ha. You get Wiley." This is the stuff of which lifetime traumas are made.

Many gym teachers, realizing this, now assemble teams randomly by counting off by twos or fours (or two-by-fours). If you're one of the captains choosing up sides, strike a blow for kindness. Tell the other captain (discreetly) to pick people in reverse order. Start with the worst players. Of course, everyone will know what you're doing. But I guarantee you that the people usually picked last will worship you for life. And the star athletes will get a useful lesson in humility as they experience what it feels like to stand in the dwindling line as everyone else high-fives their way onto the team.

Well, that just about covers etiquette on the playing field. A few final suggestions:

- If you mistakenly kick the goalie's head instead of the ball, say "Excuse me" or "Sorry!"
- If you tackle someone, upon removing your cleats from his groin and your fingers from his eyeballs, it's a nice gesture to help him up.
- In basketball, don't pull down anyone's shorts as he or she goes up for a jump shot.

"My school forces students to take showers after gym class. I HATE it. People say rude things and make comparisons about people's . . . you know."

It's very impolite to make disparaging remarks about the sports equipment of others.

How Rude!

Let's begin with a basic fact: Teenage boys and girls are often sensitive about their body's development, or perceived lack thereof. This sensitivity is heightened when you're naked in front of 90 classmates. Perfectly normal teenagers can feel too fat or too thin, too short or too tall, too big or too small. It's important to remember that the development of secondary sex characteristics in kids typically starts anywhere between the ages of 9 and 15. This causes great curiosity as to who's matured how far. Such interest is natural but must be pursued discreetly so as not to cause offense. After all, it's rude to stare.

The operative rule for locker room etiquette is *Look, but don't touch.* The corollary to this is *Don't get caught looking.* Therefore, these are the Top Ten rules that should be posted in every locker room:

1. Don't hang people up by their underwear.
2. Don't snap your towel at anyone.
3. Don't run unless you enjoy slipping and hitting your head on a bench.
4. Don't lock anyone in his or her locker.
5. Don't drip on anyone.
6. Don't hide anyone's clothes or towel.
7. Don't point, laugh, gape, or giggle at unclad classmates.
8. Don't make comments about anyone's body or body parts.
9. Don't bend over without saying "Excuse me, do you mind my butt in your face?"
10. Don't bring a tape measure or magnifying glass into the showers.

If you're self-conscious about changing in the locker room, you can wear your gym clothes under your regular clothes. You can also protect yourself from mean-spirited classmates by sticking close to your friends. Grab lockers that are next to each other. Go as a group into the showers. And remember, the students who make the comments are usually those who are most insecure about themselves. If someone offers a disparaging remark about your anatomy, you can ignore it or respond by smiling and saying "I wouldn't talk if I were you." ◆

Cafeteria Courtesies

Throwing food. Spitting. Screeching. Chewing with their mouths open. Are we in the monkey cage? No, we're in the typical school cafeteria.

It's no wonder that students at lunchtime act like they're in a zoo. After all, they've been kept in cages all morning. Pent-up energy and chipped beef on toast are a dangerous combination. While good table manners are always preferable, there are factors in the school environment that mitigate against them. For instance, if you only have 11 seconds to eat lunch and get caught up on the latest news, the pressures to combine chewing with talking are enormous. Best behavior is not encouraged by the sight of boiled hot dogs and barfaroni. Jello that's still alive invites remarks of dubious taste, particularly if the droopy whipped cream has the consistency of skim milk.

School Rules

Nonetheless, you can rise to the challenge and resist these downward forces. Here are some etiquette tips for feeding time:

- Always be kind to food servers and other lunch counter personnel.
- Don't dump anyone's tray.
- Don't trip or tickle anyone carrying a tray.
- Don't laugh, clap, or cheer if somebody drops a tray or glass.
- Ask permission before you grab food off of anyone's plate. On second thought, don't grab. Allow it to be passed to you.
- Schedule jokes and disgusting remarks so they don't occur when your luncheon companions are drinking. This will minimize those occasions upon which milk comes snorting out of someone's nostrils.
- Throw out your trash. Don't, however, fling objects halfway across the room so their trajectory passes over others. Nobody wants your "miss" in their lap.
- Be inclusive. It's natural to want to eat with your friends. The tradition of "reserved" seats and designated tables exists in many schools. If someone who's not part of your circle sits down at your table, be friendly. Staring, holding your nose, making snide remarks, or telling the person to get lost is rude, crude, and bad attitude, dude.
- As you leave the cafeteria, give thanks that you don't have to wash the dishes.

Applying to Colleges

One day before too long, many of you will start applying to colleges. Most colleges require applicants to write an essay describing their interests, goals, and/or reasons for wanting to go there. Some ask prospective students to relate an experience from which they learned something. If you find yourself facing the latter type of essay question, you may wonder how truthful to be. Is this a case where honesty isn't necessarily the best policy?

In fact, there are times when the truth, the whole truth, and nothing but the truth could lead to that Great Rejection Pile in the Sky rather than the Land of Fat Acceptance Envelopes. Telling a college that your major interests

How Rude!

are sex and getting away from home is not the way to win the heart and mind of an admissions officer.

The key to applying to college is the key to life: *Balance.* You want to say what they want to hear without sounding phony. You want your application to stand out without drawing attention to the fact. You want to elucidate your achievements without appearing boastful. You want to show that you have the motivation to make a success of yourself (i.e., you'll be able to contribute to Alumni Giving Campaigns) without coming across as money-grubbing. In short, you want to present yourself as:

- creative but not flaky
- cooperative but not spineless
- independent but not rebellious
- confident but not cocky
- principled but not intolerant
- enthusiastic but not ditsy
- well-rounded but not unfocused
- socially aware but not self-righteous.

Thus, the act of applying to a school is the culmination of everything you've learned (and are learning) about good manners: Present yourself as a sincere, tolerant, observant, secure individual who, while marching to your own drumbeat, is ever mindful of the rights and sensibilities of others. Towards that end, here are six tips for school applications and interviews:

Remember that the purpose of filling out an application is to get into that school. It is not to commence an autobiography entitled *Confessions of a Young Miscreant.* Anything you include that reflects negatively on yourself must be portrayed as a profound learning experience from which you have grown.

Dress appropriately for interviews. College admissions officials have no interest in seeing the top six inches of your underwear or the bottom six inches of your cleavage. Wear something casual enough to help you feel comfortable and natural, yet formal enough to show that you respect the occasion and have made an effort to look nice.

Be on your best behavior. This is the time to pull out all the manners stops. Rise when the interviewer comes to greet you. Offer a firm handshake. Look 'em in the eye. Use "Sir" and "Ma'am." Sit up straight. Try not to fidget. When the interview concludes, thank the admissions official and say that you enjoyed talking with him or her.

Show enthusiasm. It's not a good sign if your interviewer falls asleep in the middle of your interview. Don't be a lifeless lump. Speak up. Put a sparkle in your eyes. Don't mumble. Convey the kind of energy you will apply to your studies. No, on second thought, better not.

School
Rules

Demonstrate knowledge of the institution. Show that you've read the catalog. It would be embarrassing to reveal a passion for architecture and then learn that the college to which you're applying because your father went there doesn't have a design school.

Come with questions. It never hurts to have a few intelligent queries ready in case the interviewer asks if you have any questions. You can inquire about the curriculum, cultural life, volunteer programs, academic policies, sports requirements, social opportunities, etc. Try not to ask anything that would be obvious to anyone who'd done her homework (as in "How many years does it take to get a degree?").

There are several fictions to the application process that both sides agree not to examine too closely. For example, applicants pretend that all of their extracurricular activities were motivated by altruism and love of learning, rather than by the craving to get into college. They also pretend that the college they are currently considering is their first choice. Meanwhile, colleges pretend that the decisions they make are objective. They aren't. Most students are amply qualified to attend the schools to which they apply. The choice of whether to accept the straight-A student who loves history, captains lacrosse, plays flute, and works with the homeless, or the straight-A student who loves math, captains tennis, plays guitar, and works with inner city youth, is arbitrary. The ultimate decision is not going to be made on the basis of you, but on the basis of how the tennis and lacrosse teams have been doing. Therefore, while an acceptance should make you feel proud, deserving, and successful, a rejection should never be taken personally.

In sum, applying to college is like going on a first date. You want to be honest about who you are. At the same time, you don't want to reveal anything less than salutary about yourself until the relationship has reached a point where your deficiencies will be seen in the light of your many fine qualities.

CHAPTER QUIZ

How Rude!

Keep your eyes on your own paper. You may begin.

1. *Your school springs a random drug test on you. What's the proper response?*
    a) don't take it sitting down
    b) stand up for your rights
    c) grin and bare it.

2. *You're taking a final exam. The student in the seat next to yours is trying his hardest to copy your paper. Do you:*
    a) hand it to him so he doesn't strain his eyes
    b) yell "Brian's cheating, Brian's cheating!" or
    c) use your arm to shield your paper?

3. *A teacher wrongly accuses you of cheating. Do you:*
    a) slap him with a wet noodle
    b) slap him with a sexual harassment suit, or
    c) go up to him after class and calmly make your case?

4. *Your teacher is out sick and you have a new sub for the day. Classroom etiquette requires you to:*
    a) switch seats so she won't know who sits where
    b) hang a jock strap from the fluorescent lights
    c) make a special effort to be cooperative.

5. *It's especially crowded in the cafeteria one day. An unpopular student has to sit at the table usually reserved for you and your friends. The polite response would be to:*
    a) throw coleslaw at her
    b) pinch your nose and say "What's that rotten smell?"
    c) engage her in friendly conversation.

7

Friends, Romance, Countrymen

Lend Me Your Peers

Adolescence is a time of many firsts—and lasts. Adults, having repressed their own painful memories, often describe the teenage years as the "best years of your life." But teenagers know firsthand the worry, cruelty, and competition; the pressures and responsibilities; the fears and confusions; the humiliations and torments; the jealousies and rivalries. They know how deep their feelings go; that it's *not* just a crush, they *won't* get over it, it *was* real love.

The greatest pleasures of adolescence are usually linked to one's social life—and so are the greatest pains. A lot of the aches and embarrassments

How Rude!

could be eliminated if teenagers behaved politely towards one another. The very idea of being polite to one's peers may generate hoots of derision in some circles. This is because many teens seem to feel that the best way to avoid getting hurt is to get the first punch in. They don't want to be teased, taunted, badmouthed, and ostracized, so they tease, taunt, badmouth, and ostracize others.

Teenagers who practice good manners with their peers can dodge much of the suffering and anxiety that runs rampant in school corridors. And they will enjoy closer and more rewarding relationships with their friends and romantic interests. Let's look at some of the ways you can put politeness to work with your peers.

The Etiquette of Friendship

MAKING NEW FRIENDS

Is there a proper way to make new friends? Yes: *Act as if you already have as many as you need.*

This may seem like strange advice. But, for some reason, teens are turned off by people who seem desperate to have friends. Maybe they figure that if you want to be friends with *them*, there must be something wrong with *you*. (That's what low self-esteem does for people.)

So do your best to exude confidence. Be relaxed, yet respectful. Cool, but without an attitude. Eager, but not fawning. Mysterious, but not aloof. Smile enough to show you're at peace, but not so much as to suggest you're coming unglued. Once your aura is properly adjusted, you can commence operations.

1. Observe. Get a sense of who's who. Check out the pecking orders and group affiliations (jocks, troublemakers, druggies, wannabees, artists, school leaders, middle-of-the-road good kids, etc.). This will give you a better idea of people you'll want to steer clear of and people you'll want to approach.

2. Inquire. In a low-key way, ask questions. These can be procedural ("How do you think the teacher wants us to do these papers?") or personal ("What sport did you letter in?"). Since most teenagers find themselves interesting, they appreciate anyone who asks them questions.

3. Compliment. If someone says something noteworthy in class, wears a nice outfit, or makes a good play, tell him so. We all like to be around those who recognize our fine qualities.

4. Join. Go out for the team, audition for the band, sign up for the school paper, get involved with the service club. Being with people who share your enthusiasms is one of the best ways to find kindred spirits and new friends.

5. Resist. You may be approached by teens who are looking for new partners in crime. These are the kids who'll be your friends if you'll be mean to their preselected targets, or if you'll use drugs or cut school with them. These are the sorts of friends you can do without.

6. Nurture. Friendships require time to develop and maintenance to thrive. Once you make a new friend, give her your support, encouragement, loyalty, and empathy. These are things we all wish to receive. And when we do, we keep coming back to the well that provides them.

Friends,
Romance,
Countrymen

"I try to be polite and to think about how my actions affect other people. But I get teased a lot for having good manners, even by my friends. Why is it considered bad to be polite?"

There are still a few bugs to work out in teenage human software. One is the tendency to put people down for being smart, well-behaved, industrious, and moral. The idea is, if you devalue those traits in others, you don't have to feel bad about not possessing them yourself.

Don't ever apologize for being polite, principled, responsible, or virtuous. Those very friends who tease you now will discover later on—when it may be too late—how valuable those characteristics are. While they desperately play catch-up to try to acquire them, you'll already be reaping the benefits. ◆

"Is teasing always rude?"

It's sometimes okay to tease people about their positive attributes—looks, accomplishments, popularity, etc. This form of teasing, if done with a light, affectionate touch, is usually intended and taken as a backhanded compliment.

It's never okay to tease people about aspects of their appearance, background, or behavior that they can't help and/or feel self-conscious about—an accent or stutter, poor grades, a parent in prison, etc.

How do you know whether someone is pleased or embarrassed to have attention drawn to, for example, good grades or a British accent? You just know! A teenager's most highly developed radar is the one that detects the sensitive spots of others. ◆

How Rude!

COPING WITH CLIQUES

You may think (and you may be right) that cliques are the height of rudeness. It's fine if people want to be with their friends. There's nothing wrong with that. But do they really have to treat everyone else like dirt?

Of course they don't—and they shouldn't. But knowing that won't make them stop. So what are your alternatives when you're faced with (or shut out by) a clique?

- You can start by understanding why some people form cliques. Many teenagers are unsure of themselves socially. They lack self-confidence and certain social skills. Cliques and gangs (which are really just cliques carried to an extreme) furnish love, approval, protection, and support. The more a clique's members put other people down, the cooler they think they are.

- You can decide whether belonging to a particular clique is really that important to you. What, if anything, do they have that you want? When you closely examine a particular clique, you may find that they're not as special or elite as they'd like you to believe.

- If you're convinced that your life will be meaningless and empty if you're not part of a certain clique, then do what you can to join. You can try making friends with one member. (**TIP:** Approach the person when he or she isn't surrounded by other members. Your chances of being scorned and rejected will be somewhat reduced.) Maybe you have interests in common. Once you've established that friendship, you may find that you're automatically part of the clique. (And once you're in, you can try to influence the clique to stop being so nasty to outsiders.)

Of course, you have another alternative: You can ignore the clique. Follow the steps in "Making New Friends" on pages 224–225. Find other people who are warm, interesting, inviting, and open-minded. The chances are excellent that they'll welcome you and return your friendship.

Handling Friendship Problems Politely

PEER PRESSURE

What if you learn that the people you hang out with do things that are questionable or against the law? How can you avoid getting involved without seeming holier-than-thou?

Just say no.

"But," you protest, "the 'Just Say No' campaign didn't work!"

True . . . but that's because they didn't say "No, *thank you.*"

Saying no is the ultimate act of personal control. When pressured to do something you don't want to do, simply respond with one of these phrases:

"No, thank you."
"I'd prefer not to."
"Count me out."
"No can do."

Beyond that, you don't owe anyone an explanation. With certain people, in certain situations, you may wish to provide one. For example, you might want to explain to someone with whom you've been seriously involved why you don't want to have sex. Otherwise, he or she might take your refusal in a way you don't intend. Or you might try to dissuade friends from spray painting racist or anti-Semitic graffiti on the walls of the school by explaining why you won't do it.

Whatever the circumstances, stand firm. Nobody can make you do anything you don't want to do. And you may discover that the minute one brave soul (namely you) says no, others will follow.

"I've decided that I don't want to use drugs. But some of my friends keep pressuring me to get high with them. What's the polite thing to say in these circumstances?"

You can take some comfort in the fact that at least your friends have been taught to share. But when they offer you something you wish to decline—whether it's a joint or a jelly sandwich—simply say "No, thank you." If the person who's inviting you to get high has good manners, the matter will go no further. Since we both know the likelihood of that, the next question is: What do you do when the person persists? Watch:

"Wanna get high?"
"No, thank you."
"Why not?"
"I'd prefer not to, thank you."
"Whatsa matter, ya scared?"
"I'd prefer not to, thank you."
"Oh, come on."

"I'd prefer not to, thank you."
"It's not gonna kill ya."
"I'd prefer not to, thank you."
"Just try it."
"I'd prefer not to, thank you."
"Oh, forget it!"

You see the power of good manners. Just remember that you don't owe anybody an explanation for your decision. In fact, it's rude of the person to ask. Responding to such pressure just prolongs the discussion and puts you on the defensive. See what happens if you try to answer the questions:

"Wanna get high?"
"No, thank you."
"Why not?"
"Because I don't want to."
"Whatsa matter, ya scared?"
"No, I'm not scared."
"Then what?"
"I just don't want to."
"Have you ever tried?"
"No."
"Then how do you know?"
"I've never jumped off a cliff, but I know I don't want to."
"That's different. Jumping off a cliff could kill you."
"So could drugs."
"How do you know? You think you know everything?"
"I didn't say that."

And so on.

If you stand firm and show no room for debate, you'll wear your interrogator down. This strategy can be used to decline participation in any event:

"I'm sorry, but I'd prefer not to shoplift, thank you."
"I'm just not able to smash mailboxes, but thank you for asking."

"Hmmm, rob the First National Bank this afternoon? Thank you for asking, but I have other plans."

As a matter of etiquette, it's not your responsibility to make judgments or point out dangers associated with those behaviors in which you're asked to participate. As a matter of friendship, it may be. ◆

DRINKING AND DRIVING

You and your friend go together to a party. He drives. Alcohol is available, and your friend partakes. As the party comes to an end, he grabs his coat, fumbles for his keys, and says "Lesh go, hokay?"

He's so far out of his gourd that he doesn't know which end is up, he's about to turn 4,000 pounds of steel into a lethal weapon, and he expects *you* to sit in the passenger seat. You haven't been drinking, so you're still mindful of your obligation to exercise good manners. You say:

> *"No way. I'll talk to the host. I'm sure you can just spend the night here."*
>
> *"You really don't look well. Come. I'll show you where you can lie down."*
>
> *"I know you think I'm overreacting, but I could never forgive myself if I let you drive and something happened. You're simply going to have to indulge me."*
>
> *"Amy said she'll take you home. We'll arrange for you to get your car tomorrow. I'll get a ride with Peter."*
>
> *"Hand me your keys, please. I'll call a cab."*

Or, if you're a licensed driver:

> *"Hand me your keys, please. I'll drive you home and return your car to you first thing in the morning."*

If these approaches don't work, gather several of your largest friends. Then sit on the person and pry the keys out of his fingers. This is not impolite. Etiquette grants considerable leeway to those engaged in the saving of lives. For example, shoving a total stranger would, in normal circumstances, be bad manners. Doing so to move him out of the path of an oncoming bus would be a heroic act.

Don't worry about being seen as rude. It's likely the person won't even remember what was said or done. And if, the next day, he should give you a hard time, simply put on a resolute, I'll-have-none-of-that air and say:

> *"Your friendship and safety are so important to me that I'm happy to put up with your anger. And I'll do it again if it will keep you from killing yourself or someone else."*

BACKBITING

You've just heard that one of your friends has been saying mean things about you behind your back. Understandably, you're hurt and upset. Should you say something or drop him as a friend? That depends.

You have only the word of the person who told you—who spoke behind the back of the friend who allegedly spoke behind *your* back. But where did Person B (the tattler) get the news about Person A (your friend)? Did he hear it directly from your friend (A)? Or from someone else (C) who heard it from someone else (D) who heard it from someone else (E) who heard it from your friend (A)? In other words, how many people were involved in passing this information along to you?

It's best to receive this sort of communication with skepticism. You have no idea what your friend actually said. To put this another way, imagine that he bakes a big plate of brownies as a gift for you. He hands the plate to a friend and says "Please give these to Jeff." The friend figures no one will miss one brownie, so he takes one and hands the plate to another friend with instructions to "Give this to Jeff." The plate goes through 12 more people, and each takes a brownie, rearranges the remainder, and passes it on. By the time it gets to you, there's just a bunch of crumbs. And you think *What kind of a lousy cheap present is this?*

Now watch what happens when words instead of brownies get passed along:

Andy: *"I'm worried about Jeff. His parents are getting a divorce, and he seems pretty upset. I wish there was something I could do to help."*

Sandy: *"Andy's really upset that Jeff's parents are divorcing. He wishes he could do something to help Jeff."*

Mandy: *"Andy said that Jeff's parents are really upset about getting divorced. Apparently Jeff's been getting some kind of help."*

Randy: *"According to Andy, Jeff's parents are getting divorced because Jeff is in some kind of trouble and needs a lot of help."*

And this is what finally reaches Jeff:

Candy: *"Andy's been telling people that it's all your fault that your parents are getting divorced and that you're going to have to go to this special school that helps kids who are in trouble."*

The only way to check out the backbiting rumor is to talk to your friend. He probably said *something*. But there may have been a context, or additional remarks, that didn't get passed along. Give him the benefit of the doubt. Tell him what you heard and how it made you feel:

"I can't believe that you'd say something like that, so I wanted to ask you about it."

You may discover that the whole thing was just a misunderstanding. Or you may find that your friend is guilty as charged. In that case, you'll have to decide whether and/or how things can be patched up.

SHUNNING

One day, for no apparent reason, your friends start acting like jerks. They don't return your calls, and when you see them in school, they don't stop to talk. You know they're getting together without you. What's up . . . and what can you do?

It can feel very lonely and disorienting when people you like and trust suddenly give you the cold shoulder. If *one* friend does this, maybe he *is* a jerk and you should just write him off. But if you're having problems with *all* of your friends, it may be because of something you did (or they mistakenly think you did).

Take a close look at yourself. Has your behavior changed? Have you been upset, negative, or cranky? Have you said or done anything that might have hurt someone or caused offense? Even if your friends are behaving badly towards you—even if they're being selfish, snooty, or petty—make the effort to consider your own words and actions. Keep in mind that you can't control your friends; you can only control *yourself*. The way to get other people to change their behavior is to change your own. This works with friends, parents, teachers, bosses—anybody.

If you can't identify any reasons for the way your friends are treating you, seek out the one friend you trust the most. Approach her when she isn't with the rest of the group and doesn't have to put up a front. Tell her that you value her friendship, but you've noticed that she and the others don't seem to want you around lately. Explain that this has upset you, and you wonder if you've done something to alienate them. She may give you some feedback that will point the way to changes you can make, or reveal a misunderstanding that you can set straight.

It's also possible that you're simply out of favor. Sad but true, relationships among teenagers can be fickle, painful, and short-lived. Friends drop friends for reasons both good and lousy. If this particular group has decided to reject you, you can't force them to take you back. But you can hold your head high and make new friends. If your old group should later decide that they want to include you again, you can choose to resume those friendships or not. But whatever you do, don't drop your new friends. You know how much that can hurt.

How Rude!

"I did something terrible to one of my friends. We've been avoiding each other ever since. I'd apologize, but I don't think it will help. What should I do?"

The only thing you *can* do is apologize. You can do this in person (if she's willing to talk to you) or by writing a note. Don't hedge your apology. Don't make excuses, or minimize what happened, or place any blame on your friend for "being too sensitive" or "not being able to take a joke." Take full responsibility for the terrible thing you did, and make it clear that you're profusely and abjectly sorry. Say that the last thing you'd ever want to do would be to hurt or embarrass a friend; that you don't know how you could have been so careless, unthinking, and inconsiderate; that you can understand if she never wants to see you again; that you'd give anything to turn back the clock and erase the event; and that you know you don't deserve it, but you hope she'll be able to forgive you.

If your friendship is strong, your friend *will* forgive you. After hearing how miserable and guilty you've been feeling over the incident, she may even console you. ◆

TAKING SIDES

If you have more than one friend (and let's hope you do), chances are that at some point two of them won't get along. And each will want you to take sides against the other.

Adults face this same situation when couples they have been friends with divorce, and each spouse tries to convince his or her friends that it was the other person's fault. It's best to stay out of the crossfire. Friendship doesn't obligate you to enlist every time one of your friends goes to war.

When your friends begin to badmouth each other, simply hold up a hand and say:

"Stop! I'm very sorry that you and Meg are angry with each other, and I know how upsetting that must be. But I like you both too much to get caught in the middle or choose sides. I'm sure that if you and Meg sit down and talk about the problem, you can resolve it."

This doesn't mean that you can't use information you glean from one or the other to try to affect a rapprochement. For instance, if one of your friends said "You know, if she'd just apologize, I'd be willing to forget the whole thing," you could mention to the other friend "You know, I'm sure if you'd just apologize, Meg would be willing to forget the whole thing."

TELLING SECRETS

Have you ever had a friend (note the past tense) who couldn't keep a secret? This is one of the most serious—and most common—of all friendship problems. Keeping secrets is difficult, and the temptation to share them is great, because information is power. When someone blabs a secret, they're saying "I know something you don't know. I'm 'in the loop' and you're not."

Not all secret spillers are intentionally malicious. In their mind, they're not really breaking a confidence, because they're only telling a friend they know they can trust. Of course, that friend tells *her* best friend, who tells *her* best friend, and before you know it, your secret makes the rounds of the entire school.

There's only one surefire way to keep someone from spilling one of your secrets: Don't tell it in the first place. But if you must tell someone, make sure it's a person who's told *you* a lot of secrets. This is known as *mutual deterrence*. It's what two countries do when they point nuclear weapons at each other. Since either has the power to destroy the other, neither makes the first move.

"This so-called friend of mine read my diary and told everyone what I'd written about them. I'm so embarrassed I could die. But first I want to kill him. Why are people so mean?"

All thoughtful, moral people ask this question at some point in their lives. The answer has to do with evolution, human nature, psychology, genes, temperament, self-image, the environment in which one lives, and how one was brought up. You can even bring religion or spirituality into the discussion by rephrasing the question as "If God is good and loving, why is there so much meanness in the world?" Add in the fact that not all meanness is equal, and the issue gets even more complicated. Dumping someone's books is mean, but it's nowhere near as mean as taunting someone because of his ethnic background, which is nowhere near as mean as executing all of the people in a village because of their religious beliefs.

Meanness is usually the result of:

Thoughtlessness. People may be "sloppy" about the way they go through life. They don't take the time to think before they speak or act.

Lack of empathy. People may be self-centered and fail to consider how things look from someone else's perspective.

Intolerance. Children learn intolerance from their parents, political and religious leaders, societal messages, prior generations, etc. Prejudiced people,

233

because they're self-righteous, wouldn't call their behavior "mean." But of course it is—and worse.

Entitlement. People who feel that life has treated them unfairly may believe that they're entitled to take what they want and abuse others. They see this as "righting the scales," not as being mean.

Poor self-image. People who hurt others are often in great pain themselves. Putting others down is a power trip that masks their own insecurities.

How Rude!

None of these "causes" of meanness is an excuse for being mean. But each helps us to understand it—and ourselves—a little better.

Meanness is an extreme form of rudeness. In the case of your "friend's" betrayal, you have three choices:

1. You can make a conscious decision to drop him.
2. You can wait and see what happens. The friendship may dry up and die on its own; it may return to normal with time; your own feelings may change; or your friend may apologize.
3. You can try talking to your friend. Tell him how you feel about what he did. Don't accuse or attack. Focus on your own shock, embarrassment, and hurt. He may be feeling terribly remorseful, and your overture may give him the opportunity to apologize. ◆

DODGING A DEBT

You're a kind and generous person, so you occasionally agree to loan money to a friend. But what should you do when the friend doesn't pay you back? Since dodging a debt is rude, you can treat this as a "responding to rudeness" situation.* You might say:

> *"You know that ten dollars I loaned you last week? I'm sure it's just slipped your mind, but I need it back."*

By giving your friend the benefit of the doubt, you offer her a face-saving way out. If she says she doesn't have the money right now, try to set up a payment plan in which, for example, she gives you two dollars a week. You'll quickly learn whether she intends to repay you or string you along with a bunch of excuses. If she's a bad debt, you may have to absorb your loss.

When loaning money to friends whose creditworthiness hasn't yet been established, it's a good idea to see whether they repay their *first* loan before you agree to a second (or a third). This way, you cut your losses early. For

---

* For a refresher on the best ways to respond to rudeness, see pages 19–21.

larger loans (for example, the $50 or $100 a friend needs for a new pair of track shoes), draft a letter stating the amount and outlining a payment schedule. This prevents misunderstandings and impresses upon both parties the businesslike nature of the transaction.

Many friends loan money back and forth to tide each other over during lean periods. This is fine, as long as things stay relatively even. If, however, you keep coming up on the short end of the deal, you may need to cut off the cash flow.

"You're my best friend. Of course I'll lend you the money. Introductory interest rate of 5.9% for the first three months, 18.9% for the next three months, monthly P&I payments amortized over 15 years, $10 late fee, balloon for the balance in six months. Sign here."

"I have this friend I really like, but she stays at my house forever—even when I hint that it's time for her to go. How can I get her to leave without being rude? She also keeps me on the phone forever when we talk."

You'll have to be a bit more assertive—and forearmed. When you issue an invitation, include an end time. Say:

"Do you want to come over this afternoon? I have to start my homework at 6:00. But you could stay until then."

For those never-ending phone calls, have an arsenal of excuses handy:

"I have to eat dinner now."
"I need to make another call before it gets too late."
"My dad has to use the phone."
"My mom asked me to help her with something."

How Rude!

When you offer an excuse, preface it politely. As in:

"I wish you could stay longer, but . . . ."
"I'd love to talk more, but . . . ." ◆

JEALOUSY

Sometimes it may seem as if your friends are better than you. Maybe they're winning more prizes or getting better grades or wearing cooler clothes. Perhaps they're more popular or attractive or smart. In any case, you wake up one day feeling like a total loser—and jealous besides.

It's difficult when other people seem to have all the luck and success, especially when they're your friends. It's natural to feel jealous. But you're overlooking one thing: They have chosen *you* for their friend. Do you think they'd hang out with a total loser? No way. This means there must be something wonderful in you that they see and you don't.

People are successful in all sorts of different ways. Maybe you're a terrific "people person"—considerate, well-mannered, responsible, trustworthy, helpful, empathetic, caring, loyal, supportive, and fun to be with. Those are *real* talents. They're just not as easy to quantify as grades or votes or numbers of goals scored. You may tell yourself that those things don't count. But they do. In fact, you'll go a lot farther in life, and find a lot more fulfillment, than will people who are great students or athletes but lack those skills.

Being a friend means showing pleasure in your friends' prizes, trophies, and honors—even when you're hurting inside. But that hurt will go away if you take the friendship of these high achievers for the compliment it is. Focus on the strengths and talents you have, rather than the ones you may not have.

TRUE CONFESSIONS

Do your friends bring their problems to you? This can be a compliment—and a burden. Sometimes you might not know what to say, or you might be afraid of saying the wrong thing.

Chances are you're already saying the right things, or you wouldn't have so many friends confiding in you. For everyday problems and normal teenage mood swings, here are some good ways to respond:

Be a shoulder. Most people, when they have problems, just want somebody to listen. They're feeling isolated, abnormal, confused, or afraid. If you lend an attentive and empathetic ear, you might give your friend 90 percent of what she needs. If you've dealt with a similar problem in your own life, share your experience. If you see a possible solution, suggest it.

Friends, Romance, Countrymen

Ask questions. This is a good way to help people get their troubles in perspective. Essentially, what you're doing is leading a problem-solving session.* First, help your friend to define the problem. (Often we just feel overwhelmed. Once we get a handle on the problem, it becomes less scary or upsetting.) Then let your friend brainstorm attitudinal and/or practical ways to deal with it. Encourage her to pick the best ideas and to make a plan of action. You can then help her to follow through.

Be sure not to minimize the problem. In an effort to make your friends feel better, you may say things to comfort them that end up belittling their feelings or situation:

> *"You'll get over it."*
> *"It's not that big a deal."*
> *"You'll get another chance."*
> *"That happens to lots of people."*
> *"It'll be all right."*

Of course, these things may all be true. But people who are upset don't want logic or platitudes. They want sympathy, love, understanding, and acceptance. They want you to know that they're hurting. To be a real friend, show that you know and give them what they need.

For example, if a friend says that her father has to have an operation for cancer, don't say "Oh, I'm sure it will be fine." Even though you're saying it to cheer her up, you don't know how the operation will turn out. Neither does she, and that's why she's scared to death. Say "That must be really frightening" or "I'd be so worried if my father had to have an operation."

Offer assistance. When friends come to you with problems, ask them if there's anything you can do to help. They'll probably respond "No." When they do, say "Okay, but promise you'll tell me if there is. I really want to help." When you make your caring explicit, it lets your friends know that they're not alone.

Show that you're not afraid to talk about difficult things. Sometimes, after sharing a problem, teenagers will feel embarrassed or wish they could take back what they said. The next time you talk to your friend, tell her how

---

* For a refresher on how to do this, see pages 128–129.

glad you were that she told you about her troubles. Then ask her how she's feeling and how it's going. If it's obvious that she doesn't want to talk about it anymore, let it pass.

Be alert to the possibility that there's more to the story than you're being told. Friends with serious problems will sometimes only tell you the tip of the iceberg. They may be in denial; they may be ashamed; they may be hesitant to spill a family secret.

For example, someone says that his parents aren't getting along, but what's really happening on the home front are knock-down-drag-out fights. Or someone says he's been experimenting with drugs when in fact he's been using them daily for six months.

If you suspect that you're not getting the whole story, you'll need to encourage your friend to say more. Asking "Do you want to talk about it?" makes it easy for him to say "No." Instead, try saying "Sounds like things are pretty rough. I'd really like to listen. Please tell me what's going on." In your friend's mind, this turns talking from a self-indulgence into a kindness he can do for you.

Know when you need to turn to others. The approaches described above should work for most everyday problems. But what about a friend who says she's going to kill herself? What about a friend you suspect is being abused at home? What about a friend who's shooting heroin? These are terribly difficult situations, and you shouldn't expect or attempt to solve them by yourself.

Your friend may be confiding in you in the hope (conscious or not) that you'll "force" her to get help. Even if she resists, try to get her to see a counselor, talk to a trusted adult, or contact a hotline. Explain that you're very concerned about her and will do everything you can to help. If your friend refuses or makes you swear not to tell, don't back off or let it go. Talk to your parents or another trusted adult. Tell them what you know about your friend and ask for their help.

It's worth risking the friendship if your friend's life or health are in danger. She may be angry at first. But if she gets the help she needs, she'll eventually think of you as the best friend she ever had. And if she drops you or comes to greater harm, at least you'll know you did everything you could to help.

"What are you supposed to say if a friend tells you he's gay?"

It depends on how and why it's said. If it's just mentioned in passing—as in "I'd love to come to your party, but my boyfriend and I will be attending the Gay Pride rally that day"— treat it as you would any other piece of information. Say "We'll miss you" or "Have a good time!" or "You'll have to tell me how it went."

If it's said to set things straight (so to speak), say "You're very kind to tell me."

Friends, Romance, Countrymen

If it's said as a proud disclosure of identity, offer the person your best wishes for a life full of much love and happiness.

If it's said in confidence by a friend who's troubled by his sexuality, respond with warmth, support, and empathy. Encourage him to talk. Ask questions and use active listening.* If specific things are upsetting him (for example, how to tell his parents, or harassment at school), help him to explore options for dealing with these issues. If your school is "gay-friendly," he may find a student support group and/or empathetic counselors. He could also look in local bookstores for some of the excellent books written for gay and lesbian teens. Most larger cities have gay- and lesbian-themed bookstores and newspapers, which are other good sources of information. Support groups for gay and lesbian youth can be found by looking in the Yellow Pages under "Gay Organizations" or "Social and Human Services" or by calling a hotline. Finally, if your friend has access to a computer and the Internet, there are sites on the World Wide Web for, about, and by gay teens.

There's no need for a gay or lesbian teenager to deal with these issues alone. The best thing you can do for your friend is see that he doesn't have to. ◆

Getting Along with Roommates

You're thrown into a cabin at Camp Meneemoskeetoes with seven kids you can't stand. Or you go away to school and get stuck with the dork from New York. If you're lucky, these loathsome creatures will become your best friends. If you're not, they'll make your life a living hell.

When it's time for you to have a roommate, ideally you'll be matched with people with whom you have something in common. Realistically, you might find yourself sharing close quarters with beings who, like you, are air-breathing bipeds—and that's where the similarity ends.

Roommates can be soul mates—simpatico companions you end up loving as much as (or more than) your siblings.** Or they can be schmucks who charge you for a stamp, leave crumbs on your bed, take your things without asking, and tell you to get lost so they can make out with their boyfriend or girlfriend.

---

* To learn how to use active listening, see pages 349–351.
** For a refresher on rooming with siblings, see pages 127–130.

Improve your chances of getting along by doing your part. Start by respecting your roommate's privacy. It's very important for roommates to respect each other's privacy because there isn't any. Since *physical* privacy is usually impossible to achieve, you have to create *psychological* privacy. Here's how:

- Never read your roommate's letters, email, journals, or papers.
- Stay out of your roommate's desk and bureau drawers.
- Always ask permission before borrowing your roommate's possessions.
- Don't reveal personal things you learn from living with your roommate. ("Hey, did you guys know that James drools in his sleep?")
- Never rat on your roommate unless his transgressions harm you personally, or place him or others in physical, legal, emotional, or reputational danger.

Non-Rattable Offenses	Rattable Offenses
Your roommate sneaks out during every full moon to sing Verdi under the stars.	Your roommate sneaks out during every full moon to get drunk and play chicken with freight trains.
Your roommate uses cheat sheets for French quizzes.	Your roommate deals drugs from your room.

Of course, it's best for your relationship if you first try to deal directly with your roommate about even the rattable issues.

If you're scrupulous about honoring these principles, your roommate is likely to follow suit. Setting a good example is better than saying "Mess with my things and I'll pull your tongue out." Since people have different attitudes towards sharing, it's also perfectly fine to establish limits: "You're welcome to play my CDs, but I'd appreciate it if you'd check with me before using my toothbrush." You can also negotiate such things as who gets the upper bunk, whether you sleep with the window open, and what to do when your roomie's clothes take up the whole closet.

Another way to create the illusion of privacy is to make your presence invisible when circumstances require. Let's say your roommate is in the middle of a private and painful conversation with a friend. You'd leave the room except you're waaaay behind schedule on a paper and you have to keep working at your computer. Your roommate would leave except it hasn't occurred to her. Therefore, create the illusion of privacy by intensifying your concentration. This will reduce the self-consciousness your roommate would feel if you made faces in response to the conversation, or even entered into it. When the friend leaves, your roomie will probably want to talk about what transpired. Even though *she* knows *you* know that something went down, let her tell you what happened. It reinforces the illusion of privacy.

A final aspect of roommate privacy involves respecting routines. Let's say you go to soccer practice every afternoon between 3:00 and 4:00. One day your coach is sick and practice is canceled. You head back to your dorm barely five minutes after having left it. Your roommate, however, may be counting on having an hour of private time. If you barge in unexpectedly, you might catch him doing something that he'd be very embarrassed to have you discover—like, say, studying. Therefore, when you get near your door, bang against it. Fumble with your keys. Drop your books. Yell "Hi!" to a friend. Take a lonnnnnnnnng time to open the door. Your roommate will appreciate this act of courtesy.

Friends,
Romance,
Countrymen

"What do you do when your roommate is a jerk? I mean, this guy is hopeless."

Whoa. Let's back up for a minute. First, we need to confirm that your roommate really *is* a jerk, because sometimes the label is unfairly applied. For example, these characteristics might be misinterpreted as jerkdom when really they're a matter of perspective and preference:

- lines pencils up by height
- wears funny glasses
- has a weird hairdo
- studies too hard
- doesn't study hard enough
- writes letters to his or her parents
- uses a knife and fork to eat an apple
- likes Donny Osmond.

In contrast, these characteristics indicate that you're dealing with a genuine jerk:

- spreads malicious rumors about people
- bullies new kids
- takes your sweater without asking
- refuses to do his or her fair share of cleaning

- spits on someone's tuna sandwich as a joke
- refuses to turn off music so you can sleep
- blabs your secrets to everyone
- likes Donny Osmond.

You can see that the first list reflects the intolerance of the beholder rather than the jerkiness of the beheld. These surface behaviors have nothing to do with the substance of a person. Judging people in this manner is *character bigotry*. It says "If you don't do things my way, you're a jerk." Isn't that the very attitude teenagers hate so much in adults?

The second list portrays a bona fide, Class A jerk. These behaviors are not harmless superficial traits. They are acts of aggression. People get hurt. This person is self-centered and inconsiderate.

The first thing you need to do is diagnose your roommate's jerkiness. Is he just different, or is he a certifiable jerk? If it's the former, suspend your judgment long enough to get to know him. You may discover a terrific person beneath those uncool (to you) surface characteristics.

If, however, the person is truly a jerkmeister, you have three choices:

1. **Set him straight.** If you're willing to invest some time and energy, you can use your insight and people skills to try to help your roommate. Maybe he doesn't know how to make friends. Maybe he feels awkward and stupid. Maybe nobody's ever told him how his actions affect others. Maybe he's hurting from something in his background or home life. Be his friend. It could work wonders.

2. **Maintain your distance.** Be polite. Stay cool. Establish limits as to what you will and won't tolerate in your roommate's behavior. And count the days until you and he part ways.

3. **Change roommates.** Most school and camp officials would probably say that learning to get along with people you don't like is a valuable life lesson. That's all well and good, but they don't have to live with them. If you've really tried to handle the situation, if your roommate is really making life miserable for you and others, there's no reason to put up with it. Talk to your advisor or counselor. It may be possible to engineer a roommate swap or move one of you to a different room. ◆

The Etiquette of Romance

During elementary school, most kids' energy goes into the three R's. But once junior high rolls around, a fourth R is added: *Romance*. Hormones start percolating, and suddenly the world looks very different. Obnoxious boys turn into *cute* obnoxious boys; giggly girls turn into *cute* giggly girls. The fear of cooties is set aside and the hunt is on.

Romance doesn't just happen. It takes careful strategizing and armies of friends to pull it off. This is because junior high etiquette doesn't permit the couple-to-be to negotiate on their own behalf. The reason: the fifth R—*Rejection*—which must be avoided at all costs.

Here's how the ritual works: A guy calls up a girl. He pretends that he has questions about homework or carpool. Then, with all the offhandedness he can muster, he says "By the way, I was wondering . . . do you like Tim?"

The girl is *absolutely bonkers wild in love with Tim.* So she says "He's okay." And the conversation continues:

> *"Well, do you like him?"*
> *"Why, does he like me?"*

Since this could go on all evening, the guy tries a different tack:

> *"If he asked you to go with him—and I'm not saying he would—but if he did, would you?"*
> *"I might."*
> *"Well, would you?"*
> *"Probably."*
> *"Probably yes?"*
> *"Yeah, I guess."*
> *"So you would, right?"*
> *"Yes."*
> *"Well, I just wondered. Hey, you'll never believe this, guess who just walked in the door, it's Tim—Tim, you won't believe who I'm talking to, it's Beth, you wanna talk to her?"*

At this point, Tim quietly puts down the extension on which he's been listening the whole time and, now that he knows he won't be rejected, asks Beth to go with him. By 8:20 the next morning, the news is all over school. Tim and Beth are seen holding hands. Their friends are free to spread rumors and participate in all the major and minor crises of the relationship.

Which probably won't last very long, because nobody wants to be dumped. And the only way to avoid getting dumped is to dump the other person before he or she dumps you. So, at the first signs of strain, boredom, or wandering eyes in the relationship, one of the parties will enlist a friend to

How Rude!

tell the other "You're dumped." The dumpee can then either deny having been dumped or use being dumped as a way to get sympathy and attention. Friends will rally 'round, be extra nice, and say nasty things about the dumper. The school will have a new source of drama, and local phone lines will buzz all night.

From an etiquette standpoint, this system leaves a lot to be desired. In an effort to spare one person from hurt, it inflicts hurt on others. It opens personal matters up to widespread scrutiny and gossip. But in junior high (and sometimes into high school), it's the way things tend to happen.

The first steps towards a new skill—be it reading, riding, or romancing—are often awkward and scary. As you start down the rocky road to love, you can expect to undergo a period during which your relationships are orchestrated by emissaries. You might compare this to training wheels. When you first learned to ride a bicycle, they kept you up and running with maximal speed and minimal injury. But if you use them longer than you need them, they can foster a dependence that ultimately slows your future progress. Therefore, training wheels—and emissaries—should be discarded at the first opportunity.

"Girls are always falling in love with me. How do I let them know I'm not interested without hurting their feelings?"

Assuming that the infatuated ones are asking you out, the simplest way to deflect their affections is by being "too busy." (There's no need to issue preemptive rejections to anyone rumored to be swooning over you.) Simply say:

"I'm sorry, but I have plans for that night."

If they ask again, respond with the same statement. If they call, say:

"I'm sorry, but I'm busy and can't talk."

It should soon become clear that you're too engaged to squeeze them into your life. If they press you further ("Is there *any* time in the next five years when you don't have plans?"), say:

"I'm afraid I'm just too busy to have much of a social life."

Of course, they'll eventually realize that you find time to go out with *other* girls. So a feeling of rejection is unavoidable. But etiquette doesn't erase hurt from the face of the earth; it merely tries to minimize it. And those who refuse to take face-saving hints only open themselves up to greater hurt. ◆

"There's a boy I really love, but he doesn't even know I exist. How can I get him to like me?"

If there's anything worse than being in love with someone who doesn't know you exist, it's being in love with someone who knows and doesn't care. Romance would be easier and less heartbreaking if we could *will* people to like us.

It might also be less fun.

You can't "get" him to like you. But you *can* try to attract his attention—and eventually, maybe, win his affection—by being your best self. Don't show off. Don't force yourself on him. And follow the strategies outlined in the answer to the next question. ◆

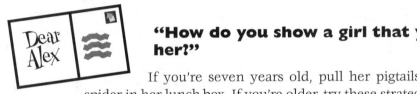

"How do you show a girl that you like her?"

If you're seven years old, pull her pigtails and put a spider in her lunch box. If you're older, try these strategies instead:

Pay attention to her. Smile. Say "Hello!" Ask questions about her classes, teachers, friends, parents, interests, siblings, and experiences. Showing interest in another person says *I like you.*

Spend time with her. Do things together. Walk with her between classes. Carry her books. Call her on the phone. Wanting to be with someone says *I like you.*

Treat her with respect. Say "Please" and "Thank you." Show pleasure in her accomplishments. Comfort her when she's disappointed. Never say anything behind her back you wouldn't say to her face. Being supportive and trustworthy says *I like you.*

Be thoughtful. Bring her a flower. Write a note. Listen carefully to everything she says. Give her a small gift that follows up on an offhanded remark she makes. Being sensitive and attentive says *I like you.*

Get the word out. Have *your* friends make it known to *her* friends that you like her. This is the sort of thing that makes school so interesting.

Tell her! The direct approach works wonders. Say "I really like you." If that seems too forward, say "I really like being with you," or "I really like it when we do things together." ◆

How Rude!

ASKING SOMEONE OUT

Before you plant, you must prepare the soil. Similar groundwork must be undertaken before asking someone for a date. Here are nine tips that will increase your chances of success:

1. Get to know the person first. Invitations out of the blue are usually rejected because most of us are taught never to go anywhere with strangers. So take the time and make the effort to learn about the other person—and give him or her a chance to learn something about you. Talk in class (but not during class). Sit together at lunch. Hang out in the same group(s). See if you have things in common and if you enjoy each other's company. If all systems are go . . .

2. Ask early. Give the person advance notice—three to four days for informal dates such as dinner, a movie, or paintball. This allows her plenty of time to check with her parents, earn some extra money, reschedule an appointment, decide what to wear, etc. Of course, she also has plenty of time to look forward to being with *you.*

Last-minute invitations are likely to be rejected. Either the person has other plans, or the person doesn't have other plans and wants to hide the fact, or the person assumes (rightly or wrongly) that you couldn't get anyone else to go.

There is an exception to the ask-early rule: an occasion that couldn't have been anticipated. As in:

"I just found out that my uncle is sailing his boat up tomorrow. Do you want to go out on the bay with us?"

3. Don't ask *too* early. Being overeager isn't attractive. Also, it makes both parties involved feel silly:

"Would you like to go to the senior prom with me?"

"Gee, I don't know. I'm really flattered that you asked. Let's see how we're feeling about each other in two years."

4. Choose the right moment. You know how important timing is when asking your parents for permission to do something. The same holds true for asking someone out on a date. You don't want to pop the question if your intended is upset, distracted, surrounded by other people, or rushing madly to class. Wait for a calm, private moment.

5. Do the asking yourself. Throughout history, certain individuals have willingly done the dirty work of others. In the adult world, these people are called *lawyers.* In the teenage world, they're called *friends.*

Obviously, rejection is easier to take if it comes secondhand. If you don't do the actual inviting, you have what's known as *plausible deniability*. When the rumors of your rejection start to fly, you can say "What do you mean? I never asked him out." Despite this advantage, using friends as proxies can backfire for three reasons:

- *Secondhand invitations make you look like a wuss*—someone who's scared or lacking in confidence. Of course, you may actually be scared and lacking in confidence on certain occasions. That's perfectly natural. But courage means taking action in spite of your fears. It's an attractive, admirable quality—one we like to see in people whose dates we accept.

- *Secondhand invitations promote miscommunication.* Are you positive your friend said just what you told her to say? Did she get the day and time right? Did she ask at a good moment? And if your invitation was rejected, was it with an "I-never-want-to-go-out-with-him" no or an "I-might-go-out-with-him-but-not-to-that" no or an "I'd-love-to-go-out-with-him-but-can't-that-night" no?*

- *Secondhand invitations encourage gossip and rumors.* If you ask someone out and get turned down, only two people know. It's a private matter. There's a good chance that the respect you've shown in asking the person yourself will be reciprocated by her not blabbing all over creation. If, however, you get a friend to do the asking, it becomes a public matter. Your friend may tell a friend, your prospective date may tell a friend, and before you know it, the gory details are all over school.

So resist the temptation to use friends as social secretaries. Issue your invitations face-to-face, phone-to-phone, or in writing.

6. Go s-l-o-w-l-y. Some people (there are three in North America) have no trouble asking for a date. Full of confidence and charm, they pick up the phone, propose a wonderful evening, wait for the yes, and carry out their plans with aplomb.

Most people are a bit less sure of themselves. You know what that can be like. You agonize for weeks or months: *Does she like me? What if I don't have anything to say? What if the answer's no? What if I make a fool of myself? Where would we go?* Finally, you muster the courage to pop the question. With pounding heart and flip-flopping stomach, you pick up the phone and dial. And slam it down again. After eleven tries, you let it ring. She answers. And in a firm, confident voice, you say "Gulp."

---

* For more on the variations of the deceptively simple word "no," see pages 251–252.

How Rude!

When you ask someone out for the first time, take it easy. Think date with a small *d*. Don't plan a six-hour evening where you'll be all alone in new or stressful circumstances. Do something low-key and informal. Go to a basketball game with a group of friends. Play tennis. Go skating. See a movie. Do some shopping. Your comfort and friendship will grow, and you'll know when the time is right to ask for a date with a capital *D*.

You may be thinking *But I'm cool. I can handle anything.* That may be true, but your date might not feel the same way. Take things slowly for her sake.

7. Be specific. If you issue a vague invitation, you're asking for it. Not a date—a major hurt. As in:

"You wanna go out sometime?"
"No."

Even if the person replies "Sure," she may be thinking *In a hundred million years.* And you have no way of knowing.

Here's the difference between being vague and being specific:

Vague—No!	**Specific—Yes!**
"What're ya doin' Friday night?"	"Are you free Friday night to go ice-skating?"
"Ya wanna go out with me?"	"Would you like to go to the Halloween Dance with me?"
"How 'bout doin' somethin' sometime?"	"I'm wondering if you'd like to see that new documentary on bighorn elks at the Rialto. Maybe this Saturday? It's only showing for a week."

Once you've issued the invitation, you can provide further details on time, place, mode of transportation, curfews, special clothing or equipment required, etc.

8. Be positive. Negative invitations plant the idea of rejection in the mind of the person you're asking. And they make it easy to say no in response.

"You wouldn't want to go to the movies with me, would you?" (No, I wouldn't.)
"I don't suppose you're free next Thursday?" (No, I'm not.)

Negative invitations soften the blow of rejection ("I got turned down, but at least I guessed right!"). They also tend to be self-fulfilling prophecies. Because they reveal your lack of confidence, they require the person to contradict you in order to accept, and that's too confusing and too much work.

"You wouldn't want to go to the movies with me, would you?" (Well, yes, I would, but if you think I wouldn't, then maybe I shouldn't.)

"I don't suppose you're free next Thursday?" (Actually, I am, but if you think I'm not, then I probably shouldn't be, because what does that say about my social schedule? So I'd better find something else to do.)

Friends, Romance, Countrymen

Remember that an invitation from you is a compliment. It says *I and my wonderful self desire your company.* Let that be your message. If you still get turned down, at least you gave it your best shot.

9. Be up-front about money. Let's say you want to invite someone out but you don't have enough moola. Should you forget about asking? Or you've been invited to a concert but the tickets cost $35—too much for you. Do you say no? Either way, don't let money keep you from extending or accepting invitations. It's normal for teenagers to be flush one week and broke the next.

If you're doing the inviting, you can signal your intentions with certain words and phrases. For example, if you plan on paying, you can say:

"My treat."

"Would you be my guest for . . . ?"

"I just got my birthday money, and I'd love to take you to . . . ."

If you don't have the bucks, you can mention that you'll have to "go Dutch," which means each person pays his or her way.* Or you might say "I can cover the tickets if you can spring for the food."

If you're on the receiving end of the invitation, don't be embarrassed about raising the question of who pays. If money isn't an issue, you can just bring some to cover your expenses should the need arise. If it is an issue, say "I'd love to go, but I'm short on funds right now." That will get things out into the open.

BEING ASKED OUT

Someone you know has just asked you out. It's Decision Time! What you say and how you say it will depend on whether you like the person, whether you like the person enough to go out with him or her, whether you're free to date, and about a zillion other factors. But basically your answer will be "Yes," "Maybe," or "No." Let's look at the protocols of each.

---

* For more on "going Dutch," see page 299.

If your answer is "Yes" . . .

Shout it from the rooftops of your heart. Say:

>*"I'd love to!"*
>*"That sounds great!"*
>*"I've always wanted to do that!"*
>*"I was hoping you'd ask me!"*

Convey enthusiasm, appreciation, anticipation, eagerness, and anything else you can think of along those lines. The person who asked you probably sweated bullets for three weeks before popping the question. He or she deserves more than:

>*"Okay."*
>*"Sure."*
>*"I guess."*
>*"Why not?"*

Never accept an invitation and back out later unless there's an emergency or you become ill. It's not fair to leave your date high and dry. He or she might have already made arrangements, spent money, or told other people. Your reversal might be inconvenient and/or embarrassing. And it would give you a reputation for being hurtful and unreliable.

"Oh, man, if only she'd ask me to the Turnabout Dance this Saturday, my life would be perfect. I'd be the happiest guy on the planet. Please, oh please, let her ask me."

If your answer is "Maybe" . . .

Sometimes you'll need to check with your parents or reschedule a conflict before you can accept an invitation. If this is the case, convey your enthusiasm, just as you would if you answered "Yes." Then, in a verbal footnote, explain the catch. Let the person know when you'll have a definite answer. Don't invent a phony excuse to keep someone on hold for days while you wait to see if a better offer comes along.

"Hi, Luke. Would you like to go to the Turnabout Dance with me?"
"I dunno. Maybe. When is it?"

250

If your answer is "No" . . .

There are three types of no:

Friends, Romance, Countrymen

1.   The "I'm-hoping-someone-else-will-ask-me" no. Let's say you've been invited to a school dance by someone you feel lukewarm about. You're hoping someone else will ask you. You can't say "I'm holding out for someone better" or "I'll go with you if no one else asks" because that would hurt the asker's feelings. And you can't say "Sorry, but I'm going to be away that weekend" because then, if you turn up at the dance, you'll be caught in your lie. So there's only one thing you *can* say, and that is:

> *"I'm sorry, but I already have plans for Saturday. Thank you for asking."*

If you show up at the dance with someone else, it'll be apparent what those other plans were.

It would be rude for anyone to ask what your plans are. Should this happen, you're under no obligation to respond. Just be a parrot and repeat what you said about already having other plans. Eventually the person will give up.

2.   The "I'd-love-to-but-I-can't" no. The key here is to make sure the person knows that you really *want* to be asked again. When you refuse the invitation, make sure you convey your regret, dismay, disappointment, and heartbreak:

> *"Oh, Nigel, I'm soooo sorry, but that's the night I have my acupuncture sessions and I just can't get out of them. But please ask me again. I'd love to do it some other time."*

3.   The "I-wouldn't-go-out-with-you-for-a-billion-dollars" no. The first time someone in this category extends an invitation, you can use the "I already have plans" response or "Thank you, but I'm not free that evening." Be polite. There's no need to carve the person's feelings into mincemeat with a reply such as "Are you kidding? What makes you think *I* would ever go out with *you?*"

The second time this person extends an invitation (which may occur then and there—"Well, how about *next* Saturday?"), you can respond in the same way. If after several refusals he or she still doesn't get the hint, you'll need to be more direct, but in a gentle, considerate manner:

> *"I'm very flattered that you keep asking me, but I just don't see us going out together."*

If the person presses you for a reason, take it upon yourself:

> *"I'm just not the person for you."*
> *"I'm interested in someone else."*
> *"I'm not dating anyone these days."*

This type of response accomplishes two good things. First, it respects the other person's feelings. And second, it closes the door to rebuttals. Only someone who's completely clueless will fail to take the hint.

Finally, don't blab. If you asked someone out and got turned down, you'd feel hurt or disappointed. Imagine how much worse you'd feel if the person went around telling everybody. There's not much you can do to stop others from indulging in such rudeness. But you can make sure that *you* never do it yourself.

"Is it okay to go out with someone if your friend likes him, too?"

If your friend is currently going out with him, no. If neither of you is seeing him, talk to your friend before taking any action. It's difficult to maintain a friendship when you're both competing for the same guy.

You might try to find out how he feels about you and your friend. If he doesn't like either of you, or he just likes one of you, knowing that might save you some needless conflict. Once you've got the lay of the land, you can negotiate with your friend about the best way to proceed. For example, you might decide that the person who's liked him longest gets first dibs.

Sometimes sensitive teens voluntarily refrain from going out with their friends' ex-boyfriends or crush objects. But one should never ask somebody to do this. It's hard enough to manage one's own social life without trying to run the social lives of others. ◆

"When my boyfriend picks me up to go out, he just sits in his car and honks. My parents get mad at me because he won't come into the house. He gets mad at me because I tell him he should come in. And I get mad at everyone. What does etiquette say about this?"

Etiquette says "Young man, get out of that car this instant!" A gentleman *always* comes to the door the first time he picks up a young lady at her home. He does this for three reasons:

1. so the girl's parents can meet him
2. as a sign of respect for his date, and
3. so he can wear a T-shirt that says "I Met My Girlfriend's Parents and Survived."

You're beyond the first date stage, but it's not too late to amend the situation. Tell your boyfriend that the next time he picks you up, he *will* and *must* get out of his car and come into your house.

You can ensure that the occasion will go smoothly by doing a little prep work. Tell your parents a few things about your boyfriend:

> *"Henry is on the chess team. He spent last summer on an archaeological dig in Levittown."*

This way, they'll have some leads for conversation. Coach your boyfriend in the same manner:

> *"My dad helped design the Space Shuttle. My mom is a crime reporter for* The Journal. *They just built a new addition on our house. Tell them you like it."*

Greet your boyfriend personally when he arrives. None of this up-in-your-room-still-getting-dressed business. Instead, make introductions and let the conversation flow. If your parents are the sort who really push their luck, they may invite you to sit in the living room for a few minutes. Once you've done this, you're free to depart.

On subsequent dates, you can watch for your boyfriend from a window and go out to meet him when he drives up. It's not necessary for him to come to the door. But a wise young gentleman will do so anyway. And this goes for young ladies who take gentlemen on dates, too. ◆

"If somebody sets you up on a blind date and you meet the person and don't like her, is it okay not to go through with the date?"

No. That would be rude and hurtful. You can, however, take certain steps to minimize the awkwardness:

- Only go out on blind dates in a group. This doesn't mean that you audition four hopefuls at once. Instead, it means that you go out with several other couples or friends. This allows you to dilute the contact with your date, if need be.

- Pick an activity that doesn't force you to talk or stare into each other's eyes all night. A movie, ice-skating, or a football game all fit the bill.

A blind date can be fun and interesting if you go with the right attitude. At best, it can result in a wonderful new friend. At worst, it's a great chance to practice your patience, tolerance, and charm. ◆

How Rude!

"Sometimes my boyfriend comes over to my house, and I'll cook a snack or a meal. He never helps. He won't even do the dishes. He says it's the woman's job. Another thing I don't like is when I'm with him and we run into people he knows, he never introduces me. Other than those two things, I love him."

If your boyfriend has an allergy to kitchen work, you might overlook it as long as he does the laundry. But it sounds as though he has an allergy to respecting women. He wants you to serve him in private and stand in his shadow in public. If you probe your relationship, you may find other examples of this attitude.

Your boyfriend is living in a time warp. He'd probably love the following advice, taken from a 1950s home economics textbook:

How to Be a Good Wife

Have dinner ready. Most men are hungry when they come home, and the prospect of a good meal is part of the warm welcome needed.

Minimize the noise. At the time of his arrival, eliminate all the noise of the washer, dryer, dishwasher, or vacuum. Try to encourage the children to be quiet. Greet him with a warm smile and be glad to see him.

Some don'ts: Don't greet him with problems and complaints. Don't complain if he is late for dinner. Count this as minor compared to what he might have gone through that day. Make him comfortable. Have him lean back in a comfortable chair or suggest that he lie down in the bedroom. Have a cool drink ready for him. Arrange his pillow and offer to take off his shoes. Speak in a low, soft, soothing and pleasant voice.

Make the evening his. Never complain if he does not take you out to dinner or to other pleasant entertainment. Instead try to understand his world of strain and pressure, his need to unwind and relax.

You're excused if you need to go puke or laugh yourself silly. This sort of sexist garbage was actually taught in home ec classes all across America. But that was then, and this is now, and there's no excuse for such Neanderthal behavior.

There's nothing wrong with being sensitive and considerate to someone you love. This is the bedrock of good manners and successful relationships. But it has nothing to do with gender—and it works both ways. Since you say you love your boyfriend, it's probably worth making the investment to try to bring him out of the Stone Age. Don't attack him. Simply tell him how you feel. Say what you need in order for things to work out between you:

"I need to feel that you respect me as an equal."

"I need us to share responsibilities without regard to gender."

He may not have a clue what you mean. In that case, you'll have to be more explicit. If he begins to come around, be supportive and encouraging. If he doesn't, drop him. But don't get discouraged yet. He's young, and he may still be teachable. ◆

DANCE DECORUM

You're at a school dance. The band is playing a song you like. The mirror ball suspended from the ceiling is casting sparkly confetti through the air. You're tired of hanging around the food table. How do you ask someone to dance?

You say "May I have this dance?" You don't say "Wanna dance?" unless you're willing to hear "Sure, with that gorgeous guy over there!"

How do you refuse if someone asks *you* to dance? Believe it or not, this is trickier than doing the asking. First, you never *refuse*. You *decline,* which is more polite. You do this by invoking one of the following:

1. A physical incapacity. As in:

. . . I'm feeling a bit tired right now."

"I'm sorry, but . . . . . . I'm just too overheated."

. . . I think I slipped a disc on that last dance."

Honor demands that your subsequent behavior be that of one who is too tired, overheated, or out of alignment to dance. After a reasonable period of recuperation (for example, 10–15 minutes), you can consider yourself back to speed and return to the dance floor.

2. An urgent mission elsewhere. As in:

. . . I simply must get some air."

"I'm sorry, but . . . . . . I have to make a phone call."

. . . I'd like to freshen up a bit."

Here, too, you need to disappear for a few moments to uphold your integrity.

How Rude!

3. A prior obligation. As in:

> *. . . I promised this dance to someone else."*
> *"I'm sorry, but . . . . . . I told Mrs. Lilliliver I'd help with the punch."*
> *. . . I said I'd show Mindy how to do the tango."*

You're probably wondering why, if someone asks you to dance, you can't just say "No, thank you." Picture this:

> You say: *"May I have this dance?"*
> The other person says: *"No, thank you."*
> You think: *What th' . . . ?*

And you stand there for a minute or two—perplexed, hurt, not knowing what to say. Then you slink away wondering *Why not? Is there something wrong with me? Am I too sweaty? Is it my dancing? Should I ask again?*

In other words, a polite excuse—*even if it's not really true*—allows both parties to maintain their dignity and self-respect. And that's the essence of good manners.

 **"I've been taught that if someone asks you to dance and isn't a total loser, it's polite to accept. But the problem is how to get rid of them afterwards. I'm willing to be polite, but I'm not willing to go steady based on one dance, if you know what I mean."**

Use the same strategies you would to decline a dance in the first place. The only difference is that you excuse yourself from the field rather than the sidelines. Thank your partner for the dance, then declare a physical incapacity, urgent mission elsewhere, or prior commitment. You might also smile warmly, say "Thank you for the dance. Excuse me," and then make your exit. ◆

 **"I'm taking my girlfriend to a fancy school dance. Do I have to buy her those flowers you pin on?"**

No, you don't "have to." You're perfectly free to bring your date unadorned. Let her look like a patch of crabgrass while the other girls burst forth in the blossoms of spring.

If, however, you wish your relationship to flower, a *corsage* is just what the gardener ordered. Before the dance, ask your date the color of her dress so you can order one that matches (no, not a *dress* that matches, a *corsage* that matches). For example, if she's wearing a plaid dress, you won't want to bring a polka-dot corsage.

"But," you say, "won't knowing about the corsage ahead of time spoil the surprise?"

No. Tradition demands that the young lady act surprised when she receives it.

Now comes the hard part—pinning it on. Start by asking your date where she would like it. Corsages can be pinned up near the shoulder (make sure her dress actually goes up that far before pinning) or at the waist (try not to crush it when dancing). Or she may prefer that her corsage be pinned on the fancy little evening bag she's carrying.

Once you've determined the proper location, follow these simple steps:

1. Hold the corsage so the flowers are at the *top*.

2. Take the pin (the long, nasty-looking one that should have come with the corsage) and push it *horizontally* into the dress and back out through the fabric at one side of the stem of the corsage.

3. Slide the pin *over* the stem, then back *into and out of* the fabric. This not only holds the corsage securely, but creates four holes in the dress. (**TIP:** Some corsages come with two pins, supposedly so you can crisscross them and hold the flowers more securely. But the real reason is so you can make *eight* holes in your date's dress.)

Right

Wrong

257

How Rude!

Some girls—perhaps those who don't like mutilating their dresses— prefer to receive a *wristlet* (a corsage worn around the wrist like a bracelet) or a *nosegay* (a little bouquet of flowers meant to be carried). If you want to know which your date prefers, ask.

Your date may present you with a *boutonniere*—a small flower to be pinned on your jacket lapel where the buttonhole is (or would be if your jacket had one). It's pinned on in the same manner as a corsage, except the pin goes *through* the flower stem rather than over it.

The reason a young lady gives her date a boutonniere is not, as you might think, to be kind. It's to get even for all those holes you've just poked in her dress. ◆

BREAKING UP

You've been going with the same person for a month (or a week, or a year). For whatever reason—boredom, a new love on the horizon, changing interests, incompatibility, unhappiness—you think it's time to break up. But you're a thoughtful, sensitive individual, and you'd rather not trash the other person in the process. What's the best way to behave?

It's kind of you to ask. This means that you're willing to take the appropriate steps to minimize pain and suffering. Whether you wish to break off all contact or redefine the relationship as "just friends," the technique is the same:

1. **Do it face-to-face.** This will be difficult, but presumably you did other things face-to-face. Don't send an emissary or write a letter. Find a private moment when you can speak without an audience present.

2. **Don't accuse or lay blame.** Either will only increase the hurt and the likelihood of an argument. Saying "You never pay any attention to me" or "I'm fed up with your drinking" gives the other person the chance to say "You're misjudging me" or "I'll change!"

3. **Avoid "making a case."** You want the breakup to seem fated, not the result of anyone's behavior. Simply say "I want to go out with other people" or "I guess I just don't feel the way I used to." Make it clear that your feelings have changed and you're responsible for them. It's not the other person's fault.

There's no magic formula for breaking up. Ending a relationship can be messy and painful. But if you do it quickly, directly, and resolutely, you'll lessen the suffering and may even stay friends.

"I just learned that my girlfriend dumped me. She sent her best friend to tell me that she doesn't want to go out with me anymore. What's the best way to get even?"

Friends, Romance, Countrymen

It's unfortunate that your girlfriend chose to convey the news in such a rude manner. You have every right to be hurt and angry. The best way to get even is to . . .

. . . respond with perfect graciousness. Show that your poise and confidence exist apart from any relationship. Since your friends and classmates will know you were dumped, they'll be watching to see how you react. If you fly into a rage or badmouth your girlfriend, you'll be playing into her hands. She might even say "That's why I didn't tell him myself. I knew he'd turn ugly." Other girls may hesitate to go out with you if they see you as vengeful and out of control.

Be calm, philosophical, and understanding. If friends press you for a response, you can say:

"People change. Life goes on."
"I'll always cherish the memories of our time together."
"I wish her all the best in her future relationships."

Your impeccable politeness will indirectly highlight your girlfriend's bad manners. When she learns how "well" you're taking it, she'll probably feel low, cowardly, and guilty, proving once again that politeness is the best revenge.

P.S. When you get home, by all means, rant, rave, and beat up your pillow. Cry yourself to sleep. Talk with a best friend. But then get back on the horse. Stay active and involved. Don't let yourself get isolated. Spend time with your friends. Do something nice for yourself. Your friends will admire you for the stoic, upbeat way you carry on with a broken heart. Keep it up and you may find yourself in a new relationship sooner than you think. ◆

BEYOND RUDE: ABUSIVE RELATIONSHIPS

You know when someone treats you right: You feel valued and respected and cared for. But it's not so easy to know when someone treats you wrong. Teenagers are often confused about what's normal or acceptable in a relationship. Those who grow up in a home with two adults who love and respect each other have a model for what a healthy relationship looks like; those who grow up in a home with parents who fight a lot may think *that's* normal.

How Rude!

If you're wondering about your relationship and you want to understand it better, here are some questions you can ask yourself. They apply to any relationship and can be asked by boys or girls.

Does your boyfriend or girlfriend . . .

. . . put you down in front of other people?

. . . publicly tease or embarrass you?

. . . demean your ideas?

. . . disregard your feelings?

. . . badmouth people or things you care about?

. . . use alcohol or other drugs as an excuse for his/her behavior?

. . . try to cut you off from your friends?

. . . take things out on you?

. . . get angry at you when you don't know why?

. . . treat you poorly, apologize, promise he/she'll never do it again—and do it again?

. . . blame you for things he/she has done?

. . . deny that he/she has hurt you?

. . . make it clear that he/she calls the shots?

. . . threaten or intimidate you to get his/her way?

. . . use physical force or violence against you?

. . . make you engage in sexual activity you don't enjoy or aren't ready for?

If you answered yes to one or more of these questions, it means that you're almost certainly in an abusive relationship. Of course, an otherwise wonderful, loving person might have the *one* annoying habit of telling embarrassing stories about you in public or the *one* flaw of an authoritarian streak that he or she needs to work on. A caring boyfriend or girlfriend, if told that his or her behavior upsets you, will make a genuine effort to respect your needs and feelings. So you'll have to use your judgment in assessing how these issues apply to your situation.

In general, though, answering yes to these questions suggests that you're in trouble. Abuse can be emotional or psychological as well as physical. If you think you might be in an abusive relationship, get help. Talk to your parents, a teacher, or a school counselor, or contact a teenage or domestic violence hotline. Another person's bad behavior is never your fault. And you don't have to take it anymore.

Sex-Ediquette

Most etiquette books steer clear of sex. That's generally because the behavior of consenting adults in the privacy of their bedrooms is their own business. But this is a book for teenagers, which allows a certain license (as opposed to licentiousness).

Friends,
Romance,
Countrymen

Whether teenagers should or shouldn't be sexually active isn't our topic here. What you decide for yourself is up to you and your partner. Your decision will depend on your values, maturity, religious beliefs, self-image, aspirations, and personal morals. It will depend on what your parents have taught you, what you've learned on your own, and ultimately what you feel is right for you. It should *not* depend on what your friends think, what your boyfriend or girlfriend wants, or what the advertising media tell you in the myriad mixed messages they send.

Now that we've made these disclaimers, let's focus on what *is* our topic here: the etiquette related to sex.

If you plan to be (or are) sexually active, it's beyond rude to:

- give someone the HIV virus
- transmit a venereal disease
- get someone pregnant
- trick someone into getting you pregnant
- bring a child into the world before you're financially, emotionally, or logistically able to care for it
- expect society or your parents to assume the responsibility for such a child
- pressure someone to have sex
- force someone to do sexual things that make him or her uncomfortable
- use alcohol or other drugs to weaken someone's resistance or awareness
- ignore the word "No"
- use, abuse, and lose someone
- say things you know aren't true just to get someone into bed
- spill intimate secrets or spread sexual rumors
- have sex with your best friend's partner
- sexually harass someone*

---

* For more on sexual harassment, see pages 206–208.

- make disparaging comments about someone's body or sexual performance.

If you plan to be (or are) sexually active, it's essential that you:

- treat your partner with respect and kindness
- make every effort to be honest in your relationship
- show sensitivity to the wishes and signals of your partner
- go no further or faster than your partner wishes
- always use condoms and other forms of protection to lessen the chance of disease and/or pregnancy
- refrain from blabbing intimate details about your relationship.

"One of my friends has just been diagnosed HIV-positive. My parents told me I can't see him anymore. I don't believe this. We've been friends since kindergarten. There's no way I'm not going to see him. What can I do to get my parents to listen?"

You're right to want to be there for your friend. It would be rude, as well as uncaring, to drop him because he has the virus associated with AIDS. Your parents are probably frightened because they know there isn't a cure for AIDS yet. This fear, coupled with their love for you, has led to their prohibition.

If you haven't done so already, explain the medical facts to your parents. Tell them that the only way HIV can be transmitted is by the exchange of bodily fluids. These include semen, blood, vaginal secretions, and saliva (although the possibility of acquiring the virus from saliva is considered very remote). This means that it can only be passed from one person to another through oral, anal, or vaginal sex; tainted blood transfusion; the commingling of blood (as in "blood brother" rituals); or sharing needles. As long as you don't take drugs intravenously, have sex, or exchange blood, you're protected against AIDS. You can't get AIDS from toilet seats or swimming pools. You can't get AIDS by dancing or holding hands. You can't get AIDS by hugging, sleeping next to, or being breathed upon by a person with AIDS.

Once the shock of the news wears off, your parents may relax their prohibition. It wouldn't hurt to leave some medical pamphlets around for them to read. In the meantime, you have a difficult decision to make. Should you ignore your parents' wishes and keep seeing your friend, even if it involves subterfuge on your part? This is an issue for your conscience and morals to decide. As far as etiquette is concerned, it would be terribly rude and hurtful to shun a good friend just because he has a virus. ◆

"My boyfriend wants me to have sex with him. He says there's no way he could have AIDS, so he doesn't want to use a condom. Could this be true? Can you know for sure that you don't have AIDS?"

Someone who has *never* had sex, shared needles, received a blood transfusion, or otherwise exchanged bodily fluids with anybody can be sure he or she doesn't have AIDS. If your boyfriend has engaged in any of those activities, he could be carrying HIV. He could even be carrying it if he just had a test saying he was HIV-negative! (This is because it can take some time before the virus is detectable.)

Most people who are HIV-positive don't know it. People who say they couldn't possibly have AIDS may be speaking the truth, or they may be deluded, in denial, or ignorant of the facts. If your boyfriend had sex just once with just one person, he could have acquired the virus. If, five years ago, he and a friend cut their palms with a pocketknife and shook hands to signify everlasting friendship, he could have acquired the virus.

Even if your boyfriend doesn't have AIDS, condoms offer additional protection against pregnancy and sexually transmitted diseases. It's a mark of good manners to do whatever one can to make a sexual partner feel comfortable and safe. Therefore, your boyfriend should use a condom if for no other reason than you asked him to. If it turns out you didn't "need" to, no harm has been done. If, however, you needed to and didn't, a lot of harm may have been done.

Trust is critical to any healthy relationship. And you probably wouldn't want to have a sexual relationship with a boy you didn't feel you could trust. But remember, more lies have been told to get someone into bed than for any other reason. ◆

"Who's supposed to bring the condom, the boy or the girl?"

An excellent question, because no teenager today who chooses to be sexually active should have intercourse or oral sex without protection.

Traditionally, the man brought the condom. This goes back to the days when men were considered the initiators of sex. It would have been scandalous for a woman to acknowledge having a sex life, let alone buy condoms. In today's world of changing attitudes and sex roles, this tradition no longer makes sense. Unless you have an explicit division of responsibilities—for example, you bring the condoms and your partner brings the breath mints—it's the responsibility of *both* partners to ensure that they take every precaution, every time, to protect themselves and each other against pregnancy and/or disease. ◆

A Brief History of the Condom

Since you were wondering, it was a 16th-century Italian physician named Gabriel Fallopius (of Fallopian tube fame) who is generally credited with designing the first male prophylactic. Its purpose was not to prevent pregnancy, but to combat the epidemic of venereal disease ravaging Europe. Dr. Fallopius's invention quickly led to the manufacture of medicated linen sheaths a uniform eight inches long. They were secured to the base of the penis with a pink ribbon (cute). In the mid-1600s, King Charles II of England supposedly asked his personal physician to devise a method of protection against syphilis. Legend has it that the doctor created a sheath out of oiled sheep intestine. His name? Dr. Condom.

MAKING OUT IN PUBLIC

You're waiting at a bus stop with your boyfriend, and the bus isn't due for another ten minutes. You kiss him, he kisses you back, and nine minutes later you come up for air—and dirty looks from the other people at the bus stop.

You might ask *Why is it rude to make out in public? With all the violence in the world, what's wrong with showing a little love?* Good questions. But the fact remains that what you call "showing love," others call "disgusting behavior."

While affection in general is to be applauded, affection in public is to be avoided. Why? Because nobody likes a show-off. It's rude to rub people's noses in the fact that you have something they don't.

This isn't about holding hands, kissing good-bye, hugging at the airport, or strolling arm-in-arm with the one you love. It's about physical contact that's basically sexual in nature. The kind that makes your heart beat faster and your blood pressure rise. (And that's just for the people who are watching.) Things like petting. Tongue wrestling. Rounding the bases between first and home.

Making out is a wonderful thing to do with someone you care about. But it should be done in private. When you do it in public, you force people to witness behavior that may be distracting or discomforting. And that, as you know, violates the basic principles of etiquette.

P.S. The prohibition against public displays of affection is lifted under certain situations. For example, as long as it's raining, couples are permitted to kiss passionately along the Seine River in Paris during the entire month of

April. Similar license is granted to those watching the sunset by the ocean in Key West. You may apply to me if you wish to propose additional exceptions for consideration.

TRUE STORIES FROM THE MANNERS FRONTIER
PDA

I was downtown when I saw this young couple, hands plunged in each other's rear pockets, locked in an embrace. At first I thought they were trying to dry-clean each other's blue jeans. But then, after watching for 45 minutes, I became convinced that they were doing something entirely different.

I found the entire episode highly distracting, and it made me late for where I was going.

"My boyfriend is a terrible kisser.* Is there a polite way to tell him this?"

No. How would you feel if he told *you* something similar? If you enjoy his company in other ways, if you're a good match in terms of your personalities and interests, then you can probably assume that he *wants* to please you. Use his desire as a teaching tool. Don't say "Ewwww!" or "You kiss like a fish." Instead, say "I love it when . . ." or "Do you think you could . . . ?" On the other hand, if he has no desire to please you, you might want to send him out to pasture. ◆

BEING DISCREET

If you've dated, you've had this experience: You go out with someone, and the next day all of your friends ask nosy questions. Like "How far did you get?" and "Did you _____?"

It's not surprising that your friends would feel they have the right to know such intimate details. After all, look at the bad example set by politicians who feel they have the right to legislate people's love lives. Nevertheless, you have the right to privacy. So when your friends pry into your personal affairs, smile and reply:

---

* Or whatever.

How Rude!

"A gentleman [or a lady] never tells."

"I prefer not to discuss things of that nature."

"I can't imagine why you would be interested in things of such a personal nature."

The more secretive you sound, the more—or less—they'll assume you did. But you can't be held responsible for other people's assumptions.

"My boyfriend and I are in love, and we had sex. Now he's told everybody about it and he's ignoring me."

Nothing ruins a good relationship like sex. Some boys (not all) view sex as a conquest. It's a notch they put on their belt once it's back around their waist. In laying the groundwork for sex, they may even convince themselves (and you) that they're in love. After the sex, however, they discover that it wasn't love but horniness, and they're no longer interested in the relationship. So they move on to another conquest.

Of course this is terribly hurtful. If your boyfriend's behavior was unintentional, it's a sign of immaturity and insensitivity. Immature, insensitive people shouldn't be having sex. If your boyfriend's behavior was deliberate and manipulative, it's a sign of unforgivable rudeness and disrespect. Either way, you're better off without him. ◆

CHAPTER QUIZ

1. *You've just started attending a new school, and you're eager to make new friends. Do you:*
   a) hand out $10 bills,
   b) offer to do everyone's homework, or
   c) project a confident air, ask questions, and join clubs and groups?

2. *You have a friend who always overstays her welcome. The polite way to get her to leave is:*
   a) put a Carpenters album on your stereo
   b) toss a tear gas canister at her feet
   c) say "I wish you could stay, but I have to do something with my mother."

3. *Your best friend informs you that he's gay. Do you:*
   a) tell him it's just a stage he's going through
   b) say "I'm feeling a bit giddy myself," or
   c) reassure him of your friendship and thank him for telling you?

4. *Your roommate takes things from your desk without permission. The best way to get him to stop is to:*
   a) throw out your desk
   b) set a mousetrap in the top drawer
   c) request that he ask permission before going through your things.

5. *Half of the boys in school want to go out with you. Do you:*
   a) tell them to take a number
   b) print up little rejection cards and pass them out in study hall, or
   c) use "having plans" and "being busy" as polite excuses when turning down requests for dates?

6. *You're in love with a girl who doesn't know you exist. The best way to get her attention is to:*
   a) push her down the stairs
   b) do a striptease in the cafeteria
   c) maneuver into her vicinity and start a conversation.

7. *When a boy pins a corsage on a girl, it's essential to:*
   a) check it for bugs
   b) offer the young lady an antihistamine
   c) confirm that the place you're about to stick the pin is a shoulder strap and not a tan line.

8. *Public displays of affection aren't bad manners as long as:*
   a) you keep three feet on the ground
   b) one of you remains fully clothed
   c) you're both on the honor roll.

8
Eat, Drink, and Be Wary

Tabled Manners and Food for Thought

Ever since the first caveman threw a few dino-chops in the microwave and invited the neighbors over for dinner, eating has been the central social event in people's lives. Whether a romantic dinner, a wedding banquet, a power lunch, or a Thanksgiving feast; whether a sacrificial slaughter, a Passover seder, a funeral wake, or a two-straw shake at the mall, food and drink play a part in virtually every human activity. No wonder so many rules and rituals have evolved around the what, when, where, and how of eating.

It's important to learn the food-related rituals and practices of any culture you live in or visit. Bad table manners can get you chewed out by your mom, embarrassed in front of your friends, or dumped by your date. First impressions are often formed around a dinner table. And if the impression you give makes people sick, you won't be invited back. So here are the ABCs of minding your peas and cukes.

Place Settings: Cracking the Code

Eat, Drink, and Be Wary

You've been invited to a formal dinner party at your girlfriend's house. She's told you that her parents are going all out, and you're already nervous. You arrive on time, and after a brief period of chitchat in the living room, dinner is announced.

The moment you catch sight of the table, you know you're in trouble. Deep trouble. You've never seen so many dishes, plates, glasses, bowls, knives, forks, and spoons in your life—and that's just *your* place setting. Your whole body breaks out in a sweat. There's nowhere to run, nowhere to hide. Within 30 seconds, you'll be revealed as an ignoramus.

Wake up! It's only a bad dream. Cracking the code of the formal place setting isn't as hard as it looks. Read on to learn everything you need to know to be suave, sophisticated, and self-assured at even the most daunting dinner table.

SETTING THE WELL-MANNERED TABLE

To avoid awkward moments in other people's homes, start by practicing in your own. Take out your family's best dishes (ask first) and announce that you've decided to learn how to set a proper table. Once your parents recover from their initial shock, they may even offer to help you (or learn along with you).

It's easy to set a table correctly. In fact, the basic rules are so simple that even an adult can understand them:

- Set out only what you need for that meal.
- Place the silverware* and glassware so people work their way *from the outside in* as the meal progresses.

Like this:

1. Forks go to the *left* of the plate (except for that tiny seafood fork, which goes to the *right* of the spoons).
2. Knives go to the *right* of the plate, with their sharp edges facing in.
3. Spoons go to the *right* of the knives. Dessert spoons are set *above* the plate, or they can make a grand entrance later with the dessert.
4. Salad plates go to the *left* of the forks (unless the salad is served as a separate course).
5. Bread-and-butter plates go *above* the forks.
6. Glasses go *above* the knives.

If you're a dinner guest in somebody's home, you'll start with the silverware farthest from your plate for the first course. Once that's cleared away,

---

* Silverware not actually made of silver should, strictly speaking, be called *flatware*.

you'll use the silverware that's *now* farthest from your plate for the second course, and so on. Of course, if your hosts have taken liberties with the arrangement, all bets are off. You'll have to watch them for cues as to which utensils to use, or you might end up trying to cut your steak with a spoon.

A FORMAL DINNER, COURSE-BY-COURSE

Since learning about proper place settings and how to use them can be a lot to digest, let's imagine you're back at your girlfriend's house, only now you know what you're doing. (NOTE: A less formal family dinner would be similar to the one described here, except some of the courses and place setting pieces would be eliminated.)

The Initial Service

Dinner begins with raw oysters. Of course you're not going to have any, but you should still know about that tiny fork to the right of your plate. That's what you'd use if you weren't so busy thinking *Ewwww, I'm gonna puke if I have to keep looking at these slimy things.* Fortun-

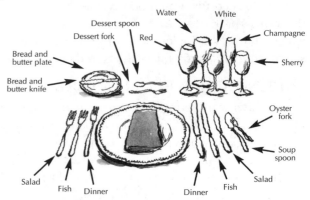

ately, your neighbor says "If you're not going to eat those, can I?" and quickly swaps plates with you. This, at a formal dinner party, is a lapse of both manners and grammar. But who's picky in an emergency like this? Finally, the oyster plates are cleared away. (**TIP:** Throughout any meal, dishes are cleared from the *right* and served from the *left.*)

Soup's On

Next up is a soup. Since you don't eat soup with a fork, you look to the far right, *et voilà*, there's your soup spoon.

By now you might be wondering *Isn't there usually a teaspoon on the far right?* And the answer, bouillon brain, is: Yes, there is. And it's not supposed to be there! That tea-

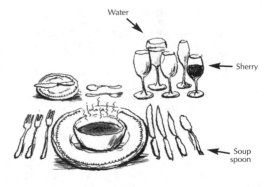

spoon has no business on the table unless tea is the first course. So ignore it. If you're the one who's setting the table, leave it in the drawer.

As for your soup: Don't slurp.

The Salad Course

Still hungry? Of course you are! Never fear; it's salad time. A small fork on the far left is rarin' to go, as well as a salad knife on the right for those who need it. Lettuce proceed.

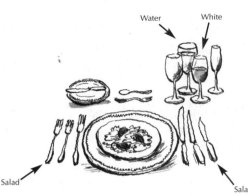

Something's Fishy

After the salad comes a fish course. With the salad fork retired to the great dishwasher in the sky, next up on the far left is the fish fork. On the far right you'll find the fish knife.

Let's take a breather as you dab your mouth with a napkin and join the chorus of compliments offered to the host and hostess.

Once the fish plates and utensils are cleared away, clean plates are set in front of you. It's time for . . .

The Meaty Course

A platter of thick, sizzling venison is brought to the table. (Oh, deer, it's Bambi's great, great, great grandson.) The proper knife and fork for the meat course have now reached the head of the utensil line. *Bon appétit.*

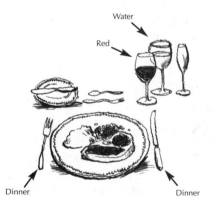

NOTE: During dinner, your hosts will serve those beverages that best accompany each course: sherry with the soup, white wine with the fish, red wine with the meat, and champagne with the dessert. And, since the table was correctly set, you'll find just the right glass each time you move along the lineup of glassware from the outside in.

271

What if you're not old enough or you prefer not to drink alcohol? No problem. When you're served, simply decline by saying "No, thank you." Don't place your hand over the glass or turn it upside down on the table.

Just Desserts

Since everybody knows that the purpose of dinner is to whet one's appetite for dessert, you're probably in a panic because you've used up all your silverware and the *pièce de résistance* has yet to arrive. Fear not. See that spoon and fork lying facedown above the space where your plate used to be? That's your dessert service.* Notice that the spoon is not a teaspoon. (Teaspoons are used for tea!) Dessert spoons are larger.

A 22-layer pecan torte with a dollop of white chocolate ice cream soon arrives. It's history in no time. You turn to the neighbor who saved you from oyster hell and say "Excuse me, if you're not going to eat that, may I?" It's still a lapse of manners, but at least your grammar's good. No one's looking—quick—you swap plates.

"What should you do if you use the wrong fork?"

Just keep using it. If you're feeling particularly daring and you're in a private home, wait until no one is looking, then lick it clean and put it back where you found it. ◆

"I'm not a very religious person. What should I do if I'm at someone's house for dinner and they say grace? I know I shouldn't start eating, but do I have to bow my head, say 'Amen,' or hold hands with the people on either side of me?"

Etiquette insists that you follow the "when in Rome . . ." principle and do as your host family does. But all that's required of you is the *appearance* of

---

* If it's not there, be patient. It will be coming with the finger bowl. (See page 281 for fingerbowl facts.)

respect for their tradition; you don't have to convert to their religion. So bow your head, join the circle of hands, and mutter "Amen." If, in the process, you figure out some batting averages, no one will be the wiser. In the future, try to sit next to those persons whose hands you would most like to hold. ◆

"I'm going out with this girl, and my parents want me to invite her over for dinner. I keep putting them off because she has the world's worst table manners and my parents would fall out of their chairs if they saw them. Even I, who's been known to put an elbow or two on the table, am pretty disgusted. How can I tell my girlfriend that her table manners are terrible?"

Pointing out flaws in a person's manners, behavior, and/or character is always risky and often rude. Most people can handle the news that they have gravy on their chin. It's a bit harder to swallow the notion that one isn't fit to be taken out in public.

Try this: Tell your girlfriend that she's the most wonderful creature on the face of the planet, that you love her more than words can say, and that you soooo want your parents to like her. Then, in an embarrassed tone of voice, confide that they have this weird thing for table manners. Mention a few of the behaviors that drive your parents up the wall: using fingers as utensils, sucking entire strands of spaghetti into one's mouth, talking while chewing, etc. Ask your girlfriend if, as a special favor to you, she'd make a point of being extra careful when she comes over for dinner.

And in case you need to polish your own table manners, read on for a refresher course. ◆

Basic Table Manners

You've just learned how to navigate your way through a formal table setting. But there's more to table manners than using the correct fork or saying "Excuse me" if you bump into a sideboard.

Following are some rules and guidelines that will give you food for thought. Abide by them at other people's homes, in restaurants, and, if you want to amaze your parents, at your own dinner table.

PLAYING WITH FOOD

It's never proper to catapult pudding across the dinner table (something I learned as a child when I responded to my grandfather's teasing in such a manner), nor shall peas and other tiny vegetables be used as artillery against one's siblings. As for all those other imaginative things you can do with your food while eating, now that you've thought about them, forget about them. Playing with food is not allowed.

PUSHING FOOD AROUND ON YOUR PLATE

If you're having fun, this counts as playing with food and isn't allowed—no matter how artistic your arrangement may be. This means no making mashed potato dams or clearing paths with sausage plows.

There's one exception to this rule:

FOOD YOU DON'T LIKE

When you're a guest in somebody's home, you may be served food you don't like. It's rude to leave your plate untouched. If your dislike is mild, try to eat as much as you can. If you absolutely can't bear to consume a single morsel, move your food around on your plate so it appears to have seen some action. Tuck a little slice of liver under the lettuce. Cut a few more bites and slip them in with the green beans. Try to reduce the overall surface area of the food. Meanwhile, engage in animated conversation so people will look at your brow, not your chow.

You don't want anyone to notice that you're not eating; this defeats the purpose of surreptitious food relocation strategies. And if someone is so rude as to ask "Don't you like the liver?" or "Aren't you eating?" just smile and say "It's delicious."

"I'm a vegetarian, and when my friends invite me to dinner, they usually serve meat. What's the polite thing to do?"

Take the opportunity of the invitation itself to explain your food preferences. Tell your friend that you don't eat meat, then hasten to explain that you'll be perfectly satisfied with the salad, vegetables, rice, and/or other nonmeat items people normally serve along with the meat course. In other words, they don't have to change their menu just for you. Then simply pass the meat plate when it comes your way.

In time, most of your friends (and their parents) will remember that you're a vegetarian, and they might even prepare vegetarian meals when you're their guest. Especially if your manners are so impeccable and your conversation so engaging that they can't wait for you to grace their table again. ◆

"My parents force me to eat things I don't like. Isn't that rude?"

Children shouldn't be forced to eat things that make them gag, vomit, and keel over at the table. And parents shouldn't have to cook five different entrées to satisfy the finicky eating habits of family members. What's needed is a middle ground—somewhere between the parent who insists that a child eat eggplant and the child who claims that she'll never eat anything but fish sticks for the rest of her life.

Here are Seven Reasonable Rules for Happy Home Dining:

1. Children must try a bite of a new food before they can proclaim that they don't like it.

2. Parents must respect the right of underage taste buds to declare certain foods off-limits.

3. Children who reject certain foods must not expect parents to prepare alternate meals for them.

4. Parents must make good faith efforts to prepare meals that all family members like.

5. Children must recognize that microwaved burritos are not nature's only food group and try to eat a well-balanced diet.

6. Parents must recognize that children can go quite a few days without vegetables or fruit before they begin to waste away.

7. Children and parents together shall determine household food policies to address the following questions:
   - Can a child who doesn't like something make something else?
   - Can a child who doesn't finish his dinner have dessert?
   - Who determines the portions of food served?
   - Can a child who doesn't eat her dinner cook something later?
   - Can a child snack between meals if it spoils his appetite? ◆

SELF-SERVICE

A platter of food from which you're supposed to serve yourself normally arrives from your *left*. If it sits on the table (rather than being held for you), make sure it sits *on* the table. Otherwise the Escalope de Veau on Rice may end up as Escalope de Veau on Floor.

How Rude!

Use the serving utensils provided (never your own silverware) to take a portion. Often there are two utensils that look like a spoon and fork on steroids. Use the spoon to (duh) spoon out a portion. Use the fork to steady it from the top or side. Place the utensils securely back on the platter. If someone has been holding the dish for you, say "Thank you."

Some items will come to you in ready-made portions dictated by the recipe (Eggs Benedict, Salmon in Pastry Puffs, etc.). Don't cut yourself a half-portion or scoop off the toppings and leave the foundation behind. Take a whole portion of what's being served, even if you know you won't eat it all.

For all other dishes, take only as much as you can finish. In fact, when a platter of food arrives, do a quick mathematical calculation. Place yourself in the numerator. You're #1. (Don't let it go to your head.) In the denominator, enter the number of people dining minus the number of people who have already taken portions. If there are eight people dining and you're the first to be served, you would enter an 8 (8 – 0 = 8). If three people have already been served, you would enter a 5 (8 – 3 = 5). The resulting fraction (in this case, 1/5) represents the maximum amount of food you're allowed to take.

And you thought math was useless.

"What should you do if you drop food on the floor?"

If the family dog is nearby, do nothing. He'll gladly take care of it for you. If the dog is absent and the food is of the nonmessy variety (such as a string bean or an apple slice), you can bend down, pick it up, and place it discreetly on the edge of your plate. (The same thing applies if you drop things on the table, although you can eliminate the bending down part.)

Messier droppings (such as chili or creamed corn) may require excusing yourself, saying "How could I be so clumsy?" and zipping into the kitchen for a spoon, sponge, or paper towel (unless you're advised to leave it until after dinner).

If you're at home and you drop a utensil, pick it up, excuse yourself, and get a clean one from the kitchen. In a restaurant, it's okay to leave it on the floor (unless you think someone might slip on it) and ask the waiter for a new one. You can also leave food you drop on the floor. ◆

Who's on First?

If you're like most people, you've bolted upright from a sound sleep wondering about the correct order for serving people at a family dinner. Here it is:

- adults before children*
- females before males
- unrelated (guests) before related (family members), and
- older before younger.

If you're not sure of someone's age or gender, don't ask. Guess.

Thus, the oldest adult female who's not related to your family would be served first, followed by the next oldest. Once you run out of unrelated females, you turn to related ones such as grandmothers, aunts, etc. Once you run out of those, you serve females in your immediate family, such as mothers and sisters one would no longer consider children. (The point at which a child ceases to be a child is often a matter of dispute. The sensitive host knows that he can win an admirer for life by conferring adult status on older adolescents.) When you've finished with the women, you turn to the men and start over again.

Once all the adults are salivating at the food they're not yet allowed to eat, it's time to serve the children: girls first, guests first, oldest first, and then the boys. The person preparing each plate serves himself or herself last.

Sometimes people are determined to confound etiquette, and the person for whom the plate is intended insists on passing it to someone else, who in turn sends it on. If you're not careful, the same plate can circle the table four or five times. An experienced server often announces the destination of each plate by saying "This is Aunt Mary's."

Children shouldn't feel slighted by this system. Rather, they should feel privileged that their status allows them to exercise such generosity toward their elders.

---

* Children too young to be able to wait should be served first.

Eat, Drink, and Be Wary

PLEASE PASS THE . . .

Usually the things you want or need during dinner are stacked up in front of somebody at the far end of the table. If you want something, don't reach. Ask:

"Could you please pass the Mushrooms à la Grecque?"

Sometimes a dish being passed 'round the table comes to a complete halt in front of one oblivious soul. In such a case, it's perfectly fine to say:

How Rude!

"Excuse me, Natasha, are you finished with the Mushrooms à la Grecque?"*

Natasha will turn red in the face and pass the dish. She's allowed to take some before passing it because you phrased your request as a question.

It's improper to intercept an item being passed to someone who requested it. For example, if the gravy is traveling from person A to person F, persons C and E can't halt its journey. When F has finished, C and E can put in their own bids and wait their turns.

Items with handles (pitchers, serving utensils, gravy boats) should be passed so the handle is presented to the recipient.

"Are there rules about passing food?"

Platters of food should make their rounds from left to right counterclockwise around the table. Most people are right-handed, and it's easier to serve yourself by reaching across your plate to a dish positioned to your left. Attendees at a Convention of Left-Handers would be correct in passing food in the opposite direction.

When you're somebody's dinner guest, the food-passing route isn't up to you. If a platter blows in from the east instead of the west, don't reverse its direction—unless the dinner party is boring and you want to liven things up a little. ◆

"Why are you supposed to pass BOTH the salt and pepper if somebody just asks for one of them?"

Because condiments have feelings, too. They get lonely without each other. And if they stay together, you'll never have to send a search party across the tabletop to find the one that's missing. ◆

ASKING FOR SECONDS

Don't ask for seconds if you're a guest in somebody's home. Your hosts may not have any, or they may be in a rush to finish up, or they may be counting on leftovers for tomorrow's supper.

If you're *offered* seconds as a guest at an informal dinner, it's usually all right to accept. Especially if you know that others will be doing the same. At a formal dinner, you're better off declining. This way, you avoid the risk of being the only person having a second helping while 11 other guests have to wait for the next course until you finish.

---

* Translation: "Natasha, get with the program and stop hogging the mushrooms."

OFFERING DRINKS

When you're hosting guests, don't say "What do you want to drink?" This can lead to awkward exchanges:

Eat, Drink, and Be Wary

> You: *"What do you want to drink?"*
> Guest: *"How about some tomato juice?"*
> You: *"We don't have any tomato. Would you like some cranberry juice?"*
> Guest: *"Oh, I'll just have a diet Coke, then."*
> You: *"I don't think we have any diet sodas. Is Pepsi all right?"*
> Guest: *"Do you have some tonic water?"*
> You: *"No, but we have club soda. Only I think it's flat."*

It's much better to say:

> *"What would you like to drink? We have orange juice, apple cider, ginger ale, and I can make a mean chocolate milk."*

"Why do you have to hold your pinkie in the air when you drink tea?"

You don't. The reason people used to do this centuries ago was because cups didn't have handles. Since a cup of boiling water was HOT, the more fingers you kept away from it, the fewer got burned. Once handles were invented, there was no longer any reason to fly superfluous fingers in the wind. The custom, however, has been slow to die out. Therefore, many people, if served a dainty cup of tea, still hold their pinkies in the air. ◆

ELBOWS OFF THE TABLE

This is a much misunderstood point of etiquette. When parents say "Elbows off the table!" what they really mean is:

- Don't lean on the table.
- Don't rest your head in your hands.
- Don't eat with your elbows glued to the tablecloth.

These are all reasonable expectations.

You may, however, set the undersides of your forearms gently on the table while resting between courses or conversing since, technically speaking, these aren't your elbows.

As long as we're on the topic of elbows, keep yours *down and at your sides* while cutting and eating food. No flapping or jabbing your neighbors allowed.

How Rude!

GETTING FOOD ONTO THE FORK

Forks were designed to capture food without any help from bread, knives, or fingers. The combination of those handy little spears for stabbing, that long edge for pursuing, and that flat surface for shoveling provide all the tools you'll ever need to transfer food from plate to mouth.

Occasionally you'll encounter some defiant holdouts who refuse to board. Usually these are peas or beans, the very things your parents admonish you to finish if you want your dessert. If this should happen, tell your parents that you've done the best you can without committing an etiquette violation.

EATING WITH YOUR FINGERS

At informal family dinners or picnics, it's okay to eat the following foods with your fingers: chicken (unless it's in a thick, gooey, sauce); crisp bacon; fish sticks; shrimp cocktails; pizza; spareribs; chop bones (after you've eaten the meat with a knife and fork); artichoke leaves; crisp asparagus; corn on the cob; french fries; pickles; crudités (cold vegetables); fruit (apples, oranges, watermelon, bananas, etc.); and, of course, things set out without any silverware in sight, such as chips, nuts, olives, cheese and crackers, hors d'oeuvres, tiny sandwiches, and so on.

If you're a guest at an informal dinner at somebody's house, watch what your host family does and follow suit. If you're at a formal dinner, you're unlikely to be served any of these foods. But if, for example, a little gourmet pizza is presented as an appetizer, use a knife and fork.

"Is it okay to eat chicken with your fingers?"

Yes. But I prefer to eat my fingers plain, with just a touch of lemon. ◆

"Is it okay to blow on your food?"

Only if it spontaneously combusts. If it's merely too hot, allow it to cool. Soup may be gently aerated by stirring. ◆

SOPPING UP SAUCE

It's not proper to take a piece of bread and hydroplane across a lake of gravy. Still, it's a basic human drive to want to soak up that last bit of sauce. So, if you must, here's a compromise:

1. Break off a small piece of bread.
2. Place it on your dinner plate.
3. Delicately spear it with your fork.
4. Make like a sponge and mop. Gently.

Meanwhile, don't stare at your handiwork. Make it seem as if the bread has a mind of its own, like a Ouija Board pointer. And don't worry about capturing every speck of sauce. Your plate will still end up in the dishwasher, even if it sparkles by the time you're through with it.

Eat, Drink, and Be Wary

DUNKING

Almost everyone dunks at one time or another. It's a natural and satisfying human urge, and the pleasures it yields should not cause anyone to feel guilty. However, the joys of dunking are best reserved for private moments at home. It's simply not considered proper for anyone over the age of four to plunge donuts, cakes, or other soakables into milk or coffee in the company of others.

Finger Bowl Facts

Chances are you'll get through life without ever encountering a finger bowl. But if you should meet one in a dark alley some evening, here's what you need to know: A finger bowl is a small bowl, usually glass, in which you place finger bones.

Ha, ha. Let's start again.

It's a small bowl, half filled with water and set on a doily, that arrives with the dessert setting. It may have little things floating in it. These are not insects. They are flower petals.

If you want your dessert, you now have to work for it. Remove the finger bowl and doily and set it to the left of your dessert plate. Remove the dessert fork and spoon which came along for the ride, and place them, respectively, to the left and right of your plate.

Don't drink from the finger bowl or try to drown the flowers. Just barely dip your fingers into it, one hand at a time, and then dry them on your napkin.

Finger bowls are really quite silly. They're never around when you need 'em, like after a picnic of fried chicken and barbecued spareribs. Instead, they only show up at formal dinners, where fingers aren't likely to be messy in the first place. Go figure!

How Rude!

EJECTING INEDIBLES

Sometimes what goes in must come out again. Inedible food debris leaves the mouth by the same method it enters. In other words, a bite of steak delivered by fork, upon being recognized as a piece of gristle, exits the mouth by fork. This is best done at a moment when all eyes aren't on you. Discreetly place the half-chewed glob back on your plate. If you can tuck it under a piece of lettuce, so much the better.

An olive popped in by hand returns its pit to the world by hand. Exceptions:

- *Fish bones.* Fish flesh enters by fork, but the bones leave by hand. This is because the skinny little vertebrae tend to stick to lips and forks if you try to remove them by utensil. They don't stand a chance against fingers.

- *Watermelon seeds.* Although they sneak into the mouth via hand-delivery, watermelon seeds may, by unanimous consent of all present, leave by oral projectile. This approach is known as a spitting contest. It's restricted to outdoor locations and must never be tried inside.

EATING OUT OF CONTAINERS

I confess: I eat ice cream out of the carton. But I only do it when I'm by myself. As far as good manners go, this transgression doesn't exist. Similarly, if nobody sees you having an open-refrigerator-door buffet, sampling from this container and that, polite society won't be offended. If your mother sees you, that's a different story.

Concerning containers on the table, the High Etiquette rule is simple: Don't. Never bring a milk carton, a pickle jar, or a cardboard silo of parmesan cheese to the table when serving company. Transfer the milk to a pitcher, the pickles to a small platter, and the cheese to a serving dish with a spoon.

But High Etiquette often goes on hiatus when the family sits down to dinner. This is because serving foods in the containers they come in cuts down on preparation time, cleanup time, and dishwashing time. Your family will have to seek its own comfort level regarding such things as pizza and cereal boxes, carryout Chinese food, jam jars, and ketchup bottles.

The Breakfast Club

Breakfast differs from other family meals in that many rules of conduct are relaxed. This is because people clawing their way to consciousness are in a fragile emotional state. Children and parents about to head off, respectively, to school and bullies, work and bosses, need to indulge in certain ritualized eccentricities if they are to face the day. These include:

continued

- arriving and departing at different times
- reading at the table
- sitting in dazed silence, and/or
- consuming the identical menu day after day.

This need not be the same menu as anyone else's, since definitions of break-fast in most families range from light (toast and coffee) to hearty (pancakes, scrambled eggs, bacon, juice, cereal, and French toast).

While conversation isn't necessary (or, in some families, advisable), good mornings and good-byes are. Under no circumstances shall critical comments be made that would undermine any family member's belief that he or she is a lovable and capable human being. This will happen soon enough after leaving the house.

BUFFET BEHAVIOR

The world is divided into two types of people: those who pig out at buffets and those who don't. Whichever category you fall into, there are three rules to follow when you're dining the buffet way:

1. Don't sneeze on it.
2. Don't bring your dirty plate back to it for refills. Get a clean one each time you go up.
3. Don't get more than one course ahead of the other people you're with. Wait until everyone is finished before you go up for dessert.

LEAVING THE TABLE

One leaves the table when everyone is through with the final course. A host might signal this moment by saying "Why don't we move into the living room?" and a parent by "Whose turn is it to do the dishes?"

If you're a guest and you must leave the table for any reason, simply say "Excuse me" and depart. At home, it's proper to ask "May I please be excused?" (Children who say "may I" as opposed to "can I" receive bonus points.)

"If you're eating over at a friend's house, should you help clear the table?"

Follow your friend's lead. If he gets up to clear, you get up to help. If a chorus of protests tells you to stay seated, that's what you should do. After dinner, offer to help your friend with any dishwashing or drying chores he may have been assigned. ◆

How Rude!

The Eight Dinnertime Duties of Children and Teens

1. To come when called. (Astute parents will issue five-minute, three-minute, and "You'd-better-get-down-here-right-now-or-else" warnings.)

2. To present yourself at the table clean and clothed.

3. To wait until your parents sit down before starting to eat, unless they insist otherwise. For extra credit, hold your mom's chair and push it in for her when she sits down at the table.

4. To use good table manners.

5. To contribute to the conversation with:

   • topics of general interest (for example, a supply-side economics analysis of how the new unified European currency will affect bond rates in the Tokyo stock exchange); and/or

   • narratives of personal experience (for example, how you saved your best friend's life on the way to school this morning).

6. To listen (or give the appearance of listening) to the conversation of others.

7. To remain at the table until permission is granted to leave.

8. To participate cheerfully in postdinner cleanup chores as requested.

You may be thinking *Ha, ha, ho, ho. I don't really have to do all that.*

Yes, you do. If it's your parents' responsibility to bring home the bacon, it's your responsibility to not be a pig while eating it.

"My parents nag me about not talking with my mouth full, but every time I take a bite of something they ask me a question. How can I answer without talking with my mouth full?"

If you're caught *in flagrante mouthful,* try to park the chew in your cheek long enough for a brief response. Some people consider this cheating, but if you can do it without spraying food particles, nobody will object and it's a handy skill to master.

If all that's required is a yes or no, nod or shake your head.

More detailed responses require a different approach: signaling to the questioner that a reply is forthcoming as soon as you swallow. You do this by raising your hand, index finger extended, as if testing for wind. Such a gesture, when accompanied by gleefully raised eyebrows, says *I can't wait to answer your question—but you're going to have to—since you wouldn't want me to talk with my mouth full, would you?*

Or you can take smaller bites. This way, your mouth is more conversation-ready at any given moment. ◆

"I hate eating dinner with my parents. Every two seconds it's 'Hold your fork right,' 'Sit up straight,' 'Don't talk with your mouth full.' What should I do?"

Hold your fork right. Sit up straight. And don't talk with your mouth full. ◆

"My parents are always making snide comments about how much me and my friends eat. It's not our fault we're hungry. Don't you think this is rude?"

Look on the bright side. Your parents could be making snide comments about your grammar.

The truth of the matter is that the feeding habits of the adolescent are astonishing to behold. Like sharks, teenagers just open their jaws and consume whatever is in their way: cold pizza, chocolate fudge peanut butter ice cream, leftover Chinese food, 30 gallons of milk. And that's just for breakfast! These creatures usually forage in packs, drawn to the kitchen by familiar scents (brownies baking, sauces simmering) and sounds (the slam of the silverware drawer, the sizzle of bacon frying).

If dinner is still 20 minutes away, this means there's time for a snack: pretzels, bagels, microwaveable pizza, microwaveable soup, mircrowaveable ravioli, microwaveable waffles. In the old days, a teenager could starve to death between the onset of hunger and the end of sandwich-making. Nowadays, a 12-course dinner can be zapped in less time than it takes to say "Medium high."

Of course, the remarkable feeding habits of adolescents don't justify rudeness on the part of those who track them. Your parents should pick their jaws up off the floor, stop gaping, and say nothing to your guests other than "Another piece of pie, boys?"

But this isn't likely to happen. Because the real reason parents tease their kids about the amount of food they eat is: It drives them crazy that you can consume 15,000 calories a day and not gain a pound! ◆

How Rude!

Napkin Niceties

Here's everything you always wanted to know about napkins but were afraid to ask:

- Place your napkin on your lap as soon as you sit down. It's not a waiter's job to do this. He has no business in your lap. Some restaurants fold their napkins into cone shapes; resist the temptation to put these on your head.

- Huge napkins may be left folded in half. Small napkins should be fully unfolded.

- Don't hold your napkin out to the side and unfurl it with a chivalrous flourish as if you were Henry VIII's barber.

- Never tuck your napkin under your chin. Bibs were invented for this purpose, and they are meant only for children under three and persons eating lobster who don't mind feeling foolish if it will spare their upper garments from attack.

- Use your napkin to dab at your mouth, not scrub the skin off of your face.

- Don't use your napkin to blot lipstick, clean eyeglasses, or wipe off silverware between courses.

- If you get up during dinner, leave your napkin on your chair until you return. If dinner is over, leave your napkin loosely folded on the table to the left of your plate (or where your plate used to be).

- Never use napkin rings with company. It's a common mistake to assume that these little devices were originally intended as a decorative way to present napkins and impress guests with how much silver one owned. Actually, they were designed as a way to tell family members' napkins apart in the days before paper napkins and washing machines. It was impractical for most families to wash cloth napkins after every use; thus, each person had a napkin ring engraved with his or her own initials or symbol. This permitted bonding between increasingly soiled napkins and their respective owners until the relationship was ripped asunder on wash day.

- Finally, never use your napkin as a handkerchief. If you blow your nose into your napkin, everyone else at the table will spend the rest of the evening picturing your slimy snot slowly solidifying and will experience the same reaction you're having now.

Utensil Essentials

There are three ways to hold and use silverware while cutting and eating your food: the American Way, the Continental Way, and the Wrong Way. Left-handers may reverse the following instructions for left and right. They should not, however, reverse the actual place setting.

Eat, Drink, and Be Wary

The American Way	The Continental Way	The Wrong Way
1. Hold the fork in your left hand, tines down. Use your index finger to steady it and apply pressure. Cup the handle in your palm.	**1–3.** Hold and use the fork and knife as you would in the American Way, but think Continental thoughts.	**1.** Hold the fork in your left fist.
2. Hold the knife in your right hand, sharp edge down.		**2.** Hold the knife in your right fist. (Picture yourself gripping a pair of toothbrushes.)
3. Slice gently. Don't saw. Keep the knife close to the fork or you risk flinging your filet across the table.		**3.** Saw away. Flap your elbows and slop food over the edges of your plate.
4. Set the knife at the top of your plate so the blade faces inward.	**4.** Continue to hold the knife or set it down, depending on how soon you'll need it again.	**4.** Using both your knife and your fork, shovel food into your mouth.
5. Transfer the fork to your right hand, tines facing up. Lift or spear a bite of food.	**5.** With the fork still in your left hand, tines down, spear a bite of food.	**5.** Talk with your mouth full.
6. Raise fork to mouth. Eat.	**6.** Raise fork to mouth. Eat.	**6.** Ask your dinner partners why they are leaving the table before the meal is through.

SILVERWARE SIGNALS

Silverware has its own body language. Here's what various positions mean:

"I'm still eating."

"I'm about to pass my plate for seconds."

"I'm done."

"I'm a slob."

USING CHOPSTICKS

If the chopsticks are stuck together, separate them. You'll notice that they taper at one end. Use the smaller, narrower ends for picking up food; usually they're round, while the top ends are square. You'll hold the chopsticks about half to two-thirds of the way up, keeping the ends even.

Hold the upper chopstick—the one that moves—as if it were a pencil (almost). Support it between your second and third fingers, but extend them a bit straighter than if you were writing.

Don't rest the upper chopstick in the hollow between your thumb and index finger, as you would a pencil. That's where you'll rest the upper half of the bottom chopstick. Support the lower half with the tip of your ring finger. The bottom chopstick stays fixed, while the upper chopstick pincers up and down when you move your second and third fingers.

On second thought, never mind. It's impossible to explain how to use chopsticks. Get a friend to show you—or ask the waiter for a fork.

Eat, Drink, and Be Wary

The Do's and Don'ts of Delightful Table Manners

Do . . .

. . . wait to sit until everybody is present and all ladies have been seated
. . . wait to eat until everybody is served—unless your hostess tells you to please start
. . . take small portions when food is passed
. . . offer to pay the dry cleaning bill of anyone upon whom you spill food
. . . learn to talk with a little food in your mouth and your lips closed (this skill will serve you well at business lunches)
. . . finish swallowing one mouthful before taking another (or a sip of your beverage)
. . . take small bites and chew with your mouth closed
. . . pace your eating so you don't get ahead of or behind the others in your group
. . . sit up straight and lean slightly over the table when putting fork to mouth
. . . keep your humming to a minimum.

Don't . . .

. . . redip the bitten ends of veggies or chips into the communal bowl of dip (you may redip the other ends)
. . . pick your teeth at the table

continued

289

How Rude!

. . . reach across another person to get something (ask for it to be passed instead)

. . . smack your lips (although an ecstatic "mmmm" may be exhaled in the direction of the host)

. . . use common serving utensils (sugar spoons, butter servers) to stir your own tea or butter your own bread

. . . tilt your chair

. . . mop the table with your napkin if you spill water (just right the glass—and don't mop your dinner partner if you spill water on her)

. . . hold your silverware in a fist

. . . gesture with a knife or fork in your hand

. . . play footsie unless you're very sure whose feet belong to whom.

How to Eat

1. Open mouth.
2. Insert food.
3. Chew and swallow.

Beyond these rudiments, you may have questions about the proper way to eat certain types of foods. From Artichokes through Spaghetti, the chart on the next six pages tells you everything you want and need to know.

Dining Out

You'd like to take your girlfriend to a fancy restaurant for dinner. You've never done this before, and you're not quite sure how to go about it. Here's precisely what to do to ensure that a good time is had by all.

When you pop the question, give your girlfriend clues for how to dress. If you want to surprise her with your choice, you can say:

"Are you free for dinner Saturday night? I'd like to take you to this fancy little place I know."

Or you can be more direct and ask:

"Would you like to go to Le Snob on Saturday night?"

continued on page 297

Food	Do's	Don'ts	Fine Points
Apple or pear	Hold. Bite. Chew. Swallow.	Don't eat an apple or pear by hand in a formal setting. Stab it with your fork. Then cut it in quarters and eat bite-sized pieces by fork.	If you swallow a seed, it takes approximately 60 years for an orchard to grow in your stomach.
Artichoke	Pull off a leaf. Dip the pulpy end into the sauce. Slowly draw the leaf through your teeth. Repeat until you finish or get fed up with so much effort for so little return. When all leaves are gone, you come upon a tender heart surrounded by tough bristles. Use your knife and fork to cut off the fuzzy "choke." Eat your heart out.	Don't stick the whole artichoke in your mouth.	Leaves that you have scraped clean or rejected may be stacked on the plate.
Asparagus	Use your knife and fork to cut and capture bite-sized morsels.	Don't stick the spears in your ears.	According to etiquette, crisp asparagus may be eaten with the fingers. Few people know this, so you may not want to try it in a fancy restaurant.
Baked beans	Consume with a fork, but only when you anticipate being by yourself for the next 24 hours.	Beans should never be eaten with the fingers.	Ask yourself: Why are beans primarily cooked on camping trips, where you'll be sleeping in a closed tent with 12 other bean-digesting campers?
Banana	Hold by the bottom. Strip the peel a little bit at a time. Eat the fruit.	Don't lick a banana as if it were a lollipop.	At a formal dinner, peel the banana all at once and eat it with a knife and fork.

291

Food	Do's	Don'ts	Fine Points
Berries and cherries	Use the fingers to grasp the stem. Insert the berry/cherry into mouth. Clamp lips. Pull on stem with hand. Berry/cherry should pop off. Place stem on plate, in trash, or gently upon Mother Earth. Remove pits, if any, from mouth by hand.	Never spit pits at your dinner partner.	Formal settings require the use of a spoon. Use the tongue to re-deposit pits on the spoon.
Bread and butter	Break off a small piece of bread by hand. Butter it. Eat it. Repeat. (Exception: Toast may be buttered all at once.) If you don't have a bread plate, place the bread (or roll) on the edge of your dinner plate.	Never stuff an entire buttered slice or roll into your mouth. Never hold the bread in the palm of your hand while slathering gobs of butter on it.	When taking a pat of butter from the butter dish, use the butter knife traveling with it. Place the butter on your butter plate (or dinner plate, if a butter plate is not provided). Then use your own knife to butter your bread.
Cake	Eat with a fork. True aficionados always begin at the point of the triangle.	Don't eat cake with your fingers, unless you're sneaking a piece in the kitchen.	Cake left sitting on the counter quickly disappears, despite the fact that nobody's had any. This is because everyone who takes some thinks his or her slice is too thin to be detected.
Candy	All teenagers are genetically pro-grammed to know how to eat candy.	Don't leave telltale chocolate smears on your face.	With boxed candy, you must "take the one you touch," and *only* one, unless your host insists that you take several. (This would be the mark of a *very good* host.) The little paper tray comes along for the ride and may be placed in a nearby ash-tray or candy-wrapper-discard-dish.

Food	Do's	Don'ts	Fine Points
Cherry tomatoes	Small cherry tomatoes should travel by fork to the mouth and be eaten in one bite, thus producing a squirt of tomato seeds inside your cheek. Larger cherry tomatoes should be cut in half.	Never bite into a cherry tomato unless your mouth is fully closed.	Cheery tomatoes should be eaten with a big grin and a happy disposition.
Club sandwich (and other food too tall to fit in your mouth)	Discreetly compress the sandwich. Eat over the table so falling food will land on your plate and not in your lap. Use your fork to pick up the droppings.	Never stand on a club sandwich to flatten it.	The toothpicks with shrubbery on top are not meant to be eaten.
Corn on the cob	Ears are eaten from left to right. You may nibble horizontally (the "typewriter" method) or vertically (the "rotary" method).	Making typewriter sounds is forbidden.	These methods are designed to maximize the number of corn bits that get stuck in your teeth.
Fish	Use the fish fork, tines down, to anchor the fish. Holding the fish knife as you would a pencil, cut through the skin from left to right. Lift up the top flap of skin and eat from left to right. Then lift the bottom flap and repeat. Break off the fish meat carefully so you don't pry up any bones. The backbone will now be exposed. Gently remove it and place it on the edge of your plate. The fish's other flank is now available for eating.	Never use a toy guillotine to decapitate the fish. If you can't stand the sight of a fish head, cover it with your lemon.	While fish may come to the table with their heads on, it's considered rude for them to wear hats.

Food	Do's	Don'ts	Fine Points
Grapefruit	There's no way to eat a grapefruit properly unless you're furnished with a serrated grapefruit spoon, or the sections have been previously loosened in the kitchen.	Try not to squirt people in the eye while eating grapefruit.	Someday when you're bored, try to figure out how grapes and grapefruit are related.
Grapes	Use your fingers to place grapes in your mouth one by one. Remove any seeds by hand.	Don't pick single grapes off of a communal bunch. This leaves an unappetizing graveyard of stems for others.	If a bowl of grapes is passed, use your fingers or the scissors (if provided) to break off a small bunch.
Ice	Consume with an iced tea spoon. Or hold the glass to your lips *after* the liquid has been consumed, tilt, and pop cube into mouth.	Don't chew the ice. You'll sound like a trash compactor.	Ice is a refreshing, no-calorie, highly underrated treat.
Ice Cream in a Bowl	Eat with a spoon and a rapturous look on your face.	Don't mush it into ice cream soup. If you really can't eat it any other way, wait patiently while it starts to melt. Then allow your spoon to travel in genteel circles around the bowl until the ice cream reaches the desired consistency.	Greedy children who gulp down their ice cream are punished with headaches.
Ice Cream in a Cone	Immediately attack the overhanging lip to prevent drips. Push the scoop into the cone with downward tongue pressure to prevent tearful "scoop-on-the-sidewalk" scenes. Be gentle to avoid agonizing "my cone broke" scenes.	Don't work your way up from the bottom.	Dripless and dropless techniques must be practiced and mastered in order to maximize carryout cone-in-the-car opportunities.

Food	Do's	Don'ts	Fine Points
Ice Cream Soda	The only way to eat an ice cream soda is with two straws, two spoons, and somebody you really like.	It's acceptable to slurp up the last remains of soda and melted ice cream—but the sound must not be audible to those in the next booth.	Always offer your date the cherry on top.
Lemon	When squeezing a lemon wedge, use your other hand as a shield to prevent lemon spritzes from flying into people's eyes.	Don't bite into a lemon wedge in company. This will make everyone pucker up.	When life gives you lemons, make lemon chiffon pie.
Orange	Either cut in quarters and burrow your face in the fruit, or peel by hand and separate into sections.	Never tell "Knock, knock" "Who's there" "Orange" "Orange who?" "Orange you glad . . ." jokes at formal dinners.	In a fancy restaurant, eat the fruit with a fork.
Peas	Consume with a fork. The last few peas may be cornered against a wall of mashed potatoes. If the peas are the only food remaining on the plate, the holdouts are generally impossible to catch and must be sacrificed.	Never use bread, fingers, or a knife to push peas onto your fork.	Parental commands to "Finish your peas!" are unreasonable unless permission is granted to snare the stragglers using improper methods.
Pizza	For informal occasions, pizza may be lowered into the mouth from above for that first delicious bite of the triangle. The remaining wedge may be kept flat or folded by breaking the spine of the crust with your forefinger.	Don't pull long strings of cheese with your teeth.	For formal occasions, use a knife and fork. If you must pick off the olives, do it with your fork.

Food	Do's	Don'ts	Fine Points
Salad	Use a salad fork and knife if provided. Otherwise use your main course utensils. Large pieces of lettuce may be cut with your knife.	Refrain from cutting your lettuce so fine that it looks like it went through a shredder.	In Europe, salads are typically served *after* the main dish; in America, before.
Soup	Hold the soup spoon so its length runs parallel to the table edge. Fill by submerging the far side first and moving the spoon toward the back of the bowl. Sip from the *near side* of the spoon, not the tip. Pour the liquid into your mouth. Tilt the soup plate *away* from you to get the last drops.	Don't put the spoon in your mouth unless it has chunky goodies on it. Don't suction the contents of your spoon as if you're cleaning out a septic tank. Don't crumble crackers into the bowl. Don't use a knife to cut things in your soup; use the edge of your spoon. Don't drink from the bowl unless it has handles or the soup arrives in a mug.	When pausing or finishing, leave your spoon in the bowl if the bowl is large, or on the saucer underneath if the bowl is small.
Spaghetti Etiquetti	Capture a few strands in the tines of your fork and twirl. (Not you. The spaghetti.)	Don't slurp or lower linguini into your mouth as if it's feeding time at Sea World. Don't sever strands with your teeth so they fall onto your plate.	It's not considered proper to twirl spaghetti on a spoon. It doesn't matter if everybody does it.

Next, make a reservation. It's not necessary to speak French. Call the restaurant. Tell them you'd like a table for two on Saturday night at 8:00. If you have any special requests (for example, a table near the window, or a birthday cake) make them known at this time.*

When you arrive, you'll be greeted by the maitre d'. State your name and say that you have a reservation. He'll check to make sure that you do, then lead the two of you to your table. Your girlfriend should go first—after the maitre d'. So you don't get lost, you should follow her. If there's any problem with the table (too close to the kitchen, in a draft, next to neighbors who look like they'll eavesdrop, etc.), politely request a different one. You have every right to do this.

The maitre d' will either pull out the woman's chair for her to sit down, or, if your table is a banquette (a bench against the wall instead of chairs), slide out the table so she can gracefully scoot in. Once your girlfriend is seated, you may sit down.

Menus come next. If you want to communicate subliminally to your girlfriend that she'd better not order the most expensive item on the menu, you can mention dishes that look interesting to you. She will then check them out, note their prices, and order accordingly.

As long as you don't eat with your fingers or use the tablecloth as a handkerchief, there's no need to feel uncomfortable in a fancy restaurant. Snootiness isn't the same as elegance; disdain isn't the same as good service. If a restaurant indulges in either, it's the restaurant, not the patrons, who are rude. Demonstrate your opinion of their behavior by never returning.

"What are you supposed to do with those pretty little things that come with your plate of food?"

I assume you're referring to the garnishes. It's perfectly fine to eat the various sprigs and ferns that doll up a dish. Do, however, keep a sharp lookout for miniature Oriental parasols, plastic palm trees, and toothpicks with greenery on top. While nonfattening, these are not readily digestible. ◆

"How do you decide who gets the best seat when you go out to dinner?"

This is usually determined by clever planning and quick footwork, since possession is nine-tenths of the law.

---

* If the restaurant is especially popular or very small, make the reservation *before* asking your girlfriend. You can always cancel your first reservation and make another one if she's already busy that night. But DO call to cancel your first reservation. No-shows are rude.

Traditionally, the woman was given the "best" seat—the one against the wall, from which you can look out and see everything. This left the man better positioned to pay the bill, taste the wine, and beckon the waiter. Since women today perform many of these tasks, there's no longer any gender-based reason for who sits where. People who go out together frequently can alternate "best" seats. ◆

DECIDING WHAT TO ORDER

When someone takes you to dinner, what should you order? Why, the most expensive thing.

Just kidding.

It's best to order something in the mid-price range. If you order the cheapest item, your host will think you think he's cheap. If you order the most expensive, he may wish you thought he was cheap.

Listen for clues. If your host says "This place is famous for the lobster" or "I think I'll have the chicken, but I hope you'll try the steak," he's giving you permission to order whatever you want.

If he puts you on the spot with "What do you think you're going to have?" you can say "Everything looks good. What are *you* thinking of having?" Similarly, if a friend's parents take you out, ask if there's anything in particular they'd recommend. Even if they've never been to the restaurant before, they'll mention some items that sound good, and you'll get the menu guidance you need.

"I was invited to dinner at a country club. My menu didn't have any prices on it. I was afraid of ordering the most expensive thing by mistake. What's the polite thing to do when this happens?"

The idea behind the "priceless" menu is that it's gauche for hosts to let on exactly how much their generosity is costing them. (We remove price tags from gifts for the same reason.) This makes sense in a country club, where it's assumed that the members will pay for their guests. In public restaurants, however, there's no way (short of mind reading) for waiters to know who the lucky check picker-upper will be. It's the height of sexism to give menus with prices to men and menus without prices to women.

If you're handed a menu without prices, use the strategies discussed above to solicit clues and suggestions. Generally speaking, things like lobster, seafood, shellfish, and fine cuts of meat are more expensive than chicken, pasta, salads, and sandwiches. ◆

TRUE STORIES FROM THE
MANNERS FRONTIER
Beaucoup de Bucks

Eat, Drink,
and Be Wary

I was once taken out to dinner at a three-star Michelin restaurant in Paris. It was the kind of place where you could spend more on lunch than most countries spend on defense.

Our party consisted of three men and a lady. As the men stared at the menu prices in stunned silence, the lady exclaimed "Doesn't this look fabulous! We must try the lobster-stuffed raviolis, and the crab timbale, and the salmon, and —" on and on through half the items on the menu. We were a bit surprised at her extravagance, until we discovered that her menu had no prices.

It was at this moment that the brothers Slobola walked in. No, not really; it was at this moment that the waiter arrived. We ordered everything we wanted. And then we economized by eating dry cereal for the next eight days.

GOING DUTCH

Going Dutch doesn't mean dining in Amsterdam. It means that each person pays his or her own share of the bill. The tricky thing is, if you're invited out, how do you know if it's Dutch or not?

If you're lucky, the person will make it clear by saying "Let's have dinner together Saturday, my treat" or "I have some good news and some bad news. The good news is I'm inviting you to go out to dinner with me. The bad news is I'm flat broke, and we'll have to go Dutch."

If you're not sure who's paying, you can:

- wait and see, being sure to have enough money with you in case you need to cover your share, or
- say "I'd love to go, but I'm out of funds until next Friday." This will generate either "Oh, that doesn't matter, I'm paying" or "Why don't we wait 'til then, okay?"

If you do go Dutch, split the bill evenly by the number of people. This saves endless hassles over who had coffee and whose appetizer cost 35 cents more. If, however, you know that your share came to much more than anyone else's, you should insist on putting more money in.

How Rude!

"What can you do if you order something in a restaurant and you don't like it?"

If the item is well-prepared, you're probably stuck. You could see if anyone at your table wants to swap with you, or you could order a different dish. A truly classy restaurant might not charge you for the order you didn't eat, but don't count on it.

If you order something and it's unsatisfactory, discreetly bring it to your waiter's attention. Say:

"Excuse me, I ordered my steak rare. This one is well-done."

"The soup is delicious, but I wonder if you could have it warmed up."

As long as you're polite, the restaurant should agree to make things right. If you don't get satisfaction from the waiter, ask to speak to the headwaiter or manager.

It's also perfectly proper to ask the waiter to replace dirty forks, dishes, or glassware. ◆

"Why are waiters so rude to teenagers?"

Because *some* teenagers are very rude and rowdy in restaurants. They yell, swear, make out, blow bubbles in their drinks, snort through their noses, play with their food, throw things, create salt mountains on the tablecloth, treat servers with contempt, leave little or no tip, and even bolt from the restaurant without paying. Unfortunately, their behavior puts *all* teenagers under suspicion. Therefore, some waiters groan inside when a group of teenagers sits down at one of their tables. This doesn't excuse rude service, but it may help to explain it.

Naturally, when *you* dine out, your behavior should be exemplary. Use your best table manners, treat the staff with respect, tip well,* and leave the restaurant intact when you depart. The next time you visit that establishment, the waiters will fight for the right to serve you. Look on the next page for a summary of acceptable vs. unacceptable acts. ◆

---

* For tipping tips, see pages 302–304.

It's okay to:	It's not okay to:
request a particular table	rearrange the room
ask for descriptions of menu items	ask the waiter to repeat them more than once
ask the prices of specials	blurt "What a rip-off!"
send back an improperly prepared dish	stomp into the kitchen and throw your plate against the wall
address a request to any staff person who serves your table or passes within its vicinity	yell across the room "What do I have to do to get some service around here?"
ask for a doggie bag	ask for a barf bag
glance at the check to make sure there are no errors	bring along your accountant
discreetly apply a little lipstick at the table.	comb your hair, apply full makeup, or squeeze zits at the table.

"Is it proper to hand plates to a waiter?"

Only if you're tucked away in an awkward corner and the waiter would have to reach over other diners to take your plate. Otherwise it might be seen as an affront to his professionalism. On a similar topic: Never stack the dishes at your table. Let the staff do it when they clear them away. ◆

SHARING FOOD

You're at a restaurant with a friend, your orders arrive, and you notice that her onion rings look spectacular. Meanwhile, your french fries are especially crisp and golden. You wonder if it's all right to share.

If she agrees, it is. But ask first. Or, better yet, wait until she offers. Don't just reach across the table. (If she's slow to offer, you might casually remark "Boy, those rings look good. How are they? By the way, want some of my fries?")

Although it's rude to pass mashed potatoes from one person's mouth to another in public, it's acceptable to share some types of food at restaurants. For example, grub that's brought in communal serving dishes—sesame

How Rude!

shrimp, pizza, big bowls of pasta—is meant to be enjoyed by all. In fancy restaurants, where one oohs and ahhhs and thinks *six dollars* every time you take a bite, you may put a taste of food on your fork and pass it to a close friend or loved one. For people you know less well, samples should be delivered on their forks.

If you plan to go halvesies on two entrées or split one, tell the waiter when ordering. Many restaurants will make the division in the kitchen. This might upset the chef's carefully laid out squiggles and sprinkles, but every artist needs to be challenged once in a while.

Tipping Tips

In a perfect world, there would be no tipping. Workers would be paid a fair wage to do their jobs. Instead, they get caught between cheap employers ("Yeah, but you'll make a fortune in tips") and cheap customers ("Tip? They earn a good salary"). The fact is that people in service jobs earn very low base salaries—often below minimum wage. They depend on tips for their income. If a waitress serves a party of 12 businessmen who hog three tables all night, run up a bill of $1,000, and leave a $10 tip, that waitress has been stiffed for her work. Imagine if you baby-sat for an entire evening and got paid a quarter.

The first rule of tipping is that it's *not* optional. If the hairdresser cuts off your ear, or the cabby runs over your foot, you can leave a small tip—or none at all. But you should make it known why you aren't leaving a standard tip. In Europe, a service charge is added to the bill in most restaurants, and it's perfectly acceptable to leave without tipping anyone. In America, the convention is different. Tipping is an "honor system" in which customers are trusted to ante up most of the worker's wage.

Teenagers tend to leave low tips. Often it's because their own funds are limited or because they don't know how much to give. But it's not fair to penalize workers who are trying to make a living. So here are the rules for being a tip-top tipster wherever you go:

Restaurants. Tip 15 percent of the bill—20 percent if the service is exceptional or the restaurant fancy. (Figuring these amounts is another reason for taking math in school.) Never leave less than a quarter, even if all you had was a cup of coffee and it means you're leaving a 50 percent tip.

If the food was bad, don't take it out on the waitress. She didn't prepare it. As long as she or the manager were responsive to your complaints, you should still leave a tip. Just don't go back to that restaurant again.

If you're part of a large group, check to make sure that the restaurant didn't already add the tip (sometimes referred to as a "service charge" or "gratuity") to your check. Otherwise you'll end up tipping twice.

Sorry, but you still need to leave a full tip in buffet-style restaurants where you serve yourself.

Eat, Drink, and Be Wary

It's not necessary to tip the maitre d' or headwaiter if all he does is show you to a table, pull out your chair, and hand you a menu. If, however, he provides a special service (rearranging tables, securing a birthday cake, squeezing you in without a reservation), a tip of $5 to $10 is customary. This should be discreetly slipped into his hand as you leave.

The *sommelier* (wine steward) need not be tipped if all he does is serve the bottle ordered. If, however, he helped with the selection, a tip of 15 percent of the wine bill is appropriate.

Rest room attendants. These are people whose job is to listen to you pee. If the attendant does nothing for you, no tip is required. If he or she hands you a towel, tip 50 cents to $1.

Checkroom attendants. You can usually tell if tipping is expected by the presence of a little tray full of money on the counter. Don't be fooled by any large bills you see. They represent what the person would like to get, not what you're obliged to give. The going rate for checking a coat or parcel is 50 cents to $1 per item, depending on the fanciness of the place.

On a personal note, I'm happy to tip checkroom attendants in restaurants, museums, galleries, and concert halls. I refuse to tip in stores that presume me to be a thief upon entering and require me to leave my parcels or bags.

Airport skycaps. $1 per bag is standard.

Hotels. If you stay in a fancy hotel, you should arm yourself with a roll of dollar bills. These can be handed out to bellhops ($1 a bag) and doormen ($1 for strenuous cab hailing). Now you know why motels were invented.

For hotel maids, leave $1 per day in your room when checking out. Few people observe this custom. Be one of them.

The *concierge* (which is French for Person Who Knows Everything) may perform a special service for you, such as obtaining tickets for a sold-out show or finding a psychiatrist for your homesick dog. A gratuity of $5 to $10 is standard.

Many hotels add a 15 percent service charge to the bill for room service. Check your bill, and if this has been done, no further tip is required when your breakfast or midnight snack is delivered to your door.

The pizza guy or gal. Usually $1 per pizza, up to $5. Be a bit more generous if you live in a sixth floor walk-up or the delivery person had to trudge through snow-drifts to find you.

Taxi drivers. The minimum tip is 50 cents. For fares over $3, tip 15 percent. No tip is necessary if the driver runs out of gas and you miss your flight.

Shoe shiners. If you ever have time on your hands and want to get those Nikes shined up, tip 50 cents for shoes and $1 for boots.

"Keep the change."

Hairdressers and manicurists. Tip 15 to 20 percent of the bill. Give the shampooist a buck.

Wandering musicians. I have often been tempted to offer them a dollar if they will stop playing. No tip is required if a strolling musician just stops by your table, plays, and moves on. If you make a request, tip a dollar. More requests, more dollars. Pay when he or she leaves.

Valet parking. Tip $3 in great metropolises, $2 in lesser ones—as you leave. No tip is necessary if your car is returned with 200 more miles on the odometer than when you left it.

Owners. Don't tip the owners of establishments when they provide services to you (for example, Jean-Louis himself cuts your hair, or Mel of Mel's Deli personally brings you your Reuben). Instead of money, give profuse thanks and many referrals.

Tour guides. Museum docents and sightseeing tour guides are sometimes tipped. Watch what others do. For a short tour, $1 is adequate. If someone has been your tour bus guide for three weeks through Siberia, a much larger tip would be proper.

And finally:

Never tip a **police officer.** For some reason, this is interpreted as a bribe. Others who should never be tipped include flight attendants, bus drivers, train conductors, pilots, elevator operators (if there are still any left), government officials, teachers, and owners of bed-and-breakfast establishments.

CHAPTER QUIZ

Eat, Drink, and Be Wary

1. *You're at a dinner party. You ingest a mouthful of soup and discover that it's burning hot. Do you:*
   a) spit it out
   b) sue your hostess for $4,000,000, or
   c) quietly breathe air into your mouth to cool it?

2. *You're having dinner at the home of some friends of your parents. When the main dish is brought from the kitchen, you realize that it's something you don't like. Do you:*
   a) knock it out of your hostess's hands and hope she'll serve something else
   b) say "Yiccch. I hate that!" or
   c) take a small portion and eat as much as you can?

3. *A vegetarian comes to your house for dinner. She loads up on the salad and pasta but doesn't touch the meat. The proper thing to say is:*
   a) "If humans were meant to be vegetarians, animals would be made out of rice."
   b) "Have you ever had scurvy?"
   c) nothing.

4. *You're having lunch in the school cafeteria. While munching on a morsel of Salisbury steak, you encounter a huge piece of gristle. Do you:*
   a) throw it at the gym teacher
   b) go "ARRRGH, ARRRGH, ARRRGH" and try to swallow it, or
   c) deposit it on your fork when no one is looking and transfer it to your plate?

5. *Etiquette permits family members to read at the table so long as they:*
   a) don't move their lips
   b) provide plot summaries for one another
   c) are eating breakfast.

6. *You're dining out at a fancy restaurant. The waiter brings your entrée, and it's not what you ordered. The best response is to:*
   a) dump it on the floor
   b) try to jerk the tablecloth out from under the dishes
   c) say "Excuse me, but I ordered the duckling."

9
On Your Best Behavior

Etiquette for the Milestones and Celebrations of Life

Life is full of special events: weddings, funerals, bar mitzvahs, graduations. Some of these are happy occasions; others are sad. But they all have one thing in common: uncomfortable seats. So you don't trip the groom, tickle the bride, or fill your canteen from the baptismal font, here are some tips for minding your manners at the milestones of life.

"What are you supposed to do at a funeral?"

Just lie still. ◆

Funerals

The thought of attending a funeral or memorial service may make you uncomfortable. You may think *I won't know what to say. I won't know anybody there. What if I cry? What if I laugh?*

Our culture is squeamish about death. People don't like to talk about it, and most people grow up without knowing how to deal with grief—whether their own or somebody else's. While it's natural to feel ambivalent about going to a funeral, it's important that you do attend. It's a way of supporting the bereaved, consoling yourself, and honoring the dearly departed. You never get a second chance to go to someone's funeral. Here's what to do and why:

Dress conservatively. You don't have to wear black, but loud, attention-getting outfits are out of place. This isn't the time for fashion statements other than one of respect for the solemnity of the occasion and/or the traditions of the family.

Sign the registry. There should be a book at the church or funeral home for guests to sign. Presumably its purpose is to allow the family of the deceased to appreciate those who attended rather than depreciate those who didn't ("And after everything Harry did for him!").

Respect the rites. The death of a person can involve many separate events: a viewing of the body, a religious service, a procession, a burial, a wake, a messy lawsuit over the will. Depending on the family's cultural and religious traditions, there may be wailing and keening—or stiff upper lips; there may be wild, life-affirming parties—or subdued reminiscing. You aren't required to participate in behaviors that are foreign or objectionable to your culture, language, religion, or relationship to the deceased. For example, nobody would expect you to make the sign of the cross, to kiss the corpse, to recite a prayer in a language you don't know, or to become hysterical. What you can always do, however, is be observant and respectful. Stand and sit when others do. Try to blend in with the tone and traditions of the occasion.

Feel free to decline. You may be asked to throw dirt on the coffin. You may be asked to say a few words. (Tributes and recollections from people who knew the departed are included in some services.) You may be offered an opportunity to view the body. Such rituals are never obligatory, and you won't cause offense by declining. A simple "No, thank you" should suffice. If asked to speak, you could say "Oh, I'd love to, but there's no way I could get through it."

If you're asked to be a pallbearer, however, it's *not* considered proper to decline—unless you recently dislocated your shoulder.

How Rude!

Don't be too jolly. Let's say the father of one of your friends has just died. You feel for your friend, but you didn't know his father. At the funeral are many of your classmates. Since you're not grieving yourself, it might seem natural to greet them jubilantly and engage in animated conversation. Don't. Behavior that's too upbeat might be misinterpreted as a lack of respect for the somber nature of the occasion. While you don't have to put on fake grief, you do have to maintain a subdued decorum to show your empathy.

Express your sympathy. Right after the service, guests usually form a receiving line to extend their condolences to the family. This is the moment most people have in mind when they worry about what to say.

Stop worrying. *All you have to say to each person as you pass through the line is "I'm sorry."* If this taxes your tongue too much, you don't have to say anything. If the person is someone you know well, you can simply hug him or her. If it's someone you don't know at all, you can engage in a mournful handshake. Instead of a vigorous up-and-down squeeze, embrace the person's hand between your own two hands, as if you were holding a bug. Either a hug or a handshake can be accompanied by a sad look that says "I feel for your pain."

Probably more important than knowing what to say is knowing what *not* to say. Avoid any and all of the following:

> *"I know just how you feel."*
> *"You must be heartbroken."*
> *"It's much better this way."*
> *"At least he's out of his pain."*
> *"Now you can get on with your life."*
> *"You never liked her much anyway."*
> *"I suppose you'll get the house?"*
> *"Your parents can always have another kid."*
> *"I'm sure he wouldn't want us to be sad."*

These sentiments are inappropriate because:

- They presume to tell others what their emotions or grieving process should be.
- They put words and thoughts into the mouths of those who can no longer speak for themselves.
- They frame the death in terms of its impact on you.
- They suggest that people who die can be replaced as easily as lightbulbs.

Send flowers. It's traditional to send flowers to the church where the funeral will be held, or to the family of the deceased. Of course, if 300 people do this, there'll be so many flower arrangements that it will look like . . . a funeral. No one will be able to get in the door.

This is why many families ask that, in lieu of flowers, contributions be made to the deceased's favorite charity. Giving the money to a good cause is not only a lovely, lasting tribute to the one who was called away, but also a kindness to hay fever sufferers.

Write a letter of condolence. This, like a thank-you note, is nonnegotiable. Write it by hand, in ink, on good quality personal note paper. Do *not* send one of those tacky store-bought sympathy cards with canned messages:

> Roses are red,
> Violets are blue,
> Sorry he's dead,
> Boo-hoo, boo-hoo.

Instead, send a short, warm note. Acknowledge the death. Include a fond recollection. Close with an expression of sympathy. Avoid euphemisms such as "passed away" or "left us." These suggest that the deceased just overtook a slow-moving car or stepped out of the room for a moment.

Dear Mr. and Mrs. Bereaved,

I was so sorry to hear the sad news of Billy's death. His friendship was very special to me. When I came to Buford in the middle of my freshman year, he went out of his way to make me feel welcome. I don't know what I would have done without his friendship (and his answers in math!). Please accept my deepest sympathy.

Sincerely yours,
Arthur Graves

Let it out. Somebody's death, even if you didn't know the person, can set off all sorts of feelings. Don't keep them bottled up inside. Write them down in a journal. Talk to people about how you feel, about the person who died. If you don't find the comfort or support you need from your family or friends, talk to a teacher, counselor, or member of the clergy.

"Is it true that when a person is cremated, people at the funeral have to spread the ashes?"

How Rude!

If the person who died was cremated, there may be a ceremony in which her ashes are scattered. This doesn't usually take place at the time of the funeral, since ashes flung around the church would just end up in a vacuum cleaner. Most people who are cremated make it known (*before* they die) where they would like their ashes scattered. It's usually a place that holds special meaning for them (for example, the White Mountains, the Tiber River, or the Food Lion parking lot). If you participate in one of these ceremonies, you don't have to dish out the dust. But if you choose to do so, stand upwind. ◆

"I have this friend whose mother died about six months ago. I'm feeling guilty because I haven't seen much of my friend since then. She isn't much fun to be around anymore, plus I don't know what to say. How much longer do you think she'll be like this?"

There's no way of saying, because there's no "correct" way to mourn a death. Some people cry; others don't. Some people become depressed for a long time; others snap out of it quickly. Some people go through periods of anger and guilt for having done (or not done) something to or for the deceased. Some people may even be angry at the person who died—for dying. What you see on the surface may bear little resemblance to what a person feels inside.

Your friend had the rug pulled out from under her life. Her mother's untimely death will be a part of her identity forever—long after her acute feelings of grief and sadness have subsided. Six months ago, her friends and relatives probably rallied to offer their love and support. They came to the funeral, brought food, sent flowers—and then disappeared. The bereaved are often abandoned, emotionally if not physically. Other people expect them to "get on with their life," or they assume that those who have suffered a loss want to be left alone, or they are simply uncomfortable being around someone in so much pain.

The best thing you can do for your friend—and yourself—is to *be* her friend. Call her, spend time with her, and include her in social gatherings. If she hesitates or declines, apply a little pressure. Tell her you miss doing things together. Don't make her feel she has to put on a happy face. Let her know you want her company just the way she is.

When you're together, ask her how she is, how things are at home, and how her family is doing. Get her talking. People who suffer loss often feel isolated from those around them—because they have experienced something others haven't, and because people tend to avoid the subject. It's okay to talk about your friend's mother. Share some memories you have of her. Bringing them up won't make your friend feel worse by "reminding" her. She's already thinking about her mother all of the time.

If your friend starts to share her feelings, just be a good listener.* Don't try to cheer her up or talk her out of her feelings. If she speaks of problems at home, or if she seems terribly troubled or inconsolable, encourage her to talk to a counselor or another trusted adult. ◆

On Your Best Behavior

Religious Services

Presumably you know how to behave at your own house of worship, provided you attend one. In the event you're invited to attend a religious service outside your faith—perhaps for a special occasion—follow these guidelines to avoid offending the Higher Powers-That-Be:

- Respond promptly to the invitation.**
- Arrive on time.
- Don't skip the ceremony and just go to the party.
- Don't talk during the service unless audience participation is an integral part. (Whispered requests for a prayer book or page number are fine.)
- If you have to go to the bathroom, there's no need to raise your hand until the priest or rabbi calls on you. Simply exit quietly—preferably during a boisterous moment in the ceremony.
- Don't tell jokes. No environment is more conducive to uncontrollable fits of giggling than a house of worship. Should you suffer an attack, bite the insides of your cheeks. Whatever you do, don't look at your friend while he's reading from the Torah. If he breaks up, all is lost.
- Dress appropriately. Your friend and/or other classmates who belong to the same church or synagogue can advise you.
- Participate in the rituals. You don't have to take communion, kneel while praying, or immerse yourself in the baptismal font if these rituals are foreign to your faith. But you should stand when others stand, sing when others sing, and honor the traditions of worship practiced by that congregation.
- Don't take the money. At some services, a plate full of money will be passed. This is not an hors d'oeuvres tray of free samples; it's a collection plate to raise money for the church. If you feel so inclined, you may make a donation.

---

* For tips on listening, see pages 349–351.
** For tips on responding to invitations, see pages 153–158.

How Rude!

- Send a gift.* Honoring your friend and the occasion with a gift is a thoughtful thing to do. It's best if you don't bring your present to the church or synagogue. Send it to your friend's home ahead of time, or take it with you to the party later in the day. Checks and cash may be passed discreetly immediately following the service.

BAR AND BAT MITZVAHS

A bar mitzvah (bat mitzvah for girls) is a religious ceremony that occurs shortly after a Jewish child's 13th birthday. It marks the child's initiation as a full-fledged adult into the Jewish faith.** The service, which takes place at a synagogue, is open to the congregation as well as to the invited guests of the bar (bat) mitzvah and his (her) family. (The name applies both to the ceremony and the person being initiated into religious adulthood.) After the service, there's usually a reception at the synagogue, during which people offer their congratulations and consume large amounts of herring.

Later in the day, there's often a more elaborate by-invitation-only party. This is for relatives, family friends, and classmates. I attended numerous such events myself between ages 12 and 14, as I was blessed with many Jewish friends. My respect for religion grew by leaps and bounds as I realized that sacred traditions could be celebrated by bowling, swimming, skating, dining, doing the limbo, and sneaking onto the golf course to discuss theology with a member of the opposite sex.

If you're a bar (bat) mitzvah, fulfilling the following responsibilities will reinforce your newly minted adult status:

Prior to the event . . .

- Show your maturity by recognizing your family's financial limitations. Bar (bat) mitzvah parties are not a competitive sport. Just because some other kid's parents hired a Grammy-winning rock band to perform live is no excuse for saying "If you loved me, you'd take out a second mortgage."

- When your parents and siblings propose inviting certain of their friends as guests, try not to say "Ewwww, do they HAVE to come?" Instead, encourage them. This ensures that your family members will be occupied while you spend time with your friends.

- Reciprocate by inviting classmates who asked you to their bar (bat) mitzvahs. If you're limited in the number of guests you can invite to the party, at least issue invitations to the service itself.

---

* For the nitty-gritty on gift-giving, see pages 34–35.
** In the Christian faith, a confirmation ceremony admits a young person to membership in the adult congregation. If you're invited to attend a confirmation, or if you're being confirmed, many of the suggestions in this section will apply to you, too.

On the day of the event . . .

On Your Best
Behavior

- Enjoy being the center of attention, but do so with grace, charm, and modesty. Recognize that even though it's your day, you must still honor your social obligations.
- Great all guests with warmth and joy, even the ones your parents made you invite. Say "It's so nice to see you. Thank you for coming."
- Try not to grimace when kissed by relatives you don't know or like.
- Don't interrupt the festivities to announce that you've passed the $1,000 mark in gifts received.
- Introduce your friends to your relatives, to your parents' friends, and to each other.
- Be patient with adults who say "My, how you've grown" and "How does it feel to be an adult?"

"My, how you've grown!"

"My, how you've grown!"

"My, how you've grown!"

"My, how you've grown!"

How Rude!

- Write your thank-you notes pronto.* The longer you delay, the harder it gets. Begin each note with an expression of delight at having seen (or regret at not having seen) the person you're writing to. Never begin with "Thank you for the . . . ."
- Thank your parents for everything they did to make the day so special. Thank the rabbi, thank the cantor, thank Moses—make it an all-inclusive list.
- Leave some strudel for others.

"I've been invited to a friend's bar mitzvah. I'm not Jewish. Do I have to wear one of those beanies?"

If you're referring to a beanie with a propeller on top, certainly not. If you're referring to the small cap worn by men and boys of the Jewish faith, then you mean a *yarmulke,* not a beanie.

Do you have to wear one upon penalty of being shot? No. Is it okay to wear one if you're not Jewish? Yes. It's a mark of respect, much like rising when others rise during a church service. ◆

The Debut

First, *debut* is pronounced "day-byoo," not "duh-but." Knowing this ahead of time will save you from awkward moments like:

> You: *"Dearest Amelia! I can't wait to see your duh-but."*
> Amelia: *"My butt? Why would you want to see my butt?"*

A debut is the occasion upon which a young lady (the *debutante*), having attained the age of 18, is presented to society at a formal dance (the *debutante ball*). This ritual was much more prevalent in days of yore (that period when strenuous efforts were made to keep a woman's ankles from being viewed by the opposite sex). Because young ladies were kept sheltered from society, it made sense to have an event at which they were unveiled (the young ladies that is, not their ankles). This is why debuts were often referred to as "coming out" parties. Today, the custom has become so outmoded that most people, if invited to a "coming out party," would expect something quite different.

The declining popularity of the debutante ball is related to the declining popularity of courtship. It used to be that a gentleman wouldn't dream of

---

* For tips on writing thank-you notes, see pages 40–42.

speaking to a young lady before they were properly introduced. Courtship was the period during which, and the process by which, he then showed his interest and affection for her, with the intention (if all went well) of eventually marrying her. The debutante ball was the perfect setting for making introductions and getting the word out that a young lady's hand (and presumably the rest of her) was available for marriage. The debutante's parents would invite their friends, particularly those with handsome, honorable, and financially well-endowed sons. Since the parents knew the families of the young men in attendance, they could rest assured that all contenders would pass inspection.

Things today are quite different. The strictures against people getting together without being properly introduced have disappeared. This means that a young gentleman can approach a young lady in a laundromat, say "Yo, borrow your Clorox?" and three days later they're in Las Vegas being married by an Elvis impersonator. Potential partners can meet at the gym ("Spot me while I work on my pecs?"), at bars ("Are you going to eat that olive?"), and through personal ads ("Fun-loving professional, age 28, looks 27 . . .").

It's not surprising that fewer parents are going to the trouble and expense of presenting their daughters to society (and that fewer daughters wish to be so presented). Where the custom does persist, it's usually stage-managed by a *cotillion committee*. These self-appointed social arbiters screen and select each season's candidates and orchestrate the event. With several dozen young ladies all making their bows at the same time, the tradition has been updated to resemble the modern assembly line—and enjoys similar cost and production benefits.

At least two or three male escorts are required for each debutante. This is so the young ladies will feel in great demand, and also so there will be enough young men to dance with their sisters, mothers, and great aunts. If the debutante has been properly protected up to her 18th birthday, she won't know three eligible escorts. Therefore, the cotillion committee must find them for her. This is accomplished by a careful computer search that cross-checks the senior class of St. Smithereens School for Boys against social register, country club, and Forbes 400 membership lists. Those boys whose families show up on all lists are invited. If this fails to produce enough eligible young men, a "Free Punch" sign is placed outside the ballroom.

If you're a young woman whose parents are planning to debut you, here are your responsibilities (please note that they are remarkably similar to those of the bat mitzvah):

- Be mindful of your family's financial limitations. It just may not be possible to charter a Virgin Airways jet to take your friends to the Bahamas for a postball beach brunch.

How Rude!

- Remember that the true purpose of a coming out party is to present you to your parents' society. This means they have every right to invite their friends (and even have them outnumber your friends) without your saying "Why do THEY have to come?"

- Find a common denominator for music and food so members of all generations present will be able to partake without shocking themselves or others.

- Welcome and chat with all guests, be they young or chronologically challenged. Tell them how pleased you are that they could come.

- If you aren't an innocent young child who's being cast, eyelashes a-fluttering, into the adult world, pretend that you are.

- Dress properly. Typically this means wearing a white gown, not cutoffs.

- Introduce your friends to your family, to your parents' guests, and to each other.

- Pay attention to all of your escorts. Dance with fathers, grandfathers, cousins, and family friends in such proportion as to pay equal homage to duty and pleasure.

- Smile and be patient with adults who say "Whatever happened to the little girl I used to know?"

- Acknowledge all presents promptly.

- Thank your parents.

If you're a young man who's been recruited from St. Smithereens or elsewhere to tour the debutante circuit, here are your responsibilities:

- RSVP promptly.*

- Dress appropriately. (Proper dress is usually indicated on the invitation.)

- Anoint your deb with a floral arrangement.**

- As there shall be no wallflowers, do your part to see that all ladies who wish to dance have the opportunity.

- Engage in charming conversation with the hosts and their invited guests.

- Flirt with grandmothers.

- Maintain sobriety.

- Send a thank-you note to your hosts.

---

* For a refresher on RSVP-ing, see pages 153–158.
** A.k.a. a corsage. See pages 256–257.

Graduation

Twelve long years of school—worrying, struggling, hassling, dreading, hating, hoping, helping, longing, pleading, praying—and that's just what your parents have been through! No wonder they're so excited about their, er, your high school graduation. This is the moment they've been waiting for. Free at last! No more tests. No more homework. No more meetings with the vice principal. Now they can sit back, relax, and look forward to . . . *four more years?!!!*

On Your Best Behavior

Graduation may be your triumph, but it's payback time for your parents. They'll be so giddy with pride and joy that they'll forget about the backpacks left on buses, lost gym shorts, stolen sneakers, broken eyeglasses, misplaced notebooks, and report cards that never made their way home. In this euphoric, all-is-forgiven state, they may also do silly things. Like ask to be introduced to your friends. Or want to see your locker. Or insist that you stand on the steps of the school for the longest minute on record as they aim the camera, forget to remove the lens cap, re-aim the camera, forget to advance the film, re-aim the camera, focus, brush a fly from their forehead, re-aim the camera, tell everyone to smile, wait for your little brother to look, and then, with all 380 of your classmates watching, take a picture.

Yes, graduation is a day you'll always remember. To be sure it's a day you'll *want* to remember, here are some pointers for proper commencement behavior:

Send out invitations. Typically, these are provided by the school. They look something like this:

The Headmaster, Faculty, and Graduating Class
of the
Bedlam School
request the pleasure of your company
at
Commencement Exercises
Saturday, the 20th of May
at one o'clock
on the Academy Lawn

How Rude!

If you just stick this in an envelope, the recipient will have no idea who the lucky graduate is. Therefore, include your card along with the invitation. What? No card? Then buy some blank ones. In your most calligraphic scrawl, handwrite your name. If you and a number of friends all wish to invite the same person (for example, your soccer league coach), you may send one invitation. Just enclose all of your cards. That way, his mailbox won't get overstuffed.

Because seating is usually limited at commencement exercises, you may not be able to invite as many people as you wish. In this case, you'll have to prioritize. Start with anyone likely to give you a car. Then invite your immediate family and closest relatives. If you still have some seats left, you can broaden the net to include mentors, friends, and distant relatives.

Send out announcements. These you send to friends and relatives who would be thrilled to hear of your accomplishments. This list might include tutors, coaches, piano teachers, scout leaders, and treasured baby-sitters from your childhood. If you had hoped to invite them to the graduation but were unable to do so because of limited seating, include a note to that effect. Let them know how much their support and/or friendship have meant to you over the years.

Don't fish for presents. It's tacky to blanket the populace with news of your graduation. Don't send invitations or announcements to the diaper service driver or the doctor who removed your tonsils—unless they went on to become your close friends.

Be tolerant of parents and relatives. Your folks will be bursting with pride. This means that they'll stalk you with a camcorder, reveal your family nickname, leave lipstick on your cheek, and talk about you to anyone who will listen. Don't be embarrassed by your parents' behavior. Your friends have parents, too.

Shake, don't stir. When you go up to receive your diploma, restrict physical contact with the principal to a handshake. No hugs, playful slugs on the shoulder, or European air kisses allowed.

Thank your parents.

"Does it matter what you wear under your gown at graduation?"

The safest bet is to follow your school's dress code for the occasion.

You might wonder *But if you can't see it, what difference does it make?* In theory, it makes no difference. People attending a graduation ceremony should pay attention to the speeches, not speculate on what their classmates have on beneath their robes. In other words, as long as what you're wearing (or not wearing) under your gown doesn't distinguish you from classmates who are properly attired, you're within the bounds of etiquette. ◆

On Your Best Behavior

"Is it rude to protest at graduation exercises?"

Some adults get teary-eyed at the sight of a class of graduating seniors standing with their backs turned to a distinguished speaker. For them, it evokes that Golden Age of protest known as "The Sixties." (You can read more about that time period in a textbook on Ancient History. Or ask your parents.) Nevertheless, such behavior is inexcusable. Commencement exercises aren't designed as forums for individual expression, whether artistic or political. Unless you go to the High School for the Artsy-Craftsy, where it's traditional for graduates to decorate their caps and gowns to look like postmodern cooking appliances, nix on the buttons, stickers, posters, placards, and pins.

Small ribbons, worn by group consent in loving memory of the 12 graduating seniors who were eaten by alligators on a field trip, would be an appropriate exception to this rule. ◆

"My school has invited a commencement speaker who's very controversial. Many students, myself included, are thinking of walking out. Would this be a breach of etiquette?"

How Rude!

Statements of personal belief—be they moral, political, or religious—by anyone other than a graduation speaker are inappropriate at a commencement. (The wise speaker knows to tread carefully in these domains.) Walking out, booing, hissing, or wearing incendiary slogans on your cap would all constitute breaches of etiquette. Since talking while someone else is talking is also rude, heckling and chanting belong on the list of unacceptable behaviors.

Virtually any speaker, with the possible exception of Mr. Rogers, is going to say *something* with which some audience members will disagree. Imagine the chaos that would result if students shouted, stomped, strolled in and out, and bobbed up and down every time they heard something they didn't like. (Imagine the fun!)

To be brutally frank, the individual student and what he or she thinks don't count for beans at a graduation. This is a ceremony of, by, and for the community. It's for the families and the faculty; for tradition and knowledge; for the graduating class as a whole. You have a lifetime in which to proclaim your individuality, express your opinions, and fight for the causes of your choice. But until the ceremonies are over, you must squash, squelch, and grind under your feet any such noble tendencies—even if the speaker expresses controversial beliefs that run counter to your own.

There's one exception to this rule: hate speech. If a commencement speaker engages in verbal violence or sullies the dignity of the occasion by attacking members of the community, the community doesn't have to take it lying down (or slouching in their chairs). A calm, strong response to verbal abuse isn't rudeness, it's limit setting. The more dignified your response is, the more power it will have.

A quiet turning of backs or a solemn procession out of the auditorium would be a proper and restrained reaction to such provocation. A student who stood up and said "Sir, these attacks are hateful, and they dishonor this institution and occasion. I must ask you to stop them" would forever be a hero in my book. ◆

"Do you have any tips for giving a valedictory address without offending anyone?"

Keep it short. Don't swear. Hurt no one. Tell a few inside jokes. Radiate idealism. Thank all parents and teachers. Don't trip when you leave the stage. ◆

Weddings

You've been invited to a wedding. And you've been asked to be a bridesmaid or an usher. Here's what you need to know:

On Your Best
Behavior

BEING A BRIDESMAID

Despite their title, bridesmaids don't scrub floors and iron blouses for the bride. Rather, their duties are to look pretty and support the dress industry.

All you have to do to be a wonderful bridesmaid is show up and follow directions. For a wedding with all the trimmings, you'll need to attend a fitting for your gown (which you'll be expected to pay for), bridal showers (bring an umbrella), prenuptial parties, photography sessions, wedding rehearsals, and postnuptial receptions and parties. (Don't forget to go to the wedding.) You'll be told, via spoken and written words, everything you need to know about where to be when and what to do where.

BEING AN USHER

If you're asked to be an usher, it's an honor, and you must accept unless there's a good reason why you can't. (A football game that's on TV at the same time as the wedding doesn't count.) Your main responsibilities as an usher are to look handsome, act charming, and escort guests to their seats as they arrive.

You'll probably need to rent formal wear for the occasion. The best man and/or head usher will tell you the various times and places where your presence is required. These include dinners and parties before and after the wedding, the fitting for your penguin suit, photography sessions, the wedding rehearsal, and the wedding itself.

You'll need to show up at the church an hour before the ceremony, doff your coat and hat, don your gloves, pick up your boutonniere, and station yourself to the left of the entry door inside the church. The head usher will give you instructions on how people are to be seated (usually on their butts).

The bride's family and friends sit on the *left* side of the church; the groom's family and friends sit on the *right*.

- If a lady arrives by herself, offer her your right arm. (She must give it back, though.)
- If a group of ladies arrives, offer your arm to the eldest. (You may guess their ages but never ask them.)
- If a lady arrives with a male escort, the escort should follow meekly in your wake.

- If a male guest arrives, there's no need to offer him your arm unless he needs assistance.
- If a family arrives, escort the mother. Hubby and kids will follow.

Engage the being whose hand is stuck through your arm in gracious conversation. Even though the line of guests waiting to be seated is stacking up at the entry, don't rush. Act as if you have all the time in the world.

If the bridegroom has no friends and his section is empty, the head usher will ask you to start seating the bride's guests on the other side of the aisle. This is so the church doesn't tilt to the left.

If there are enough ushers to seat guests in a timely fashion, you may escort young ladies in the 10- to 15-year-old age range. This will be a thrill they'll never forget.

When everyone is seated, there will be a processional of ushers and bridesmaids (and other minor figures like the bride and groom) up the aisle. After the ceremony, there will be a recessional. These traditions follow the same basic principle of digestion: What comes in must go out. The head usher will tell you your responsibilities for crowd management during and after the recessional.

"What are you supposed to say when you go through the receiving line at a wedding?"

"I'm so sorry."

Oops, wrong occasion.

You congratulate the groom. To do this, say "Congratulations." You never congratulate the bride. Instead, you extend your best wishes for her happiness, as in "I wish you all the happiness in the world."

To those who had a minor role in bringing the occasion about as the result of certain exertions 25 or so years ago, you give your name and say "How do you do," "It's a pleasure to meet you," or "The ceremony was beautiful, just beautiful" as if you're still entranced by the breathtakingly magical occasion. ◆

Visiting the Sick

Sooner or later, the body of someone you know will suffer some sort of mechanical breakdown. Let's hope it's not serious and they get better quickly. You'll want to visit them (or won't want to, but will feel you should). Good manners are indispensable to a healthy hospital visit. Here's what they are:

Ask first. Sometimes people don't want visitors. This may be because they're too ill, too embarrassed, or too intent on enjoying the first peace and quiet they have had in years. Respect their wishes. Call the patient or the patient's family to ask permission to come before putting in an appearance.

On Your Best Behavior

Leave the room at appropriate times. Honor the dignity of the person you're visiting. Leave the room when nurses come in, unless they're just dropping off a pill or the *Wall Street Journal.* Sponge baths, bedpans, and the rears of people in hospital gowns were never designed for public viewing.

Bring a gift. Or don't. In other words, it's optional—nice, but not required. How many balloons, flowers, or boxes of candy does somebody really need? If you do deliver flora, make sure it's ready to view and easy to carry. No cut flowers unless you also provide the vase.

Be sensitive in your gift selection. A box of cigars to a patient with lung cancer is a no-no. Books and magazines are usually appreciated, particularly if they're the trashy, gossipy type one would never buy but reaches for first in the doctor's waiting room. Homemade cards and artwork are always big hits.

Be imaginative. If the hospital will allow it, arrange for a band of school friends to play a concert for the wing. Bring in your VCR, hook it up to the hospital TV, then each day rent a different video for your friend to watch.

Ask the patient what she would like. An imported pepperoni pizza may be the thing she wants most in life at that moment.

Be upbeat. You're there to offer support, sympathy, and good cheer. Don't talk about how hard your life has been, or your aches and pains, or how serious or trivial the patient's problems are. Tell the patient he's looking well. This will cheer him up if he thinks he looks terrible. Follow the patient's lead as to whether it's okay to discuss his condition. Some patients want to talk about nothing but; others want to talk about everything but. Pay attention so you'll know whether the patient views his situation as humorous or tragic. Respond in kind.

Don't overstay. Patients may be medicated, tired, or in pain. They may have work to do or other visitors coming. Don't stay more than 20 minutes. If your imminent departure is greeted with a desperate plea of "Nooooo, don't go, please, please, please stay, I'm going crazy I'm so bored in here," you can allow your arm to be twisted. But not so much that it breaks.

CHAPTER QUIZ

How Rude!

1. *The reason you sign the registry at a funeral is:*
   a) to get in the running for the door prize
   b) to practice your signature
   c) to show your respect and extend your condolences.

2. *You've been invited to a friend's bar mitzvah. Unfortunately, it conflicts with your recital that same Saturday morning. The best way to handle this is to:*
   a) ask your friend to change his bar mitzvah to Sunday
   b) wear a yarmulke to your recital
   c) send profuse regrets and a lovely gift to your friend.

3. *You'll be serving as an escort at a debutante ball. Your duties include:*
   a) spiking the punch
   b) setting out whoopee cushions
   c) being a charming dancer and conversationalist.

4. *The commencement speaker at your graduation is a politician whose views you strenuously disagree with. The proper response is to:*
   a) moon him
   b) bombard him with tomatoes
   c) listen politely but withhold your applause.

5. *You're attending a wedding. You like the groom, but you don't approve of the bride. Should you:*
   a) step on the train of her dress
   b) push her into the cake, or
   c) be friendly and courteous despite your opinion?

6. *One of your schoolmates had a bike accident and is lying with his arms and legs in traction in the hospital. When you go to visit, the polite thing to do is:*
   a) tickle him in the ribs
   b) place a spider on his nose
   c) ask if there's anything he'd like you to bring on your next visit.

10
Talking Headiquette

The Art of Conversation

Rudeness comes in many forms. It can be physical (someone on a skate-board slams into you on the sidewalk); symbolic (wearing a National Rifle Association T-shirt to the funeral of a gunshot victim); behavioral (tail-gating on the freeway); or omissional (not offering your seat to a person on crutches). And it can be verbal. All some people have to do is open their mouths and out pops a rude, insensitive remark:

"Can't you see I'm busy?"
"I wish I'd never had you."
"Who cares what you think?"
"Maybe Billy would like to tell the class what he finds so amusing."

How Rude!

Insults. Put-downs. Slurs. Sarcasm. People who cut you off, interrupt, ask nosy questions, say mean things. People who accuse, criticize, whine, and compare. People who never say "Please," "Thank you," or "Excuse me."

Virtually every human, every day, interacts with other people—whether in person, over the phone, or by letter. The nature of these communications goes a long way towards determining the quality of our day and our relationships. If our interactions are pleasant and polite, we're likely to feel good about ourselves and the world we live in. If our interactions are disagreeable and rude, we're likely to feel angry and mistrustful.

What this means is that everyone needs to know the basics of courteous communication. Here they are.

Telephone Etiquette

Whether you're the caller or the callee, it pays to be well-mannered on the phone. So put down those potato chips, park your gum, deposit 25¢, and pay attention, please.

MAKING A CALL

Ask politely for your party. If the person you wish to speak to doesn't answer the phone, you'll need to ask for her. Say:

> *"May I please speak to Muffy?"*

Don't say:

> *"Is Muffy there?"*

I learned this the hard way when I telephoned a friend and his four-year-old son answered the phone. "Is your daddy there?" I asked. "Yes," the boy said. After five minutes went by with no sign of Daddy, insight dawned. "Could you please get him?" I said. "Okay," the boy replied.

It's not necessary to tell the person who answers the phone who you are. In fact, it's a breach of etiquette for her to ask (unless she's been instructed to do so by a higher power, such as a parent or boss). If you know the person, it's a friendly gesture to say:

> *"Hi, Mrs. Beeswax, this is Mortimer Snerdhopper. May I please speak to Jack?"*

Your friends' parents will adore you for this courteous acknowledgment of their existence.

Identify yourself when you reach your party. This has probably happened to you: Someone telephones, starts talking, and you don't have the faintest idea who it is. Unless you're calling a soul mate who would recognize your voice in a hurricane at 500 yards, say who you are. It could save you both from embarrassment.

Talking Headiquette

Don't call at inconvenient times. Since households eat and go to bed at all sorts of different hours, find out from your friends when it's okay and not okay to call. Many families don't appreciate interruptions during dinner or at two in the morning. It never hurts to ask "Is this a good time to talk?" or "How late is it okay to call?"

Ask permission to use the phone. If you're a guest in someone's home, say "May I please use your phone?" before making any calls. Keep your calls short. If you're dialing long-distance, use a calling card or call collect. Clever guests make innocent remarks such as "It's so hard to remember all these access numbers" or "Have you tried the new Save-a-Bundle phone card?" to reassure their host that he won't get stuck with the bill.

TAKING A CALL

Say "Hello." A cheerful "Hello" is all you need when answering a residential phone. It's not necessary to say "Pedigree residence, Bartholomew speaking" or "Murray's Mortuary, you stab 'em, we slab 'em."

Your parents may want you to answer the phone in a particular way. If so, do as they ask.

Don't screen other people's calls. If you answer the phone and it's for someone else, it's none of your business who's calling, no matter how curious you are. Don't inquire about the caller's identity unless your parents or siblings specifically ask you to. In that case, say to the caller "May I tell them who's calling?"

Don't yell. It bugs parents no end when their kids answer the phone and scream "MA! TELEPHONE! IT'S THAT LADY!!!" While yelling is one way to get a message from point A to point B, moving your body is another. If you need to alert someone to a phone call, relocate yourself more proximitously to the party whose attention you're trying to catch. Then say "Ma, telephone. It's that lady."

Never give out personal information. For safety's sake, don't reveal to strangers whether your parents are home or not. Don't give out your address or credit card numbers. And whatever you do, don't say that your dad is in the bathroom. People are never "in the bathroom" to callers. They are "unable to come to the phone."

Give the caller your full attention. It's rude to talk to someone while watching TV, carrying on other conversations, or typing away at your computer keyboard. If you can't focus on the phone call, tell the person that you're in the middle of something and will have to call back later.

How Rude!

TRUE STORIES FROM THE MANNERS FRONTIER
Sorry, Wrong Number

The other day my phone rang. I picked it up and said "Hello." A voice said "Who's this?" *How rude,* I thought. "To whooooom do you wish to speak?" I said. This firm yet polite response made the caller realize his phone faux pas. It also taught him a thing or two about grammar.

If you get a wrong number or a strange voice answers the phone, never hang up or say "Who's this?" Instead, ask for the person you're trying to call. If it turns out that you reached a wrong number, apologize. You may want to verify the number with the person who answered. That way, you'll know whether the number itself is wrong or you just misdialed.

And now, if you're ready for today's truth-is-stranger-than-fiction bulletin, my phone just rang, affording us an invaluable opportunity for seeing these principles at work as I reproduce the entire conversation for your enlightenment:

> *<Ring. Ring.>*
> Alex: *"Hello."*
> Caller: *"Meat Department."*
> Alex: *"Hello?"*
> Caller: *"What store is this?"*
> Alex: *"I think you have the wrong number."*
> Caller: *"I apologize."*
> Alex: *"That's all right."*
> *<Click.>*

All in all, it was a lovely exchange that reaffirmed my faith in etiquette.

CELLULAR PHONES

The day they offer surgical telephone implants, half of America will sign up. It's a mystery why so many people are so eager to expand the ways in which bill collectors can reach them.

328

The ubiquity of beepers affects us all. Even if you don't indulge, you're still exposed to secondhand sound. You can't go anywhere anymore without hearing so many chirping phones you'd think you were at a cricket convention. You're with somebody at a restaurant, and instead of talking to you he talks on the phone. Or there you are, trying to sleep on an airplane, and the guy next to you is yelling in your ear:

Talking Headiquette

"A MILLION TELEDEX, SHORT 'EM AT 29, AND TELL BEVERLY TO GET THE POOL CLEANED. OF COURSE I'M CALLING FROM THE PLANE. OF COURSE I'M SHOUTING. HOW ELSE WILL EVERYONE KNOW WHAT AN IMPORTANT PERSON I AM?"

All public spaces should be required to have phoning and nonphoning sections. Until that day comes, here are the two basic rules of cell phone etiquette:

1. Turn off all beepers and ringers when you're at an event or place where quiet and/or respect are required: places of worship, libraries, concerts, plays, lectures, funerals, restaurants, private dinners at someone's home, etc. Silent ringers—the kinds that vibrate to let you know you have a call—are allowed. But you're still not permitted to take the call. Instead, follow proper rules of etiquette for having to get up and leave during such an event.

2. Recognize that people talking to themselves—and that's how you appear to others, despite the piece of plastic growing out of your ear—are a distraction. Therefore, unless the call is of interest or relevance to everyone present (for example, a business negotiation or a loved one in common), take it to a private spot where your conversation won't intrude on those of others.

"Phoning or nonphoning?"

How Rude!

TELEMARKETERS

In case you're unfamiliar with the term, *telemarketers* are total strangers who have been trained to act as if they're your best friend in order to sell you something of dubious value. They're instructed to call at the precise moment when you've just sat down to dinner:

"Hello Alex how are you tonight that's great because this is your lucky night you have definitely won one of the following great prizes that's right you have won either a brand-new Rolls Royce or a Lear Jet or ten million dollars or a genuine artificial tin-plated fake diamond pendant and all you have to do to claim your prize is purchase a vacation package for six hundred dollars so if you'll just give me the credit card number to which you want to charge your vacation I'll tell you which of these four fabulous prizes you've won."

Telemarketing is rude. But two rudes don't make a right. Therefore, the proper response to these unwanted invasions of privacy is a polite "Thank you, but I'm not interested." Since telemarketers are trained to keep you on the line, they will respond, not by respecting your courteous attempt to end the conversation, but by escalating their pitch:

"Are you telling me you don't want to win ten million dollars?"

At this point you may issue a firm "Good-bye" and hang up.

CALL WAITING

When someone with call waiting puts me on hold, I count to 20. That's ample time for the person to tell the second caller "I'm sorry, but I'm on the other line. I'll call you back in a few minutes." What usually happens, though, is that caller #2 goes to the head of the queue, while caller #1 (yours truly) continues to wait. At the end of 20 seconds, I hang up the phone.

This isn't rude since I'm not hanging up on anyone. I'm hanging up on *no one,* which is the whole point. Before I learned this technique, I would often be put on hold two, three, even four times during the course of a 15-minute conversation. And, as often as not, I'd be calling long-distance.

People with whom you use this strategy will call you back and say "I guess we got cut off." To which you may reply "Yes, it appears we did." In time, the coincidence of how often you get cut off will encourage these people to ignore call waiting when talking to you.

Call waiting is r-u-d-e. One expects to be put on hold when telephoning a business. One understands that the person one needs to speak to may already have another customer on the line. No such justification exists for putting personal callers on hold. It won't kill anyone to hear a busy signal, or to leave a message on voicemail.

You're doubtless aware of all the justifications for call waiting:

- so someone can reach you in case of an emergency
- so you can use the phone while expecting an important call
- so parents, children, or business acquaintances can get through when the line is tied up.

Talking Headiquette

Too bad. Rudeness often comes with its own rationalization(s). Putting people on hold is a way of saying "My time is more important than your time." In a genuine emergency, an operator can cut into a call.

If your parents insist that your home phone be equipped with call waiting, you're stuck with it. But you can still behave politely in response to those obnoxious little clicks. Here's how:

1. Tell the person you're speaking to that you're expecting a call, and if another call comes in you're going to have to see who it is.
2. If a call comes in, excuse yourself to caller #1.
3. Tell caller #2 you'll have to get back to him or her.
4. Return as quickly as possible to caller #1. Apologize and continue your conversation.

Or:

4. Put caller #2 on hold. Return to caller #1. Say "I'm so sorry, but this is the call I need to take. May I call you back?" Then return to caller #2.

When rudeness is anticipated and apologized for in advance, it sometimes mutates into something we call *consideration*.

TIP: The only time it's *not* rude to use call waiting is with telemarketers. It's perfectly proper to put them on hold if another call comes in. Or even if it doesn't. You'd be amazed by how impatient telemarketers are. Most of the time, they're gone by the time you get back to them!

ANSWERING MACHINES

Prior to the invention of telephones, people would go "calling." They would show up at each other's houses unannounced. It was understood that these visits wouldn't always lead to an audience with the person one wished to see; he or she might be sleeping, entertaining, eating, practicing the lute, or painting his or her toenails. The housekeeper or butler would inform the visitor that "Madam is not at home." This had nothing to do with Madam's whereabouts; it was simply the convention for letting people know that Madam was not available. The visitor would leave a card, and Madam would know who had called on her.

How Rude!

Today, of course, we have the telephone answering machine. Think of it as an electronic butler. Surely you have the right to interruption-free moments in the privacy of your own home. Surely you have the right to know who's there before opening the telephonic door. Thus, there's nothing rude about using answering machines to screen calls, as long as you follow these guidelines:

Keep your recorded greeting short. Unless your caller has been living on Pluto for the past century, he knows what to do when encountering an answering machine. It's not necessary to issue such detailed instructions as:

"Hello, you've reached the answering machine of Bill, Mary, Grandpa, Fido, Curly, Larry, and Moe McCarthy at nine-six-six two-three-five-one. We're sorry, but we're unable to come to the phone or we're away from our desks or we're in the middle of dinner, but your call is really important to us so please leave a message including your name, time of call, phone number, shoe size, person you're calling, reason for calling, and the best time to reach you and we'll try to get back to you as soon as possible. Remember to wait for the beep, which will come in approximately three point two seconds if this machine is working or in eleven seconds after five beeps and a screeching eight-second noise if it isn't. Have a great day and thanks for calling!"

Neither is it necessary to record Mahler's Symphony No. 2 or Lincoln's Gettysburg Address as your greeting. People, especially those calling long-distance, don't appreciate having to twiddle their thumbs while some answering machine gets its musical, political, or comedic jollies off. A simple "You've reached 401-9999. Please leave a message after the tone" is more than adequate.

Keep your message short. Occasionally, you may need to leave a lengthy, complicated message. Whenever possible, however, try to keep your messages brief. And remember that people other than the intended recipient may hear them. It's also a good idea to leave your phone number unless you're positive the person knows it by heart. This is because people often call in for messages when they're away from their home or office. Speak slowly and clearly. Otherwise, someone may have to play back your message 37 times to decipher the number.

The Ten Commandments
of Telephone Etiquette

THOU SHALT NOT . . .

. . . make or accept calls during dinner.

. . . eat while talking on the phone.

. . . carry on conversations with people in the room while talking on the phone.

. . . make prank phone calls.

. . . screen other people's calls unless asked to do so.

. . . hog the phone.

. . . listen in on the conversations of others.

. . . interrupt someone who is on the phone unless it is an emergency.

. . . neglect to give the messages thou takest.

. . . beep, whistle, and pretend to be an incoming fax.

How Rude!

"My parents are always picking up the phone while I'm talking to someone. Isn't this rude?"

No, it's inevitable—especially if you're on the phone a lot. It's unrealistic for people to do a reconnaissance of all the extensions in the house before making a call. So this is bound to happen from time to time.

If you're the picker-upper, simply hang up right away. If you're the picker-upped-upon, say "I'm on the line." At this point, the picker-upper has the option of saying "Sorry" or "Excuse me" before hanging up. Except in an emergency, the picker-upper may not interrupt the conversation with questions ("How long are you going to be on?") or statements ("I have to use the phone. Would you please get off!"). These must be delivered in person, by note, or whispered so as not to embarrass those already on the line. ◆

"Suppose someone calls me long-distance and I can't talk right then. Is it okay to ask them to call me back, or do I have to call them back?"

This is one of those tricky situations where etiquette must work hand-in-hand with the size of your allowance. The most gracious thing to do is say:

"I'm so sorry, but I can't talk right now. May I call you back in an hour?"

However, the fact that someone has chosen to call you long-distance shouldn't require you to spend money you don't have or would rather not spend. Many people, for example, write letters precisely because they wish to avoid big phone bills. Therefore, it's permissible to say:

"I'd love to talk, but I can't right now. Do you think you could call me back in an hour?"

Sensitive callers will happily accede to your request. (After all, they were prepared to pay for the call in the first place.) If, however, your finances are in decent shape, it's considerate for friends who talk long-distance to keep the costs in rough balance—but without giving the slightest indication that anyone is keeping score. ◆

"People in my house always forget to give me my phone messages. Sometimes I'll be talking about a friend and my mother will say 'Oh, by the way, she called you yesterday.' This is so annoying. What should I do?"

Talking
Headiquette

You'll need a combination of high- and low-tech strategies to solve this problem. Start by getting an answering machine or voicemail system with separate "mailboxes" for each family member. Your friends can leave messages directly in your box, and other family members can listen to their messages without touching yours.

But what if a live human being answers your phone? Since most messages get lost because people don't write them down, this calls for a low-tech solution. Place by every phone a pad of paper and a pen or pencil that can't be removed. Only a total dolt would stand by the phone, listen to a request to "Please tell her that Fran called," and not write down *Phran cald.*

Visual checks of message pads, combined with the occasional "Did I get any calls?" should take care of the problem, provided the dolt factor in your household isn't too high. ◆

COMPUTERIZED VOICE MESSAGING SYSTEMS

It seems as if every time you make a call these days, you're presented with a menu of prerecorded choices ("Press 1 for . . . . Press 2 for . . . . Press 3 for . . . ." *ad infinitum*). As soon as you make your first selection, you're presented with 500 more options, and then 500 more, and then 500 more.

The good news is: Computerized voice messaging systems aren't inherently rude. In fact, most prerecorded messages are quite polite ("We're sorry, but all our representatives are assisting other customers"). They even say "Please" and "Thank you." They're a lot more considerate than humans who snap "Please hold" and then disappear from your life.

But that doesn't mean you have to *like* spending half a morning pressing numbers on your telephone. Especially when you also have to listen to horrible music that keeps you from concentrating on whatever you could be working on while holding if you weren't listening to horrible music. So I'm going to let you in on one of my most precious and, until now, closely held secrets: When I encounter one of those endless, multitiered computerized voice messaging systems, *I pretend I'm on a rotary phone.*

If you listen closely to the recorded message that lists your first set of options, you'll often hear "Stay on the line if you're calling from a rotary phone." All those other choices are just a way of keeping you busy while you

How Rude!

wait to talk to the same person everybody ends up talking to eventually. So don't press 1, 2, 3, or any other number. Just stay on the line. There's no way anyone on the other end can tell that you're actually calling from a touch-tone phone.

At least, that's what *I* think. And it seems to me that I reach an operator faster when I use this minor deception than when I wade through 18 layers of menu options. Even if I'm wrong, at least I feel better. We humans need to outsmart a machine every now and then.

One day, though, I expect to hear the prerecorded voice say "Sir, please don't pretend to be on a rotary phone," and the jig will be up.

"All service representatives are currently helping other customers.
Please stay on the line and your call will be answered shortly."

OBSCENE PHONE CALLS

It's never rude to hang up on an obscene phone caller. In fact, that's the best thing to do. Don't talk or stay on the line, no matter how bizarre the noises you hear. If the calls persist, contact the phone company. They have ways of tracking those people down.

Letter Etiquette

Letter writing is becoming an increasingly scarce art form. In days of yore, letters were the only means of getting a message from, say, Alexander the Great to Alexander Hamilton. And if one of them didn't like the message, he might kill the messenger. This was the origin of the expression "Hey, don't kill *me*, I'm just the messenger."

Today, of course, we have many additional methods of communication: email, telegrams, telephones, faxes. These instant forms of communication are certainly handy. If you want to contact your neighbor across the valley, you can simply pick up the phone or log on to the Internet. It's no longer necessary to write a letter and wait three days for an answer just to find out if you can borrow an ox.

Because so few people write personal letters anymore, the pleasure in receiving one is all the greater. Which makes *your* heart beat faster? A fat envelope full of Valu-Coupons addressed to "Occupant" or a scented purple envelope with your name and address handwritten in ink?

You should practice the art of letter writing for at least three reasons:

Talking Headiquette

1. You'll please and impress people.
2. You'll bring joy to the recipients of your elegantly written epistles.
3. You'll get letters back.

There are as many different types of letters as there are human sentiments. There are love letters and thank-you letters; letters to say hello; letters to say good-bye; and letters of condolence, apology, inquiry, pleading, or complaint. No matter what the purpose of your letter may be, certain rules of etiquette come into play. Let's start with . . .

LETTERS TO YOUR PARENTS

Writing home, whether from school, camp, or vacation, is a nonnegotiable tradition of the parent-child relationship. The parent who screams "I can't wait until you go back to school!" is the same parent who, two days after you've left, sits tearfully in your room stroking your trophies. Your letters will provide your parents with a treasure chest of memories they can carry into their old age. They'll also provide you with a literary time capsule you can open in years to come whenever you feel like cringing at what you used to be like.

Every proper letter from a child to a parent should contain these three elements:

1. something to make your parents proud
2. something to make your parents worry
3. something to make your parents send you money.

Mixed in with these essentials should be news, affection, chitchat, progress reports, social commentary, philosophical musings, and lots of questions that show you take an interest in your parents' lives. Everyday aspects of your existence—friends, teachers, outings, studies, grades, athletic competitions, intrigues, aspirations—are all grist for the quill. So are questions or issues raised in your parents' letters.

Think about what you would say in a phone call. Then just say it—on paper.

How Rude!

Dear Mom and Phil,

What's happenin', dudes? Since I know how much you miss me, I thought I'd say hello. Guess what? I've joined the X-treme Club here at school. It's a group of students who go out every weekend to ride mountain bikes off cliffs. But don't worry. Our faculty adviser (he's this neat guy we call "The Torso" because he lost all his arms and legs trying to dive through a turbo engine) insists that we wear bungee cords. (He holds them.) So it's really perfectly safe.

You know that French test? I aced it. I guess you guys were right when you said all I had to do to get good grades was put my derrière on the chair! I've volunteered to teach French to kids at the county juvenile detention center. But I have to learn some new words first, like "incarceration" and "probation."

I've been going to the canteen a lot for serious snacking purposes. It's a little embarrassing because my friends always pay for me 'cause they know my funds are a bit tight. One day I hope to be able to treat them if I can manage to save some money. Or maybe next time I'm home I could bring back some of Mom's triple-fudge brownies to share with them.

How did Phil's speech go? Did Mom get the commission she was telling us about? How's the painting coming along? Tell Katie she can wear my shirt, but only if she promises not to drool on it.

Well, I gotta go study, so I'd better sign off.

Love,

Bentley

disguised affection

news

something to make your parents worry

something to make your parents proud

something to make your parents send you money

hint, hint

shows interest in your parents and kid sister

Try not to be self-conscious about your letters. Of course, you'll want to make them as presentable as possible. After all, they do indicate whether your parents are getting their money's worth from sending you away to school. But what matters most is not *what* you say, but *that* you are saying it. Wise parents cherish any communication from their children. And they know that it's forbidden to make any comments regarding spelling or grammar.

Talking Headiquette

"My parents have said I can go to camp, but only if I promise to send them a letter twice a week. Isn't blackmail bad manners?"

This question calls for a lesson in life as well as etiquette. Many eons ago, a Stoic philosopher by the name of Epictetus said "Men are not disturbed by things, but by the view they take of them." Similarly, Shakespeare observed in *Hamlet* that "There's nothing either good or bad but thinking makes it so." In other words, our feelings are caused more by our *attitudes* towards life than by life itself.

You can see the truth of this if you imagine that you've been waiting over an hour for your mom to pick you up. If you *think* she's just been flaky and has forgotten about you, you'll feel angry. If you *think* she's had an accident, you'll feel worried or panicked. If you *think* the car broke down or she's caught in rush hour, you'll feel sympathetic. The attitude you take towards this or any event (being dumped, wanting friends, flunking a test) determines to a large extent how you'll feel about it. You can *choose* whether to have an attitude that is hopeful or despairing, understanding or intolerant, realistic or irrational—and your feelings will follow.

What does this have to do with your situation? You can call your parents' request for letters "blackmail"—or you can call it "fondness." Change your feelings by changing your thoughts. Instead of feeling angry, feel loved. Instead of thinking of letter writing as a chore, think of it as an opportunity to convey news, affection, and requests for food.

The duty to write letters home also gives you a great line to use when getting to know someone you like at camp. Simply approach your target, make a face, and groan. Then say "I HATE having to write letters. Do your parents make you do it, too?" If she says "I consider it a privilege to communicate with my beloved mater and pater," you're in a bit of trouble. But if she says "I know. I CAN'T STAND writing home either," you're in fat city. Say "I'm heading down to the lake to write one now. Do you want to write to your parents and we'll suffer together?" ◆

How Rude!

"I go to boarding school. I get letters from my parents almost every week, and I feel terrible because I don't write back very often. It isn't that I don't want to, it's just that I never know what to say. Is it bad manners if I call instead of write?"

Is that a *collect* call? Phoning home is never rude as long as:

- you don't do it at 3:00 A.M., and
- you disguise the request that's your main reason for calling.

Failing to respond to the warm, written overtures of your nearest and dearest—whether by letter or phone call—is most certainly a breach of etiquette. It's like ignoring someone who's speaking to you. Not to mention paying your school bills. ◆

MAIL MANNERS

Courteous correspondents honor the following rites of writing:

Respect the recipient's privacy. No matter how curious you are, never open or peek at mail that isn't yours. This includes postcards (but not underwear catalogs). It's also improper to take note of who's gotten mail from whom. Thus, you would never ask your sister "What did your ex-boyfriend want?" as this suggests you know something that etiquette prevents you from knowing.

Respect the sender's privacy. If you get a great letter from somebody, it's natural to want to share it with others. Before you do, think carefully about whether the writer would want you to. The letter may contain things that are very personal and were meant for your eyes only. If in doubt, err on the side of caution. Keep the letter to yourself until you can obtain permission to show it to others.

Be creative. Never begin a letter with "How are you? I'm fine." It's not that these aren't noble sentiments, it's just that they've been done before—about 896,443,221,909 times. Instead, try something like this:

> *Dear Grandma and Grandpa,*
>
> *I just blew my nose into one of the beautiful handkerchiefs you gave me for my birthday, which got me thinking of you. How have you been? Is Grandpa over the flu? My hay fever has been real bad this season, but thanks to you I don't have to use my sleeve anymore. That was some tornado you had. Has anyone come yet to get the cow out of the pool?*

STATIONERY

First things first: How can you remember that the station<u>e</u>ry you write on is spelled with an "e" and the station<u>a</u>ry that keeps you in your place is spelled with an "a"? The following mnemonic is offered as a public service:

Talking Headiquette

Ask yourself "What do you do with stationery?"

Write letters.

"And what vowels are in the word 'letter'?"

Eeeeees.

Since eeeeees are in "letter," you use an "e" for the stationery you write on. Class dismissed.

The kind of stationery you use depends on the kind of letter you're writing:

- For letters to your friends, you can use just about any stationery or writing implement you fancy—up to and including purple ink on lime-green paper with glow-in-the-dark pictures of bunny wabbits all over.

- For letters to businesses, schools, and representatives of the Real World, skip the wabbits and wainbows. These letters should be legibly handwritten, typed, or laser-printed on good quality 8½" by 11" paper. No garish colors; just your basic white, cream, or very light gray.

- Personal letters to adults, relatives, and/or peers who aren't close friends should be handwritten in black ink on note-size paper or blank cards. (If your handwriting is illegible, you may type a personal letter. The joy of getting your epistle will be diminished if the recipient can't read it.) Make sure that any artwork on the front of the card doesn't offend the recipient or clash with the purpose of your communication. For example, don't send a get-well card with a picture of food to someone in the hospital who's just had his stomach removed.

If you're prone to mistakes and changing your mind about what you want to say, you'll need to write a first draft. Once you've got your content, spelling, and grammar down, create your final draft.

Try not to get ink on your fingers, or you'll smudge the paper and people will start to call you Inky. Fold your letter only as much as necessary to get it into the envelope, which usually means into halves or thirds. A letter should not be folded until it's the size of a microchip.

SALUTATIONS

Virtually all letters begin with "Dear." What's next? That depends on the person you're writing to. Specifically:

How Rude!

- If you're writing to a man whose name you don't know, use "Dear Sir."
- If you're writing to a woman, write "Dear Madam."
- If you're writing to someone of unknown gender, write "Dear Madam or Sir" and hope they make up their mind.
- If you wish to give old-world charm to your letters to loved ones and close friends, you may use "Dearest," as in "Dearest Mother."

For business correspondence, end your salutation with a colon (:). For personal correspondence, use a comma (,).

Love letters (more about those shortly) allow greater creativity, since it's assumed that no one but the beloved will be privy to your sappiness. Therefore, greetings like "My darling of delight," "Sweetie-Weetie," and "Honey bunny bear" fly below the radar of etiquette and are beneath comment.

"I just got an invitation addressed to 'Master' with my name after it. What's that supposed to mean?"

"Master" is used when addressing an envelope to a boy eight years old or younger. (Some people say it's okay to use it with boys as old as 10 or 12.) In the British educational system, a "Master" is a male teacher—think of the words "Headmaster" or "Housemaster."

Here's a rundown on how envelopes should be addressed:

For Boys and Men	For Girls and Women
Up to age 8: Master Jay Jehosophat	*Up to high school:* Miss Kay Kalamazoo
Ages 8–18: Jay Jehosophat	*High school and beyond:* Ms. Kay Kalamazoo
Ages 18 and up: Mr. Jay Jehosophat	*Those who are married:* Mrs. Kay Jehosophat

Exceptions: Some married women prefer to be addressed by their husband's first and last names—for example, "Mrs. Jay Jehosophat." If that's what they want, honor their wishes. Some women choose to keep their birth name (a.k.a. maiden name) rather than take their husband's name when they marry. Often this means that they retain the "Ms." rather than opting for "Mrs." ◆

CLOSINGS

"Sincerely" is the all-purpose closing. Along with its cousins—"Sincerely yours," "Yours sincerely," "Yours truly," and "Very truly yours"—it's appropriate for both business and personal use. If the personal correspondence involves close ties and/or loving feelings, you may elect to close with "Love," "Affectionately," or "Fondly." If you're in junior high school, you may close with hearts, XXXOOO, and "Luv," but try not to.

Talking Headiquette

For business correspondents with whom you have a prior relationship of trust, respect, friendship, and/or positive exchange, you may wish to employ a closing from the "regards" family:

> *Kind regards,*
> *Warm regards,*
> *Best regards,*
> *Beauregards.*

These breezy sign-offs split the difference between "Sincerely" and "Love." They're the literary equivalent of air kisses, halfway between a handshake and a smooch. You can use them with your agent, attorney, and/or stockbroker.

If you're going through a stage of Victorian formality, you may close letters to your parents with "Your devoted daughter" or "Your loving and affectionate son." Don't use "Your most humble and obedient servant" unless you want more chores to do.

LOVE LETTERS

Let's assume for a moment that there's a girl you really like and you want to write her a love letter. What's the best way to go about this?

V-e-r-y c-a-r-e-f-u-l-l-y. In fact, you might want to think twice about whether to write it at all.

It's admirable that you wish to convey your affection. The problem is, the minute you do so, you'll also convey it to half of the students at your school. This is because the young lady, if she reciprocates your sentiments, will gleefully show your letter to all her friends. (If she can't stand your guts, she'll do the same—but with even greater relish, and what a pickle you'll be in then.) If this show-and-tell occurs at school, chances are someone will grab the letter from her hand and read it aloud to the assembled masses in the cafeteria. Emmm-barrassing!

Even though your love is undying and eternal, in adolescence "eternity" usually translates as "two weeks." Thus, it's possible that in less time than it takes to dissect a frog, your feelings may shift to a new object of affection. If this happens, will you want a chain of love letters in the public domain by which historians can trace your romantic evolution? Probably not.

How Rude!

Therefore, it's best that declarations of love be issued by mouth rather than by hand. *Tell* her how you feel. You can do this directly or indirectly. Directly means saying "I really like you." Indirectly means giving compliments, asking questions, spending time together, treating your beloved with kindness and respect—*behavior* that says "I really like you." This is far more romantic than sending a letter. And in the likely event that you'll break up, because nothing's in writing, you can deny having said all the mushy things you said.

Now that you know all of the above, you're still determined to write your love letter. Sigh. Here's how:

1. Choose romantic stationery.

Good	Bad
high-quality note paper and envelope	lined yellow legal paper folded and taped shut

If you choose a card with a photograph:

Good	Bad
snuggling puppies	chemical storage tanks

2. Use ink.

It's the proper thing to do, plus it prevents anyone from tampering with your words.

3. Convey the magnitude of your longing, but don't come across as a wussy, lovesick, protoplasmic mess.

You can see the difference:

Example #1: Lovesick

Sitting here in Chem Lab, I don't know how I can live without you. I can't concentrate. I feel hollow. My existence is as empty as a politician's promise. Without you, I am nothing.

The reaction to this is likely to be "Get a life, would ya."

Example #2: Lovely

Sitting here in Chem Lab, I watch the sulfur burn. And I think of how bright the flame of my love burns for you. It's hard to imagine I won't see you for 37 minutes and 14 seconds. But, with the vision of your soft smile and silky hair to sustain me, I shall endure.

The reaction to this is likely to be "Oh, my gentle little hunkie-poo." This is because your sensitive, empathetic, romantic soul is revealed in the context of your strength, courage and stoicism. It's a highly attractive combination, *n'est-ce pas?*

Speaking of French, you can never go wrong with a touch of the Gallic (not to be confused with a touch of the garlic). This is because the French, having invented the French kiss, are properly associated with love. (Why do you think French is considered a Romance language?) Therefore, feel free to sneak a little French (*chérie, l'amour, je t'aime, moutarde*) into your love letters.

Talking Headiquette

The Well-Mannered Conversation

Every relationship—whether between friends, lovers, or colleagues—begins with the people not knowing each other. They may meet by chance. They may be introduced by mutual friends or a task in common. But the way they get to know each other is invariably the same: through *conversation*. Following are some tips and guidelines that will make you a talented talker.

HOW TO START A CONVERSATION

Lots of people feel awkward or shy when starting a conversation. That's natural. But anyone can do it if they know the secret of successful small talk, which is . . . sorry, it's a secret.

Oh, all right, here it is: The secret is to *ask questions*. That's all you have to do to get a conversation going. The best questions are those with open-ended answers. Questions with yes-or-no answers are okay, but they make your work harder.

Here's what happens when someone trying to start a conversation offers personal opinions and yes-or-no questions:

"Great music."
"Yeah."
"Do you like the Empty Bladders?"
"Yeah."
"Cool party."
"Yeah."
"You a friend of Mike's?"
"Yeah."
"Cool."

How Rude!

Now watch how much better the conversation flows if the questions are more open-ended:

"What do you think of the music?"

"Rave totale. Compliments to the chef de musique. This DJ's waaaaay."

"Waaaaay?"

"Yeah, you know. Waaaaay. He was the spinologist at another festivity I went to last weekend. Total Empty Bladders freak, this guy."

"Where was the other party?"

"Lacey Kingman's abode of habitation. A sugary coming-of-automotivity party."

"Huh?"

"Sweet sixteen."

"What was it like?"

"Very waaaaay. Verrr-ry. A lot of the same revelers but the muncholinos tonight are mucho more magnifico."

"Knowing the way Mike eats, that doesn't surprise me. How do you know Mike?"

"Actually, it's his sibling of the female persuasion I am privileged to know. We were in the Convent of Our Lady of Parallel Parking together."

"Huh?"

"Driver's Ed, my man."

"I've got to take that next semester. What do they make you do?"

At this point, you're home free. You'll get a blow-by-blow description of Driver's Ed. Like it or not.

When meeting people your own age, there are a million things you can ask questions about: schools, teachers, classes, interests, hobbies, current events, sports, movies, TV shows, travel, music, people you know in common. Be alert to visual clues. You can ask someone wearing a Lakers cap about basketball, or someone with lift tickets dangling from his or her parka about skiing.

Talking with adults is no different. If you're visiting the home of a friend, you'll see things in the house that you can ask her parents about: curious objects, posters, books, hobbies, souvenirs from places they've visited. You can ask about the work they do or even their experiences when they were younger. As long as your questions are sincere and respectful—and you listen to the answers—people will be flattered by and appreciate your interest. After all, it takes a lot of pressure off of them. If they're good conversationalists, they'll ask *you* lots of questions. As the Q's and A's fly back and forth, you'll suddenly discover that you're having an easy, pleasant talk.

Now that you know the basics, here are a few conversation fine points:

Talking Headiquette

Remember that good conversation is an art, not a science. Keeping a conversation going is a bit like driving a car. You don't just aim and floor it. You have to make constant adjustments in response to the route and driving conditions. The same holds true when you're chattering away. Be alert to body language and verbal cues you receive. You may discover that certain topics go nowhere; if that happens, slam on the brakes and try a new tack. Or, if someone really starts to bubble with enthusiasm, you've got a green light to put your pedal to the metal as far as that subject is concerned.

Stay away from gossip and rumors. When you dish dirt, you get covered in it yourself. This happens because people think *Gee, if she says such mean things behind so-and-so's back, how do I know she won't do the same thing to me?* Backbiting can also get you into some very awkward positions.

Watch how easily this can happen:

You're at a party at Tim Devlin's house. You don't know him well, but since you're on the swim team together, you got an invite.

You notice Jill Banks standing on the opposite side of the room. She's generally regarded as the class airhead.

You start a conversation with Tim:

"Great party."
"Thanks."
"Hey, isn't that Jill Banks? Man, I can't believe she actually found your place. I mean, the directions you gave, you had to know left from right. I guess in this age of diversity, every party has to have a moron. I'm kind of surprised you invited her."
"I didn't."
"You mean she just crashed?"
"No. She lives here. She's my stepsister."

Oops.

Don't be nosy. When striking up a conversation, you want to show interest without sticking your nose where it doesn't belong. This can be a tricky tightrope to walk. You'd like to ask a question, but you're not sure if it's too personal. How do you know? Ask yourself how *you* would feel if someone asked the question of *you*—and *everyone in the room could hear your answer.* If you'd feel comfortable, chances are the question's okay.

In our culture, certain topics are considered off-limits by many people. You wouldn't ask someone you've just met about their religion or sexuality, or

How Rude!

how much money they make, or if they've cheated on their spouse, or why they don't have children.

By the same token, it's a good idea to avoid questions that have an implied judgment or criticism. Examples:

"How can you drive such a gas guzzler?"

"Don't you think it's wrong to go out with Jeffrey after telling Brad you'd go steady with him?"

Although these are reasonable questions for your little gray cells to ponder, it's bad form to ask them. Of course, the rules change if you're talking to a friend. Close relationships allow for more confiding and challenging—but you still should be kind and respectful.

Don't get drunk. Nothing ruins a good conversation faster or more permanently. Getting drunk is one of the rudest things you can do to your host or social companions. One must remain in control of oneself in order to follow the Four Simple Rules of Polite Conversation:

1. Don't make speeches.
2. Don't say hurtful things.
3. Don't reveal secrets.
4. Tread very carefully when discussing controversial social, political, moral, and religious issues about which people have strongly held (and often irrational) views.

 TRUE STORIES FROM THE MANNERS FRONTIER

Tanks for Nothing

Recently, I went out to dinner with a small group of friends. The husband of one of them got tanked up and proceeded to rant and rave about anything and everything.

He violated just about every rule of polite social exchange: He monopolized the conversation so nobody else could speak; he shouted and swore so other diners stared at our table; he mortified and verbally abused his wife; he held forth on politics, the economy, money, welfare, and how everybody who wasn't pulling their weight should be blown off the planet.

It was ugly, embarrassing, and hurtful. I completely lost my appetite, and the sheep brains I was so looking forward to eating sat untouched.

"My parents don't speak English. So at home we use our native language. I've never invited any friends over because I figure it would be rude if they don't know what anybody's saying. Is it impolite to speak a foreign language in front of guests?"

Talking
Headiquette

If that's all you did, it would be rude. Imagine the discomfort a guest would experience if everybody at the dinner table chattered away in a language he didn't understand. He'd feel excluded and might even think you were talking about him.

However, if you're willing to serve as a translator, this can be a wonderful experience for everybody. You can be an intermediary between your friend and your folks. You and your family can even teach your friend expressions and traditions from your native culture, and vice versa. Since a lot of communication occurs through facial expressions, gestures, and ritual, you can all have a fine old time even if you don't speak the same language. Just keep your hearts warm and your sense of humor engaged. ◆

THE ART OF POLITE LISTENING

Has this ever happened to you? You're talking away, only to realize that your so-called "listener" isn't paying any attention to what you're saying. You might as well be addressing a lamppost. This is very disconcerting, since very few people like to talk to lampposts.

Courteous conversationalists use many techniques to show that they're paying attention. Like what? Well, think of everything you *could* do if someone (like a parent or a teacher) gave you a Big Lecture: You could slouch, sigh extravagantly, roll your eyeballs, stare at the ceiling, doodle, tap your foot, drum your fingers, shift your position, and/or consult your watch. This is known as Communicating Total Indifference. Polite listeners do the opposite. They:

- sit or stand erect
- look the speaker in the eye
- avoid tapping, squirming, or fidgeting
- grunt, nod, emit, and emote (all signs that show they're paying attention). Plus they cheer people on with such expressions as:

"Hmmm."

"No kidding?"

"Wow!"

"And then?"

"Cool!"

"No way!"

"Surely you jest."

How Rude!

The above attitudes, gestures, and responses show that you're *hearing* what the person is saying. But that's only part of courteous listening. You also want to show that you *understand*, that you *care*. You do this by pretending you're a mirror and reflecting the speaker's words back to him or her.

When engaged in "lite" talk, it's generally most appropriate to reflect the *informational* content of the speaker's words:

Lou: *"Nice weather we're having."*

You: *"It's great to have some sun after all that rain."*

Lou: *"I'm not used to so much rain. I've been living in the Sahara."*

You: *"Wow! You lived in the desert? What was that like?"*

You show Lou that you're listening by making appropriate comments and asking relevant questions. If you respond to "Nice weather we're having" with "I prefer jelly donuts myself," Lou will rightly assume that you haven't been listening (and also that you have jelly for brains).

When engaged in "heavy" talk, it's best to reflect the *emotional* content of the speaker's words:

Sue: *"I HATE rain. The worst things in my life all happened on rainy days."*

You: *"Rain reminds you of a lot of bad memories?"*

Sue: *"My dog died. My gerbil died. My turtle died. My baby-sitter died. My uncle died."*

You: *"Rain must bring back a lot of sadness."*

You pick up on the fact that Sue isn't talking about the weather per se, but about some powerful associations she has with rain. You prove that you're listening by reflecting the feelings behind her words. Your show of empathy will keep Sue talking. She'll sense your support and understanding and feel safe about revealing herself.

You can see how inappropriate it would be to reply to Sue's statement as if it really were just about the weather:

Sue: *"I HATE rain. The worst things in my life all happened on rainy days."*

You: *"I don't mind the rain. But then again, my great-grandfather was a duck—quack, quack."*

When you clue in to what a speaker is saying and respond accordingly, you're using "active listening." This simple strategy says *I hear you, I understand how you feel, and I acknowledge your right to have those feelings.*

Talking Headiquette

There will be times when you don't agree with the speaker's feelings, or you don't think those feelings are justified. Especially when you're the target of anger or hostility. Instead of arguing or lashing out, listen even more carefully. Try to uncover the feelings *behind* those the speaker is expressing. This is a great way to defuse potentially explosive situations and avoid conflict. Watch:

Your father says: *"Where have you been?!? It's past midnight, and if you think you can just waltz in here—"*

You say: *"You must have been so worried about me."*

What was your father feeling? Anger, yes. But anger is usually a mask for some other feeling. In this case, your dad was worried out of his gourd. Just imagine all the horrible scenarios that flashed through his mind as he waited for you to come home.

Or consider this example:

Your friend says: *"How could you?!? I told you that was a secret. Now everybody knows!"*

You say: *"I didn't mean to tell. It just slipped out. I know it was a terrible thing to do, and I can understand it if you never trust me again."*

Here, too, there's a lot of anger. But underneath are feelings of hurt and betrayal. This is what you'll need to acknowledge in order to mend the broken faith between you and your friend.

In any conversation that seems to be heading for disaster, reflect the emotions *first* in order to calm things down. Then, if you think the problem stems from a misunderstanding, check the facts and assumptions behind the speaker's words. You can do this with statements like:

"It sounds as if you think that I intentionally disobeyed you."

"Are you saying that you think I left the lawnmower outside?"

"I was the last person in your room, so you believe I took your new CD?"

"You were under the impression that you had already won the game?"

"Is it bad manners to listen in on other people's conversations as long as they don't know you're doing it?"

351

How Rude!

If the other people believe that they're speaking without being overheard, yes. This is a gross invasion of privacy called *snooping*. To understand the felonious nature of snooping, imagine how you'd feel if you learned that your parents listened in on your telephone calls or read your journal.

Sometimes it's impossible not to overhear a conversation. Like when the couple at the next table is having an argument, or two kids on a bus are swapping the latest gossip. Listening in on such occasions isn't snooping, it's *eavesdropping*. This is how one learns about life and gathers material for a novel. Since eavesdroppees have no expectation of privacy in a public space, eavesdropping isn't bad manners so long as you hide the fact that you're doing it. This means keeping your nose in your book. Concentrating on buttering your dinner roll. Adopting a meditative demeanor that suggests you're visiting a distant plane of consciousness.

Truly conscientious eavesdroppers make sure that their presence is known. For example, if your parents are having a private conversation in the kitchen, they may not realize you're in the family room. Clear your throat. Bump a chair. You may lose your chance to eavesdrop, but you're doing the right thing. If you don't make any noise, you're snooping. ◆

CORRECTIONS AND CONTRADICTIONS

What do you do when you're talking with someone and she says something you *know* is wrong? You can think *You blithering idiot! How can you be so stupid?* But you can't *say* it. Similarly, you can think *You clumsy oaf!* to the apologetic person who just stepped on your toe, but what you should *say* is "That's all right. No harm done."

Etiquette doesn't ask you to censor your thoughts. It asks you to resist the temptation to voice them. It's rude to correct or contradict someone in public—especially an adult. (And adults need to realize that it's equally rude to treat children this way.) Most of the errors people make in conversation are of little consequence. They are slips of the tongue, insignificant errors of fact, or minor mistakes of pronunciation or grammar. Someone may say "Alan Burr" instead of "Aaron," or get a date wrong, or confuse one event with another. It's not worth correcting the person because the matter is trivial. And if the person is profoundly wrong about something important, chances are her mind is closed to enlightenment. So it's usually best to let it go unless doing so will cause harm.

If you feel that you must issue a correction, here are some guidelines:

Do it in private. Spare the person from embarrassment by ensuring that no audience is present.

Do it with modesty. Approach the point in question as if *you* might be the one in error. You might say:

"Isn't that interesting. I was taught that George Washington was the father of our country. But maybe it's Dolly Madison. Now you've got me curious. I'll have to look it up."

Talking Headiquette

Often, if you're gentle and respectful in your correction, the person in error will say:

"You know, now that you mention it, I think you may be right."

Siblings and close friends who disagree may simply say—

"Is."

"Is not."

"Is."

"Is not."

—for however long it takes until one of them gets tired and gives up.

"My aunt tells the same stories over and over again. They're boring the first time and even more boring the fifth time. How can you shut people up when they do this?"

Your aunt doesn't mean to bore you. People often repeat themselves. For the elderly (anyone over 29), this is because they're down to their last three brain cells and have trouble remembering. For the young, it's because they have so many friends they can't remember to whom they've told what.

If someone starts to tell a story you've heard before, you have a window of about two seconds in which you can say:

"Oh, I remember that story. It was absolutely the most hilarious/sad/ touching thing I've ever heard."

The degree to which the story delighted or moved you must be stated extravagantly. This is so your enthusiasm will overwhelm any embarrassment the speaker might feel upon being unmasked as a twice-told taleteller. If others are present, you may follow your remark with:

"Wait 'til you hear this story. It's so great, you're going to love it. I'm just going to excuse myself for a moment while Auntie Alice tells it."

If you didn't manage to nip the story in the bud, you've lost your chance. You must now listen politely, giving no indication that you're bored to tears. Nod (but don't nod off), smile pleasantly, chuckle when others do, and use the time to meditate or put together a shopping list in your head. ◆

How Rude!

"I have a friend who stutters. If I know what he means to say, is it okay to finish a sentence for him?"

No. In polite conversation, you wait for the other person to finish before speaking. In this case, you simply have to wait a little longer. Do nothing to indicate your awareness of his stuttering. Maintain eye contact. Refrain from twiddling your thumbs. ◆

THE ART OF POLITE EXPRESSION

If you wish to be a courteous and effective conversationalist, here are some rules you'll need to follow:

Use the magic words. The magic words are "Please," "Thank you," and "Excuse me." They have the power to make people do your bidding; to help you escape from tight spots; to cause problems to disappear. In case you're a little rusty, here's how to work a little magic every time you open your mouth:

1. Include the word "Please" in any requests.
2. Always say "Thank you" when someone gives you something or does something for you.
3. Learn and master the many forms of "Excuse me."

"Excuse me!"	said with a bright lilt in your voice	means	*"Coming through!"*
"Oh, excuse me!"	accompanied by a sharp intake of breath, a look of mortification, and a hand placed over your heart	means	*"How clumsy/careless of me!"*
"Ex-cuuuse me?"	said sternly with raised eyebrows and ascending pitch	means	*"You'd better undo what you just did— fast!"*
"Excuse me."	said with demure matter-of-factness	means	*"Sorry about that there belch."*
"Excuse me . . ."	as the preface to a remark	means	*"Please forgive me for interrupting, but . . ."*

Choose your moment. You wouldn't have a heart-to-heart with someone during the bottom of the ninth with the score tied 3–3. And you wouldn't ask your parents for a new CD player an hour after denting your dad's car. Why not? Because timing is everything. If you want to be heard, if you want your requests to be granted, you have to speak up when your targets are in receptive listening mode. This means when they are relaxed, cheerful, and not in the middle of something.

Talking
Headiquette

Don't interrupt. If two people are having a conversation and you need to butt in—don't. Instead, wait for a pause or for one of them to turn to you. Then say "Excuse me" and whatever else you want or need to say.

"What if you really need to interrupt a conversation, and you stand a few feet away waiting for a moment to interrupt, but they act as if you're not even there?"

Your body language is saying *I'm waiting for a chance to interrupt you.* Their body language (and perhaps also their facial expressions) are saying *We're not open to being interrupted.* Maybe they're being rude, but don't automatically assume that. Maybe they're involved in a heavy conversation and really can't be interrupted. Or maybe they're so engrossed in their conversation that they simply haven't noticed you.

Since you haven't been acknowledged, you could wander off and try again later. Or you could say:

> *"Forgive me for interrupting, but my carpool is leaving. Did you want that address now or should I call you with it later?"*

Then start to leave. If they need the information you're offering, they'll pause their conversation to get it. ◆

"What if you're talking and someone interrupts? There's a girl at school who does this all the time."

You have three choices:

1. Just keep talking. This is the equivalent of ignoring the rudeness. It can be a lot of fun, because you won't believe how hard it is to keep it up if the other person continues to talk. Sometimes, she'll get the point and yield to

How Rude!

your right-of-way. Usually, she won't. So you'll end up giving her the floor, but spectators will be very aware of the rudeness committed and your graciousness in allowing the interruption.

2. Say "Just let me get out this one last thought" or "Please let me finish what I was saying."

3. Speak to the interrupter in private. Use the cardinal principles of correction: the assumption that the other person must not realize what she's doing, and the ownership of the issue as one of your sensitivity:

"Jill, I'm sure you're not aware of this, but sometimes you interrupt me when I'm talking. I'd really appreciate it if you could try not to. I'm such a scatterbrain at times that I need all the help I can get remembering what I want to say." ◆

Conversational Conventions That Don't Cross Cultures

Every society develops conventions for addressing people, transacting business, negotiating, interacting socially, and so on. Here are some typical American practices that may cause confusion or offense if practiced with people of different cultural backgrounds:

- In America, it's increasingly common to call one's elders and total strangers by their first names. In most other countries, this is considered disrespectful. In fact, in some cultures, people avoid using names entirely. They refer to each other as "Sister" or "Brother" or "Lili's mother."

- In the United States, a person's family name (surname) goes last (e.g., John Wilkes Booth). In many Asian countries, such as Vietnam, Korea, and Cambodia, the last name goes first (e.g., Booth John Wilkes). Thus, Park Young Sam would be Mr. Park, not Mr. Sam.

- Americans usually address married women as "Mrs." plus their husband's last name. Wives in Korea, China, Vietnam, and Cambodia usually retain their maiden names. Mr. Park's wife would not be addressed as Mrs. Park, but by her maiden name, Mrs. Kim.

- American slang such as "tied up at the moment," "having a cow," and "chill" are so common that we don't realize that others may have no idea what they mean. Similarly, Americans who travel to England—where they speak English!—would be confused if they were asked for a "fag" (a

continued

cigarette), shown to the "loo" (bathroom), or cautioned to "mind their head" (don't bump it). In England, "willy" is slang for penis. (Imagine the guffaws when the American movie *Free Willy* was released over there.)

- Americans are usually delighted to receive praise. Many Asians feel embarrassed and uncomfortable when someone praises them. In their culture, praise *now* suggests that their performance *before* might have lacked something. Also, being singled out for attention could alter relationships with work colleagues, possibly triggering jealousy or competition.

Talking Headiquette

BAGGING THE BRAGGING

You're a person of many accomplishments, and you're right to think that everyone should know all about them. You may think that the best way to spread the news is to do it yourself.

Don't. Tooting one's own horn is never good form. It's much better to let your actions speak for themselves. There's no need to tell the world about your great save in the game or the prize you won at assembly. Other people were there. They saw it. And if it's something that didn't occur in the public eye, there's another way for word to get out—friends.

Yes, that's what friends are for. Any friend worth his salt will say "Did you hear? Bilbo bagged the bantamweight belt." Any friend *really* worth his salt will say it ten times fast.

When people offer their hearty congratulations, respond with disbelief and demurral:

"I was so lucky."
"The others deserved it just as much as I did."

You cover yourself with modesty because people who say "Aw, shucks" are much more attractive than those who say "Ain't I grand!"

How do your friends find out about your successes? You tell them—in a way that reveals your surprise and appreciation:

"Guess what? You know that essay contest I entered? I actually won! I can't believe it!"

It's okay to do this because there's a difference between bragging (a form of conceit) and sharing one's joy (a form of giving). You owe the latter to your close friends and family.

How Rude!

"There's this kid in my school who always brags. I like her, but it really gets boring, and I hate to be around my other friends when she's doing it. I don't want to give up being her friend, but sometimes I think I will."

It helps to understand that when people brag, it's often because they have a low opinion of themselves. They try to boost their self-esteem by telling other people how great they are. Of course, this has the effect of driving people away. Rejection then causes the braggart to feel even worse, leading to more bragging and more rejection. You can see the kind of nasty cycle this can turn into.

Etiquette doesn't require you to address the psychosocial problems of your classmates. You can ignore your friend's bragging and maintain the status quo, you can gently bow out of the relationship, or you can tackle the issue head-on by saying:

"I think you're a wonderful person—otherwise I wouldn't be friends with you. But I get the feeling it turns people off when you talk about yourself so much. I know it's kind of a habit because sometimes I do it myself. But I thought, if you wanted to do something about it, we can have a signal so that if I hear you bragging, I can let you know without anyone else knowing."

Your friend may feel a little hurt at first. But if you bring the subject up gently and follow through with humor and sensitivity, she'll know she's lucky to have you by her side. ◆

HOW TO END A CONVERSATION

Now that you know how to get into a conversation and handle some of the fine points and rough spots, you need to know how to get out of one gracefully. This comes in handy when you have to talk to someone else, attend to a personal matter, or escape the clutches of the world's greatest bore.

There are many strategies you could employ. For instance:

- You could point to a distant spot in the room and say "Isn't that Bertie Wooster?" When the person goes to look, you disappear. By the time he or she turns back, you're long gone.

- If a very large person walks between you, you could slip away by using him or her for cover, in much the same way that cowboys used to ride out of town hidden behind the flanks of a horse.

The problem with these two techniques is that they're rude, rude, rude. In contrast, here are two socially acceptable methods for getting out of a conversation:

Talking
Headiquette

1. The Foist-'em-Off Ploy. In one-on-one conversations at a social event, it's impolite to simply walk away from someone, even if there's a pause in the conversation. But it's permissible to hand her off to someone else. You do this by saying something like this:

> *"Oh, you just have to meet Clarence Darrow. Let me introduce you."*

Approach Clarence, make a proper introduction, give good clues to get the new conversation started ("Clarence has just taken on a new case you may have read about"), and then excuse yourself and leave. Clarence may never speak to you again, but at least you're a free agent.

2. The "Please Excuse Me" Ploy. It's okay to abandon someone as long as you offer an excuse. The ideal excuse leaves the impression that, if it weren't for fate or duty, you'd love to spend the rest of your life talking to the person. Here are some tried-and-true excuse me's:

> *"Please excuse me, but . . .*
> *. . . I must catch Madonna before she starts singing."*
> *. . . my ride is about to leave."*
> *. . . I have to make a call."* (This is preferable to "I have to go pee.")

Choose your excuse carefully, because you must follow it through (or at least give the appearance of doing so). It would hurt someone's feelings if you said you had to leave and then hung around the party for another two hours.

If you're on the receiving end of an excuse, accept it at face value. For example, if someone says "Excuse me, I'm going to step outside for some fresh air," don't say "Good idea. I think I'll join you." If he wanted your company, he'd say "Would you like to come outside for some fresh air?"

You can duck out of group conversations a lot more easily. Since the discussion will continue without you (although at nowhere near its former sparkle), you can just say "Excuse me" and depart. This form of "Excuse me" means "I wouldn't dream of interrupting, so you people should all just carry on without me."

How Rude!

"How do you get out of a conversation with someone who doesn't give you a moment's breather to say anything?"

How do you extricate yourself from a conversation with a compulsive talker who, for those of you who may be unfamiliar with the term, is an individual who neither comes up for air when speaking nor speaks, as most of us do, in sentences punctuated with pauses the purpose of which is to invite the listener to reply, but rather utilizes epic nonstop linguistic constructions that go on forever, one idea following the next, a sort of ceaseless drone, a mind-numbing succession of verbal paragraphs that quickly lose meaning and induce feelings of sleepiness, fantasies of escape, and visions of violence on the part of the hapless listener trying to be polite but feeling more and more trapped by the minute?

Believe me, I know how difficult this can be.

Faint

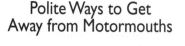

Polite Ways to Get Away from Motormouths

Disappear

Create a diversion

If you're unable to find an opening, you must make one. Politely. While trapped as a listener, you'll have ample time to come up with an excuse (your bus is about to leave; you have to get to a shop before it closes; etc.). Decide whether you'll need visual or tactile assistance to accomplish your break-in (an expression of sudden surprise as if you just remembered something; a gentle hand placed on theirs). Then say:

Talking Headiquette

"Mrs. Motormouth, I hate to interrupt because I do so enjoy our conversations, but I just remembered that I promised my mother I'd be home by four."

Get up, start walking away, and set your exit in inviolate motion.

What if she follows you, still talking? This is such an outrageous breach of etiquette that you have no choice but to do the only sensible thing under the circumstances: Run! ◆

Dealing with Rude Adults

Americans love children. That's why we're cutting back on so much spending on their behalf. Wise grownups know that hardship builds character. If we provided better schools and health care, we could easily spoil an entire generation. Therefore, caring adults recognize that the interests of the young are best served not by putting our money to work, but by putting our mouths to work.

You wouldn't believe the things some adults say to kids. Then again, maybe you would:

"My, how you've grown."

"You're almost as pretty as your sister."

"Look at those freckles."

"You must be awfully nearsighted to have to wear those glasses."

"Aren't you a bit old to be in the tenth grade?"

"The camp you're going to—is it a camp for overweight children?"

"How did you ever get to be so tall?"

It may take a whole village to raise a child, but some of the villagers should keep their mouths shut. Insensitive remarks aren't necessarily meant to be unkind. It's simply that most adults develop total amnesia about childhood once they leave it behind. They forget what it feels like to have adults scrutinizing your behavior and appearance 24 hours a day. Imagine what would happen if adults said to their peers the sorts of things they say to children:

How Rude!

"You're as pretty as Jim's last wife."

"Look at those stretch marks."

"My, I think you've put on at least 30 pounds since I last saw you."

"Aren't you a bit old to still be assistant manager?"

So what do you do when grownups make rude or intrusive remarks? You have three choices:

1. You can make a snappy comeback.
2. You can reply with patience, good humor, respect, and a smile.
3. You can assert yourself without being rude.

The second choice drives adults crazy. Watch:

EXAMPLE #1
**An adult says "That's the third piece
of cake you've had."**

Snappy Comeback	Polite Reply
You say: "It'll look a lot better on me than on you."	*You say:* "How kind of you to point that out. In all honesty, Ma'am, I was so busy enjoying it that I hadn't noticed."
Analysis: The snappy comeback leaves the adult feeling that her intrusion was justified. Not only are you a pig, you're a *rude* pig. And the behavior of impolite children must be closely monitored and corrected.	*Analysis:* The polite reply leaves the adult scratching her head. You expressed appreciation for her kind attentiveness. You confessed to your own lapse in monitoring your food consumption. So how come she feels put in her place? Because your exemplary good manners reveal her remark for what it was—bad manners. Don't you love it?

EXAMPLE #2
An adult says "So tell me, is there a special little girlfriend in your life?"

Talking
Headiquette

Snappy Comeback	Polite Reply
You say: "No, but is there one in yours?" ***Analysis:*** You might experience a moment of satisfaction as the adult turns red in the face and sputters off, wondering just how much you do know about his life. But all you've accomplished is to create an uncomfortable situation and establish yourself as disrespectful.	***You say:*** "I'm blessed with many friends, both girls and boys." ***Analysis:*** With immaculate politeness, you slam the door in the face of this nosy question. Hidden within your reply, deep enough to shield you from accusations of disrespect but shallow enough to be felt by your questioner, is the message *None of your business.* Game, set, and match to politeness.

EXAMPLE #3
An adult says "I don't know why you young people do such things to your hair."

Snappy Comeback	Polite Reply
You say: "At least we *have* hair." ***Analysis:*** Nothing is gained or learned from such an exchange. The adult's stereotype of teenagers is reinforced.	***You say:*** "And I worked so hard to try to look nice tonight! I'd love to hear about the styles when you were my age." ***Analysis:*** When delivered with a forlorn, injured expression, your reply will cause the adult to backpedal quickly, insisting that he never meant to imply that you don't look nice. And then, as he recounts the fashion fads of his youth, he'll recognize the folly of his comment. Your triumph will be complete.

How Rude!

When responding to ill-mannered questions and remarks, the basic principles are these:

- Rudeness returned is the least effective rejoinder to bad manners.
- Don't feel you have to answer a nosy question just because it was asked.
- Respond to rudeness by making a gracious, general statement:

"You're very kind to tell me that."
"Thank you for bringing that to my attention."
"I'll give that some thought."
"That's not something I'm comfortable discussing."
"Do you really think so?"
"I'm always interested in hearing another opinion."

Of course, you may need to modify these principles to fit the specifics of the situation. But you can see them at work in the following examples:

Adult: *"In today's world, you'll never make it as an artist."*
Child: *"Thank you for bringing that to my attention."*

Adult: *"You really should treat your parents with more respect."*
Child: *"Do you really think so? I'll give that some thought."*

Adult: *"In my opinion, you're much too young to travel by yourself."*
Child: *"I'm always interested in hearing another opinion."*

Now let's look at the third choice: asserting yourself without being rude. Maybe you've heard the old saw "It's not *what* you say, it's *how* you say it."* In fact, if you know *how* to say things, you can say almost anything without offending anyone. This comes in handy when you're dealing with boorish people. You can see from the following examples that polite phraseology is much more powerful than discourtesy:

Rude	**Politely Assertive**
"You said no such thing."	"I must have heard you wrong."
"What an ignorant, bigoted thing to say."	"I beg your pardon?"
"You're a liar."	"I believe you're mistaken."
"Mind your own business."	"That's not something we discuss outside of the family."

---

* Maybe you've heard it a hundred million times from your parents. Even so, it's worth hearing again, because it's true.

"I was adopted three years ago by an American family. Because there are obvious differences in appearance between my family and me, people can tell I'm adopted. I don't mind that, but I do mind all the questions they ask. Sometimes even waiters do it. What should I say? Is it considered rude in America to ask questions of this nature?"

Talking
Headiquette

Apparently not. Otherwise we wouldn't have so many ill-mannered people doing it. But it *is* rude. It is *so* rude, in fact, that you have very special latitude in dealing with such boorish busybodies:

To someone who says . . .	You may reply . . .
"Those can't be your real parents."	"Oh, they're very real to *me.*"
"Why didn't your parents want you?"	"Isn't it interesting to speculate on why parents do the things they do? For example, did your parents want *you,* or were you an accident?"
"How come you were adopted?"	"Why do you wish to know?" OR "I prefer not to discuss personal matters with people I don't know well."

You may also, if you feel up to it, give the real reason—not because it's anybody's business, but because it reveals the inexcusable intrusiveness of the question:

"Why was I adopted? Because my parents were dragged from our house in the middle of the night, tortured, shot, and dumped in a shallow grave. After that, they were no longer able to care for me."

You may wish to consider the context in which the question is asked before deciding how to respond. For example, a classmate or teacher who inquires about your family may be trying to build a friendship. You may decide to speak openly about your feelings and history. A waiter, however, is more likely to be scratching the itch of curiosity. He deserves to be put in his place, politely but pointedly.

Responding in such a manner isn't rudeness. It's a public service. It may cause these people to hold their tongues the next time they're tempted to intrude into the personal lives of people they barely know. ◆

How Rude!

WHEN PARENTS ARE RUDE

Strangers, nonrelatives, and casual acquaintances aren't the only adults who are rude to children and teenagers. Parents—perhaps including *your* parents—can be shockingly rude. This may have to do with the confusion between "company manners" and "being real."* Or it may be linked to the mistaken belief that honesty is always the best policy.** Whatever the cause, parental impertinence is as much a breach of etiquette as teenage impudence.

When parents are rude, it's usually in the area of criticizing their children. Admittedly, some criticism is deserved and, when it's constructive, can even be welcome. But criticism is bad manners if the remark is unnecessarily harsh, unkind, or intrusive. For example, there's no excuse for saying "Can't you do anything right?" when the same idea could be expressed as "Let me show you how I learned to do that." Nothing in the parent-child contract excuses parents from showing the same degree of respect and politeness *towards* their offspring that they expect *from* their offspring.

Often the problem is one of definitions. As you can see from the following examples, parents and children use very different dictionaries when it comes to defining behavior:

What parents call . . .	Children call . . .
guidance	criticism
reminding	nagging
for your own good	unfair
ignoring	forgetting
slamming	shutting

The next time your parents call you on the carpet, say "You're absolutely right. I'm sorry. I'll try to do better." This stops criticism dead in its tracks. I guarantee it.

---

* This concept, along with other examples of parental (and teen) rudeness, was discussed earlier in Chapter 4.
** Be patient. A thorough examination of this assumption lies ahead.

The Survey Says . . .

Talking Headiquette

Here, according to our survey of *teenagers,* are 40 Rude Things Parents Say to Teens:

1. "How can you be so dumb?"
2. "You don't try hard enough."
3. "What's wrong with you?"
4. "You little @$#!%&!"
5. "Don't you ever think?"
6. "You'll never amount to anything."
7. "You should have known better."
8. "You're wearing that to school?!"
9. "Get over here."
10. "Get off the phone."
11. "Get out of my sight."
12. "Go to your room."
13. "Listen when I'm talking to you."
14. "Turn off that TV."
15. "Do what I say."
16. "No, and that's final."
17. "Don't you ever talk to me that way again."
18. "Don't cry or I'll hit you even harder."
19. "I don't know why I bother trying."
20. "I don't want to be around you for a while."
21. "I don't believe you."
22. "I don't love you."
23. "I don't care."
24. "It doesn't matter what you want."
25. "It's all your fault."
26. "It's none of your business."
27. "How can I ever trust you again?"
28. "I can't wait for you to leave home."
29. "I wish I'd never had you."
30. "I hate your friends."
31. "Why can't you be like so-and-so?"
32. "If so-and-so jumped off a bridge, would you?"
33. "Act your age."
34. "You're so immature."
35. "What do you know? You're just a child."
36. "You're too young to understand."
37. "Because I said so."
38. "Because I'm your mother/father."
39. "After all of the things I've done for you . . ."
40. "When I was your age . . ."

The Survey Says . . .

Because fairness is our goal, here, according to our survey of *parents,* are 40 Rude Things Teenagers Say to Parents:

1. "Leave me alone."
2. "Mind your own business."
3. "Get out of my face."
4. "Get out of my life."
5. "Stay out of my room."
6. "Shut up."
7. "@$#!%&! you."
8. "You're the world's worst parent."
9. "I wish you weren't my mother/father."
10. "I wish I was never born."
11. "I wish you were dead."
12. "I hate being part of this family."
13. "I don't need you."
14. "You don't own me."
15. "I don't have to."
16. "I don't care."
17. "You can't tell me what to do."
18. "What about *you?*"
19. "YOU do it!"
20. "Forget you."
21. "I'll do what I want."
22. "I'll do it when I feel like doing it."
23. "I don't need your help."
24. "You never do anything for me."
25. "You're so unfair."
26. "You're a nag."
27. "You're too old to understand."
28. "I don't want to be seen with you in public."
29. "Don't buy me clothes. You have horrible taste."
30. "Give me money."
31. "It's my life."
32. "So?"
33. "Who says?"
34. "Fine!"
35. "Yeah, right."
36. "Big deal."
37. "Do I have to eat that?"
38. "This dinner is gross."
39. "I hate you."
40. "You don't care about me at all."

"My father says that all I do is complain and I don't appreciate what I have. That's not true. I do appreciate what I have. What am I supposed to do? Go around saying 'Gee, I'm so lucky, oh wow, this is great?'"

Talking
Headiquette

What we have here is the proverbial failure to communicate. You appreciate your good fortune, you take pleasure in the world, yet your dad isn't getting the message. This happens in a lot of families. For some reason, humans seem more readily disposed to complain than to praise, to express displeasure rather than delight. There's probably some evolutionary basis for this. After all, one is more likely to live to see tomorrow by saying "I hate it when you throw boulders at me" than "My, what a pretty dandelion."

What you need to do is let out all that appreciation. Politeness demands that you convey genuine pleasure when you feel it—as well as when you don't. To examine how this is done, let's look at the three forms of pleasure:

1. **Pleasure in anticipation.** This is what you experience when you look forward to and/or are asked to participate in some future event. This brand of pleasure is expressed with comments such as:

   "Oh boy! That'd be great!"
   "I'd love to!"
   "I can't wait!"
   "Thank you for asking me."

2. **Pleasure in the moment.** This is what you feel when you're having a good time. A quick change of tense and we get:

   "Oh boy! This is fantastic!"
   "I love this!"
   "What fun!"
   "I'm so glad you asked me."

3. **Pleasure reflected upon.** This is what we experience in the afterglow of an enjoyable event. You convey this with comments such as:

   "That was super!"
   "I had a fabulous time!"
   "I hope we can do this again."

Why should you communicate your delight? First, because it's the polite thing to do. Second, because it brings great joy to those who care about your

How Rude!

welcome. And third, because a grateful, enthusiastic response increases the likelihood that the behavior that provoked it will be repeated. ◆

"My mother refuses to talk to me when I 'whine'—as she puts it. I think if someone is talking to you, it's impolite to ignore them."

Your mother isn't ignoring you. She's doing you a favor. "Whining" is the name we give to speech that's repetitive, singsongy, demanding, complaining, and selfish. Such language patterns are associated with small children who, through no fault of their own, haven't yet learned to consider their needs in fair balance with the needs of others. If your mother listened to you, she'd have to conclude that you were behaving in a childish manner. Therefore, you wouldn't stand a chance of getting or doing whatever it is you're whining about not being able to get or do. By refusing to acknowledge you, she's hoping that you'll adopt a more mature perspective and tone of voice so that she might accommodate your wishes. With that in mind, go give your mother a big kiss right now. ◆

Is Honesty Always the Best Policy?

One of the first lessons parents teach their children is "You must never tell a lie." Invariably, a neighbor comes to visit shortly thereafter. Mommy says "Would you like to give Mrs. Sweetums a kiss?" And little Johnny, mindful of his parents' wise counsel, replies "No. She's ugly and smells bad."

As soon as Mrs. Sweetums is out the door, Johnny learns the second lesson parents teach their children: "You must never tell a lie, but you must not always tell the truth." The parent proceeds to explain that there's a difference between *lying to stay out of trouble* (which is bad) and *lying to avoid hurting someone's feelings* (which can be good).

Knowing when to tell the truth and when to take creative liberties is at the heart of good manners. Because this issue is so important, we wanted to learn what teenagers thought about it. So we asked them "Is honesty always the best policy?"

Here's what the teenagers we surveyed said:

Yes	39%
No	61%

And here are some reasons they gave:

"Honesty is always the best policy because . . ."

"If you're honest, your parents will trust you."

"People will like you."

"When you're honest, you never have to remember any lies. The truth always stays the same."

"If you're not honest, it will eventually come back to you in a bad way."

"Telling a lie will push your guilt button, and that's a yucky feeling."

"In my experience, if you lie you always get found out, and then you get in trouble for lying as well as for doing the thing you lied about."

Talking
Headiquette

One teenager put it this way:

"Honesty is the best policy. But it's not always the most convenient policy."

"Honesty isn't always the best policy because . . ."

The teenagers who responded this way to our survey fell into two camps. There were those who saw lying as a way of avoiding hassles:

"You can get away with things when you don't tell the truth."

"Honesty isn't the best policy—at least, not with parents."

"Honesty may get you into more trouble than you need."

"If the other person will never know the difference and the truth will hurt you, zip your lip."

"If someone offers you a drug, you might have to lie to get out of that situation."

And there were those who saw lying as a way of preventing hurt feelings:

"When giving opinions, lying is better than criticizing, but only because people are so damned sensitive!"

"I wouldn't want to tell someone they're ugly or look nasty."

"Honesty can sometimes make people commit suicide, cry, get hurt emotionally, or want revenge on you."

"If you're too honest, you can hurt a friend."

"Telling someone EXACTLY what you think is never good. You should use discretion."

So, is honesty always the best policy or not? The answer is "It depends." The teenagers who said "Yes" realized that telling the truth leads to self-respect, a clear conscience, and the trust of others. They were aware that lies can trip you up and get you into trouble. They were looking at the issue from the *moral* angle.

Most of the teenagers who said "No" were looking at the issue from the *etiquette* angle. They recognized that there are situations where telling the truth

How Rude!

can be cruel, antagonizing, and purposeless. This doesn't mean that it's okay to lie. It means that it's sometimes okay to substitute good manners for the literal truth. Here are a few examples:

- You're feeling lonely and depressed and you have a stomachache. A friend of your mother's drops by the house and asks "How are you?" You say "Fine, thanks." This isn't considered a lie, even though it's not the truth. You understood that the question was a social pleasantry rather than an earnest inquiry into your health.

- You have dinner at a friend's house. The food tastes so bad you can barely get it down. When it's time to leave, you say "Thank you so much for having me over for dinner. I really enjoyed it." You don't say "Your cooking was terrible and I almost threw up." This is because you're not a food critic. You're a sensitive human being who wishes to thank people for the social kindnesses they extend to you.

- A classmate invites you to a dance. What goes through your mind is *I think you're gross and dull, and I wouldn't be caught dead at a dance with you.* What you say is "I'm sorry, but I already have plans." Even if you don't. This is because the question being asked is "Will you go out with me?" and not "What do you think of me?" Thus, the relevant truth is most politely conveyed by using an untruth.

"What are you supposed to say when someone asks you if they look fat?"

You say "Certainly not! Whatever gave you such an idea?" People who ask this question are seeking reassurance, not honesty. They're saying *Please help me to feel okay about myself.*

It's important to be able to recognize questions like these when you hear them. Sometimes they're disguised as declarative statements ("I look so fat"). And sometimes they're introduced with "I want your honest opinion . . . ." But don't be fooled. The last thing the person wants is your honest opinion.

Since these questions are often asked by our closest friends and loved ones, you need to know how to respond when the trap is laid. Here are some practice questions. For each one, pick the answer you think is best:

"Do I look all right?"

a) "That depends on what you consider all right."

b) "You look terrific."

"Is my hair okay?"

a) "It is if you're a rat looking for a nest."

b) "Your hair is fine."

"I messed up so bad in my piano recital."

a) "I'll say. Thirty people walked out."

b) "Oh, no, it sounded wonderful."

**Talking
Headiquette**

In every example, the proper answer is b. But you knew that.

Are there ever times when it's okay to give an honest reply to a question about someone's looks or performance? Absolutely. So how do you know when to be honest and when to be, er, "reassuring"? Here's how:

Be honest when . . .	Be reassuring when . . .
The statement or question seeks specific information. "Is my tie on straight?" "Do I have bird doo-doo in my hair?"	*The statement or question is vague or broad.* "Nobody likes me." "Do you think I'm a nice person?"
The statement or question implies that the person wishes for, and is motivated to make, some change. "Do you think I'd have more friends if I could control my temper better?"	*The statement or question refers to something the person can't easily change about herself.* "I hate being this tall. I look so dumb."
The statement or question addresses an event in the future. "How would I look if I shaved my head?"	*The statement or question addresses an event from the past.* "When I blew the final debate, everybody thought I was a total dork."
An honest answer could lead to positive action or save the questioner from embarrassment, injury, or trouble. "Yes, I *do* think you tend to bully people." "There *is* a huge rip in your bathing suit."	*An honest answer could not be acted upon.* "Yes, girls *would* like you better if you were three years older."
An honest answer, while hurtful, would serve a greater good. "You weren't invited because you drink too much, and people are sick of having their parties ruined."	*An honest answer would be hurtful without doing any good.* "I think you're right. Nobody will ever want to go out with you."

How Rude!

It's especially important to follow these guidelines if the asker is a close friend. And even when honest input is appropriate, criticism should be expressed as positively as possible. This means, if you're out helping a friend buy a new outfit, you say "The green dress is very slimming" as opposed to "The blue dress makes you look like a cow." ◆

"What's the point of asking 'How are you?' Everybody just says 'Fine.' It's so fake."

Would you prefer "My hemorrhoids are killing me, thank you"?

You're right. It *is* fake. People who ask "How are you?" are no more interested in hearing your medical history than you are in reciting it. What they're really saying is *Hey, here we are, two human beings in this cold, cruel world. Let's share a few mindless pleasantries to acknowledge our encounter and leave each other feeling a little warmer than before.* Maybe an electric blanket could accomplish the same thing, but it wouldn't make for a very interesting lunch date.

Human beings have social rituals. So do animals. But humans, instead of sniffing or bleating upon greeting fellow members of the species, prefer to shake hands and say things like "How are you?" and "Have a nice day." It would be a mistake to take all of these phrases at face value. Their actual meaning is symbolic and may even be quite different from what the words literally say. ◆

Polite Profanities

There's no such thing as a polite profanity. If you're prone to imprecations, maledictions, and naughty words, you may include them in the Great American Novel you're writing. But they have no place in polite conversation.

It's not that swearing is "bad" in the sense that if you do it, you'll go to H-E-double-toothpicks for eternity and never be able to watch MTV again. But there are three reasons why it's a bad idea:

1. **Excessive swearing makes your mind go soggy.** People who swear all the time are tiresome to listen to:

    "%#@&!-in'-A, man! I'm so %#@&!-in' mad. %#@&! him! I'm gonna %#@&! that &#@&!-er over, he won't know what the %#@&! hit him."

    A nine-word vocabulary doesn't allow for the expression of much insight, wit, intelligence, or empathy. If your speech is lazy, vague, and unimaginative, your mind is sure to follow.

2. **Excessive swearing takes the shock value out of profanity.** The whole purpose of swearing is to have a few words available for those occasions when all others are insufficient. If you say "&@#&!" when you drop a sandwich, what do you say when an airplane drops a 300-pound block of frozen waste on your foot?

3. **Swearing in public is considered impolite because it's insensitive to the feelings of others.** Many people find profanity offensive. It wasn't that long ago that nobody (except the most vulgar people imaginable) ever swore. To do so in the presence of a lady was unthinkable. Children had their mouths washed out with soap for saying "damn." Some of us learned very young that Dial tastes better than Ivory Soap.

What's that you say? "But it's only words?" Yes, but the images those words conjure up—things one might be full of, or be asked to do to oneself or a close relative—aren't what most people want playing on their mental multiplexes. ◆

"Every time I swear, my parents make me give them ten cents. Do you think this is fair?"

Certainly not. Your parents deserve at least a quarter. ◆

CHAPTER QUIZ

How Rude!

1. *You're home alone when the phone rings. You pick it up and discover that it's an obscene caller. Do you:*
   a) say "Excuse me, I have another call coming in" and put the person on hold
   b) ask the caller to pant a little louder, or
   c) hang up immediately?

2. *You're having lunch with someone who keeps taking calls on his cell phone. You have every right to:*
   a) throw the phone in his soup
   b) do your impersonation of an answering machine
   c) excuse yourself, go to a pay phone, call him, and say you're going home.

3. *A love letter meant for someone else ends up in your locker by mistake. Do you:*
   a) open it, read it, and toss it in the trash
   b) make a hundred copies and plaster them all over the school, or
   c) hand it discreetly to the proper recipient and say "I found this in my locker. I think it's really for you"?

4. *You're at a party where you don't know anybody. The best way to start a conversation with somebody is to:*
   a) throw a drink in the person's face
   b) start singing excerpts from *Cats*
   c) ask some open-ended questions.

5. *Your father drags you up to his boss and says "Mr. Addlebury, I'd like you to meet my son, Ted." Mr. A. responds "My, aren't you a big boy!" Do you:*
   a) punch him out
   b) scowl and say nothing, or
   c) smile and say "Healthy genes"?

11
Netiquette

*Going Online Without
Getting Out of Line*

The reason grownups have children is to ensure that somebody in the house will know how to work the computer. Computer-savvy kids love to help their parents out:

> *"Billy, come quick!"*
> *"What is it?"*
> *"I just deleted all my files."*
> *"Again?!?! I'd love to help you, Ma, but I'm so distracted these days worrying about how I'm gonna get to Sandy's this weekend if you won't lend me the car."*

Computers are not only changing parent-child relationships, they're changing the world! Can you think of another invention, with the possible exception of nose-hair trimmers, that has had such a great impact on life and language? Booting up no longer means putting on footwear. Crashing has nothing to do with cars. People speak of MUDs, MUCKs, MOOs, and MUSEs; Macs and PCs; USENET, BITNET, INTERNET, HAIRNET; RAM, ROM, BIX, FAQ, ALT, DOS—and *other people actually know what they're talking about!*

It's estimated that 40 million people are now hooked into the Internet, and that in just a few years there may be 500 million. Think about it! Half a billion people—old and young, techie and newbie—sending email, hacking, conferencing. Why, the possibilities for rudeness boggle the mind.

If you're out there surfing the cyberwaves, what you have to remember is that there is no Internet President, no central governing board, no manager, no bureaucracy, no single set of rules or laws. This, of course, explains why the Internet works so well. But it also means it takes a bit of doing to learn the customs and protocols of online behavior. Some of these you already know—they're just common courtesy. Others you'll discover. (For example, you don't have to take your boots off in the MUD room.)

Want to know more? ASCII, and ye shall receive.

Discussion Group Decorum

You may spend a lot of your online time in newsgroups. These are discussion forums, and thousands are available on the Internet and through commercial services such as CompuServe, America Online, and Prodigy. No matter what your interest, chances are you'll find people who share it.

Newsgroups are like interactive bulletin boards. People post messages. Others respond to them. If you're new to newsgroups, the main thing to remember is that courtesy is courtesy, whether online or off. You build a good reputation and reveal a winning personality over the Net just as you would face-to-face—by being thoughtful, reasonable, and considerate. First impressions count. Swearing online is considered unimaginative—the product of a lazy mind. People who brag, lie, and put others down are as unwelcome in a newsgroup discussion as they would be in your living room.

While most netniks happily make allowances for newbies (newcomers to the Net), you don't want to strain anyone's tolerance. Here's how to get in on the fun without putting your foot in your mouse:

Practice. Commercial online services often have "test" discussion groups where you can practice posting and receiving messages. Check 'em out.

Lurk before you leap. You'll hear this phrase a lot. What does it mean? If you went to a new school, you'd probably keep a low profile for a while. You'd observe, read the rule book, and find out who's who and what's what in order to learn the customs and expectations of your new environment. The same thing applies online. When you travel the information highway, pretend you're a car at a railroad crossing: Stop. Look. Listen.

Before you ask questions or post messages, scope out the content and behavior of discussion groups you'd like to join. One good way of doing this is to . . .

Netiquette

Get the FAQs. FAQs are <u>F</u>requently <u>A</u>sked <u>Q</u>uestions. These are documents that set out the ground rules and operating procedures of a discussion group. For example, some discussion groups limit postings to news and facts; others welcome opinions and debate. FAQs are wonderful sources of information that will answer many, if not most, of your questions as a newcomer to a group. FAQs also spare group members from having to answer the same questions over and over and over and over and over and over and over again.

Read the Rules of the Road. Online service providers establish their own policies for members. America Online, for example, disallows any conduct that "restricts or inhibits any other Member from using or enjoying AOL." This includes posting "unlawful, harmful, threatening, abusive, harassing, defamatory, vulgar, obscene, hateful, racially, ethnically or otherwise objectionable Content." Download your system's Terms of Service files and become familiar with them. If you find them too censorious, you may want to consider using a provider that doesn't restrict content or access.

Watch what you say. You are what you post. Once your words are out there, you can't get them back. They become public. There are even services that gather, organize, and distribute network messages for years after they first appear. So be prudent about what you say and how you say it. Don't post secrets. Don't spread rumors. Don't say anything you wouldn't feel comfortable saying to someone's face.

Respect the focus of a group. You wouldn't go to a club that played music you didn't like. If you don't like the general content or point of view of an online group, don't go there to be a pest. Just avoid it.

Be nice. Online discussions are conversations. Use the same courtesies you would in a face-to-face exchange. Say "Please" when making requests; thank people for their insights and information; apologize if you commit a gaffe. If you disagree with someone's opinion, respond with respect and reason, not insult and tirade.

Don't blather. You know, like, how, um, someone will go, like, in real life I mean, like talking, you know, two people having a conversation, um, and it

How Rude!

takes, like, so long, I mean, like so much time, um, you know, for the person who is talking, to like, um, get to the point, that, it's been so long, I mean, getting there, you know, like, um, from the beginning, that by the time he gets there, the point where he is, after so long, it's like, you couldn't care less, like you're so totally bored, that now that he's like, um, finally finished, you know, done, all you can think is, like, *Please, God, don't let me ever have to talk to this person again?*

Same thing online. If you want to be welcome as a conversationalist, be brief.

Check your spelling and grammar. The Internet ain't no English test, but propper speling, punkchooashun, and grammer do make it ezier for peepel to reed and understand yor comunikashuns. As a mark of courtesy to your correspondents, check your writing for mistakes. Don't sweat it, though. We all make ocasional errors. And whatever you do, don't chastise others for their mistakes. Blooper watchdogs quickly wear out their welcome.

Be tolerant. Everyone was a newbie once. If newcomers ask stupid questions, be kind. Either ignore them or gently take them aside via email and point out the faux pas they're committing.

Don't break the law. The Internet is policed. Things that would get you in trouble offline will get you in trouble online. Don't threaten the President, issue bomb threats, or harass anyone. Don't violate copyright laws.

Don't confuse hacking with cracking. Hacking is creative; cracking is criminal. Hacking is mischievous; cracking is malicious. Hacking is for the good of all; cracking is for the good of one. Hacking is fooling around, seeing what you can do, using your imagination to come up with something new and better. Cracking is spreading viruses, breaking in where you don't belong, pirating, vandalizing, impersonating, destroying. Cracking can land you in jail—the ultimate downtime.

Mind your format. If your margins are set so you type more words than can fit on someone
else's screen, they'll wrap around like this and be a real pain for someone to read. What's more, if the
recipient goes to print out what you sent him, it will print the same way, which will be an even greater
pain and waste lots of paper. So the thing to do is set your margins so that you'll have no more than 60
to 80 characters per line. How do you do that? DON'T ASK ME!! I've been trying to figure this out for
ages. In fact, if you know, would you please tell me?

Think globally. Keep in mind that the Internet transcends national boundaries. The messages you post may be read by people on the other side of the world. If your forum has an international membership, it's courteous to avoid expressions or references that would be hard for people from other countries and cultures to understand.

Netiquette

Dump with dignity. If you're talking to someone at a party and you wish to end the conversation, you can simply say "Excuse me" and head for the food. It's a little trickier online. Unwanted correspondents can flood you with email. If someone is bothering you or your discussion group, send him a private message. You can say something like:

"Thank you for your email, but I don't wish to continue our conversation."

Or:

"Thank you for your comments. I don't think your interests or point of view are in keeping with our discussions. I would appreciate it if you looked for another group."

If this doesn't work, see if your system allows you to set up a *bozo filter* (a.k.a. *kill file*). This is a way to screen out messages from people whose mail you don't wish to receive. It's like having a security guard who checks guests against a guest list.

Give back. The Net is a grand and sometimes bizarre bazaar where people exchange all sorts of wares. It works best when there's a balance of give-and-take. Use it to get what you need, but give back so that others may get what *they* need. Answer questions. Steer people in the right direction. Do your part to make it a friendly place.

Respect the ecology of the Net. On planet Earth, certain resources are finite and it's important to conserve them. On the Net, time and bandwidth are limited resources. Netniks who consume more than their fair share of either quickly become nudniks. Since there are only 24 hours in a day, and only so much information that can be carried over the wires at any given time, it's important to conserve time and bandwidth. You can do your part if you keep the following rules in mind:

- Say what you have to say in as few words as possible.
- If a question has been asked and answered by others, don't add your own two cents worth unless it contains information or views not previously expressed.
- Don't post information to the group if it would be more appropriate to send it to an individual.
- Don't copy or forward mail unless there's a good reason to do so.

- Keep test messages short. A friend of mine wanted to practice sending files via email, so he sent me a file 140 pages long. It took about 140 minutes to download it, and it came through as gibberish. I could have told him that from one page.

- Design a fast-loading Web page. You've probably noticed how quickly text loads and how l—o—n—g it takes to load graphics. If you have a Web page, balance your text and graphics so people can load it without having to take the afternoon off.

- Beware of registering with corporate Web sites. You may get a lot of junk email that overloads the system for everybody.

- Don't be lazy. The Internet is a fabulous resource for information, but it's not a personal research assistant. Don't expect strangers to do your homework. Questions like *Hey, I gotta write a paper on Lewis and Clark. Anybody know anything about them?* are not appreciated. Specific questions like *Does anybody know if Lewis and Clark ever stayed at a Motel 6?* are always welcome.

- Use catchy titles. Try to let browsers know what your message is about from the title. That way, they'll be able to decide if it's of interest to them without having to load it.

Email Manners

Email stands for Eeee-lectronic mail. With email, you can send and receive messages via the Internet. This means no postage or envelopes. No paper cuts on your tongue. No wondering where the stamp has been before you lick its backside. No more yicchy glue aftertaste.

Here's the lowdown for sending and receiving emissives:

Use proper addresses. Internet addresses follow a strict format:

name@organization.domain

Examples:

Peewee@aol.com
president@whitehouse.gov
fifi@stateuniv.edu

The *name* identifies the individual or group. You would never have two accounts with the same name served by the same Internet provider, since there would be no way of knowing whose mail is whose. This would be like having two Daffy Ducks both living at 111 Elm Street.

A name can be virtually anything. It can be a real name: *joe_schmo, moe_schmo, schlomo_schmo.* (Underscores are used to indicate the spaces between words.) It can be a handle: *Yogurtman, Pieface.* It can be a number or the name of a company.

After the name comes the *organization.* This usually identifies an institution, a business, or the service providing access to the Internet.

Netiquette

Finally, you have the *domain.* The six primary domains are:

1. mil = military
2. gov = government agencies and departments
3. net = networks
4. edu = educational institutions
5. com = commercial businesses
6. org = nonprofit organizations.

Because an Internet address can be a bit complicated, always double-check that you've got it right. One typo or misplaced "dot" may send your message to the far side of Uranus instead of to its intended recipient.

Don't be too forward. When forwarding mail to someone else, it's a courtesy to delete the headers—those lines of gobbledygook that describe the path the message took to get to you. This way, people won't have to wade through 18 screens of

> *emout.12.mail.aol.com (7.5.14/6.3.12 id 0BB0344812 mx [by arl.14.NAA2753@mail.com] 17:54:04) <940571833_1158962357>*

to get to the three-line joke you and your friends are passing along the Net. So stamp out those unnecessary headers.

Think "typewriter." With current email technology, it's impossible to italicize, boldface, or underline words the way you would with word-processing software. In fact, old-fashioned typewriters* are capable of more "special effects" than email.

To get around the limits of email technology, certain conventions have developed. To emphasize a word as if it were *italicized*, put asterisks around it. How's *that* for a solution! To underline a word or series of words, such as a book title, surround it with underscores: _Huckleberry Finn_.

Don't Shout! The use of CAPITAL LETTERS FOR EMPHASIS is the email equivalent of shouting and is therefore RUDE. Of course, if something has happened that necessitates a bit of shouting, go right ahead:

---

* Typewriters are ancient writing machines your parents used after walking home from school through 10-foot snowdrifts.

How Rude!

"YOU THIMBLE-BRAIN! YOU WART ON THE FACE OF HUMANITY! HOW COULD YOU POST MY EMAIL ON THE MESSAGE BOARD?!?"

Don't be an emoti-conman. Just when you thought you'd seen the last of those obnoxious smileys, they're ba-ack—and they're called *emoticons*. These are little sideways faces you create with letters and/or punctuation. People use them online as shorthand for emotions and facial expressions. Examples:*

:-)	I'm smiling, laughing, just kidding
:-(	I'm frowning, unhappy, bummed out
;-)	I'm winking, making a pun or joke
:-O	"WHAT?!?!" I'm shocked! Yelling!
==:-O	I'm so shocked that my hair is standing on end
:-D	I've got a HUUUUUGE grin
:-P	I'm sticking out my tongue or giving you a raspberry *(phphpht)*
:'-)	I'm crying happy tears
%-(	I'm unhappy and confused
:-#	I'm wearing braces
:-X	My lips are sealed
{:{)	I have a toupee and mustache

Admittedly, some of these are kind of cute. And I admire the creativity of those who think them up. But with over 600,000 words available to all of us free of charge, can't we say what we mean without burping little bug-eyed faces all over the screen? Do we need to dumb down the language even more than it already has been? Shakespeare didn't write:

To be or not to be, that is the question. %-(

And Dickens didn't end *A Christmas Carol* with:

God Bless Us, Every One! :'-)

Do you know why? Because they didn't need little pixel-pusses to convey emotion. They did it with *words*.

Emoticons are like a new toy that everybody wants to try out. And sometimes you may want to use one to be sure your message isn't misunderstood. But relying on them encourages lazy thinking and lazy writing. It's like sending someone a greeting card with a ready-made message instead of your own carefully chosen words. Which would you rather get from your true love? I rest my case.

---

* Turn the book 90 degrees clockwise to see the faces.

384

Don't overdo it. People want to get their signature just right. Perhaps it's this motivation to make a statement with one's John Hancock that causes many people to go overboard when creating signature files. These are lines of information that automatically appear at the end of any email you send (assuming your system allows them).

Netiquette

A basic signature file is like a return address. It contains the name of the person or company; his or her address, phone and/or fax number; and perhaps a small logo or slogan.

However, some people turn their signature file into an extravaganza of silly pictures, jokes, quotations, and unnecessary minutiae that waste bandwidth and time. It's a bit like people who make you wade through three minutes of instructions, dialogue, and music before you can leave a message on their telephone answering machine.

Network protocol frowns on show-offy signatures. In fact, some Internet sites limit you to no more than four lines. If you create a signature file for yourself, keep it short. Remember, less is more.

Give to get. The best way to get a lot of email is to send a lot of email—if getting a lot of email is what you want. Some people enjoy receiving dozens or hundreds of emails each day. Others would prefer not to spend 60 hours per week reading and answering their email.

Be discreet. Even though email feels very private, it isn't. Hackers, "Big Brother," and people with whom you share a computer or Internet account can all peek at your email. Recipients can forward your messages to someone else. Unless you use encryption programs, anything you write is prey to prying eyes.

TRUE STORIES FROM THE
MANNERS FRONTIER
Memail

It's easy to send email to the wrong person. Just the other day, I accidentally sent a message meant for Paula to myself!! Imagine my surprise when I checked my email later in the day and discovered that I had new mail from ME!

At least no harm was done. But if I had sent Paula's message to Pegeen by mistake—oh, boy, I'd be in big trouble. So be extra careful about what you write—and to whom you send it. And, since email can go astray, read on.

How Rude!

Don't assume your message has gotten through. Systems crash. And, believe it or not, there are bozo-brains who send mail to the wrong address or forget to click "send" in the first place. If you don't get a response to one of your emails, check to see that your message was received—*before* you assume that the intended recipient is an inconsiderate, slothful, procrastinating jerk.

Count to ten. Let's say a friend sends you a letter in the mail that really upsets you. You write an angry reply. But you can't find a stamp, and your friend didn't put her return address on the envelope. By the time you dredge up the address and walk to the post office, you begin to cool down and have second thoughts about what you wrote. So you decide to wait a day before sending the letter. And are you glad you did, because 24 hours later you see things differently. You tear up the letter and write a more balanced, thoughtful response.

Now let's say your friend's letter arrives as email. You read it. You're furious and upset. You whip off a hurtful, accusatory reply and click "send" and it's outta there. Later that day, you wonder if maybe you took what she wrote the wrong way, and maybe you were partly to blame, and maybe she didn't mean it the way you thought she did, and maybe what you wrote is only going to make things worse, and if only you could take it back—TOO LATE—your message is long gone, the damage done.

Email makes communication such a snap that it's easy to "send" before you comprehend. Count to ten, or a hundred, or ten thousand before replying to email that upsets you. Remember, electronic communication doesn't provide the visual or vocal clues you get in face-to-face conversations. It's prone to misinterpretation. Don't be so quick on the draw that you say something you might regret later.

Give people adequate time to respond. Email is so convenient that it's natural to expect people to drop whatever they're doing to reply to your missives. Be patient. If days or weeks pass without a response, send a polite follow-up query to be sure they got your message. If they did, they'll get your message.

Stay away from chain gangs. Chain letters are scams. Have you ever in your whole life known anyone who actually got 14,789 dollar bills in the mail, let alone one lousy postcard? Most commercial networks outlaw chain letters. If you get one, ignore the instructions. I promise you won't be cursed with an eternity of bad luck. For good luck, forward the letter to the administrators of your system. Ask them to clamp down on the person who sent it. You'll save a lot of suckers from being fleeced.

Don't post or forward email without permission. You wouldn't tack a personal note somebody sent you on the bulletin board of your neighborhood supermarket. If somebody sends you something that you'd like to share with others, always ask for permission before doing so.

TO FLAME OR NOT TO FLAME

Netiquette

Flaming doesn't refer to setting someone's computer on fire. Rather, flaming is verbal fisticuffs. Digital duking. Flaming is meant to cause arguments, provoke reactions, get people stirred up. It's a Net tradition. People get flamed for being too dumb or too smart, too silly or too serious, too involved or too indifferent. They get flamed for wasting time, grossing someone out, asking stupid questions, giving stupid answers, and even for flaming. In short, people get flamed for anything and everything.

At its best, flaming elevates argument to an art form. World-class flamers use wit, intelligence, and laser-like linguistic precision to destroy their opponent's point of view. At its worst, flaming is like a barroom brawl: ignorant, destructive, and out of control.

So, is flaming good or bad? Look at it this way: Let's say you're eating dinner at a friend's house. Somehow, the topic of politics comes up, and it turns out that your friend's parents are planning to vote for two different candidates in an upcoming election. A discussion gets going, and before you know it, your friend's parents are putting down each other's candidates and political beliefs. But they're doing it with great style. It's sport, they're having fun, there's a twinkle in their eye, they respect each other's right to have an opinion—*no matter how stupid it is.* The back-and-forth is so stimulating that you and your friend are drawn into the discussion. By the time you leave the table, you're full of new ideas, new respect for your friend's family, new pride in yourself, and too much lasagna. This was a good flame. Score one for civilization.

Now let's say the discussion had gone the other way—that it had degenerated into an ugly slugfest of name calling, accusations, and attack. It got mean and personal with everyone shouting and no one listening. The mood was spoiled. You felt uncomfortable and embarrassed. You wanted to get up and leave. This was a bad flame. Score one for boorishness.

It's silly to debate whether there should or shouldn't be flaming on the Net. As long as people gather, there will always be flames—civilized and otherwise. What you can do, though, is use the following six guidelines to uphold the finest traditions of flaming:

1. Avoid cheap flames. Choose targets who deserve your wrath. Don't flame the poor newbie for a stupid question. Don't flame people for their spelling or grammar.

2. Don't get caught by flame-bait. Some people cruise the Net for the sole purpose of trying to stir up trouble. They post messages designed to ignite

How Rude!

flame wars: homophobic remarks on gay and lesbian bulletin boards, anti-Semitic tirades on Holocaust discussions, cat meat recipes on friends-of-felines forums. These people aren't looking for intelligent discussion. They're looking for attention.

If you come across flame-bait, ignore it. There's no more powerful reply. This doesn't mean, however, that you can't address prejudice or ignorance when you encounter it. Don't expect miracles, though. Most bigots never let the facts get in the way of their opinions. But at least you'll have tried to shine some light into the dark cavities of their mind.

You can also respond to flame-bait in several other ways:

- Use a kill file to screen out any messages from that person.
- Send a note to the flamer. Tell him that his message was inappropriate. Request that he refrain from posting anything like it again. The flamer may slink off in shame. He may apologize. Or he may escalate his abuse. If this happens . . .
- Rat on him. Send a note to the administrators of the flamer's service provider. Advise them of the problem and ask that they take steps to curb their pixellated pit bull.

3. Don't post things just to get flamed. Online arsonists quickly wear out their welcome, especially if they're ill-informed. If you have a strong opinion, fine. Put it out there. But be prepared to back it up with facts and experience or you may get burned.

4. Don't get caught in the middle. Sometimes the person who tries to stop a fight becomes everyone's target. If you advise flamers to take their dispute out of the group and into email, you may end up with a plague from both their houses.

5. Mark your flames. You can let people know you're about to flame by writing "FLAME ON" before you start your tirade. When you're through, you can write "FLAME OFF." That way, nobody can accuse you of taking them by surprise.

6. Beware of flame wars. Nothing destroys a discussion group faster than an ugly, personal, protracted flame war. If you're one of the participants, it's considered proper form to take the debate to email, where bystanders won't be hit by flying venom. If you're one of the spectators, don't add fuel to the fire by taking sides.

The Safety Net

Netiquette

As long as there are people, there will always be jerks. And if you navigate the Net, you may encounter the occasional Bad Apple—and by that I don't mean a Macintosh with a personality disorder.

There's no need to be paranoid, or to imagine that behind every pixel lurks a candy-bearing pervert who wants to entice you into an oven in his house in the woods. But you need to exercise the same caution online that you would in the "real" world.

Your parents have probably admonished you not to talk to strangers from the time you were old enough to understand. If, however, you're active on the Internet, you'll "talk" to strangers every day via email and newsgroups. The thing to keep in mind is that these people aren't necessarily who or what they say they are. Sometimes this is part of the fun—for example, in simulation games where players are encouraged to create characters for themselves. Occasionally, though, someone you meet online may be hiding behind a false front in order to scam, harass, or seduce you. You can easily protect yourself if you follow a few basic rules:

Beware of false intimacy. The anonymity of online communication makes it very easy to share personal information that you would never reveal in a face-to-face conversation. While this has its rewards, it also has its risks. Watch out for PC-pals who get very friendly very quickly—people who want to know what you look like, who want to meet you right away, who ask questions about your sexual interests, fantasies, or experiences, or who share theirs.

These are perfectly reasonable topics, and you might want to talk about them online. And there are certainly many kind, trustworthy, empathetic individuals—peers and adults—with whom you could safely share your thoughts, questions, or concerns. What you need to do is follow your instincts, just as you would in "real" life. If it feels weird, it probably is. And if it feels okay, it probably is. But just in case it isn't . . .

Never go alone to meet someone in person you've met online. Let's say you've met a fellow Harley enthusiast and he invites you over to his place to look at his bikes. This could be a great opportunity and the start of a true friendship. Nevertheless, you're not 100 percent sure who this person is. So the first time you go, go with a friend. Go with several friends. Go with several BIG friends. Be sure your parents know where you're going. Be sure the Harley guy knows that your parents know where you're going. Good people won't be offended by your caution in checking them out. They'll understand and be impressed.

389

This doesn't mean you have to approach everyone as if he (or she) is a serial port ax murderer. You may chat up someone through a school network, and it'll be obvious from her knowledge of teachers and fellow classmates that she's on the level. In that case, it's fine to arrange to meet without a phalanx of bodyguards.

Play your cards close to your chest. Sad to say, but wherever humans congregate, there are low-life weasels out to steal your money and your innocence. You can avoid these sharks by keeping your address and phone number to yourself. Don't use a credit card number online unless you want to end up with a $127,986 bill next month. Never tell anyone your password. Change it often. Don't fall for the old con that there's "trouble with your system" and "we're checking to confirm passwords if you'll just tell us what yours is." If anyone asks for your password, report it to your system administrator.

Don't be a compuholic. Computers are great, but don't OD on yours. An online social life should be an addition to, rather than a replacement for, face-to-face interaction. You need to

You Know You're a Compuholic When . . .

Your friends take your keys away.

You wake up with a strange computer and don't know how you got it.

You hide laptops all over the house and deny any knowledge of them.

exercise more than just your brain and your fingers. If there's mold growing on your hair, it could be a sign you need to get out in the sun—and taking your laptop to a park doesn't count. Get a reality check from parents, siblings, or friends as to whether you're spending too much time in cyberland. If the answer is yes, you'll need to cut down.

Start by trying to understand your computer addiction. Why are you hooked? Are you an online participant, or spectator? When do you use your computer? What does it take the place of? How do you feel when you're using it or not using it? Depending on what you discover, you may need to make new friends, get some counseling, do volunteer work, or find new interests and activities. Connect with other kids who are recovering computer junkies—just don't do it online. It's easier to cut down if you have the support and empathy of like-minded individuals.

Netiquette

Family Shareware

The family that computes together disputes together—*if* family members forget to mind their PC p's and q's. For keyboard harmony in the household, here are the common courtesies of computer sharing:

Wash your hands. Nobody wants to be able to tell what you had for lunch by looking at the keyboard. So keep your sticky fingers away from the P, B, and J, as well as all the rest of the keys. Even the most mild-mannered parents go berserk when QWERTY gets dirty.

TRUE STORIES FROM THE
MANNERS FRONTIER
Baby Blues

The only time a gentle, loving mother I know ever swatted her child on the behind was when the little tyke smeared chocolate all over the keyboard.

"I just saw red and lost it," the mother confessed.

"The chocolate was red?" I said.

Of course, the poor mother has suffered eternal self-damnation for her brutal loss of self-control. But the keyboard has remained fudge-free ever since.

Don't spill coffee on the CPU. Computers don't know how to swim.

Clean house frequently. Don't let your hard disk turn into a graveyard. Get rid of files that are ancient history and only clutter up the machine for others.

How Rude!

Back up your files. Just in case your little sister accidentally deletes your term paper, wouldn't you rather say "Don't worry, I've got it on a floppy" than "I'm going to KILL YOU!!!!"? In fact, make *two* sets of backup disks for important files. Keep one set at home. Keep the other set off premises—in your school locker or at a friend's house. This way, if there's ever a fire, burglary, or earthquake or your house gets swallowed by a sinkhole, you'll still have a copy safe and sound.

Paranoid? Perhaps. But for the few seconds and few pennies this extra protection costs, isn't it worth it?

Use antivirus software. If you're an active downloader, sooner or later your computer is going to get blasted with a virus. Be sure you protect the computer and everybody's files by using software that will guard you against viruses. Otherwise, your family is going to blast *you*.

Don't tie up the phone. If your modem operandi is to rack up hours of connect time every day, this may cause conflict with the rest of your family. With the phone tied up, they won't be able to make or receive calls. (Plus you'll need to disable call waiting if you don't want incoming calls to crash your connection.)

Before trouble brews, work out a fair-use plan with your clan. Your best bet may be to install a separate line dedicated to computer use. You can split the cost. If there's competition for using the computer, you may need to work out a schedule so everyone gets the time they need.

Respect people's privacy. Your computer may enable users to lock their files under a secret password. But that shouldn't be necessary. Snooping is a major breach of etiquette. Your family, with you leading the way, can affirm that no one will ever look at anyone else's email or files. This policy can be facilitated by creating hard disk subdirectories and email file cabinets for each family member.

"I'm the technically gifted one in my family, and everyone (especially my parents) comes to me with their computer questions. I can have friends over or be doing my homework and my parents expect me to drop everything just because they hit the wrong key or deleted a file or tried to download something and ended up with some disk error message that has them convinced their computer is going to self-destruct in thirty seconds. Is there anything I can do to discourage this dependence on me?"

Discourage it? You want to *encourage* it with every fiber of your being. You're in an enviable position.

To begin with, you can use your superior knowledge to get your parents to buy all sorts of software and hardware you've been dying to have. You can say to your mom:

> *"You know, your work would go ten times faster if you got a single-pass 30-bit color scanner with custom gamma adjustment and SCSI-2 interface."*

Netiquette

Or to your dad:

> *"The only thing that will solve your problem once and for all is a dedicated computer telephone line, antivirus software, a 128 MB RAM memory upgrade, and a 20" multi-frequency, anti-reflection monitor with full-function remote control, LCD display, and 1600 x 1280 resolution."*

Dad might scratch his head and say:

> *"I need all that just because my computer won't boot up?"*

To which you would confidently reply:

> *"Well, you could just remove your floppy from the A-drive and hit 'enter,' but I think this would work a lot better, Dad."*

You also have a priceless opportunity to model proper teaching behavior for your parents. This, of course, will take a great deal of patience on your part. Adults tend to ask silly questions, rush ahead without reading directions, and get defensive when being corrected. Here are the best techniques for instructing adults without hurting their feelings or injuring their self-confidence:

Be tolerant. Grownups just aren't as experienced as kids in many areas. Computer-ease is one of them. It's not your parents' fault that they're cybernetically challenged. Treat them with respect. Assume that they have the ability to learn. At all costs, avoid remarks such as "How could you be so dumb?" or "Can't you do anything right?"

Be patient. Experience is the best teacher—even if it means making mistakes. When you see your parents head off in the wrong direction, resist the temptation to jump in and take over. If they're about to nuke the hard disk or something equally irrevocable, you can usually prevent it by saying "Let's just consider this for a minute before proceeding." Then ask questions to help them think through their actions before taking them. Most adults will make responsible decisions if trusted to do so.

How Rude!

Be encouraging. In the face of their children's techno-brilliance, many parents lack confidence, feel stupid, and get easily discouraged. You must counter these feelings. Be a cheerleader for your folks. Say:

"You're doing great!"
"Keep up the good work!"
"Look out, Bill Gates!"

If you practice these teaching methods diligently, you'll find that your parents' computer knowledge will increase to the point where they'll be less dependent on you for help. And, given your shining example, they may start to use these methods of instruction with you. ◆

CHAPTER QUIZ

What do these emoticons mean?

1. {: --------

    a) my nose is running
    b) I told a fib
    c) I was a lollipop in a previous life.

2. |
    {: -
    |

    a) I love to pump iron
    b) I was born with a pole through my head
    c) I have *very* large ears.

3. {: >>>>>

    a) I'm gonna hurl lunch
    b) each of my five chins has a goatee
    c) I just swallowed a V-chip.

12
Clothes-Minded

You Are What You Wear

Each day, when you wander to your closet, dresser, or Everest-size heap of clothes on the floor, you're not just deciding what to wear. You're deciding what you want to tell the world about yourself. When you walk out the door, your clothes will say:

"I'm cool"	or	*"I'm trying to be cool."*
"I take pride in my appearance"	or	*"I'm a slob."*
"I spend a lot of money on clothes"	or	*"I shop at thrift stores."*
"I want to be noticed"	or	*"I want to blend in."*
"I'm trying to look older"	or	*"I'm trying to look younger."*
"I respect social traditions"	or	*"I thumb my nose at society."*

How Rude!

Of course, your clothes might also say:

University of Chicago
Tommy Hilfiger
Grateful Dead
My parents went to Tobago and all I got was this lousy T-shirt.

Clothes can tell you whether someone is a police officer, Girl Scout, aging hippie, soldier, flight attendant, nurse, convict, businessperson, or baseball player. And because clothes make such powerful statements, the way you dress can be a source of conflict with your parents, teachers, peers, or employers. So let's take a look at some of the issues involved.

Why Clothes Matter

Why does everybody make such a big deal about clothes? If you wear certain things, it's because you like them, right? Not because you're angry or rebelling or making a statement. As long as you're not going around naked, why does it matter what you wear?

It matters because clothes are symbolic. They make a statement about your attitudes, status, and self-image, even if that's not your intent. When you say that you "like" certain clothes, what do you like about them? Probably the way they look and feel. Which means that you like the way they make *you* look and feel. Consciously or not, you're attracted to the associations those clothes trigger in your mind: *I'm artistic; I'm tough; I'm laid back; I'm sexy; I'm politically correct; I'm totally uninterested in clothes.*

Fashion Tip for Teens #1:
Beachwear should never be worn in church.

Fashion Tip for Teens #2:
Always wear an apron while barbecuing
in gym class.

Fashion Tip for Teens #3:
Remove all rings before stepping through airport security.

Clothes-Minded

Because clothing is an external, visual representation, there's no way you can avoid being judged by what you wear. Before the first word pops out of your mouth, your clothes and appearance have already said quite a bit about you. The problem is, what they say may not be true. For example, you could go out this afternoon, shave your head, get a swastika tattoo, put on boots and camouflage gear, and the world would think you're a neo-Nazi skinhead. You'd still be your same sweet self, but your image would say otherwise—and people would react accordingly. This is why the first thing a defense attorney does is a client makeover. The serial murderer who, when arrested, looked like a cross between Bigfoot and the Big Bad Wolf will enter the courtroom looking like Santa Claus on his way to church.

You have the right to dress any way you like. But if you defy social standards, as is your privilege, people will make judgments accordingly, as is their privilege. It's up to you to determine whether what you wear will hurt you or help you.

"I wear nice clothes, but I never feel that I look good. It's not like I'm ugly. I just don't like the way I feel."

You probably look wonderful. But what can you do to help yourself feel that way?

First, you need to recognize that the way people feel involves much more than the clothes they wear. Feeling smart and snazzy is a function of self-confidence, personal hygiene, and overall mental and physical health. To get a handle on the source of your malaise, write down as many words as you can to describe how you feel. Then analyze them.

Do the words suggest that your problem is one of *attitude* (you feel "uncool," "dumb," "clumsy," "self-conscious")? Or one of *grooming* or *posture* (you feel "sticky," "sloppy," "frizzy," "unkempt")? Or that the problem may be *physical* or *health-related* (you feel "uncoordinated," "tired," "depressed," "achy")?

How Rude!

If the problem seems to originate in your head, that's where you should go to look for a solution. You don't feel you look good because you don't feel good about *yourself*. Teenagers often get down on themselves because of the pressures of measuring up. Get a reality check from a close friend, sibling, parent, or adult you trust. Talk to your school counselor. Explain how you've been feeling. Find out why you're so hard on yourself, then work to improve your self-esteem.

If the problem seems to be one of grooming, you may need to wash, shower, and clean your hair more often. Try new body gels, lotions, powders, and scents. Take a toothbrush to school and brush after lunch.

If you think the way you feel has to do with your overall health, see a doctor. You may have a physical problem that's sapping your energy and making you feel dull. You may have mono or a low-grade infection. You may be depressed and need some counseling or medication. You may need to work on your posture, exercise more, or change your eating habits. Get your eyes checked. See a dentist. All of these things can affect the way you feel.

Finally, experiment with the clothes you wear. Different clothes have different "feels." For example, heavy boots may be in, but you might feel snappier if you don't clunk around in 20 pounds of footwear. Try being dressier. Or more casual. Try looser clothes or tighter clothes. Try fabrics that are softer or starchier. You may discover that a change in look will create a change in the way you feel. ◆

"There's a girl at school who wants to be friends with me. I'm popular and I like her, but she wears the most uncool clothes. People tease her a lot, and I'm afraid if I hang out with her they'll tease me, too. How can I tell her without being rude that she has to change the way she dresses if she wants to have friends?"

Assuming that the girl you describe is neat and clean in her grooming, and that her clothes, while not in keeping with prevailing fashion fads, are presentable and appropriate for school, the dilemma you face presents you with a choice—one that you're likely to encounter repeatedly throughout life:

1. Do you allow the snobbish, intolerant standards of a peer group, in combination with the fashion industry's self-appointed arbiters of taste, in cahoots with greedy clothing manufacturers using child slave labor, to dictate what's important to you and who your friends are?

OR:

2. Do you stand up for the right of people to be judged on who they are and what they do rather than on how they look?

Clothes-Minded

As you can see, this isn't about clothes. It's about *values*.

There's no polite way to tell someone you don't like the way she dresses. What you *can* do, though, is work both sides of the issue. You can tell your friends that the girl is really a lovely person and they shouldn't judge her because of her clothes. If you're popular, your opinion should carry some weight. At the same time, as you get to know the girl, you can find out more about how she feels about her dress and image.

The next time you go shopping for yourself, invite her along. The conversation will naturally include talk about clothing likes and dislikes, and you'll get a better understanding of her situation. Maybe her family can't afford to buy her clothes. Maybe she feels perfectly fine about what she wears. Maybe she's clueless about how to create a look.

Depending on what you learn about her, you may want to suggest a makeover—gently, discreetly, and politely. This could build a friendship and help a friend. Or you might find yourself back at square one, having to decide between friendship and fashion. ◆

The Age of Entitlement: Choosing Your Own Clothes

When should children be able to choose their own clothes? Generally, they should be given some say when they're old enough to dress themselves. At this tender age, they'll be malleable to their parents' definitions of practicality and good taste. Parents should take advantage of this opportunity to imprint proper standards of dress on their offspring, who can usually be satisfied with being allowed to decide whether they want choo-choo trains or dancing bears on their pajamas. It's only when they get older that they'll question whether they want pajamas at all.

Children old enough to go shopping by themselves come under a different set of rules: those of the Parent-Child Dominant Peer Group Appropriate Dress Treaty. Briefly stated, this pact stipulates the following:

1. When in the company of peers, the child may dress any way he or she likes.
2. When in the company of parents, the child must conform to adult interpretations of appropriateness.
3. When in the company of both peers and adults, the decision goes to whichever generation can make a better claim for ownership of the event.

How Rude!

In other words, a child accompanied by parents to a school basketball game would be permitted to dress as he wishes. A child accompanying her parents to an office picnic would have to dress in accordance with their wishes.

"My mother insists on going clothes shopping with me. (I'm fifteen.) We have these big arguments because she won't let me get any clothes with designer names or company logos. I don't think this is fair."

You're right. It isn't fair. Calvin Klein has to pay through the nose when he puts a 12-story underwear billboard on Times Square. Why should teenagers provide advertising space for free?

But fairness isn't the issue here, and it's not a good argument to pose to parents (who are likely to reply "So what? Life isn't fair"). Your goals for any clothes-buying trip with your mother should be to:

- avoid needless argument
- show that you're willing to be financially aware and responsible, and
- end up with a wardrobe that makes you both happy.

As a first step, take an inventory of your closet. Determine the articles and outfits you'll need to purchase for the next six months or year. Divide these into two categories:

1. those you'll wear primarily in the company of your peers, and
2. those you'll wear primarily in the company of adults.

Next, establish with your mother a budget for each category. Then approach her with this proposal:

As long as you stay within budget and reason, Category #1 items are yours to buy without your mother's approval, and Category #2 items are to be selected jointly, with your mother's wishes given priority.

In addition, you're free to use your allowance or earnings to buy clothing of your own choosing.

This solution is likely to work because:

- it respects both viewpoints (yours and your mom's)
- it recognizes that teenagers and adults have different tastes and operate in different worlds, and

- it requires maturity, compromise, and generosity of spirit on everybody's part.

In other words, *it's fair.* ◆

"How much should a clothing allowance be?"

Let's acknowledge that not all parents wish to give their children clothing allowances or can afford to do so. If your parents do and can, your clothing allowance should be enough to buy everything you need, but not everything you want, with a little left over for something you'd really like. ◆

"Do you see anything wrong with boys wearing an earring?"

I see absolutely nothing wrong with boys wearing a discreet earring—as long as it doesn't look like a Calder mobile and is worn according to the terms of the Parent-Child Dominant Peer Group Appropriate Dress Treaty (see page 399).

In fact, I've often thought it unfair that women can adorn themselves with any number of rings, necklaces, baubles, pearls, diamonds, earrings, and brooches while men must make do with a lousy tie tack. ◆

The Big Three Clothing Categories

You probably have a regular uniform of jeans, T-shirt, and sneakers. Or cut-offs, T-shirt, and sandals. Or Dockers, Gap T-shirt, and Hush Puppies. But the day will come before too long (if it hasn't already) when you'll be required to wear something else.* For example, you might receive an invitation in the mail with the words "Black tie," "White tie," or "Black-tie Optional." Rather than stand before your closet in quiet desperation, read on.

Most people recognize three categories of clothing: *casual, semiformal,* and *formal.* Trying to define them is a bit like trying to define *inexpensive, moderate,* and *expensive* in relation to restaurant prices. The boundaries are fuzzy and constantly subject to debate. In fact, one could argue that there are really

---

* Prudent pointers on proper attire have also been provided in previous chapters. You may wish to peruse pages 48–49, 159, and 220.

How Rude!

fourteen categories which, in descending order of dressiness, are:

14. coronation stuffy formal

13. inaugural populist formal

12. white-tie ultraformal

11. black tie

10. lowbrow formal

9. Hollywood formal

8. high semiformal

7. traditional semiformal

6. nontraditional warm-climate semiformal

5. dressy casual

4. standard casual

3. grungy casual

2. grungy, and

1. "Where do you think you're going dressed like that?"

But we'll stick to the Big Three.

CASUAL

Generally speaking, *casual* refers to your nicer everyday clothes—the types of things you'd wear to school, the dentist, a recital, and your mom's office. These include khakis, sport shirts, sweaters, slacks, blouses, and skirts.

Most people allow themselves one or more categories of dress below casual—the kinds of things you'd wear to clean out the basement, mow the lawn, or hang around the house or the beach, including T-shirts, jeans, cutoffs, and tank tops.

Parents are usually satisfied to be seen at the supermarket or the doctor's office with children in casual dress. Casual clothes don't have to mean casual manners.

SEMIFORMAL

To most people, *semiformal* means dresses for girls, suits and ties for boys. (The arguments begin when someone asks "Well, then, what do you call it when a boy wears a navy blue blazer, a white shirt, a tie, gray flannel slacks, and dress shoes?" Call it "spiffy" and leave it at that.) Thus, teenagers would wear semiformal clothes to school dances, fancy dinners out, job interviews in the business world, etc.

Parents may require semiformal dress when taking their children to the opera, the office Christmas party, a worship service, or to meet their friends.

FORMAL

Formal refers to long dresses for girls and black tie for boys. Formal is harder to define for girls than for boys. This is because the fashion industry changes the lengths, colors, fabrics, and styles of women's clothing almost daily. For men, *black tie* means formal evening wear—black dinner jackets with the shiny lapels, white shirts with studs instead of buttons, black pants with zippy stripes running down the sides, cummerbunds, black bow ties, shiny black shoes—you know the look. One would never, ever wear this during the daytime.

Clothes-Minded

Even more formal for evening wear is *white tie*. This is the outfit that makes you look like a butler. You trade in the black tie for a white one and wear a long jacket with tails.

Formal wear during the day is called *morning dress*. This doesn't mean you have to put on a dress. It means wearing a *cutaway*—a long coat with striped gray trousers. This is what you'd wear if you were an usher at a formal daytime wedding.

Black-tie Optional indicates that the hosts couldn't make up their minds what they wanted. This shouldn't be confused with Clothing Optional.

In general, formal wear isn't considered appropriate for young men under the age of 18, so why are we even discussing it?

The Three Categories of Dress

Casual

Semiformal

Formal

How Rude!

"I hate wearing ties. Does etiquette say I have to wear them? What purpose do they serve?"

Historically, etiquette has said a great deal about clothing, most of which may be summarized by one simple statement: *The more uncomfortable, the better.* This has been demonstrated down through the ages by such bizarre inventions as powdered wigs, corsets, suits of armor, wool underwear, lederhosen, thongs, bustles, high-heeled shoes with pointy toes—and neckties.

Ties serve absolutely no purpose.* So how did they come about? In the 1660s, Croatian soldiers wore scarves around their necks. Nobody seems to know why. The French thought this a delightful touch, and soon began to sport long, knotted-at-the-neck scarves themselves. The fad spread to England, where Charles II made it a fashion staple of the court. The citizens of London, who had just endured a great plague and fire, needed something to take their minds off of death and destruction. Neckties provided it, and the rest, as they say, is history.

Men began wearing neckties for formal, ceremonial, and business-oriented occasions. As a result, ties came to symbolize respect and professionalism. Of course, this was all arbitrary. If history had gone a little differently, wearing a dollop of molasses on your nose could just as easily have been the means of conveying such a message.

Today, etiquette doesn't require you to dress up in stiff formal clothes and be uncomfortable. It requires you to dress appropriately. And that means making sure that the symbolism of your clothes is in keeping with the occasion. Thus, it's just as much an error to wear a jacket and tie to a swim class as it is to wear a bathing suit to church or temple.

Formality doesn't have to be boring or uncomfortable. You can always add a dash of your own individuality to any outfit. Try a splash of color or re-interpret an old symbol in a new and unique way. For example, I once wore a white, double-breasted linen suit with a delicate green pinstripe to an outdoor summer wedding. Only instead of a conventional shirt and tie, I wore a white shirt open at the neck, with a light orange knit tie loosely knotted like an ascot. I can't tell you how many marriage proposals this generated. ◆

---

* Although in a hurricane you could always use one to lash yourself to a tree.

School Uniforms

Clothes-Minded

Should children and teenagers be required to wear uniforms in school? (That is, other than jeans, T-shirts, and baseball caps?) Depends on who you ask. Some school authorities have decided that the only thing wrong with our educational system is the way kids dress. So, instead of dealing with crumbling buildings, overworked teachers, inadequate resources, and parental apathy; instead of demanding that communities and politicians address the relationship between poverty, crime, drugs, dysfunctional families, and the discipline and learning problems of youth, what do they do? They send parents and kids on a shopping spree to Wal-Mart.

Proponents of uniforms claim that academic performance increases, and disciplinary problems decrease, when schools make kids dress alike. This may be true. *But it's not because of the uniforms.* It's because schools that require standardized dress are likely to be schools where teachers and administrators respect students and expect them to behave responsibly, where parents are involved in their children's education, where conflict resolution and peer mediation programs are in place, and where community values are articulated and enforced—in short, where the school climate is based on the highest principles of good manners. If you took away the flannel pants, those schools would function just as well (although kids might complain about their legs being cold).

Children and teens opposed to school uniforms claim that they infringe upon their inalienable rights to life, liberty, and the pursuit of designer labels. Fashion, they say, is a means of self-expression—it's their very individuality. What some of these libertarians overlook is that freedom of dress, like other freedoms, must be exercised responsibly. The role of fashion in determining school pecking orders can be so extreme that kids spend more time each day choosing outfits than doing homework. Families that can barely put food on their table buy $150 sneakers so their child won't be a social outcast. When the symbolism of clothing is used to convey disrespect, promote snobbery, exclude, and embarrass, this is neither well-mannered nor conducive to a positive school climate.

Ultimately, the issue of school uniforms is one of politics, pedagogy, and power, not etiquette. If students don't want to be dressed alike, they should stop shooting each other over their clothes and stop judging each other by the price of their jeans. And if school authorities want to do a makeover, let them do it on the school rather than on the student.

HATS IN SCHOOL

You may have heard that a number of schools are banning baseball caps inside the building. Your own school might be among them. Some students

How Rude!

are asking "Does this violate our rights? Should we take the school board to court?" These students are missing the point. This isn't a legal issue, it's an *etiquette* issue.

Baseball caps are grand. They're functional, jaunty, and, when worn with the visor to the rear, they make you look like your head's on backwards. Personally, I'm all for them—just not in school.

Why not? *Because etiquette demands that gentlemen remove their hats when they are indoors.* This makes sense. Hats were designed to:

1. keep your head warm
2. protect you from sun and precipitation
3. keep your hair from blowing all over creation, and
4. hide baldness.

Since you're not yet follicularly challenged, your only justification for wearing a hat would be to protect you from the elements. Unless your school has no roof, it would be inappropriate to wear a hat in the classroom.

Your school may have additional reasons for not wanting students to wear hats indoors. For one thing, a hat prevents teachers from seeing your eager little face. It's not very rewarding to teach a class of visors. Caps also make it hard for teachers to identify students when they raise their hands. It depersonalizes the learning environment if students are referred to as Bulls, CAT, John Deere, and No Fear.

Your school may also be concerned about gang warfare. The color or tilt of a cap can be used to identify oneself as a member of a particular gang, or to challenge someone in another gang. Wear the wrong cap and you could end up getting beaten or shot. This is disruptive to the educational process. If nobody is allowed to wear caps, it eliminates the problem—at least within the school building.

The final reason for banning baseball caps in schools is a practical one: As your head fills with knowledge, it must have room to expand.

"I know you're not supposed to wear hats at church or inside someone's house, but is it okay to wear them inside stores and other public places where nobody knows you?"

Once and for all, here are the rules about hats:

A gentleman, regardless of his age, is expected to take off his hat indoors. Indoors means houses, places of worship, restaurants, stores, elevators,

406

theaters, schools, airports, trains, tanning salons, etc. This is considered a sign of respect. The only exceptions are:

1. A gentleman may wear his hat at indoor sporting events such as hockey games or wrestling matches, even while brawling.

2. A gentleman may keep his hat on in spaces which, while indoors, serve "outdoor" functions (e.g., a shopping mall concourse, train station platform, or glass-sheltered bus stop).

3. A gentleman may keep his head covered indoors if the traditions of his religion require it.

A lady may keep her hat on indoors (even in churches, restaurants, and private homes) provided she is dressed up in formal daytime clothes. Hats worn on these occasions usually look like fruit baskets or nesting birds. Ladies may also wear hats during dressy evening events. These hats are more elegant. The exceptions for women are:

1. A lady may not wear a hat indoors at her own home.

2. A lady may not wear a baseball cap indoors. This is because baseball caps are considered unisex and women wearing them must abide by the same rules that apply to men. ◆

Clothes-Minded

Well-Mannered Warnings

How do you tell someone that his fly is open? Or that her skirt is caught in her underwear, revealing her Jockeys for Her to the world? Or that a friend has unwittingly committed some other sartorial slip-up?

Carefully and discreetly, as follows.

If you know the person very well, you can say (mix-and-match as appropriate):

"Sweetums,		*fly*		*full of lint."*
"Honeybunch,		*zipper*		*undone."*
"Darling,	*your*	*bellybutton*	*is*	*falling off."*
"Dogface,		*slip*		*showing."*
"Dad,		*strap*		*coming apart."*

If you don't know the person well (or at all) and the problem is non-embarrassing, you can tell him or her regardless of your sex. This would apply to things like buttons about to fall off, belts caught in car doors, labels showing, etc.

If the problem is of an intimate or personal nature (i.e., involving clothing or body parts considered "private"), it's best to have someone of the same sex deliver the news. This lessens the embarrassment quotient. Thus, a male could approach another male on a subway and say:

"Excuse me, sir, in case you weren't aware of it, I thought you might like to know that your fly is open."

If, however, you're a male and you see a woman in need of a private word, you can go up to an approachable-looking female and say:

"Excuse me, Ma'am, I wondered if you'd feel comfortable letting that woman know that her skirt is caught in her undergarments."

Braces

If you wear braces, you've probably already been the butt of jokes. Your friends make fun of you because exhibiting extreme cruelty towards peers is one of the favorite leisure activities of the young and the restless.*

It's only natural that braces draw a certain amount of attention. Adults are famous for such stunning observations as "Oh, you got braces." This is not said out of rudeness, it's said out of shock. They see the bulk of a family's financial assets in a child's mouth and think *There but for the grace of an overbite go I.*

When your peers call you "tinsel teeth" or hum the *Jaws* theme in your honor, don't take the bait. Flash a sparkling smile and say "Yes, I'm so glad I've gotten braces. My teeth will be beautiful." By placing subtle emphasis on the word "my," you can suggest the obvious implication without being rude.

As a wearer of braces, however, you have certain responsibilities. You must conduct all maintenance tasks in private. This means never removing or installing retainers at the dinner table, in the classroom, or anyplace else where spectators are present. Equipment should be kept out of sight and therefore out of mind. Would you want to have your grandfather's false teeth staring at you from his butter plate all through dinner?

"Is it okay to ask someone about their braces? Or is that like asking someone about a disability?"

Wearing braces isn't considered a disability, except in the presence of saltwater taffy. Polite inquiries ("Who's your orthodontist?" "How long

---

* It's my sincere hope that this book will cut down on that deplorable practice.

do you have to wear them?") are perfectly appropriate for casual conversation among peers and/or fellow sufferers, er, wearers. ◆

Umbrellas

Teenagers don't seem to use umbrellas much. Maybe it's because they're more rain-resistant than adults. Or maybe it's because they figure *Why bother? When I take one it never rains. And when I don't, it does! So I can't win either way.* True, true. But just in case you do find yourself with an umbrella in the middle of a downpour, here are some *parapluie* pointers:

Try not to poke anyone's eye out. If you're carrying an umbrella, particularly on a crowded sidewalk, you need to constantly adjust its height, tilt, and wind expansion vector so you don't gouge an eyeball or collide with another umbrella. Watching a procession of hundreds of bobbing umbrellas on a crowded sidewalk can be quite inspiring, as it reminds the viewer of what humans can accomplish through cooperation. It's also an excellent exercise for developing hand-eye coordination.

Unfurl your umbrella *after* you step outside. Most buildings have awnings or overhangs that permit you to do this without getting wet. You've probably heard that it's unlucky to open an umbrella indoors. This has nothing to do with superstition. Rather, it has to do with the reaction you'll incur from the innocent bystander whose cheek you stab. When carrying an umbrella indoors, keep it close to you.

Know how to share. When the umbrella is used to shield more than one person, it should be held by the taller of the two, unless one person enjoys walking with his or her arm extended at full mast. It's perfectly fine to offer shelter to a stranger. Particularly one you hope to know better.

Know how to shake. Humans shaking water off of their umbrellas should follow the same rules as dogs shaking water off of their coats, namely:

1. Do it away from people.
2. Do it outside. When approaching a building or residence that has an overhang, shake the umbrella before entering. In a public building such as a mall or a bank, you may also shake it indoors if the building has an entry vestibule or rubber-floored area clearly intended as a transition between outside and inside. Umbrellas shouldn't be shaken once you've stepped into a private residence or restaurant. Instead, look for an umbrella stand or ask your host or maitre d' where it would be best to berth your bumbershoot.

CHAPTER QUIZ

How Rude!

1. *Tight clothes shouldn't be worn by teenagers because:*
    a) they cut off circulation
    b) they take too long to wiggle in and out of
    c) they make parents insanely jealous.

2. *You have a clothing allowance of $100 a month. The best way to spend it is on:*
    a) candy
    b) a pair of John Lennon's underwear
    c) overpriced designer items that will be out of fashion in three weeks.

3. *You arrive at a school dance to discover that you are waaaay overdressed. Your best bet is to:*
    a) crawl under the refreshments table
    b) grab the school banner and turn it into a toga
    c) find a kid wearing VERY baggy pants and ask if you can jump in.

4. *The purpose of a tie is to:*
    a) make you late for dressy occasions
    b) keep your Adam's Apple from dropping down your throat
    c) secure your head to your body in the event of high winds.

5. *Your school has just announced that all students must wear a uniform. The proper response is to:*
    a) refuse to wash yours
    b) wear your Spiderman pajamas underneath it
    c) dye it pink and say your dog did it.

6. *Your friend's family has invited you to spend a weekend with them at a nudist camp. As a first-time guest, it's best to bring:*
    a) a bathing suit
    b) a bathrobe
    c) the bare minimum.

13

Ahh, Ahh, Ahh—CHOOOOOO!!!!

Body Talk, Hygiene, and Disgusting Habits

A-CHOO!!

The body is a marvelous, miraculous invention. For centuries, it has inspired great works of art, dance, literature, and Spandex. It's capable of breathtaking feats of skill and endurance. Is there anything else on the planet that can do a three-and-a-half double-reverse gainer, leap across a stage while singing Italian, scarf down 14 Big Macs at a sitting—and then go home to reproduce itself? Yes, bodies should be celebrated and well cared for. They are nature's finest work.

Some people feel that because bodily functions are "natural," it's okay to exhibit them in public. Well, earthquakes, monsoons, and eating one's off-spring are natural occurrences, too. But that doesn't mean we want to witness them in our daily lives. If ever.

How Rude!

There's no reason to feel embarrassed or ashamed about the natural noises and emissions of your body. But, as the old saying reminds us, there's a time and a place for everything. Knowing when and where is the key to keeping a well-mannered body.

Bodily functions tend to fall into two categories:

1. **Things you do to your body.** Usually these are things you can control (picking your nose, cracking your knuckles, going to the bathroom), although your ability to do so may vary with your age and how many sodas you've had to drink.

2. **Things your body does to you.** These are events and occurrences (sneezing, yawning, hiccuping) over which you have little or no control.

Etiquette divides these categories further. There are things that befall people in public that, while natural, are considered socially unacceptable. Farts, for example, Do Not Exist as far as society is concerned.* They are acknowledged by neither perpetrator nor bystander. Burps, on the other hand, are acknowledged by the burper ("Excuse me") but not the burpee. Other bodily trumpetings, such as sneezes, are acknowledged by sneezer and sneezee alike ("Gesundheit." "Thank you.")

Bodily functions carried out in the privacy of one's bedroom or bathroom are just that—private. Therefore, in the eyes of society, they Do Not Exist. As such, they are nobody's business. Certain politicians would be well-advised to remember this most basic form of good manners.

If this seems a bit confusing, don't be alarmed. We'll take (almost) all of the things bodies do and consider them one by one. But please, let's try to be mature about it. Hee, hee, hoo, ha, ha.

Things You Do to Your Body

NOSE PICKING

Digital roto-rooting is a natural, necessary maintenance task one must perform to keep the breathing apparatus in tip-top form. In fact, archaeologists (people who like to dig) have established that nose picking began in ancient Egypt during the Pharocious Period, which occurred approximately 3000 B.C. (Before Cable).

---

* The word "fart" is today considered vulgar by many people. But it wasn't always so. Chaucer and other early English writers used the word often and without shame. It even appeared in the respected *Oxford English Dictionary* until the onset of the Victorian era.

All that sand blowing across Egyptian mucous membranes led to major booger production. This was a problem for the workers who were building the Pyramids, since they had to stop every few minutes to excavate the Nubian nostrils. It also upset the Pharaohs, since the mucous mining was putting Pyramid construction waaaay behind schedule.

Ahh, Ahh, Ahh— CHOOOOOO!!

So Queen Nasaltiti, the wife of King Toot-and-Come-In, decreed that people picking their noses in public would have a 2,000-ton pyramid stone dropped on their proboscises. As a result of this edict, the citizens of Egypt learned that it was neither polite nor healthy to pick their noses in public. (This is why so many Egyptians are depicted with flattened noses on ancient vases.)

It's practically and aesthetically wise to navigate one's nasal passages in private. Etiquette demands the use of a handkerchief, which is later washed, or a tissue, which is subsequently discarded in an official waste receptacle. Because so few people today carry handkerchiefs or tissues, avoid running your hands along the undersides of desks and car seats.

TEETH FLOSSING

Let's now turn to flossing conventions. No, these are not large gatherings where people discuss the relative merits of waxed vs. unwaxed dental tape. Rather, they're rules that govern the use of said tape for the purpose of removing chow crumbs from between one's teeth. Here are all the dental dictums you need to know:

1. Never pick your teeth or floss your fangs in public.
2. If you floss your teeth as a guest in someone's home, be kind and clean the mirror.
3. Don't floss your teeth before having sex. This is not a joke. This is a genuine Safer Sex Health Bulletin. It's meant neither to encourage you to engage in sex nor to abstain from flossing, but simply to apprise you of the facts. HIV, which most scientists believe causes AIDS, is transmitted via the exchange of bodily fluids. Flossing often results in small cuts to and bleeding from the gums, which may put you and/or your partner at risk.

ZIT POPPING

Pimples are properly popped in private.* Squeeze with eeze, but pleeze, keep it a secret between you and your mirror. And wipe said mirror off when you're done.

---

* Some people say that they shouldn't be popped at all. But I have yet to meet anyone who has ever followed that advice.

How Rude!

SPITTING

It used to be perfectly acceptable to spit in public. Back in the 17th century, when floors were made of dirt or stone or rushes, people even spit indoors. But as furnishings and floor coverings became fancier, anyone with a hankering for hawking was expected to hang on to a hankie.

Samuel Pepys, who kept a diary during that time,* wrote on January 28, 1661, of an experience he had while attending the theater. He was sitting in a dark corner when a "lady spit backwards upon me by mistake, not seeing me; but after seeing her to be a very pretty lady, I was not troubled at all."

Times have changed. Most people today would be deeply troubled if they were spat upon, no matter how pretty the lady. If you need to spit and a spittoon isn't available, your best bet is to go to a private spot such as a bathroom and spit into the toilet. If privacy isn't an option, your next best bet is to spit (when no one is looking) into a handkerchief or someplace where others won't have to see it or come into contact with it. This doesn't mean behind the bookshelf. It means in the gutter, down a storm drain, or onto the grass.

In an emergency, such as an open-mouthed head-on collision with a fly, you may either swallow the tasty little critter for extra protein or spit it out. The edicts of etiquette are waived as long as you're outdoors and you aim away from people.

Never spit into a water fountain. And if you ever spit out the window of a moving vehicle, make sure the car behind you isn't a convertible.

On occasion, you may be asked to spit. People who issue these requests are called *dentists*. It would be rude and leave a bad taste in your mouth to reject their kind invitation. So spit away. Just do it in the shiny round sink with the funny noises and water swirling round—not on the dentist.

Finally, if you should need help remembering these rules, here's a song from my childhood, sung to the tune of that great refrain from the opera *Carmen:*

> *Tor-e-a-dor,*
> *Don't spit on the floor,*
> *Use a cus-pi-dor.*
> *That's what it's for.*

---

* This is a famous diary, and you may read it if you like. It's called *The Diary of Samuel Pepys* (duh). When you ask for it at the library, don't say "Do you have a copy of *The Diary of Samuel PEPISS*?" Instead, say "Do you have a copy of *The Diary of Samuel PEEPS*?" The librarian will be impressed that you've pronounced the name correctly.

TRUE STORIES FROM THE
MANNERS FRONTIER

Great Expectorations

Ahh, Ahh,
Ahh—
CHOOOOOO!!

For some people, spitting is a nervous habit. They have a windup longer than a major league pitcher's as they dredge the spittle up from their toes. HAGGGGHHHHKKKK, HAGGGGHHHHKKKK, HAGGGGHHHHKKKK, PTOOOEY. A projectile wings through the air and lands splat on the sidewalk, where it waits for somebody to step in it.

You can't possibly win friends and influence people if you spit in public. Just the other day, when I was riding the bus, the rear door opened. A fellow passenger poked his head out and dribbled a stream of drool onto the sidewalk. I suppose I should have been grateful that he didn't do it inside the bus. But I'd rather he hadn't done it at all.

SCRATCHING

If the itch is on your arm, leg, shoulder, or back, go ahead and scratch. Just try not to look like a monkey. But if the itch is in a more private area, front or rear, you may not scratch in public.* Times like these call for covert scratching techniques.

GOING TO THE BATHROOM

Every human being is allotted three years during which his or her bathroom goings-on are a matter of public record. Ideally, these should be the first three years. After that, your activities in this domain should be a matter of no one's concern but your own.

Schools are the biggest violators of this rule. Children shouldn't be forced to reveal the status of their bladder to the entire class by having to ask the teacher for permission to go to the bathroom. They should be allowed to slip out

Covert Scratching, Posterior Itch

---

* This rule is suspended for baseball players, who are paid large sums of money to scratch their privates in public.

How Rude!

of the room discreetly, take care of their need, and come right back. Since they aren't, is it any wonder that so many American adults feel compelled to announce their bathroom comings and goings to anyone who will listen?

"Nature calls, heh, heh."
"I'm going to the john."
"I gotta take a whiz."

Here's how to be on your best bathroom behavior:

If you're in a group of people and you need to relieve yourself, don't declare your intentions. Simply get up, say "Excuse me," and leave. Most people are imaginative enough to figure out where you've gone. If you're not sure where the bathroom is, ask your host, a friend, or a waiter. When you return, make sure your hands are dry in case you have to shake hands with anybody.

Put the toilet seat up, boys. (Unless you have to sit down.) In case the logic behind this has never been explained to you, it's because if you don't, the seat is likely to get wet. The next person to use the bathroom will either get a wet behind or be required to clean up after you. When you're through, put the seat back down. If you're in a public bathroom and don't want to touch the seat, you can use the side of your shoe to lift it. This is an excellent exercise for improving one's balance, overall body tone, and hamstrings.

Protect your seat. If you're in a public bathroom and need to sit down and there's no toilet seat protector dispenser at hand, you can tear off three strips of toilet tissue to place on the seat. If the toilet paper is of the single-sheet variety, you'd better not be in a hurry, because you're going to have to balance about 20 pieces.

Wash your hands. Something like 94 percent of all Americans claim to wash their hands after going to the bathroom. But scientists have discovered that only 60–70 percent actually do wash their hands. How, you might ask, did they discover that? By stationing someone in the bathroom to count.*

These fascinating facts aside, *not* washing your hands is a prime means of contracting various diseases that can make you very ill or even very dead. No joke! So, for your own health as well as that of your fellow planeteers, give your hands the old scrub-a-dub after you go to the bathroom. This doesn't mean waving them in the vicinity of a faucet. It means energetic rubbing with soap and water.

---

* This, curious reader, is called *research*. Next question: How many of the people observed told building security about the weirdo hanging around the bathroom with a clipboard?

As you leave the bathroom, ponder this: What's the point of washing your hands if, as you open the door, you have to grab the door pull that the slob before you who didn't wash his hands just touched? You see the problem. And here's the solution: Public rest rooms should be required to have little towelette dispensers right by the door. Upon exiting, you'd grab a towelette and use it to open the door. And when you were through, you'd deposit the used towelette in the receptacle provided for that purpose right outside the door. As these devices become ubiquitous throughout the land, just remember where you first heard about the idea.

Ahh, Ahh, Ahh— CHOOOOOO!!

Never pee in a pool. It's rude to litter. Besides, some people put a chemical in their pools that turns the water dark if it comes into contact with urine. "Oh, that's just a legend," you say. Are you willing to put it to the test?

If you're traveling and you come across a bathroom, always use it. You never know when you'll see one again.

If, before you go out with your family, your parents ask "Do you have to use the bathroom?" always say "No." To do otherwise would violate one of the most sacred parent-child covenants.

Flush. Unless you're a guest in a home with sewer problems and your host has specifically instructed you otherwise.

"What do you do if you use the bathroom at somebody's house and really stink it up?"

Hold your nose? Americans are so finicky when it comes to odors associated with the body. If God hadn't meant us to smell each other, he wouldn't have issued schnozzolas. Still, you'd like to leave the bathroom in the same olfactory condition in which you found it. That's because you're a considerate guest.

Since going to the bathroom is a private activity which falls into the Does Not Exist category, so would taking a discreet look under the sink to see if there's a can of air freshener available. If so, a quick spray should do the trick. If there's no can in the can, there's not much you can do except leave the fan on or otherwise ensure maximum air flow.

Don't be embarrassed. There's no such thing as immaculate evacuation. And, with any luck, someone else will use the bathroom after you, thus lengthening the list of suspects.

Incidentally, it's silly to run water to mask the sounds you make. Good manners already prevent anyone from hearing them. And all it does is make people think *He's running the water to try to cover up those noises he's making.* ◆

KNUCKLE CRACKING

Cracking your knuckles is the same as scraping your fingernails across a blackboard. It sends shivers down the spine. Therefore, it's to be done only when you're alone or in the company of like-minded individuals. But if your knuckles swell to the size of golf balls or your fingers fall off someday, don't say you weren't warned.

GUM CHEWING

Smack, chomp, clop, POP! How attractive. Gum chewing offers the imaginative teen endless opportunities for grossing people out. You can chew so loudly that it sounds like a regiment of soldiers marching through mud. You can pull out long strands and swing them to and fro like a pendulum. You can fill the air with sweet, noxious fumes. You can blow bubbles that burst in your face and adhere to your nose and cheeks. Of course, this is what makes gum chewing so much fun. Feel free to indulge whenever you're in the company of fellow masticators.

But if you don't want to gum up your reputation for good manners, here are some suggestions to chew on:

Be discreet. While some arbiters of etiquette insist that gum chewing is never acceptable in public, I say it is—*if* others in the vicinity can't tell you're doing it. Clandestine gum chewing falls into the realm of etiquette offenses that Do Not Exist.

To accomplish this deception, don't actually *chew* your gum. Instead, fondle it with your tongue. Wedge it in your cheek. Turn it over with your teeth. But no smacking, blowing, pulling, or popping allowed. If you find it impossible to restrain yourself, it may mean that you were a cow in a previous life. Seek professional help.

Never spit out or drop your gum on the ground. The reason for this is obvious: In today's ecology-conscious world, gum should be recycled. Do you think someone else is going to want to chew it if it's been on the ground? Also, people are liable to step on it, and we all know what a pain that can be.

Never dispose of gum by sticking it under a seat or desk. This is very rude because when other people drop off *their* boogers and gum, they'll get *yours* all over their fingers. Gum that has expired should be placed in a wastebasket or trash barrel. If the container isn't lined with a plastic bag, wrap the gum in paper or tissue first.

TRUE STORIES FROM THE
MANNERS FRONTIER

Ahh, Ahh,
Ahh—
CHOOOOOO!!

Confessions of a Secret Snacker

I was a stealth gum chewer all through my school days. I went through a Dentyne period, a Juicy Fruit phase, and a Doublemint obsession (when I wanted to double my fun). I tried chewing bubble gum, but to my great shame I was never able to blow bubbles. It took many years in therapy to work this through and become the Carefree guy I am today.

I also used to snack on peanut M&M's in class. Once, the bag broke and a waterfall of M&M's came pouring out of the two drainage holes in the bottom of my desk. But that's another story.

NAIL BITING

In a perfect world, there would be no nail biting. People would be serene, life's pressures would be manageable, and children wouldn't labor under a crush of anxiety and unrealistic expectations.

If nail biting must be done at all, it should be relegated to the private realm. The problem, of course, is that nail biting (and its cousin, cuticle picking) is a nervous habit. You may be several minutes into the activity before you even realize you're doing it.

Since it's rude to mutilate oneself, you should try to break the habit. If you're a chronic nail biter, there are many things you can do to help yourself stop. Wear gloves. Try hypnosis. Put Band-aids around your fingertips. Sit on your hands. Join a 12-Step support group like Cuticles Anonymous. Keep your mouth busy by chewing gum. Keep your hands busy with a hand squeezer or those silver Chinese anti-stress balls. Apply that foul-tasting chemical that's supposed to discourage nail biting (check with your pharmacist). Put lotion on your hands to keep them smooth; this minimizes the little dried skin flaps that are so appealing for picking. Or, better yet, look for the sources of stress in your life and see what you might do to reduce or eliminate them.

How Rude!

TRUE STORIES FROM THE MANNERS FRONTIER

Eeeyouch!

As a recovering nail biter myself, I am well aware that stopping this noxious habit is easier said than done. But the consequences of not trying can be severe.

Once, in my youth, I got an infected finger from chomping on my claws. I had to go to the doctor to have it lanced. The physician stuck a sharp metal V-shaped spike into my finger, at which point I promptly fainted. Fortunately, he broke my fall by grabbing my hair. But that's another story.

COMBING HAIR AND APPLYING MAKEUP

The brushing of hair and applying of makeup should be done in private or semiprivate settings. Private settings include your bathroom, bedroom, or boudoir; semiprivate settings include public rest rooms and cars. Lipstick may be applied at the table in a restaurant. Never comb or brush your hair in the vicinity of food. Locks in the lox spoil the appetite.

PRODUCING FRENCH HORN-LIKE SOUNDS FROM UNDER ONE'S ARMS

This should only be done during band practice. People who make popping sounds by placing a finger in their mouth may join in if invited.

Things Your Body Does To You

Some of these involuntarily events should be acknowledged by perpetrators and bystanders alike. Others should be acknowledged by perpetrators only. Still others should be ignored by all. Read on to learn which is which and why.

SNEEZING

"Ahh, ahhh, ahhhhh—CHOOOOOOO!!!!"

The responsibility of the sneezer is to cover his nose with a handkerchief. (It never hurts to include the mouth, too.) Don't study what you've produced, no matter how proud you feel. If you don't have a handkerchief or tissue, create a little tent with your hands by putting your fingertips together. Place it over your nose and mouth like a gas mask, then sneeze into that. (Next time, carry a handkerchief!) Ideally, you'll be able to wash your hands immediately following the sneeze. If this isn't possible, use clandestine cleanup strategies. (Shaking someone's hand doesn't count.) Wait a suitable length of time so that when you eventually place your hands in your pockets, or rub them on the nubby sofa cushion, nobody will associate these actions with the sneeze.

The sneeze observer's responsibility is to convey sympathy. This is done by saying "God bless you," "Gesundheit," "Que Dieu te benisse," and the like. The sneezer may then respond "Thank you," "Danke," or "Merci."

Ahh, Ahh, Ahh— CHOOOOOO!!

Serial sneezes. It's not unusual for hay fever sufferers to sneeze dozens of times in a row. If you witness a display such as this, don't acknowledge more than two or three sneezes. Otherwise, the hapless hayseed will feel self-conscious, and you and she will spend the day saying:

"Ah-choo!!!"
"Gesundheit."
"Thank you."
"Ah-choo!!!"
"Gesundheit."
"Thank you."
"Ah-choo!!!"
"Gesundheit."
"Thank you."

Advanced Body Etiquette Tip #1:
If you must sneeze in the vicinity of a buffet,
always turn your head.

Instead, smile sympathetically after your first or second "Gesundheit" and say "Hay fever, huh?" The sufferer will nod gratefully and continue to sneeze.

Sudden sneezes. Sometimes a sneeze comes upon you before you can produce your handkerchief. If that happens, the proper thing to do is to whip it out anyway. You can use it to mop up and, in the tradition of better late than never, at least it shows that you meant well.

NOSE BLOWING*

When you blow your nose in public, do so into a handkerchief or tissue. Try not to honk. Refrain from strenuous wiping during the final cleanup.

---

* Although nose blowing is a voluntary action, it's done in response to something your body has done to you. Hence its placement in this part of the chapter. In case you were wondering.

Otherwise, it looks as though you're unscrewing your nose. If you're discreet about carrying out this perfectly normal function, others will respond by not noticing.

How Rude!

TRUE STORIES FROM THE
MANNERS FRONTIER
He Blew It

Once upon a time, I had a farm. And on that farm there was a—well, that's beside the point.

The point is that I was sitting on the veranda one afternoon, surveying the rolling hills and pastoral beauty, when a guest walked to the edge of the porch, placed his index fingers on both sides of his nose, and blew. Two streams of you-know-what cascaded to the ground.

I suppose he was overcome by all the natural splendor. I was overcome by nausea.

THROWING UP

Throwing up is like growing up. Both activities, through no fault of your own, sometimes create messes that others have to clean up for you. An unscheduled upchuck presents well-mannered persons with a unique paradox. On the one hand, etiquette insists that a ralph-a-rama be ignored. On the other hand, it's impossible to ignore.

Here's how these seemingly irreconcilable demands may be met:

- If you make it to the bathroom in time, the entire event is overlooked. It took place offscreen and therefore Did Not Exist in any social sense. Concerned parents, hosts, and/or close friends may inquire discreetly "Are you all right? Is there anything I can do?" either through the door or afterwards. No such remarks are permitted of others. Unless you're too sick to do so, you must remove any telltale traces from chin and bathroom before rejoining society.

- If you don't make it to the bathroom on time, you must appear wretched and allow yourself to be ushered to more comfortable and less vulnerable quarters. If possible, utter in deathbed tones "I'm sorry. I don't know what came over me. I feel just terrible about it." Meanwhile, any onlookers should act as if nothing happened. The host, relative, or concerned friend who must mop up the mess focuses on consoling you by saying:

"Don't you worry."
"It happens to everybody."

"You just lie down."

"I had fourteen children, so this doesn't bother me a bit."

The bottom line is: No rebuking for puking.

Ahh, Ahh, Ahh— CHOOOOOO!!

COUGHING

The lone cough, along with the minimal multiple cough, need not be recognized by cougher or coughee. The cougher must, however, make a loose fist with her hand and place it over her mouth.

Extended coughing fits may be acknowledged by asking the cougher if she's okay. Any inability on the cougher's part to answer indicates that she's not. At this point, you might want to consider the possibility that she may be . . .

CHOKING

Chokers not at risk of death (i.e., the soda went down the wrong way) should say "Excuse me," once they have recovered. Observers need not say anything.

Chokers turning blue in the face (i.e., those with chicken bones stuck in their windpipe) should point to their throat and hope that someone nearby knows the Heimlich maneuver. When breathing resumes, they should say "Thank you for saving my life."

The response "It was nothing," might be misconstrued. Therefore, it's better to simply say "You're welcome."

BURPING AND BELCHING

We are referring here to the involuntary burp. Those talented souls who can belch on command should do so in the barn and only in the company of like-minded individuals.

If you're the perpetrator of an accidental burp, place your hand to your mouth. (This confuses inattentive listeners into thinking they may have heard a cough, which is considered more socially acceptable than a burp.) Then say "Excuse me."

Advanced Body Etiquette Tip #2:
Belching contests are not permitted during the cadenza.

423

How Rude!

YAWNING

People yawn for one of three reasons:

1. They're tired.
2. They're bored.
3. They see someone else yawn.

Yawning is highly contagious. If you don't think this is true, watch someone yawn. I guarantee you'll soon be yawning yourself.

Cover your mouth when you yawn. Interesting as your uvula is, most people would just as soon not see it. It's also impolite to indicate your boredom with present company or proceedings. Your hand helps to disguise what the mouth cannot deny.

Yawners and yawnees alike need never comment on the event. However, if you're a guest and your host exhibits chronic yawning syndrome, you should say "My goodness, I had no idea it was so late. I really must be going." Then go.

STOMACH RUMBLINGS

The human digestive system was designed to growl during tests and other periods of silent prayer. Should your stomach ever attempt such a communication, adopt a tranquil, meditative expression. This suggests that the noise was either a figment of the listener's imagination or a paranormal acoustical phenomenon involving the ozone layer. Whatever it was, it clearly had nothing to do with you.

PASSING WIND

It sounds so lovely. The perfect thing to do on a summer day. You can just imagine a friend returning from an outing to the beach:

"Oh, we had a great time. Dale and I spent the afternoon surfing, listening to the waves, enjoying the breeze, and passing wind."

In case you didn't know it, "passing wind" is a euphemism for farting.* The release of bodily gas is nothing to be ashamed or embarrassed about. Chimneys smoke, kettles steam, and humans fart. It's the natural order of things.

Teenagers often see possibilities for humor, creativity, and social sanction in farts that would go right over the heads of most adults. One properly consummated fart is good for at least ten minutes of distraction in the average

---

* Because it pays to build an extensive vocabulary, other euphemisms for farting include "breaking wind," "passing gas," and "cutting the cheese."

classroom. At a sleepover, one good fart deserves another, and hours of entertainment can be derived from the production, analysis, and, believe it or not, lighting of farts.*

What does etiquette say about farting?

Speak no evil. Hear no evil. Smell no evil.

Perpetrators of, and witnesses to, vacated vapor must convey the following in their body language and facial expressions:

Perpetrator: *I didn't do that.*

Bystander 1: *I didn't hear that.*

Bystander 2: *I didn't smell that.*

This rules out behaviors such as giggling, groaning, fainting, fanning, and saying "EEEEE-yoooooo" while looking at the dog. Furthermore, it's absolutely forbidden to engage in conversations such as:

"Oooo-ooo, Brandon cut one."

"He who smelt it, dealt it."

"Oooo Brandon."

"I DIDN'T DO IT!"

"Did too."

"Did not."

"Did too."

"Did not."

Advanced Body Etiquette Tip #3:
Deny everything.

Thus, the only reaction anyone can have when a butt bomb goes off is: None. The first few seconds are the hardest. During this time, the perpetrator tries not to blush, and the bystanders try not to breathe. Once this initial period has passed, it's fine to roll down a window, make an unscheduled exit from the elevator, or suddenly remember an errand you have to run.

---

* Regrettably, this topic is beyond the scope of our discussion, but an excellent review of the literature in this area may be found in an article by Dr. Frederick Fumes, S.B.D., entitled "Combustion Properties of Natural Gas" (*International Journal of Petroleum Jelly,* January, 1988).

How Rude!

HICCUPING

The hiccup is a practical joke the body likes to play. You never get the hiccups when it's fourth-down-goal-to-go in the last ten seconds of the Superbowl and everybody's yelling their heads off. You always get them right after the teacher says "Class, I don't want to hear a peep out of anyone."

"Hic.

Hic.

Hic.

Hic."

The proper response for anyone in the presence of a hiccup is to ignore it. This is difficult, since hiccups are timed to go off just after you've forgotten about the last one. Nonetheless, the etiquette is to forgetiquette.

The hiccuper shall do nothing to draw attention to herself. If you wish to stand on your head, gargle, drink water upside down from a glass, eat a spoonful of sugar, hold your breath until you turn blue, and/or sing the National Anthem while a friend smacks you on the back, take it someplace private. Upon your return, be prepared for the assembled masses to be eagerly awaiting your next hiccup.

The hiccupee shall do nothing to focus attention on the hiccuper. This means no laughing, no fake hiccup echoes, and no trying to scare the hiccuper out of her wits.

HORMONAL HAPPENINGS

The male organ, especially during its owner's adolescence, often elects to stand up for itself at the most inconvenient times. Such "elections" should never be remarked upon or pointed out by witnesses. Other than for the embarrassed one, they Do Not Exist.

If you're of the gender for which the words "rise and shine" have special meaning in the morning, you may wish to avail yourself of those fashion styles designed as protective covering for adolescent boys, such as baggy pants and long flannel shirts that go down to your knees. One hopes that your parents and teachers will have the sensitivity not to insist that you tuck in your shirt.

"How do you tell someone they have body odor or bad breath?"

From upwind.

First, you should know the person or at least have a vested interest in his or her ability to go through life without offending those who are near or dear.

426

This category include friends, relatives, and people you must sit next to on a regular basis. It doesn't include strangers on the bus.

Second, the problem should be ongoing. If the whiff you sniff is situational—i.e., the person just finished cutting the lawn on a 110° day—don't say anything unless he's about to go on a date or you're really hard up for conversation.

Once you decide to break the news that someone's body or breath has the bouquet of swamp gas, keep in mind that few people enjoy being told that they stink. Therefore, you need to exercise utmost tact. Bring up the subject in private. There are several approaches you can take:

Ahh, Ahh, Ahh— CHOOOOOO!!

Direct: *"I hope you don't mind my saying this, but your breath is very strong."*

Indirect: *"You might want to get that jacket cleaned. I think it's picked up a very strong odor."*

Confidential: *"I sometimes have a problem with this myself, so I thought I'd let you know that you have body odor. There's this great new antiperspirant I've been using that lasts all day and is strong enough for a woman yet gentle enough for today's sensitive guy."* ◆

"Should you tell someone they have something stuck between their teeth?"

This question has plagued humankind since the dawn of time. Is it *our* responsibility to apprise others that they have spinach in their teeth, milk in their mustache, and boogers dangling from their nose? I say "Yes!"—for otherwise we are no different from the lowest animal.

If you're polite and discreet in pointing these things out, most people will be grateful, preferring a moment of embarrassment to a day of humiliation. If a bright-eyed, respectful youth came up to me and said "Excuse me, sir, but you have a roll of toilet paper trailing from your pants," I'd reply "Thank you for telling me, young sir" and hand him a gold coin.

So, by all means, if it shows, tell. Before you do, though, make sure it's correctable. There's no point in alerting someone to something they can't do anything about at the time—like a run in their stocking or a stain on their shirt. Also, for certain really personal or embarrassing things, you might, if you're not of the same gender as the target, ask someone who is to break the news.

Here's how to handle your garden-variety spinach-on-the-chin dilemma:

Let's say you're at Taco Bell with your 11-year-old brother and he's eating rather messily. It's fine to say "Excuse me, Ivan, but you have some salsa in

How Rude!

your beard." You can use this *Excuse me, but you have . . .* technique for just about anything. Sometimes it's helpful to point to the location of the offense on yourself. This way, instead of saying "Excuse me, but you have a dried booger hanging out of your left nostril," you can say "Excuse me, but you have a little something here" while gently touching your own left nostril.

Taking this one step further, many couples, through years of intimacy, develop sign language for alerting each other to errant dribbles. I can remember sitting at the dinner table as a child on occasions when we had company. Once in a while, a little bead of gravy would squat on my father's chin. I would watch with fascination, wondering how long it might remain in residence. But invariably, if I turned toward my mother, I would see her catch his eye and subtly brush her chin twice with a finger. My father would take his napkin and dab at the corresponding location on his face. Thus I learned the benefits of being in a relationship. ◆

 **TRUE STORIES FROM THE MANNERS FRONTIER**

The Price Is Right

Recently, I was waiting in line at the video store. The woman in front of me was wearing a beautiful silk scarf from Neiman-Marcus that cost $295. How did I know that? From the price tag. Good Samaritan that I am, I said "Excuse me, Ma'am. I wasn't sure if you knew, but the sales tag is still on your scarf." She gave me an icy stare and replied through pursed lips "Thank you."

Although it's pleasing when virtue is rewarded, I remained undaunted by the rebuff and set off to do another good deed. After all, the world is full of people with their flies open.

CHAPTER QUIZ

Ahh, Ahh, Ahh— CHOOOOOO!!

1. *It's okay to pick your nose in public as long as you:*
   a) wear white gloves
   b) raise your pinky
   c) do it one nostril at a time.

2. *You're paying rapt attention as your English teacher recites a poem by Emily Dickinson. An unpleasant odor wafts across your nasal radar screen, suggesting that one of your nearby classmates has passed wind. Do you:*
   a) jump out of your seat, fling open the windows, and shriek "AIR RAID!!"
   b) point at your neighbor and yell "Billy cut the cheese, Billy cut the cheese!" or
   c) ignore it, silently reminding yourself that "There but for the grace of baked beans go I"?

3. *Your mother asks you to pass some hors d'oeuvres at a party she's giving. You're standing in the hallway, conversing with a guest, the tray in your hands, when suddenly you get this wicked itch on your backside. Do you:*
   a) drop the tray, make gorilla sounds, and scratch energetically
   b) turn around, bend over, and say to the person "Excuse me, could you please scratch my butt?" or
   c) surreptitiously use the banister to massage your behind?

4. *You're at a family picnic in the park. Your cousin Cindy sits across from you and a couple of seats down. You notice that she has a big kernel of corn clinging to her chin. Do you:*
   a) say "Hey, everyone, look at the corn booger on Cindy's chin!"
   b) take out your slingshot and try to knock the kernel off with a pea, or
   c) catch Cindy's eye and discreetly point to your own chin?

14
I Beg My Pardon

Being Polite to Yourself

Here we've spent a whole book talking about how important it is to be polite to your family and friends, to teachers and employers, even to total strangers you'll never see again. But we've left out the one person for whom you should always be on your best behavior: *Yourself*.

What does it mean to be polite to yourself? Certainly it means saying "Excuse me" if you accidentally step on your toe. And getting up to give yourself a seat on a bus. But it also means being kind to yourself. Taking good care of yourself. Treating yourself with the same tolerance and understanding you extend towards others.

How do you know if you're treating yourself with respect and consideration? When you make a mistake, do you think *I'm such an idiot. How can I be so dumb? I can't do anything right!* If so, how rude! Do you ever look in a mirror and say *I'm so ugly. I hate the way I look!* If so, how rude! Do you ever do things that could get you into serious trouble or harm your health or body? If so, how rude!

Why should you be polite to yourself? For the same reasons you're polite to others: Because it feels good. Because it demonstrates respect. And because people will enjoy your company. (You *do* want to enjoy your own company, don't you?)

Many teenagers don't treat themselves with the kindness they deserve. If you're one of them, if you're constantly dissing and dismissing yourself, you need to stop being so rude and start being more courteous.

How can you do this? To find out, we surveyed hundreds of teenagers across the land. Except for one boy who said "I don't get offended, so it isn't necessary to be polite to myself," most teens who responded offered sensible suggestions for self-courtesy:

"I keep myself looking good."

"I take care of my hair."

"I brush my teeth."

"I do my nails."

"I wear nice clothes."

"I take showers."

"I exercise."

"I meditate."

"I eat good food once in a while."

"I don't smoke or do drugs."

"I give my body and mind rest."

"I compliment my looks."

"I set aside time to relax and think."

"I look both ways when crossing the street."

When you're frazzled and hassled, it's easy to let your most basic needs slide. Not sneakers and CDs, but exercise, proper nutrition, good hygiene, and plenty of rest. All of which help you to feel, be, and do your best.

There's a famous Latin saying: *mens sana in corpore sano.* It means *a sound mind in a sound body.* The early Romans recognized the importance of mental and physical hardiness. In fact, their system of educating the young—cold showers and lessons with Nero—was based on this concept. It's no wonder the Romans left so many lasting contributions to the world, such as togas and marinara sauce.

If you mean to leave your mark on the world, you must keep your mind and body in tip-top condition *(mens tiptopa in corpore tiptopo).* Here's how.

How Rude!

Exercise

It's a well-known fact that today's teenagers are in poorer physical condition than their parents and grandparents were when they were children. This is because prior generations had to get up to change channels. Advances in technology have made it easier for the youth of today to be less physically active. Exertion to them means surfing the Net. But the more energetic you are, the more energy you'll have. (This is called a *paradox*, which is Latin for *two ducks.*)

So unless you're already playing on a school team or working out or swimming laps, it's time to get the ticker ticking and the endorphins flowing.

As long as your doctor gives you the okay, get a strenuous aerobic workout for at least 20–30 minutes three times a week or more. Do some heavy-duty bike riding or inline skating. Jog. Run up and down a flight of stairs 40 times. In addition to your aerobic workout, take up a sport. Play basketball or tennis. Join a soccer or baseball league. Challenge your parents or siblings to a game of badminton or base running. And if you hate sports, go dancing (which counts as exercise as long as you're not just slow dancing). Or take long walks. If you make several nonstop window-shopping circuits of a major mall, that's a couple of miles right there.

The physical benefits of exercise are obvious, especially to those admiring your finely toned bod. But there are other benefits as well. Research shows that exercise reduces depression, generates feelings of well-being, promotes sound sleep, and enhances one's sex life. What more could you ask for?

Eat Right

This means making sure that your daily diet includes all four basic food groups: pizza, candy, nachos, and Coke.

Ha, ha. Just kidding. Machines need proper fuel in order to run properly. If you fill up on ice cream, or don't fill up at all, you're not going to have the energy you need to get through the day.

Check with your parents, physician, school nurse, or local library for the lowdown on healthy eating habits. There are four reasons why you should consume regular, balanced, nutritious meals:

1. You'll look good.
2. You'll feel good.
3. You'll live longer.
4. You'll be able to cheat with junk food.

Keep It Clean

The problem with hygiene is the word itself. It sounds so . . . sanitary. Like something you'd have to do with a clothespin on your nose when no one's looking. So let's come up with a new concept: *self-detailing.* Surely you deserve as much care as the family car. Before you set off for the day, pull in for a pit stop and run through your checklist:

I Beg My Pardon

- ❑ **BODY:** Washed? Sweet-smelling?
- ❑ **FACE:** Scrubbed? Shaved? Made-up?
- ❑ **HAIR:** Cleaned? Conditioned? Combed?
- ❑ **TEETH:** Brushed? Flossed? De-bugged?
- ❑ **FINGERNAILS:** Trimmed? Filed? Painted? Polished?
- ❑ **NOSTRILS:** Emptied?
- ❑ **EARS:** De-waxed?
- ❑ **SKIN:** Oiled? Lotioned? Perfumed? Sunblocked? Stridexed?
- ❑ **CLOTHES:** Laundered? Ironed? Ripped only where intended?

If you treat yourself to this sort of daily detailing, you'll run better, last longer, and turn heads when you drive, er, walk by.

Do Nothing

A lot of teenagers feel pressured to do things that will help them to get into college: lessons, dance, music, sports, extra courses, school clubs, student councils, mentoring, etc. These activities are great if you love what you're doing and don't feel overextended, exhausted, and stressed.

How Rude!

But there's no law that says you have to spend every waking moment being productive. Make sure you leave some time to do nothing. I'm not talking about being lazy, irresponsible, or slothful; I'm talking about being *idle*. Relaxed. Laid back. Carefree. Loose. Cool.

Take a moment to smell the roses. Be still. Meditate. Lie on your bed and stare at the dead flies in the ceiling light fixture. Sit on a bench and watch the people go by. Enjoy the sunset. Look at the stars. Listen to the wind. Let your mind wander.

Why is it so important to do this from time to time? Because, as a teenager I know once said, "If you don't daydream, you'll never get anywhere in life."

Do Something

Some teenagers find that instead of having too much to do, they have too little. Time wears heavily. So they hang out at malls, cruise in cars, drink, use drugs, and get into trouble. And, chances are, they don't feel very good about themselves.

This is because humans were designed to learn and love and grow and give. Teenagers who keep busy, who open themselves up to new people and adventures, tend to feel self-confident, happy, and hopeful. Teenagers who use only a fraction of their capabilities, who get into ruts, who don't try new things, tend to feel aimless and unhappy.

While it's important to schedule some downtime into your week, most people feel best about themselves and their lives when they're connected and creative. So discover your passions. Learn a musical instrument. Make a film. Take up a sport and experience the joy of total physical exhaustion. Read. Paint. Draw. Make models. Get active with a cause. Take a stand. Volunteer. Build connections to old people, young people, homeless people, people who are doing things you want to do; open yourself up to nature, to spirituality, to the mysteries of the universe, to love. You'll find that the more you get outside of yourself and the more you give to others, the richer you'll feel. And that's a very nice thing to do for yourself.

Do Unto Others

Popular teenagers tend to be friendly, outgoing, and empathetic. They're upbeat, considerate, and involved. No wonder other kids like to be around them. Here's what the teenagers we surveyed said about themselves:

"I try to be nice to people so I can have friends."
"I help others."

"I ignore a fight waiting to happen."

"I'm polite to others so others are polite to me."

Now that you've read this book,* you know almost everything you need to know about treating others well. Etiquette is all about doing unto others. Keep that in mind and you can't go wrong.

I Beg My Pardon

Plan Ahead

Treating yourself with respect also means thinking about tomorrow, and the next day, and the next several years of your life. As the teenagers we surveyed said:

"I work hard for my future."

"I take in knowledge."

"I stay in school."

"I do my homework."

"I try to get good grades."

"I keep myself well organized."

"I carry myself in a professional manner."

Do yourself a favor and learn the basics of goal setting (if you haven't already). Spend some quiet time thinking about what's important to you. Then follow these steps:

1. Write down all of the things you'd like to accomplish during the next 10 years. These are your *long-range* goals. Be specific and thorough.

2. When you complete your list of long-range goals, prioritize them. Select the 3–4 that are most important to you.

3. Write down all of the things you'd like to accomplish during the next 3–5 years. These are your *intermediate* (medium-range) goals. Prioritize them and select the top 3–4. **TIP:** Your intermediate goals should help you achieve your long-range goals.

4. Write down all of the things you'd like to accomplish within the next year or so. These are your *immediate* (short-range) goals. Prioritize them and select the top few. **TIP:** Your immediate goals should relate directly to your intermediate goals.

5. Write your prioritized lists in a small spiral-bound notebook and date them. Carry your notebook with you and consult your lists regularly—

---

* You *have* read it, haven't you?

once a day (best) or once a week (minimum). When you reach a goal, write down that date in your notebook.

6. Revise your lists as needed. Some of the goals you have today will stay the same for years to come; others will change as you change.

This system will help to get you on track and keep you on track. Make a promise to yourself to try it for at least three weeks.

Give Yourself Presents

Giving yourself presents is a very polite thing to do. The teenagers we surveyed reported that they often use incentives to pat themselves on the back or get through a difficult time:

> *"If I've had a good week, I try to reward myself by going out."*
> *"I treat myself to candy."*
> *"I go on trips."*
> *"I take myself shopping."*
> *"I hang out with my friends."*
> *"I have fun."*

Just remember that if you give yourself a present, you have to write a thank-you note.

TRUE STORIES FROM THE
MANNERS FRONTIER
In Record Time

When I was in high school and all stressed out because of, say, some upcoming tumbling exam in gym class, I used to tell myself *All right, Alex, if you practice hard and don't roll off the mat in the middle of a somersault, you can buy yourself a record when it's all over.* (Records were these primitive round disks that played music.)

Of course, if I flunked the test and was totally depressed, then I'd buy a record to cheer myself up.

All told, it was an excellent system.

Think Well of Yourself and the World

How would you feel if someone criticized you nonstop 24 hours a day?

"You're such a loser! You're so stupid! Look at you. What a mess! Nobody's ever going to like you. You're a total failure."

I Beg My Pardon

You'd feel sad, hopeless, and hurt. It would be a struggle to get through each day.

Fortunately, most teenagers aren't exposed to relentless criticism of this sort. At least, not from the outside. But a lot of kids have an *inner* voice they can't shut off. Their mind blabbers on incessantly:

"I HATE myself. I'll never have any friends. I HAVE to be popular. Nobody likes me. I can't stand school. I'm going to flunk. Nothing will ever change. It's not fair. If I don't get invited to the dance, I'll die. I'm never going to amount to anything. I'm a rotten, terrible kid. I HATE my life. I HATE it! I HATE it!"

Imagine what life would be like if your mind was your best friend instead of your worst enemy. Imagine if it functioned as your personal cheering squad. A conscience that prevented you from hurting yourself or others. A rudder that kept you steady and on course. A source of dreams, fantasies, and comfort. Here's what a mind like that would say:

"Take it easy. Stay calm. Deep breaths. Worrying won't help. You don't have to prove anything. You're a good person. You've come through things like this before. You have a lot going for you. Even if you blow it, it's not the end of the world. Believe in yourself. You can do it!"

It should be easy to get your mind on your side. But your mind has a mind of its own. And it's been barraged with messages ever since you were a little kid. These messages—from the media, television, advertising, family, friends, organized religion, and other societal institutions—can lead you to create expectations for yourself and others that are unrealistic and nearly impossible to meet.

From television, for example, your mind learns to expect instant solutions and rewards. (After all, people in sitcoms solve their problems in 30 minutes, with time off for commercials.) The message from movies and ads is that there's something wrong with you if you don't have a fancy car and a million bucks by the time you're 25, or that sex is always spectacular and without consequences. Some religions lay down such rigid absolutes for behavior that the internal conflict kids experience when they don't "measure up" can create deep feelings of guilt and shame.

How Rude!

These irrational and unhealthy attitudes lay the foundation for driving yourself crazy. How? By filling your mind with "musts":

1. I must do well.
2. I must have the approval of others.
3. Others must do right by me.
4. The conditions of the world must be fair and easy.

When we're driven by "musts," we take reasonable desires—for success, approval, love, money, pleasure, friendship—and turn them into absolute needs: *I MUST be liked by everybody. I MUST be thin. I MUST be rich.* And then, when we don't get what we want, when our needs are thwarted by reality, we view this as the worst calamity that could possibly happen. We become angry, resentful, and depressed. We "awfulize" the consequences of having our needs unmet:

I'll die if I don't get the part.
Everybody will hate me if I don't break the record.
I won't be able to stand it if we move to another town.

When we have unrealistic needs and awfulize the consequences of their being unmet, we worry endlessly about getting what we want, about not getting what we want, and about keeping what we get if we *do* get what we want. And that's not all. When we can't fulfill all of our (irrational) desires, we conclude that *we're* at fault. We must be dumb, worthless, undeserving. And we blame the world, which must be cruel, unfair, and out to get us. This three-part process—being driven by "musts," awfulizing, and dumping on oneself—is one of the things minds do to drive their owners crazy.

You can tell your mind to shape up and stop being silly. This is what kids who are polite to themselves do. In fact, the teenagers who responded to our survey reported all sorts of strategies for keeping their mind on their side:

"I compliment myself."
"I trust my feelings."
"I value myself for who I am."
"I encourage myself."
"I respect myself."
"I keep my confidence and self-esteem high."
"I judge myself fairly."
"I try to be calm and take things step-by-step, because if I do things in a hurry I'll mess up."
"I don't hurt myself."

"I try not to swear in my thoughts."

"I think positive."

"I try not to believe in things I know aren't true (about me)."

"I avoid putting myself down."

"I tell myself not to listen when people tease me."

"I love myself."

"I smile at myself in the mirror."

I Beg My Pardon

You might want to borrow some of these techniques and try them in your own life. Or come up with ideas of your own. Put your mind to it!

"It's a pleasure to see you again."

More Ways to Be Polite to Yourself

Watch out for "shoulds." Like "musts," "shoulds" can turn reasonable desires into unrealistic needs: *I should be able to do this; I should know this; I should understand this; I should be this kind of person or that kind of person.* Certainly, there are some "shoulds" that are worth following through on: *I should be kind and civil to others; I should keep my promises; I should behave responsibly.* But don't be guided by demands that lead to guilt, shame, and feelings of failure.

Hold realistic expectations. Don't torture yourself because you can't live up to impossibly high standards. You're a human being, not a machine. You're going to discover that you have strengths and weaknesses, and you're going to make mistakes.

Give yourself credit. You know those things you "can't stand"? The things that "drive you crazy"? Guess what? You're standing them and you're not crazy. In other words, you're a lot stronger than you think.

Thank yourself. When other people extend themselves on your behalf, you thank them. Do the same for yourself:

"I just wanted to thank me for the way I stuck up for myself today. I gave myself that extra effort. Good going!"

439

Develop your special talents. Pursue your passions. Schools teach many things. If you're lucky, you'll get turned on by a lot of them. But it's also possible that your interests and gifts lie outside the classroom. There are a lot of valuable things to learn that never find their way into the typical school curriculum. Make room in your life for the things you enjoy.

Surround yourself with positive people. Hang out with friends who are doing things and going places. Their positive outlook will help you to excel and handle the obstacles and bummers life throws your way.

Avoid people who are going nowhere fast. This doesn't mean shunning friends who sometimes get into trouble. It doesn't mean snubbing those who are unpopular, hurt, or underachieving. Everybody has problems, and it's important to be there for your friends when they need a helping hand. But some kids are going down, and they want to take you with them. They're proud of their attitude and lack of motivation. Misery loves company, and people who smoke, get drunk, use drugs, shoplift, tease, bully, and join gangs need to find others who will validate their behavior. Don't be duped into thinking it's cool to destroy your life or the lives of others.

Dispute negative thinking. Critiquing the errors and incidents of your life is one of the best ways to learn and grow. But don't let your own mind put you down. Don't let one event define your self-image. When your inner voice starts working overtime with negative blather, shout it down with some positive pepping up. Examples:

Negative Self-Talk	Positive Self-Talk
"Everybody hates me!"	"That's not true. Terry likes me. My parents like me. Grandma likes me. Mr. Reed likes me. It sure would be nice to have more friends, though."
"I can't do anything right!"	"That's not true. I'm good at lots of things. Just because I didn't make the team doesn't mean I'm a failure. I can try again next year."
"I can't stand it when people tease me!"	"But it happens to a lot of kids. I guess it's just part of life. I *can* stand it. I'll just ignore it and stay strong."

Don't give other people and events the power to control your feelings. Most people believe that feelings are the result of what happens to us. We feel good or bad based on events, on what others do or say. A teacher who praises us makes us feel proud; a parent who grounds us makes us feel angry. You can see these beliefs at work every time you hear statements like "You kids are driving me crazy" or "She made me so mad!"

If someone you love dies, or a friend dumps you, or a roommate loses your jacket, it's normal and healthy to feel sad, hurt, or annoyed. But often we let others push our buttons. We get consumed with anger or other self-defeating emotions because of the way we choose to look at the things that happen to us. We turn our confidence and serenity over to things we can't control.

Why give other people and events such power over you? Instead, control your *feelings* by controlling your *thoughts*.* Negative thoughts lead to negative feelings; positive thoughts lead to positive feelings. Examples:

I Beg My Pardon

The Event	Ways to Look at It	Likely Results
Your teacher catches you passing a note and sends you to detention. Meanwhile, other kids get away with it.	**1.** *I hate him. He has no right to do that. He's the worst teacher in the world. Why should I have to go to detention when no one else does? It's not fair.*	**1.** Fury. Frustration. Resentment.
	2. *I did pass the note. I wish I hadn't been caught. Oh, well, it's just one afternoon. I guess I can use the time to do homework.*	**2.** Acceptance. Less stress. Most of your homework done by 4:30 P.M.
There's someone in school you really like. You ask her out on a date—and she turns you down.	**1.** *This is awful. I can't stand being rejected like this. What's wrong with me? Nobody will ever want to go out with me.*	**1.** Hurt. Shame. Isolation. Self-doubt.
	2. *Man, that hurts. I really like her. Too bad I can't make her like me. But there are 878 other kids in this school. I'll hang in there. If Mortimer Snerdhopper can get dates, so can I!*	**2.** Disappointment— but you'll get over it. Courage to try again. A date next weekend.

---

* The idea that feelings are caused more by our thoughts about life than by life itself lies at the heart of a method of psychotherapy called *rational-emotive therapy*. It was developed by Albert Ellis, a clinical psychologist. If you want to learn more about it, check out his books.

How Rude!

Don't let other people's opinions get to you. Sometimes, other people can offer valuable feedback that will help you to solve a problem or work on yourself. But often, other people's opinions are pretty worthless. Think of all the people who once swore that the earth was flat. That humans could never fly. That individuals would never want computers in their homes. The people who are most successful and creative are those who believe in themselves, who forge ahead despite the so-called wisdom of others.

Ask yourself a question. When you're worried about something, it's often because you're projecting dire consequences into the future. Next time this happens, ask yourself *What's the worst thing that could happen?* You'll probably discover it's nowhere near as bad as you imagined.

Solve the problem. Many people let their problems simmer and stew instead of trying to solve them. When you have a personal problem or a conflict with somebody in your life, sit down with yourself. Take out a piece of paper and a pencil. Go through the five-step problem-solving strategy.* It will help you to solve almost any problem you encounter—and understand which ones really *can't* be solved, which is a good thing to know.

Build your self-esteem. Some adults believe that the way to do this is by looking in a mirror and repeating self-congratulatory mantras. They teach kids to tell themselves *I'm great at math. I'm lovable and good.* This can, in fact, raise self-esteem—to the point at which many nasty, selfish kids who are flunking math start to feel good about themselves. But this is just a mind trick. *The way to build genuine self-esteem is by doing esteemable things.* Care, give, treat others with kindness and tolerance, be honest but gentle with yourself, do the best you can in the things that really matter. You'll build your self-esteem—and it will be genuine and deserved.

Admit when you're wrong. People spend enormous amounts of time and energy protecting their pride. If you make a mistake, 'fess up. Do what you can to repair the damage. You'll be amazed by how liberating it can be to assume responsibility for your actions.

Keep a diary or journal. Many teenagers like to record their thoughts and feelings. Keeping a diary or journal is an excellent way to catch your breath and reflect on the people, events, and moods you experience. It's also a way to release feelings that might otherwise stay bottled up inside.

Use good manners. By being grateful, appreciative, courteous, tolerant, and polite, you can create an aura of goodness that will allow you to observe the

---

* See pages 128–129.

442

selfishness and thoughtlessness of others with philosophical acceptance rather than anxious outrage. This is much better for your blood pressure.

Each day, you make choices. Some are small and inconsequential: Vanilla or chocolate? Seven-thirty or nine-thirty? Gray or black? Others can affect the rest of your life (or end it): How hard should I work in school? Should I try cocaine? Should I wear my bicycle helmet? Should I have sex without a condom?

How do you know what to decide?

It usually comes down to this: Do you want to be polite or rude? Do you want to respect yourself or disdain yourself? Forgive yourself or berate yourself? Protect yourself or harm yourself?

There's only one person in the world whose behavior you can control. And that's you. So why not treat yourself with the courtesy and respect you deserve?

"Does using good manners always work? I want to know—is this 100 percent positive?"

There are no guarantees in life other than death, taxes, and being called on when you're daydreaming. But in most situations, with most people, good manners are definitely the way to go. People with good manners are far more likely than those with bad manners to like themselves, have friends, and live to see tomorrow. And they're far more likely to get others to stop being rude.

Think of manners as you would seatbelts. Sometimes they take a little getting used to. Sometimes you forget to use them. Sometimes they confine you more than you'd like. But they're the best system we have for keeping you in the driver's seat and out of trouble. ◆

CHAPTER QUIZ

How Rude!

1. *If other people put you down, the best response is to:*
   a) call out the custard pies
   b) give them a wedgie
   c) ignore them.

2. *One builds self-esteem by:*
   a) hiring a good carpenter
   b) repeating "I'm so great!" 10,000 times
   c) behaving honorably and giving to others.

3. *Keeping a journal is a good idea because you can:*
   a) blackmail your friends
   b) leave it where your parents will find it
   c) record your thoughts, feelings, and experiences.

4. *Which of the following are unhealthy "musts"?*
   a) I must be thin
   b) I must be rich
   c) I must my hair.

5. *When negative self-talk threatens, you should:*
   a) gag yourself
   b) scream "Shut up!"
   c) seek a rational, balanced perspective.

6. *Being polite to yourself means:*
   a) getting up when you enter a room
   b) looking yourself in the eye when you speak
   c) treating yourself with kindness, patience, and understanding.

Answers to the Chapter Quizzes

Chapter 1: Minding Manners (page 23)

1. d. Although it's never permissible to bolt upright in your coffin during the funeral. (For more on funeral etiquette, see pages 307–309.)
2. a, b, and c are all correct, unless someone is having a *really* bad hair day, in which case d would also be correct.
3. d.
4. None of the answers is correct. Only dead people can be rude back. (See question #1.)

Chapter 2: Social Interactions 101 (page 59)

1. c.
2. c.
3. c.
4. c. As long as the owner doesn't hear you, you may ask the parrot directly if it knows any swear words.
5. c.

Chapter 3: Uncommon Courtesies (page 105)

1. c. If the elderly woman says "Yes" when you ask her if she would like a seat, don't say "Well, I hope someone offers you one."
2. c.
3. None of the answers is correct. Only *foreign* cars may be frontside bluntsided if you are to remain within the bounds of propriety.
4. c.
5. None of the answers is correct. Oranges must be *six* for a dollar or less.

Chapter 4: Family Life and Strife (page 151)

1. c. *Then* you may laugh.
2. c. If that doesn't work. you may run his underwear up the flagpole as long as it's clean.
3. c.
4. c. As an alternative, you may drench the bathroom with Lilac Fresh-Hint-of-Spring Air Freshener. Just don't announce it to everyone.

How Rude!

Chapter 5: Artful Lodgers (page 179)

1. All of the answers are correct.
2. All of the answers are correct. (Just checking to see if you're awake. Of course, *none* of the answers is correct. The only acceptable response would be to respectfully decline the invitation.)
3. Either c or a—if you use a frozen *egg roll.*
4. None of the answers is correct. You may only bring your pet to someone's house if *his or her pet* extends the invitation.
5. The proper response is to spit immediately at the kid who asked and say "I won."
6. Every written invitation should include the nature of the event, the date and time, and a crisp $50 bill.

Chapter 6: School Rules (page 222)

1. c. You may add Red Dye #9 to your specimen.
2. c. Or, as an alternative, write *wrong* answers in big handwriting, let him copy, and then change your answers right before the bell rings.
3. c. You may then throw Styrofoam peanuts at him.
4. c.
5. c.

Chapter 7: Friends, Romance, Countrymen (pages 266–267)

1. c. Answer a is close, but still incorrect. You need to hand out *counterfeit* $10 bills. That way you won't go broke.
2. c. But if you want her to leave in a hurry, put on a Carpenters album and sing along.
3. c.
4. c. Alternately, you may set a mouse in the top drawer.
5. c. Although you may stand up during assembly and ask the *other* half of the boys in school what's wrong with them.
6. c. If that doesn't work, do a striptease on the stairs.
7. c. If you *must* pin the corsage to a tan line, always disinfect the area first.
8. None of the answers is correct. You must keep *five* feet on the ground.

Chapter 8: Eat, Drink, and Be Wary (page 305)

1. c. Whatever you do, don't spit it out *on* your hostess.
2. c.
3. c. You may hum the "Rice-a-Roni" theme song under your breath.
4. c.
5. c. However, it's forbidden to read aloud from cereal boxes, as severe brain damage may result.
6. c. If this doesn't work, call the restaurant a dump, the waiter a jerk, and duck.

Chapter 9: On Your Best Behavior (page 324)

1. c.
2. c.
3. c. Bonus points if you come dressed as Whoopi Goldberg.
4. c.
5. c. If you really, really don't like the bride, you may step on the cake.
6. c. Then try to remember to bring it.

Chapter 10: Talking Headiquette (page 376)

1. c.
2. None of the answers is correct. Instead, throw the person in his soup.
3. c. If the recipient opens it, reads it, and tosses it in the trash, you may retrieve it and peruse it at your leisure.
4. c. If the person fails to respond, you may answer the questions yourself.
5. c.

Chapter 11: Netiquette (page 394)

1. c.
2. None of the answers is correct. The emoticon means *I was born with a pole through my very large ears.*
3. None of the answers is correct. The emoticon means *Has anyone seen my Siamese twin? He looks like this:* < < < < : }.

Chapter 12: Clothes-Minded (page 410)

1. c.
2. c. Although if you can find items that will be out of fashion in two weeks, so much the better.
3. c is close. Find a kid wearing VERY baggy pants and turn him into a toga.
4. b and c are both correct.
5. None of the answers is correct. The proper response is to dye your dog pink and say Spiderman did it. This way, you'll probably get sent to another school.
6. None of the answers is correct. First-time guests traditionally bring the volleyball.

Chapter 13: Ahh, Ahh, Ahh—Chooooooo!!! (page 429)

1. a.
2. c. Alternately, you may point at your book and yell "EMILY did it!"
3. c. For *really* nasty itches, you may slide down the banister.
4. c. If Cindy doesn't get it, you may want to stick a large kernel of corn to your own chin and point to that.

How Rude!

Chapter 14: I Beg My Pardon (page 444)

1. c. And then eat a custard pie.
2. c. Or, for *really* high self-esteem, say "I'm so great!" 1,000,000 times.
3. c. Although you may choose to keep a journal so you can blackmail your friends' parents.
4. a, b, and c are all correct.
5. c. Although eating a half gallon of Cherry Garcia ice cream sometimes helps.
6. c. But the supreme act of politeness would be to turn to page 1 and read this book all over again.

Bibliography

Axtell, Roger E. *Gestures: The Do's and Taboos of Body Language Around the World* (New York: John Wiley & Sons, 1991). Read this book to learn more about the meanings of different gestures in various cultures.

Brainard, Beth, and Sheila Behr. *Soup Should Be Seen, Not Heard: The Kids' Etiquette Book* (New York: Dell, 1990). This colorful, profusely illustrated guide to proper behavior is just the ticket for little kids who need to learn good manners but aren't yet mature enough for a sophisticated book like *How Rude!*

Dresser, Norine. *Multicultural Manners: New Rules of Etiquette for a Changing Society* (New York: John Wiley & Sons, 1996). Read this book to learn lots about manners in different cultures.

"Guidelines for Reporting and Writing about People with Disabilities," Fifth Edition (Lawrence, KS: The Research and Training Center on Independent Living, 1996). You already know that words such as "harelip," "retard," "psycho," and "spastic" are very rude. This handy little pamphlet gives you a straightforward, sensitive working vocabulary of words and phrases to use when writing about or talking with people with disabilities. To learn how to get a copy of the Guidelines, contact: RTC/IL, 4089 Dole Center, University of Kansas, Lawrence, KS 66045; telephone (785) 864-4095.

Krementz, Jill. *How It Feels to Be Adopted* and *How It Feels When Parents Divorce* (both New York: Knopf, 1988). In these excellent and inspiring books, children talk about what it was like to go through these challenging experiences. The stories and advice are particularly helpful to those in similar situations. The series also includes *How It Feels When a Parent Dies* and *How It Feels to Live with a Physical Disability*.

Mandel, Thomas, and Gerard Van der Leun. *Rules of the Net: Online Operating Instructions for Human Beings* (New York: Hyperion, 1996). A good resource for an expanded discussion of online etiquette.

Martin, Judith. *Miss Manners' Guide to Excruciatingly Correct Behavior* (New York: Warner Books, 1988) and *Miss Manners Rescues Civilization: From Sexual Harrassment, Frivolous Lawsuits, Drive-by Shootings & Other Lapses in Civilization* (New York: Crown, 1996). For those adults in your life who could use a remedial course in manners, these etiquette books are the way to go. They're witty, informative, and very heavy. Whether you buy one or borrow

How Rude!

it from the library, never give it directly to a parent. Instead, leave it lying around or inside one of your dresser drawers, where your parents are bound to find it.

Panati, Charles. *Panati's Extraordinary Origins* (New York: HarperCollins, 1989). This book is jam-packed with explanations of how manners and many other things came to be. For example, you can learn the origins of Silly Putty, potato chips, toilet paper, Groundhog Day, nursery rhymes, underwear, lipstick, etc.

Shea, Virginia. *Netiquette* (San Francisco: Albion Books, 1994). Another good resource for an expanded discussion of online etiquette.

Singer, Bennett L., and David Deschamps, eds. *Gay and Lesbian Stats: A Pocket Guide of Facts and Figures* (New York: The New Press, 1994). A wide-ranging and comprehensive compendium of statistics about gay men and lesbians, drawn from hundreds of sources.

Strauss, Susan, with Pamela Espeland. *Sexual Harassment and Teens: A Program for Positive Change* (Minneapolis: Free Spirit Publishing, 1992). Written for educators, this book includes much information about sexual harassment that you should know.

Wildeblood, Joan. *The Polite World: A Guide to English Manners and Deportment* (London: Davis-Poynter, Ltd., 1973). This delightful book takes a look at the history of manners in England. For example, in the 19th century, houseguests ". . . arriving with children and horses . . . were even more awkward for the hosts, and to arrive without mention of them in advance, would be in still worse taste."

Index

How Rude!

Index

How Rude!

Index

How Rude!

and survival of
    human race, 61
teaching of, 1
ten reasons to have,
    3–4
waivers, 17–21
See also Etiquette;
    specific circum-
    stances, i.e., Public
    events; School rules
Martin, Judith, 449
Meals. *See* Diet and nutri-
    tion; Foods; Restau-
    rants; Table manners
Meanness, 233–234
Meat, 271
Mediterranean, 33
Men, as subculture, 7
Mens sana in corpore sano,
    431
Menus, 297, 298, 299
Messiness, vs. neatness,
    111, 131–132, 174
Michelangelo, 28
Middle Ages, 8, 28, 31, 134
Middle East, 6, 33
Minorities, as subculture,
    7
Miss Manners, 2, 449–450
Modesty, 352–353
Money
    being up-front about,
        249
    clothing allowance, 401
    debts, 234–235
    Dutch treat, 249, 299
    loaning to friends, 234–
        235
    tipping, 300, 302–303
Mooching, 153
Morning dress, 403
Motormouths, 360–361
Movie theaters, 90–92
Music listening, 84, 96–97
Musicians
    as subculture, 7
    tipping, 304

N

Nail biting, 419–420
Napkin rings, 286
Napkins, 286
Nasaltiti, Queen, 413
National Anthem, 92
Neatness, vs. messiness,
    111, 131–132, 174
Neckties. *See* Ties
Negative thinking,
    negating, 440
Negative self-talk, 440
Negotiation, family
    manners, 83, 127–128
No, types of, 247, 251–252
Noise pollution, 84, 96–97,
    130–131, 172
Nose blowing, 8, 421–422
Nose picking, 11, 412–413
Nosegays, 258
Nosiness, 347–348
Nutrition. *See* Diet and
    nutrition

O

Obscene phone calls, 336
Offering someone your
    seat, 65–66
On Civility in Children
    (Erasmus), 8–9
Online etiquette. *See*
    Computers; Email;
    Internet
Opera, 88
Oranges, 295
Order for serving people
    at family dinner, 277
Overnights, 7, 162–164,
    166–167, 171–172, 425
Owners of establishments,
    tipping, 304
Oxford English Dictionary,
    412
Oyster/seafood forks, 269,
    270
Oysters, 270

P

Packer, Alex J., 464
Panati, Charles, 450
Parent-Child Dominant
    Peer Group Appro-
    priate Dress Treaty,
    399, 401
Parents
    as rude, 366–367
    surveys, 21, 107–108,
        145–146, 150, 367–368
    worries of, 82–83
Parking lots, 102
Passing food, 155, 278
Passing wind/passing gas.
    See Farting
Patience, 393
PDAs. *See* Public displays
    of affection
Pears, 291
Peas, 295
Peer pressure, 226–229
People with disabilities,
    53–58, 449
    birth defects, 58
    blindness, 56
    physical disabilities,
        57–58
    preferred terminology,
        54–55
    wheelchair users, 55–56
Pepys, Samuel, 414
Perfectionism, 4
Pets, 174–178
Piercings, 51. *See also*
    Earrings
Pinkie finger, raising
    when drinking, 2, 279
Pizza, 295
    tipping for delivery, 304
Place settings, 269–273
Plates, 269, 270, 272, 301
Plausible deniability, 247
Playing tricks, on sleeping
    people, 166–167
Please, use of, 354

Index

How Rude!

How Rude!

Index

About the Author

Alex J. Packer (but you may call him "Alex") is a very polite educator, psychologist, and screenwriter. He is the author of the award-winning *Bringing Up Parents, Highs!, 365 Ways to Love Your Child, Parenting One Day at a Time,* and *The Nurturing Parent.* His articles have appeared in *McCall's, Child, U.S. News and World Report,* and the *Harvard Graduate School of Education Bulletin.*

Alex prepped at Phillips Exeter Academy, where he never once referred to kitchen personnel as "wombats" (although he *was* told to get a haircut by his dorm master). He then went to Harvard, where he pursued a joint major in Social Relations and Finger Bowls. A specialist in adolescence, parent education, and substance abuse, Alex received a Master's Degree in Education from the Harvard Graduate School of (duh) Education, and a Ph.D. in Educational and Developmental Psychology from Boston College, where he always held doors for his professors.

For eight years, Alex was headmaster of an alternative school for children ages 11–15 in Washington, D.C. He has since served as Director of Education for the Capital Children's Museum. He is currently President of FCD Educational Services, Inc., a leading Boston-based provider of drug education programs to schools and colleges worldwide. When asking kids to not use drugs, Alex always says "please."

Although it's rude to talk behind someone's back, reliable sources report that Alex flies ultralight aircraft, spends several months a year in France, drives a 28-year-old sports car, and chews with his mouth closed.

When asked to supply a photograph, Alex refused, saying "What!?!?! And never be able to go out to a restaurant again without hordes of adoring teenagers asking me which fork to use?"

Other Great Books from Free Spirit

Bringing Up Parents
The Teenager's Handbook
by Alex J. Packer, Ph.D.
Straight talk and specific suggestions on how teens can take the initiative to resolve conflicts with parents, improve family relationships, earn trust, accept responsibility, and help to create a happier, healthier home environment. For ages 13 & up.
$15.95; 272 pp.; softcover; illus.; 7¼" x 9¼"

HIGHS!
Over 150 Ways to Feel Really, REALLY Good…Without Alcohol or Other Drugs
by Alex J. Packer, Ph.D.
This book describes safe, creative ways to find peace, pleasure, excitement, and insight. Because most teens are stressed out, the author starts with serenity highs: breathing and meditation. Then he describes highs related to sports and exercise, food, the senses, nature, creativity, family, friends, and more. For ages 13 & up.
$15.95; 264 pp.; softcover; illus.; 7¼" x 9¼"

What Are My Rights?
95 Questions and Answers About Teens and the Law
by Thomas A. Jacobs, J.D.
Teens need to know about the laws that affect them to make informed decisions about what they should and shouldn't do. This fascinating book helps teens understand the law, recognize their responsibilities, and appreciate their rights. For ages 12 & up.
$14.95; 208 pp.; softcover; 6" x 9"

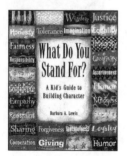

What Do You Stand For?
A Kid's Guide to Building Character
by Barbara A. Lewis
This book empowers children and teens to identify and build character traits. Inspiring quotations, activities, true stories, and resources make this book timely, comprehensive, and fun. For ages 11 & up.
$19.95; 284 pp.; softcover; B&W photos and illus.; 8½" x 11"

To place an order or to request a free catalog of SELF-HELP FOR KIDS® and SELF-HELP FOR TEENS® materials, please write, call, email, or visit our Web site:

Free Spirit Publishing Inc.
217 Fifth Avenue North • Suite 200 • Minneapolis, MN 55401-1299
toll-free 800.735.7323 • local 612.338.2068 • fax 612.337.5050
help4kids@freespirit.com • www.freespirit.com

NURSING TODAY

NINTH EDITION

TODAY

TRANSITION and TRENDS

JoAnn Zerwekh, EdD, RN

President/CEO
Nursing Education Consultants
Chandler, AZ;
Nursing Faculty
Online Campus
University of Phoenix
Phoenix, Arizona

Ashley Zerwekh Garneau, PhD, RN

Nursing Faculty
GateWay Community College
Phoenix, Arizona

ELSEVIER

ELSEVIER

3251 Riverport Lane
St. Louis, Missouri 63043

NURSING TODAY: TRANSITION AND TRENDS
NINTH EDITION

ISBN: 978-0-323-40168-5

Notices

Knowledge and best practice in this field are constantly changing. As new research and experience broaden our understanding, changes in research methods, professional practices, or medical treatment may become necessary.

Practitioners and researchers must always rely on their own experience and knowledge in evaluating and using any information, methods, compounds, or experiments described herein. In using such information or methods they should be mindful of their own safety and the safety of others, including parties for whom they have a professional responsibility.

With respect to any drug or pharmaceutical products identified, readers are advised to check the most current information provided (i) on procedures featured or (ii) by the manufacturer of each product to be administered, to verify the recommended dose or formula, the method and duration of administration, and contraindications. It is the responsibility of practitioners, relying on their own experience and knowledge of their patients, to make diagnoses, to determine dosages and the best treatment for each individual patient, and to take all appropriate safety precautions.

To the fullest extent of the law, neither the Publisher nor the authors, contributors, or editors, assume any liability for any injury and/or damage to persons or property as a matter of products liability, negligence or otherwise, or from any use or operation of any methods, products, instructions, or ideas contained in the material herein.

Library of Congress Cataloging-in-Publication Data

Names: Zerwekh, JoAnn Graham, editor. | Garneau, Ashley Zerwekh, editor.
Title: Nursing today : transition and trends / JoAnn Zerwekh, EdD, RN
    President/CEO Nursing Education Consultant Chandler, AZ, Nursing Faculty
    Online Campus University of Phoenix, Phoenix, Arizona, Ashley Zerwekh
    Garneau, PhD, RN, Nursing Faculty, GateWay Community College Phoenix,
    Arizona.
Description: Ninth edition. | St. Louis, Missouri : Elsevier, [2018] |
    Includes bibliographical references and index.
Identifiers: LCCN 2016056532 | ISBN 9780323401685 (pbk.)
Subjects: LCSH: Nursing--Vocational guidance. | Nursing--Social aspects.
Classification: LCC RT82 .N874 2018 | DDC 610.7306/9--dc23
LC record available at https://lccn.loc.gov/2016056532

Senior Content Strategist: Sandra Clark
Senior Content Development Manager: Laurie Gower
Content Development Specialist: Jennifer Wade
Publishing Services Manager: Hemamalini Rajendrababu
Book Project Manager: Divya Krishna Kumar
Designer: Patrick Ferguson

Printed in Canada

Last digit is the print number: 9   8   7   6   5   4   3   2   1

CONTRIBUTORS

Susan Ahrens, PhD, RN
Associate Professor
Department of Nursing
Indiana University—Purdue
    University of Fort Wayne
Fort Wayne, Indiana
Chapter 22: Quality Patient Care
Chapter 25: Workplace Issues

Nikki Austin, JD, RN
Consultant
Phoenix, Arizona
Chapter 20: Legal Issues

**Julie V. Darmody, PhD, RN,
ACNS-BC**
Clinical Associate Professor
College of Nursing
University of Wisconsin-Milwaukee
Milwaukee, Wisconsin
*Chapter 16: Economics in
    the Health Care Delivery System*

**Michael L. Evans, PhD, RN,
NEA-BC, FACHE, FAAN**
Dean and Professor
School of Nursing
Health Sciences Center
Texas Tech University
Lubbock, Texas
*Chapter 17: Political Action in
    Nursing*

**Ashley Zerwekh Garneau,
PhD, RN**
Nursing Faculty
GateWay Community College
Phoenix, Arizona
Chapter 1: Transitions
*Chapter 2: Personal
    Management: Time and
    Self-Care Strategies*
*Chapter 4: Mentoring,
    Preceptorship, and Nurse
    Residency Programs*
Chapter 8: Nursing Theories

**Ruth I. Hansten, RN, BSN,
MBA, PhD, FACHE®**
Principal Consultant
Hansten Healthcare PLLC
Port Ludlow, Washington
*Chapter 14: Delegation in the Clinical
    Setting*

**Peter Melenovich, PhD,
RN, CNE**
Nursing Faculty
GateWay Community College
Phoenix, Arizona
Chapter 19: Ethical Issues
*Chapter 21: Cultural and Spiritual
    Awareness*
*Chapter 24: Using Nursing
    Research in Practice*

**Cheryl D. Parker, PhD, MSN,
RN-BC, FHIMSS**
Contributing Faculty
College of Nursing
Institution Walden University
State Minneapolis, Minnesota
*Chapter 23: Nursing
    Informatics*

**Jessica Maack Rangel, MS,
ASPPS, RN**
Southwest Zone Director—
    Performance Improvement
Texas Health Resources
Arlington, Texas
*Chapter 11: Nursing Management
    Skills*

**Margi J. Schultz, PhD, RN,
CNE, PLNC**
Director, Maricopa Nursing
Maricopa Community College
District Tempe, Arizona
*Chapter 9: Image of Nursing: Influences
    of the Present*

**Susan Sportsman, PhD, RN,
ANEF, FAAN**
Director
Consultation and Services
Elsevier
Forestburg, Texas
*Chapter 15: The Health Care
    Organization and Patterns
    of Nursing Care Delivery*

Gayle P. Varnell, PhD, MSN, RN, CPNP-PC

Nursing Consultant for
   Education
Texas Board of Nursing
Austin, Texas
Chapter 7: Nursing Education

Joann Wilcox, RN, MSN, LNC

Continuing Education Director
Creative Training Solutions
Kansas City, Missouri
*Chapter 10: Challenges of Nursing
   Management*
Chapter 18: Collective Bargaining

JoAnn Zerwekh, EdD, RN

President/CEO
Nursing Education Consultants
Chandler, Arizona;
Nursing Faculty
Online Campus
University of Phoenix
Phoenix, Arizona
Chapter 1: Transitions
*Chapter 4: Employment Considerations:
   Resumes and Interviewing*
*Chapter 5: NCLEX-RN® and the
   New Graduate*
*Chapter 6: Historical Perspectives:
   Influences of the Present*

*Chapter 12: Effective Communication
   and Team Building*
Chapter 13: Conflict Management
Chapter 26: Emergency Preparedness

Tyler Zerwekh, DrPH, REHS

Administrator, Environmental
   Health Services Bureau
Shelby County Health Department
Memphis, Tennessee
Chapter 26: Emergency Preparedness

REVIEWERS

Faisal H Aboul-Enein, DrPH, MSN, MPH, RN, FNP-BC, FRSPH, FACHE
Professor
School of Nursing
Walden University
Minneapolis, Minnesota

Ruth Gladen, RN, MS
Associate Professor
Nursing Department
North Dakota State College of
   Science (NDSCS)
Wahpeton, North Dakota

Mary Annette Hess, PhD, FNP-BC, CNS
Assistant Professor/Family Nurse
   Practitioner
Department of Acute, Chronic, and
   Continuing Care
University of Alabama at Birmingham
   School of Nursing
Birmingham, Alabama

Julie Lyndsay, MSN, RN
Nursing Program Director
Nursing Department
Blackfeet Community College
Browning, Montana

Denise McEnroe-Petitte, PhD, MSN, BSN, AS, RN
Associate Professor, Nursing
Nursing Department
Kent State University Tuscarawas
New Philadelphia, Ohio

Lorraine Mainer, RN, MSN
Nursing Program Director/Instructor
Moraine Park Technical College
Marian University
Heartland Hospice
School of Nursing
Fond-du-Lac, Wisconsin

Renne Mielke, MSN, RN, CNE
Nursing Professor
Nursing Department
Kellogg Community College
Battle Creek, Michigan

Duane Napier, MSN, RN
Director
Nursing Department
University of Charleston
Charleston, West Virginia

Laura A. Steadman, EdD, CRNP, MSN, RN
Assistant Professor
Department of Adult/Chronic Care
   and Foundations
University of Alabama at Birmingham
   School of Nursing
Birmingham, Alabama

Nursing Today: Transition and Trends evolved out of the authors' experiences with nursing students in their final semester and the students' transition into the realities of nursing practice. With the changes in health care and the practice of nursing, there is even more emphasis on the importance of assisting the new graduate through the transition from education to practice. Nursing education and the transition process are experiencing a tremendous impact from changes in the health care delivery system.

In this ninth edition, we provide several new features that we feel are vital to the professional development and success of our future generation of nurses. For the soon-to-be nurse, we have added tips for studying effectively in groups, strategies for maximizing your time effectively, online resources for improving your time-management skills, as well as popular apps for organizing documents in Chapter 2, *Personal Management: Time and Self-Care Strategies.* We have provided findings from the National Council State Boards of Nursing (NCSBN) *Transition to Practice* study and have examined how these findings influence new graduates entering practice. We have provided updated information on transition programs and have included characteristics of effective transition programs in Chapter 3, *Mentorship, Preceptorship, and Nurse Residency Programs.* We have continued to provide the graduate nurse with information on nursing informatics and management and have continued to increase the focus on the use of information technology for the transitioning graduate by including new content on telemedicine and updated information on point-of-care electronic documentation as these areas relate to providing data tracking and analysis for improving patient care. Chapters related to current issues in health care, such as Chapter 15, *The Health Care Organization and Patterns of Nursing Care Delivery*; Chapter 16, *Economics of the Health Care Delivery System*; Chapter 18, *Collective Bargaining: Traditional (Union) and Nontraditional Approaches*; Chapter 19, *Ethical Issues*; Chapter 20, *Legal Issues*; Chapter 21, *Cultural and Spiritual Awareness*; Chapter 22, *Quality Patient Care*; Chapter 25, *Workplace Issues*; and Chapter 26, *Emergency Preparedness*, have been expanded. We kept the same easy reading style to present timely information, along with updated information on the 2016 NCLEX-RN® Detailed Test Plan and samples of the alternate-item format test items appearing on the NCLEX-RN® Exam. One of our goals with this book is to provide graduating nurses with practical guidelines that can be implemented in their transition from nursing students to effective entry-level nursing practice. Additionally, we have provided foundational content that will serve as a resource for graduating nurses continuing their nursing education.

For these reasons, we have introduced key differences among evidence-based practice, research utilization, and nursing research in Chapter 24, *Using Evidence-Based Practice and Nursing Research.* Compassion fatigue and strategies for preventing burnout are introduced in Chapter 2, *Personal Management: Time and Self-Care Strategies.* Recognizing the need for new graduate nurses to develop leadership skills, we have updated information on leadership and followership in Chapter 10, *Challenges of Nursing Management, and Followership.* New content on interprofessional practice and communication, along with best practice measures for using human patient simulation to improve interprofessional education, can be found in Chapter 12, *Effective Communication, Team Building, and Interprofessional*

Practice. Updated information on TeamSTEPPS as a tool for improving interprofessional communication has also been added to Chapter 11, *Building Nursing Management Skills.*

The classic findings and experience of Marlene Kramer and her research on reality shock, and Patricia Benner's work on performance characteristics of beginning and expert nurses, continue to affect the need for transition courses in nursing education programs. These courses focus on trends and issues to assist the new graduate to be better prepared to practice nursing in today's world. With the increased demands and realities of the health care system, it is necessary for the new graduate to make the transition rapidly to an independent role. We have written this book for use in these transition courses and to assist individual students in anticipating encounters in a rapidly changing, technologically oriented work environment.

We have revised and updated each chapter to reflect the changes in the health care delivery system and have maintained recommendations from the 2010 Institute of Medicine *Future of Nursing* report. To illustrate this, results of initiatives based on the recommendations from the *Future of Nursing* (2010) report have been included in Chapter 15, *The Health Care Organization and Patterns of Nursing Care Delivery*; initiatives focusing on improving the health needs of the lesbian, gay, bisexual, and transgender community are explored in Chapter 21, *Cultural and Spiritual Awareness*; methods for evaluating patient care, patient satisfaction, and quality outcome measures in today's redesigned health care system have been highlighted in Chapter 22, *Quality Patient Care*; issues in emergency preparedness education and training, and patient triage have been expanded in Chapter 26, *Emergency Preparedness*. Some of the lengthy tables and figures have been moved to Evolve Resources to keep the material intact and to make the reading easier. We have maintained and added additional cartoons drawn by C.J. Miller, BSN, RN. We feel they add a smile and perhaps make the difficult information a little easier to comprehend.

Each chapter begins with Learning Objectives and a quote as an introduction to the content. Within each chapter, there is a practical application of the concepts discussed. Critical Thinking boxes in the text highlight information to facilitate the critical thinking process. Using a question approach, material is presented in a logical, easy-to-read manner. There are also opportunities to respond to thought-provoking questions and student exercises to facilitate self-evaluation. Research for Best Practice boxes have been incorporated to provide implications for nursing practice and opportunities for discussion on how to incorporate the information into the practice setting. We have continued to provide online resources and relevant websites for each chapter.

The student receives an overall view of the nursing profession from historical events that influenced nursing to the present-day image and also the legal, ethical, political, and on-the-job issues confronting today's nurse. Communication in the workplace, time management, how to write an effective resume, interviewing tips, guidelines for using social media as a professional, employee benefits, and self-care strategies are among the sound career advancement tools provided.

FOR NURSING FACULTY

Our key goal in developing this book has been to provide timely information that is applicable to current practice and is fun to read. An Instructor's TEACH for Nurses lesson plan manual, which is web-based, is available from the publisher on the Evolve website to assist faculty in planning and promoting a positive transition experience. This valuable website contains suggestions for classroom and clinically based student activities. Additionally, we have included the 2016 Accreditation Commission for Education in Nursing (ACEN) Standards throughout each TEACH for Nurses lesson plan manual among other curriculum standards (i.e., QSEN, BSN Essentials).

At the request of nursing faculty using our book, we have continued to provide a secure, updated web-based Test Bank and have developed more than 300 questions, with detailed rationales included on higher order level test questions; text page references indicating where the correct answer can be obtained in the chapter have been provided for all test items. Additional alternate-format test items have also been added to the Test Bank. We have provided students with over 100 NCLEX-style questions that test their knowledge of the chapter content. We have also provided suggested responses for selected critical thinking questions threaded throughout each chapter. We have included accompanying textbook appendices and have expanded the content within Evolve, which supports the textbook, that includes PowerPoint presentations with audience-response questions, sample NCLEX-style questions, including alternate-format items, and case studies. The Evolve website will continue to provide updated information as new trends and issues affect the practice of nursing.

Please consult your local Elsevier representative for more details.

JoAnn Zerwekh
Ashley Zerwekh Garneau

ACKNOWLEDGMENTS

The success of previous editions of this book is a result of the contributions and efforts of our chapter contributors, who provided their expertise and knowledge, and our book reviewers, who provided their insights and suggestions on pertinent issues in nursing practice. This new edition is no exception. We thank the staff at Elsevier for their assistance and guidance during the revision of the ninth edition: Sandy Clark, Senior Content Strategist, and Jennifer Wade, Content Development Specialist. We also extend our gratitude to Divya Krishna Kumar, Team Leader, Book Production, and Minerva Irene A. Viloria, Book Project Manager, for monitoring the production of this book to ensure its delivery on schedule; a special thank you to Patrick Ferguson, Design Direction, for the overall book layout and design.

I would like to thank my children, Tyler and Ashley (my coauthor!); their spouses (Cassi Zerwekh and Brian Garneau); and my grandchildren (Maddie and Harper Zerwekh, Ben Garneau, Alexis and Brooklyn Parks, Owen and Emmett Masog) for putting a smile on my face and coaxing me to step away from the computer during those challenging times in the revision process. I would also like to thank my stepchildren, Carrie Parks and Matt Masog, and their spouses, Scott Parks and Becky Masog, for their support and great friendship and also for blessing me with more grandchildren. Finally, I would like to thank my husband, John Masog, for unending support, patience, and sense of humor during the revision of the ninth edition. I appreciate your willingness to complete the additional "honey-do" lists (especially trips to the grocery store!) that I managed to compile for you while I was entrenched in the book revision.

— **JoAnn**

To my husband, Brian, for unwavering support, unconditional love, wittiness, and for always being able to recognize when I needed a brain break from the computer. Thank you for keeping me grounded and balanced. To my son, Ben, who amazes me every day with how he sees the world around him. Last, I would like to thank my Mom, JoAnn, for her kindred spirit and for inspiring me to pursue the profession of nursing. You are my confidant, mentor, and the Nurse I aspire to be.

— **Ashley**

CONTENTS

UNIT II: NURSING: A DEVELOPING PROFESSION

UNIT III: NURSING MANAGEMENT

CONTENTS

Professional Growth and Transition

1

Role Transitions

JoAnn Zerwekh, EdD, RN, and Ashley Zerwekh Garneau, PhD, RN

(e) http://evolve.elsevier.com/Zerwekh/nsgtoday/.

When you're finished changing, you're finished.
Benjamin Franklin

Role transition can be a complex experience.

After completing this chapter, you should be able to:

- Discuss the concept of transitions.
- Identify the characteristics of reality shock.
- Compare and contrast the phases of reality shock.
- Identify times in your life when you have experienced a reality shock or role transition.
- Describe methods to promote a successful transition.

Welcome to the profession of nursing! This book is written for nursing students who are in the midst of transitions in their life. As a new student, you are beginning the transition to becoming indoctrinated into nursing, and sometimes it is not an easy transition. For those of you who are in the middle of nursing school, do you wonder if life even exists outside of nursing school? To the student who will soon graduate, hang on; you are almost there! For whatever transition period you are encountering, our goal is to help make your life easier during this period of personal and professional adjustment into nursing. We have designed this book to help you keep your feet on the ground and your head out of the clouds as well as to boost your spirits when the going gets rough.

As you thumb through this book, you will notice that there are cartoons and critical thinking questions that encourage your participation. Do not be alarmed; we know you have been overloaded with "critical thinking" during nursing school! These critical thinking questions are not meant to be graded; instead, their purpose is to encourage you to begin thinking about your transition, either into nursing school or into practice, and to guide you through the book in a practical, participative manner. Our intention is to add a little humor here and there while giving information on topics we feel will affect your transition into nursing practice. We want you to be informed about the controversial issues affecting nursing today. After all, the future of nursing rests with **you**!

Are you ready to begin? Then let's start with the real stuff. You are beginning to experience transitions—for some of you, just getting into nursing school has been a long struggle—and you are there! For others, you can see the light at the end of the tunnel, as graduation becomes a reality. Nursing is one of the most rewarding professions you can pursue. However, it can also be one of the most frustrating. As with marriage, raising children, and the pursuit of happiness, there are ups and downs. We seldom find the world or our specific situation the exact way we thought it would or should be. Often your fantasy of what nursing *should* be is not what you will find nursing to be.

> You will cry, but you will also laugh.
> You will share with people their darkest hours of pain and suffering, but
> You will also share with them their hope, healing, and recovery.
> You will be there as life begins and ends.
> You will experience great challenges that lead to success.
> You will experience failure and disappointment.
> You will never cease to be amazed at the resilience of the human body and spirit.

TRANSITIONS

What Are Transitions?

Transitions are passages or changes from one situation, condition, or state to another that occur over time. They have been classified into the following four major types: developmental (e.g., becoming a parent, midlife crisis), situational (e.g., graduating from a nursing program, career change, divorce), health/illness (e.g., dealing with a chronic illness), and organizational (e.g., change in leadership, new staffing patterns) (Schumacher & Meleis, 1994).

> Transitions are complex processes, and a lot of transitions may occur at the same time.

What Are Important Factors Influencing Transitions?

Understanding the transition experience from the perspective of the person who is experiencing it is important because the meaning of the experience may be positive, negative, or neutral, and the expectation may or may not be realistic. The transition may be desired (e.g., passing the NCLEX® Exam) or undesirable (e.g., the death of a family member, after which you have to assume a new role in your family).

> Often, when you know what to expect, the stress associated with the change or transition is reduced.

Another factor in the transition process is the new level of knowledge and skill required, as well as the availability of needed resources within the environment. Dealing with new knowledge and skills can be challenging and stressful and can lead to a variety of different emotions related to the expectation of the new graduate to be competent (Box 1.1). This will resolve as your confidence grows and you have more understanding of the concept of how to "think like a nurse."

Transitions are a part of life and certainly a part of nursing. Although the following discussions on role transition and reality shock focus on the graduate nurse experience, there are many applicable points for the new student as well. As you learn more about transitions, reality shock, and the graduate nurse experience, think about how this information may also apply to your transition experience into and through nursing school (Critical Thinking Box 1.1).

Looking back, what transitions have you experienced? What transitions are occurring in your life now? Has your entry into, as well as progress through, nursing school caused transitions in your personal life? Has your anticipated job search caused transitions in your professional as well as personal life?

Transitions in Nursing

The paradox of nursing will become obvious to you early in your nursing career. This realization may occur during nursing school, but it frequently becomes most obvious during the first 6 months of your first job.

Health care organizations are very concerned about your transition experience and job satisfaction during that first 6 months of employment. Have you been hearing about "evidence-based

---

BOX 1.1   STRESSES REPORTED BY NEW GRADUATES RELATED TO 6 CRUCIAL COMPETENCY AREAS

1. Communication
   - Calling or talking with a physician, completing shift reports, addressing patient requests, and resolving conflict
2. Leadership
   - Lack of delegating skills
   - Anxiety associated with collaborative teamwork
3. Organization
   - Lack of organizational and management skills to prioritize care
4. Critical thinking
   - Difficulty with clinical decision making
   - Feeling unprepared to meet the challenges of the workplace
   - Deficits in clinical knowledge
5. Specific situations
   - Lack of confidence when dealing with acutely ill patients, emergency situations, and end-of-life scenarios
6. Stress management
   - Unfamiliarity with stress management techniques
   - Lack of social support

From Theisen, J., & Sandau, K. (2013). Competency of new graduate nurses: A review of their weaknesses and strategies for success. *Journal of Continuing Education in Nursing, 44*(9), 406–414. doi: dx.doi .org/10.3928/00220124-20130617-38.

> ## ❓ CRITICAL THINKING BOX 1.1
>
> What is your greatest concern about your transition? Is it personal or work transitions because you are a student nurse, or is it your transition from school to the practice setting?

practice?" Well, it is working for you now! During the first 6 months of employment, new graduates need a period of time to develop their skills in a supportive environment. Employee retention and job satisfaction are key issues with the hospital; confidence in performing skills and procedures, nurse residency programs, and dependence versus independence are key graduate nurse issues driving this research. The well-being of the graduate nurse and the ability to deliver quality nursing care during the transition period have sparked research to validate the need for special considerations of the graduate nurse experiencing transition (Casey et al., 2004; Godinez et al., 1999; Lavoie-Tremblay et al., 2002; Steinmiller et al., 2003; Duchscher, 2008; Duchscher, 2009; Varner and Leeds, 2012; Spector, 2015a). With identification of the basic problems encountered by new graduates during this first 6 months, there is a concerted effort to begin to meet the special needs of the graduate nurse and assist him or her to "think like a nurse" (Research for Best Practice Box 1.1).

The role-transition process that occurs on entry into nursing school and the process from student to graduate nurse do not take place automatically. Having the optimal experience during role transition requires a great deal of attention, planning, and determination on your part. How you perceive and handle the transition will determine how well you progress through the process. It is important that you keep a positive attitude. The challenges and rewards of clinicals, tests, and work situations will cause your emotions to go up and down, but that is okay. It is expected, and you will be able to deal with it effectively. It is important that you keep a positive attitude. The wide range of emotions experienced during the transition process can often affect your *emotional and physical well-being;* check out the discussion of self-care strategies in Chapter 2.

So, let's get started. Reality shock is often one of the first hurdles of transition to conquer in your new role as a graduate nurse or registered nurse (RN or Real Nurse ☺).

REALITY SHOCK

What Is Reality Shock?

Reality shock is a term often used to describe the reaction experienced when one moves into the workforce after several years of educational preparation. The recent graduate is caught in the situation of moving from a familiar, comfortable educational environment into a new role in the workforce in which the expectations are not clearly defined or may not even be realistic. For example, as a student you were taught to consider the patient in a holistic framework, but in practice you often do not have the time to consider the psychosocial or teaching needs of the patient, even though they must be attended to and documented.

The recent graduate in the workplace is expected to be a capable, competent nurse. That sounds fine. However, sometimes there is a hidden expectation that graduate nurses should function as though they have 5 years of nursing experience. Time management skills, along with the increasing acuity level of patients, are common problems for the new graduate. This situation may leave you with feelings of powerlessness, depression, and insecurity because of an apparent lack of effectiveness in the work environment. There are positive ways to deal with the problems. You are not alone! Reality shock is not unique to nursing. It is present in many professions as graduates move from the world of academia to the world of work and begin to adjust to the expectations and values of the workforce.

RESEARCH FOR BEST PRACTICE BOX 1.1

Role Transition: Think Like a Nurse

Practice Issue

Students report that when they first entered their nursing courses they were unaware of the complexity of thinking and problem solving that occurs in the clinical setting. They often are unable to "think on their feet" and change a planned way of doing something based on what is happening with a specific patient at any given moment. Research supports the finding that the beginning nursing graduate continues to have difficulty making clinical judgments (i.e., thinking like a nurse). Graduates with baccalaureate degrees in nursing were interviewed three times in 9 months to determine their perceptions of how they learned to think like nurses (Tanner, 2006). In a later simulation study by Ashley and Stamp (2014), thinking like a nurse was one of the major themes that emerged when comparing sophomore and junior students. During simulation, the sophomore student approached the clinical scenario more as a layperson than as a professional with specialized knowledge, which was exhibited by little preplanning and the expectation that the clinical problem would be self-evident and would require nothing more than common sense to achieve an outcome.

Implications for Nursing Practice
Clinical Judgments—Thinking Like a Nurse

- Nursing students and new graduates are often unaware of the level of responsibility required of nurses and lack confidence in their ability to make clinical judgments.
- The process of learning to think like a nurse is characterized by building confidence, accepting responsibility, adapting to changing relations with others, and thinking more critically.
- Multiple clinical experiences, support from faculty and experienced nurses, and sharing experiences with peers were critical in the transition from student nurse to beginning practitioner.
- Nursing education must assist nursing students to engage with patients and act on a responsible vision for excellent care of those patients and with a deep concern for the patients' and families' well-being. Clinical reasoning must arise from this engaged, concerned stance.

Considering This Information

What types of resources will you utilize as a nursing student to improve your clinical reasoning skills? What characteristics have you observed in staff members who effectively "think like a nurse"? How can you begin to incorporate these aspects into your practice as a new graduate nurse?

References

Ashley, J., & Stamp, K. (2014). Learning to think like a nurse: The development of clinical judgment in nursing students. *Journal of Nursing Education, 53*(9), 519-525. doi: dx.doi.org/10.3928/01484834-20140821-14.

Etheridge, S.A. (2007). Learning to think like a nurse: Stories from new nurse graduates, *Journal of Continuing Education in Nursing, 38*(1), 24-30.

Tanner, C.A. (2006). Thinking like a nurse: A research-based model of clinical judgment in nursing, *Journal of Continuing Education in Nursing, 45*(6).

What Are the Phases of Reality Shock?

Kramer (1974) described the phases of reality shock as they apply to nursing (Table 1.1). Although she identified this process in 1974, these phases remain the basis for understanding the implications of reality shock and successfully progressing through the process. In our current world of nursing, we are still dealing with this same process. Adjustments begin to take place as the graduate nurse adapts to the reality of the practice of nursing. The first phase of adjustment is the honeymoon phase (Fig. 1.1). The recent graduate is thrilled with completing school and accepting a first job. Life is a "bed of roses" because everyone knows nursing school is much harder than nursing practice. There are no more concept care maps to create, no

TABLE 1.1	**PHASES OF REALITY SHOCK**	
HONEYMOON	**SHOCK AND REJECTION**	**RECOVERY**
Sees the world of nursing looking quite rosy Often fascinated with the thrill of "arriving" in the profession	Has excessive mistrust Experiences increased concern over minor pains and illness Experiences decrease in energy and feels excessive fatigue Feels like a failure and blames self for every mistake Bands together and depends on people who hold the same values Has a hypercritical attitude Feels moral outrage	Beginning to have sense of humor (first sign) Decrease in tension Increase in ability to be objective

FIG. 1.1 Reality shock. The honeymoon's over.

more nursing care plans to write, and no more burning the midnight oil for the next day's examination. No one is watching over your shoulder while you insert a catheter or administer an intravenous medication. You are not a "student" anymore; now you are a nurse! During this exciting phase, your perception of the situation may feel unreal and distorted, and you may not be able to understand the overall picture.

HONEYMOON PHASE

I just can't believe how wonderful everything is! Imagine getting a paycheck—money, at last! It's all great. Really, it is.

The honeymoon phase is frequently short-lived as the graduate begins to identify the conflicts between the way she or he was taught and the reality of what is done. Every graduate nurse will have a unique way of coping with the situations; however, some common responses have been identified. The graduate may cope with this conflict by withdrawing or rejecting the values learned during nursing school. This may mark the end of the honeymoon phase of transition. The phrase "going native" was used by Kramer and

Schmalenberg (1977) to describe recent graduates as they begin to cope and identify with the reality of the situation by rejecting the values from nursing school and beginning to function as everyone else does.

SHOCK AND REJECTION PHASE

Mary was assigned 10 patients for the morning. There were numerous medications to be administered. It was difficult to carry all of the medication administration records to each room for patient identification. Because she "knew the patients" and because the other experienced nurses did not check identification, she decided she no longer needed to check a patient's identification before administering medication. Later in the day, she gave insulin to Mrs. James, a patient she "knew"; unfortunately, the insulin was for Mrs. Phillips, another patient she "knew."

With experiences such as this during transition, graduates may feel as though they have failed and begin to blame themselves for every mistake. They may also experience moral outrage at having been put in such a position. When the bad days begin to outnumber the good days, the graduate nurse may experience frustration, fatigue, and anger and may consequently develop a hypercritical attitude toward nursing. Some graduates become very disillusioned and drop out of nursing altogether. This is the period of shock and rejection.

I had just completed orientation in the hospital where I had wanted to work since I started nursing school. I immediately discovered that the care there was so bad that I did not want to be a part of it. At night, I went home very frustrated that the care I had given was not as I was taught to do it. I cried every night and hated to go to work in the morning. I did not like anyone with whom I was working. My stomach hurt, my head throbbed, and I had difficulty sleeping. It was hard not to work a double shift because I was worried about who would take care of those patients if I was not there.

A successfully managed transition period begins when the graduate nurse is able to evaluate the work situation objectively and predict the actions and reactions of the staff effectively. Prioritization, conflict management, time management, and support groups (peers, preceptors, and mentors) can make a significant difference in promoting a successfully managed transition period.

Nurturing the ability to see humor in a situation may be the first step. As the graduate begins to laugh at some of the situations encountered, the tension decreases and the perception increases. It is during this critical period of recovery that conflict resolution occurs. If this resolution occurs in a positive manner, it enables the graduate nurse to grow more fully as a person. This growth also enables the graduate to meet the work expectations to a greater degree and to see that she or he has the capacity to change a situation. If the conflict is resolved in a less positive manner, however, the graduate's potential to learn and grow is limited.

Kramer (1974) described four groups of graduate nurses and the steps they took to resolve reality shock. The graduates who were considered to be most successful at adaptation were those who "made a lot of waves" within both their job setting and their professional organizations. Accordingly, they were not content with the present state of nursing but worked to effect a better system. This group of graduates was able to take worthwhile values learned during school and integrate them into the work setting. Often they returned to school—but not too quickly. Since Kramer's original work, students are now encouraged to go back to school fairly quickly, especially with the emphasis from the IOM report of encouraging more advanced degrees in nursing.

RECOVERY PHASE

I am really glad that I became a nurse. Sure, there are plenty of hassles, but the opportunities are there. Now that I am more confident of my skills, I am willing to take risks to improve patient care. Just last week my head nurse, who often says jokingly, "You're a thorn in my side," appointed me to the Nursing Standards Committee. I feel really good about this recognition.

Another group limited their involvement with nursing by just putting in the usual workday. Persons in this group seldom belonged to professional organizations and cited the following reasons for working: "to provide for my family," "to buy extra things for the house," and "to support myself." Typically, this group's negative approach to conflict resolution leads to burnout, during which time the conflict is turned inward, leading to constant griping and complaining about the work setting.

> I was so happy, at first. Gee, I was able to buy my son all those toys he wanted. But things here always seem to be the same—too many patients, not enough help. I get so upset with the staff, especially the nursing assistants, and the care that is given to patients. I wonder whether I will ever get the opportunity to practice nursing as I was taught. Well, I'll hang on until my husband finishes graduate school; then I'll quit this awful job!

Another group of graduates seemed to have found their niche and were content within the hospital setting. However, their positive attitude toward the job did not extend to nursing as a profession; in fact, it was the opposite. Rather than leave the organization during conflict, these "organization nurses" would change units or shifts—anything to avoid increasing demands for professional performance.

> During those first few months as I was just getting started, I sure had a tough time. It was difficult learning how to delegate tasks to the aides and practical nurses. But now that I have started working for Dr. Travis, everything is under my control. I just might go back to school someday.

The last group of graduates frequently changed jobs. After a short-lived career in hospital nursing, this group would pirouette off to graduate school, where they could "do something else in nursing" (meaning, "I can't nurse the way I've been taught, so I might as well teach others how to do things right"). Achieving a high profile in professional nursing organizations was common for these graduates, along with seeking a safer, more idealistically structured environment in which the values learned in school prevail.

> Finally, I got so frustrated with my head nurse that I just resigned. What did she expect from a recent graduate? I couldn't do everything! Cost containment; early discharge; no time for teaching; rush, rush, rush, all the time. Well, I've made up my mind to look into going back to school to further my career.

The job expectations of the hospital administration or the employing community agency and the educational preparation of the graduate nurse are not always the same. This discrepancy is considered to be the basis of reality shock. Relationships among the staff, nursing professionalism, job satisfaction, and employee alienation were studied by Roche and colleagues (2004), Casey and colleagues (2004), and Varner and Leeds (2012). What is interesting is that the issues of reality shock and role transition described by Kramer in the early 1970s are still around. We (nurses) have entered the 21st century with many of the same issues we had in the 20th century.

It might seem to you right now, after reading all of this information, that reality shock is a life-threatening situation. Be assured, it is not. You may, however, experience some physical and psychological symptoms in varying degrees of intensity. For example, you may feel stressed out or have headaches, insomnia, gastrointestinal upset, or a bout of poststudent blues. Just remember that it takes time to adjust to a new routine and that sometimes, even after you have gotten used to it, you still may feel overwhelmed, confused, or anxious. The good news is that there are various ways to get through this critical phase of your career while establishing a firm foundation for future professional growth and career mobility. Try the assessment exercise in Critical Thinking Box 1.2.

CRITICAL THINKING BOX 1.2

Reality Shock Inventory

All students, as well as new graduates, experience reality shock to some extent or another. The purpose of this exercise is to make you aware of how you feel about yourself and your particular life situation.

Directions: To evaluate your views and determine your self-evaluation of your particular life situation, respond to the statements with the appropriate number.

1 Strongly agree	4 Slightly disagree
2 Agree	5 Disagree
3 Slightly agree	6 Strongly disagree

1. I am still finding new challenges and interests in my work.
2. I think often about what I want from life.
3. My own personal future seems promising.
4. Nursing school and/or my work has brought stresses for which I was unprepared.
5. I would like the opportunity to start anew knowing what I know now.
6. I drink more than I should.
7. I often feel that I still belong in the place where I grew up.
8. Much of the time my mind is not as clear as it used to be.
9. I have no sense of regret concerning my major life decision of becoming a nurse.
10. My views on nursing are as positive as they ever were.
11. I have a strong sense of my own worth.
12. I am experiencing what would be called a crisis in my personal or work setting.
13. I cannot see myself as a nurse.
14. I must remain loyal to commitments even if they have not proven as rewarding as I had expected.
15. I wish I were different in many ways.
16. The way I present myself to the world is not the way I really am.
17. I often feel agitated or restless.
18. I have become more aware of my inadequacies and faults.
19. My sex life is as satisfactory as it has ever been.
20. I often think about students and/or friends who have dropped out of school or work.

To compute your score, reverse the number you assigned to statements 1, 3, 9, 10, 11, and 19. For example, 1 would become a 6, 2 would become a 5, 3 would become a 4, 4 would become a 3, 5 would become a 2, and 6 would become a 1. Total the number. The higher the score, the better your attitude. The range is 20 to 120.

Modified from White, E. (April 23, 1986). Doctoral dissertation, *Chronicle of Higher Education*, p.28. Reprinted with permission.

ROLE TRANSFORMATION

Remember when you first started nursing school? The war stories everybody told you? The changes that occurred in your family as a result of your starting nursing school? Are you in the midst of that now, or does it seem like a long time ago? Can you really believe where you are now and where you were when you first began nursing school, those first nursing courses, and clinicals? It has taken a lot of work and sacrifice to get to where you are now. Believe it or not, you have already experienced a role transition—you successfully transitioned to a student nurse. Now, as you draw nearer to the successful completion of that experience, you are ready to embark on a new one. Take a minute to read the thoughts of one of your peers about her transition into nursing. I'm sure you will smile at her satire (Critical Thinking Box 1.3).

Give yourself a well-deserved pat on the back for what you have accomplished thus far. It is important to learn early in your practice of nursing to take time to reflect on your accomplishments. Now, back to the present. Let's look at the current role-transition process at hand, from student to graduate nurse RN.

⚡ CRITICAL THINKING BOX 1.3

Survival Techniques from one who has Survived

You finally did it; you have decided nursing is what you want to do for the rest of your life. After all, who would go through all this anguish if you only wanted to do this as a pastime? If you are taking this like everyone else, you are probably going to do this by trial and error, "war" stories, or by helpful hints from the nursing staff.

You need to prioritize your time. This is a familiar and much used term that you will hear often. It is also easier said than done. If you are single, you have an advantage—maybe. You can decide right now that single is "where it's at" and stay that way for the duration. Of course this means literally living the "single" life. There are no "dinners-for-two," no telephone conversations, no movies at the cinema (rarely any TV)—in other words, no physical contact with the opposite sex. I know you were not thinking about it anyway, but in case you are studying anatomy and physiology, and hormonal thoughts pervade your consciousness, dismiss them.

If you are married, I am not suggesting divorce, just abstinence. Hopefully, you kissed your spouse good-bye when you came to school for your first day of class because your next chance will be on your breaks or when you graduate.

If you happen to be a parent, do as I did. I put pictures of myself in all rooms of my house when I started to school so that the kids would not forget me. My children, in return, helped me by plastering their faces in my fridge (they know I'll look there) or on my mirror (another sure spot). I have acquired a son-in-law, a daughter-in-law, and five grandchildren in the past 2½ years, and I usually do not recognize them if I run into them on the rare occasions when I go to the store for essentials (like food) or out to pay our utility bills. Christmas is fun, though, because each year I get to spend a few days getting to know the family again. But we all must wear name tags for the first day!

If your children are small, buy them the Fisher Price Kitchen and teach them how to "cook" nourishing "hot" cereal on the stove that does not heat up. For the infant, hang a TPN (hint: Total Parental Nutrition) of Similac with iron at 40 mL/hr that the baby can control by sound! Crying should do it! Instead of a needle, use a nipple....

Diapers—what would we do without those disposable diapers that stay dry for 2 weeks at a time? You can even buy the kind that you touch the waistband, and Mickey Mouse and his friends jump off to entertain your baby.

Some of you may feel guilty about not fixing those delicious meals your family once enjoyed. Do not! We get two "breaks" a year, and during that time, fix barrels of nourishing liquid (you can add a few veggies). When your family gets hungry, just take out enough to keep fluids and lytes balanced. Remind them that this is only going to last another year or two.

Have I covered everything? Oh I forgot dust.... Dust used to bother me, but not anymore. I use it to write notes to my 17-year-old, to let him know what time I am going to be in the house, so he will not mistake me for a burglar, and to say "I Love You."

On a serious note, each semester you will get regrouped with new classmates. They will become your family, your support group. You will form a chain, and everyone is a strong link. This is a group effort. These are people who will laugh with you and cry with you. You will form friendships that will last a lifetime. Take advantage of these opportunities.

On a closing note, do not listen to all the "war stories" that go around—just to the credible ones like mine!

From Beagle, B. (May/June, 1990). Survival techniques, *AD Clinical Care*, p.17. Reprinted with permission.

When Does the Role Transition to Graduate Nurse Begin?

Does the transition begin at graduation? No. It started when you began to move into the novice role while in your first nursing course (Table 1.2). According to Benner (1984,p.20):

> Beginners have no experience of the situation in which they are expected to perform. To get them into these situations and allow them to gain experience also necessary for skill development, they are taught about the situation in terms of objective attributes, such as weight, intake/output, temperature, blood pressure, pulse, and other objective, measurable parameters of a patient's conditions—features of the task world that can be recognized without situational experience.

For example, the instructor gives the novice or student nurse specific directions on how to listen for bowel sounds. There are specific rules on how to guide their actions—rules that are very limited and fairly inflexible. Remember your first clinical nursing experiences? Your nursing instructor was your

TABLE 1.2   FROM NOVICE TO EXPERT

STAGE	CHARACTERISTICS
NOVICE	
Nursing student Experienced nurse in a new setting	• No clinical experience in situation expected to perform • Needs rules to guide performance • Experiences difficulty in applying theoretical concepts to patient care
ADVANCED BEGINNER	
Last-semester nursing student Graduate nurse	• Demonstrates ability to deliver marginally acceptable care • Requires previous experience in an actual situation to recognize it • Begins to understand the principles that dictate nursing interventions • Continues to concentrate on the rules and takes in minimum information regarding a situation
COMPETENT	
2-3 years' clinical experience	• Conscientious, deliberate planning • Begins to see nursing actions in light of patients' long-term plans • Demonstrates ability to cope with and manage different and unexpected situations that occur
PROFICIENT	
Nurse clinicians Nursing faculty	• Ability to recognize and understand the situation as a whole • Demonstrates ability to anticipate events in a given situation • Holistic understanding enhances decision making
EXPERT	
Advanced practice nurse clinicians and faculty	• Demonstrates an understanding of the situation and is able to focus on the specific area of the problem • Operates from an in-depth understanding of the total situation • Demonstrates highly skilled analytical ability in problem solving; performance becomes masterful

Modified from Benner, P. (2001). The Dreyfus model of skill acquisition applied to nursing. In *From novice to expert,* Commemorative Edition, Menlo Park, CA: Addison-Wesley.

shadow for patient care. As nursing students enter a clinical area as novices, they have little understanding of the meaning and application of recently learned textbook terms and concepts. Students are not the only novices; any nurse may assume the novice role on entering a clinical setting in which he or she is not comfortable functioning or has no practical experience. Consider an experienced medical-surgical nurse who floats to the postpartum unit; she would be a little uncomfortable in that clinical setting.

By graduation, most nursing students are at the level of advanced beginner. According to Benner (1984, p.20):

> Advanced beginners are ones who can demonstrate marginally accepted performance, ones who have coped with enough real situations to note (or to have pointed out to them by a mentor) the recurring meaningful situation components....

To be able to recognize characteristics that can be identified only through experience is the signifying trait of the advanced beginner. Thus, when directed to perform the procedure of checking bowel sounds, the students at this level are learning how to discriminate bowel sounds and understand their meaning. They do not need to be told specifically how to perform the procedure.

Let's look at what you and your nursing instructors can do to promote your well-being and success during the role-transition experience. These activities reinforce your progress and movement along the continuum from advanced-beginner to competent nurse (see Table 1.2).

How Can I Prepare Myself for This Transition Process?

During the last semester of nursing school, it is very advantageous to have as much clinical experience as possible. The most productive area for experience is a general medical-surgical unit, which will have a variety of patient cases. This will help you ground your assessment and communication skills, as well as help you to apply principles that are most often tested on the NCLEX Exam. This is also the area in which you will most likely be able to obtain some much needed experience with basic nursing skills.

Begin Increasing Independence

It is time to have your nursing instructor cut the umbilical cord and allow you to function more independently, without frequent cueing and directing during the last semester of your clinical experience.

More Realistic Patient-Care Assignments

Start taking care of increasing numbers of patients to help you with time management, prioritization, and work organization. Evaluate the nursing staff's assignments to determine what a realistic workload is for a recent graduate.

Clinical Hours That Represent Realistic Shift Hours

Obtain experience in receiving shift reports, closing charts, completing patient care, and communicating with the oncoming staff and other health care professionals involved in providing patient care.

Perform Nursing Procedures Instead of Observing

Take an inventory of your nursing skills, and be sure to have this available for potential employers so they can see what skills you are familiar with. If there are nursing skills you lack or procedures you are uncomfortable with, take this opportunity while you are still in school to gain the experience. Identify your clinical objectives to meet your personal needs. Request opportunities to practice from your instructor and staff nurses. Casey and colleagues (2004) identified skills that were challenging for the graduate nurses in the first year of practice. These skills included code blues, chest tubes, intravenous skills, central lines, blood administration, and patient-controlled analgesia (PCA). While it is important for you to be proficient and safe in performing skills, Theisen and Sandau (2013) pointed out in their review that new graduate nurses lack competency in communicating with the health care team, delegating, resolving conflict during stressful situations (i.e., end-of-life care, deteriorating patient), prioritizing patient care, and critical decision making. Make an effort to gain experience in these areas while you are still in school; you will be more comfortable in your nursing care as a graduate.

More Truth About the Real Work-Setting Experience

Identify resource people with whom you can objectively discuss the dilemmas of the workplace. Talk to graduates: Ask them what they know now that they wish they had known the last semester of school.

Look for Opportunities to Problem Solve and Practice Critical Thinking

Actively seek out learning opportunities in both the clinical and classroom setting to exercise your critical thinking skills and decision making. Now is the time to stand on your own two feet while there is still a backup—your instructor—available. Look for opportunities to communicate with the interprofessional team.

Request Constructive Feedback from Staff and Instructors

Stop avoiding evaluation and constructive criticism. Find out now how you can improve your nursing care. Ask questions and clarify anything that is not understood. Evaluate your progress on a periodic basis. The consequences may be less severe now than later with your new employer.

Request Clinical Experience in an Area or Hospital of Interest

If you have some idea of where you would like to work, it is very beneficial to have some clinical experiences in that facility the last semester of school. This gives you the opportunity to become involved with staff nurses, identify workload on the unit, and evaluate resources and support people. It also gives the employing institution an opportunity to evaluate you—Are you someone that institution would like to have work for them?

> Attitude is the latitude between success and failure.

Think Positively!

Be prepared for the reality of the workplace environment, including both its positives and negatives. You may have encountered by now the "ol' battle ax" who has a grudge against new nursing graduates.

> I do not know why you ever decided to be a nurse. Nobody respects you. It's all work, low pay. I guess as long as you've got a good back and strong legs, you'll make it. Boy, do you have a lot to learn! I wouldn't do it over again for anything!

When you find these nurses, tune them out and steer out of their way! They have their own agenda, and it does not include providing supportive assistance to you. Eventually, you will learn how to work with this type of individual (see Chapter 12), but for now, you should concentrate on identifying nurses who share your philosophy and are still smiling.

> Surround yourself with nurses who have a positive attitude and are supportive in your learning and growing transition.

Another way to keep a positive perspective is to focus on the good things that have happened during the shift rather than on the frustrating events. When you feel yourself climbing onto the proverbial "pity pot," ask yourself "Who's driving this bus?" and turn it around!

Anticipate small irritations and disappointments, and keep them in perspective. Do not let them mushroom into major problems. Turn disappointments and unpleasant situations into learning experiences. Once you have encountered an unpleasant situation, the next time it occurs you will recognize it sooner, anticipate the chain of events, and be better able to handle it.

> Do not major in a minor activity.

Be Flexible!

Procedures, policies, and nursing supervisors are not going to be the same as those you experienced in school. Be prepared to do things differently from the way you learned them as a student. You do not have to give up all the values you learned in school, but you will need to reexamine them in light of the reality of the workplace setting. Flexibility is one of the most important qualities of a good nurse!

School-learned ideal. Sit down with the patient before surgery, and provide preoperative teaching.

Workplace reality. One of your home care patients is receiving daily wound care for an extensive burn. You receive a message that the patient has been scheduled for grafting in the outpatient surgery department and is to be a direct admit at 6 AM the next morning. You have two more home visits to make: one to hang an intravenous preparation of vancomycin and the other a new hospice admission, which you know will take considerable time.

Compromise. You delegate to one of the home care practical nurses to take the preoperative teaching and admission instructions to your patient. Later on, you make a telephone call to your preoperative patient and go over the preoperative care teaching information from the home care practical nurse. You make arrangements to meet this patient at home immediately after the grafting procedure is complete.

Get Organized!

Does your personal life seem organized or chaotic, calm or frantic? Sit back and take a quick inventory of your personal life. How do you expect to get your professional life in order when your personal life is in turmoil? For some helpful tips on organizing your personal life, check out the personal management chapter (see Chapter 2).

Stay Healthy!

Have you become a "couch potato" while in school? Are you too tired, or do you lack the time to exercise when you get home from work? Candy bars during breaks, pepperoni pizza at midnight, and Twinkies PRN? How have your eating habits changed during your time in school? Your routine should include exercise, relaxation, and good nutrition. Becoming aware of the negative habits that can have detrimental effects on your state of mind and overall physical health is important in developing a healthy lifestyle.

Find a Mentor!

Negotiating this critical transition as you begin your nursing career should not be done in isolation. Evidence suggests that close support relationships, mentors, and preceptors are key, if not essential, ingredients in the career development of a successful, happy graduate (Casey et al., 2004; Roche et al., 2004). For additional tips on finding a mentor as you begin your professional practice, take a look at the mentoring chapter (see Chapter 3). In addition to your family and close nursing school friends, it will be important to develop professional support relationships.

Find Other New Graduates!

Frequently, several new graduates are hired at the same time. Some of them may even be your classmates. Find them and establish a peer support group. Sharing experiences and problems and knowing that someone else is experiencing the same feelings you are can be a great relief!

Have Some Fun!

Do something that makes you feel good. This is life, not a funeral service! Nursing has opportunities for laughter and for sharing life's humorous events with patients and coworkers. Surround yourself with people and friends who are lighthearted and merry and who bring those feelings out in you. Remember, the return of humor is one of the first signs of a healthy role transition. Loosen up a little bit. Go ahead, have some fun! Check out the information in Chapter 3 for more on selection of mentors and preceptors.

Know What to Expect!

Plan ahead. Plan your employment interviews; ask to talk to nurses on the units and find out how nursing care is delivered in the institution. The length of orientation, staffing patterns, opportunity for internship, areas where positions are open, and resources for new graduates are all important to establish prior to employment. This helps you know what to expect when you go to work. Work satisfaction is a positive predictor of a successful role transition during the first year (Roche, 2004). Know what is expected of you on your work unit. How can you expect to do a job correctly if you do not know what the expectations are? Learn the "rules of the road" early. This may be in the hospital, doctor's office, or community setting. While still in school, you may find it helpful to interview nurse managers to determine their perspectives on the role of the graduate nurse during the first 6 months of employment. This will give you a base of reference when you interview for your first job. How do you measure up to some of the common expectations nurse managers may be looking for in a graduate nurse?

Are you:

- Excited and sincere about nursing?
- Open-minded and willing to learn new ideas and skills?
- Comfortable with your basic nursing skills?
- Able to keep a good sense of humor?
- Receptive to constructive feedback?
- Able to express your thoughts and feelings?
- Able to evaluate your performance and request assistance?
- Comfortable talking with your patients regarding their individual needs?

What Is the Future of Role Transition?

At the August 2008 annual meeting of the National Council of State Boards of Nursing (NCSBN), the Practice and Education Committee reported "there was adequate evidence to support a regulatory model for transitioning new graduates to practice" (NCSBN, 2008a, p.259). The committee noted that the need for a transition regulatory model has grown from the changes occurring in health care over the past 20 years, not from deficiencies in nursing education and/or unrealistic expectations of the workplace. In the report from the committee to the NCSBN, the goal for the transition to practice regulatory model is "to promote public safety by supporting newly licensed nurses in their critical entry and progression into practice" (NCSBN, 2008b, p.262). In 2009, the NCSBN finalized the design of an evidence-based "transition to practice" regulatory model (Fig. 1.2) that includes modules on communication and teamwork, patient-centered care, evidence-based practice, quality improvement, informatics, and an additional module of preceptor training. A Transition to Practice toolkit is available at the NCSBN website (https://www.ncsbn.org/687.htm) that provides links to all of the modules.

The results from the national Transition to Practice (TPP) study in hospital settings conducted by the NCSBN have been reported (NCSBN, 2015), which addressed questions about the effectiveness of the NCSBN's TTP program and whether or not TTP programs make a difference in new graduate outcomes in terms of safety, competence, stress, job satisfaction, and retention (Research for Best Practice Box 1.2).

> What is happening in your state regarding the Transition to Practice model?

The TTP model recommends a 9- to 12-month internship, so the new graduate receives continued support during the vulnerable period from 6 to 9 months. For the transition process to be effective, it should occur across all settings and at all education levels. This would include both the

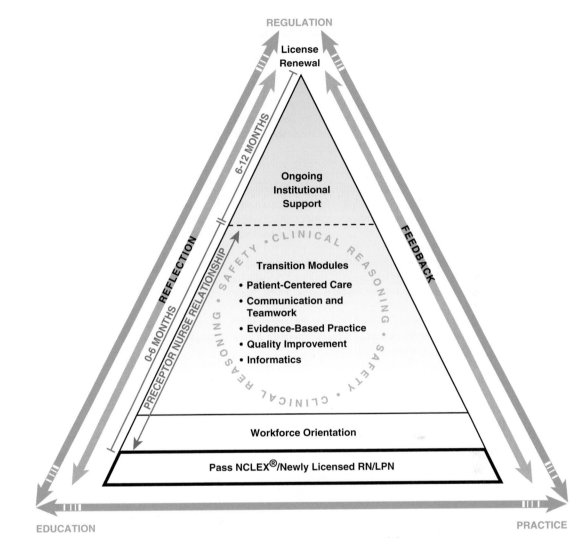

FIG. 1.2 Transition to Practice model.

RN and the LPN/LVN. To promote safer nursing practice through a regulatory transition period, practice, education, and regulation all must work together on the development of a model that will effectively support the new nurse in his or her transition to safe practice (Spector, 2015b).

In response to the 2010 Institute of Medicine (IOM) report, the Robert Wood Johnson Foundation has developed the Initiative on the Future of Nursing (2011) to address the IOM recommendations for the nursing profession. One recommendation is to implement nurse residency programs for new graduate nurses to acquire skills and develop competency as nurses in providing care to today's complex and diverse health care population. Since the IOM report, state boards of nursing, nursing education programs, and health care institutions have joined together and developed nurse residency programs to prepare the future nurse—that's you! For additional resources and research on nurse residency programs, check out the mentoring, preceptorship, and nurse residency program chapter (see Chapter 3).

🔍 RESEARCH FOR BEST PRACTICE BOX 1.2

Role Transition

Practice Issue

With the increased complexity of the health care environment, new graduates struggle with the transition into clinical practice. This matter is related to several issues: sicker patients in an increasingly complex health care setting, the shortened gap between taking NCLEX and being licensed, variable transition experiences, increased patient workload due to the nursing shortage, high job stress and turnover rates in new graduate RNs (approximately 25% of new nurses leave their position within the first year of practice), and practice errors.

Implications for Nursing Practice

- Transition experiences of new RNs vary across practice settings.
- Health care agencies with formalized transition programs have noted a marked drop in new graduate attrition, along with improved patient outcomes when a transition program has the following characteristics.
- A preceptorship with the preceptor receiving education for the preceptor role.
- Program is 9-12 months in length.
- Program content includes patient safety, clinical reasoning, communication and teamwork, patient-centered care, evidence-based practice, quality improvement, and informatics (QSEN competencies).
- New graduates are given time to learn, apply content, obtain feedback, and share their reflections about the transition process.
- Programs are customized so the new graduate learns specialty content in the areas where they are working.
- At 6 months, when new graduates typically become more independent there is an increase in errors, a decrease in job satisfaction, and an increase in work stress.
- At 12 months in practice, work stress and reported errors decrease and job satisfaction increases; research findings support need for ongoing support during first year of practice.
- The 6- to 9-month period of practice is the most vulnerable time for new graduates.

Considering This Information

What can you do to ease your transition process?

References

NCSBN. (2016). *Transition to practice.* Retrieved from https://www.ncsbn.org/transition-to-practice.htm.

Spector, N. (2015a). The National Council of State Boards of Nursing's transition to practice study: Implications for educators. *Journal of Nursing Education, 54*(3), 119-120. http://dx.doi.org/10.3928/01484834-20150217-13. Retrieved from http://www.healio.com/nursing/journals/jne/2015-3-54-3/%7Bc25037ac-f3b7-4a30-a64c-2a8556b783de%7D/the-national-council-of-state-boards-of-nursings-transition-to-practice-study-implications-for-educators

Spector, N., et al. (2015b). *Transition to practice study in hospital settings.* Retrieved from https://www.ncsbn.org/Spector_Transition_to_Practice_Study_in_Hospital_Settings.pdf.

CONCLUSION

What will be the direction for role transition of graduate nurses? Will your state adopt the Transition to Practice model? How will preceptors be selected, and will they be credentialed? As you progress through the chapters in this book, you will find references to the Institute of Medicine (IOM), The Joint Commission (TJC), and other health care resources concerned with the safety of patients, the reduction of errors, and the economic impact of errors, retention of nurses, and cost of health care. These are key players and important considerations in the new nurse's transition to safe nursing practice.

As you progress through your own personal transition into nursing practice, the "rules of the road" for transition can be likened to traffic signs (Fig. 1.3). Check out the following signs that will help you to direct your transition experience. Fig. 1.4 gives additional advice from graduates who have successfully made the transition.

Look for the humor in each day and take time to laugh. You will be surprised by how good it makes you feel!

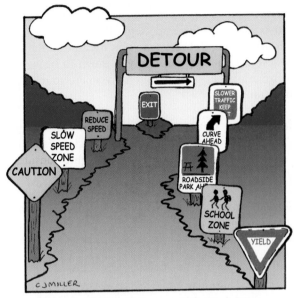

FIG. 1.3 "Rules of the road" for transition.

FIG. 1.4 Advice for the new grad.

RULES OF THE ROAD

 Stop. Take care of yourself. Take time to plan your transition. Get involved with other recent graduates; they can help you. Do not be afraid to ask questions, and do not be afraid to ask for help.

 Detour. You will make mistakes. Recognize them, learn from them, and put them in the past as you move forward. Regardless of how well you plan for change, there are always detours ahead. Detours take you on an alternate route. They can be scenic, swampy, or desolate, or they can bog you down in heavy traffic. Do not forget to look for the positive aspects—the detour may open your eyes to new horizons and new career directions.

Curve ahead. Get your personal life in order. Anticipate changes in your schedule. Be adaptable, because the transition process is not predictable.

Yield. You do not always have to be right. Consider alternatives and make compromises within your value system.

Resume speed. Maintain a positive attitude. As you gain experience, you will become better organized and begin to really enjoy nursing. Be aware; sometimes as you resume speed, you may be experiencing another role transition as your career moves in a different direction.

Exit. Pay attention to your road signs; do not take an exit you do not really want. Before you exit your job, critically evaluate the job situation. "Look before you leap" by making sure the change will improve your work situation.

 Slow traffic, keep right. You may be more comfortable in the slower traffic lane with respect to your career direction. Take all the time you need; it is okay for each person to travel at a different speed. Do not get run over in the fast lane.

School zone. Plan for continuing education, whether it is an advanced degree program or one to maintain your clinical skills or license. Allow yourself sufficient time in your new job before you jump back into the role of full-time student.

 Slow speed zone. Take time to get organized before you resume full speed! Have a daily organizational sheet that fits your needs and works for you both in your job and your personal life.

Caution. Do not commit to anything with which you are not professionally or personally comfortable. Think before you act. Do not react. Do not panic. If in doubt, check with another nurse.

 Roadside park ahead. Take a break, whether it is 15 minutes or 30 minutes a day to indulge yourself—or a week to do something you really want to do.

⊕ RELEVANT WEBSITES AND ONLINE RESOURCES

NCSBN (2016)
Transition to Practice. https://www.ncsbn.org/transition-to-practice.htm.

Robert Wood Johnson Foundation (2016)
Initiative on the Future of Nursing campaign. IOM Recommendations. http://campaignforaction.org/abo ut-us/campaign-history.

Robert Wood Johnson Foundation (2015)
Value of Nursing Education and Nurse Residency Programs. http://campaignforaction.org/resource/val ue-nurse-education-and-residency-programs.

University Healthsystem Consortium (UHC) & American Association of Colleges of Nursing (AACN) (2015)
Nurse Residency Program Participants. http://www.aacn.nche.edu/education-resources/NRPParticipants.pdf.

BIBLIOGRAPHY

Beecroft, P. C., Dorey, F., & Wenten, M. (2008). Turnover intention in new graduate nurses: A multivariate analysis. *Journal of Advanced Nursing, 62,* 41–52. http://dx.doi.org/10.1111/j.1365-2648.2007.04570.x.

Benner, P. (2001; 1984). *From novice to expert.* Menlo Park, CA: Addison-Wesley; Commemorative edition, Upper Saddle River, NJ: Prentice-Hall.

Berkow, S., Virkstis, K., Stewart, J., & Conway, L. (2008). Assessing new graduate nurse performance. *Journal of Nursing Administration, 38*(11), 468–474. http://dx.doi.org/10.1097/01.NNA.0000339477.50219.06.

Candela, L., & Bowles, C. (2008). Recent RN graduate perceptions of educational preparation. *Nursing Education Perspectives, 29,* 266–271.

Newton, J. M., & McKenna, L. (2007). The transitional journey through the graduate year: A focus group study. *International Journal of Nursing Studies, 44*(7), 1231–1237. http://dx.doi.org/10.1016/j.ijnurstu.2006.05.017.

Casey, K., et al. (2004). The graduate nurse experience. *Journal of Nursing Administration, 34*(6), 303–311.

Duchscher, J. B. (2008). A process of becoming: The stages of new nursing graduate professional role transition. *Journal of Continuing Education in Nursing, 39*(10), 441–450.

Duchscher, J. B. (2009). Transition shock: The initial stage of role adaptation for newly graduated Registered Nurses. *Journal of Advanced Nursing, 65*(5), 1103–1113.

Institute of Medicine of the National Academies. (2011). *The future of nursing: Leading change, advancing health.* Retrieved from http://www.nap.edu/catalog/12956/the-future-of-nursing-leading-change-advancing-health.

Kramer, M. (1974). *Reality shock.* St. Louis: Mosby.

Kramer, M., & Schmalenberg, C. (1977). *Path to biculturalism.* Rockville, MD: Aspen.

Lavoie-Tremblay, M., et al. (2002). How to facilitate the orientation of new nurses into the workplace. *Journal for Nurses in Staff Development, 18*(2), 80–85.

National Council of State Boards of Nursing (NCSBN). (2008a). *2008 business book. Report from Transitions to Practice Committee* (pp.259–295). Nashville, TN: Annual meeting. Retrieved from www.ncsbn.org/2008_BusinessBook_Section2.pdf.

NCSBN. (2008b). *NCSBN transition to practice report.* Retrieved from www.ncsbn.org/388.htm.

Oermann, M. H., Alvarez, M., O'Sullivan, R., & Foster, B. (2010). Performance, satisfaction, and transition into practice of graduates of accelerated nursing programs. *Journal for Nurses in Staff Development, 26*(5), 192–199. http://dx.doi.org/10.1097/NND.0b013e31819b5c3a.

Robert Wood Johnson Foundation. (2011). *Value of nursing education and nurse residency programs.* Retrieved from http://campaignforaction.org/resource/value-nurse-education-and-residency-programs.

Roche, J., Lamoureux, E., & Teehan, T. (2004). A partnership between nursing education and practice. *Journal of Nursing Administration, 34*(1), 26–32.

Schumacher, K. L., & Meleis, A. I. (1994). Transitions: A central concept in nursing. *Image, 26*, 119–127.

Spector, N. (2008). *Toward an evidence-based regulatory model for transitioning new nurses to practice.* Retrieved from www.ncsbn.org/Pages_from_Leader-to-Leader_FALL08.pdf.

Spector, N., et al. (2015a). *Transition to practice study in hospital settings.* Retrieved from https://www.ncsbn.org/Spector_Transition_to_Practice_Study_in_Hospital_Settings.pdf.

Spector, N. (2015b). The National Council of State Boards of Nursing's transition to practice study: Implications for educators. *Journal of Nursing Education, 54*(3), 119–120. http://dx.doi.org/10.3928/01484834-20150217-13. Retrieved from http://www.healio.com/nursing/journals/jne/2015-3-54-3/%7Bc25037ac-f3b7-4a30-a64c-2a8556b783de%7D/the-national-council-of-state-boards-of-nursings-transition-to-practice-study-implications-for-educators.

Steinmiller, E., Levonian, C., & Lengetti, E. (2003). Rx for success. *American Journal of Nursing, 103*(11), 64A–66A.

Theisen, J., & Sandau, K. (2013). Competency of new graduate nurses: A review of their weaknesses and strategies for success. *Journal of Continuing Education in Nursing, 44*(9), 406–414. http://dx.doi.org/10.3928/00220124-20130617-38.

Varner, K. D., & Leeds, R. A. (2012). Transition within a graduate nurse residency program. *Journal of Continuing Education in Nursing, 43*(11), 491–499.

Personal Management: Time and Self-Care Strategies

Ashley Zerwekh Garneau, PhD, RN*

ⓔ http://evolve.elsevier.com/Zerwekh/nsgtoday/.

Gain control of your time, and you will gain control of your life
Anonymous

Is time managing you, or are you managing time?

After completing this chapter, you should be able to:

- Identify your individual time style and personal time-management strategies.
- Discuss strategies that increase organizational skills and personal priority setting.
- Describe early signs of compassion fatigue and burnout.
- Describe how compassion fatigue and burnout affect nurses.
- Discuss the importance of caring for yourself.
- Identify strategies for self-care.

There are so many activities that individuals need to accomplish at any one time that deciding "how to get it all done" and "what to do when" is a daily challenge—one that can sometimes be overwhelming. Nursing school complicates the daily routine. This relentless competition for our attention is described by the term *timelock* (Keyes, 1991).

MANAGING YOUR TIME

Regrettably, there is no way to alter the minutes in an hour or the hours in a day. Although we cannot create more actual time, we can alter how we use the time we have available.

* We would like to thank Sharon Decker, PhD, RN, ANEF, FAAN, for her previous contributions of this chapter.

Employers of new graduates have identified lack of organizational and time-management skills as areas in which new nurses frequently need the most improvement and assistance. The methods and strategies identified by time-management experts can help you cope with timelock.

This section introduces you to the principles of effective time management. You will learn how to gain control of your time, increase your organizational skills, and reduce wasted time to your advantage. You will learn strategies for using those newly acquired hours to achieve your personal and professional goals.

Balance Is the Key

Making time to meet your individual, family, and professional needs and goals is vital to your overall success. If you neglect your health maintenance needs, completing school may be jeopardized. Integrating the principles of time management into your daily life can help you achieve both your personal and professional goals.

What Are Your Biological Rhythms, and How Do You Use Them?

Individuals have different biorhythms that affect their energy levels during the day and can even vary from season to season. Rest and sleep are essential for optimal health and emotional and physical responsiveness.

> Whenever possible, schedule difficult activities when you are most productive.

When possible, get eight solid hours of sleep. Maintaining a regular sleep-wake rhythm (circadian rhythm) with adequate hours of sleep has both physiological and psychological restorative effects. Disruption of this rhythm causes chronic fatigue and decreases one's coping abilities and performance. Factors affecting rest and sleep include anxiety, work schedules, diet, and the use of caffeine, alcohol, and nicotine.

Fatigue, which can lead to impaired decision making, can occur with changes in the circadian rhythm and sleep deprivation. Physiological, psychological, and emotional problems have also been correlated to sleep deprivation; these include ischemic disease, increased peptic ulcers, indigestion, increased susceptibility to viral and bacterial infections, weight gain, sleep disturbances, and mood disorders. Therefore, if situations occur that interfere with your normal circadian rhythm, it is important to take measures to prevent these possible complications. Self-care tips to prevent complications caused by interferences in the normal circadian rhythm are presented in Box 2.1. Try these strategies, tossing out those that do not work for you.

> Engage in a relaxing activity 1 hour before going to bed; for example, take a warm bath, read an interesting novel, or learn to initiate progressive relaxation techniques.

What Is Meant by Right- and Left-Brain Dominance, and Where Is My Brain?

People think about and manage time differently, depending on their characteristic brain dominance—left, right, or both (Fig. 2.1).

Left-brain–dominant people process information and approach time in a linear, sequential manner. Their thinking structures time by minutes and hours. They tend to schedule activities in time segments and perform them in an ordered sequence. Left-brain–dominant people like to know the rules and play by them. They are usually able to meet their goals, but if this behavior is carried to

BOX 2.1   SELF-CARE TIPS WHEN CIRCADIAN RHYTHMS ARE DISRUPTED

- Reserve the bedroom for sleeping.
- Avoid watching television or using the computer while in bed.
- Leave your stressors at the door, and pamper yourself just before sleeping by reading; stretching; meditating; or taking a warm, scented bath.
- Establish and maintain a consistent bedtime routine.
- Decrease noise or create "white noise" in the bedroom (e.g., use a bedroom fan).
- Charge or place your smartphone or mobile device in another room.
- Sleep with earplugs.
- Darken and cool down your sleeping environment.
- Use eye shields.
- Maintain a diet high in protein and low in carbohydrates to support your immune system.

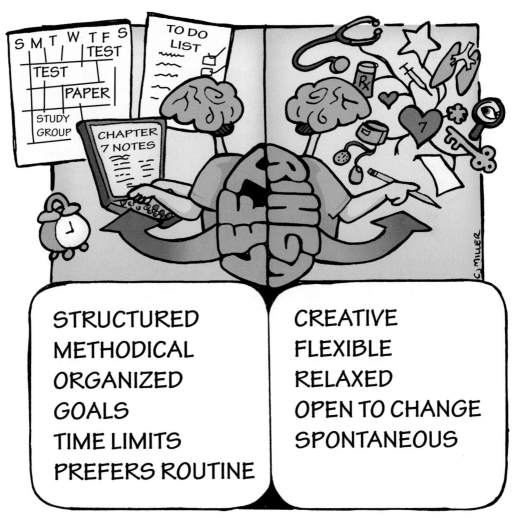

FIG. 2.1 Are you right- or left-brain–dominant?

an extreme, the individual is in danger of overwork at the expense of creative, artistic, and relaxing activities.

Right-brain–dominant people resist rules and schedules. They prefer to look at a project as a whole and to complete it in their own way and time. These are creative, flexible thinkers. However, if their behaviors are taken to an extreme, they can fail to meet needed completion times, which can induce guilt.

Some people are neither left-brain–dominant nor right-brain–dominant; hence they are more mixed in their behaviors. In fact, everyone uses both sides of the brain to some extent, thus tapping into the benefits of the brain's full capacities. The use of lists and calendars engages the left brain, whereas techniques such as the use of colored folders and whimsical office supplies helps individuals to use right-brain holistic thinking to solve problems.

Which Are You?

(Check out the Hemispheric Dominance Inventory at http://capone.mtsu.edu/studskl/hd/learn .html.)

- I am left-brain–dominant.
- I am right-brain–dominant.
- I am left-brain–dominant and right-brain–dominant.

In addition to assessing your own dominant time style, it is helpful to be aware of the time styles of the people with whom you live and work. Rigid rules on a right-brain–dominant person will lead to increased resistance and frustration for everyone. Better to assign tasks such as cleanup of the kitchen or utility room to be completed by a specific time and inform them of the consequences of its not being done. It would be appropriate to have some right-brain–dominant persons on the recruitment and retention committee and some left-brain–dominant persons on the policy and procedures committee.

Knowing your time style can help you maximize your strengths and modify your weaknesses. Individual time styles can be modified, but it is wasted energy to fight or work against natural inclination. After you are aware of your time style, you can begin to create more time for what you want to do and need to do by increasing your organizational skills.

How Can I Manage My Physical Environment?

A place for everything and everything in its place.

Organizing and maintaining your physical environment at home, school, and work can dramatically reduce hours of time and the emotional frustration associated with "looking for stuff" (Fig. 2.2).

At home, set up a specific work area for such things as school supplies, papers, and books. A separate area or corner should be established where you can pay bills, send letters, order take-out food, and take care of other household chores. When studying or working on major projects, find a space that provides a comfortable, but not too cozy, area. This space should have adequate lighting and be as free from distractions as possible. If you are studying, break your time into 50-minute segments followed by 10-minute breaks. Before beginning each study session, gather the appropriate tools—textbooks, paper, pens, highlighters, laptop, smartphone or handheld device, and reference material—to avoid wasting time searching for these items after you begin your work.

	Start an ongoing list of "Things to Do." It feels so good to cross off the task as you complete it.
	If you don't already have a file folder (either paper or electronic version), then start one immediately. If you can't keep up with the magazine and journal articles or if you don't have time to put your notes together, then file them. Get to them when you can.
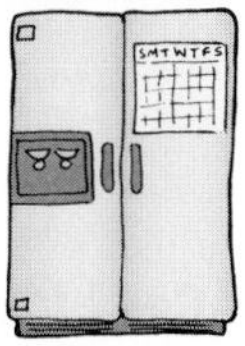	Post a large calendar on the refrigerator door. It is a great way to keep track of a busy family's schedule. Assign each person to write down his or her meetings, practices, and other activities in a different colored ink.
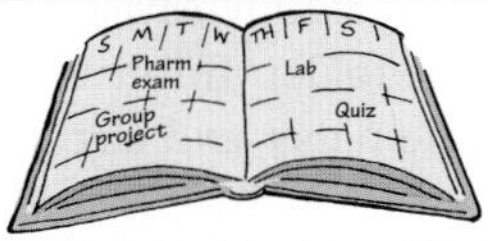	Post a desk calendar at your workspace that shows due dates for assignments, exams, or important projects.
	Don't spend a lot of time in card shops searching for birthday and anniversary cards. Keep a supply of attractive blank cards on hand for these last-minute greetings to be a made, or buy a bunch of greeting cards and keep them in a letter holder with dividers indicating the month and day that cards should be mailed.
	Set a timer on your phone, and make time for yourself. Tell the children that this is your time to read, watch television, and relax.
	Neighborhood teenagers are often willing to run errands, mow lawns, wash cars, or clean house. Call on them.
	Check to see whether you cleaners, drug store, or grocer has free delivery, and then use it.
	Do your shopping online, by phone, or mail. Make use of the numerous catalogs that are around; sign-up for specials or promotions from your favorite shopping stores, and by from the convenience of your mobile device or office chair.
	Learn to say, "No." Remember that "No" is a complete sentence! It's so easy to get involved in too many activities. Set priorities, and do just one to two activities that please you, then say "No" to the rest.

FIG. 2.2 Ten suggestions for organizing yourself.

Compartmentalize

Place pens, notebooks, your smartphone or handheld device, or other reference materials in a designated holder or in a specific area of your workstation for quick access.

Color-Code

Do this for your files, keys, and whatever you can. Office supply stores are good sources of color-coded items. For example, color-coding keys with a plastic cover enables you immediately to pick out your car key or house key.

Convenience

Move and keep frequently used items nearest to where they are used.

Declutter the Clutter

At work, as well as at home, regularly clear your study and work areas.

What About All the Paperwork and/or Electronic Requests—How Can I Manage It?

Handling each piece of paper or electronic request only one time is a great time-saver. Whenever possible, spend 30 seconds filing important information in the appropriate folder. This technique can save you time when you need the information again. Five ways to handle paper and electronic requests follow: Read each item, and then:

- File it.
- Forward it.
- Respond to it—on the same sheet if possible.
- Delegate it.
- Discard it.

> One time-management principle is, "Don't agonize. Organize!"

What About Managing the Telephone?

Polite comments at the beginning and end of a telephone conversation are necessary to maintain positive interpersonal communications. However, when time limits are necessary, focus the conversation on the business at hand. Some possible phrases to move things along include "How can I help you?" or "I called to …." To end the conversation, summarize the actions to be followed through: "I understand. I am to find out about … and get back to you by the end of the week. Thanks for calling." Professional courtesy demands that you turn off your cellular phone while at work, in the classroom, during clinical rotation, and while attending a workshop.

Allocate a specific time during the day for business- or school-related telephone calls. Plan these calls by identifying key points that need to be discussed during the conversation. If you need to leave a message, provide enough detail, with the time and date, and a time when the individual can contact you. When making a call, (1) introduce yourself and your business or relationship to the individual, (2) relax—speak as if the individual is sitting in the room beside you, (3) smile—smiling will modify the tone of your voice, (4) keep the conversation short and to the point, and (5) summarize the conversation, review any action items, and thank the individual for his or her time.

Having conversations to maintain friendships, to touch base with a relative, to relax yourself, to vent your emotions, or to serve similar social purposes can be combined with routine housekeeping duties. Who has not swept the floor, put away dishes, sorted mail, or cleaned out a drawer while chatting with a friend?

What About All That E-Mail, Texting, or Social Media?

Restrict work- or school-related communications to one account, with another account designated for personal use. Turn off the notification chime, and set aside a specific time during the day to read and answer your e-mail or texts instead of answering each one as it arrives. This could be the first task in the morning while you are enjoying your coffee. Do not let e-mail pile up in your inbox. Read it, answer it, and, if important, transfer it to a designated folder. Activate the junk e-mail function on your computer or read the subject line, determine whether a message is "junk," and delete it without even taking the time to read it. Your e-mail program may have parameters that allow you to designate specific messages to be sent directly into a special file. This helps move information out of the inbox and keeps you organized. Spend some time investigating the various features of your e-mail. Use your e-mail to your best advantage, because e-mail can become your best friend in terms of helping you organize your messages in folders. Specific tips for effective use of e-mail are provided in Box 2.2.

When communicating with your instructor by e-mail, be sure that you include your class number or title in the subject line. Many instructors manage their e-mail by sorting messages according to class, so a standardized subject line saves your instructor time. Identify yourself in the e-mail, and be sure to include a signature line with your contact information.

> Use your delete key aggressively, and eliminate junk e-mail without reading it.

How Can I Manage My Time?

Time management is a skill and involves planning and practice. Multiple time-management worksheets are available to assist in completing a personal analysis of your time. For example, the website *Mind Tools: Essential Skills for an Excellent Career* at http://www.mindtools.com/index.html provides multiple tools, worksheets, and strategies to assist in developing and refining time-management skills.

Calendars are available to schedule to-do activities by the month, week, and day. You gain control of your life by completing a schedule (Table 2.1). Scheduling provides you with a method to allocate time for specific tasks and is a constant reminder of your tasks, due dates, and deadlines.

BOX 2.2   TIPS FOR EFFECTIVE ELECTRONIC COMMUNICATION

- Turn off those constant alerts and reminders.
- Check e-mail and texts at a specific time rather than constant monitoring.
- Take control—access an app that pushes messages at a designated time, or explore features available through your current system that allow you to manage your inbox.
- Before sending, texting, or posting (committing)—THINK—could what you say be misinterpreted? Could it result in a misunderstanding?
- If it is in writing, you are accountable.
- Communication through electronic media (e-mail, texting) is not necessarily confidential.
- Use the "SUBJECT" line when appropriate.
- Proofread before you send or post.
- Follow the same principles of courtesy as you expect in face-to-face communication.
- Respect others' time and bandwidth.
- Keep flaming responses under control.
- Send responses to appropriate individuals only.
- Be brief, and always close with a farewell.
- Social media can drain your time—be aware of "friends" who are negative.

TABLE 2.1	**WEEKLY PERSONAL CALENDAR**			
MONDAY	**TUESDAY**	**WEDNESDAY**	**THURSDAY**	**FRIDAY**
Cleaners 9 AM workout	Pick up health-insurance forms 3:30 PM carpool	4 PM workout 5:30 PM T-ball practice	4-7 PM Professional organization meeting	9 AM workout

Schedule only what can realistically be accomplished, and leave extra time before and after every major activity. Tasks, meetings, and travel can take longer than anticipated, so give yourself some time to transition from one project to another. Schedule personal time in your calendar. If someone wants to meet with you during this time, just say, "Thank you for the invite; however, I've got an important appointment. When would be another convenient time?" Or ask, "Could we meet tomorrow afternoon?" Color-code your appointments according to priorities or specific roles to stimulate the right side of your brain.

> Leave white space (nothing) in your schedule so you will have time for yourself and family, or schedule uninterruptible time for both.

At the beginning of each week, review the week's activities to avoid unexpected "surprises." Overscheduling of more tasks than any human being can do in a single day inevitably leads to frustration. Build in some flexibility. It will not always be possible to follow your schedule exactly. However, when you do get "derailed," having a plan will help you get back on track with minimal time and effort (Critical Thinking Box 2.1).

[?] CRITICAL THINKING BOX 2.1

Develop your time calendar—will it be a week-at-a-glance or a month-at-a-glance? Think about what works the best for you.

> Strategy: Leave some extra time before and after every major event to allow for transition.

MANAGING TASKS

How Do I Deal With Procrastination?

Everyone procrastinates, especially when a task is unpleasant, overwhelming, or cannot be done perfectly. Procrastination can lead to last-minute rushes that cause unnecessary stress. The time spent stressing about doing something takes more time than actually doing it! The anticipation itself can also be worse than the actuality, draining your energy and accomplishment. Alternatively, procrastination can lead to multitasking, which can impact your ability to give 100% of your attention to a task or project. Mokhtari, Delello, and Reichard (2015) surveyed college students by asking them if multitasking interfered with their ability to focus on their academic studies and guess what—multitasking was reported as a distractor to their learning. Considering this, here are some tips for preventing procrastination.

Consider the Consequences

Ask yourself what will happen if you do something and what will happen if you do not. If there are no negative outcomes of not doing something, there is no point in spending time doing it. You can eliminate that activity!

If something will happen because you don't do it, then, of course, you need to get started.

The Earlier, the Better

Most projects take longer than planned, and glitches happen; for example, coffee spills all over your study notes the night before the test, your computer crashes, or your dog eats your notes. To compensate for the inevitable delays and to avoid crises, start in advance and plan for your project to take three times longer than you think. Be realistic and use your common sense in scheduling this time frame.

Schedule times to work on your project, and track your progress on a calendar.

"By the Inch, It's a Cinch"

Break projects into small, manageable pieces; gather all the resources required to finish the project; and plan to do only the first step initially. For example, to study for a test, first collect all the related notes and books in one place. Next, review the subjects likely to be tested. If you are having difficulty getting started, plan to work on these steps for only 5 to 10 minutes. (Anybody can do just about anything for 5 to 10 minutes, eh?) Frequently, this will create enough momentum to get you going. When you have to stop, leave yourself a note regarding what the next steps should be. Here are some hints for effective studying.

- Study difficult subjects or concepts first.
- Study in short "chunks" of 50 minutes each.
- Take a brief 10-minute break after every 50 minutes of studying.
- Schedule study time when you are at your best (be aware of your internal clock).
- Use waiting times. (Compile and carry 3 × 5 note cards or use Notes on your cell phone to organize critical information that you can review wherever you go—even when you are standing in that long line at the checkout counter.)
- Keep a calendar for the semester that includes all of your assignments, tests, and papers. Use a different color for entering deadlines for each course.
- Make a weekly to-do list. Prioritize this list and cross off each task as you complete it.
- Before beginning a project, know what you are doing. Determine the goals, benefits, costs, and timetable for the endeavor. If you are working in a group, at the beginning of the project, make sure everyone understands his or her responsibilities. You should also designate someone to be in charge of organizing group meetings. Leave time during the project for unexpected delays and to revisit and modify your goals. Be flexible.

If you are taking an online or web-enhanced course, remember these courses take as much, if not more time, than traditional face-to-face classes.

Here are some hints to assist with your time management related to online courses:

- Print the syllabus, and place deadlines on your calendar before the first course meeting.
- Identify how to contact your instructor, and schedule online office hours in your calendar.
- Schedule daily times for logging into the class website.
- Schedule a time for class work, and select a specific site.
- Cultivate collegial support groups with individuals who provide support and are good listeners.
- Form an online or face-to-face study group with one or two peers. In your study group, make sure that all members are involved and your expectations for the study group align with your

peers. One way to maximize a study group session is to come prepared to "teach" a section of the class material to your study group. Do not waste time reviewing your notes in the study group—you can do this by yourself.

- Be active in the course by participating appropriately in discussion groups.
- Establish an evidence-based file to download important articles (pdf format).
- Bookmark websites (but before bookmarking these, review the information—Don't assume all sites are up-to-date and evidence-based).
- There are online sites that offer online storage and retrieval of documents and files. Check out the following links for more information on storing files via the Internet: www.justcloud.com, www.icloud.com, www.google.com/drive, and www.dropbox.com.

Reward Yourself

Bribing yourself with a reward can help you get started and keep going: "If I concentrate well for 1 hour on reading the assigned chapter, then I can watch my favorite television show guilt-free." Often, the stress reduction that comes from working on the project that has been put off is a reward in itself (Critical Thinking Box 2.2).

> **? CRITICAL THINKING BOX 2.2**
>
> What do you do to reward yourself for a job done well?

> Schedule a time for celebration and self-reward with all of your projects.

Avoid the Myth of Perfection

Many of us were brought up with the well-intentioned philosophy that "Anything worth doing is worth doing well." Unfortunately, this is often interpreted as "Anything worth doing is worth doing *perfectly*." The fear of not doing something well enough or perfectly also feeds the tendency to procrastinate.

Certainly, everyone needs to make the best effort possible, but not everything needs to be done perfectly. Consider what the expected standard is—not the standard of perfection possible—and how you can meet it with a minimum amount of time and effort. Effective procrastination (i.e., procrastination that is used appropriately) is recognizing when a task should be purposefully postponed. This technique is a conscious decision and is used when time is needed to accomplish a task with a higher priority. Priority setting, delegating tasks when possible, eliminating wasted time by avoiding excessive social telephone calls, breaking tasks into separate small steps, and establishing realistic short-term goals are some additional strategies for managing procrastination.

MANAGING OTHERS

Communicating and getting along with other people can be challenging. Most people are supportive and easy to be with. They add to your energy and ability to function effectively, and they contribute to your goal attainment. However, some individuals drain energy from you and jeopardize organizational accomplishment through their whining, criticizing, negative thinking, chronic lateness, poor crisis management, overdependency, aggression, and similar unproductive behaviors. Avoid those individuals both online (through social media, texting, and e-mail) and in person. Occasional exhibitions of such behavior in relation to a personal crisis can be understood. Even in the best of human

---

BOX 2.3   TIPS FOR MANAGING TIME AND MANAGING OTHERS

- Analyze how you spend your time.
- Maintain a "to-do" list.
- Organize material into files.
- Use an activity planner or calendar (paper copy or on your smartphone)—review it daily.
- Prioritize your activities.
- Make use of "mini" or waiting-time periods.
- AVOID PERFECTIONISM.
- Take "mini" vacations such as walk or do a load of laundry throughout the day to refresh your brain.
- Be aware of your internal clock—do critical tasks when you are most alert.
- Minimize the time spent with individuals who constantly complain and criticize.
- Use assertive communication with individuals with whom you are having a problem.
- Develop rituals (such as changing clothes) when you get home that say "I'm off duty."
- Avoid always saying yes. Before agreeing—take a deep breath—think about the real expectation of the project.
- Delegate when appropriate.
- Use technology.
- Don't let your e-mail, social media, and cell phone manage you and your time.
- Recognize "multitasking" as an excuse for "poor planning"—no one can do multiple tasks successfully and exceptionally.

---

relationships, conflict and extreme emotions are inevitable. However, when people use these behaviors as their everyday *modus operandi* (method of operating), they interfere with attainment of individual and organizational goals. To protect your time and achieve your goals, it may be necessary to limit your time with such individuals. Learning to say "no" and practicing assertive communication can help as well. Chapters 12 and 13 provide assistance in learning these communication skills. Box 2.3 provides some hints for managing others.

What About Delegation and Time Management?

You do not have to handle everything personally. Use your delegation skills at home to identify tasks and activities that can be completed by others, leaving you more time to study and concentrate on important projects. The website *Mind Tools: Essential Skills for an Excellent Career*, at http://www.mindtools.com/index.html, provides multiple strategies related to delegation and a delegation worksheet to assist in determining whether a task can be delegated and to whom (see Chapter 14).

MANAGING YOUR GOALS

Goals are the incremental steps required to achieve long-term success. Personal and professional goals are critical to lifestyle management. Keeping your goals in mind enables you to plan and perform activities that contribute to your goals and eliminate or reduce those that do not. Be realistic when setting your goals: allow enough time to complete them appropriately. Activities that contribute to goals are your high-payoff, high-priority activities; those that do not are low-payoff, low-priority activities. Your goals should be demanding enough that completion provides a feeling of satisfaction.

Many goal-directed activities need to be scheduled with completion times. This is sometimes called *deadlining* the to-do list. All kinds of calendars are available to schedule to-do activities by the month, week, and day. There are organizer apps available for your smartphone (check out www.rememberthemilk.com). It is also easy to make your own forms. Knowing your goals and priorities promotes flexible rescheduling, resulting in more effective time management and successful accomplishment.

Begin by Listing

It will be helpful to list all your goal-related activities on a master to-do list. Using all of the features of Microsoft Outlook by identifying tasks in the e-mail and/or calendar program and setting up reminders will be helpful for both tasks that are listed and tasks based on e-mails received or sent (e.g., assignments). Cross out items on your to-do list, your cards, and your schedule as you do them. This will give you immediate, positive feedback—an instant reward for your efforts and progress. When the inevitable interruptions occur, scan the to-do list and reevaluate your priorities in relation to your remaining time.

> Reward yourself as you cross out items on your to-do list.

Prioritize With the ABCD System

Other people are constantly demanding your time and energy; therefore you need to establish priorities but also be flexible. Being flexible will allow you to change your priorities throughout the day as situations change. Additionally, as you work, always try to combine activities (multitask) or delegate tasks in an effort to manage your time appropriately.

Scan your to-do list and decide which are A, B, C, or D items (Box 2.4). The activities that are most closely related to your goals are the high-payoff ones; these are A priorities. Effective use of your time-management skills demands that you focus most of your energy on A-priority items. List these according to the urgency of the time limits. Train yourself to do the hardest task first. Attending to the most difficult activity first reduces the nagging, anxiety-provoking thought that you "should be doing ___ instead" and helps you make early progress in identifying, gaining control of, and possibly preventing additional problems. This is an example of the classic time-management principle known as Pareto's 80/20 Rule.

According to Pareto, an early 1900s economist, 20% of the effort produces 80% of the results. For example, spending 20% of your time studying the most difficult course can produce 80% success. In your home, 80% of what needs to be cleaned is in the kitchen and bathroom; spend 20% of your cleaning time on these two rooms and 80% of the cleaning will be done. Likewise, 80% of your nursing care will be with 20% of your patients. This illustrates that there are proportionally greater results

---

BOX 2.4 PRIORITIZATION USING THE ABCD SYSTEM

A Absolute (immediate priority)—do it now or as soon as possible
B Better (as soon as possible)—necessary, but it can be done later
C Can wait until later—or when you get around to it
D Don't worry about it—let someone else take care of it
   OR ... the 4 Ds
   Do it.
   Delay it (to a specific time).
   Dump it (unimportant; doing it just wastes your time).
   Delegate it.

in concentrating at least 20% of your efforts on higher payoff priorities. You will need to balance your priorities, because it is impossible to achieve our best at all times.

The B items on your list also contribute to goal achievement; thus, they are high-payoff items but are generally less urgent than A items and can be delayed for a while. Eventually, many B items become A items, especially as completion times approach. It is also possible to "squeeze in" some B items in short periods of time—for instance, reading an article as you wait in a long line or as you "waste" time waiting for someone.

Items that do not substantially contribute to goals or do not have to be accomplished within a specific time frame are C items. These activities really can wait until you get around to them; they are things to be done when, or if, time permits. Of course, some C items become B or A priorities. However, many C items will fit the "nothing will happen if you do not do something" category and become D items. D items are those "nice to do" but not necessary. Some of these items could be classified as time wasters and can be ignored when you have only a limited amount of time (Box 2.5).

Keep It Going

Continuously review your lists, schedules, and outcomes, and reward yourself for achieving your goals. No one is perfect. Omissions and errors will occur, and these are good learning experiences. Do not waste time regretting failure or feeling guilty about what you did not do; consider these as learning experiences of "what not to do" and opportunities for learning "what to do." Remind yourself that there is always time for important things and that if it is important enough, you will find the time to do it.

SELF-CARE STRATEGIES

The most beautiful people we have known are those who have known defeat, known suffering, known struggle, known loss, and have found their way out of the depths. These persons have an appreciation, a sensitivity and an understanding of life that fills them with compassion, gentleness, and a deep loving concern. Beautiful people do not just happen.

**   Elizabeth Kübler-Ross**

As a professional nurse, you will be involved with providing care to individuals at their most vulnerable times. You will experience stressful and emotionally charged situations with your patients and their families that may leave you feeling emotionally and physically exhausted, resulting in compassion fatigue. Compassion fatigue has been extensively reported in nursing practice as the distress experienced by nurses who assume caregiving roles of patients experiencing pain and suffering from debilitating medical conditions (Figley, 2002; Yoder, 2010; Berger et al., 2015). Compassion fatigue can lead to burnout, dissatisfaction with work, and high nurse turnover. Therefore, it is important that you

---

BOX 2.5 TIME WASTERS

- Engaging in idle gossip
- Constantly checking and responding to text and instant messages
- Checking and responding to personal communication and social media sites (Facebook, Twitter, G-chatting) religiously
- Multitasking
- Watching TV, gaming, or online browsing/shopping instead of completing your "to-do" list

FIG. 2.3 Self-care strategies.

practice self-care measures to maintain your overall well-being, so that you are able to provide quality care to your patients (see Fig. 2.3).

Self-care, the practice of engaging in activities that promote a healthy lifestyle, is the foundation that will assist you in thriving in nursing instead of just surviving. Engaging in the practice of self-care requires knowledge, motivation, time, and effort, but it is mandatory in your ability to manage stress. Self-care practices that decrease stress-related illness can be learned. Physical illnesses correlated to stress include cardiovascular problems, migraine headaches, irritable bowel syndrome, and muscle and joint pain. Mental health problems include unresolved anxiety, depression, and insomnia. Finally, stress and burnout among nursing personnel can contribute to organizational problems and attrition.

Is Burnout Inevitable for Nurses?

Much has been written about the concept of burnout in nurses. In early research, burnout was thought to be a problem within a nurse or a problem inherent in the nursing profession. However, the stressors in the current workplace caused by staffing shortages, along with an increase in patient acuity and the accelerated rate of change in the health care environment, have increased the potential for burnout among nurses. Nurses have learned to recognize and manage burnout related to caring too much for their patients. What nurses are currently struggling with is that they may be working in environments that are not congruent with their personal philosophies of nursing care.

Burnout associated with job stress can leave nurses vulnerable to depression, physical illness, and alcohol and substance abuse. Symptoms include a loss of energy, weariness, gloominess, dissatisfaction, increased illness, decreased efficiency, absenteeism, and self-doubt. Burnout typically progresses through five stages that are particularly notable within the work setting: an initial feeling of enthusiasm for the job, followed by a loss of enthusiasm, continuous deterioration, crisis, and finally devastation and the inability to work effectively. Box 2.6 lists early warning signs of burnout.

BOX 2.6 EARLY WARNING SIGNS OF BURNOUT

- Irritability
- Weight changes
- Frequent headaches and gastrointestinal disturbances
- Chronic fatigue
- Insomnia
- Depression
- Feeling of personal inadequacy
- Negativity
- Cynicism
- Angry outbursts
- Withdrawn
- Decreased engagement and productivity at work

The increase in patient acuity, coupled with shortened hospital stays, is not compatible with the emphasis on high-quality, safe patient care and consumer satisfaction. These opposing philosophies create conflict for nurses and lead to burnout that is not as easily remedied as burnout caused by internal factors. Therefore, it is important to recognize clearly the mission of the hospital or corporation when you apply for your first job. Is their mission similar to yours? Will you be able to give the quality care that you want to deliver, or will you be required to compromise your values to fit into the system?

There are many strategies designed to combat burnout, and many of them are detailed in this chapter. However, nurses need to determine whether their burnout is caused by internal or external factors. A nurse who neglects his or her own needs can develop feelings of low self-esteem and resentment. These feelings could affect the care you provide to others. Therefore, by taking care of yourself, you are ultimately able to provide better care for others. In some cases, it may be necessary for the nurse to relocate to a place of employment that is more in line with her or his personal belief system.

Empowerment and Self-Care

Learning about self-care is really about empowerment. To empower means to enable—enable self and others to reach their greatest potential for health and well-being. However, the concept of "enabling" is seen in a negative light, because it refers to doing things for others that they can do for themselves. Actually, preventing friends and loved ones from dealing with the consequences of their behavior is very disempowering.

With empowerment comes a feeling of well-being and effectiveness. There are times and situations in our lives when we feel more or less powerful. Examples of occasions when one feels powerful or powerless are listed in Box 2.7. You may find as you read through these lists that there are some situations in your life in which you do feel powerful and some in which you do not. Self-assessment of our sense of well-being and self-esteem helps us to know where to begin. Because change is a constant, and all of us are in varying states of emotional, physical, and mental change at any given time, it is important to assess ourselves on a regular basis. As a matter of fact, knowing one's self is the very first step in learning to care for one's self. Empowerment in all spheres of our being is very important. Examine the Holistic Self-Assessment Tool (Critical Thinking Box 2.3), which includes measures of our emotional, mental, physical, social, spiritual, and choice potentials.

Emotional wholeness is about our ability to feel. The ability to express a wide range of emotions is indicative of good mental health. Nurses are often very good at helping their patients

BOX 2.7   EXAMPLES OF TIMES WHEN ONE FEELS POWERLESS OR POWERFUL

I Feel Powerless When
- I'm ignored.
- I get assigned to a new hospital unit.
- I can't make a decision.
- I'm exhausted.
- I'm being evaluated by my instructor.
- I have no choices.
- I'm being controlled or manipulated.
- I have pent-up anger.
- I don't think or react quickly.
- I don't speak loudly enough.
- I don't have control over my time.

I Feel Powerful When
- I'm energetic.
- I receive positive feedback.
- I know I look good.
- I tell people I'm a nurse.
- I have clear goals for my career.
- I stick to decisions.
- I speak out against injustice.
- I allow myself to be selfish without feeling guilty.
- I tell a good joke.
- I work with supportive people.
- I'm told by a patient or family that I did a good job.

Adapted from Josefowitz, N. (1980). *Paths to power.* Menlo Park, CA: Addison-Wesley, p.7. Reprinted with permission.

⍰ CRITICAL THINKING BOX 2.3

Holistic Self-Assessment Tool

Directions: Place a check mark in the space before the statement that applies to you.
Emotional Potential
_____ I push my thoughts and feelings out of conscious awareness (denial).
_____ I feel I have to be in control.
_____ I am unable to express basic feelings of sadness, joy, anger, and fear.
_____ I see myself as a victim.
_____ I feel guilty and ashamed a lot of the time.
_____ I frequently take things personally.

Social Potential
_____ I am overcommitted to the point of having no time for recreation.
_____ I am unable to be honest and open with others.
_____ I am unable to admit vulnerability to others.
_____ I am attracted to needy people.
_____ I feel overwhelmingly responsible for others' happiness.
_____ My only friends are nurses.

Physical Potential
_____ I neglect myself physically—overweight/underweight, lack of adequate rest and exercise.
_____ I feel tired and lack energy.
_____ I am not interested in sex.
_____ I do not engage in regular physical and dental check-ups.
_____ I have seen a doctor in the past 6 months for any of the following conditions: migraine headaches, backaches, gastrointestinal problems, hypertension, or cancer.
_____ I am a workaholic—work is all-important to me.

CRITICAL THINKING BOX 2.3

Holistic Self-Assessment Tool–cont'd

Spiritual Potential

_____ I see that events that occur in my life are controlled by external choices.

_____ I find the world a basically hostile place.

_____ I lack a spiritual base for working through daily problems.

_____ I live in the past or the future.

_____ I have no sense of power greater than myself.

Mental Potential

_____ I read mostly professional literature.

_____ I spend most waking hours obsessing over people, places, or things.

_____ I am no longer able to dream or fantasize about my future.

_____ I can't remember much of my childhood.

_____ I can't see much change happening for myself, either personally or professionally.

Choice Potential

_____ I have difficulty making decisions, I am prone to procrastination, and I am frequently late for personal and professional appointments.

_____ I find it difficult to say no.

_____ I find myself unwilling to take reasonable risks.

_____ I find it difficult to take responsibility for myself.

From Zerwekh, J., & Michaels, B. (1989). Co-dependency: Assessment and recovery, *Nurs Clin North Am, 24*(1), 109–120.

"feel" their feelings but often have a difficult time feeling and expressing their own. Nurses frequently neglect their physical health. We make certain that our patients receive excellent health education and discharge instructions and worry when they are noncompliant. As nurses, however, we do not always follow through when it comes to such things as physical examinations, mammograms, and dental health for ourselves. We work long hours and do not plan adequate time for physical recuperation.

Because our profession is such a demanding one, we often do not take the time to cultivate our social potential. When we do spend time with friends, it is because they "need" us. When we get together with friends who are also nurses, we spend the time together talking about work. Spiritual potential simply means that we have a daily awareness that there is something more to living than mere human existence. With spiritual potential, nurses' lives have meaning and direction.

The ability to know that we have choices in life is the final area of the assessment tool. Nurses without "choice power" see life as black-and-white, with little gray in the middle. Awareness of our choices eliminates the black-and-white extremes and enables us to act rather than react in situations. Nurses with choice power are able to make decisions, take risks, and feel good about it.

Remember to use this tool not only to assess the negatives in your life but also to assess areas in which you are experiencing growth. You cannot survive nursing school, for example, without experiencing growth in all areas.

Suggested Strategies for Self-Care That Are Based on the Holistic Self-Assessment Tool

Not having life in a state of balance and not having a vision for the future often reflect a state of poor self-esteem. Nathaniel Branden (1992), who is often referred to as the "father of the self-esteem

Exercises to Help Access and Acknowledge Feelings

1. Turn your attention to how you are feeling. What part of your body feels what?
2. Acknowledge that this is how you are feeling, and give it a name. If you hear an inner criticism for feeling this way, just set it aside. Any feeling is acceptable.
3. Allow yourself to experience the sensations you are having. Separate acknowledging these feelings from having to do anything about them.
4. Ask yourself whether you want to express your feelings now or some other time. Do you want to take some other action now or later? Remind yourself that you have choices.

movement," has identified several factors found in individuals with healthy self-esteem. These include the following:

- A face, manner, and way of talking and moving that project the pleasure one takes in being alive
- Ease in talking of accomplishments or shortcomings with directness and honesty
- An attitude of openness to and curiosity about new ideas, new experiences, and new possibilities of life
- Openness to criticism and comfortable about acknowledging mistakes, because one's self-esteem is not tied to an image of perfection
- An ability to enjoy the humorous aspects of life in one's self and others (Branden, 1992, p.43)

The key to developing a healthy self-esteem is to become aware of the areas that need the most repair and to work on them. However, it is essential to maintain a sense of balance; going overboard in one or two areas is counterproductive. For example, a nurse who exercises five times a week, follows a healthy diet, and sleeps well but is emotionally numb and does not have a clear vision for her future, is out of balance.

Am I Emotionally Healthy/Emotionally Intelligent?

Being emotionally healthy means that you are aware of your feelings and are able to acknowledge them in a healthy way. In the best-selling book *Emotional Intelligence*, Goleman (1995) states that emotional intelligence consists of the following five domains: knowing one's emotions, managing emotions, motivating one's self, recognizing emotions in others, and handling relationships.

Nurses who have good emotional health know when they are feeling fearful, angry, sad, ashamed, happy, guilty, or lonely, and they are able to distinguish these feelings. They have found appropriate ways to express their feelings without offending others. When feelings are not expressed or at least acknowledged, they frequently build up, which results in emotional binging. Sometimes our bodies take the brunt of unacknowledged feelings in the form of headaches, gastrointestinal problems, anxiety attacks, and so on.

Feelings or emotions are neither good nor bad. They are indications of some of our self-truths, our desires, and our needs. Critical Thinking Box 2.4 is an exercise to help access and acknowledge feelings.

What About Friends and Fun? How Do I Find the Time?

An occupational hazard of nursing is overcommitting, both personally and professionally. Nurses who do this frequently have difficulty in meeting their social potential.

Student nurses often say they do not engage in recreational activities because of the cost and that all their money goes toward living expenses. First, it is important to include some money in your monthly

---

BOX 2.8 SOME PLEASURABLE ACTIVITIES

- Go on a picnic with friends.
- Invite friends over for a potluck dinner.
- Go to a movie.
- Plan celebrations after exams or completion of a project.
- Introduce yourself to three new people.
- Visit a new city.
- Call an old friend.
- Play with your children.

- "Borrow" someone else's children for play.
- Volunteer for a worthwhile project.
- Get involved in religious or spiritual activities.
- Spend some time people-watching.
- Take up a new hobby.
- Invite humor into your life.

❓ CRITICAL THINKING BOX 2.5

What am I doing that interferes with my health and well-being?

---

budget for fun. Depriving yourself of time for recreation on a regular basis may lead to impulsive recreational spending, such as a shopping binge with credit cards or with money allotted for something else. Second, there are many pleasurable things to do and fun places to go that do not cost a lot of money. Several examples are found in Box 2.8.

Another social area in which many nurses have difficulty is in forming relationships outside of nursing. If you spend all your free time with nurses, chances are that you will "talk shop." Nursing curricula are very science-intensive, because there is so much to learn in such a short time. Cultivate some friends who have a liberal arts or fine arts background. Choose friends who have different political opinions or come from a different part of town, a different culture, or a different socioeconomic class.

How Do I Take Care of My Physical Self?

Nurses are great when it comes to patient education; it is one of the strengths of the nursing profession. Sometimes, though, we have difficulty applying this information to ourselves. Taking care of ourselves physically is extremely important. Our profession is both mentally and physically challenging. This physical self-care entails getting the proper nutrition, maintaining a healthy weight, obtaining adequate sleep, quitting smoking, limiting alcohol consumption to one drink daily, and exercising on a regular basis (Critical Thinking Box 2.5). Engaging in some form of relaxation will trigger the relaxation response, which prevents chronic stress from harming your health (Stark et al., 2005). According to Kernan and Wheat (2008), health and learning are linked; optimal learning cannot be achieved unless the environment is supportive and promotes the development of effective learning skills. They identified mental health concerns (stress, anxiety), respiratory tract infections, interpersonal concerns, and sleep difficulties as the greatest threats to academic success.

Self-Care Activities

Physical exercise. Incorporate 30 minutes or more of moderate-intensity physical activity, such as walking, into your schedule (preferably daily). A good exercise program is one that includes activities that foster aerobic activity, flexibility, and strength. A very important part of an exercise program is that it be a regular habit. To be effective, the program should take 3 to 6 hours a week. And it does not have to cost money. You do not need to belong to a gym or invest in exercise equipment. Aerobic activities include walking, jogging, swimming, bicycling, and dancing. Minimal fitness consists of raising your heart rate to 100 beats/min and keeping it there for 30 minutes. Other strategies to increase your physical activity could include the following:

- Park your car farther away from the entrance door.
- Use the stairs instead of the elevator whenever possible.
- Stretch during your breaks from homework or housework.
- Take your dog for a walk (or volunteer to walk someone else's pet).

Laughter. Seek 20 minutes of laughter every day. Laughing promotes deep breathing and releases neuropeptides that decrease stress and lower blood pressure. (Check out www.laughteryoga.org for inspiring thoughts and affirmations.)

Mental exercise. Engage in some activity daily for at least 30 minutes that challenges your way of thinking. This activity will increase the number of connections between your brain cells (rewiring your brain). Activities that could promote brain function include:

- Take a walk in the park to stimulate all your senses.
- Try out a new restaurant.
- Listen to new music.
- Try brain games (see www.lumosity.com).

Motivate yourself. In the morning, read an inspiring quote, listen to upbeat music, or do stretching exercises. Take time for a balanced breakfast, and visualize your day. Take periodic breaks or switch activities throughout your day to maintain a high energy level. Tension can be released by simple stretching exercises and laughter.

Schedule idle time. We live in a time in which any moment can be interrupted by individuals, e-mail, texting, or phone calls. We need to give ourselves permission to relax—to unwind. Take care of your physical and mental health by scheduling idle time. Idle time is time you schedule away from interruptions: no phone calls—no e-mail—no texting. This is time in which you disconnect from technology to think and reflect. Take a walk in the park, just sit in your backyard and listen to the birds, or get a massage, but turn all your electronic devices off.

> Alternate mental and physical tasks. This strategy includes taking periodic breaks from studying to engage in a short game of basketball or a short run with the vacuum cleaner.

Strategies to Foster My Spiritual Self: Does My Life Have Meaning?

People who have a sense of spiritual well-being find their lives to be positive experiences, have relationships with a power greater than themselves, feel good about the future, and believe there is some real purpose in life. If we find that our lives lack meaning and our spiritual health is lacking, how do we go about finding spiritual well-being?

Daily prayer and meditation are very important in maintaining a spiritual self. Reading religious or philosophical material and studying the great religions are two examples of ways to foster spiritual growth.

In addition to reading what others have written about the subject, many people access their spiritual selves with the practice of meditation. Meditating allows us time to become quiet, heal our thoughts and bodies, and be grateful. The engagement of daily prayer or meditation allows for a time of self-reflection.

How Do I Increase My Mental Potential? Is It Okay to Daydream?

Nursing students are afforded considerable opportunity to exercise their mental potential while they are in nursing school. This activity, however, is primarily in the form of formal education. There are many other ways to exercise this potential. One of the first ways is to concentrate on removing negative

FIG. 2.4 Daydream: Send up your brain balloons!

thoughts or self-defeating beliefs from our minds. Here are some examples of statements that nursing students frequently make:

- "I must make *A*s in nursing school."
- "I must have approval from everyone, and if I don't, I feel horrible and depressed."
- "If I fail at something, the results will be catastrophic."
- "Others must always treat me fairly."
- "If I'm not liked by everyone, I am a failure."
- "Because all my miseries are caused by others, I will have no control over my life until they change."

If you relate to any of these statements, you have some work to do on your belief system. You are setting yourself up for failure by having extremely high expectations of yourself. You are also giving other people power over your destiny. Remember, you cannot change others. The only person you can change is yourself. Wolf, Stidham, and Ross (2015) contend that using coping strategies such as positive thinking may be beneficial for reducing stress (specifically, for nursing students—that's you!)

One way that we can change these internal beliefs of negativity into positive thinking is to learn how to give ourselves daily affirmations—or daydream a little (Fig. 2.4). Simply put, affirmations are powerful, positive statements concerning the ways we would like to think, feel, and behave. Some examples are "I am a worthwhile person"; "I am human and capable of making mistakes"; and "I am able to freely express my emotions." Always begin affirmative statements with "I" rather than "you." This practice keeps the focus on self rather than others and encourages the development of inner self-worth.

The power of affirmation exercises lies in consistency—repetition encourages ultimate belief in what is being said. Begin each day with some affirmations. Try some of the examples in Box 2.9. These enable us to feel better about ourselves and consequently raise our self-esteem. Stand in front of a mirror and tell yourself that you are a special person and worthy of self-love and the love of others. Another suggestion is to record some positive affirmations on your telephone answering machine and call your telephone number in the middle of the day or when you are having a slump or

BOX 2.9   AFFIRMATIONS

- I am a worthwhile person.
- I am a child of God.
- I am willing to accept love.
- I am willing to give love.
- I can openly express my feelings.
- I deserve love, peace, and serenity.
- I am capable of changing.
- I can take care of myself without feeling guilty.
- I can say no and not feel guilty.
- I am beautiful inside and out.
- I can be spontaneous and whimsical.
- I am human and capable of making mistakes.

- I can recognize shame and work through it.
- I forgive myself for hurting myself and others.
- I freely accept nurturing from others.
- I can be vulnerable with trusted others.
- I am peaceful with life.
- I am free to be the best me I can.
- I love and comfort myself in ways that are pleasing to me.
- I am automatically and joyfully focusing on the positive.
- I am giving myself permission to live, love, and laugh.
- I am creating and singing affirmations to create a joyful, abundant, fulfilling life.

? CRITICAL THINKING BOX 2.6

What are some positive affirmations that work for you? How can you increase the effectiveness of these affirmations?

attack of self-pity; hearing you own voice say you are okay can have a very positive effect. For example, "Hello—Glad you're having a great day, please leave a message" (Critical Thinking Box 2.6).

What Are My Choices, and How Do I Exercise Them?

Many of us negotiate our way through life never realizing that we have many choices. In his best-selling book *Seven Habits of Highly Effective People*, Stephen Covey (1989, 2004) states that the very first habit we must develop is to be proactive. We stop thinking in black-and-white and come to realize that in every arena of our lives, we have choices about how to respond and react. Covey differentiates between people who are proactive and people who are reactive. Examples of proactive versus reactive language are included in Box 2.10. Pay attention to your own language patterns for the next few weeks. Are there times when you could say "I choose"? You can choose to respond to people and situations rather than react. Exercising our choice potential also entails that we act responsibly toward others. We recognize that other people have the right to choose for themselves and to be accountable for their own behavior.

CONCLUSION

Before we can act responsibly toward others, we must first act responsibly toward ourselves. This involves self-acceptance and self-love. In his book *Born for Love: Reflections on Loving*, Leo Buscaglia (1992) states this very eloquently:

> *Being who we are, people who feel good about themselves are not easily threatened by the future. They enthusiastically maintain a secure image whether everything is falling apart or going their way. They hold a firm base of personal assuredness and self-respect that remains constant. Though they are concerned about what others think of them, it is a healthy concern. They find external forces more challenging than threatening. Perhaps the greatest sign of maturity is to reach the point in life when we embrace ourselves—strengths and weaknesses alike—and acknowledge that we*

BOX 2.10 **EXAMPLES OF REACTIVE AND PROACTIVE LANGUAGE**

Reactive	Proactive
There's nothing I can about do about it.	Let's look at our alternatives.
That's just the way I am.	I can choose a different approach.
He makes me so mad.	I control my own feelings.
They won't allow that.	I can create an effective presentation.
I have to do that.	I will choose an appropriate response.
I can't.	I choose.
I must.	I prefer.
If only.	I will.

are all that we have; that we have a right to a happy and productive life and the power to change ourselves and our environment within realistic limitations. In short, we are, each of us, entitled to be who we are and become what we choose (p.177).

When you get your personal life organized, you will become effective in getting priorities accomplished at home. When you get your school activities organized, you will study more effectively, be less stressed, and be able to prioritize more effectively. With these two areas organized, there will be more time for you to spend on yourself! You will find that after you get organized with your clinical schedule, you will become a more effective nurse and begin to have the time to perform the type of nursing care that you were taught. Often you will hear nurses complain about not having enough time in clinicals to provide the type of bath or teaching they would like to do because of the lack of time. Check them out; often they are the most guilty of wasting time (e.g., taking time to gossip after report, wasting time complaining that they do not have enough time, not delegating effectively, allowing unnecessary interruptions, not organizing their patient care, or not delegating when appropriate). Wow, all the things that this chapter is about!

🌐 RELEVANT WEBSITES AND ONLINE RESOURCES

Dartmouth College (2015)
Managing your time. http://www.dartmouth.edu/~acskills/success/time.html.

MindTools.com (2015)
https://www.mindtools.com/.

QS Top Universities (2015)
Top time management apps for students in 2015. http://www.topuniversities.com/blog/top-time-management-apps-students-2015.

BIBLIOGRAPHY

Berger, J., Polivka, B., Smoot, E. A., & Owens, H. (2015). Compassion fatigue in pediatric nurses. *Journal of Pediatric Nursing, 30*(6), e11–e17.
Branden, N. (1992). *The power of self-esteem.* Deerfield, FL: Health Communications.
Buscaglia, L. (1995). *Born for love: Reflections on loving.* Thorofare, NJ: Random House.

Covey, S. (2004). *Seven habits of highly effective people*. New York: Simon & Schuster.

Figley, C. (2002a). Compassion fatigue: Psychotherapists' chronic lack of self-care. *Psychotherapy in Practice*, *58*(11), 1433–1441.

Goleman, D. (1995). *Emotional intelligence*. New York: Bantam Books.

Hopper, C. (2007). *Hemispheric dominance inventory*. Retrieved from http://capone.mtsu.edu/studskl/hd/learn.html.

Kernan, W. D., & Wheat, M. E. (2008). Nursing students' perceptions of the academic impact of various health issues. *Nurse Educator*, *33*(5), 215–219.

Keyes, R. (1991). *Timelock: How life got so hectic and what you can do about it*. New York: HarperCollins.

Knox, K. C. (2013). Getting a handle on email. *Information Today*, *30*(1), 21.

Lerner, R. (1985). *Daily affirmations*. Pompano Beach, FL: Health Communications.

Lumosity. (2015). *Brain training games*. Retrieved from http://www.lumosity.com/.

Mokhtari, K., Delello, J., & Reichard, C. (2015). Connected yet distracted: Multitasking among college students. *Journal of College Reading and Learning*, *45*(2), 164–180.

Peck, M. S. (1978). *The road less traveled*. New York: Simon & Schuster.

Remember the Milk. (2015). *The best way to manage your tasks*. Retrieved from http://www.rememberthemilk.com/.

Stark, M. A., Maning-Walsh, J., & Vliem, S. (2005). Caring for self while learning to care for others: A challenge for nursing students. *Journal of Nursing Education*, *44*(6), 260–270.

Wolf, L., Stidham, A., & Ross, R. (2015). Predictors of stress and coping strategies of us accelerated vs. generic baccalaureate nursing students: An embedded mixed methods study. *Nurse Education Today*, *35*(1), 201–205.

Yoder, E. A. (2010). Compassion fatigue in nurses. *Applied Nursing Research*, *23*(4), 191–197.

3

Mentorship, Preceptorship, and Nurse Residency Programs

Ashley Zerwekh Garneau, PhD, RN

ⓔ http://evolve.elsevier.com/Zerwekh/nsgtoday/.

Mentoring is a brain to pick, an ear to listen, and a push in the right direction
John Crosby

Mentoring is one of the broadest methods of encouraging human growth and potential.

After completing this chapter, you should be able to:

- Describe the difference between mentoring, coaching, and precepting.
- Identify characteristics of effective mentors, mentees, and preceptors.
- Implement strategies for finding a mentor.
- Discuss the types of mentoring relationships.
- Examine components of a nurse residency program.

■ *Ashley*

It was my first day as a nurse extern in a busy medical intensive care unit. As I walked into my new place of work, I observed nurses on the phones, talking with doctors, and running in and out of patients' rooms with stern looks on their faces. So many questions were going through my head. Which one of these nurses was my preceptor? What would my preceptor expect from me? Would he or she be receptive to helping me develop into my role as a professional nurse? I entered the room where the nurses receive hand-off report from the night staff. It was there that I had my first encounter with Julie, who would become my preceptor, nursing role model, and mentor in the months ahead.

HISTORICAL BACKGROUND

Did you ever wonder where the word *mentor* originated? It originated from Greek mythology. Mentor was the name of a wise and faithful advisor to Odysseus. When Odysseus (or Ulysses, as the Romans called him) left for his long voyage during the Trojan War, he entrusted the direction and teaching of his son, Telemachus, to Mentor. According to mythology, through Mentor's guidance, Telemachus became an effective and beloved ruler (Shea, 1999). Mentor's job was not merely to raise Telemachus but to develop him for the responsibilities he was to assume in his lifetime. Mentoring is one of the broadest methods for encouraging human growth and potential.

WHAT MENTORING IS AND IS NOT

A definition of mentoring in nursing is captured by Meier (2013) as "a nurturing process in which a more skilled or more experienced person, serving as a role model, teaches, sponsors, encourages, counsels and befriends a less-skilled or less-experienced person for the purpose of promoting the latter's professional and/or personal development" (p.343). Oftentimes, the term *mentoring* is confused with *coaching* or *precepting*. Coaching is an approach to assisting an individual's growth through partnership with a colleague or other individual who is an equal. In coaching, one person focuses on the unique and internal qualities observed within the other person that may not be recognized or appreciated (MindTools, 2016). In the business world, executives often refer to themselves as coaches rather than managers, thus fostering a collaborative team-oriented approach. The International Coach Federation (2016) defines coaching as a partnership that enables and motivates the individual receiving coaching to attain his or her highest achievement in all areas of life. From a nursing perspective, the term *health coaching* describes the partnership between the nurse and patient, where the nurse assists the patient in identifying and engaging in healthy lifestyle choices. Olsen (2014) offers an operational definition of health coaching as "a goal-oriented, client-centered partnership that is health-focused and occurs through a process of client enlightenment and empowerment" (p. 24). From these definitions, it is clear that coaches help individuals find new ways to solve problems, reach goals, and design plans of action to motivate people to participate in activities that will advance and fulfill all aspects of their lives. According to Guest, "The strength of mentoring lies in the mentor's specific knowledge and wisdom, in coaching it lies in the facilitation and development of personal qualities. The coach brings different skills and experience and offers a fresh perspective, a different viewpoint. In both cases one-to-one attention is the key" (1999, p.7). An effective coach does not need to have experience in the activities or context of what he or she is teaching. Rather, an effective coach has a unique set of qualities for coaching individuals in achieving knowledge and skills in a particular area.

Based on these definitions, coaches possess characteristics of mentors, and mentors share attributes of coaching. Considering this, mentoring and coaching complement one another and are often used concurrently in assisting individuals to grow both professionally and personally.

What about preceptors? The term *preceptor* simply means "tutor" and generally refers to a more formal arrangement that pairs a novice with an experienced person for a set time period, with a focus on policies, procedures, and skill development. Preceptors serve as role models and precept during their regularly scheduled work hours, which is part of their work assignment, in contrast with mentors, who are chosen, not assigned, and focus on fostering the mentee's individual growth and development during an extended period. Mentors develop a professionally based, nurturing relationship, which generally occurs during personal time (Fig. 3.1).

MENTOR	VS	PRECEPTOR
Occurs over time		Has set time limit
No termination date		Termination date
Sought out by mentee		Assigned
Teaches networking		Formalized orientation
Shares personal experiences		Assists in fine tuning skills
Experiences are personal		Offers suggestions
Mentoring relationship may be personal, academic, or work-related.		Work-related focus

CJMILLER

FIG. 3.1 Mentor versus preceptor.

What Is Preceptorship?

A preceptorship is a clinical teaching model in which a student is partnered with a preceptor and a faculty member, usually during the student's last semester of nursing school (Billings & Halstead, 2016; Bott, Mohide, & Lawlor, 2011). Nursing schools sometimes use the term *capstone course* synonymously with the term *preceptorship*. In a capstone course, the senior-level student works one-on-one with a preceptor who is a competent and experienced registered nurse (Fig. 3.2). The preceptor guides, observes, and evaluates the student's ability to perform clinical skills with competency and to begin applying critical thinking and organization skills in managing a group of patients in a specific setting. The preceptor and the nursing student identify goals and work in a collaborative fashion toward meeting the goals. During a traditional preceptorship, the nursing student identifies an area of interest that he or she anticipates working in following nursing school, because it provides an opportunity for the student to acquire and master nursing skills common to the specialization area and to begin practicing clinical decision making and prioritization (Emerson, 2007). The preceptorship experience promotes role transition and socialization for the nursing student while fostering professional leadership skills in the preceptor. For example, a student may begin to role-model characteristics of prioritizing patient care based on observations of how the preceptor plans and prioritizes patient-care activities. In turn, the preceptor gains leadership traits by communicating and role-modeling professional behaviors. Preceptors have been referenced in the literature as clinical coaches where they foster critical thinking, safe practice, and socialization during the first year of practice for the new nurse (Bratt, 2009).

FIG. 3.2 Capstone course.

What Happens If I Experience a Challenge During My Preceptorship?

When the time arrives for you to complete your preceptorship at the end of your nursing education program, rest assured that those feelings of uncertainty and anxiety that you experienced on your first day of nursing school are normal and will subside with time. As you establish a professional relationship with your preceptor, it is important to understand your role and responsibilities as preceptee as well as the preceptor's role and responsibilities. But what happens when you are placed with a preceptor who doesn't share the same excitement and interest as you do in participating in the preceptorship? Or what happens when your personalities do not blend well? What do you do?

First, it is important to identify the issues you are having with your preceptor. It may be helpful to write down what is concerning you and share this information with your clinical site supervisor before communicating your concerns to the preceptor. *A word of advice: Never approach an issue with anyone (this includes your preceptor) when your emotions are running high. Give yourself a little time to cool off.*

After you have discussed your concerns with the clinical supervisor, arrange a time to meet with your preceptor to communicate your concerns in a professional manner, while also providing suggestions for a possible solution to the issue(s) you are having with your preceptor. Oftentimes, expressing your concerns to your preceptor will help the preceptor recognize and see your perspective on an issue. Equally important is for you to provide an opportunity for the preceptor to provide you feedback and offer suggestions on any concerns or issues related to the preceptorship experience. If neither you nor the preceptor is able to resolve the issue(s), then reach out to your clinical faculty for guidance and support. For additional conflict resolution strategies, refer to Chapter 13, Conflict Management.

A preceptorship has also been identified as a nurse residency program, where a new graduate nurse completes a formalized residency at his or her first place of employment as a professional nurse. Nurse residency programs are now being implemented across many practice settings to ensure that new graduates deliver safe patient care.

WHAT IS A NURSE RESIDENCY PROGRAM?

The moment has finally arrived; you have passed the NCLEX-RN® and obtained your RN license. Now the next step in your professional career path as a nurse begins as you land your first position as a professional nurse. Making this step (what might feel like a big leap!) in your nursing career is like a moment of passage. Gone are the days of nursing school; you are no longer a student but a competent professional nurse. To that end, it is no surprise that you might be feeling a little bit scared or anxious as you start your first day working on the unit at your new place of employment. Remember your first day of nursing school? Similar feelings are sure to surface again as you begin working as a new graduate nurse.

In an effort to ease the transition into the clinical practice setting and reduce job-turnover rates of new graduate nurses, nurse residency programs are now being employed by many health care organizations as a requirement for all newly hired graduate nurses. You might be asking yourself, what exactly is a nurse residency program? A nurse residency program is a formalized orientation that varies in length (anywhere between 6 and 18 months, but usually for about 1 year), where a new graduate nurse works full-time on the unit where he or she will be working following completion of the residency program. Nurse residency programs vary at each institution but essentially serve the same purposes, which are to assist the new graduate nurse with transitioning into the nursing role by providing orientation to the unit to which the new graduate nurse is hired and working with a dedicated and experienced nurse throughout the residency who serves as both a mentor and a coach. In addition, residency programs provide additional specialty training, certification, and courses that may be a unit-specific requirement for the newly hired graduate nurse. Twibell et al. (2012) added that nurse residency programs include a focus on curriculum and specific clinical experiences grounded in evidence-based practice as well as offer new graduate nurses an opportunity for professional growth and socialization as members of the health care team (see the end of the chapter for a list of relevant websites and online resources). Following completion of a nurse residency program, the nurses will work on the unit where they completed the residency. The American Association of Colleges of Nursing offers a listing of nationally accredited nurse residency programs.

Further support for requiring all new graduate nurses to complete a nurse residency program following completion from a prelicensure degree program has been proposed by the Institute of Medicine (IOM). The IOM in collaboration with the Robert Wood Johnson Foundation conducted a 2-year initiative examining how nursing practice and education will transform the delivery of health care. In the 2010 IOM report, *The Future of Nursing: Leading Change, Advancing Health,* the IOM recommended that the following actions should be taken to implement and support nurse residency programs:

- State boards of nursing, in collaboration with accrediting bodies such as The Joint Commission and the Community Health Accreditation Program, should support nurses' completion of a residency program after they have completed a prelicensure or advanced practice degree program or when they are transitioning into new clinical practice areas.
- The Secretary of Health and Human Services should redirect all graduate medical education funding from diploma nursing programs to support the implementation of nurse residency programs in rural and critical access areas.
- Health care organizations, the Health Resources and Services Administration and Centers for Medicare and Medicaid Services, and philanthropic organizations should fund the development and implementation of nurse residency programs across all practice settings.

🔍 RESEARCH FOR BEST PRACTICE BOX 3.1

Nurse Residency Program

Practice Issue

The clinical environment presents an engaging and rewarding experience for nursing students to begin applying nursing concepts and skills learned in the classroom setting to the practice setting. However, changes impacting health care, decreased clinical site availability, increased student enrollment, and faculty shortages have required key stakeholders in both academia and practice to develop alternative models of clinical education that will prepare tomorrow's professional nurse to practice competently and safely. Nurse residency programs are a move in that direction, where a graduate nurse participates in a 1-year program that fosters role transition and clinical decision-making skills grounded in evidence-based practice. Providing a smooth transition into practice has also contributed to increased retention of new graduate nurses and decreased job burnout following completion of the nurse residency program (UHC/AACN, 2016a).

Implications for Nursing Practice

- Health care organizations consider adopting a nurse residency program new graduate nurses are required to complete at the beginning of their employment.
- Implement an evidence-based curriculum under the nurse residency program that focuses on development of critical thinking behaviors and aligns to established core competencies implemented by the health care institution.
- Collaborate with academic institutions to align nurse residency program objectives with nursing educational program outcomes.
- New graduate nurses who have completed the 1-year nurse residency program reported an increase in confidence, competence, organization and prioritization, communication, leadership, and a reduction in stress levels (UHC/AACN, 2008, pp. 5–6).
- Since its inception, UHC/AACN's nurse residency programs have an average retention rate of 95% for first-year employed nurses (UHC/AACN, 2016b).

Considering This Information

What are your thoughts on completing a nurse residency program as a requirement of your employer following graduation from nursing school?

References

University HealthSystem Consortium (UHC), American Association of Colleges of Nursing (AACN). Executive Summary. (2008). Retrieved from http://www.aacn.nche.edu/leading-initiatives/education-resources/NurseResidencyProgramExecSumm.pdf.

University HealthSystem Consortium (UHC), American Association of Colleges of Nursing (AACN). Nurse Residency Program. (UHC/AACN, 2016a). Retrieved from http://www.aacn.nche.edu/education-resources/nurse-residency-program.

University HealthSystem Consortium (UHC), American Association of Colleges of Nursing (AACN). UHC/AACN Nurse Residency Program Overview. (UHC/AACN, 2016b). Retrieved from https://www.uhc.edu/docs/3333-24-9492_UHCAACNNurseResProgInfoSheetSept2014.pdf.

- Health care organizations that offer nurse residency programs and foundations should evaluate the effectiveness of the residency programs in improving the retention of nurses, expanding competencies, and improving patient outcomes (IOM, 2010, p.12).

In 2008, the American Association of Colleges of Nursing (AACN), in collaboration with the University HealthSystem Consortium (UHC), developed a nurse residency program for postbaccalaureate nurses following completion of their educational programs. The UHC/AACN nurse residency program is 1 year long and uses an evidence-based curricular framework for preparing new graduate nurses to transition from their role of novice to competent practitioner. At the time of this publication, 187 practice sites in 32 states currently offer the UHC/AACN nurse residency program (UHC/AACN, 2016a) (Research for Best Practice Box 3.1). The benefits of a nurse residency program have also been extensively studied by the National Council State Boards of Nursing (NCSBN).

The NCSBN implemented a transition to practice study for new graduate nurses employed in their first nursing position (NCSBN, 2016). The aim of the study was to examine the effectiveness of a

> ### BOX 3.1   ESSENTIAL ELEMENTS OF TRANSITION PROGRAMS
>
> - Be formalized in the institution, and have support and involvement of key stakeholders (chief nursing officer and administration)
> - Be at a minimum 6 months in duration
> - Include a preceptorship program into the transition program
> - Include QSEN competencies of patient safety, teamwork, evidence-based practice, communication, informatics, quality improvement, clinical reasoning, and patient-centered care
> - Be customized to the learning needs of the new graduate working on the unit
> - Allow ample time for new graduates to learn and apply content, obtain feedback, and share their reflections.

Adapted from Spector, N., Blegan, M.A., Sivestre, J., Barnseiner, J., Lynn, M.R., Ulrich, B., Fogg, L., & Alexander, M. (2015). Transition to practice study in hospital settings. *Journal of Nursing Regulation, 5*(4), 24–38.

transition to practice program on new graduate outcomes with regard to safety, competence, stress, job satisfaction, and retention as compared to current onboarding programs used by hospitals participating in the study (Spector et al., 2015, p.26). The NCSBN Transition to Practice Model (TTP) employed in the study consisted of an extensive institution-based orientation program, trained preceptors who assisted the new graduate with onboarding processes specific to the unit he or she was working in, and Quality and Safety Education for Nurses (QSEN) online educational models that the new graduate nurses completed during the study. Findings from this study support the utilization of transition to practice programs to improve new graduate readiness for practice and increase retention. Based on findings from the study, researchers (Spector et al. 2015) suggest that nurse transition programs have essential elements that are evidence based (Box 3.1). As you begin your career as a professional nurse, here are additional questions you may want to ask your employing institution or agency:

- Is a formalized orientation program, preceptorship, internship, and/or nurse residency program available to graduate nurses? If so, what is the duration of the nurse residency program?
- Will I be paired with one or several preceptors?
- What is the structure of the nurse residency program? Face-to-face? Online? Hybrid? Simulation?
- Is the nurse residency program nationally accredited?

■ *Ashley*

When I was in nursing school, I thought that a preceptor was fancy terminology for mentor. However, I found out that these two terms are very different from each other.

In nursing, the word *mentor* has become synonymous with trusted advisor, friend, teacher, guide, and wise person. There have been many attempts at deriving a single definition of mentoring. Gibbons (2004) provides a detailed listing of 16 (yes, 16!) different definitions for *mentor*. What makes mentoring so different, so "special," and more encompassing than precepting and coaching?

- Mentoring requires a primary focus on the needs of the mentee and an effort to fulfill the most critical of these needs.
- Mentoring requires going the extra mile for someone else. The rewards of mentoring are enormous: a sense of personal achievement, mentee appreciation, and a sense of building a better organization.

- Mentoring is a partnership created between two people; the mentor possesses the educational degree to which the mentee aspires (Shea, 1999).

> As you read through this chapter, begin to develop your own definition of a mentor.

Since the beginning of time, storytelling has been an important way to teach one another. A story about a starfish follows:

> A beachcomber is walking along the beach one morning when he sees a young man running up and down by the water's edge throwing something into the water. Curious, he walks toward the runner and watches him picking up the starfish stranded by the tide and tossing them back into the ocean. "Young man," he says, "there are so many starfish on the beach. What difference does it make to save a few?" Without pausing, the young man picks up another starfish and, flinging it into the sea, replies, "It made a difference for this one."

> That is what mentors do. They make a difference for one person at a time.

According to Peddy, the process of mentoring can be described in eight words, "Lead, follow, and get out of the way" (2001, p.16). What does this mean?

Lead

Mentors are leaders. They encourage another's growth and development, professionally and personally. Mentors help and inspire mentees by acting as role models. The focus is on wisdom and judgment. The mentor plays a very active role: teaching, coaching, and explaining, while supporting and shaping critical thinking skills, providing invaluable advice when asked, and introducing the mentee to committees, advancements, and honors.

Follow

This is where mentees need to "get their feet wet." At this stage, the mentor and mentee walk the path together, but the advisor (mentor) assumes a more passive role. It is now up to the learner (mentee) to seek actively the advice or listening ear of the mentor.

Get Out of the Way

This means knowing when it is time to let go. If you have ever taught a child to swim or ride a bike, you know how hard it is to "let go" and let the child soar on his or her own. A helping relationship is a freeing relationship. This does not mean the relationship has to end; you share common values and beliefs in lifelong learning.

This process of mentoring is dynamic, not static. A mentor's task of self-development, learning, and mastery is never done. Each person in the mentoring process has a role. Mentors generally have more experience and are dedicated to helping mentees advance in their careers, especially in work and/or life skill issues. Mentoring is a two-way street, a partnership, with both parties freely contributing to the relationship as equals—working together in mutual respect.

■ *JoAnn*

On a personal note, when I think about mentors that I have had, one person comes to mind: Satora. She was my first mentor when I started working in the ICU after graduating with my diploma in nursing. She personified all that a new graduate would want in a mentor. She was understanding, patient, and compassionate, and she possessed extensive experience. She had an important, long-lasting impact on my nursing career. She nurtured me and encouraged me to reach within myself to become the nurse that I am today. I will never forget her.

Approximately 25 years after I left the ICU, I had the opportunity to talk with Satora by phone. It was one of those coincidences or synchronistic moments in which I was able, via a mutual friend, to find out where she was working. I had lost contact with her over the years in the several moves that I had made to different places. She was so surprised that I had called, and I shared with her how important our mentoring relationship had been to me. It made me feel good to pass along my gratitude for her willingness to mentor me.

How to Find a Mentor

The key to finding a mentor is having an open mind, being flexible, and remaining optimistic. As you finish nursing school and while you are in school, write down the goals you feel a mentor might help you achieve. Keep this list of goals with you while you are working, and try to get a feel for the different personality types that you will see as a nurse among your coworkers.

■ *Ashley*

During my orientation program as a newly licensed professional registered nurse, my mentor Julie shared with me a saying that I will share with you: "Always remember, the patient comes first." This stuck with me because it helped me gain greater awareness of the profound impact that we, as nurses, have in our patients' lives and in assisting them to an optimal level of wellness.

As you progress through your nursing program, consider establishing a mentoring relationship. Having the feeling of comfort and building trust with this person is crucial to the process of mentoring. Here are some ideas and strategies to think about:

- Look for common background in either nursing education or an area of expertise/practice or interest.
- Tell the person about yourself. When you disclose something about yourself, it is especially helpful if you can laugh about yourself in a given situation. This sets the tone of the interaction. It is helpful to keep it light, friendly, and positive.
- Find out the best mode for communicating (e.g., in person, by e-mail, phone) with your mentor.
- Ask broad, open-ended questions such as, "How are things going?" that stimulate open discussion rather than direct questions such as "Do you like working here?" or "What kinds of problems are you having?" that may make the other person feel vulnerable.
- By starting out with these basic questions, you can begin to determine a level of comfort about the person. Next, let us examine the characteristics of a successful mentor.

What Are the Characteristics of a Successful Mentor?

When I think about the desired characteristics or competencies of a successful mentor, the following qualities come to mind:

- A mentor communicates **high expectations**. Mentors push mentees and provide avenues and opportunities for them to grow. They allow the mentees to learn through many of their own failures. The mentee grows and develops through active listening, role modeling, and open communication with the mentor. When mentors act as sources of intellectual stimulation and encouragement, they encourage their mentees to trust their own abilities and skills. Mentors open doors and encourage their mentees to search out and seek professional avenues that mentees might not have known about or would have taken longer to discover on their own. Rather than being the "sage on the stage," the mentor is the "guide on the side."

- A mentor is also a **good listener**. Mentors provide a nonjudgmental, listening ear (without taking on the mentee's problems, giving advice, or joining the mentee in a game of "Ain't it awful?"). This can serve as a powerful aid to a mentee. Many mentors believe that respectful listening is the premier mentoring act. When two people really listen to each other, a wonderful sense of synergy is created.
- A mentor has **empathy**. A mentor possesses a degree of sensitivity and perception about the needs of the mentee and has an ability to teach others in an unselfish, respectful way that does not blame but stays neutral. Mentors know what it is like to be the "new kid on the block."
- A mentor offers **encouragement**. By providing subtle guidance and reassurance regarding decisions made by the mentee, the mentor values the mentee's experience, ideas, knowledge of how things work, and special insights into problems. Mentors strive to promote independence in their mentees by offering suggestions but not pushing—mentors know that growth depends on the mentee solving his or her own problems.
- A mentor is **generous**. Mentors are willing to share their time and knowledge with others. Much of what the mentor offers is personal learning or insight (Shea, 1999) (Critical Thinking Box 3.1; Fig. 3.3).

? CRITICAL THINKING BOX 3.1

- Which of these traits appeals to you the most?
- Which ones would be the most important for your mentor to have?

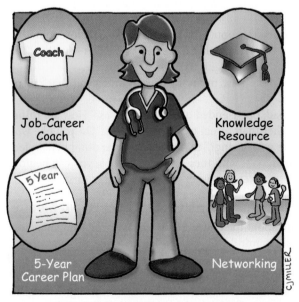

FIG. 3.3 Expectations of a mentor.

What Is a Mentoring Moment?

Have you ever experienced a flash of insight or revelation? Peddy (2001) calls this a "mentoring moment." How do you know when that moment arrives? Someone once said, "When the student is ready, the teacher appears" (Peddy, 2001, p.52). According to Peddy, mentoring is often built on a just-in-time principle, whereby the mentor offers the right help at the right time. A potential mentor must recognize when the mentee feels free to expose a deep-felt need, thereby enabling the mentor to provide the right help at the right time to the best of the mentor's ability.

When Do We Need Mentors?

A mentor is an established professional (selected by you) who takes a long-term personal interest in your nursing career. The mentor not only serves as a role model or counselor for you but also actively advises, guides, and promotes you in your career. A mentor can be any successful, experienced nurse who is committed to a professional career and to being a key figure in your life for a number of years while you are going through school, as well as when you graduate. Mentors should have your best interest at heart and should bolster your self-confidence. Mentors should be able to give feedback in a highly constructive, supportive atmosphere. As a result, trust and caring are hallmarks of the bonding that occurs between mentor and mentee. In short, a mentor is "a wise and trusted adviser" who can serve you well as you experience both professional and personal growth (Fig. 3.4).

A mentoring relationship is an evolving, personal experience for both mentor and mentee. It involves a personal investment of the mentor in the direction of the mentee's professional development. The mentor also benefits from the association by gaining an awareness and perspective of the recent mentee's role in nursing. Take note of the characteristics of successful mentors listed in Box 3.2.

FIG. 3.4 The mentor role.

BOX 3.2 **CHARACTERISTICS OF SUCCESSFUL MENTORS**

- Make a personal commitment to be involved with mentee for an extended period of time
- Be trustworthy and sincere
- Show mutual respect
- Do not be in a position of authority over the mentee
- Promote an easy give-and-take relationship, and be flexible and open
- Listen and accept different points of view
- Be experienced
- Have values and goals compatible with those of the mentee
- Be able to empathize with mentee's struggles
- Be nurturing
- Have a good sense of humor, and enjoy nursing

? CRITICAL THINKING BOX 3.2

- What are my objectives for developing this mentoring relationship?
- What are my goals?
- How can a mentor help me achieve my professional and personal goals?
- What is the best way for me to approach a possible mentor to gain his or her interest in developing a mentoring relationship?

What Is the Role of the Mentee?

As a mentee, you will be learning and absorbing the useful information that the mentor provides. Before seeking a mentor, there are a few questions you may want to ask yourself that may help you get exactly what you need from the mentoring relationship (Critical Thinking Box 3.2) (Shea, 1999).

What Are the Characteristics of the Mentee?

Just exactly what are important characteristics that you, as a mentee, should project in your interpersonal communications with your mentor? Use the checklist in Table 3.1 to answer the questions in the table.

How did you score? Are there areas in which you need to improve your interpersonal skills as a mentee?

What Are the Types of Mentoring Relationships?

There are several types of mentoring relationships that you may experience when you develop an active relationship with your mentor (Table 3.2). Formal, informal, and situational mentoring relationships are three types that are commonly encountered (Shea, 1999).

Mentoring Through Reality Shock

The hospital setting is the largest setting where nurses work. In this setting, formal preceptorship programs are usually established, and a mentoring environment is fostered so the new graduate can address the issues of reality shock. This type of mentoring setting appeals to many new graduates, because it provides support from other health care team members. Remember Kramer's phases of reality shock in Chapter 1? Let us see how an effective mentorship relationship could address each of the phases.

TABLE 3.1 MENTEE CHECKLIST

WHEN MEETING WITH YOUR MENTOR, DO YOU ...	ALWAYS	FREQUENTLY	USUALLY	SELDOM	NEVER	SCORE
Communicate clearly						
Welcome your mentor's input (express appreciation or tell him or her how it will benefit you)						
Accept constructive feedback						
Practice openness and sincerity						
Take initiative to maintain the relationship with your mentor						
Actively explore options with your mentor						
Share results with your mentor						
Listen for the whole message, including mentor's feelings						
Be alert for mentor's nonverbal communication, and use it as data						

Score yourself as follows: *Always*, 10; *frequently*, 8; *usually*, 6; *seldom*, 4; *never*, 2. According to Shea, a score of 80 or better means you are among the limited group of individuals who have good mentee interaction skills (Shea, 1999, p.46).
Adapted from Shea, G.F. (1999). *Making the most of being mentored: How to grow from a mentoring relationship*, Lanham, MD: Crisp Publications.

TABLE 3.2 TYPES OF MENTORING RELATIONSHIPS

	FORMAL	INFORMAL	SITUATIONAL
Structure	Traditional/structured	Voluntary/very flexible	Brief contact/often casual
Characteristic	Driven by organizational needs	Mutual acceptance of roles	A one-time event
Effectiveness	Results measured by organization frequently	Periodic check-ups by supervisors	Results assessed later

Adapted from Shea, G.F. (1999). *Making the most of being mentored: How to grow from a mentoring partnership*, Lanham, MD: Crisp Publications, pp.73-75.

Honeymoon Phase

The mentor can be supportive by listening and understanding when the mentee shares the excitement of starting the new position and passing the NCLEX Exam. The mentor can act as an intermediary with other staff members and as a professional role model.

Shock or Rejection Phase

Mentors can encourage mentees to discuss their feelings of disillusionment and frustration, as well as share their own personal transition processes through this phase. Asking mentees to write down their feelings (keep a reflection journal) or sharing ideas for a possible resolution to a situation can be helpful in mitigating the feelings associated with this phase.

Recovery Phase

The mentor's role during this phase, as mentees begin to accept the reality of the situation and put issues in perspective, is to maintain an open channel of communication and encourage mentees to "step outside their comfort zone" and try new things without stifling the mentee's transition as a new graduate nurse.

Resolution Phase

Mentors are instrumental during this phase to reinforce positive qualities that the mentee possesses and to encourage the mentee in solving problems related to any issues involving the desire either to change nursing positions or to stay put.

What Does the Future Hold?

The future of mentoring programs is changing. Because of technological advancements that have made it possible to offer nursing programs online, a new wave of mentoring has evolved, known as e-mentoring. The term *e-mentoring* simply means any type of mentoring partnership that takes place in an online modality (NHLBI [National Heart, Lung, and Blood Institute], 2012). The NHLBI has launched an e-mentoring program for all college students and graduate students continuing their education in a science-related field (NHLBI, 2012). An advantage of e-mentoring is that mentoring can occur at any time; there are no time or physical constraints that may occur in a face-to-face mentoring partnership (Research for Best Practice Box 3.2).

Peer mentoring programs are developing on campuses throughout the United States. These programs allow senior-level nursing students to mentor entering freshman nursing students. Peer mentoring can be an effective collaborative clinical teaching model for use as a capstone course or preceptorship for senior-level nursing students (Research for Best Practice Box 3.3).

🔍 RESEARCH FOR BEST PRACTICE BOX 3.2
E-Mentoring

Practice Issue

Formalized orientation programs traditionally are offered onsite at the new graduate nurses' employing institution following their hire. Throughout the orientation, the new nurse is paired with a preceptor and begins to acquire increased confidence and problem-solving abilities by working with the preceptor in delivering patient care, performing nursing skills, delegating, and communicating with other members of the health care team for a set period of time. A shortage of nursing staff, coupled with an increase in the number of nurses retiring from the workforce and limited educational resources, pose as a myriad of factors affecting the new graduate nurse's transition into practice.

Implications for Nursing Practice

- Develop or adapt an e-mentoring model where a portion of the new graduate nurse's orientation program occurs in a blended learning environment consisting of both an online component and onsite at the institution.
- The online component would consist of the new graduate nurse and mentor. Seek mentors for the online course who possess leadership skills and are committed to communicating with the new nurse in an online environment, who maintain professionalism, and who are familiar with using the technology (e.g., e-mail, posting discussions in an online discussion thread).
- Miller and colleagues (2008) conducted a study on the effectiveness of e-mentoring in public health nursing by evaluating experiences gained both of students and of mentors, and they concluded that the students (practicing nurses completing a public health nursing course) gained greater confidence in understanding population-based practice and developed skills "in problem-solving, coordinating, and identifying best practices" (p.397) in public health nursing.
- Pietsch (2012) noted that nurses who had previously received e-mentoring were more likely to view future e-mentoring encounters as positive and beneficial for their professional growth. The author also suggested that the term *i-mentoring* may be a more comprehensive term to describe online mentoring via the Internet, as the term *e-mentoring* may limit the online mentoring structure to only two people (the sender and recipient of information) in an online environment.

RESEARCH FOR BEST PRACTICE BOX 3.2—cont'd

E-Mentoring

Considering This Information

What are your thoughts on e-mentoring? What strategies would you use to maintain a consistent and open line of communication with your e-mentor? Would you prefer a more traditional e-mentoring partnership where you communication with one person or a more innovative approach where you have access to a community of mentoring resources and online mentors? What do you feel will benefit you the most as a mentee using an e-mentoring approach?

References

Miller, L., et al. (2008). E-mentoring in public health nursing practice. Journal of Continuing Education in Nursing, 39(9), 394–399. doi: http://dx.doi.org/10.3928/00220124-20080901-02.

Pietsch, T.M. (2012). A transition to e-mentoring: Factors that influence nurse engagement. *CIN: Computers, Informatics, Nursing*, 30(12), 632-639. http://dx.doi.org/10.1097/NXN.0b013e318266cbc5.

RESEARCH FOR BEST PRACTICE BOX 3.3

Peer Mentoring

Practice Issue

Peer mentoring involves a shared learning experience where a senior nursing student mentors a beginning or freshmen nursing student in fine-tuning nursing skills, assisting with test-taking strategies and study tips, and in sharing strategies for success in nursing school. According to Dennison (2010), peer mentoring has the potential to address clinical site shortages and decreased number of clinical faculty by having senior nursing students' clinical experience include a peer mentoring role in the nursing laboratory where he or she works with first- and second-semester nursing students in learning how to operate medical equipment and perform nursing skills.

Implications for Nursing Practice

- The mentors (junior and senior nursing students) gain leadership skills and professional role development behaviors by mentoring other nursing students in the clinical setting (Li, Wang, Lin, and Lee, 2011).
- The mentor maintains competency with nursing skills as he or she is continually teaching the skills to mentees in the nursing laboratory.
- The mentees (beginning or second-year nursing students) gain experience in learning nursing skills and may be more comfortable performing these skills in front of a student than a clinical instructor (Dennison, 2010).
- The mentee can take advantage of working one-on-one with a mentor in the nursing lab.
- Including peer mentoring as a component of the student's capstone course addresses decreased clinical site availability.

Considering This Information

What attributes would you look for in a peer mentor to assist you in performing various nursing functions in the skills lab? What do you feel might be a potential challenge(s) in working with a peer mentor? How will you plan to overcome these challenges?

References

Dennison, S. (2010). Peer mentoring: Untapped potential. *Journal of Nursing Education*, 49(6), 340–342. doi: http://dx.doi.org/10.3928/01484834-20100217-04.

Li, H., Wang, L. S., Lin, Y., & Lee, I. (2011). The effect of a peer-mentoring strategy on student nurse stress reduction in clinical practice. International Nursing Review, 58(2), 203–210. http://dx.doi.org/10.1111/j.1466-7657.2010.00839.x.

CONCLUSION

Here is one final note about mentorship: There is a short anecdotal story about "Everybody, Somebody, Anybody, and Nobody" that has become part of Internet lore. I think you will understand that Everybody has to realize the importance of advancing the field of nursing through mentorship; your task will be to find that Somebody who is willing to extend a hand to guide you through the process.

There was an important job to be done, and Everybody was sure that Somebody would do it. Anybody could have done it, but Nobody did it. Somebody got angry about that, because it was Everybody's job. Everybody thought Anybody could do it, but Nobody realized that Everybody wouldn't do it. It ended up that Everybody blamed Somebody, when Nobody did what Anybody could have.

Mentoring is a complex, interpersonal, emotional relationship. All parties involved in a mentoring relationship benefit from a mutual exchange of information, life experiences, and diversity. *Mentoring* is defined as a developmental, empowering, and nurturing relationship that extends over time (Vance and Olson, 1998). It involves mutual sharing, learning, and growth that occur in an atmosphere of respect and affirmation (Bower, 2000). A mentor has been described as a role model and guide who encourages and inspires. We leave you with this thought:

"There are two ways of spreading light: to be the candle or the mirror that receives it."

Edith Wharton

🌐 RELEVANT WEBSITES AND ONLINE RESOURCES

American Association of Colleges of Nursing (AACN) and University HealthSystem Consortium (UHC) (2012)
Nurse Residency Program. http://www.aacn.nche.edu/education-resources/nurse-residency-program.

American Association of Colleges of Nursing (AACN) (2010)
Accredited Nurse Residency Programs. http://apps.aacn.nche.edu/CCNE/reports_residency/resaccprog.asp.

Institute of Medicine of the National Academies (IOM) (2010)
The Future of Nursing: Leading Change, Advancing Health (Consensus report). http://www.iom.edu/Reports/2010/The-Future-of-Nursing-Leading-Change-Advancing-Health.aspx.

NHLBI (National Heart Lung and Blood Institute) (2012)
eMentoring: An Online Mentoring Initiative. http://www.nhlbi.nih.gov/ementoring/index.htm.

Twibell, R.. St. Pierre, J., Johnson, D., Barton, D., Davis, C., Kidd, M., & Rook, G. (2012)
Tripping over the welcome mat: Why new nurses don't stay and what the evidence says we can do about it. http://www.americannursetoday.com/article.aspx?id=9168&fid=9138.

U.S. Department of Health & Human Services (2012)
HHS Mentoring Program: Become a Mentor/Mentee. https://mentoring.hhs.gov/mentors.aspx.

BIBLIOGRAPHY

Billings, D., & Halstead, J. (2016). *Teaching in nursing: A guide for faculty* (5th ed.). St. Louis, MO: Elsevier.

Bott, G., Mohide, A., & Lawlor, Y. (2011). A clinical teaching technique for nurse preceptors: The five minute preceptor. *Journal of Professional Nursing, 27*(1), 35–42. http://dx.doi.org/10.1016/j.profnurs.2010.09.009.

Bower, E. (2000). Mentoring others. In E. L. Bower (Ed.), *Nurses taking the lead* (pp.11–14). Philadelphia: Saunders.

Bratt, M. (2009). Retaining the next generation of nurses: The Wisconsin nurse residency program provides a continuum of support. *Journal of Continuing Education in Nursing, 40*(9), 416–425.

Emerson, R. J. (2007). *Nursing education in the clinical setting*. St. Louis, MO: Elsevier.

Gibbons, A. (2004). *Mentoring definitions*. Retrieved from http://www.coachingnetwork.org.uk/information-portal/Articles/ViewArticle.asp?artId=54.

Guest, A. B. (1999). A coach, a mentor…a what? *Success Now 13*. Retrieved from http://www.coachingnetwork.org.uk/information-portal/Articles/ViewArticle.asp?artId=72.

Institute of Medicine of the National Academies. (IOM). (2010). *The Future of Nursing: Leading Change, Advancing Health (Consensus report)*. Retrieved from http://www.iom.edu/Reports/2010/The-Future-of-Nursing-Leading-Change-Advancing-Health.aspx.

International Coach Federation. (2016). *What is professional coaching?* Retrieved from http://www.coachfederation.org/need/landing.cfm?ItemNumber=978&navItemNumber=567.

Meier, S. R. (2013). Concept analysis of mentoring. *Advances in Neonatal Care, 13*(5), 341–345. http://dx.doi.org/10.1097/ANC.0b013e3182a14ca4.

MindTools. (2016). *What is coaching?* Retrieved from https://www.mindtools.com/pages/article/newTMM_15.htm.

National Council of State Boards of Nursing (NCSBN). (2016). *Transition to Practice. Why Transition to Practice (TTP)?* Retrieved from https://www.ncsbn.org/transition-to-practice.htm.

National Heart Lung and Blood Institute (NHLBI). (2012). *eMentoring: An Online Mentoring Initiative*. Retrieved from http://www.nhlbi.nih.gov/ementoring/index.htm.

Olsen, J. M. (2014). Health coaching: A concept analysis. *Nursing Forum, 49*(1), 18–29. http://dx.doi.org/10.1111/nuf.12042.

Peddy, S. (2001). *The art of mentoring*. Houston: Bullion Books.

Shea, G. (1999). *Making the most of being mentored: How to grow from a mentoring relationship*. Lanham, MD: Crisp Publications.

Spector, N., Blegan, M. A., Sivestre, J., Barnseiner, J., Lynn, M. R., Ulrich, B., Fogg, L., & Alexander, M. (2015). Transition to practice study in hospital settings. *Journal of Nursing Regulation, 5*(4), 24–38.

Twibell, R., & St. Pierre, J. (2012, June). Tripping over the welcome mat: Why new nurses don't stay and what the evidence says we can do about it. *American Nurse Today, 7*(6). Retrieved from https://americannursetoday.com/tripping-over-the-welcome-mat-why-new-nurses-dont-stay-and-what-the-evidence-says-we-can-do-about-it/.

Vance, C., & Olson, R. K. (1998). Discovering the riches in mentor connections. *Reflections on Nursing Leadership: Sigma Theta Tau International Honor Society of Nursing, 26*(3), 24–25.

4

Employment Considerations: Opportunities, Resumes, and Interviewing

JoAnn Zerwekh, EdD, RN

(e) evolve.elsevier.com/Zerwekh/nsgtoday/.

School is almost over and the dream of being paid as an RN (Real Nurse) will soon come true!

Nursing offers more job possibilities than any other aspect of health care. So if your first choice doesn't work out, select another specialty!

After completing this chapter, you should be able to:

- Assess trends in the job market.
- Identify the primary aspects of obtaining employment.
- Describe the key aspects of an e-portfolio and a resume.
- Describe the essential steps involved in the interviewing process.
- Discuss the typical questions asked by interviewers.
- Analyze your own priorities and needs in a job.
- Develop short-term career goals.

With graduation in sight, you are excited but probably a little anxious about moving into the workplace, looking for the perfect match to your hard-earned degree. As you consider possible employment opportunities, prepare for the upcoming job search as you would any graded class assignment: Do your homework! Careful preparation is the key to finding a job you really want. Very few worthwhile job offers come to someone who just happens to walk into the human resources department. The continued expansion of the health care field and the growing nursing shortage have created tremendous opportunities for recent graduates. You have developed marketable skills that are in demand, but to sell yourself successfully to prospective employers and get the job you really want, you must do some homework.

> Take some time to brainstorm about a career—if you could go anywhere you wanted to in nursing, where would it be?

In addition to evaluating the possibilities and limitations of the job market under consideration, give yourself plenty of time to consider what type of position you want and need, in addition to the possibilities and limitations of the job market under consideration. You can compare the process with the selection of a marriage partner, car, home, or any other major life choice. It is important for nurses to take the time to create a career plan. Your first professional position is a stepping stone in a long nursing career; it will help define who you are and influence your career path. Only *you* can determine the path you want to travel, so it is important that you become informed and selective in the process. Too often, new graduates accept their first job without sufficient awareness of their own needs or knowledge about the employer they select. Your work is a major factor in your life. If you simply go to work every day, put in your time, and go home, then your job will manage you. If your work enriches your life, is exciting, and you have a feeling of fulfillment, then you are in charge. As a graduate nurse, you have a choice—to do nothing or to take charge of the direction you want to go. However, as the Cheshire Cat was well aware, only Alice could make the choice as to the direction she should go (Fig. 4.1). Although there is no guarantee that a job will be a perfect fit, career dissatisfaction and turnover can be decreased if careful consideration is given to possible job selection *before* you send out your resume and schedule an interview.

This chapter provides some guidelines to a thorough background preparation for your job search. Critical Thinking Box 4.1 will help you identify your clinical interests and the possible

FIG. 4.1 Choose carefully where you want to go.

reasons for these preferences. Hint: This will also help you answer interview questions about your professional interests.

WHAT IS HAPPENING IN THE JOB MARKET?

For the past few years it has been impossible to read an article about the health field that does not mention the nursing shortage, the "looming nursing shortage," or the "worst nursing shortage in U.S. history." The U.S. nursing shortage is projected to grow to 260,000 registered nurses (RNs) by 2025. Let's look at a chronological order of current and projected shortage indicators that have been published since Buerhaus et al.'s (2009) statement about the current easing of the nursing shortage due to the recession.

- 2010—The Institute of Medicine (IOM) *Future of Nursing* report called for increasing the number of baccalaureate-prepared nurses in the workforce to 80% and doubling the population of nurses with doctoral degrees. Only 55% of registered nurses are prepared at the baccalaureate or graduate level.
- 2012—In the January 2012 issue of *American Journal of Medical Quality* a group of researchers used projected changes in population size and age to develop demand and supply models to forecast the RN job shortage in each of the 50 states in the publication, "United States Registered Nurse Workforce Report Card and Shortage Forecast." The number of states with a significant RN shortage ratio will increase from 5 in 2009 to 30 by 2030, for a total national deficit of 918,232 RN jobs. Their findings note a significant RN workforce shortage throughout the country in 2030, with the western states having the largest shortage ratio.

? CRITICAL THINKING BOX 4.1

Assess Your Wants and Desires, Likes and Dislikes

Identify your interests and the possible reasons for them.

INTERESTS	REASONS
1. I prefer to work with patients whose age is _____.	
2. I prefer to work in a small hospital versus a large medical center _____.	
3. I prefer rotating shifts versus straight shifts _____.	
4. I prefer an internship versus general orientation _____.	
5. I prefer to have a set routine or a constantly changing environment _____.	
6. I prefer these areas (e.g., geriatrics, pediatrics, community, health, medical) _____.	
7. Which of my religious or cultural beliefs or values might have an impact on where I work? _____.	

- In the Bureau of Labor Statistics' Employment Projections 2012–2022 released in December 2013, registered nursing is listed among the top occupations in terms of job growth through 2022. From 2.71 million expected nurse positions in 2012 to 3.24 million needed in 2022, the predicted increase is 19%, or an increase of 526,800 RNs. Approximately 1.05 million nurses will be needed in 2022 to cover the number of job openings for RNs due to growth and replacements (AACN, 2014).

Over the past three decades the Health Resources and Services Administration (HRSA) has reported every 4 years on the supply of RNs through the National Sample Survey of Registered Nurses (NSSRN). Data collection from the most recent, and final, NSSRN was completed in 2008. The 2008 survey noted that the average age of all licensed RNs increased to 47 years in 2008 from 46.8 in 2004, which represents a stabilization after many years of continuing large increases in average age. Nearly 45% of RNs were 50 years of age or older in 2008, a dramatic increase from 33% in 2000 and 25% in 1980 (HRSA, 2010).

In 2015, the National Council of State Boards of Nursing (NCSBN) and the National Forum of State Nursing Workforce Centers worked together to conduct a survey to provide data on the national nursing workforce. The publication is titled *The National Council of State Boards of Nursing and the Forum of State Nursing Workforce Centers 2015 National Workforce Survey for RNs* (NCSBN, 2015). Their findings include:

- Male RNs are a growing minority in the workplace.
- Half (50%) of those working in nursing were age 50 or older, which is down from 53% in 2013.
- Approximately 19.5% of responding RNs were from a minority population, with newly licensed nurses having a more diverse racial/ethnic composition.
- 6.7% of the RN workforce were foreign educated.
- 42% of RNs had a BSN or higher degree as their initial credential, while 65% had obtained a baccalaureate or higher degree (in any field) as their highest level of education (NCSBN, 2015).

The graying of the American population will have a large impact on the health care industry. There will continue to be a substantial increase in the number of older patients, and their levels of care will vary widely from assisted living settings to high-technology environments. This impacts the growing need for nurses in the geriatric setting. As the general population is aging, so are nurses.

What will happen with nursing employment, the job market, and health care when a large percentage of nurses become part of the older generation? What effort will hospitals make to retain older nurses as the economic recession recovers? Who will mentor the new nurses and help them develop critical decision-making skills at the bedside? How will the role of simulation help bridge the gap between textbook learning and clinical decision making? According to the Bureau of Labor Statistics *2014-2015 Occupational Outlook Handbook*, "Employment of registered nurses is projected to grow 19 percent from 2012 to 2022, faster than the average for all occupations. Growth will occur for a number of reasons, including an increased emphasis on preventative care; growing rates of chronic conditions, such as diabetes and obesity; and demand for healthcare services from the baby boomer population, as they live longer and more active lives." The current and continuing shortage in nursing personnel in some areas of the country will dramatically heighten the need for increased efficiencies in clinical education for new graduates. How will the job market continue to evolve for the graduate nurse during the next 5 years? Only one thing is certain—everything will continue to change at an increased pace (Critical Thinking Box 4.2).

> **? CRITICAL THINKING BOX 4.2**
>
> What changes have you observed as a result of the nursing shortage? What impact has the shortage had on salaries and staffing in your community? If the signs of a nursing shortage were beginning to surface as far back as the late 1990s, why haven't we (education, health care employers, government) created effective solutions to this growing problem yet?

SELF-ASSESSMENT

What Are My Clinical Interests?

Begin by jotting down possible settings where you could pursue your areas of clinical interest. Depending on your interests, there will be a number of possible paths to pursue. As you identify clinical areas that interest you, try to prioritize them. This step may seem like a nonissue if you tend to "eat, sleep, and drink" one nursing specialty; however, many people have two or more strong interests, and this step helps to outline some increased possibilities. Believe it or not, some graduating students confess to liking *every* clinical rotation and feel pulled in multiple directions when they consider where to begin a job search. If that description fits you, hang in there—you are not alone! Keep in mind that all nursing experiences, both negative and positive, can contribute to your career in a productive way. The more areas you sample, the broader your knowledge base as you gradually build a career.

Recruiters like to see flexibility in new graduates, but let us try to narrow your professional interests just a bit before your actual job search. Perhaps you can identify what you liked about each clinical rotation through reflective journaling and then prioritize possible interests or identify common experiences.

What Are My Likes and Dislikes?

Another way to approach self-assessment involves identification of your likes and dislikes in the work setting. This is related to interests but on a more personal level. The job you eventually select may have some drawbacks, but it should meet many more of your likes than dislikes in order to be a good "fit" (Fig. 4.2).

Write out your responses to the following questions:

1. **Do you enjoy an environment that provides a great deal of patient interaction, or do you thrive in a technically oriented routine?** Think back to your clinical rotations and see if you can find a pattern to what was most enjoyable or disagreeable.
   - I liked opportunities for using many technical skills.
   - I was bored with slower-paced routines (e.g., mother-infant care).
   - I liked to see the results of care as soon as possible (e.g., PACU).
   - I disliked the constant turnover of patients every day (e.g., ED).
2. **Do you enjoy caring intensively for one or two patients at a time with a high acuity level and a potential rapid change in patient status, or do you prefer a patient assignment less acute with opportunities for family education and observing increased patient independence? Why did you like or dislike one type or the other?** Discuss your responses with some friends who may have had other experiences and get their opinions. Consider how you will explain your preferences to a nurse recruiter on the phone, in an online cover letter, or in person.
3. **Do you learn best in a highly structured environment or in more informal on-the-job training situations?** Knowing your learning style can guide your interest and narrow your selection of an internship or orientation program. For example, internships range from formal classes with lengthy preceptorships to more informal orientations of fairly short duration. Remember, a

FIG. 4.2 Assessing personal needs and interests. Is the job a good fit?

program that meets your needs may not be the answer for your best friend. Write down what you would like from an orientation or internship program. Look over your list and prioritize what you need and want most.

4. **Do you feel comfortable functioning with a significant degree of autonomy, or do you want and need more direction and supervision at this point in your professional development?** Shortly, you will have completed nursing school, backed up by employment on a telemetry unit throughout your senior year. Are you ready to be a charge nurse on the 3 to 11 pm shift in a small rural hospital, or do you want a slower transition to such responsibility? If this situation was offered, would you be flattered, frightened, or flabbergasted? Write down your reaction and consider how you would respond to the recruiter who offers you such a position.

5. **How much physical energy are you able and willing to expend at work?** Running 8 to 12 hours a day may or may not act as a tonic. Think back to the pace of your clinical rotations, and consider how your body reacted (minus the anxiety associated with instructor supervision, if you can!). Would you prefer a unit that has some predictable periods of frenzy and pause, or do you thrive on the unpredictable for your entire work shift?

6. **Are you a day, evening, or night person? Are there certain times of the day when you are at your peak of performance? How about your worst?** Be honest and realistic with your answers. Very few people are equally efficient and effective 24 hours a day. If your body shuts down at 10 pm, or you resist all efforts to wake up before 9 am, a certain shift may need to be eliminated. However, if the job market is tight in your area of interest, the available positions may be on a less desirable shift, and you may need to make adjustments in other areas of your life to temporarily acclimate better to a professional position.

7. **Do you like rotating shifts, or, perhaps more realistically, can you work rotating shifts?** One aspect of reality shock for many new graduates is the realization that working the day shift may have ended with the last clinical rotation in school. Hospital and long-term care staffing is 24 hours a

day, 7 days a week. It is a "24/7 profession"—a possibly unpleasant aspect of nursing, but a real one nonetheless. Assess your ability to work certain shifts and try to strike a flexible approach before you speak with nurse recruitment. Working 12-hour shifts (7 AM to 7 PM or 7 PM to 7 AM) can be very demanding on the days assigned, but this option is very popular with many nurses because of the increased days off.

8. **Consider the impact of these choices on your family, your social life, and other needs.** If there are certain shifts you must rule out, recognize that this may limit your job choices and plan accordingly. Giving some thought to your flexibility ahead of time will help you avoid committing to any and all shifts during an interview and will facilitate your job hunt. On the other hand, it is probably not realistic to request a Monday-through-Friday schedule in an acute care setting unless the organization has a separate weekend staff or a high level of personnel who request to work only weekends. Shift patterns may vary significantly within a city—and in different areas of the country as well—so do your homework online or through job fairs about available shifts before you go in for an actual interview.

9. **Can you work long hours (e.g., 12-hour shifts) without too much tension and fatigue?** The 12-hour staffing option offers flexibility (e.g., six 12-hour days of work in an 80-hour pay period) but leaves some people exhausted and irritable. Consider your personal needs outside of work when you respond to this item. Can you climb into bed or put your feet up after a nonstop 12-hour shift, or do you need to pick up family responsibilities as soon as you walk in the door? The 4 days off may well compensate for 3 days of fatigue, but map out your needs before you begin your job search.

10. **Do you like making decisions quickly or generally favor a more relaxed approach to clinical problems?** In general, ICU and step-down units require more immediate reactions than an adolescent psych unit or orthopedics. Does the ICU environment excite or overwhelm you? Would you prefer a slower pace? Do not criticize yourself for your likes or dislikes. Slower-paced units require different strengths, not less knowledge. You have nothing to gain by working in an ICU if you dislike the setting. Meet your own needs, not someone else's. You will spend a great deal of your time at work. Make the choice for you, not someone else's idea of the perfect job.

11. **What do you need in a job to be happy?** This question does not mean money or benefits but rather the sense that the job is worth getting excited about. Think about past employment you have had, whether in health care or not. What did you like or dislike about the job? What made you stay? Possible answers include opportunities for growth, advancement, working with people you respect, or collegiality. Remember, your answers should include things that are important to you. These are the kinds of issues that make you eager to go to work or to help you work through difficult clinical days. You may want to compare your answers with those of others whose opinions you value to gain a broader perspective.

After thoroughly reflecting on the questions listed, it will be necessary to reflect on yourself as a person and explore what interests you have in the many facets of nursing.

What Are My Personal Needs and Interests?

A third aspect of self-assessment focuses on personal needs and interests. How much time and effort are you willing and able to give to your career at this point in time? Will work be a number-one priority in your life, or does family or continued education take precedence?

Is relocation a possibility? If you are considering relocation, decide how you will gather information on possible job opportunities in the area or areas under consideration. Include Internet websites, professional journals, and professional and family contacts as possible sources of information.

In addition to reviewing online job possibilities, research the hospital's website for details about the organization's overall philosophy, its department of nursing, and a sense of "fit." Prospective employers want to know that applicants have taken the time to become knowledgeable about them and appreciate when applicants ask more informed questions about employment.

If this is a voluntary move, develop a list of pros and cons for each location under consideration. Include your personal interests in the decision (e.g., cost of living, commuting time, possible relocation allowance, access to recreational activities, opportunities for advanced education, and clinical opportunities).

What salary range are you willing to consider? Although starting salaries for new graduates are generally nonnegotiable, differentials for evenings, nights, and weekends create a range of salary possibilities. If you want an extended internship, a lower starting salary may be offered. Are you willing and able to trade this for the benefits of an extended internship? The quality of the internship may be worth a lower salary temporarily because of later advancement opportunities. Some areas of the country offer considerably higher salaries than others, but factor in the cost of living before you move out of town. You may be unpleasantly surprised by a monthly rent that swallows up a significant percentage of your salary.

What Are My Career Goals?

The final step of your self-assessment is the development of career goals. Yes, you really do need to have some goals! You are the architect of your professional future, so take pen to paper or fingers to the keyboard and start designing. Consider your answers to the following questions.

What do you want from your first nursing position? Possible answers might include developing confidence in decision making, more proficiency with technical skills, increased organizational abilities, and gathering skills to move into a more favorable position.

What are your professional goals for the first year? Third year? Fifth year? If you cannot imagine your life, let alone your career, beyond 1 to 2 years, relax. Many people feel uneasy planning beyond their initial position and first paid vacation.

Develop a comfortable response to a question regarding your goals for the first year, and consider what you might want to be doing after that time. Remember, it is far easier to gauge how your career is progressing if you have established some benchmark goals to which you can refer. This is also a favorite question posed during interviews, so spend some time thinking about it! Recruiters are interested in nurses with a plan.

RESEARCHING PROSPECTIVE EMPLOYERS

What Employment Opportunities Are Available?

You have a world of nursing to choose from; there are opportunities available to begin your practice as a graduate nurse. The largest employers are hospitals or acute care facilities. In hospitals, a wide variety of positions are available, although new graduates are almost always placed in staff nurse positions. If it is a general hospital, you need to choose what areas interest you most. Your first position may not be exactly what you want, but remember, it is the first step toward your career goal. As you build your competence and self-esteem, you may find just the position you want. In many hospitals, staff positions represent different levels of proficiency, especially if the hospital participates in clinical or career ladders (Fig. 4.3).

> The staff nurse position can be one of the most challenging. It can also be like an "incubator" from which to develop your nursing career.

FIG. 4.3 Ways to research prospective employers.

Charge nurse positions may involve responsibility for a particular staff or a particular day, or they may involve managing staff for an entire unit. New graduates should not be placed in charge positions until they have mastered a staff nurse role, but the marketplace may result in new graduates being offered the charge position, especially in more rural settings. If this is a situation that you will face soon after graduation, make sure that you identify your resources and consider whom you can contact for professional support and backup. Do not allow your ego to let you accept an unsafe position that could endanger patients and your hard-earned nursing license.

Entry-level positions in the hospital are usually staff nurse positions. Staff nurse positions in medical-surgical nursing are some of the most demanding—and rewarding—positions. Frequently, nurses begin their careers here with the intention of moving on to greener pastures; however, the rewards and challenges may more than fulfill their needs. It is important that your first position offers you an opportunity to further develop your nursing skills. Surely, you have heard at least one person in nursing school say to you, "You should get a year's experience in Med-Surg first." Is this a true statement? Yes and no. Yes, if you want to work in a medical-surgical field, and no, if you do not. Yes, the experience will help sharpen assessment skills and some technical skills, but every area of work has advantages and potential drawbacks. If you know in your heart that med-surg makes you miserable, turn around and go in a different direction. Life is too short to be miserable for 8 to 12 hours a day. Furthermore, chances are that you will not give your best to the patients if you are unhappy.

Whether it is working in the emergency department, day surgery, specialty units, or medical-surgical units, staff nurse positions give you a very valuable opportunity to polish your time management, patient care organization, and nursing skills. Once you are confident with skills, procedures, and the overall practice of nursing, you may be ready to move on to new challenges. This may take 6 months for some recent graduates. For others, it may take a year or more. Take the time to reinforce your nursing competencies; it will prepare you for your future practice in nursing. Other areas in which nurses may find employment include community health, home health care, and nursing agencies. Working in the community in such positions as occupational health, school health, and the military may require a bachelor's degree in nursing and at least 1 year of hospital nursing. If you want to work in a community setting, concentrate initially on refining your assessment and critical thinking skills in the acute care setting, because the autonomy of the community setting means more decision making on your own without the immediate backup of experienced peers who are usually available in the acute care setting.

What About Advanced Degrees in Nursing?

There are many advantages to earning an advanced degree in nursing (review Chapter 7 for the different choices). One of the most important aspects of obtaining an advanced degree is using your experience as a nurse to help you determine in what direction you want to go. If you have an associate's degree, you might want to consider the basic requirements for your baccalaureate's degree, including what schools are available and what their requirements are. This is an area you can begin to work on immediately after graduation. As you interview for jobs, ask whether the prospective employer will work with your schedule if you decide to go back to school and if they provide tuition reimbursement for continuing education.

HOW DO I GO ABOUT RESEARCHING PROSPECTIVE EMPLOYERS?

Employment Considerations: How Do You Decide on an Employer?

In your search for a job, it is important to look for organizations and hospitals that create a work environment that supports professional nursing practice. In 1980, the American Academy of Nursing identified criteria for the designation of "magnet hospitals." This designation recognized certain hospitals for their lower turnover rates, their visionary leaders, the value they placed on education, and an ability to maintain open lines of communication. To identify magnet hospitals in your area, check the website http://www.nursecredentialing.org/Magnet/FindaMagnetFacility (ANCC, 2015). Inquire about the last accrediting agency survey results. This may be a state survey in long-term and subacute care or The Joint Commission in acute care. The survey results will give you information about the quality of care delivered at that employment agency. Showing an interest in being a part of a quality organization will convey a positive light as a candidate for hire. In your search for a job, it is important to look for organizations and hospitals that create a work environment that supports professional nursing practice. In the current job market, locating magnet hospitals in your community is an important consideration in your job search.

Media Information

Newspapers. Although many people no longer look at the newspaper for information, preferring the Internet for data, the newspaper is still a good place to access useful information about jobs, as well as articles about hospitals or other health care employment opportunities. This will vary considerably depending on the area of the country where you are hoping to work. Scan the advertisements to see whether any are targeted specifically to graduating seniors. Focus on these initially because they will include information on possible job fairs, internships, or specialized orientations, in addition to specific openings for graduate nurses.

Online searches. Electronic job searches have replaced newspapers for many people as the top place to start looking for employment. This is an efficient way to search because you can access information for both local and distant nursing opportunities with the ease of a few clicks, assuming that sites are kept current. As a new graduate, consider the value of looking at employer websites rather than generic nursing employment sites because employer sites are better focused for new graduates. Additionally, many employer websites offer services for building a profile that allows you to customize based on the department or unit you are interested in working for. It is also a terrific way to review the positions available within the entire organization. If you intend to use this method to follow up on a job posting, be prepared to submit your flawless resume electronically—and be sure to spell-check all of your correspondence before you click the "Send" button! Many organizations now require electronic applications, occasionally raising issues of software compatibility for applicants. Know and be prepared to comply with human resources requirements for submitting your resume and cover letter. Patience in the application process is essential for your professional success. With the availability of computer spell-checking and editing support, there is no excuse for a poorly written resume or cover letter. Take the time to review your documents for errors. Recruiters pay attention to these details.

Social networking. Social networking is the way the 21st century seems to communicate with each other in online websites that consist of a community of individuals with like-minded interests. According to the January 2015 PEW Research Center report, 52% of online adults now use two or more social media sites, a significant increase from 2013, when it stood at 42% of Internet users. For the first time, more than half of all online adults 65 and older (56%) use Facebook, which acts as a social media "home base." This represents 31% of all seniors. Also for the first time, more than half of Internet using young adults ages 18 to 29 (53%) use Instagram, with almost half of all Instagram users (49%) using the site daily. Internet users with college educations using LinkedIn reached 50%. There is an increase of 23% of online users currently using Twitter. Approximately 36% of Twitter users visit the site daily, but this actually represents a 10-point decrease from the 46% who did so in 2013. About 17% of users visit Pinterest daily, with the majority of them being young women (Duggan et al., 2015).

Thus, if you are trying to make a good impression, then your appearance on the social networking website will be what an employer first sees. Begin by doing an Internet search on yourself and fix anything that may have a negative reflection of yourself. Be sure to use a professional photo, perhaps just a headshot, and make your Facebook account private to prevent employers from searching for you, if you want to use the Facebook account for family and friends. Potential employers may dismiss you as a candidate after viewing inappropriate photographs or information. A study by Careerbuilder (2014) noted that more employers are using networking sites to obtain additional information about a potential applicant. Approximately, 51% of employers who research job applicants on social media said they've found content that caused them to eliminate the candidate, up from 43% in 2013 and 34% in 2012.

As the amount of personal information available online grows via sources such as Facebook, Twitter, and the like, first impressions are being formed long before the interview process begins, warns David Opton, ExecuNet CEO and founder. "Given the implications and the shelf-life of Internet content, managing your online image is something everyone should address—regardless of whether or not you're in a job search," he says (Lorenz, 2009).

LinkedIn (2015) operates the world's largest professional network on the Internet with over 400 million members in over 200 countries and territories. LinkedIn has become the place for reconnecting with colleagues and classmates, as well as powering your career with a vast network of contacts and employers looking for the right employee. Recruiters often search this site. If you do not have a profile on LinkedIn, you may be left out of finding the right type of position. LinkedIn® allows you to link to your professional Twitter™, Facebook, or blog pages and upload your resume to your profile, which definitely comes in handy for interested employers.

Job fairs/open houses. You may have the opportunity to attend a nursing job fair or hospital open house as a soon-to-be graduate nurse. Take advantage of these opportunities to collect information about specific employers and possibly make initial contacts for later interviews. Leave your jeans and tennis shoes at home on these occasions, and put on your professional best. Take some time with your appearance, because first impressions are important (Fig. 4.4)!

Employee contacts. If you have a friend or family member—or simply know someone—who works at an organization you are considering for employment, make an effort to speak with him or her about the job environment. As an insider, this person may be able to provide you with a perspective about the employer that the advertisement, recruiter, or interview cannot. Possible questions you may want to ask such an insider may include these: "Why do you enjoy working there? What was orientation like? How is employee morale? What is the turnover rate for nursing or for other employees? Does management show appreciation for employee effort and welcome employee input?"

Recruitment Contacts

Letter-writing campaign. Plan to send your resume with a cover letter and triple-check both documents for grammatical errors. Your resume and cover letter are the first impression you will make with a prospective employer. Make it a positive one!

Telephone contact. Before you pick up the telephone, get out your calendar and start planning likely dates for possible interviews, as well as the approximate date you want to begin working. Armed with this information, you can comfortably answer questions beyond the fact that you would like the employer to send you a brochure and an application. Depending on the organization you contact, the human resources or nurse recruitment department may want you to first submit a resume online or may ask you to set up an appointment for an interview. Do not commit to an interview if you are not ready.

Personal contact. If you plan to just stop by human resources or nurse recruitment for a brochure and an application, make sure you give some thought to your appearance. Tee shirts, shorts, and jeans are not appropriate and have caused otherwise well-qualified applicants to be passed over for further consideration. Again, remember that first impression!

FIG. 4.4 The first impression is a lasting one, so make it count for you, not against you.

WHAT DO I NEED TO KNOW TO ASSESS THE ORGANIZATION?

Now that you have described yourself and have thought about the kind of setting in which you work best, continue these exercises on a consistent basis. This ongoing analysis will help you make decisions about the kind of organization that is best for you and put you in a position to determine what kind of organization fits you.

How Do You Go About Assessing an Organization to Find What You Want?
Talk to People in the Organization

One obvious answer is to ask the people who work in that organization. When you interview for a position, you can meet people who work in the specific setting in which you are interested. Ask questions that will help you learn about certain situations. Take some time to think about questions and situations you would like to present when you talk to people in various facilities. Keep in mind that the values of the organization will affect your work on a daily basis. If both patients and employees are valued, you will see this reflected in the quality of patient care and in the retention of nurses.

Read and Analyze the Recruitment Materials

Organizations also present themselves to you through their documents. Carefully analyze the materials presented to you—this is another way of determining the values the organization lives by and deems important. All of these materials are intended to make a statement to you about who they are.

Review the Mission or Philosophy Statement

There are other written documents to examine. For example, a specific nursing unit may have a mission statement that tells you who they are and what they are about. The department of nursing will have a philosophy statement or possibly a nursing theory that should be the organizing framework around which the members structure themselves in delivering nursing care. In some organizations, the staff knows what this mission statement says and how it provides direction to them. In other organizations, the staff will be unfamiliar with the statement of philosophy and may react with confusion when you ask them. All of these written materials should send a message to you about the organization. Do your observations during the interview process support the organization mission/philosophy statements (Critical Thinking Box 4.3)?

❓ CRITICAL THINKING BOX 4.3

What are some observations that you could have during your interview process that would cause you to have second thoughts about accepting a position at the organization?

Evaluate the Reputation of the Leadership

Organizations are guided by people at the top and take on the characteristics these people support. What do you know about the chief executive officer (CEO)? This person sets the stage and the direction for the organization. You can gather information about the CEO by checking the organization's website and asking people during the interview what this person is like. People in the community will also be familiar with this person and can give you insight into the values and characteristics that this person represents.

> ### BOX 4.1   PORTFOLIO SUPPORTING DOCUMENTATION
>
> - Degree from nursing school attended
> - Clinical evaluation document for all clinical rotations that includes a narrative notation from the clinical instructor(s) about your progress in the clinical and simulation setting
> - Documentation of nursing skills list
> - Group projects or assignments demonstrating your involvement in working with a team
> - Certificates of attendance for any nursing student or professional development conferences attended
> - Supporting documentation for any service learning projects that you planned or participated in (i.e., health fair, flu vaccination clinics)

The same can be said for the chief nursing officer (CNO). This person sets the direction for the nursing organization, either by active design or benign neglect, and sets into motion an organization that structures the beliefs about patients, staff, and nursing. It is important to talk with nurses who are working with the CNO to determine how they feel about the leadership in the organization. Has he or she had a successful track record? Is this person well respected? Can people point to a strategic direction and philosophy this person has given to the organization?

PORTFOLIOS

Portfolios have been used in nursing education to document a student's knowledge, skills, abilities, and learning to track the progress within a curriculum, along with monitoring and evaluating a student's performance at strategic checkpoints. A professional portfolio is like a scrapbook that is a collection of past events, documents, certificates, and other artifacts (term given to all information, documents, etc. placed in the portfolio). Portfolios take time to develop and maintain; however, the payoff is that the collection of information is available for job seeking, promotion, and evaluation. Don't confuse a portfolio with a resume. The resume is a component of the professional portfolio. If you haven't already started a portfolio during your nursing program, you can start by compiling the supporting documents to include in the portfolio. Box 4.1 provides a list of supporting documents to include in the portfolio. As you collect your documents, it is prudent to scan them into an electronic format and keep a backup on either a removable disk drive or in the "cloud." By having your portfolio documents in electronic format, you can create an e-portfolio.

What Is an E-portfolio?

The electronic portfolio, or e-portfolio, is a relatively new tool being used by students to secure their first position after graduation by showcasing their talents and skills and focusing attention on what unique attributes they have for the prospective employer and desired position. In addition, the e-portfolio clearly demonstrates the new graduate's web writing skills and ability to create and update their e-portfolio website. Many health care employers use the portfolio as an additional tool to review the prospective employee in the pre-hire period beyond the resume, employment application, and interview (McMillan, Parker, & Sport, 2014) (see Critical Thinking Box 4.4). As you acquire e-portfolio

> ### ❓ CRITICAL THINKING BOX 4.4
>
> Are you wondering where to find a website or hosting for your e-portfolio? Type the following in your web browser, "free e-portfolio website providers," to locate some suggestions. What obstacles do you feel you will encounter in creating your e-portfolio?

documents, now is a good time (if you have not already started) for developing your resume to showcase your academic, professional, and past employment experience. So, let's focus on resumes.

TRADITIONAL AND EMPLOYER-FOCUSED RESUMES

A trend in writing a resume is the employer-focused resume, which basically has the same elements as the traditional resume but requires a change in focus. The traditional resume provides an inventory of your professional work background and skills and highlights the background first, followed by matching it to attributes noted for a desired job position. The employer-focused resume approach requires the prospective job applicant to know the audience (employing agency) and what they want, so that the resume can be written to demonstrate that the applicant has the required competencies for employment (i.e., the applicant is a "good fit" for the agency). Let's look at some techniques in writing an effective resume.

How Do I Write an Effective Resume?

> Design your resume by using the KISS principle: Keep It Simple, Sincerely! (That is, use concise wording and make it easy-to-read, informative, and simple.)

Your resume is the first introduction a prospective employer will have to you. It will give the employer a basic idea of who you are professionally and what your objectives are for your nursing career. While defining your strengths, it is important not to overstate your skills. Everything that you include on your resume should be true. Expect the employer to check all facts. Do not jeopardize a job possibility by intentional misstatements or careless attention to dates of prior employment or education.

Most employers are willing to train you on all or some of the components of the position you are applying for. A resume is a concise, factual presentation of your educational and professional history (Box 4.2). Do not be surprised if a recruiter suggests other areas to you in addition to what you have initially indicated on your resume or in your interview. Be open to suggestions; they may have some ideas or considerations you have not even thought about.

What Information Is Necessary for a Resume?

Here are the components of a resume. Be sure to proofread what you write for correct spelling and grammar. Do not forget that this is the first impression someone may have of you.

Demographic Data: Who Are You?

Your name, address, telephone number, and e-mail address should be at the top of the page. Be sure to give correct, current information so that the employer can easily contact you. If you need to give an alternative telephone number or e-mail address, provide the prospective employer with the contact person's name and advise the person that a potential employer may be calling for you. Keep in mind that you never put personal information such as your social security number, marital status, number of children, or picture on a resume. Your e-mail address conveys a message, so do not include anything that sends a "cutesy" or possibly offensive message to a prospective employer. Consider the image you want to convey.

Summary of Qualifications (Professional Objective): What Position Are You Applying For?

There is a wide variety of ways to address this element. With the traditional resume, it is important that you describe the position you are applying for and specify what department or area of nursing you are interested in. The professional objective statement focuses on the job applicant's wishes and needs and not on the prospective employer's needs. With the widespread use of the Internet, it is easy to view job

---

BOX 4.2   RESUME GUIDELINES

- Catch all typos and grammatical errors. Have someone proofread your resume.
- Present a clear summary of qualifications that emphasize your skills and strengths.
- A good first impression is critical, so if written, your resume should be neat and printed on white or off-white paper.
- Avoid using "I" or "me" in your resume.
- Keep the information concise, preferably limited to one or two pages.
- The rule of thumb on work experience is to show most current work experience. This generally means the last 10 to 15 years unless there is something in your more distant background that is critical to note.
- Do not try to impress anyone with big words. Jargon specific to the profession is okay if everyone knows what it is.
- Do not inquire about salary or benefits in your resume. It is not the right time or place for that.
- Do not exaggerate about what you can and cannot do, because the potential employer will check it out.
- Present yourself in a positive light.
- Your resume should be neat and visually appealing. If sending by email, save to a PDF file to preserve formatting.
- Do not list all of your references. Be prepared to provide them on a separate list when asked. You may want to have different references for different types of positions.

Linda Smith

123 Any Street

Dallas, TX 77777

972-555-5555

E-mail: lsmith@hotmail.com

Objective:

To obtain a staff nurse position in Hematology-Oncology

Education:

Memorial High School, Dallas, Texas, graduated 5/2008

El Centro College, Dallas, Texas

ADN, awarded February, 2014

Experience:

10/2008 to present–Baylor Hospital, Dallas, Texas–nurse tech, part-time

9/2005 to 5/2008–Kroger's Supermarkets, cashier

Licensure:

Eligible for NCLEX May 2014 (Texas)

Certifications: CPR expires 3/30/2015

Professional Organizations:

Texas Nursing Students Association

References: On request

FIG. 4.5 Resume.

openings and be more educated and decisive about what you are looking for. This is the first step in developing your employer-focused resume by determining what the employer wants in a job applicant. The **summary of qualifications** has become more common today than the professional objective. The qualification summary notes the specific skills and competencies you have that fit the job position. Typically, the qualification summary is 5 to 10 lines or bullet points providing a brief overview of your critical skills and competencies. The qualification summary functions like an abstract for a journal article (Welton, 2013). See Fig. 4.5 for an example of the summary of qualifications.

Education: Where Did You Receive Your Education?

List your education in chronological order, beginning with the most recent. List the month and year of graduation and what degree you received, if any. If you have degrees other than nursing, include these in the chronological order in which you received them. This section will contain any certifications (BLS, ACLS, PALS) and special training you have received, where you received them, and the date you completed them. If you are currently enrolled in school, be sure to include that as well.

Professional Experience: What Do You Know How to Do?

"Easy to read" is the goal. It is very important to put this section in chronological order beginning with the present. You want the prospective employer to see what you have been doing most recently. List your current or previous employer, position held, dates from and to, and a brief description of your responsibilities. This is a good place to reinforce special skills that you highlighted in your summary of qualifications that you feel may be important to your prospective employer. This section will differ for an experienced nurse versus a recent graduate nurse. However, it is important to list your employment history through the past 7 years, including those areas of employment that may not be associated with nursing or the health care field. All the experiences you have had as an employee help to demonstrate your ability to work with people, handle stress, be flexible, and so forth. It is not necessary to list clinical rotations you have completed during nursing school, which are mostly standardized. If you have not had any work experience and this will be your first job, state that also. It is important for managers and staff educators to be aware of the levels of experience of recent graduates they consider. If you had an opportunity to take a clinical elective in a specialty area, include that information because it may enhance your application, especially if you apply for a position in that specialty.

Licensure: What Can You Do and Where Can You Do It?

This is a very important area of information for nurses. With the implementation of the multistate Nurse Licensure Compact (see Chapters 5 and 17), you may only need to be licensed in one state. It is your responsibility to know which states will honor your license and which ones will require you to obtain a separate license. As a general rule, you will be required to be licensed in the state of your residence, and possibly in another state of practice, depending on the licensure compact of the states involved. List the state in which your license was issued and the expiration date. For security reasons, do not list your license number.

Professional Organizations: What Do You Belong To?

You may list organizations in which you are a member or have held an office. You should list professional and community groups. Include any certifications that you have obtained (BLS, ACLS, PALS). This section is optional.

Honors and Awards: What Did You Receive Recognition For?

If you have received recognition for special skills or volunteer work, you may want to include it here. You may also include any scholarships you have received. This is also an optional section.

References: Who Knows About You?

Be prepared to provide a separate typed sheet that lists at least three references. Provide the names and telephone numbers of three professionals with whom you have worked. These professionals need to be able to say something positive about you, so give careful consideration to whom you choose. Always notify your references that you have listed them and that they may receive a telephone call about you. Look at the example of a resume in Fig. 4.5, and adapt it to what works best for you. Make every effort as a new graduate to keep your resume on one page because recruiters generally scan the resume in less than 2 minutes. As you gain professional experience a longer resume may become necessary. If you need further examples of resumes or formats, check the Internet for samples (www.resume.monster.com). Many word processing programs also have resume formats that you can access.

What Else Should I Submit With My Resume?

Along with your resume, you should enclose a cover letter that serves as a brief introduction (Box 4.3). Summarize your important strengths or give information regarding change of specialty, but remember that this letter should be brief—about three to five well-written paragraphs on one or two pages (www.csuchico.edu/plc/cover-letters.html). If you have spoken with a recruiter and have a specific name, address the letter to him or her. However, you do not have to address it to a specific person; it will be distributed to the recruiter who handles the units in which you have indicated an interest. Simply addressing it to "Nurse Recruitment" will usually ensure that it gets to the right person. Large organizations may have several recruiters, so a general address to recruitment will often suffice. However, if you have spoken with a recruiter and have a specific name, address your letter to that person.

BOX 4.3 REMINDERS FOR COVER LETTERS

Content and Format
- Business letter format
  Date
  Employer's Name and Title
  Company Name
  Address
- Salutation: Use person's name and title (e.g., Mr. John Smith, Outpatient Supervisor)
- Opening Paragraph: Should state what position you are interested in and how you heard about it.
- Middle Paragraph: Should detail how you are qualified for the position based on experience, skills, and abilities. Discuss your interest in working for this agency. Carefully check for grammar, as the cover letter provides a short glimpse of your writing skills.
- Closing Paragraph: Refer the person to your resume and focus on the steps or actions that need to be taken to initiate an interview.

If Mailed
- 8½- by 11-inch paper—white, off-white, or light blue
- Typed, with no mistakes (your first opportunity to wow them with professional style)
- No smudges
- 1½- to 2-inch margins on all sides
- Signed, usually in black ink
- No abbreviations
- Business letter format

If E-mailed
- Follow good writing skills.
- Create resume in a Word document using standard fonts (Times New Roman, Arial, Helvetica), and save to PDF to preserve formatting.
- Attach the cover letter and resume or complete forms on an agency human resources website.
- Save files using your name and date (e.g., John-Adams_resume_5-2017; John-Adams_coverletter_5-2017).

What Are the Methods for Submitting Resumes?

There are a variety of ways to submit a resume: hand-carry it, submit it electronically by means of e-mail or the hospital website, or mail it through the post office. Your prospective employer will likely have a preferred method for submission. If their website states that electronic submission is required, do not place a printed version in the mail. It is likely to be ignored. One of the most popular methods for nurses to send resumes is through the website of the medical organization where they are interested in obtaining an interview. This is an excellent way to submit your resume, but remember to follow up with a telephone call if you have not heard from a recruiter within 1 week. You can also directly e-mail your resume to a recruiter. E-mail addresses are readily available through business cards, websites, and word of mouth. If you email your resume, be sure to convert it to a PDF file to preserve the formatting to make it easy to read. But beware: Your e-mail first page will serve as the cover letter when you submit your resume by using an e-mail attachment of the PDF file. The same resume-writing principles apply to all electronically submitted resumes because your resume will be printed for review.

There are also many large job-search websites available on the Internet. You can post your resume on any of these by using their specific formats, but remember that businesses must pay a fee to search for applicants. It is important to remember that not all of the organizations belong to every job-search website. Use discretion regarding where you want to post your resume; if you are interested in a specific organization, it is best to review their website directly for positions available and guidelines for submitting resumes.

Now that you have your resume ready to submit, you will need to identify prospective employers. Remember, one of the first things you can do is network. Networking is contacting everyone you know and even some people you do not know to get information about specific organizations or institutions. Places where you can network are at your facility during clinical, at nursing student organization programs, at career days at colleges, and at career opportunity fairs. Attend local chapter meetings of nursing organizations. Read nursing journal employment sections. When you have identified the organizations where you would like to discuss possible employment, send them your resume. If you have not heard from them within 7 to 10 days, give them a call to make sure your resume was received and to schedule an interview. Keep a record of contacts and resumes sent so that you will have easy access to all of this information (Fig. 4.6). It will be important to document your follow-up actions and results—do not forget to keep copies of correspondence and notes about any conversations with potential employers. Date all entries, briefly note any information received, and indicate all interviews requested and granted, resumes sent, and job offers received. Box 4.4 presents a summary of the steps to finding the job you want.

Employer Address and Phone Number	Interviewer and Title	Date Resume Sent	Date and Time of Interview	Inquiry of Application Letter	Application Submitted	"Thank You" Letter Sent After Interview	Job Offer Received	Confirmation of "No Thank You" Letter Sent	Comments or Notes

FIG. 4.6 Record of employer contacts and resumes sent.

BOX 4.4   YOUR CHECKLIST FOR FINDING A JOB

- Define your goals.
- Develop your resume.
- Identify potential employers.
- Send your resume and cover letter.
- Return a follow-up phone call.

- Schedule an interview.
- Send a follow-up letter.
- Keep a record of employer contacts (see Fig. 4.6).
- Make an informed decision where to work.

THE INTERVIEW PROCESS

How Do I Plan My Interview Campaign?

Set up Your Schedule

Keep the following points in mind:

- Agencies usually have specific dates for orientations, internships, and preceptorships.
- Identify when you want to begin employment, and mark your calendar.
- Work backward from this date to plan dates and times for interviews.
- Plan no more than two interviews in 1 day. If you do, beware of information overload and the risk of being late for at least one interview. Have two or three possible dates available on your calendar before calling the human resources or nurse recruitment office. Advance planning will keep you from fumbling on the telephone when they tell you that your first choice is unavailable! It is also a good idea to get a contact name and phone number in the event that you need to reschedule the interview.

While you are on the telephone, ask questions about the interview process. How much time should you plan for the interview? It may range from under 1 hour to a half day. If you have not already read the job description in the newspaper or online, ask where you can access it when you call. Becoming familiar with both the job description and the prospective employer is critical to interview success.

What does the interview process involve? It may involve tours and multiple interviews including human resources, nurse recruitment, one or more clinical managers, and, possibly, staff nurses. If you are applying for an internship, it is not unusual to be interviewed by a panel of three or four people. Knowing this ahead of time may increase your anxiety, but it is less stressful than being surprised by this fact at the door.

Will more than one interview be required? Some organizations will use the first interview as a screening mechanism. You may be asked to come back for a follow-up interview.

How do you get to the human resources or nurse recruitment office? Ask for directions ahead of time if you are unfamiliar with the area. Have a good idea of the time involved for travel. Arriving late for an interview may create a very poor initial impression.

Will you be able to meet with clinical managers from different areas on the same day? Are there new graduates in the area with whom you can talk? This is important if you are interested in more than one clinical area. Will a tour of the unit be included? If this is not a standard part of the interview process, express interest in having one so that you can get a more realistic idea of the setting and possibly meet some of the staff.

Prepare to Show Your Best Side

Develop your responses to probable interview questions. If you do not plan possible responses, you run the risk of looking wide-eyed as you fumble for an answer or ramble on around the subject. Despite the reality of a nursing shortage in most areas of the country, organizations still give considerable

? CRITICAL THINKING BOX 4.5

Sample of Interview Questions

The following is a sample list of interview questions you should be familiar with. Prepare your responses.
1. What area or areas of nursing are you interested in and why?
2. Tell me about your clinical experiences. Which rotations did you enjoy the most? Why?
3. What is the biggest mistake you ever made, and how was the problem resolved?
4. Tell me about yourself. What do you see as your strengths? Why?
5. How about your weaknesses? Why?
6. Tell me about a staff nurse who most impressed you and why.
7. How would your most recent nursing instructor describe your performance in the clinical setting?
8. Tell me about your most challenging clinical assignment and what you learned from it.
9. What skills do you feel you have gained from your past work experiences that may help you in this position?
10. Tell me a little about yourself. How would others describe you?
11. What are your future career plans? Where do you expect to be in 2 or 3 years? In 5 years?
12. We do not have any openings at the present time in the areas in which you have indicated an interest. Would you be willing to accept a position in another area? If so, what other areas interest you?
13. Tell me about a time when you had to establish priorities during one of your clinical experiences.
14. Tell me about a time when you went out of your way to assist a family or patient, even though you really did not have the time.

(Spend some time looking over your answers. Do they describe you accurately? Rework your answers until you feel comfortable with them, but do not try to memorize the words. They should serve as a guide for the upcoming interview.)

weight to the interview, and an employment offer is far from automatic to anyone who walks in the door with a diploma or license in hand.

Critical Thinking Box 4.5 includes examples of interview questions with which you should be familiar. How would you answer these questions?

Rehearse the Interview

If you role-play a possible interview, it will probably increase your comfort level for the real thing. Following are some suggestions for a rehearsal:
- Dress for the part. It will add some authenticity to the situation.
- Choose a supportive friend, recently employed new graduate, or family member to role-play the interview while video recording, which will allow you to view your nonverbal communication. Sometimes we make facial expressions and display body language that may be unfavorable.
- Practice your verbal responses to sample questions in front of the mirror.
- Ask for constructive feedback regarding your appearance, body language, and responses.

Many applicants say they have no questions at the end of the interview. This may be true, or it may reflect the urge to end the interview and relax! Some words of advice: Prepare a few questions! This will be your opportunity to gather important details and possibly impress the interviewer with your interest. The following is a sampling of possible questions:
- What are your expectations for recent graduates?
- What is your evaluation process like?
- Who will evaluate me, and how will I get feedback about my performance?
- I would like some more information about your preceptorship program. How long will I have a preceptor, and what can I expect from the preceptor?
- What is the nurse-to-patient ratio on each of the shifts I may be working?
- What is your policy regarding weekend coverage?

BOX 4.5   THE *DOS* AND *DON'TS* OF DRESSING FOR INTERVIEWS

Do

- Look over your wardrobe and select a conservative outfit. The tried-and-true rule for job interview attire is this: Dress conservatively and professionally. Although a nursing shortage may loosen the rules a bit, the impression you convey by your appearance is likely to be remembered. Also, remember that you may be touring the facility, so wear comfortable shoes.
- Cover any body art and remove any visible jewelry piercings.
- Women: If you own a suit, consider wearing it, but do not blow your budget buying something you will never wear again. Other acceptable outfits include a business-type dress or skirt with coordinated top. Dress pants and a conservative blouse are also acceptable. Also, remember that you may be touring the facility, so wear comfortable shoes.
- Be conservative with your perfume, makeup, and hairstyle.
- Wear minimal jewelry; you do not want to jingle and rattle with every move.
- Wear hose with a skirt or a dress; bare legs may be fashionable, but they are not appropriate for a professional interview.
- Men: Consider wearing a suit or jacket with coordinated slacks and shirt, but do not blow your budget buying something you will never wear again. A tie is optional. A dress shirt and slacks are also acceptable. Be conservative with your cologne, after shave, and hairstyle.
- Take a few minutes to look yourself over in the mirror.

Don't

- Wear casual clothes such as tee shirts, jeans, tennis shoes, or sandals. They may reflect the "real" you, but this is not the place to show that aspect of your personality.
- Be guilty of poor grooming or hygiene.
- Chew gum during the interview.
- Wear brand-new shoes, which may turn your day into a "painful" experience.
- Bring your children with you. Do not expect the staff to act as babysitters.
- Wear wrinkled or revealing clothing.

- What opportunities are there for professional and leadership development?
- When do you plan to fill the position?
- How will I be notified if I am offered the position?

Strategies for Interview Success

One of the most important strategies for successful interviewing is to dress for success (Box 4.5). Pay attention to your interviewing etiquette; your nursing instructors have taught you professional standards, and this is an opportunity to put that education to good use. Also, make sure you know the name and title of the individual who is scheduled to meet with you.

CRITICAL FIRST 5 MINUTES!

> The decision to hire or not is usually made within the first 60 seconds. You will need to put your best foot forward from the start. Show up at least 10 to 15 minutes early. Smile at everyone you meet, and shake hands firmly (Restifo, 2002).

Arriving early may give you a chance to look over additional information about the organization or possibly give you more time for your interview. If you are delayed or cannot keep the appointment, call the interviewer as soon as possible to reschedule. Under no circumstances should you present yourself for an interview with your children or spouse in tow. They do not belong at a job interview and will create a negative impression with the interviewer. Human resources cannot provide babysitting services, and the presence of children in the waiting area is a safety concern without adult supervision. If you experience a childcare emergency, call and reschedule the interview.

Be aware of your body language; establish eye contact with the interviewer and maintain reasonable eye contact during the interview. Try to avoid or minimize distracting nervous mannerisms. Keep your hands poised in your lap or in some other comfortable position. If you tend to "talk with your hands," try not to do this continually. If you cross your legs, do not shake your foot. If offered coffee or another drink, decide whether this will relax you or complicate your body language. Show enthusiasm in your voice and body language. Do not chew gum or have anything in your mouth. Give a winning smile when you are introduced, and offer to shake hands.

Demonstrate interest in what the interviewer has to say. Do not argue with or contradict the interviewer! Wait to ask about salary and benefits until all other aspects of the interview have been completed, including your other questions! Salary and benefits are important aspects, but they should not dominate your conversation. If the salary offer is lower than you expected, do not argue with the interviewer. You may point out that another organization is offering a higher starting salary, but do not try to use this information as a form of harassment or coercion. If you want to take some notes during the interview, ask the interviewer if he or she minds. This is generally quite acceptable. Bring along your list of questions, and if you cannot recall them when given the chance, ask to take out your list. Do not check off information during the interview as if you were grocery shopping!

PHASES OF THE INTERVIEW

The interview is generally divided into three areas, each of which serves a particular purpose. The first few minutes constitute the introduction. This is a "lightweight" section that is designed to help put you somewhat at ease. Some effort to "break the ice" will be made, and the communication may focus on the traffic, the weather, or the excitement you probably feel about your upcoming graduation. Take some slow, deep breaths, and make a conscious effort to relax.

The second phase involves fact finding. Depending on the skill and style of the interviewer, you may be unaware of the subtle change in conversation, but questions about you will most likely now be asked. Your resume may be used as a source of questions, so make sure you can speak about its contents and that every item on the resume can be verified. Be prepared to offer your references and possibly explain why you have selected these particular individuals. If you have a tendency to give short responses or avoid answering questions, a skilled interviewer will reword the question or possibly note that you do not answer questions well. Interviewers strive to have the applicant talk about 90% of the time, so consider this your audition. Be prepared to explain how you fit into carrying out the mission and values of the agency. They are really interested in getting to know you as a prospective "fit" with their organization, so you should be both enthusiastic and honest. Although many organizations offer a prolonged internship or preceptorship to increase both your confidence level and practical skill set, the interviewer is looking for prospective employees who are capable of being assertive team players—people who can be flexible but persistent. Critical Thinking Box 4.5 offers sample questions that you can practice with. Consider how you can best portray your background and experiences for the recruiter. Explaining how you have gone the extra mile for patients in a challenging situation is what a recruiter and nurse manager want to hear.

Some organizations are asking students or recent graduates to bring in a portfolio reflecting their school experiences. Included in this portfolio might be your skills check-off sheet, exemplar nursing care plans/concept maps, and any educational materials that showcase your best work. This is particularly beneficial if it is signed by the faculty with occasional positive comments.

The closing is the last phase of the interview process. The interviewer may summarize what has been discussed and give you some ideas about the next step in the process (e.g., a tour, a meeting with clinical managers, or a follow-up interview). This is your time to ask questions. However, if you feel full of facts and unable to ask any questions at this time, leave the door open to future contacts by saying, "I believe you answered all my questions at this time, but may I contact you if I have some questions later on?"

After the initial interview, you may have the opportunity to tour the area in which you will work. Show interest when this tour is offered, and use it as a chance to observe the surroundings for such things as professional behaviors as well as organizational and environmental factors. If you have the chance, interact with the staff, especially with recent graduates. Ask what they enjoy about their unit and job position. Before leaving, make sure you thank the interviewer for his or her time and interest.

HOW DO I HANDLE UNEXPECTED QUESTIONS OR SITUATIONS?

So, you did your homework and you are prepared for anything, but out of the blue you are asked a question you never expected. What should you do? Saying "No fair" is not a good answer! Take a deep breath, pause, and consider saying something like this: "That's an interesting question. I'd like to think about my answer for a minute if you don't mind. Can we come back to that subject later in the interview?" Given a temporary break, you will have time to develop your thoughts on the subject. Do not ignore the question, however, because a good interviewer will most likely bring it up again. Suppose you answer the question but feel your response was incomplete or off the mark. Look for an opportunity at the end of the interview to bring up the subject again, saying something like, "I've had some time to think about an earlier question and want to add some additional information if you don't mind" (Box 4.6).

Now Can We Talk About Benefits?

At some point during the interview process, the interviewer might open the discussion on the salary and benefits the hospital has to offer. Salary, job responsibilities, and facility location are not the only major considerations in choosing an employer; do not forget to consider the total compensation package (that is, your benefits). Often, benefits are overlooked by new graduates because their value is less visible than an exciting new salary. Some organizations spend as much as 40% of their total employee payroll to provide this extra compensation. You should consider benefits as your "hidden paycheck" (Box 4.7).

BOX 4.6 KEY POINTS TO REMEMBER ABOUT YOUR RESPONSES DURING AN INTERVIEW

- Answer honestly.
- Do not brag or gloat about your achievements, but do show yourself in a positive light. It might be helpful to have your portfolio available from your prelicensure nursing program to showcase your clinical experiences, exposure to nursing skills, and other academic accomplishments.
- Remember that you are your best salesperson!
- Do not criticize past employers or instructors. It is more likely to reflect unfavorably on you than on them.
- Do not dwell on your shortcomings. Turn them into areas for future development: "I want to improve my organizational skills. Managing a group of patients will be a challenge, but I am looking forward to it."
- Demonstrate flexibility and a willingness to begin work in an area of second or third choice if the job market is limited in the area in which you are applying.

BOX 4.7   BENEFIT PACKAGE OPTIONS

Check with human resources regarding which benefits you are eligible to receive and when they are effective.

- Health and life insurance
- Accidental death and dismemberment coverage
- Sick or short-term disability pay
- Vacation pay
- Retirement plan
- Long-term disability leave
- Dental and/or vision care
- Parking
- Tuition reimbursement
- Loan programs
- Dependent care programs
- Health and wellness programs

Sign-on Bonuses

This has become a marketing tool for some organizations. Be cautious: carefully read and evaluate what is connected with the sign-on bonus. How long will you have to work for the employer to receive any or all of the bonus, and when will it be paid? Is the sign-on bonus in any way tied to the area in which you will be working? If you originally wanted to work in an intensive care unit but decided after 6 months that was not the area for you, can you transfer to another unit without losing your sign-on bonus?

When doing your job search, reviewing benefits is a major part of your decision. Therefore, as a new graduate, be sure to familiarize yourself with all the options that are available to you. The human resources department of the hospital or organization will be able to answer your questions. The decisions you make soon after graduation and in the early months of employment will have a far-reaching effect on your future.

JOB OFFERS AND POSSIBLE REJECTION

Let us consider a positive outcome first. If you are offered a position during or at the end of the interview, you are likely to have one of three possible reactions:

1. You are not ready to say yes or no. This is your first interview, and you have two more interviews scheduled.
2. You would like very much to work here. The job offer is just what you are looking for.
3. You do not want the position. It is not what you thought it would be, or something about the organization has created a negative impression.

Whichever decision you make about the job offer, the following are helpful tips for forming a response:

- Be honest. If you have other interviews to complete, say so. Be prepared to tell the interviewer when you will make your decision about the job offer.
- Avoid being pressured to say yes if you are not ready to commit to the job or feel that the position does not meet your needs.
- Be polite. Ask for some time to consider the offer if you are unsure of what you want to do at present.
- If you know the offer does not interest you, decline the offer graciously and express appreciation for the company's interest in you.
- Accept the offer and smile!

Suppose you receive a rejection or no job offer for the position, despite your interest and preparation. Before you leave in a state of dejection, find the courage to ask for a possible explanation if it has not been made clear at this point. If you do not find out about the rejection until later, consider calling the interviewer for this information. Check the following list for common reasons an organization may not offer you a job. Consider whether any of these factors might apply to you:

- *Lack of opening for your interests and skills.* They liked you but could not find a spot right now, or a more qualified candidate was selected for the position.

- *Poor personal appearance, including inappropriate clothes.* You stopped by for the interview on your way to the gym.
- *Lack of preparation for the interview.* You were unable to answer questions intelligently or showed lack of knowledge of, or interest in, the employer. Your answers were superficial or filled with "I don't know."
- *Poor attitude.* You conveyed an attitude of "What's in this for me?" instead of "How can I contribute to the organization?" Your first question focused on salary and perks.
- *Your answers and behavior reflected conceit, arrogance, poor self-confidence, or lack of manners or poise.* They should hire you just because you showed up! Or you submitted a resume and responses that did not reflect initiative, achievements, or reliable work history.
- *You have no goals or future orientation.* After all, you just want a job, and they should hire you because there is a nursing shortage.
- *Perceived lack of leadership potential.* You like being a follower in all situations and do not want to make decisions. If this scenario sounds like you, rethink your approach. All nurses are expected to be leaders, whether in a formal or informal role. In your next interview, ask the interviewer how the organization supports the development of leadership in new graduates.
- *Poor academic record without a reasonable explanation.* You worked as hard as you could in school, but the teachers did not like you; you lacked appropriate references; or your references were not available or did not reflect favorably on you. All experiences provide us with an opportunity for growth, especially the negative ones. Avoid blaming others for your shortcomings, and look for ways to grow from the experience.
- *Lack of flexibility.* You were unwilling to begin work in an area that is not your first or second choice. Consider how rigid you can afford to be at this particular point in time or at this organization.

> If at first you don't succeed, try, try again.

Postinterview Process

Now that the interview is over, you may want to relax, celebrate, or jump in your car to make your next interview appointment. However, stop for a few minutes and jot down some notes about the interview. This is particularly important if you have another interview the same day. Critique the interview you just had. Consider the following questions:

1. What do you think were your strengths and weaknesses?
2. Is there anything you wish you had or had not said? Why?
3. Were there any surprises?
4. How do you feel you handled the situation?
5. What can you do differently the next time?

Write down details about the job that will help you decide on its relative merits and drawbacks. If you do not do this, you may not be able to distinguish job A from job B by the time the interviews are finished. You may experience information overload after a number of interviews, but if you have taken notes about each, the sorting-out process will be easier.

After the interviews are over, rank your job offers against your personal list of priorities to make an informed choice. This may be an unnecessary step for you if you were sold on a particular interview. However, it is a good idea to consider interviewing with at least two organizations, if only to strengthen your decision about the first interview. It will help eliminate possible doubts about your choice later on. If there is a job you think you are really interested in, do a couple of other interviews first. This will give you some experience in interviewing. You may then be able to conduct a more positive interview for the position in which you are most interested. More interviews may also open your eyes to other possibilities.

Follow-up Communication

Remember how nice it is to get a thank-you note in the mail or a telephone call of appreciation? Well, the same idea carries over to the work world: Write those letters!

Follow-up Letter

Take a few minutes to write a note of thanks to the interviewer for the time and interest spent on your behalf. You may want to include additional information in the note: your continuing interest in the position if you hope an offer will be made, the date you will be making your job decision, additional thanks for any special efforts extended to you (lunch, individualized tour), and any change in telephone numbers and appropriate times when you can be reached. Use plain thank-you note cards, not frilly or cute ones. This is a situation where a handwritten note is certainly acceptable; just make sure it is legible and neat. Recruiters frequently comment on the positive aspect of a follow-up letter, and this attention to interpersonal communication may serve to keep your name at the top of the list. This step also helps to "separate you from the pack of applicants."

An electronic note of thanks is acceptable (www.jobsearch.about.com/od/thankyouletters/a/samplethankyou.htm). However, in the blur of daily e-mail, a personal handwritten note will particularly stand out.

Letters of Rejection

As soon as you make up your mind regarding job offers, notify other prospective employers of your decision. Decline their job offer graciously, and include an expression of appreciation for their interest in you. The format for this letter should follow the standard rules of business letters. Remember, you have accepted a position elsewhere, but your career could take a turn in the future that may bring you back to the organization you are now declining. Leave a positive impression with human resources and recruitment.

Telephone Follow-up

On the basis of the interview, you should have a pretty clear idea of the "how" and "when" of further contact. A telephone call may be appropriate when you have not heard from a recruiter by an agreed-upon date. You can contact a recruiter or interviewer by telephone to decline a job offer, but a personal letter is preferable to leaving a telephone message. Remember to be unfailingly polite to everyone you speak to on the telephone. Administrative assistants and other support personnel will remember and pass on unfavorable impressions to their superiors. Recruiters do not want to hire staff members who are rude or impatient. They know that this behavior is likely to be shown toward patients and families as well. Administrative assistants often act as gatekeepers for their boss and can be counted on to report both positive and negative perceptions of the job applicants with whom they have contact.

What If I Do Not Like My First Position?

It is not uncommon to experience frustrations during your first work experience. Return to Chapter 1 on transitions and reality shock, and review it for some suggestions on how to handle your situation. You also need to keep in touch with the nurse recruiter who hired you. Nurse recruiters can offer further support and assistance. Recruiters know where other recent graduates are working in the organization and may provide you with a network of individuals who can offer suggestions and support to improve your situation. In addition, recruiters know the staffing needs of other areas in the hospital and may suggest transferring. A good way to get an idea of other areas where you may be interested in working is to "shadow" a staff nurse in that

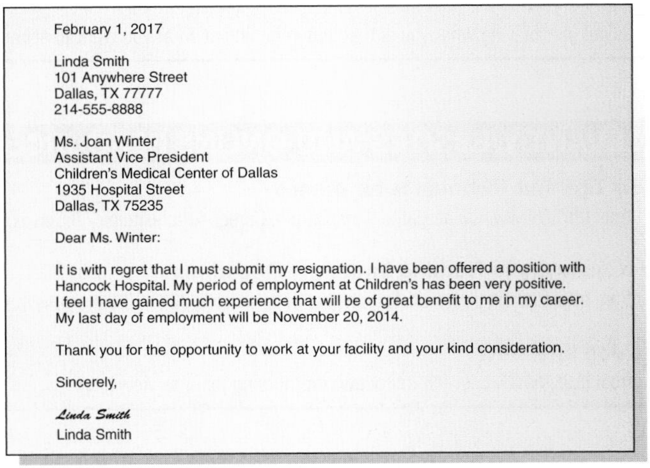

February 1, 2017

Linda Smith
101 Anywhere Street
Dallas, TX 77777
214-555-8888

Ms. Joan Winter
Assistant Vice President
Children's Medical Center of Dallas
1935 Hospital Street
Dallas, TX 75235

Dear Ms. Winter:

It is with regret that I must submit my resignation. I have been offered a position with Hancock Hospital. My period of employment at Children's has been very positive. I feel I have gained much experience that will be of great benefit to me in my career. My last day of employment will be November 20, 2014.

Thank you for the opportunity to work at your facility and your kind consideration.

Sincerely,

Linda Smith
Linda Smith

FIG. 4.7 Letter of resignation.

area. This means you would spend a day observing this staff nurse performing his or her job. This provides you with a good insight as to what the job requires and the working conditions of that area. When you take your first position, plan on staying there for at least a year. You want to avoid "job hopping", or changing jobs whenever you do not like what is going on with your current position. Remember, other positions have their benefits and problems; the grass may not be greener on the other side of the fence.

> Don't trade one set of problems for another set that may be even more difficult.

What If It Is Time for Me to Change Positions?

If you think it is time to change positions or explore other options, it is important to submit a letter of resignation (Fig. 4.7). Give at least 2 weeks' notice. Check your contract to see whether you agreed to give more than that; if so, give 4 weeks' notice if possible. If you are leaving on less than amicable terms, do not express this in your resignation letter. You can always report grievances to the personnel or human resources department. As a means of improving retention, many organizations conduct an exit interview or call former employees sometime after resignation to explore reasons for leaving. If you are provided this opportunity, make every effort to provide objective feedback and avoid character assassination. Do not "burn any bridges" since you may want to work at the organization again later in your career. Maintain a professional attitude as you develop a network of contacts. Always "take the high road" and avoid petty comments.

CONCLUSION

Searching for and finding your niche in the workplace can sometimes be overwhelming. Take the plunge and start looking. Keep a positive outlook because the job you are looking for is out there. This is one of those situations in which a little preparation and investigation go a long way toward finding what you want. Get your resume together and start investigating what is out there for you. A basic understanding of the process of job hunting can minimize the frustrations and promote a positive first-job experience. Take a look below for additional online resources for interviewing and securing a job position. Good luck with your job search!

Success lies not in achieving what you aim at, but in aiming at what you want to achieve.

RELEVANT WEBSITES AND ONLINE RESOURCES

Interview Tips and Techniques for nurses
Retrieved from http://www.nursetogether.com/Career/Career-Article/itemid/786.aspx.

10 Worst Answers to Nursing Interview Questions
Retrieved from http://nursinglink.monster.com/benefits/articles/8211-10-worst-answers-to-nursing-interview-questions.

Nursing Job Interview
Retrieved from http://www.best-job-interview.com/nursing-job-interview.html.

BIBLIOGRAPHY

American Association of Colleges of Nursing. (2014). *Nursing shortage*. AACN. Retrieved from http://www.aacn.nche.edu/media-relations/fact-sheets/nursing-shortage.

American Nurses Association. (2015). *Nursing career center*. Retrieved www.nursingworld.org/career-center.

American Nurses Credentialing Center. (2015). *Find a magnet organization*. Retrieved from http://www.nursecredentialing.org/Magnet/FindaMagnetFacility.

Andre, M., & Heartfield, K. (2011). *Nursing and midwifery portfolios: evidence of continuing competence* (2nd ed.). Sydney: Elsevier Publishing. Retrieved from. http://www.us.elsevierhealth.com/media/us/samplechapters/9780729540780/Andre_Nursing&MidwiferyPortfolios_Sample.pdf.

Budden, J. S., Zhong, E. H., Moulton, P., & Cimiotti, J. P. (2013, July). Highlights of the national workforce survey of registered nurses. *Journal of Nursing Regulation, 4*(2), 5–13. Retrieved https://www.ncsbn.org/JNR0713_05-14.pdf.

Buerhaus, P. I., Auerbach, D. I., & Staiger, D. O. (2009). The recent surge in nurse employment: Causes and implications. *Health Affairs, 28*(4), 657–668.

Bureau of Labor Statistics. (2014). *U.S. Department of Labor, Occupational Outlook Handbook, 2014-15 Edition, Registered Nurses*. Retrieved from http://www.bls.gov/ooh/healthcare/registered-nurses.htm.

Careerbuilder. (2014). *Number of employers passing on applicants due to social media posts continues to rise*. Retrieved from http://www.careerbuilder.com/share/aboutus/pressreleasesdetail.aspx?sd=6%2F26%2F2014&id=pr829&ed=12%2F31%2F2014.

Doyle, A. (2015). *Thank you letter: Job interview*. Retrieved from http://jobsearch.about.com/cs/thankyouletters/a/thankyou.htm.

Duggan, M., Ellis, N. B., Lampe, C., Lenhart, A., & Madden, M. (2015). *Social media update 2014*. Pew Research Center. January 9, 2015. Retrieved http://www.pewinternet.org/2015/01/09/social-media-update-2014/.

Health Resources and Services Administration. (2010). *The registered nurse population: initial findings from the 2008 national sample survey of registered nurses*. Retrieved from http://bhpr.hrsa.gov/healthworkforce/rnsurvey/initialfindings2008.pdf.

Juraschek, S. P., Zhang, X., Ranganathan, V., & Lin, V. W. (2011, November). United States registered nurse workforce report card and shortage forecast. *American Journal of Medical Quality, 27*(3), 241–249. http://dx.doi.org/10.1177/1062860611416634.

LaMaster, M. A., & Larsen, R. A. (2010). Prepare for a behavioral interview, then ace it! *American Journal of Nursing, 110*(1) 8,10.

Linked-In. (2015). *About Us*. Retrieved from https://press.linkedin.com/about-linkedin.

Lorenz, K. (2009). *Warning: Social networking can be hazardous to your job search*. Retrieved from http://www.careerbuilder.ca/blog/2006/07/12/cb-warning-social-networking-can-be-hazardous-to-your-job-search/.

McMillan, L., Parker, F., & Sport, A. (2014). Decisions, decisions! E-portfolio as an effective hiring assessment tool. *Nursing Management, 45*(4), 52–54. http://dx.doi.org/10.1097/01.NUMA.0000444882.93063.a7. Retrieved from http://journals.lww.com/nursingmanagement/Fulltext/2014/04000/Decisions,_decisions__E_portfolio_as_an_effective.11.aspx.

National Council of State Boards of Nursing (NCSBN). (2015). *National nursing workforce study*. Retrieved from https://www.ncsbn.org/workforce.htm#7313.

Restifo, V. (2002). *The successful interview how to market yourself for career advancement*. NSNA Imprint, 37–41. Retrieved from www.nsna.org/Portals/0/Skins/NSNA/pdf/Career_successint.pdf.

Smith, L. S. (2011). Professional growth: Showcase your talents with a career portfolio. *Nursing 2011, 41*(7), 54–56.

Welton, R. H. (2013). Writing an employer-focused resume for advanced practice nurses. *AACN, 24*(2), 203–217.

NCLEX-RN® Examination and the New Graduate

JoAnn Zerwekh, EdD, RN

(e) http://evolve.elsevier.com/Zerwekh/nsgtoday/.

The way I see it, if you want the rainbow, you gotta put up with the rain.
Dolly Parton

After completing this chapter, you should be able to:

- Discuss the role of the National Council of State Boards of Nursing (NCSBN).
- Discuss the implications of computer adaptive testing.
- Identify the process and steps for preparing to take the National Council Licensure Examination for Registered Nurses (NCLEX-RN® Examination).
- Identify criteria for selecting a NCLEX-RN® examination review book and review course.
- Identify the characteristics of the alternate item format questions on the NCLEX-RN® examination.

Don't take any chances…understand the NCLEX-RN® examination process.

The National Council Licensure Examination for Registered Nurses (NCLEX-RN® Examination)—this is the really big test for which you have been preparing since you entered nursing school. Consider the opportunity to take the NCLEX-RN® Examination a privilege; it took a lot of hard work to achieve this level, and you should have confidence you are prepared to pass the NCLEX-RN® and begin your professional practice as an RN. As with other aspects of transition, planning begins early, before you graduate. Planning ahead will help you develop a comprehensive plan for how to attack that mountain of material to review. When you plan ahead and know what is expected, your anxiety about the examination will be decreased. Being prepared and knowing what to expect will help you maintain a positive attitude.

THE NCLEX-RN® EXAMINATION

Who Prepares It and Why Do We Have to Have It?

The National Council of State Boards of Nursing (NCSBN) is the governing body for the committee that prepares the licensure examination. Each member board or state determines the application and registration process as well as deadlines within the state. The NCLEX-RN® examination is used to regulate entry into nursing practice in the United States. It is a national examination with standardized scoring; all candidates in every state are presented with questions based on the same test plan. Every state requires the same passing level or standard. There is no discrepancy in passing scores from one state to another. In other words, you cannot go to another state and expect the NCLEX-RN® examination to be any easier.

According to the NCSBN, the NCLEX-RN® examination is designed to test "knowledge, skills, and abilities essential to the safe and effective practice of nursing at the entry level" (NCSBN, 2016a). On successful completion of the examination, you will be granted a license to practice nursing in the state in which you applied for licensure. The status of state licensure continues to be in a transition process of its own. There are many nurses who maintain a current license in multiple states. The increase in nursing practice across state lines, the growth of managed care, and the advances in telehealth medicine prompted a research project conducted by the NCSBN in the late 1990s. Results of the research resulted in the development of the Mutual Recognition Model for Multistate Regulation. This is now referred to as the *Nurse Licensure Compact (NLC)*. As of January 2016, the NLC has been enacted through the legislatures of 25 states (NCSBN, 2016h).

How Will the Nurse Licensure Compact Affect Your License?

The nursing license in the participating compact states will function much like a driver's license. The individual holds one license issued in the state of residence but is also responsible for the laws of the state in which he or she is driving. The individual nurse will be licensed to practice in his or her state of residence but may practice nursing in another state; however, the nurse must comply with the Nurse Practice Act of the state in which he or she practices. The transition process for the Nurse Licensure Compact began in 2000 and is continuing to progress. The Nurse Licensure Compact must be passed by the state legislature in each participating state. Watch your state nursing organization and Board of Nursing newsletters, or check the NCSBN website (www.ncsbn.org) to see where your state is in the process of implementing the NLC (Critical Thinking Box 5.1).

Before the Nurse Licensure Compact is implemented, the respective states will continue to require the nurse to be licensed in the individual state of practice. Transfer of nursing licenses between states is a process called "licensure by endorsement." If you wish to practice in a state in which you are not currently licensed, you must contact the State Board of Nursing in the state in which you wish to practice. The State Board of Nursing will advise you of the process to become licensed in that state (see Appendix A, State Boards of Nursing, on the Evolve website). Transferring your license to practice from one state to another does not negate your successful completion of the NCLEX-RN® examination, nor do you have to take the examination again. All states recognize the successful completion of the NCLEX-RN® examination, regardless of the state in which you took the examination or where your initial license was issued. You can get the most recent list of state boards of nursing from the NCSBN website (https://www.ncsbn.org/contact-bon.htm).

? CRITICAL THINKING BOX 5.1

What is the status of the Nurse Licensure Compact in your state?

What Is the NCLEX-RN® Examination Test Plan?

The content of the NCLEX-RN® examination is based on a test blueprint that is determined by the National Council of State Boards of Nursing (NCSBN). The blueprint reflects entry-level nursing practice as identified by research published in an RN practice analysis study of newly licensed registered nurses. The NCSBN conducts this research study every 3 years. The RN practice analysis research in 2014 indicated that the majority (72%) of new graduates was continuing to work in hospitals with approximately 14% working in long-term care and 10% in community-based facilities. A slight shift was noted in newly licensed RNs working acute care and long-term and community facilities since the previous practice analysis study. The overall practice settings were in medical-surgical (27.7%) and critical care settings (18.7%), which represent a decrease in these settings from the previous practice analysis study in 2011. There was an increase in nursing home, skilled or intermediate care (from 9.5% to 11.2%), and rehabilitation (from 4.9% to 5.5%) settings. Additionally, the *2014 RN Practice Analysis: Linking the NCLEX-RN® Examination to Practice* reflected two new categories, Short Stay/Observational (1.2%) and Step-Down Progressive Care (4.3%), which affected the decrease in medical-surgical and critical care practice settings. Most entry-level nurses indicated that they cared for acutely ill clients. The majority of entry-level nurses indicated they cared for adult and geriatric clients who were acutely ill, as well as adults and geriatric clients with stable and unstable chronic conditions. The majority of the new graduates surveyed responded that they were receiving some form of formal orientation. Hospitals and long-term care facilities were the primary employers of new graduates. Respondents (43.4%) reported having a primary administrative position. Newly licensed RNs working in long-term care facilities were more likely to report having primary administrative responsibilities than those working in hospitals (60.6% in long-term care versus 9.4% in hospitals). The test plan in this chapter was implemented in April 2016 and will be used until April 2019. A new test plan is implemented every 3 years. This represents the time required to conduct the research, analyze the data, and implement the new test plan for the NCLEX-RN® examination (NCSBN, 2015).

The examination is constructed from questions that are designed to test the candidate's ability to apply the nursing process and to determine appropriate nursing responses and interventions to provide safe nursing care. The distribution of content is based on the areas of client needs. The nursing process is integrated throughout the exam. There are four levels of client needs identified in the *2016 NCLEX-RN® Detailed Test Plan* (NCSBN, 2016a). Each level of client need is assigned a percentage that reflects the weight of that category of client need on the NCLEX-RN® examination. The approximate percentages of each area are as follows:

Safe, Effective Care Environment

Management of care	17%-23%
Safety and infection control	9%-15%
Health promotion and maintenance	6%-12%
Psychosocial Integrity	6%-12%

Physiological Integrity

Basic care and comfort	6%-12%
Pharmacological and parenteral therapies	12%-18%
Reduction of risk potential	9%-15%
Physiological adaptation	11%-17% (NCSBN, 2016a)

In April 1994, the NCSBN implemented computer-adaptive testing (CAT) for the NCLEX-RN® examination for both practical/vocational nurses (NCLEX-PN/VN®) and registered nurses

(NCLEX-RN®). The information presented here is a brief introduction to the NCLEX-RN® computer adaptive test (CAT). It is important that you download the Candidate Bulletin for your testing year from www.ncsbn.org and carefully follow the instructions; you will receive additional information from your state board of nursing.

Pearson VUE is the company contracted by the NCSBN to schedule candidates, administer, and score the NCLEX-RN® examination. The NCSBN is responsible for the content and development of the test questions, the test plan, policies, and requirements for eligibility for the NCLEX-RN® examination. Pearson VUE will assist you in scheduling your examination and will provide a location and equipment for the administration of the examination.

What Does CAT Mean?

With CAT (computer adaptive test), each candidate receives a different set of questions via the computer. The computer develops an examination based on the test plan and selects questions to be presented on the basis of the candidates' responses to the previous question. So, every time a candidate answers a test question, the computer re-estimates the candidate's ability based on all the previous answers and the difficulty of those items. The number of questions each candidate receives and the testing time for each candidate will vary. As candidates answer questions correctly, the next question will be either a degree of difficulty equal to the previous question or a higher level of difficulty. All of the questions presented will reflect the categories of the NCLEX-RN® examination test plan (NCSBN, 2016a).

"Pretest" questions have been integrated into the examination in the past and will continue to be integrated into the current examination. The NCSBN Examination Committee evaluates the statistical information from each of these "pretest" questions to determine whether the question is valid and to identify the level of difficulty of the test item (NCSBN, 2016a). Do not be alarmed—these questions are not counted in the grading of your examination, and time has been allocated for you to answer these questions. It is impossible to determine which questions are "pretest" questions and which ones are "scored" test questions, so it is important that you answer every question to the best of your ability. These pretest items ensure that each question that counts toward your score has been thoroughly evaluated for content as well as statistically validated.

What Is the Application Process for the NCLEX-RN® Examination CAT?

In the beginning of the semester in which you will graduate, your school of nursing will have each student complete an application form and send it to the state board of nursing. When you complete the nursing program, the school will verify your graduate status with the state board of nursing. After the forms have been processed, you will receive an Acknowledgement of Receipt of Registration. You will then receive by e-mail the Authorization to Test (ATT) with instructions regarding how to schedule your examination with Pearson VUE. You cannot schedule your examination until you have received your ATT. Read your instruction packet and your *Candidate Bulletin* carefully (the *Candidate Bulletin* may be found at www.ncsbn.org, navigate to NCLEX Examination Candidates). All registrations must be processed via the Pearson VUE website or through the Pearson VUE call center. After you schedule your appointment, you will be emailed a Confirmation of Appointment from Pearson VUE. First, verify that all information is correct. Then, call or go online to check that your appointment has been scheduled/rescheduled. If you do not receive a confirmation every time that you schedule or reschedule an appointment, contact Pearson VUE NCLEX Candidate Services immediately to correct any errors to the appointment (NCSBN, 2016c). Your ATT will contain your authorization number, candidate ID number, and an expiration date. The expiration date cannot be extended for any reason; *you must test within the dates on the ATT.* It is to your advantage to schedule your examination date shortly after receiving your ATT—even if you do not plan to take the test for several weeks. Testing centers tend to fill up early; if you wait too long you may not be able to get your desired testing date. Pearson VUE will email a confirmation of your testing appointment. As a first-time test taker, you will be offered an appointment within 30 days of the request to schedule an appointment (NCSBN, 2016e).

When you provide an email address at the time you register for the NCLEX-RN® examination, all future correspondence from Pearson VUE will be via email, regardless of whether you registered by telephone or via the Internet. To gain access to the NCLEX-RN® exam, you must present one form of identification that matches exactly the name they provided when registering. The first and last name on your identification must match exactly the name you provided when registering. You will be required to provide your digital signature and a palm vein scan and will have your photograph taken (NCSBN, 2016e).

Where Do I Take the Test?

There are testing sites in every state. A candidate may take the test at any of the Pearson VUE testing sites listed in the *Candidate Bulletin*. However, the license to practice will be issued only in the state where the candidate's application was submitted. Information regarding the location of the centers can be found at the candidate area on the NCSBN website. There will be multiple testing stations at each center.

When Do I Take the Test?

After receiving the ATT, a candidate may contact the examination Candidate Services at the phone number provided in the *Candidate Bulletin* or go to the NCLEX examination area of the Pearson VUE website (www.pearsonvue.com/nclex) to schedule the examination. The location and telephone numbers of the testing centers will be included in the information from the NCSBN. Remember, you *must* test within the dates on your ATT. You may schedule your examination as soon as you receive the emailed ATT. This means that you could receive the ATT on Wednesday, call or go online to the location of your choice, and if you wish, take the examination the next day, if there is space available. Or you can call and/or go online and schedule your examination date within the next 2 to 3 weeks.

During the last 2 months of school, begin to make plans for when you would like to take the examination. The examination should be taken within approximately 4 to 6 weeks of graduation. Allow for some study time, and consider whether you want to take a formal review course. It is important that you take the examination soon after graduation. If you wait too long, your level of comprehension of critical information will be decreased. Finish school, take a review course if you desire, obtain your ATT, and go take the examination. This is not a good time to plan a vacation, get married, or engage in other activities that could cause a crisis in your life (Critical Thinking Box 5.2).

How Much Time Do I Have and How Many Questions Are There?

Each candidate is scheduled for a 6-hour time slot. You should plan to be at the site for 6 hours. Each candidate must answer at least 75 questions. Within those first 75 questions, there are 15 pretest items

? CRITICAL THINKING BOX 5.2

When do you want to take your NCLEX-RN® examination? Refer to this book's *Evolve* website for information on selecting an NCLEX-RN® examination review course to help you start thinking about this process and assist you in deciding how to select a review book.

that are not scored on your examination. The number of questions you answer and the length of time that you test are not indications of whether you will receive a pass or fail score. The length of your examination depends on how you answered the questions. When the computer indicates that you are finished, regardless of how long you have been testing or how far past 75 questions you have gone, it just means you have "turned your test in," and your test is completed. The examination will end when the student:

- Measures at a level of competence above or below the established standard of competency and at least 75 questions have been answered
- Completes a maximum of 265 questions
- Has been testing for the maximum time of 6 hours (NCSBN, 2016f)

Do I Have to Be Computer Literate?

It is not necessary to study from a computer, nor is it necessary that you be "computer literate." Research has demonstrated that candidates who were not accustomed to working on a computer did as well as those who were very comfortable with the computer (NCSBN, 2016g). So, previous computer experience is not a prerequisite to passing the NCLEX-RN® examination!

How Will I Keep the Computer Keys Straight and Deal With a Mouse?

At the testing site, each candidate is given a tutorial orientation to the computer. This tutorial will introduce you to the computer; demonstrate how to use the keyboard and the calculator, as well as how to use the mouse to record your answers (Fig. 5.1). It will also explain how to record the answers for the alternate item format items (more about this later). If you need assistance with the computer after the examination starts, a test administrator will be available. Every effort is made to ensure that you understand and are comfortable with the testing procedure and equipment.

There will be only one question on the screen at a time. You will read the question and select an answer. After the answer is selected, select "enter" from the lower right corner of the screen, and the computer will present another question. Previously answered questions are not available for review. There is an onscreen optional calculator built into the computer. The tutorial program will demonstrate the use of the calculator in calculating numerical answers.

FIG. 5.1 As of 2002, the use of the computer mouse makes navigating the CAT easier. (From Zerwekh, J. (2016). *Illustrated study guide for the NCLEX-RN® exam* (9th ed.). St. Louis: Mosby.)

What Is the Passing Score?

Every state has the same passing criteria. Specific individual scores will not be available to you, your school, or your place of employment. You cannot obtain your results from the testing center. Your score will be reported directly to you as pass or fail. A composite of student results will be mailed to the respective schools of nursing. There is no specific published score or number that represents passing.

How Will I Know I Have Passed?

The examination scores are compiled at the Pearson VUE center and are transmitted directly to state boards of nursing. Most boards of nursing can advise the candidates in writing of their results within 4 to 6 weeks of taking the examination. Some states allow you to access your "unofficial" results after 48 business hours through the quick results service of Pearson VUE. There is a small fee for this service. Check your *Candidate Bulletin,* as well as online verification from your state board of nursing, regarding the availability of results online or from an automated telephone verification system. *Do not call* the state board of nursing, NCLEX Examination Candidate Services, or the Pearson VUE Professional Centers to inquire about your pass or fail status; they cannot release information over the telephone.

What Types of Questions Will Be on the NCLEX-RN® Examination?

Most of the questions are in multiple-choice format, with four options. Each question will stand alone and will not require information from previous questions to determine the correct answer. All of the information for the question will be available on the computer screen. You will be provided an erasable board for any notes or calculations you would like to make. You may not take calculators into the examination; the "drop-down" calculator will be available on the screen for math calculations. Everyone will be tested according to the same test plan, but candidates will receive different questions. There is only one correct answer to each question; you do not get any partial credit for another answer—it is either right or wrong. All questions must be answered, even if you have to make a wild guess. The computer selects the next question based on your response to the previous question. (You do not get another question until the one on the screen is answered.) You will not be able to go back to a previous question after that question is removed from the screen. (This means you cannot go back and change your answer to the wrong one!) There will be an optional 10-minute break after 2 hours of testing. If you need to take a break before the 2 hours, notify one of the testing center administrators. A second optional break is offered after 3½ hours of testing. The tutorial and all breaks are considered part of the 6 hours allowed for testing (NCSBN, 2016b).

There is not much storage space at the testing sites. There are some small lockers for your personal items. Therefore, do not take your textbooks, your notes from school, your lucky stuffed bear, or any other materials you have been carrying around in that pack for the past 2 years! All electronic devices (cell/mobile/smartphones, tablets, pagers, or other electronic devices) are required to be sealed in a plastic bag provided by the Pearson VUE Testing Center. If you refuse to store your mobile device(s) in the plastic bag provided, you will not be allowed to take the exam and will be required to repay a $200 examination fee and reschedule to take the exam (NCSBN, 2016i).

What Are Some of the Other Things I Really Need to Know About the NCLEX-RN® Examination?

What If I Need to Change the Time or Date I Have Already Scheduled?

You can change your testing date and time if you advise NCLEX examination Candidate Services 24 hours or 1 full business day before your scheduled examination appointment. You may go to the NCLEX candidate website (www.Pearsonvue.com/nclex) to reschedule or you may speak with an agent at Pearson VUE and receive confirmation of the unscheduled/rescheduled appointment letter.

The phone number will be listed in your *Candidate Bulletin*. You can then reschedule the test at no additional cost. If a candidate does not reschedule within this time frame or does not come at the scheduled testing time, the ATT is invalidated, and the candidate will be required to reregister and repay the $200 registration fee. There are *no exceptions* to this policy (NCSBN, 2016c).

What About Identification at the Testing Site?

At the testing site, you will submit a digital signature and will be digitally fingerprinted and photographed. An additional security screening is the palm vein screening. It will be required for admission to the exam. You will also be required to provide one form of identification. All identification documents must be in the original form; no copies will be accepted. Be sure that the first and last name printed on your identification match exactly the first and last name printed on your ATT. The following are acceptable forms of identification (must be in English, valid and not expired, with a photograph and a signature):

- U.S. driver's license
- U.S. state-issued identification
- Passport
- U.S. military identification (NCSBN, 2016f)

What Are the Advantages of CAT for the Candidate?

The environment is quiet and conducive to testing. The work surface is large enough to accommodate both right-handed and left-handed people, with adequate room for the computer. Each candidate can work at his or her own pace and is allowed to test up to 6 hours. Each candidate has his or her own testing station or cubicle. There should be a minimal amount, if any, of distraction by the other candidates who are testing at the same time. If a candidate has to retake the examination, the parameters for retesting are established by the respective state board of nursing. The NCSBN requires the candidate to wait at least 45 days before rescheduling the examination. Some individual boards of nursing require a waiting period of 90 days after the first examination before scheduling. Candidates who take the examination again will not receive the same questions (NCSBN, 2016f).

PREPARING FOR THE NCLEX-RN® EXAMINATION

Where and When Should I Start?

Six Months Before the NCLEX-RN® Examination

Make sure you know the dates and deadlines in the state in which you are applying for licensure. Your school will advise you of the specific dates the forms are due to the state board of nursing. If you are registering individually, contact the state board of nursing in your state of residence (or in the state where you wish to file for licensure) and find out the filing deadlines. Make sure you follow the directions exactly. State boards of nursing will not accept applications that are not submitted on time or are submitted in an incorrect format. A listing of the state boards of nursing can be found on the Evolve website. If you plan to apply for licensure in a state other than the one in which you are graduating, it is your responsibility to contact the board of nursing in that state to obtain your papers for application. Plan early (at least 6 months ahead) to investigate the feasibility of taking the examination in another state.

Investigate review courses. Review courses can be an excellent resource in your preparation for the NCLEX-RN® examination. Review courses will assist you in organizing your study materials and identifying areas in which you need to focus your study time. These courses will help you to understand the NCLEX-RN® examination test plan. Understanding the test plan will help you to prioritize your studying.

Plan an expense account for the end of school and for the NCLEX-RN® examination. Frequently, students face unexpected expenses at the end of school; one of these expenses may be the fees for the NCLEX-RN® examination. Start a small savings plan—maybe $10 a week—to help defray these expenses. For family and friends who want to give you something for graduation, you might tell them of your "wish list," including those expenses incurred at graduation (Box 5.1).

Two Months Before the NCLEX-RN® Examination: What Do I Need to Do Now?

If you have a job, discuss your anticipated NCLEX-RN® examination test date with your employer. You can estimate your test date by checking your graduation date, determining from previous students or nursing faculty the approximate time to receive the ATT in your state, and then considering review courses and study time and how these might affect when you want to schedule your examination. Remember, you can change your testing appointment without penalty, as long as you do it within 24 hours (or one full business day) of your scheduled appointment and within the dates on the ATT. Submit your request for days off work in writing as soon as you have confirmed your examination date. This is something you want to make sure that your manager understands. Plan to take off the day or two before the examination and, if possible, the day after as well. This will allow you time to relax and, if necessary, travel to and from the testing site.

BOX 5.1   BUDGET FOR THE END OF SCHOOL AND THE NCLEX-RN® EXAMINATION

How Much Is It Going to Cost Me to Complete School?

Required Expenses
Graduation fees from college or university _____
Application fees for NCLEX-RN® examination _____

Expenses to Take NCLEX-RN® Examination
Travel (e.g., car, bus, airfare) _____
Hotel accommodations at NCLEX examination testing site _____
Miscellaneous (e.g., food, cab fare, parking) _____

Optional Expenses
School pin _____
Uniform or cap and gown for graduation _____
Graduation expenses passed on to graduate _____
Graduation pictures (class or individual) _____
Graduation invitations _____
Commercial exit testing _____
NCLEX-RN® examination review course (need to plan this before school is out) _____
NCLEX-RN® examination review books (get these early—they really help with the last year of nursing school!)
_____

Expenses After Graduation (It's Not Over Yet!)
Professional organizations (most organizations will give a new membership discount to the graduate nurse)
_____
Professional journals _____
Uniform, scrub suits, and shoes to begin new job _____
Professional liability insurance (check with the school regarding transfer from school policy to individual policy)
_____

Decide how you are going to get to the test site and whether it will be necessary for you to stay overnight. If the closest testing site is not easily accessible, is more than an hour's drive away, or involves driving through a heavily congested traffic area, you may consider staying overnight in a hotel close to the site. For some graduates, this will prevent unnecessary hassle and may alleviate anxiety on the day of the examination.

Are you going with a group or by yourself? How will you feel if the group is finished and you are still working on your examination? Will you feel rushed because everyone is waiting for you? Do not create a situation that will increase your anxiety at one of the most important times of your nursing career. If you are okay with the group waiting for you, and everyone understands the situation, then it may be a source of support for you. If a group of graduates is traveling together, and everyone is able to schedule the examination on the same day, consider planning hotel accommodations if they are necessary. Do not have a crowd in your room. Five people in a room designed for two or four will not be conducive to sleep the night before the examination. If you are rooming with another person, select someone you like and can tolerate in close quarters for a short period of time. Surround yourself with people who have a positive attitude; you do not need complainers and negative thinkers.

Develop a plan for studying. Do you need to study alone, or do you benefit from group study time? Set yourself a study schedule that you can realistically achieve. About 2 to 3 hours a day for 2 or 3 days a week is realistic; 8 hours a day on your days off does not work. If you take a formal review course, plan your study time to gain the most from the course. A review course is not meant to be your only study time. When you finish a review course, you should have a much better idea of what is going to be tested, how it will be tested, and where you need to focus some study time. Priority areas to study are those in which you are the weakest; focus on those first.

The Day Before the BIG DAY

Make sure you have your identification required for admission. Read your *Candidate Bulletin* again. The information that you receive should have all of the necessary information and directions needed for the test site. Check whether there is anything else you will need to take with you to the site.

Make a "test run" the evening before the test. Go to the site and evaluate traffic patterns and driving time. Find the parking area. If your hotel is within four to six blocks of the test site, walk to the site; this is a terrific way to help reduce anxiety and get the blood circulating to your brain! Whether you drive or walk to the site, go the day before to make sure you know where you are going.

Go to bed early; do not study, cram, or party! Plan to eat a light dinner, something that will not upset your stomach—you do not need to be up half of the night with heartburn and/or diarrhea!

The BIG DAY Is Here

Eat a well-balanced breakfast, not sweet rolls and coffee. Protein and complex carbohydrates will help sustain you during the examination. Eat light, something that is nourishing but not heavy. Do not drink a lot of coffee; you do not need to have the caffeine jitters or be distracted by frequent bathroom trips.

Dress comfortably, but look nice. Anticipate that the temperature at the testing sites will be a little cool rather than too warm. Do not wear tight clothes that restrict your breathing when you sit down! Dress casually and comfortably; you may not wear hats, scarves, or jackets in the testing room. The NCSBN requests that you arrive at the testing site about 30 minutes early. This will allow you time to get checked in and prevent anxiety about being late. If you arrive more than 30 minutes after your scheduled appointment, you may be required to forfeit your examination appointment, as well as the examination fees (NCSBN, 2016b).

How Do I Select an NCLEX-RN® Examination Review Course?

There are many review courses available to assist the graduate nurse in preparing for the NCLEX examination. Before you sign up, evaluate which course will be most beneficial to you. In considering a review course, remember that the objective is review, not primary learning. (See the Evolve website for selecting an NCLEX-RN® Examination Review Course.)

What Types of Review Courses Are Available?

Live (face-to-face) review courses. Evaluate your geographic location. Which review courses are easily accessible? Are you considering traveling to another city to attend a review course? If you have a prospective employer, check with the nurse recruiter to determine whether the facility provides a review course. Collect data on all of the courses; then compare them to see which one best meets your needs and budget. Also, check with the nurse recruiter or the nursing manager regarding time off and scheduling. Plan ahead and make an intelligent decision regarding review courses. Do not feel that you must sign up with the first review company that contacts you!

NCLEX-RN® examination online review courses. How well do you study at the computer? If you find studying at the computer is very easy for you, then you may want to consider an online review course. When investigating online review courses, determine whether the course provides an online book, study questions, additional online study materials, as well as the availability of a review faculty. Most students need a resource person or faculty to answer questions (either about nursing content or the NCLEX-RN® examination) and to assist in developing a study plan. Consider the length of time the online course is available—is it over several weeks, or is it an indefinite time? With online courses, it is critical to set aside study time, plan how you are going to progress through the course, and evaluate how long you think you will need to complete the course. Online review courses can be beneficial if you plan your study time, take advantage of the course resources available, and follow the suggested activities within the online course.

Carefully evaluate your need for a review course. Are you the type of student who can plan study time, establish a study review schedule, and stick to it? Were you in the top 25% of your graduating class? Have you had experience working in a hospital with adult medical-surgical clients, other than while you were in school? As a new graduate, do you feel prepared for this examination? If you can answer "yes" to all of these questions, you may not need to consider a review course in your preparation for the NCLEX-RN® examination. Most graduates can say "yes" to one or two of these questions but not to all of them.

What Are the Qualifications of the Review Course Instructors?

To teach a review course effectively, the instructor needs to be familiar with the NCLEX-RN® examination. That ability is most often found in instructors who have teaching experience in a school of nursing. Some hospitals provide in-house review courses taught by excellent educators and clinical specialists. Determine whether these instructors are familiar with the NCLEX-RN® examination test plan. Information that is not a focus of the NCLEX-RN® examination test plan does not need to be included in a review course. It is also important to find out whether the review course instructor is from a school of nursing in your immediate area. It is possible that you will be paying for a review course to be taught by someone from your nursing school faculty. A review course may be more effective if someone other than your school faculty teaches it. You need to hear information from a different perspective. This helps to anchor information and reinforce previous learning. Look for a course that brings faculty in from areas outside your school.

What Types of Instructional Materials Are Used in the Course?

Are the materials required for the course an additional expense (or part of the registration fee)? Do you get to keep the materials after the course is finished? Can you print copies of the materials if you are taking an online course? Are handouts, workbooks, CDs, audiotapes, books, and other materials used to enhance learning? Be concerned if there are no course outlines, workbooks, handouts, or books; you might spend all of your time writing and miss listening to the necessary information. Do the course materials include practice test questions that are similar in format to the NCLEX-RN® examination? Ask about the format used to organize the material (e.g., integrated, blocked, systems). How does the format compare with the NCLEX-RN® examination plan of client needs and nursing process that is described in your *Candidate Bulletin* from the NCSBN?

Does the Course Include Instruction in Test-Taking Skills and Testing Practice?

Test-taking skills and testing practice are very important aspects of a review course. Graduates need to practice test-testing strategies and use them in answering questions written by someone other than their nursing school faculty. This is important to evaluate in the face-to-face review as well as in the online review.

How Much Does the Course Cost?

Most review courses cost between $300 and $500. Frequently, there is a discount for early registration, and there may also be a discount for group registration. Make sure you understand and review company policy regarding deposit, registration fees, and cancellation policy. Check out the possibility of organizing a group; some courses give a free review or a discount to the group organizer.

How Long Does It Last?

Is the face-to-face course 3, 4, or 5 consecutive days? Is it offered only in the evenings? Is it taught only on the weekend for 6 weeks? The answers to these questions are very important to determine early in your evaluation of review courses. Notify your employer as soon as possible if you need to fit the review course into your work schedule. Most hospitals will arrange the new graduate's schedule to allow attendance at a review course. It is important to provide adequate advance notice to your employer so that staffing schedules may be planned.

If you are considering an online course, how long will it take you to work through the course? Is the course set up in "real time" similar to the face-to-face review, or is it self-paced? How long does the provider recommend that you spend in the course? Do you want to study for 2 to 3 hours every day for 4 weeks, or do you want to work faster and study 4 to 6 hours a day and complete it in 2 weeks? If you plan to study 4 to 6 hours in 1 day, you should not plan to work that day.

Some hospitals even provide a review course or reimburse the review course registration fee as a benefit to the graduate nurse employee! After you have determined which review course, as well as what type of review course, you wish to take, discuss it with your prospective employer or notify your current employer as soon as possible.

Where Is the Face-to-Face Course Held?

Are you going to have to drive for an hour every day? Will you need to arrange for a hotel room? Ask about parking. What is the availability of inexpensive restaurants in the area? These are additional expenses you must consider if you plan to take a live review course.

What Are the Statistics Regarding the Pass Rate for the Company?

It is appropriate to inquire how the review company determines the pass rate statistics. Check the NCSBN website (www.ncsbn.org/index.htm) to determine the most current statistics for passing the NCLEX-RN® examination. The review company must obtain NCLEX-RN® examination results directly from course participants. The NCSBN or a school of nursing will not provide this information to review companies. Find out whether the advertised pass rate is based on actual responses from participants or on projected figures from the company.

Does the Review Company Offer Any Type of Guarantee?

Some review companies will offer a guaranteed "refund," a free review course, or further assistance if you are not successful on the examination. Find out what the guarantee means and who is eligible for it. Sometimes the "guaranteed refund" is not easily obtainable and may require completing 100% of the course resources and additional materials. Make sure you obtain in writing what you must do to be eligible and to file for the benefit.

When Is the Course Offered?

Some graduates prefer to take a review course just before the examination so that the information is still fresh in their minds. Most graduates prefer to take the review within 1 to 2 weeks before the examination. This time frame generally works very well; the review course may be scheduled during the time you are waiting for your Authorization to Test (ATT). When you receive your authorization, you have completed your review course, and you are ready to schedule the examination. This schedule allows time to organize and study those areas that are your weakest. If you have only one review course available, how does it fit with your plans for scheduling the examination? Another aspect to consider is your employment schedule. Arrange your review course time so that you can truly focus on the material. If you have to work nights or evenings during the course, you will not benefit as much from the review.

Call the review company for answers to your questions. Does the representative spend time on the telephone with you, or does he or she rush you off the telephone? Or do you get an automated response instead of a live conversation? Is the company representative friendly and knowledgeable, and does that person demonstrate concern for answering all of your questions?

The online review course eliminates the problem of scheduling a specific time for you to take a review course. However, you must still plan the time to spend working through the online course in order for the review to be beneficial. Ultimately, each graduate must decide whether to take a review course and what type of review course to take. The more informed you are regarding a review course, the more intelligent your decision.

NCLEX-RN® Examination Review Books: Which One Is Right for You?

It is important to select a review book that meets your study needs. The first step is to check out your choices. Nursing faculty, friends who have review books, the school library, and the local bookstores that stock nursing textbooks are all sources of information regarding review books. There are two types of nursing review books: those with content review and those that consist totally of review test questions. Evaluate how you are going to use the book. Is it for study during school, or is it specifically for review for the NCLEX-RN® examination? For example, if you bought the review book to study pediatric nursing, you may be disappointed. The focus of the NCLEX-RN® examination is not on pediatrics; therefore, pediatrics is not often a strong component in review books. If you wish to use a review book to identify priority aspects of care in the medical-surgical client, a review book can be of great benefit. The following discussion of review book selection is directed primarily toward review books that contain content review. Take notes as you read the different selections; it is hard to remember all the positive and negative points of each book (Box 5.2) (see "Selecting a Review Book: Where Do I Start?" in the Evolve resources). Frequently, students find the review books to be of great benefit during school in assisting them to organize and consolidate a large amount of information. Plan to purchase a review book while you are still in nursing school.

BOX 5.2 SELECTING AN NCLEX-RN® EXAMINATION REVIEW COURSE

Here are some questions to consider:

Where Am I Going to Work?
Will the institution pay for the review? _____
Will the institution pay the initial fee, or do I need to plan for reimbursement? _____

Does the Institution Provide an On-Site Review?
Who teaches it? _____
Is it organized and presented by an independent company or by hospital employees? _____

Review Course Instructors
Who will teach the class? Your faculty from school? Or review course faculty trained by the review company?
_____

What Type of Instructional Material Is Used?
Does it cost extra beyond the registration fee? _____
If it is additional to the registration fee, where do I get it? _____
Can I keep all of the instructional materials (e.g., books, testing booklets, online modules, DVDs, CDs)?
_____
Does the instructional material include practice test questions in the NCLEX-RN® examination format?
_____

How Are the Classes Conducted?
How many days? _____
Are days consecutive or spread across several weeks? _____
What are the hours each day? _____
What is the teaching style (e.g., group work, lecture, home study, group participation, testing practice, online)?
_____
What is the average size of the class for the area? _____

How Much Does It Cost?
What is the total price? _____
Does this include all of the class materials? _____
Are there group rates? If yes, what are they? _____
Does the group organizer receive a special rate? _____
Are there early registration discounts? _____
When does the money have to be in? _____
Are there any "extra incentives"? _____

How Do I Pay for It?
Is there a payment plan? _____
Can I make an early deposit to hold my space? _____

BOX 5.2   SELECTING AN NCLEX-RN® EXAMINATION REVIEW COURSE—cont'd

When is the deposit due? When is the final amount due? _____

If I change my mind after I make the deposit, can I get the deposit back? _____

Is There a Guarantee?

What is the guarantee? _____

Can I take the review again? _____

Does it have to be in the same location as the first time? _____

What do I have to do to qualify for the guarantee? _____

What Is the Pass Rate, and How Is It Determined?

How does the company determine the pass rate for the review course? (Remember—the review company does not have access to NCLEX-RN® examination results.) _____

Is the pass rate determined by a company survey of review participants after the NCLEX-RN® examination?

_____

Is it based on all participants or only the first-time takers? _____

Is it based on the company's projected success rate? _____

Did the review company answer all of my questions in a courteous manner, and did they seem interested in my business?

_____

Do you know anyone who has taken a review? What are their recommendations? _____

Scan the Table of Contents

Is the information presented in a logical sequence? How is the information organized? It is important that the information be organized in a manner that is logical to you. The NCLEX-RN® examination is based on an integrated format, with a focus on the nursing process and client needs. Read the introduction to see how these areas were considered in the organization of the text. Quickly scan the table of contents and check the number of pages in various areas of subject material. Where is the focus of the material?

Evaluate Chapter Layout

How well is the material organized within the chapter? Are there major headings and subheadings to assist you in finding information quickly? Some texts use boxes or color to highlight divisions of content or priority information. These characteristics help to decrease the monotony of constant reading, and they help increase interest in the material presented.

Evaluate Content

Select a topic or topics you would like to read about in each of the review books you are considering. Select the priority nursing concepts and interventions you want to identify (e.g., nursing care of a client with diabetes). Evaluate the information regarding the adult, pediatric, and obstetric client. How does the information compare in the review books you are considering? Is the material logically organized? Does it contain the major concepts of care for that particular example? The focus of the review book should be toward nursing concepts and delivery of safe nursing care. In evaluating the currency of content, keep in mind that you cannot expect information that came out last month to be reflected in any textbook. The purpose of the NCLEX-RN® examination is to determine whether a candidate can perform safely and effectively as an entry-level nurse. This is the content that should be included in the review book. Based on the detailed test plan and the areas where new graduates are employed, the NCLEX-RN® examination is more heavily weighted toward the medical-surgical adult client.

Evaluate the Index

Look up several common topics in the index. A good index is critical to finding information in a timely manner.

Test Questions

Are test questions included in the text? Questions may be found after each of the main chapters or grouped together at the end of the book. Check to see if a rationale for the correct answer is included for each question and the rationale for why the other options are incorrect. Does a computer disk of questions or an online test bank come with the book? How many questions are available? Are alternate item format test questions included?

Test-Taking Strategies

Does the book include information on test-taking strategies for multiple-choice and alternate item format questions? Test-taking strategies help you to be more "test-wise." These strategies can be of great benefit while you are still in school, in addition to practicing them as a method to prepare for the NCLEX-RN® examination.

Test Anxiety: What Is the Disease? How Do You Get Rid of It?

Frequently, students and graduates focus on their "test anxiety" as the reason for not doing well on examinations. Test anxiety is something that only you can change. You are the one allowing the anxiety to affect you in a negative way. The only person responsible for your test anxiety is you, and the only one who can do anything about it is you. Address your test anxiety while you are still in school. Look at some simple steps to decrease your anxiety regarding testing.

- **Plan ahead.** Do not wait until the last minute to read 150 pages in your textbook, all your classroom notes, and the 10 articles assigned for the test. Plan study time, and stick to it!
- **Set aside study time for when you are at your best.** Frequently, study time is squeezed in only after everything else (laundry, meals, housecleaning, yard work, and so on) has been completed. You are defeating your purpose and increasing your anxiety when you try to study at a time when you are tired and not receptive to learning.
- **Study smart.** Plan for 45 minutes to an hour of review on the day after a 90-minute class lecture. This will greatly enhance your retention of the classroom information. Plan for an hour to review/ scan assigned reading or information before class so that you will know where information is located and what you will need for note-taking in class.
- **Give yourself a break!** Plan your study time to include a break about every hour. Your retention of information begins to decrease after about 30 minutes and is significantly decreased after an hour.
- **Think positively!** If your friends are "negative thinkers," do not plan to study with them. Go to the movies or play sports with them, but do not study with them. Anxiety and negative thinking are contagious—do not expose yourself to the disease!
- **Do not cram.** Whether you are studying for a unit examination in school or for the NCLEX-RN® examination, cramming is not an effective study method, and it will increase your anxiety. The NCLEX-RN® examination is not written to evaluate memory-based information. Test questions focus on the higher levels of cognitive ability. Application of principles and the analysis of information will be required to determine an appropriate nursing response or action. Do not jeopardize your critical thinking skills by staying up late and cramming.

Just thinking about an examination can cause some students an increase in anxiety. It seems as though during the last year of school, particularly the last semester, tests become a major source of anxiety. Everyone knows fellow students who become obsessed with the idea that they are going to fail an important examination. View an examination as a positive step—an opportunity to demonstrate your knowledge.

> Put yourself in charge of your feelings.
>   Get rid of those negative thought "tapes"!
>   Replace negative thoughts and ideas with positive ones:
>   I WILL pass this test!
>   I will be so glad to get this test behind me.

Write down positive affirmations, and put them on your bathroom mirror, on your refrigerator, anywhere you will see them often. Potential employers, state boards of nursing, your spiritual advisers, and your neighbors are not going to think less of you if you are not at the top of the class. Keep in mind that your employers and the state boards do not care what your grades were in school or on the NCLEX-RN® examination—they just want to know that you can pass the NCLEX-RN® examination and practice nursing safely. Give yourself permission to be in the middle—an average student on grades but one who is concerned about professional, safe nursing practice.

What Kinds of Questions Can I Expect on the NCLEX-RN® Examination?

On the NCLEX-RN® examination, it is anticipated that most of the questions will be in a multiple-choice format; they have a stem in which the question is presented and four options from which to choose an answer. Of these four options, three are meant to distract you from the correct answer. With the four-item, multiple-choice questions, there is only one correct answer. The multiple-choice NCLEX-RN® examination questions provide a choice of four answers, not a combination of the four options (Fig. 5.2).

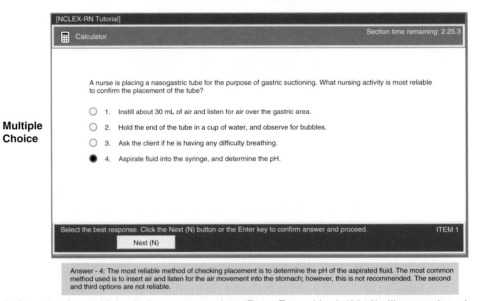

FIG. 5.2 Sample of a multiple-choice test question. (From Zerwekh, J. (2016). *Illustrated study guide for the NCLEX-RN® exam* (9th ed.). St. Louis: Mosby.)

The focus of the NCLEX-RN® examination is on nursing care. The questions ask you to use nursing concepts and judgment in the situation presented.

What Are Alternate Item Format Questions and Why the Big Fuss About Them?

In October 2003, different types of questions (other than four-option multiple-choice questions) were introduced as "scored" questions on the NCLEX-RN® examination. These questions are frequently referred to as "alternate item format" questions and are included in the test bank of questions that will be used to select the test items for a candidate's examination. There is no preset number of alternate item format questions that will be presented to a candidate; the question or items will be randomly selected as the adaptive testing process selects questions that meet the parameters of the test plan.

There is no special or additional nursing knowledge needed to answer the alternate item format questions. There is no attempt to hide or camouflage the questions; they are randomly selected to be included in a candidate's exam. The same nursing concepts are being tested, and the questions are based on the same test plan. The question is simply asked in a different format. All test item types may include multimedia, such as charts, tables, graphics, sound, and video. You do not need to do anything differently with regard to the alternate item format questions; just be aware of types of alternate item format test questions, and implement good testing strategies to answer the question (NCSBN, 2016d).

What Are the Different Types of Alternate Item Format Questions?

Fill-in-the-blank. A short answer is required for fill-in-the-blank questions. These may be questions that require a drug calculation, an intake and output calculation, or an assessment scoring. In these questions, only the numbers should be entered in the space provided. No units of measurement can be included with the answer, because the unit of measurement is already on the screen (Fig. 5.3).

Multiple-response item. This is a different type of multiple-choice question. There will be more than four options presented, and the question will very clearly ask you to select all of the options that correctly answer the question. With the mouse, you will select each option you want to include in the answer, and then click *enter* to confirm your answers and continue to the next question. There is only one correct combination of answers (Fig. 5.4).

Hot spot. These items present a diagram or a graphic and require you to select an area on the diagram to answer the question. For example, let's assume that the diagram is an illustration of the anterior thorax. The question for this diagram might ask you to click on the area where you would place the stethoscope to listen for the apical heart rate or where you would listen for the characteristic sounds of the mitral valve (Fig. 5.5).

Ordered response (drag-and-drop). For this type of question, you will be presented with a list of activities, clients, or steps in a procedure. The question will ask you to click on each item and "drag" it to another area of the screen, placing the items, for instance, in the order in which they would be performed or in order of priority of care. Pay close attention to how the question asks you to rank the options. After you have determined how your answer should be ranked, click on the option you want to place first, "drag" that option over, and place it in the box. You will then select the next option you want to place second, "drag" that option over, and place it in the box. You will continue this process until you have used all of the options available. You can change your answer

Fill in the Blank

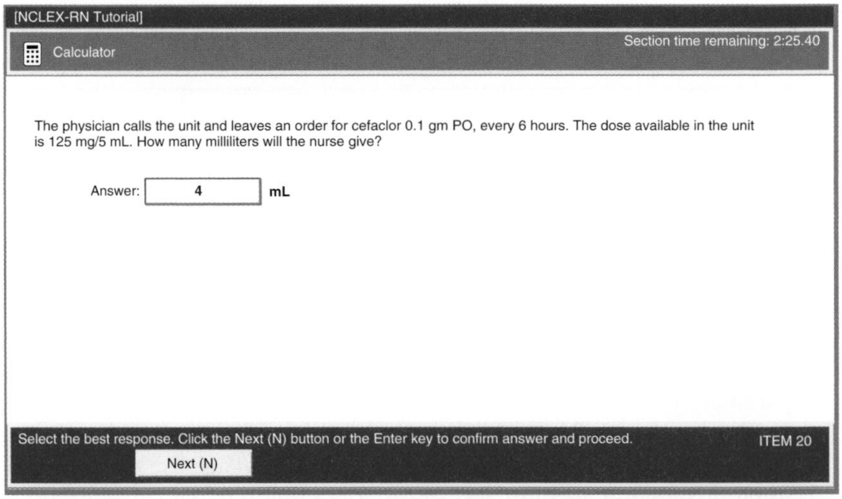

[NCLEX-RN Tutorial]

Calculator   Section time remaining: 2:25.40

The physician calls the unit and leaves an order for cefaclor 0.1 gm PO, every 6 hours. The dose available in the unit is 125 mg/5 mL. How many milliliters will the nurse give?

Answer: [4] mL

Select the best response. Click the Next (N) button or the Enter key to confirm answer and proceed.   ITEM 20

Next (N)

Answer - 4 mL: Rationale: 1 gm = 1000 mg, therefore 0.1 gm = 100 mg   125 mg : 5 mL :: 1000 mg : x mL
Formula: 125 x X = 125X (Note: Multiply the two outside numbers of the ratio equation together, then the two inside numbers; solve for X by dividing the total of the inside numbers by the outside numbers.)
5 x 100 = 500   X = 500/125 = 4 mL

FIG. 5.3 Fill-in-the-blank. (From Zerwekh, J. (2016). *Illustrated study guide for the NCLEX-RN® exam* (9th ed.). St. Louis: Mosby.)

Multiple Response

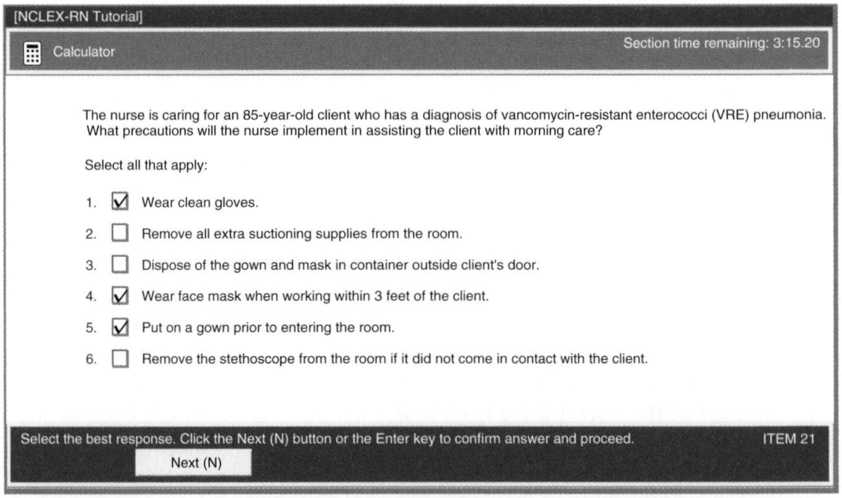

[NCLEX-RN Tutorial]

Calculator   Section time remaining: 3:15.20

The nurse is caring for an 85-year-old client who has a diagnosis of vancomycin-resistant enterococci (VRE) pneumonia. What precautions will the nurse implement in assisting the client with morning care?

Select all that apply:

1. ☑ Wear clean gloves.
2. ☐ Remove all extra suctioning supplies from the room.
3. ☐ Dispose of the gown and mask in container outside client's door.
4. ☑ Wear face mask when working within 3 feet of the client.
5. ☑ Put on a gown prior to entering the room.
6. ☐ Remove the stethoscope from the room if it did not come in contact with the client.

Select the best response. Click the Next (N) button or the Enter key to confirm answer and proceed.   ITEM 21

Next (N)

Answer: The answer is based on standard precautions, plus respiratory precautions for the pneumonia. Nothing should be removed from the room and the gown should be removed prior to leaving the room, not outside the room.

FIG. 5.4 Multiple response. (From Zerwekh, J. (2016). *Illustrated study guide for the NCLEX-RN® exam* (9th ed.). St. Louis: Mosby.)

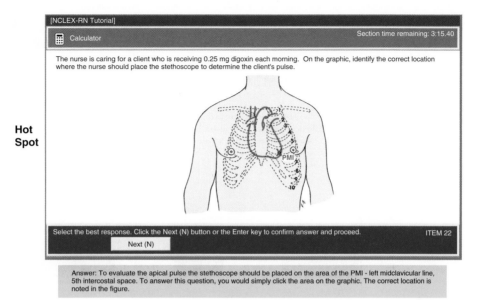

Hot Spot

[NCLEX-RN Tutorial]

Calculator   Section time remaining: 3:15.40

The nurse is caring for a client who is receiving 0.25 mg digoxin each morning. On the graphic, identify the correct location where the nurse should place the stethoscope to determine the client's pulse.

Select the best response. Click the Next (N) button or the Enter key to confirm answer and proceed.   ITEM 22

Next (N)

Answer: To evaluate the apical pulse the stethoscope should be placed on the area of the PMI - left midclavicular line, 5th intercostal space. To answer this question, you would simply click the area on the graphic. The correct location is noted in the figure.

FIG. 5.5 Hot spot. (From Zerwekh, J. (2016). *Illustrated study guide for the NCLEX-RN® exam* (9th ed.). St. Louis: Mosby.)

Drag and Drop

[NCLEX-RN Tutorial]

Calculator   Section time remaining: 2:15.20

The nurse is caring for a client with pneumonia. He is dyspneic, his temperature is 102°F orally, and he is complaining of chest pain. In what order would the nurse provide care for this client?

Place all of the actions below in the order of priority for nursing care. Use all of the options.

Unordered options:

| Encourage clear fluids |
| Administer humidified oxygen |
| Place in semi-Fowler's position |
| Administer antipyretic medication |
| Instruct client regarding risk factors |

Ordered Response:

| Place in semi-Fowler's position |
| Administer humidified oxygen |
| |
| |
| |

Select the best response. Click the Next (N) button or the Enter key to confirm answer and proceed.   ITEM 23

Next (N)

Need to know: Review each of the items in the list. Determine what is the most important action to take first, then second, etc. This question is asking you to provide care for a client who is experiencing difficulty breathing and has chest pain. The dyspnea and chest pain are most likely a result of the client's pneumonia. Position is the first thing that you can do that will benefit the client the most, then begin the oxygen, administer the antipyretic medication, encourage clear liquids, and teaching is last. Remember Maslow when setting priorities.

FIG. 5.6 Drag and drop (ordered response). (From Zerwekh, J. (2016). *Illustrated study guide for the NCLEX-RN® exam* (9th ed.). St. Louis: Mosby.)

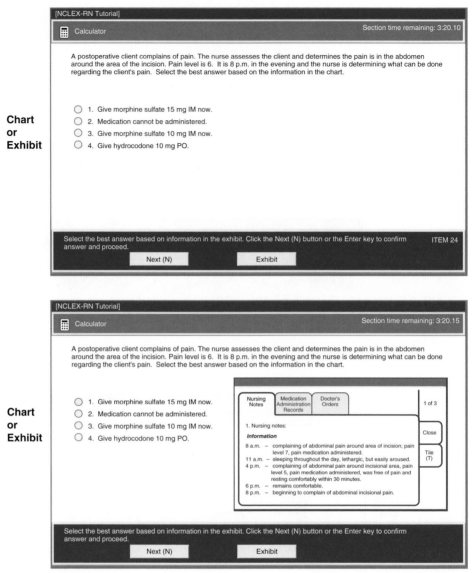

FIG. 5.7 Exhibit. (From Zerwekh, J. (2016). *Illustrated study guide for the NCLEX-RN® exam* (9th ed.). St. Louis: Mosby.)

any time before you click the Next button. This type of question is called an "ordered response" (Fig. 5.6).

Chart/exhibit item. These questions will present a problem and then provide exhibit information stored in tabs. You will click on each tab to find information that will assist you in solving the problem that is presented. The tabs frequently contain information from a chart or data collection from the client. There will still be four options from which to select the correct answer, but you

[NCLEX-RN Tutorial]

Calculator   Section time remaining: 3:20.15

A postoperative client complains of pain. The nurse assesses the client and determines the pain is in the abdomen around the area of the incision. Pain level is 6. It is 8 p.m. in the evening and the nurse is determining what can be done regarding the client's pain. Select the best answer based on the information in the chart.

Chart or Exhibit

○ 1. Give morphine sulfate 15 mg IM now.
○ 2. Medication cannot be administered.
○ 3. Give morphine sulfate 10 mg IM now.
○ 4. Give hydrocodone 10 mg PO.

| Nursing Notes | Medication Administration Records | Doctor's Orders | | 2 of 3 |

Close
Tile (T)

2. Medication administration record (MAR):

Morphine sulfate 10 mg IM administered at 8 a.m.

Hydrocodone 10 mg, PO administered at 4 p.m.

Select the best answer based on information in the exhibit. Click the Next (N) button or the Enter key to confirm answer and proceed.   ITEM 24

Next (N)   Exhibit

[NCLEX-RN Tutorial]

Calculator   Section time remaining: 3:20.30

A postoperative client complains of pain. The nurse assesses the client and determines the pain is in the abdomen around the area of the incision. Pain level is 6. It is 8 p.m. in the evening and the nurse is determining what can be done regarding the client's pain. Select the best answer based on the information in the chart.

Chart or Exhibit

○ 1. Give morphine sulfate 15 mg IM now.
○ 2. Medication cannot be administered.
○ 3. Give morphine sulfate 10 mg IM now.
○ 4. Give hydrocodone 10 mg PO.

| Nursing Notes | Medication Administration Records | Doctor's Orders | | 3 of 3 |

Close
Tile (T)

3. Doctor's orders:

Orders for the last 24 hours include:

Morphine sulfate 10-15 mg q 3-4h PRN severe pain.

Hydrocodone 10 mg PO, every 3-4 hours moderate pain.

Select the best answer based on information in the exhibit. Click the Next (N) button or the Enter key to confirm answer and proceed.   ITEM 24

Next (N)   Exhibit

FIG. 5.7, Cont'd

will need to evaluate the data in each of the tabs to determine the correct answer. Do not attempt to select the correct answer without evaluating all of the information provided on each of the tabs (Fig. 5.7).

Audio item. In this type of item, you will be presented with a question that has an audio component. You will put on the headset provided and click the Play button to listen to the audio for the information required to answer the question. The volume may be adjusted, and you can click the Play button to repeat the audio information. Listen carefully to the audio clip, and select the option that best answers the question (Fig. 5.8).

[NCLEX-RN Tutorial]

▦ Calculator   Section time remaining: 3:20.40

A postoperative client complains of pain. The nurse assesses the client and determines the pain is in the abdomen around the area of the incision. Pain level is 6. It is 8 p.m. and the nurse is determining what can be done regarding the client's pain. Select the best answer based on the information in the chart.

○ 1. Give morphine sulfate 15 mg IM now.
○ 2. Medication cannot be administered.
○ 3. Give morphine sulfate 10 mg IM now.
● 4. Give hydrocodone 10 mg PO.

Select the best answer based on information in the exhibit. Click the Next (N) button or the Enter key to confirm answer and proceed.   ITEM 24

[Next (N)]   [Exhibit]

Chart or Exhibit

Need to know: Analysis of information.
Client received morphine sulfate 10mg IM at 8 a.m., and he was lethargic and sleeping for the next 5 hours. He received hydrocodone PO at 4 p.m., and he was comfortable for the next 4 hours. The doctor's orders are current for both the IM and the PO medication for pain. Give the hydrocodone PO for pain at this time. It held him for 4 hours the last time, and the doctor's order is current.

FIG. 5.7, Cont'd

[NCLEX-RN Tutorial]

▦ Calculator   Section time remaining: 5:59.33
                                                                7 of 8

A client is one day postoperative following an abdominal exploratory laparotomy. The nurse auscultates the abdomen and hears the following:

Listen to the audio clip.
What would be an appropriate nursing intervention?

1. ○ Begin clear liquids, as ordered.

2. ○ Notify the physician.

3. ○ Reinsert nasogastric tube.

4. ○ Keep client NPO.

Audio

Select the best response. Click the Next (N) button or the Enter key to confirm answer and proceed.
[Next (N)]

Answer 1: Bowel sounds are noted on the audio clip, which means that peristalsis has returned to the gastrointestinal tract and the client can begin a clear liquid diet. If bowel sounds are present, there is no need to notify the physician; keep the client NPO or reinsert the nasogastric tube. Laparoscopic procedures are associated with lower rates of postoperative complications, earlier diet progression, and shorter hospital stays.

FIG. 5.8 Audio. (From Zerwekh, J. (2016). *Illustrated study guide for the NCLEX-RN® exam* (9th ed.). St. Louis: Mosby.)

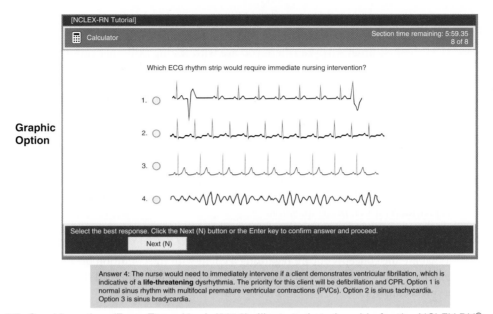

FIG. 5.9 Graphic option. (From Zerwekh, J. (2016). *Illustrated study guide for the NCLEX-RN® exam* (9th ed.). St., Louis: Mosby; rhythm strips from Lewis, S.L., et al. (2014). *Medical-surgical nursing* (9th ed.) St. Louis: Elsevier, pp 799, 793, and 800, respectively.)

Graphic options. The graphic option type of alternate item format presents you with graphics instead of text for the answer options. You will be required to select the correct answer from the graphics presented at the end of the question (Fig. 5.9).

As the NCSBN continues to research the development of test items that evaluate the reasoning and nursing judgment of nursing graduates, other types of alternate item format questions will be developed. Don't be alarmed if you encounter one of these alternate item format questions—focus on what the question is asking, follow the directions, and select the option that reflects the best client care.

What Difference Do Test-Taking Strategies Make?

Knowing how to take an examination is a skill that is developed through practice. Look back at the beginning of nursing school and your first nursing examination; you have come a long way from there! How many times during school have you reviewed a test and discovered you knew the right answer but marked the wrong one? Nursing faculty and those responsible for the NCLEX-RN® examination are not sympathetic to your claim that you "really meant this answer and not the one I marked." How many times did you go back and change an answer from the correct response to the wrong one? If these are common errors you experience during nursing school, you need to incorporate test-taking strategies into your testing skills. Some of the testing practices you have developed through the years may be positive, whereas others may be negative. Information on test-taking strategies can be of benefit to you now and later. Start using testing strategies while you are still in school. This will help you with your current examinations, and the testing strategies will be second nature by the time you take the NCLEX-RN® examination. Take the time to implement good testing practices—get the question right the first time! Analyze where you are with testing skills, get rid of the negative, and retain the positive.

What Are Strategies for Answering Multiple-Choice Questions?
Read the Question (Stem) Carefully
Do not read extra meaning into the question. Avoid asking yourself, "What if the client should …?" Or, "What if the client does …?" Make sure you read the "stem" correctly and understand exactly what information is being requested. (Do you tend to make the client sicker than he really is by the time you finish the question?) Do not add information to the question or think about a client whom you cared for during clinicals or at your job. All the information you need to answer the question correctly is provided for you in the question.

Create a Pool of Information
What are the concepts of care regarding a client with the condition or problem presented? Get a general idea of the condition and type of care required before you read the options. Do not try to predict a correct answer.

Look for Critical Words
Evaluate the question for critical words that make a difference in what the question is asking. Watch for *priority, initial, first action, side effect,* and/or *toxic effect.*

Evaluate All the Options in a Systematic Manner
Focus on what information is being requested, and then carefully go through each option. Do not stop with the first correct answer; the last option may be more correct or more inclusive of information.

Eliminate Options You Know Are Not Correct
And leave them alone! After you have eliminated an option, do not go back to it unless you have gained more insight into the question. Frequently, your initial response in evaluating an option is correct. Go through all of the options, and eliminate incorrect ones. What is left is frequently the correct answer, even if it is not what you were looking for.

Identify Similarities in the Options
Look for an option that is unique from the rest. For example, in a question dealing with a low-residue diet, three of the options might contain a vegetable with a peel, but one might not—that one is probably the correct answer. Evaluate options that contain several suggested client activities. Are three of the activities similar and one different from the rest? The option that is different may be the correct answer.

Evaluate Priority Questions Very Carefully
Keep in mind the nursing process and Maslow's hierarchy of needs. You must have adequate assessment information before proceeding with the nursing process. If assessment information is presented in the stem of the question, then the answer may require a nursing intervention. If a client in the question is presented as experiencing severe chest pain, it would not be appropriate to conduct a cardiac

assessment before putting the client to bed and starting the oxygen! (*If in distress, don't assess!* — If a client is presented in a distressed condition, then adequate assessment data have already been provided in the stem of the question, so you will need to look for an immediate nursing intervention to address the problem). According to Maslow, physical needs must be met before psychosocial needs—the physical needs of your mental health client must be met before you can focus on the mental health needs. When considering the physical needs, respiratory needs are a priority. (You've got to breathe first!) But as a word of caution—do not give a client a respiratory problem if he does not have one!

Select Answers That Focus on the Client

Choices that focus on hospital rules and policies are most often not correct. Consider that you have enough time and adequate staff to perform whatever action is necessary for safe client care.

Analyze your testing skills so that you will know where to start to improve them. After you have identified your testing weaknesses, organize a plan to correct the problem areas. One of the most difficult things to do is to change the way you are used to doing something, even when the change makes life easier. Get an early start on evaluating testing skills; it can make a significant difference in the remaining examinations in nursing school.

NCLEX-RN® Examination Testing Tips
NCLEX Hospital

For the NCLEX-RN® examination to be appropriate to all candidates nationwide, it is important that there be a base for the vast knowledge that is to be tested. Therefore, when you are taking the NCLEX-RN® examination, consider yourself as working in the "NCLEX Hospital." It is a great place to work; everything you need is provided—great equipment that works the way it is supposed to, plenty of staff, and enough time to provide the best and safest nursing care possible. The clients (*patients* are most frequently referred to as *clients* on the NCLEX-RN® examination) all have conditions that respond just as the book says they are supposed to respond. Study according to your textbooks. Your clinical experience is complementary with your academic study. Do not focus on the unusual, unexpected, or strange things that happened to you during clinical rotations. Avoid thinking "this is the way we actually do it where I work."

NCLEX Clients

Focus on the client in the question you are working on. As far as the NCLEX Hospital is concerned, that is the only client you are to be concerned about. Do not worry about the five or six other clients you may have assigned to your care. In the NCLEX Hospital, you are taking care of one client at a time, unless it is stated otherwise. Your priority concern is the client in the current question you are trying to answer.

Medication Administration

Know the Six Rights and the common nursing implications of medications. The generic name will be in the question, because it is more consistent while a brand or trade name may vary (NCSBN, 2016g). A good strategy is to study the medications according to the classification. For example, study the nursing implications regarding administration of corticosteroid medications, and be able to identify the generic name of common corticosteroid medications and their nursing implications.

Calling for Assistance

Be careful with questions for which the right answer appears to be to call someone else to take care of the problem. This is a nursing examination; therefore, identify the best nursing management. This includes questions that include calling the doctor, respiratory therapist, housekeeping, chaplain, or social worker. Be sure there is not something you need to do for the client before notifying someone else regarding the problem. If the client is experiencing difficulty, her condition is changing, and there is nothing you can do, call the doctor. This is particularly true in situations in which the client is experiencing a problem with circulatory compromise. However, if the client is having difficulty breathing, the priority focus may be to position the client to maintain an open airway and/or to begin oxygen as well as to assess quickly the status of the client before calling the doctor.

Positioning

Watch for questions that have particular positions in the stem of the question or those that include positions in the options. Is the client's position necessary to prevent complications or to treat a current problem, or is it primarily for comfort? As you are reviewing, be aware of questions that include conditions that require a specific position in the care of that client.

Delegation and Supervision

The NCLEX-RN® examination includes questions in these areas. Check out the decision tree for delegating to nursing assistive personnel in the *Transition to Practice* materials of the NCSBN (https://www.ncsbn.org/Preceptor-DelegationProces.pdf). Some common considerations to make when evaluating these questions include:
- Delegate to someone else the care of the most stable client with the most predictable response to care.
- Delegate tasks to the most qualified person to perform the task.
- Delegate to nursing assistants those tasks that have the most specific guidelines (e.g., collecting a urine sample, feeding, providing hygiene, ambulating).

Setting Priorities With a Group of Clients

A question may present a group of clients and ask you to determine which client you would take care of first or to rank the clients according to when you would take care of them. Determine the most unstable client who requires nursing care to prevent immediate problems—take care of this client first. Keep in mind Maslow's hierarchy of needs.

Prescriber's Orders

For most of the questions, you can consider that you have a prescriber's order to perform any of the options presented in the question. However, you should watch for questions that may specifically ask for a "dependent nursing action" where you will have to consider whether you need a prescriber's order to perform the nursing action. It would be difficult to present questions while continuing to repeat that a physician's or health care provider's order was present. Standing orders and state nurse practice acts all have implications on orders. This is a standardized test that is administered nationally, and, therefore, there has to be consistency; consequently, unique aspects of nurse practice acts and standing orders are not tested.

> Be aware that the answer you are looking for is frequently not included in the options! This is not uncommon on NCLEX-RN® examination questions. Consider the principles and concepts of care for a client with the problem presented. Eliminate the wrong answers, and evaluate what is left.

CONCLUSION

Wow! NCLEX-RN® examination deadlines, review courses, testing skills, review books, money, license—and you thought all you needed to do was graduate from nursing school! A lot happens between graduating from nursing school and being successful on the NCLEX-RN® examination. The key to surviving it all with a smile is careful planning and implementing those plans during your role transition. (That sounds a lot like the nursing process, doesn't it?) The NCLEX-RN® examination is one of the most incredible opportunities of your life. This examination will open the doors for you as you begin one of the most fantastic experiences of a lifetime: a career in nursing. A listing of relevant websites and online resources follows.

Just say to yourself, "I can do it. I WILL pass the NCLEX-RN® examination!"

🌐 RELEVANT WEBSITES AND ONLINE RESOURCES

National Council of State Boards of Nursing (NCSBN)
http://www.ncsbn.org.

Candidate Bulletin
(updates every year in January: https://www.ncsbn.org/1213.htm). 2016 Bulletin: https://www.ncsbn.org/089900_2016_Bull etin_Proof3.pdf.

Detailed Test Plan
https://www.ncsbn.org/2016_RN_Test_Plan_Candidate.pdf.

Pearson VUE Testing
This is also the location for the Online Tutorial for the NCLEX Exam. http://www.pearsonvue.com/nclex/.

BIBLIOGRAPHY

National Council of State Boards of Nursing. (2015). *2014 RN Practice analysis: Linking the NCLEX-RN® examination to practice.* Retrieved from https://www.ncsbn.org/15_RN_Practice_Analysis_Vol62_web.pdf.

National Council of State Boards of Nursing. (2016a). *2016 NCLEX-RN® detailed test plan.* Retrieved from https://www.ncsbn.org/2016_RN_Test_Plan_Candidate.pdf.

National Council of State Boards of Nursing. (2016b). *2016 NCLEX examination candidate bulletin.* Retrieved from https://www.ncsbn.org/089900_2016_Bulletin_Proof3.pdf. https://www.ncsbn.org/2013_NCLEX_Candidate_Bulletin.pdf.

National Council of State Boards of Nursing. (2016c). *Registration.* Retrieved from https://www.ncsbn.org/1202.htm.

National Council of State Boards of Nursing. (2016d). *Alternate item formats frequently asked questions.* Retrieved from https://www.ncsbn.org/2334.htm.

National Council of State Boards of Nursing. (2016e). *Authorization to test.* Retrieved from https://www.ncsbn.org/1212.htm.

National Council of State Boards of Nursing. (2016f). *NCLEX candidate frequently asked questions.* Retrieved from https://www.ncsbn.org/2321.htm.

National Council of State Boards of Nursing. (2016g). *NCLEX exam development frequently asked questions.* Retrieved from https://www.ncsbn.org/2324.htm.

National Council of State Boards of Nursing. (2016h). *Nurse licensure compact.* Retrieved from https://www.ncsbn.org/nurse-licensure-compact.htm.

National Council of State Boards of Nursing. (2016i). *The eight steps of the NCLEX examination process.* Retrieved from https://www.ncsbn.org/16_NCLEXinfo_factsheet.pdf.

Pearson V.U.E. (2013). *State of the art identification: Palm vein pattern recognition for the NCLEX examination.* Retrieved from www.pearsonvue.com/nclex/NCLEX_PalmVeinFAQ.pdf.

Pearson V.U.E. (2015). *The NCLEX examination.* Retrieved from http://www.pearsonvue.com/nclex/.

Nursing:
A Developing Profession

Historical Perspectives
Influences on the Present

JoAnn Zerwekh, EdD, RN

ⓔ http://evolve.elsevier.com/Zerwekh/nsgtoday/.

History repeats itself because each generation refuses to read the minutes of the last meeting.
Anonymous

After completing this chapter, you should be able to:

- Explain the early European contributions to nursing.
- Explain the events that have affected the roles of American nurses.

Nursing has come a long way; it is not what it used to be.

So, you have to study the history of nursing. Generally, the topic is considered boring. Well, be prepared for a different approach to the topic. Knowing the history of our profession guides our understanding of why we do what we do today. This understanding can be useful to us as we set our professional goals. Threads of nursing history can be found throughout the book. Understanding the history can often help in deciding what changes are needed, what changes are helpful, and what changes may be unnecessary. Let us begin with a look at where nursing began.

NURSING HISTORY: PEOPLE AND PLACES

Where Did It All Begin?

Most nursing historians agree that nursing, or the care of the ill and injured, has been done since the beginning of human life and has generally been a woman's role. A mother caring for a child in a cave and someone caring for another ill adult by boiling willow bark to relieve fever are both examples of nursing. The word *nurse* is derived from the Latin word *nutricius,* meaning "nourishing."

Roman mythological figures included the goddess Fortuna, who was usually recognized as being responsible for one's fate and who also served as Jupiter's nurse (Dolan, 1969). Even before Greek and Roman times, ancient Egyptian physicians and nurses assembled voluminous pharmacopoeia with more than 700 remedies for numerous health problems. Great emphasis was placed on the use of animal parts in concoctions that were generally drunk or applied to the body. The physician prescribed and provided the treatments and usually had an assistant who provided the nursing care (Kalisch & Kalisch, 1986). Some ancient medicine was based on driving out the evil spirit rather than curing or treating the malady (i.e., condition or illness). The treatments were often very foul and frequently included fecal material. By now you may be thinking of the saying, "The treatment was successful, but the patient died."

Advancement of medical knowledge halted abruptly after the Roman Empire was conquered and the Dark Ages began. Any medical and health care knowledge that survived these dark times did so only through the efforts of Jewish physicians who were able to translate the Greek and Roman works (Kalisch & Kalisch, 1986). One bright spot was in Salerno, where a school of medicine and health was established for physicians and women to assist in childbirth. In fact, a midwife named Trotula wrote what may be considered the first nursing textbook on the cure of diseases of women (Dalton, 1900). Generally, nursing was performed by designated priestesses and was associated with some type of temple worship. Little information has survived about this early period. Historians have assumed that women assisted Hippocrates, but there is little information to support that. From these roots, nursing began to develop as a recognized and valued service to society (Jamieson & Sewall, 1949).

Why Deacons, Widows, and Virgins?

Paralleling the fall of the Roman Empire was the rise of Christianity. The early organization of the young Christian church, which was directly affected by the vision of Paul, included a governing bishop and seven appointed deacons. These individuals assisted the apostles in the work of the Church (the word *deacon* means "servant"). The deacon was directly responsible for distributing all the goods and property that apostles relinquished to the Church before they "took up the cross and followed." The apostles were required to give up all material resources to achieve full status in the Church.

Women sympathetic to the Christian cause of aiding the poor were encouraged in this work by the bishops and deacons. Eventually, the deacons relinquished this work to women and established the position of deaconess for that purpose. To maintain a pure heart, these women were required by the Church either to be virgins or widows. The stipulation for widows, however, was that they had to have been married only once (Jamieson & Sewall, 1949). The deaconesses carried nursing forward as they ministered to the sick and injured in their homes. Phoebe, a friend of Paul's and the very first deaconess in the young Christian church, has been called the first visiting nurse (Dana, 1936).

Treatments continued to be a mixture of scientific fact, home remedies, and magic. Eventually, an order of widows evolved that was composed of women who were free from home responsibilities and thus able to commit fully to working among the poor. The widows, although not ordained, continued to do the same work as the deaconesses. This was soon followed by the creation of the Order of Virgins as the Church began placing greater value on purity of body. Although deaconess orders were abolished in the Mediterranean countries, they thrived in other European countries. The traditional commitment to care for the poor and sick became invaluable in a society that generally had neither the time nor the inclination to aid them. Eventually, these women became known as *nuns* (from *non nuptae*, meaning "not married").

This was a time of tremendous upheaval in the world. Wars, invasions, and battles were constant, and as a result of these encounters, the number of widows was significant. Society during this time did not have the sophistication or the means to handle the dependents of the soldiers killed in battle. As a means of survival, women joined the nuns as a form of protection from starvation and poverty. This was a dark and dreary time in which superstition, witchcraft, and folklore were predominant influences. Because of the need for physical protection, convents were built to shelter these women (Jamieson & Sewall, 1949). The convents became havens into which women could withdraw from ignorance and evil and be nurtured in traditional Christian beliefs (Donahue, 1985). The deaconesses, widows, and virgins continued to minister to and nurse the ill within the safety of the convent.

How Did Knighthood Contribute to Nursing?

The Holy Wars furthered the development of nursing in an interesting way. Because many Christian crusaders became ill while in Jerusalem, a hospital known as the Hospital of St. John was built to accommodate them. Those who fought in these Holy Wars had taken oaths of chivalry, justice, and piety and were known as knights. Often men trained in the healing arts accompanied the knights into battle. These male nurses cared for wounded or otherwise stricken knights. They usually wore a red cross emblazoned on their tunics so that in the heat of battle they could be easily identified and thus avoid injury or death (Bullough & Bullough, 1978).

The Hospital of St. John provided excellent nursing care. Many of the nurses who survived stayed to work with the hospital organizers. As the battles in the Holy Land continued, the nurses and knights organized a fighting force with a code of rules and a uniform consisting of a black robe with a white Maltese cross, the symbol of poverty, humility, and chastity. They ventured out to rescue the sick and wounded and transport them to the hospital for care; thus they became known as the Hospitalers (Kalisch & Kalisch, 1986). Male nurses dominated these orders. Other orders that emulated the Hospitalers developed in Europe, and more hospitals were opened based on the Hospital of St. John model (Donahue, 1985).

The altruistic spirit of nursing was also seen in the craftsmen's guilds. Although their primary purpose was to provide training and jobs through the practice of apprenticeship, the guilds provided care and aid for their members when they became old and could no longer work at their trade. The guilds also assisted members and their families in times of illness and injury. The apprenticeship system—in which experience is gained on the job but no formal education is provided—once served as a model for the training of nurses (Donahue, 1985). This system is no longer used and is now considered to have been detrimental to the evolution of nursing.

What nursing gained during this period of history was status. The altruistic ideal of providing care as a service performed out of humility and love became the foundation for nursing. The recognition of the value of hospitals grew; all across Europe, cities were building their own hospitals. A general resurgence in the demand for trained doctors and nurses contributed to the building of medical schools and the development of university programs in the art and science of healing.

What About Revolts and Nursing?

Revolts—not the kind that led to battles but revolts of a social nature—were common. There were battles, too; however, the social revolts had a more direct impact on nursing. The revolution of the spirit, more commonly known as the Renaissance, ushered in new concepts of the world: the discovery of the laws of nature by Newton, the exploration of unknown lands, and the growth of secular interests (humanism) over spiritual ones. In this era emerged several outstanding humanists who were to become saints (Donahue, 1985). Interestingly, these saints are shown in depictions as needing nursing care or as giving care to a wounded or injured person.

In Europe, the Protestant Reformation began primarily as a religious reform movement but ended with revolt within the Church. Many hospitals in Protestant countries were forced to close, and those loyal to the Church that operated them were driven out of the country, resulting in a significant shortage of nurses (mostly nuns) to care for the ill and injured. The poor and ill were considered a burden to society, and those hospitals that remained operational in the Protestant countries became known as "pest houses." To fill the need for nurses, women (many of whom were alcoholics and former prostitutes) were recruited. Generally, during this period, a nurse was a woman serving time in a hospital rather than a prison (Donahue, 1985; Jamieson & Sewall, 1949).

The industrial and intellectual revolutions that followed the Reformation all had significant impacts on nursing. During the Industrial Revolution, as production of much-needed goods was streamlined through industrial innovation, craftsmen left the rural life to work in factories. The intellectual contributions of scientists, many of whom were physicians, combined with the inventions of the microscope, thermometer, and pendulum clock, advanced our knowledge and understanding of the world. The invention of the printing press allowed for easier sharing of information, which further contributed to experimentation. Finally, a disease that was feared worldwide was conquered when Edward Jenner (1749–1823) proved the effectiveness of the smallpox vaccination.

Throughout these revolutions, however, the maternal and infant death rates continued to be high. In fact, before his pioneering work in antisepsis in obstetrics, Ignaz Phillipp Semmelweis (1818–1865) observed that patients giving birth in hospitals under the care of educated physicians had significantly higher death rates than women giving birth at home or in clinics with the assistance of midwives.

Despite all the knowledge gained during this time of revolution, society was generally callous toward the plight of children. Children were abandoned without apparent remorse, and poor families who were desperate to reduce the number of mouths to feed practiced infanticide. These families had no reliable form of birth control except abstinence. Because it was common practice for the woman hired as a wet nurse to sleep with the infant, many infants were inadvertently suffocated. Donahue (1985) reported that, during this period, 75% of all children baptized were dead before they reached the age of 5 years. Because of the persistence of these sad conditions, children's and foundlings' hospitals were established. Eventually, laws were enacted to aid these unfortunate victims (Donahue, 1985).

Existing health care conditions for the ill and injured continued to contribute to high mortality rates. Some sources reported hospital mortality rates as high as 90%. Conditions in the armies were no better. In any military action, mortality rates were high. Reports from the battlefront during the Crimean War suggested that battles were postponed because there were too few able-bodied soldiers to fight. Dysentery and typhoid were the military's nemeses. If a soldier was wounded, infection invariably resulted. Hospitals generally offered no guarantee of survival. In any event, these occurrences had a serious effect on military strategies. If men are ill or injured, battles cannot be won.

Upon this scene entered Florence Nightingale.

Florence Nightingale: The Legend and the Lady

First, let us discuss the legend. Published works about Florence Nightingale before the 1960s generally presented the legend. Most authors agreed that she was beautiful, intelligent, wealthy, socially successful, and educated. She certainly had an ability to influence people and used every Victorian secret to accomplish her desires. Although Nightingale believed it improper to accept payment for her services, she did demand financial support for materials, goods, and staff to accomplish her programs and goals. Some historians believe that it was through Nightingale's influence that Jean Henri Dunant, a Swiss gentleman, provided the aid to the wounded that laid the foundation for the organization of the International Red Cross (Bullough et al., 1990; Dodge, 1989; Dossey, 2000).

Regardless of what actually happened between Dunant and Nightingale, her interest and ambition lay in becoming a nurse. Her family was upset because of this decision. As described by Dossey (2000), Florence (or "Flo" as her family and friends called her) began her journey as a mystic when she was 16 years old. Her experience of a sudden, inner "knowing" took place under two majestic cedars of Lebanon in Embley (England), one of her sacred spots for contemplation. She claimed to receive the following in her awakening moment: "That a quest there is, and an end, is the single secret spoken." Energized by her contact with the Divine Reality or Consciousness, Florence "worked very hard among the poor people" with "a strong feeling of religion" for the next 3 months (Dossey, 2000, p. 33) (Critical Thinking Box 6.1, Fig. 6.1, and Box 6.1).

? CRITICAL THINKING BOX 6.1

Consider all that you have heard about Florence Nightingale. Now, think about the idea that she was a mystic. What does that mean?

FIG. 6.1 Florence Nightingale: The legend (mystic, visionary, healer) and the lady.

BOX 6.1 NIGHTINGALE AND MYSTICISM

What is mysticism? It is considered to be a universal experience of enlightenment obtained via meditation or prayer that focuses on the direct experience of union with divinity, God, or Ultimate Reality, and the belief that such experience is a genuine and important source of knowledge. It is characterized by a call to personal action, because the person is uncomfortable with the world as it is. Underhill (1961) describes five (nonlinear or nonsequential) phases in the spiritual development of a mystic: awakening, purgation, illumination, surrender, and union.

Awakening: At age 16, Nightingale experienced her first call from God and on three other occasions later in life when she heard the voice of God again.

Purgation: Nightingale spent her later teen years and young adulthood (approximately 17 years) separating herself from the affluent lifestyle and worldly possessions that characterized her early life.

Illumination: For Nightingale, this period began when she accepted her first superintendent position at Harley Hospital in London, which propelled her to battle for better conditions during the Crimean War invasion and later, when she returned to England, to fight for reform of the army medical department.

Surrender: This "dark night of the soul" period for Nightingale is thought to have begun approximately 6 years after the Crimean War when she was in her late 30s and continued to her late 60s, a time characterized by her chronic ill health and episodes of stress, overexertion, and depression.

Union: The last 20 years of Nightingale's life (ages 70 to 90) were engendered with an appreciation of the blessings in her life and feelings of peace, joy, and power. Social action and issues no longer spurred the driving force in her life.

Data from Dossey, B. (2005). *Nursing as a spiritual practice: The mystical legacy of Florence Nightingale.* Retrieved from www.altjn.com/perspectives/spiritual_practice.htm; Underhill, E. (1961). *Mysticism.* New York: Dutton.

Nightingale's parents felt that hospitals were terrible places to go and that nurses were, in most cases, the dregs of society. Hospitals were certainly not places for women of proper social upbringing. Although she was forbidden to do so, Nightingale studied nursing (in secret). After a fortuitous meeting, a relationship developed between Nightingale and Sidney and Elizabeth Herbert, an influential couple who were interested in hospital reform. Impressed with Nightingale's analytical mind and her ability to apply nursing knowledge to the critical situation in the hospitals (Bullough & Bullough, 1978; Bullough et al., 1990), they encouraged her to study nursing at Kaiserswerth School, run by Lutheran deaconesses (Dolan, 1969). Her family, of course, was very unhappy. In fact, Dodge (1989) reported that the event precipitated a family crisis, because they threatened to withdraw financial support.

Nightingale accepted a position as administrator of a nursing home for women, the Institution for the Care of Sick Gentlewomen in Distressed Circumstances. She hired her own chaperone and went to work at reforming the way things were done. Nightingale's interest in hospital reform was insatiable. She visited hospitals and took copious notes on nursing care, treatments, and procedures. She sent reports on hospital conditions to Sidney Herbert, the British Secretary of War. Secretary Herbert then assigned her other hospitals to review. The reviews always included recommendations for improving nursing care. From this early background of experiences, Nightingale was now ready for her greatest mission—the Crimean War. The legend was on the way (Bullough et al., 1990).

In 1854, soldiers were dying, more from common diseases than from bullets. Bullough and colleagues (1990) reported that the Crimean War was a series of mistakes. No plan was made for supplying the troops, no plan was in place to maintain the environment in camps, and no provisions were available to care for the injured after the battle. When Herbert appointed Nightingale as head of a group of nurses to go to Crimea, she had already developed a plan of action. In fact, some historians believe that she was already planning to go in an unofficial capacity. The announcement caused a sensation, and when Nightingale began a rigorous selection process for accepting nurses, many volunteered, but few were chosen. She cleaned up the kitchens, the wards, the patients, and improved the general hygiene. From there, the legend grew.

She was clever; after demonstrating the effectiveness of her methods, she withdrew her services. Naturally, all that she had accomplished was done under the scrutiny, skepticism, suspicion, and anger of the physicians. Without the services of the nurses, the abominable conditions quickly returned, and finally the physicians begged her to do whatever she wished—just help! Nightingale responded to the pleading. The actual number of soldiers who benefited from the care of her nurses was immeasurable.

> The nurses made rounds day and night, and the legend of the lady with the lamp was born.

Nightingale's great success prompted her to begin developing schools of nursing based on her knowledge of what was effective nursing. Eventually, many schools in Europe and America used the Nightingale model for nursing education. The program was generally 1 year in length, and classes were small. Many women wanted to become nurses; however, only 15 to 20 applicants were accepted for each class. The goals of her programs included training hospital nurses, training nurses to train others, and training nurses to work in the district with the sick poor (Dolan, 1969). Nightingale had changed society's view of the nurse to one of dignity and value and worthy of respect. As a tribute to Nightingale, Lystra Gretter, an instructor of nursing at the old Harper Hospital in Detroit, Michigan, composed "The Nightingale Pledge," which was first used by its graduating class in the spring of 1893. It is an adaptation of the Hippocratic Oath taken by physicians (Box 6.2).

BOX 6.2   NIGHTINGALE PLEDGE

I solemnly pledge myself before God and in the presence of this assembly, to pass my life in purity and to practice my profession faithfully. I will abstain from whatever is deleterious and mischievous, and will not take or knowingly administer any harmful drug. I will do all in my power to maintain and elevate the standard of my profession and will hold in confidence all personal matters committed to my keeping and all family affairs coming to my knowledge in the practice of my calling. With loyalty will I endeavor to aid the physician, in his work, and devote myself to the welfare of those committed to my care.

In any legend, the truth is often mixed with myth. The stories surrounding Florence Nightingale are many. What is interesting is that, before the 1970s, authors tended to deify Nightingale or establish her as a saintly person. These myths make for interesting reading. Early nurse historians also contributed to these myths by their interpretations of Nightingale's work. But myths have a purpose. They can be used to explain worldviews of groups of people or professions at a given time, and they provide explanations for practice beliefs or natural phenomena. Myths tend to maintain a degree of accuracy when the truth is lost. The trick is to separate myth from fact and story from legend and to draw conclusions regarding the occurrences. This is no easy task when one studies Florence Nightingale. Therefore, it is important to read a variety of studies across several time periods before drawing conclusions about the legend and the lady.

In summary, Florence Nightingale had certain characteristics that assisted her in becoming successful during the strict Victorian times in which she lived. She was extremely well educated for her time. She had traveled throughout the world and had the advantage of personal wealth and a gift for establishing relationships with persons of influence and philanthropic spirit. Most portraits depict her as an attractive woman with pleasant features. Contemporary historians agree she had tremendous compassion for all who suffered. She was very strong-willed, a characteristic that carried her through the period of the Crimean War. She had the ability to analyze data and draw relevant conclusions, on which she based her recommendations. Her students of nursing received better preparation than most physicians. She was 36 at the end of the war, and when she returned home, she became a virtual recluse until she died at age 90. She did have some physical ailments: Crimean fever, sciatica, rheumatism, and dilation of the heart, each of which could have crippling side effects and contributed to her becoming bedridden (Bullough et al., 1990). According to Dossey (2000), "In 1995, D.A.B. Young, a former scientist at the Wellcome Foundation in London, proposed that the Crimean fever was actually Mediterranean fever, otherwise known as Malta fever; this disease is included under the generic name brucellosis" (p. 426). Because of the widespread Crimean fever that the soldiers encountered, it is thought that Nightingale was most likely exposed to this disease through ingesting contaminated food, such as meat or raw milk, cheese, or butter. It seems a logical assumption that Nightingale's 32-year history of debilitating, chronic symptoms is compatible with a diagnosis of chronic brucellosis. In any event, the legend and the lady had a significant effect on American nursing as we know it today (Bullough & Bullough, 1978; Bullough et al., 1990; Dodge, 1989; Dolan, 1969; Dossey, 2000).

AMERICAN NURSING: CRITICAL FACTORS

What Was It Like in Colonial Times?

In colonial times, all able-bodied persons shared nursing responsibilities; however, when there was a choice, women were preferred as nurses. Early colonial historians described care for the ill and house chores as the responsibilities of nurses. Although most women of this era were considered dainty (Bradford, 1898), nurses were usually depicted as willing to do hard work. Some colonies organized nursing services that sought out the sick and provided comfort to those who were ill with smallpox and other diseases (Bullough & Bullough, 1978). There were few trained nurses, however, and most of the individuals who delivered nursing care in the five largest hospitals were men (Dolan, 1969). Eventually, women were hired at the command of George Washington to serve meals and care for the wounded and ill. The era ended with the enactment of the first legislation to improve health and medical treatment and to provide for formal education for society as a whole (Dolan, 1969).

What Happened to Nursing During the U.S. Civil War?

The period of the U.S. Civil War witnessed an improvement in patient care through control of the environment in which the patient recovered. The greatest problems for the Army stemmed from the poor sanitary conditions in the camps, which bred diseases such as smallpox and dysentery. The results were many deaths from inadequate nutrition, impure water, and a general lack of cleanliness.

Nurses who had some formal training were recognized as being major contributors to the relative success of hospital treatments. It was in this era that the value of primary prevention, or the prevention of the occurrence of disease by measures such as immunization and the provision of a pure water supply, became understood. Volunteer nurses, mostly women, served in hospitals caring for those wounded soldiers fortunate enough to have survived the trip from the battlefield. Their patients were nursed in a clean environment and were provided with adequate nutrition. The likelihood of their recovering was significantly improved. Astute physicians observed that patients cared for by nurses generally recovered well enough to return to the battlefield. Families, too, saw that when nurses had control over the environment, their ill or injured loved one was more likely to recover—and return home.

As the United States moved into the industrial age of the early 1900s, Victorian values began to permeate the middle and upper middle classes. Social concerns focused on protecting families from the diseases of the crowded urban areas, and the demand for improved health care increased.

How Did the Roles of Nurses and Wives Compare During the Victorian Era?

The Victorian era had a significant effect on nurses, primarily because they were women. The parallelism between the idealized view of the Victorian woman and the traditional nurse is stunning. The effect of many of the values and beliefs of this era, some historians report, is still felt by women today.

The typical upper-class Victorian household consisted of a husband, who earned a living outside of the home and maintained total control of the family finances, and his wife, who maintained harmony within the home and raised their children. Women's work was generally restricted to philanthropic and voluntary work; women attended teas and other social functions to raise money for organizations and people in need.

Most women were considered fragile and dainty. They were often ill. It has been suggested that some women used illnesses and frailty as a form of birth control to prevent the numerous pregnancies that most women experienced. Some historians concluded that it was through their weaknesses that women gained control and attention. If the wife was ill or frail, maids or servants were hired, but if the wife was healthy, the husband would expect more from her. The Victorian wife was expected to "be good." She was esteemed by her husband but had limited power within the confines of the home and society. She was expected to be hardworking and able to maintain harmony while at the same time being submissive to the demands of her husband. Generally, this fostered dependence on the dominant male figure—the Victorian husband (Rybczynski, 1986).

Let us examine nursing during this same time, especially within the hospital organization. Nurses generally were women who wanted to avoid the drudgery of a Victorian marriage. They were required to be single to make a complete commitment to their vocation. Schooled in submission, women were expected to be equally accommodating within the hospital organization. A good nurse worked for harmony within the hospital. She was expected to be hardworking and submissive. The doctor and the hospital administrator were frequently the same person, usually a man who expected position and power to go hand in hand. Patients were admitted only if they had income and could afford to pay for the services. It was the physician who generated income, and good nurses were expected to help him continue to maintain power. Because the system rewarded people for being ill, there was little incentive to be healthy. Social values contributed to dependence on the health care system. From this milieu came the reformers (Bullough & Bullough, 1978; Davis, 1961; Kalisch & Kalisch, 1986; Stewart, 1950).

Who Were the Reformers of the Victorian Era?

The Victorian era, although a time of repression for women, was also a time of reform. A list of important names in nursing reform includes M. Adelaide Nutting, Minnie Goodnow, Lavinia L. Dock, Annie W. Goodrich, Isabel Hampton Robb, Lilian D. Wald, Isabel M. Stewart, and Sophia Palmer, among others (Jamieson & Sewall, 1949; Kalisch & Kalisch, 1986). These women, who had in common a comfortable upper middle-class background, intelligence, and education, also had in common a desire to reach beyond the constraints that society imposed on them. As society began to realize the important role that nurses played in treating the ill and injured, it also began to understand the need for training programs that would better educate nurses. Reformers focused on establishing standards for nursing education and practice. Among their accomplishments were the organization of the American Nurses Association and the creation of its journal (until 2006, when *American Nurse Today* became the official journal of the ANA), the *American Journal of Nursing*, and the enactment of legislation to require the licensure of prepared nurses. This protected the public from inadequate care provided by people who were not trained as a nurse (Maness, 2006; Christy, 1971; Dock, 1900).

What Were the Key Challenges and Opportunities in Twentieth-Century Nursing?

Wars, influenza, the Great Depression, HIV/AIDS, and rapid technological advancements during the twentieth century affected the nursing profession. Table 6.1 summarizes some key historical and nursing events along a timeline.

How Did the Symbols (Lamp, Cap, and Pin) of the Profession Evolve?

As mentioned previously, Florence Nightingale acquired the nickname "Lady with the Lamp" while caring for soldiers during the Crimean War. Throughout the night, she would carry her lamp while checking on each soldier. For many historical scholars, this image of Nightingale more accurately represents Longfellow's poetic imagination in his 1857 Santa Filomena than the historical record (Grypma, 2010). Here is a link to this famous poem: www.theatlantic.com/past/docs/unbound/poetry/nov1857/filomena.htm.

The nurse's cap design evolved from the traditional garb of the early deaconesses or nuns who were some of the earliest nurses to care for the sick. More recently, the cap's use was to keep a female nurse's hair neatly in place and present a professional appearance. There were two types of cap styles: one was a long nurse's cap, which covered most of the nurse's head; the other was a short nurse's cap, which sat on top of the head. The design of the cap identified the nurse's alma mater, which differentiated graduates from their respective nursing programs. Typically, a black band sewn on the cap signified a senior-level student or graduate status and sometimes identified the head nurse on a clinical unit. The origin of the black or navy band is unknown; some historical scholars believed the black band was a sign of mourning for Florence Nightingale. By the late 1970s, the hat had disappeared almost completely, as have "capping" ceremonies when the new students passed a probationary period of the program to receive their nursing cap. Also, the rapid growth of the number of men in nursing necessitated a unisex uniform.

The nursing pin is a 1000-year-old symbol of service to others (Rode, 1989). The Maltese cross worn by the knights and nurses during the Crusades is considered the origin of the nursing pin. The most recent ancestor of the pin is the hospital badge that has been worn to identify the nurse since its inception more than 100 years ago. The nursing pin was given by the hospital school of nursing to the graduating students to identify them as nurses who were educated to serve the health needs of society. As schools of nursing flourished, each designed their own unique pin to represent their unique philosophy and beliefs. The pin is still worn as part of the nurse's uniforms today.

What Are the Key Events and Influences of the Twenty-First Century?

The beginning of the current millennium was marked with the Year 2000 problem, or Y2K, signifying problems that originated from mainframe computers that were keeping computer documentation data in an abbreviated two-digit format (98, 99, 00) rather than a four-digit year (1998, 1999, 2000). The computer would interpret 00 as 1900 rather than 2000. In newspapers and magazines, there were reports of widespread fear and concern that a massive computer calamity would lead to a global financial crisis, hospital support system shutdown, nuclear meltdowns, collapse of air-traffic control systems, loss of power, and so on. Throughout the world, organizations had to fix and upgrade their computer systems.

Dramatic events following the World Trade Center attacks in New York City on September 11, 2001, affected all aspects of life, including more focus on nursing disaster management and emergency preparedness. Natural disasters, such as Hurricane Katrina in 2005 (Gulf Coast) and Superstorm Sandy in 2012 (East Coast) called on nurses to respond to events that they had not previously experienced. The Ebola outbreak that began in West Africa and spread to the United States in the fall of 2014 pushed nursing to focus on early identification, isolation, monitoring, and quarantine (CDC, 2014).

In early 2010, the passage of the Affordable Care Act, also referred to as "health care reform" or "Obamacare," was signed into law. Although it will take 10 years to fully implement the reform, it provides for a comprehensive national health insurance program. There continues to be controversy since the passage of the act, with some states suing the federal government, stating that it is unconstitutional to mandate that individuals buy health insurance. The Supreme Court ruled that the health

TABLE 6.1   TIMELINE OF EVENTS IN THE 20th AND 21st CENTURIES

1900-1910	1910-1920	1920-1930	1930-1940	1940-1950
1820-1910 Influence of Florence Nightingale 1900 First publication of the *American Journal of Nursing* 1901 U.S. Army Nurse Corps established 1908 U.S. Navy Nurse Corps established 1909 American Red Cross Nursing Service formed 1909 University of Minnesota establishes the first baccalaureate nursing program 1910 Florence Nightingale dies	1914-1918 World War I 1918-1919 21.5 million people died as a result of the 1918-1919 pandemic. More recent estimates have placed global mortality from the 1918-1919 pandemic at anywhere between 30 and 50 million	1923 Goldmark Report—study focused on nursing student preparation in hospital programs and faculty preparation 1924 Yale School of Nursing becomes the first autonomous school of nursing in the U.S. with its established nursing department meeting the standards of the university 1925 Establishment of the Frontier Nursing Service—first organized midwifery program 1925 Establishment of the Frontier Nursing Service—first organized midwifery program 1929 Stock market crashes, leading to the Great Depression	1932 Teachers College establishes the first EdD in nursing 1934 First PhD program in nursing started at New York University 1935 Social Security Act enhances and promotes public health nursing	1939-1945 World War II 1943 Nurse Training Act provided federal funding for nursing education 1943 U.S. Cadet Nurse Corps established During this decade the rise of "team nursing" occurs because of a shortage of nurses

RESOURCES

American Association for the History of Nursing (2016). *Nursing history calendar.* Retrieved from http://www.aahn.org/nursinghist orycalendar.html.

American Journal of Nursing (1952). *The state board test pool exam, 52*(5), 616, 1952. Retrieved from http://www.jstor.org/ discover/10.2307/3468023?uid=3739552anduid=2129anduid=2anduid=70anduid=4anduid=3739256andsid=21101634154573.

American Nurses Association (2016). Historical review. Retrieved from http://www.nursingworld.org/FunctionalMenuCategories/ AboutANA/History/BasicHistoricalReview.pdf.

Haase, P.T. (1990). *The origins and rise of associate degree nursing education.* Durham and London: Duke University Press.

National Council of State Boards of Nursing. (2016): *NCSBN historical timeline.* Retrieved from https://www.ncsbn.org/70.htm.

Texas Organization for Associate Degree Nursing. (n.d.). *History.* Retrieved from http://www.toadn.org/history/index.php?PHPSES SID=53455f97767bc71c0a89009780fb7676.

1950-1960	1960-1970	1970-1980	1980-1990	1990-2000	2000 to current
1950 Associate degree education for nursing began as part of an experimental project at Teachers College, Columbia University, New York 1950-1953 Korean War 1953 Establishment of the National Student Nurses' Association 1950 Nursing became first profession to use the same licensing exam in all states, called the State Board Test Pool Exam 1952 Publication of first issue of *Nursing Research* 1959 Beginning of the Vietnam War that would last until 1975	1964 Nursing Training Act— first federal law to give comprehensive assistance for nursing education 1965 Medicare and Medicaid Acts 1965 ANA's "Position Paper on Educational Preparation for Nurse Practitioners and Assistants to Nurses" 1965 Establishment of the first nurse practitioner (NP) role, developed jointly by Loretta Ford, a nurse educator, and Henry Silver, a physician at the University of Colorado 1968 Adoption by ANA of a new Code for Nurses	1973 Establishment of the American Academy of Nursing 1978 First test-tube baby born 1978 Establishment of the National Council of State Boards of Nursing (NCSBN) to lead nursing regulation 1985 Establishment of the American Association of Nurse Practitioners (AANP)	1981 Release of the first IBM personal computer 1982 Centers for Disease Control and Prevention (CDC) begins formal tracking of all AIDS cases 1984 Formation of Texas Organization of Associate Degree Nursing (TOADN) 1985 Establishment of the National Institute of Nursing Research (NINR) at the National Institutes of Health (NIH) 1986 National Organization for the Advancement for Associate Degree Nursing (NOAADN) is established	1991 American Nurses Credentialing Center operational 1990 Explosion of medical technologies and the access to information via the Internet 1994 NCSBN Implements computer adaptive test (CAT) for nurse licensure 1996 Publication of a free online electronic journal, *Online Journal of Nursing Issues (OJIN)*	2000 NCSBN initiates the Nurse License Compact (NLC) 2001 9/11 Terrorist attack 2004 American Association of Colleges of Nursing (AACN) recommends all advanced practice nurses earn a Doctor of Nursing Practice (DNP) 2010 Affordable Care Act signed into law 2012 Canada chooses to use the NCLEX exam for licensing

Kansas University Medical Center. (n.d.). *100-year timelines of world history, nursing, medicine, science & industry advances, U.S. economic & healthcare market, U.S. social policy, and U.S. presidents*. Retrieved from http://www2.kumc.edu/instruction/nursing /pqe/timelinehistory.htm.

National Institute of Nursing Research. (n.d.). *Important events in the National Institute of Nursing Research History*. Retrieved from https://www.ninr.nih.gov/aboutninr/history.

U.S. Department of Health & Human Services. (n.d.). *The great pandemic: The United States in 1918-1919*. Retrieved from http:// www.flu.gov/pandemic/history/1918/.

University of Minnesota School of Nursing. (2013). *School of nursing: About*. Retrieved from http://www.nursing.umn.edu/about/in dex.htm.

care law was constitutional in 2012; however, politicians and the public still have dividing opinions on the implementation of the reform.

HISTORY OF NURSING EDUCATION

What Is the History of Diploma Nursing?

The oldest form of educational preparation leading to licensure as an RN in the United States is the diploma program. Education in diploma schools emphasized the skills needed to care for the acutely ill patient. Graduates received a diploma in nursing, not an academic degree. From 1872 until the mid-1960s, the hospital diploma program was the dominant nursing program. Currently, there are approximately 42 diploma programs accredited by the Accreditation Commission for Education in Nursing (ACEN); this represents the smallest percentage of all basic RN programs (ACEN, 2016). Perhaps one of the reasons for this decline was that the courses offered by hospitals frequently did not provide college credit. Although most diploma programs are associated with institutions of higher learning, where the graduates receive some college credit, graduates still may not receive college credit for the nursing courses.

What Is the History of Associate Degree Nursing?

The associate degree nursing program has the distinction of being the first and, to date, only educational program for nursing that was developed from planned research and controlled experimentation. Since its beginning in 1951, the associate degree nursing program has grown to more than 1092 programs, producing more graduates annually than either diploma or baccalaureate programs (NLN, 2014).

In 1951, Mildred Montag published her doctoral dissertation, *The Education of Nursing Technicians*, which proposed education for the RN in the community college. Dr. Montag suggested that the associate degree program be a terminal degree to prepare nurses for immediate employment. According to Dr. Montag, there was a need for a new type of nurse, the "nurse technician," whose role would be broader than that of a practical nurse but narrower than that of the professional nurse. The technical nurse was to function at the "bedside." The duties of the technical nurse, according to Dr. Montag, would include (1) giving general nursing care with supervision, (2) assisting in the planning of nursing care for patients, and (3) assisting in the evaluation of the nursing care given (Montag, 1951).

In 1952, the American Association of Junior Colleges established an advisory committee. Along with the National League for Nursing (NLN), this committee was to conduct cooperative research on nursing education in the community college. The goals of this Cooperative Research Project were threefold: (1) to describe the development of the associate degree nursing program, (2) to evaluate the associate degree graduates, and (3) to determine the future implications of the associate degree on nursing. The original project was directed by Dr. Montag at Teachers College of Columbia University and included seven junior colleges and one hospital from each of the six regions of the United States.

In the proposed technical nursing curriculum, there was to be a balance between general education and nursing courses. Unlike the diploma programs, the emphasis was to be on education, not service. At the end of 2 years, the student was to be awarded an associate's degree in nursing and would be eligible to take the state board examinations for RN licensure (now called the NCLEX-RN® Exam).

What Is the History of Baccalaureate Nursing?

The early baccalaureate nursing programs were usually 5 years in length and consisted of the basic 3-year diploma program with an additional 2 years of liberal arts. In 1909, the University of Minnesota offered the first university-based nursing program. It offered the first Bachelor of Science in Nursing degree and graduated the first bachelor's degree–educated nurse. By 1916, there were 13 universities and 3 colleges with baccalaureate nursing programs. A 2014 survey conducted by the American Association of Colleges of Nursing (AACN) found that total enrollment in entry-level nursing programs leading to the baccalaureate degree, was 189,729—up 4.2% from the previous year and a 10.4% increase in RN-to-BSN programs (AACN, 2014). The increased enrollment in the RN-to-BSN programs marks the twelfth year of enrollment increases, which is evidence of the priority that RNs place on continuing their education. According to NLN's (2014) biennial survey of schools of nursing, there are 740 baccalaureate nursing programs.

What Is the History of Graduate Nursing Education?

Graduate nursing programs in the United States originated during the late 1800s. As more nursing schools sought to strengthen their own programs, there was increased pressure on nursing instructors to obtain advanced preparation in education and clinical nursing specialties.

The Catholic University of America, in Washington, DC, offered one of the early graduate programs for nurses. It began offering courses in nursing education in 1932 and conferring a master's degree in nursing education in 1935.

The NLN's Subcommittee on Graduate Education first published guidelines for organization, administration, curriculum, and testing in 1957. These guidelines have been revised throughout the years and reflect the focus in master's education on research and clinical specialization.

Until the 1960s, the master's degree in nursing was viewed as a terminal degree. The goal of graduate education was to prepare nurses for teaching, administration, and supervisory positions. In the early 1970s, the emphasis shifted to developing clinical skills, and the roles of clinical specialists and nurse practitioners emerged. By the late 1970s, the focus again shifted back to teaching, administration, and supervisory positions (McCloskey & Grace, 2001).

In response to health care reform, the number of master's programs has increased. Enrollments in master's degree programs rose by 6.6%, and by 3.2% in research-focused and 26.2% in practice-focused doctoral programs (DNP). In 2014 NLN reported that 113,788 students were enrolled in master's programs, 5290 were enrolled in research-focused doctoral programs, and 18,352 were enrolled in practice-focused doctoral programs in nursing (AACN, 2014).

THE NURSE'S ROLE: THE STRUGGLE FOR DEFINITIONS

What Do Nurses Do?

As a student, you study nursing texts that explain theories, skills, principles, and the care of patients. Every text has at least one introductory chapter that describes nursing and its significance. By examining many of these introductory chapters of nursing texts, you can generate a rather extensive list of roles (Anglin, 1991). From this list of roles, six major categories can be determined (Table 6.2). The most traditional role for nurses is that of caregiver. The nurse as teacher or educator is often referred to when discussing patient care or nursing education. The role of advocate had been very controversial in the early 1900s; however, patient advocacy has become the essential nursing role since the 1980s and has become more of a priority of the profession (Hanks, 2008). Nurses were also expected to be managers ever since the first formal education or training program was instituted. Another interesting role for the nurse is that of colleague. The final role is that of expert.

What Is the Traditional Role of a Nurse?

The role of the nurse as caregiver has engendered the least amount of controversy. This role has been thoroughly documented, not only in writing but also through art, since early times. Nurses

TABLE 6.2	**WHAT NURSES DO**				
CAREGIVER	**EDUCATOR**	**ADVOCATE**	**MANAGER**	**COLLEAGUE**	**EXPERT**
Care provider	Patient educator	Interpreter	Administrator	Collaborator	Academician
Comforter	Family educator	Learner	Coordinator	Communicator	Historian
Healer	Counselor	Protector	Decision maker	Facilitator	Nursing instructor
Helper	Community	Risk-taker	Evaluator	Peer reviewer	Professional
Nurturer	teacher	Change agent	Initiator	Professional	educator
Practitioner			Leader	Specialist	Researcher
Rehabilitator			Planner		Research consumer
Support agent					Teacher
					Theorist
					Practitioner
					Leader

and nursing leaders agree that this is their primary role. As students, your caregiving skills will be measured constantly through skill laboratories, clinical evaluation proficiency, and, eventually, through licensure testing and staff evaluations. All of these mechanisms are used to evaluate your ability to be a caregiver.

> Caregiving is probably the only role about which there is agreement as to what it means and how we do it.

Imagine a nurse providing care. Generally, the picture that most often comes to mind is someone, usually female, in a white uniform caring for a patient who is ill. This picture is the romanticized version of caregiving continually portrayed in movies, television, and novels. We know that caregiving takes place in many settings: clinics, homes, hospitals, offices, businesses, and schools, among others. We can probably agree that caregiving is an important role for nurses and that it is why most of us chose nursing. Studies examining the role of caregiver continue to be undertaken, and our understanding of the role is expanding (Benner, 1984; Leininger, 1984; Watson, 1985). Without a doubt, caregiving is an important role, one that is essential to nursing.

Did You Know You Would Be a Teacher or Educator?

Teaching patients about their therapy, condition, or choices is critical to the successful outcome of some prescribed treatments. For example, nurses have learned through research that knowledge can reduce anxiety before and after surgery. Teaching becomes especially important when patients have to make treatment choices and decisions about their care. With the volumes of information available regarding health care, it is even more important that nurses help patients understand what they need to know to make wise decisions regarding their health. Discharge plans also provide an opportunity for patient education. Home care includes teaching as a reimbursable activity. Agency charting procedures all require documentation of patient education. All nursing textbooks include sections on what the nurse needs to emphasize regarding patient education. With all this evidence, there is little doubt that the educator role is an important one for the nurse (Fig. 6.2).

Teaching is planned to strengthen a patient's knowledge regarding making decisions about treatment options, and it is an essential nursing intervention (Alfaro-LeFevre, 1998). In many ways, the nurse as an educator is also an interpreter of information, and this leads us to the next role for discussion.

FIG. 6.2 Did you know you would be a teacher?

When Did the Nurse Become an Advocate? Nurse in the Role of Advocate

A useful definition of the term *advocate* is "one who pleads a cause before another." The first advocacy issue, arising early in the 1900s, concerned nursing practice. Public health and visiting nurses were the majority (approximately 70%), and hospital nurses were the minority (approximately 30%) of working nurses. Working as a private duty nurse or visiting nurse was a source of income for women who had no other means of support. Because there was no way to determine the credentials of the visiting nurse, many impostors worked in that capacity. Lavinia L. Dock, Sophia Palmer, and Annie W. Goodrich, three nursing leaders, deplored this situation and endeavored to protect the public from unscrupulous "nurses" (Dolan, 1969; Goodnow, 1936). Dock was an excellent nurse who believed in fairness to qualified nurses and to the public. She advocated that all practicing nurses be measured by a "fair-general-average standard," as determined by written examination, and be rewarded with licensure on attainment of the standard (Christy, 1971).

Palmer's proposed solutions were similar. Many hospitals were sending out inexperienced undergraduates to do private duty nursing while not reporting the income. She advocated a training school in which students of nursing would learn to provide care under a qualified nurse, and she supported the implementation of a registration process for all qualified nurses to protect the public from incompetent, unqualified nurses.

Goodrich advocated compulsory legislation that would ensure that graduates or trained nurses would be the only ones who could work as nurses. She pleaded for the registration of qualified nurses, not only for the protection of the nurse but also for the protection of the community. Goodrich also fought against correspondence or home-study programs for nurses, which were a greater menace to the public's safety than people realized. Such legislation, she believed, would encourage talented young women who were intellectually prepared for scientific education to select nursing as a career. The role of the advocate, as understood by these three early nursing leaders, was to protect the public from unqualified nurses (Christy, 1969; Dock, 1900; Palmer, 1900).

From this beginning, the role of advocate grew. Public health nurses served as advocates in factories and communities during the Industrial Revolution. Many municipal boards of health hired visiting nurses to work as inspectors in the factories to protect the workers from health hazards and to help prevent accidents. Communities were finding that the nurse as advocate for the factory worker had inestimable value. Visiting nurses were also proving very effective in preventing the spread of communicable diseases. Hospital nurses also worked as advocates for the patients while giving care. Nurses were crucial in protecting patients from harm when they were too ill to protect themselves. Nurses were also responsible for providing measures to relieve pain, and they strove to make their patients happy and comfortable, even if it meant breaking the rules sometimes (Hill, 1900). During the 1970s and 1980s, the responsibility of the nurse as advocate was expanded to include speaking for their patients when they could not speak for themselves (Sovie, 1983). Nurses returned to work in churches in the primary role of advocate under the Granger Westberg model for parish nursing. The members of the congregation where a parish nurse practiced found affirmation and support as they reached to improve their physical, emotional, and spiritual health (Striepe, 1987).

Historically, consumers, administrators, and courts have not shared the perception of the nurse as advocate. The findings of a study done in 1983 indicated that consumers did not recognize the nurse as an initiator of health care (Miller et al., 1983). Consumers also believed that physicians would protect the rights of the patient. Miller and colleagues (1983) concluded that although nurses were serving as mediators between patients and institutions, changes rarely occurred within the institutions as a result of this role. Patient advocacy was directly related to the power and authority allowed the nurse by the particular system. Nurses generally became advocates whenever the issue involved patient care; however, they had little power to be truly effective as an advocate when the concerns involved the medical regimen or health care services (Miller et al., 1983). Examples of advocacy included questioning doctors' orders, promoting patient comfort, and supporting patient decisions regarding health care choices.

> Advocacy is a critical role for nurses today. Nurses are in a vital position to be effective in this role.

With the need for informed consent, advance directives, and treatment choices, patients more than ever need an advocate to interpret information, identify the risks and benefits of the various treatment options, and support the decision they make. However, nurses are extending their roles as advocates in providing patient care to initiatives that improve patient safety and recognize the nursing profession as a key player in providing all individuals access to quality health care.

For example, the American Nurses Association (ANA) has endorsed the *Registered Nurse Safe Staffing Act of 2015*. If passed, this law would require Medicare-funded hospitals to develop and implement safe staffing plans for nurses. Nurses providing direct patient care along with nurse managers would comprise a nurse staffing committee that would evaluate staffing needs of the health care institution with an overall goal of ensuring nurse-to-patient acuity ratios are optimal to deliver safe patient care, reduce patient readmissions, and improve nursing staff retention (ANA, 2015). With the inception of the Affordable Care Act, ensuring access to health care for the public remains an ongoing concern.

Considering this, the Coalition for Patients' Rights (CPR) consists of over 35 organizations with dedicated members who are on the frontline in ensuring that all health care professionals be able to practice fully to the extent of their education, scope, and practice in providing quality health care (CPR, 2016). With registered nurses comprising the largest group of health care professionals, CPR in collaboration with several professional nursing organizations recognize that nurses are and will continue to play an integral role in providing quality health care to the public. For a complete listing of current CPR coalition members, check out http://www.patientsrightscoalition.org/Main-Menu/About-Us/List-of-Coalition-Members.html.

What Is the Role of Manager of Care?

Even Florence Nightingale recognized the need for nurses to be managers. She insisted that nurses needed to organize the care of the patient so that other nurses could carry on when they were not present. There were four major eras in the development of the nurse as manager. During the first period, lasting until about 1920, a nurse manager was known as the *charge nurse*. Charge nurses were responsible for teaching the nursing students what they needed to know and for directing the care that the students provided. The charge nurse was autocratic. This nurse had absolute authority over the student.

During the second era, lasting until 1949, the term *supervisor* was used to describe the role of nurse manager. The supervisor continued to be responsible for the students; however, the role had expanded to include enforcing agency policies, developing improvements in the care of the ill, and being responsible for the effective use of the ward's resources. Nurses were more involved in the patient care process. Hospital administrators were relying on nursing expertise to establish policies for patient care and hospital administration. This era ended with the publication of Esther Lucille Brown's report (1948) recommending that nursing education be separated from hospital administration.

During the third period, lasting until 1970, the nurse was referred to as a *coordinator*. The nurse coordinator no longer had responsibility for the nursing education of the students but was expected to motivate staff, be innovative, and solve problems. Coordinators were active in improving patient care and were expected to maintain harmony within the institution. Many nurse coordinators had few skills in and little knowledge of middle management. They basically learned by trial and error how to be effective.

The last period, from 1970 to the present, is a series of waves. Nurses gained recognition as managers and were able to function in that role. Hospital nurses gained middle-management positions and proved their abilities. The period before diagnostic-related groups (DRGs) saw escalating hospital costs and growth in the numbers of employees and services. From this growth came significant efforts to control the costs of health care. The term *manager* is used most often now in the nursing literature, but you may find it used to describe any of the four periods.

> No matter what era in history you study, the expectation is that the nurse-manager will coordinate patient care and supervise nurses in the delivery of quality care.

Can Nurses Be Colleagues?

The role of colleague is a vital one in any profession. The status of colleague within health care generates pictures of nurses, doctors, and pharmacists discussing, on an equal basis, problems and concerns related to health care. In nursing, we have made great progress in achieving the status of colleague. Interprofessional collegial relationships are strengthening, due in part to the increasing utilization of health care-related services taking place in community and homecare settings (Naylor, 2011). Interprofessional collaboration is essential to the changes taking place with health care delivery models.

Between 1960 and the present, the term *collaborator* has been adopted for this role. The definition of this word means "a person who works jointly on an activity or project; an associate." A secondary definition means "a person who cooperates traitorously with an enemy; a defector."

The primary definition may be the most fitting description of the role. Nurses are interested in developing collaborative relationships with doctors, pharmacists, and other health professionals.

The literature is abundant with discussions of these relationships and consistently describes these relationships as collaborative (Hahm & Miller, 1961; Kelly, 1975; Quint, 1967; Seward, 1969; Tourtillott, 1986; Wisener, 1978).

Where Does This Leave the Role of Colleague?

Nursing education has promoted the term *collaborator* over *colleague*. Students in their educational experiences are seldom offered the opportunity to practice the role of colleague and therefore have only a vague understanding of the role. However, public health nurses throughout American history have not only understood the role but probably have attained a greater degree of collegiality than any other practice area of nursing. Public health nurses are not the majority within the profession. Nevertheless, they continue to enjoy and maintain the essence of the role (Anglin, 1991). As a colleague, one recognizes nurses with expertise and relies on those nurses for their expertise in the interest of improving patient care and advancing the profession. The essence of the role is mutual respect and equality among professionals, both intradisciplinary and interdisciplinary (Anglin, 1991). The Interdisciplinary Nursing Quality Research Initiative (INQRI) recognizes the valuable role nurses play in advancing and improving patient care and continues to validate the nurse as a deliverer of quality patient care through conducting extensive interdisciplinary research (INQRI, n.d.).

What About Experts?

There is one other role in which nurses are often found. This role is called *expert*. It is a conglomerate of advanced formal or informal education, certification, and acquired or recognized expertise. The role includes academicians, historians, nursing educators, clinicians, professional educators, researchers, research consumers, theorists, nurse technologists, and the leaders within the profession. The American Academy of Nursing recognizes some of these individuals and votes to bestow on them the honor of Fellow. There are many nurses who are experts in an area of practice, whether it be in clinics, at the bedside, in nursing homes, or in other settings. As nurses with special expertise, they are called on to provide testimony in courts and at government hearings or to share information and knowledge with other nurses, which is their obligation to the profession. This sharing can be done through mentoring, guest speaking, performing in-services, offering continuing-education programs, contributing to publications, and writing technical articles. These experts are usually the nurses who create the momentum that moves the profession forward. This is a role that should be recognized, encouraged, and rewarded.

CONCLUSION

The history of nursing provides a wealth of knowledge about where we have been and illustrates for us the lessons that have been learned. Few of us know the specifics of how nursing evolved into the discipline that it is today; however, the study and review of our rich history provides the context for where we will be tomorrow. At the end of this chapter is a listing of relevant websites and online resources on the history of nursing.

So history naturally informs nursing knowledge, both imaginatively and practically. As historian Joan Lynaugh observed, nursing history is "our source of identity, our cultural DNA." Nurses love nursing history when it illuminates their imaginations and they can feel its meaning in their bones. Indeed, nursing history offers all nurses an exciting future in ideas (Meehan, 2013, p. 13.)

What do nurses do? There is no simple answer. We agree that nurses care for patients—hence nurses are caregivers. We agree that nurses teach patients what they need to know to make informed choices—and therefore nurses are educators. We also agree that the role of manager exists in some form, and so we manage our practice and patients' care. We can even define the role of advocate. The role of colleague is gaining clarity with an increased focus on nurses' role in interprofessional collaboration. We are consistent in using the term *collaborator*; however, the term *colleague* is frequently referenced in nursing education and research, as compared to clinical practice, but progress is being made in recognizing the nurse as a colleague in all settings where nurses practice.

Finally, we have experts whom we may or may not recognize—and on whom the profession depends to provide the leadership for the whole. These roles merely provide a beginning for you to understand the profession you have chosen—nursing. May you become proficient in these roles and develop into an expert who will then provide the leadership for nursing in the future.

> *The future is not the result of choices among*
> *Alternative paths offered;*
> *It is a place that is created,*
> *Created first in the mind and will,*
> *Created next in activity.*
> *The future is not some place we are going to,*
> *But one we are creating.*
> *The paths to it are not found, but made.*
> *And the activity of making them*
> *Changes both the maker and the destiny.*
>
> *Anonymous, 1987*

🌐 RELEVANT WEBSITES AND ONLINE RESOURCES

American Association for the History of Nursing
http://www.aahn.org/.

Black Nurses in History
http://libguides.rowan.edu/blacknurses.

Canadian Association for the History of Nursing
http://cahn-achn.ca/.

Clendening History of Medicine Library—Florence Nightingale Resources
http://clendening.kumc.edu/dc/fn.

Frontier Nursing Service
http://www.frontiernursing.org.

Images from the History of Medicine
http://www.ihm.nlm.nih.gov/.

Margaret M. Allemang Society for the History of Nursing (Canadian)
http://allemang.on.ca/.

Museum of Nursing History
http://www.nursinghistory.org/.

Nursing History and Health Care
www.nursing.upenn.edu/nhhc.

BIBLIOGRAPHY

Accreditation Commission for Education in Nursing (ACEN). (2016). *Online directory of accredited programs.* Retrieved from http://www.acenursing.us/accreditedprograms/programSearch.htm.

Alfaro-LeFevre, R. (1998). *Applying nursing process: A step-by-step guide.* New York: Lippincott Williams & Wilkins.

American Association of Colleges of Nursing. (2014). *2014-2015 Enrollment and graduations in baccalaureate and graduate programs in nursing.* Author: Washington, DC.

American Nurses Association. (nd). In review. Retrieved from http://www.nursingworld.org/FunctionalMenuCategories/AboutANA/History/BasicHistoricalReview.pdf.

American Nurses Association. (2015). *Safe staffing.* Retrieved from http://www.rnaction.org/site/PageNavigator/nstat_take_action_safe_staffing.html.

Anglin, L. T. (1991). *The roles of nurses: A history, 1900 to 1988.* Ann Arbor, MI: University of Michigan.

Benner, P. (1984). *From novice to expert: Excellence and power in clinical nursing practice.* Menlo Park, CA: Addison-Wesley.

Bradford, W. (1898). *History of Plymouth plantation: Book II (1620).* Plymouth, MA: Wright & Potter.

Brown, E. L. (1948). *Nursing for the future.* New York: Russell Sage Foundation.

Bullough, V., & Bullough, B. (1978). *The care of the sick: The emergence of modern nursing.* New York: Prodist.

Bullough, V., Bullough, B., & Stanton, M. P. (1990). *Florence Nightingale and her era: A collection of new scholarship.* New York: Garland.

CDC. (2014). *Cases of Ebola diagnosed in the United States.* Retrieved from http://www.cdc.gov/vhf/ebola/outbreaks/2014-west-africa/united-states-imported-case.html.

Christy, T. E. (1969). Portrait of a leader: Isabel Hampton Robb. *Nursing Outlook, 17*(3), 26–29.

Christy, T. E. (1971). First fifty years. *American Journal of Nursing, 71*(9), 1778–1784.

CPR. (2016). *Coalition for Patients' Rights.* Retrieved from http://www.patientsrightscoalition.org/.

Dalton, R. (1900). Hospitals: Their origins and history. *Dublin Journal of Medical Science, 109*(3), 17–19.

Dana, C. L. (1936). *The peaks of medical history.* New York: Paul B. Hoeber.

Davis, M. D. (1961). I was a student over 50 years ago. *Nursing Outlook, 61,* 62.

Dock, L. (1900). What may we expect from the law? *American Journal of Nursing, 1,* 9.

Dodge, B. S. (1989). *The story of nursing* (2nd ed.). Boston: Little, Brown and Company.

Dolan, J. A. (1969). *History of nursing.* Philadelphia: Saunders.

Donahue, M. P. (1985). *Nursing: The finest art.* St. Louis: Mosby.

Dossey, B. (2000). *Florence Nightingale: Mystic, visionary, healer.* Springhouse, PA: Springhouse.

Goldmark, J. (1923). *Nursing and nursing education in the United States: Report of the Committee for the Study of Nursing Education.* New York: Macmillan.

Goodnow, M. (1936). *Outlines in the history of nursing.* Philadelphia: Saunders.

Grypma, S. (2010). Revis(it)ing nursing history. *Journal of Christian Nursing, 27*(2), 67.

Hahm, H., & Miller, D. (1961). Relationships between medical and nursing education. *Journal of Nursing Education, 39,* 849–851.

Hanks, R. G. (2008). The lived experience of nursing advocacy. *Nursing Ethics, 15*(4), 468–477. http://dx.doi.org/10.1177/0969733008090518.

Hill, J. (1900). Private duty nursing from a nurse's point of view. *American Journal of Nursing, 1*(2), 129.

INQRI. (n.d.). *Program overview. The Interdisciplinary Nursing Quality Research Initiative.* Retrieved from http://www.inqri.org/about-inqri/program-overview.

Jamieson, E. M., & Sewall, M. F. (1949). *Trends in nursing history.* Philadelphia: Saunders.

Kalisch, P. A., & Kalisch, B. J. (1986). *The advance of American nursing.* Boston: Little, Brown and Company.

Kelly, L. Y. (1975). *Dimensions of professional nursing* (3rd ed.). New York: Macmillan.

Leininger, M. (1984). *Care: The essence of nursing and health.* Thorofare, NJ: Charles B. Slack.

Maness, P. F. (2006). Introducing the new voice of nurses. *American Nurse Today, 1*(1). Retrieved from https://americannursetoday.com/introducing-the-new-voice-of-nurses/.

Meehan, T. C. (2013). History and nursing knowledge. *Nursing History Review, 21,* 10–13.

McCloskey, J., & Grace, H. K. (2001). *Current issues in nursing* (6th ed.). St. Louis: Mosby.

Miller, B. K., Mansen, T. J., & Lee, H. (1983). Patient advocacy: Do nurses have the power and authority to act as patient advocate? *Nursing Leadership, 6*(2), 56–60.

Montag, M. L. (1951). *The education of nursing technicians.* New York: GP Putnam's Sons.

National League for Nursing (NLN). (2014). *Number of Basic RN Programs, Total and by Program Type: 2005 to 2014.* Retrieved from http://www.nln.org/docs/default-source/newsroom/nursing-education-statistics/number-of-basic-rn-programs-total-and-by-program-type-2005-to-2014.pdf?sfvrsn=0.

Naylor, M. D. (2011). *Viewpoint: Interprofessional collaboration and the future of healthcare.* Retrieved from http://www.americannursetoday.com/viewpoint-interprofessional-collaboration-and-the-future-of-health-care/.

Palmer, S. (1900). The editor. *American Journal of Nursing, 1*(4), 166–169.

Quint, G. C. (1967). Role models and the professional nurse identity. *Journal of Nursing Education, 6*(1).

Rode, M. W. (1989). The nursing pin: Symbol of 1000 years of service. *Nursing Forum, 24*(1), 15–17.

Rybczynski, W. (1986). *Home: A short history of an idea.* Middlesex, England: Penguin.

Seward, J. M. (1969). Role of the nurse: Perceptions of nursing students and auxiliary nursing personnel. *Nursing Research, 18*(2), 164–169.

Sovie, L. (1983). Nursing. In N. Chaska (Ed.), *The nursing profession.* New York: GP Putnam's Sons.

Stewart, I. M. (1950). A half-century of nursing education. *American Journal of Nursing*, p. 617.

Striepe, J. (1987). *Nurses in churches: A manual for developing parish nurse services and networks.* Spencer: Iowa Lake Area Agency on Aging.

Tourtillott, E. A. (1986). *Commitment—a lost characteristic.* New York: JB Lippincott.

Watson, J. (1985). *Nursing: Human science and human care—a theory of nursing.* East Norwalk, CT: Appleton-Century-Crofts.

Wisener, S. (1978). *The reality of primary nursing care: Risks, roles and research. Role changes in primary nursing.* New York: National League of Nursing.

Nursing Education

Gayle P. Varnell, PhD, MSN, RN, CPNP-PC

ⓔ http://evolve.elsevier.com/Zerwekh/nsgtoday/.

Education should not be a destination—but a path we travel all the days of our lives.
Anonymous
Unless we are making progress in our nursing every year, every month, every week, take my word for it we are going back.
Florence Nightingale

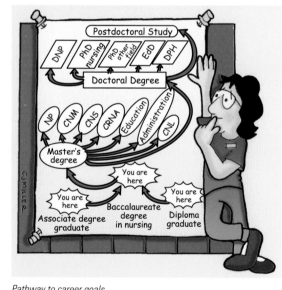

Pathway to career goals.

After completing this chapter, you should be able to:

- Compare the various types of educational preparation for nursing.
- Describe the educational preparation for a graduate degree.
- Compare nontraditional pathways of nursing education.
- Describe the purpose of nursing program accreditation.
- Set personal educational goals for yourself.

What an exciting time to be a nurse. Never before have the doors been so open for nurses to further their education. The Institute of Medicine (IOM) report, *The Future of Nursing: Leading Change, Advancing Health* (2010), set forth recommendations that would change the future of nursing and nursing education in ways never dreamed possible. Recommendation 4 discussed increasing the number of nurses with baccalaureate degrees to 80% by the year 2020, whereas Recommendation 5 proposed to double the number of nurses with doctorate degrees by 2020. Recommendation 6 explained the need for nurses to engage in lifelong learning. Based on these three recommendations alone, educational systems across the country began diligently brainstorming and working collaboratively to address these goals.

A Joint Statement on Academic Progression for Nursing Students and Graduates (2012) was made by the Tri-Council for Nursing policy (2010) and endorsed by both community college–registered and university-registered nursing programs with the understanding that both student nurses and practicing nurses need to be encouraged and supported to achieve higher levels of education (AACN, 2012a). What does all this mean to you as a nurse? It means that educational programs as well as employers throughout the country are striving to find ways to make it easier for nurses to further their education. More community colleges and universities are expanding their nursing programs to meet the needs for health care reform. Add to this the advancing computer technology that makes it easier to provide comparable education via distance learning and simulation, and you have an environment that beckons nurses to further their education. Whatever your basic nursing education program, you will now find it easier to advance in your profession. Instead of seeing roadblocks, you will see more doors and windows opened to allow you to advance your education. Are you ready for the challenge?

After struggling to complete your basic educational preparation for nursing, you are probably looking forward to that first paycheck as a registered nurse. The last thing on your mind is returning to school for more education! The purpose of this chapter is not to discuss the issue of entry into practice or to debate which educational program is best. Instead, the goal of this chapter is to help you look at where you are educationally and to offer direction regarding educational opportunities to enhance your career goals and to continue on the path of lifelong learning. Before looking down the path at the variety of educational offerings available to help you meet those goals, let us look at the variety of pathways that lead to the basic educational preparation for an RN.

Which path did you travel? There are three primary paths (diploma, associate's degree, and bachelor's degree) that lead to one licensing examination: the National Council Licensure Examination for Registered Nurses (NCLEX-RN® Examination). These programs usually require a high school diploma or the equivalent for admission. Some of the other paths include master's and doctoral nursing degree programs, both of which accept college graduates with liberal arts majors. Other paths are becoming more popular, including career ladder programs (from practical nurse to associate degree or baccalaureate degree nurse), concurrent enrollment program (from associate's degree to bachelor's degree), accelerated baccalaureate program for non-nursing college graduates, entry-level master's and doctorate programs, and community college–based BSN programs. Still another source for nursing education is the online option. Online programs are particularly popular for people who are place-bound and unable to travel to distant sites to obtain or continue their education. Some of these programs require brief visits to a campus, whereas others are completely online.

The distribution of the RN population according to basic nursing education is illustrated in Fig. 7.1. In 1980, the diploma education track was the highest level of education for most nursing graduates. Since 1996, there has been a continued increase in the number of RNs receiving their initial preparation in either an associate's degree or a baccalaureate program. The *National Workforce Survey of Registered Nurses* (2013) indicates that initial preparation in a diploma program accounted for 18%, the associate's degree accounted for 39%, and the baccalaureate degree program accounted for 36% of the registered nurses. Furthermore, it is estimated that 3% of RNs received their initial nursing education at either a master's or doctoral level (Budden et al., 2013, p.7).

PATH OF DIPLOMA EDUCATION

What Is the Educational Preparation of the Diploma Graduate?

The current preparation of a diploma nurse varies in length from 2 to 3 years and takes place in a hospital school of nursing. This type of program may be under the direction of the hospital or

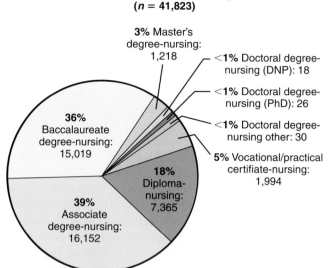

Type of Nursing Degree/Credential that Qualified Respondents for First U.S. Nursing License
(n = 41,823)

3% Master's degree-nursing: 1,218

<1% Doctoral degree-nursing (DNP): 18

<1% Doctoral degree-nursing (PhD): 26

<1% Doctoral degree-nursing other: 30

5% Vocational/practical certifiate-nursing: 1,994

36% Baccalaureate degree-nursing: 15,019

18% Diploma-nursing: 7,365

39% Associate degree-nursing: 16,152

FIG. 7.1 Type of nursing degree/credential that qualified respondents for first U.S. nursing license. (Adapted from Budden, J., Zhong, E., Moulton, P., & Cimioti, J. (2013). Highlights of the national workforce survey of registered nurses. *Journal of Nursing Regulation, 4*(2), 5–13.)

incorporated independently. The diploma program may include general education subjects such as biology and physical and social sciences, in addition to nursing theory and practice. Graduates of diploma programs are prepared to function as beginning practitioners in acute, intermediate, long-term, and ambulatory health care facilities. Because there is a close relationship between the nursing school and the hospital, graduates are well prepared to function in that institution. On graduation, many diploma graduates are employed by that same hospital and therefore may experience an easier role transition.

Standards and competencies for diploma programs are developed and maintained by the National League for Nursing (NLN) Council of Diploma Programs. Graduates of diploma programs are awarded a certificate and are eligible to take the NCLEX-RN® Examination for licensure.

PATH OF ASSOCIATE DEGREE EDUCATION

What Is the Educational Preparation of the Associate Degree Graduate?

The current preparation of an associate degree nurse usually begins in a community college, although some programs are based in senior colleges or universities. The associate degree program lasts 18 to 21 school calendar months. The NLN recommends that associate degree nursing programs consist of 60 to 72 semester credits (90 to 108 quarter credits) and that there is a balanced distribution of no more than 60% of the total number of credits allocated to nursing courses (NLN, 2001). In some programs, the student must complete the general education and science course requirements before beginning the nursing courses. At the end of the program, the student receives an associate's degree in nursing (ADN) or Associate in Applied Science (ASN or AAS).

Associate degree nursing education has helped to bring about a change in the type of student who enrolls in nursing programs. Before the emergence of associate degree nursing programs, nursing students were traditionally single white females younger than 19 years of age who came from middle-class families (Kaiser, 1975). Associate degree programs attract a more diverse student population that includes older individuals, minorities, men, and married women from a variety of educational and economic backgrounds. Many of these individuals have baccalaureate and higher degrees in other fields of study and are seeking a second career. Along with their maturity, these students bring life experiences that are applicable to nursing. The students tend to be more goal oriented and have a more realistic perspective of the work setting. The community college curriculum is conducive to students who want to attend school on a part-time basis. Graduates of associate degree programs are eligible to take the NCLEX-RN® examination for licensure.

Dr. Montag's (1951, 1959) original proposal for the associate degree program to be a terminal degree is no longer applicable. In 1978, the American Nurses Association proposed a resolution regarding associate degree programs that recommended they be viewed as part of the career upward-mobility plan rather than as terminal programs. Recommendation 4 of the recent IOM report, proposing to increase to 80% by 2020 the proportion of nurses with BSN degrees, further supports the need for ADNs to consider advancing their educations (IOM, 2010). The associate degree program has provided students with the motivation to further their education and the opportunity for career mobility. Although many nursing students end their education with an associate's degree, many others enter the associate degree program with every intention of continuing their nursing education to the baccalaureate level or even further.

PATH OF BACCALAUREATE EDUCATION

In this discussion, only the "generic" baccalaureate programs are addressed. A generic student is one who enters a baccalaureate nursing program with no training or education in nursing. A traditional generic baccalaureate program includes lower-division (freshman and sophomore) liberal arts and science courses with upper-division (junior and senior) nursing courses. RNs entering baccalaureate programs are discussed later in this chapter.

What Is the Educational Preparation of the Baccalaureate Graduate?

The current preparation of a baccalaureate nurse is 4 to 5 years in length (120 to 140 credits) and emphasizes courses in the liberal arts, sciences, and humanities. Approximately one-half to two-thirds of the curriculum consists of non-nursing courses. To qualify for a baccalaureate program, the student must first meet all of the college's or the university's entrance requirements. Usual entrance requirements include college preparation courses in high school (e.g., foreign language, advanced science, and math courses) and a specified cumulative grade-point average (GPA). Most colleges also require a college entrance examination such as the Scholastic Aptitude Test (SAT) or the American College Test (ACT).

During the first 2 years of a traditional baccalaureate nursing program, the student is usually enrolled in liberal arts and science courses with other non-nursing students. It is usually not until late in a student's sophomore or early junior year that nursing courses are introduced. However, some baccalaureate programs incorporate nursing courses throughout the 4-year nursing curriculum. The emphasis in the baccalaureate nursing program is on developing critical decision-making skills, exercising independent nursing judgment, and acquiring research skills.

The graduate of a baccalaureate program must fulfill both the degree requirements of the nursing program and those of the college. On completion of the program, the usual degree awarded is a Bachelor of Science in Nursing (BSN).

The graduate of a baccalaureate program is prepared to provide health promotion and health restoration care for individuals, families, and groups in a variety of institutional and community settings. Graduates of baccalaureate nursing programs are eligible to take the NCLEX-RN® examination for licensure. BSN graduates are also prepared to continue their education by moving directly into graduate education. An increasing number of BSN graduates are continuing their nursing education by going directly into graduate programs.

OTHER TYPES OF NURSING EDUCATION

What Are the Other Available Educational Options?

In the 1960s, baccalaureate programs made it very difficult for the RN to return to school to earn a baccalaureate in nursing. Most of the time, these nurses found themselves receiving no credit for their past education or experience. A resolution was passed in 1978 by the American Nurses Association (ANA) that helped to change this philosophy. This resolution urged the creation of quality career-mobility programs with flexibility to assist individuals desiring academic degrees in nursing. Following the IOM report, developers of nursing educational programs have been challenged to rethink nursing education. The Tri-Council's 2010 statement for access to nursing education for all nurses, providing for a seamless academic progression (AACN, 2012a), has further widened the pathways toward advanced education. It is anticipated that nursing education will be transformed to create a health care workforce that is better prepared in ways that can only be imagined at this time.

Besides the traditional pathways for entering the nursing profession such as diploma, associate degree, and baccalaureate programs, new pathways are emerging. Entry-level master's programs, accelerated programs for non-nursing graduates, community college–based baccalaureate programs, and registered nurse degree completion programs for licensed practical nurses and other health care providers are a few of the many options, and it is anticipated that there may be others in the near future.

Just as there are new pathways to enter the nursing profession, there are also new pathways for those nurses who are interested in advancing their nursing education including baccalaureate to doctoral programs, master's degrees for advanced generalist roles, such as the clinical nurse leader (CNL), as well as the Doctor of Nursing Practice (DNP).

It truly is an exciting time to be in nursing, and there is no one right career pathway for everyone. Each person needs to consider what his or her professional end goal is and what works best for him or her. Is an online program that provides more flexibility in scheduling for family and work obligations the best choice or perhaps a blended or hybrid program? Is the program respected in the nursing community and known for producing great nurse educators, researchers, or advanced practice nurses? Is it an accredited program? Will course work transfer? It is important to ask yourself what you are willing to invest in your education besides the time and monetary expenses.

In assessing the available educational options, one source of information is the American Association of Colleges of Nursing (AACN) website (http://www.aacn.nche.edu/students). There is a section for students that includes information on nursing careers, financial aid, scholarships, and nursing programs. Potential students should also contact individual schools for information regarding their particular programs. After you are ready to begin the application process, you will also find that the Nursing Centralized Application Service (CAS) has simplified the process by providing a service for students to use to apply to nursing programs at participating schools nationwide (http://www.aacn.nche.edu/nursingcas). At the end of this chapter is a complete list of additional relevant websites and online resources for advancing your nursing education.

The career ladder or bridge concept focuses on the articulation of educational programs to permit advanced placement without loss of credit or repetition. There are many variations on this type of program. Multiple-exit programs provide opportunities for students to exit and reenter the educational system at various designated times, having gained specific education and skills. An example is a program that ranges from practical nurse to RN at the associate's, baccalaureate, master's, and doctoral levels. A student in such a program may decide to leave the educational system at the completion of a specific level and be eligible to take the licensure examination applicable to that educational level. On termination, the student may choose to work for a while and later return for more education at the next level without having to repeat courses on previously acquired knowledge or skills. Information on the three types of articulation agreements—individual, mandated, and statewide—can be found on the AACN website. Growing numbers of basic nursing education programs within the community college setting are beginning to offer career ladder programs and concurrent enrollment programs, affiliating themselves with upper-division colleges in the area. A student can enter the community college to spend 1 year studying to become a practical or vocational nurse. After a year, the student can decide to stop and take the practical nurse licensure examination or continue and complete the associate's degree in nursing. At the end of the second year, the student is eligible to take the RN licensure examination and may choose either to exit with an associate's degree or to attend an affiliated upper-division college to obtain a bachelor's degree (Fig. 7.2).

What Is a BSN/MSN Completion Program?

A BSN-completion program is a baccalaureate program designed for students who already possess either a diploma or an associate's degree in nursing and hold a current license to practice as an RN. Depending on the part of the country, these programs may also be known as RN baccalaureate (RNB) programs, RN/BSN programs, baccalaureate RN (BRN) programs, two-plus-two programs, or capstone programs. There are more than 679 BSN-completion programs. In addition to the BSN-completion programs, 209 RN-to-master's degree program options are available, and there are 28 additional nursing schools planning to implement a BSN and 31 planning to implement an MSN completion program in the near future (AACN, 2015c). In most of these programs, nurses receive transfer credit in basic education courses taken at other institutions plus either some transfer credit for their previous nursing courses or the opportunity to receive nursing credit by passing a nursing challenge examination.

The usual length of such programs is 1 to 3 years, depending on the number of course requirements completed at the time of admission to the program. To meet the needs of the returning student, many BSN-completion programs offer flexible class scheduling, which allows the student to continue working while going to school. Another innovation being implemented to address the needs of individuals seeking baccalaureate degrees in outlying geographic areas is telecommunication-assisted studies and Internet courses. More than 400 programs have part of their curriculum online, whereas an increasing number of programs are available completely online (AACN, 2015c).

What Is an External Degree Program?

In the early 1970s, the external degree program was a nontraditional program that allowed a student to gain credit, meet external degree requirements, and obtain a degree from a degree-granting institution without attending face-to-face classes. One of the earliest external degree (or distance education) programs was offered through the New York Board of Regents external degree programs (REX), which is now Excelsior College. External degree programs may offer an ADN as well as a BSN and a master

FIG. 7.2 What are other available education programs?

of science in nursing (MSN). These programs are designed to allow individuals to obtain degrees in nursing without leaving their jobs or their communities.

Nursing education online is a rapidly expanding part of the Internet. In the past these programs were called external degree or distance education; however, more commonly now the programs are considered nursing online education. Online nursing programs are accredited either by the Accreditation Commission for Education in Nursing (ACEN) (formerly the National League for Nursing Accrediting Commission [NLNAC]), National League for Nursing Commission for Nursing

Education Accreditation (CNEA), or by the Commission on Collegiate Nursing Education (CCNE), which is an autonomous accrediting agency associated with the AACN. In the undergraduate nursing programs, all students are required to pass specific college-level tests and performance examinations in two components: general education and nursing. On completion of the undergraduate external degree programs, students are eligible in most states to take the RN licensure exam. One of the largest CCNE-approved programs for BSN completion and graduate education is the University of Phoenix online campus.

Online (Web-Based) Programs

More and more traditional colleges and universities are offering courses and even entire programs through the Internet. In fact, it is possible to earn ADN, BSN, master's, and doctoral degrees in web-based or web-enhanced formats. At times, it can be confusing and overwhelming to find the right programs. Several sites are available to help users locate specific web-based or web-enhanced courses (and course descriptions). See the Internet resources listed on this book's *Evolve* website. It is important to take into consideration the cost not only of an online program but also of out-of-state tuition when considering which program is the best fit for your career goals.

Proprietary Nursing Schools

In addition to the colleges and universities that are offering these types of courses, an influx of new proprietary nursing programs has emerged. A proprietary nursing school is a for-profit school with a nursing program. Many proprietary schools have nursing programs in more than one state. Since not all nursing boards have the same requirements for licensure, it is important to review the requirements in your state to make sure that you will be eligible for licensure once you complete the program. A prospective student should also make sure that the program is accredited and ask about the pass rates on the NCLEX examination for their graduates.

What Is an Accelerated Program?

Accelerated programs are offered at both the baccalaureate and master's degree levels; they are designed to build on previous learning to help a person with an undergraduate degree in another discipline make the transition into nursing. In 2013, there were 293 accelerated baccalaureate programs and 62 accelerated master's programs available at nursing schools nationwide. In addition, 13 new accelerated baccalaureate programs are in the planning stages, and 9 new accelerated master's programs are also taking shape (AACN, 2015b).

NONTRADITIONAL PATHS FOR NURSING EDUCATION

What About a Master's Degree as a Path to Becoming an RN?

MSN programs are particularly attractive to the growing number of college graduates who decide later in life to enter nursing. Generally, the program is 24 to 36 months long. Upon graduation these students are expected to demonstrate the same entry-level competencies in nursing as baccalaureate graduates. MSN graduates from these programs are then eligible to take the NCLEX-RN® examination. Currently, there are 62 entry-level master's programs in the United States (AACN, 2015b).

What About a Doctoral Path to Becoming an RN?

The last and least common path leading to the RN licensure examination is the doctoral degree, where the graduate has a non-nursing baccalaureate degree. This program began in 1979 at Case Western Reserve University in Cleveland, Ohio. Rush University in Chicago initiated a similar program in

1988, and the University of Colorado began one in 1990 (Forni, 1989). These programs, such as the one at the University of Texas at Austin, provide basic nursing courses, along with advanced nursing courses. Upon completion, the graduate is eligible to take the NCLEX-RN® examination. There are currently 81 baccalaureate to research-focused doctoral programs (PhD) and 153 practice-focused baccalaureate to doctoral programs (DNP) (AACN, 2014a).

GRADUATE EDUCATION

What About Graduate School?

Whatever path you chose to become an RN, one thing was certain: It was not easy! After putting life, liberty, and the pursuit of happiness on hold while you worked toward becoming an RN, it may seem like pure insanity to subject yourself to more education!

Graduate nursing education, like other graduate programs, is responding to changes in social values, priorities in the public sector, and student demographics, in addition to technological advances, knowledge development, and maturity of the profession. According to the 2013 *National Nursing Workforce Survey of Registered Nurses* (NCSBN, 2013), there is an increase in the percentage of nurses who indicate a BSN as their initial education. Approximately 36% reported their initial education as BSN, while 3% reported their initial education as a graduate degree. After initial licensure, 24% of the nurses went on to receive advanced formal education (NCSBN, 2013), indicating that RNs in the workforce are recognizing the need for additional education and are returning to college to further their education either in nursing or nursing-related fields such as public health and health care administration.

Graduate education programs are available on either a part-time or a full-time basis. Graduate programs require a good GPA at the undergraduate level. Prerequisites for most graduate programs are satisfactory scores on the Graduate Record Examination (GRE) or the Miller Analogies Test (MAT). Although an increasing number of graduate programs are waiving the entrance examination requirements, it is strongly recommended that all students, whether they plan to pursue graduate studies or not, take the GRE after completing their undergraduate studies. Taking another test may be the last thing you want to do, but it is much easier to do it now, while the information is current in your mind, than later when you decide that you want to continue your education.

Why Would I Want a Master's Degree?

You've got to be kidding! More school?

Sure, an advanced degree may not be in your career plans right now, but later, after you have been practicing nursing, you may change your mind. Policy statements from the nursing profession reflect the need for more education in preparation for the changing role of nursing, a result of health care reform. As care delivery moves increasingly from the acute care center to the community setting, there will be an increased need for advanced clinical practice nurses. Nursing programs are already responding to this changing need.

Master's nursing programs vary from institution to institution, as do the admission and course requirements and costs. The master of science (MS) and the master of science in nursing (MSN) are the most common degrees. The usual requirements for admission include a baccalaureate degree from an ACEN, CCNE, or Commission on Nursing Education Accreditation (CNEA, the accrediting body of the NLN since 2013) accredited program in nursing, licensure as a registered nurse, completion of the GRE or MAT, and a minimum undergraduate GPA of 3.0.

The majority of programs are at least 18 to 24 months of full-time study. Unlike undergraduate students, master's students usually choose an area of role preparation, such as education or administration, as well as an area of clinical specialization, such as pediatrics or adult health. Some of the more common areas of role preparation include education, administration, case management, health policy/health care systems, informatics, and the increasingly popular advanced clinical practice roles.

An evolving area of role preparation is that of the clinical nurse leader (CNL). The CNL role is different from the role of manager or administrator. The CNL is prepared at the master's level as a generalist managing the health care delivery system across all settings. Any person interested in the CNL role is encouraged to read the *Competencies and Curricular Expectations for Clinical Nurse Leader Education and Practice* (AACN, 2013) found on the AACN website. Upon completion of a formal CNL program, a graduate is eligible to take the CNL Certification Examination. In Fall 2014/ Winter 2015, 109 of 229 nurses taking the CNL certification exam passed, for a pass rate of 68% (AACN, 2015a).

Areas of specialty within the master's nurse practitioner programs include family, acute care, pediatric, psychiatric, and adult-gerontology nursing practice. There are more family nurse practitioner programs than any other program. The AACN supported the position of the practice doctorate (DNP) as the entry level for the advanced practice registered nurse (APRN) by the year 2015 (AACN, 2015d). Although there is a growing number of DNP programs, less than 25% of the schools with nurse practitioner programs have met this goal (Martsolf et al., 2015). An excellent resource for nurses who are considering becoming an APRN can be found at the American Association of Nurse Practitioners website http://www.aanp.org/education/student-resource-center/planning-your-np-education.

The National Council of State Boards of Nursing APRN Advisory Committee and leading professional nursing organizations formed an APRN Consensus Work Group to work toward establishing clear expectations for LACE (**l**icensure, **a**ccreditation, **c**ertification, and **e**ducation) for APRNs. This work group has been meeting for several years, and in July 2008 the landmark document, *Consensus Model for APRN Regulation: Licensure, Accreditation, Certification, & Education,* was finalized. This document will be used to shape the future of APRN practice across the nation and to allow APRNs to practice to the full extent of their education. APRNs will be educated in one of the four roles, certified registered nurse anesthetist (CRNA), certified nurse-midwife (CNM), clinical nurse specialist (CNS), or certified nurse practitioner (CNP), and in at least one of six population foci: family/individual across the lifespan, neonatal, pediatrics, adult-gerontology, women's health/gender-related, or psych/ mental health. All four of these roles will be given the title of advanced practice registered nurse (APRN). It is important for all potential APRNs to read this document, because it will change how APRNs are educated in the future (www.aacn.nche.edu/education-resources/APRNReport.pdf). See Table 7.1 for typical educational preparation and responsibilities of various advanced practice nurses.

According to *The U.S. Nursing Workforce: Trends in Supply and Education* report (2013), there has been a rapid growth of 69% in the number of nurse practitioner graduates from 7261 in 2001 to 12,273 in 2011. During that same time period, there also was a 111.1% increase in CRNAs from 1159 to 2447 graduates, although CNMs have not experienced as much of an increase from 285 in 2007 to nearly 400 in 2011.

In the more traditional master's degree programs, the student takes the courses required for the degree and then, depending on institutional requirements, may also be required to take a written or oral comprehensive examination or write a thesis, or both. There are also nontraditional models that include outreach programs, summers-only programs, and programs for RNs who have bachelor's degrees in other fields.

Advances in technology have also made it possible for graduate programs to become more creative in the way courses are being offered. It is now possible for students to obtain all or part of their course

TABLE 7.1   ADVANCED PRACTICE NURSING

	EDUCATION	WHAT THEY DO
Nurse practitioner (NP)	Most of the approximately 350 NP education programs in the United States today confer a master's degree. In the future, the DNP will be the entry level for an NP. The majority of states require NPs to be nationally certified by ANCC, ACNP, or a specialty nursing organization. In 2014, more than 205,000 of advanced practice nurses were NPs.	Working in clinics, nursing homes, hospitals, HMOs, private industry or their own offices, NPs are qualified to handle a wide range of basic health problems. Most have a specialty—for example, an adult, family, or pediatric health care degree. At minimum, NPs conduct physical examinations, take medical histories, diagnose and treat common acute minor illnesses or injuries, order and interpret laboratory tests and radiographs, and counsel and educate patients. In all states they may prescribe medication according to state law. Some work as independent practitioners and can be reimbursed by Medicare or Medicaid for services rendered.
Certified nurse-midwife (CNM)	An average 1.5 years of specialized education beyond nursing school, either in an accredited certificate program or at the master's level. In 2015, there were an estimated 11,018 nurses prepared as CNMs in the United States (ACNM, 2015).	CNMs are well known for delivering babies in hospitals, homes, well-woman gynecological and low-risk obstetrical care, including prenatal, labor and delivery, and postpartum care. The CNM manages women's health care throughout the lifespan, including primary care, gynecological exams, and family planning. CNMs have prescriptive authority in all 50 states.
Clinical nurse specialist (CNS)	CNSs are registered nurses with advanced nursing degrees—master's or doctoral—who are experts in a specialized area of clinical practice such as psychiatric/mental health, adult/gerontology, pediatric, women's health, and neonatal health. There are approximately 72,000 CNSs in the United States (NACNS, 2014).	Most CNSs work in the hospital setting, full time, and have responsibility for more than one department. CNSs can also work in clinics, nursing homes, their own offices, and other community-based settings, such as industry, home care, and HMOs. They conduct health assessments, make diagnoses, deliver treatment, lead evidence-based practice projects, and develop quality-control methods. In addition to delivering direct patient care, CNSs work in consultation, research, education, and administration. Some work independently or in private practice and receive reimbursement. Based on state laws where the CNS practices, CNSs are authorized to prescribed medications (NACNS, 2014).
Certified registered nurse anesthetist (CRNA)	CRNAs are registered nurses who complete a graduate program and meet national certification and recertification requirements. There are an estimated 39,410 CRNAs in the United States (Bureau of Labor Statistics, 2015).	In this oldest of the advanced nursing specialties, CRNAs safely administer approximately 40 million anesthetics to patients each year in the United States. In some states, CRNAs are the sole anesthesia providers in rural hospitals (AANA, 2015). This enables health care facilities to provide obstetrical, surgical, and trauma stabilization services. CRNAs provide anesthetics to patients in collaboration with surgeons, anesthesiologists, dentists, podiatrists, and other qualified health care professionals.

offerings by means of the Internet, distance learning, computer-based programs, and teleconferencing. This flexibility makes it easier for students in rural communities and part-time students to obtain advanced degrees.

How Do I Know Which Master's Degree Program Is Right for Me?

Your career goals and interests will help you to determine which choice is best for you. Do some reading on your area of special interest and find out how advanced education would help you to obtain your career goals. As an example, in most nursing programs, a nurse with a non-nursing master's degree would need to complete a master's in nursing to become an advanced practice nurse. If you think that you might want to become a nurse practitioner at some point in your life, be sure that you obtain your master's in nursing. You can always go back and obtain a post-master's certificate as a nurse practitioner. If your master's degree is in another field, this may not be possible, as most programs require a master's in nursing. Although the movement to change the entry level for an APRN to a DNP by the year 2015 did not materialize, it is important to note that this may be a reality in the future, and you might want to consider this as you set your educational goals.

After you have decided on a master's degree, there are several resources available online, such as the *Peterson's Guide* (www.petersons.com), to help you find the right school. Consider all the options, and do your homework. If you are considering an advanced practice degree, be sure to check with the Board of Nursing for the state in which you reside to see what the requirements are to be recognized as an APRN in your state. Believe it or not, the requirements are *not* the same for every state. After all, if you are going to expend the time, energy, and finances to obtain a graduate degree, you want to get the most from it.

Why Would I Want a Doctoral Degree?

Power, authority, and professional status are usually associated with a doctoral degree. Nurses with doctoral degrees provide leadership in the improvement of nursing practice and in the development of research and nursing education programs. It is no secret that the role of the nurse is changing and will continue to change as health care reform continues to be implemented. There is a growing need for administrators, policy analysts, clinical researchers, and clinical practitioners in the community and in governmental agencies. Nurses need to position themselves to take on these new leadership roles, and the way to do this is through advanced education, particularly at the doctoral level.

Until recently, there were two basic models of doctoral education in nursing: the academic degree, or Doctor of Philosophy (PhD), and the professional degree, or Doctor of Nursing Science (DNS, DSN, or DNSc). For either of these degrees, you must first have a master's in nursing. Nurses have other doctoral degree options available to them, such as the Doctor of Education (EdD), the Doctor of Public Health (DrPH), the Doctor of Philosophy (PhD) in a discipline other than nursing, the nontraditional external degree doctorate, and the practice-focused Nurse Doctorate (ND), which was initiated as an entry-level degree.

In October 2004, the AACN published a position statement on the practice doctorate in nursing (DNP). The term *practice doctorate* would be used instead of *clinical doctorate*, and the ND degree would be phased out. The DNP would become the educational preparation for all advanced practice nurses. This move toward a DNP is to take place throughout a 15-year period. There are currently 243 DNP programs with more than 70 additional nursing schools that are considering starting a DNP program (AACN, 2014a).

How Do I Know Which Doctoral Program Is Right for Me?

As with the master's degree, it is important to look at your career goals before deciding which doctoral program is best for you. To help you with that task, look at the NLN and AACN publications specific to doctoral education. Ask yourself how much time you can devote to obtaining a doctorate degree. Can you be a full-time student, or must you continue to work? What do you plan to do with the degree after you obtain it?

Is there an institution available to you that offers a doctorate in nursing, or would you have to consider moving? What are your career and professional goals? Do you want to teach? The PhD is considered the research-focused degree. It prepares an individual for a lifetime of intellectual inquiry and has an increased emphasis on postdoctoral study. In contrast, the DNP is viewed as the practice-focused degree. The goal of this program is to prepare an advanced practitioner for the application of knowledge with an emphasis on research. The original intent of the DNS was to prepare nurses to perform clinical research. The August 2015 Report from the *Task Force on the Implementation of the DNP* (AACN) is an excellent resource for those considering a DNP.

At the end of this chapter are additional relevant websites and online resources for continuing your nursing education.

CREDENTIALING: LICENSURE AND CERTIFICATION

What Is Credentialing?

In the early days of nursing before the Nightingale era, anyone could claim to be a nurse and practice the "trade" as he or she wished. It was only during the past century that nursing became a credentialed profession. A credential can be as simple as a written document showing an individual's qualifications. A high school diploma is a credential that indicates a certain level of education has been attained. A credential can also signify a person's performance. The attainment of a title—such as Fellow of the American Academy of Nursing (FAAN)—signifies excellence in performance; a postgraduate degree from an institution of higher learning (PhD or EdD) indicates success in terms of academic achievement and advanced nursing knowledge.

In nursing, the educational credentials that an individual holds indicate not only academic achievement but also the attainment of a minimum level of competency in nursing skills. An ADN, a diploma in nursing, or a baccalaureate degree in nursing (BSN or BS) represents academic achievement. After academic preparation and successful completion of the NCLEX, you will have a legal credential—your nursing license—that permits you to practice as an RN. Additional nursing credentials may reflect practice in special areas, such as Critical Care Registered Nurse (CCRN) and Certified Addictions Registered Nurse (CARN).

What Are Registration and Licensure?

Licensure affords protection to the public by requiring an individual to demonstrate minimum competency by examination before practicing certain trades. By 1923, 48 states (Alaska and Hawaii did not become states until much later) had some form of nursing licensure in place. Nursing licensure is a process by which a governmental agency grants "legal" permission to an individual to practice nursing. This accountability is maintained through state boards of nursing, which are responsible for the licensing and registration process. Boards of nursing vary in structure and are based on the design of the nurse practice act within each state. State boards of nursing also exercise legal control over schools of nursing within their respective states. In 1978, all boards of nursing formed a national council, the

National Council of State Boards of Nursing (NCSBN), to present a more collective front on nursing education and licensure.

Foreign nurse graduates who want to practice nursing in the United States must contact the board of nursing in the state in which they want to practice to obtain licensure, because each state controls its own requirements for licensure. The state's board of nursing will review the candidate's nursing education and determine requirements needed to obtain a license in that respective state. Most states require that foreign nurses take the Committee on Graduates of Foreign Nursing Schools (CGFNS) examination before the NCLEX-RN® examination. This examination determines proficiency both in nursing and the English language, thus assisting in the prediction of success on the NCLEX-RN® examination. All foreign graduates, regardless of licensure in their home countries, must successfully complete the NCLEX-RN® examination.

What Is Certification?

In the classic article on credentialing published by the ANA in the late 1970s, certification is defined as a "voluntary process by which a nongovernmental agency or association certifies that an individual licensed to practice a profession has certain predetermined standards specified by that profession for specialty practice" (ANA, 1979, p. 67). Certification is a different credential from licensure and has a variety of interpretations—both for the nursing profession and the public.

The movement toward certification in nursing practice areas has grown significantly within the past 40 years. In 1946, credentialing was first required for entry into practice as a nurse anesthetist (i.e., CRNA). Twenty-five years later, nurse-midwives followed suit, needing certification through the American College of Nurse Midwives as an entry-level credential.

> The nursing license is recognized as indicating minimum competency, whereas the certification credential indicates preparation beyond the minimum level.

Since the establishment of the first certification program by the ANA in 1973, certification is the credential that provides recognition of professional achievement in a defined functional or clinical area of nursing practice. Credentials, such as professional certification, are the stamps of quality and achievement to communicate professional competence. The process of becoming certified engages a full circle of accountability to patients and families, along with professional colleagues. There are over 33 areas of specialty certification available from the ANCC (2014). In addition, magnet hospitals are more likely to have nurses that are specialty certified (McHugh et al., 2013).

What Is Accreditation?

The term *accreditation* is often confused with certification. The term is defined as "a process by which a voluntary, nongovernmental agency or organization approves and grants status to institutions or programs (not individuals) that meet predetermined standards or outcomes." The accreditation of nursing programs by either the Accreditation Commission for Education in Nursing (ACEN) or the Commission on Collegiate Nursing Education (CCNE) is an activity that you, the recent graduate, may have been involved with during your nursing education.

Accreditation is a peer-review and voluntary process. Member schools for the peer-review evaluation process support the use of standards and criteria. The process of accreditation is similar for both accrediting organizations—the CCNE and the ACEN. The National League for Nursing Commission for Nursing Education Accreditation (CNEA) is a newly formed accrediting body that will begin the process of accrediting all types of nursing programs (PN/VN, diploma, associate's, bachelor's, master's, post-master's certificate, and clinical doctorate [DNP]) in 2016. The process of accreditation for NLN CNEA is similar to CCNE and ACEN.

Why should you be concerned whether the nursing program you are attending, or thinking about attending, is accredited? Accreditation assures you, the student, and the public that the program has achieved educational standards over and above the legal requirements of the state. It guarantees the student the opportunity to obtain a quality education. Accreditation is strictly a voluntary process. The U.S. Department of Education approves the professional association that is allowed to accredit nursing schools. Until 1997, the National League of Nursing (NLN) was the only accrediting body for nursing programs. In 1997 the National League for Nursing Accrediting Commission (NLNAC) was established, and responsibility for all accrediting activities was transferred to this new independent subsidiary. In 2013 the name was changed to ACEN.

Some graduate nursing programs require completion of an ACEN or CCNE-approved undergraduate program as a prerequisite for admission to their master's or doctoral program. Both the ACEN and CCNE publish annually an official complete list of accredited programs. Accreditation becomes a major concern as more and more courses and programs are offered by means of distance learning.

With different organizations offering accreditation to schools of nursing, it was difficult for schools of nursing to develop competency statements that were consistent. Rather than listing competency statements for three levels of nursing, the competency statement accepted by the 1996 annual meeting of the NCSBN is presented. According to the NCSBN, "Competence is defined as the application of knowledge and the interpersonal, decision-making and psychomotor skills expected for the practice role, within the context of public health, safety and welfare" (NCSBN, 1996, p 47). The NCSBN continues to work on the concept of continued competence as it explores its regulatory role.

> Boards of nursing cannot go it alone. This has to be a collaborative effort. Nurses, employers, educators, nursing organizations, CE providers, consumers, and boards of nursing are all stakeholders and have perspectives to share and expertise to offer. Stakeholder buy-in to any regulatory model is important. But the bottom line is that only governmental licensing boards have the authority to enforce change (NCSBN, 2005).

The promotion of competency requires a collaborative approach; it involves the individual nurse, employers of nurses, nursing educators, and the regulating board of nursing. The roles of each of these in competence accountability are described in Fig. 7.3.

NURSING EDUCATION: FUTURE TRENDS

Education is a lifelong process and an empowering force that enables an individual to achieve higher goals. Student access to educational opportunities is paramount to nursing education. A chapter on nursing education would not be complete without taking a look at the future.

The Changing Student Profile

Future nursing programs will need to be flexible to meet the learning needs of a changing student population. It has previously been stated that there is a growing population of nontraditional students—individuals who are making midlife career changes in part because of job displacement or job dissatisfaction. The student population tends to be older, married, and with families. Minority individuals, foreign students, and the poor are looking toward nursing education for career opportunities. There are a growing number of students choosing to attend school part time.

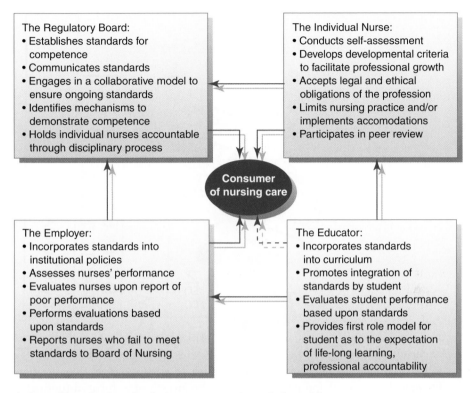

The Regulatory Board:
- Establishes standards for competence
- Communicates standards
- Engages in a collaborative model to ensure ongoing standards
- Identifies mechanisms to demonstrate competence
- Holds individual nurses accountable through disciplinary process

The Individual Nurse:
- Conducts self-assessment
- Develops developmental criteria to facilitate professional growth
- Accepts legal and ethical obligations of the profession
- Limits nursing practice and/or implements accomodations
- Participates in peer review

Consumer of nursing care

The Employer:
- Incorporates standards into institutional policies
- Assesses nurses' performance
- Evaluates nurses upon report of poor performance
- Performs evaluations based upon standards
- Reports nurses who fail to meet standards to Board of Nursing

The Educator:
- Incorporates standards into curriculum
- Promotes integration of standards by student
- Evaluates student performance based upon standards
- Provides first role model for student as to the expectation of life-long learning, professional accountability

Actions of boards of nursing that ensure competence to the public:
1. Establish competence requirements for safe and effective practice.
2. Communicate standards to the consumers, nurses, nursing educators, employers, and other regulators.
3. Hold individual nurses accountable for continued competence.
4. Engage in collaborative activities with nurses, educators, employers, and consumers to ensure nurses practice safely and effectively.
5. Identify a variety of techniques nurses may use to demonstrate competence.
6. Discipline nurses who fail to meet standards for safe and effective practice.
7. Inform the public of disciplinary actions taken against nurses.
8. Establish nondisciplinary model to monitor and/or limit the practice of nurses who demonstrate an inability to carry out essential nursing role functions.

FIG. 7.3 Competence accountability. (From National Council of State Boards of Nursing (1996). Annual meeting. In *Book of reports,* Chicago: National Council of State Boards of Nursing, p 51.)

These changes mean that nurse educators will have to address even further the needs of the adult learner. More programs will be needed that permit part-time study and allow students to work while attending school. One option may be for more night or weekend course offerings. There will continue to be a need for emphasis on remedial education such as developmental courses in math, English, and English as a second language. The diversity in the student population means diversity in learning rates, which may be addressed with more self-paced learning modules (Fig. 7.4).

Educational Mobility

Educational mobility will also need to be addressed further. A growing number of individuals in health care are seeking more education. The issue is not one of entry into practice but rather of how

FIG. 7.4 The changing student profile.

to best facilitate the return of these individuals to nursing school for educational advancement that fits their professional and personal needs. The growth of web-based (online) courses may facilitate educational mobility.

A Shortage of Registered Nurses

According to the Health Resources and Services Administration (HRSA, 2014), there are approximately 2.9 million nurses employed in 2012, and it is projected that the number will increase to 3.8 million by 2025, which is a 33% increase nationally. Although these projections indicate that there will not be a nursing shortage nationwide, it is predicted that 16 states (10 states in the west, 4 in the south, and 2 in the northeast) will still be experiencing a nursing shortage. Even though these projections seem very positive, factors such as early retirement or increased demand may nullify any positive gains.

A Shortage of Qualified Nursing Faculty

Data on the nursing faculty shortage reported by the AACN in their *2015-2016 Salaries of Instructional and Administrative Nursing Faculty in Baccalaureate and Graduate Programs in Nursing* (2016) indicate that the "average ages of doctorally prepared faculty holding the ranks of professor, associate professor, and assistant professor were 62, 57, and 51 years, respectively." There are fewer nurses entering the profession who are choosing a teaching role. Because of decreased numbers of new teachers, along with the number of current faculty retiring, the number of qualified faculty will continue to decline.

The ability to earn more in the clinical and private sector is also attracting potential nurse educators to leave academia (AACN, 2015e). The American Academy of Nurse Practitioners (AANP) gives the average salary of a nurse practitioner as $91,310, whereas the AACN reported that master's-prepared faculty had an annual income of $73,633. In addition, the shortage of nursing faculty was the primary reason that 13,444 qualified master's program applicants and 1844 qualified doctoral program applicants were not accepted into their respective graduate programs (AACN, 2014c).

Technology and Education

Educational learning will continue to change with advances in telecommunication and technology. Nurses and nurse educators will need education to implement these advances into the curriculum and into nursing practice. Cable television, the Internet, computer tablets, and smartphones have significantly extended the boundaries of the classroom; these technologies will facilitate the offering of courses to meet the lifestyle of the changing student population.

Changing Health Care Settings

There has been a major shift from inpatient to outpatient nursing services as health care and nursing focus on maintaining health rather than handling illness. However, with an increase in the age of the population, more inpatients have multiple chronic health problems. Society is now developing a variety of new health care settings. Are nurses educated for these new roles? What will the role of the advanced nurse practitioner be? Will there be enough nurses educationally prepared to meet these new challenges?

The Aging Population

There is a growing aging population. According to the Administration on Aging (2014), by 2040 there will be about 82.3 million older persons, over twice their number in 2000. The population age 65 and over has increased from 35.9 million in 2003 to 44.7 million in 2013 (a 24.7% increase) in just 10 years and is projected to more than double to 98 million by 2060. Currently, the older adult population represents 14.1% of the U.S. population, which is about one in every seven Americans. The 85+ population is projected to triple from 6 million in 2013 to 14.6 million in 2040. This is more than twice the number in 2000. Naisbitt and Aburdene stated in their book *Megatrends 2000*, published in 1991, "If business and society can master the challenge of daycare, we will be one step closer to confronting the next great care giving task of the 1990s—eldercare" (p 83). This is still a critical issue in the 21st century. In 2010, it was reported that the United States had well over 4600 adult daycare centers (35% increase since 2002), with a current estimate of more than 5000 currently operating (MetLife, 2010). Nursing educators need to address the provision of health care to the elderly and include it in the curricula.

> What great opportunities in nursing!

CONCLUSION

The future of nursing looks bright and exciting. With the inception of the Affordable Care Act, technological advances, changes in health care settings, and increased demand for the services of the RN, nurses now have increased opportunities to chart their own destinies.

Nurses who have career plans and career goals will see the future trends in health care as a challenge and an opportunity for growth in roles such as case manager, independent consultant, nurse practitioner, nursing educator, nursing informatics, policy maker, and entrepreneur. In contrast, nurses without career goals may find themselves displaced or obsolete. There has never been a more exciting time to be entering the profession of nursing than right now. Opportunities in nursing are wide open to those with the sensitivity and the creativity to embrace the future.

I challenge you to get out a piece of paper and put your educational goals down in writing. After you do this, set some deadlines for when you want to achieve these goals. Place this piece of paper in a prominent place where you will see it every day.

What's talked about is a dream,
What's envisioned is exciting,
What's planned becomes possible,
What's scheduled is real.

Anthony Robbins

🌐 RELEVANT WEBSITES AND ONLINE RESOURCES

American Academy of Nurse Practitioners (2015)
Planning your NP education. http://www.aanp.org/education/student-resource-center/planning-your-np-education.

American Association of Colleges of Nursing (2015)
Your nursing career. http://www.aacn.nche.edu/students/your-nursing-career.

National Council of State Boards of Nursing (2016)
Consensus model for APRN regulation: Licensure, accreditation, certification & education. https://www.ncsbn.org/736.htm.

American Colleges of Nursing (2015)
- List of schools that offer accelerated baccalaureate programs for non-nursing college graduates. http://www.aacn.nche.edu/leading-initiatives/research-data/BSNNCG.pdf.
- List of schools that offer entry-level or second-degree master's programs. http://www.aacn.nche.edu/leading-initiatives/research-data/GENMAS.pdf.

National League for Nursing (2015)
http://www.nln.org/.

Nursing's Centralized Application Service, Nursing CAS (2015)
Offers prospective students a convenient way to apply to nursing programs at participating schools nationwide. http://nursing cas.org/.

BIBLIOGRAPHY

Administration on Aging. (2014). *Profile of older Americans.* Retrieved from http://www.aoa.acl.gov/Aging_Statistics/Profile/2014/3.aspx.

American Association of Colleges of Nursing (AACN). (2007). *White paper on the education and role of the clinical nurse leader* (Revised and approved by AACN Board of Directors July 2007). Retrieved from. http://www.aacn.nche.edu/publications/white-papers/cnl.

American Association of Colleges of Nursing (AACN). (2012a). *AACN and community college leaders join together to support academic progression and provide joint statement on academic progression for nursing students and graduates.* Retrieved from http://www.aacn.nche.edu/news/articles/2012/academic-progression.

American Association of Colleges of Nursing (AACN). (2012b). *Leadership, collaboration, innovation: Advancing higher education in nursing 2012 annual report.* Retrieved from http://www.aacn.nche.edu/aacn-publications/annual-reports/AnnualReport12.pdf.

American Association of Colleges of Nursing (AACN). (2013). *Competencies and curricular expectations for clinical nurse leader education and practice.* Retrieved from http://www.aacn.nche.edu/cnl/CNL-Competencies-October-2013.pdf.

American Association of Colleges of Nursing. (AACN). (2014a). *Annual report 2014: Building a framework for the future.* Retrieved from http://www.aacn.nche.edu/aacn-publications/annual-reports/AnnualReport14.pdf.

American Association of Colleges of Nursing (AACN). (2014b). *Fact sheet: The impact of education on nursing practice.* Retrieved http://www.aacn.nche.edu/media-relations/EdImpact.pdf.

American Association of Colleges of Nursing (AACN). (2014c). *Nursing shortage fact sheet.* Retrieved from http://www.aacn.nche.edu/media-relations/fact-sheets/nursing-shortage.

American Association of Colleges of Nursing (AACN). (2015a). *CNL statistics.* Retrieved from http://www.aacn.nche.edu/leading-initiatives/cnl/cnl-certification/pdf/CNLStats.pdf.

American Association of Colleges of Nursing (AACN). (2015b). *Fact sheet: Accelerated baccalaureate and master's degrees in nursing.* Retrieved from http://www.aacn.nche.edu/media-relations/fact-sheets/accelerated-programs.

American Association of Colleges of Nursing. (AACN). (2015c). *Fact sheet: Degree completion programs for registered nurses: RN to master's degree and RN to baccalaureate programs.* Retrieved from http://www.aacn.nche.edu/media-relations/fact-sheets/degree-completion-programs.

American Association of Colleges of Nursing (AACN). (2015d). *Report from the Task Force on the Implementation of the DNP.* Retrieved from http://www.aacn.nche.edu/aacn-publications/white-papers/DNP-Implementation-TF-Report-8-15.pdf.

American Association of Colleges of Nursing (AACN). (2015e). *Nursing faculty shortage.* Retrieved from http://www.aacn.nche.edu/media-relations/fact-sheets/nursing-faculty-shortage.

American Association of Colleges of Nursing (AACN). (2016). *2015-2016 Salaries of instructional and administrative nursing faculty in baccalaureate and graduate programs in nursing.* Retrieved from http://www.aacn.nche.edu/research-data/standard-data-reports.

American Association of Nurse Anesthetists (AANA). (2015). *Certified Registered Nurse Anesthetists fact sheet.* Retrieved from http://www.aana.com/ceandeducation/becomeacrna/Pages/Nurse-Anesthetists-at-a-Glance.aspx.

American College of Nurse-Midwives (ACNM). (2015). *Essential facts about midwives.* Retrieved from http://www.midwife.org/Essential-Facts-about-Midwives.

American Nurses Association (ANA). (1979). *The study of credentialing in nursing: A new approach.* Kansas City, MO: American Nurses Association.

American Nurses Credentialing Center (ANCC). (2014). *2014 Annual Report.* Retrieved from http://www.nursecredentialing.org/Documents/Annual-Reports-Archive/2014-AnnualReport.pdf.

APRN Consensus Work Group and the National Council of State Boards of Nursing APRN Advisory Committee. (2008). *Consensus model for APRN regulation. Licensure, accreditation, certification, and education.* Retrieved from http://www.aacn.nche.edu/education-resources/APRNReport.pdf.

Budden, J., Zhong, E., Moulton, P., & Cimioti, J. (2013). Highlights of the National Workforce Survey of Registered Nurses. *Journal of Nursing Regulation, 4*(2), 5–13. Retrieved from https://www.ncsbn.org/JNR0713_05-14.pdf.

Bureau of Labor Statistics. (2015). *Occupational employment statistics, May 2015: 29-1151 Nurse Anesthetists.* Retrieved from http://www.bls.gov/oes/current/oes291151.htm.

Forni, P. R. (1989). Models for doctoral programs: First professional degree or terminal degree? *Nurs Health Care, 10*(8), 429–434.

Health Resources and Services Administration (HRSA) Bureau of Health Professions National Center for Health Workforce Analysis. (December, 2014). *U.S. nursing workforce: Trends in supply and education.* Retrieved from http://bhpr.hrsa.gov/healthworkforce/supplydemand/nursing/workforceprojections/nursingprojections.pdf.

Institute of Medicine. (2010). *The future of nursing: Leading change, advancing health.* Retrieved from https://iom.nationalacademies.org/Reports/2010/The-Future-of-Nursing-Leading-Change-Advancing-Health.aspx.

Kaiser, J. E. (1975). *A comparison of students in practical nursing programs and in associate degree nursing programs.* National League for Nursing Publication No. 23-1592. New York: National League for Nursing.

Martsolf, G., Auerbach, D., Spetz, J., Pearson, M., & Muchow, A. (2015). Doctor of nursing practice by 2015: An examination of nursing school's decisions to offer a doctor of nursing practice degree. *Nursing Outlook, 63*(2), 219–226.

McHugh, M. D., Kelly, L. A., Smith, H. L., Wu, E. S., Vanak, J. M., & Aiken, L. H. (2013). Lower mortality in magnet hospitals. *Med Care, 51*(5), 382–388. http://dx.doi.org/10.1097/MLR.0b013e3182726cc5.

MetLife Mature Market Institute. (2010). *The MetLife national study of adult day services*. Retrieved from https://www.metlife.com/assets/cao/mmi/publications/studies/2010/mmi-adult-day-services.pdf.

Montag, M. L. (1951). *The education of nursing technicians*. New York: GP Putnam's Sons.

Montag, M. L. (1959). *Community college education for nursing*. New York: McGraw-Hill.

Naisbitt, J., & Aburdene, P. (1991). *Megatrends 2000: New directions for tomorrow*. New York: William Morrow.

National Association of Clinical Nurse Specialists (NACNS). (2014). *Key findings from the 2014 Clinical Nurse Specialist census*. Retrieved from http://www.nacns.org/docs/CensusInfographic.pdf.

National Study of Adult Day Services (NSADA). (2002). *National study of adult day services, 2001-2002. Winston-Salem, North Carolina: Partners in caregiving: The adult day services program*. Wake Forest University School of Medicine. Retrieved from http://www.nadsa.org/consumers/overview-and-facts/.

National Council of State Boards of Nursing. (1996). *Definition of competence and standards for competence, National Council of State Boards of Nursing annual meeting, Book of reports*. Chicago: National Council of State Boards of Nursing. Retrieved from https://www.ncsbn.org/1996_Part3.pdf.

National Council of State Boards of Nursing. (2005). *Meeting the ongoing challenge of continued competence*. Retrieved from https://www.ncsbn.org/Continued_Comp_Paper_TestingServices.pdf.

National Council of State Boards of Nursing. (2013). The National Council of State Boards of Nursing and the Forum of State Nursing Workforce Centers 2013 National Workforce Survey of RNs. *Journal of Nursing Regulation, 4*(Suppl.) S1–S72.

National League for Nursing. (2001). *Council of associate degree nursing competencies task force: Educational competencies for graduates of associate degree nursing programs, book code 1404-6*. New York: National League for Nursing.

Tri-Council for Nursing. (2010). *Tri-Council for Nursing issues news consensus policy statement on the educational advancement of registered nurses*. Retrieved from http://www.aacn.nche.edu/education-resources/TricouncilEdStatement.pdf.

Nursing Theory

Ashley Zerwekh Garneau, PhD, RN

ⓔ http://evolve.elsevier.com/Zerwekh/nsgtoday/.

The only good is knowledge and the only evil is ignorance.
Socrates (BC 469–399)

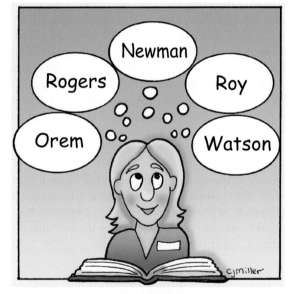

There are many nursing theories available to help guide my practice.

After completing this chapter, you should be able to:

- Identify the purposes of nursing theory.
- Distinguish between grand theory, middle-range theory, and practice theory.
- Describe the origins of nursing theory.
- Describe key concepts associated with nursing theory.
- Identify some of the more well-known and well-developed nursing theories.
- Discuss some of the main points of each of these theories.

Just mentioning the word theory, let alone nursing theory, can make many nurses' yawn reflexes start to work overtime. What is theory? Who are nursing theorists? What are the different nursing theories? Nursing theories are a way to organize and think about nursing, and the people who wrote theories are part of our nursing history. Theory provides an overall "theme" to what nurses do. In this chapter, the key words related to theory are defined, and the main elements of eight nursing theories are summarized. Buckle your seatbelts—we might be in for a bumpy ride. And no yawning!

NURSING THEORY

What Is Theory?

Quite simply, theories are words or phrases (concepts) joined together in sentences, with an overall theme, to explain, describe, or predict something. A more complex definition of a theory is "a set of interrelated concepts, definitions, and propositions that present a systematic way of viewing facts/ events by specifying relations among the variables, with the purpose of explaining and predicting the fact event" (Kerlinger, cited in Hickman, 2003).

Theories help us understand and find meaning in our nursing experience and also provide a foundation to direct questions that provide insights into best practices and safe patient care. You might see theory referred to as a conceptual model or a conceptual framework in nursing textbooks and journals. Meleis offered a definition of nursing theory with the following: "an articulated and communicated conceptualization of invented or discovered reality in or pertaining to nursing for the purpose of describing, explaining, predicting or prescribing nursing care" (cited in Hickman, 2003, p.16).

The bottom line is that words and phrases (concepts) are put together into sentences (propositions that show the relationships among the words/concepts), with an overall theme, to create theories. Theories also have some basic assumptions (jumping-off points; what is assumed to be true), such as the idea that nurses contribute to the patient's wellness and recovery from illness. Nursing theories also define four metaparadigms (metaparadigms refer to big, comprehensive concepts) and address the nursing process. Finally, nursing theories can be categorized as grand theory, middle-range theory, or practice theory. Each theory level is based on the abstractness of the concept or phenomena presented. For example, grand theories offer broad and abstract concepts about nursing practice, research, and education, which provide a more global view of nursing. Middle-range theories are not as abstract as grand theories; their focus is concentrated on the relationship between concepts with a narrower scope. Last, practice theories guide nursing practice by examining specific issues in nursing practice (Research for Best Practice Box 8.1).

What Nursing Theory Is Not

Nursing theory is *not* managed care, primary nursing, team nursing, or any other more business-related method of delivering care. Nursing theory is *not* obstetric nursing, surgical nursing, home health nursing, or any other nursing specialty; however, nursing theory can be applied to all areas of nursing, including administration, education, patient care, and research. Nursing theory is by nurses and for nurses, providing quality care to their patients, either directly or indirectly.

Why Theory?

Consider all that you do as a nurse. What you do is based on principles from many different professions, such as biology, sociology, medicine, ethics, business, theology, psychology, and philosophy. What is specifically based on nursing? Also, if nursing is a science (and it is), there must be some scientific basis for it. Furthermore, theory helps define nursing as a profession (Fig. 8.1).

Theory is a means to gather information, to identify ideas more clearly and specifically, to guide research, to show how ideas are connected to each other, to make sense of what we observe or experience, to predict what might happen, and to provide answers. A nurse is not a "junior physician," although for years nursing care has been based on the medical model. Because nursing is a science (as well as an art) and a unique profession in its own right, nurses need nursing theory on which to base their principles of patient care (Critical Thinking Box 8.1; Research for Best Practice Box 8.2).

🔍 RESEARCH FOR BEST PRACTICE BOX 8.1

Practice Theory

Practice Issue

There are a limited number of studies reporting an examination of the use of a nursing theory to guide the care of school-age children with special health care needs in a school setting. Using Orem's Self-Care Deficit theory, Green (2012) discussed how school nurses can assist children with special health care needs in gaining independence with self-care and daily activities. Using Orem's Self-Care Deficit theory, researchers Wong, Wan, Choi, and Lam examined the relationship between basic conditioning factors (BCFs), self-care agency, and self-care behaviors in adolescent girls with dysmenorrhea (Wong et al., 2015). Findings from the study suggest that BCFs such as age, knowledge about medications used to treat menstrual pain (self-medication), and educational level of parents, along with self-care agency can influence an adolescent with dysmenorrhea to perform self-care measures associated with menstruation problems.

Implications for Nursing Practice

Application of Orem's self-care deficit nursing theory can be used by school nurses to identify, plan, and implement nursing care measures that will assist children with special health care needs and their families in developing independence with self-care needs. School nurses can educate adolescent girls on common health-related issues such as menstruation, so that the adolescent is informed about self-care measures that can be used to alleviate associated symptoms of dysmenorrhea.

 In practice settings where vulnerable populations are present (such as school nursing), use of a nursing theory serves as an ideal theoretical framework for the nurse to identify self-care needs of the population and provide optimal nursing care with a goal of promoting self-care.

References

Wong, C. L., Wan, Y., Choi, K. C., & Lam, L. (2015). Examining self-care behaviors and their associated factors among adolescent girls with dysmenorrhea: An application of Orem's self-care deficit nursing theory. *Journal of Nursing Scholarship, 47*(3), 219–227.

Green, R. (2012). Application of the self-care deficit nursing theory to the care of children with special healthcare needs in the school setting. *Self-Care, Dependent-Care Nursing 19*(1), 35–40.

FIG. 8.1 Theory guides both research and nursing practice.

? CRITICAL THINKING BOX 8.1

What advantages and disadvantages do you see for using nursing theory in your nursing practice?

Q RESEARCH FOR BEST PRACTICE BOX 8.2

Nursing Theory

Practice Issue

Although the focus of health care institutions in improving patient outcomes is based on evidenced-based practice, little research has investigated the use of a theoretical framework guided by nursing theory in examining patient perceptions in living and managing a medical condition.

Desanto-Madeya (2006) examined perceptions of family members of individuals who had sustained a spinal cord injury about the "meaning of living" (p.240) using Roy's Adaptation Model. In her qualitative ethnographic study, seven themes emerged from the data analysis in addressing the following research question of what the meaning of living is to the family of an individual with a spinal cord injury.

"The seven themes were (a) looking for understanding to a life that is unknown, (b) stumbling along an unlit path, (c) viewing self through a stained-glass window, (d) challenging the bonds of love, (e) being chained to the injury, (f) moving forward in a new way of life, and (g) reaching normalcy" (Desanto-Madeya, 2006, p.241). Using Roy's adaptation model, each theme was categorized into one or more modes of adaptation.

Seah and Tham (2015) suggested that the use of Roy's Adaptation Model could be used by nurses in managing patients with bulimia nervosa. The authors contended that Roy's Adaptation Model supports a multidisciplinary team approach in the context of providing patient care.

Implications for Nursing Practice

Implementation of a nursing theory to examine patient and family experiences when faced with an illness or injury that may cause both physical and emotional life-altering changes can serve as a framework for nurses in guiding their practice.

As part of the multidisciplinary health care team, nurses can assist patients and their families in adapting to the physiologic and psychosocial factors affected by a life-altering injury and/or illness.

Nursing theories can assist nurses in providing holistic nursing care.

References

DeSanto-Madeya, S. (2006). A secondary analysis of the meaning of living with spinal cord injury using Roy's adaptation model. *Nursing Science Quarterly 19*(3), 240–246.

Seah, X. Y., & Tham, X.C. (2015). Management of bulimia nervosa: A case study with the Roy adaptation model. *Nursing Science Quarterly 28*(2), 136–141. doi:10.1177/0894318415571599

What Is the History of Nursing Theory?

In studying nursing theories and the people who created them, it is important to look at the background of the theorist, as well as how life experiences, beliefs, and education influenced the resulting theory. What are the overall theme and main ideas of the theory, and how does the theorist define the four nursing metaparadigms (Box 8.1)?

The four metaparadigms for nursing are nursing, person, health, and environment.

Florence Nightingale is considered to be the first nursing theorist. She saw nursing as "A profession, a trade, a necessary occupation, something to fill and employ all my faculties, I have always felt essential to me, I have always longed for; consciously or not. … The first thought I can remember,

---

BOX 8.1   DEFINITION OF METAPARADIGMS

Person

Individuals, families, communities, and other groups who are participants in nursing and who receive nursing care.

Environment/Situation

The patient environment includes any setting and influencing factors that can alter the setting where the patient receives care. Factors influencing the environment include room temperature, family members' presence or lack of presence in the plan of care, work, and school.

Health

The patient's state of well-being. A patient's health is influenced by many physical and psychosocial factors.

Nursing

Nursing involves the use of the nursing process to assess, diagnose, plan, implement, and evaluate an individualized plan of care for providing patient care and education.

From Potter, P. A., Perry, A. G., Stockert, P., Hall, A., & Ostendorf, W. R. (2017). *Fundamentals of nursing* (9th ed.), St. Louis: Elsevier, p.42.

and the last was nursing work…" (Florence Nightingale as cited in Dunphy, 2015, p.38). Now, you might not feel as dedicated as she, but Nightingale also stated, "Nursing is an art. … It is one of the Fine Arts; I had almost said, the finest of the Fine Arts" (Florence Nightingale, as cited in *Una and the Lion*, 1871, p.6).

Nightingale had various influences, including her education (which was fairly comprehensive for a 19th-century English woman), her religion (Unitarianism), the history of the time (the Crimean War and invention of the telegraph), and her social status. The Unitarian belief involved salvation through health and wholeness, or our modern-day "holism." Nightingale believed that there was no conflict between science and spirituality. Science was necessary for the development of a mature concept of God (Dunphy, 2015). She also studied many other religions throughout her life, including Anglicanism, and considered starting a Protestant religious order of nuns.

Nightingale came from a very wealthy, prominent family and enjoyed traveling throughout Europe, one of the destinations being Kaiserwerth in Germany, where she observed and was moved by nuns caring for the ill. Nightingale felt a "calling" to care for others and began training with various groups, usually nuns who cared for the sick. When the Crimean War broke out, Nightingale was asked and volunteered to go to care for the wounded English soldiers. The Crimean War was the first war after the invention of the telegraph, so news of the war was more immediately circulated than had been previously experienced (Dunphy, 2015).

The overall theme of Nightingale's theory was that the environment influences the person. When she went to help soldiers during the Crimean War, her initial intent was to feed the soldiers healthy food, maintain cleanliness in the barrack hospital, and ensure proper sanitary and hygiene care (Dunphy, 2015) (Fig. 8.2). When soldier mortality rates fell, a legend was born!

Nightingale believed that nursing was separate from medicine and that nurses should be trained (although we prefer the word *educated*). She also believed that the environment was important to the health of the person and that the nurse should support the environment to assist the patient in healing (Dunphy, 2015).

To define the metaparadigms, Nightingale noted that the person is the center of the model and incorporated a holistic view of the person, someone with psychological, intellectual, and spiritual components. The nurse was a woman (because only women were nurses in Nightingale's day) who had

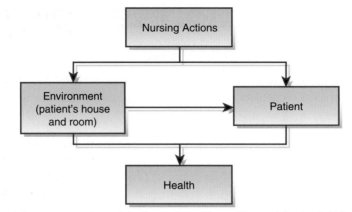

FIG. 8.2 Nightingale's conceptual model of nursing. (From Fitzpatrick, J., & Whall, A. (1996). *Conceptual models of nursing: Analysis and application* (3rd ed.). Stamford, CT: Appleton & Lange, p.38.)

charge of the health of a person, whether by providing wellness care, such as with a newborn, or by providing care to the sick. Health was the result of environmental, physical, and psychological factors, not just the absence of disease (Dunphy, 2015).

No other theories were identified or published until the 1950s when Peplau published her theory based on the interpersonal process. Other nurses were working on theories during that time and into the 1960s. In the 1970s, nursing was beginning to see itself as a scientific profession based on theoretical ideas. Nursing theory continues to influence health. For example, health care institutions seeking Magnet recognition are required to adopt a nursing theory or framework that guides nursing practice (Smith & Parker, 2015) (Table 8.1).

TABLE 8.1 **NURSING THEORIES**		
YEAR	**THEORIST**	**THEORY DESCRIPTION**
1860	Florence Nightingale	Although her model did not have a specific name, the basic underpinnings revolve around how a person is influenced by the environment. Nursing was a "calling" to help the patient in a reparative process by directly working with the patient or indirectly by affecting the environment to facilitate health and recovery from illness.
1952	Hildegard Peplau	Interpersonal Relations Model—describes the four phases of the dynamic relationship between nurse and patient: orientation, identification, exploitation, and resolution.
1960	Faye Abdellah	Patient-Centered Approach—develops a list of 21 unique nursing problems related to human needs; promoted the use of a problem-solving approach to the practice rather than merely following physicians' orders. Responsible for changing the focus of nursing theory from a disease-centered to a patient-centered approach and moved nursing practice beyond the patient to include care of families and the elderly.
1961	Ida Jean Orlando	Theory of Deliberative Nursing Process—focuses on the interpersonal process between nurse and patient through a deliberative nursing process; most concerned with what was uniquely nursing.
1966	Virginia Henderson	One of her main topics is the "unique functions of nurses." All of her materials provide a focus for patient care via 14 basic needs.

TABLE 8.1   NURSING THEORIES—cont'd

YEAR	THEORIST	THEORY DESCRIPTION
1969	Myra Estrin Levine	Conservation Model—focuses attention on the wholeness of the person, adaptation, and conservation, which is guided by four principles (conservation of energy, structure, personal integrity, and social integrity).
1970	Martha Rogers	Science of Unitary Human Beings—an abstract model addressing the complexity of the "unitary human being," which allows for the examination of phenomena (energy fields, paranormal) that other theories do not describe, as nurses promote synchronicity between human beings and their environment/universe.
1971	Dorothea Orem	Self-Care Nursing Theory—three interwoven theories of self-care, self-care deficit, and nursing system help the nurse identify strategies to meet the patient's self-care needs.
1971	Imogene King	Theory of Goal Attainment—patient goals are met through the transaction between nurse and patient involving three systems (personal, interpersonal, and social).
1972	Betty Neuman	Neuman Systems Model—focuses on wellness and mitigating stress within three levels of prevention: primary, secondary, and tertiary.
1974	Sister Callista Roy	Roy's Adaptation Model—individual seeking equilibrium through the process of adaptation; identified six physiological needs (exercise and rest; nutrition; elimination; fluid and electrolytes; oxygenation and circulation; and regulation of temperature, senses, and endocrine system).
1976	Josephine Paterson and Loretta Zderad	Humanistic Nursing Theory—focuses on the nurse and the patient; dignity, interests, and values are of greatest importance; belief that there is more to nursing that is not explainable by scientific principles.
1978; 1991	Madeline Leininger	Theory of Culture Care Diversity and Universality—a grand theory that considers the impact of culture on the person's health and caring practices.
1979	Margaret Newman	Theory of Health as Expanding Consciousness—every person in every situation is ever-changing in a unidirectional, unpredictable, all-at-once pattern involving movement, time, space, and consciousness; emphasizes the importance of viewing patients in the context of their holistic patterns.
1979	Jean Watson	Theory of Human Caring—identifies 10 "carative" factors focusing on the interactions between the one who is caring and the one who is being cared for.
1980	Dorothy Johnson	Behavioral Systems Model—focuses on human behavior rather than the person's state of health; this theory helped clarify the differences between medicine and nursing.
1981	Rosemarie Rizzo Parse	Theory of Human Becoming—focuses on the human-health-universe; views nursing as a participation effort with the patient that focuses on health.
1983	Helen Erickson, Evelyn Tomlin, and Mary Ann Swain	Modeling and Role Modeling Theory—uses the understanding of the patient's world to plan interventions that meet the patient's perceived needs and that will assist the patient to achieve holistic health; focus is on the person receiving the care, not the nurse, not the care, and not the disease.
1984	Pat Benner	Professional-Advancement Model—applies the Dreyfus model of skill acquisition to nursing; area of concern is not how to do nursing but rather, "How do nurses learn to do nursing?"; identifies seven domains: practice-helping, teaching/coaching, diagnosing and monitoring, managing changes, administering and monitoring therapeutic interventions, monitoring quality care, and organizing to enact the work role.

Data from Fawcett, J. (2005). *Analysis and evaluation of contemporary nursing knowledge: Nursing models and theories*. Philadelphia: FA Davis; Alligood, M. R. (2014). *Nursing theorists and their work* (8th ed.). St. Louis: Mosby.

Among the best known and best formulated theories or models are those by Dorothea Orem, Martha Rogers, Sister Callista Roy, Dorothy Johnson, Betty Neuman, Imogene King, Jean Watson, and Madeleine Leininger (see the *Definitions of the Metaparadigms* by these theorists in the *Evolve* website). Each theory has been around for over 30 years, and each theorist has practiced nursing at the bedside, in the community, and in administration or education. At the end of this chapter are listed relevant websites and online resources related to each nursing theory and associated nursing theorist.

WHO ARE THE NURSING THEORISTS?

Selected Nursing Theorists

Dorothea Orem—Self-Care Nursing Theory

Orem's theory includes the overall theme of self-care. She sees the person as composed of physical, psychological, interpersonal, and social aspects. Nursing consists of those actions to overcome or prevent self-care limitations (self-care deficits) or to provide care for someone who is unable to perform self-care. A nurse may need to do everything for the patient (wholly compensatory, such as for a patient who is under general anesthesia or a newborn), to do some things for the patient (partly compensatory, such as with a patient who is 2 days postop and may be able to do some things, but not everything, independently), or to educate the patient (supportive educative, such as with postpartum parents). Orem added that self-care requisites (food, water, air) are universal basic needs that individuals need to sustain life. Health, to Orem, is the internal and external conditions that permit self-care needs to be met (Hood, 2014). The environment is anything outside of, or external to, the person. Thus, in assessing a patient, a nurse using Orem's theory would ask, "What can the patient do for himself or herself? And what do I, as the nurse, need to do for the patient? What are the patient's self-care deficits (or things that he or she cannot do)? What nursing functions can be provided to the patient to assist in self-care and promote recovery?"

Orem's nursing process includes assessing the patient, deciding whether nursing care is needed, and, if so, determining which self-care deficits are present. Does the patient need wholly or partly compensatory or supportive-educative nursing care? The nurse needs to identify interventions and decide which interventions the patient can do (if any) and which interventions the nurse will do. The nurse describes which helping methods are used for the interventions (acting for or doing for another, guiding and directing, providing physical or psychological support, providing a therapeutic environment, or teaching) (Foster & Bennett, 2003). And all interventions fall under one of those five helping methods (Figs. 8.3 and 8.4).

Martha Rogers—Science of Unitary Human Beings

Martha Rogers was one of the most original thinkers of the nursing theorists. Her overall theme is that the person and the environment are one thing and cannot be separated. Rogers takes holism to a new level. The person, for Rogers, is an energy field that exhibits patterns (think of electrocardiogram [ECG] patterns, fetal heart rate patterns, biorhythms, auras). Health is an "index of field" (Rogers as cited in Hood, 2014, p.141). Rogers, however, did not like to define the word *health,* because she believed it was a value judgment (e.g., what your patient thinks is healthy about himself may not be what you think is healthy about the patient). The environment for Rogers was also an energy field that was interacting constantly with the energy field of the person (similar to what Nightingale thought). The role of nursing was to repattern the person and environment to achieve maximum health potential for the person. Although this may all sound a little far-fetched, many nurses, when first entering a patient's room in a hospital, will assess the patient and rearrange or clean up the room to make things more convenient or therapeutic for caring for the patient. That is, the patient and environment are "repatterned" to achieve maximum health for the patient (Hood, 2014).

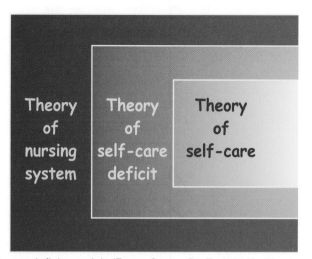

FIG. 8.3 Orem's self-care deficit model. (From Orem, D. E. (2001). *Nursing concepts of practice* (6th ed.). St. Louis: Mosby, p.141.)

Rogers' theory is grounded in the science of physics and the ideas of matter and energy. Rogers was very interested in space travel and envisioned nurses as providing care for people on earth or in space. She felt that some pathologies were a result of our being earthbound (e.g., osteoporosis and arthritis) but that these diseases would not be an issue in outer space because of the changes in gravity. Rogers also believed in the value of nurses using creative therapies, such as touch, color, sound, motion, and humor. The use of complementary therapies (guided imagery, biofeedback, meditation, yoga, Reiki) fits very well with Rogers' ideas. The nursing care plan that Rogers developed, but was not sold on, included Pattern Manifestation Knowing-Assessment (our idea of *assessment*), Voluntary Mutual Patterning (whereby the nurse and patient pattern the environmental energy to promote health—or interventions), and Pattern Manifestation Knowing-Evaluation (our idea of *evaluation*) (Muth Quillen, 2003).

Rogers' theory entitled, "Principles of Homeodynamics" examines the wholeness of humans and their interactions with the environment. Under homeodynamics, three principles exist that further define the environmental conditions that humans experience, and they are resonancy, integrality, and helicy. Resonancy is the "continuous change from lower- to higher-frequency wave patterns in human/environmental fields" (from Rogers in *Nursing Science and the Space Age,* as cited in Alligood, 2014b, p.248).

Integrality looks at how human beings and the environment are continuously and simultaneously interacting. This interaction influences the changing life process that humans experience in their everyday activities. Helicy looks at the continuous and evolving pattern changes that exist between humans and their environment (Fig. 8.5).

Sister Callista Roy—Adaptation Model

Sister Callista Roy saw the person as a biopsychosocial being (yes, it does seem as if these theorists make up their own words) who is seeking equilibrium. Her overall theme was adaptation. The four adaptation modes represent the behavior responses exhibited by the individual and include "physiological-physical, self-concept–group identity, role function, and interdependence" (Tiedeman, as cited in Fitzpatrick & Whall, 2005, p.152). As nurses, we are to assess how well the person is coping and adapting to stimuli. The stimuli could be any stressors that are making a person ill or causing

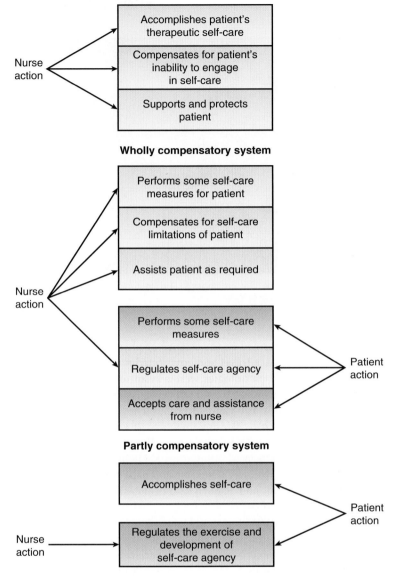

Wholly compensatory system

Partly compensatory system

Supportive-educative system

FIG. 8.4 Orem's basic nursing systems. (From Orem, D. E. (2001). *Nursing concepts of practice* (6th ed.). St. Louis: Mosby, p.351.)

FIG. 8.5 Roger's science of unitary human beings. (From Fitzpatrick, J., & Whall, A. (1996). *Conceptual models of nursing: Analysis and application* (3rd ed.). Stamford, CT: Appleton & Lange.)

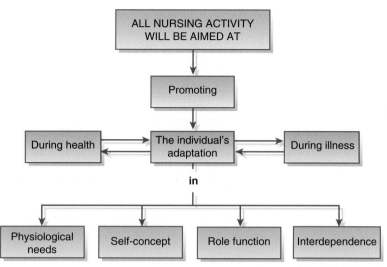

FIG. 8.6 Roy's adaptation model. (From Pearson, A., Vaughan, B., & Fitzgerald, M. (2005). *Nursing models for practice* (3rd ed.). Edinburgh: Butterworth & Heinemann, p.129.)

the person to not adapt. The stimulus could be focal (the stimulus that is the greatest concern at the moment—e.g., labor pain), contextual (all other stimuli in the area that contribute to the effect of the focal stimulus, such as noise in the background), or residual (a stimulus that is unknown to the nurse but is bothering the patient—e.g., memories of past labors and births).

Health is defined as successful coping with stressors, and the environment is defined as the influences that affect the development of a person. Illness is unsuccessful coping. The nursing process is a problem-solving approach that encompasses steps to gather data, identify capacities and needs of the human adaptive system, select and implement approaches for nursing care, and evaluate the outcome of the care provided. In Roy's nursing process, she adds two assessment parts: (1) What is the stimulus? and (2) What is the person's response to the stimulus? The nurse's role is to influence stimuli to improve successful coping (Alligood, 2014a) (Fig. 8.6).

Dorothy Johnson—Behavioral Systems Model

Dorothy Johnson was one of Roy's teachers at UCLA. Johnson's theme was balance; her theory is that the person is a behavior system and a biological system seeking balance (George, 1995). The environment is anything outside the person or behavior system. Health is balance or stability. The nurse's role is to restore or maintain the balance in the person or behavior system. A visual example would be learning to use crutches after a leg fracture. The person needs to learn to balance (literally) on crutches but also needs to learn to "balance" the other aspects of his or her life that are affected by the broken leg.

Johnson views the nursing process as assessment, diagnosis, intervention, and evaluation. The person's eight subsystems are assessed. These subsystems are the achievement subsystem, which includes mastery or control of the self or environment; the aggressive/protective subsystem, which includes protecting oneself or others; the dependency subsystem, which includes obtaining attention or assistance from others; the eliminative subsystem, which includes not only physical elimination from the body but also being able to express one's feelings or ideas; the ingestive subsystem, which includes eating, as well as "taking in" other things such as pain medication or information; the affiliative subsystem, which includes relating to others or achieving intimacy; the sexual subsystem, which includes activities related to sexuality, such as procreating and sexual identity; and the restorative subsystem, which focuses on measures such as rest and relaxation to optimize mind and body restoration (Holaday, 2015) (Fig. 8.7).

> Consider how patients for whom you care would fall into each of these seven subsystems or which subsystems would most apply to the patients for whom you provide care.

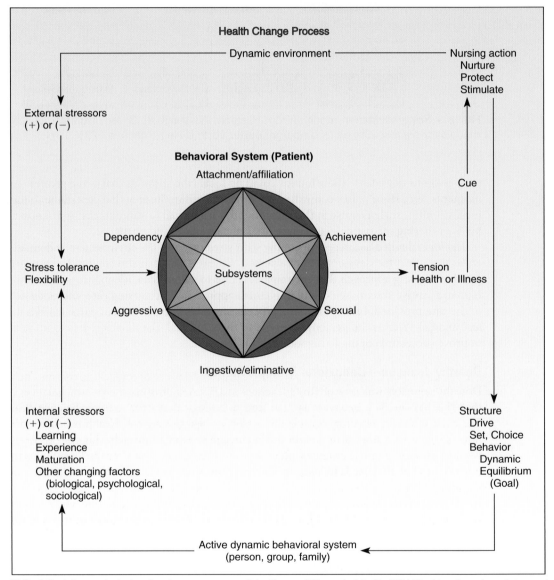

FIG. 8.7 Johnson's behavioral systems model. (From Alligood, M. R. (2016). *Nursing theorists and their work* (8th ed.). St. Louis: Mosby, p.338.)

Betty Neuman—Systems Model

Betty Neuman's conceptual model focuses on prevention, or prevention as intervention, as a response to stressors. Primary prevention is what a person does to prevent illness—for example, exercise, sleep 8 hours, eat a balanced diet. Secondary prevention is what is done when an illness strikes. For example, when a person with a myocardial infarction comes into the emergency department, what is done by the staff to prevent this person from dying or from having further heart damage? Tertiary prevention is what is done to rehabilitate a person after an illness or accident, such as cardiac rehabilitation or stroke rehabilitation. Tertiary prevention can move the person back to primary prevention again. The nurse's role is to help reduce the stressors through the three levels of prevention.

Neuman also talks about the flexible lines of defense, the normal lines of defense, and the lines of resistance. The flexible lines of defense are the outermost boundary and serve as the initial response to stressors. Neuman describes these lines as accordion-like, in that they can expand and contract depending on our health practices (e.g., lack of sleep, lack of eating well). Our normal lines of defense are what usually protect us from stressors—for example, our age, physical health, genetic makeup, spiritual beliefs, and gender. When the flexible lines of defense and the normal lines of defense can no longer protect us from stressors, our equilibrium is affected, and a reaction occurs. The lines of resistance come into play to help restore balance, similar to how the body's immune system works. The person, for Neuman, may be an individual (i.e., patient), family (i.e., parents of a chronically ill child), group of people (i.e., pregnant women), or a community (i.e., residents in an assisted-living facility) and has physiological, psychological, sociocultural, developmental, and spiritual variables (Alligood, 2014a).

Think of how Neuman's ideas accurately portray the life of a student. The student struggles to keep up with coursework, work, and family life but may find himself or herself sleeping less, eating less or eating poorly, and then getting sick or having less energy. Neuman's nursing process has just three steps: diagnosis, nursing goals (interventions are included with this step), and nursing outcomes. Neuman also has a unique way of looking at the environment, which she identifies as the internal, the external, and the created environment. The created environment is developed by the patient and serves as his or her protective device (Alligood, 2014a). The created environment can be a healthy adaptation (e.g., someone relaxing through visualization), or it can be maladaptive (e.g., someone with a type of psychosis, such as schizophrenia) (Fig. 8.8).

Imogene King—Goal Attainment Model

The theme of Imogene King's theory is interaction and goal attainment. The person interacts with the environment, and health is a dynamic state of well-being. The nurse interacts with the patient to set mutually agreed-upon goals for the patient's health. The nurse and the patient are each recognized as bringing his or her own set of knowledge, values, and skills to the interaction. King also emphasizes that the nurse and patient usually first come together as strangers and through the interactions, both verbal and nonverbal, develop a relationship based on their perceptions (Alligood, 2014b). King's nursing process looks very similar to that with which nurses are already familiar: assessment, diagnosis, planning, intervention, and evaluation. King would like her model to be used as the basis of the U.S. health care system and would like a person's entry into the health care system to be by means of nursing assessment (Sieloff & Frey, 2015)! King's vision of the future of nursing is a move in the right direction (Fig. 8.9).

Jean Watson—Theory of Human Caring

Jean Watson's theory is all about caring—finally, a theory about caring. Watson sees the person as a mind–body–soul connection. Health is unity and harmony within the mind, body, and soul. The

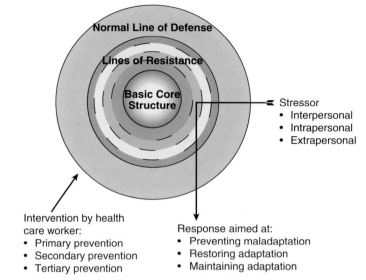

FIG. 8.8 Neuman systems model. (From Alligood, M. R. (2014). *Nursing theorists and their work* (8th ed.). St. Louis: Mosby, p.287.)

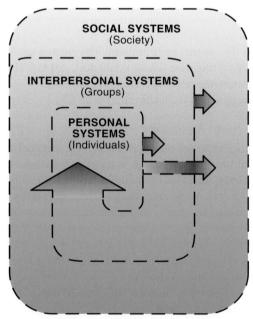

FIG. 8.9 King's goal attainment model for nursing. (From Pearson, A., Vaughan, B., & Fitzgerald, M. (2005). *Nursing models for practice* (3th ed.). Edinburgh: Butterworth & Heinemann, p.162.)

nurse comes in contact with the person during a "caring occasion" or "caring moment" and promotes restoration of a sense of inner harmony through Watson's 10 "carative" factors. To Watson, caring is a moral idea rather than an interpersonal technique (Alligood, 2014b).

Here are Watson's 10 carative factors (with each one, see what nursing interventions you can identify):

1. The formation of a humanistic–altruistic system of values
2. The instillation of faith–hope
3. The cultivation of sensitivity to one's self and to others
4. The development of a helping–trust relationship
5. The promotion and acceptance of the expression of positive and negative feelings
6. The systematic use of the scientific problem–solving methods for decision making
7. The promotion of interpersonal teaching–learning
8. The provision for a supportive, protective, and corrective mental, physical, sociocultural, and spiritual environment
9. Assistance with the gratification of human needs
10. The allowance for existential–phenomenological forces (Alligood, 2014b)

Madeleine Leininger—Culture Care Theory

Madeleine Leininger's overall theme is culture. Leininger is the "Margaret Mead of the health field" and has traveled widely and studied many cultures. She sees the person as caring and capable of being concerned with the welfare of others. Nursing is a transcultural caring discipline and profession. Nurses need to be mindful of folk practices or generic health care practices. (Think of health care practices that were practiced when you were a child that would be considered folk or generic health care practices—e.g., Vicks VapoRub applied to your chest for a cold; depending on the illness, not drinking either hot or cold beverages; not sitting too close to the TV because it was "bad" for your eyes.) The nurse needs to be aware of and use culture care data that are influenced by religion, kinship, language, technology, economics, education (both formal and informal), cultural values and beliefs, and the physical (or ecological) environment. Leininger believes that there can be no curing without caring. Health is culturally defined (Alligood, 2014b).

The health care professional needs to examine the prescribed health care requirements and decide if there can be culture care preservation or maintenance (where the relevant care values can be retained), or if there needs to be culture care accommodation or negotiation (where the cultural practices need to be adapted or negotiated to return the patient to health), or if culture care repatterning or restructuring is required (where the patient needs to change or significantly alter culturally based health practices to promote good health). Leininger's theory can be summarized in her Sunrise Model. Leininger replaced the word *model* with the term *enabler* "to clarify it as a visual guide for exploration of cultures" (Alligood, 2014b, p.354) The upper half of the sunrise enabler (model) represents the various cultural factors that impact a person's views toward health. The lower half is for decision making between the health care professional and the person (Fig. 8.10).

CONCLUSION

In reviewing these nursing theories, you may find that some especially appeal to you and others do not. That is okay. What is important is to understand that nursing theories are a rich part of our nursing history and that they are a way to organize, deliver, evaluate, and ultimately improve the care we provide to the patient populations we serve (Critical Thinking Box 8.2).

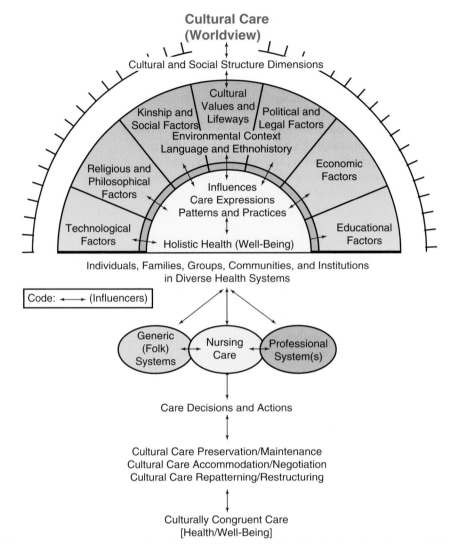

FIG. 8.10 Leininger's sunrise enabler. (From Alligood, M. R. (2014). *Nursing theory: Utilization and application* (5th ed.). St. Louis: Mosby, p.355.)

The future of nursing theory is at a turning point. Nursing theory has and will continue to guide nursing practice. Given the increasing complexity of the health care environment, nursing theory can contribute to the use of evidence-based nursing practice by linking theory with research and practice (Research for Best Practice Box 8.3).

❓ CRITICAL THINKING BOX 8.2

In reviewing the theories, which one would best fit in your clinical practice?

Which theory most appeals to you and why?

Which theory/theories would fit best with the following patient settings and why?

- Perioperative patient
- Obstetrical patient
- Psychiatric patient
- Nursing education
- Managing a nursing unit
- Community health
- Organizing a computer-generated acuity form
- Pediatric patients
- Home health
- Hospice care
- Long-term care facility
- Rehabilitative therapy

🔍 RESEARCH FOR BEST PRACTICE BOX 8.3

Future of Nursing Theory

Practice Issue

Given the changes facing health care in the twenty-first century, examination of trends in nursing theory has not been explored within the past decade.

Implications for Nursing Practice

Based on their review of literature, Im and Chang (2012) suggested that the profession of nursing continues to link nursing theory to research and practice and to expand use of nursing theory internationally and embrace international collaborative processes to gain awareness and understanding of international nursing perspectives. Im and Chang (2012) added that nursing theories remain in coexistence, so that a multiple range of theories can be applied in various practice and academic settings.

  McCrae (2011) suggested that nursing theory in undergraduate curriculum is critical to advancing the practice of nursing.

References

Im, E. O., & Chang, S. J. (2012). Current trends in nursing theories. *Journal of Nursing Scholarship, 44*(2), 156–164. doi:10.1111/j.1547-5069.2012.01440.x.

McCrae, N. (2011). Whither nursing models? The value of nursing theory in the context of evidence-based practice and multidisciplinary health care. *Journal of Advanced Nursing 68*(1), 222–229. doi:10.1111/j.1365-2648.2011.05821.x.

🌐 RELEVANT WEBSITES AND ONLINE RESOURCES

American Association for the History of Nursing (2007)
Bibliography. https://www.aahn.org/methodology.html.

Cardinal Stritch University (2016)
Nursing theorists overview. http://www.stritch.edu/Library/Doing-Research/Research-by-Subject/Health-Sciences-Nursing-Theorists/Nursing-Theorists/.

Clayton State University (2015)
Nursing theory link page. http://www.clayton.edu/nursing/Nursing-Theory.

Continued

⊕ RELEVANT WEBSITES AND ONLINE RESOURCES—cont'd

Current Nursing (2010)
Nursing theories. http://currentnursing.com/nursing_theory/.

Hahn School of Nursing and Health Science (2016)
Nursing theory and research. http://www.sandiego.edu/nursing/research/nursing-theory-research.php/.

Nurses Info (2010)
Nursing Theories A-Z. http://www.nurses.info/nursing_theory.htm.

Petiprin, A. (2015)
Nursing theory. http://www.nursing-theory.org/.

BIBLIOGRAPHY

Alligood, M. R. (2014a). *Nursing theorists and their work* (8th ed.). St. Louis: Mosby.

Alligood, M. R. (2014b). *Nursing theory: Utilization and application* (5th ed.). St. Louis: Mosby.

Dunphy, L. H. (2015). Florence Nightingale's legacy of caring and its application. In M. C. Smith, & M. E. Parker (Eds.), *Nursing theories and nursing practice* (4th ed.) (p 37–54). Philadelphia: FA Davis.

Foster, P. C., & Bennett, A. M. (2003). Dorothy E. Orem. University of Phoenix College of Health Sciences and Nursing (Ed.). In *Theoretical foundations of nursing practice* (pp. 137–168). Boston: Pearson Custom Publishing.

George, J. B. (1995). *Nursing theories: The base for professional nursing practice* (4th ed.). Norwalk, CT: Appleton & Lange.

George, J. (2003a). Betty Neuman. University of Phoenix College of Health Sciences and Nursing (Ed.). In *Theoretical foundations of nursing practice* (pp. 243–267). Boston: Pearson Custom Publishing.

George, J. (2003b). Madeleine M. Leininger. University of Phoenix College of Health Sciences and Nursing (Ed.). In *Theoretical foundations of nursing practice* (pp. 289–303). Boston: Pearson Custom Publishing.

Hickman, J. S. (2003). An introduction to nursing theory. University of Phoenix College of Health Sciences and Nursing (Ed.). In *Theoretical foundations of nursing practice* (pp. 15–28). Boston: Pearson Custom Publishing.

Holaday, B. (2015). Dorothy Johnson's Behavioral system model and its application. In M. C. Smith & M. E. Parker (Eds.), *Nursing theories and nursing practice* (4th ed.) (pp. 89–104). Philadelphia: FA Davis.

Hood, L. J. (2014). *Leddy and Pepper's conceptual bases of professional nursing* (8th ed.). Philadelphia: Lippincott.

Nightingale, F. (1871). *Una and the lion.* Cambridge: Riverside Press.

Sieloff, C. L., & Frey, M. A. (2015). Imogene King's theory of goal attainment. In M. C. Smith & M. E. Parker (Eds.), *Nursing theories and nursing practice* (4th ed.) (pp. 133–151). Philadelphia: FA Davis.

Smith, M. C., & Parker, M. E. (2015). *Nursing theories and nursing practice* (4th ed.). Philadelphia: FA Davis.

Muth Quillen, S. (2003). Rogers' model: Science of unitary persons. University of Phoenix College of Health Sciences and Nursing (Ed.). In *Theoretical foundations of nursing practice* (pp. 309–323). Boston: Pearson Custom Publishing.

Tiedeman, M. E. (2005). Roy's adaptation model. In J. J. Fitzpatrick & A. L. Whall (Eds.), *Conceptual models of nursing: Analysis and application* (pp. 146–176). Upper Saddle River, NJ: Prentice Hall.

Image of Nursing: Influences of the Present

Margi J. Schultz, PhD, RN, CNE, PLNC

ⓔ http://evolve.elsevier.com/Zerwekh/nsgtoday/.

Unless we are making progress in our nursing every year, every month, every week,
take my word for it, we are going back.
Florence Nightingale

Nursing image—how is it perceived?

After completing this chapter, you should be able to:

- Discuss the effect of image on the public perception of nursing.
- Describe different sociological models that characterize "professionalism."
- Apply Pavalko's characteristics as a framework to describe modern nursing practice.
- Identify the impact that nursing organizations have on professional practice.
- Describe the role of credentialing and certification in professional practice.

Nursing image—how is it perceived? What does it mean to be a professional nurse? How does the public view nursing? How does nursing define and view itself? What role does the public image of the nursing profession play in our current nursing climate? What do you do to further the image of a professional nurse?

Historically, nurses have struggled to define the image of nursing and the professional role of the nurse. There are many different views and opinions, but nurses are definitely gaining ground when it comes to defining the profession of nursing. The annual Gallup survey for professions noted that for honesty and ethical standards, nursing has been rated at the top of the list for the past 13 years. In 2014, 80% of the American public rate the standards held by nurses as either high or very high; this rates the nursing profession 15 percentage points above any other profession (ANA, 2014). The image of nursing is evolving and changing, with nursing being promoted and viewed as an intellectual, autonomous profession that demands a high level of commitment, focus, and a dedication to advancing education and scholarly activity.

Modern-day nursing has many dimensions, one of which includes the debate surrounding its identification as a profession. One ongoing challenge in nursing is to diligently foster and enhance the public image and the self-image of the nurse. In this chapter, the development of nursing into a profession is discussed, and the present and future dimensions of nursing's "image" are explored. The lasting impact of the 2010 Institute of Medicine report on *The Future of Nursing* and other significant position statements and reports on the profession will be discussed. Historical knowledge about our "rites of passage" provides an appreciation of the path nursing has taken as a profession and what the future of nursing may hold for the recent graduate in this complex and evolving health care world.

PROFESSIONAL IMAGE OF NURSING

What Do We Mean by the "Image" of Nursing?

Santa Filomena
Lo! in that hour of misery
A lady with a lamp I see
Pass through the glimmering gloom,
And flit from room to room.

Longfellow, 1857

Nursing has been identified as an "emerging profession" for at least 150 years. The historical context of nursing's image is often traced back to Florence Nightingale, the "founder of nursing." Florence Nightingale is recognized as a nurse, statistician, and writer who became known for her groundbreaking work during the Crimean War. Nurse Nightingale was also called the "Lady with the Lamp," as she was reported to have made rounds on her patients at night by the light of a lantern. International Nurse's Day is celebrated each year on her birthday, May 12, and the Nightingale Pledge is still recited by new nursing graduates around the world, often with the accompaniment of flickering candles in symbolic lamps. Even though much has been written about Florence Nightingale's many contributions, she is undeniably remembered as the pioneer of nursing education (Bostridge, 2008).

I attribute my success to this—I never gave or took any excuse.
Florence Nightingale

Do you feel most nurses portray a professional image? If so, what qualities do they possess to project this image? If not, what is lacking?

The image of professional nursing continues to evolve and is significantly affected by the media, women's issues and roles, and an ever-evolving high-technology health care environment. How nursing views itself in the evolution of the profession and how actively nurses are involved in the definition process will continue to determine the image and role of nursing in the future.

In a 2008 study on public perceptions of nursing and factors that influence these insights, the study determined a personal experience with nurses either as a patient or with a family member was the leading influence on perceptions of nurses and the profession of nursing (Donelan et al., 2008).

There is a new, innovative approach to recruiting and retaining more men into nursing, seeking a more gender-neutral attitude. The American Assembly of Men in Nursing (AAMN) has initiated the marketing campaign "Advancing Men in Nursing" with materials highlighting the camaraderie and opportunities available to men entering the profession. The professional, skilled, compassionate male image portrayed in posters and advertising is designed to break down the stereotypes typically associated with men in nursing (Stokowski, 2012). As more men enter the profession and there is a push to increase minorities in nursing, will the image of nursing change (Critical Thinking Box 9.1)?

❓ CRITICAL THINKING BOX 9.1

Think Quick!

Picture in your mind your image of a nurse—did you just think of a female, tidy hair, professional looking uniform, serviceable white shoes, stethoscope around the neck, determined look in the eyes, energetic walk, clipboard in hand? Or did you just envision a male nurse with many of those same attributes? The image of nursing is changing, and many media depictions now include men as nurses. There have always been men in nursing, but with the increasing respect for the profession, and the high touch, high technicality in the field of nursing, more men than ever are looking to become nurses. Indeed, many men who enter nursing are interested in fighting the same stereotypes that woman have battled through the years. The term "male nurse" is considered an unnecessary distinction, much like saying a "female physician"—the gender bias is simply not a critical element (Wilson, 2009). The first step in turning the tide of thought about gender in nursing is for members of the profession to alter their own perceptions.

Nurses should be thought of as autonomous and competent decision makers within their nursing practice areas. Throughout the 1990s, a nationwide advertising campaign supported by the National Commission on Nursing Implementation Project produced radio and television ads that said, "If caring were enough, anyone could be a nurse." Nurses of America, an advocate organization sponsored by the National League for Nursing (NLN), implemented a very successful program directed toward improving the image of nursing as depicted on television, on radio, in print, and on lecture circuits. Consultants were contracted to work with executives, politicians, and celebrities to present nursing in a positive manner. This approach reinforced the image of the modern professional nurse as having critical thinking, evidence-based decision-making, and problem-solving skills.

At a nursing symposium in May 2012, it was noted that while the depiction of nurses in the media can affect how the public views nurses, it is truly up to each individual nurse to be proactive in presenting nursing as a respected profession (Muehlbauer, 2012). The American Academy of Nursing (http://www.aannet.org/raisethevoice, 2014) through the Raise the Voice campaign has brought nursing policy innovators to the forefront of health care policy debates. A concentrated effort by individuals and organizations is raising awareness of what nurses do and heightening the image and voice of nursing as a profession. As noted by Groves (2007), accurate portrayals of nurses as professional members of the health care team are rare, but it takes time to change perceptions. The continued trend of building a positive, intelligent, competent, and professional image of nursing must continue. Nurses who are new to the profession need to be aware of the extraordinary challenges and opportunities that they will face. It is equally important for nurses to improve the self-image of the professional nurse. The behaviors and ethics displayed by nurses on a day-to-day basis can do much to elevate the present and shape the future image of nursing (Cohen & Bartholomew, 2008).

Nursing associations are working together to promote a positive image and to handle nursing shortage issues. Nurses for a Healthier Tomorrow, an alliance of 43 nursing and health care organizations, has launched a national media campaign that demonstrates, through print and broadcast media, the many opportunities for the career of nursing. One tangible example of this effort is the website www.nursesource.org. Sigma Theta Tau International, the international honor society for nursing, is the coordinator of Nurses for a Healthier Tomorrow. Review their website at www.nursingsociety.org. The American Nurses Association published a flyer titled *Every Patient Deserves a Nurse*, along with other promotional materials for the lay public. The promotional message of these materials reinforces the positive image of nurses as patient advocates and critical resources both to patients and families, while also emphasizing the right of people to a safe health care environment.

In 2002, the Johnson & Johnson Company developed a nationwide campaign to support the nursing profession. This program, titled "The Campaign for Nursing's Future," was developed along with health care leaders and nursing organizations such as the National Student Nurse's Association (NSNA), the American Nurse's Association (ANA), the American Organization for Nurse Executives (AONE), the National League for Nursing, and Sigma Theta Tau. The goal of this program is to increase the number of young adults entering nursing through raising the visibility of nurses of varied races, gender, and roles. The website for the campaign can be found at www.discovernursing.com.

The negative images of nursing, those of the "naughty nurse" or the "Nurse Ratchet" that are depicted in the media, are still prevalent, but these erroneous portrayals do offer professional nurses the opportunity to educate the public about what nurses truly do. Nursing is not the only profession that struggles with a skewed media image. Some of these erroneous depictions may be related to the largely female population who seeks these professions; consider the sexual media images that are often illustrated by flight attendants, massage therapists, or secretaries. Other occupations that suffer from poor media portrayals include the "mad scientist" role (chemist or researcher), construction worker (often a sexual male image), or consider the negative images that both female and male lawyers are often faced with! Devaluation of the nursing profession by demeaning or comical images only extends the nursing shortage and further discourages talented people from entering the nursing profession. It is up to each individual to continue to display professional role modeling and provide public education on what nurses really do to empower the professional image of nursing (Cohen & Bartholomew, 2008).

How can nurses change the image of nursing? How can the image of nursing become more congruent with the actual role the nurse plays in today's rapidly evolving health care environment? Nurses outnumber all other professions in health care. Mee (2006) suggests that nurses can promote the professional image of nursing by doing the following.

Patient Interactions

One by One. During the first 60 seconds that a patient sees the nurse, a lasting impression may be formed. Take a moment before meeting a new patient to portray confidence in your role and a respect for the patient from the beginning. Many health care institutions require nurses to wear nursing uniforms of a distinct color that separates them from nurse assistants and respiratory therapists.

Personal Interaction With the Public

Have a professional response ready in case someone asks about nursing. Present nursing's image positively, and relate what an important role nurses have in society as health care providers. Nursing advocacy starts with *you*! Every professional nurse has the responsibility to educate the public about what nurses do and the amount of education and dedication it takes to be a nurse. Believe in yourself, and project the image you want the public to see (Jacobs-Summers & Jacobs-Summers, 2011).

Public Speaking and Community Activities

Consider speaking at or visiting schools on Career Day. You don't have to be an expert at public speaking to discuss the role of the nurse with local community groups. A brief, interactive presentation at an elementary or high school can stimulate interest in nursing early—for both male and female students.

Participation in Political Activities

Increase the positive visibility of nurses through politics by becoming actively involved as a nurse lobbyist. Be aware of the current health care issues on the community, state, and national levels. Get to know the elected officials, and talk to them about the role of the nurse. This may be a valuable opportunity to present nursing in a very positive manner. Remember that most elected officials do not understand the role nurses play in health care (Mee, 2006).

The image of nursing continues to evolve as the many roles of nurses are portrayed through the media in the restructuring of health care environments and in a variety of settings, from emergency rooms to war zones. Studies continue to verify that competent nursing care affects mortality rates in critical care patients, and the future for many nursing jobs lies in the expanding role of nursing into emergency and disaster preparedness and integration of technology and informatics into practice settings (Health Resources and Services Administration [HRSA], 2010). The role and image of the nurse will continue to change as the many facets of health care delivery evolve during this century. The current nursing shortage will play a significant future part in the creation of the image and role of the nurse. How will nurses respond to these changes? How will you present yourself as a professional?

What Constitutes a Profession?

There are many ways to describe a "professional." What meaning does the word have for you as a graduate professional nurse? Controversy about the definition of the term *professional* as it relates to nursing is not a new issue. Strauss (1966), a noted sociologist, found the word *professional* used in reference to nursing in a magazine article published in 1892 titled "Nursing, a New Profession for Women." The nurses of the 20th and 21st centuries owe a great deal to Isabel Adams Hampton (later Isabel Hampton Robb) for her visionary focus in the late 1800s. She was an outstanding advocate for the professionalization of nursing. In the textbook *Nursing Ethics* (1900), she wrote:

> *The trained nurse, then, is no longer to be regarded as a better trained, more useful, higher class servant, but as one who has knowledge and is worthy of respect, consideration, and due recompense.... She is also essentially an instructor; part of her duties have to do with the prevention of disease and sickness, as well as the relief of suffering humanity.... These are some of the essentials in nursing by which it has become to be regarded as a profession, but there still remains much to be desired, much to work for, in order to add to its dignity and usefulness.*

In Caplow's classic work from the early 1950s, *The Sociology of Work* (Caplow, 1954), several steps in the process of "becoming professional" were defined further, and the value of forming an association that defined a special membership was addressed. Caplow suggested that making a name change to clarify an area of work or practice would subsequently produce a new role. With the creation of this new role, the group would then establish a code of ethics and legal components for licensure to practice and educational control of the profession (Caplow, 1954). This process of becoming professional was taking place in nursing in 1897 with the establishment of the ANA. Other aspects of professionalization were also beginning to develop. For example, the *Code for Nurses* was suggested as early as 1926, although it was not written or published by the ANA until the early 1950s. Revisions were made in 1956, 1960, and 1976, with changes made in 1985 that included interpretative statements. In the summer of 2001 at the ANA convention, delegates again updated the code and changed the name to the *Code of Ethics for Nurses with Interpretive Statements*. The American Nurses Association deemed 2015 the Year of Ethics and issued an updated *Code of Ethics with Interpretive Statements* found at http://nursingworld.org/MainMenuCategories/EthicsStandards.

Almost 20 years after Caplow's work, Pavalko (1971) described eight dimensions of a profession. Pavalko's dimensions of a profession and their specific application to nursing are examined in more detail later in this chapter. Nursing continues to apply these dimensions to support nursing's move away from the occupational focus to a professional focus. Is nursing a profession or semiprofession?

By responding to the questions in Critical Thinking Box 9.2 (which presents Levenstein's model, a fourth model of professionalism), you will identify common themes in describing a profession. What are your thoughts about the nursing profession in light of these criteria?

❓ CRITICAL THINKING BOX 9.2

Levenstein's Characteristics of a Profession

What do you think about …
- The element of altruism
  How do you define caring in your clinical practice?
- Code of ethics
  Are you familiar with the ANA Code of Ethics?
- Collaboration with groups and individuals for the benefit of the patient
  What other groups do you work with in your clinical setting that affect the health needs of the patient and family?
- Colleagueship demonstrated by
  An organization for licensing
  - What is the role of the State Board of Nursing in your state?
  A group that helps ensure quality
  - Are you aware of the role of national nursing organizations that accredit nursing programs?
  - There are two national nursing organizations that accredit nursing programs; do you know what they are?
  Peer evaluations of practitioners
  - What is the role of job evaluations in terms of professional growth?
- Accountability for conduct and responsibility for practice decisions
  Who monitors professional conduct issues from a legal and ethical point of view?
  Does shared governance reflect more control of one's nursing practice?
- Strong research program
  Are you aware that a national center for nursing research is now operating in Washington, DC?

Others have written about professions and their development, but these sociological models present some logical characteristics for you to use to examine professionalism. According to Henshaw, a noted nursing leader and researcher, a profession includes "self-regulation and autonomy with ultimate loyalty and accountability to the professional group" (cited in Talotta, 1990). Nursing is a dynamic profession and continues to strive to enhance a professional image—which leads us to the next question.

Is Nursing a Profession?

Eunice Cole, a past president of the ANA, described nursing as a dynamic profession that has established a code of ethics and standards of practice, education, service, and research components. The standards for both the professional and practical dimensions of nursing are continually reviewed and updated. Nurses, strong in numbers but splintered professionally in many ways, represent the largest group of health care providers in the United States.

There are approximately 2.9 million registered nurses in the workforce with an average age of all licensed RNs increasing by about 2 years for RNs, and about one-third of the current nursing workforce is older than 50. The RN supply is anticipated to grow by 952,000 full-time equivalents (FTEs)—from 2,897,000 FTEs in 2012 to 3,849,000 FTEs in 2025—a 33% national increase (U.S. Department of Health and Human Services, 2014).

The majority of nurses (59.7%) complete their initial education preparation at the associate degree level. Currently, approximately 55% of the RN workforce holds a bachelor's or higher degree. Additionally, there has been a substantial increase (86.3%) in the number of RN-BSN graduates over the past few years, noting a trend of increasing postlicensure education. There was significant growth (a 67% increase from 2007 to 2011) in the numbers of RNs with a master's or doctoral degree in nursing or a related field (HRSA, 2013).

In October 2010 the IOM released its report, *The Future of Nursing*, initiated by the Robert Wood Johnson Foundation, which called for increasing the number of baccalaureate-prepared nurses to 80% and doubling the population of nurses with doctoral degrees. The current nursing workforce falls short of these recommendations, with approximately 50% of registered nurses prepared at the baccalaureate level. Nursing leaders, educators, and practice partners are working to increase the number of baccalaureate-prepared nurses using innovative educational strategies for advancement.

The key to addressing the need to increase the educational preparation of the nursing workforce is progression. In 2012, the Organization for Associate Degree Nursing (OADN), joined with nursing educators, community leaders, college presidents, and other national organizations to endorse a Joint Statement on Academic Progression for Nursing Students and Graduates (http://www.aacn.nche.edu/news/articles/2012/academic-progression).

Examine the issues that challenge nursing as a profession by using Pavalko's eight dimensions to describe a profession.

1. A Profession Has Relevance to Social Values

Does nursing exist to serve self or others? Nursing historically had its roots in true altruism with lifelong service to others. As nurses, we focus not only on the treatment component of patient care as a part of our nursing practice but also on wellness and health promotion issues. The goal is to shift the focus of health care so that primary prevention becomes more valued. As this shift occurs, nurses will become increasingly important because of their ability to be teachers of health promotion activities and managers of wellness, which are activities that have an impact on social values.

2. A Profession Has a Training or Educational Period

According to Florence Nightingale, a nurse's education should involve not only a theory component but also a practice component. An educational process for any professional is critical, because it transmits the knowledge base of the profession and, through research and other scholarly endeavors, advances the practice of the profession. The diversity of educational pathways for nurses has stimulated debate regarding the entry practice level for registered nurses. The Institute of Medicine report (2010), the OADN progression statement (2012), the National League for Nursing (2011), and the Carnegie Foundation Report on the Advancement of Teaching (2010) all speak to the issue of advancing nursing education and entry into practice (see the end of this chapter for a list of relevant websites and online resources). Some questions surrounding the issues include the following:

- What changes will shape the future of associate degree nursing programs?
- Will diploma or hospital-based nursing programs remain?
- How critical is it to complete a bachelor of science in nursing (BSN) program to handle the challenges of the health care environment, complex patient–family needs, and the expanding community-based settings for clinical work?
- Is a "ladder" approach or a concurrent enrollment program (CEP) to advanced education the best pathway for you?
- Will the practice doctorate in nursing (DNP) degree clarify or confuse advanced-practice roles in nursing?

These questions have been debated since the publication in 1965 of an ANA position paper that charged the profession with the goal of establishing nursing education at the baccalaureate level within 25 years. Almost 40 years have passed since then, and the issue continues to challenge the profession. The inability of nursing organizations and educational systems at all levels to come to agreement on this issue continues to affect the solidarity of the profession.

In the mid-1990s, some states (e.g., Maine and Idaho) engaged in debate about regulatory issues concerning the BSN as the entry credential. Beyond this generic-degree controversy are the issues associated with specialization: With the momentum from the AACN, the DNP has been established as the clinical practice degree for advanced practice. What should be the focus of the MSN degree or PhD degree? How will those degrees integrate into nursing education?

3. Elements of Self-Motivation Address the Way in Which the Profession Serves the Patient or Family and Larger Social System

In 1990, the Tri-Council of Nursing, along with the American Association of Colleges of Nursing, designed a "Nursing Agenda for Health Care Reform" to express collectively the views of nurses concerning health care. Endorsed by 39 major specialty nursing organizations, along with the ANA and the NLN, the Tri-Council emphasized a restructured health care system that would provide universal access to health care, direct health care expenditures toward primary care, and reduce costs.

Political activity is a way of translating social values into action. Nursing faces special challenges when, for example, nurses must go on strike for better pay and benefits or demonstrate a united front to gain federal funding rather than continuing a passive role in such issues. It is time for the nursing profession to define a new narrative that reflects how much the profession has changed, how critical nursing skills are to today's patient care, how the profession has stayed abreast of medical and technological innovation, and what nursing is going to look like in the future (Kaplan, 2005).

4. A Profession Has a Code of Ethics

Nursing, like other professions, has ethical dimensions. As noted earlier in the chapter, the nursing *Code of Ethics* published by the ANA dates to the 1950s. Key points of the code are provided in Box 9.1. The *Code of Ethics* is discussed in more detail in Chapter 19.

5. A Professional Has a Commitment to Lifelong Work

By this statement, Pavalko means that a professional sees his or her career as more than just a stepping stone to another area of work or as an intermittent job. Government data show that 83% of the nearly 2.9 million registered nurses work in health care (HRSA, 2010). Nursing constitutes the largest health care occupation, and more jobs are expected for registered nurses than for any other occupation. This faster-than-average growth is being driven by technological advances. Thus, nursing as a career has great potential for financial rewards, involvement in a variety of professional endeavors, several different areas of practice, and a commitment to lifelong work.

6. Members Control Their Profession

Nurses are not entirely autonomous. Although nurses have the challenge to ensure that members of the profession honor the trust given them by the public, they also work under professional and legislative control. Among these controls are the 50 state boards of nursing, which regulate the scope of nursing practice within each state, and the professional practice standards that are supported both at local and national levels. In 1973, the ANA wrote the first *Standards of Nursing Practice* and since then has had a leadership role in the development of general and many specialty nursing practice standards. Moreover, specialty organizations maintain standards for certification.

BOX 9.1   CODE OF ETHICS FOR NURSES

The ANA House of Delegates approved these nine provisions of the new Code of Ethics for Nurses at its June 30, 2001, meeting in Washington, DC. In July 2001 the Congress of Nursing Practice and Economics voted to accept the new language of the interpretive statements, resulting in a fully approved revised Code of Ethics for Nurses with Interpretive Statements, as follows:

1. The nurse, in all professional relationships, practices with compassion and respect for the inherent dignity, worth, and uniqueness of every individual, unrestricted by considerations of social or economic status, personal attributes, or the nature of health problems.
2. The nurse's primary commitment is to the patient, whether an individual, family, group, or community.
3. The nurse promotes, advocates for, and strives to protect the health, safety, and rights of the patient.
4. The nurse is responsible and accountable for individual nursing practice and determines the appropriate delegation of tasks consistent with the obligation to provide optimum patient care.
5. The nurse owes the same duties to self as to others, including the responsibility to preserve integrity and safety, to maintain competence, and to continue personal and professional growth.
6. The nurse participates in establishing, maintaining, and improving health care environments and conditions of employment conducive to the provision of quality health care and consistent with the values of the profession through individual and collective action.
7. The nurse participates in the advancement of the profession through contributions to practice, education, administration, and knowledge development.
8. The nurse collaborates with other health professionals and the public in promoting community, national, and international efforts to meet health needs.
9. The profession of nursing, as represented by associations and their members, is responsible for articulating nursing values, for maintaining the integrity of the profession and its practice, and for shaping social policy.

Reprinted with permission from American Nurses Association. (2015).: *Code of ethics for nurses with interpretive statements*, Silver Spring, MD: Author. Retrieved, nursebooks.org.

Another publication by the ANA, the *Standards of Clinical Nursing Practice* (2003), discusses the use of nursing process and professional practice standards. The development of professional practice standards indicates to the larger social system that nursing can define and control its quality of practice. These national standards are incorporated into institutional standards to help guide nursing practice. Most recent publications by the ANA can be found on their website (www.nursingworld.org). The issue at hand, however, is that these professional practice standards authorize nurses to practice nursing. Nurses are expected to take responsibility for their own actions and not just follow orders without thinking critically.

Nurses practice in varied settings, and the advanced practice nurse functions in a more autonomous professional role, such as the nurse-midwife, psychiatric clinical specialist, nurse practitioner, or certified nurse educator. In 1992, there were 100,000 advanced practice nurses in the United States. Among practicing RNs, 55% achieved a baccalaureate or higher degree in nursing or a nursing-related field in 2010, compared to 27.5% in 1980 (HRSA, 2013). These changes represent the largest growing segment of specialty nursing practice. Advancing education and knowledge levels often allows for increased autonomy.

Most nurses in the United States work within a structured setting; three out of five jobs are in hospital, inpatient, or outpatient settings. Trends in those settings are slowly changing to give nurses a stronger voice. For example, nursing care delivery systems that have case management and shared governance reflect more progressive and autonomous environments (see Chapter 15). Nursing can control its scope of practice through professional organizations and published documents, along with an active voice in regulatory bodies, such as state boards of nursing.

7. A Profession Has a Theoretical Framework on Which Professional Practice Is Based

Nursing continues to be based in the sciences and humanities, but nursing theory is evolving. It was not until the 1950s that nursing theory was "born." In 1952, Dr. Hildegard Peplau published a nursing model that described the importance of the "therapeutic relationship" in health and wellness. Since then, other nursing theorists such as Martha Rogers, Sister Callista Roy, Dorothea Orem, and Betty Neuman have contributed to our evolving theory-based nursing science.

8. Members of a Profession Have a Common Identity and a Distinctive Subculture

The outward image of nursing has changed remarkably within the past 50 years. Nurses were once identified by how they looked rather than by what they did. The nursing cap and pin reflected the nurse's school and educational background. The modern-day trend emphasizes that it is not what is worn but what is done that reflects one's role in the nursing profession. The struggle to shift out of rigid dress codes was a major issue in the 1960s. Clothing and other symbols identify a subculture, and changes in that identification process occur slowly. What kind of image do you want to project as a professional nurse (Critical Thinking Box 9.3)?

Nursing colleagues reflect attitudes and values about the profession. Many schools of nursing have alumni associations, student nurse associations, and nursing honor societies or clubs on campus. These groups provide social interaction during the nursing education years and are great ways to network later in one's career. Belonging to a professional organization (such as the ANA) or a specialty organization helps professional nurses maintain certifications and network with peers, and it enhances collegiality and scholarship.

> Nurses should choose optimism, making positive strides each day to celebrate who they are and the differences they make. Just a nurse—no, never.
>   Melissa Fitzpatrick, 2001

> **? CRITICAL THINKING BOX 9.3**
>
> ***What do you Think?***
>
> **What Kind of Image Do You Want to Project As a "Professional"?**
> - Should nurses wear visible body jewelry, piercings, or have tattoos?
> - Are the doctors on your unit called by their first or last names? How are *you* addressed in a professional setting?
> - Are your credentials visible to indicate additional degrees or certifications? If not, why not? Is it the policy of the agency or facility where you work to display these?
> - Are the nurses on your unit certified in their specialty areas? Is this recognized by your facility?
> - What do your peers wear?
> - Do you think scrubs look professional?
> - Can a nurse wearing cartoon-character scrubs be taken seriously? Why? Why not?
> - Should nurses leave the hospital in their scrubs and go run errands?
> - What other professions are associated with a "uniform"?

When will the conflicts in educational preparation be resolved? How will we use further refinement and application of nursing theories in our clinical practice? What can nurses do to have more control of nursing practice regardless of the clinical setting? Will there be an increase in the percentage of people who are choosing nursing as a career? What are the forces that will help nursing "come together" and become not only a true profession but the largest and most powerful of all the health care professional groups? (Remember, there is always strength in numbers.)

NURSING ORGANIZATIONS

What Should I Know About Professional Organizations?

Nursing organizations have significant roles in empowering nurses in their emerging professionalism (Fig. 9.1). Yet many nurses do not belong to a national organization such as the ANA, or to their state affiliate organization, or even to specialty-focused groups such as the American Association of Critical-Care Nurses (AACN) or the National Black Nurses Association (NBNA). Of the 3.4 million registered nurses, membership in the constituent associations in ANA represents less than half of the nurses (ANCC, 2015; HRSA, 2010). During the past few years, researchers have examined the issue of belonging to a professional organization. Although there are no conclusive findings regarding why or how nurses choose nursing organizations, some have suggested that organizations representing nursing as a whole, such as the ANA and the NLN, do not meet the needs of the individual nurse practicing in today's changing health care environment.

Affiliation with a nursing organization to facilitate networking with colleagues is a valuable resource. As a recent graduate, you will need to examine your options for joining a professional group and then demonstrate your professional commitment by active participation. The question should be "Which ones should I join?" rather than "Should I join an organization?" (Box 9.2). In the next section, various organizations are reviewed, with historical notes to assist you in making the best choice as you begin your nursing career. A more complete directory of nursing organizations can be found on the *Evolve* website.

What Organizations Are Available to the Recent Graduate?

A few of these key professional organizations for individual and organizational membership are described in this section in alphabetical order. Many of these organizations publish a newsletter or professional journal, and most have websites. Individual memberships in your professional

FIG. 9.1 There is a nursing organization to fit your needs.

BOX 9.2   THE BENEFITS OF BELONGING TO A PROFESSIONAL NURSING ORGANIZATION

- Representation and influence in the legislature
- Continuing education
- Develop leadership skills
- Participate in research
- Resources
- Personal benefits
- Networking
- Playing a part in reshaping the future of nursing

---

nursing organization and a specialty organization are great ways to maintain current knowledge about changes in your career field and create networking opportunities for both new graduate nurses and experienced nurses seeking to find a new position or to increase their knowledge (see Box 9.2).

American Nurses Association

The ANA is identified as the professional association for registered nurses. It was through the early efforts of Isabel Hampton Robb and others that the Nurses Associated Alumnae of the United States and Canada was formed. At the World's Fair in 1890, a group of 15 nursing leaders began discussions about forming a professional association. Six years later, alumnae from the training schools organized the professional association now known as the ANA. Canadian members split from the original group in 1911 and formed their own professional association. The organizational structure of the ANA has undergone many changes through the years.

Currently, when an individual joins the ANA, he or she joins the national organization along with the constituent associations at the state and local levels. This method geographically groups smaller clusters of members together according to their practice interests. According to the ANA website, the current membership is almost 180,000 individual registered nurses (ANA, FAQ—Membership, 2010).

In 1974, the Employee Retirement Income Security Act (ERISA), an amendment to the Taft-Hartley Act, allowed professional nursing organizations to be considered labor unions. United American Nurses is the collective bargaining organization representing the ANA. After this significant event, some nursing administrators and managers withdrew their memberships from ANA because of the potential conflict of interest between professional affiliation and the workplace. However, this change generated the development of other major nursing organizations: the Center for the American Nurse (CAN) and the American Association of Nurse Executives (AONE).

The ANA has been at the forefront of policy issues and represents nursing in legislative activities. The cabinets and councils of the ANA have provided standards of practice for both the generalist and the specialist. The 1988 *Social Policy Statement* document defined nursing practice at both the generalist and specialist levels; this is echoed in the current 2010 *Social Policy Statement*. The certifying organization of the ANA is the American Nurses Credentialing Center (ANCC), which has certified more than 250,000 RNs in different practice areas at both the generalist and specialist levels, along with more than 75,000 advanced-practice nurses (ANCC, 2015). The ANCC, a subsidiary of the ANA since 1991, identifies its mission as improving nursing practice and promoting quality health care service through several types of credentialing programs. The ANCC has created a modular approach to certification that enables the nurse to be recognized for multiple areas of expertise, not simply for competency in a core clinical specialty. There are 27 generalist care clinical specialties, 12 nurse practitioner certifications, 10 clinical nurse specialist certifications, and an interprofessional certification (ANCC, 2015). As a result of their "open door 2000" program, all qualified registered nurses, regardless of their educational preparation, can become certified as generalists in any of the following specialty areas: ambulatory care, home health, informatics, gerontology, medical-surgical, pediatrics, perinatal, and psychiatric-mental health nursing to name a few (ANCC, 2015). Check out the available nursing specialty certifications at http://www.nursecredentialing.org/Certification.aspx.

> Have you considered attaining a specialty certification? If so, what certification would you like to obtain?

In addition to certifying individual nurses, the organization also accredits educational providers (i.e., organizations that issue continuing education credits for professional programs), recognizes excellence in magnet nursing services through the ANCC Magnet Recognition Program®, and educates the public about credentialing and professional nursing. This organization is electronically linked on the home page of the ANA (www.nursingworld.org).

American Nurses Foundation and the American Academy of Nursing

Two other organizations associated with the ANA are the American Nurses Foundation, founded in 1955, and the American Academy of Nursing (AAN), founded in 1973. Briefly described, these organizations serve special purposes in support of research and recognition of nursing colleagues. The American Nurses Foundation was established as a tax-exempt corporation to receive money for nursing research. With the establishment of the National Nursing Research Institute, the focus has changed to one of support in the areas of policy making and research or educational activities. The AAN has a membership of more than 1500 nursing leaders and was established as an honorary association for nurses who have made significant contributions to the nursing profession. When a nurse is elected to the AAN, she or he is called a Fellow, and the credential following the nurse's name is FAAN. You may have had instructors who were faculty in the American Academy of Nursing, or you may be working with a nurse who is a FAAN. These nurses can provide valuable mentorship for the new graduate. The official publication of this organization is *Nursing Outlook.*

International Council of Nurses

The International Council of Nurses (ICN), established in 1899, is the international organization representing professional nurses. The focus of this nursing organization is on worldwide health care and nursing issues; it meets every 4 years and is headquartered in Geneva, Switzerland. The ICN has been involved in the development of ethical guidelines for the recruitment of nurses from low-income nations. Many European nations have adopted an ethical code and restrict their recruiting from 150 low-income nations (Anderson & Isaacs, 2007).

National League for Nursing

The NLN was established in 1952; however, the beginning of NLN can be traced back to the 1893 organization of the American Society of Superintendents of Training Schools for Nurses of the United States and Canada. Between the late 1800s and the early 1900s, seven nursing organizations formed and joined under the collective name and function of the NLN. One of the unique features of the NLN is that both individuals and agencies are members. The NLN adopted a strategic plan in 1995 to place community-based health care education and health care delivery at the center of its focus and activities (NLN, 1995). The NLN continues to foster improvement in nursing services and nursing education and offers annual educational summits so that nursing faculty and leaders in all types of nursing education programs can come together. Non-nurses can also join the NLN, fulfilling its purpose of promoting the consumer's voice in some nursing policies. The NLN has a biennial convention and publishes *N&HC: Perspectives on Community* (called *Nursing & Health Care* before 1995), *NLN Update*, and numerous other publications that can be obtained by calling 800-669-1656 or by visiting their website at www.nln.org.

Before 1997, the NLN functioned as an accrediting body in all levels of nursing education. In 1997, the NLN created an independent organization called the National League for Nursing Accrediting Commission (NLNAC) to accredit educational and professional nursing programs. This organizational change was in response to new standards established by the U.S. Department of Education (USDOE). This step was taken to separate accrediting activities from membership activities and to respond to the Higher Education Act Amendment of 1992. In 2013, NLNAC changed its name to the Accreditation Commission for Education in Nursing (ACEN) to maintain continued recognition by the USDOE as a Title IV Gatekeeper. This recognition by the USDOE ensures that nursing students enrolled in an accredited nursing education program continue to receive Federal Student Aid. Also during 2013, the National League for Nursing Commission for Nursing Education Accreditation (NLNCNEA) was established as another accreditation service of the NLN, which is **not** for Title IV purposes. Is your school an ACEN or CNEA-accredited institution? To find out, visit their websites at http://acenursing.org/or http://www.nln.org/accreditation-services/.

National Student Nurses' Association

The National Student Nurses' Association is a fully independent organization with a membership of approximately 60,000 nursing students throughout the United States. NSNA mentors the professional development of future nurses and facilitates their entrance into the profession by providing educational resources, leadership opportunities, and career guidance.

The organization was formed in 1952. Becoming a member of the NSNA may be viewed as a way to begin the "professional" socialization process. There are local school chapters as well as state and national level memberships. Often, members of the NSNA serve on selected committees of the ANA and speak to the ANA House of Delegates regarding student-related issues. The quarterly journal, *Imprint*, is published by the NSNA. Visit their website at www.nsna.org.

Organization for Associate Degree Nursing

This group was organized in 1986 as an outgrowth of several state organizations. Texas was the first state to have a chapter, which was started in 1984. Membership in the Organization for Associate Degree Nursing (OADN) is open to associate degree nursing graduates, educators, and students. Individuals, states, agencies, and other organizations may also join. There are state and national chapters. The mission of this organization is to be the advocate for associate degree nursing education and practice while supporting advanced nursing education through academic progression. OADN strives to maintain eligibility for RN licensure for graduates of associate degree (AD) programs, to promote AD nursing programs in the community, to provide a forum for discussion of issues affecting AD nursing, to develop partnerships and increase communication with other health care professionals, to increase public understanding of the AD nurse, to participate at state and national levels in the formation of health care policies, and to facilitate legislative action supporting the activities of OADN. Visit their website at http://oadn.org/.

American Association of Colleges of Nursing

This organization is the national voice for university and 4-year college educational programs in nursing and has a membership of more than 500 colleges. The mission of the organization is to serve the public interest by assisting deans and directors in improving and advancing nursing education, research, and practice. This organization publishes a newsletter and a bimonthly nursing journal called the *Journal of Professional Nursing*. In the past few years, it has formed a subsidiary for credentialing purposes. That organization is the Commission on Collegiate Nursing Education (CCNE). This autonomous accreditation agency serves only baccalaureate and higher degree programs in the accreditation process. Additional information on either organization can be found at www.aacn.nche.edu.

American Board of Nursing Specialties

Significant growth in specialty practice in nursing has been evident since the late 1990s. Throughout the 1980s and 1990s, specialty organizations met annually as the National Federation of Specialty Nursing Certifying Organization to discuss issues in certification and nursing practice. This organization dissolved, and many of the specialty organizations joined the American Board of Nursing Specialties (ABNS) in 1991. The ABNS was established to create uniformity in nursing certification; it now represents more than 25 specialty nursing organizations that promote specialty practice and address certification issues associated with specialty practice. The ABNS functions as a consumer advocate in promoting nursing certification.

As a recent graduate, are you interested in a particular specialty nursing practice area? How and when do you anticipate obtaining specialty certification? How will you include membership in a professional organization in your 5-year career-educational plan? Do you know the benefits of being a certified nurse? Do you work with nurses who are certified in their specialties?

American Assembly for Men in Nursing (Formerly Known As the National Male Nurses Association)

The purpose of AAMN is to recruit men into the profession of nursing, support men who are nurses in professional growth endeavors, and provide a framework for nurses to influence factors that affect men as nurses. At the time of this publication, the AAMN has chapters in 30 states (AAMN, 2015).

The American Red Cross

The American Red Cross is an international organization of approximately 120 Red Cross organizations around the world. Nurses of the American Red Cross pioneered public health nursing in the early 1900s. The American Red Cross is a voluntary agency that is supported by contributions and plays an important role in providing disaster relief and education in first aid and home health and in organizing volunteers to assist in hospitals and nursing homes. Nurse volunteers with the Red Cross play a significant role in assisting those who have been affected by natural disasters.

In summary, professional organizations play a significant role in enhancing the image of nursing. Their impact is seen in both educational and practice issues for generalist and specialist nurse roles. Organizations provide a voice for nursing in policy issues and serve to unite nurses as a group of professionals. Ultimately, it may be nursing organizations that will serve as the catalyst for change in the health care system, and their impact will be felt in the next century.

CONCLUSION

Throughout the past century, the image of nursing has undergone many changes. The portrayal of nurses in the media has impacted the public perception of both male and female professional nurses. How will nurses continue to refine, intensify, and manage the image of nursing for the future? Will the self-image of nursing change public perception? Nursing is defined as a profession. Participation in the political side of health care, active involvement in professional organizations, a dedication to furthering academic advancement through progression of all nurses, and a commitment to the improvement of nursing's self-image are all ways to meet the upcoming challenges both in the nursing profession and in this dynamic health care environment.

The questions will go on and on, and the answers will come from nurses in clinical practice, education, and research. These issues, which have a significant impact on nursing's professional image, must be resolved so nursing continues to move forward as a profession. As a recent graduate, you are the future of this exciting transition. The question to ask yourself is, what can I do to improve and maintain the image of nursing and the integrity of the profession? Change can and does begin with one person who is willing to step forward and make a difference. Is that you?

⊕ RELEVANT WEBSITES AND ONLINE RESOURCES

Carnegie Foundation for the Advancement of Teaching (2010)
Book highlights from educating nurses: A call for radical transformation. http://archive.carnegiefoundation.org/elibrary/educating-nurses-highlights.

Institute of Medicine (2010)
The future of nursing: Leading change, advancing health. http://www.iom.edu/Reports/2010/The-Future-of-Nursing-Leading-Change-Advancing-Health.aspx.

Future of Nursing; Campaign for Action (Update 2015)
Academic progression in nursing education. http://campaignforaction.org/apin.

American Association of Colleges of Nursing
Joint statement on academic progression for nursing students and graduates. http://www.aacn.nche.edu/aacn-publications/position/joint-statement-academic-progression.

BIBLIOGRAPHY

Accreditation Commission for Education in Nursing (ACEN). (2013). *NLNAC changes name to ACEN*. Retrieved from http://www.acenursing.net/acenursing/ACENrom/.

American Academy of Nursing. (2014). *Raise the voice*. Retrieved from http://www.aannet.org/raisethevoice.

American Assembly for Men in Nursing (AAMN). (2015). *Advancing men in nursing*. Retrieved from http://aamn.org/index.

American Nurses Association. (2015). *Code of ethics for nurses with interpretive statements*. Silver Spring, MD: ANA. Retrieved from nursebooks.org.

American Nurses Association. (2014). Public ranks nurses as most honest, ethical profession for 13th straight year (12/18/14). Retrieved from http://nursingworld.org/Nurses-MostHonestEthicalProfession.

(2013). *Standards of clinical nursing practice*. Kansas City, MO: ANA.

American Nurses Association. (2010). Frequently asked questions. Retrieved from www.nursingworld.org/FunctionalMenuCategories/FAQs.aspx#about.

American Nurses Association. (2010). *Social policy statement*. Kansas City, MO: ANA.

American Nurses Association. (n.d.). The importance of belonging to your professional nursing organization. PowerPoint presentation. Retrieved from www.nursingworld.org/EspeciallyForYou/Educators/TheImportanceofBelonging.aspx#276.

American Nurses Credentialing Center. (2015). *ANCC certification center*. Retrieved from http://www.nursecredentialing.org/Certification.aspx.

Anderson, B., & Isaacs, A. (2007). Simply not there: The impact of international migration of nurses and midwives—perspectives from Guyana. *Journal of Midwifery & Women's Health, 28*(6), 392–397. Retrieved from http://web.ebscohost.com.ezproxy.baylor.edu/ehost/detail?vid=11&hid=102&sid=04252468-7087-4df4-84a1-f2f55dc652ec%40sessionmgr104.

Bostridge, M. (2008). *Florence Nightingale: The woman and her legend*. London: Viking Press.

Caplow, T. (1954). *The sociology of work*. Minneapolis: University of Minnesota.

Cohen, S., & Bartholomew, K. (2008). *Our image, our choice: Perspectives on shaping, empowering, and elevating the nursing profession*. Marblehead, MA: HCPro.

Donelan, K., Buerhaus, P., Desroches, C., Dittus, R., & Dutwin, D. (2008). Public perceptions of nursing careers: The influence of the media and nursing shortages. *Nursing Economics, 26*(3), 143–150, 165. Retrieved from http://www.medscape.com/viewarticle/576950_4.

Groves, B. (2007). An image problem: From TV to silver screen. *The Record*. Retrieved from http://www.nursingadvocacy.org/news/2007/may/06_record.html.

Health Resources and Services Administration. (HRSA). (2010). *HRSA study finds nursing workforce is growing and more diverse*. Washington, DC: HRSA. Retrieved from http://www.hrsa.gov/about/news/pressreleases/2010/100317_hrsa_study_100317_finds_nursing_workforce_is_growing_and_more_diverse.html.

Health Resources and Services Administration. (HRSA). (2013). *The U.S. nursing workflow: Trends in supply and education*. Washington, DC: HRSA. Retrieved from http://bhpr.hrsa.gov/healthworkforce/reports/nursingworkforce/nursingworkforcefullreport.pdf.

Jacobs-Summers, H., & Jacobs-Summers, S. (2011). *The image of nursing: It's in your hands*. Retrieved from http://www.nursingtimes.net/nursing-practice/clinical-zones/educators/the-image-of-nursing-its-in-your-hands/5024815.article.

Kaplan, M. (2005). Speech: Why isn't nursing more newsworthy? Medscape Nursing. Retrieved from www.med scape.com.

Mee, C. (2006). Painting a portrait: How you can shape nursing's image. *Imprint, 53*(5), 44–49.

Muehlbauer, P. (2012). *How can we improve the way media portrays the nursing profession?*. Retrieved from http ://connect.ons.org/issue/december-2012/a-closer-look/how-can-we-improve-the-way-the-media-portrays-the-nursing.

National Organization for Associate Degree Nursing. (2012). *Joint statement on academic progression for nursing students and graduates*. Retrieved from https://www.noadn.org/dmdocuments/120918_Joint_Statement_Academic_Progression.pdf.

Nursing-Informatics. (2003). The in/visibility of nurses in cyberculture. Retrieved from http://visiblenurse.com/visiblenurse1.html.

Pavalko, R. (1971). *Sociology of occupations and professions*. Itasca, IL: Peacock.

Peplau, H. (1952). *Interpersonal relationships in nursing*. New York: Putnam Press.

Robb, I. H. (1916). *Nursing ethics: For hospital and private use*. Cleveland, OH: E. C. Koeckert.

Strauss, A. (1966). *The structure and ideology of American nursing: an interpretation in the nursing profession*. New York: Wiley.

Stowkowski, L. A. (2012). Just call us nurses: Men in nursing. Medscape Nurses. Retrieved from http://www.me dscape.com/viewarticle/768914_7.

Talotta, D. (1990). Role conceptions and professional role discrepancy among baccalaureate nursing students. *Image: Journal of Nursing Scholarship, 22*(2), 111–115.

U.S. Department of Health and Human Services, Health Resources and Services Administration, National Center for Health Workforce Analysis. (2014). *The future of the nursing workforce: National- and state-level projections, 2012-2025*. Rockville, MD: Author.

What's the big deal about naughty nurse images in the media? (2010). Retrieved from www.truthaboutnursing .org/faq/naughty_nurse.html.

Wilson, D. (2009). Meet the men who dare to care. *Johns Hopkins Nursing, VII*(2). Retrieved from http://web.jhu.edu/jhnmagazine.

Nursing Management

Challenges of Nursing Management and Leadership

Joann Wilcox, RN, MSN, LNC

ⓔ http://evolve.elsevier.com/Zerwekh/nsgtoday/.

Leaders don't force people to follow—they invite them on a journey.
Charles S. Lauer

Outstanding leaders go out of their way to boost the self-esteem of their personnel. If people believe in themselves, it's amazing what they can accomplish.
Sam Walton

"I need help on the night shift!"

After completing this chapter, you should be able to:

- Differentiate between management and leadership.
- Describe theories of management and leadership.
- List characteristics of an effective manager and an influential leader.
- Discuss the elements of transformational leadership.
- Identify distinguishing generational characteristics of today's workforce.
- Differentiate between leadership and followership.
- Differentiate the concepts of power and authority.
- Apply problem-solving strategies to clinical management situations.
- Identify the characteristics of effective work groups.
- Discuss the change process.
- Discuss the value of using evidence-based management actions.

A s you move closer to meeting your goal of becoming a graduate nurse, give consideration to understanding the role of the nurse as a manager and as a leader. You might be thinking:

I do not want to be a manager; I am just a recent graduate!
OR
I want to take care of patients, not be a paper pusher!
OR
Am I ready to be followed by others?

Nursing, in any role, is a *people business. Management* is the process of effectively working with people. When you accept your first position as a graduate nurse, it is important to realize that you are becoming a part of a work group where members spend at least a third of their day interacting with each other. Therefore, registered nurses must be prepared to use varying levels of management skills, enhanced by interpersonal, followership, and leadership skills, to be effective in their role as a provider of patient care and as member of the care team.

There are multiple levels of management that a registered nurse can practice. The specific level depends on the experience, competency, and defined role of the individual nurse. For example, as a recent graduate, you will have *primary management* responsibility for the patients for whom you will be providing care. This will include planning and coordinating the care with other nursing personnel, with health care staff, and with the patient and family members. Provision of this level of management is expected from all registered nurses who practice in the acute-care environment.

MANAGEMENT VERSUS LEADERSHIP

What Is the Difference Between Management and Leadership?

Although the terms *management* and *leadership* are frequently interchanged, they do not have the same meaning. A leader selects and assumes the role; a manager is assigned or appointed to the role. Leaders are effective at influencing others; managers, as providers of care, supervise a team of people who are working to help patients achieve their defined outcomes. Managers also have responsibility for organizational goals and the performance of organizational tasks such as budget preparation and scheduling. Although it is desirable for managers to be good leaders, there are leaders who are not managers and, more frequently, managers who are not leaders! So, let us discuss the actual differences in more detail.

The Functions of Management

Management is a problem-oriented process with similarities to the nursing process. Management is needed whenever two or more individuals work together toward a common goal. The manager coordinates the activities of the group to maintain balance and direction. There are generally four functions the manager performs: *planning* (what is to be done), *organizing* (how it is to be done), *directing* (who is to do it), and *controlling* (when and how it is done). All of these activities occur continuously and simultaneously, with the percentage of time spent on each activity varying with the level of the manager, the characteristics of the group being managed, and the nature of the problem and goal.

According to Rothbauer-Wanish (2009), planning is generally considered a basic management function and one on which managers should spend a significant part of their time. The foundation for all planning begins with the development of goals that reflect the mission and vision of the organization and defining strategies that will be implemented to meet and maintain that mission and vision. The next level of planning is used daily as a part of determining the requirements for accomplishing the work to be done and ensuring that what is needed is available. This planning must be congruent with the strategies for meeting the mission and vision of the organization. Along with this approach, a manager must also be able to plan for contingencies, which, if not addressed, will interfere with accomplishing what needs to be done. When managing a patient-care unit, which needs specific resources 24 hours a day, one can be certain that the unexpected will happen. Being prepared for the unexpected is a key function of a nurse manager.

Staff nurses practice the elements of planning as the plans of care for each patient are developed. For this process, the patient's current status and goals are assessed to determine what needs to occur during the time one is assigned to provide that care. The interventions needed are selected to advance the patient to the point of meeting his or her defined goals. This process of management of patient care uses the same planning skills as those used by someone who has the responsibility of managing staff.

Organizing occurs as the manager aligns the work to be done with the resources available to do that work (Rothbauer-Wanish, 2009). This requires knowledge of all parts of the work, as well as a clear understanding of the competencies required of those who will be performing the assigned work. The manager must consider not only the licensing regulations but also the facility's policies when organizing the assignment of work. For example, licensing regulations may allow a licensed practical nurse to administer defined intravenous medications, but the facility policy may not allow that level of employee to perform that procedure. Another example would be that the licensing regulations for registered nurses do not specify that a newly licensed nurse cannot be assigned to work in a critical care unit. However, facility policy may state that registered nurses who wish to work in a critical care unit must gain 1 year of other experience before being assigned to critical care service. Knowing this information prevents the manager from making decisions that may be unacceptable.

The next phase of management is providing direction or supervision. The manager retains accountability for ensuring the work is completed in a timely and competent manner. Additionally, staff members need to complete assigned work according to standards, policies, and procedures with the understanding that the manager will provide sufficient observation and assessment of care being delivered to ensure that the care provided is safe and complete. When patient care falls below minimum standards, the manager has two actions to take. The first is to make certain the care and safety of the patient are addressed by ensuring the proper care is provided, and the second is to address the performance of the staff who did not provide the care as assigned. Managers need to be able to make decisions regarding the level of supervision needed by each staff member. Managers must also be able to motivate staff toward reaching their full competence to perform the assigned work with minimal observation and direction.

Staff nurses who are managing the care of patients need to have a clear understanding of the relevant policies and procedures related to the care provided and must be confident that he or she is competent to provide that care. The staff nurse must be cognizant of the expected outcomes of the care to be provided and how to determine if progress toward those outcomes is occurring. Actions to take when outcomes are not being met must be understood by the staff nurse who is managing the care.

Controlling is the last aspect of the planning function of the nurse manager. Most of the controls in health care facilities exist because health care is a highly regulated system, and much of what must be done is dictated by governments, insurers, evaluating agencies, health policy, and institutional policy. The effective manager needs to be cognizant of the regulations that affect his or her area of practice and must be able to clearly communicate the essence of these regulations to the staff. Staff members need to have a thorough understanding of regulations and implications of noncompliance with these regulations. An example of external controls imposed because of regulations is the elimination of the use of certain dangerous abbreviations when a physician writes a medication order (see Chapter 11 for a list of abbreviations). This regulation is a part of The Joint Commission (TJC) Standards, as well as Standards from the Centers for Medicare & Medicaid Services (CMS). Although the initial focus of this regulation is on the physician, registered nurses may not implement an order that includes these eliminated abbreviations.

Control by the manager may also be demonstrated through data collected when reviewing quality of care to determine the level of compliance with standards and other quality monitors. These data give the manager the ability to validate observations, because these observations can represent the outcomes of care that has been provided. For instance, if the rate of hospital-acquired infections continues to be above the expected level, the manager has the information needed to implement and mandate interventions to reduce the number of infections.

> Florence Nightingale was an early nursing leader. What characteristics of a manager did she also demonstrate?

What Are the Characteristics and Theories of Management?

Active interest in management as a separate entity was first noted as part of the industrial revolution. The *traditional theory* developed at that time was based on the premise that there was a need to have the highest productivity level possible from each worker (Wertheim, n.d.). This theory is the basis for the hierarchy that has dominated much of management theory for almost two centuries. This type of management is also known as the bureaucratic theory of management, defined as "dividing organizations into hierarchies, establishing strong lines of authority and control. He [Weber, the author of this theory] suggested organizations develop comprehensive and detailed standard operating procedures for all routinized tasks" (McNamara, n.d.). The manager who functions under the traditional theory follows rules closely and understands the concept of the division of labor and the chain-of-command structure. Historically, this kind of functioning was thought to be efficient and clear and was considered necessary to attain the most work from each employee. Throughout nursing history, this has been the theory on which the work of nurse managers was based. Since the mid-1990s, movement from this traditional theory has occurred, and more appropriate theories have been put into practice in multiple health care settings across the country.

Following the development of traditional theory of management was *behavioral theory* (also called *human-interaction theory*). This evolved as it became more evident that the humanistic side of management needed to be addressed (Hellriegel et al., 1999). Employees seeking recourse from some of the rules of hierarchy looked for assistance outside of their place of work, for instance, in the growing labor unions. Employers recognized the need to consider the human side of productivity so as to maintain a stable, satisfied work force.

This was followed by the introduction of *systems theory*, which considers inputs, transformation of the material, outputs, and feedback (Hellriegel et al., 1999). Systems theory is implemented when consideration is given to the impact of decisions made by one manager on other managers or on parts of the system as a whole. This is important in health care, because it helped management move from making decisions in the traditional manner, in which departments functioned as though they were independent, to recognizing the interdependence of departments on each other. Recognizing that patients cannot be treated as though they are a number of separate and distinct parts has promoted the understanding and importance of systems theory. Whereas behavioral theory as it relates to management considers the attitudes and needs of the employee, systems theory examines the possible outcomes of all individuals affected by a decision.

The last theory of management to be considered is the *contingency theory*, which is also referred to as the *motivational theory* (Hellriegel et al., 1999). This theory focuses on the manager being able to blend the elements of the earlier theories, using those elements to determine what motivates people to make choices and leading to the most effective methods to complete the work that needs to be done. All of these theories are directed toward ways to ensure that employees are as productive and timely as possible when working to meet the organizational goals or targets.

> Consider how you might gain information about the management theory used in the facility in which you are seeking employment. What questions would you ask as a part of the interview process? Why is this important to you?

What Is Meant by Management Style?

You will experience a variety of management styles in your nursing practice. These styles follow a continuum from *autocratic* to *laissez-faire* (Fig. 10.1).

FIG. 10.1 Management styles.

The *autocratic manager* uses an authoritarian approach to direct the activities of others. This individual makes most of the decisions alone without input from other staff members. Under this style of management, the emphasis is on the tasks to be done, with less focus on the individual staff members who perform the tasks. The autocratic manager may be most effective in crisis situations when structure and control are critical to success, such as during a cardiac arrest or code situation. In general, however, the autocratic manager will have a difficult time in motivating staff to become part of a satisfactory work environment, because there is minimal recognition of the contributions of staff to the work that needs to be done and minimal focus on the necessary relationships that make up the successful health care team. Many individuals, particularly those from generations after the Baby Boomers, will not stay in a position in which autocracy is the major style of management.

On the other end of the continuum is the *laissez-faire manager*, who maintains a permissive climate with little direction or control exerted. This manager allows staff members to make and implement decisions independently and relinquishes most of his or her power and responsibility to them.

Although this style of management may be effective in highly motivated groups, it may not be effective in a bureaucratic health care setting that requires many different individuals and groups to interact.

In the middle of the continuum is the *democratic manager*. This manager is people-oriented and emphasizes effective group functioning. The goals of the group are identified, and the manager is perceived as a group member who is also its organizer who keeps the group moving in the defined direction. The environment is open, and communication flows both ways. The democratic manager encourages participation in decision making; he or she recognizes, however, that there are situations in which such participation may not be appropriate, and the manager is willing to assume responsibility for a decision when necessary. The democratic style is the blend of autocracy and laissez-faire with assurances that the extreme ends of the continuum are rarely, if ever, necessary.

One example of a democratic manager following either the behavioral or contingency theory would be a manager who creates a Nurse Practice Committee on his or her unit. This committee would have some defined authority and responsibility to address specific items in the practice environment, such as schedules and practices on the unit. This type of committee supports the idea that staff and management are interdependent in governing the successful practice environment (Tonges et al., 2004).

To be a successful manager in today's hierarchical organizations, the nurse manager will need to adopt a democratic style of management, one that is flexible enough to adapt to the changing roles of nursing staff. The nurse manager should be willing and able to share power with the same people whom he or she will supervise. The successful manager will also need to acquire an element of laissez-faire style for those components of governance that will be under the auspices of the staff. It will be important for staff nurses to develop a balanced combination of autocracy and laissez-faire as they implement shared governance (stakeholder participation in decision making) that will include quality of care and peer review (Institute of Medicine, 2004).

As is evident, the continuum of management styles ranges from what might be considered total control to complete freedom for subordinates. In choosing a management style, the manager must decide on levels of control and freedom and then determine which trade-offs are acceptable in each situation. Behaviors vary from telling others what to do, to relinquishing to another group within the organization the authority for portions of the work to be done. As a new staff nurse, your initial involvement in management occurs when you manage the care of a group of patients. The next involvement may be as a part of the shared governance model that may be developing in your facility. As you gain experience and knowledge, it is important for you to develop an understanding of which style you should use, depending on what you hope to be able to achieve.

> Look at managers on the units where you are assigned for clinical practice. How do they fit into these categories?

Leadership, in contrast, is a way of behaving; it is the ability to cause others to respond, not because they have to but because they want to. Leadership is needed as much as management for effective group functioning, but each role has its place. The manager determines the agenda, sets time limits, and facilitates group functioning. The leader "models change, establishes trust, sets the pace, creates the vision, [provides] focus, and builds commitment" (Manion, 1996, p.148).

What Are the Characteristics and Theories of Leadership?

The many attempts to define what makes a good leader have resulted in a variety of studies and proposals. Researchers have tried to identify the characteristics or traits necessary to be a good leader. Several of these studies have defined the concept of a *born leader,* implying that the desired traits are inherited. This is often referred to as the "Great Man" theory, because it was first identified when leadership was generally thought to be a male quality, particularly as it related to military leadership (Van Wagner, 2007). With later research, it became clear that desired leadership traits could be learned through education and experience. It also became clear that the most effective leadership style for one situation was not necessarily the most effective for another and that the effectiveness of the leader is influenced by the situation itself. As leadership theories continue to develop, emphasis is more on what the leader does rather than on the traits the leader possesses.

Several other theories of leadership are worth discussing. The first is *contingency leadership,* which says that leadership should be flexible enough to address varying situations. Although this may sound complicated, it can be compared with your approach to patient care. As a nurse, you individualize a patient care plan based on the needs of the individual. Then the plan is implemented using available resources. The effective leader, using contingency leadership, brings the same flexible approach to each individual situation where leadership is required.

Situational leadership theory resulted from the study of the contingency theory. Under situational leadership theory, the leader attempts to function more closely in the situation being addressed. Blanchard and Hersey (1964) define the situational leader as one who analyzes the needs of the current situation and then selects the most appropriate leadership style to address that particular situation. The selected style depends on the competencies of each employee who will be helping address the current situation. The authors state that a good situational leader may use different styles of leadership for different employees, all of whom are involved in addressing the same situation. This is not unlike what you, as a team leader, will be doing when assigning work to members of your work team. The assignments will need to be individualized based on the competencies of each member of the team to help ensure the patient-care goals can be met.

Interactional leadership is the next theory to consider. With this theory, the focus is on the development of trust in the relationship (Marquis & Huston, 2003). Interactional leadership includes concepts of behavioral theories, which begin to address the theory that leaders are *made* and not *born*, because the needed behaviors can be taught and learned. Individuals who function based on the theory of interactional leadership use democratic concepts of management and view the tasks to be accomplished from the standpoint of a team member.

Leadership theory can also be described as *transactional,* noting that the transactional leader is one who has a greater focus on vision, defined as the ability to envision some future state and describe it to others so they can begin to share that vision. The transactional leader holds power and control over followers by providing incentives when the followers respond in a positive way to the leader's vision and the actions needed to reach that vision. The basis for the relationship between leader and follower is that punishment and reward motivate people. Transactional leaders seek equilibrium so the vision can be reached and he or she only intervenes when it appears that goals will not be attained (Sullivan & Decker, 2012).

This leadership theory does not sound like one that many would be encouraged to embrace or follow, as the rewards are ultimately one-sided. However, the transactional approach to leadership still exists in most organizations, generally at the management level as incentives are provided to gain a defined level of productivity. One may believe that this approach is closer to management than leadership, which may explain why it might not be effective at other levels in the organization.

Transformational leadership occurs when the leader has a strong, clear vision that has developed through listening, observing, analyzing, and finally by truly buying into the vision to change dramatically the way things are currently done (Bass, 1990). This theory was introduced as early as the 1970s and is still in its infancy of use by particular industries such as health care. However, this theory of leadership is a "major component of the Magnet model developed by the American Nurses Credentialing Center" (Sherman, 2012, p.62).

According to Sherman (2012), there are four key elements that characterize the transformational leadership style. The first element is idealized influence, meaning that the transformational leader is a "role model for outstanding practices which in turn inspires followers to practice at this same level." Inspirational motivation, the second element, is demonstrated by the leader being able to "communicate a vision" in a manner that others understand. Intellectual stimulation and individual consideration are the last two elements and address the fact that the leader values staff input and creativity while continuing to coach and mentor staff, recognizing there are both group and individual needs and issues to consider (Sherman, 2012, p.64).

Characteristics of transformational leaders, according to Tichy and Devanna (1986), are that these leaders are courageous change agents who believe people will do what is right when provided direction, information, and support. They are also value-driven visionaries, lifelong learners, and individuals who can successfully handle the complexities of leadership. To accomplish their goals, they effectively change the traditional way of leading, which is often from the office, to leading from the place where the action is occurring.

Transformational leadership will be implemented when it is clear to the strong, visionary leaders that the current situation(s) cannot be "fixed" using the traditional methods that have worked in the past. In the early 1990s, Leland Kaiser, a renowned health care futurist, discussed transformational leadership, identifying the transformational leader as the primary architect of life in the 21st century. Many of the predictions made by Kaiser are now being recognized as part of transformational leadership. An example of this is what has occurred at Virginia Mason Medical Center, as the leadership of that organization took on the task of transforming health care at that facility (Kenney, 2011). The entire leadership team has worked together to ensure that this transformation occurred as envisioned.

If transactional leadership involves the use of leadership power over rewards and punishments, transformational leadership can be characterized as a process whereby leader and followers work together in a way that changes or transforms the organization, the employees/followers, and the leader. It recognizes that real leadership involves transformation and learning on the part of follower *and* leader. As such, it is more like a partnership, even though there are power imbalances involved.

Whereas transactional leadership involves telling, commanding, or ordering (and using contingent rewards), transformational leadership is based on inspiring, getting followers to buy in voluntarily, and creating common vision. Transformational leadership is what most of us refer to when we talk about great leaders in our lives and in society.

The nurse shortage is a good example of a problem in which the solution will most likely be found by transformational leaders. It is evident that the old ways of fixing the nurse shortage have not been effective. Managers, lawmakers, and organizations have tried increasing wages, paying bonuses, recruiting foreign nurses, mandating staff-to-patient ratios, adding nurse-extenders, and implementing flexible shifts. None of these methods has had any long-lasting effects, because they do not address the conflicts that have occurred as newer generations of nurses have reached the level where they want control of their practice as granted by education and licensure. A transformational leader understands the basis for these conflicts and develops a vision, which will address the needs of the people involved in the conflict.

One might anticipate that the Chief Executive Officer and the Chief Nursing Officer of a hospital would both be transformational leaders. These leaders have a responsibility to see the bigger picture and to be able to describe that vision or picture to others. Porter-O'Grady (2003a) describes this type of leader as one who can "stand on the balcony" (p.175). From this position, the leader can monitor the ebb and flow of the organization and determine in which direction the organization is moving. To be effective, the transformational leader must have a vision that can be put into words for others to understand. Check out the relevant websites and online resources at the end of the chapter for additional information on transformational leadership.

Although most leaders tend to lean toward one of the theories discussed here, fluctuations from one to another can occur, depending on the particular situation. In the health care setting, good leaders carefully balance job-centered and employee-centered behaviors to meet both staff and patient needs effectively (Critical Thinking Box 10.1).

> ### ❓ CRITICAL THINKING BOX 10.1
>
> Consider your educational and clinical experiences. What leadership theories and styles have you observed? What management styles have you observed? Are there specific personality traits that enhance a person's performance in these two roles?

An effective leader works toward established goals and has a sense of purpose and direction. She or he must also be aware of how her or his behavior impacts the workplace. Emotions, moods, and patterns of behavior displayed by the leader will create a lasting impression on the behavior of the team involved. It is critical for the leader to be aware of this impact if she or he is going to be effective in managing and leading a team (Porter-O'Grady, 2003b). Rather than push staff members in many directions, the effective leader uses personal attributes to organize the activities and *pull* the staff toward a common direction.

The most current theory addressing the changing environment in which we work is the *complexity theory* of leadership. The complexity theory addresses the "unpredictable, disorderly, nonlinear, and uncontrollable ways that living systems behave" (Burns, 2001, p.474). This theory indicates that we need to look at systems, such as those in health care organizations, as patterns of relationships and the interactions that occur among those in the system.

Complexity theory is complex! However, the basis of the thinking can most easily be understood by comparing traditional ways of analyzing an organization to the ways in which this analysis would be accomplished using the complexity theory. The traditional method used to understand an organization is to "break a system into smaller bits and when we believe we understand the bits we put them all back together again and draw some conclusions about the whole" (IOM, 2004). Complexity theory examines the whole rather than the sum of its parts, because breaking a system apart removes all the impact of the human relationships that affect the whole.

Smyth (2015) asked, "Why do we struggle to achieve our goals in clinical outcomes, safety and financial performance in [health care facilities] when these facilities are chockfull of brilliant, well-intentioned people?" It is because those people bring factors such as varying levels of competence and performance and differing emotional states—all of which can have an unpredictable impact on the outcome. In general, most health care organizations work solely through hierarchies, which does not allow for the openness needed to achieve the best solutions to problems being addressed.

Following complexity theory, one understands that organizations are "organic, living systems" (Anderson et al., 2005) in which people act quickly and use knowledge sharing and patterns of relationships rather than the rules of a hierarchy. When leading according to the principles of complexity, change is understood as successful when accomplished by individuals as they adapt to variations in the environment and not as the linear managers dictate. "However, we are still mired in the hierarchical structures we have lived with for more than fifty years—going up and down the chain of command to make decisions…" (Smyth, 2015).

As we complete the discussion on the theories and characteristics of leaders and managers, it becomes evident that there are more differences between these two groups than those briefly identified in the opening paragraph of this discussion. According to Manion (1998), the major differences are

- Leaders focus on effectiveness, and Managers focus on efficiency.
- Leaders ask what and why, and Managers ask how.
- Leaders deal with people and relationships, and Managers deal with systems, controls, and policies.

- Leaders initiate innovation, and Managers maintain the status quo.
- Leaders look to the horizon, and Managers look to the bottom line (pp.3–7).

Management Requires "Followership"

Individuals can manage things, processes, and people. When thinking of nurse managers, it is generally assumed they are managing people, who are managing the care of patients. When being managed, one is in the role of a follower—an essential role in the safe and effective delivery of patient care. The role of the follower is not always considered when discussing management functioning, but it is obvious that those who are expected to follow the direction of the manager are essential to the success of the manager.

Followership is "the ability to take direction well, to get in line behind a program, to be a part of a team and to deliver what is expected of you" (McCallum, 2013). There cannot be a truly effective leader without competent followers since if the followers fail in the work they are doing, the manager will not be able to successfully complete the assigned work.

From the above information, it appears there are significant differences between leadership and followership. While this is true, the interconnections between these two functions make the differences almost irrelevant. "You can't have one without the other!" truly applies. They need each other to exist and to have a purpose.

While many believe followers are subservient to leaders, leaders are beholden to followers for both leaders and followers to be successful. Followers must have the ability to think critically and actively participate in the successful completion of the leadership directions/goals (Miller, 2007).

When assessing the success of a team or group of staff, it is important to remember that, at times, individuals assume either leadership or followership roles or assume both leadership and followership roles during the completion of required tasks. A successful leader understands the role of followers and recognizes that followers should receive credit for the success of the team/group just as the leader receives this credit (Miller, 2007).

THE TWENTY-FIRST CENTURY: A DIFFERENT AGE FOR MANAGEMENT AND FOR LEADERSHIP

The face of leadership is changing, and this is very evident in nursing and health care. Changes in health care are altering some of the foundations of nursing practice. Shorter hospital stays and emerging therapeutics require less, but perhaps more intense, clinical time and challenge the need for certain nursing interventions that have become routine over time. Nurses are becoming increasingly frustrated with the reality that the nursing care they were taught to provide—and they feel they need to provide—is not possible given the decreased time spent with their patients (Porter-O'Grady, 2003c). This dissatisfaction may be compounded by the conflict between established nurses and upcoming generations of nurses. In general, younger generations of nurses have accepted the newer foundations of practice, whereas these changes are often resisted by tenured staff. Thus the task of learning how to bridge the gaps in a multigenerational staff must be added to the nurse manager's other responsibilities.

> "For the first time in decades, there are four separate and distinct generations potentially working together in a stressful and competitive nursing work-place" (Boychuk-Duchscher & Cowin, 2004, p.493).

The generations that have retired or will soon retire in the nursing profession include those born during the 1920s, 1930s, and early 1940s, sometimes referred to as the Silent Generation or the Veteran Generation. The generations currently active in the nursing profession include the Baby Boomer Generation, born more or less between 1945 and 1960; Generation X, born between 1960 and 1980; and the Millennial Generation, born between 1980 and 2000 (Carlson, 2014).

The leadership of health care in the 21st century has been and will continue to be significantly affected by the diverse generations in today's workplace. These generational groups have major differences in communication styles, in what motivates them, in what turns them off, and in their workplace ideals (Boychuk-Duchscher & Cowin, 2004; Martin, 2004). Great diversity also exists in the beliefs, attitudes, and life experiences of these various generations (Scott, 2007). As such, generational diversity has been recognized as one of the major factors precipitating conflict in the workplace. Box 10.1 lists time frames of each generation as well as the percentage of each generation in the workforce.

BOX 10.1 CHARACTERISTICS OF GENERATIONS

Silent or Veteran Generation: Born between 1925 and 1942—account for 10% of the current workforce
Baby Boomers: Born between 1943 and 1960—account for 45% of the current workforce
Generation X: Born between 1961 and 1979—account for 30% of the current workforce
Generation Y: Born between 1980 and 2000—account for 10% of the workforce
Generation Now/Gen Z: Born between 1995 and now—the newest group to the job market

---

"I honestly think there has always been a general tension among different generations, but it has never had a 'voice' like it has now" (Wieck, cited in Trossman, 2007, p.8).

The Silent or Veteran Generation

This oldest generation of nurses, which is also the group that is retiring or retired, was taught to rely on tried, true, and tested ways of doing things. Because of early experiences with economic hardship and living through the Great Depression of the 1920s and 1930s with their families, these nurses place high value on loyalty, discipline, teamwork, and respect for authority (Boychuk-Duchscher & Cowin, 2004). Nurses from this generation have always worked within the hierarchy of management and diversity of leadership and are accustomed to the autocratic style of leaders and managers.

The Baby Boomers

The Baby Boomers make up the largest group of nurses working today, and the majority of nurse management positions are filled by Baby Boomers. Members of this group have a multitude of family responsibilities, frequently spanning three generations. In fact, this group is frequently referred to as the "sandwich generation," because these people are caught between caring for their children while also caring for their own aging parents. Nurses in this group are very ambitious. They put in long hours and have a strong sense of idealism, both at home and at work. Baby Boomers value what others think, and it is important that their achievements be recognized. They have set and maintained a grueling pace between their family and employment responsibilities. This group has embraced technology as a method to increase productivity and to have more free time (Cordeniz, 2003).

The individuals of the Baby Boomer generation are also most accustomed to working with autocratic leaders so they remain products of the hierarchical theory of leadership and management but are beginning to recognize and ask for some of the elements of the behavioral theory. They are also frequently challenged by nurses of younger generations, who see little value in hierarchical leadership in a system such as health care, which includes multiple groups and professions, some of whom have autonomy by licensure that is not recognized in a leadership hierarchy. By contrast, Baby Boomers are focused on building careers and are invested in organizational loyalty (Scott, 2007).

Generation X

Members of Generation X grew up in the information age; they are energetic and innovative. They are also hard workers, but unlike Baby Boomers, Gen X employees have little loyalty to, or confidence in, leaders and institutions. They value portability of their career and tend to change jobs frequently; they will stay in a position as long as it is good for them. This generation saw the downsizing of the 1990s, when organizational loyalty did not protect workers from loss of jobs or retirement. Thus they tend to have little aspiration for retirement. The use of technology has initiated an expectation of instant response and satisfaction. Technology has shaped their learning style; they want immediate answers from a variety of sources (Scott, 2007). They want different employment standards, such as opportunities for self-building and responsibility for work outcomes. They want extensive learning and precepting, and they want their questions answered immediately.

Gen X nurses value their free time; therefore, flexible scheduling and benefits (daycare centers, liberal vacations, working from home) are important. They claim to be motivated by work that agrees with their values and demands (Cordeniz, 2003). This group wants to work under motivational leadership with a democratic manager. If they do not find that kind of environment, they will have little reason to maintain employment in that institution.

Because most of the leaders and managers in health care are from the Baby Boomer generation, the conflict between these generations is certainly a significant contributor to the high turnover rate among younger nurses and the high rate of nurses finding employment outside of the hospital setting.

Generation Y

Members of Generation Y (also known as Generation Net, Nexters, or the Millennium Generation) were born between 1980 and 2000. This is the largest group, perhaps three times the size of Generation X; as such, this generation is having a formidable impact on the employment market. Those in their 20s and 30s are beginning to have an influence on how organizations are managed. This generation represents a large number of the children of the Baby Boomers. While the Baby Boomers were trying to master Windows and now the iPhone, these kids were playing with computers in kindergarten!

The impact of this generation is still being defined, but with the speed of generational changes, the impact of Generation Y may soon be integrated with the newest generation, currently labeled Generation Now. The Y Generation is smart and believes education is the key to success. For this group, diversity is a given, technology is as transparent as air, and social responsibility is a business imperative (Martin, 2004). Members of Gen Y are optimistic and interactive; yet they value individuality and uniqueness. They can multitask, think fast, and are extremely creative.

Managing this group will require a vastly different set of skills than what exists in the market today. Generation Y nurses are not team players. They are in the driver's seat—they know that work is there for them if they want it. Focusing on understanding their capabilities, treating them as colleagues, and putting them in roles that push their limits will help managers recognize the potential of this group to become the highest producing workforce in history (Martin, 2004). This is the most educated generation ever. Gen Y employees believe that they can either "start at the top or be climbing the corporate ladder by their sixth month on the job" (NAS, 2006, p.6). They learn quickly and adapt quickly. Research by a leadership development company found that "while just 48% of millennials hold a leadership title, 72% of them consider themselves a leader in the workplace" (Fallon, 2014). The hierarchy of health care leadership and management is generally not what they are seeking as a part of their employment, because they will develop their own leadership position in whatever they are doing. How they function in the role of follower is still being determined, and the role of follower will likely be redefined by this fast-moving generation.

Generation Now or Gen Z

The newest generation is being called Generation Now, the I Generation, or Gen Z. They have never lived without the Internet and other forms of rapid communication. This means they have never known a world without immediacy (IMedia Connection, 2006). The impact of this generation is already being felt in all aspects of our society and world. The way those in Gen Now/Gen Z think, act, find information, negotiate, and make decisions may make our present theories of leadership and management obsolete and just a part of our long history. Is this part of what Leland Kaiser envisioned when he talked about transformational leadership occurring when we were ready, or does Gen Now/Gen Z represent the emergence of a new leadership theory?

The challenge to nursing will be to develop a workplace, as well as a profession, that will be attractive to all these generations, particularly those who represent the mainstream of the workforce. Equally important is consideration by nurse leaders and managers of the unique differences that exist between each generation (Critical Thinking Box 10.2). According to Lynn Wieck, who has been studying the

---

? CRITICAL THINKING BOX 10.2

What are the main issues, as stated by Shah (2015), of five generations at work, and what are the implications?

Do employees understand customer needs?

Do employees understand how to interact with staff from the different generations?

How important is interaction among staff from different generations on patient satisfaction?

Do employees understand the workplace styles of different generations?

Example: A registered nurse from the Baby Boomer generation believes that when he/she gets a call to work on his/her day off, he/she should do this unless it is not possible from a family perspective. A registered nurse from Generation Y does not feel the same "level" of obligation to the workplace. The Baby Boomer "lives to work," whereas to Gen Y "works to live."

How does a leader address this difference to avoid an interstaff conflict?

How does the solution reflect staff understanding of patient satisfaction and outcomes, interaction with other staff members, and the differences among generations that are real and need to be respected and understood?

Shah, R. (2015). Working beyond five generations in the workplace. Retrieved from http://www.forbes.com/sites/rawnshah/2015/02/23/working-beyond-five-generations-in-the-workplace/#7568c4e13702.

---

different generations and the impact they have on nursing, "The younger nurses also want to know who, what, and why a policy was decided, and they want input into the process" (cited in Trossman, 2007, p.8). Wieck's research has validated the generational differences and the impact these differences are having on nursing (Trossman, 2007). The key is to learn the art of compromise as these generations continue to learn to work together, calling on the wisdom of the more experienced generation and the enthusiasm of the youngest of us to demonstrate that excellent care can be provided while making the work "more ergonomic, economical and eco-friendly" (Malleo, 2010, para 9). Gen Now/Gen Z staff can show a new way to accomplish the work that is different from the task orientation of the older generations—both of which were, and are, appropriate for the system at the time. They perceive themselves to be leaders versus followers, which means management will need to do what can be done to "equalize" the perception of leaders and followers.

Initially, there must be a focus on recruiting the younger generations into the health care fields, specifically into nursing. Emphasis must also be placed on retention of experienced nurses. These nurses are necessary to mentor the younger generations, and their experience is invaluable. Eric Chester works with young people and has outlined strategies for managing and motivating the younger generations (Boxes 10.2 and 10.3). Review these strategies—they are not new, nor are they exclusive to young employees. These strategies make sense for every generation and every organization at any time (Verret, 2000) (Critical Thinking Box 10.3).

BOX 10.2 MOTIVATIONAL STRATEGIES FOR GENERATIONS X AND Y

1. Let them know that what they do matters.
   - When was the last time a letter from a patient who was very pleased with the care on a unit was shared with the staff? When was the last time management sat down with all of the unit personnel to tell them they are doing a good job? When was the last time the Chief Executive Office complimented the staff on a job well done?
2. Tell them the truth.
   - When did the managers on a unit acknowledge to the staff exactly what was going on? For example, the surgery schedule is going to be heavy this next week, there are going to be a lot of new admissions, as well as a lot of patients who will be going home. Acknowledge that the work level is going to increase, and ask whether any of the staff have suggestions for improving the coordination and workload assignments.
3. Explain why you are asking them to do it.
   - When a difficult time is anticipated, explain to the staff what is happening and why. Maybe a particular area of the hospital is overloaded, and additional staff are being pulled from their regular units to help. These patients must be accommodated and cared for—this is why the hospital is there, and maintaining patient census is what pays the bills.
4. Learn their language.
   - When was the last time the unit manager, head nurse, or other manager actually sat down with the staff (all levels) to find out who they are and what they like to do? What are their priorities? Their family situations? What do they do on their days off?
5. Look for rewarding opportunities.
   - When did a staff member handle a particularly difficult patient situation very well with acknowledgment at that time given to the staff member? Give positive feedback when opportunities arise. Do not wait for a performance evaluation to do so.
6. Praise them in front of their peers and other staff.
   - Acknowledge a job well done at a staff meeting or in the presence of people who are important to that person.
7. Make the workplace fun.
   - Making the hospital work environment fun can sometimes be a little difficult, but there are opportunities for humor if we just look for them. Patients share a lot of humor with the staff. Is the staff encouraged to share that humor with the rest of the unit personnel? When something funny happens to staff, are they encouraged to laugh and share with others?
8. Model behavior.
   - Does the behavior of the unit manager or head nurse model the behavior the manager is expecting others to exhibit? What about confidentiality? Is it expected of the personnel? Does the manager practice it as well?
9. Give them the tools to do the job.
   - What about effective communication skills or, perhaps, good customer service skills? The health care industry is in the business of providing a service for the customer—the patient. Training is offered for the technical skills—new equipment, procedures, policies—but what about training for the skills necessary to handle people? How about skills to deal effectively with the angry patient, the difficult doctor, the outraged family (Verret, 2000)?

These strategies are from Eric Chester, as presented by Carol Verret in Verret, C. (2000). *Generation Y: Motivating and training a new generation of employees.* Retrieved from www.hotel-online.com/Trends/CarolVerret/GenerationY_Nov2000.html.

BOX 10.3 MOTIVATIONAL STRATEGIES FOR GENERATION NOW/GEN Z

In addition to Box 10.2, consider these strategies specific to Generation Now:
1. Look at where they are going for information.
   - They are always on the lookout for something new. It is the job of the leader or manager to stay current to keep up with them.
2. Make your message relevant.
   - They know when they are being "talked to." They consider their time precious, and they want you to use their time wisely.

The changes in the way the younger generations relate to leadership and management may well be part of the reason more hospitals are becoming Magnet certified. Magnet is a comprehensive program relating to many aspects of nursing and nursing practice, but the basis for most of the success of the program is the acceptance of a change in the way practice is governed and controlled. Magnet facilities demonstrate a true implementation of shared governance in which the nursing staff has control of the clinical practice of nursing and practice aspects of the work environment (HCPro, 2006).

Up to this point, leadership has been considered primarily as a part of management. In 2004, the American Association of Colleges of Nursing (AACN) brought a group together to develop a position of clinical nurse leader (CNL) (Stanley et al., 2008). The rationale for this position was that, with the changing health care needs of this society, the system does not seem to be "making the best use of its resources leading to a need to educate future practitioners differently" (Stanley et al., 2008, p.615). It was thought that this was critical to addressing successfully the many significant clinical issues facing the system during a time when resources are becoming limited. Having a highly prepared individual in the clinical setting is meant to impact positively the current patient safety issues by identifying and managing risk while meeting standards of quality clinical care.

As stated by Tornabeni and Miller (2008), "Improved patient care requires more nurses, better educated nurses and revised systems and environments for delivering patient care" (pp.608–609). Many factors support this need; it is known that with shorter lengths of stay and increasing complexity of care and treatment, stability in the delivery of nursing care is essential for reaching the defined outcomes of that care. This also has to be accomplished in a manner that maximizes the use of available resources while minimizing patient hand-offs and risks as these outcomes are reached. The clinical nurse leader is a master's degree–prepared registered nurse who is expected to

- Improve the quality of patient care through evidence-based practices
- Improve communication among all team members
- Provide guidance for less experienced nurses
- Assure that the patient has a smooth flow through the health system (Stanley et al., 2008, p.618).

This role is a combination of a bedside nurse, case manager, clinical educator, and team leader. The introduction of the clinical nurse leader role also addresses a long-standing complaint about acute-care nursing practice. Within the clinical setting, the two major opportunities for advancement were to assume a management position or to become a clinical educator. Both essentially remove individuals from the bedside, which is the heart of our practice. With this new clinical role, nurses who wish to advance to a different role while providing direct patient care now have the opportunity to do so.

An example of the success of the CNL role follows. Measurable performance measures for the staff practicing on the surgical unit were identified as a part of the quality review program. These performance measures were antibiotic use and venous thromboembolism prophylaxis. To effectively transform the nurses' thought processes and gain buy-in to this performance improvement, the need for a cultural change was identified. A clinical nurse leader was made available to assist the staff in understanding the need for this change and the benefits that would come about after this change was implemented. The CNL is a transformational leader who uses more than one style of leadership to motivate his or her employees to perform at a level of excellence. The styles of leadership used to adequately improve the performance on the surgery unit were affiliative and democratic (Landry, 2000–2016).

POWER AND AUTHORITY IN NURSING MANAGEMENT

Do You Know the Difference Between Power and Authority?

To have power means having the ability to effect change and to influence others to meet identified goals. Having authority relates to a specific position and the responsibility associated with that position. The individual with authority has the right to act in situations for which one is held responsible within the institutional hierarchy. This is a role most often assumed as a part of management.

> Power and responsibility always go hand in hand!

What Are the Different Types of Power?

There are many different types of power, so let us discuss those that are most common. *Legitimate power* is power connected to a position of authority. The individual has power as a result of the position. The head nurse has legitimate power and authority as a result of the position held.

Reward power is closely linked with legitimate power in that it comes about because the individual has the power to provide or withhold rewards. If supervisors have the power to authorize salary increases or scheduling changes, then they have reward power. *Coercive power* is power derived from fear of consequences. It is easy to see how parents would have coercive power over children based on the threat of punishment. This type of power can also be used toward staff members when, for example, there is the threat of receiving unfavorable assignments. However, in considering the characteristics of the upcoming generations, this sort of power may not be effective with them.

Expert power is based on specialized knowledge, skills, or abilities that are recognized and respected by others. The individual is perceived as an expert in an area and has power in that area because of this expertise. For instance, the enterostomal therapist has expertise in the care of individuals who have had ostomies. Therefore, staff nurses seek out the therapist as a resource and use the expert's knowledge to guide the care of these patients. The clinical nurse leader is another example of a nurse-expert who has responsibility to act as a resource for others.

Referent power is power that a person has because others closely identify with that person's personal characteristics; they are liked and admired by others. Individuals who have knowledge that is needed by others to function effectively in their roles possess *information power*. This type of power is perhaps the most abused! An individual may, for example, withhold information from subordinates to maintain control. The leader who gives directions without providing needed information on rationale or constraints is abusing information power.

Leadership power is the "capacity to create order from conflict, contradictions, and chaos" (Sullivan & Decker, 2012). This is possible when the staff or people involved in the conflicts have a trust in that leader who is able to influence people to respond because they want to respond!

Leaders and managers need to understand the concept of power and how it can be used and abused in working with others. Nurses, on the whole, need to identify ways to increase their power within the health team. Graduate nurses need to be aware of and willing to implement methods and resources to increase their personal power. As they gain experience in the staff nurse role, they can develop expert power by increasing competency in their roles and clinical skills.

> If you really want to see the best use of power, see a nurse who is actually providing the care that a patient needs and how many times he or she has to manage the system, massage the system, and find ways through the system just to get good care for patients. That's power.
>
> **Beverly Malone, PhD, RN, FAAN (cited in Mendez, 2006, p.55).**

Refining interpersonal skills that enhance the ability to work with others can expand many types of power, such as information, referent, and leadership power. These skills include clearly and completely communicating information that people need to know while gaining support for work to be done either through delegating or by encouraging staff to step forward to do what's necessary to accomplish the stated goals. Demonstrating a willingness to give and receive feedback while providing positive communication is also important when working to develop and enhance power in working with others.

It is also important to recognize what detracts from power. Impressing others as disorganized, either in personal appearance or in work habits, engaging in petty criticism or gossip, and being unable to say *no* without qualification are some of the behaviors that can detract from power.

Today there is much discussion in nursing about the importance of power and the concept of *empowerment*. To *empower* nurses is to provide them with greater influence and decision-making opportunities in their roles. The realization of greater power in the profession depends on the willingness of administrators to allocate this power and of nurses to accept it, along with the accompanying responsibility.

There are some people in the health care system who believe nurses are powerless—among these people are many nurses who " feel powerless in their jobs, unable to act autonomously or even speak up about concerns or suggestions" (Garner, 2011). Part of this perception of powerlessness is related to the fact that minimal time is spent learning leadership skills and more than 50% of nurses are not educated at the baccalaureate level where most of the leadership skills are discussed and practiced.

It is essential that nurses, who spend more time than others at a patient's bedside, feel confident in identifying "activities that can improve patient care or help the unit run more smoothly" (Garner, 2011). The growth in the number of Magnet hospitals is making a significant difference and decreasing the number of nurses who are hesitant to let their power show!

The basis for practice in Magnet-credentialed facilities is the empowerment of staff to make decisions that directly affect the practice of registered nurses who are providing direct care. This is accomplished through the development of a culture supporting the decentralization of management, power, and authority in all places in which registered nurses are providing care. A clearly delineated structure for accomplishing the appropriate decision making and clearly communicating these decisions must be in place and accessible to all registered nurses in the organization. Additionally, the responsibility for monitoring compliance and outcomes is also shared by the registered nurse staff rather than leaving this important function solely to management.

MANAGEMENT PROBLEM SOLVING

How Are Problem-Solving Strategies Used in Management?

Management is a *problem-oriented process*. The effective manager analyzes problems and makes decisions throughout all the planning, organizing, directing, and controlling functions of management. Problem solving can be readily compared with the nursing process (Table 10.1). This is because the nursing process is based on the scientific method of problem solving. The two are essentially the same, as can be seen by comparing the steps of one with the other.

As with the nursing process, problem solving does not always flow in an orderly manner from one step to the next. Throughout the process, feedback is sought, which may indicate a need for altering the plan to reach the desired objective. The most critical step in either process is identifying the problem (identified as the *nursing diagnosis* in the nursing process). Frequently what was originally identified as *the problem* may be too broad or unclear. Only the symptoms of the problem may be seen initially, or there may be several problems overlapping. If an approach is used to relieve only the symptoms, the problem will still exist. The good manager will guide the process of identifying the problem by asking questions such as "What is happening?" "What is being done about it?" "Who is doing what?" and

| TABLE 10.1 **NURSING PROCESS VERSUS PROBLEM SOLVING** ||
NURSING PROCESS	**PROBLEM SOLVING**
Assessment	Data gathering
Analysis/nursing diagnosis	Definition of the problem
Development of plan	Identification of alternative solutions
Implementation of plan	Implementation of plan
Evaluation/assessment	Evaluation of solution

"Why?" It is important to differentiate among facts and opinions and to attempt to break down the information to its simplest terms. Think of it as being a detective looking for every clue!

After the problem is clearly identified, the group should *brainstorm* all possible solutions. Often the first few alternatives are not the best or most practical. Identifying a number of viable alternatives usually provides more flexibility and creativity. All possible solutions must fall within existing constraints, such as staff abilities, available resources, and institutional policies. The more complex the problem, the more judgment is required. In some cases the problem may extend beyond the manager's scope of responsibility and authority; therefore, it may be necessary to seek outside help.

After identifying all the alternatives, each must be evaluated in relation to changes that would be required in existing policies, procedures, staffing, and so forth, as well as what effect these changes would have. Ask "What would happen if …" questions to clarify the short- and long-term implications of each alternative. Keep in mind that the perfect solution is not possible in most situations.

Problem solving represents a choice made between possible alternatives that are thought to be the best solutions for a particular situation. At its best, problem solving should involve ample discussion of the possible solutions by those who are affected by the situation and who possess the knowledge and power to support the possible solution. After an alternative has been selected, it should be implemented unless new data or perspectives warrant a change. Feedback should be sought continuously to provide ongoing evaluation of the effectiveness of the solution. Remember that simply choosing the best alternative does not automatically ensure its acceptance by those who work with it!

Evidence-Based Management Protocols and Interventions

Just as nurses are expected to practice using evidence-based protocols and interventions for clinical decision making, managers are expected to use those management practices that are based on demonstrated outcomes. This may be difficult to accomplish, because management practices are often deeply imbedded in the culture of an organization. Changing these practices to what is known to work from those that may have worked in the past may be considered as a challenge to the core philosophy of that organization.

Pfeffer and Sutton (2006) state:

> *If a manager is guided by the best logic and evidence and if they relentlessly seek new knowledge and insight, from both inside and outside their organizations, to keep updating their assumptions, knowledge and skills, they can be more effective.*

To accomplish this, the manager needs to be able to develop a commitment to searching for, and using, processes and solutions that are factually based, leading to the ability to make decisions that lead to intended outcomes (Pfeffer & Sutton, 2006). It is believed that there is much peer-reviewed information regarding managing organizations that is not used because of the desire to do things as they have always been done—knowing that they do work some of the time.

The example provided in an article in the *Harvard Business Review* relates to the use of stand-up meetings versus the traditional sit-down meetings. Evidence indicates that during stand-up meetings it took 34% less time to make decisions (Pfeffer & Sutton, 2006). Using this model could save an organization many hours a year that could be put to another productive use or could be eliminated from the payroll. However, very few organizations use this model for meetings, even in the face of the clear evidence regarding the impact it would have on the organization.

Appropriate hand washing between patient encounters is a problem that has affected health care since the 1850s. The solution sounds simple—wash your hands between patient encounters—but history has demonstrated that having leaders/managers who require this solution has not been effective. Random surveys of staff in health care facilities demonstrate that rates of hand washing average "about 37.5%" (WHO in Armellino et al., 2011).

A study conducted in 2009 to 2010 by Armellino et al. used "remote video auditing with and without feedback" to determine the rate of hand hygiene among the staff in an intensive care unit (2011). The prefeedback period demonstrated a hand-hygiene rate of 10%. The visualization of performance with feedback resulted in a hand-hygiene rate of 81.6%. The evidence from this study demonstrates that staff are more compliant when they are aware they are being observed and also when they receive feedback regarding these observations.

Although this study pertained to hand hygiene, the elements of observation and feedback can be assumed to increase compliance with other aspects of practice that require minimal variation in the practice. Secondarily, one can take this evidence a bit further and correlate the infection rate in this intensive care unit during the period in which the 81.6% hand-hygiene compliance occurred. Consider what changes in patient status and hospital costs would be noted if an 81.6% hand-washing compliance resulted in a major reduction in hospital-acquired infections.

What other aspects of practice can you think of that can be measured using direct observation? Using regular feedback?

Nurses who have been prepared to practice using evidence-based clinical information may find that using these same skills and approaches to management is the norm. This will require a collaborative working relationship with the tenured management staff who may see this result in a shift of power to the staff who do use evidence-based management practices as a regular part of decision making.

Frequently, implementing the solution to a problem causes several other problems to arise. This can be avoided if the selected solutions are evidence-based and if they are tested before implementation to identify any areas that may be negatively affected by the new solution. This testing should be a formal process following the steps of a Failure-Mode-Effects-Analysis, which is meant to identify and address those risk points that may not have been evident when the solution was selected. Many of you will be given the opportunity to work with others to complete an analysis of new procedures, for example, before that new procedure is fully implemented. If problems arise after the analysis, testing, and implementation, the new problems should not be allowed to impede the implementation process. Instead, pause and consider each problem individually, solve it, and then return to the plan that was tested. The old adage "If at first you don't succeed, try, try again" is most appropriate when applying the problem-solving process, but using evidence-based solutions should keep repeat trials to a minimum. Remain positive, confident, and flexible! Let us apply the process to an actual problem.

John is the head nurse on a busy medical-surgical unit with 32 patients. Staff members have complained to him that too much time is being spent during the morning change-of-shift report. After asking questions and seeking additional information, John determines that a clearer definition of the problem is that the night charge nurse does not give a clear, concise report. Researching the peer-reviewed literature for solutions addressing end-of-shift communication and involving the night charge nurse in the problem-solving process help to define the problem. Is it because the nurse does not have adequate knowledge of how to give a change-of-shift report? Or is it a flaw in the report system that does not allow for adequate communication to occur?

Can you see how, after the problem has been clarified, it becomes more amenable to an acceptable, and perhaps even easy, solution?

How Are Problem Solving and Decision Making Related?

By definition, problem solving and decision making are almost the same process, with one very notable difference. Decision making requires the definition of a clear objective to guide the process. A comparison of the steps of each illustrates this difference (Table 10.2). Although both problem solving

TABLE 10.2   PROBLEM SOLVING VERSUS DECISION MAKING

PROBLEM SOLVING	DECISION MAKING
Define problem	Set objective
Identify alternative solutions	Identify and evaluate alternative decisions
Select solution and implement	Make decision and implement
Evaluate outcome	Evaluate outcome

and decision making are usually initiated in the presence of a problem, the objective in decision making may not be to solve the problem but only to deal with its results. It is also important to distinguish between a good decision and a good outcome. A *good outcome* is the objective that is desired, and a *good decision* is one made systematically to reach this objective. A good decision may or may not result in a good outcome. Although it is desirable to have both good decisions and good outcomes, the good decision maker is willing to act, even at the risk of a negative outcome.

Susan is the evening charge nurse on a medical unit that has a total of 24 patients. One of the patients is terminally ill and seems to be having a particularly difficult evening. The patient requires basic comfort measures but little complex care. Susan has a choice of assigning the patient to another RN or delegating care to a nursing assistant. If she assigns the RN, the workload for the other staff will be heavier, and she herself will be assigned to the terminally ill patient, to provide the care that cannot be delegated to the nursing assistant. Susan decides to assign the RN, because this patient requires the emotional and physical support best provided by an RN. During the shift, the RN spends time sitting with the patient. Close to the end of the shift, the patient dies. Was this a good decision with a bad outcome or a good decision with a good outcome?

Decision making is values-based, whereas problem solving is traditionally a more scientific process. Efforts to acquire evidence-based information as one is identifying alternative solutions to problems move the decision making process into the scientific arena. Nurses will continue to make decisions based on personal values, life experiences, perceptions of the situation, knowledge of risks associated with possible decisions, and their individual ways of thinking, but these factors will be influenced by the availability of information and solutions that have been scientifically tested. Because of these variables, two individuals given the same information and using the same decision-making process may arrive at different decisions, but the probability should be lower after evidence-based information is available.

In today's ever-changing health care environment, it is important for nurses and nurse managers to be effective in both problem solving and decision making. The good manager will evaluate the problem-solving or decision-making process based on criteria that provide a view of the big picture. These criteria include the likely effects on the objective to be met, on the policies and resources of the organization, on the individuals involved, and on the product or service delivered.

The quality of patient care is dependent on the ability of the nurse to effectively combine problem solving with decision making. To do so, nurses must be attuned to their individual value systems and understand the effect of these systems on thinking and perceiving. The values associated with a particular situation will limit the alternatives generated and the final decision. For this reason, the fact that nurses typically work in groups is beneficial to the decision-making process. Although the process is the same, groups generally offer the benefits of a broader knowledge base for defining objectives and more creativity in identifying alternatives. It is important for nurses to understand the roles of individuals within the group and the dynamics involved in working in groups to take full advantage of the group process. Chapter 11 focuses on communication, group process, and working with teams.

What Effect Does the Leader Have on the Group?

The leader's philosophy, personality, self-concept, and interpersonal skills all influence the functioning of the group. A leader is most effective if members are respected as individuals who have unique contributions to make to the group process. Can you remember our earlier discussion of the characteristics of a good leader? The ability to influence and motivate others is particularly important in the group process.

Whenever the combination of people in a group is altered, the dynamics are changed. If the group is in the working phase, it will revert to the initiating phase when a new person or persons are added and will remain there until they have been assimilated into the group and a new dynamic has been formulated. The most effective groups are those that have had consistent membership and are highly developed. These groups demonstrate friendly and trusting relationships; the ability to work toward goals of varying difficulty; flexible, stable, and reliable participation of members; and productivity with high-quality output. Leadership within these groups is democratic, and the members feel positive about their participation and the outcomes of the group process. Now let us apply these principles to a real situation!

When you graduate and accept a nursing position, you will become a new nurse in the work group, causing it to regress to the initiating phase. This is your opportunity to demonstrate to the members of the group that you are worthy of being included in the group. If this is your first nursing position, you will also demonstrate to the group that you are worthy of entering the nursing profession. During this time, you may experience feelings of loneliness, isolation, and distance that accompany the initiating phase. However, your feelings of pride, excitement, eagerness, and accomplishment should quickly eradicate those feelings of distance, because there is much to gain and much to offer when entering a new group with common goals.

Put your energy into forming supportive professional relationships, including the social aspects of these relationships. Seek and use feedback, and ask for help in areas that are not as familiar to you, such as priority setting. As you contribute your individual talents to the group, you will move from being a dependent new person to full group membership. It is important that you do not underestimate the length of time that may be needed to accomplish this task! Group processes proceed very slowly in some cases, and it may be 6 months or more before you are accepted as a full member of the work group. Do not be discouraged! Instead, use this opportunity to gain information regarding what you can offer to the next new member of the group and what you can do to make transitioning from school to practice a positive experience.

Management skills come with experience in nursing, so do not be too hard on yourself during the transition phase. Identify experienced staff nurses who are effective at managing the care of their assigned patients, and identify nurse managers who have the skills you would like to incorporate into your management style. Look at the positive side of working with staff nurses and various nursing managers as a means to assist you in the development of your personal management style. Develop the ability to think like a manager as you perform your assignments—always look at the big picture.

THE CHALLENGE OF CHANGE

How many times have you heard staff nurses complain about how powerless they feel about the lack of control they have over their work environment? They say they are frustrated with the amount and quality of patient care they are able to deliver and that staffing patterns are placing undue stress on them. Some will talk about leaving the acute-care environment to try some other aspect of nursing (perhaps home health) as a less stressful option. Why do they run from finding a situation, rather than thinking about how they can act to change it? Do they feel powerless to do so? Is it easier to withdraw and escape?

One thing we all know is that change is inevitable, particularly in today's health care delivery system. Economic factors have taken center stage, and cutbacks in all aspects of health care services are occurring. Additionally, the Patient Protection and Affordable Health Care Act of 2010 will bring changes to many aspects of health care as this act is incrementally implemented (Focus on Health Reform, n.d.). A major aspect of this act is that all Americans will have some type of health insurance coverage. Consider the kinds of changes this can bring on an almost immediate basis. Are you prepared to accept the challenges ahead while continuing to provide quality care as a part of your professional obligation? Change can be like a truck with no driver at the wheel: It moves slowly and steadily toward you (Fig. 10.2). You have three options: you can move out of the situation and perhaps miss some opportunities; you can just stand there and withdraw, doing what you are told just to avoid conflict; or you can start to run with it, jump on, and try to steer it in a positive direction.

So, how do you begin to direct the change that is on the horizon? The first thing to know about the change process is that it, too, has similarities to problem solving and the nursing process. Let us lay them out and compare the two processes (Table 10.3).

Look familiar? Maybe it is not that hard to take control and be a change agent! The first thing you need to know about the change process is that resisting change is a natural response for most people. All of us are most comfortable in our state of equilibrium, where we feel in control of what we are doing. To handle change effectively, it is important to understand that every change involves adaptation. It requires a period of transition in which the change can be understood, evaluated in light of its impact on the individual, and, one hopes, eventually embraced.

There are various reasons for people's resistance to change, and understanding them will help you to implement the change process more effectively. Following are the most common factors that cause resistance to change:

- A perceived threat to self in how the change will affect the individual personally
- A lack of understanding regarding the nature of the change
- A limited ability to cope emotionally with change
- A disagreement about the potential benefits of the change
- A fear of the impact of the change on self-confidence and self-esteem

Kurt Lewin (1947) sought to incorporate these concepts in his Change Theory. He identified three phases in an effective change process: *unfreezing, moving,* and *refreezing.* In the *unfreezing phase,* all of the factors that may cause resistance to change are considered. Others who may be affected by the

FIG. 10.2 Change: React, don't react, or jump on board.

TABLE 10.3 **NURSING PROCESS VERSUS CHANGE PROCESS**	
NURSING PROCESS	**CHANGE PROCESS**
Assessment	Recognition that a change is needed; collect data
Identification of possible nursing diagnoses	Identification of problem to be solved
Selection of nursing diagnosis	Selection of one of possible alternatives
Development of plan	Implementation of plan
Implementation of plan	Implementation of plan
Evaluation	Evaluation of effects of change
Reassessment	Stabilization of change in place

change are sought out to determine whether they recognize that a change is needed and to determine their interest in participating in the process. You will need to determine whether the environment of the institution is receptive to change and then convince others to work with you.

The *moving phase* occurs after a group of individuals has been recruited to take on responsibilities for implementing the change. The group begins to sort out what must be done and the sequence of actions that would be most effective. The group identifies individuals who have the *power* to assist in making the plan succeed. *(What types of power would be most effective?)* The group also attempts to identify strategies to overcome the natural resistance to change—and how to achieve a cooperative approach to implement the change. Once developed, the plan is then put into place.

The *refreezing phase* occurs when the plan is in place and everyone involved knows what is happening and what to expect. Publicizing the ongoing assessment of the pros and cons of the plan is an important part of its ultimate success. Be certain someone is responsible for continuing to work on the plan so that it does not lose momentum. Finally, make the changes stick—or *refreeze*. This will make the change a part of everyday life, and it will no longer be perceived as something new. Now let us apply this process to a real situation!

Patti is working in a medical-surgical unit at a 200-bed acute-care hospital. She constantly hears her peers complaining about the lack of adequate nursing staff, and during the previous 3 months, two full-time staff nurses have resigned. To cover the unit, part-time staff from temporary agencies and from the hospital staffing pool are being used to supplement the remaining regular staff. Because these staff members have little orientation to the unit and are frequently assigned where they are needed the most, the continuity of care and a potential for increased errors in patient care became a major concern.

Rather than continuing to complain about the situation or considering leaving, Patti decided to act and try to steer the change truck. She approached a few of the nurses and initiated a discussion about the changes in staffing and how scheduling had become a nightmare for the charge nurse. She enlisted the support of several members of the staff to begin problem solving possible solutions. They agreed that increased staffing was probably not a possible immediate solution and agreed to work within the constraints that they had.

Several of the pool nurses were receptive to requesting that their assignment be limited to this one unit, and they agreed to schedule their hours to complement each other. This, in essence, would add a shared full-time position, at no additional cost, and would also provide consistency of patient care. When the proposal was presented to administrators, they agreed to support the idea based on its economic and patient-centered benefits.

Who Initiates Change and Why?

Another aspect to consider when evaluating change is to determine who wants the change and why. Is it the system? Is it management? Is it you, the nurse? Or is it the patient? There should be a specific rationale for change, and the identified change should be carefully planned, implemented, and evaluated to ensure the outcome is as anticipated. By identifying who is initiating the change and the reason for the change, the implementation plan can be better defined and understood, particularly regarding how implementation will affect the staff or the system.

The Change Truck—how will you respond?

React—move out of the way. Let the truck (change) pass you by. However, opportunities may be missed.

Do not act—just stand there and let the truck run over you. It will leave you behind and, more than likely, in worse shape than when you started.

Act—start running when you see it coming. Pace with it until you can decide when to jump on and steer it in the direction you want to move.

System

The most common reason for change is that what you did before is no longer effective. For example, the electronic medical record is largely replacing the handwritten medical record system, because the old system does not allow for the integration of the information in the record. The handwritten record generates volumes of paper and is not adequate to keep pace with the number of patients and the need to access key information quickly from various individuals both inside and outside of the traditional hospital (home health nurse or hospice nurse at the patient's home).

Management

Change frequently occurs when new regulations are developed by agencies that license or approve the facility. This provides a new perspective and view regarding how the system currently operates and what part of the system needs to be changed for compliance with the new regulation. A significant change in almost all areas of the hospital occurred with the implementation of the HIPAA regulations. Employees at all levels needed to know "How will the implementation of HIPAA change my job? Do I know how to respond to a request for information?" (See Critical Thinking Box 10.4.)

? CRITICAL THINKING BOX 10.4

What changes have you made in your life?

How long did one situation last before it changed again?

You have just learned to deal successfully with the changes associated with being a student. Now you are facing the challenge of change again as you prepare for your role as a practicing registered nurse.

Patient

When customers are not happy, something within the system needs to change. What are the specific patient problems, and how can they be resolved? The fact that medical errors continue to occur at a high rate is of concern to patients or to people who may become patients. This has been publicized in the mainstream media for several years with minimal evidence that errors have been reduced. This makes the public a group who wants change and who expects the system, management, and staff to create the solutions to this problem. Does change at this level require the use of transformational leadership and evidence-based decisions?

Yourself

Sometimes we impose change on ourselves. We may or may not like it, but we see a need for some aspect of change to occur (Table 10.4). Who has ever enjoyed being transferred to a different unit if the one we are working on is slated to close? Stop to consider how you are going to implement the change. How will your work environment be affected? If change involves other employees, include them as a part of that change. Gain the power that comes from working as a team.

Only when you feel threatened by a change will you go through the steps (i.e., resistance, uncertainty, assimilation, transference, integration) to conquer it (Wilson, 1996) (Fig. 10.3). All change will elicit some type of resistance. It is up to you to increase the impetus for change while decreasing resistance. The decision to be involved with change will help steer you in a direction that will be most beneficial.

TABLE 10.4   EMOTIONAL PHASES OF THE CHANGE PROCESS

PHASE	CHARACTERISTICS	INTERVENTIONS
Equilibrium	High energy; feelings of balance, peace, and harmony	Explain how changes will affect the status quo.
Denial	Denies reality that change will occur; experiences negative changes in physical health, emotional and cognitive behavior	Actively listen, be empathetic, and use reflective communication. Offer stress-management programs.
Anger	Blames others; may demonstrate envy, rage, or resentment	Be assertive and assist with problem solving. Encourage employee to determine the source of his or her anger.
Bargaining	Efforts made to eliminate the change; frequently talks in terms such as "If only"	Search for real needs and problems and explore ways to achieve outcomes through conflict management and win–win negotiation skills.
Chaos	Diffused energy; feelings of powerlessness and insecurity and a sense of disorientation	Encourage quiet time for reflection as inner search for identity and meaning occurs.
Depression	No energy left; nothing seems to work; sorrow, self-pity, and feelings of emptiness	Encourage expression of sorrow and pain. Exhibit patience as employees learn to let go.
Resignation	Lack of enthusiasm as change is accepted passively	Allow employees to move at own pace.
Openness	Some renewal of energy and willingness to take on new roles or assignments resulting from change	Patiently explain again, in detail, the desired change.
Readiness	Willingly expends energy to explore new events that are occurring; reunification of emotions and cognition	Assume a directive management style; assign tasks, provide direction.
Reemergence	Feelings of empowerment as new project ideas are initiated	Mutually explore questions and develop an understanding of role and identity. Employees take actions based on own decisions.

Adapted from Perlman, D., & Takacs, G. J. (1990). The ten stages of change, *Nurs Manag, 21*(4), 34.

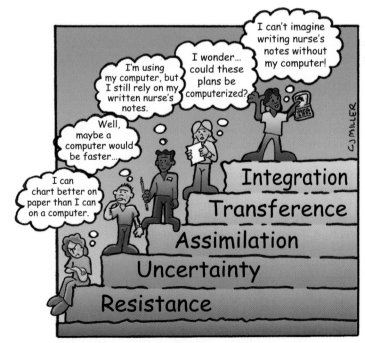

FIG. 10.3 Five steps toward conquering change.

CONCLUSION

As a new graduate, you will be facing many transitions, including the transition from a "newbie" providing direct care for assigned patients, to managing the care for a group of patients, to a team leader role where you are managing the care of a group of patients through a team of staff members. You may also be appointed to a formal management position or may assume the role of an informal, but powerful, leader. All of these phases or roles require the characteristics of a leader who can influence others, including patients, to respond because they want to respond.

Think about the characteristics of your generation—will these influence your management style as you consider how you will positively engage with all the members of your staff? How will you contribute to the resolution of some of the differences in the nursing environment? Will you research the literature to find those actions that have proven effective, or will you do what has always been done? Understanding management and leadership along with your generational characteristics will facilitate the development of a leadership and management style that is a reflection of you. Improving your ability to reach out to those outside the organization through communication and the use of the literature will provide you with the tools to build effective nursing management practices while also leading a successful team.

🌐 RELEVANT WEBSITES AND ONLINE RESOURCES

Duke University School of Nursing (2013)
Redefining what leadership means for the next generation of nurses. https://nursing.duke.edu/news/redefining-what-leadership-means-next-generation-nurses.

Riggio, R. E. (2009)
Are you a transformational leader? http://www.psychologytoday.com/blog/cutting-edge-leadership/200903/are-you-transformational-leader.

Sherman, R. O.
Becoming a transformational nurse leader. http://www.emergingrnleader.com/transformational-nurse-leader/.

BIBLIOGRAPHY

Anderson, R. A., Crabtree, B. F., Steele, D. J., & McDaniel, R. R. (2005). Case study research: The view from complexity science. *Qualitative Health Research, 15*(5), 669–685.

Armellino, D., Hussain, E., Schilling, M., Senicola, W., Eichorn, A., & Dlugacz, Y. et al. (2011). Using high-technology to enforce low-technology safety measures: The use of third-party remote video auditing and real-time feedback in healthcare. *Clinical Infectious Diseases Advance.* Retrieved from http://www.ncbi.nlm.nih.gov/pubmed/22109950.

Bass, B. (1990). From transactional to transformational leadership: Learning to share the vision. *Organizational Dynamics, 19*–31.

Blanchard, K., & Hersey, P. (1964). *Management of organizational behavior: Leading human resource.* New York: Morrow.

Boychuk-Duchscher, J., & Cowin, L. (2004). Multigenerational nurses in the workplace. *Journal of Nursing Administration, 34*(11), 493–501.

Burns, J. (2001). Complexity science and leadership in healthcare. *Journal of Nursing Administration, 31*(1), 474–482.

Carlson, K. (2014). *Nurses learn to work through generational diversity.* Retrieved from http://exclusive.multibriefs.com/content/nurses-and-generational-diversity.

Cordeniz, J. (2003). Recruitment, retention, and management of generation X: A focus on nursing professional. *Journal of Healthcare Management, 47*(4), 237–249.

Fallon, N. (2014). How millennials really feel about leadership. *Business News Daily*. Retrieved from http://www.businessnewsdaily.com/7328-millennials-leadership-development.html.

Focus on health reform. (n.d.). *Affordable Healthcare for America Act*. Retrieved from http://www.hhs.gov/healthcare/about-the-law/index.html.

Garner, C. (2011). *Powerlessness is bad practice: Any nurse can be a facilitator of change*. American Sentinel University. Retrieved from http://www.americansentinel.edu/blog/2011/04/11/facilitating-change-white-paper/.

HCPro. (2006). *Magnet status: A guide for the nursing staff*. Marblehead, MA: HCPro.

Hellriegel, D., Jackson, S., & Slocum, J. (1999). *Management* (8th ed.). Reading, MA: Addison-Wesley.

IMedia Connection. (2006). *Talking to generation now*. Retrieved from http://www.imediaconnection.com/content/12412.asp.

Institute of Medicine. (2004). *Keeping patients safe: Transforming the work environment of nurses*. Washington, DC: National Academies Press.

Kenney, C. (2011). *Transforming health care*. New York: Taylor & Francis Group.

Landry, C. (2000–2016). Clinical nurse leadership and performance improvement on a surgical unit. *RN Journal*. Retrieved from http://rnjournal.com/journal-of-nursing/clinical-nurse-leadership-and-performance-improvement-on-surgical-unit.

Lewin, K. (1947). Group decisions and social change. In Newcomb, T. M. and Hartley, E. L. (Eds), Readings in Social Psychology. New York: Henry Holt.

Malleo, C. (2010). Each generation brings strengths, knowledge to nursing field: A nurse's journal. Retrieved from http://www.cleveland.com/healthfit/ index.ssf/2010/02/each_generation_brings_strength.html.

Manion, J. (1996). *Team-based health care organizations*. Gaithersburg, MD: Aspen Publishers.

Manion, J. (1998). *From management to leadership*. Chicago: American Hospital Publishers.

Marquis, B. L., & Huston, C. J. (2003). *Leadership roles and management functions in nursing* (4th ed.). Philadelphia: Lippincott Williams and Wilkins.

Martin, C. (2004). Bridging the generation gap. *Nursing*, *34*(12), 62–63.

McCallum, J. (2013). Followership—the other side of leadership. Ivey Business Journal. Retrieved from http://iveybusinessjournal.com/publication/followership-the-other-side-of-leadership/.

McNamara, C. (n.d.). *Historical and contemporary theories of management*. Retrieved from http://managementhelp.org/management/theories.htm.

Mendez, L. C. (2006). Beverly Malone: An image of leadership. *Imprint*, *53*(5).

Miller, M. (2007). Transformational leadership and mutuality. *Transformation*, *24*(3/4), 180–192.

NAS. (2006). *Generation Y: The millennials. Ready or not, here they come. NAS insights,* NAS Recruitment Communications. Retrieved from www.nasrecruitment.com/TalentTips/NASinsights/GenerationY.pdf.

Pfeffer, P., & Sutton, R. (Jan. 1, 2006). Evidence-based management. *Harvard Business Review*.

Porter-O'Grady, T. (2003a). A different age for leadership. Part 1: New context, new content. *Journal of Nursing Administration*, *33*(2), 105–110.

Porter-O'Grady, T. (2003b). A different age for leadership. Part 2: New rules, new roles. *Journal of Nursing Administration*, *33*(3), 173–178.

Porter O'Grady, T. (2003c). Researching shared governance: A futility of focus. *Journal of Nursing Administration*, *33*(4), 251–252.

Rothbauer-Wanish, H. (2009). *Four functions of management*. Retrieved from http://businessmanagement.suite101.com/article.cfm/four_functions_of_management.

Scott, D. (2007). The generations at work: A conversation with Phyllis Kritek. *American Nurse Today*, *39*(3), 7.

Shah, R. (2011). *Working with five generations in the workplace*. Retrieved from http://www.forbes.com/sites-/rawnshah/2011/04/20/working-with-five-generations-in-the-workplace.

Sherman, R. O. (2012). What followers need from their leaders. *American Nurse Today*, *7*(9), 62–64.

Smyth, R. (2015). *Applying complexity theory to healthcare delivery is not complicated*. Forbes/Pharma & Healthcare. Retrieved from http://www.forbes.com/sites/roysmythe/2015/01/08/applying-aspects-of-complexity-theory-to-health-care-delivery-its-not-complicated/.

Stanley, J., Gannon, J., Gabuat, J., et al. (2008). The clinical nurse leader: A catalyst for improving quality and patient safety. *Journal of Nursing Management*, *16*, 614–622.

Sullivan, E., & Decker, P. (2012). *Effective leadership and management in nursing* (8th ed.). Prentice-Hall.

Tichy, N., & Devanna, M. (1986). *The transformational leader*. New York: John Wiley & Sons.

Tonges, M., Baloga-Altieri, B., & Atzori, M. (2004). Amplifying nursing's voice through a staff-management partnership. *Journal of Nursing Administration, 34*(3), 134–139.

Tornabeni, J., & Miller, J. (2008). The power of partnership to shape the future of nursing: The evolution of the clinical nurse leader. *Journal of Nursing Management, 16*, 608–613.

Trossman, S. (2007). Talkin' bout my generation: Gaining awareness of differences key to easing workplace tensions. *American Nurse, 39*(3), 1–2.

Van Wagner, K. (2007). *Leadership theories: Eight major leadership theories*. Retrieved from http://psychology.about.com/od/leadership/p/leadtheories.htm.

Verret, C. (2000). Generation Y: Motivating and training a new generation of employees. Hotel Online: ideas and trends. Retrieved from http://www.hotel-online.com/Trends/CarolVerret/GenerationY_Nov2000.html.

Wertheim, E. G. (n.d.). *Historical background of organizational behavior*, College of Business Administration, Northeastern University. Retrieved from https://www.scribd.com/doc/6926402/Historical-Background-of-Organizational-Behavior.

Wilson, P. (1996). Empowerment: Community economic development from the inside out. *Urban Studies, 33*(4-5), 617–630.

Building Nursing Management Skills

Jessica Maack Rangel, MS, ASPPS, RN

(e) http://evolve.elsevier.com/Zerwekh/nsgtoday/.

Example is not the main thing in influencing others; it is the only thing.
Albert Schweitzer

Communication should be clearly stated and directed to the appropriate, responsible individual.

After completing this chapter, you should be able to:

- Analyze effective communication as it relates to patient safety.
- Analyze TeamSTEPPS Tools as an evidence-based teamwork system to optimize patient outcomes.
- Identify current methods of transcribing physicians' orders.
- Use a standardized hand-off communication tool (SBAR or I-SBAR-R) for receiving and giving change-of-shift report.
- Discuss strategies to manage and prioritize your time in the clinical setting.
- Identify criteria for supervising and delegating care provided by others.

The entry-level nurse is expected to demonstrate competence as a manager of patient care. The process of building nursing management skills encompasses effective communication, management of prioritization in the clinical setting, and management of other members of the health care team to maintain patient safety and prevent harm. The topics in this chapter will be helpful in your development of management skills that keep patients safe while you are a student, as well as during your transition period as a new graduate.

233

COMMUNICATION AND PATIENT SAFETY

We have all learned different ways of communicating. Our tone, inflections, and decibel level are all learned. Roles with perceived authority differences have a significant impact on how we communicate and how much information we communicate. This is called an authority gradient, that is, the balance of decision-making power or the steepness of command hierarchy in a given situation (AHRQ, 2015). Even gender plays a large part in how we communicate information. Consider asking a female colleague how her day was yesterday (or about a particular movie). Then ask a male colleague the same question. Chances are, the information you receive will vary greatly in the amount of detail and the number of words it takes to tell the story.

The same is typically true in the medical field where perceived authority gradients exist between physician and nurse, supervisor and direct report, expert and novice. How and to what degree information is shared will vary. This is why team building and simulation are so important: to break down perceived barriers to communicate effectively. Consider how you might share information regarding a patient's condition with a colleague with whom you've worked and trusted; then consider how you might communicate this same information to the chief of staff who happens to be the primary physician on this case. Do you think the volume and detail of information might differ? Additionally, nurses and physicians are trained to communicate quite differently. Nurses are taught to be broad in their narrative. They give a descriptive picture of the clinical situation. Physicians, on the other hand, learn to be very concise—they want the facts and the important points. Whether under stress or relaxed, nurses must find effective ways to communicate critical information in very short periods of time.

> Communication failures are the root cause for the majority of sentinel events (an unexpected occurrence that reaches the patient and results in severe temporary or permanent harm or death (TJC, 2015).

A 2010 study by The Joint Commission (TJC) reported that communication failure was a primary contributing factor in almost 80% of more than 6000 adverse events. Another TJC study into fundamental reasons for failure or inefficiency of processes that led to patient harm validated that communication continued to be in the top three root causes in sentinel events from 2013 to 2015. Integrating teamwork and effective communication into day-to-day practice can help to eliminate errors. Through exercises in teamwork, cultural sensitivity, and self-awareness/situational awareness techniques, health care providers learn skill sets that promote expeditious and appropriate care. The Department of Defense (DoD) Patient Safety Program in collaboration with the Agency for Healthcare Research and Quality developed an evidence-based teamwork system in 2007 that focused on improving communication and teamwork skills in the health care industry to improve patient outcomes (AHRQ, 2013). The result was TeamSTEPPS—Team **S**trategies and **T**ools to **E**nhance **P**erformance and **P**atient **S**afety (Box 11.1).

BOX 11.1   TEAM STEPPS

TeamSTEPPS provides higher quality, safer patient care by:
- Producing highly effective medical teams that optimize the use of information, people, and resources to achieve the best clinical outcomes for patients.
- Increasing team awareness and clarifying team roles and responsibilities.
- Resolving conflicts and improving information sharing.
- Eliminating barriers to quality and safety.

Communication challenges in practice were identified early by The Joint Commission. The National Patient Safety Goals were developed for implementation beginning in 2003 with the expectation of full implementation and compliance as a condition of accreditation. Failures in communication involved *incomplete* communication among caregivers. The Joint Commission issued National Patient Safety Goal #2: *Improve the effectiveness of communication among caregivers.* Specifically, "Get important test results to the right staff person on time" (The Joint Commission, 2015). It is now an expectation that facilities have embedded a standardized approach to hand-off communication, including passing information regarding orders and test results.

How Can I Improve My Verbal Communication for Patient Safety?

Let us focus on a couple of communication techniques that can improve the accuracy of the care we provide. First, The Joint Commission notes that there is a big difference between verbal orders and telephone orders. Orders received verbally (with the physician present) should never be accepted except in an emergency or during a procedure where the physician is in a sterile procedural environment and read-back verification techniques are utilized to assure accuracy. There is too much opportunity for transmitting and transcribing the order incorrectly. Telephone orders are acceptable, because the physician is simply not present to input the orders himself or herself. To make this even safer, practice a "read-back." In other words, handwrite or input into the electronic health record the order or test results given to you, and read them back to verify accuracy of the orders and to confirm that they were understood correctly. As many as 50% of all medication errors have been directly attributed to the failure to communicate information *at the point of transition* (Institute for Healthcare Improvement, 2008). Specifically, any hand-off of communication is a point of vulnerability, whether it is a telephone communication, a written communication, communication of a critical test result, or a shift-change report. All have been shown to be critical points in the patient's journey. Points of transition in communication encompass all disciplines.

Consider how often we miscommunicate with each other casually and think of the implications for the clinical setting. Your friend asked you to stop by the store and pick up bread, eggs, and milk, but you forgot to pick up the milk because you didn't write it down, you thought you had committed it to memory. You had other things on your mind and you haven't been able to get much sleep lately, which you already know impairs your memory. What other areas of your life might be impacted from your lack of sleep and stress?

These variables are called "human factors," and they often influence the communication transition between different parties. These are the very same factors that can and do affect your ability to recall information you just received.

How much more effective would it have been had you actually *written down* what you were told to bring home and then *read that list back* to the person who gave it to you? Fatigued, distracted, worried, or sleepy—had you repeated the written list back to the other person, chances are the milk would have made it home, too! This is precisely how to manage the verbal and telephone transmission of information from caregiver to caregiver (Box 11.2).

BOX 11.2 SAFETY STEPS FOR VERBAL AND PHONE ORDERS

Step 1: Order is communicated verbally.
Step 2: Order is documented verbatim.
Step 3: Documented order is read directly back to the person who gave it for confirmation that it is accurate and understood correctly.

It's that simple! This process minimizes errors of omission and commission, and it eliminates the need to rely on memory to recall an order accurately. Your patients' lives depend on it!

How Can I Improve My Written Communication for Patient Safety?

The next communication concern is how we write and document in the electronic health record (EHR) to communicate essential information. Legibility and clarity are nonnegotiable essentials. Remember, the written or typed word is another point of transmission that has proven to be a root cause of many catastrophic errors. How often has a medication ordered at 5.0 mg been mistaken for 50 mg, because the decimal point was too light to be noticed? Consider instead .5 mcg being mistaken for 5 mcg. The resultant overdose could have devastating consequences. When documenting numbers, the trailing "0" *must be eliminated* to avoid the confusion between 5.0 mg and 50 mg. Likewise, the insertion of the "0" before the decimal is crucial to differentiate 0.5 mcg from 5 mcg. In 2003, TJC released a Sentinel Event Alert that is still being addressed today regarding these very documentation issues that have led to grave miscommunications and includes strategies to eliminate harm. Although the EHR has helped to mitigate many of these issues, the risk is ever present.

Furthermore, many written abbreviations used to designate dosage frequency must be eliminated. Abbreviations such as Q.D. for "daily" have become targets for clarification, because they can be easily misunderstood (Q.D. has been mistaken for Q.I.D. meaning "four times a day"). Many facilities have disallowed the use of these "unsafe" or "unapproved" abbreviations because of their potential for causing errors leading to harm for a patient.

Organizations within the health care delivery system will have their own abbreviations, acronyms, and symbols that should not be used. These abbreviations and symbols may be in addition to the recommendations from The Joint Commission. It is imperative that you become familiar with the approved abbreviations, symbols, and acronyms that you can use. The Joint Commission has mandated that these dangerous abbreviations be eliminated from any documentation, printed or written, when communicating patient-care issues (Critical Thinking Box 11.1, Table 11.1).

❓ CRITICAL THINKING BOX 11.1

What happens when an unsafe abbreviation is found in a patient order?
- Step 1: Notify the prescriber of the order containing the unsafe abbreviation.
- Step 2: Ask for a clarifying order to clear any misinterpretation of the order.
- Step 3: Document the clarification.

Once again, it's that simple! However, one more word of caution must be added for written communication when dealing with patients. Cultural variances of the written word must be acknowledged and minimized. Consider a prescription for a primarily Spanish-speaking patient that reads, "Take once daily for 5 days." The word *once* in Spanish means eleven! Interpretive services must be accessed if the language spoken and written is not the patient's primary language. Direct and succinct written and verbal communication in a language that is clearly understood by the patient is essential to appropriate and safe care. Remember that just because the patient can speak English, it does not mean that the patient can read English, or any language at all. It's important to use a TeamSTEPPS strategy "check-back." A check-back is a closed-loop communication strategy used to verify and validate information exchanged (AHRQ, 2013). Simply put, ask

TABLE 11.1	THE JOINT COMMISSION OFFICIAL "DO NOT USE" LIST OF ABBREVIATIONS*	
DO NOT USE	**POTENTIAL PROBLEM**	**USE INSTEAD**
U, u (unit)	Mistaken for "0" (zero), the number "4" (four) or "cc"	Write "unit"
IU (International Unit)	Mistaken for IV (intravenous) or the number 10 (ten)	Write "International Unit"
Q.D., QD, q.d., qd (daily)	Mistaken for each other	Write "daily"
Q.O.D., QOD, q.o.d., qod (every other day)	Period after the Q mistaken for "I" and the "O" mistaken for "I"	Write "every other day"
Trailing zero (X.0 mg)†	Decimal point is missed	Write X mg
Lack of leading zero (.X mg)		Write 0.X mg
MS	Can mean morphine sulfate or magnesium sulfate	Write "morphine sulfate"
MSO$_4$ and MgSO$_4$	Confused for one another	Write "magnesium sulfate"

*Applies to all orders and all medication-related documentation that is handwritten (including free-text computer entry) or on preprinted forms.
†**Exception:** A "trailing zero" may be used only where required to demonstrate the level of precision of the value being reported, such as for laboratory results, imaging studies that report size of lesions, or catheter/tube sizes. It may not be used in medication orders or other medication-related documentation.
From The Joint Commission. (2016; 2004). *Official "Do Not Use" List.* Retrieved from https://www.jointcommission.org/topics/patient_safety.aspx

the patients to repeat back to you what they understood— for example, discharge instructions, how to take their medication, how to do their dressing change, and so forth. The Centers for Medicare & Medicaid Services (CMS) requires organizations to provide language services for all patients who need them (Critical Thinking Box 11.2).

? CRITICAL THINKING BOX 11.2

Role-play with a partner the transcription of verbal physician orders and the reading back of those orders for clarity and accuracy. Can you identify any potential miscommunications?

Health care literacy has become a focal point across the nation. It is staggering how many patients, who are seemingly literate, simply do not understand their discharge instructions or medication administration directions. The National Library of Medicine (2012) reported that reading abilities of adults are typically three to four grade levels behind the last year of school completed. A high-school graduate typically has a seventh- or eighth-grade reading level. Therefore, it is essential for the health care provider to ask patients to repeat back what they understand about their condition, medications, education, and discharge instructions (a check-back). As a health care professional, you now speak a language that is unfamiliar to the public. Consider that you and the patient's physician may refer to the patient's high blood pressure condition as hypertension. Does the patient realize that hypertension and high blood pressure are the same things, or does he or she think that hypertension is a "hyper" condition in which the person cannot sit still? You might be surprised when you hear what the patient understands about his or her own condition!

Transcribing Written Orders

In the process of providing safe patient care, it is essential that physician or health care provider orders be communicated clearly and correctly to the health care team. The physician order must clearly indicate what is to be done, when it should be done, and how often it should be done. All orders must include the patient's identifying information and the current date and time. Table 11.2 provides a summary of the various types of orders. The process for transcribing orders may involve other health team members, such as the unit secretary, but it is the nurse's responsibility to verify that the orders are implemented correctly. This involves making sure that the order is clearly understood and documented accurately. If any component of the order is not clear, the physician should be contacted for clarification (Box 11.3).

The computer prescriber order entry (CPOE) is an electronic means for entering a physician order. This system has the benefit of reducing errors by minimizing the ambiguity of handwritten orders, as well as intercepting errors when they most commonly occur—at the time the order is written. The system also has the added benefit of allowing a new order to be entered from multiple locations. This in turn decreases the need for telephone orders, as the person writing the order can use any computer terminal within the system to do so (and sometimes smartphone technology is utilized to facilitate remote order entry). The CPOE system is integrated with other patient information, including laboratory information, diagnostic results, and medication records. Even with all the advantages of the electronic health record, in the event the systems shut down, the

TABLE 11.2   TYPES OF WRITTEN ORDERS

TYPE	DESCRIPTION
One-time-only order	An order for a medication or procedure to be carried out only one time.
PRN order	An order to be carried out when the patient needs it, not on a scheduled basis. For example, a PRN pain medication order.
Standing order	A physician's routine set of orders for a specific procedure or condition. For example, a surgeon may have standing preoperative and/or postoperative orders for an abdominal surgery patient.
STAT order	An order that is to be implemented immediately. Usually, it is a one-time order. The term is derived from the Latin word *statim*, which means "immediately."

BOX 11.3   STEPS IN TRANSCRIBING ORDERS

1. Read all of the order(s).
2. Determine whether all request forms (laboratory, medication, diagnostic test) and/or contacts have been initiated.
3. Review notes for order entries.
4. Follow institution policy for rechecking orders and signing off.

best practices related to transcription of orders, accuracy of orders, and legibility of orders cannot be forgotten.

COMMUNICATING WHEN IT IS CRITICAL—WHAT DO YOU NEED TO DO?

Critical Patient Tests

Communication of critical test results is yet another vulnerable time when errors can occur. Critical test results warrant expeditious communication to the responsible licensed caregiver without delay. This includes not only laboratory panic values but also other diagnostic test results specifically defined by the institution. The primary goal is to transmit the critical information to the person who can most quickly fix the problem. Documentation of how this was accomplished is essential to promoting and providing validation that the critical test result was communicated and, if needed, acted on.

Often, nurses are notified of a critical test result without passing that communication along to the practitioner who has the scope and authority to act on that result. Assumptions are sometimes made that the physician is aware of the test result or that notifying the nurse is enough. The licensed independent practitioner in this case is the individual who is able to act on the result of the test. The nurse is NOT that person. The physician who ordered the test IS.

"When in doubt, call it out" to the physician, and document the results of that conversation when clarifying ambiguous orders.

Managing critical information regarding a patient's test result is all about getting the information to the right person. What should be done if you cannot reach the physician who ordered a test with critical results? As a nurse, you may find it necessary to initiate the chain-of-command or chain-of-resolution policy. Most institutions have a process that identifies a step-by-step method of whom to contact in case the physician cannot be reached. The nurse continues to care for the patient, documenting the care that has been provided and all attempts that were made to contact the physician. Finally, the nurse is responsible for determining that resolution has occurred and for documenting the resolution in the medical record. It is vital that you become aware of the chain-of-command or chain-of-resolution policy at your place of employment and understand situations that warrant its initiation. Merely documenting in the patient's chart that you tried to notify the physician does not take responsibility for the patient's current health status away from you. You are the advocate for the patient and are responsible to assure communication has taken place.

Critical Hand-Off Communication

The Joint Commission's National Patient Safety Goal #2 clearly states that health care facilities must implement a standardized approach to communications. The implementation of a hand-off communication tool helps to reinforce to clinicians that they have a responsibility to provide succinct, accurate information and safe, quality care throughout the patient's period of hospitalization through a safe discharge, thus making the patient's hospital journey a safe one.

One of the communication modalities that is often employed in the health care setting is called "I-SBAR-R Communication." Originally, this tool was called SBAR, and now it has been updated to I-SBAR-R to reinforce the importance of patient safety goal #2 (read-back communication) and patient identification. Integrating I-SBAR-R techniques into your communication with other team members will organize your discussion and promote patient safety (Grbach, 2008).

Scenario: Mrs. Smith is an 84-year-old patient who was admitted with a diagnosis of uncontrolled diabetes. It's 2:00 AM, and the nurse notices the patient in respiratory distress. She assesses Mrs. Smith and calls the physician:

"Dr. Brown, I'm Nancy Jones, RN **(I)**, and I've been caring for Mrs. Jane Smith, an 84-year-old female in room 302 who was admitted tonight, who is experiencing increased shortness of breath and is very anxious. **(S)**

"She's not ever had an episode like this before. She has no history of respiratory distress, asthma, or COPD. She was sitting up in bed and had a sudden onset of shortness of breath. She does have a history of thrombophlebitis. **(B)**

"She is breathing 42 breaths a minute. Her pulse oximeter is showing an oxygen saturation of 86% on room air. She has bilateral breath sounds with some expiratory wheezes in all lobes. Her skin is pale, cool, and clammy. She is oriented but very anxious. She is afebrile, pulse of 120, and blood pressure of 92/60. Her glucose is 130. She is sitting up in bed; compression stockings are in place. **(A)**

"I've called a rapid response team. Would you like me to obtain arterial blood gases or administer some oxygen? Could you come in and see her?" **(R)**

Dr. Brown states, "Thanks for the update on Mrs. Smith's condition. Please initiate oxygen at two liters per nasal cannula. Let's order arterial blood gases. I'll be in within the next hour to see her but call me with any changes or concerns." **(R)**

"I will place the order for arterial blood gases to be drawn and administer oxygen at two liters per nasal cannula and will call you back with any changes or concerns." **(R)**

Imagine how differently this conversation could have gone had the nurse not had an organized manner to communicate this urgent situation, especially in the middle of the night when the physician may have been asleep!

I-SBAR-R provides a common and predictable structure and can be used in virtually any clinical setting. Use of I-SBAR-R also refines critical thinking skills; *before* communication is delivered, the person initiating the communication makes an assessment of the patient and provides a recommendation for ongoing care. I-SBAR-R is a communication strategy that helps organize and focus on critical information (Box 11.4). Additionally, the use of a standardized communication and reporting method may help alleviate anxiety that students and new graduate nurses experience during hand-off communication (Kostiuk, 2015). A recent initiative from The Joint Commission encourages the use of the acronym SHARE to promote effective hand-off communication (Box 11.5).

BOX 11.4   SITUATION-BACKGROUND-ASSESSMENT-RECOMMENDATION (I-SBAR-R) TOOL

I = Identification: Identify yourself and your patient (two identifiers are used).
S = Situation: What is happening at the present time?
B = Background: What are the circumstances leading up to this situation?
A = Assessment: What do I think the problem is?
R = Recommendation: What should we do to correct the problem?
R = Read-back or Response: Receiver acknowledges information given: What is his or her response?

Grbach, W. (2008). *Reformulating SBAR to "I-SBAR-R," QSEN.* Retrieved from http://qsen.org/reformulating-sbar-to-i-sbar-r/.

Shift Change—So Much to Say … So Little Time

Any time there is an exchange of information, there is a possibility for miscommunication either by omission (forgetting to share something important) or by simply focusing on the things that are not as essential as others (the patient's nephew who is coming to visit versus the pending critical test result). How can the nurse possibly begin to decide what is important to discuss in the short amount of time provided for the change-of-shift report? With a standardized method to hand off or communicate the care of the patient to another clinician, a miscommunication of information is less likely. This means for the nurse that any time a report is transferred from one person to another (even a colleague who covers another for a break), the adopted method for communicating information must be followed.

Some of the most critical elements in a change-of-shift report using the patient's medical record include:

- Two patient identifiers (typically name and date of birth)
- Current medical diagnoses
- Physician(s) on the case
- Pertinent medical/social history

BOX 11.5 **HAND-OFF COMMUNICATION**

The Hand-off Communications Targeted Solutions Tool™

- Facilitates the examination of the current hand-off communication between two settings of care from the viewpoints of both the senders and receivers involved in the process.
- Provides a tested and validated measurement system that produces data that support and drive the need for improving the current hand-off communication processes.
- Identifies areas of focus, such as the specific information needed for the transition that is being measured. For example, the information needed for a hand-off from the emergency department to an inpatient unit differs from that needed for a hand-off from a hospital to a skilled nursing facility.
- Provides customizable forms for data collection to fit the specific needs of the transition being measured.
- Provides guidelines to determine the most appropriate and realistic hand-off communication process for a given transition, while also empowering the staff involved in the process.

The Joint Commission Hand-off Communication Acronym: SHARE

To improve effective patient hand-offs, The Joint Commission recommends following the "SHARE" acronym, which stands for:

- **S**tandardize critical content: Make sure a patient's history and other key information are readily available and easy to comprehend.
- **H**ardwire within your system: Identify new and existing technologies to aid in a patient's hand-off.
- **A**llow opportunity to ask questions: Rather than take all information about a patient at face value, check and double check with others involved in the patient's care to ensure accuracy.
- **R**einforce quality and measurement: Essentially, hold your colleagues (as well as yourself) accountable for actions taken and for monitoring compliance.
- **E**ducate and coach: Teach all colleagues the ins and outs of successful hand-offs.

From: The Joint Commission (2010). *Joint Commission Center for Transforming Healthcare tackles miscommunication among caregivers.* Retrieved from http://www.centerfortransforminghealthcare.org/assets/4/6/CTH_Hand-off_commun_set_final_2010.pdf.

The Joint Commission. (2012, June). Center for Transforming Healthcare released a new Hand-off Communications Targeted Solutions Tool (TST). Retrieved from http://www.centerfortransforminghealthcare.org/center_transforming_healthcare_tst_hoc/

- Current physical condition (review of systems)
- Resuscitation status (no resuscitation, full resuscitation)
- Nutritional status (nutritional intake, NPO, supplements)
- Pending or critical issues and tests

When appropriate, a bedside report that involves the patient has demonstrated greater satisfaction and improved outcomes for the patient, because the patient is an active member of his or her own health care team! This provides the opportunity for the patient and the family to greet the oncoming caregiver and for both caregivers to assess the patient together, especially where there may be skin integrity issues or wounds involved. When I-SBAR-R guidelines are consistently used, the shift report and patient transfer are organized, thorough, and yet concise. Furthermore, important information is not forgotten, and the transition of care is then more complete and safer for everyone involved.

How Can I Deal With All the Interruptions?

Interruptions are one of the major threats to effective time management and patient safety. Each interruption during medication administration was associated with a 12.1% increase in procedural errors and a 12.7% increase in clinical errors. It was noted that interruptions occur in 53.1% of all administrations (Westbrook et al., 2010). Not only is time taken away from goal-directed activities, but clearly interruptions create patient safety hazards! Of course, some interruptions are inevitable, but they are manageable. Begin by recognizing when *you* are permitting interruptions. Do you start one task and then begin another rather than concentrating on completing the first? Do you respond to added distractions (e.g., television, ringing telephones, and chatty colleagues) at times when task completion is required? When possible, in nonemergency situations, use your time-management strategies and communication skills to remain focused on the task at hand. Colleagues and visitors will accept that you may need to get back to them when you have finished what you are doing. Write down when and where you can reach them, and then follow through.

Responding to interruptions can also mean you are doing your job. For example, when you are interrupted to answer a patient's call light or answer a physician's telephone call, you are doing your job. These activities are part of your nursing responsibilities. They may not be of an urgent nature and can be delayed a short time, or they may be urgent and necessitate immediate response—either way, you will need to handle them eventually. Rather than feeling that you have been interrupted, remind yourself that what you are doing is accomplishing part of your job. There are many aspects of your job that you cannot control, but you can always choose how to respond.

Evidence has demonstrated that medication administration and shift report are critical times to minimize interruptions. To signify the need not to interrupt the caregiver engaging in these critical tasks, facilities are employing various strategies to alert others that the nurse is involved in a critical task. Many clinical settings have created a "no-interruption zone" around medication administration dispensing areas and educate visitors on honoring this time for the sake of patient safety. Others have tried having the staff wear brightly colored vests while giving report or medicating patients until the task is complete. This way, everyone, from the physician to the families, is aware that the caregiver is engaged in a critical task that requires his or her full attention (Pape & Richards, 2010). Working with your team and creating a list of those tasks that are best served by minimal interruptions can facilitate effective teamwork. Prioritizing what is most important will keep you and your colleagues on task.

Everyone needs some totally uninterrupted time to relax, refocus, and re-energize. During clinical experience, or while you are at work or at home, spend a few minutes in a quiet place by yourself (e.g., the nurses' lounge, the chapel, an empty patient room, a bedroom at home) to evaluate what is happening or what needs to happen next. Take several deep, slow breaths; read; meditate; relax; or get in touch with yourself. (Parents with small children can take turns watching the children so each adult can have some uninterrupted private time.)

What Skills Do I Need to Use the Telephone Effectively?

Many nurses spend time on the telephone talking with physicians, patients, their families, and other health care personnel. Here are some tips for making telephone communication productive. It is honoring of others' time and priorities to ask the person you are calling if this is a convenient time to talk based on the urgency. If you anticipate your conversation will involve complex information, make notes ahead of time so that you can keep your conversation as focused and brief as possible. Go ahead and try organizing your conversation in the I-SBAR-R communication format. After discussing detailed, critical information on the telephone, it is wise to follow up with a documented communication to the other person. This helps clarify and confirm the information discussed. If your telephone conversation requires a follow-up action, you need to document that.

It is difficult to focus on a telephone conversation if you are doing something else at the same time. Your communication will be more effective if you do one thing at a time. (Case in point: How often do you pass people on the road who are driving recklessly only to see they are talking on a cellular telephone or texting?) Recent graduates often experience a challenge when communicating with physicians, especially on the telephone. Box 11.6 highlights some helpful tips.

MANAGING TIME IN THE CLINICAL SETTING

One of the main sources of job dissatisfaction reported by nurses is too little time to provide their hands-on care. This "limited time" to provide patient care has been accelerated by the nursing shortage combined with cost-effective staffing, the increase in numbers of patients, and the higher acuity of these patients. In response to this issue, nurses must develop competent skills in time management and priority setting. Nurses can use several techniques to maximize the time spent providing patient care. Remember Pareto's 80/20 Rule. In this case, 20% of your patients

---

BOX 11.6   TIPS FOR COMMUNICATING WITH PHYSICIANS ON THE TELEPHONE

1. Use the I-SBAR-R technique.
2. Say who you are right away.
3. State your business briefly but completely.
4. Ask for specific orders when appropriate.
5. If you want the physician to assess the patient, say so.
6. If the physician is coming, ask when to expect him or her.
7. If you get cut off, call back.
8. Document all attempts to reach a health care provider. If you cannot reach a health care provider or get what you need, notify your chain of command or chain of resolution.

will require 80% of your time! Those 20% should be the sickest patients. When their care and needs are met first, the rest of your assignment is much easier. It is important to determine which patients require the most time (80%). Then ask yourself—Do they require time that can be delegated to someone else, or do they require the time because they are the most unstable and ill patients? It is essential to communicate any concerns regarding unsafe patient assignments through the chain of command or chain of resolution so that care can be effectively managed (Critical Thinking Box 11.3, Fig. 11.1).

> Request consistent patient assignments whenever possible. This allows you to develop relationships with your patients and their families and promotes time management, because you become familiar with the special needs of these patients.

? CRITICAL THINKING BOX 11.3

Develop a flow sheet to organize your time and patient care for your clinical schedule. Obtain an assignment for an RN on one of the units to which you are assigned for clinical. Can you prioritize and delegate this RN's assignment appropriately?

Get Organized Before the Change-of-Shift Report

Develop your own work organization sheet, or use one provided by the agency to document information you will need to begin coordinating care for a group of patients. Modify this form as you discover areas that need improvement. Avoid distractions as you receive a report, and begin to fill out your time management (or work organization) form. Get the information needed to plan the care for your patients, and begin to organize your shift activities (Fig. 11.2).

FIG. 11.1 Can you work overtime?

Name: Susan

Time	Activities	Room 416	Room 417	Room 418
7–8	✓ MAR Shift report ✓ vitals	✓ Bld sugar 7:30 insulin	IV. @ 125/hr. turn ✓ pulses	7:45 pre-op NPO ✓ consent form
8–9	assessments meal trays	meds x3–9 up for meals	meds x2–9 If leg dsg. assist c̄ meal	To OR
9–10		shower chg bed ✓ pain meds	complete bath ✓ pulses turn	
10–11	Chart			Chg bed
11–12	meal trays lunch	up for meals ✓ Bld sugar insulin?	turn ✓ pulses assist c̄ meal	
12–13	Chart assessment	meds x2–12	IVPB–12	Return fm OR? N.G. suction I.V.
13–14		diabetic teaching	turn ✓ pulses If. leg dressing change	
14–15	I & O's IV's report info			

FIG. 11.2 Work organization sheet.

Prioritize Your Care

Setting priorities has become difficult in light of the dichotomy between the expected outcomes of efficiency and effectiveness and the perceived limitations of resources, including time. Priority setting is not only based on patient needs; it is also influenced by the needs of the organization and the accountability of the nurse. Priorities are established and reprioritized throughout the day according to patients' assessed needs and unscheduled interruptions, both minor and emergent. Plan your day around the patient you perceive to be the sickest. This is the patient who is at the greatest risk from harm if you do not address his or her needs first.

> Prioritize patients by using the ABCD system or Maslow's hierarchy of needs. Of highest priority are the patients with problems or potential problems related to the airway. Next are those having any difficulty with breathing and then those with circulation problems. When using Maslow's hierarchy of needs to assist with prioritization, you need to meet physiological needs first: that is, resolve any difficulty with oxygenation first. Be flexible and reprioritize as emergencies occur.

Prioritize your patients after you receive report and immediately proceed to the patient whom you have placed highest on your priority list. Remember that this prioritization may change as you complete your initial assessments. Additional modifications will be made according to the location of patients' rooms to avoid wasted time and movement. When you first enter a patient's room, introduce yourself, perform hand hygiene measures, and complete a quick environmental assessment. Think about any supplies you will need when returning to the room. Complete the focused assessment, validate the safety of your patient, and proceed to your next patient. After you have completed your initial rounds, reassess your initial prioritization, modify according to your assessments, and plan your day.

For example, a characteristic assignment for the day could be:
- A patient who is 1 day postoperative and wants something for pain
- A geriatric patient who is vomiting
- A patient with diabetes who is angry about the care from the last shift
- A geriatric patient whose bed is wet because of urine incontinence

Which of these patients needs your immediate attention and which tasks could be expeditiously completed by delegating? Most likely the one who is vomiting needs the nurse's attention first, because this patient is at increased risk for aspiration. Next is probably the patient who is in pain. You could possibly delegate the bath and bed change of the geriatric patient who has soiled the bed with urine. Assisting your colleagues in their assignments if yours are completed is another technique in TeamSTEPPS called Task Assistance, also known as "no one sits until we all sit."

Identify the busiest times on the unit; do not schedule a dressing change when medications need to be given. Research any medications with which you are unfamiliar before they are due. Do not procrastinate; start early. If you have dressing changes for several patients, start with the cleanest and progress to the more contaminated wounds (Critical Thinking Box 11.4).

> **❓ CRITICAL THINKING BOX 11.4**
>
> How do the efficient nurses on your clinical unit prioritize their time and their patients' needs?

Watch those nurses who always seem to get everything done, done well, and still enjoy nursing. Ask them about their "secrets" of time management, and try out some of their tips.

Organize Your Work by Patient

By organizing work by patient, the nurse maximizes the number of tasks that can be accomplished with each visit to the patient. The nurse thinks strategically: "How can I multitask or accomplish several objectives in one visit to the patient?" By using this technique, the nurse can combine assessment, administration of medications, and teaching during one patient visit (see Fig. 11.2).

Another way to organize and coordinate the needs of the patient is by implementing hourly rounds. This is where the caregivers (both nursing and ancillary help) can alternate visiting the patients every hour to verify that patients' needs are met proactively. This is often referred to as meeting the "three Ps": pain, position, and potty. Is the patient in pain? Does the patient need assistance in changing position? Does the patient need assistance in toileting? By implementing this strategy, patients use call bells less, have fewer falls, and have higher patient satisfaction. It also assists the nurse in attending to prioritized tasks with minimal interruptions (Fig. 11.3).

THREE Ps OF NURSING ROUNDS

FIG. 11.3 "Three Ps" of hourly rounds.

MANAGING OTHERS

Communicating and getting along with other people are always challenging tasks. Most people are easygoing, straightforward, and supportive. They add to your energy and ability to function effectively, and they contribute to your goal attainment. However, if you experience a phone call or visit from someone who just wants to talk when you are busy, you need to avoid being trapped. Tell that person, "Now is not a good time. Could we discuss this later?" or even "I've got another appointment. Could we postpone this conversation until tomorrow?" Some individuals drain energy from others and from organizational accomplishment through their whining, criticizing, negative thinking, chronic lateness, poor crisis management, dependency, aggression, and similar unproductive behaviors. Occasional exhibitions of such behavior in relation to a personal crisis are understandable. However, when people use these behaviors as their everyday *modus operandi* (method of operating), they interfere with attainment of individual and organizational goals. Even in the best of human relationships, conflict and extreme emotions are inevitable. To protect your time and achieve your goals, it may be necessary to limit your time with such individuals. Avoidance is one strategy. Learning to say "no" and using assertive communication can help as well. Setting clear boundaries is essential and demonstrates respect for both yourself and the other person.

What About Delegating and Time Management?

You may have observed nurses performing non-nursing activities during your clinical experience, which include but are not limited to cleaning, running errands, clerical duties, and stocking supplies. Appropriate delegation of non-nursing tasks can provide the nurse with additional time to dedicate to patient care. Even some patient care tasks can be delegated after verifying the training and competence of unlicensed personnel. These requirements vary in different states and institutions. Review Chapter 14 for more specifics on delegation.

Delegation includes more than asking someone to do something. The American Nurses Association (ANA) and the National Council of State Boards of Nursing (NCSBN) have defined delegation as "the transfer of responsibility for the performance of an activity from one individual to another, with the former retaining accountability for the outcome. The RN may delegate components of care but does not delegate the nursing process itself … nursing judgment cannot be delegated" (ANA & NCSBN, 2005). This definition emphasizes that delegation increases the responsibility and accountability of the registered nurse (RN). Be sure you know the delegation rules and regulations of your state's nursing practice act. Additionally, you will need to know the delegation policies and job descriptions of nursing team members in your employing agency and department as job descriptions can vary from one department to another.

In general, most caregivers are by nature people-pleasers. We are even taught to anticipate and meet the needs of others. Because of this, we tend to have great difficulty in sharing and delegating the multitude of responsibilities given to us. Delegation is a learned skill and is essential for us to adopt to be successful and to help others grow in their skill sets.

To increase delegation skills, it is sometimes necessary to overcome the myth of perfection. When you teach or train someone else to do a delegated task, initially that person may not be able to perform the activity perfectly or as well as you can. That is not important. What is important is that the person is able to meet the standards required to complete the task and to delegate appropriately to others. With experience, most people will improve in their skills (and may even surpass you). Simulation and team building practice can help with this. You are not only helping them grow, you are freeing up your time to tend to more involved tasks (Critical Thinking Box 11.5).

> ### ❓ CRITICAL THINKING BOX 11.5
>
> On your clinical unit, how many levels of personnel provide patient care? How is the nursing care of patients delegated?

Determine which patients are the most stable and whose positive progress can be anticipated. The stable patients with predictable progress should be the first whose care is delegated. The care of unstable, unpredictable patients should only be delegated to an RN. An RN should also be assigned to any patient who is undergoing a procedure or treatment that may cause the patient to become unstable.

When you are working with unlicensed assistive personnel (UAP), you can delegate to them those activities that have specific guidelines that are unchanging. For example, feeding, dressing, bathing, obtaining equipment for the nursing staff, picking up meal trays, refilling water containers, straightening up cluttered rooms—all of these activities should have guidelines according to institutional policies, should fit within the job description, and should be followed by the unlicensed assistive personnel. To the extent it is possible, involving the UAP in bedside report is optimal.

Patient teaching and discharge planning are also the responsibility of the RN. RNs are responsible for determining the patient's learning needs and establishing a teaching plan. It is also the RN's responsibility to coordinate and implement the discharge planning. The RN should request input from all nursing personnel who have assisted in providing care for the patient or who have been otherwise involved (e.g., dietary, physical therapy) in the patient's care. After the RN implements the teaching plan, it is important that the other RNs, licensed practical nurses, vocational nurses, and unlicensed assistive personnel are aware of what the patient has been taught so that they may follow up and report any pertinent observations to the RN (Critical Thinking Box 11.6). Thorough discharge planning that is understood by the patient can prevent unnecessary readmissions and harm to the patient.

> **? CRITICAL THINKING BOX 11.6**
>
> Determine how and to whom patient care is delegated on your current clinical unit. What guidelines are implemented? Is it within the nursing scope of practice?

Nursing care makes a difference in patient outcomes. This care is more than performing tasks. It incorporates assessment, care planning, and initiation of interventions, interdisciplinary collaboration, and outcome evaluations. It includes patient and family teaching, therapeutic communication, counseling, discharge planning, and teaching. To maximize the impact that nursing care can have on patient outcomes, nurses must develop and integrate multiple strategies to promote effective time management.

Supervising and Evaluating the Care Provided by Others

To meet the demanding and complex needs of the public for safe and good-quality patient care, it is imperative that the use of all nursing resources be maximized. The licensed practical nurse and other unlicensed personnel can function as extensions to the RN as providers of care if definitive supervision and evaluative guidelines are established. State boards of nursing are responsible for articulating those guidelines.

> Unlicensed personnel: An individual not licensed as a health care provider; a nursing student providing care that is not a part of his or her nursing program.

Supervision entails providing direction, evaluation, and follow-up by the RN for nursing tasks that have been delegated to unlicensed personnel. The following criteria apply to the RN who functions in a supervisory capacity:

- Provide directions with clear expectations of how the task is to be performed.
- Verify the task is being performed according to standards of practice.
- Monitor the task being performed; intervene if necessary.
- Evaluate the status of the patient.
- Evaluate the performance of the task.
- Provide feedback as necessary.
- Reassess the plan of care and modify as needed.

These criteria apply to RNs who delegate nursing care for patients with acute conditions or those patients who are in an acute-care environment. The continued growing need for unlicensed personnel, as well as the role of the practical nurse in providing care, will require the RN to serve in the supervisor and evaluator roles and to be accountable and responsible for those assigned nursing tasks.

It is never easy to provide constructive feedback regarding a deficiency or an area needing improvement; however, sandwiching the constructive feedback between layers of recognition and positive reinforcement makes the communication more palatable and more effective. Keep in mind that when providing constructive feedback, you are simply providing your evaluation of an individual's performance, not his or her character. Here's an example of how a supervisor effectively used the "sandwich" method for providing constructive feedback.

Carrie is a new graduate who has completed the first 6 weeks of employment. She is consistently tardy and delays shift report. When Carrie arrived in the supervisor's office for her evaluation, the supervisor was very nice in her approach to talking with her. The supervisor reviewed with Carrie the progress she has made in orienting to the unit and managing the care for a group of patients. Carrie was pleased with the recognition of her progress. Next, the supervisor addressed Carrie's tardiness on the unit and how it has affected the shift report. Carrie acknowledged this as a problem and discussed the situation, making some suggestions to alleviate the problem. The supervisor was supportive of Carrie's suggestions and her initiative to examine the tardiness issue.

When providing constructive feedback, one should
- Actively listen to the individual's perception of the situation
- Focus on the facts
- Provide an opportunity for the individual to self-reflect
- Support the individual

When providing constructive feedback, one should not
- Argue with the individual's perception of the event
- Reprimand, scold, or belittle the individual
- Offer unsolicited personal advice (e.g., "This is what I think you should do…")
- Coerce or make intimidating statements to demonstrate your authority

CONCLUSION

Building nursing management skills that promote patient safety is a new task for the graduate nurse. Implementing management skills in the clinical setting is challenging. By using effective communication, time management in the clinical setting, and managing other members of the health care team, the new graduate can begin to grow professionally and personally. See additional relevant websites and online resources for developing management skills.

After your clinical schedule is organized, you will become a more effective nurse and will begin to have the time to provide safe nursing care, which leads to positive patient outcomes.

🌐 RELEVANT WEBSITES AND ONLINE RESOURCES

Nurse Together (2013)
6 Time management tips every nurse should have. Retrieved from http://www.nursetogether.com/6-time-management-skills-every-nurses-should-have.

American Nurses Association (2010)
Developing delegation skills. Retrieved from http://nursingworld.org/MainMenuCategories/ANAMarketplace/ANAPeriodicals/OJIN/TableofContents/Vol152010/No2May2010/Delegation-Skills.html.

The Joint Commission (2016)
Sentinel event alert. Retrieved from https://www.jointcommission.org/sentinel_event.aspx.

BIBLIOGRAPHY

Agency for Healthcare Research and Quality (AHRQ). (2013). *TeamSTEPPS™. Strategies and tools to enhance performance and patient safety.* Retrieved from www.teamstepps.ahrq.gov.
Agency for Healthcare Research and Quality (AHRQ). (2015). *Patient safety network glossary 2015.* Retrieved from http.psnet.ahrq.gov/glossary.

American Nurses Association & National Council of State Boards of Nursing. (2005). *Joint statement on delegation.* Retrieved from www.NCSBN.org/Joint_Statement.pdf.

Grbach, W. (2008). *Reformulating SBAR to "I-SBAR-R."* Retrieved from www.qsen.org/teachingstrategy .php?id=33.

Institute for Healthcare Improvement (IHI). (2008). *IHI saving lives web & action programs: preventing adverse drug events through medication reconciliation.* Retrieved from www.IHI.org.

Kostiuk, S. (2015). Can learning the ISBARR framework help to address nursing students' perceived anxiety and confidence levels associated with handover reports? *Journal of Nursing Education, 54*(10), 583–587. doi http:/ /dx.doi.org/10.3928/01484834-20150916-07.

National Library of Medicine. (2012). *Health literacy.* Retrieved from http://nnlm.gov/outreach/consumer/hlthl it.html.

Pape, T., & Richards, B. L. (2010). Stop "knowledge creep." *Nursing Management, 41*(2), 8.

The Joint Commission. (2010). *Advancing effective communication, cultural competence, and patient and family-centered care.* Oakbrook Terrace, IL: Joint Commission Resources.

The Joint Commission. (2010). *Handoff communication.* Retrieved from www.centerfortransforminghealthcare .org.

The Joint Commission. (2012). *Facts about the do not use abbreviation list,* Oakbrook Terrace, IL. Retrieved from http://www.jointcommission.org/about_us/patient_safety_fact_sheets.aspx.

The Joint Commission. (2015). *Sentinel event data root causes by event type 2004-Q2 2015.* Retrieved from www .jointcommission.org/assets/1/18/Rootcauseeventtype.pdf.

Westbrook, J., Woods, A., Rob, M., Dunsmuir, W. T., & Day, R. O. (2010). Association of interruptions with an increased risk and severity of medication administration errors. *Archives of Internal Medicine, 170*(8), 683–690.

Effective Communication, Team Building, and Interprofessional Practice

JoAnn Zerwekh, EdD, RN; Ashley Zerwekh Garneau, PhD, RN

ⓔ http://evolve.elsevier.com/Zerwekh/nsgtoday/.

To effectively communicate, we must realize that we are all different in the way we perceive the world and use this understanding as a guide to our communication with others.
Anthony Robbins

High-functioning teams require collaboration between physicians, nurses, pharmacists, social workers, clinical psychologists, case managers, medical assistants, and clinical administrators.
Department of Veterans Affairs, 2010, p. 2

Communication should be clearly stated and directed to the appropriate, responsible individual.

After completing this chapter, you should be able to:

- Describe the basic components of communication.
- Identify effective ways of communicating with the health care team.
- Describe an assertive communication style.
- Apply effective communication skills in various nursing activities.
- Identify different types of groups and explain group process.
- Discuss team building, group problem solving, and interprofessional practice.
- Analyze components of interprofessional practice.

Communication is like breathing—we do it all the time, and the better we do it, the better we feel. At times communication can be so subtle that others are not able to comprehend the communicator. Communication between people in everyday life is an exercise in subtleties and interpretations. The more personal the information, the more indirect and obscure the message becomes. In nursing, indirect communications and obscure terminology can be the difference between life and death. When you say, "I want to be clear when I communicate with others," it is no different from washing windows. The clearer the window, the better we see. Communicating with the health care team and teaching patients what they need to know is part of the foundation of nursing care (Critical Thinking Box 12.1).

? CRITICAL THINKING BOX 12.1

Try This ...
1. How many different ways can you communicate this sentence to change its meaning or tone? "I do not care how you've done that procedure before; do it my way now."
2. The instructor says to you, "Come to my office at 2:00. There's something I want to talk to you about." What are some possible interpretations of this message?
3. A patient's spouse says to you, "I do not need your help when we go home." How many possible explanations can you come up with regarding the meaning of the communication?

COMMUNICATION IN THE WORKPLACE

Sharing information with the health care team requires different approaches. This communication on a daily basis may involve delegation of a nursing procedure to nursing personnel, clarification of a physician's orders, reevaluation of a patient-care assignment of another health care team member, or coordination of various hospital departments (e.g., radiology, dietary, pharmacy, surgery, laboratory) to provide nursing care. Create role-playing situations with your peers by taking turns acting in the supervisor and subordinate roles (Critical Thinking Box 12.2).

? CRITICAL THINKING BOX 12.2

Try This ...
Role-play these situations with your classmates. Try taking turns acting in the supervisory and subordinate roles.
1. The charge nurse has asked the team leader and the nurse providing care to Mr. Smith to provide an update on his progress and anticipated discharge date.
2. You are the team leader giving bedside report to two nursing assistants and one LPN who will be working on your team today.
3. You are caring for a patient who has been newly diagnosed with Type 2 diabetes. You discuss the patient's care with the dietitian, the social worker, and the patient's wife.

How Can I Communicate Effectively With My Supervisor?

Upward communication with supervisors takes on a formal nature. It is important to learn and use the channels of communication. For example, you may share information with your designated team leader on the unit. The team leader shares information with the nursing supervisor or nurse manager, who shares information with the assistant vice president of nursing, who shares information with the vice president of nursing, and so on. From this example, you can see the communication approach taken with the appropriate chain of command.

Do you remember the game you played as a child in which someone whispers a secret to the next person, and each person repeats the secret down the line until the last person speaks the secret aloud? The secret may have started out as "Jenny was out picking berries today so she can bake a pie." By the end of the line, it may have become "Jenny is so allergic to cherries that she breaks out into hives." The point is that messages can become very distorted when they travel through the chain of command in the upward flow of communication. Arredondo (2000) says that when communicating with superiors it is important to state needs clearly, explain the rationales for requests, and suggest the benefits to the larger unit. It is also important to listen objectively to the response of the supervisor, because there may be good reasons for granting or not granting the request.

Arredondo (2000) gives the following tips for talking to your supervisor:

1. Keep your supervisor informed of potential or upcoming issues.
2. If a problem is developing, make an appointment to talk it over. Have specific information available, especially written documentation of facts. Focus on resolving the problems, not just the problems.
3. Show that you have important information to share and a sense of responsibility.
4. Be careful which words you use. Avoid blaming others, exaggerating, and using overly dramatic expressions.
5. Do not talk to your supervisor when angry, and do not respond with anger. Use "I" statements, and explain what you think in a professional manner.
6. If you want to present a new idea, give your supervisor a written proposal, and then set up a meeting to discuss it after the supervisor has read it.
7. Accept feedback, and learn from it through self-reflection.
8. Never go above or circumvent the chain of command; this includes your supervisor. Always communicate directly with your supervisor first before going farther up the chain of command.
9. Do not engage in sharing the details of your conversation with others who do not have a stake in the issue.

How Can I Communicate Effectively With Other Nursing Personnel?

When you speak with other professional nurses, you communicate using a lateral, or horizontal, flow of information. This flow is based on a concept of equality, in which no person holds more power than the other. This type of communication is best achieved in a work climate that promotes a sense of trust and respect among colleagues. When nurses work effectively together, their cohesiveness makes success more likely. This takes work and the deliberate use of facilitative messages (Northouse, 2015).

Ideally, professional nurses should view themselves as equals in their interactions with members of other health care disciplines, and their approach to communication should be a lateral one, even with physicians. The basis of this communication is the ability of the nurse to see himself or herself as competent and worthy of being an equal to physicians, social workers, dietitians, and others. Gaining this self-confidence is a major goal of every recent graduate. Using effective communication practices, as described in this chapter, and communication reporting tools (see Chapter 11 for information on hand-off communication) will help you achieve that goal.

Even a recent graduate will soon be providing direction to licensed nursing personnel and unlicensed assistive nursing personnel (see Chapter 14 for further information on delegation). It is important to remember that these people have needs for satisfaction and self-esteem, too. Directions do not need to be given in the form of authoritative commands unless an emergency demands immediate action in a prescribed way. Marquis and Huston (2014) suggest that when you provide direction, you need to think through exactly what you want to be done, by whom, and when. You need to get the full attention of the other person so you know that he or she hears you accurately. You should provide clear, simple instructions in step-by-step order, using a supportive tone of voice. Before the other person goes to do the task, ask for feedback to verify that he or she has accurately heard your instructions. Follow-up is necessary to be sure your directions were followed and to find out what happened, in case something more needs to be done. Involving personnel who are at other levels of nursing care in the planning and evaluation of patient care will increase those associates' sense of responsibility for the outcomes and will help you to seem less authoritarian. Refer to the checklist in Critical Thinking Box 12.3 to identify areas needed for growth.

❔ CRITICAL THINKING BOX 12.3

Facilitation Skills Checklist

Directions: Periodically during the clinical experience, use this checklist to identify areas needed for growth and progress made. Think of your clinical patient experiences. Indicate the extent of your agreement with each of the following statements by marking the scale: SA, strongly agree; A, agree; NS, not sure; D, disagree; SD, strongly disagree.

1. I maintain good eye contact.	SA	A	NS	D	SD
2. Most of my verbal comments follow the lead of the other person.	SA	A	NS	D	SD
3. I encourage others to talk about feelings.	SA	A	NS	D	SD
4. I am able to ask open-ended questions.	SA	A	NS	D	SD
5. I can restate and clarify a person's ideas.	SA	A	NS	D	SD
6. I can summarize in a few words the basic ideas of a long statement made by a person.	SA	A	NS	D	SD
7. I can make statements that reflect the person's feelings.	SA	A	NS	D	SD
8. I can share my feelings relevant to the discussion when appropriate to do so.	SA	A	NS	D	SD
9. I am able to give feedback.	SA	A	NS	D	SD
10. At least 75% or more of my responses help enhance and facilitate communication.	SA	A	NS	D	SD
11. I can assist the person to list some alternatives available.	SA	A	NS	D	SD
12. I can assist the person to identify some goals that are specific and observable.	SA	A	NS	D	SD
13. I can assist the person to specify at least one next step that might be taken toward the goal.	SA	A	NS	D	SD

Adapted from Myrick, D., & Erney, T. (1984). *Caring and sharing*, Minneapolis: Educational Media Corporation, p. 154.

WHAT DOES MY IMAGE COMMUNICATE TO OTHERS?

> Remember that old saying, "Do not judge a book by its cover."

Unfortunately, we know that most people do not follow that suggestion. People develop impressions about us from the way we look, sound, talk, and act. Often we are less careful about the messages we send with our appearance and behavior than we are when we choose our words. But our image may speak louder than our words. Think about it. Would you feel comfortable accepting nutritional advice from a 300-pound nurse? How would you like it if your instructor criticized your professionalism while wearing dirty shoes, a wrinkled uniform, bright red nail polish, and four earrings in each earlobe? What would you think about a physician whose progress notes contain many misspelled words and poor grammar?

Your credibility is enhanced by good communication. Your image will help you communicate your professional credibility. Maintaining personal hygiene and grooming is essential. Your appearance at work should conform to the norms for professionals in your work setting; save your individuality for your personal time away from work.

Another aspect of your image is your depth and breadth of knowledge of your particular area in nursing. However, you also need to be familiar with a wide variety of subjects so that you can have conversations with people beyond nursing. When people discover common interests, they are more willing to communicate with you.

Flexibility is necessary for effective communication with different kinds of people. This means that you are willing and able to adapt your behavior to relate more comfortably or effectively with others. Flexibility is part of a positive image and says to people that you are willing to accept responsibility for changing your behavior to meet the professional needs or requirements of others. Take an inventory of your appearance, knowledge, and attitude. If you are not sure what kind of image you are communicating, ask several trusted friends.

How Do Gender Differences Influence Communication Styles?

Men and women view their work environments from different perspectives (Vengel, 2010; Mindell, 2001). Men often see the world from a logical, sequential, focused perspective. Women often tend to see the big picture and to seek solutions based on what makes people feel comfortable. Subtle communication differences can create barriers to open, healthy communication between men and women in the workplace. Within the workplace, the dominant communication style is direct, confident, and assertive. This style may be more familiar to men, because they are often raised hearing more aggressive, direct language from their parents, whereas many women may be more used to a soft, supportive tone of voice and choice of words. Cultural values learned in childhood also play a role in the communication style a person chooses. This style may have to be modified to make interactions more successful. A woman who is communicating with a man may need to be more direct and assertive than usual, whereas a man may need to learn to be less aggressive in many situations.

To summarize, men and women have innately different communication styles, often developed from their childhood experiences and environment. To be successful in the workplace, we all have to learn as much as we can about communication differences, identify our own styles, and have the flexibility to use other communication techniques as situations warrant.

What Should I Know About the "Grapevine"?

> The grapevine is like the tabloid newspapers. Would you bet your job on the accuracy of a rumor? So, when in doubt, check the facts out!

In addition to formal messages, communication can be informal. This type of communication flows upward, downward, and horizontally and is known as the *grapevine*. Whereas some people think of this kind of communication as gossip, others say it is the way things really get done. No matter how we describe the grapevine, we know it flourishes in all settings. People enjoy the satisfaction of the social interaction and recognition associated with the grapevine. It also provides information to employees that may not be easily obtained in any other way. It may be the quickest way to find out what the supervisor really values or what new job openings are available (Marquis & Huston, 2014) (Fig. 12.1).

Mindell (2001) provides the following tips for controlling the grapevine:

1. Provide factual information to answer questions before they are asked. Few employees get all the information they feel they need.

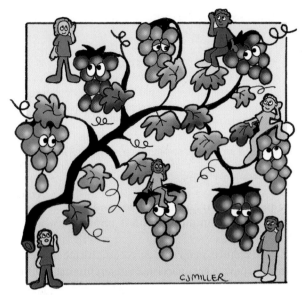

FIG. 12.1 What should you know about the grapevine?

2. Communicate face-to-face whenever possible. Do not trust the accuracy of messages conveyed through a third party.
3. Whenever rumors are running through the grapevine, hold a meeting to provide information and answer questions.
4. Do not spread rumors. Make sure you have all the facts from their source.
5. Enlist the support of respected leaders to spread the truth.
6. Address significant issues as soon as possible with your manager so that negative feelings can be defused.
7. Make sure what is put in writing is clear and accurately understood.

How Can I Handle Cultural Diversity at Work?

Giger (2013) tells us that culture is a pattern of values and beliefs reflected in the behaviors we demonstrate. Whenever a group of people spends an extended period of time together, that group develops a culture. Each of us comes from a cultural background, and we have beliefs, values, and behaviors that result from that background. In our workplaces, we will encounter many different types of people coming from diverse cultural backgrounds. To communicate effectively, we need to understand our own culture as well as the other person's culture. In addition, we must acknowledge and adhere to the cultural norms or rules that have developed in our workplace.

We must be aware of stereotypes that may interfere with our ability to see people as individuals. If we view people according to stereotypes, we might limit the way we perceive their communication. Even positive stereotypes make assumptions about people that may be inaccurate and thus may limit the nurse's ability to use all of his or her work skills effectively (Critical Thinking Box 12.4).

According to Arredondo (2000), communication goes through many filters when a person interacts with someone whom he or she perceives as different. Some of those filters are related to culture, gender, education level, age, and experience. When messages go through these filters, the messages may change because the actual communication symbols are interpreted

? CRITICAL THINKING BOX 12.4

Try This …

As you go about your work, take note of the various people you interact with and your reactions to them. Write these observations down so that you can reflect on them later. What kinds of thoughts come to mind when you see a female executive, an older woman, or a handsome man dressed in a suit? What kinds of thoughts come to mind when you see people of ethnic origins that differ from your own? How do your initial impressions affect the way you communicate with each of these people? Now picture yourself in the homes of five of your patients. Choose people from different cultural backgrounds. How are their homes different? In what ways do their homes reflect their culture? How does the family communicate in the home? What do you need to know about each culture so that you can provide culturally congruent care effectively while avoiding any stereotyped beliefs?

according to a person's own cultural values and beliefs. This change may lead to misperceptions and misinterpretations. Communication is improved when we become more aware of the filters we use.

Within the work culture, people often communicate using jargon, inside jokes, or slang unique to the work setting. Acronyms are an example of jargon that health care workers understand but patients may not. It may seem to patients and their families that we are speaking in a code or foreign language. To interact effectively, we need to speak clearly, avoid jargon or slang, and keep our communication short and to the point. Long explanations with lengthy terminology can be confusing to people who are not familiar with the health care culture.

Differences in the cultural backgrounds of workers can be a real asset. Sometimes we may have to provide care to patients who speak languages other than English, and we may need to enlist the skills of co-workers to translate or interpret, especially when cultural values influence the interpretation of the patient's behavior. We need to understand and respect cultural differences in patients. We can learn how to do this by learning about the differences among our co-workers. Respect and empathy enhance communication with people from other cultures, whether those people are patients or co-workers (Giger, 2013).

COMPONENTS OF EFFECTIVE COMMUNICATION

How Can I Communicate Effectively in Writing?

Communication takes place not only when words are spoken but also when they are written and then read by someone else. A big part of a nurse's overall effectiveness depends on the ability to write effectively. This includes written treatment plans, progress notes, job descriptions, consultation requests, referrals, and memos. Some of you may even write articles for nursing journals or chapters for textbooks!

Mindell (2001) provides some guidelines for writing. First, determine whether you need to write in a formal way. Most upward communication needs to be formal, which means you should use proper titles, format, grammar, spelling, and punctuation. Never allow something you have written to be sent without careful proofreading. Nothing creates a negative impression faster than sloppy work, misspelled words, or poor grammar. If you need to, ask someone else to do this proofreading; be sure it is done well. Take the time to make necessary revisions before sending your written work to others.

Also decide what your purpose is before you write (Marquis & Huston, 2014). This will help you to organize your thoughts so that everything you write helps to meet your purpose. Learn to write exactly what you mean. Choose words that are clear and specific. Often this means simple, small words. Be careful to use technical words only when you are sure you are choosing the correct words and your reader will understand you. Keep your sentences short and simple, with only one idea in each sentence.

> Try using the KISS principle: Keep It Short and Simple.

When you learn to be clear and concise, you will write the essential information without many lengthy phrases. Your readers will be very grateful if they can follow your thoughts easily. Make sure the first sentence in each paragraph identifies the key point for that paragraph. The reader should not have to guess what you are trying to say. Use a format that guides the reader. This means that main points on each page are easy to locate visually, and concepts are identified by headings or titles. Remember, how well you write strongly influences how you are evaluated. What you put down on paper makes a lasting impression, and people will make judgments about your credibility and professionalism for a long time after you have actually written the words.

How Can I Learn to Speak Effectively?

From giving a change-of-shift report to another nurse, to explaining your plans for a new protocol on the unit, to the organization's administration, you will have many opportunities speaking to individuals or an entire audience! Even now as a student, you may have the opportunity to make a presentation to your fellow peers.

> The first step in making effective presentations is to develop a positive attitude.
> ACCENTUATE the POSITIVE!

Many of us let our anxiety intimidate us when it comes to public speaking. However, public speaking can be a great chance to show off our skills, our ability to be creative, and our willingness to be a star entertainer. Think of your presentation as a wonderful opportunity to have the attention of others on just you, even if only for a few minutes (Arredondo, 2000).

> The second guiding principle in making good presentations and speaking in front of an audience is practice.
> PRACTICE makes PERFECT!

A well-planned rehearsal provides the chance to see how long it will take you to say what you want, and it will help you feel more comfortable saying the words easily. Here are some tips on presentation preparation from Kushner (2004) and Peoples (1992).

Analyze Your Audience

What do they already know, and what do they need to know? Have a few objectives for what you want your audience to receive from your presentation.

Do Your Homework

Know enough about your subject to make your talk clear and believable. Make sure you can answer at least a few questions.

Plan the Presentation

This includes making an outline of the content and the teaching strategies you might use. Visual aids or activities may be used to involve the audience in active participation. Visual aids should keep the presentation focused and organized. They should help you hold your audience's attention (**Plus, you are more likely to persuade with visual cues.**)

FIG. 12.2 Engage your audience.

Add Spice to the Presentation

The more active your audience's participation, the longer they will pay attention. Choose at least one presentation strategy that involves them, such as question/answer, role playing, or small-group discussion. Highlight visually on slides or using other types of media the key points you want your audience to remember. Pecha Kucha is an innovative format for developing presentations. A Pecha Kucha is essentially a slideshow presentation where you show 20 slides, each for 20 seconds (Pecha Kucha, 2016). Check out the following video from University of North Dakota for details on developing a Pecha Kucha (https://www.youtube.com/watch?v=32WEzM3LFhw) (Fig. 12.2). **Use an attention grabber at the beginning** to make sure your audience is listening. This may be a friendly greeting, a stimulating question, a startling statistic, a relevant story, or a quote by an expert. Then, in brief and concise words, tell your audience the purpose of the presentation and what it will cover.

Create Cheat Sheets

Cheat sheets are your clues—jot down the first couple of words around a topic to help you remember what to say or what questions to ask, or include small pictures or drawings to jog your mind during the presentation in case you stumble and fumble with your thoughts and words. If the speech or presentation is an important one and is fairly formal, you may want to prepare a script. This means you write out exactly what you will say and have it typed double-spaced, with a wide margin on the left side. Here you can write notes to yourself about when to use your visual aids or when to pass out materials for the audience. Even if you choose to write a script, **be sure to memorize the first 2 minutes of what you are going to say!**

The Closing

In your closing, review what you have said, summarize the benefits or implications of what you have said, and reiterate any action you want taken. **(Design your closing FIRST, because it is the most important part of the formal presentation. It may sound crazy to work backward, but the closing is what the audience will hear last and remember. Write it out and memorize it!)**

Final Details

Be familiar with the room and equipment you will use prior to the presentation. Determine that everything you need is there before you begin. Make sure the spelling is correct on your visual aids and handouts. Speak with confidence and enthusiasm, while making as much eye contact as you can. Walk around the room and use your hands and arms to make dramatic gestures. They add energy and interest. Most important—relax and have some fun. If you make a mistake, learn to laugh at yourself and move on. Your audience will forgive you. They may not be any more comfortable with public speaking than you are and will generally reach out and be supportive of you.

What Listening Skills Do I Need to Develop?

Listening effectively is one of the most powerful communication tools you can have. It is more than just hearing the words of others. Listening involves concentrating all your energy on understanding and interpreting the message with the meaning the sender intended. Of the four verbal means of communication—writing, reading, speaking, and listening—listening requires most of our communication time. Yet we often pay the least attention to our listening skills (Mindell, 2001). It has been estimated that people actually remember only one-third of the messages they have heard, although they spend 70% of their time listening (Marquis & Huston, 2014).

> Did you know? People speak at 100 to 175 words per minute, but they can listen intelligently at 600 to 800 words per minute (Fowler, 2016).

There are reasons that people are not good listeners (Arredondo, 2000). We simply do not pay enough attention; we hear what we want to hear and filter out the rest. Listening requires concentration, and that means doing nothing else at the same time. Some people think of listening as a passive behavior; they want to be in control by talking more. We think a lot faster than people speak, so we often think way ahead, think about other things, or daydream. Maybe too many distractions are interfering with listening, such as background noises or movements.

One of the most problematic reasons for ineffective listening is that people allow their emotions to dictate what they hear or do not hear. If the message is making demands on us to do more, change what we do, or do better, we may stop listening and start dealing with our own feelings of anger, guilt, or anxiety. We may start planning our own defensive response while the other person is still talking.

Think about situations where you've had difficulty listening, understanding, or remembering what was said. Consider these examples:

- A psychiatric patient who has recently been admitted displays acutely psychotic thought processes by talking rapidly in pressured speech, using words and phrases so loosely connected that the whole conversation is disorganized and incomprehensible.
- A charge nurse spends 5 minutes screaming at her team leader, criticizing everything she has done that day, and then asks the team leader to carry out a very specific and detailed change in the physician's orders for a patient.
- Another nurse asks you to hang an intravenous solution for the patient in Room 1253 while you are writing some progress notes on a patient's chart. When you finish, you cannot remember the room number where you agreed to hang the intravenous solution.

It becomes essential to develop effective listening skills (Arredondo, 2000). Here are some tips:

Make Sure You Can Hear What Is Being Said

Move closer, eliminate distracting noises, and most important of all, do not talk. You cannot hear someone else when you are talking.

Focus Your Attention on What Is Being Said

Actively concentrate by analyzing the key points as they are being said. Take notes. Do not do anything else while you are listening except to concentrate on hearing and understanding what is being said.

Recognize and Control Your Emotional Response to What Is Being Said

Focus on hearing and seeing accurately what is being communicated. You will have time to ask questions and explore your feelings after the other person finishes. As Vertino (2014) pointed out, if you feel threatened during communication with others, step back, and take a few minutes to calm down before responding.

Make the Decision to Listen and Accept the Other Person's Needs and Feelings, Whatever They Are

Improved understanding of the other person is gained through listening, and this understanding will help you to be more effective in solving problems and eliminating negative feelings.

Pay Attention to Nonverbal Communication as You Listen to the Words

Much of a message's meaning is communicated through the sender's tone of voice, facial expressions, and body movements. You must listen with your eyes and your ears.

Fight Off Distractions

Do not let the speaker's style of communicating, his or her mannerisms, or other interruptions such as telephone calls or another person vying for your attention break your concentration.

Take Notes

If a lot of factual, important information is being shared, take notes—but just jot down key words or numbers, or the note-taking itself will become a distraction. You may also ask the speaker to put in writing what he or she has said.

Let the Speaker Tell the Whole Story

Make it a point not to interrupt. Do not assume you know what is going to be said. Don't formulate criticisms as you listen.

React to the Message, Not the Person

Ask yourself, "Are my feelings or biases interfering with my listening?" Seek clarification of your understanding by verifying what you have heard.

Respond Positively to the Feelings Being Communicated

Empathy and acceptance will make it easier for the communication to continue. Maintain a positive attitude about listening. Recognize that listening is necessary for success. Allow yourself to hear all sides of an issue.

Identify the characteristics of your listening skills in Critical Thinking Box 12.5.

How Can I Use Nonverbal Communication Effectively?

Nonverbal communication uses movements, gestures, body position, and voice tone to transmit messages (Arredondo, 2000). To convey confidence and leadership ability, it is necessary to learn to use certain nonverbal signals effectively. Here are some tips.

Make Eye Contact With the Person With Whom You Are Talking

This helps the person interpret your message more favorably and says that you are giving your full attention to the conversation.

Stand Up Straight, With Shoulders Back

You may want to lean slightly forward toward the other individual to convey your interest. Stand with your toes pointed slightly outward and slightly apart and approximately 18 inches to 4 feet from the person you are talking to so that you do not invade personal space. Avoid personal contact unless you know the person well and it is a casual conversation.

Use an Assertive Voice Without Pauses to Suggest Confidence

Avoid a whining, nagging, or complaining tone. You may need to listen to your recorded voice to gain some insight into how you sound to others.

Watch for Distracting Behaviors

Avoid negative behaviors that detract from your verbal messages: nodding constantly, yawning, playing with your hair, checking messages on your phone, looking away from the other person, or constantly shifting your weight from one foot to the other. When you use your hands in gestures, keep your forearms up and the palms of your hands open. Avoid making a fist or shaking a pointing finger at the other person.

How Can I Communicate Effectively by Using Technology?

Many of us are learning to use the technology that is changing our workplace and making communication easier. Although cell phones, e-mail, text messaging, tablets, and other mobile devices may be

---

 CRITICAL THINKING BOX 12.5

Try This …

Develop a listening action plan.
1. I listen most effectively when ….
2. I have difficulty listening when ….
3. My best listening skills are ….
4. To improve my listening skills, I will ….

conveniences, they must be used thoughtfully to make a positive contribution to your overall image as an effective communicator. Believe it or not, there is an actual term for properly communicating online—*netiquette*. Deep and Sussman (1995) give the following netiquette tips.

Do Not Misuse or Overuse E-mail and Text Messaging

Review the tips for effective use of e-mail and text messaging. If you need to send a long document or detailed message, use e-mail.

Learn to Use Computer Software

Using technology can make not only your work but also your communication easier and more effective. Integrated computer systems on hospital units, electronic health record systems, passive infrared tracking of patients and nurse locations along with enhanced nurse-call systems, wireless in-house telephone systems, and web-based electronic grease boards to track patients throughout their days of scheduled surgeries, diagnostic tests, and so forth, can be viewed on computer monitors in patients' rooms or from large display monitors strategically located throughout a department (Bahlman & Johnson, 2005).

When You Send E-mail Messages

If you are sending messages by e-mail, be sure to perform a grammar and spellcheck, and read your words carefully before sending them. Because you are sending words without the benefit of clarifying nonverbal communication, the likelihood of being misinterpreted is greater. Make sure your messages are as clear as they can be. Include your name and subject in the e-mail note.

Do Not Send an Emotional Outburst in an E-mail

These messages can seem more hostile than you intended, and you can alienate or anger many people. If you would not say these words in person, then do not send them by e-mail (Box 12.1).

BOX 12.1   TIPS FOR USING E-MAIL EFFECTIVELY

1. STOP, THINK ABOUT WHAT YOU WANT TO SAY, *THEN WRITE*.
   - Be sure to determine whether an e-mail is the appropriate communication medium. E-mail is meant for quick, simple communication. Ask yourself whether a phone conversation or face-to-face meeting would be more appropriate.
2. INCLUDE A DESCRIPTIVE SUBJECT LINE.
   - In the subject line of the e-mail note, place a description of what the e-mail is about. Be specific—for example, Quarterly QA Report or Case Study Assignment—Informatics.
3. MAKE YOUR E-MAIL NOTE EASY TO READ.
   - Use short paragraphs, usually no more than two or three paragraphs at most—get to the point, quickly. Consider that most people have a limited attention span with e-mail, especially if they are receiving a lot of messages.
   - Have ample white space on the page. Usually five to seven lines of text are best for a paragraph.
   - Use bullets or numbers to guide the reader.
   - Carefully choose your font size, type, and color. Using a bright color (such as purple) may not convey as professional a tone as a standard black or navy font would. Very large fonts (14-point or more) might make your message seem "loud" and accusatory. A sans serif font, such as Arial or Tahoma 10-12 point, is easier to read on the computer screen than a serif font such as Times Roman.
4. BE PRECISE, CONCISE, AND CLEAR.
   - Use a conversational writing style.
   - If responding to multiple questions embedded in a large e-mail, copy the questions into your e-mail and write your answers next to them.
   - When replying to a message, include enough of the original e-mail note to provide context to your response.

BOX 12.1 TIPS FOR USING E-MAIL EFFECTIVELY—cont'd

- If in doubt, spell it out—limit your use of jargon or abbreviations.
- Always spellcheck and proof your e-mail before you send it.

5. DEMONSTRATE NETIQUETTE—BE PROFESSIONAL AND MAINTAIN APPROPRIATE ONLINE TONE.
   - Do not type in all CAPS! Capitals can be used for emphasis, but ALL CAPS LOOKS LIKE YOU'RE YELLING AT THE PERSON. If you emphasize everything, then nothing is considered as more important than the rest.
   - Do not type in all lowercase—this violates the rules of English grammar and usage. Keep in mind that you are not texting a friend.
   - If a communication is upsetting to you, keep calm and collected. Your emotional state can slip into an e-mail without notice, in the form of curt sentences, skipped pleasantries, and blunt comments.
   - Remember, unlike telephone and personal conversations that fade from the memory with time, impulsive e-mail responses have "staying power"—meaning the e-mail is readily available in e-mail boxes, can be printed out, distributed to others, and attain a level of importance that was never intended.
   - A word about flaming (which is the expression of extreme emotion or opinion in an e-mail message, often derogatory)—be polite and pleasant, and consider whether you want to respond to a "flaming" e-mail.

6. BE CAREFUL WITH ATTACHMENTS.
   - Open attachments only if you trust the source, because attachments can contain executable files that can spread viruses and slow down processing.
   - Consider the size of the attachments—large files (greater than 1000 KB or 1 MB) can clog up networks and rapidly fill your Inbox. Many servers prohibit the sending and receiving of large e-mail file attachments.
   - Use spam filters and delete chain e-mails or other scams—do not open the document or have the viewing pane open, because this can perpetuate the spam.

7. WATCH HUMOR.
   - Find different ways to express emotion, body language, and intonation, when warranted. Use "smileys," also called emoticons, to convey feelings in your message; however, be mindful not to overuse them.
   - As in any setting, humor can be misconstrued, so be extra careful, and use taste and discretion before transmitting any humor.

8. INCLUDE A SIGNATURE.
   - Include a signature with your e-mail, usually no more than four to six lines of text. Remember, this part of your message is the last thing the receiver will read.
   - Include your name, title, contact information, and e-mail address or URL. Many e-mail programs can be set up to attach automatically a default signature or signature file to the end of all your outgoing messages (including replies).

9. REVIEW YOUR MESSAGE BEFORE SENDING.
   - Remember, e-mail is not confidential—do not send personal or sensitive e-mail, because there is no "secure" e-mail system.
   - Review and proof your message before clicking "Send."

10. RESPOND TO E-MAIL.
    - Make an effort to respond to e-mail within 24 hours. Otherwise, use the auto-reply function to inform the person when you will respond.

11. TEXT MESSAGING
    - Keep in mind that most agencies do not want you texting during your clinical experience. Check with faculty about using your smart phone in the clinical area.

When You Leave a Voice Mail Message for Someone, Speak Slowly and Distinctly

This is especially important when you are leaving your telephone number so that the other person can return your call. It is frustrating to receive a message but not be able to understand the name or have to replay the message to get all of the digits in the phone number. Make your voice mail message brief but complete, saying when you called, what you want the other person to do, and when you can be reached.

If You Are Using Call Waiting, Do Not Leave Callers on Hold

Explain to the first caller that you must briefly answer another call, then take the number of the second caller, with the assurance that you will call back as soon as you finish your first call. This interruption should last no longer than 10 seconds. Be sure to write down the telephone number of the second caller so that you do not forget it by the time you finish the first call.

When You Call Someone, Ask If He or She Has Time to Talk, and Offer to Call Back at a More Convenient Time If Necessary

People appreciate this courtesy and will be more likely to have a positive conversation with you if it is conveniently timed and is respectful of their busy schedules.

If You Are Conducting a Conversation or a Meeting With a Speaker Telephone or by Means of a Teleconference, Make Sure That Each Party to the Call Is Introduced to the Other People

Do not use the speaker telephone unless you are including a group in the conversation. Even with a conference call, there should be some structure to the discussion, including an agenda or a specified purpose and time for the call. Learn how to "mute" a conversation, especially when there is considerable background noise.

When You Need to Send a Personal Message, Especially a Reminder or a Thank-You Note, the Most Powerful Way Is to Send a Handwritten Note

This conveys the importance you connect with the message and continues the interpersonal aspect of the communication. If you need to communicate something that you expect will have a significant emotional impact, do it face-to-face. This communication style also allows you an opportunity to read the other person's nonverbal communication and offers a chance to negotiate a comfortable understanding following your message delivery.

GROUP COMMUNICATION

What Is Group Process?

When we discuss the dynamics and communication patterns in groups, it is important to note that personality conflicts may develop during the different cyclical phases of the group. In **forming** the group, think back to orientation day for nursing school. You sit surrounded by some people you have never seen before and some you have known from your prenursing classes. A common bond is that you are all there for well-defined reasons, including finding out who is in your clinical group and who the instructors will be. Of course, the orientation is mandatory. You sit in the auditorium or classroom talking, listening, and watching those around you, playing your part in a form of controlled pandemonium. The pandemonium can actually be considered the storming phase. In the **storming** phase, you begin to act out the roles you normally portray in the presence of your peers, as you discuss your fears, fantasies, and hopes for a successful outcome to your nursing program (Tuckman & Jensen, 1977).

Next, you are divided into clinical groups. You now begin to reevaluate the personality composition of the new groups. As you begin to react to your new relationships, you start to exhibit personality traits to establish the role you would like to be identified with in the group setting. Unfortunately, your unconscious defense mechanisms surface in the form of competitive conflict or one-upmanship within the group, and your hope is that your response will secure the desired role in the group. It is at this time that **norming** begins to develop among members of the group, with the help of the instructors. Norming occurs during the development of mutual goals and guidelines that help to redefine your behavioral roles in the group. This can allow agreement in performing activities to help establish a purposeful clinical experience that involves interdependence and flexibility.

During the **performing** phase, everyone knows one another, is able to work together, and trusts one another. The group works together and makes changes in a seamless way, because there is a high degree of comfort among the group members that funnels all of the energy of the group toward the tasks at hand—getting through nursing school. Later Tuckman and Jensen (1977) added the final stage, **adjourning,** which has been called *deforming* and *mourning* by others. This phase is about completion and disengagement, both from the tasks and from the group members. Many of you have experienced or will experience the adjourning phase as you move from one clinical group to another or during the transition from student to graduate, as you are nearing completion of your nursing program.

Groups can be multipurpose and multidynamic, as are the basic role choices of each participant in a group. When working in a group, the real fun and excitement start when group members begin responding to and dealing with the unconscious and semiconscious defense mechanisms of the individuals who are using these mechanisms in the roles they play in the group. The responses of the defensive individual tend to be unproductive, time-consuming, and inappropriate to the harmony and overall function of a group effort. In my years of nursing and group participation, the following tend to be my favorite dysfunctional group personalities.

The **self-servers** feel that the rules of the group do not apply to them. They show up late. They are usually unprepared to work. At times they will walk in and out of the group for superficial reasons, while appearing preoccupied with unrelated work or issues from outside of the group. When they do participate, their contributions are of little consequence. If they refuse to be functional members of the group, you may need to ask them to leave the group.

The first response of a **critical conservative** to a creative suggestion can be, "No, it won't work," or "But it's always been done this way," or "How can you people succeed if you've never done this before?" They seem to have a criticism for any suggestion other than their own. If it is not done their way, it just is not right. They are obsessively negative and fearful of changes. It is important to recognize the lessons of experiences and outcomes, but it is equally important to find new approaches to old problems.

The **motor mouths** talk just to hear themselves talk. They interrupt at any given moment to make statements or deliver a verbose response, possibly because they feel they have been quiet for too long. Even when another person is talking, motor mouths will talk over the speaker's words just to be the center of attention. These people may begin to make a statement, only to ramble in and out of the group's issue, and end up talking about unrelated issues that are usually about themselves. I suggest redirecting their conversation to focusing on the issue and periodically asking them for a short critical assessment of the issues in question.

The **mouse** is the silent observer who is fearful of voicing an opinion. Usually, the mouse sits transfixed, watching other individuals take risks and responsibility for their input to the group. The mouse nods his or her head at appropriate times and answers questions in one or two words. The mouse may be a real addition to the group, especially if others in the group are able to find ways to engage and encourage the mouse to voice opinions and feelings about the group issues. It is important to remember that these people may be some of the best observers and listeners; ask them for their input. You may find them to be a valuable asset to your team. Regardless of where you choose to work or the type of care delivery system you are in, these group members are always there!

How Can You Improve Communications in Group Meetings?

Nurses participate in many meetings, from patient-care conferences to more formal committee meetings. Communication within a group of people can be an opportunity to influence the quality of care provided to patients. When you participate as a member of a group, the following are positive behaviors that will help you to communicate effectively and will also help the group to accomplish its tasks more efficiently:

- Come prepared. Bring all the "stuff" you need.
- Listen. Be open to other viewpoints.
- Keep on track. Do not visit or chit-chat or bring other work to do.
- Present your ideas or opinions. Ask other members for theirs.
- State disagreements. Be able to back them up.
- Clarify as needed. Do not assume.

All of us have been to and participated in meetings that were disorganized, confusing, and a waste of time. Critical Thinking Box 12.6 will help you to identify some unpleasant group meeting experiences and give you the opportunity to change future meetings.

? CRITICAL THINKING BOX 12.6

Try This ...

Think of particularly unpleasant experiences you have had at meetings. You might think about meetings involving your clinical group or study group. Develop a list of ideas about what was wrong with those meetings.

The key to effective meetings is the planning and organization that occurs before the meeting is actually held. An effective technique using de Bono's (1999) Six Thinking Hats can spur a group meeting to better productivity and problem solving (Box 12.2). Planning should allow the leader to think through what the meeting is for, who should be there, and how it should run (Huber, 2014). There should be a clear purpose for every meeting and every item on the agenda. Every item should require some action by the group. If making a telephone call or sending a memo could achieve the purpose in another way, there should be no meeting.

If you are making a formal presentation, some audiovisual equipment will be necessary, and chairs will need to be arranged so that everyone can see the presenter and the audiovisuals. If the meeting is for discussion and decision making, a table at which everyone can sit face-to-face is more effective, and someone needs to take meeting minutes. Look at Fig. 12.3. This type of note taking clarifies who is responsible for what activities. At the conclusion of the meeting, summarize the decisions, and identify the plan of action. At the end of the meeting, the time should be established for the next meeting. All members should receive a copy of the meeting minutes.

TEAM BUILDING AND INTERPROFESSIONAL PRACTICE

What Is Team Building?

Team building is a deliberate process of unifying a group of individuals into a functional working unit, accomplishing specific goals (Farley & Stoner, 1989). Another definition of a team is "a small number of people with complementary skills who are committed to a common purpose in performance of common goals, for which they hold themselves mutually accountable" (Katzenbach & Smith, 2003, p. 45). Katzenbach and Smith state that the right mix of attributes is needed in three categories that help ensure a highly complementary and functional team. The three categories described are

BOX 12.2 EDWARD DE BONO'S SIX THINKING HATS: LOOKING AT A DECISION AND WORKING THROUGH A PROBLEM CONSIDERING SIX POINTS OF VIEW

Six Thinking Hats is an important and powerful technique created by Edward de Bono that can be used as an effective group process tool in meetings that get bogged down with diverse views and adamant positions. It offers a strategy to "think outside the box" by challenging the group to think or see all sides of an issue. Each "Thinking Hat" represents a perspective or way of thinking. During a meeting, a "different color hat" can be put on or taken off to indicate the type of thinking the person is using. By putting on a different hat in a particular sequence, problem solving is encouraged.

White Hat: Neutral, Objective, Concerned With Facts and Figures, *The Fact Hat*

Used to think about facts, figures, and other objective information (think of a scientist's white lab coat).

- What facts and data are available?
- What facts would help me further in making a decision?
- How can I get those facts?

Red Hat: The Emotional View, *The Emotional Hat*

Used to elicit the feelings, emotions, and other nonrational but potentially valuable senses, such as hunches and intuition (think of a red heart). Encourages people to express their feelings without the need for apology, explanation, or attempt to justify them.

- How do I really feel?
- What is my gut feeling about this problem?

Black Hat: Careful, Cautious, *The "Devil's Advocate" Hat*

Used to discover why some ideas will not work, this hat inspires logical negative arguments (think of a devil's advocate or a judge robed in black). Helps you to see problems in advance (spot flaws in thinking), prepare for potential difficulties, and prepare contingency plans to counter the issues.

- What are the possible downside risks and problems?
- What is the worst-case scenario?
- What are the weak points of the plan? It allows you to eliminate them, alter them, or prepare contingency plans to counter them.

Yellow Hat: Sunny and Positive, *The Optimistic Hat*

Used to obtain a positive, optimistic outlook, this hat sees opportunities, possibilities, and benefits of a decision (think of the warming sun). Keeps you going when the going gets tough.

- What are the advantages?
- What would be the best possible outcome?

Green Hat: Associated With Fertile Growth, Creativity, and New Ideas, *The Creative Hat*

Used to find creative new ideas (think of new shoots sprouting from seeds).

- What completely new, fresh, innovative approaches can I generate?
- What creative ideas can I dream up to help me see the problem in a new way?
- Are there any additional alternatives or can this be done in a different way?
- Could there be another explanation?

Blue Hat: Cool, the Color of Sky, *The Organizing Hat*

Used as a master hat to control the thinking process (think of the overarching sky, or a "cool" character who's in control).

- Review my thoughts—it suggests the next step for thinking.
- Sum up what I have learned and think about what the next logical step is—asks for summaries, conclusions, and decisions.

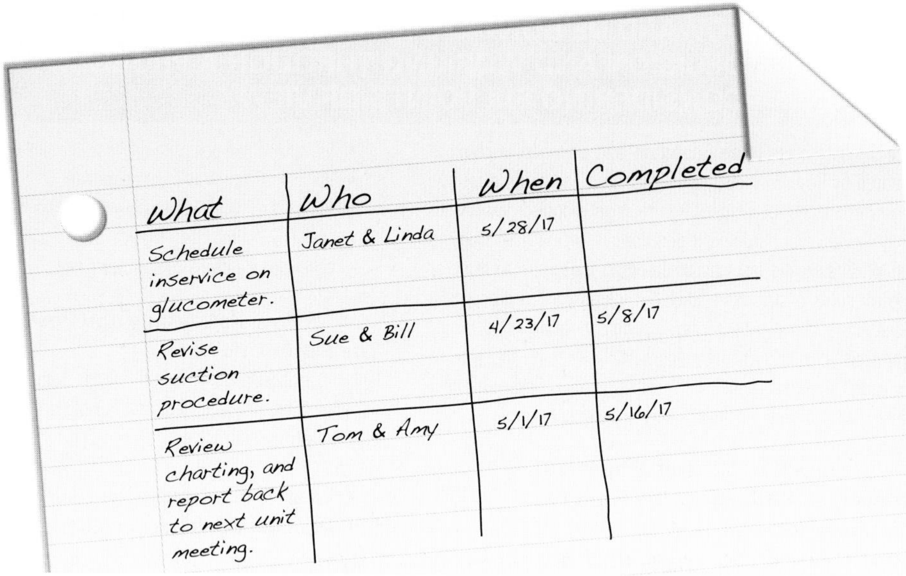

FIG. 12.3 Action timeline for meetings.

? CRITICAL THINKING BOX 12.7

Think About ...

Try to assess and come to your own conclusion regarding the following hypothetical problem by picturing in your mind the *who,* *what,* and *why* before you read what the experts in the field would say:

You will be responsible for the care of your critically ill parent during his or her stay in the hospital during the next 2 months. Assemble a team of your nursing peers to deliver care to your parent. The care will be based on the highest level of difficulty because of the serious nature of the diagnosis.

- What nurses would you choose to help you?
- Why would you choose those specific nurses?
- What qualities would you want them to have when caring for your family member?
- What skill level would you want them to possess to perform the overall treatment plan?
- If some of them lacked the skill levels to meet the treatment plan criteria, what would be an appropriate approach to this inadequacy?

---

interpersonal skills, problem-solving and decision-making skills, and technical or functional expertise (Critical Thinking Box 12.7).

Teams are a formal way to actualize collaboration. Collaboration is at the heart of successful decision making. Collaboration among team members leverages skills, time, and resources for the benefit of the team and that of the organization. If you examine the word *collaboration,* you will see that "co-labor" is the core of the word—meaning "working together toward some meaningful end."

There are many health care professionals who play an integral role in providing quality patient care. Think about what health care professionals you would be collaborating with in the following patient scenario.

You are providing care to a patient with a diagnosis of chronic bronchitis and heart failure. The patient requires nebulizer treatments and has orders for CPAP. Arterial blood gases have been ordered, and the lab personnel has just called you to confirm that the patient is in the room. A physical therapy (PT) evaluation and a low-sodium cardiac diet have been ordered by the cardiologist. The patient's spouse is concerned that she will be unable to provide care for her husband after discharge, as she works full-time and they have no family nearby to care for him during the day while she is at work.

Well, how many health care professionals did you come up with?

It is a fact that as nurses you will be part of the health care team. This will require you and other health care professionals to collaborate, communicate, and coordinate delivering safe and effective patient care. Not only will you need to have an understanding of nursing practice, but you must have a foundational understanding of the responsibilities and roles of other health care professions, because they will be part of the health care team that you are working with.

What Is Interprofessional Practice?

As its name implies, interprofessional practice involves health care professionals across disciplines working together in providing patient care. The World Health Organization (WHO) offers the following definition: "When multiple health workers from different professional backgrounds work together with patients, families, caregivers, and communities to deliver the highest quality of care across settings" (WHO, 2010, p. 13). Regardless of what type of health care setting you work in as a professional nurse, you will be working with others, including the patient and their family, as well as the community at large. As you know by now, collaborating and communicating with others is a skill, and it takes time and deliberate practice to develop.

During your clinical rotation, have you communicated with other non-nursing health care professionals (respiratory therapist, registered dietitian, physical therapist, phlebotomist, etc.) involved in your patient's care? If you answered no to this question, you are not alone. Nevertheless, it is not too early to begin honing your interprofessional practice skills. In fact, you can begin right now while you are still in your nursing program by engaging in learning experiences and activities with students from other health care disciplines on your campus (Research for Best Practice Box 12.1).

🔍 RESEARCH FOR BEST PRACTICE BOX 12.1

Interprofessional Practice Using Human Patient Simulation

Practice Issue

The current health care climate requires health care professionals to work together as an interprofessional team. Health professions students from various disciplines (nursing, respiratory, dentistry, medicine, physical therapy, etc.) have limited opportunities in the clinical practice setting for engaging in team-based experiences to further their knowledge and understanding of interprofessional practice. Considering this, health education programs are exploring various learning opportunities for students across health care arenas to work together as a routine part of their education. As the IPEC has pointed out, "The goal of this interprofessional learning is to prepare all health professions students for *deliberately working together* with the common goal of building a safer and better patient-centered and community/population oriented U.S. health care system" (IPEC, 2011, p. 3). While didactic and laboratory instruction is essential to foundational concepts and skills, in each respective health education program, interprofessional education is difficult to employ in these learning environments. However, the use of human patient simulation offers health professions students an opportunity to collaborate and communicate with each other during a simulated clinical patient scenario.

Rossler and Kimble (2016) conducted a study examining readiness for interprofessional learning and collaboration among prelicensure nursing, respiratory therapy, health administration, and physical therapy students. The authors' findings suggested

Continued

🔍 RESEARCH FOR BEST PRACTICE BOX 12.1—cont'd

Interprofessional Practice Using Human Patient Simulation

that all students gained an appreciation and understanding of their role in working on a team as well as the responsibilities of each team member outside of their discipline. Student participants also reported that the simulation experience provided them an opportunity to practice interprofessional communication.

Implications for Nursing Education and Practice
- Nursing and allied health programs can introduce students to interprofessional practice concepts through human patient simulation.
- Rotating team roles among students will assist students in acquiring knowledge of the various responsibilities of each team member's role.
- Implementing interprofessional practice activities can improve communication and collaboration among health care professionals.

Considering This Information
Can you identify additional activities or educational opportunities for promoting interprofessional practice?
  What potential challenges do you feel may surface when working with other health professions students?
  How can you overcome these challenges?

References

Interprofessional Education Collaborative Expert Panel (IPEC). (2011). *Core competencies for interprofessional collaborative practice: Report of an expert panel.* Washington, D.C.: Interprofessional Education Collaborative.
Rossler, K. L., & Kimble, L. P. (2016). Capturing readiness to learn and collaboration as explored with an interprofessional simulation scenario: A mixed-method research study. *Nurse Education Today, 36*, 348–353.

When Nurses Work As an Interprofessional Team, Everyone Involved Benefits!

In health care, the imperative is on the quality of care and interprofessional teams, as reported by the Institute of Medicine (2003) and other leaders in health care education (Interprofessional Education Collaborative Expert Panel, 2012). It is also clear that interprofessional teamwork is essential in care delivery outcomes and cost control (Fig. 12.4).

One of the most important ingredients in the team approach to delivering patient-centered care is a positive psychological and emotional bond between members of the team, which helps to develop more cohesiveness among the individuals of the team. Without a positive cohesive bond, there can and will be limits to the overall quality and function of the team. You as nurses are the unknown intervening variables that either make or break the quality of the team-nursing concept. You and your colleagues, as an interprofessional team, have the skills necessary to handle the multitudes of problems associated with care delivery. You may want to ask yourselves:

- Are you as an individual mentally and emotionally prepared for providing team-based care?
- Can you reflect and make changes on your individual performance as well as the overall team's performance in care delivery?
- Is your attitude about yourself and your peers conducive to support interprofessional teamwork?
- Are you willing to make difficult decisions in directing team care delivery and be accountable?
- Are you willing to relinquish control of those under your direction when necessary?
- Are you adaptable to changing your role on a team and in different health care settings?

Nurses read and do research to help formulate problem solving and innovative approaches in the establishment of functional care-delivery models. What is frequently left out of the equation is the extent of the role that management is willing to play in helping to ensure the success of the new

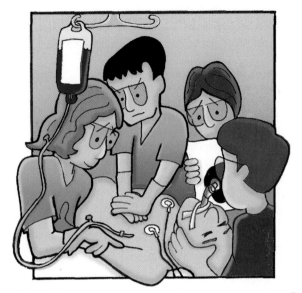

FIG. 12.4 When nurses work as a team, everyone benefits.

ideas. Is management willing to share control and leadership to help ensure a successful outcome in nurse-managed teams? I have been witness to the creation of nursing leadership roles—some consisting of team nursing care delivery, decentralization of authority, and shared governance—only to have them fail because of limitations and perceived liabilities placed on the nursing staff by management. At other times, failures were caused by the last-minute intervention of management, usurping the managerial authority of the nursing teams. Some other factors responsible for group or team failure are

- Nursing staff being unprepared or lacking the interpersonal communication skills needed to work with other staff members in a unified team setting.
- Nurses unwilling to move in and out of leadership roles to ensure the unity of the group and best possible outcomes.
- Management being pressured by upper management for faster adaptation to cost-cutting poli-cies, which usually causes communication between management and nursing to consist of veiled threats, innuendoes, mixed messages, and other subtle negative forms that affect the morale of the nursing staff.
- Nursing supervisors and administrative staff who appear to support shared governance but are unwilling to relinquish actual control of the nursing staff.

Actions always speak louder than words. Work toward transparent communication with admin-istrators. Try to meet them halfway and find out what they are willing to do to support your teams or groups. How much interest do they have in the actual quality of health care delivery? Are they interested in learning the dynamics of your role as a nurse or the role of the interprofessional team? Let them know what type of support you need from them. Explain to them the importance of mutual respect and support in the overall quality of nursing care.

When forming teams, realize that perfection is an illusion created in the mind of a critic. All of us have different skill levels. To function as a unified team, you will need to work with peers whose skills may need to be enhanced. You can help your peers by working side by side with them to build confidence while sharing in learning situations. Find ways to make the learning situations enjoyable,

BOX 12.3   BASIC ROLES OF GROUP MEMBERS

The following are some roles that individuals adopt when participating in a group. Each member may adopt more than one role.

- Opinion giver—states beliefs or values
- Opinion seeker—asks for clarification of beliefs or values
- Information giver—offers facts or personal experience
- Information seeker—asks for facts pertinent to what is being discussed
- Initiator—proposes new ideas on how the goal can be reached or how to view the problem
- Elaborator—expands on the idea of another; takes the idea and works out what would happen if it were adopted
- Coordinator—brings together ideas and suggestions
- Orientor—keeps the group focused on goals or questions the direction taken by the group
- Evaluator or critic—examines possible group solutions against group standards and goals
- Clarifier—checks out what someone said by restating or questioning
- Recorder—acts as the group's memory (e.g., takes notes)
- Summarizer—pulls together related ideas, restates suggestions, and offers decisions or conclusions

From Sullivan, E. J., & Decker, P. (1997). *Effective leadership and management in nursing* (4th ed.). Menlo Park, CA: Addison-Wesley, p 144.

show a sense of humor, and give positive reinforcement whenever possible. Fear and guilt undermine confidence and destroy the cohesiveness of a team or group.

In the formation of any team or group, the mental and emotional stability of the individuals who make up the team or group will be reflected in the quality of their work under stress and their ability to focus during care delivery and to establish a working rapport with the other team members. It is important for the stronger team members or group members to provide support and guidance as needed. The attitude of the stronger members of the team can go a long way in building confidence in the other team members. The level of quality for any team is increased substantially by the level of comfort and camaraderie among the individuals who make up the team.

The mix of complementary skills and experience can also help to give strength to the overall group. Taking inventory of technical and communication skills helps identify where weaknesses and strengths need to be considered before assigning individual duties to the team members. All team members should receive learning opportunities, support, and guidance to strengthen the cohesiveness of the team. Realizing the importance of collaborative practice in health care, leaders from dentistry, medicine, nursing, pharmacy, and public health united to develop the Interprofessional Education Collaborative (IPEC), to advance interprofessional education and practice (AACN, 2012). The IPEC Expert Panel (2012) report identified four competency domains for improving interprofessional collaboration and practice, which include values/ethics for interprofessional practice, roles/responsibilities, interprofessional communication, and teams/teamwork. Under each domain are additional sub-competencies and skills that further describe attributes of the domain (pp. 15–16). Their report notes that high-functioning interprofessional teams in health care must exhibit features of good team function in all four key domains.

Working on a team will require you to have an understanding of your own role as well as other health care professionals who comprise your team. Recognizing each team member's role is vital to ensuring that the health care needs of the patient are being met (Interprofessional Education Collaborative Expert Panel, 2012). It will be important for the team members to communicate with one another to ensure the high quality and continuity of care to be delivered (Box 12.3 and Fig. 12.5).

FIG. 12.5 We work as an interprofessional team!

ASSERTIVE STYLES OF COMMUNICATION

All of us have a style or way of communicating with others that is often based on our own personality and self-concept. In other words, the kind of people we are and the way in which we see ourselves influence the process of communication. This style can be divided into three common types: passive or avoidant, aggressive, and assertive (Marquis & Huston, 2014). The following are some characteristics of each style:

People who tend toward **passive** or **avoidant behavior** let others push them around. These people do not stand up for themselves; do what they are told regardless of how they feel about it; are not able to share their feelings or needs with others; have difficulty asking for help; and feel hurt, anxious, or angry at others for taking advantage of them.

Aggressive behavior means that a person puts his or her own needs, rights, and feelings first and communicates that in an angry, dominating way; attempts to humiliate or "put down" other people; conveys a righteous, superior attitude; works at controlling or manipulating others; is seen by others as punishing, threatening, demanding, or hostile; and shows no concern for anyone else's feelings.

Assertive behavior means that a person stands up for himself or herself in a way that does not violate the basic rights of another person; expresses true feelings in an honest, direct manner; does not let others take advantage of him or her; shows respect for other's rights, needs, and feelings; sets goals and acts on those goals in a clear and consistent manner and takes responsibility for the consequences of those actions; is able to accept compliments and criticism; and acts in a way that enhances self-respect.

See if you can match the person with his or her style after you have read the descriptions.

■ *Jane*

Jane is a very shy, quiet senior nursing student who can't think straight when her instructor asks her questions in the clinical area. She wishes she could be more like her classmates, who seem to find it easy to talk about their experiences during clinical conference. During her evaluation, her instructor says she doesn't know enough theory and can't handle the pressures of the clinical unit. Jane says nothing and signs her evaluation. When she gets back to her room alone, she cries uncontrollably.

■ *Susan*

Susan is a senior nursing student who is highly verbal with her classmates. She is known to be opinionated, and in every conference with her clinical group she finds a chance to criticize someone. She blames the nursing staff on the clinical unit for making her look bad by giving her too much work to do and not enough time or help. When her instructor tells her she has not integrated sufficient theory in her written assignments, she says, "It's not my fault; you should have told me sooner."

■ *Mark*

Mark is a senior nursing student who is described by his clinical group as goal-oriented and confident. He wrote learning objectives for himself at the beginning of the last clinical experience and brought them with him, along with a self-evaluation for his final evaluation conference. He listened to his instructor's suggestions, thanked her, and said, "I appreciate your concern for the quality of my nursing skills. I'm aware now of what I need to pay attention to in the first few months in my new job."

If you decided that Jane used a passive or avoidant style, Susan used an aggressive style, and Mark used an assertive style, you were right. Congratulations!

How Can Nurses Be More Assertive?

It seems as though many nurses do not consistently act or communicate in an assertive way. Some have a hard time believing in their own rights, feelings, or needs. This difficulty may have started in childhood through exposure to many negative statements or experiences. It is important to recognize that communication style is learned and reinforced through time. While in nursing school and working in the nursing profession, additional experiences or comments may reinforce those negative messages about self-worth. It can be very difficult to change behavior, especially when taking risks is necessary. The first step is to recognize what the barriers are. What is it that prevents you from being more assertive? Is it previously learned behavior, or are you afraid of the repercussions of assertive communication? Check the list in Box 12.4. If this list includes statements you feel are true, then you have identified some roadblocks to your ability to develop more assertive communication.

Look over this list of barriers to assertive communication and think about yourself. Do any of these explain your feelings? Assertiveness takes self-awareness and practice. It will help you if you identify and accept your position right now with regard to assertiveness so that you can make a plan to develop this skill.

What Are the Benefits of Assertiveness?

Assertive communication is the most effective way to let other people know what you feel, what you need, and what you are thinking. It helps you to feel good about yourself and allows you to treat others

---

BOX 12.4   BARRIERS TO ASSERTIVENESS

Barriers to assertiveness include the following beliefs:
- Assertive communication should not threaten others.
- If you do not have anything nice to say, do not say anything at all.
- If you feel uncomfortable when presenting your position or stating your feelings, then you are nonassertive.
- Assertiveness should come easily and spontaneously.
- Health care facilities do not promote or support assertive behavior.
- You cannot be assertive and consider another person's feelings and behavior at the same time.
- Assertive behavior is just another way of complaining.
- If I am assertive, I will lose my job.
- There is no difference between assertiveness and aggressiveness.

with respect. Being assertive helps you to avoid feeling guilty, angry, resentful, confused, or lonely. You have a greater chance to get your rights acknowledged and your needs met, which leads to a more satisfying life.

What Are My Basic Rights as a Person and as a Nurse?

As an adult human being, you have some legitimate rights. You may have to do some work to allow yourself to believe in your rights. You may have learned other values that make it difficult to accept the validity of these rights. But belief in your own value as a separate individual and confidence in the positive concepts associated with assertiveness as a communication style will help you to believe in your rights.

Consider the rights and responsibilities of the nurse. The issue of rights can become one-sided. When nurses consider rights, responsibilities must also be included. These rights are yours as a registered nurse; acquiring them and holding them are your responsibility (Chenevert, 1997).

How Can I Begin to Practice Assertive Communication?

There are a variety of ways to learn to be more assertive in your communication style, but they all involve self-awareness and practice. It may not feel totally comfortable at first, but as you work at it, assertive communication will come more naturally.

> Changing one's behavior requires a conscious decision.

At first, it is helpful to practice being assertive by yourself. Rehearse what you might say by talking to yourself while looking in a mirror. After you feel more comfortable, ask a friend to help you practice. The two of you can role-play some assertive conversations. You may even want to video or audio record your practice so you can get an idea of how you look and how you sound. If sharing your feelings with your instructor or charge nurse makes you extremely uncomfortable, set the situation aside. You can work on it after you are more confident. You should practice being assertive in a situation in which there is minimal risk to you, so you can experience success. Share your feelings and practice being assertive with someone with whom you are comfortable. Personal risk should be at a minimum. When you are ready, try out your new assertive communication skills in a mildly uncomfortable situation you would like to change. Pay attention to how you feel. Ask for feedback from the other person. You will then be able to evaluate your progress and decide what other information you want to practice.

What Are the Components of Assertive Communication?

Assertive communication is a technique used to get one's needs met without purposely hurting others. It incorporates the principles of therapeutic communication, active listening skills, and willingness to compromise. When you use these skills, you will be able to express yourself more effectively during challenging situations and handle confrontation in a professional manner. When you are confronted by a situation that provokes anger, take a deep breath, pull yourself away, get your emotions under control, and then approach the individual privately in a nonthreatening manner. The following are some hints for using assertive communication:

- Use "I" statements: "I am really upset about …."
- Describe the behavior that has upset you and focus on the present: "You have been texting and talking on your personal cell phone on the unit several times in the past 2 days."

- Discuss the consequences of the behavior: "This behavior is contrary to the agency policy and could result in …."
- State how the behavior needs to be modified and the time frame for this change: "You must immediately stop this interruption to your work and only use your cell phone off the unit while on your breaks."

The following strategy is a way to think about expressing your feelings and needs that will assist you to communicate assertively: **I feel … about … because ….**

Let us look at an example:

- I feel tired and cranky, because I'm not paying enough attention to my family's needs.
- I feel hurt and angry about Dr. Jones yelling at me in front of you, because I need to feel competent and respected at work.

These statements are most successful when you maintain direct eye contact, stand up straight, and speak in a clear, audible, firm tone of voice. After expressing your own feelings and needs, it is helpful to seek clarification of the other person's feelings or needs. This can be done with the following questions:

"How do you feel about that?"

"What were you thinking and feeling at that time?"

"How would that affect you?"

With skillful listening and clear communication, the problem can be defined without placing blame or putting down the other person. Notice the use of "I" messages—that indicates willingness to accept responsibility for the process of defining the problem and negotiating a workable solution. To find a compromise, you have to be willing to meet the other person halfway. You may agree to try it your way one time and the other person's the next. Or you may both agree to change or give up something. You may do something for him or her if he or she does something else for you. Remember that in the work setting you cannot always have things exactly as you want them. You must be willing to change and compromise (Elgin, 2000).

When to Use Assertive Communication

Here are some examples of situations in which assertive communication would be helpful.

■ *Communicating Expectations*

Supervisor: "You're being pulled to the orthopedic unit today because they're short-staffed."

Nurse: "I expect to be oriented into the unit and the equipment before I give nursing care, because I haven't worked on that unit in more than a year."

■ *Saying No*

Physician: "Come with me right now. I need some help doing a procedure on Mr. Smith."

Nurse: "I can't come with you right now. Let me have the nursing assistant get Mrs. Anderson back to bed, and I'll help you then."

■ *Accepting Criticism*

Head Nurse: "It seems to me that you are having difficulty updating your nursing care plans and getting the changes on the electronic medical record before the end of the shift."

Nurse: "I have been falling behind on updating my care plans in the electronic medical record. I need to work on better time management. Do you think you could help me with that?"

■ *Accepting Compliments*

Home Care Patient's Spouse: "My wife feels very comfortable when you are here taking care of her. It's obvious you know what you're doing."

Nurse: "Thank you. Your feedback is important to me."

■ *Giving Criticism*

Nurse: "I want to talk with you about your care of Mrs. Samuelson. I found her sitting in a wheelchair alone in the hallway. It is your responsibility to make sure that she is not left alone, so that nothing happens to her."

Aide: "I do not think that's my job."

Nurse: "We talked about your responsibilities of caring for Mrs. Samuelson this morning when you received your assignment. If you have difficulty in carrying out this assignment, I expect you to ask for help."

■ *Accepting Feedback*

Head Nurse: "I wanted to tell you that I have noticed an improvement in your communication with Dr. Turner. He has not complained about his patient's care for 2 weeks, and yesterday he told me that he had a positive discussion with you about home health care options for Mrs. Atkins."

Nurse: "Thank you. I have been working very hard at not responding angrily to his sarcastic comments and criticisms."

■ *Asking for Help*

Nurse: "I am having a hard time with Mr. Jones. He seems to have a way of pushing my buttons, so I get angry. It is hard for me to ask for help, because I expect myself to care for all patients without difficulty."

Community Health Nurse Supervisor: "Mr. Jones can be a difficult patient. Can I help you?"

Nurse: "Yes. I need help in understanding why I get so angry at him, and I want to know how to handle him in a more positive way."

Remember that you need to evaluate how your assertive communication feels to you and to seek feedback from others about how you are being interpreted. You need to know whether people perceive you as aggressive rather than assertive. It may mean modifying your communication to make sure you are standing up for yourself without violating the rights of others.

It should also be noted that some situations will not be resolved just because you communicated assertively. Finding a workable solution is a process involving other people who must take responsibility for their own feelings and needs. When others are unable to acknowledge their feelings, to listen, or to negotiate a compromise, your assertive communication may make you feel better about yourself, but it may not produce an immediate solution. But keep trying. Persistence pays off.

Remember, too, that there are some situations in which you must simply follow orders. You cannot always meet your own needs; you must do what a physician or your head nurse tells you to do. Sometimes you must put aside your own needs to meet the needs of the patients for whom you are caring. However, your judgment will increase as you gain experience, and you will recognize ways to communicate your needs and feelings, with the goal of improving the processes and procedures used in your work setting.

CONCLUSION

Interpersonal skills, effective communication, group process, team building, and interprofessional practice are important for the nurse because they form the foundation for creating an effective working environment and delivering quality care. Well-planned, well-executed, and well-validated communication, along with a caring and positive attitude, will foster motivation, success, and satisfaction for the nurse in both the student role and as a new graduate.

Now that you have learned more about communicating effectively, try doing the student exercise in Critical Thinking Box 12.8, and review the relevant websites and online resources that follow. Happy communicating!

? CRITICAL THINKING BOX 12.8

Communication Exercise

Directions: Use the following situations to reflect on key points covered in this chapter. Think of a way to communicate effectively in each situation. You may want to consider your own individual solutions and then role-play or discuss your ideas with a group of your classmates.

1. Develop a list of 10 patients who are hospitalized on your unit. For each patient, provide some personal information, a diagnosis, and some data about his or her progress during the previous 24 hours. Use the information you have listed to give a change-of-shift report to the four staff members who will be caring for these patients during the next 8 hours.

2. You have asked to speak to Dr. Sanders about your concerns in caring for one of her patients who has required much physical care since she has gone home from the hospital. Dr. Sanders has a reputation for being cold, aloof, and sarcastic. You have never spoken directly to her alone before.

3. You are a member of the home health care agency's procedures committee. After attending the last meeting, you have been given the responsibility for drafting a revision to the procedure used when administering controlled substances. You know that you need more information before you can begin your work. Send a memo to at least three different members of the agency staff identifying what information you would like them to provide for you. Make a follow-up phone call to make sure they received the memo.

⊕ RELEVANT WEBSITES AND ONLINE RESOURCES

American Academy of Communication in Health Care (2016)
Retrieved from http://www.aachonline.org/

American Association of Colleges of Nursing (2016)
Interprofessional education. Retrieved from http://www.aacn.nche.edu/ipe.

Interprofessional Professionalism Collaborative (n.d.)
Retrieved from http://www.inter professionalprofessionalism.org/

Mind Tools: Essential Skills for an Excellent Career (2016)
Assertiveness: Working with people, not against them. Retrieved from http://www.mindtools.com/pages/article/Assertiveness.htm.

BIBLIOGRAPHY

American Association of Colleges of Nursing (AACN). (2012). *AACN advances nursing's role in interprofessional education.* Retrieved from http://www.aacn.nche.edu/news/articles/2012/ipec.

Arredondo, L. (2000). *Communicating effectively.* New York: McGraw-Hill.

Bahlman, D. T., & Johnson, F. C. (2005). Using technology to improve and support communication and workflow processes. *Association of Perioperative Registered Nurses Journal, 82*(1), 65–73.

Chenevert, M. (1997). *Pro-nurse handbook* (3rd ed.). St. Louis: Mosby.

Deep, S., & Sussman, L. (1995). *Smart moves for people in charge.* Reading, MA: Addison-Wesley.

Elgin, S. (2000). *The gentle art of verbal self-defense at work.* Paramus, NJ: Prentice Hall.

Farley, M. J., & Stoner, M. H. (1989). The nurse executive and interdisciplinary team building. *Nursing Administration Quarterly, 13*(2), 24–30.

Fowler, K. (2016). *Active listening, MindTools.* Retrieved from www.mindtools.com/CommSkll/ActiveListening.htm.

Giger, J. N. (2013). *Transcultural nursing* (6th ed.). St. Louis: Elsevier/Mosby.

Huber, D. (2014). *Leadership and nursing care management* (5th ed.). St. Louis: Elsevier/Saunders.

Institute of Medicine. (2003). *Health professions education: A bridge to quality.* Washington, D.C: The National Academies Press.

Interprofessional Education Collaborative Expert Panel (IPEC). (2011). *Core competencies for interprofessional collaborative practice: Report of an expert panel.* Washington, D.C.: Interprofessional Education Collaborative.

Katzenbach, J. R., & Smith, D. K. (2003). *Wisdom of teams.* New York: HarperBusiness.

Kushner, M. (2004). *Presentations for dummies.* New Jersey: Wiley Publishing.

Marquis, B., & Huston, C. (2014). *Leadership roles and management functions in nursing: Theory and application* (8th ed.). Philadelphia: JB Lippincott.

Mindell, P. (2001). *How to say it for women: Communicating with confidence and power using the language of success.* Paramus, NJ: Prentice Hall.

Northouse, P. (2015). *Leadership theory and practice* (7th ed.). Thousand Oaks, CA: Sage.

Peoples, D. A. (1992). *Presentations plus.* New York: John Wiley & Sons.

Pecha Kucha. (2016). *Pecha Kucha 20 × 20.* Retrieved from http://www.pechakucha.org/.

Tuckman, B., & Jensen, M. (1977). Stage of small group development revisited. *Group and Organization Studies, 2,* 419–427.

Vengel, A. (2010). *The influence edge: How to persuade others to help you achieve your goals.* San Francisco, CA: Berrett-Koehler Communications.

Vertino, K. (September 30, 2014). Effective interpersonal communication: A practical guide to improve your life. *OJIN: The Online Journal of Issues in Nursing, 19*(3). http://dx.doi.org/10.3912/OJIN.Vol19No03Man01.

World Health Organization (WHO). (2010). *Framework for action on interprofessional education & collaborative practice.* Retrieved from http://apps.who.int/iris/bitstream/10665/70185/1/WHO_HRH_HPN_10.3_eng.pdf?ua=1.

Conflict Management

JoAnn Zerwekh, EdD, RN

ⓔ http://evolve.elsevier.com/Zerwekh/nsgtoday/.

Everything that irritates us about others can lead us to an understanding of ourselves.
Carl Jung

There is a better approach to conflict resolution than fighting it out.

After completing this chapter, you should be able to:
- Identify common factors that lead to conflict.
- Discuss five methods to resolve conflict.
- Discuss techniques to use in handling difficult people.
- Discuss solutions and alternatives in dealing with anger.
- Identify situations of sexual harassment in the workplace, and discuss possible solutions.

Can you imagine a world without conflict? Why, it would be a world without change! Conflict is inevitable wherever there are people with differing backgrounds, needs, values, and priorities.

A stereotypical perspective of conflict related to nursing is that "nice" nurses avoid conflict. According to Beauregard and colleagues (2003), although caricatured images of the nurse may encompass the "old" battle-ax, the control freak, the naughty nurse, or the doctor's handmaiden, the primary perception of the nurse by the public is one of the caring angel who is gentle and kind. Conflict within the nursing profession has traditionally generated negative feelings to the extent that many nurses use avoidance as a coping mechanism because of their feeling that the "public's stereotypical image of them demanded that they be 'nice,' self-sacrificing, and submissive nurses and that if they engaged in conflict they would be branded emotional or unfeminine women" (Kelly, 2006, p. 27).

The presence of conflict in a situation is not necessarily negative but may, in fact, have some positive results. As a process, conflict is neutral. Following are some possible outcomes of conflict:

- Disturbing issues are brought out into the open, which may avert a more serious conflict.
- Group cohesiveness may increase as individuals resolve issues.
- New leadership may develop as a consequence of resolution.
- The results of conflict can be constructive, occurring when productive outcomes are achieved, or destructive, leading to poor communication and creating dissatisfaction.

CONFLICT

What Causes Conflict?

Let us look at some common factors of conflict as they relate to nursing.

Role Conflict

When two people have the same or related responsibilities with ambiguous boundaries, the potential for conflict exists. For example, a nurse on the 11 PM to 7 AM shift may be uncertain whether he or the nurse on the 7 AM to 3 PM shift is responsible for weighing a patient.

Communication Conflict

Failing to discuss differences with one another can lead to problems with communication. Communication is a two-way process; when one person is unclear in a communication, the process falls apart. A recent graduate may find that with a busy schedule, numerous patient demands, and a shortage of time, it is easy to forget to notify a patient's family of a change in visiting hours—a great annoyance to the family members who cannot visit when they arrive.

Goal Conflict

We all have unique goals and objectives for what we hope to achieve in our places of employment. When one nurse places his or her personal achievement and advancement above everyone else's, conflict can occur. An example of this can be seen in the newly graduated nurse who pursues an advanced nursing degree immediately following undergraduate education; the experienced nurse in the unit may feel that the new graduate nurse requires a minimum length of time at the bedside before advancing his or her education.

Personality Conflict

Wouldn't it be great if we got along with everyone? Of course, we all know that there are just some people with whom we have a difficult time. The situation is all too familiar, and many times we may find ourselves with such thoughts as "I'll try to overlook her negative, lousy behavior; after all, she doesn't have much of a family life." Trying to change another person's personality is like guaranteeing an unhappy ending to a story.

Ethical or Values Conflict

During a cardiac arrest, a graduate nurse has a conflict with the physician's order of "No Code," on a young adolescent patient. She has difficulty taking care of the adolescent, because he reminds her of her younger brother who died tragically in an automobile accident.

Conflicts in nursing may fit into one or more of the aforementioned categories. Consider some common areas of conflict among nursing staff, including scheduling days off, determining vacation leave, assigning committees, patient care assignments, and performance appraisals, to name just a few.

What Are Common Areas of Conflict Between Nurses and Patients—and Between Nurses and Patients' Families?

Guttenberg (1983) identifies five common areas of conflict among nurses and their patients and families.

1. **Quality of care.** This is by far the most common area of conflict and the easiest to remedy. Families typically are concerned with how well their loved one is being attended to, how friendly the nurses are, how well the hospital or home health services are provided and coordinated, and how flexible the hospital is with visiting hours and meeting their special needs.

2. **Treatment decisions.** This area of conflict often arises between the family of an older adult and the nurse. A physician may order a treatment with which the family does not agree. In this situation it is very important that the nurse not defend the physician's orders or attempt to persuade or convince the family that the physician or nurse knows what's best for the patient. In these situations, the issue is rarely the treatment itself but rather the family's desire to decide what is right for the loved one. Be sure to clarify the orders and explain to the family that you are supposed to carry them out unless the family negotiates directly with the physician to change them. Conflict may also exist between the nurse and physician regarding care of older adults. For example, a physician may decline to perform a medical procedure on an older patient secondary to advanced age or preexisting comorbidities.

3. **Family involvement.** For example, when a young adult is diagnosed with cancer, numerous issues may arise concerning the presence of family members during procedures and the extent of their involvement in the overall care. Such issues are based on the family's real need to feel significant and adequate in meeting the young adult's needs.

4. **Quality of parental care.** This can become an issue when nurses are unhappy with how parents are participating in their child's care. It is helpful to offer parenting classes that can encourage parents to meet other parents and can model positive parenting techniques. Fear of being a bad parent, by not responding to every cry an infant makes, is a good example of an area where the nurse can educate the parents on responding to their infant's physical and emotional needs.

5. **Staff inconsistency.** This is another issue that is easily prevented. Make sure that staff members on each shift are consistent in enforcing hospital policies and that they notify other shifts of any attempts at manipulation by family members or patients.

CONFLICT RESOLUTION

What Are Ways to Resolve Conflict?

Unresolved conflicts waste time and energy and reduce productivity and cooperation among the people with whom you work. In contrast, when conflicts are resolved, they strengthen relationships and improve the performance of everyone involved (Kim, Nicotera, & McNulty, 2015). The key to managing conflict successfully is tailoring your response to fit each conflict situation instead of just relying on one particular technique. Each technique represents a different way to achieve the outcome you want and to help the other person achieve at least part of the outcome that he or she wants. How do you know which technique to use? That depends on the following:

- How much power do you have in this situation compared with the other person?
- How much do you value your relationship with the person with whom you are in conflict?
- How much time is available to resolve the conflict?

An example of a model for conflict resolution can be found in Fig. 13.1. This model incorporates several views of conflict resolution. Filley (1975) described three basic strategies for handling conflict, according to outcome: win-win, lose-lose, and win-lose. Various others have identified the following five responses to resolve conflict: competition, accommodation, avoidance, compromise, and cooperation. In a recent study, the prevalent style for conflict resolution used by nursing students was compromise, followed by avoidance (Hamilton, 2008). As noted in this research study, compromise attempts to meet the needs of individuals on both sides of a conflict, whereas collaboration, which may take more time, offers the best avenue or approach to settling the conflict that will satisfy both participants (win-win solution). A research study by Iglesias and Vallejo (2012) examined predominant conflict resolution styles used by a sample of Spanish nurses in two work settings, academic and clinical, in order to determine differences between these environments. Their findings indicated that conflict management styles varied according to work setting, with nurses in an academic environment using most frequently the compromising style and nurses in the clinical environment using the accommodating style most frequently.

Let us look at an example and apply the model.

Suppose the charge nurse on your unit has posted the vacation schedule for the month of December. You, as a recent graduate, have requested to be off during the week of Christmas. You notice on the schedule that none of the recent graduates has received the Christmas holidays off. You feel that this is unfair, because you will not have an opportunity to be with your family during the Christmas holidays. How can you resolve this conflict?

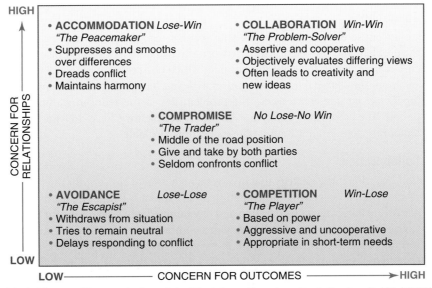

FIG. 13.1 Model for conflict resolution. (Modified from Douglas, E., & Bushardt, W. (1988). Interpersonal conflict: Strategies and guidelines for resolution, *J Am Med Rec Assoc 56*(18); Sullivan, E., & Decker, P. (1988). *Effective management in nursing*. Menlo Park, CA: Addison-Wesley.)

Competition

This is an example of the *win-lose* situation. In this situation, force—or the use of power—occurs. It sets up a type of competition between you and your charge nurse. Typically, competition is used to resolve conflict when one person has more power in a situation than the other. *In the given situation, the charge nurse refuses your request for Christmas vacation, explaining that the staff members with more seniority have priority for vacation at Christmas time.*

Avoidance

Avoidance is unassertive and uncooperative and leads to a *lose-lose* situation. In some situations, avoidance is not considered a true form of conflict resolution because the conflict is not resolved and neither party is satisfied. *In the given situation, you would not have approached the charge nurse with the Christmas schedule issue.* Usually, both persons involved feel frustrated and angry. There are some situations in which avoiding the issue might be appropriate, such as when tempers are flaring or when strong anger is present. However, this is only a short-term strategy; it is important to get back to the problem after emotions have cooled.

Accommodation

Accommodation is the *lose-win* situation, in which one person accommodates the other at his or her own expense but often ends up feeling resentful and angry. *In the given situation, the charge nurse would put her own concern aside and let you have your way, possibly even working for you during the scheduled slot. The charge nurse loses and the graduate nurse wins in this situation, which may set up conflict among staff and other recent graduates.* When is accommodation the best response? Is it when conflict would create serious disruption, such as arguing, or when the person with whom you are in conflict has the power to resolve the conflict unilaterally? In this response to conflict, differences are suppressed or played down while agreement is emphasized.

Compromise

Compromise or bargaining is the strategy that recognizes the importance of both the resolution of the problem and the relationship between the two people. Compromise is a moderately assertive and cooperative step in the right direction, in which one creates a *modified win-lose* outcome. *In the given situation, the charge nurse compromises with you by allowing you to have Christmas Eve off with your family but not the entire week.* The problem lies in the reduced staffing that will occur for a short period. The compromise may not be totally satisfactory for either party, but it may be offered as a temporary solution until more options become available.

Collaboration

Collaboration is the strategy that involves a high level of concern for the problem, the outcome, and the relationship. It deals with confrontation and problem solving. The needs, feelings, and desires of both parties are taken into consideration and re-examined while searching for proper ways to agree on goals. Collaboration is a *win-win* solution with a commitment to resolve the issues at the base of the conflict. It is fully assertive and cooperative. *In the given situation, you and the charge nurse discuss the week of Christmas vacation and the staffing needs and agree that you will work the first three days of that week and the charge nurse will work the second half of that week. You also agree to be there the first part of the week to complete the audit on the charts from the previous week for the charge nurse. In this situation both persons are satisfied, and there is no compromising what is most important to each person. That is, the charge nurse gets her audit completed, and the recent graduate is able to spend half of the Christmas week with her family.* What is your particular style for resolving conflict? (See Critical Thinking Box 13.1.)

? CRITICAL THINKING BOX 13.1

Conflict Questionnaire

Directions: Consider situations in which you find your wishes differing from those of another person. For each of the following statements, think how likely you are to respond to each situation in the manner described. Check the rating that best corresponds to your response.

	VERY UNLIKELY	UNLIKELY	VERY LIKELY	LIKELY
1. I am usually firm in pursuing my goals.				
2. I try to win my position.				
3. I give up some points in exchange for others.				
4. I feel that differences are not always worth worrying about.				
5. I try to find a position that is between others' and mine.				
6. In approaching a negotiation, I try to consider the other person's wishes.				
7. I try to show the logic and benefits of my position.				
8. I always lean toward a direct discussion of the problem.				
9. I try to find a fair combination of gains and losses for both of us.				
10. I attempt to work through our differences immediately.				
11. I try to avoid creating unpleasantness for myself.				
12. I might try to soothe others' feelings and preserve our relationship.				
13. I attempt to get all concerns and issues immediately out.				
14. I sometimes avoid taking positions that create controversy.				
15. I try not to hurt the other's feelings.				

SCORING: Very Unlikely = 1; Unlikely = 2; Likely = 3; Very Likely = 4.

	ITEM:	ITEM:	ITEM:	
COMPETING:	1 _____	2 _____	7 _____	TOTAL _____
COLLABORATING:	8 _____	10 _____	13 _____	TOTAL _____
COMPROMISING:	3 _____	5 _____	9 _____	TOTAL _____
AVOIDING:	4 _____	11 _____	14 _____	TOTAL _____
ACCOMMODATING:	6 _____	12 _____	15 _____	TOTAL _____

From Thomas, K. W. (1977). Toward multidimensional values in teaching: The example of conflict behaviors, *Academy of Management Review, 2*, 487.

What Are Some Basic Guidelines for Choosing the Technique to Use?

In some situations, certain techniques and responses work best. You may have to use accommodation or avoidance when you lack the power to change the situation. When you have conflict in a relationship that you value, it might be more helpful to use accommodation, compromise, or collaboration. When there is no immediate, pressing sense of urgency to solve an issue, then any of the five techniques can be used. However, when you are facing an emergency situation or a rapidly approaching deadline, your best bet is to use competition or accommodation. Just remember the following key behaviors in managing conflict:

- Deal with issues, not personalities.
- Take responsibility for yourself and your participation.
- Communicate openly.
- Avoid placing blame.
- Listen actively.
- Sort out the issues.
- Identify key themes in the discussion.
- Stay focused in the present; don't dwell on the past.
- Weigh the consequences.
- Identify resolution options.
- Develop an outcome and obtain consensus.

Suppose that you follow all of these suggestions and you still are confronted with that difficult situation or that difficult person. Read on.

DEALING WITH DIFFICULT PEOPLE

What Are Some Techniques for Handling Difficult People?

Now that we have discussed types of conflict-management techniques, we are ready to look at techniques for handling difficult people. How do you deal with an abusive physician or supervisor? How do you react when someone constantly complains and gripes about something? How do you handle the know-it-all who will not even listen to your thoughts about an issue? (See Research for Best Practice Box 13.1 for suggestions on managing difficult employees.)

I am sure, if you have not already, you will run into in the near future a Sherman tank (Fig. 13.2). According to Bramson (1981), Sherman tanks are the *attackers*. They come out charging and are often abusive, abrupt, and intimidating. But more important, they tend to be downright overwhelming.

Remember Dr. Smith, who flew into a tirade because you forgot to have a suture removal set at his patient's bedside at 8 AM sharp? Remember how you felt? "My heart was beating so loud I could hear it, and I was sure everyone else around could hear it, too. I was so furious at him for the comments he made."

In understanding Sherman tanks, it is important to realize that they have a strong need to prove to themselves and to others that their view of the situation is right. They have a very strong sense of what others ought to do but often lack the caring and the trust that would be helpful in getting something done. They usually achieve what they want, but to do so causes them a lot of disagreements, lost friendships, and uncomfortable relationships with their co-workers. Sherman tanks are often very confident and tend to devalue those whom they feel are not confident. Unfortunately, they demean others in a way that makes them look very self-important and superior. How do you cope with a Sherman tank? The most important thing is to keep your fear and anger under control

RESEARCH FOR BEST PRACTICE BOX 13.1

Managing Difficult Employees

Practice Issue

Nurse managers are often faced with a difficult employee. The difficult employee's negative conflict behavior affects team performance effectiveness, job satisfaction, and turnover intention. According to Pareto's 80/20 rule, 20% of employees/workers will cause 80% of the problems, which means that a small number of issues are responsible for a large percentage of the effect.

In an environment of team collegiality, there is less negative conflict, increased commitment to the organization, and greater satisfaction, autonomy, and control over practice. In professional practice environments, nurses experience constructive conflict approaches, and effectiveness is enhanced in the workplace.

It is part of the nurse manager role to create an environment that facilitates professional practice. This type of environment requires that employees are socialized to their nursing role. In these professional practice environments, the unique preferences, perspectives, opinions, concerns, and choices of the individuals are recognized and valued. During nursing school, professional role socialization ("think like a nurse") is initiated and later solidified during the early years of practice when the new graduate incorporates knowledge, skills, attitude, and affective behavior associated with carrying out the expectations of the nursing role.

Additionally, nurse managers may encounter conflict among employees in which the nurse manager needs to serve as a mediator among the employees involved in an argument or disagreement. The role of a mediator is to assist disputants in coming to a resolution or agreement. The mediator assists the parties involved by "defining problems, enumerating priorities, exploring alternatives, and facilitating resultant negotiations" (Cheng, 2015, p. 311).

Implications for Nursing Practice

Effective role socialization occurs when the nurse engages in actions that benefit other nurses and/or patients and families by helping, supporting, and encouraging mutual goal accomplishment and/or well-being.

- There needs to be positive interdependence among the nursing staff.
- Nurses need to understand and use constructive conflict-management skills.
- Employ mediation techniques when disputes arise between employees and/or patients and their families.
- There needs to be high trust among the nursing staff.
- Prosocial behavior should be noted among staff with the feeling of "sink or swim together" versus "you sink and I swim."
- Do not procrastinate in dealing with difficult employees, patients, or their families.
- A high basic self-esteem is noted among nursing staff in an empowering, healthy workplace environment.
- The conflict negotiation strategy used may be collaboration (win-win) or mediation.

Considering This Information

How might you use some of the strategies listed in this chapter to handle a difficult employee? What types of activities are you involved in as a student that promote a positive professional practice environment? What essential skills would be important for a nurse to possess to serve as a mediator?

References

Arnold, E., Pulich, M., & Wang, H. (2008). Managing immature, irresponsible, or irritating employees. *Health Care Manager, 27* (4), 350–356.

Cheng, F. K. (2015). Mediation skills for conflict resolution in nursing education. *Nurse Education in Practice, 15* (4), 310–313. http://dx.doi.org/10.1013/j.nepr.20115.02.005.

Cornett, P. A., & O'Rourke, M. (2009). Building organizational capacity for a healthy work environment through role based professional practice. *Critical Care Nursing Quarterly, 32* (3), 208–220.

Cornett, P. A. (2009). Managing the difficult employee: A reframed perspective. *Critical Care Nursing Quarterly, 32* (4), 314.

Hader, R. (2008). Workplace violence survey 2008: Unsettling findings. *Nursing Management, 39* (7), 13–19, 326.

Middaugh, D. J. (2015). Managing the 80/20 rule. *Medsurg Nursing, 24* (2), 127, 129.

Rondeau, A. (2007). 57% of managers time is spent dealing with difficult staff. Retrieved from http://www.selfgrowth.com/articles/57_of_ Managers_Time_is_Spent_Dealing_With_Difficult_Staff.html.

Siu, H., Laschinger, H. K. S., & Finegan, J. (2008). Nursing professional practice environments: setting the stage for constructive conflict resolution and work effectiveness. *Journal of Nursing Administration, 38* (5), 250–257.

FIG. 13.2 Sherman tank.

and to avoid an outright confrontation about who is right and who is wrong. The following are some specific things you should do:

- Do not allow yourself to be run over; step aside.
  - Stand up for yourself. Defend yourself, but without fighting. Seek support when warranted.
  - Give them a little time to run down and express what they might be ranting about.
  - Sometimes, it is necessary to be rude; get your word in any way that you can.
  - If possible, try to get them to sit down. Be sure to maintain eye contact with them while you are assertively stating your opinions and perceptions very forcefully.
  - Do not argue with them or try to cut them down.
- When they finally hear you, be ready to be friendly.

Next to the Sherman tanks are the *snipers* (Fig. 13.3). The snipers are the pot-shot artists. They are not as openly aggressive as the Sherman tanks. Their weapons are their innuendoes, their digs, and their nonplayful teasing, which is definitely aimed to hurt you. Snipers tend to choose a hidden rather than a frontal attack. They prefer to undercut you and make you look ridiculous. So, when you are dealing with snipers, remember to expose the attack, that is, "smoke them out." Ask them very calmly:

"That sounded like a put-down. Did you really mean it that way?" Or you might say, "Do I understand that you don't like what I'm saying? It sounds as if you are making fun of me. Are you?"

When a sniper is giving you criticism, be sure to obtain group confirmation or denial. Ask questions or make statements such as, "Does anyone else see the issue this way?" "It seems as though we have a difference of opinion," or "Exactly what is the issue here? What is it that you don't like about what occurred?" One way to prevent sniping is by setting up regular problem-solving meetings with that person.

FIG. 13.3 The sniper.

Also difficult to cope with are the *constant complainers*. These people often feel as though they are powerless, so they draw attention—but seldom action—to their problem. A complainer points out real problems but does it from a very unconstructive stance. Coping with a complainer can be a challenge. First, it is important to listen to the complaints, acknowledge them, and make sure you understand what the person said by paraphrasing it or checking out your perception of how the person feels. Do not necessarily agree with the person; with a complainer, it is important to move into a problem-solving mode by asking very specific, informative questions and encouraging him or her to submit complaints in writing. For example, try communicating with the constant complainer in the following manner:

"Did I understand you to say that you are having difficulty with your patient assignment?"
"Would it be helpful if I went to the pharmacy for you, so that you could complete your chart on your preoperative patient?"

Next are the maddening ones: the *clams* (Fig. 13.4). The clams have an entirely different tactic from the previous three. They just refuse to respond when you need an answer or want to have a discussion. It might be helpful to try to read a clam's nonverbal communication. Watch for wrinkled brows, a frown, or a sigh. How to deal with clams? Try to get them to open up by using open-ended questions and waiting very quietly for a response. Do not fill in their silence with your own conversation. Give yourself enough time to wait with composure. Sometimes a little "clamming" on your own part might be helpful by using the technique called the "friendly, silent stare," or FSS. The way to set up the FSS is to have a very inquisitive, expectant expression on your face with raised eyebrows, wide eyes, and maybe a slight smile—all nonverbal cues to the clam that you are waiting for a response. When clams finally open up, be very attentive. Watch your own impulses—do not bubble

FIG. 13.4 The clam.

over with happiness just because they have finally given you two moments of their time. Avoid the polite ending; in other words, get up and say, for example:

"This was important to me. I'm not going to let this issue drop. I'll be back to talk to you tomorrow at 2 o'clock." Do not be the nice guy and say, "Thanks for coming in. Have a nice weekend. I'll see you tomorrow."

Be very direct and inform the clam what you are going to do, especially if the desired discussion did not occur.

What Is Anger?

Anger is something that we feel. Usually when we become angry, we assume it is because we are upset about what someone has done to us. Often we want to pay them back or take out our rage on them. Usually when anger occurs, it is difficult to see beyond the moment, because most people are consumed with thoughts of revenge or the wrongdoing that has occurred to them. Weiss and Cain (1991) state that "Anger is often a cover-up emotion … that disguises what is really going on inside you." But anger is a signal, and according to Lerner (1997), it is "one worth listening to" (p. 1). She goes on further to say that:

> Our anger may be a message that we are being hurt, that our rights are being violated, that our needs or wants are not being adequately met, or simply that something is not right. Our anger may tell us that we are not addressing an important emotional issue in our lives, or that too much of ourselves—our beliefs, values, desires, or ambitions—are being compromised in a relationship. Our anger may be a signal that we are doing more and giving more than we can comfortably do or give. Or our anger may warn us that others are doing too much for us, at the expense of our own competence and growth. Just as physical pain tells us to take our hand off the hot stove, the pain of our anger preserves the very integrity of our self. Our anger can motivate us to say "no" to the ways in which we are defined by others and "yes" to the dictates of our inner self. (p. 1)

No matter what, when feelings of frustration, disappointment, or powerlessness take over, there is no doubt that anger is in the making. Anger seems to begin in situations fraught with threats and anxiety.

Anger has two faces. One is *guilt,* which is anger aimed inward at what we did or did not do, and the other is *resentment,* which is anger directed toward others at what they did or did not do.

> The following is true about both guilt and resentment: They both accumulate over time and lead to a cycle of negative energy that poisons our relationships and stifles our personal growth.

There is another side of the coin, however. If feeling angry signifies a problem, then ventilating anger does not necessarily solve it. Actually, ventilating anger may serve to maintain it if change and successful resolution do not occur. Tavris (1984) suggests that we learn two things about handling anger: first, how to think about anger, and second, how to reduce the tension. More about this later in the chapter.

Box 13.1 shows a summary of different anger styles. Just think about anger from a cardiovascular point of view. Most authorities consider anger one of the most damaging and dangerous emotions, because your pulse and blood pressure become elevated, sometimes to dangerous heights.

What Is the Solution for Handling Anger?

> Change the image of it!

Stop

Appraise the situation. Do not do a thing. You are at a pivotal point. You have two ways to go: One is to become angry; the other is to reevaluate the situation. Try to look at a way to reinterpret the annoying comment. Consider the following example:

"Who does that charge nurse think she is to treat me like I'm a dummy!" or "How could someone be so thoughtless as to not remember my birthday!" You can reinterpret these and say to yourself, "Maybe if she weren't so unhappy, she wouldn't have considered doing such a thing" or "Maybe that person's having a rough day." The important thing here is to empathize with the person and to try to find justifications for the behavior that was so annoying to you.

Look

What image about yourself or another is about to be or has been breached—what *should*s, *must*s, or *need to*s have been violated? In other words, what has just occurred that has led you to feel angry with yourself or with another?

After receiving the end-of-shift report and making patient rounds, a recent graduate goes into a patient's room to take vital signs. Within moments the patient has a cardiac arrest. Two hours later, while completing her charting, the recent graduate states guiltily, "I should have taken those vital signs earlier. It just needs to be the first thing I do when I get on the unit. I should have been on top of this. I must do better." Notice the self-criticism in the recent graduate's comments. Guilt, like resentment, can be a habit. It demonstrates—too clearly—how we respond to a situation in a negative manner. To help you get in touch with these feelings, try eliminating the words "must" and "should" from your vocabulary for just an hour. It is quite surprising to find out how frequently we use these terms.

BOX 13.1   ANGER CHARACTERISTICS AND TRIGGERS

What Is Your Anger Style?
Passive Characteristics
- Avoidance—no eye contact or avoiding communicating with others; "silent treatment or cold shoulder"
- Withdrawing emotionally
- Becoming ill or anxious
- Sitting on the fence and not making a decision
- Talking about frustrations but showing no feelings
- Doing little or nothing or putting things off to thwart other's plans
- Not feeling anger when something is wrong

Aggressive Characteristics
- Acting out or lashing out at another person; out of control behavior
- Bullying
- Incivility—offensive, intimidating, or hostile action
- Explosive, sudden outburst and release of feelings
- Taking anger out on someone or something else (i.e., kicking the dog, breaking things)
- Violence—getting physical or hurting people
- Bringing up old grievances

Passive-Aggressive Characteristics
- Resenting and blaming others; opposition to the demands of others
- Hidden action to get back at someone; conscious revenge
- Procrastination and intentional mistakes in response to others' demands; intentional inefficiency; "forgetting" to do things and using forgetfulness as an excuse
- Cynical, sullen, or hostile attitude
- Frequent complaints about feeling underappreciated or cheated; self-deprecating

What Are Red Flags and Long-Standing Issues That Trigger Anger?
- Experiencing feelings of being discounted, threatened, humiliated, rejected, insecurity
- Having to wait a long time for a person or an appointment
- Getting caught in traffic congestion or crowded buses, airplanes, or other similar frustrating situations
- Joking comments made about sensitive topics
- Friends borrowing items and not returning them or returning them in disrepair
- Friends borrowing money and not paying you back
- Being wrongly accused of some action or comment
- Having to clean up after someone who does not keep things as tidy as you expect
- Having a neighbor who plays loud music or is engaged in other behavior that is inconsiderate
- Being placed on hold for long periods of time while on the telephone
- Having your computer crash and losing valuable data
- Being given wrong directions when asking for assistance
- Having money or property stolen
- Being taken for granted by family and friends

Valentine, P. E. (2001). A gender perspective on conflict management strategies of nurses. *Journal of Nursing Scholarship, 33* (1), 69–74.
Vivar, C. (2006). Putting conflict management into practice: A nursing case study. *Journal of Nursing Management, 14,* 201–206. doi: 10.1111/j.1365-2934.2006.00554.x

Change

How do you change the image? One of the ways is to use humor. Humor makes the anger (guilt and resentment) tolerable. Remember that it is difficult to laugh and frown at the same time. (It only takes 15 facial muscles to laugh, but twice that many to frown.) If reappraising the situation and using humor both fail as ways to manage your anger, some suggest venting the anger—for example, by getting mad, yelling, shouting, telling someone off, or breaking things. Although this might make us feel better momentarily, in the long run such outbursts make us feel worse.

Why does this method of venting anger, that is, letting it all hang out, make us feel worse? First, think of all the physiological changes that are occurring in your body: blood pressure, pulse, and respirations increase; the muscles contract; and adrenalin is released. Sound familiar? It is the "fight or flight" adrenal response. Can it be healthy to maintain a constant state of stress and readiness to respond? Another disadvantage of an uninhibited outburst of anger is that it may lead the other person to retaliate.

It might be important to recognize the difference between venting and acknowledging our anger. A typical expression of anger might be something such as the following:

"Hey, you turkey, what do you think you're doing? Don't you know how to put that catheter in? Are you stupid or something? Either you figure it out, or you get out of here. You hear me?"

This approach is insulting, demeaning, and accusatory. It is also likely to lead to some type of provoking response. In contrast, when we acknowledge our feelings, we make statements such as *"I feel angry about …"* or *"I feel hurt about …"* or *"I feel guilty about ….."* The use of "I" statements is our first step toward taking responsibility for ourselves by owning up to our own feelings instead of blaming others.

Venting anger simply does not work unless you want to intimidate those around you, coerce them into submission with a hot temper, or, even worse, look childish while ranting, raving, and beating the floor or each other with foam bats. So, what does work? *Face it, embrace it, and erase it!*

First, acknowledge the anger (*face it*): Ask "What am I feeling? Anger? Guilt? Rage? Resentment?"

Second, identify the provoking or triggering situation (*embrace it*): Ask "What caused this feeling? Whose problem is it?"

Third, determine what changes need to occur (*erase it*): Ask "What can I change? Can I accept what I cannot change?" Then take action and let go of the rest. Other ways to handle anger and remove yourself from the vicious cycle of guilt and resentment are in the following sections.

Move.

Get Active

Try exercise or anything involving physical activity, such as walking, aerobics, and running. Clean the garage or a kitchen drawer. If you are sitting, get up. If you are in bed, move your arms around. Just get active and do something!

Focus.

Refocus on Something Positive

Think of your cup as half full, not half empty. Look at the provoking situation: "My charge nurse won't give me Christmas off. However, I am not scheduled to work either Christmas Eve or New Year's Eve. So, by working Christmas Day, I'm assured the other days off."

> Breathe.

Pay Attention to Your Breathing

Slow it down. Take deep, slow breaths, feeling the air move through your nose and down into your lungs. Check out your body for areas of tenseness. Often anger can be felt as tightness in the chest and abdomen.

Conflict is an inevitable part of our day-to-day experience. How we negotiate and handle conflict and anger may not always be easy. You might be thinking right now "This looks good on paper, but in real life, it is not that easy to put into practice." If you are feeling this way, take a risk and try changing your approach and viewpoint.

> The important thing is learning about yourself.

How do you cope with conflict? How do you handle difficult people? How do you respond when angry?

SEXUAL HARASSMENT IN THE WORKPLACE

In today's world, sexual harassment as a source of conflict has been taken seriously, as evidenced by the widespread visibility and increased recognition of the issue. The potential impact of harassment on nursing students both in the classroom and in the practice area is significant. According to Dowell (1992), nursing administrators and educators must be proactive in writing and implementing policies regarding sexual harassment. Valente and Bullough (2004) concur that employers should outline consequences and infractions of sexual harassment in their policies, as well as provide ongoing education about what constitutes sexual harassment and enforce a "no tolerance" policy (pp. 239–240). In a study by Libbus and Bowman (1994), 70% of female staff nurses surveyed reported sexual harassment by male patients and co-workers, with the most common complaint being sexual remarks and inappropriate touching. In addition, in a survey of nursing administrators, 68.8% of those who responded reported sexist attitudes among employees in their organizations, and 47.7% reported observing instances of sexual harassment (Blancett & Sullivan, 1993). These studies reflect the prevalence of sexual harassment in health care settings during the 1990s. With the introduction of sexual harassment awareness and training instituted by health care agencies, since this time, there have been few if any research studies reflecting the prevalence or sexual harassment in today's health care workplace. Valente and Bullough (2004) have also noted that sexual harassment cases are often unreported by the victim. This might also explain why there is limited data on sexual harassment in the workplace setting.

The issue of sexual harassment came to the forefront during the 1991 confirmation hearings of Supreme Court Justice Clarence Thomas (Allen, 1992). A once-secretive problem is now openly discussed in newspapers and by the media. As awareness about sexual harassment increased, we all realized how little we knew about it and what we could do about it. The majority of cases involve women who report being harassed by men, but the reverse has also occurred. In nursing, the stereotypical situation of sexual harassment involves a nurse (i.e., a woman) and a doctor (i.e., a man) because of the large number of nurses who are women. However, with the increase in the number of men entering the nursing profession, there is the potential for men to experience sexual harassment in the workplace. Roth and Coleman (2008) agree that actual and perceived barriers exist that prevent men from entering the nursing profession. In an effort to remove existing barriers and attract more men into the nursing profession, the authors recommend that the image of men in nursing and the media's depiction of male nurses should be showcased as positive and that increasing staff diversity by recruiting men within the nursing workforce should be embraced by both the public and nursing profession (Fig. 13.5).

FIG. 13.5 Sexual harassment.

What Is Sexual Harassment?

According to Friedman (1992), "sexual harassment refers to conduct, typically experienced as offensive in nature, in which unwanted sexual advances are made in the context of a relationship of unequal power or authority" (p. 9). He goes on to explain that victims of sexual harassment are subjected to sexually oriented verbal comments, unwanted touching, and requests for sexual favors. The typical problem, known as *quid pro quo harassment*, arises when unwelcome sexual advances have been made and an employee is required to submit to those demands as a condition either of employment or of promotion. "Hostile work environment" has been used as a legal claim to show that "the atmosphere in the work (or other) environment is so uncomfortable or offensive by virtue of sexual advances, sexual requests, or sexual innuendoes that it amounts to a hostile environment" (Friedman, 1992, p. 16). Hershcovis and Barling (2010) succinctly state, "Sexual harassment has been described in terms of its three subcomponents: gender harassment, unwanted sexual attention, and quid pro quo" (p. 875). Let us look at hypothetical examples of how sexual harassment can affect nursing.

Samantha, a recent graduate, was receiving continued requests from a male patient to provide him with a complete bed bath. However, when a male nurse was assigned to this patient the following day, the patient reported to the male nurse that he was capable of bathing himself and proceeded to take a shower.

Lisa, the evening charge nurse, was quite excited that Tom, a recent graduate, was going to work on her unit. Lisa pursued Tom by repeatedly asking him for assistance with patient care, and, when she called him into her office, she would touch him inappropriately.

What Can I Do About It?

There are two ways to handle this type of workplace conflict: informally and formally through a grievance procedure. Start with the most direct measure. Ask the person to STOP! Tell the harasser in clear terms that the behavior makes you uncomfortable and that you want it to stop immediately. Also, you might want to put your statement in writing to the person, keeping a copy for yourself. Tell other people, such as family, friends, personal physician, or minister, what is happening and how you are dealing with it. Friedman (1992) suggests keeping a written journal of harassing events, including all attempts used to try to stop the harassment. The need to exercise power and control, rather than sexual desire, is frequently the motive of the sexual harasser (perpetrator). If sexual harassment is occurring as a result of miscommunication and misinterpretation of actions and is primarily sexually driven, not power driven, then telling the perpetrator to stop will often clear up any misconceptions. However, if the perpetrator is power driven, the harassment will continue as long as he or she views the victim as passive, powerless, and frightened. What may be most difficult for the recent graduate is facing the fear that surrounds threats of job insecurity or public embarrassment (Friedman, 1992).

If a direct request to the perpetrator to stop does not work, then an informal complaint may be effective, especially if both parties realize a problem exists and want it to be solved. The goal of the informal method is to stop the harassment but not to punish the perpetrator. This method assists the person filing the complaint in maintaining some type of harmonious relationship with the perpetrator. According to Friedman (1992), "a formal grievance usually requires filing a written complaint with an official group such as a hearing" (p. 65). This is a legal procedure that is guided and regulated by federal and state laws specific to this type of grievance. Before a 1991 amendment to the Civil Rights Act (Title VII), the means of correcting this bad situation—making it right or compensating the victim for difficulty encountered—were quite restricted. What has occurred as a result of this act is that victims of intentional discrimination may now seek compensatory and punitive damages. Each state has an Equal Employment Opportunity Commission, which has as its specific charge the enforcement of Title VII.

Unfortunately, sexual harassment may be a form of conflict you are faced with in the workplace. It is important to learn to deal with your feelings and to be aware of actions to take in case this happens to you. When this type of situation is resolved in a constructive, positive manner, it allows you an opportunity to feel better about your ability to manage conflict.

CONCLUSION

Most of us have experienced conflict. Building effective conflict-management skills is key to working with patients, staff, and physicians. Various models exist to provide a framework for effective conflict resolution; the "win-win" model of *collaboration* is the strategy that aims for the highest level of resolution and is fully assertive and cooperative in approach. It requires creative nursing management and understanding to recognize and acknowledge that conflict will exist whenever human relationships are involved. This needs to be tempered with open, accurate communication and active listening by maintaining an objective, not emotional, stance as conflict resolution strategies are implemented. Review the Relevant Websites and Online Resources.

🌐 RELEVANT WEBSITES AND ONLINE RESOURCES

Community Tool Box (2015)
Section 6. Training for Conflict Resolution. Retrieved from http://ctb.ku.edu/en/table-of-contents/implement/provide-information-enhance-skills/conflict-resolution/main.

Conflict Resolution Network (2015)
http://www.crnhq.org/.

Lutz, K. (2013)
Conflict resolution lessons from the home: How conflict management skills transform discord into harmony. Retrieved from http://www.pon.harvard.edu/?p=34983/?mqsc=E3519589.

MindTools (2013)
Conflict resolution. Resolving conflict rationally and effectively. Retrieved from http://www.mindtools.com/pages/article/new LDR_81.htm.

Segal, J., & Smith, M. (2013)
Conflict resolution skills. Retrieved from http://www.helpguide.org/articles/relationships/conflict-resolution-skills.htm.

Webne-Behrman, H. (2013)
Conflict resolution. Retrieved from https://www.ohrd.wisc.edu/home/HideATab/FullyPreparedtoManage/ConflictResolution/tabid/297/Default.aspx.

BIBLIOGRAPHY

Allen, A. (1992). Equal opportunity in the workplace. *Journal of Postanesthesia Nursing, 7*(2), 132–134.

Beauregard, M., etal. (2003). Improving our image a nurse at a time. *Journal of Nursing Administration, 10,* 510–511.

Blancett, S. S., & Sullivan, P. A. (1993). Ethics survey results. *Journal of Nursing Administration, 23*(3), 9–13.

Bramson, R. (1981). *Coping with difficult people.* New York: National Press Publications.

Dowell, M. (1992). Sexual harassment in academia: Legal and administrative challenges. *Journal of Nursing Education, 31*(1), 5–9.

Filley, A. C. (1975). *Interpersonal conflict resolution.* Glenview, IL: Scott Foresman.

Friedman, J. (1992). *Sexual harassment: What it is, what it isn't, what it does to you, and what you can do about it.* Deerfield Beach, FL: Health Communications.

Guttenberg, R. M. (1983). How to stay cool in a conflict and turn it into cooperation. *Nurse Life, 3*(3), 25–29.

Hamilton, P. (2008). Conflict management styles in the health professions. *Southern Online Journal of Nursing Research, 8*(2), 2.

Hershcovis, M. S., & Barling, J. (2010). Comparing victim attributions and outcomes for workplace aggression and sexual harassment. *Journal of Applied Psychology, 95*(5), 874–888. http://dx.doi.org/10.1037/a0020070.

Iglesias, M., & Vallejo, R. (2012). Conflict resolution styles in the nursing profession. *Contemporary Nurse, 43*(1), 73–80. http://dx.doi.org/10.5172/conu.2012.43.1.73.

Kelly, J. (2006). An overview of conflict. *Dimensions of Critical Care Nursing, 25*(1), 22–28.

Kim, W., Nicotera, A., & McNulty, J. (2015). Nurse's perceptions of conflict as constructive or destructive. *Journal of Advanced Nursing, 71*(9), 2073–2083. http://dx.doi.org/10.1111/jan.12672.

Lerner, H. (1997). *The dance of anger: A woman's guide to changing the patterns of intimate relationships.* New York: Harper & Row.

Libbus, M. K., & Bowman, K. G. (1994). Sexual harassment of female registered nurses in hospitals. *Journal of Nursing Administration, 24*(6), 26–31.

Roth, J., & Coleman, C. (2008). Perceived and real barriers for men entering nursing: Implications for gender diversity. *Journal of Cultural Diversity, 15*(3), 148–152.

Tavris, C. (1984). Feeling angry? Letting off steam may not help. *Nurse Life, 4*(5), 59–61.

Valente, S. M., & Bullough, V. (2004). Sexual harassment of nurses in the workplace. *Journal of Nursing Care Quality, 19*(3), 234–241.

Weiss, L., & Cain, L. (1991). *Power lines: What to say in problem situations.* Dallas: Taylor.

Delegation in the Clinical Setting

Ruth I. Hansten, RN, BSN, MBA, PhD, FACHE®

ⓔ http://evolve.elsevier.com/Zerwekh/nsgtoday.com/.

Let whoever is in charge keep this simple question in her head (NOT how can I always do the right thing myself but) how can I provide for this right thing always to be done?
Florence Nightingale

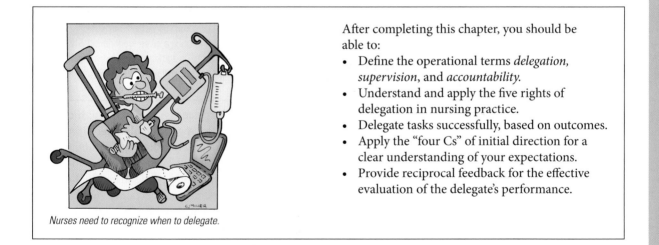

Nurses need to recognize when to delegate.

After completing this chapter, you should be able to:

- Define the operational terms *delegation, supervision*, and *accountability*.
- Understand and apply the five rights of delegation in nursing practice.
- Delegate tasks successfully, based on outcomes.
- Apply the "four Cs" of initial direction for a clear understanding of your expectations.
- Provide reciprocal feedback for the effective evaluation of the delegate's performance.

Expert teamwork can make (or break) patient results and our own job satisfaction. As you review the multitude of health care team members you work with, how do you determine the best use of the resources they have to offer? What is your role as the registered nurse (RN) on the team in terms of making these decisions? Your ability to delegate effectively the tasks that need to be done, based on desired outcomes, will go a long way in determining the success of the efforts of your work. As nursing leads the way to better health care across the continuum, RNs will supervise additional innovative roles of care team members as we strive to provide leadership toward cost-effective quality care for better population health (Future of Nursing™ Campaign for Action, 2015).

WHAT DOES DELEGATION MEAN?

State boards of nursing and professional associations, such as the American Nurses Association (ANA) and the National Council of State Boards of Nursing (NCSBN), have clarified definitions of the terms related to clinical leadership. Clinical delegation has been with us since the dawn of nursing, but teamwork has taken on new meaning, as many types of assistive personnel have been added to our care delivery models (Kalisch & Schoville, 2012). Current evidence points to the conclusion that inappropriate care assignments, delegation, and supervision may be leading to missed care and untoward clinical outcomes (Bittner & Gravlin, 2009; Kalisch et al., 2009; Gravlin & Bittner, 2010; Kalisch et al., 2011; Bittner et al., 2011; Hansten 2014a). Researchers reviewing failures to rescue (FTR), a situation in which patients are deteriorating but the symptoms are not noted before death, indicate that vital signs, neurological status, and urine output changes may occur up to 3 days before the final events. The RN's choice of nursing assistants, how carefully they are supervised, and how well the RN interprets patient data provided by assistive personnel, may be either life threatening or lifesaving to patients (Bobay et al., 2008). Let us define delegation and accountability to minimize RNs' confusion about their roles.

> **Delegation:** "... the process for a nurse to direct another person to perform nursing tasks and activities. National Council of State Boards of Nursing (NCSBN) describes this as the nurse transferring authority while ANA calls this a transfer of responsibility. Both mean that a registered nurse (RN) can direct another individual to do something that that person would not normally be allowed to do. Both papers stress that the nurse retains accountability for the delegation" (NCSBN, 2005, p. 1).
>
> **Assignments:** "... the distribution of work that each staff member is responsible for during a given work period. The NCSBN uses the verb 'assign' to describe those situations when a nurse directs an individual to do something the individual is already authorized to do, e.g., when an RN directs another RN to assess a patient, the RN is already authorized to assess patients in the RN scope of practice" (NCSBN, 2005, p. 1).

As you can see, these are generic definitions, used as standards across the country; most states have incorporated similar definitions into their nurse practice acts. A good deal of decision making is left to you as the RN and is also guided by your state's nursing practice act. You will be selecting the task and the situation in which to delegate or assign work. You will make a decision to delegate based on your assessment of the desired outcome and the competency of the individual delegate. These clinical decisions require complex critical thinking skills and are certainly more involved than a simple process for time management! In the pages ahead, we discuss steps that use the "five rights" that will assist you in this practice, making it easier for you to maximize safely the work of your team.

> **Supervision:** "... the provision of guidance or direction, oversight, evaluation and follow-up by the licensed nurse for accomplishment of a delegated nursing task by assistive personnel" (NCSBN, 2005, p. 1).

Nurses are often confused regarding supervision. This responsibility does not belong to only the one with the title of *manager* or *house supervisor*; rather, the expectation by law is that any time you delegate a task to someone else, you will be held accountable for the initial direction you give and the timely follow-up (periodic inspection) to evaluate the performance of the task.

The Delegation Process

In order to determine when an RN should delegate the ANA, the NCSBN, and your own state's nursing practice acts offer decision-making support. See Fig. 14.1 for the Decision Tree for Delegation by Registered Nurses to Unlicensed Assistive Personnel (ANA, 2012).

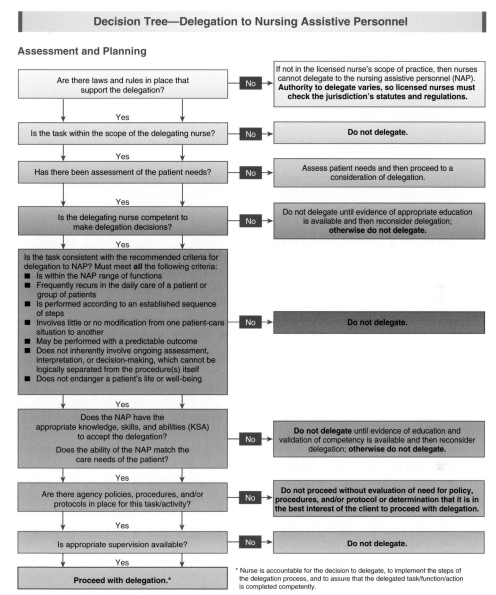

FIG. 14.1 Decision Tree for Delegation by Registered Nurses. American Nurses Association 2012. ANA's Principles for Delegation by Registered Nurses to Unlicensed Assistive Personnel (UAP). http://www.nursingworld.org/MainMenuCategories/ThePracticeofProfessionalNursing/NursingStandards/ANAPrinciples/PrinciplesofDelegation.pdf, p. 12.

After it is determined the RN is able to delegate through **assessment and planning**, then the RN must **communicate**. Initial direction and ongoing discussion must be a two-way process involving the nurse who assesses the nursing assistive personnel's understanding of the delegated task and the nursing assistive person who asks questions regarding the delegation and seeks clarification of expectations if needed.

Surveillance and supervision are ongoing through the episode of care. The purpose of surveillance and monitoring is related to the nurse's responsibility for patient care within the context of a patient population. The nurse supervises the delegation by monitoring the performance of the task or function and assures compliance with standards of practice, policies, and procedures. Frequency, level, and nature of monitoring vary with the needs of the patient and the experience of the assistant.

Evaluation and feedback can be the forgotten steps in delegation and should include a determination of whether the delegation was successful and a discussion of parameters to determine the effectiveness of the delegation (ANA & NCSBN, 2006, pp. 7–9).

> Delegation and supervision are integrated processes: After you delegate, you must supervise.

WHO IS ACCOUNTABLE HERE?

One of the biggest questions concerning teamwork and delegation is the issue of personal accountability. The definition of delegation already notes that the nurse is accountable for the total nursing care of the individuals. What does this really mean?

> **Accountability:** "Being answerable for what one has done, and standing behind that decision and/or action" (Hansten & Jackson, 2009, p. 79).
>
> **Accountability:** "Being responsible and answerable for actions or inactions of self or others in the context of delegation" (NCSBN, 1995, p. 1).

Some nurses equate accountability with "I am the one to blame." With that kind of attitude, no wonder there is reluctance to delegate! What is the point of delegating if someone else is going to make a mistake and you are going to take the blame? Let's not forget that accountability also means taking the credit for the positive results we achieve through the actions and decisions we make, as well as our freedom to act because of our licensure. Our individual choice to take actions (personal accountability) is based on our professional knowledge and judgment, unleashing the art and science of nursing as applied to real-time individual patient and family situations using the gifts and skills of team members each day (Samuel, 2006). An important reminder about accountability before you take the weight of the world on your shoulders is:

> "The delegate is accountable for accepting the delegation and for his/her own actions in carrying out the task" (NCSBN, 1995, p. 3).

It is important to focus on what you are accountable for in this process and to let the delegate also assume his or her own level of accountability. Remember, you are accountable for the following:

- Making the decision to delegate in the first place.
- Assessing the patient's needs.
- Planning the desired outcome.
- Assessing the competency of the delegate.
- Giving clear directions and obtaining acceptance from the delegate.
- Following up on the completion of the task and providing feedback to the delegate.

What if the delegate makes a mistake in completing the task? For what are you accountable? Let us consider the following example:

> It is 7 AM on your busy medical-surgical unit. You scan your assignment quickly, reviewing the high points with your nursing assistant before going into report. With trays coming at 7:30, you remind your assistant that your patient in Room 210 will be going to surgery this morning and is to have nothing to eat or drink. Coming out of report, you make brief rounds, only to find that (you guessed it!) your patient in Room 210 is happily drinking her morning coffee and eating a bagel.
> - What are you accountable for?
> - Did you delegate correctly?
> - What do you do now?

Based on a review of the previous guidelines, we can say that you did indeed delegate appropriately. Your communication may or may not have been as complete as it needed to be (more about that later). You are accountable for correcting the clinical effects of this error: Did the patient eat or drink too much, requiring the delay or cancellation of surgery? If so, you will call the operating room and make the appropriate adjustments in this patient's care based on the decision regarding her surgery time. What about the nursing assistant? You are also accountable for following up with her regarding her performance, providing appropriate feedback so that she understands her level of personal accountability as well. For more on the *how-to*s, read on as we discuss the Five Rights of Delegation.

> **The Five Rights of Delegation**
> 1. The right task
> 2. Under the right circumstances
> 3. To the right person
> 4. With the right directions and communication; and
> 5. Under the right supervision and evaluation (NCSBN, 2005, p. 2).

THE RIGHT TASK

The first part of any decision regarding delegation is the determination of what needs to be done and then the assessment of whether this is a task that can be delegated to someone else. However, personal barriers in the nurse can prevent letting go of tasks. Some suffer from "supernurse syndrome" and believe that no task should be delegated, because no one can do it better, faster, or easier than they can (Fig. 14.2). Others labor under the idea that never delegating tasks or data gathering will somehow ensure patient safety and believe their martyrdom (and overtime) is respected by their peers. Others fear offering direction and feedback and want assistive personnel to "just do their jobs" without any input from the RN, without understanding fully the RN's and team member's accountability for the tasks being performed. These issues, along with role confusion, may create care omissions (Hansten, 2014a, pp. 70–72). In their alarming report, *To Err Is Human*, the Institute of Medicine (IOM) provided statistical data on the frequency of medical errors and sentinel events occurring within the health care system. The IOM (2000) reported between 44,000 and 98,000 sentinel events as preventable adverse events. Although some patient safety progress has occurred, subsequent studies have estimated 30% of health care spending was wasted on inefficiencies and suboptimal care quality and that 75,000 deaths could have been avoided (Institute of Medicine of the National Academies, 2013).

In comparison, other nurses may be all too eager to delegate the least desirable tasks to someone else. A word of caution is necessary here: If we focus only on making task lists for people to do, we eliminate the very core of our purpose. Remember, your role as the RN on the team involves

FIG. 14.2 Many nurses suffer from "supernurse syndrome."

the coordination and planning of care, with your primary focus on identifying, with the patient and the physician, the desired outcomes for your patients. Once determined, interventions will be readily apparent, and the decision regarding possible delegation of these tasks must be made.

Reflection: Do I personally tend toward being a "supernurse" or "supermartyr" wanting to do everything myself, because I won't let go of nursing tasks? Or do I tend to be a "dumper" who would rather let the assistive personnel do all messy or difficult tasks? Or do I tend to be afraid to give direction and correct others for fear of not being "liked"? What kind of feedback could I ask for that would help me monitor my tendencies and improve my leadership?

WHAT CAN I DELEGATE?

Fortunately, there are several reference sources to assist you in making this determination. The first place we recommend looking is in the nurse practice act for your state. Each state board of nursing has a nursing practice act that guides nursing decisions about what to delegate to nursing assistive personnel. Be sure you become familiar with your state's nursing practice statute, regulations, rules, policies, and advisory opinions.

Considering this, a professional registered nurse CAN DELEGATE:
- Discrete tasks or data retrieval based on patient condition and planned outcome.
- Tasks that the delegate is competent to do and is allowed to do according to your state regulations and organizational job descriptions and skills checklists.
- Tasks that the competent delegate has also agreed to do and understands preferred outcome, parameters, and how and when to report to the delegating RN.

At this point, the majority of state boards have addressed the issue of delegation or assignment and have developed rules that may offer information regarding who can do what. The scope of practice for each care-provider level usually includes a description of the processes that may be performed at that level. In an attempt to clarify the role of the licensed practical nurse (LPN), the National Council of State Boards of Nursing constructed the Practical Nurse Scope of Practice White Paper (NCSBN, 2005), calling for nursing education programs, regulatory agencies, and practice settings to educate nursing professionals about the differences in LPN and RN roles and to articulate clearly the LPN and RN scope of practice regulations. Traditionally, clinical experiences have provided students an opportunity to observe how registered nurses communicate and delegate tasks to LPNs. However, clinical site availability in settings where LPNs are employed has dramatically decreased, preventing the students from observing the delegation of tasks by the registered nurse to the LPN (Garneau, 2012). Therefore, decreased clinical site experiences, coupled with unfamiliarity regarding the scope of practice regulations for the LPN, have also contributed to ineffective delegation (Mole & McLafferty, 2004; NCSBN, 2006).

> If you work with licensed practical nurses (LPNs) or licensed vocational nurses (LVNs), please consult your specific state's rules and regulations along with your organization's job descriptions. LPN practice varies from state to state.

A key distinction between RNs and LPNs is related to the first step of the nursing process: assessment. The LPN collects data during the health history and physical examination, whereas the RN conducts a comprehensive physical assessment and develops a plan of care for the patient based on assessment findings. Moreover, the RN initiates and provides patient teaching and discharge planning, as well as evaluates the patient's response to the plan of care and his or her understanding of the information provided (NCSBN, 2016a). The LPN contributes to the development and/or updates the plan of care and reinforces patient teaching and discharge instructions (NCSBN, 2014). In the midst of health care payment reform and attempts to connect all parts of the care continuum for the provision of better health care for entire populations, state practice rules for care providers may be changing quickly. For example, more states have recently promulgated rules related to certified medication aides in long-term care or community settings. These aides are certified nursing assistants who may, with additional training and certification, administer some routine medications, functioning under the supervision of an RN (or possibly LPN, depending on the state). In addition, community health care lay assistants are often deployed out of medical homes (ambulatory care clinics) or public health departments. These workers, following procedural rules, may function as case finders or perform such tasks as vital signs or home checks in the community. An RN or a physician supervises these community health aides. Medical assistants (MAs) in ambulatory clinics are not always specifically addressed by state practice regulations and have functioned under the direct supervision of physicians in their offices, but presently their roles are being regulated in some states. Creative roles will emerge in the future as states and municipalities attempt to find better, more cost-effective ways to deliver care. RNs should remain tuned in to their state's health division's regulatory changes as new roles and responsibilities emerge. Whatever roles appear, RNs remain accountable for the nursing care of their patients, even though those they supervise actually may complete tasks. One of the causes of disciplinary action that is listed in many nurse practice codes under "professional misconduct" is "delegating to an unlicensed person activities that can only be performed by licensed professionals" or "failure to adequately supervise or monitor those to whom care has been delegated" (Brous, 2012, p. 55).

The next place to look is in your organization, obtaining a copy of the job description, nursing responsibilities, and the skills checklist for each care provider. This will give you a very specific list of tasks from which to work, but remember, there are other considerations. Simply because the skills checklist includes ambulation of patients, it may not be advisable to delegate the first ambulation of a postoperative total hip replacement patient to the new patient care assistant (Critical Thinking Box 14.1).

If you have questions and need clarification for your state, go online to your board of nursing to consult statutes, rules, regulations, and advisory opinions or call your nursing regulatory body for assistance. (See www.ncsbn.org for links to your state's nursing regulatory commission.) Be aware that your

❓ CRITICAL THINKING BOX 14.1

In Your Organization, Could You Delegate the Following Tasks?

	YES	NO
Bladder retention catheter insertion	☐	☐
Taking vital signs	☐	☐
Feeding a patient	☐	☐
Hygienic care	☐	☐
Medication administration	☐	☐
Discontinuing an intravenous line	☐	☐
Teaching insulin administration	☐	☐

state may have introduced or passed a bill that may affect your practice in relation to residents of neighboring states. As of July 2015, 25 states had passed legislation approving interstate compact licensure regulation legislation designed to allow nurses to practice across state lines because of e-consultation, telenursing, or other technology that would broadcast nursing practice across state borders, and 7 more states had pending legislation (NCSBN, 2016b).

Beyond the law, your employer will have job descriptions and skills checklists that may clearly define the role of the caregiver. If you have not seen these documents, be sure to review them soon. This is the baseline for determining "who does what" and selecting the right task to delegate. As many organizations develop creative assistant roles to leverage the professional judgment of registered nursing personnel, the scope of practice of each role is defined first by law. If the organization extends the role of a patient care technician to include preoperative teaching, you want to be aware that this is clearly an RN function and by law is not allowed to be delegated to the technician.

> A job description or policy should never override the legal limits of the scope of practice.

Is There Anything I Cannot Delegate?

Again, your first resource is the law. Many states are very specific in their descriptions of what duty cannot be delegated and belongs only to the RN's scope of practice. The NCSBN reminds us that:

Nursing is a knowledge-based process discipline and cannot be reduced solely to a list of tasks. The licensed nurse's specialized education, professional judgment, and discretion are essential for quality nursing care.... While nursing tasks may be delegated, the licensed nurse's generalist knowledge of client care indicates that the practice-pervasive functions of assessment, evaluation, and nursing judgment must not be delegated (NCSBN, 1995, p. 2).

According to nurse-attorney Joanne P. Sheehan, nurses cannot delegate the following:
- Assessments that identify needs and problems and diagnose human responses
- Any aspect of planning, including the development of comprehensive approaches to the total care plan
- Any provision of health counseling, teaching, or referrals to other health care providers
- Therapeutic nursing techniques and comprehensive care planning (Sheehan, 2001, p. 22) (Critical Thinking Box 14.2).

> **? CRITICAL THINKING BOX 14.2**
>
> ### Where to Look for Determination of the Right Task
>
> State nurse practice act, rules, policies, advisory opinions
> Employee job description
> Skills checklist
> Demonstrated competency

With the right task selected according to state scope of practice, the policies in your agency, and your assessment of the situation, there is still work to be done.

> **DO NOT DELEGATE**
> - Professional nursing judgment
> - The RN nursing process: Data gathering and some tasks or interventions can be delegated (see Right Task) but the comprehensive assessment, nursing diagnosis, care planning, evaluation, and care coordination may not be delegated.
> - With patient education, there is some variance by state regulation, but patient education planning and comprehensive patient education are generally reserved for RNs.

THE RIGHT CIRCUMSTANCES

Next, "Right Circumstances—appropriate patient setting, available resources, and consideration of other relevant factors" (NCSBN, 1995, p. 2) suggests that the staffing mix, community needs, teaching obligations, and the type of patient receiving care should also be considered. Different rules for delegation may apply regarding what and how an RN must delegate in-home care, long-term care, or care in community homes for the developmentally disabled or group boarding homes for assisted living (Hansten et al., 1999; Hansten & Jackson, 2009).

Emergency departments may have different rules for delegation, such as in Montana's Advanced Delegation to UAPs with additional emergency training (Administrative Rules of Montana, 2006). Other settings such as correctional facilities, ambulatory care clinics, or assistive living long-term care may have state rules related to medication aides, medical assistants, or other technicians (Research for Best Practice Box 14.1).

How Can I Determine the Strengths and Weaknesses of Team Members?

Often motivated by the fear that a delegate may make a mistake in an assigned task, nurses focus on the potential weaknesses of their team members. As nurses, we are educated to anticipate the worst so that we can prevent accidents, adverse drug reactions, and negative impacts from disease processes and treatments alike. As prudent as this approach may be for the safety of all concerned, it is worthwhile to discuss the advantages of recognizing the strengths of the team members as well.

Recall the last time you were given specific, positive feedback about your performance during your clinical experience as a nursing student. How did you feel? Most of us are energized and restored by the reinforcement that our hard work has been recognized. Recognition of strengths will begin to get us on the right track in our relationship.

Assigning tasks on the basis of the strengths of the person will allow the patient to experience the very best care—and allow the delegate to provide the very best care. As a supervising RN, you are

🔍 RESEARCH FOR BEST PRACTICE BOX 14.1

Delegation and Supervision

Practice Issue

Changes in health care reimbursement and care delivery reforms would indicate that nurses are dreaming if they believe they will be able to practice effectively without proficient delegation skills. Nurses will need to exhibit expert leadership at the point of care so as to use our nation's human and material resources cost-effectively to improve the health of our communities. Compounding the fractures that can occur in teamwork when multiple individuals must communicate in a complex situation, early discharges, advances in technology, increased RN autonomy, better informed consumers, and expanded legal definitions of liability all increase the need to use the best delegation and supervision techniques (Croke, 2003).

A study geared to understand the critical thinking processes of nurses in delegation showed that nurses often expected assistive personnel to have a higher degree of knowledge and skill than they possessed or were licensed to perform, such as the nursing process, prioritizing, and assessment (Bittner & Gravlin, 2009; Hansten, 2014a). Nurses report difficulty with delegating because of the structure of care delivery, with multiple assistive personnel reporting to multiple RNs, and challenges in how to communicate what needs to be done as well as how to follow up without offending co-workers (Standing & Anthony, 2008). However, difficulties with delegating appropriately mean that there is missed care, leaving hospitalized patients in jeopardy because of the consequences of omissions, such as hospital-acquired pressure ulcers, infections, and errors, as well as failures to rescue deteriorating patients (Kalisch et al., 2009). Many insurers will not reimburse these hospital-acquired conditions and errors, and they cost the patient/family and health care organizations billions per year nationally (Virkstis et al., 2009).

Review of care issues involving cases in which the five rights of delegation and supervision were not followed showed that problems were related to RNs not providing the right direction or communication (13.9%) or supervision (12.4%). A total of 60.6% of deficiencies were related to the UAP not following through with a task that was delegated or not following unit/department procedures (Standing et al., 2001).

To help nurses learn how to work effectively within teams at their worksites, organizations have provided in-depth education in applying the principles of delegation at work, and they have combined the training with a consistent care delivery structure. At the end of 16 weeks of instructor-guided self-study, professional practice skills have improved up to 37%, and the use of supervision checkpoints by RNs with team members has doubled in frequency (Hansten, 2008a; Hansten, 2009; Hansten, 2014a, 2014b).

Implications for Nursing Practice

- There is a need for ongoing education for nurses regarding team leadership skills and unit practices that create care delivery models supporting nurses in delegating and supervising effectively in highly complex work (Hansten, 2005; Hansten & Jackson, 2009; Standing & Anthony, 2008; Hansten, 2009; Hansten, 2014a, 2014b).
- Each health care team must create a care delivery model that includes a clear plan for the day, proper times for initial direction and ongoing supervision, and updating of clinical and performance information (Hansten, 2008a, 2008b).
- Communication lapses have been a frequently reported root cause of sentinel events from 2013 to 2015 (2015a). The Joint Commission's (TJC) National Patient Safety Goals have included a need to develop a standardized approach to hand-off communication. Although many hospitals have interpreted the term hand-off to consist of the information shared between shifts and at patient transfer, the need for accurate ongoing updating of patient data during a team's shift or episode of care would also apply. TJC continues to incorporate improved patient/family and care provider communication in their standards (2015b).
- Missed care resulting from poor-quality delegation and supervision skills and unclear assignments can result in health care–acquired conditions that will no longer be paid for by insurers. These conditions cost the patients and their families more than dollars, including untoward pain and suffering. The reimbursement losses and costs from poor quality can provide the motivation to sink scarce funds into the development of delegation and teamwork skills (Bittner et al., 2011; Hansten, 2014b).

🔍 RESEARCH FOR BEST PRACTICE BOX 14.1—cont'd

Delegation and Supervision

Considering This Information

What education and orientation processes are in place in your organization to promote effective delegation and supervision? If these processes are not present now, how can you be involved in their development? What unit processes could be created that would help teams collaborate throughout the shift?

References

Alfaro-LeFevre, R. (in press, 2017). *Critical thinking, clinical reasoning, and clinical judgment: A practical approach* (6th ed.). St. Louis: Elsevier Saunders.

Bittner, N., & Gravlin, G: (2009). Critical thinking, delegation, and missed care in nursing practice. *Journal of Nursing Administration, 39*(3), 142–146.

Bittner, N., Gravlin, G., Hansten R., & Kalisch, B. (2011). Unraveling care omissions. *Journal of Nursing Administration, 41*(12), 510–512.

Croke, E. (2003). Nurses, negligence, and malpractice. *American Journal of Nursing, 103*(9), 9.

Hansten, R. (2005). Relationship and results oriented healthcare: Evaluate the basics. *Journal of Nursing Administration, 35*(12), 522–525.

Hansten, R. (2008a). *Relationship & results oriented healthcare planning & implementation manual*. Port Ludlow, WA: Hansten Healthcare PLLC.

Hansten, R. (2008b). Why nurses still must learn to delegate. *Nursing Leadership, 10,* 19–25.

Hansten, R. (2009). A bundle of best bedside practices. *Health Care Management, 28*(2), 111–116.

Hansten, R. (2014a). Coach as chief correlator of tasks to results through delegation skill and teamwork development, *Nurse Leader 12*(4), 69–73.

Hansten R. (2014b). *The master coach manual for the relationship & results oriented healthcare program*. Port Ludlow, WA: Hansten Healthcare PLLC.

Kalisch, B., Landstrom, G., & Williams, R. (2009). Missed care: Errors of omission. *Nursing Outlook, 57,* 3–9.

Kalisch, B. (2006). Missed nursing care. *Journal of Nursing Care Quality, 21*(4), 306–313.

Kalisch, B., & Begeny, S. (2005). Improving nursing unit teamwork. *Journal of Nursing Administration, 35*(12), 550–556.

Standing, T., & Anthony, M. (2008). Delegation: What it means to acute care nurses. *Applied Nursing Research, 21,* 8–14.

Standing T., Anthony M., & Hertz, J. (2001). Nurses' narratives of outcomes after delegation to unlicensed assistive personnel. *Outcomes Management for Nursing Practice, 5*(1), 18–23.

The Joint Commission. (2016). *2016 National Patient Safety Goals*. Retrieved from http://www.jointcommission.org/standards _information/npsgs.aspx.

The Joint Commission (2015a). *2015 Sentinel Event Data Summary*. Retrieved from http://www.jointcommission.org/sentinel _event.aspx.

The Joint Commission (2015b). *Hand-off Communications Targeted Solutions*. Retrieved from http://www.centerfortransforming healthcare.org/projects/detail.aspx?Project=1

Virkstis, N. D., Westheim, J., & Boston-Fleischhauer, C. (2009). Safeguarding quality: Building the business case to prevent nursing-sensitive hospital-acquired conditions. *Journal of Nursing Administration, 39*(7–8), 350–355.

in a new position with respect to the long-term performance of delegates. If assistive personnel are assigned only those tasks in which they perform well, they may not grow in their abilities and skills. This mistake is exemplified by a hospital that had created a new multiskilled patient care assistant (PCA) role with certified nursing assistants (CNAs). These CNAs had been trained to do phlebotomies as well, as authorized by the state board. Phlebotomists had been eliminated but were given the option of training for the new PCA role. When all of the PCAs worked together, those who had been phlebotomists, because they were more comfortable with that skill, drew the lab tests. When all the PCAs who were former phlebotomists were off on vacation and maternity leave, none of the other PCAs had become proficient at this skill. Recognize strengths, and encourage the best patient care possible by using them, but also challenge delegates to grow.

Asking the right questions before delegating can often prevent dreaded performance gaps. Nurses can be reluctant to ask float personnel or agency replacement staff whether they feel comfortable in completing the assignment they have received. Float and temporary personnel tell us that they would prefer being asked about their competency at the beginning of a shift or assignment, with the offer of help and clarification, rather than having to locate an RN later to request information. The American Nurses Association (ANA) Code of Ethics states, "The nurse is responsible and accountable for individual nursing practice and determines the appropriate delegation of tasks consistent with the nurse's obligation to provide optimum patient care" (ANA, 2015). Be assured that although it is the responsibility of the RN to assess the competency of those they supervise, the delegate must be "accountable for accepting the delegation and for his/her own actions in carrying out the task" (NCSBN, 1995, p. 1). The RN who is familiar with the situation, however, must ask the correct questions to determine whether the person is competent.

For example, if an RN were planning to ask a nursing assistant to feed a baby who has respiratory difficulties, based on the team's plan that the baby would be able to ingest 12 ounces of formula this shift, what questions might the RN ask to determine the potential strengths and weaknesses? If the individual has not had experience in this procedure, how could the nurse ensure future competency? In this situation, an RN would certainly ask questions about past experiences with feeding babies who had difficulty swallowing. If the delegate assures the RN that she or he is competent, the RN may go further in asking what the CNA would do if coughing or choking occurred. Depending on the situation, the RN would probably want to demonstrate feeding techniques and observe the skills to ensure the competency of the delegate.

What Are the Causes of Performance Weaknesses?

Let us look at an example of a performance weakness and try to determine what the potential causes may be.

In this scenario, you are an RN working a night shift on a hematology-oncology unit, and an agency nursing assistant, Pam, comes to work with you this shift. Pam is excited about the possibilities of interviewing for a regular night-shift position and would love to work extra on holidays and weekends. As you begin to discuss her assignment for the night, she states, "Oh, I forgot to tell you, I do not ever care for bloodborne pathogen positive patients! Ever!"

There are some potential costs and benefits to your response to this statement. As the nurse, you could ignore this statement and continue with your work. You may decide this person has problems, and you may elect to deny her request for an interview. Or, you may determine there is something behind her refusal. How you respond may cost you a potentially valuable staff member and could upset the other members of your staff and the patients. Avoiding the problem or accommodating her refusal could become a terrible headache when making assignments and would be contrary to the mission of your organization.

Experience has shown that there are several potential causes of performance inadequacies (Critical Thinking Box 14.3). One of the most common causes is that employees are not aware of what is expected of them. Does Pam know that it is part of your policy at this facility for everyone to take care of all patients, whether or not they are known to be HIV- or hepatitis C–positive?

> **? CRITICAL THINKING BOX 14.3**
>
> *Potential Sources of Performance Weakness*
>
> - Unclear expectations
> - Lack of performance feedback
> - Educational needs
> - Need for additional supervision and direction
> - Individual characteristics: past experiences, motivational or personal issues

Perhaps being aware of this expectation would assist Pam in making her decision about whether to apply for work on this unit.

Often, being clear about expectations is not enough. All of us have some blind spots in our own performance. Perhaps we think we are doing just fine, meeting performance competencies and beyond, but colleagues have noted that we are not performing procedures according to policy. So another common cause of performance difficulties is that others have not shared their perceptions of our performance with us. If these observations are not shared, we will blithely believe we are doing great. Pam may have adopted this attitude regarding bloodborne pathogen patients in other work settings, but because of the desperation for her help, no one had shared the fact that this behavior falls short of competencies in her job description.

Another common origin of performance weakness is an educational need. Does Pam need more education about how bloodborne infection is transmitted and how it is prevented? Surely, she had to complete some infection control content in her CNA certification course, but it seems she did not internalize this content. Or is there a personal problem? She may have just witnessed the death of a loved one from hepatitis or AIDS and feels unable to cope with seeing others with this disease at this time.

The amount of supervision needed can be another source of performance problems. As an RN, you must determine the degree of "periodic inspection" needed for the delegate. Some people require additional direction but are still able to do the job competently. In the absence of that direction, they will be unable to create positive patient outcomes. Nurses tell us they wish that the assistive personnel on their staff would be self-directed and take initiative without being told. We question whether an RN's hope that all will do their jobs without interaction or supervision on his or her part fits with the definition of supervision! Again, as leader, the RN must determine how much supervision is needed for the individual delegate, just as we determine the degree of observation needed for each patient based on our assessment of the patient's needs. In Pam's case, her reluctance to work with bloodborne pathogen patients may have nothing to do with supervision but may reflect a need for guidance, education, or a frank discussion of expectations.

As the RN who is supervising Pam, what steps would you take to determine the cause of her performance weakness—her assertion that she refuses to care for particular patients? What questions would you ask? How would you respond so that you could continue to use Pam's services during this shift, maintain the integrity of your mission, and preserve the potential for hiring a new employee?

Matching the right person with the right task is the third step in the circular process of delegation. This process includes planning and articulating priority patient outcomes, assessing the competency of the delegate to perform the task, determining the potential strengths and weaknesses of the assistive personnel, and planning how much supervision is needed. To ensure that the right person will perform the right task, additional clarification of expectations, performance feedback, and planning for educational needs may be necessary; these steps will promote the long-term success of the team.

THE RIGHT PERSON

After you have determined that a task can be delegated, matching the task to the right person involves the definition of delegation once again. Nurses must select the right task for a competent person in a *selected* situation. We have already discussed how you would determine the correct task. But how do we select the right person in the right situation (Fig. 14.3)?

PT Needs
218 New IV
219 ROM
220 Teaching
211 Needs Reassurance

CJMILLER

FIG. 14.3 It can be difficult to know who is the best person to handle a given situation.

How Can I Use Outcomes in Delegating?

In planning for the right person to handle a task, focusing on outcomes is essential (Critical Thinking Box 14.4). Alfaro-LeFevre's (2017) evidence-based critical thinking indicators are outcome-focused guides appropriate for delegation as well as critical thinking in nursing (p. 12).

> **? CRITICAL THINKING BOX 14.4**
>
> **Talking About Outcomes: What's in It for Me?**
>
> - Provides a method to decide appropriate assignments: who should be doing what task?
> - Gives you a sense of purpose for the shift (short-term and long-term)
> - Enhances your ability to motivate co-workers along a track to achieve the outcomes
> - Clarifies your role as leader of the team
> - Verifies and clarifies patient/family expectations when outcomes are discussed and planned with them
> - Promotes job satisfaction and collaboration for the whole team

For example, two patients are admitted to a hospital. Each individual will need hygienic care today (task), but who will give the baths is related to the outcome you are trying to achieve. For Mr. Peterson, who has been homeless and is in dire need of a bath so that you can perform a complete and accurate skin assessment, the priority outcome you and your patient desire is that Mr. Peterson will be clean. With Ms. Ibutu, who is a paraplegic, today is the day that her caregivers and she will demonstrate how they will assess her skin for areas of breakdown and how to perform range of motion to her lower extremities. The RN's decision about who will do which task is dependent on the plan of care and the goals that the team has established in the discussion with the patient or family (Table 14.1).

This same logic applies when you have heard in report that a patient, Mr. Handelsky, is unstable. In your current care delivery system on your unit, the licensed practical (or vocational) nurse (LPN or LVN) may handle the initial gathering of vital sign data in your postoperative intensive care unit (ICU). Suppose, for example, that the report you received stated that there had been increasing cherry-red drainage in the chest tube and that the patient's cardiac monitor showed supraventricular tachycardia, with increasing respiratory rate. Based on the outcome for the shift, Mr. Handelsky will maintain cardiorespiratory homeostasis and continue on a critical path for the first day post thoracotomy. Using your insight that his condition may be deteriorating, you may make a different decision regarding who will be there for initial patient contact. If the assistant working with you today is an experienced team member, you may choose to send him or her in to see the patient immediately while you check on another critical patient. Or if the assistant is a "float" from an agency, known to you only by initial questioning, you may immediately make a visit to see Mr. Handelsky and begin to set up the plan for the data gathering and schedule for reporting that you will expect from your assistant. This would be a very different process if the outcome you wanted to achieve was pain relief and comfort for a terminal patient.

If you are working in an ambulatory care clinic or doctor's office setting, consider a situation in which you would use outcomes to change your delegation decision. Normally the MA may gather information and vital signs for all patients, obtaining their chief reason for coming in for their appointment today. However, the community health care worker told you that she had encouraged an anxious young teen to come in to obtain accurate pregnancy and STD testing. You are aware that this teen may bolt at the slightest provocation. You tell the MA that you would like to be notified immediately when the patient arrives after school and that you will meet with her first to establish a trusting relationship. Intended outcomes would be to obtain definitive tests and to create a plan for carefully relaying the news. Longer term results would be that the patient would learn about safe sex practices. Your normal daily routines would be altered because of the patient's needs and would require the RN's interventions, teaching, and relationship-building rather than business as usual.

TABLE 14.1   USING OUTCOMES IN DELEGATING

PATIENT	OUTCOME	TASK/PROCESS	WHO WILL PERFORM IT?
Mr. Peterson	Patient will be clean.	Bath	Nursing assistant or other care associate
Ms. Ibutu	Patient and caregivers will know how to perform skin assessment and range of motion.	Bath with education regarding home care	RN: teaching plan; OT, PT, or rehabilitation aide may also assist
Mr. Handelsky	Patient will maintain cardiorespiratory homeostasis and continue on care path day 1.	Initial baseline vital signs and assessment, close monitoring	RN: assessment and interpretation of data LPN: data-gathering and reporting
	Patient will be free of pain and comfortable for this shift. Long-term outcome: pain-free death.	Pain assessment and treatment, comfort measures (repositioning, skin care)	RN: initial plan for comfort measures and pain assessment Assistant: comfort measures, report of progress

LPN, Licensed practical nurse; *OT*, occupational therapist; *PT*, physical therapist; *RN*, registered nurse.

Take a moment to consider the outcomes for a particularly difficult patient you have been dealing with lately. Were you clear on outcomes? If so, have you shared them with colleagues? Focusing on outcomes takes time, but remember, "If you fail to plan, you plan to fail." Why should an RN focus on outcomes? Discussion of goals not only establishes who should be doing what task but also allows RNs to motivate others. How many of us jump on a train if we do not know where it is going? A purpose and a destination allow all team members to function more effectively. When assistive personnel are given the same assignment daily, without variation, without any understanding of why they are doing what they are doing, it is similar to being an assembly line worker putting widgets in a machine. Satisfaction and motivation of co-workers generally come from the feeling that they are making a difference in the lives of their patients.

In a similar manner, you as the leader of the team would feel much better at the end of your shift or assignment if you could feel comfortable with the outcomes you have assisted the patient in achieving. You could actually verify the patient/family's priorities and plan with the patients, much as you were always told to do by the teachers in your nursing program! Streamlining the care to match the patient's expectations saves much time (Hansten, 2009).

Again, the RN is accountable for the patient, for determining the situation in which delegation will be used, and for the selection of the right person to do the right task, in addition to the periodic inspection and follow-up of those they supervise. The right communication will begin that clarification process, bringing us to the next step in the five rights of delegation.

THE RIGHT DIRECTION AND COMMUNICATION

How Can I Get the Delegate to Understand What I Want?

No matter what, it always comes back to communication. How clear you make your initial direction will be the cornerstone in determining the success of your delegated task and, ultimately, the performance of your team. The bottom line, which is whether the patient outcome was achieved, hinges on your ability to provide initial direction that clearly defines your expectations of the delegate in performing the assigned task. It is not surprising that this is a step that is often done poorly or left out entirely, because the assumption is made that the individual "knows what the job is and should just do it."

The first component of supervision, according to its definition, is the provision of initial direction. Achieving a balance in which we provide enough information for the person to understand the request without overstating the case and risking confusion or condescension requires that we tread a fine line. The use of the "four Cs" of initial direction will help you to plan your communication (Critical Thinking Box 14.5). Many hospitals are now performing shift reports or handovers at the bedside, engaging the patients in the discussion of their priorities, the plan for care, and what each person will do for them during the shift (Hansten, 2008a).

? CRITICAL THINKING BOX 14.5

The Four Cs of Initial Direction

CLEAR: Does the team member understand what I am saying?
CONCISE: Have I confused the direction by giving too much unnecessary information?
CORRECT: Is the direction according to policy, procedure, job description, and the law?
COMPLETE: Does the delegate have all the information necessary to complete the task?

Data from Hansten, R., & Jackson, M. (2014). *Clinical delegation skills: A handbook for professional practice,* (4th ed.). Sudbury, MA: Jones & Bartlett, pp. 287–288; LaCharity, L., Kumagai, C., & Bartz, B. (2014). *Prioritization, delegation, assignment,* (3rd ed.). St. Louis: Mosby Elsevier, p. 6.

Let us assume that you are working in a home health agency and you are planning the care for a patient with heart failure (HF). You have made your initial visit, assessing the patient and planning the outcomes that you and the team will work toward in the next 3 weeks. Your patient is taking diuretics, antihypertensives, heart medications, and potassium supplements, in addition to being on a restricted diet. She is frequently short of breath and requires an assistant three times per week for hygienic care. In addition to providing hygienic care, you would like that assistant to monitor the blood pressure and check the patient's weight on the days you are not making a visit and to notify you if the blood pressure is outside of the range of 120 to 170 systolic and 50 to 90 diastolic or if there is any weight fluctuation. Using the four Cs listed, you can evaluate your communication.

Mrs. Jones has a heart condition and high blood pressure that requires medication and constant monitoring. One of our goals is to help Mrs. Jones have a stable blood pressure in a range that is normal for her. On the days that you are visiting and giving the patient her bath, I would also like you to take her blood pressure. If it is outside the range of 120 to 170 systolic and 50 to 90 diastolic, I would like you to let me know. We may need to adjust her medication, change her diet, and call her physician or the HF clinic for different orders. I would also like you to check her weight and let me know about any changes of more than 2 pounds from her home health admission weight of 185, so let me know if she weighs 187 or more. This will help us determine if she is retaining fluid.

Clear: Does the home health aide understand what is being asked of her? This direction is fairly straightforward—an easily understood instruction of taking the blood pressure. Is it clear that the aide is to determine and report the patient's weight?

Concise: Have you confused the assistant by giving too much information? Or is it enough information for her to complete the task? Only the assistant can help you with this determination. You will need to ask directly, "Am I confusing you?" or "Do you have enough information to do the job?" Every individual has different needs. However, you will want to make certain to check this out; some people will not be honest or accurate in their assessments of their understanding or abilities, leading to trouble later. Many of us are reluctant to ask questions, being afraid to admit our need for additional information. (We do not want to look like we do not know what we are doing!) This reluctance can ultimately result in harm to the patient, because assumptions are made that the direction was understood when, in fact, it was not.

Correct: Is a home health aide able and allowed to monitor blood pressures? Where would you look for additional information if you were not sure? Is the location of the scale identified? Does the time of day of the visit make any difference?

Complete: Does the assistant have enough information to fulfill your expectations? Once again, you will need to ask the delegate for clarification of his or her understanding of what you are asking. If you also expect this assistant to note the respirations and alert you to increased effort of breathing, have you shared that in your initial direction? Or did you assume she would naturally observe all vital signs because you alerted her to the patient's condition (and besides, she is a good assistant)? In our attempts not to appear condescending (I do not want to insult this assistant by reminding her to note the respirations—she might think I do not trust her to think!), we may often choose not to be as complete as we should be in communicating initial direction. What about lost weight? Is that significant to report?

Another common pitfall is the rationale that comes from working with someone over a period of time. A working relationship develops, and a routine or pattern of performance is established. When this happens, we start talking less and less to the other individual, believing that "she knows what I expect her to do." Consider the following situation:

You are working on a surgical unit in a partnership with Sam, an LPN you have been working with for the past year. Your easygoing style has led to a comfortable reliance on each other and the feeling that each knows what the other expects. On this particular evening shift, you are traveling down the hall, intent on administering medication to one of your patients. You also know a patient from the post anesthesia care unit (PACU) will soon be coming back from surgery. Seeing Sam coming your way, you state, "Sam, the postop is coming back in Room 103." Evaluate your initial direction.

Did you believe that Sam just knew that you wanted him to check on the patient, get the first set of vital signs, position the patient, check the dressing and the drains, note the status of the IV, degree of pain, and report the patient's status to you as soon as possible, until you can see the patient yourself?

Fifteen minutes later, you see Sam at the portable computer in the hallway. You ask him, "Sam, is the new postop patient in Room 103 here?" Expecting a brief report, you are surprised when Sam says, "I don't know. Is he here? I thought you were going to assess him when he got here." What went wrong?

No matter how long you have been working with someone, the right communication is essential to ensure the success of teamwork. Sam did not accept the delegated task because he did not understand what you meant. Be sure that you check the delegate's understanding of what you are saying. Failing to do this may result in unmet expectations, which lead to anger and frustration. More important, the patient will not receive the optimal care that both you and the delegate want to provide. In this case, a new postoperative patient was not fully assessed during a critical period.

You have carefully assessed the patient, determined your plan on the basis of outcomes, and selected the **right task** to delegate to the right person. You have even provided clear initial direction as part of the **right communication**. The final **right of delegation** is also a part of supervision: the periodic inspection of the actual act.

THE RIGHT SUPERVISION AND EVALUATION

How Can I Give and Receive Feedback Effectively?

Many nurses have shared their discomfort with giving and receiving feedback from co-workers. Few of us enjoy hearing about how we may have missed the mark; however, when you are supervising others, it is absolutely necessary to share feedback during your "periodic inspection." By following a formula for giving and receiving feedback and practicing it daily, RNs are assisted in the difficult job of correcting the performance of others. The reciprocal feedback process also permits you, as supervising RN, to hear how your own supervisory performance and communication affected the outcomes of the team (Critical Thinking Box 14.6).

? CRITICAL THINKING BOX 14.6

Feedback Formula

- Ask for the other individual's input first!
- Give credit for effort.
- Share your perceptions with each other.
- Explore differing points of view, focusing on shared outcomes.
- Ask for the other individual's input to determine what steps may be necessary to make certain desired outcomes are achieved.
- Agree on a plan for the future, including timeline for follow-up.
- Revisit the plan and results achieved.

Modified from Hansten, R., & Jackson, M. (2009). *Clinical delegation skills: A handbook for nurses* (4th ed.). Sudbury, MA: Jones & Bartlett.

Let's look at how this process can be used in a situation in which positive feedback is intended.

An RN (Pat) is working with a float RN (Julia) for the first time. Julia is new in the pool but is an experienced nurse. Pat is so pleased with Julia's experience and performance that she has gone off to have a nice long break and lunch with an old friend from the third floor. She has also taken time to meet with a colleague from the evening shift regarding a unit problem. Unfortunately, she has not been present on the unit much today. When Pat is having lunch with her friend, she exclaims, "That new float Julia is just excellent! If it weren't for her, I couldn't be here having lunch with you. I hope that she knows how organized and valuable she is!" Her friend, Alex, states, "Well, you know you should tell her, not just me, about this." When Pat returns to the floor, flushed with good intentions of making Julia's day with effusive praise, she tells Julia about how lucky she has been to work with her today.

Because all of us crave positive feedback, and Julia is new to your organization, will Julia tell Pat that she's been trying to find Pat for hours? Probably not. But she *may* tell others, "Pat is one of those 'dump and run' nurses. I don't want to work on that floor again!" What if Pat asked *first*, "How have things been going for you today, Julia? I know this is your first day on the unit." Julia may have determined it was possible (and expected) to give reciprocal feedback: "I've been trying to find you! I have completed everything, but it hasn't been easy. Where have you been?" The best intentions can be destroyed by not asking the other individual for input first.

If you plan to give some negative feedback to an individual, you will also need to ask for her or his input first. For example:

You have just noted that the night shift CNA did not record the intakes and outputs (I&Os) on three patients on your telemetry unit. You have called him and are thinking about how to discuss this with him in a positive manner; yet you know that he is not going to want to chat, because it is about time for him to get some rest.

If you said, "Why didn't you record the I&Os in the electronic medical record (EMR)?!" the CNA would probably react defensively. If you state, "How was your night? I don't see the I&Os in the EMR, do you remember where they were recorded?," you have allowed the person to respond with what happened. If this CNA went home early with the flu, or the unit experienced three codes, or left the data somewhere else, it would not be an effective or popular action for you to pounce on the team member for missing data entry.

The next step in the process is giving credit for what has been accomplished. At this point, Julia's input has been received. Pat can state, "Well, I can see I didn't help you as much as I should have, and I forgot to give you my phone number. But I do want you to know that I've checked on all of our patients, and they are very happy with their care today." After hearing input and giving credit where it is due, exploration of the gaps in the relationship and their communication and initial direction at the beginning of the shift can now be undertaken with an open and frank discussion.

The discussion of differences will progress most smoothly if both parties recognize that they share common objectives: safe, effective care of the patients on their unit, as reflected in the fulfillment of shared, planned outcomes or goals determined by collaborative discussion among patients and care team members. When difficulties or conflicts occur, remember the reason you are both there: the patients.

Julia and Pat may clarify what happened and what actions each may take to ensure that the missed communication does not happen in the future. Do not try to "fix" the situation for the other individual or prescribe what you will do for them. The other individual will know what he or she needs to do to achieve your shared outcomes. For example, Pat may have decided that it would fix it for Julia to convene with her an hour before shift tomorrow and go through the unit manuals and read the procedures. However, the most Julia may need is a phone number and some more discussion and planning about assignments at the beginning of the shift.

This process may seem to take too much time, because "Why wait for the others to come up with ideas when we can solve the problem for them?" RNs who lead teams throughout the nation tell us that their lives at work would be much better if everyone were behaving accountably. When we ask others for their step-by-step plan to prevent the problem in the future, it helps them determine that they are accountable for their own performance. In our scene with the missing I&O data, the RN will ask, "How can you make sure those I&Os are recorded before you leave in the future? What will work for you?" This type of statement confers the necessary respect for the delegate's ability to determine how to adapt his work performance to conditions.

Do not miss the final steps in the formula if you would like the positive changes to become embedded. Teams must agree on how they will proceed in the future and when they will revisit the problem or issue. Julia may determine that she'll remind Pat in the future when she arrives at the unit that she will need Pat's phone number and a plan for the day. When the next shift is completed, they will want to compare notes about how the shift has proceeded and whether patient outcomes have been achieved. The CNA may decide to ask the RN the following week whether she has noted any missing I&Os. The pair will be able to evaluate whether the CNA's charting plan has been effective and can proceed to celebrate the success of the plan or to try other interventions.

Practice using the feedback formula. Remember the following three most important points:

- Ask for the other person's input first.
- Give credit for accomplishments and efforts.
- Ask the other individual to come up with steps for resolving the issue.

How would you use this formula to tell a supervisor that you are concerned about how long it has been since you have heard about your intershift transfer, and you are becoming worried about whether it will take place? How would you provide positive feedback to an individual on your team who has been improving his ability to complete his shift on time? What about a delegate who is "missing in action"—the person you cannot seem to locate when you need her?

CONCLUSION

Nurses sometimes wish for an exact prescription for what to delegate—as well as when and how. Because nursing assessment and professional judgment are necessary for clinical delegation, each situation will be different. Whether you work in an intensive care unit in a large tertiary hospital, a rural long-term care facility, home health, or ambulatory care, the template of the delegation process—*in the right circumstances, matching the right task with the right delegate, communicating effectively, and offering and receiving feedback*—will be similar. With ongoing health care reform, we suspect your leadership at the point of care will include new types of care providers and new delivery models. You will need to hone your abilities to assign care tasks effectively, and to supervise the work that is being done under your direction and supervision, to help your patients and their families achieve their preferred outcomes. The health of your community will be affected by your team and your leadership. To judge your comfort and assess your ability to integrate this process in your daily work life, complete the exercise in Critical Thinking Box 14.7. Good luck!

? CRITICAL THINKING BOX 14.7

Assessing Your Delegation Skills

Assemble these documents:

- Your state nurse practice act (includes rules, policies, and advisory opinions)
- Your job description and those of co-workers and delegates
- Skills checklists
- The patient list or assignment form from your unit
- A list of the usual staffing complement for your shift
1. Using these documents, determine the short-term outcomes for an average patient assignment based on the information you have been given in a report. What tasks could be delegated to the individuals you have on staff? When will you complete further assessment of the patient situations?
2. Based on the outcomes and job descriptions, how will you determine the competency of individuals to complete the tasks you have determined could be delegated?
3. How will you communicate the team's plan using outcomes in your discussion?
4. How often will you communicate with the delegates, based on their need for supervision and patient complexity and dynamics? Have you used the four Cs?
5. How will you evaluate the effectiveness of your plan? How will you provide positive feedback to the team?
6. A delegate made a mistake. You determined that the person was competent, but the procedure was done improperly. For what are you accountable? How will you give feedback to the individual, encouraging his or her growth and accountability?
7. Have you implemented the five rights of delegation?

⊕ RELEVANT WEBSITES AND ONLINE RESOURCES

Alfaro-Lefevre, R. Promoting critical thinking in frontline nurses
Retrieved from www.AlfaroTeachSmart.com.

American Nurses Association (ANA)
http://nursingworld.org/. See: Unlicensed Personnel, Registered Nurses Utilization of Nursing Assistive Personnel in All Settings, Registered Nurse Education Relating to the Utilization of Unlicensed Assistive Personnel, Joint Statement on Delegation.

Duffy, M., McCoy, S. F. (2014)
Delegation and you: When to delegate and to whom. Silver Spring, MD: American Nurses Association. ANA You Series: Skills For Success.

Hansten, R. (2008)
Relationship and results oriented healthcare™ planning and implementation manual, Port Ludlow, WA: Hansten Healthcare PLLC. www.RROHC.com, www.Hansten.com. Check for new delegation/supervision resources.

Hansten, R. (2008)
The master coach manual for the relationship & results oriented healthcare program. Port Ludlow, WA: Hansten Healthcare PLLC.

Hansten, R., Jackson, M. (2009)
Clinical delegation skills: A handbook for professional practice (4th ed.). Sudbury, MA: Jones & Bartlett.

National Council of State Boards of Nursing
http://www.ncsbn.org, links to state boards and resources relating to delegation and supervision. Also download the ANA and NCSBN Joint Statement on Delegation.

BIBLIOGRAPHY

Alfaro-LeFevre, R. (in press, 2017). *Critical thinking, clinical reasoning, and clinical judgment: A practical approach* (6th ed.). St. Louis, MO: Elsevier Saunders.

American Nurses Association. (2015). *Code of ethics for nurses with interpretative statements*. Retrieved from http://www.nursingworld.org/MainMenuCategories/EthicsStandards/Tools-You-Need/Code-of-Ethics-For-Nurses.html.

American Nurses Association. (2012). *ANA's principles for delegation by registered nurses to unlicensed assistive personnel*. Silver Spring, MD: ANA. Retrieved from http://www.nursingworld.org/MainMenuCategories/The PracticeofProfessionalNursing/NursingStandards/ANAPrinciples/PrinciplesofDelegation.pdf, 12.

Brous, E. (2012). Professional licensure: Investigation and disciplinary action. *American Journal of Nursing, 112*(11), 53–60.

Bittner, N., & Gravlin, G. (2009). Critical thinking, delegation, and missed care in nursing practice. *Journal of Orthopedic Nursing Association, 39*(3), 142–146.

Bittner, N., Gravlin, G., Hansten, R., & Kalisch, B. (2011). Unraveling care omissions. *Journal of Nursing Administration, 41*(12), 510–512.

Bobay, K., Fiorelli, K., & Anderson, A. (2008). Failure to rescue: A preliminary study of patient-level factors. *Journal of Nursing Care Quality, 23*(3), 211–215.

Future of Nursing™ Campaign for Action. (2015). Robert Wood Johnson Foundation and AARP.

Campaign Overview Updated March 15, 2015. Retrieved from http://campaignforaction.org/sites/default/files/Campaign%20Overview%20Updated%205-13-15.pdf.

Garneau, A. M. (2012). *The effect of human patient simulation on delegation performance among associate degree nursing students*. (Doctoral dissertation). Retrieved from Proquest Dissertations and Theses. (Order Accession No: 3502633).

Gravlin, G., & Bittner, N. (2010). Nurses' and nursing assistants' reports of missed care and delegation. *Journal of Nursing Administration, 40*(7–8), 329–335.

Hansten, R. (2005). Relationship and results oriented healthcare: Evaluate the basics. *Journal of Nursing Administration, 35*(12), 522–525.

Hansten, R. (2008a). *Relationship & results oriented healthcare planning & implementation manual*. Port Ludlow, WA: Hansten Healthcare PLLC.

Hansten, R. (2008b). Why nurses still must learn to delegate. *Nursing Leadership, 6*(5), 19–25.

Hansten, R. (2009). A bundle of best bedside practices. *Health Care Management, 28*(2), 111–116.

Hansten, R., & Jackson, M. (2009). *Clinical delegation skills: A handbook for professional practice* (4th ed.). Sudbury, MA: Jones & Bartlett.

Hansten, R., Washburn, M., & Kenyon, V. (1999). *Home care nursing delegation skills: A handbook for practice*. Gaithersburg, MD: Aspen.

Hansten, R. (2014a). Coach as chief correlator of tasks to results through delegation skill and teamwork development, August/September. *Nurse Leader, 12*(4), 69–73.

Hansten, R. (2014b). *The master coach manual for the relationship & results oriented healthcare program*. Port Ludlow, WA: Hansten Healthcare PLLC.

Institute of Medicine. (2000). *To err is human: Building a safer health system*. Retrieved from http://www.iom.edu/~/media/Files/Report%20Files/1999/To-Err-is-Human/To%20Err%20is%20Human%201999%20%20report%20brief.ashx.

Institute of Medicine Report on the Future of Nursing. (2010). Retrieved from http://www.iom.edu/~/media/Files/Report%20Files/2010/The-Future-of-Nursing/Future%20of%20Nursing%202010%20Report%20Brief.pdf.

Institute of Medicine of the National Academies. (2013). *Best care at lower cost: The path to continuously learning health care in America*. In Mark Smith, Robert Saunders, Leigh Stuckhardt, & Michael McGinnism (Eds.). (pp. 2–3). Washington, DC: The National Academies Press.

Kalisch, B., Landstrom, G., & Williams, R. (2009). Missed care: Errors of omission. *Nursing Outlook, 57*, 3–9.

Kalisch, B., Tschannen, D., & Hee Lee, K. (2011). Do staffing levels predict missed nursing care? *International Journal of Quality Health Care, 23*(3), 02–308. http://dx.doi.org/10.1093/intqhc/mzr009.

Kalisch, B., & Schoville, R. (2012). It takes a team. *American Journal of Nursing, 112*(10), 50–54. http://dx.doi .org/10.1097/01.NAJ.0000421024.08037.0d.

Mole, L. J., & McLafferty, I. H. (2004). Evaluating a simulated ward exercise for third year student nurses. *Nurse Education in Practice, 4*(2), 91–99. http://dx.doi.org/10.1016/S1471–5953(03)00031-3. 2004.

National Council of State Boards of Nursing. (1990). *Concept paper on delegation.* Chicago: NCSBN.

National Council of State Boards of Nursing. (1995). *Concepts and decision-making process.* Chicago: National Council position paper. Retrieved from www.ncsbn.org/ 323.htm/definitions#definitions.

National Council of State Boards of Nursing (NCSBN). (2005). *Practical nurse scope of practice white paper.* Retrieved from https://www.ncsbn.org/Final_11_05_Practical_Nurse_Scope_Practice_White_Paper.pdf.

National Council of State Boards of Nursing. (NCSBN). (2006). Joint statement on delegation. *American Nurses Association (ANA) and the National Council of State Boards of Nursing (NCSBN).* Retrieved from https://www .ncsbn.org/Joint_statement.pdf.

National Council State Boards of Nursing. (2014). 2014 NCLEX-PN˚. *Test Plan.* Retrieved from https://www.ncs bn.org/PN_Test_Plan_2014_Candidate.pdf.

National Council State Boards of Nursing. (2016a). *2016 NCLEX-RN˚ Test Plan.* Retrieved from https://www.ncs bn.org/RN_Test_Plan_2016_Final.pdf.

National Council of State Boards of Nursing. (2016b). *Participating states in the nurse licensure compact implementation pending legislation.* Retrieved from https://www.ncsbn.org/nurse-licensure-compact.htm.

Samuel, M. (2006). *Creating the accountable organization.* Katonah, NY: Xephor Press.

Sheehan, J. P. (2001). UAP delegation: A step-by-step process. *Nursing Management, 32*(4), 22–24.

State of Montana Administrative Rules. (9/30/2006). *Nursing Subchapter 16. Delegation and Assignment. 24.159.1601-16787.* Retrieved from http://bsd.dli.mt.gov/license/bsd_boards/nur_board/pdf/NUR%20deleg ation%20rules.pdf.

Current Issues in Health Care

15

The Health Care Organization and Patterns of Nursing Care Delivery

Susan Sportsman, PhD, RN, ANEF, FAAN

ⓔ http://evolve.elsevier.com/Zerwekh/nsgtoday/.

Better Care, Better Health, Reduced Costs
Vision for the Texas Team Advancing Health Through Nursing

Health care should be within reach of everyone.

After completing this chapter, you should be able to:
- Describe challenges facing health care that impact the delivery of nursing care, including:
  - Reduction of costs
  - Evidence-based care
  - Shortage of health care professionals
  - Patient safety
  - Nurse staffing
  - Delivery changes influenced by the 2010 Institute of Medicine Future of Nursing Report
- Trace the history of the use of nursing care delivery models.
- Consider ways to structure nursing services to improve care while reducing costs, in order to insure that health care is within reach of everyone.

The U.S. health care delivery system has been changing dramatically during the past 40 years. Economic changes around the world and the passage of the Affordable Care Act of 2010, as well as the resulting political responses, have focused the country's attention on the need to revise the U.S. health care system to improve access and quality while reducing the delivery costs. Nurses practicing in such an environment must be comfortable with change and be willing to embrace the challenges that change brings.

A first step to ensuring that your nursing practice evolves in a positive direction is to be knowledgeable about these changes.

WHAT ARE SOME IMPORTANT CHALLENGES CURRENTLY FACING HEALTH CARE?

Cost of Health Care

High health expenditures in the United States have long been a national problem. There are a number of reasons for this continued growth in the cost of health care, including expansion of prescription of drugs and new medical technologies, as well as administrative costs. The rise in the incidence of chronic disease, which accounts for a large portion of national health care expenditures, is also a major factor. For the past 30 years, various strategies have been instituted to halt this escalation in health care costs. One of the major approaches to reduce costs has been managed care.

Managed Care

In the early 1900s, patients or their families paid the physician or the hospital directly for the care they received. As health care insurance became an employment benefit after the Second World War, third-party payers became more common. These third-party payers paid the provider an agreed-on fee for each service provided. The more the provider charged, the more the payer paid.

In the early 1980s, Medicare introduced the prospective payment system as a way of reimbursing hospitals. This marked the beginning of a movement to control health care costs. Under this system, which insurance companies soon adopted, a fixed fee was paid to the hospital according to a preset reimbursement rate for the diagnosis given at discharge. A hospital could treat a patient so that a shorter length of stay was necessary, reducing the consumption of resources. This allowed the hospital to show a greater profit or smaller loss for caring for a patient if the care was more efficient than was the prearranged rate for the diagnosis. This practice began the trend of managed care in which health care is paid at a prearranged rate rather than as billed.

In the most extreme type of managed care, called *capitation*, employers pay a set fee each month to an insurance company for each covered employee and dependent. This amount does not vary based on the care given. Potential patients may never need any health care, or they may require extensive hospitalizations. Regardless, the costs of care for all members of a particular employment group must be taken out of the set fee. Under this arrangement, there is incentive for the insurance company and the provider to work aggressively to keep patients healthy, because prevention or early intervention is likely to be less expensive than hospitalization. Conversely, if patients do not stay healthy or if they overuse hospitalization, the health care provider may actually lose money.

As a part of the managed care trend, health maintenance organization (HMO) plans became very popular as a form of insurance. In HMOs, an annual payment is made on behalf of the members to a group of providers who deliver all of the health services covered under the plan, including physician and hospital services. HMOs have grown, because they provide a strong incentive to avoid hospitalization, which consequently reduces costs. HMO members often appreciate the ease of using health care with an HMO, because there are fewer noncovered services and fewer forms to complete. However, the choice of providers is limited; members must use physicians who are part of the HMO network, and they may not see specialty physicians without a referral from their primary care provider.

The preferred provider organization (PPO) is another type of insurance plan designed to meet the goals of managed care. To avoid out-of-pocket expenses, members must use physicians who have agreed to provide services at a lower price to the insurer. However, members may use an "out-of-network" provider without a referral, if they are willing to pay more for that service.

What Impact Has Managed Care Had on Costs?

Initially, managed care reduced the cost of health care. However, costs have increased sharply in response to the backlash from restrictive managed care policies. Between 1999 and 2007, employer-sponsored health insurance premiums increased by 199%, placing cost burdens on both the employers and the workers (Kaiser Family Foundation, 2007).

Given the complexity of the issues surrounding the costs of health care, it is very difficult to say conclusively that managed care is effective, in part because the definition of "effective" may vary. Effectiveness can be measured by profit and loss, quality of care, and/or access to services. Improvement in one of these factors does not necessarily mean improvement in other factors. In addition, there are a number of stakeholders who must judge the effectiveness of care in any given situation, including the managed care organization, the employer, the Centers for Medicare & Medicaid Services (CMS), regulators, and providers, as well as individual patients, their significant others, and society as a whole. Since these groups often have different needs and agendas, one definition of efficient is difficult to agree upon.

Despite these efforts to reduce the cost of health care for the past 25 years, in the fall of 2013 at the Conference on the Brookings Paper on Economic Activity (BPEA), Chandra, Holmes, and Skinner noted that health care consumes nearly 18% of the U.S. gross national product (GNP), making the U.S. the world's leader in both the level and growth rate of spending in health care. While there has been a moderation in health care spending since 2009, the authors predict that it is unlikely there will be a permanent "bending of the health care cost curve" going forward. The authors predicted that health care will grow at the level of the GDP level, plus 1.2% for the next few decades. Concern over the impact of long-term technology pipeline that could deliver new and expensive technology with very low medical or financial benefits, coupled with high labor costs will likely fuel this continued increase (Chandra, Holmes, & Skinner, 2013).

AFFORDABLE CARE ACT

On March 23, 2010, the Affordable Care Act (ACA) was passed, providing regulations to reduce health care costs, as well as improve access to care. On June 28, 2013, the U.S. Supreme Court rendered a final decision to uphold this health care law. The provisions of the law were implemented over a 5-year period. Table 15.1 provides an overview of the major elements of the bill and the year in which each component was introduced. At the time of publication of this book, there was considerable discussion about repealing all or parts of the ACA.

STRATEGIES TO CONTROL COSTS

Hospital care accounts for the largest share (32.1%) of health care expenditures; physician services are second, accounting for 19.9%; and prescription drugs account for 9.8% (CDC, 2014). Reducing costs in these areas will have the greatest impact on reducing total costs. Specific efforts to reduce hospital costs that impact the delivery of nursing care include case management, evidence-based practice, appropriate staffing, improving retention of staff, use of the electronic health record (EHR), and reducing patient-care errors.

CASE MANAGEMENT

The Case Management Society of America (CMSA) notes that case (or care) managers are advocates who help patients understand their current health status, what they can do about it, and why those treatments are important. In this way, case managers guide patients through the health care delivery

TABLE 15.1	COMPONENTS OF THE AFFORDABLE CARE ACT
YEAR	**COMPONENT OF AFFORDABLE CARE ACT**
2010	• Putting health care insurance information for consumers online • Prohibiting denial of coverage of children under 19 due to preexisting conditions • Prohibiting insurance companies from rescinding coverage based on errors or technical mistakes • Eliminating insurance prohibitions from impacting life-time coverage • Provide a way to appeal insurance company decisions • Provide small business health insurance tax credit • Offering relief from Medicare prescription donut hole • Providing free preventive care • Cracking down on health care fraud • Providing access to insurance for uninsured Americans with preexisting conditions • Children can stay on parents' insurance until age 26 • Increasing incentives for primary care working in underserved areas • Holding insurance companies accountable for unreasonable rate hikes • Allowing states to cover more people on Medicaid • Increasing payments for medical care in rural health clinics • Strengthening community health center
2011	• Prescription discounted for seniors • Free preventive care for seniors • Improving health care quality and efficiency • Transition care for Medicare • Community First Choice Options • Allowing states to offer home- and community-based services to the disabled • Addressing overpayments to big insurance
2012	• Aligning payments to quality outcomes • Encouraging integrated health services • Decreasing pipeline and administrative costs • Research on health disparities • Providing new voluntary options for LTC insurance
2013	• Improving preventative health coverage • Expanding authorities to bundle insurance products • Increasing Medicaid payments for primary care doctors
2014	• Prohibiting discrimination due to gender • Eliminating annual limits to insurance coverage • Insuring coverage for individuals participating in clinical trials • Tax credits for middle class (100%-140% of poverty level) • Increasing small business tax credits • Increasing access to Medicaid to those earning less than 133% of poverty level (approximately $14,000 for individuals and $29,000 for a family of 4) • Buying basic insurance packages or pay a fee for those who can afford it
2015	• Paying physicians based on value, not volume

Adapted from the U.S. Department of Health and Human Services. (2015). *Key features of the Affordable Care Act by year.* Retrieved from http://www.hhs.gov/healthcare/facts-and-features/key-features-of-aca-by-year/index.html#.

process and provide cohesion to other professionals on the health care delivery team. The purpose of case managers is to enable their clients to achieve goals effectively and efficiently. The role may take a variety of forms but generally includes coordination of care, communication, collaboration, and attention to the transition between levels of nursing care. Social workers and therapists may also be case managers, although how they perform their role depends on the scope of practice within their discipline. All case managers must be skilled at communication, critical thinking, negotiation, and collaboration. They must be knowledgeable about resources available to patients. The case manager not only collaborates with individual patients but also with family and other support systems of the patient.

Case management is effective in providing care, but all patients do not need this intensity of interaction. To provide case management services to all patients would be wastefully expensive. Patients should be assigned a case manager only if they:

- Have complicated health care needs
- Are receiving care that is expensive as well as complicated
- Pose discharge planning problems
- Receive care from multiple providers
- Are likely to have significant physical or psychosocial problems

Case management may also be implemented in levels of care other than acute hospitals, particularly in some outpatient and short-term rehabilitative settings. In many ways, the roles and responsibilities of the case manager are the same regardless of the level of care in which they work. The differences in the emphasis of the role are often influenced by reimbursement.

Nurse navigator programs are a form of case management that is beginning to be more widely used to coordinate patient care. In 1990, Dr. Harold Freeman developed the first nurse navigator role at Harlem Hospital in New York in an effort to expedite diagnosis and treatment, while facilitating access to care for patients with abnormal breast screening results (Pedersen & Hack, 2010). Since that time, the role of the nurse navigator has been used in a variety of settings.

In 2005, the Patient Navigator Outreach and Chronic Disease Prevention Act authorized federal grants to hire and train patient navigators to help patients who had cancer and other serious chronic diseases to receive access to screening, diagnosis, treatment, and follow-up care. In 2006, the CMS funded six demonstration projects to help minority Medicare patients overcome barriers with screening, diagnosis, and treatment, and in 2007, $2.9 million was allocated to this program (Wells et al., 2008).

Although a large number of nurse navigator programs target care of the cancer patient, there is also an opportunity to implement this role when caring for other chronic diseases (Case, 2011). For example, publications show that health care facilities carry out nurse navigator programs for conditions such as high-risk OB care, osteoarthritis, HIV (Horstmann et al., 2010), and asthma (Black et al., 2010).

The navigator role was conceived to reduce patient barriers to care for vulnerable patients who may cope with delays in access, diagnosis, treatment, and/or fragmented and uncoordinated care. An analysis of evaluations of nurse navigator programs from 2000 to 2010 identified improved patient satisfaction, positive changes in patient attitudes and understanding of disease processes, and better patient perception of a timelier and more accessible treatment process (Case, 2011).

DISEASE MANAGEMENT

Disease management refers to multidisciplinary efforts to improve the quality and cost of care for patients suffering from chronic diseases. It involves interventions designed to improve adherence to appropriate scientific guidelines and treatments. The goal is similar to case management—to support patients with chronic diseases who may receive services from various levels of care (acute care to home-based care). However, it is a population health strategy as well as an approach to personal health.

A variety of national organizations involved with consumer health or the health care delivery system at large have supported the use of disease management strategies to improve health care. For example, the American Heart Association's Expert Panel on Disease Management recommends the following guiding principles for disease management initiatives.

- The main goal of disease management should be to improve the quality of care and patient outcomes. Evaluations of disease management programs should not be based solely on their ability to reduce health care expenditures.
- Scientifically derived, peer-reviewed guidelines should be the basis of all disease management programs. These guidelines should be evidence based and consensus driven.
- Disease management programs should help increase adherence to treatment plans based on the best available evidence.
- All disease management efforts must include ongoing and scientifically based evaluations, including clinical outcomes.
- Disease management programs should exist within an integrated and comprehensive system of care in which the patient-provider relationship is central (Faxon, et al., 2004).

Although disease management shows considerable promise, significant additional attention is needed in testing and demonstrating best practices and sharing information on successful components across a variety of care settings within this evolving area.

Do Disease Management Programs Reduce the Cost of Health Care?

In 2007, the RAND Health Study reported a review of all past research (317 studies) on disease management programs related to six chronic conditions: heart failure, coronary artery disease, diabetes, asthma, depression, and obstructive pulmonary disease. The interventions ranged from prerecorded telephone reminders to home visits by medical professionals. The results showed that these programs often improved the quality of the patient's care. However, there was no conclusive evidence that disease management programs actually saved money. The authors suggested that the breadth of the definition of disease management might influence the findings. For example, some programs may have been better than others, but there is not enough research to assess properly which program is the most effective or why it is effective. In addition, most of the studies followed patients for only 1 year, which may not be long enough to determine the long-term effect of the program (RAND Corp., 2007).

Similarly, in 2015, the Cameron Institute reviewed and analyzed available literature from the past decade on disease management programs with an eye to determining their effectiveness in the Medicaid population. Although it was somewhat challenging to extrapolate the studies' results to a larger context, several recurring themes emerged, which provided perspective on the current state of knowledge:

- The robust results of many studies, across disease types, show that disease management programs were most likely to be cost-effective and improve quality of care when dealing with severely ill enrollees who are at high risk for hospitalization, near term.
- Self-management and monitoring were found to be especially effective. Provider education of patients was also found to be effective in increasing medication adherence, vaccination rates, and screening.
- Telephonic care management also was found to be effective.
- Physician- and pharmacist-led interventions positively influenced prescription medication adherence and attainment of guidelines for lipid and HbA1c levels (Schatz, 2008).

What Tools Are Used to Support Care Coordination?

Clinical pathways and **disease management protocols** are similar strategies that support the work of the coordinator of care to reduce expensive variations in care.

> Clinical pathways, also known as *care maps*, are multidisciplinary plans of "best" clinical practice for groups of patients with a specific medical diagnosis.

These pathways support the coordination and delivery of high-quality care. There are four essential elements of a clinical pathway:

- A timeline outlining when specific care will be given
- The categories of care or activities and their interventions
- Intermediate- and long-term outcomes to be achieved
- A variance record

The variance record allows caregivers to document when and why the progress of individual patients varies from that outlined in the pathway. Clinical pathways differ from practice guidelines, protocols, and algorithms, because they are used by the interprofessional disciplinary team and have a focus on quality and coordination of care for individual patients. A sample of a clinical pathway can be found in the Evolve resources.

Clinical Guidelines

Both critical pathways and disease management protocols are generally based on clinical guidelines that incorporate nationally acceptable ways to care for a specific disease. The National Heart, Lung, and Blood Institute (NHLBI), a component of the U.S. Department of Health and Human Services, defines clinical practice guidelines as "practice regulations that are systematically developed statements to assist practitioner and patient decisions about appropriate health care for specific clinical circumstances." These recommendations include specific diagnostic and treatment options based on evidence from a rigorous systematic review and synthesis of the published literature. In short, they recommend practices that meet the needs of most patients in most circumstances; however, the clinical judgment is always required to fit the guideline to the individual patient (NHLBI, n.d.).

Clinical guidelines are typically developed by government agencies, such as the Agency for Healthcare Research and Quality (AHRQ), or an organization devoted to health promotion and disease prevention, such as the American Public Health Association and the Centers for Disease Control and Prevention. A website developed by AHRQ, in collaboration with the American Medical Association (AMA) and the American Association of Health Plans (now America's Health Insurance Plans [AHIP]) provides a resource for clinical practice guidelines at www.guideline.gov.

PAY FOR PERFORMANCE

Pay for performance (P4P) is increasingly being used to reduce costs and improve quality in health care. Physicians, hospitals, medical groups, and other health care providers are rewarded for meeting certain performance measures for quality and efficiencies. Disincentives, such as eliminating payments for negative consequences of care (medical errors) or increased costs, have also been proposed. An example of such disincentives includes hospitals not receiving reimbursement for care given to treat health care–associated infections (HAIs), such as catheter-acquired urinary tract infections (CAUTI) and surgical site infections (SSIs). There are several ways in which the P4P can be implemented. Chief among them is nonpayment for treatment of preventable complications such as falls and pressure ulcers (Thomas & Caldis, 2007). Although P4P continues to be considered an important approach for continuing to reduce cost while ensuring quality, there are mixed results from research regarding its effectiveness in reducing costs (Schatz, 2008; Torgan, 2013).

EVIDENCE-BASED PRACTICE

How Do We Know That Critical Pathways and Disease Management Protocols Reflect the Latest and Best Practice?

In 2000, the Institute of Medicine (IOM) released a report, "Crossing the Quality Chasm: A New Health System for the 21st Century" (IOM, 2000). This report noted that it takes 17 years for the results of research in health care to be transmitted consistently into practice.

> Evidence-based practice is one strategy to reduce the amount of time required to integrate new health care findings into practice.

Evidence-based practice is the use of the current best evidence in making decisions about patient care. It flows from clinicians asking, "What is the best way to manage a particular situation?" Melnyk and Fineout-Overholt (2011) believe that evidence-based practice uses the following steps to answer clinical questions:

- Systematic search for the most relevant evidence to the question (What is the most relevant evidence?)
- Critical evaluation of the evidence found (Is the evidence logical and valid?)
- Your own clinical experience (Does your experience fit with the evidence?)
- Patient preferences and values (Will your patients accept the recommendations drawn from the evidence?)

The answers to these questions can then be implemented in practice or incorporated into critical pathways and disease management processes.

Most nurses use their own clinical experience with patient preferences and values in planning nursing care. However, searching for the evidence to address the question at hand and critically evaluating the evidence may be more difficult. Fig. 15.1 outlines a rating system to help you know how strong the evidence from research or other sources might be.

There are a number of evidence-based nursing centers around the world that provide the best available evidence to inform clinical decision making at the point of care. One of the largest is the Joanna Briggs Institute (JBI), an international not-for-profit research and development arm of the School of Translational Science based within the Faculty of Health Sciences at the University of Adelaide, South Australia, which collaborates internationally with more than 70 entities across the world (http://joanna briggs.org/) (Critical Thinking Box 15.1). See Chapter 24 for more information on how evidence-based practice affects economics. Relevant websites and online resources are listed at the end of this chapter.

? CRITICAL THINKING BOX 15.1

What are the advantages of using evidence-based nursing care? What are the barriers? How might these barriers be overcome?

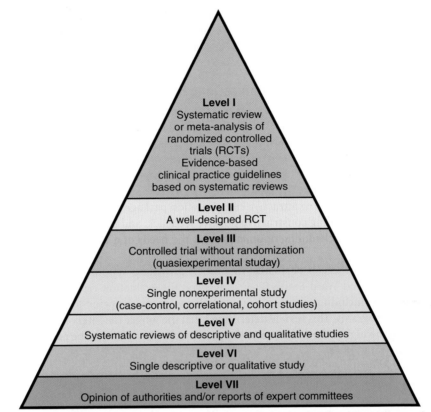

FIG. 15.1 Levels of evidence; evidence hierarchy for rating levels of evidence, associated with a study design. (From Wood, G. L, & Haber, J. (2014). *Nursing research: Methods and critical appraisal of evidence-based practice (8ed).* St. Louis: Mosby/Elsevier).

SHORTAGE OF NURSES

Although hospitals and other health care organizations have experienced nursing shortages during the past 50 years, the most recent shortage, which began in 1998, seems to be the most persistent (Buerhaus, 2009). Although the United States was in a recession in 2009, Buerhaus and colleagues found that despite the easing of the nursing shortage because of the recession, the U.S. nursing shortage is projected to continue growing. According to the Bureau of Labor Statistics' Employment Projections 2012–2022 released in December 2013, registered nursing (RN) is listed among the top occupations in terms of job growth through 2022. The RN workforce is expected to grow from 2.71 million in 2012 to 3.24 million in 2022, an increase of 526,800, or 19%. The bureau also projects the need for 525,000 replacements nurses in the workforce, bringing the total number of job openings for nurses due to growth and replacements to 1.05 million by 2022 (AACN, 2014, para 1).

According to the U.S. Registered Nurse Workforce Report Card and Shortage Forecast published in the January 2012 *American Journal of Medical Quality*, an ongoing shortage of nurses is predicted to spread across the country, especially in the South and West. In February 2012, the Bureau of Labor Statistics Employment Projections (2010–2012) indicated that the RN workforce is the top occupation for job growth, with 2.74 million jobs in 2010 growing to an expected total of 3.45 jobs in 2025, which is an increase of 26%. In addition, 495,500 RNs will retire or leave the workforce, resulting in a total number of job openings for RNs of 1.2 million by 2020 (AACN, 2014, para 2). This ongoing shortage of nurses will continue to impact the cost and quality of health care provided in the United States for the foreseeable future.

How Can Health Care Organizations Retain Nurses?

Retention of nurses in their place of employment is as important as recruitment. The number of nurses who retired during the Great Recession from December 2007 to June 2009 was significantly lower than predicted. As the economy improved, nurses in their 60s began to choose to reduce the amount of time they work each week or perhaps retire completely. In addition, the demands of the rapidly changing health care environment are reducing the satisfaction of nurses of all ages, which often drives a reduced retention rate in employment sites. To combat the need to change jobs frequently, administrators are emphasizing attractive compensation packages; focusing on a culture of training, including mentoring; providing constructive positive feedback; and providing recognition for excellence. Offering a variety of scheduling options to meet the needs of a variety of ages is also a popular retention strategy.

Currently, there is particular interest in providing support for novice nurses in their first job. McDonald and Ward-Smith (2012) reviewed the evaluation reports of transition programs for new graduates, including internships, externships (programs prior to graduation), and postorientation buddy programs. This review determined that the longer the intervention to support the novice nurse lasted, the higher the retention of the participants. In addition, the authors identified key elements of any orientation as

- Providing evaluation of baseline knowledge
- Inclusion of higher level skill practice
- Support for an experienced individual
- Providing of opportunities to clarify existing knowledge and expand knowledge
- Evaluation of individual program outcomes

Regardless of the age of the employee, addressing the negatives associated with the work environment is a key to maintaining a robust workforce.

Magnet Hospitals

Recognizing the characteristics that influence a positive work environment on nurse retention is not new. In the early 1980s, during a previous nursing shortage, the American Academy of Nursing conducted research to identify the organizational attributes of hospitals that experienced success in recruiting and retaining nurses. The American Academy of Nursing Fellows nominated 165 hospitals throughout the nation that had reputations for successfully attracting and retaining nurses and delivering high-quality nursing care. Ultimately, 41 hospitals were distinguished by high nurse satisfaction, low job turnover, and low nurse vacancy rates, even when hospitals located in the same area were experiencing nursing shortages. These hospitals were called *magnet* hospitals, because of their success in attracting and keeping nurses.

The Magnet Recognition Program identifies characteristics or outcomes, known as "Forces of Magnetism," which exemplify excellence in nursing (see Box 15.1). Ten years after the identification of the original magnet hospitals, the American Nurses Credentialing Center (ANCC) established a new magnet hospital designation process, similar to accreditation by The Joint Commission (TJC). Recently, the recognition program has been expanded to provide national recognition for excellence in long-term care nursing facilities and smaller community hospitals. In the current competitive environment, receiving the magnet status may serve as a recruiting and marketing tool for hospitals, attesting to a professional work environment and quality nursing (Critical Thinking Box 15.2).

BOX 15.1   FORCES OF MAGNETISM

Force 1: Quality of nursing leadership
Force 2: Organizational structure
Force 3: Management style
Force 4: Personnel policies and programs
Force 5: Professional models of care
Force 6: Quality of care
Force 7: Quality improvement
Force 8: Consultation and resources
Force 9: Autonomy
Force 10: Relationships between the community and the health care organization
Force 11: Nurses as teachers
Force 12: Image of nursing
Force 13: Interdisciplinary relationships
Force 14: Professional development

Data from American Nurses Credentialing Center. (2011). *Forces of magnetism*. Retrieved from http://www.nurs
ecredentialing.org/ForcesofMagnetism.aspx.

? CRITICAL THINKING BOX 15.2

What are the factors that YOU think result in a great working environment? What factors result in an unacceptable environment?

THE IMPACT OF THE 2010 INSTITUTE FOR MEDICINE FUTURE OF NURSING REPORT

The convergence of the concerns about the challenges of the U.S. health care system (high cost, primary care shortages, an aging and sicker population, health care disparities, and fragmentation of care) stimulated a national reaction regarding the need to transform the U.S. health care system. In response, the Robert Wood Johnson Foundation's Initiative on the Future of Nursing (INF) at the Institute of Medicine (IOM) was launched in 2009 (IOM, 2010).

As a part of this 2-year review process, the IOM brought together experts and thought leaders from multiple disciplines (nursing, business, law, medicine, and others) to develop a plan of action to transform the U.S. health care system. Since nurses compose the largest group of health care providers, the IOM believed that focusing on the challenges of the nursing profession would benefit the entire health care delivery system (IOM, 2010). The IOM and the Task Force held three national forums and numerous technical and policy-oriented workshops to gather insight into the challenges of nursing and to develop a transformational report on the future of nursing. On October 5, 2010, the IOM released a landmark report, *The Future of Nursing* (IOM, 2010).

The key messages of *The Future of Nursing* report (2010) include

- Nurses should practice to the full extent of their education and training through an improved education system that promotes seamless academic progression.
- Nurses should be full partners, with physicians and other health care professionals, in redesigning health care in the United States.
- Effective workforce planning and policy making require better data collection and an improved information infrastructure.

The recommendations that were derived from these key messages were as follows:

1. Remove scope-of-practice barriers.
2. Expand opportunities for nurses to lead and diffuse collaborative improvement efforts.

3. Implement nurse residency programs.
4. Increase the proportion of nurses with baccalaureate degrees to 80% by 2020.
5. Double the number of nurses with doctorates by 2020.
6. Ensure that nurses engage in lifelong learning.
7. Prepare and enable nurses to lead change to advance health.
8. Build an infrastructure for the collection and analysis of interprofessional health care workforce data (IOM, 2010).

At the time of this writing, the website Campaign for Action Dashboard (http://campaignforaction-.org/sites/default/files/2015-Dashboard-Final-5.27.15.pdf) provides the 2013 results of some of the initiatives. For example, in 2010, 49% of the RNs working held BSNs; in 2013, 51% hold this degree. A number of states have moved from a restricted scope of practice to full practice, which allows nurse practitioners (NPs) to evaluate patients, diagnose, order and interpret diagnostic tests, initiate and manage treatment, including prescribing drugs since 2010. In addition the number of DNP graduates has doubled between 2010 and 2013. There is much optimism that the Future of Nursing initiative has stimulated many stakeholders to reach for the goals established by the IOM *Future of Nursing* report.

PATIENT SAFETY

Patient safety remains an important issue in the current health care environment. In 1996, the IOM initiated a concerted ongoing effort to assess and improve the quality of care in the United States. The first phase documented the seriousness of the quality problems. In the second phase (1999–2001), two reports were released. "To Err Is Human: Building a Safer Health System" focused on how tens of thousands of Americans die each year because of medical errors (IOM, 2000). "Crossing the Quality Chasm: A New Health System for the 21st Century" defined six aims to improve health care quality, including care that is (IOM, 2001)

- Safe
- Effective
- Patient centered
- Timely
- Efficient
- Equitable

The third phase, which is going on now, focuses on determining ways that the future health care delivery system described in earlier reports can be realized. Box 15.2 outlines some of the more recent IOM reports from this initiative.

One of the IOM reports, "Keeping Patients Safe: Transforming the Work Environment of Nurses," suggests that the work environment of nurses needs to be changed to better protect patients. The report makes recommendations in the areas of (1) nursing management, (2) workforce deployment, and (3) work design and organizational culture (IOM, 2003). For example, restructuring of hospital organizations in response to managed care often has undermined the trust between nurses and administration. The report urged health care organizations to involve nurse leaders at all levels of management in decision making and to ask nursing staff their opinions about care design, because nurses are very effective in detecting processes that contribute to errors.

In 2008, The Joint Commission (TJC) published a report, "Guiding Principles for the Development of the Hospital of the Future." This report outlines principles to (1) support economic viability, (2) guide technology adoption, (3) guide achievement of patient-centered care, (4) guide design of hospitals of the future, and (5) address staffing challenges.

The concern about patient safety extends to other areas within TJC. In 2004, TJC established its National Patient Safety Goals, which have been revised each year since then. The goals and related implementation expectations are identified by program—ambulatory care, assisted living, behavioral health care, critical access hospitals, disease-specific care, home care, hospital, laboratory, long-term care, networks, and office-based surgeries (http://www.jointcommission.org/assets/1/6/2016_NPSG _HAP_ER.pdf). (See Box 22.1 for a complete list of the *2016 TJC Hospital National Patient Safety Goals*.)

One of TJC's goals is to improve the effectiveness of communication among caregivers. Although the requirements of this goal emphasize clear communication regarding physician orders and test results, there are other issues surrounding communication that may reduce patient safety and job satisfaction of nurses. A national study, "Silence Kills," sponsored in part by the American Association of Critical-Care Nurses, describes interviews with more than 1700 nurses, physicians, clinical care staff, and administrators. This study showed that fewer than 10% of those interviewed speak to colleagues about behaviors that could result in errors or other types of harm to patients.

These behaviors may include trouble following directions, demonstration of poor clinical judgment, or taking dangerous shortcuts. The results are often broken rules, mistakes, lack of support, incompetence, poor teamwork, disrespect, and micromanagement. When clinicians speak up, these conversations are called *crucial conversations* (Maxfield et al., 2005).

The authors believe that having these crucial conversations should result in significant reductions in errors, improved quality of care, reduction in nursing turnover, and marked improvement in

---

BOX 15.2 RECENT REPORTS OF HEALTH CARE QUALITY FROM THE INSTITUTE OF MEDICINE

- Preventing Medical Errors: Quality Chasm Series
- Hospital Based Emergency Care: At the Breaking Point
- Leadership by Example: Coordinating Government Roles in Improving Health Care
- Crossing the Quality Chasm: A New Health System for the 21st Century
- Ensuring Quality Cancer Care
- Envisioning the National Health Care Quality Report
- To Err Is Human: Building a Safer Health System
- Fostering Rapid Advances in Health Care
- Health Professions Education: A Bridge to Quality
- Priority Areas for National Action: Transforming Health Care Quality
- Key Capabilities of an Electronic Health Record System
- Patient Safety: Achieving a New Standard for Care
- Keeping Patients Safe: Transforming the Work Environment of Nurses
- 1st Annual Crossing the Quality Chasm Summit: A Focus on Communities
- The Healthcare Imperative: Lowering Costs and Improving Outcomes: Workshop Summary
- Value in Health Care Accounting for Cost, Quality, Safety, Outcomes, and Innovation: Workshop Summary
- Redesign Continuing Education in the Health Professions
- America's Uninsured Crisis: Consequences for Health and Health Care
- Best Care at Lower Cost: The Path to Continuously Learning Health Care in America
- Health IT and Patient Safety: Building Safer Systems for Better Care
- The Healthcare Imperative: Lowering Costs and Improving Outcomes
- The Role of Telehealth in an Evolving Health Care Environment
- Transforming Health Care Scheduling and Access: Getting to Now
- Vital Signs: Core Metrics for Health and Health Care Progress
- Assessing Progress on the IOM Report The Future of Nursing
- The Role of Public-Private Partnerships in Health Systems Strengthening: Workshop Summary

The National Academies of Science, Engineering, and Medicine. (2016). *Reports*. Retrieved from http://iom.natio nalacademies.org/Reports.aspx.

productivity (Maxfield et al., 2005). (See Chapter 11 for additional information on communication and patient safety.) In an effort to address the issues identified in "Silence Kills," the American Association of Critical-Care Nurses has established Standards for Establishing and Sustaining Healthy Work Environments. Table 15.2 identifies these standards. (Also see Critical Thinking Box 15.3.)

Building upon the 2005 "Silence Kills" study, Vital Smarts and the ANCC conducted a more extensive study, "Silent Treatment." More than 6500 nurses and nurse managers, members of the American Association of Critical Care Nursing (AACN) and/or the Association of Perioperative Registered Nurses (AORN) from health systems across the country participated in this research. The participants completed two research instruments, the "Story Collector," which collected qualitative data, and a traditional survey, which collected quantitative data. The study examined the calculated decisions that health care professionals make daily to not speak up when they see potential harm—even when they have access to safety tools to alert them. The three main reasons about which providers should have spoken up included

- Dangerous shortcuts: 84% of respondents say that 10% or more of their colleagues take dangerous shortcuts and only 17% spoke up about these practices with the colleague in question.
- Incompetence: 82% say that 10% or more of their colleagues are missing basic skills and only 11% have spoken up to identify these limitations with the incompetent colleague.

TABLE 15.2	AMERICAN ASSOCIATION OF CRITICAL-CARE NURSES STANDARDS FOR ESTABLISHING AND SUSTAINING HEALTHY WORK ENVIRONMENTS	
CATEGORY	**STANDARD**	
Skilled communication	Nurses must be as proficient in communication skills as they are in clinical skills.	
True collaboration	Nurses must be relentless in pursuing and fostering true collaboration.	
Effective decision making	Nurses must be valued and committed partners in making policy, directing and evaluating clinical care, and leading organizational operations.	
Appropriate staffing	Staffing must ensure the effective match between patient needs and nurse competencies.	
Meaningful recognition	Nurses must be recognized and must recognize others for the value each brings to the work of the organization.	
Authentic leadership	Nurse leaders must fully embrace the imperative of a healthy work environment, authentically live it, and engage others in its achievement.	

Data from American Association of Critical-Care Nurses. (2005). *AACN standards for establishing and sustaining healthy work environments: A journey to excellence.* Retrieved from http://www.aacn.org/wd/hwe/docs/hwestandards.pdf

❓ CRITICAL THINKING BOX 15.3
What Do You Think?

- How many hours are too long to work?
- Is there an increase in the number of errors made by nurses working 12 hours or longer?
- How would you handle it if the supervisor asked you to work 6 more hours after your 12-hour shift because the floor is short-staffed?
- What is your responsibility as a professional nurse when it comes to overtime?

- Disrespect: 85% of respondents say that 10% or more of the people they work with are disrespectful and therefore undermine their ability to share concerns or speak up about problems. Only 16% have confronted their disrespectful colleague (www.silenttreatmentstudy.com) (Maxfield et al., 2010).

The results of this research point to the need to overcome the reluctance of providers to speak up when there is a potential threat to patient safety.

Institute for Healthcare Improvement

The Institute for Healthcare Improvement (IHI), a not-for-profit organization founded in 1991, is also focused on improving the quality of health care. The IHI goal is to lead improvement of health care throughout the world, and it is based on the science of improvement, an applied science that emphasizes innovation, rapid-cycle testing in the field, and spread in order to generate learning. Specifically, the goal is to learn about what changes, in which context, produce improvement. It is built on the compilation of expert subject knowledge with improvement methods and tools through interdisciplinary collaboration—drawing on clinical science, systems theory, psychology, statistics, and other fields (IHI, 2016a).

An early IHI initiative that embodied these goals was the 100,000 Lives Campaign, which began in 2004 and ended in June 2006. This project was designed to engage thousands of U.S. hospitals in an effort to prevent 100,000 needless inpatient deaths by implementing improvements in care. At the end of the campaign, IHI announced that more than 3100 participating hospitals had saved an estimated 122,343 lives. Building on this success, in December 2006, IHI launched the 5 Million Lives Campaign. The focus was expanded beyond mortality to include harm also, introducing high-impact interventions that build on those of the 100,000 Lives Campaign.

The aim of the 5 Million Lives Campaign was to support the improvement of medical care in the United States, significantly reducing levels of morbidity (illness or medical harm such as adverse drug events or surgical complications) and mortality during a period of 2 years (December 12, 2006, to December 9, 2008). IHI and its partners in the campaign encouraged hospitals and other health care providers to take the following steps to reduce harm and deaths:

- Prevent pressure ulcers by reliably using science-based guidelines for preventing this serious and common complication.
- Reduce methicillin-resistant *Staphylococcus aureus* (MRSA) infection through basic changes in infection control processes throughout the hospital.
- Prevent harm from high-alert medications, focusing on anticoagulants, sedatives, narcotics, and insulin.
- Reduce surgical complications by reliably implementing the changes in care recommended by the Surgical Care Improvement Project (SCIP).
- Deliver reliable, evidence-based care for congestive heart failure to reduce readmission (IHI, 2016b).

There was also continued emphasis on strategies included in the 100,000 Lives Campaign, as follows:

- Deploy rapid response teams at the first sign of patient decline.
- Deliver reliable, evidence-based care for acute myocardial infarction to prevent deaths from heart attack.
- Prevent adverse drug events (ADEs) by implementing medication reconciliation.
- Prevent central line infections by implementing a series of interdependent, scientifically grounded steps called the "Central Line Bundle."
- Prevent surgical site infections by reliably delivering the correct preoperative antibiotics at the proper time.

- Prevent ventilator-associated pneumonia by implementing a series of interdependent, scientifi-cally grounded steps, including the "Ventilator Bundle" (IHI, 2016b).

Another IHI effort to improve safety and quality in hospitals began in 2003, when IHI, in col-laboration with the Robert Wood Johnson Foundation, developed a process for transforming care in hospital medical-surgical units. The initiative, known as Transforming Care at the Bedside (TCAB), involves a 4-point framework design theme and six core values of work redesign. Frontline staff, with the full support of the executive team, creates, designs, tests, and implements patient care improve-ments (called *tests of change*). The improvement efforts are centered on a patient's or an employee's need. Small rapid tests of change provide a mechanism for avoiding delays, discussions, debates, meet-ings, and layers of administrative sign-offs that often occur in improvement efforts. The TCAB process includes a series of steps to create a replicable approach that can be done in a short period of time:

- Clarify the current status by observations—include observations of those people involved.
- Understand the root problem to solve.
- Select a process to focus on.
- Design a prototype (plan, do, check, and act).
- Begin small (one patient, one nurse, one idea, one try) and rapidly move/test.
- Identify failures quickly and reject them.
- Determine possible improvements and quickly broaden the test of change.
- Determine definite "just do its" and quickly implement (Martin et al., 2007).

The Institute for Healthcare Improvement currently focuses on the *Triple Aim Framework* as an approach to optimize health system performance. The IHI Triple Aim is a framework developed by the Institute for Healthcare Improvement that describes an approach to optimizing health system performance through

- Improving the patient experience of care (including quality and satisfaction)
- Improving the health of populations
- Reducing the per capita cost of health care

The emphasis on safety has not only resulted in the initiation of specific programs to improve patient care but has also stimulated evaluation of those measures. For example, the IHI website high-lights examples of improving care through the reduction of costs (http://www.ihi.org/Topics/Quality CostValue/Pages/default.aspx).

THE EFFECTS OF VARIOUS PATTERNS OF NURSING CARE DELIVERY: A HISTORICAL PERSPECTIVE

Through the years, nursing care has been delivered in many ways, including total patient care (private duty model), functional, team, primary, and relationship-based care (Fig. 15.2). Although we often talk about these systems as distinct from one another, in the real world, we seldom find pure forms of these systems. Consequently, you must be prepared to work in systems that may be a combination, tailor-made to fit the needs of a specific organization.

What Is the Total Patient Care or Private Duty Model?

Originally, nursing was organized around the *total patient care* or *private duty model*. RNs were hired by the patient and provided care to one patient, typically in the patient's home. In the 1920s, 1930s, and again in the 1980s, this approach was used where one nurse assumes responsibilities for the complete care of a group of patients on a one-on-one basis, providing total patient care during the shift.

The quality of care in the total patient care model is considered to be high, because all activities are carried out by RNs who can focus their complete attention on one patient. Tiedeman and Lookinland

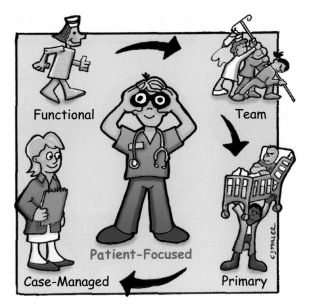

FIG. 15.2 Evolving patterns of nursing care delivery.

(2004) suggest that this model is efficient because it (1) decreases communication time between the staff caring for a patient, (2) reduces the need for supervision, and (3) allows one person to perform more than one task simultaneously. Some nurses prefer this model, because they can focus on patients' needs without the work of supervising others; others feel that their skills and time are wasted doing patient care activities that could be done by others with less skill and education. Patient satisfaction tends to be high with this model if continuity of care and communication are maintained among nurses (Tiedeman & Lookinland, 2004).

What Is Functional Nursing?

The movement toward the use of RNs as employees of hospitals came with the outbreak of World War II. RNs took over the work in the hospital, and that, coupled with the war effort, stimulated the nursing shortage of that period. This forced hospitals to develop alternative models of nursing. The positions of aides and licensed vocational/practical nurses came into being, and in some states, they were allowed to perform functions such as administration of medications and treatments. This functional kind of nursing, which broke nursing care into a series of tasks performed by many people, resulted in a fragmented, impersonal kind of care (Fig. 15.3). Fragmentation of care caused patient problems to be overlooked, because the problems did not fit into a defined assignment.

Tiedeman and Lookinland (2004) note that this assembly-line approach provided little time for the nurse to address a patient's psychosocial or spiritual needs. They cite a number of studies showing that errors and omissions increased when functional nursing was used. This approach would seem to be cost-efficient, because it can be implemented with fewer RNs. However, there are studies that suggest that the functional method, in fact, costs more than primary nursing care. In addition, patients, nurses, and physicians have been critical of this approach because of the fragmentation and the lack of accountability for the patients' total care (Tiedeman & Lookinland, 2004).

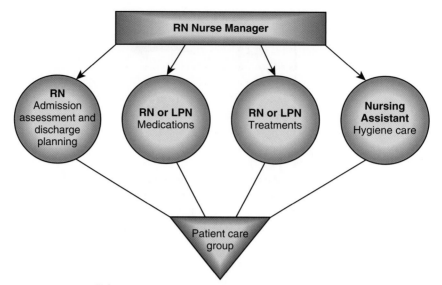

FIG. 15.3 Lines of authority: functional nursing.

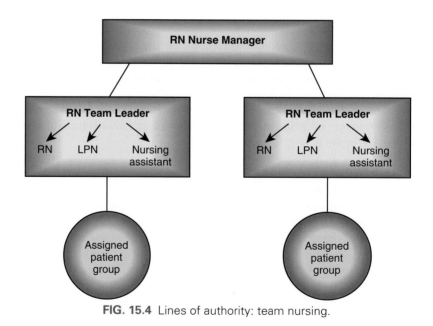

FIG. 15.4 Lines of authority: team nursing.

What Is Team Nursing?

In the 1950s, *team nursing* evolved as a way to address the problems with the functional approach. In this type of nursing, groups of patients were assigned to a team headed by a team leader, usually an RN, who coordinated the care for a designated group of patients (Fig. 15.4). The *team leader* determines work assignments for the team on the basis of the acuity level of the group of patients and the ability of the individual team members. The following is an example of the components of a team:

- An RN who is the team leader
- Two licensed vocational nurses/practical nurses assigned to patient care
- Two unlicensed assistive personnel (UAP)

The success of team nursing depends on good communication among the team members. It is imperative that the team leader continuously evaluate and communicate changes in the patient's condition to the team members. The team conference is a vital part of this approach, allowing team members to assess the needs of their patients and revise their individual plans of care on an ongoing basis.

Tiedeman and Lookinland (2004) suggest that the team model allows the nurse to know patients well enough to make assignments that best match patient needs with staff strengths. Patient needs are coordinated, and continuity of care may improve, depending on the length of time each member stays on the team. However, care can be fragmented and the model ineffective when staff is limited. In addition, the amount of time required to communicate among team members may decrease productivity (Tiedeman & Lookinland, 2004).

What Is Primary Nursing?

In the 1960s and 1970s, *primary nursing* evolved. In this system, a nurse plans and directs the care of a patient during a 24-hour period. This approach is designed to reduce or eliminate the fragmentation of care between shifts and nurses, because one nurse is accountable for planning the care of the patient around the clock. Progress reports, referrals, and discharge planning are usually the responsibility of the primary nurse. When the primary nurse is off duty, an associate nurse continues the plan of care. An RN may be the primary caregiver for some of the assigned patients, whereas an associate nurse is the primary caregiver for others. Some forms of primary nursing evolved into an all-RN staff (Fig. 15.5). You may also find primary nursing being mixed and modified with nurse extenders, such as paired partners, or partners in care. Although team nursing took the RN away from bedside care, primary and modified primary nursing puts the nurse back in close contact with the patient.

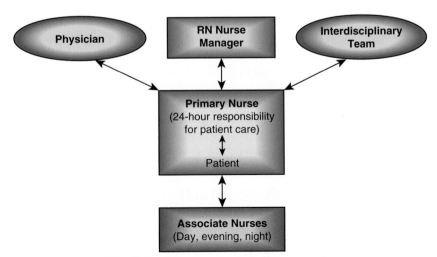

FIG. 15.5 Lines of authority: primary nursing.

Relationship-based practice is the new name for primary nursing. The RN, who may be called the care coordinator, the responsible nurse, the principal responsible nurse, the case manager, or the care manager, manages and coordinates a patient's care in the hospital, as well as coordinating the discharge plan. This nurse develops a relationship and can be identified by the patient, the patient's family, and the health care team as having the responsibility and authority for planning the nursing care that the patient is to receive.

What Is Patient-Focused Care?

Patient-focused care is another delivery system that has evolved since the late 1990s. Because of earlier nursing shortages, some traditional nursing interventions, such as phlebotomy and diet instruction, have been assigned to members of departments that do not report to nursing. These ancillary workers spend a great deal of time in transit from one unit to another. Time is also lost when there is not enough work for this single-function member to do. These tasks can be centralized on the unit under the direction of the RN. UAPs are cross-trained to perform more than one function, thus increasing the level of productivity. In this system, the patient comes into contact with fewer people, and the RN, who is familiar with the patient's plan of care, supervises the delivery of care. This model also moves RNs to a higher level of functioning, because they are now accountable for a fuller range of services for the patient. Tasks that do not require an RN can be delegated to a UAP under the supervision of the RN.

There are also models of care associated with providing care during the patient's transition to home or to another less intense level of care. Such transitional care is particularly important in today's health care environment. Peikes et al. (2012) describe three such models. The first, the *Transitional Care Model* (TCM), provides comprehensive in-hospital and follow-up care plans. The second model, *Care Transitions Intervention* (CTI), teaches self-management and communication skills to patients and caregivers so they can coordinate care. There is also a follow-up component using a home visit and telephone call. The *Re-engineered Discharge* (RED) model provides patient education, medication reconciliation and education, instruction about red flags to symptoms, teach-back learning processes, coordination of physician appointment and follow-up tests, and evidence-based written discharge plan (Peikes et al., 2012).

What Is Telehealth?

As technology has improved, the use of telehealth as a model for delivering care has expanded. *Telehealth* is the delivery of health-related services and information via telecommunications technologies. Telehealth might be as simple as two health professionals discussing a case over the telephone or as sophisticated as doing robotic surgery between facilities at different ends of the globe. Care may include preventive strategies as well as treatment of illness. In 2012, the IOM issued a report on the role of telehealth in the evolution of health care. This report provides an overview of the level of service that might integrate telehealth into their care delivery.

Telehealth, used in home and community-based care, typically focuses on chronic disease and the related education, monitoring, and management of diseases such as hypertension, heart failure, and diabetes. Telehealth can also support acute care by bringing experts to areas that may not have access to such services. Teleradiology, telepathology, and telepharmacology can also supplement care in areas with limited access (IOM, 2012).

What Is the Most Effective Model of Nursing Care?

In the past, there has been a great deal of literature published about models of care delivery. However, there is a lack of systematic evaluation regarding the use of the various models, often because of the lack of similarity in staffing and patient populations on comparison units (Tiedeman & Lookinland, 2004). As a result, it is impossible to determine the impact that inpatient models of nursing care have on patient outcomes, costs, or job satisfaction. It may be that the model of nursing care delivery is less

❓ CRITICAL THINKING BOX 15.4

What factors influence the patterns of nursing care delivery?

important than other factors, including the nurse-to-patient ratios, use of overtime, and the organizational culture in which the nurse works, in influencing outcomes (Critical Thinking Box 15.4). According to Peikes et al. (2012), there is rigorous evidence that at least some of the transitional care models are effective in improving outcomes. The impact on the reduction of cost is unclear.

The current emphasis on quality and safety of patient care has had an impact on care delivery models. Kimball and colleagues (2007) evaluated new innovative care delivery modules that have the potential to change or reinvent care delivery. Of the 45 models identified, 30 were selected for further research, including telephone interviews and review of supporting information. It was required that each of the models (1) serves primarily adult patients, (2) relies on nurses to play a primary role in care delivery, (3) includes an acute-care hospital component, (4) integrates technology, support systems, and new roles, and (5) improves quality, efficiency, and cost. The models were ranked based on (1) the model's match with the criteria, (2) the degree of innovation, (3) the level of integration with other settings and providers of care, (4) the existence of measurable results, and (5) the potential for sustainable outcomes.

Each of the models evaluated included some common elements. The first is an *elevated RN role,* which moves from traditional care delivery to serving as a "primary care manager." The second element is a *sharpened focus on the patient.* The care is nurse-managed, but patient-directed, which results in greater patient and family involvement, which in turn increases compliance and speeds recovery. The third common element includes *specialized tools for assessment, teaching, and measurement,* which ensures smooth transitions from one level of care to another. The fourth element involves *the leveraging of technology* (e.g., electronic medical records, pharmacy robots, cell phones, or walkie-talkies) to enhance communication, reduce labor-intensive documentation, improve access to information, or reduce wasted time. The fifth includes the *measurement of a broad range of clinical, quality, financial, and satisfaction indicators* to drive the redesign and to indicate viability and sustainability. The development of each of these models also involved the early and regular involvement of caregivers. Five of the models evaluated by Kimball and colleagues (2007) are described in Table 15.3.

What Is the Impact of Staffing Patterns on the Quality of Care?

Regardless of the model of care used, nurse staffing must be addressed, particularly in hospitals in which 24-hour coverage is required. In 2004 and again in 2007, the AHRQ released reports that summarized findings of AHRQ-funded research and other research on the relationship between nurse staffing levels and adverse patient outcomes. These reports included the following conclusions:

- Lower levels of hospital nurse staffing are associated with more adverse outcomes.
- Patients in hospitals today are more acutely ill than in the past, but the skill levels of the nursing staff have declined.
- Higher acuity patients have added responsibilities that have increased the nurse workload.
- Avoidable adverse outcomes, such as pneumonia, can raise treatment costs by as much as $28,000.
- Hiring more RNs does not decrease profit.
- Higher levels of nurse staffing could have a positive impact on both quality of care and nurse satisfaction (AHRQ, 2004, 2007).

TABLE 15.3	INNOVATIVE NURSING MODELS		
NAME	**DESCRIPTION**	**ROLE OF THE NURSE**	**ADVANTAGES**
The 12-Bed Hospital	Large hospital segmented into a 12- to 16-bed unit	RN is designated as a patient care facilitator who serves as a CEO of the unit. Assumes 24/7 accountability for directing and managing individualized care for each patient. Primary contact for physicians, social workers, and other members of the interdisciplinary team. Serves as a liaison for patients and families. Mentors other RNs and team members	Improved care, decreased nursing care fragmentation, improved communication and quality of patient care
Primary Care Team	Differentiated nursing practice team composed of an RN case manager, an RN or LVN/LPN, and a clinical assistant	Designed to increase the value of the experienced RN in patient care. Principles include: Team involves patient in planning by asking on each shift, "What is the most important thing I can do for you this shift?" Twice each shift, have a "Take 5 for Safety" huddle—a quick team update on patients. A unit manager and a case manager support RN care.	Decreased nursing vacancy, turnover rates; improved physician satisfaction with nursing knowledge and communication
Collaborative Patient Care Model	A multidisciplinary, population-based case management model, targeting high-volume, high-risk, and high-cost patients in disease-specific or population-based groups	RN patient care coordinators and physicians co-chair multidisciplinary practice groups.	Reduction of average acute length of stay and reduced caregiver turnover
Transitional Care Model	Provides comprehensive in-hospital planning, care coordination, and home follow-up of high-risk older adults by an interdisciplinary team.	APRNs conduct assessments and, with physicians, design and coordinate patient care and discharge plans. APRNs implement the plan of care in the home for 1 to 3 months.	Decreased total number of hospital readmissions and total health care costs
Hospital at Home	An acute home-based program of older patients with COPD, heart failure, cellulitis, and pneumonia; provides hospital-level care at home	RN is the coordinator of care for a team consisting of a physician, RN, and nursing assistant. RN observes the patient in the home during the first 24 hours—level of care is determined. Physician visits daily.	Aims to avoid many complications, including delirium resulting from the hospital admission of older patients

APRN, Advanced practice master's degree prepared nurse.
Adapted from Kimball, B., et al. (2007). The quest for new innovative care delivery models, *Journal of Nursing Administration 37*, 392–398.

The 2004 studies showed significant associations between too few nurses on a unit and higher rates of pneumonia, upper gastrointestinal bleeding, shock/cardiac arrest, urinary tract infections, and failure to rescue. Other studies in the review showed associations between lower staffing levels and pneumonia, lung collapse, falls, pressure ulcers, thrombosis after major surgery, pulmonary compromise after surgery, longer hospital stays, and 30-day mortalities (AHRQ, 2004).

In 2007, the AHRQ funded research to review studies from 11 databases to assess how nurse-to-patient ratios and nurse work hours were associated with patient outcomes in acute care hospitals, factors that influence nurse staffing policies, and nurse staffing strategies that improved patient outcomes. They found that higher RN nurse staffing was associated with less hospital-related mortality, failure to rescue, and other patient outcomes, but the higher RN nurse staffing might not be the cause of these outcomes, because hospitals that invest in adequate nursing staff may also invest in other initiatives to improve quality. Researchers also found that the effect of increased RN staffing on patient safety was strong and consistent in ICUs and for surgical patients. A larger number of RN hours spent on direct patient care were associated with decreased risk of hospital-related death and with shorter lengths of stay (AHRQ, 2007).

Determination of the number of nursing staff needed relative to the number and acuity of patients on a unit is the challenge of staffing. Since the early to mid-1990s, patient classification systems (or acuity systems) have been used to determine the number of nurses needed on a unit at any one time. Patient acuity is the measure of categorizing patients based on their nursing care requirements. Patient classification systems, particularly with increased computerization and the ability to access the system online, provide many benefits. Specifically they can be used to (1) improve patient care outcomes, (2) identify appropriate staffing, (3) track budget compliance and costs, and (4) maintain nurse retention through their ability to impact staffing through assessment of patients' conditions (Harper & McCully, 2007).

More recently, the Agency for Healthcare Research and Quality (AHRQ) implemented a longitudinal study, linking hospital nurse staffing data to AHRQ's Healthcare Cost and Utilization Project (HCUP) State Inpatient Databases from California, Maryland, and Nevada between 2008 and 2011. The purpose of the study was to assess the causal relationship between the level and skill mix of nurses, adverse events as measured by nurse-sensitive patient safety indicators, lengths of stay and cost. Increases in hospital nurse staffing levels are associated with reductions in adverse events and lengths of stay and do not lead to increased costs. Increases in nurse staffing levels were associated with reductions in nursing-sensitive adverse events and length of stay but did not lead to increases in patient care costs. Changing skill mix by increasing the number of registered nurses, as a proportion of licensed nursing staff, led to reductions in costs. This study further supported the value of inpatient nurse staffing as it contributes to improvements in inpatient care (Martsolf et al., 2014).

How Are Nursing Work Assignments Determined?

After appropriate staffing levels for a unit are determined, specific nurses must be scheduled. How work assignments are decided varies with individual organizations and is related to the model of care delivery, condition of the patient, architecture of the unit, and expertise of the staff.

> A major problem in scheduling nurses is the fact that patient acuity fluctuates dramatically from day to day and from season to season.

For example, during the Christmas holidays there is often a significant decrease in the number of elective surgeries. In response, some hospitals may close units or reduce the number of staff on any given unit. By contrast, in the middle of the influenza season, the hospital might be full and understaffed.

Nursing has tried a variety of approaches to anticipate the numbers and qualifications of nurses who will be needed for a specific period for a specific group of patients. Regulatory agencies such as The Joint Commission require that staffing be based on some sort of organized system. Staffing in organizations may be based on budgeted nursing hours per patient per day. Hours per patient per day are calculated by the number of patient care staff working during a 24-hour period and divided by the numbers of patients served in a day.

Whether nursing resource requirements are defined by nursing hours per patient days or as nurse–patient ratios, the underlying assumption is that all patients, patient days, and nursing staff are equal. In fact, the intensity of patient care needed, the length of stay of the patient, and the competency of the staff also influence the nursing resource requirement. There are three approaches to document that the organization has a minimum number of nurses to ensure safety in any given acute care unit: (1) identifying and mandating fixed staffing ratios, and (2) establishing a hospital-specific written staffing plan, which typically uses computerized patient acuity systems, or (3) reporting/public disclosure of staffing plans.

In 1999, California was the first state to pass comprehensive legislation to establish minimum nurse-to-patient ratios for RNs and LPN/LVNs in acute care, acute psychiatric, and specialty hospitals. After the bill was passed, the California Department of Health Services (CDHS) was charged with determining what the ratios in various patient care areas should be. In 2005, the governor suspended the law scheduled to take effect on January 1, 2005, which required one nurse for every five patients in medical-surgical units, which was a change from the ratio of one nurse for every six patients. A judge ruled that the governor's administration overstepped its authority and barred the administration from delaying the implementation of the staffing ratios. Although a few states have regulated the ratios in specialty areas, such as intensive care units or labor and delivery rooms, California is the only state to mandate ratios in every patient care unit in every hospital in the state (DeVandry & Cooper, 2009). Aiken and colleagues (2009, 2010) conclude that patient mortality rates have decreased and nursing retention rates have steadily increased since implementation of the mandated nurse staffing ratios in California.

In contrast to fixed nurse–patient ratios, a written plan includes the following critical factors:

- Establishing initial staffing levels that are recalculated at least annually or more often as necessary
- Setting staffing levels on a unit-by-unit basis
- Identifying ways to adjust staffing levels from shift to shift, based on intensity of patient care

Written staffing plans should be developed by an advisory committee composed of a number of RNs, a significant portion of whom are involved in direct patient care at least part of the time (Critical Thinking Box 15.5). There are also legislative initiatives to require hospitals to post or report the level of staffing to a relevant regulatory body.

Nursing organizations across the country have been involved in the legislative process to ensure that nursing staffing is safe. A federal regulation requires hospitals certified to participate in Medicare to "have adequate numbers of licensed registered nurses, licensed practical (vocational) nurses, and other personnel to provide nursing care to all patients as needed." Because of the vagueness of this regulation, the American Nurses Association (ANA) has continued to push for federal nurse staffing laws. To date, this has not occurred, and regulation to ensure that staffing is appropriate to meet patients' safety needs has been left to state legislation. Seven states (CT, IL, NV, OH, OR, TX, and WA) have regulations that require hospitals to have staffing committees responsible for plans and staffing policies. California is the only state that stipulates minimum nurse–patient ratios and Massachusetts requires that ICUs have a 1:1 or 1:3 nurse to patient ratio, depending on the patient's stability. Minnesota requires a Chief Nursing Officer or designee to develop a core staffing plan with input from others,

> **? CRITICAL THINKING BOX 15.5**
>
> How might you handle a situation on your unit where staffing is poor/What are the unit census, acuity, and patient-classification systems?
> - Does your organization have a float pool within the staff or an agency or outside staff available?
> - Check whether your part-time staff can work an extra shift.
> - Will another staff member cover the extra shift in exchange for a day off later in the schedule?
> - Can you survive with partial-shift coverage during the "peak" shift hours?
> - Ask a staff member to work a double shift—either stay late or come in early.
> - Work the shift yourself.
> - What other solutions can you think of?
> - What are the advantages and disadvantages of each of these options?

similar to the Joint Commission standard. Five states (IL, NJ, NY, RI, and VT) require some form of disclosure and/or public reporting (ANA, 2016). For more information on safe staffing legislative updates, check out the ANA's website (http://www.nursingworld.org/MainMenuCategories/Policy-Advocacy/State/Legislative-Agenda-Reports/State-StaffingPlansRatios).

The research regarding the effectiveness of the three approaches has not been conclusive, and the optimal nurse-to-patient ratio has not been determined. Until the evidence regarding staffing becomes clearer, the judgment of the competent RN is critical in making decisions regarding the necessary staff. The ANA continues to promote the position that adequate nurse staffing is critical to the delivery of quality patient care and developed the following policy statements and principles of staffing in 2004.

Policy Statements

1. Nurse staffing patterns and the level of care provided should not depend on the type of payer.
2. Evaluation of any staffing system should include quality of work life outcomes, as well as patient outcomes.
3. Staffing should be based on achieving quality of patient care indices, meeting organizational outcomes, and ensuring that the quality of the nurse's work life is appropriate.

Principles

Patient care unit related

1. Appropriate staffing levels for a patient care unit reflect analysis of individual and aggregate patient needs.
2. There is a critical need to either retire or seriously question the usefulness of the concept of nursing hours per patient day (HPPD).
3. Unit functions necessary to support delivery of quality patient care must also be considered in determining staffing levels.

Staff related

1. The specific needs of various patient populations should determine the appropriate clinical competencies required of the nurse practicing in that area.
2. Registered nurses must have nursing management support and representation at both the operational level and the executive level.
3. Clinical support from experienced RNs should be readily available to those RNs with less proficiency.

Institution/organization related

1. Organizational policy should reflect an organizational climate that values registered nurses and other employees as strategic assets and exhibit a true commitment to filling budgeted positions in a timely manner.
2. All institutions should have documented competencies for nursing staff, including agency or supplemental and traveling RNs, for those activities that they have been authorized to perform.
3. Organizational policies should recognize the myriad needs of both patients and nursing (ANA, 2004).

What About Scheduling Patterns?

Nursing has also been concerned about scheduling practices and options, because in many health care environments, nursing care must be provided 24 hours a day, 365 days per year. That is why there are numerous scheduling patterns other than the typical 8-hour shift 5 days a week. From working 10-hour days 4 days a week to the weekend alternative (known as the Baylor Plan) of two 12-hour weekend shifts for 36 hours of pay, nurses have tried numerous patterns and combinations of shifts.

What About the Use of Overtime?

With the current shortage of health professionals, employees are also encouraged and sometimes required to work overtime. In fact, Trinkoff and colleagues (2006), in a study of more than 2000 nurses across multiple care settings, found that at least one-fourth of the respondents reported working 12 hours or more per shift, one-third of the sample reported working more than 40 hours per week, and one-third reported working 6 days or more in a row at least once in the previous 6 months. Similarly, the landmark study of nurses by Rogers and associates (2004) showed that 14% of nurses in the study reported working shifts of 16 hours or longer in the previous 4 weeks; 81% of shifts ran more than their scheduled limit. This work pattern results in fatigue, which can produce performance similar to someone who is intoxicated from alcohol. Fatigue can also produce physical performance effects that inhibit critical cognitive functions, including lapses of attention, irritability, memory lapses, decreased ability to detect and react to subtle changes, slowed information processing, difficulties in handling unexpected situations, and communication difficulties (Graves & Simmons, 2009) (Research for Best Practice Box 15.1).

CONCLUSION

The emphasis on cost control and managed care has changed the way that nursing care is delivered. New models of health care delivery are being developed in which we look at the desired outcome and "manage backward" to achieve that outcome at the lowest level of expenses. Because of some of the unexpected negative consequences of managed care, there is a renewed emphasis on evidence-based care to enhance patient safety (see the Relevant Websites and Online Resources). We are continually challenged to develop more innovative and creative ways to ensure excellence in patient care with limited dollars. Nurses can meet this challenge.

🔍 RESEARCH FOR BEST PRACTICE BOX 15.1

Creating Healthy Work Environments to Retain Nurses

Practice Issue

Kramer and colleagues (2009) reviewed literature from seven professional organizations/regulatory bodies to identify structures and leadership practices that influence a healthy working environment likely to retain nurses. They also analyzed 88 additional studies to identify structures that are most helpful in supporting nurses to provide high-quality patient care. Creating healthy nursing environments improves quality patient care and employee retention.

Implications for Nursing Practice

Structures most frequently cited as influencing a healthy working environment are

- Management style of the nurse leader is visionary, visible, open and rich, and includes skilled communications.
- Opportunities for education, professional growth, development, and advancement are available, including tuition reimbursement, continuing education, and certification.
- Nurse staffing structures provide adequate numbers and flexible scheduling.
- Flat, decentralized organizational structures promote unit-based and shared decision making.
- Collaborative, interdisciplinary relationships are demonstrated through evidence such as committee membership and minutes.
- A culture of interdisciplinary collaboration, teamwork, and safety exists and is nurtured.
- Personnel policies include salary and benefits competitive for geographic area and advancement, such as career ladders.
- Quality improvement infrastructure and environment are in place, including research and evidence-based practice initiatives.
- Meaningful recognition structures are operative, including recognition of nurses' contributions and the value of these contributions; reward/pay for performance.

Structures most helpful in supporting nurses to provide high-quality patient care are

- Nurse managers who share power; request evidence used to make autonomous decisions; hold staff accountable in positive, constructive ways for decisions made; promote group cohesion and teamwork; and resolve conflicts constructively.
- Structures that support evidence-based practice teams.
- Approval from administration for nurses to make autonomous decisions, interdisciplinary collaboration, and for leadership/participation in council activities.
- Programs that help develop effective teamwork.
- Staffing structures that consider RN competence, level of patient acuity, flexible scheduling, and flexible care delivery systems.
- Availability and support for educational programs.
- Regular, interdisciplinary patient care rounds, review and critique sessions, and critical pathway and protocol development.
- Structure for regulation and determination of nursing practice by nurses at all levels of the organization.
- Development of and "living" a patient-centered culture in which values are known, subscribed to, and transmitted to newcomers.

Considering This Information

What can you do as a nursing leader to promote a healthy work environment?

Reference

Kramer, M., Schmalenberg, B., & Maguire, P. (2009). Nine structures and leadership practices essential for a magnetic (healthy) work environment. *Nursing Administration Quarterly, 34,* 4–17.

RELEVANT WEBSITES AND ONLINE RESOURCES

Agency for Healthcare Research and Quality
Retrieved from http://www.ahrq.gov.

American Association of Colleges of Nursing
Retrieved from http://www.aacn.nche.edu.

American Nurses Association
Retrieved from http://www.nursingworld.org.

Institute of Medicine
Retrieved from https://www.nationalacademies.org/hmd/.

The Joint Commission
Retrieved from http://www.jointcommission.org.

Institute for Healthcare Improvement
Retrieved from http://www.ihi.org.

Indiana Center for Evidence-Based Nursing Practice, in the Purdue University Calumet's School of Nursing
Retrieved from http://www.ebnp.org.

Joanna Briggs Institute University of Adelaide, Australia
Retrieved from http://joannabriggs.org/.

Louisiana Center for Evidence-Based Nursing at LSU HSC School of Nursing
Retrieved from https://www.lsuhsc.edu/n o/library/news/?tag=evidence-based-nursing.

TCU Center for Evidence-Based Practice and Research: A Collaborating Center of the Joanna Briggs Institute
Retrieved from http://www.harriscollege.tcu.edu/evidence-based.as.

The Academic Center for Evidence-Based Nursing (ACE) at the University of Texas Health Science Center at San Antonio
Retrieved from http://www.acestar.uthscsa.edu.

The Sara Cole Hirsch Institute for Best Nursing Practice Based on Evidence at Case Western Reserve School of Nursing
Retrieved from http://fpb.case.edu/HirshInstitute/index.shtm.

The Center for the Advancement of Evidence-Based Practice—Arizona State University
Retrieved from http://nursinga ndhealth.asu.edu/evidence-based-practice/index.htm.

BIBLIOGRAPHY

Agency for Healthcare Research and Quality. (2004). *Hospital nurse staffing and quality of care: Research in action.* Retrieved from www.ahrq.gov.

Agency for Healthcare Research and Quality. (2007). *Evidence based practice center.* Retrieved from www.ahrq.gov/clinic/epc.

Aiken, L., Clarke, S., Sloane, D., et al. (2009). Effects of hospital care environment on patient mortality and nurse outcomes. *Journal of Nursing Administration, 39*(7–8), S45–S51.

Aikin, L., Sloane, D., Cimiotti, J., et al. (2010, August). Applications of the California nurse staffing mandate for other states. *Health Services Research, 45*(4), 904–921.

American Association of Colleges of Nursing (AACN). (2014). *Nursing shortage fact sheet.* Retrieved from http://www.aacn.nche.edu/media-relations/fact-sheets/nursing-shortage.

American Association of Critical-Care Nurses (AACN). (2005). *AACN standards for establishing and sustaining healthy work environments: A journey to excellence.* Retrieved from http://www.aacn.org/wd/hwe/docs/hwestandards.pdf.

American Nurses Association. (2004). *ANA principles on safe staffing.* Retrieved from https://nursing2015.files.wordpress.com/2008/09/_17ana-principles-on-safe-staffing.pdf.

American Nurses Association. (2016). *Nurse staffing.* Retrieved from http://www.nursingworld.org/nursestaffing.

American Nurses Credentialing Center. (2011). *Forces of magnetism.* Retrieved from http://www.nursecredentialing.org/ForcesofMagnetism.aspx.

Black, H., Priolo, C., Akinyemi, D., et al. (2010). Clearing clinical barriers: Enhancing social support using a nurse navigator for asthma care. *Journal of Asthma, 47*(8), 913–919.

Buerhaus, P. (2009). *The future of the nursing workforce in the United States: Data, trends and implications.* Sudbury, MA: Jones and Bartlett.

Case, M. B. (2011). Oncology nurse navigator: Ensuring safe passage. *Journal of Oncology Nursing, 15*(1), 33–40.

Case Management Society of America. (2015). Retrieved from www.cmsa.org.

Centers for Disease Control and Prevention (CDC). (2014). *Health expenditures.* Retrieved from http://www.cdc.gov/nchs/fastats/health-expenditures.htm.

Chandra, A., Holmes, J., & Skinner, J. (2013). *Is this time different? The slowdown in health care spending.* Brookings paper on economic activity. Retrieved from http://www.brookings.edu/about/projects/bpea/papers/2013/fall-chandra-healthcare-spending.

DeVandry, S., & Cooper, J. (2009). Mandating nurse staffing in Pennsylvania: More than a numbers game. *Journal of Nursing Administration, 39*, 470–478.

Donaldson, N., Shapiro, S., Scott, M., et al. (2009). Leading successful rapid response teams: A multisite implementation evaluation. *Journal of Nursing Administration, 39*, 176–181.

Faxon, D., Schwamm, L., Pasternak, R., et al. (2004). Improving quality of care through disease management: Principles and recommendations from the American Heart Association's expert panel on disease management. *Circulation, 109*, 2651–2654. Retrieved from http://circ.ahajournals.org/content/109/21/2651.full.

Graves, K., & Simmons, D. (2009). Reexamining fatigue: Implications for nursing practice. *Critical Care Nursing Quarterly, 32*(2), 112–115.

Herbert, P., Sisk, J., Wang, J., et al. (2008). Cost-effectiveness of nurse-led disease management for heart failure in an ethnically diverse urban community. *Annuals of Internal Medicine, 149*(8), 540–548.

Harper, K., & McCully, C. (2007). Acuity systems dialogue and patient classification system essentials. *Nursing Administration Quarterly, 31*(4), 284–299.

Healthcare.gov. (2015). *Key features of the Affordable Care Act, year by year.* Retrieved from http://www.hhs.gov/healthcare/facts-and-features/key-features-of-aca-by-year/index.html.

Horstmann, E., Brown, J., Islam, F., Brick, J., & Agins, B. D. (2010). Retaining HIV infection patients in care: Where are we? Where do we go from here? *Clinical Infectious Diseases, 50*(5), 752–761. http://dx.doi.org/10.1086/649933.

Institute for Healthcare Improvement. (2016a). *About us.* Retrieved from http://www.ihi.org/Pages/default.aspx.

Institute for Healthcare Improvement. (2016b). *Protecting 5 million lives from harm.* http://www.ihi.org/engage/initiatives/completed/5MillionLivesCampaign/Pages/default.aspx.

Institute of Medicine. (2000). *To err is human: Building a safer health system.* Retrieved from http://nationalacademies.org/hmd/reports/1999/to-err-is-human-building-a-safer-health-system.aspx.

Institute of Medicine. (2001). *Crossing the quality chasm: A new health system for the 21st century.* Retrieved from http://nationalacademies.org/HMD/Reports/2001/Crossing-the-Quality-Chasm-A-New-Health-System-for-the-21st-Century.aspx.

Institute of Medicine. (2003). *Keeping patients safe: Transforming the work environment of nurses.* Retrieved from http://nationalacademies.org/hmd/reports/2003/keeping-patients-safe-transforming-the-work-environment-of-nurses.aspx.

Institute of Medicine. (2010). *Future of nursing.* Retrieved from http://nationalacademies.org/hmd/Reports/2010/The-Future-of-Nursing-Leading-Change-Advancing-Health.aspx.

Institute of Medicine. (November 2012). *Role of telehealth in an evolving healthcare environment.* Retrieved from http://nationalacademies.org/hmd/reports/2012/the-role-of-telehealth-in-an-evolving-health-care-environment.aspx.

Joanna Briggs Institute. (2016). *AboutJBI.* Retrieved from http://www.joannabriggs.org/about.html.

Kaiser Family Foundation. (2007). *U.S. health care costs: Background brief.* www.kaiseredu.org/topics_im.asp?1&;parentID=61&id=358.

Kalisch, B., & Lee, H. (2009). Nursing teamwork, staff characteristics, work schedules, and staffing. *Health Care Management Review, 34*(4), 323–333. http://dx.doi.org/10.1097/HMR.0b013e3181aaa920.

Kimball, B., et al. (2007). The quest for new innovative care delivery models. *Journal of Nursing Administration, 37*(9), 392–398.

Kramer, M., Schmalenberg, B., & Maguire, P. (2009). Nine structures and leadership practices essential for a magnetic (healthy) work environment. *Nursing Administration Quarterly, 34*(1), 4–17. http://dx.doi.org/10.1097/NAQ.0b013e3181c95ef4.

Maxfield, D., Grenny, J., McMillan, R., Patterson, K., & Switzler, A. (2005). Silence kills: The seven crucial conversations in health care. American Association of Critical Care Nurses. Vital Smarts. Vital Smart Industry Watch. Retrieved from http://www.silenttreatmentstudy.com/silencekills/SilenceKills.pdf.

Maxfield, D., Grenny, J., Lavandero, R., & Groah, L. (2010). The silent treatment: Why safety tools and checklists aren't enough to save lives. American Association of Critical Care Nursing. Association of Peri-Operative Registered Nurses. Vital Smarts. Vital Smart Industry Watch. Retrieved from http://www.silenttreatmentstudy.com/silencekills/SilenceKills.pdf.

Martin, S., et al. (2007). Transforming care at the bedside: Implementation and spread model of single-hospital and multihospital systems. *Journal of Nursing Administration, 37*(10), 444–451.

Martsolf, G. R., Auerbach, D., Benevent, R., et al. (2014). Examining the value of inpatient nurse staffing: An assessment of quality and patient care cost. *Medical Care, 52*(11), 982–988.

McDonald, A., & Ward-Smith, P. (2012). A review of evidence based practice to retain graduate nurses in the profession. *Journal for Nurses in Staff Development, 28*(1), January-February, E16-E20.

Melnyk, B., & Fineout-Overholt, E. (2011). *Evidence based practice in nursing and health care: A guide to best practice* (3rd ed.). Philadelphia: Lippincott Williams & Wilkins.

National, Heart, Lung, and Blood Institute (NHLBI). (n.d.). Retrieved from http://www.nhlbi.hih.gov.

Needleman, J., Buerhaus, P., Pankratz, V. S., Leibson, C. L., Stevens, S. R., & Harris, M. (2011). Nurse staffing and inpatient hospital mortality. *New England Journal of Medicine, 374*(11), 1037–1040.

Pedersen, A., & Hack, T. F. (2010). Pilots of oncology health care: A concept analysis of the patient navigator role. *Oncology Nursing Forum, 37,* 55–60.

Peikes, D., Zutshi, A., Genevro, J., Smith, K., Parchman, M., & Meyers, D. (February 2012). *Early evidence on the patient-centered medical home.* Final report (Prepared by Mathematica Policy Research, under Contract Nos. HHSA290200900019I/HHSA29032002T and HHSA290200900019I/HHSA29032005T). AHRQ Publication No. 12-0020-EF. Rockville, MD: Agency for Healthcare Research and Quality.

RAND Corp. (2007). *Analysis of disease management.* Retrieved from http://www.rand.org/pubs/technical_reports/TR562z15/analysis-of-disease-management.html.

Rogers, A. E., et al. (2004). The working hours of hospital staff nurse and patient safety. *Health Affair, 23,* 202–212.

Schatz, M. (2008). Does pay for performance influence quality of care? *Current Opinion in Allergy and Clinical Immunology, 8*(3), 213–221. Retrieved from http://www.medscape.com/viewarticle/576573_4.

Sharpnack-Elganzouri, E., Standish, C., & Androwich, I. (2009). Medication administration time study (MATS): Nursing staff performance of medication administration. *Journal of Nursing Administration, 39*(5), 204–210.

Thomas, F., & Caldis, T. (2007). Emerging issues of pay-for-performance in health care. *Health Care Financing Review.* Retrieved from https://www.cms.gov/Research-Statistics-Data-and-Systems/Research/HealthCareFinancingReview/downloads/07fallpg1.pdf.

The Joint Commission. (n.d.). (2016). *National patient safety goals.* Retrieved from www.jointcommission.org/PatientSafety/NationalPatientSafetyGoals.

Thomas, P. (2009). Case management delivery models. *Journal of Nursing Administration, 39,* 30–37.

Tiedeman, M., & Lookinland, S. (2004). Traditional models of care delivery: What have we learned? *Journal of Nursing Administration, 34,* 291–297.

Torgan, C. (2013). *Patient outcomes improved by pay for performance NIH research matters.* Retrieved from http://www.nih.gov/researchmatters/september2013/09232013performance.htm.

Trinkoff, A., Geiger-Brown, J., Brady, B., et al. (2006). How long and how much are nurses now working? *American Journal of Nursing, 106,* 60–67.

Wells, K. J., Bellagio, T. A., Dudley, D. J., et al. (2008). Patient navigation: State of the art or is it science? *Cancer, 113*(8), 1999–2010.

16

Economics of the Health Care Delivery System

Julie V. Darmody, PhD, RN, ACNS-BC

ⓔ http://evolve.elsevier.com/Zerwekh/nsgtoday/.

The registered nurse utilizes appropriate resources to plan and provide nursing services that are safe, effective, and financially responsible.
Standard 15, Resource Utilization, ANA Standards of Professional Nursing Practice (2010)

Value is the intersection of cost and quality in health care.

After completing this chapter, you should be able to:

- Define economics and health care economics.
- Compare the market for health care to a normal market for goods and services.
- Use a basic knowledge of health care economics to analyze trends in the health care delivery system.
- Describe what operating budget, personnel budget, and capital budget mean.
- Define economic research strategies.
- Describe what is meant by the term *fiscal responsibility* in clinical practice.
- Discuss strategies you will use to achieve fiscal responsibility in your clinical practice.

The rate of increase in U.S. national health care spending for 2013 was 3.6%, continuing a pattern of low growth following the economic recession for five consecutive years from 2009 to 2013 (Hartman et al., 2015). U.S. National health expenditures (NHE) in 2013 were $2.9 trillion, or $9255 per person, which comprises 17.4% of the gross domestic product (GDP) (Hartman et al., 2015). By the year 2024, those expenditures are projected to be $5.4 trillion and comprise 19.6% of GDP (Keehan et al., 2015).

The outcome of this large investment of resources in health and health care in the United States is variable. Many Americans do not receive the care they need, receive care that causes harm, or receive care without consideration of their preferences and values. The distribution of services is often inefficient and uneven across populations. Since 1999, annual reports by the Agency for Healthcare Research and Quality (AHRQ) have summarized the performance of the U.S. health care system and identified strengths and weaknesses (AHRQ, 2015). The specific goals are to achieve better care, smarter spending, and healthier people. The most recent report for 2014 indicates that access has improved and quality has improved for many priorities including patient safety, person-centered care, effective treatment measures for some conditions, and healthy living (AHRQ, 2015). However, many challenges remain in improving quality and reducing racial, ethnic, and income disparities (AHRQ, 2015). All of these clinical and financial measures of the health care system have implications for nursing practice.

WHAT ARE THE TRENDS AFFECTING THE RISING COSTS OF HEALTH CARE?

Both intrinsic and extrinsic factors contribute to the rising costs of health care. Intrinsic factors include characteristics of the population (the population is getting older and is requiring more of the health care system), the demand for health care, and health insurance coverage. Extrinsic factors include the availability of technology, prescription drug costs, and workforce costs (Fig. 16.1). The effects of the economic recession between 2008 and 2010 were high levels of unemployment, a decrease in private health insurance enrollment, an increase in Medicaid enrollment, and an increase in the number of uninsured people (Hartman et al., 2015). Economic trends, such as a recession, have both intrinsic and extrinsic effects.

Intrinsic Factors

The 2010 Census reported that there are 308.7 million people in the United States, a 9.7% increase from the 2000 Census (U.S. Census Bureau, 2011). Population projections based on the 2010 Census for the years 2012 to 2060 predict much slower growth during the next several decades and increased

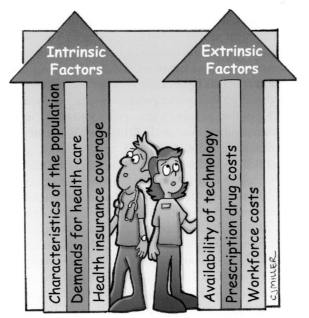

FIG. 16.1 Trends affecting the rising cost of health care.

diversity in the U.S. population (U.S. Census Bureau, 2012). According to projections for 2012 to 2060, the population over age 65 is expected to more than double, and the population of the "oldest old," over age 85, is expected to more than triple (U.S. Census Bureau, 2012). This is important information, because older people typically use increased health care resources and may not have the income to purchase them. During the projection period of 2009 to 2019, the Baby Boomers (citizens born between 1946 and 1964) will become eligible for Medicare health insurance. A critical challenge for the Medicare program will be to provide quality care for the increasingly aging population while keeping the program financially secure. The Affordable Care Act (ACA) of 2010 included reductions in Medicare payments to plans and providers and introduced system reforms including accountable care organizations (ACOs), medical homes, bundled payments, and value-based purchasing to improve quality and reduce costs (Kaiser Family Foundation Fact Sheet, 2015c). Medicare spending growth has slowed recently, averaging 4.1% between 2010 and 2014, compared to 9.0% between 2000 and 2010 (Kaiser Family Foundation Fact Sheet, 2015b).

Demand, in the economic sense, is the amount of health care services that a consumer wishes to purchase. Demand for health care may be influenced by illness, cultural-demographic characteristics, and economic factors, including income and health insurance (Feldstein, 2012). Health insurance coverage is one of the most important factors that influences the quantity of health services demanded (Feldstein, 2012). In 2014, the number of uninsured people was estimated at 32 million, a decrease of nearly 9 million since 2013 (Kaiser Family Foundation Fact Sheet, 2015a). With the 2014 implementation of the ACA Medicaid expansion and Health Insurance Marketplaces, it was estimated that 8.4 million Americans gained insurance coverage (Keehan et al., 2015). One of the first groups to gain expanded health insurance options under the ACA was young adults, age 19 to 25, who were allowed to remain as dependents on their parent's private insurance until age 26. The uninsured rate for these young adults dropped from over 30% in 2009 to 19% in 2014 (McMorrow et al., 2015).

Extrinsic Factors

The availability of new medical technology has contributed to the rising costs of health care. If an organization does not offer technology that a competitor offers, it is likely that the market share (percentage of persons in an area selecting that institution) of the organization will decline. To attain a competitive edge, an organization needs to be an early adopter of expensive, new technology. Then, thinking sequentially, someone has to pay for the technology, and this cost will be passed on to consumers in the form of higher health care costs.

After slower growth in 2012, prescription drug spending increased by 2.5% in 2013. Factors influencing the increased spending included higher prices for brand-name and specialty drugs, new medicines, and increased utilization (Hartman et al., 2015). Another factor driving health care costs is hospital care expenditures, which increased 4.3% in 2013, a slightly lower increase than the 5.7% increase in 2012 (Hartman et al., 2015). Individuals' out-of-pocket spending for health care increased to 12% of NHE in 2013 due to higher cost sharing in group health insurance plans and increased enrollment in consumer-directed health plans with high deductibles and copayments (Hartman et al., 2015). The Organization for Economic Cooperation and Development (OECD) compared health data for 34 industrialized countries in 2013 (OECD, 2015). In 2013, health spending was 16.4% of GDP in the United States, which was well above the OECD average of 8.9% (OECD, 2015). The United States spent $8713 per capita (per person) on health care in 2013, which is also well above the OECD average health spending per capita in 2013 of $3453 (OECD, 2015). In 2013, the United States continued to be number one in health care spending as a percent of GDP and also in per capita spending; however, the United States had an infant mortality rate of 6.0 deaths per 1000 live births, which is above the OECD average of 4.1, and a life expectancy of 78.8 years, which is more than 1.7 years less than the OECD average of 80.5 years (OECD, 2015).

> This has led some to question whether the United States has the best health care system in the world or just the most expensive.

WHAT IS THE EFFECT OF THE CHANGING ECONOMIC ENVIRONMENT ON CLINICAL PRACTICE?

Because nurses belong to the largest health care profession and are thus in a position to influence health care costs, it is essential that all nurses understand basic concepts of economics and fiscal (money) management. This knowledge was previously taught in graduate courses for nurse managers or nurse executives. However, the world has changed! Nurses at the point of care in all settings will be challenged to maintain caring values and practices in relationships with patients and families while maintaining financial responsibility within the economic reality of limited resources (Cara, Nyberg, & Brousseau, 2011).

> Today all nurses need to couple their clinical skills with business skills that enable them to be full participants in designing and delivering health care.

INTRODUCTION TO ECONOMICS

A simple definition of economics is the allocation of scarce resources. An analogy might be made to the income that an individual earns. The paycheck is a limited, finite amount of money, and choices must be made about how to spend, or allocate, the money. Such choices might include rent, a car payment, food, clothing, and health insurance payments. Individuals may not be able to pay for all of the goods or services that they wish to have, so decisions must be made and priorities established.

Similarly, health care is a limited resource, and choices have to be made. The choices about health care that concern economists are made at the national level. Questions include How much does the country wish to spend on health care, what services does the country wish to provide, what is the best method for producing health care, and how will health care be distributed (Feldstein, 2012)?

What Are the Choices About Amount of Spending?

Currently, the United States is spending between 17% and 18% of its income on health care. As the payer for Medicare (the national health insurance program for people aged 65 years or older, some people younger than age 65 with disabilities, and people with end-stage renal disease) and Medicaid (a joint federal and state program that pays for medical assistance for certain individuals and families with low incomes and resources), the federal government is the nation's largest purchaser of health care. Yet this amount does not fully meet the needs of the populations served under these programs, let alone provide for the health care needs of persons without insurance.

The Affordable Care Act of 2010

The ACA of 2010 was the largest mandated health care change since Medicare and Medicaid were introduced in 1965. The timeline for implementing the ACA was from 2010 through 2015. The provisions of the law addressed issues of access, quality, and cost in the U.S. health care system (Critical Thinking Box 16.1).

> **? CRITICAL THINKING BOX 16.1**
>
> What are the implications of the Affordable Care Act (ACA) for nursing practice? Suggest strategies for nurses to assist individuals and families to understand their rights and choices under this law.

The ACA created a framework for increasing access to health coverage for Americans. Key features of the Affordable Care Act include:

- Provides state and federal-based health insurance marketplaces where individuals can purchase private insurance with premium and cost-sharing assistance based on income level. Requires all health plans to provide a standardized, easy-to-read uniform Summary of Benefits and Coverage (SBC), which gives consumers consistent information and allows them to compare what health plans offer when making choices of coverage
- Prohibits denial of coverage for children with preexisting conditions beginning in 2010 and for adults with preexisting conditions beginning in 2014
- Allows young adults up to age 26 to stay on their parents' insurance policies
- Provides expanded Medicaid coverage for low-income children and adults
- Provides coverage for a range of preventive health services without any patient cost-sharing (co-payments, deductibles, or co-insurance) (Kaiser Family Foundation Issue Brief, 2015c)

Four years after its implementation, the ACA remains controversial, although progress has been made to increase access and affordability of health coverage for many Americans. Challenges include that many uninsured remain unaware of the requirement to have coverage and the subsidies available to make it more affordable, some uninsured are still left out of the expanded coverage, and there is uncertainty about the funding for maintaining coverage expansions in the future (Kaiser Family Foundation Issue Brief, 2015c).

What Are the Choices Regarding the Services Provided?

The state of Oregon passed legislation between the years 1989 and 1995 that provides an example of choices about the services provided to persons with Medicaid coverage. Consumers and providers of health and social services were charged with developing a ranked list of health care services, in the order of their benefit to the entire population being served, and reflecting community values. Coverage for all conditions at a certain level would be set by the state legislature and would be dependent on budget constraints. In the listing of services, treatment of premature infants, cleft palate, hip fracture, or stroke was covered, for example, whereas radial keratotomy, cosmetic dentistry, and treatment of varicose veins was not included (Oregon Health Authority, 2012). Although this is one type of rationing of health care, and Americans are typically opposed to any type of rationing system, it must be noted that the services denied under the Oregon plan are consistent with those denied reimbursement under other private and public insurance plans.

As it is for physicians, rationing of care is an important issue facing the nursing profession. The International Hospital Outcomes Study reported on rationing of nursing care. Researchers in Switzerland (Schubert et al., 2008) explored the association between the implicit rationing of nursing care and patient outcomes in Swiss hospitals. They found that, despite low levels of rationing of nursing care, rationing was a significant predictor for the six patient outcomes that were studied.

What Are the Choices About Methods to Produce Health Care?

One informal definition of managed care is the right care, in the right amount, by the right provider, in the right setting. This definition implies that there are several ways to provide health care. For example, a woman may choose to have an annual physical examination by a nurse practitioner, a certified nurse-midwife, a gynecologist, or a family practice physician. Each provides care from a different perspective and at a different price. In another example, certain procedures that were once performed only in hospitals are now done in outpatient settings, many with the addition of home health nursing. Lumpectomy and simple mastectomies are surgical procedures that are now handled in an outpatient setting, illustrating a different method of providing health care. Deciding the best method is subject to research and must include an analysis of the costs.

What Are the Choices About Allocation?

These decisions involve "who gets what." The underlying question is Is health care a right or a commodity (like cars or clothing) to be allocated by the marketplace? The World Health Organization (WHO) states in its constitution that the enjoyment of the highest attainable standard of health is one of the fundamental rights of every human being (WHO, 2005). The American Nurses Association Health System Reform Agenda (2008) also affirms that health care is a basic human right and that a health care system should ensure universal access to essential health care services. In another document, the ANA *Code of Ethics for Nurses* (2015) states that nurses should provide care without consideration of the patient's social or economic status. However, even if one believes that health care is a right, challenging questions remain: How much health care is a right? Who pays for the health care of people who cannot afford it? Let us assume that an instructor is teaching senior nursing students who all agree that health care is a right. The instructor then asks the students how much of their paycheck they would be willing to forfeit in taxes so that everyone could have this right to receive health care. It is rare that students are willing to subsidize others' health care at a cost of more than one third of their own salaries.

> Think about your first paycheck as a registered nurse. How much would you be willing to give up?

Even beyond the costs of care is the question of allocation decisions—that is, who decides who receives what health care. Several responses are possible: the government, payers of health care, individuals, the marketplace, or rationing systems.

Government Allocation Decisions

Through its funding of Medicare, the government has made multiple allocation decisions. The U.S. government has decided it will pay for inpatient health care and some outpatient care for patients older than 65 years of age and for selected others. Unfortunately, many of the persons covered by Medicare have come to believe that Medicare covers "everything," and this is not so. It is particularly challenging to nurses when elderly patients assume that they "have Medicare" and thus "nursing home care is paid for." This is a frequent misinterpretation of Medicare coverage. There are many limitations to the services reimbursed by Medicare and many requirements that must be met before the government will make payment (Critical Thinking Box 16.2).

Payer Allocation Decisions

The ACA of 2010 required all health plans to provide coverage for applicants regardless of health status, gender, or any other factors. In addition, the ACA requires plans to cover a range of preventive

> **? CRITICAL THINKING BOX 16.2**
>
> Hospice is reimbursed $75 per visit by Medicare Part B for home visits. For one particular group of patients, it costs hospice an average of $98 per day to provide care.
> - What are the implications for hospice?
> - What options should the hospice nurse manager and nurses consider?

health services without any patient cost sharing (Kaiser Family Foundation, 2015c). Within these overall guidelines, all insurance companies have rules about the services that will be covered or not covered and the requirements that must be met under their policies.

Most policies require preauthorization (preapproval) of services before the patient receives care, except in cases of emergency. For example, a physician's office will typically communicate the need for a surgical procedure to the insurance company and obtain this approval. If the patient is admitted to the hospital in an emergency, however, this requirement is normally waived, and the hospital has a limited amount of time to gain the payer approval or reimbursement for the care or the claim may be denied.

Another restriction on resource allocation involves the process of concurrent utilization review (UR). This is a strategy used by managed care companies to control both costs and quality. The process requires that hospital staff, typically registered nurses, communicate the plan of care for a hospitalized patient to the payer or their representative. The payer then determines whether the care is appropriate, is medically necessary, and is covered under the terms of the policy or the contract with the provider (Murray & Henriques, 2003). For example, if a patient is admitted to the hospital the day before elective surgery, that day's cost will almost certainly be denied reimbursement. Preoperative patient teaching and surgical preparation can be handled on an outpatient basis at a much lower cost than a day in the hospital.

Marketplace Allocation Decisions

A final alternative for the allocation of resources is the marketplace. This type of decision making implies that health care is a normal good, similar to a car or a piece of clothing, where an increase in income leads to an increase in demand for the good, and the rules of supply and demand apply. However, the market for health care includes some significant differences when compared to the market for normal goods.

Unpredictability of demand. The first difference in the market for health care is the unpredictability of demand. When a person is well, there is little demand for health care services. There is a great demand for health care when a person is ill, and the timing of illness is, of course, uncertain. Consider, for example, the case of a patient needing a heart transplant. A patient does not wait until the price comes down. Rather, the surgery is purchased at any price if a donor heart is available.

Consumer knowledge. Another difference in the health care market involves the knowledge of the consumer. If an individual is purchasing a coat or a car, the person usually knows a good deal about the item being purchased, or he or she consults *Consumer Reports* for further data. This is not the case in health care, about which patients tend to have limited knowledge and limited ability to interpret the available knowledge.

Barriers to entry to the market. Even if patients had sufficient knowledge to treat their own illnesses, the health care market is fraught with barriers. All providers must pass examinations and be licensed by appropriate boards. Prescriptive authority is heavily regulated and closely controlled.

Lack of price competition. The health care market, unlike the market for clothing and automobiles, does not engage in price competition. When, for example, have you heard of a sale on appendectomies or "2 for the price of 1" hip replacements? Of course, it does not happen. But more problematic is the fact that health care consumers frequently do not know the cost of their care—especially if an insurance provider is paying for it. In fact, many consumers indicate that they "never saw a bill" for their hospitalization. This is considered to be a measure of the quality of their insurance. Is there any other product that would be routinely purchased without knowledge of its price? The lack of this knowledge leads to predictable consumer health care purchasing behavior.

The classic Rand Health Insurance Experiment (Keeler & Rolph, 1983) was a controlled research study that examined the effect of different copayments on the use of health care. Participants in the study either received free care or paid copayments of 25%, 50%, or 95%. Economic theory would predict that as price increases, the purchase of goods or services would decline. That is exactly what happened. With a copayment of 25%, there was a decline in the use of health care of 19% compared with a free plan. There were even greater declines in the use of health care services at the higher rates of copayments. This consumer behavior is so predictable that health care economists have a term for it: *moral hazard.* It refers to a situation in which a person uses more health care services because the presence of insurance has lowered the price to the person.

A final method of allocating health care resources is some system of rationing. Rationing is a type of allocation decision that suggests a need-based system. One author defines rationing as a decision to "(1) withhold, withdraw, or fail to recommend an intervention; (2) informed by a judgment that the intervention has common sense value to the patient; (3) made with the belief that the limitation of health care resources is acute and seriously threatens some members of the economic community; and (4) motivated by a plan of promoting the health care needs of unidentified others in the economic community to which the patient belongs" (Sulmasy, 2007, p. 219). Americans find this inherently distasteful. One example of a rationing decision is to not perform heart transplants on patients older than 65 years, with the rationale that the money could be spent on, for example, well-child immunization programs. The major ethical questions (Sulmasy, 2007) involved in rationing decisions include (1) who makes the decision, and (2) using what criteria? However, most Americans find the concept of rationing inherently unacceptable. The counterargument to this position is that rationing occurs every day in the U.S. health care system, but the decision is currently made on the basis of the individual's ability to pay for care.

BUDGETS

A *budget* is a tool that helps to make allocation decisions and to plan for expenditures. It is important for staff nurses to understand budget processes, because these decisions directly impact their clinical practice. For example, staff nurses working on a patient-care unit may feel that there is not enough time to care for acutely ill patients on the unit. A clinical manager may respond that the "budget will not allow" additional staff. The reality is that the budget is a human-made planning tool and must be flexible to be useful. Savvy staff nurses will understand the budget process and be able to relate patient acuity to staffing needs. To engage in these discussions, all nurses need to understand basic concepts of budgets as well as different types of budgets: capital budgets, operating budgets, and personnel budgets (Fig. 16.2).

What Are the Basic Concepts of Budgets?

When preparing a budget, one must first consider the unit that the document or budget will serve. It could be an entire hospital, a department, or an individual patient-care unit. This discussion will focus on the budget of a patient-care unit, because that is the work environment of most registered nurses.

FIG. 16.2 Budget—a tool that helps make allocation decisions.

Here are the basic terms that nurses must know:

Revenue: All the money brought into the unit as payment for a good or a service. Some departments in the hospital are defined as revenue centers. Examples might include radiology or surgery. Typically, these departments generate a great deal of income for the larger organization.

Expense: All the costs of producing a product. Nursing care units are typically labeled as cost centers; that is, they do not directly generate revenue. Most hospitals have a fixed room rate that includes nursing care. Nurse leaders have questioned the appropriateness of nursing care being lumped into the room rate, but few have been able to effect a change. Some exceptions to this include nursing care to patients in the recovery room, intensive care unit, or labor and delivery area, where there is a separate charge for nursing care.

Margin (or profit): Revenue minus expenses equals margin or profit. Nurses may cringe at the thought of hospitals making a profit, but every hospital—whether it is defined as a *not-for-profit hospital* or a *for-profit hospital*—must make a profit. Profits are needed to replace equipment, purchase new technology, and, in some cases, provide care for indigent patients. In addition, for-profit hospitals must pay stockholders a return on their investment. The necessity of making a profit is so crucial to the continued existence of an organization that there is an old adage that states, "No margin, no mission." This means that if an organization does not make a profit, it is unable to fulfill the purpose or mission of the organization, no matter what it might be. The lay public will often describe hospitals as "for profit" or "not-for-profit." Often faith-based institutions are included in the latter category. In reality, all hospitals must make a profit. It is more significant how the profit is used.

What Are the Types of Budgets?

The budget process involves the development of three budget types that are combined to make an overall budget for the patient-care unit: the capital budget, the operating budget, and the personnel budget. The budget covers a 12-month period that may begin January 1, July 1, or October 1, depending on the organization.

Capital Budget

The beginning point of a budget cycle is usually the *capital budget*. Hospital administrators usually ask departments or patient-care units for a list of items that their area will need to purchase in the coming year. These items are usually restricted to equipment costing more than $5000 and lasting more than 1 year. Each manager must rank such requests for the unit and write a justification of the necessity for the item. At a unit level, for example, the nurse manager may request replacement beds, telemetry equipment, or computers. Most managers will discuss unit needs with staff nurses and seek their input. Staff nurses do the work of the organization and are in the best position to know what is needed for patient care. So be ready to make suggestions. Keep a running list of all the things you wish you had available to you to improve patient care, so when it is time to budget for the next year, and your manager asks for ideas, you will be ready to share. Next, all of the organization's needs are summarized and prioritized according to the funds available. Rarely is there sufficient capital to fund all the requests, and difficult allocation decisions and choices must be made.

Operating Budgets

This budget includes a statement of the expected expenses of the unit for a period, usually 1 year. The budget process begins with a statement of volume projections. The nurse manager projects how much patient care will be provided in the coming year. The volume that nurses are concerned with is measured in patient days, and thus the question is "How many patient days of care will be provided in the coming year?" The manager would first look at past data to examine how many days were given in the previous year. It is also helpful to look at monthly data, to determine whether there was a month that exceeded projections, perhaps a month in which there was a flu epidemic or one that had a very low number of patient days because of vacations of medical staff who admit patients. Knowledge of these trends helps the manager to project volume for the subsequent year. The manager would next consider any changes in the patient-care unit that might affect volume projections. For example, if two new surgeons were added to the staff, if the unit would begin to provide care for a new clinical population of patients, or if the unit would be newly designated as the overflow unit for same-day surgery patients, all of these factors would increase the volume projections.

In an outpatient setting, the nurse manager of a clinic considers the volume of patient-care visits. The manager carefully considers anything that might increase or decrease that volume in the coming year. This might include adding more clinic exam rooms, retirement or addition of professional providers, or events and changes within the provision of, and competition for, health care dollars in the geographic area.

In addition to projecting the patient day volume, nurse managers also examine the activity of the unit and the acuity (the intensity of care required) of patients. The activity is usually described as *admissions, discharges, and transfers* (ADTs). One measure of activity is the average daily census—that is, how many patients are occupying beds on the unit at midnight. However, this measure by itself results in an underestimation of the work of the unit. A more accurate picture is gained by the addition of the ADT data, because even though these patients may not be counted in a midnight census, they require many hours of care by registered nurses (Critical Thinking Box 16.3).

Nurse managers must also consider the acuity of the patients on the unit. In an intensive care unit, patients are extremely ill and require many hours of care per day. The number of care hours decreases as patients are moved to general patient-care units. Each organization considers the acuity of patients but may use different methods of arriving at measurements. There are several computerized software packages available, whereby nurses enter patient data and the software program produces estimates of the staffing needs of the unit. Programs are designed for each clinical population of patients (e.g., obstetrics, pediatrics, psychiatry, and the like). Nurses enter data concerning many factors, including

? CRITICAL THINKING BOX 16.3

In most hospitals, nursing care is "lumped in" with the room charge, and thus nursing care is an expense in the budget and not a revenue center. Most patients (except ICU, step-down, labor and delivery, recovery room) pay the same amount for nursing care. What are the advantages/disadvantages of this situation for nursing?

numbers of patients, functional abilities, telemetry monitoring, and postoperative day. These factors help to define how much care patients need and thus can be used to project staffing needs. At the time the budget is created, the nurse manager can review the data to see whether the staffing planned for the unit was adequate to meet patient-care needs.

On a daily basis, there may be vacant beds on a patient-care unit. However, if there were not a sufficient number of registered nurses available to provide care for the patients who *could potentially* occupy these beds, the unit would not be able to accept additional admissions. Therefore, the nurse manager frequently reports "available staffed beds" rather than "vacant beds." When there are no available staffed beds, it is a critical situation. The manager may be asked to work on increasing the supply of nurses by calling in additional staff. Another strategy might be to identify patients who could be safely discharged early if required. In the worst-case scenario, the emergency department may divert potential patients to another hospital, a situation that hospital administration executives deplore! The nurse manager must be prepared to advocate for safe patient care in these situations.

The *operating budget* also includes all of the items necessary for care on the unit. These are called *line items* in a budget and include such things as supplies, telephones, small equipment (e.g., wheelchairs, nurse pagers, fax machines, and the like), postage, and copying costs. Some of these are *variable costs*—that is, costs that change with the volume of patients cared for in a year. Some institutions would include a factor for the variable costs of housekeeping or laundry. There may be a line item for travel for staff nurses to attend clinical conferences or to pay for specialty certification of nurses. These are expenses frequently paid by employing organizations. Other costs, such as heat and electricity, are considered *fixed costs* that do not change with the number of patients. A nurse manager considers all these things when planning an operating budget (Critical Thinking Box 16.4).

Personnel Budget

The *personnel budget* for a nursing unit is the largest part of unit expenses, and nursing is the largest part of personnel expense. In most hospitals, nursing costs represent at least 50% of hospital expense budgets (Pappas, 2008). This has caused some hospital administrators, who need to reduce expenses, to state:

"Follow the dollars, and they will lead to nursing."

? CRITICAL THINKING BOX 16.4

As a staff nurse, you have been asked to serve on your unit's financial management committee. You have been told to reduce overall expenses by 3%—in any way you choose to do it.

Given the definitions of fixed and variable costs, where do you think you could begin to look for cost reductions? Develop some ideas of possible cost reductions. Remember that your commitment is to preserve the high quality of patient care.

Staff nurses need to understand how a nurse manager determines the number of nurses required for patient care. As discussed, beginning considerations are acuity of patients and the volume or number of patients. The nurse manager must also consider the clinical expertise of the nursing staff. If a unit has a high percentage of new graduates, there will be a decreased ability to safely care for a higher volume of acutely ill patients on the unit. Next, the nurse manager engages in a series of calculations, all of which are easily understood by staff nurses.

Hours per patient day (HPPD). Each patient-care unit will have a designated number of hours of care per patient day. In an intensive care unit, this might be as high as 22 hours per day; on a general surgical unit, it might be 6 to 8 hours. However, nurses need to be aware that these hours must be spread over three shifts (if the organization uses 8-hour shifts) or two shifts (in the case of 12-hour shifts). Nurse managers typically derive *staffing patterns*, that is, combinations of staff (RNs, LPNs, nursing assistants) that are needed for each shift. These may vary for weekends, nights, and even days of the week. For example, if Monday is a day when many surgical procedures are performed, staffing must include higher numbers of registered nurses to assess and monitor postoperative patients.

Full-time equivalent (FTE). An FTE represents the number of hours that a nurse employed full-time is available to perform all of the employment activities. This is calculated to be 2080 hours (52 weeks times 40 hours), but it is usually split into productive and nonproductive time (Hunt, 2001).

Productive time. This figure reflects the amount of time the nurse is available to provide care to patients. For example, one work day (8 hours) is usually considered to be 7.5 productive hours.

Nonproductive time. This time reflects the amount of time that is not available for direct care. Some examples of nonproductive time include vacations, days off, holidays, time at educational seminars, time for committee work (e.g., quality improvement), breaks, and lunch. If these factors are not calculated into the budget, staffing needs may be seriously underestimated. Skilled nurse managers know their staff and can project nonproductive time. For example, if a unit has a very senior staff that accrues annual vacations of 4 to 6 weeks, this must be considered in the budgeting process.

What Are the Economics of Caring?

As clinicians, many nurses are reluctant to incorporate knowledge of health care economics into their clinical practice, feeling that it makes them somehow less compassionate or less caring. However, it can be argued that the reason nurses must understand health care economics is that they can bring the values of nursing to the decision-making process for patient care. They can become advocates for patients in the budget process. For example, an administrator with a master of business administration degree may examine the budget of a nursing care unit and make a decision to decrease staffing. A nurse who understands the budgeting process and the research evidence about nurse staffing and patient outcomes can argue persuasively against reductions in nursing HPPD.

It is also important for staff nurses to be able to evaluate the research that provides the evidence for clinical practice change. Many nurses report that their goal is to provide "cost-effective care." However, they use this term loosely and do not understand the economic analysis strategy of cost-effectiveness analysis (CEA). This strategy provides information about the cost of an intervention and the effectiveness of an intervention.

At the level of providing care for individual patients, staff nurses must understand fiscal responsibility for clinical practice. *Fiscal responsibility* concerns a threefold responsibility: first to the patient, second to the employing institution, and finally to the payer of health care. It is defined as the duty/ obligation of the nurse to allocate (1) financial resources of the patient to maximize the patient's health benefit, (2) financial resources of the employer to maximize organizational cost-effectiveness, and (3) financial resources of the payer by using knowledge and efficiency (Fig. 16.3).

FIG. 16.3 Nurses play an important role in the economics of health care.

Fiscal Responsibility to the Patient

The primary fiscal responsibility of the nurse is always, most important, to the patient. This means that a nurse uses the most cost-efficient combination of resources to maximize the health benefit to the patient. Nurses need to understand the costs of care and different reimbursement systems, because this will affect the development of a care plan. It is important for nurses to assess the resources that patients have available to dedicate to health care. These may include not only insurance coverage, but also the availability of family members or community resources to aid in care.

For example, many churches team up to provide transportation to treatment locations for patients receiving chemotherapy. Communities vary widely in the resources they offer to patients and families. There may be free support groups, online chat rooms, or Meals on Wheels services available. All of these are valuable community health care resources that are not monetary.

In another example, when creating a discharge plan for a patient, it is essential that a nurse understand the health care resources the patient requires and how they will be paid for. A physician may write orders for prescription medications that are not covered by the patient's insurance. Patients are often reluctant to admit that they cannot afford these medications, and they may either choose not to fill the prescription or may go without other necessities to purchase the medication. Sometimes patients even resort to cutting medications in half to make them "last longer," thereby receiving only a partial dose of the medication. If nurses understand patients' insurance coverage and include this in assessment data, they can make better plans of care. It is especially important that nurses understand Medicare coverage, because in some hospitals more than 50% of patients have this coverage. Table 16.1 summarizes the basics of Medicare insurance. Nurses need to be aware that the coverage for Medicare is very complex, and the complete documentation for coverage is available online.

It is also important that nurses engage in early discharge planning, beginning the process on admission or even before admission. For example, if a patient is to have a scheduled surgery for hip replacement, the nurse in the orthopedic surgery clinic may talk with the patient about convalescence and continued physical therapy in the rehabilitation unit of a skilled nursing facility. If this process is done

TABLE 16.1 THE BASICS OF MEDICARE INSURANCE COVERAGE

WHICH PART OF MEDICARE	COST	DESCRIPTION OF COVERAGE	DOES NOT COVER
Medicare Part A	Usually no premium if the individual or the spouse paid Medicare taxes while working. Copayments, coinsurance, or deductibles may apply for some services.	Hospital care, hospice care, home health care, and inpatient care in a skilled nursing facility following a 3-day hospital stay	Custodial or long-term care in a skilled nursing facility
Medicare Part B	There is a monthly Part B premium. Most people will pay the standard premium amount, which was $166 in 2016. For covered services, enrollees must meet the yearly Part B deductible before Medicare begins to pay its share. Then, after the deductible is met, enrollees typically pay 20% of the Medicare-approved amount of the service if the health care provider accepts assignment.	Services from doctors and other health care providers, outpatient care, home health care, durable medical equipment, and many preventive services	Routine dental care, dentures, hearing aids, eye examinations for prescribing glasses, or cosmetic surgery
Medicare Part C	Medicare Advantage Plans (MAP)—a plan like an HMO, PPO or Private Fee for Service plan. Medicare will pay a fixed amount each month to the private insurance company providing the MAP.	Run by Medicare-approved private insurance plans. The MAP covers all of Part A and Part B and usually includes prescription drug coverage as part of the plan. May offer additional benefits such as hearing, vision, and dental coverage as well as health and wellness programs for an additional cost.	Might not cover if an individual goes outside of the selected provider network The individual must follow plan rules, such as obtaining a referral to see a specialist. The individual may only join a plan at certain times during the year and is expected to stay in the plan for a year.
Medicare Part D	Medicare Drug Coverage: Individual must have Part A and/or Part B. Most plans charge a monthly premium that varies depending on the plan chosen.	Prescriber must be enrolled in Medicare or have "opted-out" in order for prescriptions to be covered under Part D. There is a yearly deductible before the plan begins to pay. Copay—amounts the individual pays at the pharmacy after the deductible. Coverage gap—After the individual and the plan have paid a certain amount for covered drugs, the "coverage gap" or "donut hole" is reached. Under the ACA, in 2017, when the coverage gap is reached, the individual will pay 40% of the plan's cost for covered brand-name drugs and 51% of the plan's cost for covered generic drugs until the end of the coverage gap is reached. Not everyone will enter the coverage gap because their drug costs will not be high enough. After the yearly out-of-pocket limit is reached, the individual receives "catastrophic" insurance whereby the individual again pays only the copay for covered drugs the rest of the year.	Limits on how much medication the individual can obtain at one time Drugs not on the plan's list of approved drugs ("formulary") are not covered.

From Centers for Medicare & Medicaid Services (2016). *Medicare and You 2017*. Retrieved from https://www.medicare.gov/pubs/pdf/10050-Medicare-and-You.pdf.

before admission, the patient and the family will have the opportunity to visit several facilities and make a selection.

It is important to understand that this does not mean that patients will not receive care or medications if the patient cannot afford to pay for it. It does mean that the nurse will work to ensure that patients receive the care they need, regardless of their ability to pay. In the example of a patient who is to be discharged with a prescription that he or she cannot afford, there may be programs within the hospital that provide low-cost medications. Another alternative is to determine whether a generic drug is available at a lower cost. Some patients even choose to order their prescriptions by mail from Canada to obtain medication at lower costs. This practice is legal in some states and illegal in others. So, before you make this suggestion to a patient, make sure it is legal in your state.

It is also important that nurses understand that fiscal responsibility for clinical practice is a responsibility shared with all other health care disciplines. Nurse practitioners and physicians write orders requiring medications, diagnostic procedures, and laboratory tests. Therefore, they share fiscal responsibility. Clinical social workers have a great knowledge of health care resources available to patients both in the hospital and in the community. All members of the interdisciplinary team share this responsibility and contribute to the goal of maximizing the benefit of health care resources for patients (Fig. 16.4).

Nurses also need to advocate for staffing levels that will permit them the time they need to monitor and assess their patients, that is, time to exercise their clinical judgment. Research has demonstrated that nursing care makes a difference in preventing patient deaths and complications (Needleman et al., 2006). Using this evidence to support requests for additional nursing hours to care for acutely ill patients is a rational and respectful way to communicate.

FIG. 16.4 Advances in computer technology continue to assist the nurse, but technology cannot replace the humanistic aspect of nursing care.

Fiscal Responsibility to the Employing Organization

Nurses also have a responsibility to the organization or agency where they are employed. The most important way for a nurse to demonstrate fiscal responsibility is by providing quality patient care. For example, thorough hand hygiene and the use of sanitizing gels prevent infections that may increase patient costs. Similarly, the prevention of falls and pressure ulcers is a clinical practice that has significant cost implications (see Research for Best Practice Boxes 16.1 and 16.2).

RESEARCH FOR BEST PRACTICE BOX 16.1

The Cost of Nurse-Sensitive Adverse Events

Practice Issue

In a time of increasing health care costs and an emphasis on providing safe, high-quality care to patients, nurses need to understand the cost of complications that are related to nursing care.

Implications for Nursing Practice
- Five adverse events were studied: medication errors, falls, urinary tract infections, pneumonia, and pressure ulcers.
- For patients with health failure, the cost of an adverse event was $1029.
- For surgical patients, the cost of an adverse event was $903.
- The odds of pneumonia occurring in surgical patients decreased with additional registered nurse hours per patient day.

Considering This Information

What is an argument grounded in best practice that you can make to assure that quality care (remember this is the consideration of cost and quality) is provided to patients?

Reference

Pappas, S. H. (2008). The cost of nurse-sensitive adverse events. *Journal of Nursing Administration, 38,* 230–236.

RESEARCH FOR BEST PRACTICE BOX 16.2

Preventing Pressure Ulcers on the Heel: A Canadian Cost Study

Practice Issue

The heel is an area that is especially at risk for the development of pressure ulcers.

Implications for Nursing Practice

Two methods of preventing pressure ulcers on the heel were compared:
- Method A involved protective bandaging plus usual care.
- Method B provided a hydrocellular dressing for protection of the heel in addition to usual care.

44% of patients in the Method A group developed pressure ulcers on the heel compared with 3.3% in the Method B group. The Method B group cost $11.67 more per patient to provide than the Method A group.

Considering This Information

Based on the research, what argument can you make for the more expensive treatment?

Reference

Bou, J. E., et al. (2009). Preventing pressure ulcers on the heel: A Canadian cost study. *Journal of the Dermatology Nurses' Association, 21,* 268–272.

> Nurses who continually improve their clinical practice by using evidence-based practice or "best practice" guidelines are also engaging in quality practice that is cost-effective.

Nurses also have an obligation to use the resources of the institution wisely. The most costly health care resource that nurses allocate is their time. The nurse considers patient-care needs and prioritizes how professional nursing time shall be allocated. Although it would be ideal for nurses to have unlimited time with each patient, it is not possible. As a beginning point, the nurse knows that the most important reason that a patient is hospitalized is to receive assessment and monitoring by a registered nurse. If a patient does not need this assessment, it is likely that the patient can be safely treated in a less expensive health care setting, such as a skilled nursing facility. The care plans that nurses develop and implement include prioritizing the needs of unstable patients. At other times, it is decided that the patient and family require teaching from a professional nurse. It may also be that the patient and family require psychosocial support, a nursing intervention that requires a high level of nursing expertise.

Nurses also need to understand the *prospective payment system*. Under this system, the hospital is paid a set amount for the care of a patient with a certain condition or surgery. If the hospital engages in efficient clinical care practices, the organization makes a profit. If the hospital is not efficient, it may lose money. Medicare reimburses under this prospective system—called *diagnostic-related groups (DRGs)*—as do many private insurance companies.

This system has had a large impact on nursing practice. For example, if the nurse does not have a discharge plan in place on the day a discharge decision is made, perhaps because of the lack of planning for transportation for a patient, it may be that the patient will remain in the hospital for an additional day while arrangements are made. This incurs unnecessary costs for the hospital. From another perspective, an unnecessary hospital day is a quality issue. Patients in the hospital are subject to the possibility of infection, the hazards of immobility and bed rest, and even the potential for malnutrition. As mandated by the ACA, hospitals will not receive reimbursement for care related to "never events," such as pressure ulcers, falls, and hospital-acquired infections (Sherman & Bishop, 2012). In addition, hospitals will lose Medicare reimbursement if too many of their patients are being readmitted within 30 days of hospital discharge (Sherman & Bishop, 2012).

Another way that nurses practice fiscal responsibility is by accurately documenting the patient's condition. This must include the severity of the patient's illness as well as the plan of care. If this is not documented, insurance companies may not reimburse for the care. For example, if the nurse documents "up and about with no complaints," it is very likely that the hospital day will not be covered by insurance. However, if the nurse documents the assessments and monitoring that are being done at frequent intervals, the care will likely be reimbursed.

There are other ways in which nurses recognize institutional fiscal responsibility. For example, the nurse should be aware of bringing only the needed supplies into a patient room, because any unused supplies cannot be returned to stock. Some supplies are charged to patients when used. The fiscally responsible nurse makes this a part of practice, if required.

Another example involves breaks and meal times. The nurse takes breaks and meal times as scheduled, to remain healthy and fully functioning on the job. A shift may occasionally be hectic, and it may not be possible to take breaks, but if this is the norm, it is a situation that creates burnout and should be investigated and resolved.

Fiscal Responsibility to the Payer of Care

At present, the U.S. government is the largest single payer of health care. For government-funded care such as Medicare and Medicaid, the ultimate payer then is the taxpayer. For private insurance, the payer may be the insurance company selected by an employer or by an individual. In all cases, the nurse has the obligation to use resources efficiently and effectively. The nurse needs to provide documentation that the patient requires care in the appropriate setting. This includes communicating the severity of the patient's illness as well as the plan of care. Without this documentation, the payer may determine that a particular level of care is not necessary and may not reimburse for that care. It is also clear that the application of evidence-based practice guidelines will enable the nurse to select interventions that are cost-effective and that result in the best outcomes.

Box 16.1 summarizes some strategies to help achieve fiscally responsible clinical practice. Box 16.2 summarizes some questions that a new graduate of a nursing program might want to ask during a job interview to assess how a prospective employer views fiscal responsibility. See the end of the chapter for relevant websites and online resources regarding economics in nursing practice. These resources will be beneficial for you as you begin your profession.

BOX 16.1   STRATEGIES FOR FISCALLY RESPONSIBLE CLINICAL PRACTICE

The nurse:
- Provides quality nursing care that prevents complications
- Makes conscious decisions about the allocation of professional nursing time
- Understands Medicare and Medicaid insurance coverage
- Engages in evidence-based practice and follows best practice guidelines
- Shares information with patients and families about the costs of care and alternatives
- Assigns assistive personnel (nurse aides, certified medical assistants) appropriately to help with care and recognizes the nurse is ultimately responsible for the care provided
- Works with the members of other health care professions to promote fiscal responsibility for clinical practice
- Documents patient condition accurately
- Begins discharge planning on or before admission
- Completes charge slips for patient supplies, if required
- Avoids burnout by taking scheduled breaks, meal times, and vacations
- Engages in safe clinical practice that will avoid personal injuries

---

BOX 16.2   QUESTIONS FOR THE NEW GRADUATE TO CONSIDER ASKING DURING A JOB INTERVIEW

- How are financial concerns of patients handled? For example, if a patient is unable to afford needed medications on discharge, what resources are available to nurses to help the patient?
- How is acuity of patients assessed and factored into staffing?
- What are the budgeted hours per patient day for the unit?
- What is the turnover rate on this unit? Why do nurses stay on/leave this unit?
- How do staff nurses have input into capital budget requests for the unit?
- How are data about unit financial indicators communicated to the staff?
- What percentage of salary is used as an estimate of fringe benefits?
- What is the overtime rate on this unit?
- Can you tell me about the discharge planning process for patients on this unit?
- What is the staff development plan for professional nurses on this unit?

CONCLUSION

Given the dire predictions about health care costs being forecast for the next 10 years, it is imperative that nurses consider the economics of clinical practice. Throughout most of nursing history, nurses have not wanted to learn about the costs of care, considering such concerns about as important or as appealing as unnecessary paperwork. Nurses proclaim that they want to be caregivers, not accountants. However, nurses humanize health care institutions. Not only do they bring the values of caring and compassion to the workplace, but they represent the largest health professional group. As representatives of the largest health professional group, nurses can contribute to controlling healthcare costs by incorporating fiscal responsibility into clinical practice.

🌐 RELEVANT WEBSITES AND ONLINE RESOURCES

Dartmouth College (2015)
www.ahrq.gov.

American Nurses Association: Health Care Reform
http://www.nursingworld.org/MainMenuCategories /Policy-Advocacy/HealthSystemReform.

Centers for Medicare & Medicaid Services
www.cms.gov.

Medicare
http://www.medicare.gov/.

Medicaid
http://www.medicaid.gov/.

Health Care Reform: Affordable Care Act (ACA)
www.healthcare.gov.

Kaiser Family Foundation
http://kff.org/.

Organisation for Economic Co-operation and Development (OECD)
http://www.oecd.org/.

World Health Organization
http://www.who.int.

BIBLIOGRAPHY

Agency for Healthcare Research and Quality (AHRQ). (2015). *2014 National healthcare quality and disparities report*. Rockville, MD: AHRQ Publication No. 15-000. Retrieved from http://www.ahrq.gov/research/finding s/nhqrdr/nhqdr14/index.html.

American Nurses Association. (2015). *Code of ethics for nurses with interpretative statements*. Retrieved from http://www.nursingworld.org/DocumentVault/Ethics_1/Code-of-Ethics-for-Nurses.html.

American Nurses Association. (2008). *Health system reform agenda*. Retrieved from http://www.nursingworld .org/Content/HealthcareandPolicyIssues/Agenda/ANAsHealthSystemReformAgenda.pdf.

American Nurses Association. (2010). *Nursing: Scope and standards of practice* (2nd ed.). Silver Spring, MD: Publishing Program of ANA. Nursesbooks.org.

Cara, C. M., Nyberg, J. J., & Brousseau, S. (2011). Fostering the coexistence of caring philosophy and economics in today's health care system. *Nursing Administration Quarterly, 35*(1), 6–14.

Feldstein, P. J. (2012). *Health care economics* (7th ed.). New York: Delmar.

From Centers for Medicare & Medicaid Services (2016). *Medicare and You 2017*. Retrieved from https://www.medicare.gov/pubs/pdf/10050-Medicare-and-You.pdf.

Hartman, M., Martin, A. B., Lassman, D., Catlin, A., & the National Health Expenditure Accounts Team. (2015). National health spending in 2013: Growth slows, remains in step with the overall economy. *Health Affairs, 34*(1), 150–160.

Hunt, P. S. (2001). Speaking the language of finance. *Association of Perioperative Registered Nurses Journal, 73*, 774–787.

Kaiser Family Foundation. (2015a). *Fact sheet: Key facts about the uninsured population*. Retrieved from http://kff.org/uninsured/fact-sheet/key-facts-about-the-uninsured-population/.

Kaiser Family Foundation. (2015b). *Fact sheet: The facts on Medicare spending and financing*. Retrieved from http://kff.org/medicare/fact-sheet/medicare-spending-and-financing-fact-sheet/.

Kaiser Family Foundation. (2015c). *Issue brief: The coverage provisions in the Affordable Care Act: An update*. Retrieved from http://kff.org/health-reform/issue-brief/the-coverage-provisions-in-the-affordable-care-act-an-update/.

Keehan, S. P., Cuckler, G. A., Sisko, A. M., Madison, A. J., Smith, A. D., Stone, D. A., et al. (2015). National health expenditure projections, 2014-24. Spending growth faster than recent trends. *Health Affairs, 34*(8), 1407–1417.

Keeler, E. B., & Rolph, J. E. (1983). How cost sharing reduced medical spending of participants in the health insurance experiment. *Journal of the American Medical Association, 249*, 2220–2222.

McMorrow, S., Kenney, G. M., Long, S. K., & Anderson, N. (2015). Uninsurance among young adults continues to decline, particularly in Medicaid expansion states. *Health Affairs, 34*(4), 616–620.

Murray, M. E., & Henriques, J. B. (2003). Denials of reimbursement under managed care. *Managed Care Interface, 16*, 22–27.

Needleman, J., Buerhaus, P. I., Steward, M., Zelevinsky, K., & Mattke, S. (2006). Nurse staffing in hospitals: Is there a business case for quality? *Health Affairs, 25*, 204–211.

Oregon Health Authority. (2012). *Oregon health plan: The prioritized list*. Retrieved from http://www.oregon.gov/oha/healthplan/pages/priorlist.aspx.

Organisation for Economic Co-operation and Development (OECD). (2015). *OECD health statistics 2015*. Retrieved from http://www.oecd.org/health/health-data.htm.

Pappas, S. H. (2008). The cost of nurse-sensitive adverse events. *Journal of Nursing Administration, 38*, 230–236.

Schubert, M., et al. (2008). Rationing of nursing care and its relationship to patient outcomes: The Swiss extension of the International Outcome Study. *International Journal of Health Care Quality, 20*, 227–237.

Sherman, R., & Bishop, M. (2012). The business of caring: What every nurse should know about cutting costs. *American Nurse Today, 7*(11), 32–34.

Sulmasy, D. P. (2007). Cancer care, money, and the value of life: Whose justice? Which rationality? *Journal of Clinical Oncology, 25*, 217–222.

U.S. Census Bureau. (2011). Population distribution and change: 2000 to 2010. *2010 Census Briefs*. Retrieved from http://www.census.gov/prod/cen2010/briefs/c2010br-01.pdf.

U.S. Census Bureau. (2012). *U.S. Census Bureau projections show a slower growing, older, more diverse nation a half century from now*. Retrieved from http://www.census.gov/newsroom/releases/archives/population/cb12-243.html.

World Health Organization. (2005). *Constitution of the World Health Organization*. Retrieved from http://apps.who.int/gb/bd/PDF/bd47/EN/constitution-en.pdf.

17

Political Action in Nursing

Michael L. Evans, PhD, RN, NEA-BC, FACHE, FAAN

ⓔ http://evolve.elsevier.com/Zerwekh/nsgtoday/.

One of the penalties for refusing to participate in politics is that you end up being governed by your inferiors.
Plato

Nurses are playing a major role in the political process for planning the future of health care.

After completing this chapter, you should be able to:

- Define politics and political involvement.
- State the rationale for a nurse to become involved in the political process.
- List specific strategies needed to begin to affect the laws that govern the practice of nursing and the health care system.
- Discuss different types of power and how each is obtained.
- Describe the function of a political action committee.
- Discuss selected issues affecting nursing: multistate licensure, nursing and collective bargaining, and equal pay for work of comparable value.

Too often nurses feel that the legislative process is associated with wheeling and dealing, smoke-filled rooms, and the exchange of money, favors, and influence. Many believe politics to be a world that excludes people with ethics and sincerity—especially given the controversies in presidential administrations and political party ideologies that so often result in gridlock. Others think only the wealthy, ruthless, or very brave play the game of politics. It seems that most nurses feel that the messy business of politicking should be left to others while they (nurses) do what they do best and enjoy most: taking care of patients.

Today, however, nurses are coming to realize that politics is not a one-dimensional arena but a complex struggle with strict rules and serious outcomes. In a typical modern-day political struggle, a rural health care center may be pitted for funding against a major interstate highway. Certainly, both projects have merit, but in times of limited resources not everyone can be victorious. Nurses are now aware that to influence the development of public policy in ways that affect how we are able to deliver care, we must be engaged in the political process.

Leavitt and colleagues (2002) wrote that "the future of nursing and health care may well depend on nurses' skills in moving a vision. Without a vision, politics becomes an end in itself—a game that is often corrupt and empty" (p. 86). To demonstrate these skills, nurses must elect the decision makers, testify before legislative committee hearings, compromise, and get themselves elected to decision-making positions. Nurses realize that involvement in the political process is a vital tool that they must learn to use if they are to carry out their mission (providing quality patient care) with maximum impact.

Nurses' recognition of problems in the current health care system, and their commitment to the principle that health care is a *right* of all citizens, fuel their desire to become active in the political arena and to form a collective force to improve the health care system.

An example of the power of the nursing collective is evidenced in organized nursing's efforts to provide support and defense for a Texas nurse who was discharged from her hospital position for reporting a physician to the Texas Medical Board for medical patient care that the nurse believed was unsafe (ANA, 2010). The nurse, a member of the Texas Nurses Association and the American Nurses Association, also faced a third-degree felony charge for "misuse of official information."

The Texas Nurses Association became aware of the case and immediately offered to support the nurse involved in the case and enlisted the support from the ANA as well. The call went out from the ANA to all nurses, and more than $45,000 was donated both by individuals and organizations from across the United States to support the defense of this nurse. ANA and the Texas Nurses Association strongly criticized the criminal charges and the fact that this case could have a long-term negative impact on nurses who are acting as whistle-blowers advocating for their patients.

The case went to trial, and a jury found the nurse not guilty. The ANA President at the time, Rebecca M. Patton, RN, MSN, CNOR, said of the outcome, "ANA is relieved and satisfied that Anne Mitchell (RN) was vindicated and found not guilty on these outrageous criminal charges—today's verdict is a resounding win on behalf of patient safety in the U.S. Nurses play a critical, duty-bound role in acting as patient safety watch guards in our nation's health care system. The message the jury sent is clear: the freedom for nurses to report a physician's unsafe medical practices is nonnegotiable. However, ANA remains shocked and deeply disappointed that this sort of blatant retaliation was allowed to take place and reach the trial stage—a different outcome could have endangered patient safety across the U.S., having a potential chilling effect that would make nurses think twice before reporting shoddy medical practice. Nurse whistle-blowers should never be fired and criminally charged for reporting questionable medical care" (ANA, 2010, para 5).

It is important for nurses to join and to support nursing organizations that advocate and lobby on behalf of nurses, nursing, and quality health care. Not all nursing organizations have a governmental affairs division for lobbying. The American Nurses Association has lobbyists in Washington, DC, to advocate for the concerns of the profession. In addition, most of the constituent state nurses associations have legislative activities at the state level. (Several nursing associations, including the ANA, are described in Chapter 9.) Before joining a nursing association, you should ask whether the association lobbies on behalf of the interests of its members. The future power of nurses depends on nurses joining and supporting such associations.

> Nursing will continue to lobby for new federal and state legislation that improves the quality and availability of nursing and health care.

The nursing profession will also continue to work with the national media to portray nurses in a positive, professional light. For nurses to be effective in promoting policy, the public needs a clear picture of what nurses bring to the American health care delivery system. For example, ANA responded to an event dealing with a nurse who was competing in the Miss America contest and who was delivering a dramatic monologue about her experience as a nurse. A co-host of the television program "The View" mocked the monologue and the nurse for wearing a "doctor's stethoscope," as if the nurse were wearing a costume.

ANA led a national outcry over this situation with the message "nurses don't wear costumes; they save lives." As a result, there was so much public and advertiser backlash over this comment that the network, the television program, and the co-host issued an apology (ANA, 2015a).

WHAT EXACTLY IS POLITICS?

Politics, described by (Mason et al., 2007, p. 4), is a vital tool that enables the nurse to "nurse smarter." Involvement in the political process offers an individual nurse a tool that augments his or her power, or clout, to improve the care provided to patients. Whether on the community, hospital, or nursing-unit level, political skills and the understanding of how laws are enacted enable the nurse to identify needed resources, gain access to those resources, work with legislative bodies to lobby for changes in the health care system, and overcome obstacles, thus facilitating the movement of the patient to higher levels of health or function (Fig. 17.1).

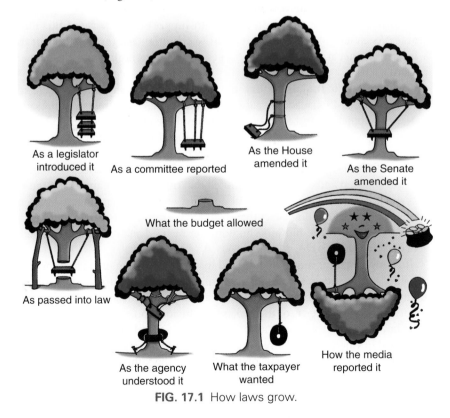

As a legislator introduced it

As a committee reported

As the House amended it

As the Senate amended it

As passed into law

What the budget allowed

As the agency understood it

What the taxpayer wanted

How the media reported it

FIG. 17.1 How laws grow.

Let us look first at the nursing-unit level:

Your hospital is in the process of selecting a new supplier of IV pumps. You and the other nurses on your unit want to have input into that decision, because IV pumps are essential to the care of your patients, and you have a definite opinion about the type of IV pump that works best. But the intensive care unit nurses, who are thought to be more important and valuable because the nursing shortage has made them as rare as hen's teeth, have the only nurse position on the review committee (and therefore, the director's ear!). You and the nurses on your unit strategize to secure input into this important decision.

Your plan might look like this:

- Gather data about IV pumps—cost, suppliers, possible substitutes, and so on.
- Communicate to the charge nurse and supervisor your concern about this issue and your plans to become involved in the decision (by using appropriate channels of communication).
- State clearly what you want—perhaps request a seat on the committee when the opportunity arises.
- Summarize in writing your request and the rationale, submitting it to the appropriate people.
- Establish a coalition with the intensive care unit nurses and other concerned individuals.
- Become involved with other hospital issues, and contribute in a credible fashion (i.e., do not be a single-issue person).

What Other Strategies Would You Suggest?

The scenario described here illustrates what a politically astute nurse would do in this situation. Although the example applies to a hospital setting, the strategies are comparable to those necessary for becoming involved on a community, state, or even federal level. Practicing at the local level will provide good experience for larger issues—one has to start somewhere. Furthermore, a nurse involved on the local level will be able to hone her or his skills, thus gaining confidence in the ability to handle similar "exercises" in larger forums.

In the previous example, the nurse was able to formulate several "political" actions to influence the outcome of the IV pump decision (Critical Thinking Box 17.1).

? CRITICAL THINKING BOX 17.1

What are some issues in your school or hospital that are examples of political issues or the result of politics?

What Are the Skills That Make Up a Nurse's Political Savvy?
Ability to Analyze an Issue (Those Assessment Skills Again!)

The individual who expects to "influence the allocation of scarce resources" must do the homework necessary to be well informed. She or he must know all the facts relevant to the issue, how the issue looks from all angles, and how it fits into the larger picture.

Ability to Present a Possible Resolution in Clear and Concise Terms

The nurse must be prepared to frame and present coherent arguments in support of the recommendation. Preparation includes anticipating questions and objections so that a rebuttal will be logical and well developed.

Ability to Participate in a Constructive Way

Too often, a person disagrees with a proposal being suggested to a hospital unit (or city council) but only gripes about it. The displeased individual seldom takes the time to study the problem or to understand its connection with other hospital departments (or city programs in a broader issue). Most important, the displeased person seldom suggests an alternate solution.

In short, if an individual's concern is not directed toward solving the problem, that person will not be seen as a team player but as a troublemaker. Constructive responses, perhaps something as simple as posing a single question such as "What solution would you suggest?" may help those involved think in positive terms and redirect energy to a more productive mode. Positive action can produce the kind of creative brainstorming that results in a solution.

> Simply complaining about something does not usually change anything. Proposing a solution is a source of power, because that solution may be chosen as the course of action.

Ability to Voice One's Opinion (Understand the System)

After the homework is done, let the *right* person know the opinion or solution that has been determined. For example, the nurse might communicate concern and knowledge about the issue to the nurse manager and supervisor. It is important, of course, to make an intelligent and well-informed decision about the person to whom it is best to voice one's opinion.

Having a confidant or mentor who knows the environment is one way to acquire this information, as he or she can provide you with insight regarding the appropriate person to whom you can express your opinion and suggestions. Another strategy is to use your listening skills. Simply standing back and listening are assets that will come in handy! Whatever the technique, studying the dynamics of the organization with all senses will help the nurse decide on the best person and the most appropriate way to communicate the proposed solution.

Ability to Analyze and Use Power Bases

While discussing issues with colleagues and studying the organization, be alert to the various power brokers. In the previous IV pump vignette, the nurse notes the VP of Purchasing is an obvious source of power in the hospital. This VP will certainly concur with, if not make, the final decision. However, be aware that power does not always follow the lines on the organizational chart. The power of the nurse aide on the oncology unit who just happens to be the niece of the newly appointed member of the Board of Trustees may escape the notice of some. This person could be used to influence a decision if necessary. Similarly, the fact that the VP of Purchasing's mother was on the unit should be filed in your memory for future use.

Understanding policy that has been promulgated by respected bodies can also be used as a power base. For example, the Institute of Medicine issued a report in 2011 called *The Future of Nursing*. One of the major tenets of this respected report is that nurses should be able to practice to the full extent of their education, licensure, and training (IOM, 2011).

If a school nurse is trying to make a point about staffing in schools or about the expanded role of the school nurse, using such information can reinforce the power behind the message (Fleming, 2012). On a more global level, using such a power base can help to make the point that the expansion of the role of advanced practice nurses can help to alleviate the massive shortage of primary care physicians and can improve care processes (Newhouse et al., 2012).

Facts may be facts, but *where* one gets information can sometimes make a statement as powerful as the information itself. Having the ability to use many different channels of information will afford the nurse the power to choose among them.

WHAT IS POWER, AND WHERE DOES IT COME FROM?

Sanford (1979) describes five laws of power. She recommends that these laws be studied to identify strategies to develop power in nursing. The laws are as follows:

Law 1: Power Invariably Fills Any Vacuum

When a problem or issue arises, the prevailing desire is for peace and order. People are willing to yield power to someone interested in restoring order to situations of discomfort. Therefore someone will eventually step forward to handle the dilemma. It may be some time before the discomfort or unrest grows to heights sufficient for someone to take the lead.

Nonetheless, a person exerting power will step forward to offer a solution. In some situations, this person may be the previously identified leader, the nurse manager, or the department chair. More often there is an official power broker influencing the action. Know that there are opportunities to exert influence—for example, by taking the leadership role (i.e., stepping forward to fill the vacuum).

Law 2: Power Is Invariably Personal

In most instances, programs are attributed to an organization. For example, the state and national children's and health associations proposed a fictitious program called ImmunEYEs. If one investigated, however, it might be found that the program began with a small group of friends talking while eating a pizza one evening, lamenting the number of infants still not immunized. In the course of their conversation, one might have said, "If we were to create a media blitz that would get the need for immunizations into the consciousness of parents—get the need for immunizations in their face!" And the next person might have said, "In their *eyes!* Yea, ImmunEYEs. Let's do it!"

Initiatives such as this start with one person creating a new approach to a problem. That person exercises power by providing the leadership or spark to create the strategy to carry out such an initiative, thus inspiring and motivating people to contribute to the effort.

Law 3: Power Is Based on a System of Ideas and Philosophy

Behaviors demonstrated by an individual as she or he exerts power reflect a personal belief system or a philosophy of life. That philosophy or ideal must be one that attracts followers, gains their respect, and rallies them to join the effort. Nurses have the opportunity to ensure that a patient's right (versus privilege) to health care, access to preventive care, and similar values are reflected in policies and procedures.

Law 4: Power Is Exercised Through and Depends on Institutions

As an individual, one can easily feel powerless and unable to handle the complex problems facing a hospital, community, or state. But through a nursing service organization, a state nurses association, or a similar organization, that individual can garner the resources needed to magnify her or his power. The person-to-person network, the communication vehicle (usually an organization's newsletter or journal), and the organizational structure are established for precisely this function—to support and foster changes in the health care system.

Law 5: Power Is Invariably Confronted With and Acts in the Presence of a Field of Responsibility

Actions taken create a ripple effect by speaking to the other nurses for whom nurses act and, most important, the patients for whom nurses advocate. The individual in the power position is acting on behalf of the group. Power is communicated to observers and is reinforced by positive responses. If the group thinks that its ideals are not being honored, the vacuum will be filled with the next candidate capable of the role and supported by the organization.

Another Way to Look at Power and Where to Get It

In a classic, much-referenced work, French and Raven (1959) describe five sources of power. They are (in order of importance) reward power, coercive power, legitimate power, referent or mentor power, and expert or informational power. These descriptions of power were presented in the discussion of nursing management in Chapter 10. The discussion there described the use of power within the ranks of nursing. Here, the use of power is presented as it applies to the political process, especially through political action in nursing.

The strongest source of power is the ability to *reward*. The best example of making use of the reward power base is the giving of money. If, for example, someone gives a decision maker financial support for a future political campaign, the recipient will feel obligated to the donor and may, from time to time, "adjust opinions" to repay these obligations! Today, because caps have been placed on campaign contributions, the misuse of this type of reward has been reduced.

An additional source of reward-based political power is the ability to commit voters to a candidate through endorsements. This illustrates the importance of having a large number of members in an organization—in other words, a large voting bloc. This reinforces the imperative for nurses to join and support nursing organizations that advocate on behalf of nurses, nursing, and quality health care.

Second in importance is the power to *coerce* or "punish" a decision maker for going against the wishes of an organization. The best example of this power, the opposite of *reward*, is the ability to remove the person from office at election time.

Third in importance is *legitimate* power, or the influence that comes with role and position. Influence derives from the status that society assigns individuals as a result of, for instance, inherited family money, membership in a respected profession, or a prominent position in the community. The dean in a school of nursing has a certain amount of influence just because of who he or she is. Right? A nurse's commitment to enhancing nursing's influence explains why nurses encourage and assist one another to achieve key decision-making positions—to build nursing's legitimate power base.

The fourth power base is that of *referent* or *mentor* power. This is the power that "rubs off" of influential people. When representatives of the student body talk with a faculty member about a problem they are having with a course, and they receive her or his support, the curriculum committee or dean is more likely to listen sympathetically than if the students were arguing only for themselves. The faculty member, joining with the students to solve their problem, adds to the students' power. The wish to build this type of power encourages nurses to join coalitions, especially those including organizations with greater power than their own.

The last and weakest of the power bases is that of *expert* or *informational* power. Nurses know about health and nursing care and are thus able to impart knowledge in this area with great confidence and style. Typically, nurses communicate this authority through letters written to legislators, testimonies presented in hearings, and through other contacts made on behalf of nursing and patients. In summary, power is derived from various sources. Nurses use, with the greatest frequency and ease, the weakest of the power bases—that deriving from their expertise. Although this is an important power base, nurses must develop and exercise the other types as well. Only then will nurses realize the full extent of their potential (Critical Thinking Box 17.2).

? CRITICAL THINKING BOX 17.2

Who are the people in positions that reflect the different power levels in your school, hospital, and community?

NETWORKING AMONG COLLEAGUES

It has been said that one should never be more than two telephone calls away from a needed resource, whether it be a piece of information, a contact in a hospital in another city, or input into a decision one is about to make. The key to successful networking is consciously building and nurturing a pool of associates whose skills and connections augment your own.

As a nursing graduate, one should begin the important task of networking by selecting an instructor from nursing school who is able to speak positively about your performance during nursing school. Ask this person if she or he would be willing to write a letter of reference for your first job. If the person agrees, nurture this contact from that time onward. Keep this individual apprised of your whereabouts, your successes, and your plans for the future. This person will be an important link not only to your school but also to your future educational and career undertakings. Then, at each future work site, find a charge nurse or supervisor willing to write a reference and with whom you can maintain contact. Keep building the network throughout your career.

Remember that this network must be nourished. Constant use of one's resources without reciprocation will exhaust them and make them unreliable sources of assistance in the future. But if properly cared for, this network will provide support for the rest of your career.

BUILDING COALITIONS

A *coalition* is a group of individuals or organizations who share a common interest in a single issue. Groups with whom nurses might form coalitions are as diverse as the topics about which nurses are concerned. For example, nurses are concerned about and lobby for adequate, safe child care, a safe environment, and women's issues. The numerous organizations interested in these diverse issues are potential candidates for a coalition with nursing organizations. It is not unusual, however, for two organizations to be in a coalition on one issue but adversaries on another. Indeed, this is common in the political arena, where negotiations and compromises are the norm.

A warning: *the selection of coalition partners should strengthen your cause or organization.* Forming coalitions is a strategy to empower oneself. Therefore, build coalitions with people more powerful than you, and build coalitions with organizations enjoying greater power than nursing, not less (Critical Thinking Box 17.3 and Fig. 17.2).

? CRITICAL THINKING BOX 17.3

What are examples of nursing coalitions in your community or state?

What About Trade-Offs, Compromises, Negotiations, and Other Tricks of the Trade?

Politics is not a perfect art or science. In the heat of battle, nurses are often called on to compromise, but if they are unwilling to bend on some principle, they sacrifice all. To hold out for the ideal typically means that no progress toward the ideal will be realized. Often, changes in health care policies are achieved in incremental steps. However, the decision to compromise a value or principle must be carefully made with full realization of the implications—not an easy decision!

FIG. 17.2 How do we build a coalition?

The political skills discussed so far apply to any situation, whether in a family, a hospital unit, or a community. The next part of the chapter is focused on skills that apply specifically to the governmental process.

How Do I Go About Participating in the Election Process?

One key to successful political activity is involvement in the election process. This is the stage where one can get to know the candidates; they also get to know you. In addition, it is a time when one makes important contacts for that network.

Getting involved in a candidate's campaign is simple. First, study the positions to be filled. Then, with the help of the local nurses' association, the local newspaper, or the county or state Democratic or Republican Party, select the candidate whose views on health care most closely match yours. Next, find the candidate's campaign headquarters. After this, contact the candidate's volunteer coordinator to see when volunteer help is needed. Most campaigns are crying for assistance with folding letters and stuffing envelopes, looking up addresses, and preparing bulk mailings. They will welcome you with great enthusiasm! Be sure to tell the campaign staff that you are a nurse and would be more than willing to contribute to the candidate's understanding of health care issues and to assist in drafting the candidate's positions on these issues (Critical Thinking Box 17.4).

> **? CRITICAL THINKING BOX 17.4**
>
> Who in your state government supports legislation that is pro nursing and pro health care?

Beware: Involvement in campaigns and party organizations can lead to catching the political "bug." Victims of the political bug are overcome by a powerful desire to make changes in the system, and they see a multitude of opportunities to educate people about the health needs of a county, state, and nation. An example of two nurses who caught the bug: During a past national presidential election, the nurses at a state caucus volunteered to write the resolution for the party's position on health care, which, if passed, would become a plank in the platform. After much work drafting the statement and bringing it before various committees, they were ecstatic when it passed and became the health statement for their party! (Review the case studies in the Evolve Resources for an example of the effectiveness of political action by nurses.)

What Is a Political Action Committee?

Another way that nurses can influence the elective process is through involvement in an organization's political action committee. Political action committees, or PACs, grew out of the Nixon/Watergate era, when Congress decided that candidates for public office were becoming too dependent on money supplied by special interests—individuals who give large political contributions and thereby exert undue influence over the elected official's decisions.

As a result, Congress limited the amount of money an individual may contribute to a candidate, established strict reporting requirements, and created a mechanism whereby individuals can pool their resources and collectively support a candidate.

The ANA National Political Action Committee is called ANA-PAC. Through this vehicle, nurses across the country organize to collectively endorse and support candidates for national offices. Likewise, state nurses associations have state-level PACs to influence statewide elections. There may be PACs in your area that endorse candidates in city elections. All PACs must comply with the state or federal election codes and report financial support given to candidates for public office.

Today, PACs play an important role in the political process, because they provide a mechanism whereby small contributors can act as a collective, participating in the electoral process when otherwise they would feel outmaneuvered by the bigger players.

The ANA's Endorsement Handbook stresses four points regarding PACs:
1. **Political focus.** The only purpose of any PAC is to endorse candidates for public office and then supply them with the political and financial support they need to win an election.
2. **No legislative activities.** A PAC does not lobby elected officials; that is the job of the ANA or the state nurses association and its government-relations arm. A PAC simply provides financial and campaign support for candidates whose views are generally consistent with those of its contributors.
3. **Not "dirty."** A PAC does not "buy" a candidate or a vote. However, the very nature of political life suggests that candidates who recognize an organization's ability to affect their electoral prospects will be inclined to listen to the group's views when considering specific pieces of legislation.
4. **Health concerns only.** Nursing PACs evaluate the candidates on nursing and health concerns only. In other words, ANA-PAC might solicit the candidates' ideas about how Congress might address the problem of older adult abuse in long-term care facilities or expanding health care insurance coverage for the uninsured. But the organization as a nursing PAC should not include questions, for instance, about the source of funding for the new cabinet on foreign commerce. The organization speaks for members only on issues covered in its philosophical statements, resolutions, position statements, legislative platforms, or other documents that its members as an organization have accepted (Critical Thinking Box 17.5).

? CRITICAL THINKING BOX 17.5

ANA-PAC, The American Nurses Association's Political Action Committee

How has ANA-PAC affected nursing on a national level? What have been the most recent activities of this organization? How does your state organization communicate or affect nursing and health care legislation in your state?

After Getting Them Elected, Then What?

Lobbying is the attempt to influence or sway a public official to take a desired action. Lobbying is also characterized as the education of the legislator about nursing and its issues. Educating officials, like educating patients, is an important part of the nurse's role.

As nurses, we can lobby in several different ways. The first and best opportunity to lobby comes when the nurse first meets the candidate and evaluates her or him as a potential officeholder. This is the time to assess the candidate's knowledge of health care issues. Take the time to teach and to learn.

A second opportunity comes when the official needs information to decide how to vote on an issue. Depending on time constraints, the issue, and other considerations, a nurse might decide to lobby the official in person or in writing. If time and financial resources permit, the most powerful type of contact is a face-to-face visit. The only way to ensure time with your senator or representative is to make an appointment. Even then, you may not be successful.

If you are making an unscheduled visit to the Capitol that precludes an appointment, the best time to catch your senator or representative is early in the day, before the legislative sessions or committee meetings start; they rarely start before 10 or 11 AM. Contact with the legislator's aid or assistant can be just as effective as time spent with the official. Busy federal and state officials depend heavily on their staff. Treat staff members with the respect they deserve! Be sure to leave a business card or your name and contact information in writing, including an e-mail address. Make sure that they know how to contact you if they should have any questions.

Finally, remember that contact should be made between legislative sessions and during holidays when the official is in her or his home district. The structure and content of the visit should be similar to that of a written contact. That is, know your issue, keep it short, identify the issue by its bill number and title, and communicate exactly what action you want the senator or representative to take. Box 17.1 is a list of specific "Dos and Don'ts When Lobbying." As you begin lobbying, add your recommendations to the list.

BOX 17.1   DOS AND DON'TS WHEN LOBBYING

Do
- Make sure your legislator knows constituents who are affected by the bill; suggest visits to programs in his or her area.
- Clearly identify the bill, using title and number if possible.
- Be specific and know about the issue or bill before you write or talk.
- Identify yourself (occupation, hometown, member of ANA).
- Use your own words; if writing, use your own stationery. No form letters!
- Send an e-mail and include your name.
- Be courteous, brief, and to the point.
- Provide pertinent reasons for your stand.
- Show your legislator how the issue relates to his or her district.
- Respect your legislator's right to form an opinion different from yours.
- Present a united front. Keep your internal problems at home.
- Write letters of appreciation or send an e-mail to your legislators when appropriate.

BOX 17.1   DOS AND DON'TS WHEN LOBBYING—cont'd

- Write letters at appropriate times or send an e-mail; for example, when a bill is in committee, request action that is appropriate for that stage in the legislative process.
- Establish an ongoing relationship with the public official.
- Know issues or problems your legislator is concerned about, and express your interest in assisting him or her.
- Attend functions sponsored by coalition members. Be seen!
- Get involved in your legislator's campaign for reelection—or his or her opponent's, if necessary!

Don't

- Write a long letter or send a lengthy e-mail discussing multiple points; deal with a single bill or concern per letter, e-mail, or contact.
- Use threats or promises.
- Berate your legislator.
- Be offended in the event of a canceled appointment. Things are unpredictable during a legislative session.
- Demand a commitment before the legislator has had time to consider the measure.
- Pretend to have vast influence in the political area.
- Be vague.
- Hesitate to admit you do not know all the facts, but indicate you will find out—and do!

BOX 17.2   EXAMPLE OF A LETTER TO A PUBLIC OFFICIAL

Ima Nurse, RN
123 Main Street
Any Town, USA 12345-6789
The Honorable U. R. Important, Jr.
United States Senate
Washington, DC 20510
Dear Senator Important:

I request your support of SB 101 regarding appropriations for nursing education and research. This bill is vital to the country's efforts to improve the number and quality of registered nurses. As you recall, the 2017 Very Important Nursing Study demonstrated the growing demand for Advanced Nurse Practitioners to work with the increasing numbers of people older than 65 years. This bill will provide funding to increase the number of faculty and student slots in the country's schools of nursing and to support nursing research in gerontological nursing. The expanding numbers of older people in our area of the country are not able to access the health care they deserve. During a trip home, I would like to take you to the Main Street Senior's Clinic. I know that you would be pleased with this service, as are the health care providers and the patients.

Will you support this bill? Do you have any questions about it? If so, please call me or call the State Nurses' Association Headquarters.

Thank you for your concern with this issue and your continuing support of health care issues.

Sincerely yours,
Ima Nurse, RN

Points to Note

Your letter or e-mail should

1. Be neat, without typos or grammatical errors
2. Be correctly addressed
3. Be on professional letterhead, if written
4. Cover only a single topic
5. Refer to the bill by number and content
6. State your request in the first sentence
7. Include brief rationale for your request
8. Use "RN" in your inside address and salutation

If you cannot visit your representative because of time or travel restrictions, a well-written letter, e-mail, or telephone call can communicate your message. Examine the sample letter in Box 17.2. Note that some pointers are listed at the foot of the page. Examples of the proper way to address a public official can be found in Box 17.3.

Letters are common methods of communicating with elected officials; however, a telephone call, fax, or e-mail is often necessary to relay your opinion when time is limited before an important vote.

BOX 17.3   HOW TO ADDRESS PUBLIC OFFICIALS

The President[1]
Writing
The Honorable (Full Name)
President of the United States
The White House
Washington, DC 20500
Dear Mr./Madam President:

Speaking
"Mr./Madam President"
"President (Last Name)"

The Vice President
Writing
The Honorable (Full Name)
Vice President of the United States
Executive Office Building
Washington, DC 20501
Dear Mr./Madam Vice President:

Speaking
"Mr./Madam Vice President"
"Vice President (Last Name)"

A Senator
Writing
The Honorable (Full Name)
United States Senate
(will have office building and room address)

Washington, DC 20510
Dear Senator (Full Name):

Speaking
"Senator (Last Name)"

A Representative
Writing
The Honorable (Full Name)
U.S. House of Representatives
(will have office building and room address)
Washington, DC 20515
Dear Mr./Ms. (Full Name):

Speaking
"Representative (Last Name)"
"Mr./Ms. (Last Name)"

A Member of the Cabinet
Writing
The Honorable (Full Name)
Secretary of (Cabinet Agency)
(will have office building and room address)
Washington, DC 20520
Dear Mr./Madam Secretary:

Speaking
"Mr./Madam Secretary"
"Secretary (Last Name)"

[1]The correct closing for a letter or e-mail to the president is "Very respectfully yours." The correct closing for all other federal officials noted here is "Sincerely yours."

The suggested format and content of the e-mail and telephone message are similar to that of a letter or face-to-face interview.

Deciding on the type of contact to make with the decision maker will vary depending on the situation. For example, if the bill is coming up for the first time in committee, the strategy may be that 10 to 15 people write letters or e-mails or call the members of the committee. At this point, the *number* of contacts with the office is important. The reason is that the legislator's assistant typically answers the telephone or opens the mail, tallies the subject of the contact, and puts a hash mark in the "Pro HB 23" or "Con HB 23" column for the bill. Therefore, a greater impact will be realized if multiple contacts pertain to one bill. Bags of form letters, however, may have a negative impact on a lobbying effort. Make sure your callers/writers understand the issue and are able to individualize their contact with the elected official. People who contact the legislator's office with a script that they do not understand will not further the lobbying efforts of an organization.

The aforementioned efforts are sufficient early in the process; however, if a major controversial bill is coming up for a final vote in the Senate, activating a statewide network and bombarding the senators with letters, e-mails, telephone calls, faxes, and telegrams—as many as possible—is a typical strategy. The bigger the issue, the bigger the campaign should be.

At several points in a lobbying season, but certainly after contacting the elected official for a major vote, a follow-up thank-you letter will strengthen your contact with the legislator and help establish you in her or his political network. In addition to reinforcing the reason for your original contact, thank the official for her or his concern with the issue and the work in solving the problem by writing the bill, voting for it (or whatever), and for paying attention to your concern (Critical Thinking Box 17.6).

? CRITICAL THINKING BOX 17.6

When are the bills that affect nursing and health care going to be presented to your state legislature? Is safe staffing on the legislative agenda?

In summary, there are specific skills to learn for effective political involvement. But remember that many of the skills needed to be politically savvy are the very ones that will serve you well in everyday professional negotiations (Fig. 17.3).

As a recent graduate who is becoming oriented to your first job and is beginning to look around at what you and your colleagues need to improve, you will agree that political involvement is necessary to reach your goals.

> Don't wait to be "allowed" to make a difference, don't wait to be invited to join, and don't let someone else do the job. Please step forward! Act like the powerful, informed, influential nurse that you are. There is much that needs to be done; be a part of the action to achieve solutions!

Margaret Mead said, "Never doubt that a small group of thoughtful, committed citizens can change the world. Indeed, it's the only thing that ever has." The nursing profession has much to accomplish in addressing the problems with affordable, readily available health care for all. Make sure you are a part of the solutions that will be discovered in the future!

FIG. 17.3 Skills to make a nurse politically savvy.

CONTROVERSIAL POLITICAL ISSUES AFFECTING NURSING

Uniform Core Licensure Requirements

What Is It?

The Nursing Practice and Education Committee, formed by the National Council of State Boards of Nursing (NCSBN), proposed the development of core licensure requirements. This was in response to an increasing concern regarding the mobility of nurses and the maintenance of licensure standards to protect the public's health, safety, and welfare. With the implementation of Mutual Recognition, it is important that health care consumers have access to nursing services that are provided by a nurse who meets consistent standards, regardless of where the consumer lives. NCSBN (2011) defines competence as "the application of knowledge and the interpersonal, decision-making, and psychomotor skills expected for the nurse's practice role, within the context of public health, welfare, and safety" (p. 3).

The competence framework is based on the recommendations from the 1996 Continued Competence Subcommittee. This framework consists of the following three primary areas:

- Competence development: the method by which a nurse gains nursing knowledge, skills, and abilities
- Competence assessment: the means by which a nurse's knowledge, skills, and abilities are validated
- Competence conduct: refers to health and conduct expectations, including assurance that licensees possess the functional abilities to perform the essential functions of the nursing role

An interesting question proposed by the committee was Do you really think nursing is that much different, that much safer on your side of the state boundary line (NCSBN, 1999, p. 3)? The summary of the proposed competencies and the 2005 Continued Competence Concept paper may be found at the National Council's website (www.ncsbn.org), which includes the rationales for the proposed requirements and a discussion of how the committee developed the recommendations.

Agreements, known as *nurse licensure compacts (NLC)*, specify the rights and responsibilities of nurses who choose or who are required to work across state boundaries and the governing body responsible for protecting the recipients of nursing care. At press time, 25 states including Arizona, Arkansas, Colorado, Delaware, Idaho, Iowa, Kentucky, Maine, Maryland, Mississippi, Missouri, Montana, Nebraska, New Hampshire, New Mexico, North Carolina, North Dakota, Rhode Island, South Carolina, South Dakota, Tennessee, Texas, Utah, Virginia, and Wisconsin have enacted nurse licensure compacts (NCSBN, 2015). Visit the NCSBN website for a map of the enacted and pending NLC states (https://www.ncsbn.org/nlc.htm).

States entering into NLC agree to recognize mutually a nursing license issued by any of the participating states. To join the compact, states must enact legislation adopting the compact. The nurse will hold a single license issued by the nurse's state of residence. This license will include a "multistate licensure privilege" to practice in any of the other compact states (both physical and electronic). Each state will continue to set its own licensing and practice standards. A nurse will have to comply only with the license and license renewal requirements of her or his state of residence (the one issuing the license), but the nurse must know and comply with the practice standards of each state in which she or he practices (NCSBN, 2015) (Critical Thinking Box 17.7).

> **? CRITICAL THINKING BOX 17.7**
>
> How will the nurse licensure compact affect the licensure and practice of nursing in your state?

As these agreements are established, experience with additional problems arising from the multistate practice of nursing will be identified and solved in amendments to state practice acts.

Nursing and Collective Bargaining

*March! There are no bunkers, no sidelines for nursing today. We find ourselves the center of atten-
tion. As the government and corporate America fight escalating health care costs, AIDS is wreaking
havoc and technology swells unchecked. Underpaid, overworked, and overstressed nurses are in the
midst of a conflagration. Nursing is in greater demand than ever before. Remember Scutari. We
must organize, unite, go on the offensive.*

Margretta Madden Styles, 1988, quoted in Hansten and Washburn, 1990, p. 53.

The National Labor Relations Act is a federal law regulating labor relations in the private business
sector (extended to voluntary, nonprofit health care institutions in 1974). This law grants employees the right to form, to join, or to participate in a labor organization. Furthermore, the law gives
employees the right to organize and bargain with their employers through a representative of their
own choosing.

Collective bargaining continues to be a point of debate among nurses. Those supporting collective
bargaining argue that it is a tool to force positive changes in the practice setting or a method of controlling the practice setting. Many positive changes in the clinical setting are attributed to advances
made during contract negotiations.

Opponents feel that as a profession, nurses should not use collective bargaining but instead should
influence the practice setting by employee and employer working as a team and not as adversaries.
They contend that a strike, the ultimate tool of any labor dispute, should not be used. Opponents further argue that practice standards are not negotiable. The points of disagreement between employer
and employee are almost always economic: pay, vacation, sick leave, and similar issues. Chapter 18
presents a more detailed discussion of collective bargaining issues. Regardless of your opinion of collective bargaining, the process will involve political action.

What do you think? A paragraph in the ANA's publication *What You Need to Know About Today's
Workplace: A Survival Guide for Nurses* summarizes the challenge for us, and the words are still accurate today:

In a work environment that is constantly changing, it is imperative that nurses are able to assess the true
merits of various labor-management structures, to evaluate the real value of proposals to upgrade compensation packages, to determine appropriate levels of participation in workplace decision-making bodies, and
to distinguish between long-range solutions and "quick fixes" to workplace problems (Flanagan, 1995, p. 5).

Equal Pay for Work of Comparable Value or Comparable Worth?

The concept of comparable worth or pay equity holds that jobs that are equal in value to an organization ought to be equally compensated, whether or not the work content of those jobs is similar. Pay
equity relates to the goal of equitable compensation as outlined in the Equal Pay Act of 1963, and "sex-
based wage discrimination" is a phrase that refers to the basis of the problems defined by Title VII of
the Civil Rights Act of 1964.

As long ago as World War II, the War Labor Board suggested that discrimination probably exists
whenever jobs traditionally relegated to women are paid below the rate of common-labor jobs such as
janitor or floor sweeper. One of the first cases was that of the *International Union of Electrical Workers
v. Westinghouse*. The union proved that male–female wage disparity existed and uncovered a policy
in a manual that stated that women were to be paid less, because they were women. Back pay and
increased wages were given in an out-of-court settlement in an appellate-level decision.

It was nurses who initiated the action in *Lemons v. the City and County of Denver*. Nurses employed by the city of Denver claimed under the Civil Rights Act that they were the victims of salary discrimination, because their jobs were of a value equal to various better paid positions throughout the city's diverse workforce. The court ruled that the city was justified in the use of a market pricing system (a form of pay based on supply and demand) even though it acknowledged the general discrimination against women. The court said that the case (and the comparable-worth concept) had the potential to disrupt the entire economic system of the United States. Because of this judgment and the fact that the nurses were unable to prepare a job evaluation program to substantiate their claim, the judge dismissed the case.

Legislative Campaign for Safe Staffing

The ANA has launched a campaign for legislative changes to address safe staffing. Safe Staffing Saves Lives is a national campaign to advocate for safe staffing legislation. As stated on ANA's website (www .safestaffingsaveslives.org), "ANA believes that staffing ratios should be required by legislation, but the number itself must be set at the unit level with RN input, rather than by the terms of the legislation" (ANA, 2008, p. 1). The position of ANA is not to demand fixed nurse–patient ratios but to develop a system that takes into account the variables that are present and to determine a safe staffing ratio. Principles that address patient safety, quality control, and patient access to care are necessary to establish a foundation for national legislation (Trossman, 2008).

In March 2008, ANA conducted a Safe Staffing Saves Lives Summit: Conversation and Listening Session. Representatives of state associations, nursing specialty, and other health care organizations, as well as representatives from health care facilities, were present. The purpose of the session was to address the issue of preventing peaks in patient flow as a method of improving the RN workload. Hospitals cannot afford to provide peak staffing 24 hours a day, 7 days a week. At Boston Medical Center (BMC), elective surgeries were scheduled to avoid peaks in patient census and to maintain a more predictable census. According to a representative from the BMC, this approach had a very positive impact on predicting and maintaining safe staffing on the nursing units (Trossman, 2008).

From the ANA website on safe staffing: "ANA's proposal is not a 'one size fits all' approach to staffing. Instead, it tailors nurse staffing to the specific needs of each unit, based on factors including patient acuity, the experience of the nursing staff, the skill mix of the staff, available technology, and the support services available to the nurses. Most importantly, this approach treats nurses as professionals and empowers them at last to have a decision-making role in the care they provide" (Trossman, 2008, p. 1).

ANA (2015b) released a study called "Optimal Nurse Staffing to Improve Quality of Care and Patient Outcomes: Executive Summary." This study conducted a targeted review of recent published articles dealing with nurse staffing and patient outcomes. A panel was also convened consisting of experts in the field of nurse staffing. ANA believes that nurses themselves should be empowered to create staffing plans due to the complex nature of staffing and the large number of variables. ANA continues to stress that staffing is too complex to simply legislatively mandate staffing ratios. The study also stresses the evidence that appropriate staffing has a demonstrated effect on a variety of patient outcomes. Nurses can use the study to advocate for and implement sound evidence-based staffing plans.

In 2013, the Registered Nurse Safe Staffing Act (H.R. 2083/S. 1132) was endorsed by ANA. This would require Medicare-participating hospitals to establish registered nurse (RN) staffing plans using a committee, comprised of a majority of direct-care nurses, to ensure patient safety, reduce readmissions and improve nurse retention. As the act moved forward it was introduced into the House of Representatives in April 2015 as the 2015 Registered Nurse Safe Staffing Act (H.R. 2083) and required amendments to title XVIII (Medicare) of the Social Security Act, requiring Medicare participating hospitals to implement hospital-wide staffing plans for nursing services among other requirements.

At the time of this publication, seven states have enacted safe staffing legislation using the Registered Nurses Safe Staffing Act's committee approach: Oregon, Texas, Illinois, Connecticut, Ohio, Washington, and Nevada (ANA, 2015c).

Much work still needs to be done in the area of safe staffing. Nurses are very concerned about staffing issues—mandatory overtime, increased numbers of assistive personnel replacing licensed personnel, and increased patient acuity are factors contributing to the problem. Changes will be achieved as we educate the public, as well as legislative representatives, and as nurses take the primary role to initiate changes in the workplace environment.

CONCLUSION

Politics, policy making, and advocating for patients are key processes for nurses to claim their "power" as a driving force in health care. Participating in ANA-PAC activities provides an opportunity to be at the grassroots level of lobbying (see the Relevant Websites and Online Resources below). Shaping policy and becoming active in the legislative area are practice roles for nurses. By having an understanding of the political process, nurses can and will make significant strides in promoting legislation that will positively affect the health of the nation.

⊕ RELEVANT WEBSITES AND ONLINE RESOURCES

ANA-PAC: Congress and Federal Agencies (2016)
http://www.nursingworld.org/MainMenuCategories/Policy-Advocacy/Federal.

American Nurses Association (2016)
http://www.nursingworld.org/MainMenuCategories/ThePracticeofProfessionalNursing.

American Nurses Association (ANA) (2016)
Official ANA position statements. http://www.nursingworld.org/positionstatements.

The American Nurse (2016)
http://www.theamericannurse.org/.

BIBLIOGRAPHY

American Nurses Association. (2008). *Safe staffing.* Retrieved from http://www.nursingworld.org/MainMenuCa tegories/ThePracticeofProfessionalNursing/NurseStaffing.

American Nurses Association. (2010). *Not guilty—Texas jury acquits Winkler County nurse.* Retrieved from http://nursingworld.org/FunctionalMenuCategories/MediaResources/PressReleases/2010-PR/Texas-Jury-Ac quits-Winkler-County-Nurse.pdf.

American Nurses Association. (2013a). *When nurses talk, Washington listens.* Retrieved from http://www.rnacti on.org/site/PageServer?pagename=nstat_take_action_activist_tool_kit&ct=1&ct=1.

American Nurses Association. (2013b). *Official ANA position statements.* Retrieved from http://www.nursingwo rld.org/positionstatements.

American Nurses Association. (2013c). *Registered Nurse Safe Staffing Bill introduced in Congress.* Retrieved from http://www.nursingworld.org/MainMenuCategories/ThePracticeofProfessionalNursing/NurseStaffing/Regist ered-Nurse-Safe-Staffing-Bill-Introduced-in-Congress.pdf.

American Nurses Association. (2015a). *ANA President Pamela F. Cipriano, PhD, RN, NEA-BC, FAAN responds to comments on ABC's "The View" (9/16/15).* Retrieved from http://nursingworld.org/FunctionalMenuCategories/Medi aResources/PressReleases/2015-NR/ANA-President-Cipriano-Responds-to-Comments-on-ABCs-The-View.html.

American Nurses Association. (2015b). *Optimal nurse staffing to improve quality of care and patient outcomes: Executive summary*. Retrieved from http://www.nursingworld.org/DocumentVault/NursingPractice/Executive-Summary.pdf.

American Nurses Association. (2015c). *Safe staffing fact sheet*. Retrieved from http://www.rnaction.org/site/DocServer/RN_Safe_Staffing_Act.pdf/2027989535?docID=2442&verID=1.

Congress.gov. (2015). H.R. 2083: Registered Nurse Safe Staffing Act of 2015. Retrieved from https://www.congress.gov/bill/114th-congress/house-bill/2083?q=%7B%22search%22%3A%5B%22%5C%22hr2083%5C%22-%22%5D%7D.

Flanagan, L. (1995). *What you need to know about today's workplace: A survival guide for nurses*. Kansas City, MO: American Nurses Association.

Fleming, R. (2012). The future of school nursing: Banishing Band-aids to improve public health outcomes. *Policy, Politics and Nursing Practice*, *13*(3), 142–146.

French, J. R. P., & Raven, B. (1959). The bases of social power. In D. Cartwright (Ed.), *Studies in social power*. Ann Arbor: University of Michigan.

Hansten, R. I., & Washburn, M. (1990). *I light the lamp*. Vancouver, WA: Applied Therapeutics.

Institute of Medicine. (2011). *The future of nursing: Leading change, advancing health*. Washington, DC: National Academies Press.

Lear, J. G. (2007). Health at schools: A hidden health care system emerges from the shadows. *Health Affairs*, *26*(2), 409–419. http://dx.doi.org/10.1377/hlthaff.26.2.409.

Leavitt, J. K., Cohen, S. S., & Mason, D. J. (2002). Political analysis and strategies. In D. J. Mason, J. K. Leavitt, & M. W. Chaffee (Eds.), *Policy and politics in nursing and health care*. St. Louis: Saunders.

Mason, D. J., Leavitt, J. K., & Chaffee, M. W. (2007). Policy and politics in nursing and health care. In D. J. Mason, J. K. Leavitt, & M. W. Chaffee (Eds.), *Policy and politics in nursing and health care*. St. Louis: Saunders.

National Council of State Boards of Nursing. (2011). *Uniform core licensure requirements: A supporting paper*. Retrieved from https://www.ncsbn.org/3884.htm.

National Council of State Boards of Nursing. (2005). *Continued competence concept paper*. Retrieved from https://www.ncsbn.org/3947.htm.

National Council of State Boards of Nursing. (2015). *Nurse licensure compact*. Retrieved from https://www.ncsbn.org/nlc.htm.

Newhouse, R. P., Weiner, J. P., Stanik-Hutt, J., White, K. M., et al. (2012). Policy implications for optimizing advanced practice registered nurse use nationally. *Policy, Politics and Nursing Practice*, *13*(2), 81–89.

Sanford, N. D. (1979). *Identification and explanation of strategies to develop power for nursing in power: Nursing's challenge for change*. Kansas City, MO: American Nurses Association.

Trossman, S. (2008). ANA's campaign to promote patient safety and quality health care. *American Nurse*, *40*(1), 1, 6.

18

Collective Bargaining
Traditional (Union) and Nontraditional Approaches

Joann Wilcox, RN, MSN, LNC

Is there a place for collective bargaining in nursing?

ℯ http://evolve.elsevier.com/Zerwekh/nsgtoday/.

It is time for a new generation of leadership to cope with new problems and new opportunities. For there is a new world to be won.
President John F. Kennedy

Difficulties are meant to rouse, not discourage. The human spirit is to grow strong by conflict.
William Ellery Channing

After completing this chapter, you should be able to:
- Identify the milestones in the history of collective bargaining.
- Compare traditional and nontraditional collective bargaining.
- Identify examples that indicate an employer's position on the role of professional nurses as it impacts practice.
- Identify conditions that may lead nurses to seek traditional or nontraditional collective bargaining.
- Identify the positive and negative aspects of traditional and nontraditional collective bargaining.
- Discuss the benefits of collective bargaining for professional groups.
- Discuss the impact of the silence of nurses in public communications and the public's perception of nurses.
- Identify barriers to the control of professional practice.

You will soon be accepting your first position as a registered nurse (RN). You will be adjusting not only to a new role but also to a new workplace. Even in these times of dramatic change in health care, many of you will start your career in a hospital. In fact, the demographics about nurses show that

- Approximately 61% of nurses in practice are providing care in hospitals (Bureau of Labor Statistics, 2016). Additionally, registered nurses are providing direct patient care in settings such as outpatient care settings, private practice, health maintenance organizations, primary care clinics, home health care, nursing homes, hospices, nursing centers, insurance and managed care companies, etc. (Potter, Perry, Stockert, & Hall, 2013; Bureau of Labor Statistics, 2016) in which care that was hospital-based in the past is now provided in these alternative settings.
- The hospital is also the most common employer of graduate nurses in their first year of practice; more than 72% of new graduates were working in a hospital in their first year of employment (NCSBN, 2015).
- Employment of registered nurses is projected to grow 16% from 2014 to 2024, faster than the average for all occupations. Growth will occur for a number of reasons, including an increased emphasis on preventative care; growing rates of chronic conditions, such as diabetes and obesity; and demand for health care services from the Baby Boomer population, as they live longer and more active lives (Bureau of Labor Statistics, 2016).

As you begin to interview for your first position in your career as a professional RN, there is no doubt you will find yourself both excited and anxious. Your prospective employer will assess your ability to think critically and to perform at a professional level in the health care setting. The potential employer will ask, "Is this applicant a person who will be able to contribute to the mission of the organization and to the quality of health care offered at this organization?"

While the employer assesses your potential to make a contribution, it is equally important that you remember that an interview is a *complex two-way* process. You will, of course, be eager to know about compensation, benefits, hours, and responsibilities. These are very tangible and immediate interests. However, these are not likely to be the best predictors of satisfaction with your practice over time, as the ability to practice your profession as defined by licensure and education will be the foundation leading to job satisfaction and professional fulfillment.

You should be prepared to assess the potential employer's mission and ability to support your professional practice and growth. It is extremely important that you gain essential information about the organization, its mission, and its culture. It is easy to overlook very significant organizational issues that will ultimately affect your everyday practice of nursing when your primary focus is on becoming employed and on wondering whether you will succeed in this first professional role. Thomas (2014) identifies several questions to keep in mind: What is the management style of the company? How is patient satisfaction measured here, and what are the most recent findings? What would you say are the top two to three qualities of the most successful nurses currently working here? Additionally, it is important to use the 2015 *Code of Ethics* for nursing to guide your questions about the role of the staff registered nurse in decision making related to the practice of nursing in the facility. "Making decisions based on a sound foundation of ethics is an essential part of nursing practice in all specialties and settings…" (American Nurses Association, 2015a).

Hospital structures and governance policies can have a dramatic influence on the effectiveness of a registered nurse and how he or she can fulfill obligations to patients and families. Registered nurses have defined the discipline of nursing as a profession, and, as members of this profession, they *must have a voice in and control over the practice of nursing*. When that voice and control are not supported in the work setting, conflicts most likely will arise. In some states, nurses have made a choice to gain that voice and assume control of their practice by using a traditional collective bargaining model, commonly known as a *labor union*. In other states, particularly those that function under the right-to-work regulations, nurses attempt to control practice through interest-based bargaining (IBB), which is a nontraditional approach to collective bargaining that is used to accomplish the provision of a voice and control over practice (Budd et al., 2004) (Box 18.1). In some states nurses use both models to meet the needs of their diverse membership.

BOX 18.1 TERMS

Traditional collective bargaining—A legally regulated collective bargaining unit or a union that assists members to gain control over practice, economics in the health care industry, and other health care issues that threaten the quality of patient care.

National Nurses United (NNU)—The new RN SuperUnion formalized in December 2009.

Nontraditional collective bargaining—Shared governance, or interest-based bargaining (IBB); a collaborative-based, problem-solving approach to assist nurses to have a voice in the workplace and control over issues that affect their practice.

Center for American Nurses (CAN)—Organization that previously represented the interests of nurses who were not formally represented by a collective bargaining unit or union (Budd et al., 2004). It is now an integral part of the ANA.

WHEN DID THE ISSUES LEADING TO COLLECTIVE BARGAINING BEGIN?

Since World War II, there have been phenomenal advances in medical research and the subsequent development of life-saving drugs and technologies. The introduction of Medicare and Medicaid programs in 1965 provided the driving force and the continued resources for this growth. This initiative opened access to health care for millions of Americans who were previously disenfranchised from the health care system.

The explosion in knowledge and technology, coupled with an expanded population able to access health care quickly, increased the demands on the health care system and many of the providers in that system. These advances required nursing to adapt as the complexity of health care and the number of patients accessing this care continued to increase. For example, at the time when the acuity of hospitalized patients increased because of shorter lengths of stay, organizations were responding to cost containment demands by downsizing the number of staff members. As more patients had access to all services in the health care system, the number of care hours available for each patient decreased, because fewer staff per patient were being hired. Overall, patients were sicker when they entered the system. Yet they were moved more quickly through the acute care setting because of such innovations as same-day admissions, same-day surgery, increased discharge to long-term care settings and early discharge. Add to these changes the periodic shortages of nurses prepared for all levels of care, the increased use of unlicensed assistive personnel to provide defined, delegated nursing care, and growing financial pressures on the health care system, and tensions became understandably high.

The time between 2000 and 2013 also brought pressures on registered nurses, as the safety of hospitalization became a paramount concern among both patients and health care staff. The publication *To Err Is Human* (Institute of Medicine, 2000, p. 31) stated that "Based on the results of the New York Study, the number of deaths due to medical error may be as high as 98,000 [yearly]." With registered nurses being at the bedside of acute care patients, their involvement in identifying and/or committing medical errors is high. Ensuring this staff has the appropriate resources to provide safe care is an issue that registered nurses need to address directly with the management of the facility and/or the collective bargaining agent for that hospital/organization. Enormous financial challenges confront health care institutions. As a registered nurse working in the health care industry, you will encounter and use newly developed and very costly health care technologies. At the same time, you will experience, firsthand, the impact of public and private forces that are focused on placing restraints on cost and reimbursement for a patient's care.

Adding to these concerns regarding safe care, new technologies, and potential staff shortages was the implementation of the Patient Protection and Affordable Care Act (PPACA) of 2010 (commonly referred to as the Affordable Care Act [ACA] or Obamacare) (U.S. Department of Health & Human Services, 2016). A significant aspect of this act is the fact that it created the requirement for almost every person in this country to be covered by some form of health care insurance, thereby increasing the numbers of people who could/would present for care from the various health care facilities.

As a professional RN, you are at the intersection of these potentially conflicting forces. For you, these forces will be less abstract; they are not just important concepts and issues facing a very large industry. As a nurse, these concepts and forces are patients with names, faces, and lives valued and loved within a family and a community. You are responsible for the care you provide and for advocating on behalf of these patients and—as you will soon discover—the health of the health care industry.

As a registered nurse, you will become familiar with how, when, and why events occur that adversely or positively affect the patient and the health of the organization. This places you in a unique position to take an active lead in developing solutions. These solutions must be good for patients and for your organization. During your interview for potential employment, while you are busy assessing the potential employer's mission and support of your practice and growth, it is easy to overlook those significant organizational attributes that will ultimately affect your everyday practice of nursing. Therefore, during your interview it would be important for you to ask those questions identified in the beginning of this chapter, particularly those that address the ethical practice of registered nurses.

THE EVOLUTION OF COLLECTIVE BARGAINING IN NURSING

In the early 1940s, 75% of all hospital-employed registered nurses worked 50 to 60 hours a week and were subject to arbitrary schedules, uncompensated overtime, no health or pension benefits, and no sick days or personal time (Meier, 2000). In 1946, the American Nurses Association (ANA) House of Delegates unanimously approved a resolution that formally initiated the journey of RNs down the road of collective bargaining. During the period between this resolution and 1999, the constituent organizations of ANA (state associations) were determined to be collective bargaining units for registered nurse members who desired this representation in the workplace. Not all states provided collective bargaining services, so the debate over the acceptance of collective bargaining as appropriate for nurses became a divisive issue in the ANA for decades.

Legal Precedents for State Nursing Associations as Collective Bargaining Agents

The legal precedent that determined that state nursing associations are qualified under labor law to act as labor organizations is the 1979 Sierra Vista decision. The important consequence of this decision that affected nurses was that they were free to organize themselves and not to be organized by existing unions (Kimmel, 2007). Many registered nurse leaders contend that these associations are not only proper and legal but are the preferred representatives for nurses in this country for purposes of collective bargaining. Ada Jacox (1980) suggested that collective bargaining through the professional organization was a way for registered nurses to achieve that collective professional responsibility that is a characteristic of a profession. It was thought by many that the state nursing association was the only safe ground that could be considered as neutral turf on which registered nurses from all educational backgrounds could meet and discuss issues of a generic nature and of importance to all registered nurses. However, as discussed in the section on the history of collective bargaining, it is beginning to appear that the preferred platform for meaningful collective bargaining for the profession is through a structure, such as the National Nurses United (NNU).

Many formally organized unions outside of the ANA have competed for the right to represent nurses. It was the opinion of many nurses that the state nurses associations were the proper and legal bargaining agents and were also the preferred representatives for nurses in this country for purposes of collective bargaining. During the late 1980s, the demand among nurses for representation continued to grow; yet efforts to organize nurses for collective bargaining were being stymied by a decision from the National Labor Relations Board (NLRB) that stopped approving the all-RN bargaining units. A legal battle then ensued, with the ANA and other labor unions against the American Hospital Association (AHA). The NLRB issued a ruling that reaffirmed the right of nurses to be represented in all-RN bargaining units.

Seeking a broader base of representation and greater support from the ANA for the collective bargaining program led activist nurses within the ANA to establish the United American Nurses (UAN) in 1999. They believed in the creation of a powerful, national, independent, and unified voice for union nurses. In 2000, the UAN held its first National Labor Assembly annual meeting. The participants in this meeting were staff nurse delegates. In February 2009, the UAN, the California Nurses Association, and the Massachusetts Nurses Association joined forces to form one new union that claims to represent 185,000 members. The new union, called the United American Nurses–National Nurses Organizing Committee, would become a part of the labor movement as an AFL-CIO affiliate union. Shortly after this move, the union was renamed the National Nurses United (NNU) (NNU, 2016).

As has been demonstrated, the representation of registered nurses for collective bargaining continues to change and grow to the point where affiliation with the ANA primarily for this purpose is no longer evident. Collective bargaining outside of ANA has become the route for registered nurses to gain the recognition many believe is essential for the growth of the profession. Others see this as the least effective way to gain recognition and benefits afforded to members of a profession.

Collective bargaining for professional groups (physicians, teachers, professors, scientists, entertainers, pilots, administrators) offers registered nurses another perspective regarding the process of collective bargaining. Identification with these professional groups can certainly help the nursing profession become accepted as a true profession with all the benefits of that identification.

Some of the differences noted between traditional collective bargaining and collective bargaining for professionals are agreeing to take lower wages in exchange for greater fringe benefits, setting a wage floor and then allowing individuals to negotiate for a salary based on individual performance and/or negotiating for merit pay for outstanding performance (DPE Research, 2015). The opportunity to develop a variety of ways to earn wages begins the recognition that, even when bargaining collectively, there are opportunities to be compensated for significant differences in performance.

Collective bargaining for professionals also offers the opportunity to designate how a proposed increase in wages can be used to address other issues that might exist within the professional group. "Registered nurses at a hospital in Michigan turned down a 3% pay raise in favor of a 2% raise and the hiring of 25 additional nurses in an effort to offer better, more professional patient care" (DPE Research, 2015, p. 5).

WHO REPRESENTS NURSES FOR COLLECTIVE BARGAINING?

Traditional and Nontraditional Collective Bargaining

The national professional organization for nursing is the ANA, with its constituent units, the state, and territorial nursing associations. Through its economic security programs, the ANA recognized state nursing associations as the logical bargaining agents for professional nurses, and the states have been the premier representatives for nurses since 1946! These professional associations are indeed multi-purpose; their activities include economic analyses, provision of related education, addressing nursing practice, conducting needed research, and providing traditional as well as nontraditional collective bargaining, lobbying, and political action.

The creation of the UAN by the ANA strengthened their collective bargaining capacity at a time when competition to represent nurses for collective bargaining was growing. The UAN was established in 1999 as the union arm of the ANA with the responsibility of representing the traditional collective bargaining needs of nurses. At the same time, a relatively new approach to collective bargaining was being developed and introduced into the labor market. This approach is a nontraditional process referred to as *interest-based bargaining* (IBB) or *shared governance* (Brommer et al., 2003; Budd et al., 2004). This is a nontraditional style of bargaining that attempts to solve problems and differences between labor and management. Although this style of bargaining and mediation will not always eliminate the need for the more traditional and adversarial collective bargaining, many believe this nonadversarial approach to negotiation may be closer to the basic fabric of the discipline of nursing and its ethical code.

The organization that represented IBB, or the nontraditional collective voice in nursing, was the Center for American Nurses (Center). This was a professional association established in 2003, replacing the ANA's Commission on Workplace Advocacy that was created in 2000 to represent the needs of individual nurses in the workplace who were not represented by collective bargaining. The Center defined its role in workplace advocacy as providing a multitude of services designed to address the products and programs necessary to support the professional nurse in negotiating and dealing with the challenges of the workplace and in enhancing the quality of patient care (The American Nurse, 2010) (Critical Thinking Box 18.1).

? CRITICAL THINKING BOX 18.1

What is the status of your state nursing association in regard to workplace issues? Is your state a member of the NNU? What is being done on a local basis that reflects the activities of your state association related to registered nurses' control over their practice?

In 2007, the American Nurses Association informed the UAN and CAN that they would not be renewing their affiliation agreement (Hackman, 2008). Following this, in 2009, the largest union and professional organization of registered nurses was officially formalized. This organization is the National Nurses United (NNU), and it is an outgrowth of the merger of three individual organizations—the California Nurses Association, the Massachusetts Nursing Association, and the United American Nurses (the former UAN) (Gaus, 2009). This NNU union includes an estimated 185,000 members in every state and is the largest union and professional association of registered nurses in U.S. history (NNU, 2016).

In 2013, what remained of the Center was integrated into the structure of ANA and is now a part of the "products and services …and valuable resources that will directly assist nurses in their lives and careers" (The American Nurse, 2010, para 2).

Whether your state is a member of ANA or NNU, or both, it is necessary to recognize that workplace advocacy is a concern that directly affects every practicing nurse. It is critical that nurses support the organizational efforts to address the growing problems regarding the safety of the workplace, as well as safe and competent patient care, managed by registered nurses.

ANA and NNU: What Are the Common Issues?

Staffing Issues

Staffing issues and policies related to nurse staffing are among the most prevalent topics discussed in any type of negotiation. There is much discussion in both the national and state legislatures regarding proposals aimed at addressing the way in which registered nurses should be staffed to be able to provide safe, as well as quality, patient care. There is also much objection to implementing mandated staffing plans rather than allowing nurses to maintain control over issues related to their professional practice. The Institute of Medicine (2004) completed a study entitled *Keeping Patients Safe: Transforming the Work Environment of Nurses*. The results of the study have led to significant recommendations that, if implemented, would begin to address the chronic shortage of registered nurse staff without resorting to mandatory regulations from the legislatures.

Staffing requirements are already mandated by various agencies. For example, Medicare, state health department licensing requirements, and The Joint Commission (TJC) each publish staffing standards that define the need to have sufficient, competent staff for safe and quality care. The ANA has launched a campaign for safe staffing: Safe Staffing Saves Lives, which encourages the establishment of safe staffing plans through legislation (Trossman, 2008). In 2015, the Registered Nurse Safe Staffing Act was introduced to Congress. If passed, Medicare participating hospitals would be required to develop safe staffing plans for each unit in the hospital. The staffing committee would be comprised of registered nurses working in direct patient care (American Nurses Association, 2015b). However, this legislation will need the factors that define safe, quality staffing as the basis for this legislation. It is also clear that staffing is more than numbers and any legislation or policy must include the fact that the registered nurses must demonstrate the competencies for the processes that are needed to provide safe care and to ensure the safety of patients. Please refer to Chapters 17 and 25 for further discussion regarding staffing issues.

Objection to an Assignment

Professional duty implies an obligation to decline an assignment that one is not competent to complete. RNs cannot abandon their assigned patients, but they are obligated to inform their supervisor of any limitations they have in completing an assignment (Fig. 18.1). Not to inform and not to complete the assignment, or not to inform and to attempt to complete the assignment, risks untoward patient outcomes and resultant disciplinary action up to and including some potential action taken by the board of nursing.

The right and the means for a nurse to register an objection to a work assignment are considered essential elements in a union contract that incorporates the values of a profession as the basis of the contract agreement. This same process must be provided to nurses not represented by a union because nurses are obligated *to only provide the care that they are competent to provide*. While they are participating in the interview process, registered nurses should ascertain the presence of a written policy regarding objections to an assignment.

Nurses are encouraged to submit reports indicating an objection to the assignment when the assignment is not appropriate. The report should follow the process defined in the contract or facility policy. These same problems should also initiate constructive follow-through by management or staff-management committees to improve the situations described in the reports. Inaction could serve as a basis for a grievance or negotiated change in a union contract or an incident or change in policy in a nonunion environment.

Concept of Shared Governance

Many facilities are implementing a variety of governance models called *shared governance, self-governance, participative decision making,* or *decentralization of management.* In its simplest form, shared governance is shared decision making based on the principles of partnership, equity, accountability,

FIG. 18.1 Declining an assignment.

and ownership at the point of service (Swihart, 2006). The purpose of shared governance is to involve nurses in decision making related to control of their practice while the organization maintains the authority over traditional management decisions. The concept of shared governance can be a concern to unions representing nurses for purposes of collective bargaining since collective bargaining is also thought to be a governance model that decentralizes aspects of management.

In general, shared governance focuses on clinical practice aspects of the registered nurse staff while collective bargaining has a major focus on work rules/policies, and so forth. While the lines separating practice from work rules is minimal at times, it can be defined by those who are truly interested in achieving outcomes that are best for all parties. The discussion and understanding that must be reached address who or what controls the practice of professional nursing.

The concept of shared governance can be a concern to registered nurses who may feel that participating in shared governance can be a disadvantage to the practicing nurse if this participation is considered an alternative to collective bargaining. Whether greater latitude in decision making could be achieved through collective bargaining is the question to be considered. However, as more facilities are moving toward Magnet certification in which shared governance is a major function, it is recognized that some unionized facilities are also embracing the concepts of Magnet as recognition of the professional aspect of bargaining when representing the profession of nursing. Either way, it is essential that the practice of nursing be defined by nursing and the structure for implementing this practice is in place in each organization where nursing care is delivered.

Clinical or Career Ladder

The clinical ladder, or career ladder, has a place in both traditional and nontraditional styles of collective bargaining (Drenkard & Swartwout, 2005). The clinical ladder was designed to provide recognition of a registered nurse who chooses to remain clinically oriented. The idea of rewarding the clinical nurse with pay and status along a specific track or ladder is the result of the contributions of a nurse researcher, Dr. Patricia Benner. Her descriptions of the growth and development of nursing knowledge and practice provided the basis for a ladder model that can be used to identify and reward the nurse along the steps from novice to expert (Benner, 2009).

Negotiations

While registered nurses in a facility have varied educational backgrounds and represent the multiple practice specialties available to nursing, there are common practice issues/processes that need to be addressed by the nursing negotiating team. Once the common issues are addressed, the differences in practice needs must then be addressed in ongoing negotiations.

Professional goals and practice needs are appropriate topics for contract negotiations. Because personnel directors, hospital administrators, and hospital lawyers may have difficulty relating to these discussions, the nurse negotiating team has to be able to provide sufficient information to help prepare these individuals to understand the inclusion of professional goals and practice needs into the collective bargaining process and as entries into the agreed-on contract. The resolution of disagreements about professional issues necessitates there be time for a thoughtful process by those who are appropriately prepared to reach agreements through the negotiating process. Perhaps the complex issues such as recruitment, retention, staffing, and health and safety are better addressed in the more collegial setting of the nontraditional model; however, many of these issues are paramount to the creation of a safe and effective work environment for nurses, and they need to be addressed in both types of negotiations (Institute of Medicine, 2004).

THE DEBATE OVER COLLECTIVE BARGAINING

Collective Bargaining: Perspectives of the Traditional Approach

Is There a Place for Collective Bargaining in Nursing?

Should registered nurses use collective bargaining if they are members of a profession? Is nursing a profession or an occupation? Those in the nursing profession have debated these questions since the late 1950s, and the discussion and debate continue today. Nurses often look for assistance outside of nursing to help resolve issues, but these two questions can and should be resolved by nurses, if registered nurses are to be recognized as independent and in control of their practice.

According to the New York Department of Labor, "A registered professional nurse is a licensed health professional who has an independent, a dependent, and a collaborative role in the care of individuals of all ages, as well as families, groups, and communities. Such care may be provided to sick or well persons. The registered nurse uses the art of caring and the science of healthcare to focus on quality of life. The registered nurse accomplishes this through nursing diagnosis and treatment of a patient's, family's or community's responses to health problems that include but are not limited to issues involving the medical diagnosis and treatment of disease and illness" (New York Department of Labor, 2014, para 1). Defining what each level of registered nurse education best prepares one to practice can also be an issue discussed and agreed to through the process of collective bargaining. However, it must be recognized that these definitions are specific to each institution as the practice of professional nursing is defined at these individual facilities. Perhaps, over time, the profession of nursing will reach consensus regarding practice and the level of education completed, and this will no longer have to be a negotiated item! Because of their expertise and the value of their service, members of a profession are granted a measure of autonomy in their work. This autonomy permits practitioners to make independent judgments and decisions on the basis of a theoretical framework that is learned through study and practice. Although there may still be some who do not agree with the need for baccalaureate education, required for nursing to be designated as a profession, consider the fact that the absence of this professional designation continues to prevent nurses from the control over and definitions of their practice and of reaching their potential contributions to patient care and the health care system in which they are practicing.

In each state, registered nursing continues to be categorized as an *occupation* by the respective labor boards, and many decisions regarding the position of nursing in an organization are based on this classification as an occupation. However, for the purposes of the discussion on traditional and nontraditional collective bargaining, the role of nursing will be addressed as that of a profession.

Registered nurses need to consider the power granted to them and to the profession when they earn their license to practice nursing. The legal authority to practice nursing is independent from any other licensed professional or regulatory organization. This power of independence includes taking the responsibility for one's practice and for the practice of others when that practice negatively impacts patients and/or the community. This power is also an important element when entering into collective bargaining, because the independently licensed registered nurse must ensure the agreement supports this independence when addressing areas of clinical practice. Conflict arises as registered nurse employees advocate for a professional role in patient care when they are not classified as a profession by labor definitions and by the hiring facilities. The health care institutions hire registered nurses as members of an occupation who are essentially managed and led by the organization's formal leaders who often focus on productivity and savings. However, the hiring organization may not put registered nurses in situations where the independent clinical responsibilities cannot be met.

This potential conflict is a factor leading registered nurses to consider unionization as the only way they can demonstrate control over their clinical practice, particularly if shared governance is not used at their place of practice.

> Nursing has used collective action to its benefit, achieving professional goals while protecting and promoting public interest through lobbying efforts in the political arena. Many registered nurses support collective bargaining in the workplace as a way to control their practice by redistributing power within the health care organization.

Registered Nurse Participation in Collective Bargaining

If the state nurses associations were considered to be logical bargaining agents for registered nurses, why do so few nurses join these associations, and why are even fewer associations pursuing collective bargaining? "ANA, a nursing organization ... reportedly represents 163,111 RNs of the almost 3 million RNs that are active in this country" (Center for Union Facts, 2016). It is important to recognize that this low membership rate is not unique to nursing but is the same for most disciplines and for society in general. However, this low membership rate may also reflect the thinking of some that the professional organization for registered nurses may not be the best organization to represent the nursing population for collective bargaining. Perhaps the conflicts that would likely arise between a professional organization and a collective bargaining organization could be avoided by not combining these two distinct processes under one umbrella.

One of the problems with association memberships is that people tend to look at these associations and organizations for "what they can do for *me*"—for the work *I* do or the benefits *I* can receive. In reality, we need to look at these associations for what they can do for the profession and the population being served by the members of the profession/occupation. We then realize that the profession is only as strong as its members and the contributions they make to that occupation/profession. Perhaps looking at it in this way will encourage more to join and become members. The professional association can provide the standards and ethical platforms for a professional practice that would then be used as the basis for a collective bargaining contract.

Collective bargaining for registered nurses occurs more frequently in states where there is significant union activity in other industries.

The current labor climate is very volatile across the country. Unions are trying to organize new categories of workers, with special emphasis on the growing health care sector in states that have not traditionally been active in the labor movement. Some state nursing associations stopped providing collective bargaining services because of external pressures, including challenges from competing unions, excessive resistance by employers, or state policies that make unionization difficult, such as right-to-work laws. In states with right-to-work laws, it is illegal to negotiate an agency shop requirement. Membership and dues collection can never be mandatory, even if the workers are covered by a collective bargaining agreement. The cost of negotiating and maintaining a collective bargaining agreement in these states is often more than the income received for providing these services. Philosophical differences regarding the benefits and risks of a professional association as the bargaining agent have also led registered nurses in some states to abandon or avoid union activities or to avoid joining the professional association.

There are 2.6 million employed registered nurses in the United States, but only a few hundred thousand are organized for collective bargaining, and only around 20% of RNs belong to a professional organization. Sixty-one percent of these registered nurses are employed by hospitals (Bureau of Labor Statistics, 2016).

How will collective professional goals be achieved if so many nurses depend on the time and finances of so few? Some believe that the profession's efforts to address workplace concerns from both the traditional and nontraditional perspectives will result in larger membership numbers in the near future. For now, there may be too few registered nurses involved in the nursing associations to make up the needed critical mass for the kinds of changes and support that need to take place. Perhaps learning that this is the case will motivate more RNs to join their professional organization to support the work that needs to be accomplished. The implementation of the National Nurses United as the "RN Super Union" (Massachusetts Nurses Association, 2016) may supplant the state nurses associations as the primary provider of collective bargaining services for registered nurses.

Where Does Collective Bargaining Begin?

As stated in the National Labor Relations Act, registered nurses in the private sector are guaranteed legal protection if they seek to be represented by a collective bargaining agent. After a drive for such representation is under way and 30% of the employed RNs in an organization have signed cards signaling interest in representation, both the employer and the union are prohibited from engaging in any anti-labor action. Employers are prohibited from terminating the organizers for union activity, and they may not ignore the request for a vote for union representation. After the organizing campaign, a vote is taken; a majority, comprising 50% plus one of those voting, selects or rejects the collective bargaining agent.

The employer may choose to bargain in good faith on matters concerning working conditions by recognizing the bargaining agent before the vote. This approach usually occurs only if management believes a large majority of potential voters support the foundation of a union. In other cases, the employer may appeal requests for representation to the NLRB. Before and during the appeal, other unions may intervene and try to win a majority of votes for representation.

As a part of this appeal process, arguments are made before the NLRB regarding why, by whom, or how the nurses are to be represented. For example, the hospital may raise the question of unit determination. The original policy interpretation of the labor law simultaneously limited the number of individual units an employer or industry would have to recognize, yet allowed for distinct groups of employees, such as RNs, to receive separate representation. Nurses historically have been represented in all-RN bargaining units, and most bargaining units throughout the country reflect that pattern.

What Can a Union Contract Do?

Generally speaking, what can a union contract do in a hospital setting? Many believe that, today more than ever, registered nurses need a strong union such as the New York State Nurses Association (NYSNA) (NYSNA, 2016). Nurse shortages and the rise of health care for profit have dramatically changed the environments in which RNs are practicing and the demands that are placed on them. Too many nurses are spending too much time on duties that can be completed by staff other than RNs. Too many nurses are enduring too much overtime and are working under conditions that are unsafe for them and their patients.

Members of the NNU believe a strong, unified workforce is the best solution to the problems facing RNs and their patients today. When RNs become members of NNU, for example, they gain the ability to negotiate enforceable contracts that spell out specific working conditions such as acceptable nurse–patient ratios, roles RNs will play in determining standards of care, circumstances under which RNs will agree to work overtime, pay scales, benefits, dependable procedures for scheduling vacations and other time off, and all other similar conditions important to nurses.

A contract can also include language related to clinical advancement, such as is measured by the use of a clinical ladder or a similar mechanism. This is one way to bring concepts that have traditionally been avoided in collective bargaining strategies into the contracts to address practice aspects of the profession. When actions such as this occur, it could be anticipated that more registered nurses will support collective bargaining.

Wages. Wages and benefits are the foundation of a contract. Wages are the remuneration one receives for providing a service and reflect the value put on the work performed. In an article on the history of nursing's efforts to receive adequate compensation, Brider (1990) reaffirmed the need to continue efforts to improve nursing salaries. The author correctly stated that "from its beginnings, the nursing profession has grappled with its own ambivalence which is how to reconcile the ideal of selfless service with the necessity of making a living" (Brider, 1990, p. 77). The article confirmed the ambivalence of the nurses who recorded both their joy in productive careers and their disappointment with the way their work was valued. Registered nursing has certainly come a long way from the $8 to $12 monthly allowance in the early 1900s, but the challenge remains to bring nursing in line with comparable careers.

As we progress through the 21st century, it is clear periods of a shortage of nurses will occur. Like other occupations and professions, when the supply and demand favor the employee, wages are more critically evaluated. More recent shortages of registered nurses seem to be less responsive to some of the traditional solutions such as wage adjustments. This likely indicates that wages are not the only, or perhaps not even the primary, reason that individuals are not choosing registered nursing as a career or that many registered nurses are choosing to leave the field.

Another aspect of registered nurse compensation involves the challenge of addressing the negative effects of wage compression. This economic concept means that registered nurses who have been in practice for 10 and 12 years may make less money than recent graduates in their first registered nursing jobs! Unfortunately, it is not uncommon during times of shortages to see hiring or relocation bonuses to attract registered nurses into new positions. It would be preferable to see those dollars redistributed for the purposes of maintaining the base that is formed by the retention of experienced registered nurses in the facility.

Job security versus career security. It is probably not news to any student enrolled in a registered nursing program that he or she has entered a field that is facing many challenges—both from within and from outside nursing. Challenges related to the need for more registered nurses will occur primarily because of technological advancements; an increased emphasis on primary and preventative care; and the large, aging Baby Boomer population who will demand more health care services as they live longer and more active lives (Bureau of Labor Statistics, 2016). Additionally, challenges related to the implementation of the Affordable Care Act of 2010 are to be expected, and planning for ways to address these challenges are under way.

> According to the Bureau of Labor Statistics' Employment Projections 2014-2024 released in December 2015, Registered Nursing (RN) is listed among the top occupations in terms of job growth through 2024. The RN workforce is expected to grow from 2.75 million in 2014 to 3.19 million in 2024, an increase of 439,300 or 16% (Bureau of Labor Statistics, 2016).

The total number of licensed registered nurses in the United States in 2016 was approximately 3.13 million (Kaiser Family Foundation, 2016). Of the 3.13 million professionally active registered nurses, 61% work in hospitals (Bureau of Labor Statistics, 2016). The need for so many additional registered nurses coupled with the anticipated growth in the profession provides an opportunity to achieve some of the professional goals that have eluded nursing thus far, including full recognition as a profession and all that entails.

According to Juraschek, Zhang, Ranganathan, and Lin (2012), a shortage of registered nurses is projected to spread across the country over the next two decades, with the South and West most heavily impacted. The researchers noted an aging population requiring health care services, health care reform legislation, and aging RN workforce as factors contributing to the nursing shortage. These new paradigms will also challenge nurses and their representatives to modify bargaining strategies and turn attention to issues of sustaining quality in nursing care in the face of shortages, to overcome negative practices such as mandatory overtime, and to advocate for health and safety initiatives.

Seniority rights. Registered nurses who remain on staff at an organization accrue seniority that is based on the length of time employed as a registered nurse at that facility. Seniority provides specific rights, spelled out in the bargaining agreement, for those who have the highest number of years of service. These rights are derived from the idea that permanent employees should be viewed as assets to the organization and should therefore be rewarded for their service. In nurse employment contracts, there may be provisions (seniority language) that give senior nurses the right to accrue more vacation time and to be given preference when requesting time off, a change in position, or relief from shift rotation requirements. In the event of a staff layoff, the rule that states "the last hired becomes the first fired" protects senior nurses. Seniority rules may be applied to the registered nursing staff of the entire hospital or may be confined to a unit. However, transfers and promotions must reward the most senior qualified nurse in the organization.

Resolution of grievances. Methods to resolve grievances, which are sometimes explicitly spelled out in a contract, are an important element of any agreement. A grievance can arise when provisions in a contract are interpreted differently by management and an employee or employees. This difference often occurs when issues related to job security (a union priority), job performance, and discipline (a management priority) arise. *Grievance mechanisms* are used in an attempt to resolve the conflict with the parties involved. The employer, the employee, or the union may file a grievance. Nurses who are covered by contracts should be represented at any meeting or hearing they believe may lead to the application of disciplinary action. A co-worker, an elected nurse representative, or a member of the labor union's staff can provide such representation.

Arbitration. If the grievance mechanism does not lead to resolution of the issue, some contracts allow referral of the issue for arbitration. A knowledgeable—but neutral—arbitrator acceptable to both parties (union and hospital) will be asked to hear the facts of the case and issue a finding. In pre-agreed, binding arbitration, the parties must accept the decision of the arbitrator. For example, some contracts require that when management elects to discharge (suspend or terminate) a nurse, the case must be brought to arbitration. Based on the arbitrator's finding, the nurse may be reinstated, perhaps with back pay, may remain suspended, or may be terminated. If the contract states that the arbitrator's decision is final and binding, there is no further contractual or organizational avenue for either party to pursue.

Arbitration has also been used to resolve issues involving the integrity of the bargaining unit. Arbitrators have been asked to decide whether nurses remain eligible for bargaining unit coverage when jobs are changed and new practice models are implemented.

Mediation, arbitration, and fact finding have all been used to resolve conflicts in union contracts.

There is strong support for the use of these three methods, but hospital management personnel often resist using them. Nurses usually fare well when contract enforcement issues are submitted to an arbitrator and facts, not power or public relations, determine the outcome.

Strikes and other labor disputes. What can nurses do in the face of a standoff during contract negotiations? The options that current RNs have are quite different from those before 1968, when nurses felt a greater sense of powerlessness. At that time, despite nurses' threats of "sickouts," walkouts, picketing, or mass resignations, the employer maintained an effective power base. Threats of group action attracted public attention, but nurses' threats had little effect on employers, because nurses who were represented through the ANA had a no-strike policy. As negotiations became more difficult, it was apparent that nurses were in a weaker bargaining position because of the no-strike policy. The ANA responded to the state nursing associations, and in 1968, it reversed its 18-year-old no-strike policy. The NNU does not have a no-strike policy.

Strikes remain rare among nursing units, but as mentioned previously, when the efficacy of patient care and patient and staff safety are at risk, registered nurses may believe they have to strike. Increased strikes were seen beginning in 2000 as facilities were imposing mandatory overtime to cover the staff shortages. Many nurses are uncomfortable with the idea of striking, believing that they are abandoning their patients. It is important for nurses who contemplate striking to discuss plans for patient care with nurses who have previously conducted strikes so that they will be assured that plans to care for patients are adequate.

When an impasse is reached in hospital negotiations, national labor law requires registered nurses to issue a 10-day notice of their intent to strike. In the public's interest, every effort must be made to prevent a strike. The NLRB mandates mediation, and a board of inquiry to examine the issue may be created before a work stoppage. The organization is supposed to use this time to reduce the patient census and to slow or halt elective admissions. In the meantime, the nurses' strike committee will develop schedules for coverage of emergency rooms, operating rooms, and intensive care areas. This coverage is to be used only in the case of real emergencies. Planning coverage for patient care should reassure nurses troubled by the possibility of a strike. Nurses who agree to work in emergencies or at other facilities during a strike often donate their wages to funds that are set up for striking nurses.

Business and labor are both in search of more positive ways to work together to be able to avoid the possibility of a work stoppage. Strikes are not easy for either side—one side is not able to provide services, and the other side is not able to earn its usual income. In the middle, when health care is involved, is the patient who loses trust in both the organization and in the body of employees who choose to strike, requiring the patient to seek care elsewhere. The Department of Labor and the Federal Mediation and Conciliation Service have sponsored national grants to undertake alternatives to traditional collective bargaining. At least two Midwestern nursing organizations have used win–win bargaining techniques and found them to be constructive methods for negotiation.

What Are the Elements of a Sound Contract?

Membership. The inclusion of union security provisions is an essential element of a sound contract (Fig. 18.2) and addresses one of the defined goals of collective bargaining (union integrity). *Security*

- Membership
- Objection to assignment
- Retirement
- Staffing
- Benefits
- Health hazards

FIG. 18.2 Effective elements of a sound contract.

provisions include measures such as enforcement of membership requirements (collection of dues and access by the union staff to the members). In a closed shop agreement, the employer agrees that they will only hire employees who are members of the union. Closed shops are generally illegal. Union shop agreements allow an employer to hire nonunion members but require the employee to join the union within a certain amount of time (usually after 30 days). In practice, though, employers are not allowed to fire employees who refuse to join the union, provided the employees pay dues and fees to the union. An *agency shop* agreement requires employees who do not join the union to pay dues and fees.

Retirement. The usual pension or retirement programs for registered nurses have been either the social security system or a hospital pension plan. Because many employers are eliminating defined pension plans, individual retirement accounts, which are transferable from hospital to hospital in case of job changes, are becoming increasingly popular. The method of addressing issues related to financial support at the time of retirement should be a topic of negotiations. The ANA has entered an agreement with a national company to provide a truly portable national plan, unrestricted by geographic location or employment site. Although this plan could be complicated by conflicting state laws governing pension plans, a precedent was set as long ago as 1976, when California nursing contracts mandated employer contributions to individual retirement accounts for each nurse with immediate vesting (eligibility for access to the fund) and complete portability for the participants (meaning that the nurse could take the established retirement account to another hospital and could continue to add to this account either directly or by rolling it over into the new employer's individual retirement account).

One of registered nursing's most attractive benefits has been a nurse's mobility, which is the opportunity to change jobs at will. A drawback of this mobility is the loss of long-term retirement funds. With financial cutbacks in the hospital industry, retirement plans are in danger of being targeted as givebacks in negotiating rights or benefits to be traded away in lieu of another issue or benefit that may be more pressing at the time. One of the major benefits of individual retirement accounts is that they do belong to the employee, and the employee's contributions to the plan plus the employer's contributions to the plan can be taken with the employee when he or she leaves that employment, assuming all the defined rules of the plan are followed.

Health insurance coverage continues to be a key concern of employees and has been at the root of the majority of labor disputes in all industries in the past few years. It is not inconceivable that nurses may be asked to trade off long-term economic security (pensions) for short-term security (e.g., health benefits, wages). There is less chance this will occur if the organization has moved from the defined pension benefit. What is more likely to occur is that the employer will ask to contribute fewer dollars to health insurance premiums and/or retirement accounts and will ask employees to contribute an increased percentage of the cost of these benefits.

Other benefit issues. Other issues that have affected RNs as employees are family-leave policies, availability of daycare services, long-term disability insurance, and access to health insurance for retirees. These are the same issues that affect many workers in this country but may have a greater impact on employees such as registered nurses because of the 24-hour-a-day/7-day-a-week coverage that needs to be provided by this professional group.

An issue of special concern to RNs involves the scheduling of work hours. Although more men have joined the nursing occupation/profession, registered nursing remains a female occupation (Kaiser Family Foundation, 2016b). This reality must be addressed by providing benefit packages that provide flexibility for women who assume multiple roles in today's society. Generally, it is women who provide ongoing care to both children and parents. The nurse in the family may be called on to do this more than the spouse or the siblings. Registered nurses are asking nursing contract negotiators to secure leave policies that permit the use of sick time for family needs, that provide flexible scheduling that is flexible, and that allow part-time employment and work sharing.

An increasing number of men are entering the nursing field. According to the U.S. Census Bureau, men comprise approximately 9% of the current RN workforce. It is also noted that males who are practicing in the nursing profession earned a median annual salary of $60,700, whereas the median annual salary for a female RN was $51,100 (Census Bureau, 2013). Would this difference exist in an organization in which there was a collective bargaining agreement? Staffing issues, such as objection to an assignment, inadequate staffing, poorly prepared staff, mandatory overtime, nurse fatigue, and health hazards, are all concerns that can be addressed in a union contract; however, these are also issues of ongoing concern for all RNs, regardless of the type of bargaining situation in their respective states or organizations. These issues are discussed further in Chapter 25.

How Can Nurses Control Their Own Practice?

The essence of the professional nurse contract is control of practice. For example, registered nurse councils or professional performance committees provide the opportunity for registered nurses within the institution to meet regularly. These meetings are sanctioned by the contract. The elected registered staff nurse representatives may, for example, have specific objectives to

- Improve the professional practice of nurses and nursing assistants.
- Recommend ways and means to improve patient care.
- Recommend ways and means to address care issues when a critical nurse staffing shortage exists.
- Identify and recommend the elimination of hazards in the workplace.
- Identify and recommend processes that work to ensure the safety of patients.
- Implement peer-review.
- Implement shared governance.

Nurse Practice Committees

Registered nurse practice committees should have a formal relationship with nursing administration. Regularly scheduled meetings with nursing and hospital administrators can provide a forum for the discussion of professional issues in a safe atmosphere. Many potential conflicts regarding contract language can be prevented by discussion before contract talks begin or before grievances arise. Ideally, all health care professionals should also be a part of these forums, because they are an integral part of the care delivery system in a hospital and in other settings. Joint-practice language has been proposed in some contracts to facilitate these discussions.

Since the recognition of Magnet hospitals by the American Nurses Credentialing Center (ANCC) began in 1994, approximately 7% of all health care organizations in the United States have achieved ANCC Magnet recognition status (ANCC, 2016; American Hospital Association, 2015). Magnet status is not a prize or an award. Rather, it is a credential of organizational recognition of nursing excellence. Approximately 20% of the organizations awarded the recognition have a collective bargaining agreement with the nurses. This helps to validate the fact that control of nursing practice by RN staff members can be successfully achieved within the context of a collective bargaining agreement when both Magnet and collective bargaining have this as a common goal.

Collective Bargaining: Perspectives of the Nontraditional Approach

Effectively addressing the concerns of workplace advocacy, higher standards of practice, and economic security are not new issues. These concerns have caused nurses in some areas of the country to organize and to use unions and collective bargaining models to address practice and economic concerns. This section is designed to provide you with information and a rationale for a different approach to the position of the traditional collective bargaining. In the end, it will be up to you and your concept of the RN's role to grapple with this issue during your professional career.

Simultaneous Debates

Registered nursing today has acquired the majority of the generally recognized characteristics of a profession. One of these characteristics is a lengthy period of specialized education and practice preparation. The activities that are performed by professions are valued and recognized as important to society. In addition, a member of a profession has an acquired area of expertise that allows the person to make independent judgments, to act with autonomy, and to assume accountability. Nurses also have specialty organizations and are eligible to receive specialty credentialing in some defined areas of practice.

Another aspect of professional registered nursing is its strongly written ethical code. It is the obligation of every licensed RN to follow the tenets of the 2015 ANA Code of Ethics for Nurses (see Chapter 19). The Code articulates the values, goals, and responsibilities of the professional practice of nursing. The provisions of the Code that outline our duties to care for, advocate for, and be faithful to those people who entrust their health care to us are well integrated into the educational preparation of the RN. They are also widely recognized and respected by the public.

Collective Bargaining: The Debate That Continues

The debate about the appropriateness of collective bargaining continues. The combination of an explosion in knowledge and technology and an expanded population able to access health care quickly brought both public and private sector payers of health care to the inevitable quest to rein in the cost of health care. This gave birth and life to a growing collection of payment systems. There are now gatekeepers, specific practice protocols, contractual agreements between payers and providers, and provider and consumer incentives that govern the place, provider, type, and quantity of a patient's care. These developments have affected everyday care in a growing number of settings. Nurses are challenged daily in practice environments that have evolved to business models to survive financially while continuing to provide care to a defined population of patients. Many registered nurses feel these business and financial environments are not conducive to the patient-focused or family-centered models of care delivery or to the ethical values that have been an inherent part of the professional education and practice preparation of nurses. All too often, the intense clinical education of the RN practicing in today's health care environment has not prepared the individual to appreciate the financial and regulatory realities of a large industry. Perhaps even more disconcerting is the fact that as RNs enter the workforce, they may not see the magnitude of their potential for leadership and problem solving within an environment that continues to evolve so quickly while the environment continues to work hard to hold on to the traditional hierarchy of medicine and health care administration.

The history of the position of registered nursing during the first half of the 20th century may, in part, explain our slow journey toward leadership and control of nursing practice. In the last half of the 20th century, some registered nurses organized and relied on collective bargaining units to speak for them. Time and energy have been spent debating who can or should best represent professional nurses in the workplace. The transition of collective bargaining from the ANA, who established the foundation for acceptance of collective bargaining by registered nurses, to the growing NNU, may signal that the journey toward gaining control of nursing practice will move more quickly. These two strong organizations could take steps to gain acceptance of the concept that control of nursing practice by registered nurses is not congruent with "holding on to the traditional hierarchy of medicine and administration."

Traditional Collective Bargaining: Its Risks and Benefits

The goal of the traditional collective bargaining model is to win something that is controlled by another. There is an "us versus them" approach. The weapon is the power of numbers. Although a desired contract is achieved, long-lasting adversarial relationships may develop between the nurses and the employer (Budd et al., 2004) (see Critical Thinking Box 18.2).

? CRITICAL THINKING BOX 18.2

With the soaring cost of health care, the changes in health care reimbursement, and the subsequent reining in of health care costs, where does that leave nursing in the collective bargaining process? Does this not further aggravate the already adversarial relationship of nurses and their employers?

Traditional collective bargaining held promise and assisted the professional nurse's evolution toward economic stability. These were important gains. However, the full power and potency of nursing as an industry leader has not emerged through traditional collective bargaining efforts. This may explain the dissatisfaction of the nurses with traditional collective bargaining or may also be an indication that the other basic debates within the body of RNs need to be resolved before nurses take the place in the industry they feel is appropriate for them.

Can nursing effectively step away from the adversarial process of traditional collective bargaining into an effective leadership role? IBB and/or processes such as shared governance may offer nurses a nonadversarial approach, but it will require nursing leaders to demonstrate an understanding of interests and outcomes that are important both to the nursing occupation/profession and to other members of the health care industry (Budd et al., 2004). As discussed earlier in this chapter, IBB is a nontraditional style of bargaining that attempts to solve problems and resolve differences between the workforce and the employer—or the nurse and the hospital. Although this style of bargaining and mediation will not always eliminate the need for the more traditional and adversarial collective bargaining, this nonadversarial approach of negotiation may be closer to the basic beliefs underlying professional nursing as well as the nursing code of ethics.

In considering nontraditional approaches, it is important to recognize state nurse associations that have made significant contributions to their local membership by offering IBB services to that membership. This has also resulted in contributions to the advancement of nontraditional, nonadversarial bargaining for the promotion of workplace advocacy on a national level (Box 18.2). Do these commitments sound familiar?

BOX 18.2 EIGHT COMMITMENTS TO WORKPLACE ADVOCACY

Workplace advocacy is a nurse-to-nurse strategy that can give RNs a meaningful voice in their workplace. As a result of Texas Nurses Association (TNA) workplace advocacy efforts in the past, Texas now has one of the strongest nursing practice acts in the country. The following are eight commitments to workplace advocacy. The Texas Nurses Association will:

Work to secure mechanisms within health care systems that provide opportunities for registered nurses to affect institutional policies. Mechanisms include:
- Shared governance
- Participatory management models
- Magnet hospital identifications
- Statewide staffing regulations

Develop with stakeholders a conflict resolution process for nurse/nurse employers that addresses registered nurse concerns about patient care and delivery issues.
- Active participation with the Texas Hospital Association and the American Arbitration Association to develop a conflict resolution process that meets the needs of nurses in resolving patient care issues.

Provide legislative solutions to Texas registered nurses by reviewing issues of concern to nurses in employment settings and introducing appropriate legislation. Previous initiatives include:
- Whistle-blower
- Safe Harbor Peer Review
- Support for Board of Nurse Examiners rules outlining strong nursing practice standards

Explore the development of a legal center for nurses that could provide legal support and decision-making advice as a last recourse in cases of unresolved workplace issues. Its purpose would be to:
- Provide fast legal assistance
- Earmark precedent-setting cases that could impact case law and health care policy

Support the RN in practice with self-advocacy and patient advocacy information by providing products that increase knowledge about:
- Laws and regulations governing practice
- Use of applicable standards of nursing practice
- Conflict-resolution techniques
- Statewide reporting mechanisms that allow the nurse to report concerns about health care institutions and professionals
- Professional behaviors, core values, and conduct that support effective negotiation

Promote to RNs those health care institutions in Texas that demonstrate outstanding nurse/employer relations.

Work with Texas schools of nursing to develop materials that incorporate self-advocacy and patient advocacy information into the nursing curriculum.

Advocate for the elimination of physician abuse of RNs with the physician community and employers by:
- Working with physician professional organizations to develop a campaign to end physician abuse of RNs
- Working with health care facilities to establish Zero Tolerance for physician abuse of RNs
- Developing model policies against physician abuse of nurses
- Encouraging nurse-to-nurse advocacy to stop abusive situations

---

Reprinted with permission from Texas Nursing Association. (2006). *Eight commitments to workplace advocacy.* Austin, TX: tna@texasnurses.org.

FUTURE TRENDS

The public should be concerned about an inadequate supply of nurses. Based on that concern, along with the multiple other issues that are impacting the provision of health care now and in the future, there is increased interest by the press and policymakers to be sure registered nurses are prepared in adequate numbers and that their working environment supports quality nursing care. This attention is helping nurses achieve improvements in overall compensation and working conditions and may also lead to support for the preparation of sufficient numbers of registered nurse faculty and methods of financial support for the education of RNs.

The nursing community should take a step back and try to identify those factors that appear to keep registered nursing from becoming a profession of choice, which should result in eliminating the continuous cycle of shortage/staff reduction/shortage. One of the classic issues is that nursing is still not considered a profession according to most definitions of a profession or according to the labor bureaus that classify employee groups. Until nurses accept the fact that we cannot just *say* we are a profession without meeting the minimum criteria for this designation, we will continue to be classified as an occupation only.

The movement to gain recognition as a profession is the next issue to be addressed in the next few years. Discussions regarding this requirement are found in Chapter 9. Another issue that must be addressed by organized nursing is the silence of nursing, as defined and discussed by Buresh and Gordon (2006). These authors completed extensive research to determine why nurses were rarely seen or heard in the various forms of media. They discovered that, for the most part, the media cannot find registered nurses who are willing to talk, to be interviewed, or to write editorials stating opinions or positions. More important, when nurses were available to talk to the media, they "too often unintentionally project an incorrect picture of nursing by using a 'virtue' rather than a 'knowledge' script" (Buresh & Gordon, 2006, p. 4). They also noted that nurses tend to downplay or devalue basic registered nursing bedside care, the heart of what we do, while focusing on the greater status of the advanced practitioner.

As with many things in life, there is a tendency to look outside of the problem to define a cause for the problem and to look to others to find a solution. Nursing, as the largest group of health care providers and as the only group of providers entrusted to implement the majority of the medical plan of care, needs to look within to find how to communicate most effectively the vital role we take in the provision of health care.

Nurses throughout the country have felt firsthand the effects of cost containment. Those effects have often been detrimental to the quality of care that RNs are charged to provide. From a professional practice perspective, mandatory overtime and short staffing are some of the factors contributing to the preponderance of medical errors documented in the Institute of Medicine report *To Err Is Human: Building a Safer Health System* (Institute of Medicine, 2000). The ANA was the initial voice in recognizing these as potential contributing factors and has led the way in encouraging research agendas that further quantify the number of work hours needed to provide safe care and further define how patient safety can be ensured. As with other major issues affecting the practice of RNs, the ANA and state nursing associations are in the lead in federal and state legislative efforts to address overtime and staffing in the context of safe patient care.

> What lies ahead for collective bargaining and all forms of collective action for nurses must be viewed within the context of the overall changes occurring in the health care system and in the financing mechanisms for that system.

As concerned nurses, we need to remain vigilant about our need to meet the basic obligation of licensure, which is to provide safe care to all patients. This issue of adequate access to health care services is one that will probably be with us for the rest of our professional careers. It is believed by many that one way to improve access to services is to deliver them in environments and by providers that have not traditionally been a part of our health care system. Each of these venues provides significant opportunities for RNs, because the essence of our work is the prevention of disease and the adaptability to chronic disease processes that will enable our patients to remain as active as possible in their own environment.

CONCLUSION

Nursing has a unique contract with society to promote effective health care and, as a natural outcome, promote the health and welfare of the nurse and the occupation/profession of nursing. The multipurpose nature of the professional nursing association will continue to work to preserve the future of nursing. This chapter cannot stand alone, nor can the nurses in the workplace stand alone if they are to offset the forces that negate the contributions of nurses. Political action and lobbying, research, and education are necessary to further the cause of nursing and to meet the health care needs of the public we serve. As nurses work to transform aspects of the health system and to improve access to care, they will continue to depend on collective action and a collective voice through the structures and functions initially established within the ANA to advocate for optimal working conditions and standards of practice. There are now multiple opportunities to continue to advance the collective voice of nursing to ensure that the profession of nursing will be available to provide the quality care and services to all those who are in need of this care and service (see the relevant websites and online resources below). Welcome to nursing! Join us in our efforts to unify our skills, knowledge, and voices as we ensure our vision is being met.

🌐 RELEVANT WEBSITES AND ONLINE RESOURCES

National Nurses United (NNU)
www.nationalnursesunited.org/.

Online Journal of Issues in Nursing
OJIN is a peer-reviewed, online publication that addresses current topics affecting nursing practice, research, education, and the wider health care sector. http://www.nursingworld.org/OJIN.

Patient Protection and Affordable Care Act
http://www.gpo.gov/fdsys/pkg/BILLS-111hr3590enr/pdf/BILLS-111hr3590enr.pdf.

IOM Report, The Future of Nursing
http://www.iom.edu/~/media/Files/Report%20Files/2010/The-Future-of-Nursing/Future%20of%20Nursing%202010%20Report%20Brief.pdf.

BIBLIOGRAPHY

American Hospital Association (AHA). (2015). *Fast facts on U.S. hospitals.* Retrieved from http://www.aha.org/research/rc/stat-studies/101207fastfacts.pdf.

American Nurses Association (ANA). (2015a). *ANA code of ethics for nurses.* Retrieved from http://www.nursingworld.org/MainMenuCategories/EthicsStandards/CodeofEthicsforNurses.

American Nurses Association (ANA). (2015b). *ANA commends introduction of the registered nurse safe staffing act.* Retrieved from http://www.rnaction.org/site/DocServer/ANARelease_RNSafeStaffingBill_2015-04-29.pdf?docID=2362.

American Nurses Credentialing Center (ANCC). (2016). *Growth of the program.* Retrieved from http://www.nursecredentialing.org/Magnet/ProgramOverview/HistoryoftheMagnetProgram/GrowthoftheProgram.

Benner, P. (2009). *Expertise in nursing practice* (2nd ed.). New York: Springer.

Brider, P. (1990). Professional status: The struggle for just compensation. *American Journal of Nursing, 90*(10), 77–80.

Brommer, C., Buckingham, G., & Loeffler, S. (2003). *Cooperative bargaining styles at federal mediation and conciliation services: A movement toward choices.* Retrieved from www.fmcs.gov/internet/itemDetail.asp?categoryID=35&;itemID=15880.

Budd, K., Warino, L., & Patton, M. (2004). Traditional and non-traditional collective bargaining: Strategies to improve the patient care environment. *Online Journal of Issues in Nursing, 9*(1), 9.

Bureau of Labor Statistics. (2016). *U.S. Department of Labor, Occupational Outlook Handbook, 2016-17 Edition, Registered Nurses.* Retrieved from http://www.bls.gov/ooh/healthcare/registered-nurses.htm.

Buresh, B., & Gordon, S. (2006). *From silence to voice.* New York: Cornell University.

Center for Union Facts. (2016). *2013 Union profiles: American Nurses Association.* Retrieved from https://www.unionfacts.com/union/American_Nurses_Association#basic-tab.

Census Bureau. (2013). *Men in nursing occupations.* Retrieved from https://www.census.gov/people/io/files/Men_in_Nursing_Occupations.pdf.

Department for Professional Employees (DPE) Research. (2015). *The benefits of collective bargaining for professionals.* Retrieved from http://dpeaflcio.org/programs-publications/issue-fact-sheets/the-benefits-of-collective-bargaining-for-professional-and-technical-workers/.

Drenkard, K., & Swartwout, E. (2005). Effectiveness of a clinical ladder program. *Journal of Nursing Administration, 35,* 502–506.

Gaus, M. (December 4, 2009). *Nurses move toward a "superunion."* Retrieved from http://www.labornotes.org/2009/12/nurses-move-toward-superunion.

Hackman, D. (2008). ANA and UAN part ways. *Georgia Nursing, 68*(4), 1. Retrieved from http://nursingald.com/uploads/publication/pdf/561/GA11_08.pdf.

Institute of Medicine. (2000). To err is human: Building a safer health system. In L. Kohn & J. Corrigan (Eds.), *IOM report.* Washington, DC: National Academies Press.

Institute of Medicine. (2004). Keeping patients safe: Transforming the work environment of nurses. In L. Kohn & J. Corrigan (Eds.), *IOM report.* Washington, DC: National Academies Press.

Jacox, A. (1980). Collective action: The basis for professionalism. *Supervisor Nurse, 11,* 22–24.

Juraschek, S. P., Zhang, X., Ranganathan, V. K., & Lin, V. W. (2012). United States registered nurse workforce report card and shortage forecast. *American Journal of Medical Quality, 27*(3), 241–249. http://dx.doi.org/10.1177/106286061146634.

Kaiser Family Foundation. (2016). *Total number of professionally active nurses.* Retrieved from http://kff.org/other/state-indicator/total-registered-nurses/#notes.

Kimmel, N. (2007). *Nurses and unions: Changing times.* Retrieved from http://ezinearticles.com/?Nurses-and-Unions--Changing-Times&id=584916.

Massachusetts Nurses Association. (2016). *Building the RN super union.* Retrieved from http://www.massnurses.org/news-and-events/national.

Meier, E. (2000). Is unionization the answer for nurses and nursing? *Nursing Economic, 18*(1), 36–37.

National Council State Boards of Nursing (NCSBN). (2015). *RN practice analysis: Linking the NCLEX-RN examination to practice.* Chicago: Author.

National Nurses United (NNU). (2016). *About NNU.* Retrieved from http://www.nationalnursesunited.org/pages/19.

New York Department of Labor. (2014). *Registered Professional Nurse.* Retrieved from http://www.labor.ny.gov/stats/olcny/registered-professional-nurse.shtm.

New York State Nurses Association (NYSNA). (2016). *What is a union?* Retrieved from http://www.nysna.org/strength-at-work/what-is-a-union#.VroVR_k4HNM.

Potter, P. A., Perry, A. G., Stockert, P. A., & Hall, A. M. (2013). *Fundamentals of nursing* (8th ed.). St. Louis: Elsevier.

Swihart, D. (2006). *Shared governance: A practical approach to reshaping professional nursing practice*. Marblehead, MA: HCPro.

The American Nurse. (November-December, 2010). *Center for American Nurses services to be integrated into ANA*. Retrieved from http://www.theamericannurse.org/index.php/2010/11/30/center-for-american-nurses-services-to-be-integrated-into-ana/.

Thomas, L. M. (2014). *15 Sample questions you should ask in a nursing interview*. Retrieved from http://www.nursetogether.com/15-sample-questions-you-should-ask-nursing-job-interview.

Trossman, S. (2008). ANA's campaign to promote patient safety and quality health care. *American Nurse, 40*. Retrieved from http://nursingworld.org/91008tan.aspx.

United American Nurses (UAN). (2008). *UAN: Power of nurses*. Retrieved from www.uannurse.org/who/history.html.

U.S. Department of Health and Human Services. (2016). *The Affordable Care Act, section by section*. Retrieved from http://www.hhs.gov/healthcare/about-the-law/read-the-law/index.html.

Williams, K. (2004). Ethics and collective bargaining: Calls to action. *Online Journal of Issues in Nursing, 9*(3). Retrieved from www.nursing world.org.

19

Ethical Issues

Peter Melenovich, PhD, RN, CNE

Ⓔ http://evolve.elsevier.com/Zerwekh/nsgtoday/.

Acting responsibly is not a matter of strengthening our reason, but of deepening our feelings for the welfare of others.
Jostein Gaarder

Ethical dilemmas are not easy situations.

After completing this chapter, you should be able to:

- Define terminology commonly used in discussions about ethical issues.
- Analyze personal values that influence approaches to ethical issues and decision making.
- Discuss the moral implications of the American Nurses Association and International Council of Nurses codes of ethics.
- Discuss the role of the nurse in ethical health care issues.
- Recognize the role of genetics and genomics in nursing practice.
- Recognize resources to assist in resolving an ethical dilemma.

In developing the content for this chapter, a deliberate effort has been made to "simplify" the presentation of ethical issues and avoid complex philosophical debate. Many nurses shy away from formal ethical discussions, because the terminology seems better suited to graduate school and a peer-reviewed journal. In reality, nurses deal with ethical issues every day in practice and need to have the tools to advocate effectively for patients, as well as for themselves. The first step in equipping oneself for ethical debate is becoming comfortable with the language and issues. Ethics refers to principles of right and wrong behaviors, beliefs, and values. Thompson et al.

(2007) add, "ethics is essentially concerned with our life as members of a community, and how we behave and function in society" (p. 36).

Concern about ethical issues in health care has increased dramatically in the past three decades. This interest has soared for a variety of reasons, including advances in medical technology; social and legal changes involving abortion, euthanasia, patient rights, end-of-life care, reproductive technology; and growing concern about the allocation of scarce resources, including a shortage of nurses. Nurses have begun to speak out on these issues and have focused attention on the responsibilities and the possible conflicts that they experience as a result of their unique relationship with patients and their families and their role within the health care team.

UNDERSTANDING ETHICS

Let us begin by defining commonly used terms (Box 19.1).

What Are Your Values?

Your values represent ideas and beliefs that you hold with high regard. Clarification of your values is suggested as a strategy to develop greater insight into yourself and what you believe to be important. Value clarification involves a three-step process: choosing, prizing, and acting on your value choices in real-life situations (Steele, 1983). Moreover, our values may impact how we practice as nurses and the decisions that we make each day in our professional practice (Wang, Chou, & Huang, 2010). Opportunities to make choices and improve your decision making are

---

BOX 19.1 DEFINITION OF TERMS

Advance directive: A written statement of a person's wishes about how he or she would like health care decisions to be made if he or she ever loses the ability to make such decisions independently.

Bioethical issues: Subjects that raise concerns of right and wrong in matters involving human life (e.g., euthanasia, abortion).

Bioethics: Ethics concerning life.

Durable power of attorney for health care: A document that allows a person to name someone else to make medical decisions for him or her if he or she is unable to do so. This spokesperson's authority begins only when the patient is incompetent to make those decisions.

Ethics: Rules or principles that determine which human actions are right or wrong.

Ethical dilemma
1. A situation involving competing rules or principles that appears to have no satisfactory solution.
2. A choice between two or more equally undesirable alternatives.

Living will: A document that allows a person to state in advance that life-sustaining treatment is not to be administered if the person later is terminally ill and incompetent.

Moral or ethical principles: Fundamental values or assumptions about the way individuals should be treated and cared for. These include autonomy, beneficence, nonmaleficence, justice, fidelity, and veracity.

Moral courage: The willingness to do what is right despite the fear of consequences.

Moral distress: Feeling of powerlessness to do what is right and ethical.

Moral reasoning: A process of considering and selecting approaches to resolve ethical issues.

Moral uncertainty: A situation that exists when the individual is unsure which moral principles or values apply in a given situation.

Values: Beliefs that are considered very important and frequently influence an individual's behavior.

included in the following pages. As you consider your values, you will, I hope, gain more understanding about the underlying motives that influence them. It is not intended as a "right" or "wrong" activity; rather, it is a discovery about the "what" and "why" of your actions. Do not be surprised if your peers or family hold different views on some topics. And remember, the values that are "correct" or "right" for you may not always be the "right" values for others, including patients and their families. Your values may also change through time as you face different life experiences.

Evaluate the critical thinking questions, write down your responses to them, and consider the possible reason or reasons for your choices. The critical thinking exercise in Critical Thinking Box 19.1 is suggested as a means of clarifying your values. Discuss your answers with peers and decide how comfortable you are in discussing and defending your values, especially if they differ from the values of your peers. Critical Thinking Box 19.2 involves reproductive issues and has been included here because of the proliferation of reproductive technology, including genetics, and the ongoing moral and political debate regarding abortion and the use of stem cells.

? CRITICAL THINKING BOX 19.1

Listing Values

List ten values that guide your daily interactions.
   Choose a partner (if available).
   Discuss with a partner each of the values you listed and how they guide your interactions.
   Compare your list of values with your partner's list, and discuss similarities and differences in the two lists.
   Prioritize your list, and discuss why you feel some are more important than others.

From Steele, S., & Harmon, V. (1983). *Values clarification in nursing* (2nd ed.). East Norwalk, CT: Appleton-Century-Crofts, p. 90; with permission.

? CRITICAL THINKING BOX 19.2

Reproductive Exercise

Identify your degree of agreement or disagreement with the statements by placing the number that most closely indicates your value next to each statement.
1 = Strongly disagree
2 = Disagree
3 = Ambivalent
4 = Agree
5 = Strongly agree

	1.	Contraception is a responsibility of all women.
	2.	Some types of contraception are more valuable than other types.
	3.	Abortion as a form of contraception is completely unacceptable.
	4.	Abortion decisions are the responsibility of the pregnant woman and her physician.
	5.	The birth of a "test tube baby" is a valuable medical advance.
	6.	Genetic screening should be done frequently.
	7.	Genetic counseling should provide information so that patients can make informed choices about future reproductive decisions.
	8.	Amniocentesis should be required as part of prenatal care.
	9.	Genetic engineering should be advanced and promoted by federal funding.
	10.	Artificial insemination should be available to anyone who seeks it.

_____	11.	Sperm used in artificial insemination should come from all strata of society as do blood transfusions.
_____	12.	Fetal surgery should be done even when it places another fetus at risk (i.e., a twin).
_____	13.	Surrogate mothers play an important role in the future of families.
_____	14.	Fetuses who survive experimentation should be raised by society.
_____	15.	Women should be encouraged to participate in fetal research by carrying fetuses to desired dates and then giving the fetus to the scientist for research.
_____	16.	Contraception is reserved for women of legal age.
_____	17.	Adolescents should require a parent's signature for abortion.
_____	18.	Information about genetically transmitted diseases should be provided to all pregnant women.
_____	19.	Women at high risk for genetically transmitted diseases should be encouraged to have amniocentesis.
_____	20.	Infants born with severe defects should be allowed to die through a natural course.

From Steele, S., & Harmon, V. (1983). *Values clarification in nursing* (2nd ed.). East Norwalk, CT: Appleton-Century-Crofts, p. 169; with permission.

Moral/Ethical Principles
What Is the Best Decision, and How Will I Know?

Despite different ideas regarding which moral or ethical principle is most important, ethicists agree that there are common principles or rules that should be taken into consideration when an ethical situation is being examined. As you read through each principle, consider instances in which you have acted on the principles or perhaps felt some conflict in trying to determine what was the best action to take (Fig. 19.1).

Autonomy: a patient's right to self-determination without outside control. Autonomy implies the freedom to make choices and decisions about one's own care without interference, even if those decisions are not in agreement with those of the health care team. This principle assumes rational thinking on the part of the individual and may be challenged when the individual infringes on the rights of others.

Consider this: What if a patient wants to do something that will cause harm to himself or herself? Under what circumstances can the health care team intervene?

Beneficence: duty to actively do good for patients. For example, you use this principle when deciding what nursing interventions should be provided for patients who are dying when some of those interventions may cause pain. In the course of prolonging life, harm sometimes occurs.

Consider this: Who decides what is good? Patient, family, nurse, or physician? How do you define good?

Nonmaleficence: duty to prevent or avoid doing harm, whether intentional or unintentional. Is it harmful to accept an assignment to "float" to an unfamiliar area that requires the administration of unfamiliar medications?

Consider this: Is it acceptable to refuse an assignment? When does an assignment become unsafe?

Fidelity: the duty to be faithful to commitments. Fidelity involves keeping information confidential and maintaining privacy and trust (e.g., maintaining patient confidentiality regarding a positive HIV test or "blowing the whistle" about unscrupulous billing practices).

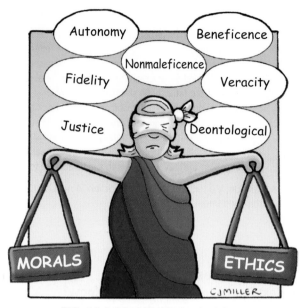

FIG. 19.1 Moral/ethical principles.

Consider this: To whom do we owe our fidelity? Patient, family, physician, institution, or profession? Who has the right to access patient medical records? When should we "blow the whistle" about unsafe staffing patterns?

Justice: the duty to treat all patients fairly, without regard to age, socioeconomic status, or other variables. This principle involves the allocation of scarce and expensive health care resources. Should uninsured patients be allowed to use the emergency department (ED) for nonemergency care—the most expensive route for delivering this type of care? Who should be paying for their care?

Consider this: What is fair, and who decides? Why are some patients labeled very important persons (VIPs)? Should they receive a different level of care? Why or why not? What kind of access to health care should illegal immigrants receive: preventive or more costly ED care?

Veracity: the duty to tell the truth. The principle of veracity may become an issue when a patient who suspects that her diagnosis is cancer asks you, "Nurse, do I have cancer?" Her family has requested that she not be told the truth, because their culture believes bad news takes away all hope for the patient.

Consider this: Is lying to a patient ever justified? If a patient finds out that you have lied, will that patient have any reason to trust you again?

Each of the aforementioned principles sounds so right; yet the "consider this" questions indicate that putting principles into practice is sometimes much easier said than done. Reality does not always offer textbook situations that allow flawless application of ethical principles. As Oscar Wilde, an Irish playwright, once said, "The truth is rarely pure, and never simple." You will encounter clinical situations that challenge the way you apply an ethical principle or that cause two or more principles to be in conflict, creating moral distress, which is often referred to as an *ethical dilemma*.

Which Principle or Rule Is Most Important?

Current thinking on the part of ethicists favors autonomy and nonmaleficence as preeminent principles, because they emphasize respect for the person and the avoidance of harm. However, there is no universal agreement, and many individuals rely on their spiritual beliefs as the cornerstone to ethical decision making.

Another possible approach to decision making is to consider the relative benefits and burdens of an ethical decision for the patient. If patients are capable of rational decision making, they may choose a different treatment approach than the care team. This fact is sometimes difficult for health care team members to accept, especially if it involves a decision to stop treatment. If patients are not capable of autonomous decision making, substituted judgment (decision making) by their designated family is then used. Problems frequently arise when family members disagree on a treatment choice or quality-of-life issues, as evidenced by the Terry Schiavo case in Florida (2003), when the husband's wishes to discontinue life support for his wife were granted after a prolonged court case that included attempted government intervention.

Traditional and contemporary models of ethical reasoning offer worldviews from which ethical principles, spiritual values, and the concepts of benefits and burdens can be derived, interpreted, and comparatively emphasized. Nevertheless, models of ethical reasoning are not without their critics, including nurses, who feel that abstract ideas about right and wrong are not helpful or "practical" at the bedside.

In recent years, nursing ethicists have advanced a new approach to ethical issues, emphasizing an ethic of caring as the moral foundation for nursing. Nurses have been encouraged to consider all ethical issues from the central issue of caring. Because caring implies concern for preserving humanity and dignity and promoting well-being, the awareness of rules and principles alone does not adequately address the ethical issues that nurses confront, such as in cases of suffering or powerlessness. Research regarding the application of caring to ethical issues is under way, but a practical model for applying this ethic of caring to clinical situations does not yet exist. Currently, the most care-centered approach to ethical dilemmas is to consider the relative "benefits versus burdens" that any proposed solution offers to the patient. Health team members need to try to consider benefits and burdens from the patient's perspective versus their own values on life, death, and the vast degrees of illness between the two. It is a difficult task to undertake.

So How Do I Make an Ethical Decision?

A number of approaches to ethical decision making are possible. The following is a brief overview of the three most commonly applied models of ethical reasoning. The first two types are considered normative because they have clearly defined parameters, or norms, to influence decision making. The third type is a combination of the other two models.

Deontological. Derived from Judeo-Christian origins, the deontological normative approach is duty-focused and centered on rules from which all action is derived. The rules represent beliefs about intrinsic good that are moral absolutes revealed by God. This approach reasons that all persons are worthy of respect and thus should be treated the same.

All life is worthy of respect.

As a result of the rules and duties that the deontological approach outlines, the individual may feel that he or she has clear direction about how to act in all situations. Right or wrong is determined based on one's duty or obligation to act, not on the consequences of one's actions. Therefore abortion and euthanasia are never acceptable actions, because they violate the duty to respect the sanctity of all life, and lying is never acceptable because it violates the duty to tell the truth. The emphasis on absolute rules with this approach is sometimes seen as rigid and inflexible, but its strength is in its unbending approach to many issues, emphasizing the intent of actions.

Teleological. Derived from humanistic origins, the teleological approach is outcome-focused and places emphasis on results. *Good* is defined in utilitarian terms: That which is useful is good. Human reason is the basis for authority in all situations, not absolutes from God. Morality is established by majority rule, and the results of actions determine the rules. Because results become the intrinsic good, the individual's actions are always based on the probable outcome.

> That which causes a good outcome is a good action.

Simplistically, this view is sometimes interpreted as "the end justifies the means." Abortion may be acceptable, because it results in fewer unwanted babies. Euthanasia is an acceptable choice by some patients, because it results in decreased suffering. Giving preference for a heart transplant to a foreign national who can pay cash and donate money for a transplant program is acceptable, because this will create a greater good for others. Using this approach, the rights of some individuals may be sacrificed for the majority.

Situational. Derived from humanistic and Judeo-Christian influences and most commonly credited to Joseph Fletcher (1966), an Episcopalian theologian, the situational view holds that there are no prescribed rules, norms, or majority-focused results that must be followed. Each situation creates its own set of rules and principles that should be considered in that particular set of circumstances. Emphasizing the uniqueness of the situation and respect for the person in that situation, Fletcher appeals to love as the only norm. Critics of this approach argue that this can lead to a "slippery slope" of moral decline.

> Decisions made in one situation cannot be generalized to another situation.

Chemically restraining a disruptive patient who has Alzheimer's disease provides a calmer atmosphere for other patients in a long-term care facility. This approach is used after all other efforts to calm the patient have failed. "Pulling the plug" on a terminally ill patient who does not want any more extraordinary care can be considered an act of compassion. Withholding or withdrawing treatment is ethically correct from the individual patient's perspective if the burden of treatment outweighs the benefit of merely extending life. Defining *burden* has to be approached from the patient's perspective, not from others who may feel burdened by the patient's need for care. Viewing a situation from the perspective of benefit versus burden can assist patients and families to make difficult decisions on the basis of the patient's clear or intended wishes discussed over a period of time. Nurses and other health care providers need to be patient advocates, speaking out for those who are disadvantaged and cannot speak for themselves.

Table 19.1 compares the relative advantages and disadvantages of each approach. Remember that there is no perfect worldview. If there were, debate would stop, and the need for continued ethical deliberation would cease. The ethical models presented here are not intended to be all-inclusive or exhaustive in depth. Rather, they should whet your appetite for further content. Many journals and texts are devoted to clinical ethics, and you are encouraged to see how ethicists apply these and other

TABLE 19.1	THREE APPROACHES TO ETHICAL DECISION MAKING: COMPARISON OF ADVANTAGES AND DISADVANTAGES	
ETHICAL APPROACH	**ADVANTAGES**	**DISADVANTAGES**
Deontological	Clear direction for action.	Perceived as rigid.
	All individuals are treated the same. Does not consider possible negative consequences of action.	Does not consider possible negative consequences of actions.
Teleological	Interest of the majority is protected.	Rights of individual may be overlooked or denied.
	Results are evaluated for their good, and actions may be modified.	What is a good result? Who determines good? Morality may be arbitrary.
Situational	This approach mirrors the way most individuals actually approach day-to-day decision making.	What is good? Who decides? Morality is possibly arbitrary.
	Merits of each situation are considered. Individual has more control/autonomy to make decisions in his or her own best interest.	Lack of rules of generalizability limits criticism of possible abuse.

models to issues that affect your area of practice. Surveys of nurses indicate an ongoing interest and an expressed need for ethical discussion and support in practice. Nurses experience ethical distress along with other health care team members, but the 24/7 experience of nursing is unique from the perspective of patient continuity and opportunities for advocacy. Nurses increasingly serve on hospital ethics committees and are encouraged to contribute their perspectives to ethical debates.

How Do I Determine Who Owns the Problem?

The decision to choose a particular model of ethical reasoning is personal (see Table 19.1) and is based on your own values. Familiarize yourself with various models to decrease your own moral uncertainty and gain some understanding of the values of others. The following guidelines are suggested as a means of analyzing ethical issues that will confront you in nursing practice. You will not be a pivotal decision maker in all situations, but these guidelines can assist you in making up your own mind and helping patients to voice their wishes and ask questions.

First, determine the facts of the situation. Make sure you collect enough data to give yourself an accurate picture of the issue at hand. When the facts of a situation become known, you may or may not be dealing with an ethical issue.

For example, as an ICU nurse, you believe that the wishes of patients regarding extraordinary care are being disregarded. In other words, resuscitation is performed despite expressed patient wishes to the contrary. You need to

- Determine whether discussion about extraordinary care is taking place among patients, their families, and health care providers.
- Clarify the institution's policy regarding cardiopulmonary resuscitation (CPR) and do-not-resuscitate (DNR) orders.
- Determine what input the families have had in the decisions—that is, whether the families are aware of the patient's wishes.
- Explore the use of advance directive documentation at your institution, and determine whether patients are familiar with the use and possible limitations of living wills.
- Share your concerns with health care providers to obtain their views of the situation. Discuss the situation with your clinical manager to clarify any misconceptions regarding policy and actual practice.

Second, identify the ethical issues of the situation. In the ICU scenario, if competent patients have expressed their wishes about resuscitation, this should be reflected in the chart. If a living will has been executed and is recognized as valid within your state, its presence in the chart lends considerable weight to the decision. The patient should be encouraged to discuss his or her decision with family to decrease the chances for disagreement if and when the patient can no longer "speak" for himself or herself. If immediate family members disagree with the living will, the physician may be reluctant to honor it, at least in part because of concern regarding possible liability. If a living will is executed without prior or subsequent discussion with the attending physician, there may be reluctance to honor the will, because the physician was not informed of the patient's decision. The physician may feel that the patient did not make an informed decision. However, a durable power of attorney for health care (DPAHC), combined with a living will completed before the patient's present state of incapacitation, would stand as clear and convincing evidence of the patient's wishes, preventing such a problem. The example of extraordinary care in the ICU illustrates the existence of values and principles in conflict. When the care team, family, and patient have different views of the situation, the patient is likely to be burdened with less than the best outcome, unless differences are resolved. The nurse can facilitate communication between the family and patient in resolving differences among all those involved. In this situation, the ethical components of this second step involve autonomy and fidelity versus beneficence.

Patient: Values autonomy, including the right to decide when intervention should stop.

Family: May value the patient's life at all costs and be unwilling to "let go" when a chance exists to prolong life regardless of life quality.

Physician: May feel that the patient has a fair chance to survive and that the living will was executed without the patient being "fully informed." The duty to care or cure may outweigh the physician's belief in the exercise of patient autonomy and fidelity.

Nurse: Values patient autonomy and the need to remain faithful to the patient's wishes. Concern for the needs of the family, in addition to respect for the physician–patient relationship, may cause some conflict.

Institution: Examination of institutional policy may show a conflict between stated policy (e.g., honoring living wills) and actual practice (e.g., performing CPR on all patients unless written physician orders indicate otherwise).

Third, consider possible courses of action and their related outcomes. Having collected data and after having attempted to discuss the issue with all involved parties, you are faced with the following three options:

1. Advocate for the patient with physicians and the family by facilitating communication.
2. Encourage the patient and family to share feelings with each other regarding desires for care.
3. Encourage the family, patient, and attending physicians to discuss the situation more openly.

If the advocacy role does not bring about some change in behavior, consider the possible input and assistance of an interdisciplinary ethics committee (IEC). In the past two decades, such committees have evolved in response to the growing number of ethical issues faced in clinical practice. Most hospitals now have an IEC, which is typically composed of physicians, clergy, social workers, lawyers, and, increasingly, nurses. Any health team member can access the committee with the assurance at least of receiving a helpful, listening ear. If necessary, the committee will convene to review a clinical case and will offer an unbiased opinion of the situation. Committee members may be helpful in clarifying issues or offering moral support; they may also be persuasive in suggesting that involved parties (i.e., family, physician, patient, and nurse) consider a suggested course of action. The authority of an IEC is usually limited, because the majority of IECs are developed with the understanding that the advice and opinions offered are not binding to the individual. However, an IEC can serve as a potent form of moral authority and influence if used.

Taking the initiative to express your values and principles is not necessarily easy. As a recent graduate, it may seem safer to "swallow hard," remain quiet, and invest your energies in other aspects of your role. You may risk ridicule, criticism, and disagreement when you speak out or have questions on an ethical issue, especially if your view is different or unpopular. However, you risk something far more important if you do not speak out and ask questions for clarification. Silence diminishes your own autonomy as a person and as a professional. Depending on the situation, you may raise eyebrows, but it is important to make your concerns known, because some values may be imposed on the patient or on you in the clinical setting, and those values may not be morally correct. You may not agree with the values or believe that they are in the best interest of the patient. Unresolved moral distress is also cited as a cause for job resignation (Pendy, 2007). Find your voice, ask questions, and speak up so you can control your practice more effectively.

Fourth, after a course of action has been taken, evaluate the outcome. In the ICU scenario, did improved communication occur among patients, families, and physicians? Were your efforts to advocate met with resistance or a rebuff? What could you try differently the next time? What values or principles were considered most important by the decision makers? What kind of assistance did you receive from the IEC? What role did nursing play in this situation, and was it appropriate?

What Other Resources Are Available to Help Resolve Ethical Dilemmas?

Nurses have several resources to assist them in resolving ethical issues that may occur in professional settings. Nurses must first consider their personal views on the issue and consider having an open and honest discussion with their peers and supervisors. After reflection and discussion, nurses may consider consulting the institution's ethics committee if the issue remains unresolved. Many professional resources are also available to provide direction about ethical issues and behavior. The first of these is the American Nurses Association (ANA) *Code of Ethics for Nurses* (2015, p. 196). The code is a statement to society that outlines the values, concerns, and goals of the profession. It should be compatible with the individual nurse's personal values and goals. The code provides direction for ethical decisions and behavior by repeatedly emphasizing the obligations and responsibilities that the nurse–patient relationship entails.

The provisions of the *Code of Ethics for Nurses* allude to the ethical principles mentioned earlier in this chapter and certainly imply that fidelity to the patient is foremost. A copy of the code with interpretive statements is available from the ANA. If you did not purchase a copy as a reference for school, consider buying it for your own use in practice. A copy of the code should be accessible within your place of employment.

Critics of the *Code of Ethics for Nurses* cite its lack of legal enforceability. This is a valid criticism, because the code is not a legal document as licensure laws are. However, the code is a moral statement of accountability that can add weight to decisions involving legal censure. Many practicing nurses claim ignorance of the *Code of Ethics for Nurses* or believe that it is a document for students only. However, the *Code of Ethics* is for all nurses and was developed by nurses. In 2001, the American Nurses Association published a *Bill of Rights for Registered Nurses*, a first ever document of "rights" in contrast to the traditional focus on responsibilities. Awareness of these rights may provide nurses with a sense of comfort in voicing their advocacy for patients as well as for themselves. Take the opportunity to become familiar with its contents (ANA, 2001). Box 19.2 presents the *International Council of Nurses*

BOX 19.2   ICN CODE OF ETHICS FOR NURSES

The ICN Code of Ethics for Nurses has four principal elements that outline the standards of ethical conduct.

Elements of the Code

1. *Nurses and People*
   - The nurse's primary professional responsibility is toward people requiring nursing care.
   - In providing care, the nurse promotes an environment in which the human rights, values, customs and spiritual beliefs of the individual, family, and community are respected.
   - The nurse ensures that the individual receives accurate, sufficient, and timely information in a culturally appropriate manner on which to base consent for care and related treatment.
   - The nurse holds in confidence personal information and uses judgment in sharing this information.
   - The nurse shares with society the responsibility for initiating and supporting action to meet the health and social needs of the public, in particular those of vulnerable populations.
   - The nurse advocates for equity and social justice in resource allocation, access to health care, and other social and economic services.
   - The nurse demonstrates professional values such as respectfulness, responsiveness, compassion, trustworthiness, and integrity.

2. *Nurses and Practice*
   - The nurse carries personal responsibility and accountability for nursing practice, and for maintaining competence by continual learning.
   - The nurse maintains a standard of personal health such that the ability to provide care is not compromised.
   - The nurse uses judgment regarding individual competence when accepting and delegating responsibility.
   - The nurse at all times maintains standards of personal conduct, which reflect well on the profession and enhance its image and public confidence.
   - The nurse, in providing care, ensures that use of technology and scientific advances is compatible with the safety, dignity, and rights of people.
   - The nurse strives to foster and maintain a practice culture promoting ethical behavior and open dialogue.

3. *Nurses and the Profession*
   - The nurse assumes the major role in determining and implementing acceptable standards of clinical nursing practice, management, research, and education.
   - The nurse is active in developing a core of research-based professional knowledge that supports evidence-based practice.
   - The nurse is active in developing and sustaining a core of professional values.
   - The nurse, acting through the professional organization, participates in creating a positive practice environment and maintaining safe, equitable social and economic working conditions in nursing.
   - The nurse practices to sustain and protect the natural environment and is aware of its consequences on health.
   - The nurse contributes to an ethical organizational environment and challenges unethical practices and settings.

4. *Nurses and Co-workers*
   - The nurse sustains a collaborative and respectful relationship with co-workers in nursing and other fields.
   - The nurse takes appropriate action to safeguard individuals, families, and communities when their health is endangered by a co-worker or any other person.
   - The nurse takes appropriate action to support and guide co-workers to advance ethical conduct.

From International Council of Nurses. (2012). *ICN Code of ethics for nurses*. Geneva: Imprimerie Fornara, with permission.

Code for Nurses. The international code is valuable because it points out issues of universal importance to all nurses.

In 1973, the American Hospital Association published a *Patient's Bill of Rights*. Now revised (Box 19.3) and called the Patient Care Partnership, this document reflects acknowledgment of patients' rights to participate in their health care and was developed as a response to consumer criticism of paternalistic provider care. The statements detail the patient's rights with corresponding provider responsibilities. Read each statement and consider whether it seems reasonable. When first developed, many of the statements were considered radical. This document reflects the increasing emphasis on patient autonomy in health care and defines the limits of provider influence and control. Earlier beliefs that the hospital and physician know best (paternalism) have been challenged and modified. This document is likely to be refined further as joint responsibilities between patients and health care providers grow.

Consider the settings in which you have had clinical experiences, and evaluate how well these rights have been acknowledged and supported. In your future practice keep these rights in mind. Observing them is not only the "right thing to do," it is enforceable by law.

As a response to the rapidly growing home health care area of community nursing, the National Association for Home Care established a *Home Care Bill of Rights* for patients and families to inform them of the ethical conduct they can expect from home care agencies and their employees when they are in the home (National Association for Home Care & Hospice, n.d.). This document is widely used and addresses the rights of the patient and provider to be treated with dignity and respect; the right of the patient to participate actively in decision making; privacy of information; financial information regarding payment procedures from insurance, Medicare, and Medicaid; quality of care; and the patient's responsibility to follow the plan of care and notify the home health nurse of changes in his or her condition. Surprising as it may seem, there are instances of nurses who have lost their licenses as a result of unethical behavior toward patients in their homes. These abuses include financial and sexual exploitation—major violations of professional boundaries.

Home care nurses often face difficult ethical dilemmas about the delivery of care to patients. For example, a patient will require or desire more care or visits than Medicare or private insurance will pay for. All home care agencies have policies written to guide them through the decision-making process when they can no longer receive reimbursement for a patient's care. Often it is the responsibility of the home care nurse to find another community agency that can meet the patient's needs at a cost the patient can afford.

An additional document with which you should be familiar is the *Nuremberg Code* (Box 19.4). This code grew out of the blatant abuses perpetrated by Nazi war criminals during World War II in the name of science. Experiments were conducted by health care professionals without patient consent, resulting in horrific mutilations, disability, and death. The *Nuremberg Code* identifies the need for voluntary informed consent when medical experiments are conducted on human beings. It delineates the limits and restrictions that researchers must recognize and respect. Because of the preponderance of research in many clinical settings, nurses have a responsibility to understand the concept of voluntary informed consent and support the patient's rights throughout the research process. After reading this code, you should have increased awareness of the patient's right to autonomy and the health care provider's responsibility to be faithful to that right.

Controversial Ethical Issues Confronting Nursing

Situations that raise ethical issues affect all areas of nursing practice. The following is a sampling of issues that consistently cause controversy.

BOX 19.3 THE PATIENT CARE PARTNERSHIP: UNDERSTANDING EXPECTATIONS, RIGHTS, AND RESPONSIBILITIES

This is an abridged text. Full text is available at www.aha.org.

Our goal is for you and your family to have the same care and attention we would want for our families and ourselves. The sections explain some of the basics about how you can expect to be treated during your hospital stay. They also cover what we will need from you to care for you better. If you have questions at any time, please ask them. Unasked or unanswered questions can add to the stress of being in the hospital.

What to Expect During Your Hospital Stay

- High-quality hospital care. Our first priority is to provide you with the care you need, when you need it, with skill, compassion, and respect. Tell your caregivers if you have concerns about your care or if you have pain. You have the right to know the identity of doctors, nurses, and others involved in your care.
- A clean and safe environment. We use special policies and procedures to avoid mistakes in your care and keep you free from abuse or neglect. If anything unexpected and significant happens during your hospital stay, you will be told what happened, and any resulting changes in your care will be discussed with you.
- Involvement in your care. Please tell your caregivers if you need more information about treatment choices. When decision-making takes place, it should include:
  - *Discussing your medical condition and information about medically appropriate treatment.* To make informed decisions with your doctor, you need to understand:
    - The benefits and risks of each treatment and whether the treatment is experimental or part of a research study.
    - What you can reasonably expect from your treatment and any long-term effects it might have on your quality of life.
    - What you and your family will need to do after you leave the hospital.
    - The financial consequences of using uncovered services or out-of-network providers.
  - *Discussing your treatment plan.* When you enter the hospital, you sign a general consent to treatment. In some cases, such as surgery or experimental treatment, you may be asked to confirm in writing that you understand what is planned and agree to it.
  - *Getting information from you.* Your caregivers need complete and correct information about your health and coverage so that they can make good decisions about your care. That includes:
    - Past illnesses, surgeries, or hospital stays; past allergic reactions; any medicines or dietary supplements (e.g., vitamins, herbs) that you are taking; and any network or admission requirements under your health plan.
  - *Understanding your health care goals and values.* Make sure your doctor, your family, and your care team know your wishes.
  - *Understanding who should make decisions when you cannot.* If you have signed a health care power of attorney stating who should speak for you if you become unable to make health care decisions for yourself, or a living will or advance directive that states your wishes about end-of-life care, give copies to your doctor, your family, and your care team.
- Protection of your privacy. State and federal laws and hospital operating policies protect the privacy of your medical information. You will receive a Notice of Privacy Practices that describes the ways that we use, disclose, and safeguard patient information and that explains how you can obtain a copy of information from our records about your care.
- Preparing you and your family for when you leave the hospital. The success of your treatment often depends on your efforts to follow medication, diet, and therapy plans. You can expect us to help you identify sources of follow-up care and to let you know if our hospital has a financial interest in any referrals. You can also expect to receive information and, when possible, training about the self-care you will need when you go home.
- Help with your bill and filing insurance claims. Our staff will file claims for you with health care insurers or other programs, such as Medicare and Medicaid. If you have questions about your bill, contact our business office. If you need help understanding your insurance coverage or health plan, start with your insurance company or health benefits manager. If you do not have health coverage, we will try to help you and your family find financial help or make other arrangements.

BOX 19.4 THE NUREMBERG CODE

The great weight of the evidence before us is to the effect that certain types of medical experiments on human beings, when kept within reasonably well-defined bounds, conform to the ethics of the medical profession generally. The protagonists of the practice of human experimentation justify their views on the basis that such experiments yield results for the good of society that are unprocurable by other methods or means of study. All agree, however, that certain basic principles must be observed in order to satisfy moral, ethical, and legal concepts:

1. The voluntary consent of the human subject is absolutely essential. This means that the person involved should have legal capacity to give consent; should be so situated as to be able to exercise free power of choice, without the intervention of any element of force, fraud, deceit, duress, overreaching, or other ulterior form of constraint or coercion; and should have sufficient knowledge and comprehension of the elements of the subject matter involved as to enable him to make an understanding and enlightened decision. This latter element requires that before the acceptance of an affirmative decision by the experimental subject there should be made known to him the nature, duration, and purpose of the experiment; the method and means by which it is to be conducted; all inconveniences and hazards reasonably to be expected; and the effects upon his health or person which may possibly come from his participation in the experiment.

2. The duty and responsibility for ascertaining the quality of the consent rests upon each individual who initiates, directs, or engages in the experiment. It is a personal duty and responsibility that may not be delegated to another with impunity.

3. The experiment should be such as to yield fruitful results for the good of society, unprocurable by other methods or means of study, and not random and unnecessary in nature.

4. The experiment should be so designed and based on results of animal experimentation and a knowledge of the natural history of the disease or other problem under study that the anticipated results will justify the performance of the experiment.

5. The experiment should be so conducted as to avoid all unnecessary physical and mental suffering and injury.

6. No experiment should be so conducted where there is an a priori reason to believe that death or disabling injury will occur; except, perhaps, in those experiments where the experimental physicians also serve as subjects.

7. The degree of risk to be taken should never exceed that determined by the humanitarian importance of the problem to be solved by the experiment.

8. Proper preparations should be made and adequate facilities provided to protect the experimental subject against even remote possibilities of injury, disability, or death.

9. The experiment should be conducted only by scientifically qualified persons. The highest degree of skill and care should be required through all stages of the experiments of those who conduct or engage in the experiment.

Reprinted from *Trials of war criminals before the Nuremberg Military Tribunals under Control Council Law.* (1949). no. 18, vol. 2, Washington, DC: U.S. Government Printing Office, p. 181.

Abortion

The debate over this issue has raged in the United States since the 1973 *Roe v. Wade* Supreme Court decision. The resolution of this case struck down laws against abortion but left the possibility of introducing restrictions under some conditions. Efforts toward that end continue today with mixed results for both pro-choice and pro-life factions. Increasing efforts are focused on the need for parental notification/consent. The right to reproductive choice and access continues to be debated, and the argument affects nursing practice in both acute care and community settings.

Historic references to abortion can be found as far back as 4500 BC (Rosen, 1967). Abortion has been practiced in many societies as a means of population control and termination of unwanted pregnancies, yet sanctions against abortion are found in both ancient biblical and legal texts. It is interesting to note that the ancient sanctions against abortion generally related to fines payable to the husband if the pregnant woman was harmed. This form of sanction derived from the concept of the woman and fetus as male property. Greek philosophers, including Aristotle and Plato, made a distinction between an unformed fetus and a formed fetus. A fine was levied for aborting an unformed fetus, whereas the aborting of a formed fetus required "a life for a life." The number of gestational weeks that determine whether a fetus was formed was not stated, although the time of human "ensoulment" was understood: Aristotle believed that a male fetus was imbued with a soul at 40 days' gestation *(quickening)* versus 90 days for a female (Feldman, 1968). The subject of ensoulment became part of the ongoing debate regarding the time when the developing fetus becomes human. In other words,

> When does life begin?

Judeo-Christian theologians generally came to identify the beginning of life as at conception or at the time of implantation. However, even within this tradition, the Jewish Talmud and Roman law stated that life begins at birth, because the first breath represents the infusion of life. These varied views continue to the present.

Social customs and private behavior regarding abortion have frequently differed from theological teaching. The first legal sanctions against abortion in the United States began in the late 19th century. Before that time, first-trimester abortions were not uncommon and, in fact, were advertised, supporting the idea that abortion before quickening was acceptable.

The ethical debate about abortion today is a continuing struggle to answer the question of when life begins and to determine an answer to the following questions:

- Does the fetus have rights?
- Do the rights of the fetus (for life) take precedence over the right of the mother to control her reproductive functions?
- When is abortion morally justified?
- Should minors have the right to abortion without parental consent or awareness?
- Should fetal stem cells be used for research, helping to end the suffering of patients with chronic disorders such as Parkinson's disease?

The struggle to answer these questions has polarized individuals into pro-life or pro-choice camps. Yet opinion polls on the subject have shown that very few people are against abortion in all circumstances or favor abortion as a mandatory solution for some pregnancies. Most Americans express views somewhere between these extremes, and the legal battle to maintain or restrict abortion access continues. The controversy has escalated into violence in some areas of the country, with abortion clinics and personnel subjected to attack; some abortion providers have been killed. This violence has resulted in the decreased availability of abortion services in many areas. In recent years, some pharmacists have refused to fill prescriptions for birth control pills and the "morning after" pill, claiming that this violates their moral beliefs, an exacerbation of the pro-life/pro-choice debate.

The Roman Catholic Church has been the religious group most frequently identified with the pro-life movement, but there are other groups—religious and otherwise—that support a ban on abortion. Pro-life proponents generally condone abortion only to save the life of the mother. These antiabortion groups are often criticized by pro-choice as extremist, anti-woman, and repressive.

The pro-choice movement is vocal in championing the woman's right to choose and promoting the safety of legalized abortion. They cite the tragedy of past "back-alley" abortions and compare restrictions on abortion to infringements on the civil liberties of women. Within the pro-choice movement are many individuals who favor restrictions on abortions after the first trimester and oppose the use of abortion as a means of birth control. Pro-life proponents often view pro-choice supporters as anti-family extremists who do not represent the views of the majority of Americans.

How does the abortion issue affect nursing?. Nurses are involved both as individuals and professionals. The following are some general guidelines to consider.

Evaluate your values and beliefs in relation to abortion and how you can best apply these values to your work and to possible political action.

If you choose to work in a setting in which abortions are performed, review Provision 1 of the ANA *Code of Ethics for Nurses*: "The nurse practices with compassion and respect for the inherent dignity, worth, and uniqueness attributes of every person" (ANA, 2015, p. 1). This statement outlines your responsibility to care for all patients. If you do not agree with an institution's policy or procedure regarding abortion, the patient still merits your care. If that care (e.g., assisting with abortions) violates your principles, you should consider changing your job or developing an agreement with your employer regarding your job responsibilities. If you cannot provide the care that the patient requires, make arrangements for someone else to do so.

You do not have to sacrifice your own values and principles, but you are barred by the ANA *Code of Ethics for Nurses* from abandoning patients or forcing your values on them. Such abandonment would also constitute legal abandonment, and you would be subject to legal action.

Some hospitals have developed conscience clauses that provide protection to the hospital and nurses against participation in abortions. Find out if your institution has such a clause.

Consider your response and the possible conflict in the following situations:

- You are a labor and delivery nurse working on a unit that performs second-trimester saline abortions in a nearby area. You are not a part of the staff for the abortion area, but today, because of short staffing, you are asked to care for a 16-year-old who is undergoing the procedure.
- You work in a family-planning clinic that serves low-income women. Because of escalating violence against abortion providers, the nearest abortion clinic is 100 miles away. You are restricted from providing information regarding abortion services because of federal guidelines.
- A 41-year-old mother of five has expressed interest in terminating her pregnancy of 6 weeks' gestation. She confides that her husband would beat her if he knew she was pregnant and contemplating abortion.
- You are teaching a class on sexuality and contraception to a group of high school sophomores. Two of the girls state that they have just had abortions. In response to your information regarding available methods of contraception, one of the girls states, "I'm not interested in birth control. If I get pregnant again, I'll just get an abortion. It's a lot easier."
- You have a history of infertility and work in the neonatal ICU. You are presently caring for a 24-week-old baby born to a mother who admits to taking "crack" as a means of inducing labor and "getting rid of the baby." The mother has just arrived in the unit and wants to visit the baby.

These sample scenarios are meant to illustrate the conflicts that personal values, institutional settings, and patients may create for the recent graduate. In your responses, consider how you might lobby or participate in the political process to change or support existing policies regarding abortion and access to such services.

Euthanasia

Euthanasia is commonly referred to as "mercy killing." It is a Greek word that means "good death" and implies painless actions to end the life of someone suffering from an incurable or terminal disease. Euthanasia has been closely tied to a "right-to-die" argument, which has gained a good deal of attention in the past decade. Euthanasia is classified as *active, passive,* or *voluntary*. *Active euthanasia* involves the administration of a lethal drug or another measure to end life and alleviate suffering.

Regardless of the motivation and beliefs of the individuals involved, active euthanasia is legally wrong and can result in criminal charges of murder if performed. In recent years, incidents of active euthanasia have become periodic news events, as spouses or parents have used measures to end the suffering of their mates or children from, for example, advanced Alzheimer's disease or persistent vegetative state. *Passive euthanasia* involves the withdrawal of extraordinary means of life support (e.g., ventilator, feeding tube). *Voluntary euthanasia* involves situations when the dying individual expresses his or her desires regarding the management and time of death to a sympathetic physician who then provides the means for the patient to obtain a lethal dose of medication.

Today, advanced technology routinely keeps alive patients who would never have survived a few short years ago. Concerns regarding prolonging life and suffering for those individuals have resulted in a movement to have right-to-die statutes and living wills accepted. In those states that have such statutes and recognize living wills, termination of treatment in such cases has become easier. Right-to-die statutes release health care personnel from possible liability for honoring a person's wishes that life be not unduly prolonged (Rudy, 1985). Many years ago, the state of Oregon enacted the Death with Dignity Act (2011), which allows terminally ill Oregonians to obtain and use prescriptions from their physicians for self-administered lethal doses of medications.

Another legal document, the DPAHC, helps ensure that a living will is carried out. The DPAHC identifies the individual who will carry out the patient's wishes in the event that he or she is incapacitated and also informs health care providers about the specific wishes of the patient regarding life-support measures.

A major impact on the availability of living wills and the DPAHC (which are referred to as *advance medical directives*) resulted from the introduction of the Patient Self-Determination Act in December 1991. Advance directives are federally mandated for all institutions receiving Medicare or Medicaid funds. On admission, information about advance directives must be offered to all competent adults. This means that all adults are told about the purpose and availability of living wills *(treatment directive)* and DPAHCs *(appointment directive)*. They are then offered assistance with completing these documents if desired. After 15 years of having advance directive information available to patients, the impact of this document on decision making is varied. It certainly has influenced the communication that many patients have with their families, physicians, and other health care providers regarding their wishes at the time of signing, but patients often change their minds when their health care status changes, frequently opting for the prolongation of life. A problem has surfaced regarding the timing of information to patients regarding advance directives. If patients first hear about advance directives on admission to an acute-care setting, anxiety about their admission and the separate concept of advance directives may seriously affect informed decision making at that time. Advance directives should ideally be discussed *before* serious illness occurs, and at the very least in a noncrisis environment to encourage nonpressured decision making. Cultural, religious, and racial issues regarding DPAHC have also surfaced and need to be researched to determine the best approaches for providing this information within a culturally diverse society. Patients and families need reassurance that declining extraordinary care does not mean the abandonment of caring and palliative care when needed. Both patients and families need to be reassured that palliative comfort care will never stop, even when aggressive curative efforts are withdrawn.

Decisions to withdraw or withhold nutrition and hydration from patients are complex and are the subject of ongoing debate by ethicists, health care personnel, and the legal system. In response to the issues of hydration and nutrition, the Ethics Committee of the ANA developed guidelines in 1988 and revised them in 1992. These guidelines state that there are instances when withholding or withdrawing nutrition and hydration are morally permissible. Although intended only as a guideline, this document provides direction for nurses who face such issues. Its wording has been both praised for its clarity and criticized for possible ambiguity. The primary exception to the withdrawal of hydration and nutrition is when harm from these measures can be demonstrated. This document is available from the ANA.

Futile Care and Physician-Assisted Suicide

Futile care (futility) and physician-assisted suicide (PAS) are two ethical and human rights issues that have drawn a great deal of attention and debate. In a survey conducted by the ANA's Center for Ethics and Human Rights in June 1994, respondents were asked to identify 10 of the most frequently occurring ethical issues. Approximately 55% identified "end-of-life decisions" as one of the top four issues, and 37% identified "providing futile care" as an important priority issue facing nursing (Scanlon, 1994). These issues continue to be at the forefront for clinicians since that time (Robichaux & Clark, 2006).

What is futility? *Medical futility* refers to the use of medical intervention (beyond comfort care) without realistic hope of benefit to the patient. *Benefit* is defined as improvement of outcome. A concrete example of futility would be the continuation of ICU care for a patient in a persistent vegetative state who would, on discharge from the hospital, return to a nursing home incapable of interacting with the environment. The futility debate concerns the very nature of the definition of *benefit*, in addition to who defines it. The economic pressure to control health care costs also causes a focus on ways to eliminate "unnecessary" intervention.

On paper, futility can be defined, but its application to diverse clinical situations remains a challenge. The debate involves multiple parties whose interests and values are not always compatible. For example, patients and families have argued both for the right to refuse care that they believe is futile and the right to receive all possible care in the face of a medical opinion of futility. This argument raises two related questions:

1. Do patients or families have the right to demand and receive treatment that health care providers believe is futile?
2. Do physicians have the right to refuse to provide treatments that they believe are futile, despite patient or family desire to initiate or continue such treatment?

Ethics committees have struggled to agree on a working definition of futility to provide support for clinicians, patients, and families who are faced with difficult decisions regarding care. Many institutions have developed guidelines for the withdrawal of treatment (except for comfort care). These guidelines emphasize the importance of clear, ongoing communication among all health care team members and with the patient and family. Accurate, compassionate discussion is essential to convey a unified approach to the realities and limitations of possible medical care. The guidelines should never be used as a threat or to imply abandonment of care. They are, as their name implies, guidelines. Lack of agreement among the patient, the family, and the health care team is likely to delay or prevent withdrawal of treatment, primarily because of the fear of liability, even in cases of brain death. Supporting the patient or family decision may be difficult because of personal values and professional opinions. It is crucial to clarify where professional loyalties should lie and to keep the discussion patient centered.

Pressures to eliminate unnecessary costs also influence the futility debate. Insurers, clinicians, and health care institutions increasingly question medical expenditures that produce futile outcomes and prolong the inevitability of impending death. Insurance reimbursement payments are likely to be further limited or denied for treatment judged to be of no benefit to the patient. A possible risk is that beneficial treatment may be eliminated or denied solely because of economic concern in cases having an uncertain outcome. Nurses need to stay informed about institutional guidelines regarding medical futility and need to communicate clearly with patients, families, and physicians regarding expected goals and likely outcomes of care. The patient's welfare—and not economic concerns—should be the primary driving force for withdrawal of treatment. Studies continue to show that nurses experience moral distress when inappropriate treatments are used to prolong the dying process. Speaking out on behalf of the patient is an essential advocacy role even if the final decision regarding care differs from what the nurse believes is appropriate. Passivity in such situations only increases frustration and a sense of professional resignation (Robichaux & Clark, 2006).

Physician-assisted suicide (PAS). PAS has gained national attention because of Dr. Jack Kevorkian's persistent efforts to publicize and bring legitimacy to a formerly taboo topic. Kevorkian assisted or attended in the deaths of more than 130 terminally and chronically ill patients (Lowes, 2011). His work caused the state of Michigan to pass legislation barring PAS. Proponents of PAS managed to put the issue on the ballot in three western states since 1991. In 1994, Oregon approved PAS legislation. It was immediately challenged in the Oregon court by right-to-life advocates, but the Death with Dignity Act finally went into effect October 27, 1997. Between 1998 and 2014, 859 people in Oregon have died as a result of prescriptions for lethal medications (State of Oregon, 2014). In 2015, California became the fifth state to legalize PAS, joining Washington, Montana, Vermont, and Oregon (Pew Research Center, 2015). For right-to-life advocates, even one of these deaths is too many and is a step down the path of state-approved murder. Quality-of-life advocates support PAS as an example of personal autonomy and control; however, the debate continues.

PAS has been debated for years, and opinions on both sides among physicians and the public are very strong. The American Medical Association opposes PAS, because it violates the most basic ethical principle: "First, do no harm." Physicians have traditionally taken care of the living patient, and support for PAS threatens to destroy this fundamental relationship. Many individual physicians have, however, changed their minds in recent years because of their work with terminally ill patients. More than a few of these clinicians have come to believe that the only option for the relief of some patients' intractable pain and suffering is death.

Although the legalization of PAS continues to be debated in the courts, the practice goes on—generally in private without headlines. Both critics and supporters of PAS state that the secrecy goes on because of the fear of arrest for homicide. There have been some court rulings supporting the right to PAS by terminally ill patients on the basis of the 14th Amendment's guarantee of personal liberty. These decisions have been assailed by right-to-life groups as an anti-life philosophy that dishonors the intrinsic value of life.

PAS affects nursing practice, because a decision to perform PAS may involve the nurse. The term *PAS* implies that the physician is the active agent, but a lethal dose may be ordered by the physician for the nurse to administer. Nurses need to be aware of the legal and ethical implications of such an order. The administration of a lethal dose for the explicit purpose of ending a patient's life is an illegal act that can be prosecuted as homicide. From an ethical point of view, many would consider this the ultimate act of mercy, yet it is an illegal act in the United States, except in Montana, Oregon, Vermont, California, and Washington State. Clinicians, ethicists, the public, and the courts continue to struggle with how best to respect the life and wishes of terminally ill patients without "doing harm." In 2013, the American Nurses Association issued a position statement prohibiting nurses from participating in any form of assisted death (American Nurses Association, 2013).

Ethicists generally agree that although the prolongation of life by extraordinary means is not always indicated, clarifying the circumstances when such care may be stopped (withdrawn) or possibly never begun (withheld) frequently creates controversy, particularly when the quality of life (coma, persistent vegetative state) is likely to be questionable.

Opponents of the right-to-die movement believe that it represents the erosion of the value of human life and may encourage a movement toward the acceptance of suicide as part of a "culture of death." They caution that the lives of the weak and disabled may come to be devalued as society concentrates on the pursuit of "quality life." If passive euthanasia achieves societal acceptance, who will speak out in favor of protecting incompetent or dependent individuals who are not living what society views as a quality life? The well-publicized Schiavo controversy demonstrates the political polarization that this topic can cause (Caplan, 2015).

Proponents of the right-to-die movement believe that it provides a more natural course of living and dying to the individual and family by avoiding the artificial prolongation of life through technology. The availability of technology to prolong life often raises the question, "We can, but should we?"

Surveys of medical and nursing school curricula in the United States continue to show minimal content on end-of-life care issues. Schools continue to focus curricula more on the curative approach to illness and disease, neglecting to address the palliative, comfort-directed needs of individuals who require care in the last months and days of their lives. This fact, combined with the aging of our population, points to the need for improvement in educating both current clinicians and students in health care institutions on ethical issues surrounding end-of-life care. A growing number of proactive clinicians and educators concerned with the quality of care provided to dying patients and their families has created an educational movement called *End-of-Life Care*. The specific program targeted for nursing is called the *End-of-Life Nursing Education Consortium Project*, targeting nursing faculty and nursing leadership in many specialty organizations. This consortium project has educated hundreds of nurses in the past few years, slowly influencing a change in both education and clinical practice. Studies of patients facing end-of-life issues indicate that pain and symptom management, communication with one's physician, preparation for death, and the opportunity to achieve a sense of life completion are the most consistently important issues (Steinhauser et al., 2000). It will be interesting to see the impact of these efforts on patient care during the next decade. As nurses, we are challenged to make this last event of life a better experience for all. The growing popularity of the palliative care movement in the United States is a significant paradigm change, acknowledging the value and complexity of supportive, noncurative care for many conditions. Supporting the broader picture of palliative interventions that may continue for months or years will increase our understanding of the needs of patients who do not have a cure awaiting them but who want to embrace the time they have left with our support.

Consider your response and possible conflict in the following critical thinking situations. Use the terms defined in Box 19.1 to guide your consideration or discussion with others:

A 22-year-old quadriplegic repeatedly asks you to disconnect him from the ventilator. His family rarely visits, and he believes that he has nothing to live for.

The spouse of a patient with advanced Alzheimer's disease states that he can no longer watch his wife of 43 years suffer. "She would not have wanted to live this way." His wife is being treated for dehydration, malnutrition, and a urinary tract infection. She is confused and is frequently sedated to manage her combativeness. The use of a feeding tube is being contemplated because of her refusal to eat.

The attending physician for a patient with terminal AIDS refuses to order increasing doses of pain medication because of her concern that it may cause a repeat episode of respiratory depression. The patient's pain is unrelieved, and he begs you for medication. "Please help me. I know I'm dying."

A patient on long-term dialysis wants to discontinue treatment, citing the side effects of dialysis and her medications. She feels that the quality of her life has disappeared. Her life partner died a year ago, and she sees no reason to continue suffering. She has been on the transplant list for 6 years. She has indicated that her last appointment will be in 1 month, and she would like to know what kind of supportive care will be available.

For each of these scenarios, consider what your reaction would be and the possible resources you would use to resolve the conflicts.

What Are the Ethical Issues Regarding Transplantation?

There are over 122,000 people on transplant lists in the United States today, and the majority of these individuals will die without a transplant because of the shortage of available organs (United Network for Organ Sharing, 2016). On what basis should someone receive an organ? Should severity of illness serve as the primary criteria, or what other factors should be taken into consideration? Should economic status be used as a contributing factor in the process? How are donors solicited? What are the religious and cultural issues that influence someone's decision to be considered as a potential donor? Should the government intervene to enlarge the donor pool by making a decision that victims of accidents imply donor consent if their driver's license does not have a statement specifically refusing donation? What protections need to be put into place to prevent coercion for organ donation, a reality in many countries where organs are paid for or where condemned prisoners are sources for donation?

All of the aforementioned questions offer a window into the complexity of issues surrounding organ transplantation. The technology exists with ever-increasing precision, but there is a tremendous scarcity of organs. On what basis do we as a society attempt to create a process of organ access that is just and equitable? Who decides?

What Is the Ethical Issue Regarding the Use of Fetal Tissue?

Fetal tissue from elective abortions has been identified as potentially beneficial in the treatment of Parkinson's disease and other degenerative disorders because of its unique embryonic qualities. Proponents argue that it is available tissue that can be put to some beneficial use in patients who at present do not have any other hope of significant improvement or cure. They further argue that the availability of fetal tissue from elective abortions is a separate issue from the later use of the tissue for stem cell research. The abortion would have occurred regardless. Later use of the stem cell derives some good from the discarded tissue.

Critics who assail the use of fetal tissue for stem cell research as a further erosion of respect for the unborn were successful in spurring a federal ban on the use of fetal tissue for research in the United States during the 1980s. They believe that the limited research that has already occurred regarding fetal tissue has created the mentality that pregnancy can be used as a means of providing parts and tissues for others. This ban was removed in early 1993 after President Clinton took office, and in 2001, use of stem cells received narrowly defined approval by the Bush administration for genetic research. Individual states also have the authority to pass laws to permit human embryonic cell research using state funding. This state right has not been overridden by any congressional ban (NIH, 2016). Access any electronic news source or a print newspaper, and you are likely to see at least one article related to the continuing debate regarding the ethics of stem cell research. As the largest group of health care providers, nurses need to be informed regarding the issues. Consider your own viewpoint and how it can affect your nursing care. Does the good (beneficence) achieved from the use of fetal tissue for patients with Parkinson's disease outweigh the harm inflicted by viewing a fetus as a source of parts?

What Are the Ethical Issues Regarding In Vitro Fertilization?

This procedure involves the fertilization of a mother's ovum with the father's sperm in a glass laboratory dish followed by implantation of the embryo in the mother's uterus. Since the birth of the first successful in vitro fertilization baby in 1978, the procedure has gained popularity as a last-chance method for some infertile couples to have a child. The availability of the technique has created a new subspecialty practice in obstetrics and has raised ethical issues for consideration. Opponents of the procedure argue that it is an unnatural act and removes the biological act of procreation from the intimacy of marriage. The cost of the procedure is also a source of criticism, calling into question whether it should be covered by insurance and whether the procedure should be available to all couples, regardless of ability to pay. Many couples are now lobbying to select the sex of their baby, choosing the desired embryo for implantation and destroying the undesired embryos. If technology can be made to meet our desires for a "designer baby," does that make it a morally correct course of action?

Questions concerning informed consent for the procedure merit attention as well. Many infertility clinics offer this service but have not been up-front about their success rates or qualifications. Standardized methods for reporting this information have just recently been established. To be ethical, all such clinics should define success the same way; for example, success equals pregnancy or success equals live birth. The two definitions are very different. Information about the qualifications of the staff should be available to patients, and the subspecialty should lobby for standards of practice that are enforceable and available to the public. Possible side effects from the drugs used to induce hyperovulation, from anesthesia, or from surgical injury during the laparoscopy should be explained.

Should anyone who desires the in vitro procedure have access, or should the procedure be limited to those in a heterosexual marriage? Most clinics have limited their services to heterosexual couples to avoid adverse publicity, but this policy is starting to change as single and lesbian women seek out avenues to become biological parents. Most important, to whom does the embryo belong, and what are the embryo's rights? There have been court cases involving marital disputes regarding the custody of frozen embryos. What are the rights of the embryos in such instances? Can a parent choose to destroy the embryos over the objection of the estranged spouse, or should one parent be able to obtain custody of the embryos when his or her spouse wants them to be thawed out and destroyed? What responsibility does the staff have for maintaining parental ownership of the embryos?

What Are Genetics and Genomics?

The study of genetics and genomics has led to the increased ability of health care professionals to assist patients in improving health outcomes and treatments of disease processes. Genetic research has led to an "improved understanding of the genetic contribution to the disease, the development of targeted drug therapy (pharmacogenomics) ... and new and better ways to treat diseases such as gene therapy" (Greco & Salveson, 2009, p. 558).

"Genetics is a term that refers to the study of genes and their role in inheritance—the way certain traits or conditions are passed down from one generation to another.

"Genomics is a relatively new term that describes the study of all of a person's genes including interactions of those genes with each other and the person's environment" (Lea, 2009, p. 2).

But what is the role of nursing in this emerging area? Nurses will provide education to patients about genetic and genomic testing, research, and treatment. As research-based improvements in the recognition of familial disease traits are identified and emerging disease treatments are discovered, nurses will play an increasingly important role in the study and application of genetic findings and the role of genetics and genomics in the health of the patients they serve. The role of genetics and genomics will undoubtedly play a significant role in current and future patient care. Nurses at all levels have the opportunity to engage in this opportunity and provide needed education, support, and treatment based in the most current research, even though ethical challenges may arise as the result of this emerging research and treatment (see the relevant websites and online resources at the end of this chapter). Kirk et al. (2011) purported that the study of genetics and genomics is one of the fastest growing areas of health care research. The authors contended that nurses must have a sound understanding of the impact of this area of health care research to provide comprehensive, effective care to their patients.

How should we use the ability to diagnose genetic defects prenatally? Genetic disorders such as Tay-Sachs disease, cystic fibrosis, Huntington's chorea, and retinoblastoma can be diagnosed early in pregnancy. As this detection technology advances, how should it be used? Should screening remain voluntary, or as some have suggested, should it be mandatory to detect fetal disorders that could be aborted or possibly treated? Should the results of such genetic screening be made available to insurance companies? Critics argue that this information could be used as a means of coercion for couples over reproductive decisions if future insurance coverage is then limited. As this technology advances, safeguards need to be applied to prevent invasion of privacy and any societal movement toward eugenics. As the human genome project allows us to become capable of knowing our genetic code and possibilities for disease, it raises the question of who should have access to that information. And for what reason(s)? If a family with a known genetic disorder chooses to have more children with that disorder, is it the obligation of society to pay for their care? Is there any reason for insurance or the government to become involved with genetic counseling, or is this a private family affair?

Allocation of Scarce Resources

When the subject of scarce resource allocation is mentioned, justice is the core issue. What is fair and equal treatment when health care financing decisions are made? Who should make such decisions and on what basis? Critics argue that health care is not a scarce resource in this country but that the *access* to such care is scarce for many. They believe that this scarcity of access could be eliminated if our priorities in governmental spending were altered. Managed care put a temporary brake on runaway costs in the 1990s, but that brake failed in the past few years. The solution to this issue remains unclear and highly politicized. In the meantime, managed care of one form or another is influencing a larger and larger share of the insured population, raising related issues of restricted access to specialized care and loss of patient and physician autonomy.

Allocation also raises a number of questions. For example, do all individuals merit the same care? If your answer is an immediate "yes," would you change your mind if the patient were indigent, with no chance of paying the bill? If you still say "yes," should this same indigent patient receive a liver transplantation as readily as someone who has insurance or cash to pay for it? Should taxpayers be responsible for the medical bills for organ transplants, cardiac bypass surgery, or joint replacements for incarcerated felons? These and other questions continue to be asked by individuals, government bureaucrats, and ethicists, in addition to health care providers. Perhaps at the core of this subject is a more fundamental question: Is health care a right or a privilege that comes with the ability to pay? If access to health care is a right that should be provided to all citizens, are we as a society prepared to pay the bill? And is there a level of health care that is essential for all, beyond which financing becomes a private matter?

The type of care that is provided and supported is another aspect of the debate. For example, should health promotion and prevention be emphasized as much as or more than illness-oriented and rehabilitative care? It is widely acknowledged that each dollar spent on preventive care (e.g., prenatal care) saves three or more dollars in later intervention (e.g., neonatal ICU), yet our national and state health care expenditures (Medicare and Medicaid) are traditionally weighted in favor of an illness model for reimbursement. Managed care is an effort to control health care costs, but it is increasingly criticized as prioritizing the financial bottom line over the quality of care.

What Are Some of the Possible Solutions Being Debated?

Some individuals have proposed the idea of health care rationing for the older adult, specifically as it relates to the use of expensive technology that often prolongs the last few weeks of life and suffering (Lamm, 1986). Proponents of health care rationing argue that high-tech "11th-hour expenditures" are unwanted by many older adults and consume disproportionate amounts of health care resources. Proponents of rationing stress the need to acknowledge the finite resources of society. As our society continues to age, younger workers will increasingly be asked to pay the costs for Medicare, Medicaid, and social security. Disparities between generations will increasingly become part of the conversation regarding health care financing.

Many believe that more vulnerable groups, such as uninsured children, should be given a more equitable portion of health care services (e.g., well-baby clinics, universal health insurance for children). Others argue that health care is already being rationed and that we should recognize this fact and articulate our priorities. Few would disagree that our present health care financing is in need of a comprehensive overhaul before we experience a chaotic breakdown.

The state of Oregon has gone one step further, imposing guidelines on the type of care that its Medicaid funds will cover. Deciding that preventive care affects a majority of its citizens, Oregon made funding for measures such as immunizations and prenatal care a priority, whereas extraordinary care that benefits only a few individuals, such as a bone marrow transplantation, is not covered (Rooks, 1990). This utilitarian approach, emphasizing the greatest good for the greatest number, is not without its critics, but it is an effort to provide direction for health care priorities. Oregon's plan was initially vetoed by the federal government and has undergone some revision, still emphasizing preventive care and treatment for disorders that affect a majority of citizens. Other states are now looking at the Oregon model as they plan health care reform. Another state to watch is Massachusetts; universal coverage was implemented in 2007 (Belluck, 2007).

Health care rationing. You may have already experienced situations of health care rationing or limited access. As a nurse you may, on one hand, feel powerless and frustrated when patients do not receive care because they cannot afford it or, on the other hand, feel angry because indigent patients are placing heavy burdens on both private and public facilities. Consider your values and professional responsibilities as you think through this issue. Efforts to address this issue include the passage of the 1986 Emergency Medical Treatment and Active Labor Act (EMTALA), which requires hospitals to provide care to anyone needing emergency health care treatment regardless of citizenship, legal status, or ability to pay. As an individual and a nurse, you need to take a stand regarding health resource allocation and support efforts to improve access, while determining in your mind what type of health care you believe to be ethically justifiable.

What Is the Impact of Social Media and Social Networking on Nursing Practice?

The use of social media and social networking sites has made it easy and convenient for nurses to stay connected to current events as well as to keep up-to-date on emerging clinical guidelines and evidence-based practice measures for implementation in the provision of patient care. However, with the increased use of technology and social media, nurses must be aware of the legal limitations for using social media in both their professional and personal lives. The National Council of State Boards of Nursing (2011) and other professional nursing organizations have developed guidelines for nurses and students to follow in an effort to avoid any potential legal ramifications (Box 19.5).

BOX 19.5   GUIDELINES FOR USING SOCIAL MEDIA

Nurses must be aware of potential patient confidentiality and privacy breaches that may occur as a result of sharing private and confidential patient information via social networking sites and on the Internet.

Here are a few points to consider:

- Any type of information, document, image, video, or material that you post on a social networking site or Internet is subject to being shared with others.
- There is no such thing as permanently deleting information from a site. Even if deleted, the information may still be accessible by others.
- It is a breach of confidentiality to discuss a patient's condition or identify the patient by another name, room number, agency location, or diagnosis, even if you do not disclose the patient's legal name.

When using social media, consider the following:

- Recall that you have an ethical obligation to maintain and protect patient privacy and confidentiality.
- Never share or post patient images, videos, or any information pertaining to a patient on any form of electronic media; this includes the use of cell phones, smart phones, cameras, and other electronic devices in the clinical setting.
- Follow the institution's policies and procedures for taking photos or videos of patients for treatment purposes on electronic devices provided by the employer.
- Do not disclose any information that may identify the patient; this includes but is not limited to biographical data (name, age, occupation), medical diagnosis, room number, implantable medical devices, and diagnostic reports.
- Do not write or verbalize negative or rude comments about a patient, family member, or health care team member.
- Do not make harassing, profane, uncivil, hostile, sexually explicit, racially derogatory, homophobic, threatening or other offensive comments about co-workers, the employing institution, patient, or patient's family.
- Recognize that professional boundaries between you, your patient, and the patient's family exist and must be carried out in both the practice setting as well as in the online environment.
- You have an ethical duty to report any type of breach of confidentiality or privacy.
- Know your employing institution's policies and procedures regarding the use of electronic media and personal devices in the workplace.
- Never speak on behalf of your employer or a co-worker unless provided authorization to do so and ensure that you follow the employer's policies and procedures.

Data from National Council of State Boards of Nursing (NCSBN). (August, 2011). *White paper: A nurse's guide to the use of social media*. Retrieved from https://www.ncsbn.org/Social_Media.pdf.

CONCLUSION

As medical technology advances, ethical issues and concerns will play an ever-increasing role in your nursing practice. The general public, health care professions, religious traditions, increasing cultural diversity, and the legal system will all influence the attempts to resolve the ethical issues affecting health care in the 21st century. Keeping an open mind in these controversial dilemmas is difficult, but it is hoped you will examine your personal values and continue to make decisions that are based on the welfare of your patients.

🌐 RELEVANT WEBSITES AND ONLINE RESOURCES

American Nurses Association (2015)
Code of ethics for nurses with interpretive statements. http://www.nursingworld.org/DocumentVault/Ethics_1/Code-of-Ethics-for-Nurses.html.

American Nurses Association (ANA) Fact Sheet (2011)
Navigating the world of social media. http://www.nursingworld.org/FunctionalMenuCategories/AboutANA/Social-Media/Social-Networking-Principles-Toolkit/Fact-Sheet-Navigating-the-World-of-Social-Media.pdf.

Social networking principles toolkit (2015)
http://www.nursingworld.org/socialnetworkingtoolkit.aspx.

ANA position statement on ethics and human rights (2013)
http://www.nursingworld.org/MainMenuCategories/EthicsStandards/Ethics-Position-Statements.

ANA: Moral courage and moral distress (2015)
http://www.nursingworld.org/MainMenuCategories/EthicsStandards/Courage-and-Distress.

Centers for Disease Control and Prevention (2013)
Public health genomics. http://www.cdc.gov/genomics/.

International Council of Nurses (2012)
The ICN code of ethics for nurses. http://www.icn.ch/images/stories/documents/about/icncode_english.pdf.

Lea, D. H. (2009)
Basic genetics and genomics: a primer for nurses, OJIN: The Online Journal of Issues in Nursing 14(2). http://www.nursingworld.org/MainMenuCategories/ANAMarketplace/ANAPeriodicals/OJIN/TableofContents/Vol142009/No2May09/Articles-Previous-Topics/Basic-Genetics-and-Genomics.html.

National Council of State Boards of Nursing (2011)
ANA and NCSBN unite to provide guidelines on social media and networking for nurses. http://www.nursingworld.org/FunctionalMenuCategories/MediaResources/PressReleases/2011-PR/ANA-NCSBN-Guidelines-Social-Media-Networking-for-Nurses.pdf

White paper: A nurse's guide to the use of social media (2011, August)
https://www.ncsbn.org/11_NCSBN_Nurses_Guide_Social_Media.pdf.

National Human Genome Research Institute (2013)
Policy, legal and ethical issues in genetic research. http://www.genome.gov/Issues/.

BIBLIOGRAPHY

American Nurses Association. (2013). *Euthanasia, assisted suicide, and aid in dying.* Retrieved from http://www.nursingworld.org/MainMenuCategories/EthicsStandards/Ethics-Position-Statements/Euthanasia-Assisted-Suicide-and-Aid-in-Dying.pdf.

American Nurses Association. (2001a). *Nurses' Bill of Rights.* Retrieved from http://www.nursingworld.org/NursesBillofRights.

American Nurses Association. (2015). *Code of ethics for nurses.* Kansas City, MO: ANA.

Belluck, P. (July 1, 2007). Massachusetts universal care plan faces hurdles. *New York Times.* Retrieved from http://www.nytimes.com/2007/07/01/health/policy/01insure.html?pagewanted=all.

Caplan, A. (March 31, 2015). *Ten years after Terri Schiavo, death debates still divide us: Bioethicist, NBC Health News*. Retrieved from http://www.nbcnews.com/health/health-news/bioethicist-tk-n333536.

Emergency Medical Treatment and Active Labor Act of. (1986). *(EMTALA)*. Retrieved from http://www.cms.gov /Regulations-and-Guidance/Legislation/EMTALA/index.html?redirect=/emtala/.

Feldman, D. M. (1968). *Marital relations, birth control and abortion in Jewish law*. New York: Schocker.

Fletcher, J. F. (1966). *Situation ethics*. Philadelphia: Westminster.

Greco, K., & Salveson, C. (2009). Identifying genetics and genomics nursing competencies common among published recommendations. *Journal of Nursing Education, 48*, 557–565.

Kaiser Family Foundation. (2016). *Key facts about the uninsured population*. Retrieved from http://kff.org/uninsured/ fact-sheet/key-facts-about-the-uninsured-population/.

Kirk, M., Calzone, K., Arimori, N., & Tonkin, E. (2011). Genetics-genomics competencies and nursing regulation. *Journal of Nursing Scholarship, 43*(2), 107–116. Retrieved from http://dx.doi.org.library.gcu.edu:2048 /10.1111/j.1547-5069.2011.01388.x.

Lamm, R. D. (1986). Rationing of health care: The inevitable meets the unthinkable. *Nurs Pract I* (57), 61–64.

Lea, D. H. (February 17, 2009). Basic genetics and genomics: A primer for nurses. *OJIN: The Online Journal of Issues in Nursing, 14*(2), 1–11.

Lowes, R. (2011). *"Dr. Death" Jack Kevorkian dies at age 83*. Retrieved from http://www.medscape.com/viewarticle/ 743977.

National Association for Home Care & Hospice. (n.d.). *What are my rights as a patient?* Retrieved from http://www.nahc.org/consumer/wamraap.html.

National Council of State Boards of Nursing. (2011). *White paper: A nurse's guide to the use of social media*. Retrieved from https://www.ncsbn.org/11_NCSBN_Nurses_Guide_Social_Media.pdf.

National Institutes of Health (NIH). (2016). *Stem cell information*. Retrieved from http://stemcells.nih.gov/Pages/ Default.aspx.

Oregon's Death with Dignity Act. (2011). *Thirteen years. CD Summary. Oregon Public Health Division, 60*(6). Retrieved from http://public.health.oregon.gov/DiseasesConditions/CommunicableDisease/CDSummary NewsletterDocuments/2011/ohd6006.pdf.

Pendy, P. S. (2007). Moral distress: Recognizing it to retain nurses. *Nursing Economics, 4*, 217–221.

Pew Research Center. (2015). *California legalizes assisted suicide amid growing support for such laws*. Retrieved from http://www.pewresearch.org/fact-tank/2015/10/05/california-legalizes-assisted-suicide-amid- growing-support-for-such-laws/.

Robichaux, C. M., & Clark, A. P. (2006). Practice of expert critical care nurses in situations of prognostic conflict at the end of life. *American Journal of Critical Care, 15*, 480–491.

Rooks, J. P. (1990). Let's admit we ration health care—then set priorities. *American Journal of Nursing, 90*, 38–43.

Rosen, H. (Ed,). (1967). *Abortion in America*. Boston: Beacon Press.

Rudy, E. B. (1985). The living will: Are you informed? *Focus on Critical Care, 12*, 51.

Scanlon, C. (1994). Ethics survey looks at nurses' experiences. *American Nurse, 26*, 22.

State of Oregon. (2006). *Characteristics of 292 DWDA patients who died during 1998-2006 after ingesting a lethal dose of medication compared with 85,755 Oregonians dying from the same underlying diseases*. Retrieved from http://public.health.oregon.gov/ProviderPartnerResources/EvaluationResearch/DeathwithDignityAct/ Documents/year9.pdf.

State of Oregon. (2014). *Oregon's Death with Dignity Act—2014*. Retrieved from https://public.health.oregon.gov/ ProviderPartnerResources/EvaluationResearch/DeathwithDignityAct/Documents/year17.pdf.

Steele, S. M. (1983). *Values clarification in nursing* (2nd ed.). East Norwalk, CT: Appleton & Lange.

Steinhauser, K. E., et al. (2000). Factors considered important at the end of life by patients, family, physicians, and other health care providers. *JAMA, 284*, 2476–2482.

Thompson, I. E., et al. (2007). *Nursing ethics* (5th ed.). St Louis, MO: Churchill Livingstone/Elsevier.

United Network for Organ Sharing. (2016). *Data*. Retrieved from www.unos.org.

U.S. Census Bureau. (2014). *Income, poverty, and health insurance coverage in the United States*. Retrieved from http://www.census.gov/library/publications.html.

Wang, K., Chou, C., & Huang, J. (2010). A study of work values, professional commitment, turnover intention and related factors among clinical nurses. *Journal of Nursing, 57*(1), 22–34.

20

Legal Issues

Nikki Austin, JD, RN

http://evolve.elsevier.com/Zerwekh/nsgtoday/.

As long as I have any choice, I will stay only in a country where political liberty, toleration, and equality of all citizens before the law are the rule.
Albert Einstein

The good of the people is the chief law.
Cicero

Knowledge is the best way to prevent poor patient and professional outcomes. Thus, knowledge is the best offense as well as the best defense.

After completing this chapter, you should be able to:

- Discuss various sources and types of laws.
- Relate the Nurse Practice Act to the governance of your profession.
- Understand the functions of a state board of nursing.
- Describe your responsibilities for obtaining and maintaining your license.
- Research and discuss scope of practice limitations on your license.
- Be able to identify the elements of nursing negligence and how each element is proven in a negligence claim.
- Incorporate an understanding of legal risks into your nursing practice and recognize how to minimize these risks.
- Discuss the concerns surrounding criminal charges in nursing practice.
- Identify legal issues involved in the medical record and your documentation, including the use of electronic medical records.
- Understand legal concepts such as informed consent and advance directives.
- Take an active role in improving the quality of health care as required by legal standards.
- Participate as a professional when dealing with nurses who are impaired or functioning dangerously in the work setting.
- Discuss the concerns surrounding at least two legal issues in nursing practice.

Generally speaking, laws are "rules of human conduct" designed to keep civilized societies from falling into anarchy. A law is a prescriptive or proscriptive rule of action or conduct promulgated by a controlling authority such as government. Because laws have binding legal force and are meant to be obeyed, failure to follow the law may subject you to a wide variety of legal consequences. The Latin phrase *ignorantia legis neminem excusat means* "ignorance of law excuses no one." It is important for all persons, including nurses, to know, understand and follow the law as it relates to their personal and professional lives.

There are many laws from a variety of sources that directly and indirectly impact the practice of nursing. Understanding these laws can have a profound effect on the way you practice nursing and may help ensure safe nursing practice. This chapter is an important start in becoming a legally educated nursing professional. Your journey does not stop here, however, because the law is always evolving and under constant scrutiny and challenge. Nursing professionals must assume ongoing responsibility for keeping up with relevant changes in the federal, state, and local laws that govern nursing practice.

SOURCES OF LAW

Where Does "the Law" Come From?

Have you ever wondered where the law comes from? Laws can be created by regulatory, legislative, and litigation processes involving different branches of government (executive, legislative, and/or judicial). There are several primary and secondary sources of law that directly and indirectly impact the practice of nursing including constitutional law, statutory law, common law, administrative law, tort law, contract law, and criminal law.

What Is Constitutional Law?

The U.S. Constitution is the supreme law of the land. *Constitutional law* refers to the power, privileges, and responsibilities stated in, or inferred from, the U.S. Constitution as well as state constitutions. Constitutions prescribe the power and responsibilities of federal and state governments. For example, the powers of the federal government are defined in Article I, Section 8 of the U.S. Constitution. These powers include such things as the power to coin money, the power to establish a uniform rule of naturalization, the power to declare war, the power to tax and spend, and the power to regulate interstate commerce. Medicare and Medicaid were enacted through the spending powers as the federal government collects the taxes and then spends them as distributions to the states to subsidize their Medicaid programs or directly to hospitals and providers as Medicare payments. The right to privacy is an example of a right inferred from the Constitution.

The Tenth Amendment to the Constitution states, "The powers not delegated to the United States by the Constitution, nor prohibited by it to the States, are reserved to the States respectively, or to the people." This means the powers of the state government include anything and everything that is not specifically described as being a power of the federal government. These powers, referred to as "police powers," include the power to license professionals, including nurses, and generally provide for public health and safety of the community. States may not pass laws or institute rules that conflict with constitutionally granted rights or powers.

What Is Statutory Law?

Statutory law is an important source of law. Statutes are created by federal, state, and local legislatures, which are comprised of elected officials who have been granted the power to create laws. It would be an impossible feat for governments to anticipate all possible scenarios in which a statute might be needed to regulate human conduct. Therefore, statutes are often written broadly enough to be applicable in a variety of situations. Courts must apply statutes, if available, to the facts of a case. If no statute exists, courts defer to *common law* (see below).

Statutory definitions are one of the most important parts of a statute. There you can find what the authors of the statute mean when they use a certain word. Because we all use words differently, a more precise understanding is necessary when reading and understanding statutory laws. (Box 20.1 lists definitions of common legal terms.) When a statute is vague or unclear, courts must engage in statutory interpretation to determine the legislature's intent.

BOX 20.1 COMMON LEGAL TERMS

Advance directive: A document made by a competent individual to establish desired health care for the future or to give someone else the right to make health care decisions if the individual becomes incompetent; examples include living wills and medical powers of attorney.

Defamation: A civil wrong in which an individual's reputation in the community, including the professional community, has been damaged.

Defendant: The person who is being accused of wrongdoing. The person then must defend himself or herself against the charges. In a negligence claim, this is the nurse or other health care provider.

Deposition: Out-of-court oral testimony given under oath before a court reporter. The purpose is to enable attorneys to ask questions and receive answers related to a case. The deposition process may involve expert witnesses, fact witnesses, defendants, or plaintiffs.

Diversion program: Voluntary, confidential monitoring programs for nurses whose practice may be impaired due to substance use disorder.

Expert witness: A person who has specific knowledge, skills, and experience regarding a specific area and whose testimony will be allowed in court to prove the standard of care.

Good Samaritan law: A law that provides civil immunity to professionals who stop and render care in an emergency. Care rendered cannot be done so in a grossly negligent manner.

Interrogatory: A process of discovering the facts regarding a case through a set of written questions exchanged through the attorneys representing the parties involved in the case.

Jurisdiction: The court's authority to accept and decide cases. May be based on location or subject matter of the case.

Malpractice: Improper performance of professional duties; a failure to meet the standards of care, resulting in harm to another person.

Negligence: Failure to act as an ordinary prudent person when such failure results in harm to another.

Plaintiff: The person who files the lawsuit and is seeking damages for a perceived wrongdoing. In medical malpractice, the patient and/or the patient's family.

Reasonable care: The level of care or skill that is customarily rendered by a competent health care worker of similar education and experience in providing services to an individual in the community or state in which the person is practicing.

Standard of care: A set of guidelines based on various types of evidence as to what is reasonable and prudent behavior for a health care professional in the same or similar circumstances.

Statutes of limitations: Laws that set time limits for when a case may be filed. These limitations differ from state to state.

Telemedicine: Using telecommunication technology, usually interactive, to provide medical information and services remotely.

Torts: Civil (not criminal) wrongs committed by one person against another person or property. Includes the legal principle of assault and battery.

Whistleblower: Individual "on the inside" who reports incorrect or illegal activities to an agency with the authority to monitor or control those activities.

Whistleblower statute: Law that protects a whistleblower from retaliation. Usually involves specific criteria about how whistle was blown.

What Is Administrative Law?

As agents for the executive branch of federal and state government, administrative agencies protect the public health and welfare. *Administrative law* is made by administrative agencies that have been granted the authority to pass rules and regulations and render opinions, which usually explain in more detail the state statutes on a particular subject.

The administrative agency that is generally most familiar to nursing professionals is the state board of nursing. Nursing boards accomplish their mission through licensing competent and qualified individuals and then regulating licensees' safeness and scope of practice as outlined in each state's Nurse Practice Act.

What Are Nurse Practice Acts?

Each state has enacted important legislation known as a Nurse Practice Act. The Nurse Practice Act in each state is comprised of both statutes and administrative rules and defines the qualifications for nursing licensure as well as establishes how the practice of nursing will be regulated and monitored within that state's jurisdiction. Nurse Practice Acts generally describe nursing scope of practice boundaries, unprofessional conduct, and disciplinary action. In most states, the Nurse Practice Act does the following:

- Describes how to obtain licensure and enter practice within that state.
- Describes how and when to renew your license.
- Defines the educational requirements for entry into practice.
- Provides definitions and scope of practice for each level of nursing practice.
- Describes the process by which individual members of the board of nursing are selected and describes the categories of membership.
- Identifies situations that are grounds for discipline or circumstances in which a nursing license can be revoked or suspended.
- Identifies the process for disciplinary actions, including diversionary techniques.
- Outlines the appeal steps if the nurse feels the disciplinary actions taken by the board of nursing are not fair or valid.

It is important to keep your state board of nursing informed of your current residence so that you receive important documents that can affect your future ability to practice in a timely fashion. Never ignore or take lightly any document received from your state board of nursing. Even if you think you have received a notice in error, contact the board of nursing immediately (Box 20.2). You also need to be informed of Nurse Practice Act requirements in a new state of residence before you begin to practice there. All Nurse Practice Acts are readily accessible online and/or easily obtained from any state board of nursing (see Appendix A on the Evolve website). If you are not familiar with the Nursing Practice Act in your state of licensure and/or state of practice, you are putting yourself and your nursing license at risk.

BOX 20.2 PROTECT YOUR LICENSE

- Periodically check to make sure that you are in good standing with your state board of nursing.
- Be sure that your state board of nursing knows whenever you change your address, whether you move across the street or across the nation.
- Know the Nurse Practice Act in your state.
- Practice nursing according to the scope and standards of practice in your state.
- Meet all renewal requirements on time.
- Always respond to correspondence from your state board of nursing.
- Know the self-reporting laws and self-report when required.

What Is Criminal Law?

Historically, nurses have been held accountable for their negligent conduct in civil actions and state licensing board disciplinary actions. However, negligent conduct can have criminal consequences as well. Whereas civil actions concern private interests and rights between individuals and/or businesses, *criminal law* involves prosecution and punishment for conduct deemed to be a crime.

Criminal negligence is based on a criminally culpable state of mind in addition to a deviation from the standard of care. The lapse in standard of care can be intentional or unintentional. For example, in November 2006, a Wisconsin nurse made an unintentional medication error that resulted in a patient's death during childbirth. The nurse was criminally charged with patient abuse and neglect causing great bodily harm, a felony that carried a penalty of imprisonment and a significant monetary fine. The nurse eventually received probation after pleading no contest to two criminal misdemeanors. Additionally, the Wisconsin Board of Nursing suspended the nurse's license for 9 months to be followed by a 2-year practice limitation (ASQ, 2007).

■ *Case study 1*

You are working in a hospital where a very well-known actor is admitted with a diagnosis of *Pneumocystis jiroveci* pneumonia. During the patient's stay, you are asked by a physician to administer an intravenous medication for purposes of conscious sedation to the patient while the physician performs a procedure. During the procedure, the patient has a respiratory arrest secondary to oversedation and dies. You are devastated and realize that you may have administered too much medication. You decide to confide in your best friend, who is also a nurse, about the incident. While speaking to your best friend, you mention the actor's name and diagnosis. Your friend says that it was "illegal" for you to administer intravenous conscious sedation and expresses concern that your actions and possible medication error might land you in trouble (Critical Thinking Box 20.1).

? CRITICAL THINKING BOX 20.1

In Case Study 1, where might you be able to search to determine whether this is true? What type of legal trouble might you have?

What Is Case Law?

The role of the judiciary (court) is to apply and interpret the law. In our judicial system, two opposing parties present evidence before a judge and/or a jury who applies the law to the facts to determine the outcome of the case. When the court's interpretation of the law leads to law itself, it is known as case law. *Case law* and *common law* are often used interchangeably to describe law that is developed by courts when deciding a case as opposed to law created through a legislative enactment or a regulation promulgated by an administrative agency. The majority of tort law is developed from case law.

Torts

Tort law, as described by Pozgar (2007), is a civil wrong committed against a person entitling the injured party to file a lawsuit to receive compensation for damages he or she suffered as a result of the alleged wrongdoing. The purpose of tort law is to determine culpability, deter future violations, and award compensation to the plaintiff if applicable. There are two categories of tort actions: unintentional and intentional. Medical negligence or professional negligence is an example of an unintentional tort and is discussed in more detail below.

What Are Intentional Torts?

Intentional torts are civil "wrongs" that are done on purpose to cause harm to another person. Instead of seeking to put the *tortfeasor* (the wrongdoer) in jail, however, an intentional tort claim attempts to right the wrong by compensating the plaintiff. These types of claims are less common than negligence claims, which are not purposeful acts and can be asserted against a nurse in some circumstances.

There are several types of intentional torts. *Assault and battery* and false imprisonment are two examples of intentional torts. *Assault and battery* are the legal terms that are applied to nonconsensual threat of touch (assault) or the actual touching (battery). Generally speaking, the practice of nursing involves a great deal of touching. Permission to do this touching is usually implied when the patient seeks medical care. All patients have the right, however, to withdraw their implied consent to medical care and refuse the procedure or treatment or medication being offered. A competent patient's refusal to consent or withdrawal of consent must be respected by the health care team or there could be legal implications. For instance, the Louisiana Supreme Court awarded $25,000 to a patient's family in a lawsuit wherein the nurses had ignored the patient's refusal of a Foley catheter. The patient was ultimately injured in the process of removing the catheter, and the court determined that the nurses had committed battery by performing an invasive procedure against the patient's wishes (*Robertson v. Provident House*, 1991). Also, a patient may wish to leave an institution "against medical advice" (AMA). If nurses use physical restraint or touching to keep this patient from leaving, these actions can lead to a civil claim of assault and battery.

False imprisonment means making someone wrongfully feel that he or she cannot leave a place. It is often associated with assault and battery claims. This can happen in a health care setting through the use of physical or chemical restraints or the threat of physical or emotional harm if a patient leaves an institution. Threats such as "If you don't stay in your bed, I'll have to sedate you" may constitute false imprisonment. This tort might also involve telling a patient that he or she may not leave the emergency department until the bill is paid. Another example is using restraints or threatening to use them on competent patients to make them do what you want them to do against their wishes. Unless you are very clearly protecting the safety of others, you may not restrain a competent adult (Critical Thinking Box 20.2) (Guido, 2013).

❓ CRITICAL THINKING BOX 20.2

In what situations would it be acceptable to restrain a patient?

In psychiatric patient populations in which patients may pose a danger to self or others, there are many very specific state and federal laws to follow as well as institutional policies. The challenge, of course, is in preventing patients from self-harm while also maintaining the patients' rights to liberty. This is not always an easy balance. There are many restrictions on the appropriate use of both hard and soft restraints and elevated scrutiny on their use in both hospital and long-term care facilities (Tolson & Morley, 2012). Claims of elder abuse have been filed for the misuse of restraints. You must be aware of the policies in your institution as well as any applicable statutory requirements.

Defamation (libel and slander) refers to causing damage to someone else's reputation. If the means of transmitting the damaging information is written, it is called *libel*; if it is oral or spoken, it is called *slander*. The damaging information must be communicated to a third person. The actions likely to result in a defamation charge are situations in which inaccurate information from the medical record is reported, such as in Case Study 1, or when speaking negatively about your co-workers (supervisors, doctors, other nurses).

Two defenses to defamation accusations are *truth* and *privilege*. If the statement is true, it is not actionable under this doctrine. However, it is often difficult to define truth, because it may be a matter of perspective. It is better to avoid that issue by not making negative statements about other people unnecessarily. An example of privilege would be required for good-faith reporting to child protective services of possible child abuse or statements made during a peer-review process. If statements made during these processes are without malice, state statutes often protect the reporter from any civil liability for defamation.

Recovery in defamation claims usually requires that the plaintiff submit proof of injury—for instance, loss of money or job. Some categories, such as fitness to practice one's profession, do not require such proof, as they are considered sufficiently damaging without it. Comments about the quality of a nurse's work or a health care provider's skills in diagnosing illness would fit in this category. You can avoid this claim by steering clear of gossip and by not writing negative documents about others in the heat of the moment and without adequate facts.

Invasion of Privacy and Breaches of Privacy and Confidentiality

A good general rule involving the sharing of patient information is always to ask yourself, "Do I have the patient's consent to share this information, or is it necessary to deliver health care services to this patient?" If the answer to either is "no," then the information should not be communicated.

Privacy regulations under the Health Insurance Portability and Accountability Act of 1996 (HIPAA) remain as a central focus for the public. There are specific privacy regulations under HIPAA that became effective in April 2003 and include an elaborate system for ensuring privacy for individually identifiable health information. Information used to render treatment, payment, or health care operations does not require the patient's specific consent for its use. This includes processes such as quality assurance activities, legal activities, risk management, billing, and utilization review. However, the rules require that the disclosure be the "minimum necessary," and a clear understanding of what information can be shared under this exception is necessary (Annas, 2003). Notice must be given to the patient regarding how the information will be used. All nurses working in health care must be aware of this law and how their institutions specifically comply with it.

Another aspect of HIPAA involves electronic information and the security measures necessary to ensure that protected patient information is not accessed by those without the right or need to know. These rules came into effect in April 2005. Each institution must have data security policies and technologies in place based on their own "risk assessment." Many institutions require that any health information transmitted under open networks, such as the Internet, telephones, and wireless communication networks, be encrypted (coded).

Many states have physician–patient privilege laws that protect communications between physicians and their patients. This enables information to pass freely between physician and patient without concern that it will be shared with those who do not need to know it. This includes law enforcement organizations. The privilege usually extends to information about a patient in the medical record or obtained in the course of providing care. Most states extend physician–patient privilege to nurses and sometimes to other health care providers as well. This privilege generally belongs to the patient and not the health care professional, which means that only the patient can decide whether to relinquish it.

As a professional it is important to observe *confidentiality* when talking about patients at home and at work (Fig. 20.1). Nurses must be very careful to keep information about the patient confidential and to share information only with health care workers who must know the information to plan or to give proper care to the patient. This is sometimes difficult to do, as seen in Case Study 1.

FIG. 20.1 Maintaining confidentiality is both an ethical and a legal consideration in nursing.

EHRs and national clearinghouses for health information present significant confidentiality concerns. Such technologies offer many advantages, including easier and broader access to needed information and more legible documentation. These same advantages also create issues, because they make it more difficult to ensure confidentiality. Many hospitals and agencies already have policies and procedures in place, such as access codes, limited screen time, and computers placed in locations that promote privacy. The nurse is still responsible for the protection of confidentiality when computers, e-mail, voice paging systems, mobile devices, or other rapid communication techniques are used.

Privacy violations can result in a legal cause of action for the tort of *invasion of privacy.* This cause of action can apply to several behaviors, such as photographing a procedure and showing it without the patient's consent, going through a patient's belongings without consent, or talking publicly about a patient.

Miscellaneous Intentional Torts and Other Civil Rights Claims Involved With Employment

The aforementioned torts and others can be relevant to nurses in relation to their employment. These intentional torts can be brought personally against the nurse. *Tortious interference with contract* is a claim alleging that someone maliciously interfered with a person's contractual (often employment) rights. This can occur, for instance, if a nurse attempts to get another nurse fired through giving false or misleading facts to a supervisor. *Intentional infliction of emotional distress* is described by its name, and it can also be attached to malicious acts in the employment setting. These and certain civil rights claims such as *sexual harassment* and *discrimination* are both rights and potential liabilities for every person in the work force. Although beyond the scope of this text, policies and information regarding these issues demand further investigation by each health care employee to ensure that their rights and the rights of others are not violated.

What Are Unintentional Torts?

The most common type of *unintentional tort* is called *negligence.* A person is considered to have acted negligently when he or she unintentionally causes personal injury or harm to property where the person should have acted reasonably to avoid such harm. Because professional negligence (also referred to as malpractice) can potentially affect every nurse, it is important to explore what this means. Before we delve into negligence, let's examine classifications of legal actions and nursing licensure.

> The most common unintentional tort action brought against nurses is a negligence claim.

COURT ACTIONS BASED ON LEGAL PRINCIPLES

There are two major classifications of legal actions that can occur as a result either of deliberate or unintentional violations of legal rules or statutes. In the first category are *criminal actions.* These occur when you have done something that is considered harmful to society as a whole. The trial will involve a prosecuting attorney, who represents the interests of the state or the United States (the public), and a defense attorney, who represents the interests of the person accused of a crime (defendant). These actions can usually be identified by their title, which will read *"State v. [the name of the defendant]"* or *"U.S. v. Smith [the name of the defendant]."* Examples include murder, theft, drug violations, and some violations of the Nursing Practice Acts, such as misuse of narcotics. Serious crimes that can cause the perpetrator to be imprisoned are called *felonies.* Less serious crimes typically resulting in fines are *misdemeanors.* The victim, if there is one, may or may not be involved in a decision to prosecute a case and is considered only a witness in the criminal trial. Laws differ in states as to victim rights and/or if the person or the state will receive any of the money from fines. In Case Study 1, your actions would not likely result in a criminal action. Recently, however, there have been instances in which a nurse was thought to have recklessly caused a patient's death, and a case was brought in criminal court for negligent homicide. The issues involved in such criminal actions will be discussed later in this chapter.

The second category of legal claims includes *civil actions.* These actions concern private interests and rights between the individuals involved in the cases. Private attorneys handle these claims, and the remedy is usually some type of compensation that attempts to restore injured parties to their earlier positions. Examples of civil actions include malpractice, negligence, and informed consent issues. The victim (patient) or victim's family (patient's family) brings the lawsuit as the *plaintiff* against the *defendant,* who may be the individual (nurse) or company (hospital) that is believed to have caused harm. In the situation presented, you might be sued for malpractice by the actor's spouse if it is felt that you acted below a standard of care and caused the actor's death.

Sometimes an event can include both criminal and civil consequences. When that happens, two trials are held with different goals. The amount of evidence required to support a guilty verdict is different for each type of trial. The criminal case requires that the evidence show that the defendant was guilty beyond a shadow of a doubt. The civil case requires only that the evidence show that the defendant was more likely guilty than not guilty. This is what makes it possible for someone such as O. J. Simpson to be found "not guilty" in a criminal trial but "guilty" or negligent in a civil trial.

NURSING LICENSURE

All states prohibit the practice of nursing without a license. Many other professional occupations require a license. Have you ever asked yourself what is the purpose of licensure and why some occupations require a license while others do not? When specialized knowledge and skill are required to perform often complex professional activities, particularly activities involving potential harm to the public, licensure is usually required. Licensure protects the public health and welfare by establishing entry-level qualifications and ongoing competencies to maintain and ensure safe practice.

A license to practice nursing is a privilege, not a right. According to the National Council of State Boards of Nursing (NCSBN, 2011a), licensure is "the process by which boards of nursing grant permission to an individual to engage in nursing practice after determining that the applicant has attained the competency necessary to perform a unique scope of practice." Each state Board of Nursing follows licensing statutes and rules designed to determine if potential applicants possess the competency and necessary skills to practice safely in their chosen field.

Even the successful completion of an educational program in nursing and/or passing the National Council Licensure Examination for Registered Nurses (NCLEX-RN®) does not guarantee that a state board of nursing will grant you a license to practice nursing. A license is granted by a state after a candidate has successfully met *all* the requirements in that particular state. Examples of these requirements may include criminal background checks and successful completion of a board-approved nursing education program.

When you graduate from nursing school and successfully complete the state licensing process to become a practical or registered nurse, you achieve professional licensure status under the law. Having a license to practice nursing brings you into close contact with laws and government agencies. Professional licensure is governed by Nurse Practice Acts that you must follow in the state(s) in which you are licensed and/or practicing nursing. Once you are licensed, the state continues to monitor your practice and has the authority to investigate complaints against your license. If you are found to have violated the Nurse Practice Act, a state board of nursing can take disciplinary action against your license.

Disciplinary Actions

Several levels of disciplinary actions can occur based on the severity of the practice act violation and the ongoing risk to the public. For instance, state boards of nursing have disciplinary power ranging from censure to probation, suspension, revocation, and denial of licensure. One of the most common reasons for state board action against nurses involves substance abuse and the diversion of prescription medications for personal use (Brent, 2001). Boards of nursing are increasingly concerned about this issue, because it has significant impact on rendering safe, effective patient care (NCSBN, 2014).

Final disciplinary actions are a matter of public record and can be accessed by contacting a state board of nursing. Additionally, final disciplinary actions are reported to governmental and nongovernmental authorities for public protection. For example, NURSYS is a nongovernmental electronic information system that includes the collection and warehousing of nurse licensing information and disciplinary actions. The Healthcare Integrity and Protection Data Bank (HIPDB) and the National Practitioner Data Bank (NPDB) are two federal data banks of information about health care providers in the United States. Adverse actions taken against a health care professional's license are required by federal law to be reported to the HIPDB and NPDB. However, the general public may not access information included in the NPDB and HIPDB, as the information is limited by law to entities such as hospitals and health plans and government agencies.

Scope of Practice

The scope of practice for professional nursing is the range of permissible activity as defined by the law; in essence it defines what nurses can and, sometimes more important, what nurses cannot do. Because the scope of nursing practice is defined by state legislation, there is great variation from state to state both in specificity and in the range of activities that are legally authorized. Many state legislatures have enacted very specific scope of practice statements whereas others have drafted very vague and broad scope of practice statements and have left the job of describing the specific activities to the state board of nursing. Some state scope of practice statements are very restrictive, whereas others allow a much broader range of activities. It is very important that a nurse become very familiar with the practice act and the scope of practice as defined by the legislature or the state board of nursing in the state where he or she intends to practice.

There is significant variability for the scope of practice of licensed practical or vocational nurses (LPN/LVN) and even more variability for the scope of practice for advanced practice nurses (nurse practitioners, midwives, anesthetists, collectively called APRN) (NPDB, 2010). Because of the restrictive nature of the scope of practice statements of many states, all APRNs are not able to practice to the full extent of their education and training.

■ *Case study 2*

After your incident with the actor, you decide to leave the state. You have to answer detailed questions on your licensure application for the new state about any previous malpractice claims. You had heard something about a claim being filed against your former hospital but had left shortly after that. Now you have received a notice from the state board of nursing of your previous residence inquiring about the incident with the actor and asking for a response within 2 weeks. The letter has taken a long time to be forwarded to you, and the 2-week deadline has passed. What should you do?

Multistate Licensure

The Nurse Licensure Compact is a "mutual recognition agreement" between states that have adopted the Compact legislation. The Nurse Licensure Compact allows both registered and practical nurses with a license in good standing in their "home state" to practice nursing in any of the other Compact states ("member states") without going through the process of obtaining additional licensure. According to the National Council of State Boards of Nursing (NCSBN), 25 states have enacted the Nurse Licensure Compact (NCSBN, 2015).

A Compact license is also known as a "multistate license." It is important to note that only nurses who declare a Compact state as their primary state of residence are eligible for a multistate license. This means that if you obtain a license in state that is not participating in the Nurse Licensure Compact, you do not have a multistate license and cannot practice nursing outside of your primary state of residency without obtaining additional licensure in a new state. It is also very important to note that when you permanently relocate to another Compact or non-Compact state, all licensure laws including the Nurse Licensure Compact require you to obtain licensure in the new state.

The APRN Compact, approved by the NCSBN on May 4, 2015, allows an advanced practice registered nurse to hold one multistate license with a privilege to practice in other Compact states. The APRN Compact is under consideration in several states.

What about Substance use Disorder in Nursing?

Substance use disorder describes a pattern of substance use behavior that encompasses substance misuse to dependency or addiction. Substances can be alcohol, legal (prescription) drugs or illegal drugs.

Substance use disorder can affect nurses and anyone regardless of their age, gender, or economic circumstances. It is a progressive and sometimes fatal disease but also one that can be treated. Boards of nursing are increasingly concerned about this issue, because it has significant impact on rendering safe, effective patient care.

The American Nurses Association (ANA) estimated that 6% to 8% of nurses abuse drugs or alcohol at a level sufficient to impair their professional judgment (NCSBN, 2011b). Many nurse practice acts have mandatory reporting obligations regarding impairment. Allowing an impaired nurse to practice not only puts the nurse and the patient at risk but also negatively impacts the facility's reputation and the nursing profession as a whole. It is important that you know what the reporting requirements are for your state board of nursing and your facility.

One of the most common reasons for state board action against nurses involves the diversion of prescription medications for personal use (Brent, 2001). Do not ever assume that you or your colleagues are immune from substance misuse, abuse, or addiction. High stress and easy access to drugs contribute to the problem for health care providers. A slippery slope occurs when a nurse first takes any medication—even an aspirin—that does not belong to him or her.

If you do find yourself in trouble with drugs or alcohol, it is advisable to voluntarily report your substance misuse or abuse to your state board of nursing and seek immediate treatment. The boards of nursing in 41 states, the District of Columbia, and the Virgin Islands have alternative monitoring programs to assist nurses with substance use disorders, which may prevent their licenses from being suspended or revoked. The nondisciplinary rehabilitative approach to substance use disorders recognizes the importance of returning a sober abstinent nurse to the work force (NCSBN, 2011b).

States with alternative monitoring programs allow enrolled nurses to meet specific behavioral criteria, such as blood or urine testing, ordered evaluations, and attendance at rehabilitation programs, either while disciplinary action is being undertaken or instead of bringing formal disciplinary proceedings. The primary concern is to ensure safe nursing practice. If a nurse is involved in a voluntary rehabilitation program through a contract with a state board and suffers a relapse or has additional problems, the board may bring formal disciplinary action against the nurse that may negatively affect licensure for the rest of his or her life.

NEGLIGENCE

■ *Case study 3*

You are a nurse working in a hospital. The physician tells you that you need to administer an injection of Vistaril (hydroxyzine pamoate). You make sure that the order is documented in the medical record. The medication comes up from the pharmacy, and you check it against the physician's order and find that it is correct. You walk into the patient's room and use at least two patient identifiers to make sure you have the right patient. You give the injection in the patient's right dorsogluteal muscle and document this in the medical record.

The patient leaves the hospital. A year later, you are told that a lawsuit has been filed against the hospital by the patient. It seems the patient is claiming that the injection you gave him caused sciatic nerve damage and his whole leg is numb (Critical Thinking Box 20.3).

? CRITICAL THINKING BOX 20.3

Who may have negligence liability in this situation and why? You? The physician? The hospital? What defenses may be available to you?

Many times nurses worry about being sued for something when, in the eyes of the law, no negligence has occurred. Not all poor outcomes are a result of negligence or are a violation of the Nurse Practice Act. A nurse also may legitimately make an error in judgment. Therefore, it is important for a nurse to know the basic elements that must be proved before negligence can occur. Then the nurse can evaluate incidents realistically.

Basic Elements of Negligence

What are the basic elements of negligence?
1. You must have a duty. In other words, there must be a professional nurse–patient relationship.
2. You must have breached that duty. In other words, you must have fallen below the standard of care for a nurse.
3. Your breach of duty must have been a foreseeable cause of the injury.
4. Damages or injury must have occurred.

There are four basic elements of negligence, all of which must be proven by the plaintiff in a negligence lawsuit in order for the plaintiff to be awarded compensation.

The job of the patient's (plaintiff's) attorney is to prove to a jury that each element of negligence has occurred. This is not always a simple straightforward process, and it can be frustrating and confusing for all involved parties. It is important for the nurse to understand the elements of negligence and how each element may be proved in a court of law.

Do You Have a Professional Duty?

Generally speaking, all persons owe a duty of "due care" to others in our daily activities and lives. This means that you must conduct yourself in a reasonable and prudent manner to avoid causing harm to another person or his or her property. The duty of due care also applies to nursing professionals who have a professional duty to act as a reasonable nurse would act in the same or similar circumstances to avoid causing foreseeable harm to patients.

To prevail in a negligence action, the plaintiff must establish that there was a nurse–patient relationship in which a professional duty was owed by the nurse to the patient. If you are working as a nurse in a hospital, the nurse–patient relationship is usually implied and you owe a professional duty of care to your patients. What if you are giving advice in your home informally to a friend, relative, or neighbor? In this setting, it may not be implied that you are acting as a nurse, particularly in the absence of payment, institution, or formal contract.

What if you stop at an accident to assist someone who is injured? Good Samaritan statutes provide immunity from malpractice to those professionals who attempt to give assistance at the scene of an accident. In essence, you do not have any professional duty to stop, although you may feel an ethical duty to do so. However, a nurse may be sued in some states for rendering Good Samaritan aid if the nurse is found to have acted in a grossly negligent manner. If you do stop at the scene of an accident to provide aid, know that in most—if not all—states you cannot be sued for malpractice for what you might or might not do, unless the aid you provide is grossly negligent. That is, you do not have a professional standard of care to adhere to unless you are a professional at the scene as part of your employment. All persons, of course, are expected not to leave a victim in a position that is more dangerous than when found. After you stop to help the injured person, stay with him or her until you are given clearance by emergency responders.

Sometimes nurses volunteer to provide nursing assistance at sporting events or other activities where it is foreseen that professional services may be needed. In thinking about this, you may see that such a situation is not quite as clear as other situations. If you are at a first-aid station or if you are wearing a badge indicating you are a nurse, then you have the appearance of a professional, and people may rely on that appearance when seeking advice or assistance.

> It is important to know your status under these various circumstances in your state. You should know whether you have immunity and whether you are covered by malpractice insurance.

Falling Below the Standard of Care: Was There a Breach of the Professional Duty?

After establishing that a professional duty is owed, the question becomes, "What is that duty?" The duty owed by a nurse to a patient is different from the duty owed to the patient by another health care discipline such as a physician or physical therapist. The duty of a nurse will be to act as a reasonable nurse would act under the same or similar circumstances. This is known as the standard of care and is a very important factor in most negligence cases. You may be asking yourself, "How will my attorney prove that I acted as a reasonable nurse and within the standard of care?"

The following aspects may be considered when attempting to establish through evidence what the standard of care for the nurse might be.

What About the Nurse Practice Act?

Perhaps the most important guideline for nurses will be the Nurse Practice Act in the state in which you are practicing. Most acts describe in fairly general terms what a nurse may or may not do. Prohibitions, or things that are considered to be unprofessional conduct, are usually more specific. A Nurse Practice Act violation means that you have fallen below a standard of care set by the state for nurses. It also may mean that you risk an action against your license. If you do not know what these prohibitions are, you are putting yourself in jeopardy. As stated previously, and as applied here to the standard of care, it is important that you obtain a copy of the Nurse Practice Act for the state(s) in which you are or will be licensed to practice, and be sure to stay current with your licensing standards. For instance, Texas now requires that all applicants for licensure pass a nursing jurisprudence examination, which is based on the Texas Nursing Practice Act and the Texas Board of Nursing Rules and Regulations (Texas BON, 2010).

What Is an Expert Witness?

The most common way to establish the duty owed by a nurse is by the testimony of a registered nurse who usually, but not always, has training and a background similar to yours. This expert witness will then testify regarding what a reasonable nurse in the same or similar circumstances would be expected to do—and, in the case of an expert witness for the plaintiff, will argue that you did not do it. If a plaintiff's attorney cannot find an expert nurse to testify that you did not act reasonably, then in most instances the case cannot go forward. In general, a patient cannot simply claim professional malpractice without having a professional witness to corroborate this.

In the same manner, if the plaintiff has an expert witness to prove you fell below the standard of care, you will need an expert witness to testify that you did not. Some nurses enjoy being expert witnesses either for the defense of a nurse or as part of the plaintiff's claim against a nurse. Either role requires both integrity and professionalism to be effective and credible in front of a jury (Di Luigi, 2004).

There is a type of malpractice case in which an expert is not required. This type of claim is called *res ipsa loquitur*, or "the thing speaks for itself." This claim is very difficult to prove, because the patient must have enough evidence to show that (1) the injury would ordinarily not occur unless someone were negligent; (2) the instrumentality causing the injury was within the exclusive control of the defendant; and (3) the incident was not a result of any voluntary action on the part of the plaintiff. If a patient can prove that all of these conditions exist, the burden then shifts to the defendant nurse to prove that malpractice did not take place. Incidents such as operating on the wrong body part or leaving a surgical sponge in a patient fall into this category of claim.

What Are Established Policies and Procedures?

Policies and procedures established by the institution in which you work are the most crucial pieces of evidence for establishing a standard of care. Most good attorneys who represent plaintiffs will request a set of hospital policies as soon as a lawsuit is filed. For instance, in Case Studies 1 and 3, a lawyer might ask for the hospital's policies on documentation and administration of medications. If you did not follow that policy, then you fell below a standard of care set by your institution.

You can see why you need to know and read the policies within your health care facility or corporation. These policies should also be a resource when you have questions about how to perform certain procedures or what your rights are in certain situations. Policies are the laws under which you must live. It is also important for you as a professional to participate in making or changing policies so that they accurately reflect what nurses are doing in your institution. In addition, the policies set standards for providing high-quality and consistent patient care. If you have followed a policy, it can be used proactively to prove that you followed the standard of care set by your institution.

What About Accreditation and Facility Licensing Standards?

Most health care facilities and other health care organizations must go through a process whereby they become licensed and/or accredited. The Joint Commission (TJC) and the National Committee of Quality Assurance (NCQA) are two such organizations that set accreditation standards for health care organizations. For instance, TJC has issued National Patient Safety Goals (NPSGs) every year since 2003 that include standards to improve safe identification of patients and their medications, prevent infections using proven guidelines, and improve communication among care providers (TJC, 2015). A state facility-licensing requirement would be that the facility develops policies and procedures to optimize patient safety when administering medications.

What About Textbooks and Journals?

Articles, textbooks, or portions of such publications may be used as evidence of the standard of care for nurses to follow. For instance, if a nursing journal has published a recent article on correct administration of intramuscular injections, that may be used to demonstrate what you should have done.

What Are Professional Standards for Nursing Organizations?

Professional nursing organizations, such as the American Nurses Association (ANA) or the Association of periOperative Registered Nurses (AORN), may publish certain standards or practice guidelines. These may be used as evidence for what a reasonable nurse should do under certain circumstances.

In summary, there are many types of evidence used by plaintiff attorneys to demonstrate an expected standard of care. The nurse needs to remember that these same documents can be used to demonstrate that you did follow the standard of care. Let us see how.

Applying the Standard of Care to the Case Study

In Case Study 3, the plaintiff will have to find a nurse who will testify about the correct method for administering intramuscular injections. If you did not give the injection in such a manner, then the jury can infer that you did not act reasonably. However, if the correct method is to give the injection intramuscularly in the right dorsogluteal site, and you have documented that you did this, the plaintiff may not be able to establish a breach of the standard of care. Also, if you can show that you followed hospital policies in the administration of the medication, again, there will be no proof of falling below the standard of care.

What if the patient attempts to claim a case using the theory of *res ipsa loquitur*? Again, the patient's lawyer must prove that the claimed injury could not have happened unless there was negligence. As demonstrated earlier, you would be able to prove through your documentation that you were not negligent. In addition, your attorney would also demonstrate your lack of liability through the third element of malpractice. Do you remember what that is?

Did the Breach of Duty Cause an Injury?

Causation is an important element that must be demonstrated in a negligence action. The plaintiff must prove that the nurse's action actually caused the injury and that the injury was a foreseeable consequence of the nurse's actions. Did the difficult birth cause the child to have cerebral palsy, or did a genetic birth defect cause the baby to experience a difficult delivery? Was the injury caused by the auto accident or by the medical care? Did the patient have the physical problem before the medical care or after? Was the injury caused subsequently by the patient's lack of compliance with the treatment plan, or did the patient subsequently injure herself after the medical care was rendered?

Applying "Causation" to Case Study 3

Returning to Case Study 3, the patient will have to prove that your injection caused the numbness in his leg. There are many intervening factors that could have caused this numbness. You do not have to prove anything, because you, as a defendant, do not have the "burden of proof." The plaintiff may have a very difficult time, especially if there are no documented complaints by the patient of problems at the time of the injection or shortly thereafter.

Just remember that a patient's claim that you or another provider caused some particular injury or problem should not automatically be assumed to be true. Although you do not have to argue the point with the patient, you also do not have to agree. Injuries have many causes and many stories behind them:

- Document the facts.
- Document what you see and do.
- Your role is to render nursing services, not to judge or give your opinion.
- Your actions and factual documentation will be your best defense.

Did the Patient Suffer Damages or Injury?

The last element that must be proved is that your breach of duty caused injury (damages) to the patient. This last element of negligence can also be overlooked when the nurse becomes distracted by the fact that he or she fell below the standard of care in making a mistake in patient care. Many practice errors, however, do not cause injury or damages. For instance, if a nurse administers a one-time dose of 650 mg of Tylenol instead of 350 mg of Tylenol, the medication error is not likely to cause permanent injury or damages. This does not mean, however, that any medication error should be ignored or taken lightly or that some medications cannot cause death or serious injury with a single mistake. Medication errors are serious breaches of the standard of care. It is very unlikely though that a malpractice claim will be brought for a medication error that does not cause injury or damages. You may still suffer an employment-related consequence such as disciplinary action for errors that do not result in patient harm.

Damages can be viewed as the sum of money a court or jury awards as compensation for a tort action. *General damages* are those given for intangibles such as pain and suffering, disfigurement, interference with ordinary enjoyment of life, and loss of consortium (marital services) that are inherent in the injury itself (Guido, 2013). *Special damages* are the patient's out-of-pocket expenses such as medical care, lost wages, and rehabilitation costs. *Punitive damages* are those damages that seek to punish those whose conduct goes beyond normal malpractice. Claims in which this might occur are rare, but they involve issues such as changed medical records, lies being told to patients, or intentional misconduct while under the influence of alcohol or drugs. Such punitive awards can add millions of dollars to an otherwise low-damage claim. Some states have limited the amount for specific types of damages that a plaintiff can receive (Critical Thinking Box 20.4).

? CRITICAL THINKING BOX 20.4

Does your state limit the amount of damages a plaintiff can receive?

Damages Applied to the Case Study

In Case Study 3, numbness of a limb may be difficult to prove. Nerve conduction studies may be performed in an independent medical examination to demonstrate that the injection could not have caused the neurologic injury about which the patient complains. Numbness also does not mean lack of function and may not usually prevent any activity of daily living. The age and status of the plaintiff would play an important role, as would your documentation of the patient's lack of complaints and ability to ambulate.

Your actions and documentation are the best defense.

WHO MIGHT HAVE LIABILITY (RESPONSIBILITY) IN A CLAIM?

■ *Case study 4*

You are a nurse working on a surgical unit in a hospital. One evening you are asked to float to pediatrics. The only experience you have had with children was when you were a student. A physician asks you to give digoxin to an infant and writes an order for 2 mL. This seems like a lot of medication to you, so you ask the head nurse on the unit about the dose. The head nurse assumes you are speaking about an oral dose of the medication and states this is normal. You give the medication by injection and shortly thereafter the child's heart stops beating and he is coded. When you attempt to use an Ambu bag, it is not on the crash cart. The child eventually recovers; however, 21 years later, you receive notice that a young man is suing you for giving him the wrong dose of digoxin when he was an infant.

Personal Liability

Who can be held accountable for your actions as a nurse? You may hear things such as, "Don't worry, I'll take responsibility for this." There is no defense called "She made me do it." For many years, physicians were seen as the "Captain of the Ship" and thus ultimately responsible for everything that happened to the patient. This doctrine is no longer true. In the eyes of the law, each individual is accountable for his or her own actions. Even if you are not personally named in a lawsuit, you will be asked to provide evidence regarding your involvement and will be expected to defend your nursing care under oath. "I was just following orders" does not explain why you, as a professional nurse, made a medication error. You are held to a professional standard of care to know about the medications you are administering, including the correct dose.

According to the NPDB 2014 report, 149,505 professional nurses had an adverse action report filed against them between the years 2001 and 2010. A professional nurse includes registered nurses, licensed practical nurses, licensed vocational nurses, nurse practitioners, nurse anesthetists, nurse midwives, clinical nurse specialists, advanced nurse practitioners, and doctors of nursing practice. There have been 6167 cases between 2003 and 2012 reported to the NPDB in which malpractice payments were made on behalf of a specifically named nurse. This does not include the number of claims naming only a facility, yet involving nursing actions. Because negligence can potentially affect every nurse, it is important to explore what this means.

In Case Study 4, who is likely to be named in a lawsuit? Who might share liability for the patient's injury? Although nurses do have a duty to follow physician's orders under most circumstances, this is never true if the nurse believes or has reason to believe that the provider's order is unsafe for the patient or not within the nurse's scope of practice. In Case Study 4, if the nurse did not know the correct dose of IV digoxin, the nurse had an independent duty to verify the correct dose.

In Case Study 1, receiving an order to give IV conscious sedation does not relieve the nurse of a duty to determine whether this is within his or her scope of nursing practice. If an order falls outside of the nurse's scope of practice, the nurse must notify the provider and refrain from carrying out the order. When accepting orders from health care providers, remember that you should only accept duties and orders that you are competent to perform and that are within your scope of practice.

Supervisory Liability

Questions often arise regarding the nurse's responsibility for the actions of others. The standard of care for a supervisor is to act as a reasonable supervisor under the same or similar circumstances. A supervisor can be expected to ensure the following:

- The task was properly assigned to someone competent to perform it safely.
- Adequate supervision was provided as needed.
- The nurse provided appropriate follow-up and evaluation of the delegated task.

As in Case Study 4, a supervisor could be expected to supervise more closely a float nurse or a recent graduate than someone who is an experienced nurse on a pediatric unit. It is also incumbent on a person being supervised to ask for assistance if that person is faced with a problem that he or she lacks the necessary skills to resolve. In Case Study 4, this was done, but the nurse administering the medication and the supervisor miscommunicated regarding the method or route of administration. How often do you think this happens in health care?

Delegation of nursing duties to unlicensed health care workers presents supervisory nurses with some special risks. Changes in health care delivery systems and financing are resulting in some unfamiliar categories of unlicensed caregivers with a wide variety of skills and expertise. Some boards of nursing have informed their licensees that each nurse remains personally liable for any task delegated to an unlicensed worker on the theory that the delegated task is considered the nurse's responsibility rather than being within the scope of practice of the unlicensed worker. Other boards of nursing have stated that they will apply to delegation the traditional standards for supervising any health care worker, as described earlier.

Certain nursing responsibilities, such as nursing diagnosis, assessment, teaching, and some portions of planning, evaluation, and documentation, should not be delegated to unlicensed staff. Contact the board of nursing in your state to understand better your responsibilities in the delegation of nursing duties.

Institutional Liability

Health care institutions such as hospitals are usually sued under a theory of *respondeat superior* for the actions of their employees. Almost all health care institutions carry insurance to cover the acts and omissions of their employees. Although institutions are often named as defendants in a lawsuit, this does not relieve the nurse from having to answer formally to the court for his or her own actions or inaction.

An institution's policies or lack thereof is also a common claim in a lawsuit. For instance, there can be a claim in Case Study 4 that the institution should have had a policy on nurses floating to other units in the hospital and that such persons should never be given the responsibility of transcribing physicians' orders. Additionally, in this case, there may be institutional liability through the pharmacy. If the pharmacy filled the wrong medication dose, and there are systems in place to check dosages, the pharmacist and/or technician may also be brought into the claim through the institution. There are certainly more systems than ever before in place in most hospitals to prevent medication errors. When they all fail, many persons can be involved in the liability.

Student Liability

Nursing students have responsibility for their own actions and can be held liable (Guido, 2013). The adage that "students practice under their instructor's license" is not true. Student nurses at all times will be held to the standard of care for the tasks they perform (Guido, 2013). It is therefore important that students never accept assignments beyond their preparation and that they communicate frequently with their instructors to obtain assistance and guidance.

Instructors and preceptors are responsible for reasonable and prudent clinical supervision. An instructor could be held liable for inadequate supervision in erroneously determining that a student was competent to perform a skill, when he or she was not competent (Shinn, n.d.).

> It is important to know your status under these various circumstances in your state and/or if you have immunity and/or are covered by malpractice insurance.

Instructors and preceptors need to remember that the level of expertise may vary for individual students, and the standard used to evaluate the students' performance usually involves more supervision than the standard used for some other, more experienced workers.

WHAT DEFENSES MIGHT BE AVAILABLE IN MALPRACTICE CLAIMS?

If the plaintiff in a malpractice claim does not prove each of the elements previously discussed, the defense can ask for a dismissal of the claim by making various motions (formal requests) to the court. There are several other issues that may have an effect on the outcome of a malpractice claim.

A *statute of limitations* is a law that sets a time period during which a lawsuit must be filed after an event. States have different statutes and case law surrounding this time limit. Usually, the limit is measured from the time of the event or incident, last date of treatment, or time the event was discovered (or should have been discovered). For minors, some states allow the time to be counted from the time they reach majority (usually 18 years old), unless a suit has already been brought on their behalf by parents or others. Therefore, in Case Study 4, a suit could be brought 2 or 3 years after a person reaches 18 years (majority) for an injury occurring as an infant. Other states do not permit this delay. Lack of mental competence will also delay the time requirements in some states.

Failure to file the lawsuit within the statute of limitations time results in the loss of the right to sue. This can be considered a defense, because filing after the date allows the defendants to have the case dismissed. It is important to know, however, that in most states, the statute starts running when the patient knows of the injury. If there is any type of cover-up regarding an incident, the statute will not run.

Proving that the patient assumed the risk of harm or that the patient contributed to the harm by his or her actions provides another type of defense. *Assumption of the risk* defense states that plaintiffs are partially responsible for consequences if they understood the risks involved when they proceeded with the action (Guido, 2013). An example would be a mentally competent patient who has been warned to use a call light but instead crawls out of bed and thus injures herself.

Contributory negligence is an older doctrine that was at one time an "all or nothing" rule. Plaintiffs who had any part in the adverse outcome were barred from compensation. Today, most jurisdictions use a comparative negligence theory and reduce the money award by the injured party's responsibility for the ultimate harm done (Guido, 2013). The results of one case indicated that a patient could be negligent and thus be at least partially responsible by (1) refusing to follow advice or instructions; (2) causing a delay in treatment or not returning for follow-up; (3) furnishing false, misleading, or incomplete information to a health care provider; or (4) causing the injury that results in the need for medical care (*Harvey v. Mid-Coast Hospital*, 1999).

COMMON CATEGORIES OF NEGLIGENCE

There are common categories of negligence and certain situations that involve a high risk for a lawsuit against nurses. These situations most often relate to failure to document, patient safety, improper treatment, problems with monitoring and reporting, medication errors, and failing to follow proper procedures and policies.

Failure to Document

Documentation is one of the best ways to protect your patient, yourself, and your license. Failure to document jeopardizes patient safety and puts you at risk should there be an adverse outcome. It is important to document all of the patient's responses to treatment as well as the patient's progress or lack of progress. Nursing assessments must be documented in the medical record in a timely manner, and any contact with any provider should be promptly and accurately noted in the medical record. Other important areas to document include time and date of nursing care provided in addition to all procedures, medications, monitoring, and interactions with the patient or his or her family.

An estimated one in four malpractice cases are decided on the basis of what is in the medical record (Sullivan, 2004). In many instances, you can become a nurse hero or be in deep trouble based on the accuracy and timeliness of your documentation in the medical record. One of the most important tools for all providers in a malpractice claim or licensure complaint is the medical record. The medical record is the first piece of evidence closely examined in any allegation of negligence. Accurate, timely, and thorough documentation is critically important. By recording the care administered, the specific time it was administered, the patient's response, and the overall status of the patient's condition, the nurse can demonstrate that the standard of care was met (Fig. 20.2).

Your defense attorney will use the medical record extensively and will make a timeline of events that surrounded the incident. Documentation regarding an incident should be thoroughly and factually done in the medical record and not in personal records or a diary (Fig. 20.3).

There is an adage that states, "If it is not documented, it wasn't done." In reality, it is simply difficult to prove something was done if there is no documentation and the plaintiff claims it was not done. It is then a "he said/she said" type of argument. A more accurate statement might be "If it is documented, it was done." When an incident is documented at the time of the event, there is a strong presumption that the documentation is accurate and whatever a patient says to the contrary is simply self-serving.

FIG. 20.2 It is critical that the nurse's notes reflect the current condition of the patient.

FIG. 20.3 Charting in the home setting can be challenging.

That is why it is so important to document extensively, accurately, and factually in the medical record (Box 20.3). This is especially true when there is an adverse event.

Forms often provide a difficult problem for defense attorneys when they are not completed properly. A blank space on the form or a box that is not checked, when it appears that the space or box was there to indicate the performance of a needed therapy, can be very detrimental to the nurse involved.

BOX 20.3   DOCUMENTATION GUIDELINES

- All entries should be timely, accurate, and factual (objective).
- Documentation should be legible, including your name and your credentials.
- Make late entries and corrections appropriately and according to agency or hospital policies. Do not ever obliterate or destroy any information that is or has been in the chart.
- All assessments, monitoring data, medications administered, plans of care and provider orders, whether verbal or written, must be noted in the medical record.
- Document all patient refusals of care and your communication with the patient's provider regarding the patient's refusal.
- Any communication with the patient's provider must be documented in the medical record including the time and date of the communication. Particularly note when the physician or health care provider visited the patient or if you had to call a physician or other provider for a problem. Record the information you communicated to the patient's physician or health care provider as well as the physician's response, your nursing actions, and the patient's response.

Most institutions are utilizing or in the process of implementing the electronic medical record (EMR) or electronic health record (EHR). The rules of documentation still apply, but additional safeguards will have to be considered. This is especially true when some of the health records are paper and some electronic. Both records will have to be accessed, coordinated, and made complete to manage and safeguard the patient. It is believed that the EHR will promote more accurate and safe record keeping.

Medication Errors

A study by the Institute of Medicine (IOM) reported that medication errors harmed 1.5 million people every year. The additional medical cost of treating drug-related injuries in the hospital was at least $ 3.5 billion per year. The study did not indicate whether the sources of the errors were nurses, physicians, and/or pharmacists. The reporting committee found that medication errors are common at every stage, from the writing of the prescription, to the filling of the prescription, to the administration of a drug and the monitoring of the patient's response (IOM, 2006). Claims involving medication errors are augmented when the nurse fails to record the medication administration properly, fails to recognize side effects or contraindications, or fails to ascertain a patient's allergies. Any initiative that improves patient safety also lowers the chance of someone being sued. At the same time, it sets a benchmark on which the standard of care may rest and thus becomes important for every nurse to know and follow.

The nurse's ability to listen to a patient or family member who notices that a medication is new, or recheck when anything such as color or amount seems unusual, may prevent a serious error. Many nurses feel rushed by the amount of work they are expected to accomplish, and they do not want to take extra time for anything. Making this check a priority will prove to be time well spent (Box 20.4). Dealing with an error and the consequences to the patient will take longer and will be more painful.

Although many medication errors do not cause permanent or serious damage to patients, there are certain medications that can. TJC standards require each institution to identify high-alert medications used in the institution and to initiate safety procedures for managing these medications (TJC, 2015a).

Whenever a medication error occurs, the source of the error and the system failure should be carefully investigated. TJC also requires that health care organizations have a plan for responding to adverse drug events and medication errors (e.g., sending reports to the Medication Error Reporting Program operated cooperatively by U.S. Pharmacopeia [USP] and the Institute for Safe Medication Practices) (IOM, 2006).

BOX 20.4 TIPS FOR BEING AT YOUR BEST WHEN ADMINISTERING MEDICATIONS

- Minimize distractions. It is important to avoid interruptions when administering medications to reduce the risk of making a medication error.
- Utilize a bar coding medication administration scanning system when available.
- Recognize fatigue. If you are fatigued, you are more likely to make mistakes. This is one of the reasons that double shifts or long shifts put patients at risk.
- Listen to your patients. Often they will tell you if what you are planning to do is different or unusual.
- Double check high-alert medications. Take the time to do a second check, and you may save yourself and your patient from a medication error.
- Ensure competence. Never do a procedure you do not know how to do at the appropriate standard of performance. It is better to admit you need help or supervision than to risk hurting someone.
- Be accountable. Never be afraid to admit you made a mistake. Prompt corrective action may stop or at least reduce patient harm.
- Take your time. Do not rush when you are especially busy because being hasty can result in errors. Set realistic priorities and ask for help.
- Keep current and up-to-date in your practice knowledge base. An article in a professional journal may keep patients safe and avoid a lawsuit.

Provide a Safe Environment

Patient safety is more and more recognized as a duty of the health care team and health care institutions. Providing a safe environment and implementing a fall reduction program were originally included in TJC's 2010 NPSGs (TJC, 2010). When a NPSG becomes a standard, the goal number is retired and is not used again. In 2010, TJC moved the goal to a standard for hospitals but kept it as a goal for long-term care facilities and home care. Ensuring patient safety includes many aspects. Nurses sometimes do not recognize the multiple roles they must play in this area. They are responsible for knowing how equipment should work and not using it if it is not functioning correctly; removing obvious hazards such as chemicals, which might be mistaken for medications; and making the environment free of hazards such as inappropriately placed furniture or equipment and spills on the floor. An additional preventive measure is knowing how to document correctly if an incident occurs, so that there cannot be a doubt regarding the facts of what happened and everything you did to protect the patient.

Patient Falls

Falls that cause serious patient injury are routinely among the Top 10 sentinel events voluntarily reported to TJC's Sentinel Event database, with the majority of falls occurring in acute care hospitals. The most common factors contributing to falls with injury are inadequate assessment, failure to communicate, failure to adhere to facility protocols and safety practices, inadequate staff supervision or staffing, lack of leadership, and physical environment deficiencies (TJC, 2015b). Additionally, the ECRI Institute (2009) reports a large number of falls in long-term care facilities and other nonhospital settings. Falls, particularly repeated falls, are serious problems and are often used as a measurement of nursing care (Dykes, 2009).

Much time and effort have been spent attempting to change patient care so that falls do not occur. Proposals coming out of such efforts range from total lack of restraints (Saufl, 2004), to comprehensive patient care plans (Dykes, 2009), to decreasing the number of certain types of medications (Haumschild et al., 2003). TJC has specific tools targeted toward preventing harm to patients as a result of falls

(TJC, 2015c). It is important to keep up with the latest information so as to prevent patient harm and avoid being caught defenseless in a claim for malpractice (Critical Thinking Box 20.5).

> **? CRITICAL THINKING BOX 20.5**
>
> What fall protocols have you observed in your clinical settings? How are they the same, and how are they different from each other? How are fall protocols in acute-care hospital settings different from long-term care settings?

Nurses are best able to defend themselves in these cases when their institution has a policy regarding protecting patients against falls, sometimes called a "fall protocol." These policies establish levels of risk in patients, such as age, confusion, sedation, and steps the nurse must take to protect the patient, such as side rails, soft restraints, or bed position. If the nurse follows such a protocol, it is difficult for a plaintiff to prove that the nurse fell below a standard of care. In developing such protocols, however, it is important to know the laws in your state, federal CMS guidelines, and TJC standards regarding restraints. Unnecessary and unsafe restraining of patients has become the focus of public and private attention, and restraint injuries can also be the basis of legal action.

Documentation is extremely important when a patient falls. Here are a few suggestions for documenting a patient fall situation; however, it is vital you follow the agency policy and procedural documentation guidelines where you are employed.

- Document the facts regarding how the fall was discovered, where the patient was found, and any other facts surrounding the fall. An example is to document that the patient was found beside the bed, with the side rails up, and the bed in the low position.
- Document the nursing assessment data, any obvious injuries, and nursing actions to maintain patient safety.
- Document what the patient says regarding the fall. A statement such as "I know you told me to put on the call light, but you all seemed so busy that I didn't want to bother you," can be of great benefit to the nurse. Of course, a patient's statement "I put on the call light, but nobody came" can have the opposite effect.
- Document whom you notified, such as the physician or the family.
- Document what was done for the patient, such as an examination, radiographs, orientation to surroundings, monitoring after the incident, restraints, and assistance with further ambulation.
- Document your adherence to any policies of the hospital regarding vulnerable patients or those at risk for falls.

In *Shaw v. Plantation Management*, a nurse found a patient on the floor with a puddle of liquid next to him. The patient stated that the liquid was urine from another patient and that this caused him to fall. The nurse assessed the patient and got him the medical attention that he needed. The patient later died after surgery for a broken hip. The nurse did not know what the liquid was, and she did not know whether or not the patient had actually urinated after he fell. The nurse only charted what she had actually seen and what she did. Her clear documentation later prevented the patient's family from being able to prove that the incident was caused by any negligence on behalf of the facility (*Shaw v. Plantation Management*, 2009).

Equipment Failure

Today many nurses feel they spend more time nursing equipment than they do patients. This can be true. What some nurses do not understand is that there is a certain standard of care connected with equipment. It must be used as directed by the manufacturer, and the nurse has a duty to know what that use is and to follow such directions. There is also a duty to make sure that the equipment is properly maintained and that records are kept of this maintenance. The equipment needs to be working properly and should not be used when a known defective condition exists. Additionally, the device must be available for use. For instance, in Case Study 4, the fact that the Ambu bag was not available can be viewed as a liability for either the nurse responsible for checking crash carts or the institution for not seeing that the carts are checked.

When there is a failure of a device or piece of equipment and a patient is injured, the focus should of course initially be on helping the patient. After that, it is extremely important that the device (e.g., catheter, pump, instrument) be sequestered and a clear record of its handling (chain of custody) be maintained. In a lawsuit, the nurse will need to prove that equipment failure, rather than human error, caused the injury. Part of the proof will rest in the piece of equipment itself. Therefore, one of the most important aspects of the defense will be not to lose or let go of the equipment or device before it is thoroughly evaluated by a neutral party after an incident. Often the manufacturer will ask for the equipment, but their interests might be adverse to yours to prove user error rather than equipment failure. Information regarding the failure can be shared, but never let the device or equipment out of the custody of the institution. In addition, the nurse should adhere to any institutional policies regarding incidents involving equipment failure.

Nurses may also have a duty to be sure their institution complies with the Safe Medical Device Act of 1990. This federal law requires that all medical device–related adverse incidents be reported to manufacturers and, in the case of death, to the U.S. Food and Drug Administration (FDA), within 10 days. The purpose of this act is to protect the public from devices that may be defective (Guido, 2013).

■ *Case study 5*

A 67-year-old woman with chronic obstructive pulmonary disease is having increasingly difficult respirations, increased cyanosis, and increased anxiety. She tells you she just cannot breathe. You have done all the measures for which you currently have orders, without her obtaining relief. It is 2 AM. You call the physician. She orders Valium 10 mg intramuscularly now. Even as a recent graduate, you know that Valium is contraindicated in a patient with this respiratory status. You call your supervisor, who tells you that Dr. Jones is a good physician and must know what she is doing. What should you do?

Failure to Assess Adequately, Monitor, and Obtain Assistance

Most often, the nurse should not delegate to another the responsibility for assessing and evaluating patient care and progress. If some portions of this duty are handled by others (e.g., another RN, LPN/LVN, unlicensed personnel), the nurse who is primarily responsible for the care of the patient must still be aware of the findings and confirm them when they indicate a change in patient condition or progress. Documentation of the changes and events surrounding the changes is critical. The accreditation standards from TJC specifically address improving the effectiveness of communication between caregivers when reporting changes in a patient's condition. Effective communication includes clear documentation of critical events.

In Case Study 5, there may also be liability for failure to challenge an inappropriate order. These areas are uncomfortable for many experienced nurses, not just for the recent graduate. Frequently, these situations involve challenging a physician or other health care professional. They require that the nurse have current and accurate information. They also require the difficult balance between assertiveness and diplomacy.

> It is not enough to identify problems. The nurse must identify the problems and contact the physician or other individuals to obtain appropriate care and follow up the chain of command as deemed necessary.

Most helpful in situations such as Case Study 5 is a policy that clearly delineates the chain of command for the institution. With a policy in place, the nurse can be clear about who must be notified about a potentially problematic order, and it can be documented appropriately. It is important the nurse be protected from any retaliation in such instances by the institution that stands to lose if the patient's safety is not put first.

Accurate documentation of the nursing assessment and of frequent monitoring will be required to prove what you have done. Flow charts and forms can be timesaving devices in this area. Electronic communications now make such time-consuming documentation more readily available. Documentation is especially important in the critical care setting and in the obstetric suite. The attachment of accurate times to such monitoring activities will be your best defense tool in many malpractice claims.

Failure to Communicate Adequately

Perhaps the most important role of everyone on the health care team is to communicate adequately. The patient's total care rests on this communication, whether it is verbal or written in the medical record.

> One of the most frequent claims against nurses in this area is the failure to communicate changes in the patient's condition to a professional who has a need to know.

Good communication is especially needed in acute-care settings during the night hours, as in Case Study 5. Communication is not always welcomed in the middle of the night and can be impaired because it is not face to face and because the receiver may not be fully awake and alert. TJC now requires a verification "read back" of all verbal and telephone orders (not limited to medication orders) by the person taking the order and the use of a standardized set of abbreviations, acronyms, and symbols throughout the organization. Thorough documentation of the communication will protect the nurse, but it should not be done defensively or thought of as a substitute for proper care.

Communication with certain hearing- and speech-impaired patients and with ethnically and culturally diverse patients will often provide a challenge to good nursing care. The Americans with Disabilities Act is a federal statute that has requirements for institutions rendering health care to have certain translators available for key health care interactions. The failure to do so may put the institution at risk for fines and penalties (*Freydel v. New York Hospital*, 2000).

Failure to Report

States have many statutes that require health care providers to report certain incidences or occurrences. If the provider fails to report as required, and a person is injured, there can be negligence per se, and no expert testimony will be needed to prove the case. In addition, both institutional and professional licensure can be affected. It is important that nurses be aware of the reporting statutes in the state in which they are practicing. In some states, it is not only a duty, but also the law to report certain incidences. The following are examples of such statutes involving a duty to report.

- A duty to self-report a criminal charge or conviction
- A duty to report other health care professionals whose behaviors are unprofessional and/or could cause harm to the public; this includes drug and alcohol abuse
- A duty to report evidence of child or adult or elder abuse and neglect, including any acts of a sexual nature against vulnerable (i.e., anesthetized) patients
- A duty to report certain communicable diseases
- A duty to report certain deaths under suspicious circumstances, including deaths during surgery

- A duty to report certain types of injuries that are or could be caused by violence
- A duty to report evidence of Medicare fraud
- Emergency Medical Treatment and Active Labor Act (EMTALA) violations

Nurses should know what to report, who should report, how the report should be accomplished, and to whom a report should be made. Institutional policies and Nurse Practice Acts on these topics are invaluable. In *State v. Brown*, criminal charges were brought against an emergency room nurse who failed to report suspected child abuse to a physician or agency when a 2-year-old boy was brought in with suspicious bruises. The trial court dismissed the charges on the grounds that the Missouri statute was unconstitutionally vague as to the term "reasonable cause to suspect"; however, the Missouri Supreme Court later reversed that decision, reinstating criminal charges against the nurse (*State v. Brown*, 2004).

Many nurses are afraid to report their employers, other professionals, or other agencies because of the possibility of retaliatory action against them. Many mandatory reporting statutes provide immunity to those who report in good faith. Some states have specific "whistleblower statutes" that not only protect nurses from retaliatory action but also may reward them. The content of the whistleblower statutes differs from state to state, so the nurse must find out whether one exists in his or her state of practice and learn what protection is provided. A federal statute, the False Claims Act, provides protection under certain situations for reporting Medicare fraud. Additionally, federal compliance standards require that institutions maintain a mechanism to report unlawful activities, such as a "hotline" where problems can be reported anonymously. In response to such reports, institutions must demonstrate that they responded appropriately and that they disciplined all individuals engaged in the illegal activities (Green, 2000) (Critical Thinking Box 20.6).

? CRITICAL THINKING BOX 20.6

Which states have "whistleblower" protection?

RELATED LEGAL CONCEPTS

Informed Consent

Consent is usually a defense to all of the aforementioned intentional torts. You cannot have a claim for assault and battery if the patient has given consent for the procedure. Likewise, there can be no invasion of privacy if the patient has given consent to share confidential information with someone else, such as his or her lawyer.

There is much confusion about informed consent in that many people believe that it must be a piece of paper with "Informed Consent" written on it. This is not always true.

> Informed consent in the health care setting is a process whereby a patient is informed of
> 1. The nature of the proposed care, treatment, services, medications, interventions, or procedures.
> 2. The potential benefits, risks, or side effects, including potential problems related to recuperation.
> 3. The likelihood of achieving care, treatment, and service goals.
> 4. Reasonable alternatives and their respective risks and benefits including the alternative of refusing all interventions (TJC, 2008a).

The nurse's role in the consent process is often confusing. It is the responsibility of the provider performing the procedure to provide the patient with information regarding risks, benefits, and alternatives. In some settings, the nurse may be responsible for obtaining the actual patient's signature on the informed consent form; however, this only occurs after the health care provider has fully explained and answered all of the patient's questions. In essence, the nurse is witnessing the patient's voluntary signature signifying informed consent before the procedure is performed. The form must be signed before the administration of preprocedure medications, which may alter the patient's judgment. Additionally, never obtain a patient's consent to a procedure that has not been fully explained to the patient by the provider.

> As advanced practice nurses perform more invasive procedures, the process of informing the patient of what is to occur is the advanced practice nurse's responsibility.

Consent forms must be signed when a patient is considered able or competent to make informed decisions and before the procedure is performed. The patient is the only person who may give consent if he or she is competent. Competency (also called "capacity") is defined differently from state to state, and the nurse should be aware of how it is defined in his or her state of practice. Competency is presumed, and therefore any claim of incompetence would have to be proved.

Some situations may require special consideration. An example would be a patient suffering from "sundowning" syndrome, who shows no signs of cognitive impairment during the day but is quite confused and/or agitated throughout the night. Although the patient may verbalize understanding of an upcoming procedure, and you believe that he is currently competent to sign a consent form, his competency could possibly be brought into question in a malpractice case if the record reflects periods of confusion.

Competent patients may always decline to give informed consent for a procedure, even if doing so may have serious consequences for their health status. This legal standard respects the fundamental liberty interest in personal autonomy protected by American jurisprudence (Moore, 1999). Consent may be withdrawn at any time before the procedure.

> Informed consent is not required if the procedure is necessary to save a life and is done during an emergency.

Advance Directives

All states have laws guiding the execution and enforcement of health care directives including living wills and medical powers of attorney. It is important to allow patients to direct the course of their care and treatment whenever possible; however, they must be protected from making harmful decisions when their cognitive status is impaired or fluctuates. States differ with regard to how consent can be given if the patient is incompetent or lacks capacity to make medical decisions. Advance directives such as a medical power of attorney or a living will may provide information about the patient's wishes. These documents allow individuals to prepare in advance for possible incompetence by formalizing their wishes in writing about their further health care decisions. The living will is used to allow a competent adult to direct what he or she wishes in regard to health care upon becoming incompetent.

Often used in conjunction with the living will is the "durable" or "medical" power of attorney. This document allows the competent adult to appoint a specific person to authorize care if he or she becomes incompetent. The durable power of attorney does not usually become effective until a person loses competency. This document may be used in conjunction with or without a living will (see Chapter 19 for more information on advance directives). Congress passed the Patient Self-Determination Act of 1990 requiring hospitals to inform their patients of the availability of advance directives. State law defines the required wording for these documents and any other formalities necessary in their preparation. Because patients must be educated on these laws and documents, so should nurses. If not, you could be caught in a violation of the law at a crucial moment of life and death.

If a family challenges a living will or a medical power of attorney, a nurse will need to go through the administrative chain of command. A general rule is for nurses to follow the advance directives unless or until there is a court order to do otherwise. This means that families need to obtain legal services and go to court to overturn or challenge these documents. All persons, no matter what their ages, should complete advance directives. The Terri Schiavo case is a sad demonstration of the difficulties faced by families when there are no documented advance directives and family members differ in beliefs about what should or should not be done. Questions then arise as to whether acts or omissions of health care providers prolong life or prolong the dying process. Judges are certainly not the preferred ultimate decision makers.

When a patient does not have an advance directive and is incompetent, there are state laws that give guidance regarding who can act as a *surrogate decision maker*. Parents must usually sign for minor children. Spouses or immediate family members may sign for unconscious adults. In other instances, if no one is available or designated, a court can appoint in a very short time someone for the purpose of making medical decisions. A special consent under stricter standards applies to research studies, and often surrogates may not be able to make such decisions (Truog, 2002).

Documentation of informed refusal should be accurate, complete, and in accordance with the policies and procedures for your facility. It should include the results of a mental status assessment to show that the patient was neurologically and psychologically capable of refusing treatment. Clearly document the information that was provided to the patient, quoting the patient's reason(s) for refusing treatment, any questions he or she may have had, and your responses (Smith, 2004).

CRIMINAL ACTIONS

Nurses who violate specific criminal statutes (such as those having to do with illegal drug use, negligent homicide, and assault and battery) risk criminal prosecution. Conviction of certain types of crimes must be reported to the state board of nursing and will usually result in a review of licensure status. You must be aware of the rules in the state in which you practice.

What Criminal Acts Pose a Risk to the Nurse?
Theft and Misappropriation of Property

- Protect the patient's property by thoroughly documenting and locking up all valuables when the patient is admitted to the facility.
- Keep all items and property owned by the facility at the facility. This includes tape, bandages, and pens, to name a few.

Sometimes, nurses fail to protect a patient's property adequately and thus open themselves up to claims of theft. Many patients bring valuables to health care facilities or think that they do. It is helpful to give clear notice to the patients before admittance to leave valuables at home. A thorough and documented list of property on admission is imperative to prevent such claims, as is the locking up of valuables. When dentures and other property have not been adequately stored or monitored, the nurse may be held responsible.

Another aspect of this problem is stealing from the employer. Because of the extensive and costly nature of this problem, many employers have developed elaborate systems to discourage theft. With an ever-increasing focus on lowering health care costs, those costs related to employee theft will not be tolerated. Occasionally, nurses accidentally leave the job with tape, bandages, or other supplies in their pockets. These should be returned. Better yet, establishing a routine of checking your pockets before leaving for home will help reduce this risk. A nurse should never intentionally take property belonging to an employer.

Nursing Practice Violations

Scope-of-practice violations that result in the death of a patient may be the result of nurses performing tasks or procedures that the state board of nursing has not accepted as being within the appropriate scope for nurses, or these violations could be a result of doing actions that have been approved for advanced practice nurses only. In some states these violations and other possible violations of the Nurse Practice Act are misdemeanors, but in other states they may be felonies.

In rare cases, charges of murder or negligent homicide may be filed against the nurse (Kowalski & Horner, 1998). In November 2000, the State of Hawaii convicted an individual of manslaughter in the death of a nursing home patient for permitting the progression of pressure ulcers without seeking appropriate medical help (Di Maio & Di Maio, 2002). In November 2006, the Wisconsin State Attorney General's Office charged a nurse with "neglect of a patient causing great bodily harm" when she accidentally connected an epidural infusion bag instead of an antibiotic to an IV, resulting in the death of the teenage mother during childbirth. The felony charge was later reduced to two misdemeanors through a plea bargain (ASQ, 2007).

This should be of concern to all nurses, because mistakes will always occur in medicine. To err is human. According to Kohn and colleagues (2000), "It may be part of human nature to err, but it is also part of human nature to create solutions, find better alternatives, and meet the challenges ahead" (p. 15). If fear of criminal prosecution and prison is added to these personal responses, how can we believe thoughtful, caring people will continue in the profession? As Curtin (1997) asks, "What conceivable social good will be achieved by putting these nurses in jail?" (Kowalski & Horner, 1998, p. 127).

Violations of the Food and Drugs Act

Participating in any activity with illegal drugs or the misappropriation or improper use of legal drugs may result in criminal action against the nurse. Conviction for a crime in this area will almost always result in action against a nurse's license. As described earlier, there is a high incidence of substance abuse in the medical profession, so nurses need to be aware of the risks and avoid them. Writing prescriptions for drugs without the authority to do so is a criminal activity. Obtaining drugs illegally for friends and/or family needs, even if they seem legitimate, will still have criminal consequences.

RISK MANAGEMENT AND QUALITY IMPROVEMENT

How Do I Protect Myself and My Patient From All These Risks?

The safety of patients often involves many different formalized processes in institutions. One involves quality and goes by many names, such as "quality assurance" (QA), "continuous quality management" (CQM), or "continuous quality improvement" (CQI). In relationship to nursing practices, *peer review* is the process of using nurses to evaluate the quality of nursing care. This means that you, as a professional nurse, will be continuously involved in evaluating the care that you and other nurses provide. In the past, this was only done through retroactive review of care using techniques such as nursing audits to evaluate care already given. The current focus is on looking for ways to do better all the time. Examples of activities that may be involved in this process include the following:

- Evaluation of what nurses are doing for patients
- Policy and procedure development
- Staff preparation, competency, and skill documentation
- Continuing education and certification

- Employee evaluations
- Ongoing monitoring, such as infection control and risk management systems

TJC requires quality measures that meet four criteria identified to produce the greatest positive impact on patient outcomes when hospital agencies demonstrate improvement: (1) research—evidence-based care process improve outcomes; (2) proximity—performing the care process is closely connected to patient outcomes; (3) accuracy—measure assesses whether or not the care process has actually been provided; and (4) adverse effects—implementing the measure has little or no chance of causing unintended adverse effects (TJC, 2015d).

Risk management is a process that becomes involved when incidents or untoward events occur that may pose a financial risk or risk of lawsuit to the institution. This department, through a risk manager, will often take the first step, which is to gather evidence surrounding the event in "anticipation of litigation." Such evidence will include interviews with those involved and physical evidence such as relevant documents. If you are being interviewed, understand that a truthful accounting is the most important aspect of this process and will best serve the institution and you.

Risk management will often then evaluate how to prevent a recurrence by changing systems that have broken down to have allowed the adverse occurrence. This might mean setting a new standard that can then be evaluated and ensured through a quality assurance process.

One tool used by a risk management team is the *incident or occurrence report*. Incident reports generate many legal concerns, because in most states they must be produced in a lawsuit and can be used as evidence against individuals and the institution (Guido, 2013). Therefore extreme caution should be used when completing an incident report, and only the person directly involved should objectively document the facts. Conclusions, opinions, defensiveness, and judgment or blame of others have absolutely no place in this document or process. In addition, the form should never be used for punitive reasons, because this will almost certainly increase the possibility that the report will not be completed honestly if at all (Kohn et al., 2000).

Although you would not mention in the medical record that you filled out an incident report, the person involved in the incident should make the same objective, factual documentation of an incident in the medical record. Lack of documentation in the face of a known occurrence will always be considered a cover-up and will thus be extremely detrimental to any subsequent legal action. Never speculate about who or what caused an incident, because this may inadvertently give the plaintiff "causation" proof, which may not be true.

An example of risk management and quality assurance working together would be the following. A fire breaks out in the operating room, and a patient is burned. Immediately after this event, a risk manager might be notified through a telephone call and then later in an incident report. The risk manager would come immediately to the scene and collect all items and/or equipment involved in the fire (evidence) to determine the cause of the fire. He or she would also interview those who saw the fire (witnesses) to determine facts involved. The risk manager may take specific actions to assist the patient and/or family, in addition to giving advice to those involved regarding documentation of the event and/or communications. Sometimes financial settlements are made very early to avoid the costly process of a lawsuit. Risk management might identify ways to prevent another occurrence, such as removal of all alcohol-based skin preparations from the operating room. The quality-assurance department may then periodically evaluate this standard to ensure the continued safety of patients.

Risk managers usually work very closely with insurance companies that cover institutions and their employees for all types of financial risk, including malpractice and general liability. The defense and prevention of many claims start with good risk management. Yet every individual on the health care team who identifies a risk to patient safety and does something constructive to correct it must also make such efforts. Several simple risk management actions by nurses can often prevent a lawsuit. These include the following:

- Approaching angry patients with an apology and an offer to help (Gutheil et al., 1984). Moving toward the patient who has experienced an unexpected outcome rather than away is always the best policy. Isolation and a feeling of abandonment in the face of an untoward event can only augment the feeling that a wrong was done.
- Sharing uncertainties and bringing patients' expectations down to a realistic level during the informed consent process can also prevent claims based on disappointment that an outcome is not perfect (Gutheil et al., 1984).
- Refusing to participate in hospital gossip, to joust in the medical record, or to judge others on the medical team will contribute to an atmosphere of teamwork and compassion rather than competition, blame, and retaliation. The latter can ultimately contribute to unsafe patient care. An inadvertent negative remark to patients and families about a physician, the pharmacy, the laboratory, or other nurses is very frequently the genesis of a lawsuit. Such remarks are often based on limited knowledge and personal bias. Making such remarks could cause you to end up as a witness in a malpractice claim against your peers and/or other medical team members. This is seldom a desirable position for anyone.

Malpractice Insurance

One of the more controversial topics for nurses involves the question whether to purchase individual malpractice insurance policies. There is often misinformation about what these individual policies will do or cover, and there is little substantiation for what most authors say. In addition, insurance companies sometimes use scare tactics to induce nurses to purchase their products.

As the nurse's role continues to expand, so does the amount of liability exposure in a medical malpractice claim. Careful consideration should be given to a decision about whether or not to carry an individual malpractice insurance policy. An informed nurse should at least know what questions to ask.

What About Individual Malpractice Insurance?

Some individual nurse policies claim that you can prevent settlement of a claim if you wish to do so (have a consent clause). However, a close reading of the policy might demonstrate that if the case is then lost at trial or settled for more than the insurance company wished to offer, the company has the right to collect that difference and the cost of defense from you. Therefore the consent you have a right to withhold may have very little meaning.

The cost for a nurse to purchase an individual malpractice policy is based on the area of nursing and the state of practice. Check your professional journals and your professional associations for insurance companies that offer malpractice insurance for nurses.

What Is Institutional Coverage?

Almost all health care corporations or institutions carry insurance policies that specifically cover acts or omissions of their employed nurses. This includes cases in which only the institution is named under the previously described *respondeat superior* doctrine or when an individual nurse employee is named. Most individual personal nursing malpractice policies are secondary to this policy. This means that they cannot be used in any manner if the institutional policy is used to cover the claim. It is not correct to assume that you can have your personal attorney present to represent your personal interests in addition to the institutional attorney. Even if you could, having two attorneys will often divide the defense.

The attorney selected by the health care institution to represent the institution is ethically required to represent both your interests and those of the institution. In addition, the institution's interests are rarely, if ever, adverse to yours.

The claim that an institution will insure you but then turn around and sue you is belied by the fact that one cannot find statistics to verify this common assumption. Institutions spend millions of dollars on insurance specifically to cover the acts of nurses. In addition, if institutions sued the nurses working for them, they would not retain many nurses.

It is true that if an employee commits a criminal act that by its nature is outside the scope of the employment, such as forced sexual intimacies with a patient, an institution may not defend the employee or cover costs. In this regard, however, criminal acts are not insurable under laws in most states and therefore are not covered by any policy (Simpson, 1998).

What Should I Ask About Institutional Coverage?

There are certain things that a prudent nurse concerned about coverage should do. All nurses should request and have a right to receive a document that provides the following information regarding their employer's insurance coverage for them:

- The name of the institution's insurance carrier, the limits of the policy, and the rating of the insurance company (Best Rating A+++ is the highest)
- Whether they are covered for all acts occurring within the scope of their employment and during the time they are employed
- The acts for which they do not have coverage
- Whether the hospital will cover them if they need to appear before the state board of nursing in relation to a malpractice claim. If not, an individual insurance policy that clearly does cover them may be valuable.
- How the nurse is covered by the institutional employer. This is particularly important if the nurse is an independent practitioner and/or in an extended practice role.

What Happens When I Go to Court?

Sometimes, despite all your efforts, you find yourself in litigation as a defendant. Know that very few claims go to trial. Therefore you do not need to picture yourself in a setting from *Law and Order* with a prosecutor tearing you apart. In reality, the majority of personal injury lawsuits are either dismissed or settled out of court, usually after an investigatory process called "discovery" (Fish et al., 1990). This involves exchanging information about the case in the form of written questions called *interrogatories*, as well as a recorded oral questioning process called a *deposition*.

Depositions are oral statements given under oath and are extremely important in any negligence claim. Depositions are used to evaluate the merits of the case, the credibility of the witnesses, and the strength of the defendants. Cases are sometimes won or lost in this process; thus with the help of your attorney, you must be prepared. If you have not been offered the chance to meet with your attorney before your deposition, request the time to do so. Being prepared ahead of time can have a significant effect on your performance under stress.

Depositions occur in a less formal setting than the courtroom. Attorneys for both sides will be present. The attorney questioning you will be the attorney for either the plaintiff or for the other defendants, or both, and their interests may be adversarial to yours. Your attorney can object to certain questions, but generally speaking you will be expected to answer the questions to the best of your recollection because in the deposition there is no judge to rule on the objections.

Remember, in a deposition you are there to answer questions in a truthful manner to the best of your recollection.

A lawsuit can be a very disconcerting and disheartening process. Your ability to realize this and not to feel alone in the process is extremely important. Often institutions mandate that persons involved in litigation receive counseling to help them resolve the anger and depression that almost inevitably occurs. Be sure to use the resources available to you, including your lawyer. Your risk management team is often a good resource as well and can usually answer questions or help resolve problems you might have in relation to the case. Remember the truth of the old adage that "this too will pass."

LEGAL ISSUES AFFECTING NURSING

Because developments and advances in medical and nursing care occur constantly, many areas of practice do not have firm rules to follow when making decisions. Changes in health care delivery and society's values have sparked controversy about a variety of issues.

Health Care Costs and Payment Issues

One example of a controversial issue is third-party reimbursement, or the right of an individual nurse, usually a nurse practitioner, to be paid directly by insurance companies for care given. Medicare has passed rules that allow nurse practitioners to bill independently under their own provider number. This is a very important step in the field of independent practice for nurses, because many health care insurers follow the lead of Medicare as related to billing issues.

In relation to the right to bill, all nurses need to understand billing and reimbursement rules so that they cannot be accused of participating in fraudulent billing schemes. For instance, although a bill can be generated for certain follow-up care performed by nurses in the outpatient clinic, as services rendered "incident to" what the physician does, there are strict requirements of physician involvement that nurses must understand. Nurse practitioners need to be careful that physicians with whom they collaborate are not also illegally billing for the nurse's services.

The seven most frequent areas where nurses can inadvertently become involved in fraud and abuse claims are the following:

1. Questionable accuracy and monitoring of physician visit coding
2. Improper use of diagnosis codes
3. Failure to provide patient care or providing patient care that is sloppy
4. Anesthesia services
5. Unneeded critical or acute-care services
6. Billing for physician assistant services
7. Improper billing of nursing or physician services (Nelson, 2005)

To avoid these areas, it is important to know about and understand your institution's compliance plan and to report suspected abuses through the required hotline or directly to nursing administration (Green, 2000).

From another perspective, the high cost of health care is also resulting in the proliferation of health care workers with less training and education than nurses, who can be hired for less money. Often these unlicensed workers have no laws circumscribing their practice and are doing tasks that have traditionally been done by RNs or LPN/LVNs, such as administering medications and giving injections.

This is an important issue for nurses, especially when asked to supervise such workers and/or compete for positions in the health care market.

Controversial legislative changes have been made in an attempt to address some of these problems. In response to concerns about whether or not increased acuity of patients, increased caregiver workload, and declining levels of training among patient-care personnel have threatened the quality of patient care, California passed Assembly Bill 394. This bill set a minimum nurse–patient ratio in acute-care general, special, and psychiatric hospitals (Lang et al., 2004). A year after it went into effect, nurses were battling Governor Arnold Schwarzenegger to keep what they fought so hard to obtain—an RN-to-patient ratio of 6 to 1 in 2004 and 5 to 1 in 2005. The controversy seems to stem from the difficulty of maintaining ratios "at all times" and in finding enough nurses to fulfill the ratios.

Related topics involve practice models and case management. Practice models involve attempts by institutions to answer what types and ratios of health care providers should constitute a patient-care team. Case management looks at how patient-care teams can best derive better outcomes and continuity for patients while effectively managing the variable costs of care delivery. Institutional decisions on these matters become policies and thus the "laws" under which you must deliver patient care.

Your knowledge of the issues, participation in the processes, and support for legislation and policies that are favorable for your profession and for patient care will be important when your state and/or institution decides such issues. Professional behavior includes concern with and participation in the direction that health care, and particularly nursing care, will take in the future.

Health Care Delivery Issues

Changes made in the types of systems used to deliver health care and in the techniques used by the systems have created many concerns for nurses. Hospitals and other expensive acute-care settings are giving way to outpatient clinics and same-day surgery centers. This means that people are being sent home while still acutely ill to take care of themselves or to be cared for by relatives without the benefit of hospital nursing services. This makes the nurse's role in discharge planning and patient education extremely important to prevent deterioration of certain health or surgical conditions in the home. In addition, it means that home health care nurses are routinely organizing care that formerly was rendered only in hospitals. For example, respirators in the home are not unusual. With this change, however, come more independent responsibilities for nurses. Responsibility can translate into liability.

Telephone nursing triage and telemedical nursing care present new and unusual legal concerns because of the difficulties of providing accurate long-distance care and the independent nature of these tasks. Although these nurses bring nursing care to many areas that have not had access to this care in the past, selecting appropriately prepared individuals to provide the care and educating them to function effectively when they cannot see the patient are challenging tasks.

HMOs and other forms of prepaid health care have helped reduce the rapidly growing costs of health care through a process called *utilization review*. Nurses hired to do this review are often asked to make judgments regarding whether or not a patient should be discharged. Early discharge of patients and limits on insurance reimbursements for certain allowable medications, equipment, and external services have sometimes caused ethical and legal problems for health care professionals.

Past laws protecting the HMOs from malpractice claims when patients were harmed because of flawed utilization review practices are now being challenged. There is a growing public concern that managed care organizations are making large profits while patients covered under their programs are not receiving adequate care.

The many changes occurring in the workplace often create levels of confusion and frustration, which make it more difficult to focus on the quality of the care being given on a day-to-day basis. These issues are examples of how legal issues interweave with all the other events in your professional life. Nurses must remain involved in these matters to stay aware of how their legal responsibilities are influenced by them.

Issues About Life-and-Death Decisions

Controversial ethical issues surrounding life and death also, of course, present controversial legal issues. Scientific research and new technologies can blur the line between life and death. As a nurse, you can often find yourself in the center of such controversies, so you need to be very aware of your state's laws at least on the following subjects.

Abortions

Where can abortions be performed? Who can perform them? When can an abortion be performed? Under what conditions? Under what, if any, conditions can teenagers obtain an abortion without parental consent?

Fetal Rights

If a fetus is born alive, what rights does it have? What rights do the parents have? What rights do health care workers have? What are the laws surrounding fetal death and/or the cessation of life-preserving treatments?

Human Experimentation or Research

What can be done legally with the products of conception? What types of consent are necessary to enroll a patient in research studies? What types of boards and oversight must be involved to approve and monitor human research studies?

Patient Rights

What rights do patients in your state have in relationship to medical records, medical information, giving consent, participating in their care, suing providers, dictating issues surrounding their death, donating organs, being protected from abuse, receiving emergency treatment, being protected from the practice of unlicensed providers, transplantation of organs, accessibility of the disabled to health care, privacy, and confidentiality?

CONCLUSION

As time goes on, laws will change and new areas will arise that nursing will have to address. Continuing education, critical thinking, and an open mind will help you to learn about, and deal with, the legal issues that will touch your professional life daily. Get involved whenever possible with patient safety, quality, and risk management processes in your institutions, and become familiar with your state's Nurse Practice Act and advisory opinions. Be someone who has an educated opinion about conflicts inherent in medicine and nursing (see the relevant websites and online resources at the end of this chapter). Take the opportunity to visit the hearings conducted by your state's board of nursing and by the state legislature. By becoming involved with the legal and disciplinary process, you will be much more aware of how you can protect yourself and your patients, and influence the direction of health care issues. After concluding this chapter, it is hoped that you also feel more confident when faced with "the law."

RELEVANT WEBSITES AND ONLINE RESOURCES

American Nurses Association (2016)
Retrieved from www.nursingworld.org.

Centers for Disease Control and Prevention (2016)
Retrieved from www.cdc.gov.

Centers for Medicare & Medicaid Services (2016)
Retrieved from www.cms.gov.

Institute for Healthcare Improvement (2016)
Retrieved from www.ihi.org.

National Academies of Sciences, Engineering, and Medicine (2016)
Retrieved from https://www.nationalacademies.org/hmd/.

National Center for Biotechnology Information (2016)
Retrieved from http://www.ncbi.nlm.nih.gov/.

U. S. National Library of Medicine (2016)
Retrieved from www.pubmed.gov.

National Council of State Boards of Nursing (2016)
Retrieved from www.ncsbn.org.

Nursys online verification (2016)
Retrieved from www.nursys.com.

National Network of Libraries of Medicine (2016)
Resources for members of the National Network of Libraries of Medicine. Retrieved from www.nnlm.gov.

National Patient Safety Foundation (2016)
Retrieved from www.npsf.org.

The Joint Commission (2016)
Retrieved from www.jointcommission.org.

U.S. Department of Health and Human Services (2016)
Agency for Healthcare Research and Quality. Retrieved from http://www.ahrq.gov/clinic/epcix.htm.

U.S. Department of Health and Human Services (2016)
Retrieved from www.hhs.gov.

U.S. Department of Health and Human Services (2016)
The Data Bank: National practitioner healthcare integrity and protection. Retrieved from http://www.npdb-hipdb.hrsa.gov.

U.S. Department of Veterans Affairs (2016)
VA National Center for Patient Safety. Retrieved from www.patientsafety.va.gov.

BIBLIOGRAPHY

Annas, G. J. (2003). HIPAA regulations—A new era of medical-record privacy? *New England Journal of Medicine, 348,* 486–1490.

American Society for Quality (ASQ). (2007). *Nurse charged with felony in fatal medical error.* Retrieved from http://asq.org/qualitynews/qnt/execute/displaySetup?newsID=1056.

Brent, N. (2001). *Nurses and the law* (2nd ed.). New York: Saunders.

Curtin, L. L. (1997). When negligence becomes homicide. *Nursing Management, 28,* 7–8.

Di Luigi, K. (2004). What it takes to be an expert witness. *RN, 67,* 65–66 (2004).

Di Maio, V. J., & Di Maio, T. G. (2002). Homicide by decubitus ulcers. *American Journal of Forensic Medicine and Pathology, 23,* 1–4.

Dykes, P. C., et al. (2009). Why do patients in acute care hospitals fall? Can falls be prevented? *Journal of Nursing Administration, 39*(6), 299–304.

ECRI Institute. (2009). *Falls.* Retrieved from https://www.ecri.org/components/HRC/Pages/SafSec2.aspx.

Fish, R. M., Ehrhardt, M. E., & Fish, B. (1990). *Malpractice: Managing your defense* (2nd ed.). Montvale, NJ: Medical Economics Books.

Freydel v. New York Hospital, No. 97 Civ. 7926 (SHS), January 4, 2000.

Green, E. (2000). Creating an effective corporate compliance program. *Drug Benefit Trend, 12,* 37–38.

Guido, G. (2013). *Legal and ethical issues in nursing* (6th ed.). Upper Saddle River, NJ: Prentice Hall.

Gutheil, T. G., Bursztajn, H., & Brodsky, A. (1984). Malpractice prevention through the sharing of uncertainty: Informed consent and the therapeutic alliance. *New England Journal of Medicine, 311,* 49–51. http://dx.doi.org/10.1056/NEJM198407053110110.

Harvey v. Mid-coast Hospital, 36 F.Supp. 2d 32 (D. Maine 1999).

Haumschil, M., et al. (2003). Clinical and economic outcomes of a fall-focused pharmaceutical intervention program. *American Journal of Health-System Pharmacy, 60,* 1029–1032.

Institute of Medicine. (2006). *New medication errors injure 1.5 million people and cost billions of dollars annually.* Retrieved from http://iom.nationalacademies.org/~/media/Files/Report%20Files/2006/Preventing-Medication-Errors-Quality-Chasm-Series/medicationerrorsnew.ashx.

Kohn, L. T., Corrigan, J. M., & Donaldson, M. S. (2000). *To err is human: Building a safer health system.* Washington, DC: National Academies Press.

Kowalski, K., & Horner, M. D. (1998). A legal nightmare. Denver nurses indicted. *American Journal of Maternal/Child Nursing, 23,* 125–129.

Lang, T. A., et al. (2004). Nurse–patient ratios: A systematic review on the effects of nurse staffing on patient, nurse, employee and hospital outcomes. *Journal of Nursing Administration, 34,* 326–327.

Moore, R. (1999). A guide to the assessment and care of the patient whose medical decision-making capacity is in question. *Medscape General Medicine, 10,* E7.

National Council of State Boards of Nursing. (2011a). *Licensure.* Retrieved from https://www.ncsbn.org/licensure.htm.

National Council of State Boards of Nursing. (2011b). *Substance use disorder in nursing: A resource manual and guidelines for alternative and disciplinary monitoring programs.* Retrieved from https://www.ncsbn.org/SUDN_11.pdf.

National Council of State Boards of Nursing. (2014). *What you need to know about substance use disorder in nursing.* Retrieved from https://www.ncsbn.org/SUD_Brochure_2014.pdf.

National Council of State Boards of Nursing. (2015). *NCSBN introduces online public access to NURSYS (letter).* Retrieved from https://www.ncsbn.org/8581.htm.

National Council of State Boards of Nursing. (2015). *Nurse Licensure Compact.* Retrieved from https://www.ncsbn.org/nlc.htm.

National Council of State Boards of Nursing. (2016). *NURSYS.com—e-verify.* Retrieved from https://www.nursys.com/.

National League for Nursing (NLN). (2008). *Workforce to practice in 21st-century.* New York: technology-rich health care environment. Retrieved from http://www.nln.org/docs/default-source/professional-development-programs/preparing-the-next-generation-of-nurses.pdf?sfvrsn=6.

National Practitioner Data Bank. (NPDB). (2010). *Fact sheet on the National Practitioner Data Bank.* Retrieved from https://www.ire.org/media/uploads/files/datalibrary/npdb/factsheet.pdf.

National Practitioner Data Bank. (NPDB). (2014). *NPDB Research Statistics for 2004-2014.* Retrieved from http://www.npdb.hrsa.gov/resources/npdbstats/npdbStatistics.jsp#contentTop.

Nelson, R. (2005). Staffing in California one year later. *American Journal of Nursing, 105,* 25z–26z.

Posgar, G. D. (2007). *Legal aspects of health care administration* (10th ed.). Sudbury, MA: Jones and Bartlett.

Robertson v. Provident House, 576 So. 2d 992 (La. 1991).

Saufl, N. (2004). Restraints use in falls prevention. *Journal of PeriAnesthesia Nursing, 19*(6), 433–436. http://dx.doi.org/10.1016/j.jopan.2004.10.002.

Shaw v. Plantation Management, 2009 WL 838680 (La. App., March 27, 2009), cited in Patient's Fall: Solid Nursing Documentation Afterward, Negligence Lawsuit Dismissed. *Legal Eagle Eye Newsletter, 17*(5), 2009. Retrieved from https://casetext.com/case/shaw-v-plantation-mgmt.

Shinn, L. J. (n.d.). Yes, you can be sued, ANA continuing education: The nursing risk management series—an overview of risk management. Retrieved from http://ana.nursingworld.org/mods/archive/mod310/cerm1ful.htm.

Simpson, K. R. (1998). Should nurses purchase their own professional liability insurance? *American Journal of Maternal/Child Nursing, 23,* 122–123.

Smith, L. S. (2004). Documenting refusal of treatment. *Nursing, 34,* 79.

State v. Brown, 140 S.W.3d 51 (Mo. 2004) No. SC85582. Retrieved from http://law.justia.com/cases/missouri/supreme-court/2004/sc-85582-1.html.

Sullivan, G. H. (2004). Does your charting measure up? *RN, 17,* 61–65.

Texas Board of Nursing (Texas BON). (2010). *Examination information.* Retrieved from www.bon.state.tx.us/olv/examination.html.

The Joint Commission. (2010). *2010 National Patient Safety Goals.* Retrieved from http://www.hcpro.com/ACC-239979-851/The-Joint-Commission-announces-2010-National-Patient-Safety-Goals.html.

The Joint Commission. (2015a). *2016 National Patient Safety Goals.* Retrieved from http://www.jointcommission.org/standards_information/npsgs.aspx.

The Joint Commission. (2015b). *Sentinel event alert.* Retrieved from http://www.jointcommission.org/assets/1/18/SEA_55.pdf.

The Joint Commission. (2015c). *Targeted solutions tool for preventing falls.* Retrieved from http://www.centerfortransforminghealthcare.org/tst_pfi.aspx.

The Joint Commission. (2015d). *Facts about accountability measures.* Retrieved from http://www.jointcommission.org/facts_about_accountability_measures/.

Tolson, D., & Morley, J. E. (2012). Physical restraints: Abusive and harmful. [Editorial]. *Journal of the American Medical Directors Association, 13*(4), 311–313. http://dx.doi.org/10.1016/j.jamda.2012.02.004.

Truog, R. (2002). *Inadequacies in use of informed consent may limit potential for research in intensive care,* 15th Annual Congress of European Society of Intensive Care Medicine. Barcelona, Spain. September 19–October 2, 2002.

Contemporary Nursing Practice

21

Cultural and Spiritual Awareness

Peter G. Melenovich, PhD, RN, CNE

ⓔ http://evolve.elsevier.com/Zerwekh/nsgtoday/.

A nation's culture resides in the hearts and in the soul of its people.
Mahatma Gandhi

Our communities need culturally competent nursing care.

After completing this chapter, you should be able to:

- Define cultural competence.
- List practice issues related to cultural competence.
- Identify challenges in defining spirituality.
- Determine the cultural and spiritual beliefs of patients in the health care setting.
- Assess the spiritual needs of patients in the health care setting.

CULTURE AND SPIRITUALITY

What Is Meant by Cultural Competence?

In today's global society, cultural competence is necessary for excellence in nursing care. People can travel like never before. Nurses are connecting to patients through the Internet. Medical "tourism" is now a reality. Individualizing the care nurses provide to patients is dependent on a thorough understanding of a person's cultural identification. These factors demonstrate the need for nurses to understand cultural and spiritual differences among themselves and others.

The American Nurses Association (ANA) affirms in the *Code of Ethics* the necessity for the nurse to be sensitive to individual needs: "The need for and right to health care is universal, transcending all individual differences. Nurses consider the needs and respect the values of each person in every professional relationships and setting ..." (ANA, 2015).

Dr. Margaret Leininger, considered a top authority on culture care diversity, proposed that cultural understanding would allow for peaceful relations among groups of people (Leininger, 2007). Some considered this philosophy so important that Dr. Leininger was nominated for the Nobel Peace Prize. Cultural competence is essential for nurses.

But what exactly is cultural competence? It is defined as "developing an awareness of one's own existence, sensations, thoughts, and environment without letting it have an undue influence on those from other backgrounds; demonstrating knowledge and understanding of the patient's culture; accepting and respecting cultural differences; adapting care to be congruent with the patient's culture" (Purnell & Paulanka, 2008, p.6).

> The culturally competent nurse has an enhanced ability to provide quality care, which fosters better patient understanding of the plan of care.

"Inattention to cultural competence in patient care leads, at best, to suboptimal patient outcomes and, at worst, to active harm," says Carla Serlin, PhD, RN, director of ANA's Ethnic/Racial Minority Fellowship Programs. "When we fail to address issues of difference such as language, ethnicity, and race, our patients will have lower levels of compliance with care instructions and longer hospital stays" (as cited in Stewart, 1998, p.1). Culturally competent nurses are accountable for assessing and recognizing not only the differences but also the variation of being the same.

The mnemonic CULTURE, developed by Zerwekh (2016), can help nurses to assess and improve their level of cultural competence (Box 21.1). In addition, nurses need to use effective cultural interviewing questions, which are best if left semistructured and open-ended. Spector (2000) has identified nine suggestions for enhancing communication when gathering cultural data (Box 21.2).

What Practice Issues Are Related to Cultural Competence?
Barriers to Cultural Competence

Two categories of barriers to cultural competence exist: provider barriers and system barriers (Mazanec & Tyler, 2003). Provider barriers are those that a nurse may have, including lack of information about a culture's customs regarding health care. System barriers are those that exist in an agency, because the agency's structure and policies are not designed to support cultural diversity (McGibbon et al., 2008).

BOX 21.1   CULTURE—A NURSING APPROACH

Consider your own cultural biases and how these affect your nursing care.
Understand the need to recognize cultural implications in planning and implementing nursing care.
Learn how to use cultural assessment tools.
Treat patients with dignity and respect.
Use sensitivity in providing culturally competent care.
Recognize opportunities to provide specific culturally based nursing care.
Evaluate your own previous encounters with patients from other cultures and backgrounds.

Zerwekh, J. (2016). *CULTURE: A mnemonic for assessing and improving cultural competence.* Chandler, AZ: Nursing Education Consultants, Inc.

> ## BOX 21.2 NINE SUGGESTIONS FOR GATHERING CULTURAL DATA
>
> 1. Determine the patient's level of fluency in English, and arrange for an interpreter if needed.
> 2. Ask how the patient prefers to be addressed.
> 3. Allow the patient to choose seating for comfortable personal space and eye contact.
> 4. Avoid body language that may be offensive or misunderstood.
> 5. Speak directly to the patient, whether an interpreter is present or not.
> 6. Choose a speech rate and style that promotes understanding and demonstrates respect for the patient.
> 7. Avoid slang, technical jargon, and complex sentences.
> 8. Use open-ended questions or questions phrased in several ways to obtain information.
> 9. Determine the patient's reading ability before using written materials in the teaching process.

Spector, R. E. (2000). *Cultural diversity in health and illness*. (5th ed.). Upper Saddle River, NJ: Prentice-Hall Health, as cited in Ignatavicius, D., & Workman, L. (2008). *Medical-surgical nursing: Critical thinking for collaborative care*. St. Louis, MO: Elsevier.

For instance, an American Indian family may wish to spend the night in the intensive care unit room with a critically ill family member. However, the room does not have a cot on which to sleep, and the waiting room is not large enough to accommodate all the family and extended family members who are present to support the patient. The community in which the hospital is located has a large American Indian population. The nurse, as an advocate for patients and their families, can intervene through activities such as joining a hospital committee focused on hospital redesign. The nurse can point out the need for space for family members to stay all night near their loved ones. In this way the nurse supports the needs of the cultural diversity in her community.

Many organizations are involved in improving cultural competency in the health care industry. One governmental organization (Office of Minority Health) provides extensive continuing education for health care professionals (U.S. Department of Health and Human Services, 2016). Through a web resource (https://www.thinkculturalhealth.hhs.gov/) and other offerings, this organization assists providers in delivering respectful, understandable, and effective care to patients of all ethnicities. This sort of education is crucial because of the increasing diversity of the American population.

Another barrier to cultural competence in the nursing profession is the need for a more diverse culture among nurses. Nursing programs have a difficult time recruiting diverse students and in some instances diversities such as English as a second language interfere with success in courses and on the NCLEX. It only makes sense that the more diverse the nursing profession, the more diverse the delivery of care, resulting in improved patient outcomes.

Health and Health Care Disparities

One of the goals of *Healthy People 2020* is to eliminate health disparities (*Healthy People 2020*, 2016a). Health disparities are inequalities in disease morbidity and mortality in segments of the population. These disparities may be a result of differences in race or ethnicity. They are believed to be the result of the interaction among genetic variations, environmental factors, and health behaviors. For instance, the infant death rate among blacks is more than double that of whites. American Indians and Alaska Natives have an infant death rate almost double that for whites. Also, their rate of diabetes is more than twice that for whites. Hispanics are almost twice as likely to die of diabetes as are non-Hispanic whites. New cases of hepatitis and tuberculosis also are higher in Asians and Pacific Islanders than in whites (*Healthy People 2020*, 2016b). Visit the website: https://www.thinkculturalhealth.hhs.gov/.

OFFICE OF MINORITY HEALTH AND DISASTER PREPAREDNESS

Office of Minority Health (OMH) is a part of the Department of Health and Human Services (DHHS). In 2009, OMH launched an initiative to help first responders better manage disasters and crises in diverse populations. Some of the issues addressed include

- Using interpreters
- Using bilingual materials
- Managing cultural variation
- Implementing culturally based standards

Inequalities in income and education are at the root of many health disparities. In general, those populations that have the worst health status are those that have the highest poverty rates and the least education. Low income and low education levels are associated with differences in rates of illness and death, including heart disease, diabetes, obesity, and low birth weight. Higher incomes allow better access to medical care, enable people to afford better housing and live in safer neighborhoods, and increase the opportunity to engage in health-promoting behaviors. Recent initiatives are focusing on genomics, sleep, social and environmental factors that promote optimal health, as well as addressing the health needs of the lesbian, gay, bisexual, and transgender (LGBT) populations (*Healthy People 2020,* 2016b).

According to the Institute of Medicine (IOM) report *Unequal Treatment,* conscious bias and unconscious bias from health care professionals affect quality of care and hence lead to health disparities (Smedley et al., 2003; White-Means et al., 2009). Some of the causes of health care disparities include provider variables and patient variables. Provider variables are provider–patient relationships, lack of minority providers, as well as provider bias and discrimination. Studies have clearly demonstrated that providers will often make different plans for different patients when the only difference is culture or skin tone. Patient variables are mistrust of the health care system and refusal of treatment (Baldwin, 2003). Often this mistrust comes from barriers in communication. For example, what types of interviewing questions would you include during an initial nursing history of a transgender patient? When obtaining a patient's sexual history, how would you address these questions to the lesbian, gay, bisexual, transgender, and queer and/or questioning (LGBTQ) community? Ignatavicius and Workman (2016) offer several interviewing questions about gender identity and sexual activity that nurses can use in their practice (Box 21.3).

The solutions to challenges of health and health care disparities are complex and are still being discovered (Critical Thinking Box 21.1). Some solutions involve increasing the diversity of health care providers; ensuring that all people have access to affordable, quality health care; promoting wellness and a healthy lifestyle; strengthening provider–patient relationships; increasing cultural competency of health care providers; and conducting research to determine why certain diseases affect minorities so greatly and to discover effective intervention strategies (Baldwin, 2003).

Culturally Diverse Work Force

To meet the health care needs of an increasingly diverse society, it would be beneficial to have such diversity represented in the nursing profession. Unfortunately, the diversity of the nursing workforce does not mirror that of the U.S. population (AACN, 2015). For instance, in 2010 the U.S. Census Bureau reported that just over one-third of the American population was from a minority background (U.S. Census Bureau, 2011). However, in 2008 the *National Sample Survey of Registered Nurses* showed that minorities accounted for 16.8% of registered nurses. It is also important for minority faculty to mentor nursing students. In 2010, 12.6% of nursing faculty reported their ethnicity as one that falls under a minority category.

BOX 21.3 RECOMMENDED PATIENT INTERVIEW QUESTIONS ABOUT SEXUAL ORIENTATION, GENDER IDENTITY, AND HEALTH CARE

- Do you have sex with men, women, both, or neither?
- Does anyone live with you in your household?
- Are you in a relationship with someone who does not live with you?
- If you have a sexual partner, have you or your partner been evaluated about the possibility of transmitting infections to each other?
- If you have more than one sexual partner, how are you protecting both of you from infections, such as hepatitis B or hepatitis C or HIV?
- Have you disclosed your gender identity and sexual orientation to your health care provider?
- If you have not, may I have your permission to provide that information to members of the health care team who are involved in your care?
- Who do you consider as your closest family members?

From Ignatavicius, D. D. (2016). Introduction to medical-surgical nursing practice. In Ignatavicius, D. D., and Workman, L. M. (Eds.), *Medical-surgical nursing* (8th ed.), p. 4. St. Louis, MO: Elsevier.

? CRITICAL THINKING BOX 21.1

Can you think of ways to decrease disparities in health and health care in your community? What projects could you do as a nursing student to make a positive impact? Could you devise a project as part of a class assignment or a Student Nurses Association activity?

The American Hospital Association (AHA) (2012) recommends that exposure to health careers begin early in the education of minority populations, as well as of males, to reach out to those who are currently underrepresented in nursing and who will account for an increasing share of the labor pool. The AHA states, "In addition to training all staff on cultural competency, look for opportunities to employ bicultural clinical and administrative staff to improve education, care delivery, and ultimately, outcomes" (p. 12). See Box 21.1 for information about culturally diverse nurse–patient interactions, and see the end of this chapter for additional relevant websites and online resources.

What Is the Meaning of Spirituality?

One of the challenges for the nurse in providing spiritual care to patients is that there is not yet a clear definition of spirituality (Gijsberts et al., 2011). Health care professionals recognize the important relationship between patient well-being and spirituality, but many feel underprepared to assist patients in incorporating this aspect of their life into the health care setting (Blaber, Jones, & Willis, 2015). Many people confuse religion with spirituality, when in fact, they can be separate entities. Pesut et al. (2008) contend that current trends in health care tend to define religion as a set of institutionalized beliefs and rituals, whereas spirituality can be defined "as an individualized journey characterized by experiential descriptors such as meaning, purpose, transcendence, connectedness and energy" (p. 2804).

McSherry (2006) presents several components of spirituality with relevance to nursing, which is a helpful framework for understanding the spirituality concept (Box 21.4). At times, a spiritual advisor or chaplain may be called on for a patient's or family's spiritual needs. But there are times when these spiritual needs may be met most appropriately by the nurse (Bokinskie & Evanson, 2009).

A definition of *spiritual nursing care* is "an intuitive, interpersonal, altruistic, and integrative expression that is contingent upon the nurse's awareness of the transcendent dimension of life but that reflects

---

BOX 21.4   COMPONENTS OF SPIRITUALITY

- Spirituality is a universal concept relevant to all individuals.
- The uniqueness of the individual is paramount.
- Formal religious affiliation is not a prerequisite for spirituality.
- An individual may become more spiritually aware during a time of need.

From McSherry, W. (2006). *Making sense of spirituality in nursing practice: An integrative approach.* Edinburgh: Churchill Livingstone, p. 48.

---

the patient's reality" (Sawatzky & Pesut, 2005, p. 23). Spiritual distress is a NANDA-approved nursing diagnosis (Ackley & Ladwig, 2014). It is essential to include the subjective spiritual assessment of patients' spiritual needs to assure there is a plan for providing ongoing interventions and evaluation of effectiveness. Examples of spiritual nursing interventions include prayer, presence, scripture reading, peaceful environment, meditation, music, pastoral care, inspiring hope, active listening, validation of patients' thoughts and feelings, values clarification, sensitive responses to patient beliefs, and developing a trusting relationship (Callister et al., 2004). To that end, nurses have many resources available to them to improve the spiritual care of their patients so that the benefits of this important aspect of patient care can be realized.

Some challenges that nursing students and nurses tend to encounter include a lack of knowledge about a spirituality unlike their own and strong convictions in their own superior being. Providing spiritual care often requires the nurse to compartmentalize his or her own beliefs and allow the patient's beliefs to prevail. For example, it may not be appropriate to provide empathy by referring to one's own source of spiritual strength. When in doubt or unsure about how one may provide spiritual support, it is appropriate to ask or verify what would be meaningful to the patient and family.

Free online services allow patients to listen to religious works such as the Bible. This is useful for the patient who is too ill to read or for family members who would like to offer this service to their loved ones (www.biblegateway.com/resources/audio).

CULTURAL AND SPIRITUAL ASSESSMENT

What Are Cultural and Spiritual Beliefs About Illness and Cures?

Patients will have different responses to illness based on their cultural and spiritual beliefs. It is vital for the nurse to be aware of the variety of responses that may be encountered (Box 21.5).

The nurse needs to be careful, however, not to stereotype a patient based on his or her cultural or spiritual background.

People of many cultures may use complementary, alternative, or integrative modalities that can affect their health status (Box 21.6). Complementary and alternative medicines are often grouped together using the acronym CAM. The National Center for Complementary and Integrative Health (NCCIH, 2015) defines complementary medicine as non-mainstream practices that are used together with conventional medicine, whereas alternative medicine is the use of non-mainstream practices in place of conventional medicine. Because the public is increasingly using complementary and alternative health approaches in the United States (Barnes et al., 2002; Clarke et al., 2012), it is vital that the nurse have a basic understanding of various therapies, as well as their benefits and risks. For instance, a patient with diabetes may be ingesting ginger for general health or to address a concern (e.g., nausea). However, the nurse needs to know that ginger may decrease blood glucose levels (Al-Amin et al., 2006). It is possible that ginger ingestion by the patient could influence the dosage of an oral antidiabetic agent needed by the

BOX 21.5 CULTURAL AND SPIRITUAL BELIEFS AFFECTING NURSING CARE

African American
Extended family has large influence on patient.

Older family members are honored and respected, and their authority is unquestioned.

Oldest male is decision maker and spokesman.

Strong emphasis on avoiding conflict and direct confrontation.

Respect authority and do not disagree with health care recommendations—but they may not follow recommendations.

Asian/Pacific Islander
Family- and church-oriented.

Extensive family bonds.

Key family member is consulted for important health-related decisions.

Illness is a punishment from God for wrongdoing or is caused by voodoo, spirits, or demons.

Illness is prevented through good diet, herbs, rest, cleanliness, and laxatives to clean the system.

Wear copper and silver bracelets to prevent illness.

Chinese
Chinese patients will not discuss symptoms of mental illness or depression, because they believe this behavior reflects on family; therefore, it may produce shame and guilt. As a result, there may be psychosomatic symptoms.

Use herbalists, spiritual healers, and physicians for care.

Hindu
Strive to live in harmony with all living things on earth.

Devout Hindus are strictly vegetarian.

Hispanic/Latino
Older family members are consulted on issues involving health and illness.

Patriarchal family—men make decisions for family.

Illness is viewed as God's will or divine punishment resulting from sinful behavior.

Prefer to use home remedies and consult folk healers known as *curanderos* or *curanderas* rather than traditional Western health care providers.

Many believe in the hot and cold theory of disease, although they may differ about what constitutes hot or cold.

Hmong
Prefer their own relatives as interpreters and may not trust a hospital-employed interpreter.

Interpreter needs to be of the same sex as the client, as intimate questions or problems are not discussed with an interpreter of the opposite sex.

Islam (Muslim)
Indians and Pakistanis do not acknowledge a diagnosis of severe emotional illness or mental retardation, because it reduces the chance of other family members getting married.

Medical beliefs are a blend of modern and traditional practice.

Preference for modesty and same-sex caregivers.

Japanese
Believe physical contact with blood, skin diseases, and corpses will cause illness.

Also believe improper care of the body, including poor diet and lack of sleep, causes illness.

Believe in healers, herbalists, and physicians for healing, and energy can be restored with acupuncture and acupressure. Their high regard for the status of physicians decreases the likelihood that they will question their care.

Use group decision making for health concerns.

Disability is a source of family shame. Mental illness is taboo.

Continued

> ### BOX 21.6 DEFINITIONS OF TERMS

> **Complementary therapies:** those that are used in conjunction with mainstream treatments.
> **Alternative therapies:** those that are used instead of mainstream medical therapies.
> **Integrative therapies:** including complementary therapies in mainstream health care.

From National Center for Complementary and Integrative Health. (2015). *What is complementary, alternative or integrative health?* Retrieved from https://nccih.nih.gov/health/integrative-health#types.

patient (Fig. 21.1). The nurse will also need to consider that ginger could increase bleeding times if the patient is taking an anticoagulant (Kee et al., 2015).

The American Holistic Nurses Association (AHNA) says that holistic nursing is defined as "all nursing practice that has healing the whole person as its goal" (AHNA, 2016). Holistic nursing is an attitude, a philosophy, and a way of being; it is not just something a person or a nurse does. Vital components of a holistic nursing assessment are the identification of cultural and spiritual practices (AHNA, 2016). Nurses need to be aware of all aspects of a patient's life, as there are many factors that must be considered for providing culturally competent nursing care (Douglas et al., 2011). Having access to a comprehensive assessment tool will assist in identifying important transcultural variations for each patient (Fig. 21.2).

The Joint Commission (TJC; formerly JCAHO) acknowledges a patient's right to receive care that respects his or her cultural and spiritual values: "JCAHO recommends that health care organizations (1) acknowledge patients' rights to spiritual care, and (2) provide for these needs through pastoral care and a diversity of services that may be offered by certified, ordained, or lay individuals" (LaPierre, 2003, p. 219). It is imperative that nurses perform a spiritual assessment to determine the patient's individual needs (Critical Thinking Box 21.2).

FIG. 21.1 Complementary health care therapy is on the rise.

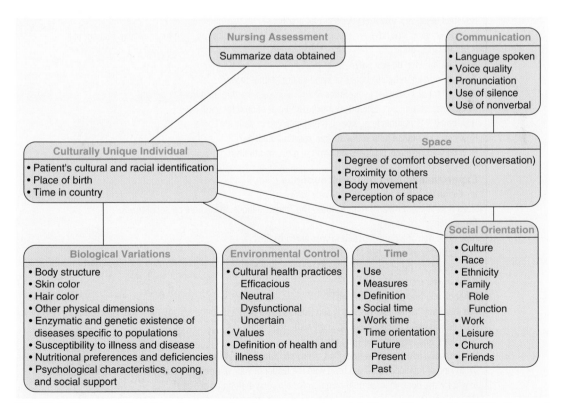

FIG. 21.2 Giger and Davidhizar's transcultural assessment model. (From Giger, J. N. (2013). *Transcultural nursing: Assessment and intervention.* (6th ed.). St. Louis. MO: Mosby/Elsevier.)

How Do You Assess Spiritual Need?

Specific spiritual assessment tools can be used by the nurse as guides to determine the spiritual needs of patients. Aspects of these tools may also be integrated into an agency assessment document or into the electronic health record. Box 21.7 lists dimensions of spirituality with corresponding assessment questions. These questions can assist the nurse in determining needs that exist in any of the six spiritual dimensions.

? CRITICAL THINKING BOX 21.2

How much knowledge do you have regarding various complementary and alternative health therapies, such as acupuncture, Reiki, yoga, herbal medicine, and aromatherapy? Use the NCCIH website https://nccih.nih.gov/health/integrative-health#types to enhance your knowledge base. Identify possible referral sources for integrative therapies in your community. You never know when a patient may ask you for information and/or a referral regarding integrative therapies.

BOX 21.7   DIMENSIONS OF SPIRITUALITY WITH CORRESPONDING ASSESSMENT QUESTIONS

Spirit-Enhancing Practices or Rituals
How do you express your spirituality (or philosophy of life)?
What spiritual or religious practices or activities are important to you?
How has being sick affected your spiritual practices?
How does being sick have an impact on your praying (or meditation, scripture reading, fasting, receiving sacraments, service attendance, etc.)?
How and for what do you pray?
What spiritual or religious books or symbols are helpful to you?
What effect do you expect your illness to have on your spiritual practices or beliefs?
What kinds of readings, artwork, or music are inspirational for you?
How do Holy Scriptures (e.g., Koran, Bible) help you in daily life?
How can I as a nurse help you with your spiritual practice?
How do your religious practices help you to grow spiritually?

Experience of God or Transcendence
Is religion important to you? Why or why not?
Does God/Higher Power/Ultimate Other/The Transcendence, etc., seem personal to you?
Do you feel close now?
How does God or a deity function in your personal life?
How is God working in your life?
How would you describe your God and what you worship?
What is your picture of God?
What do you feel you mean to God?
Are there any barriers between you and God? Is there anything for which you think that God could not forgive you?
How do you make sense of feeling angry with God?
How does God respond when you pray?
Do you feel a source of love from God or any spiritual being? Where is God in all this?
What kind of relationship do you have with the leader of your spiritual community (e.g., priest, rabbi, guru)?
In what ways does your spiritual community help you when times are bad?
What kinds of confusion or doubt do you have about your religious beliefs?
Are you having difficulty performing your religious duties?

BOX 21.7   DIMENSIONS OF SPIRITUALITY WITH CORRESPONDING ASSESSMENT QUESTIONS—cont'd

Sense of Meaning

What gives most meaning to your life? What is the most important thing in your life?

When you are sick, do you have feelings that you are being punished or that it is God's will for you to be sick?

What are your thoughts about or explanations for suffering? Are these beliefs helpful?

What do you see as the cosmic plan/God's plan or purpose for your life?

Have you been able to answer any of the "why" questions that often accompany illness?

What, if any, have been the good outcomes from having this difficult time in life?

What, if anything, motivates you to get well?

Giving and Receiving Love, or Connectedness to Self (Degree of Self-Awareness) and Others

What do you do to show love for yourself?

What are some of the most loving things that people have done for you?

What are the loving things that you do for others?How do others help you now? How easy is it to accept their help?

For what do you hope? How do you experience hope?

How have you experienced forgiveness during your life/illness (Forgiveness toward self, toward or from others and God)?

Sources of Hope and Strength

What helps you to cope now?

What (or who) is your source of hope? Of strength? How do they help?

To whom do you turn when you need help? Are they available?

What helps you most when you feel afraid or when you need special help?

How can I help you maintain your spiritual strength during this illness?

To what degree do you trust your future to God?

What brings you joy and peace in your life?

What do you believe in?

What do you do to make yourself feel alive and full of spirit?

Link Between Spirituality and Health

How does your spirituality affect your experience of being sick?

How has your current situation/illness influenced your faith?

How has being sick affected your sense of who you are (or how has being sick affected you spiritually)?

What has bothered you most about being sick (or in what is happening to you now)?

What do you do to heal your spirit?

Has being sick (or your current situation) made any difference in your feelings about God or your faith experience (or in what you believe)?

Is there anything especially frightening or meaningful to you now?

Do you ever wish for more faith to help you with your illness?

Has being ill ever made you feel angry, guilty, bitter, or resentful?

How involved in a spiritual/religious community/organization (e.g., church, temple, covenant group) are you? (As a visitor? Member? Leader?)

From Taylor, E. J. (2002). *Spiritual care: Nursing theory, research, and practice.* Upper Saddle River, NJ: Pearson-Prentice Hall, pp. 121-124.

CONCLUSION

As you enter the world of nursing, you will come into contact with patients from various cultures, and they will have many different spiritual beliefs (Critical Thinking Box 21.3). As nurses, we must be able to address these issues as they relate to health care. Nurses need to become "culturally competent" to understand better the health care needs of our vast, multicultural patient population. It will not be enough to recognize and accept these cultural implications; we must plan nursing and health care that will achieve the most positive patient results. Because of the melting pot of cultures in the patient population, nurses must increasingly implement a more holistic approach to providing health care. The place to begin is with each individual nurse, who must assess his or her own value system and become more culturally competent.

❓ CRITICAL THINKING BOX 21.3

If your patient asked you to pray with him, would you feel comfortable? If not, what other resources could you call on to meet the spiritual needs of this patient?

🌐 RELEVANT WEBSITES AND ONLINE RESOURCES

American Association of Colleges of Nursing (2008)
Cultural competency in baccalaureate nursing education. http://www.aacn.nche.edu/leading-initiatives/education-resources/competency.pdf.

Deal, B (2010)
A pilot study of nurses' experience of giving spiritual care, *The Qualitative Report 15*(4):852–863. http://www.nova.edu/ssss/QR/QR15-4/deal.pdf.

Jeffreys, M (2008)
Becoming better nurses through diversity awareness. http://www.nsna.org/Portals/0/Skins/NSNA/pdf/Imprint_NovDec08_Feat_Jeffreys.pdf.

Mayo Clinic (2015)
Spirituality and stress relief: Make the connection. http://www.mayoclinic.com/health/stress-relief/SR00035.

National Center for Complementary and Integrative Health Information (2016)
https://nccih.nih.gov/health.

The Office of Minority Health (2013)
Cultural and linguistic competency. http://minorityhealth.hhs.gov/omh/browse.aspx?lvl=1&lvlid=6.

Transcultural Nursing Society (2011)
Standards of practice for culturally competent nursing care. http://www.tcns.org/files/Standards_of_Practice_for_Cult_Comp_Nsg_care-2011_Update_FINAL_printed_copy_2_.pdf.

University of Maryland Medical Center (2013)
Spirituality. http://www.umm.edu/altmed/articles/spirituality-000360.htm.

U.S. Department of Health and Human Services (2016)
Office of Minority Health. http://minorityhealth.hhs.gov/.

In clinical settings, spiritual assessment tools can help the nurse gain a deeper understanding of the patient from a holistic perspective. However, these tools are merely guides and are not multipurpose checklists that can be completed all at once during an initial assessment period.

BIBLIOGRAPHY

Ackley, B. J., & Ladwig, G. B. (2014). *An evidence-based guide to planning care* (10th ed.). Maryland Heights, MO: Mosby.

Agency for Healthcare Research and Quality. (2016). *National healthcare disparities report 2014.* Retrieved from http://www.ahrq.gov/research/findings/nhqrdr/index.html.

Al-Amin, Z. M., et al. (2006). Anti-diabetic and hypolipidaemic properties of ginger (*Zingiber officinale*) in streptozotocin-induced diabetic rats. *British Journal of Nutrition, 96*, 660–666.

American Association of Colleges of Nursing. (2015). *Fact sheet: Enhancing diversity in the nursing workforce.* Retrieved from www.aacn.nche.edu/media-relations/diversityFS.pdf.

American Holistic Nurses Association. (2016). *What is holistic nursing?* Retrieved from www.ahna.org/AboutUs/WhatisHolisticNursing/tabid/1165/Default.aspx.

American Hospital Association. (2012). *Eliminating health care disparities: Implementing the national call to action using lessons learned.* Retrieved from http://www.hpoe.org/Reports-HPOE/eliminating_health_care_disparities.pdf.

American Nurses Association. (2015). *Code of ethics for nurses with interpretive statements.* ANA: Silver Springs, MD. Retrieved from http://www.nursingworld.org/mainmenucategories/ethicsstandards/codeofethicsfornurses.

Baldwin, D. M. (2003). *Disparities in health care: focusing efforts to eliminate unequal burdens.* Washington, DC: American Nurses Association. Retrieved from http://www.nursingworld.org/MainMenuCategories/ANA Marketplace/ANAPeriodicals/OJIN/TableofContents/Volume82003/No1Jan2003/DisparitiesinHealthand HealthCare.html.

Barnes, P., et al. (May 27, 2004). CDC Advance Data Report #343. *Complementary and alternative medicine use among adults: United States.* Retrieved from http://www.cdc.gov/nchs/data/ad/ad343.pdf.

Blaber, M., Jones, J., & Willis, D. (2015). Spiritual care: Which is the best assessment tool for palliative settings? *International Journal of Palliative Nursing, 21*(9), 430–438.

Bokinskie, J. C., & Evanson, T. A. (2009). The stranger among us: Ministering health to migrants. *Journal of Christian Nurse, 26*, 202–209.

Callister, L. C., et al. (2004). Threading spirituality through nursing education. *Holistic Nursing Practice, 18*, 160–166.

Clarke, T. C., Black, L. I., Stussman, B. J., et al. (2012). *Trends in the use of complementary health approaches among adults: United States, 2002-2012.* National health statistics reports, no. 79. Hyattsville, MD: National Center for Health Statistics. Retrieved from http://www.cdc.gov/nchs/data/nhsr/nhsr079.pdf.

Douglas, M. K., et al. (2011). Standards of practice for culturally competent nursing care: 2011 update. *Journal of Transcultural Nursing, 22*(4), 317–333. http://dx.doi.org/10.1177/1043659611412965.

Giger, J. N. (2013). *Transcultural nursing: Assessment and intervention* (6th ed.). St. Louis, MO: Mosby/Elsevier.

Gijsberts, M. J., Echteld, M. A., van der Steen, J. T., et al. (2011). Spirituality at the end of life: Conceptualization of measurable aspects—a systematic review. *Journal of Palliative Medicine, 14*(7), 852–856.

Healthy People 2020. *HealthyPeople.gov.* (2016a). Washington, DC: U.S. Department of Health and Human Services. Retrieved from http://www.healthypeople.gov/.

Healthy People 2020. (2016b). *2020 topics and objectives.* Washington, DC: U.S. Department of Health and Human Services. Retrieved from http://www.healthypeople.gov/2020/topics-objectives.

Kee, J. L., Hayes, E. R., & McCuistion, L. E. (2015). *Pharmacology: A nursing process approach* (8th ed.). St. Louis, MO: Saunders Elsevier.

LaPierre, L. L. (2003). JCAHO safeguards spiritual care. *Holistic Nursing Practice, 17*, 219.

Leininger, M. (2007). Theoretical questions and concerns: Response from the theory of culture care diversity and universality perspective. *Nursing Science Quarterly, 20*, 9–15.

Mazanec, P., & Tyler, M. K. (2003). Cultural considerations in end-of-life care: How ethnicity, age, and spirituality affect decisions when death is imminent. *American Journal of Nursing, 103*, 50–58.

McGibbon, E., Etowa, J., & McPherson, C. (2008). Health-care access as a social determinant of health. *Can Nurse, 104*(7), 22–27.

McSherry, W. (2006). *Making sense of spirituality in nursing practice: An integrative approach.* Edinburgh: Churchill Livingstone.

Migrant Clinicians Network. (2016). *Cultural competency.* Author: MCN Network. Retrieved from http://www.migrantclinician.org/services/education/training/cultural-competency.html.

National Center for Complementary and Integrative Health. (2015). *What is complementary, alternative, or integrative health?* Retrieved from https://nccih.nih.gov/health/integrative-health.

Pesut, B., et al. (2008). Conceptualizing spirituality and religion for healthcare. *Journal of Clinical Nursing, 17*(21), 2803–2810.

Purnell, L. D., & Paulanka, B. J. (2008). *Transcultural healthcare: A culturally competent approach* (3rd ed.). Philadelphia: FA Davis.

Sawatzky, R., & Pesut, B. (2005). Attributes of spiritual care in nursing practice. *Journal of Holistic Nursing, 23*, 19–33.

Smedley, B. D., Stith, A. Y., & Nelson, A. R. (2003). *Unequal treatment: confronting racial and ethnic disparities in health care, Institute of Medicine report.* Washington, DC: National Academies Press.

Spector, R. E. (2000). *Cultural diversity in health and illness* (5th ed.). Upper Saddle River, NJ: Prentice-Hall Health, as cited in Ignatavicius, D. & Workman, L. (2008). *Medical-surgical nursing: Critical thinking for collaborative care.* St. Louis, MO: Elsevier.

Stewart, M. (January–February, 1998). *Nurses need to strengthen cultural competence for next century to ensure quality patient care.* Washington, DC: NursingWorld. Retrieved from http://www.nursingworld.org/MainMenu Categories/ANAMarketplace/ANAPeriodicals/TAN/1998/TANJanFeb98FeaturesCulturalCompetence.aspx.

U.S. Census Bureau. (March 24, 2011). *2010 Census shows America's diversity.* Retrieved from https://www.census.gov/newsroom/releases/archives/2010_census/cb11-cn125.html.

U.S. Department of Health and Human Services. (2016). *Office of Minority Health.* Retrieved from http://minorityhealth.hhs.gov/.

White-Means, S., Dong, Z., Hufstader, M., & Brown, L. T. (2009). Cultural competency, race, and skin tone bias among pharmacy, nursing, and medical students. *Medical Care Research and Review, 66*, 436–455.

22

Quality Patient Care

*Susan Ahrens, PhD, RN**

ⓔ http://evolve.elsevier.com/Zerwekh/nsgtoday/.

Anyone who has never made a mistake has never tried anything new.
Albert Einstein

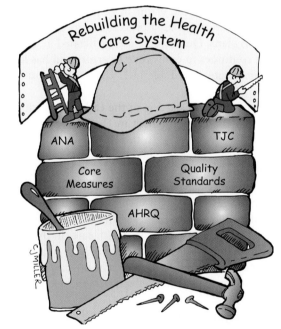

By working together using Improvement Science, we can rebuild our health care system.

After completing this chapter, you should be able to:

- Define quality standards in health care management.
- Describe the history and evolution of quality in health care.
- Define and discuss core measures.
- Identify the role of regulatory agencies in health care quality.
- Discuss the use of key indicators to measure performance.
- Describe your role in quality and performance improvement.
- Identify tools and processes for continuous quality improvement.
- Identify the role of regulatory standards and agencies.
- Incorporate successful process improvement strategies.
- Consider the value and requirements of quality credentialing.
- Synthesize understanding of the QSEN Initiative, Healthy People 2020, and The Joint Commission National Patient Safety Goals in developing a safe patient care environment.

* We would like to acknowledge **Tess (Theresa) M. Pape, PhD, RN, CNOR, CNE,** for her past contributions to this chapter.

Yₒu may wonder why nurses need to know about quality issues to provide patient care. All nurses know that an important part of their professional life is to provide high-quality care. However, many new graduates soon discover that not all nurses do the right thing all the time for the patient and family. In fact, a landmark study in 1999, called *The Quality Chasm,* estimated that the impact of poor-quality care results in almost 100,000 deaths annually in acute care settings alone. Because of the costly effects of poor care, nurses need to understand their important role in ensuring quality patient care and the actions they can take to ensure excellence. According to the Institute of Medicine (2011), the enactment of the Affordable Care Act requires nurses to play a key role in transforming health care to provide higher quality and safer care than ever before and to be involved at every level to redesign the system to improve the quality of care. As managers and providers of care, nurses can be a large part of changing health care delivery to be safer and more efficient.

> Look at almost any news show or sensational tabloid, and you will find health care errors featured. Today more than ever, these incidents seem to have become the focus of news stories. Who or what makes this happen?

Issues that are on the forefront of news will take precedence over those that are routine or commonplace. Recently, medical errors have become of primary concern. Quality-assurance departments have the job of helping nurses and health care team members avoid errors by implementing various prevention methods. They also ask for the help of nurses in mobilizing process improvement teams that work to identify risk areas and develop prevention plans. Quality care can be likened to fire prevention instead of firefighting. Illegible handwriting continues to contribute to errors and has led to regulations about what medical abbreviations are appropriate. (See Table 11.1, The Joint Commission Official "Do Not Use" List of Abbreviations.)

Hospital leaders implemented quality improvement programs starting in the early 1980s with the inception of the National Demonstration Project on Quality Improvement in Healthcare, which we know today as the Institute for Healthcare Improvement (IHI, 2016). In the late 1980s, the topic of human immunodeficiency virus (HIV) and hepatitis B virus caused an increased use of gloves to prevent the transmission of infection. The increased need for more gloves led to a need to produce them quickly, which resulted in the introduction of foreign supplies of latex gloves. More latex allergies surfaced. In the 1990s, more emphasis was placed on using needleless systems to prevent needle stick injuries, resulting in legislation to increase the number of needleless devices used. In the 2000s, there has been concern and controversy regarding the nursing shortage and access to health care. In the 2010s, increasing demands will continue for all health care providers, with the expectation of high-quality care. As knowledge development increases, new technologies and treatments mean that health care providers will need to develop quality initiatives to ensure patients receive the most effective and efficient care.

STANDARDS OF QUALITY HEALTH CARE MANAGEMENT

Several agencies have established standards that guide quality in health care. Some of these include the American Nurses Association (ANA) Standards of Nursing Care, accrediting group standards such as those of The Joint Commission (TJC), which accredits health care organizations, and the Agency for Healthcare Research and Quality (AHRQ), which has established clinical practice treatment guidelines designed to improve patient outcomes and reduce costs. In addition, another national program to ensure quality health care for the country is the Healthy People initiative. The current version of the initiative is called *Healthy People 2020.*

First outlined in 1979, a report by the U.S. Surgeon General outlined the needs of the nation for improved health. *Healthy People 2020* contains more than 1200 objectives, with each objective having a reliable data source, baseline measures, and a specific target for improvement by 2020. The objectives were prepared by experts from multiple federal agencies and made available for public comment. Agencies that support health care research often use the objectives to identify research priorities. Nursing intervention research funding requests using the *Healthy People 2020* objectives are often more likely to be awarded if all other aspects are equal.

Based on the population objectives, 12 Leading Health Indicators were identified. These indicators are used to determine whether objectives are being met or not. The data are collected over 10 years and used to update and improve the objectives for the upcoming 10 years. Major improvements in population health have been made based on this work; however, the 2010 data demonstrated the need for continued improvement (U.S. Department of Health and Human Services, 2016).

TJC is an accrediting agency that evaluates care in an organization and then determines whether the overall care meets quality care standards. TJC requires hospitals to submit error reports and identifies key "sentinel events" that have the potential for great harm and publishes a monthly sentinel event alert. A *sentinel event* is an unexpected occurrence involving death or loss of limb or function. Such events are called "sentinel," because they sound a warning of the need for immediate investigation and response (Fig. 22.1) (The Joint Commission, 2016a).

Without continual growth and progress, such words as improvement, achievement, and success have no meaning.

Benjamin Franklin

FIG. 22.1 Root causes of sentinel events.

What Is Root Cause Analysis?

When errors occur, the primary cause needs to be determined so that a solution can be found. *Root cause analysis* (RCA) is a process designed for use in investigating and categorizing the root causes of events that occur. In the health care setting, there are many factors that can contribute to the cause of errors. Rather than placing blame on any one person or thing, RCA, when conducted appropriately, can identify all factors leading to the error. A hospital's risk management department often conducts an RCA, and the results are presented to the quality improvement (QI) department for follow-up action. The role of the QI department is to be proactive at finding ways to prevent similar incidents from occurring.

Imagine an occurrence during which a nurse administers the wrong dose of a medication instead of the correct dose. In the past, the nurse (who was viewed as the last person between the medication and the patient) had sole responsibility for medication delivery. RCA has demonstrated that errors are often the result of a complex, broken system. Remedies in the past for "nurse" errors was education and sometimes discipline. RCA has shown the health care industry that medication delivery is a very complex process, and there are many things that contribute to a medication error. System issues, which are often a cause for errors that impact the delivery of medication, can be detected using the RCA process. Many things contribute to medication errors, as nurses encounter problems within the system, work-design problems, or human and environmental factors. Considering this, getting medications to the nursing unit, or medication labeling may pose medication delivery challenges.

Common causes of medication errors include wrong-dose errors, lack of drug knowledge, rule violations, carelessness, memory lapses, inadequate monitoring, misuse of infusion pumps, faulty-dose checking and failure to identify the correct drug, medication stocking problems, and using the wrong technique. System failures include lack of easy access to drug information, look-alike packaging, sound-alike drug names, transcription errors, lack of patient information, poor communication, distractions, interruptions, and excess workloads (Pape, 2003; Ehsani et al., 2013). The environment plays a part because of the many distractions the nurse must attend to in clinical practice.

The environment is as much a part of the system as are the processes within the organization. Nurses are often interrupted as they prepare medications for their patients. Sometimes the lighting is bad, or there is a great deal of noise and confusion that can distract a nurse. Technology can be helpful and is an integral part of the system components, but it cannot address the human factors and issues. Therefore, each aspect of medication errors should be considered when evaluating a cause-and-effect relationship of medication errors (Pape, 2006; U.S. Department of Health and Human Services, 2015).

A root cause factor flow diagram should be generated to find the real origin of the error. As an example, Fig. 22.2 depicts a simplified version of the root cause analysis performed. As the investigation proceeded, it became evident that a look-alike vial meant that the nurse was not entirely at fault. In addition, distractions and hurriedness also contributed to the error.

HISTORY AND EVOLUTION OF QUALITY IN HEALTH CARE

The advent of quality in health care began when hospitals found the need to look outside their own expertise for error prevention strategies. The year is not as important as the fact that health care organizations found a need to borrow from other industries that were successful at managing risk. Manufacturing industries began focusing on error prevention in the early 1920s, whereas the evolution of improved quality techniques in health care was not adopted until the 1960s, and quality techniques are still evolving.

Historically, the focus of quality improvement was in controlling processes by inspection so that errors were prevented. Later, the emphasis changed from inspection to proactive approaches to error prevention. Included with prevention are monitoring processes to control errors.

Who Are Edward Deming, Joseph M. Juran, and Philip Crosby?

Edward Deming is often considered the father of quality improvement, although quality concepts have developed and improved throughout several decades. What once began simply as a method for discovering how to prevent defects has evolved into highly skilled methods for tracking and improving quality today. Deming's teachings embraced the philosophy that quality is everyone's responsibility within an organization.

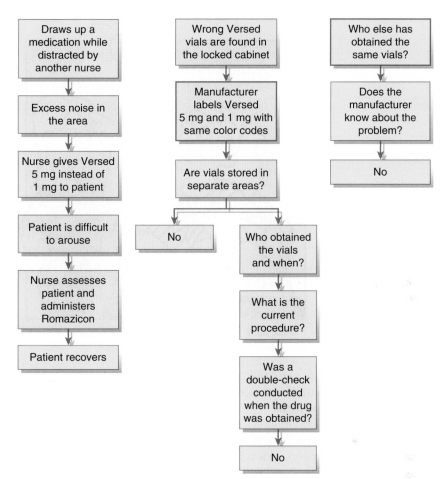

FIG. 22.2 Root cause factor flow diagram.

Another valuable forefather of quality initiatives is Joseph M. Juran, who emphasized the meaning of the Pareto principle. The Pareto principle states that 80% of problems are caused by 20% of sources, people, or things. Therefore if you can fix the 20%, you can fix almost the entire system. Juran's work marked the beginning of the idea of *total quality management* (TQM).

Philip Crosby is considered the father of *zero defects*. He often proposed simplifying things so that everyone could understand. He also believed in the importance of communicating quality efforts and their results to the entire organization. Afterward, ideas such as "lean" manufacturing, "just-in-time" product delivery, and "Six Sigma" methods crossed over into health care.

Recently, there has been a real change in how members of the health care team view quality improvement within health care settings. What once was considered work only for the QI department is now brought to the frontline workers, who can best affect the outcomes. By frontline workers, we mean the nurses at the bedside and other workers in direct patient care areas who know the problems that need to be resolved. This is also termed *Improvement Science*. An ongoing commitment to improvement strategies supports an atmosphere of teamwork. The focus is on the process and systems rather than on blaming individuals (Fig. 22.3).

Still, the regulation of health care is conducted at the national level by regulatory governmental bodies. These government agencies are responsible for approving many of the licenses for educational

FIG. 22.3 Bedside nurses often have great ideas!

institutions that educate personnel. An example of a government agency that regulates nursing is state boards of nursing. Institutional accreditation is also conducted by some government agencies such as the public health department.

As mentioned earlier, TJC, previously called JCAHO, is the primary agency used for hospital accreditation. The mere mention of a visit by TJC can elicit feelings of fear and anxiety in the minds of nurses and hospital administrators. This is because hospitals must meet certain quality standards to pass TJC's inspections to maintain accreditation, and achieving accreditation is required to receive government funding for the health care provided. In the 1990s, TJC first began to mandate the use of *continuous quality improvement* (CQI) and to recommend that organizations adopt a quality improvement model for all process improvement activities. TJC typically endorses the use of the *plan–do–study–act* cycle (PDSA) as one tool for process improvement.

Some hospital QI departments have combined newer strategies with PDSA, including *define–measure–analyze–improve–control* (DMAIC) and *rapid cycle changes* (RCCs), which further incorporate a team focus. These are components of CQI, but more discussion of these methods will come later. TJC has also mandated specific quality outcome measures for all hospitals. Outcome measures mean looking for real patient results to determine whether the organization's goals were achieved. TJC wants to know if the care that patients receive is meeting standards or is improving.

WHAT ARE CORE MEASURES?

Core measures include those for patients admitted with a diagnosis of acute myocardial infarction, congestive heart failure, community-acquired pneumonia, surgical-infection prophylaxis, pregnancy-related conditions, deep vein thrombosis, and whether specific best practices were implemented within the health care setting. These measures are those that the public consumer considers important for choosing one hospital over another.

Hospitals must continue to assess the core measures that were developed by TJC. There are 13 core measure sets (Acute Myocardial Infarction, Children's Asthma Care, Emergency Department, Hospital Outpatient Department, Hospital-Based Inpatient Psychiatric Services, Immunization, Perinatal Care, Pneumonia Measures, Stroke, Substance Use, Surgical Care Improvement Project [SCIP], Tobacco Treatment, and Venous Thromboembolism), as defined by The Joint Commission (2016b). The goal is to improve the quality of health care by implementing a national standardized performance measurement system. Key actions are listed in each category that define the best research-based care process that is appropriate for that category. By tracking these core measures, hospitals improve patient care by focusing on the results of that care.

In 2011, the Centers for Medicare and Medicaid Services (CMS) launched the Medicare Shared Savings Plan, as a requirement by the Patient Protection and Affordable Care Act, to assist all health care providers across health care settings (hospitals, doctor's offices, long-term care settings) in coordinating care for Medicare patients. Under the Medicare Shared Savings Plan, Accountable Care Organizations (ACOs), consisting of health care providers, agree to collaborate in providing patient care, versus working independently in an effort to control costs and provide quality patient care. In order for an ACO to receive financial benefits of services rendered to a Medicare patient from CMS, the ACO must demonstrate that it has met the performance standard(s) as set forth by CMS (Centers for Medicare & Medicaid Services, 2015a, p.1). There are currently 33 quality measures divided into 4 categories. This information is available from the CMS website at cms.gov (Centers for Medicare & Medicaid Services, 2016a).

WHAT IS HCAHPS?

HCAHPS refers to the Hospital Consumer Assessment of Healthcare Providers and Systems. It is a national program for collecting and providing health care information from the consumer perspective, and the results are used to improve health care services. The patient survey was developed for public reporting as a way to compare hospitals across the continuum of patient care and garner information about the overall quality of care received from the patient's viewpoint. The HCAHPS contains ratings of communication, responsiveness, pain management, discharge information, cleanliness of the hospital environment, quietness of the hospital environment, and if patients would recommend the hospital (HCAHPS, 2014).

WHAT IS HOSPITAL COMPARE?

The Hospital Compare website is designed so consumers can compare how well selected hospitals serve to provide the care recommended to their patients. This information is provided through the efforts of Medicare and the Hospital Quality Alliance so consumers make informed decisions about health care. The performance measures that can be compared include information related to heart attack, heart failure, pneumonia, surgery, and other conditions (Centers for Medicare & Medicaid Services, 2015b). Consumers can go to www.hospitalcompare.hhs.gov and search by zip code to compare hospitals and prescribers.

JUST WHAT IS THE JOINT COMMISSION?

TJC is the major accrediting body for health care institutions that are funded by Medicare and Medicaid. The CMS is a part of the U.S. Department of Health and Human Services. Both organizations set the standards for safe practice and evaluate compliance. Having TJC accreditation symbolizes the organization's commitment to quality. This means that nearly all hospitals must be TJC accredited to stay in business.

In the past, TJC standards have directly addressed patient safety in many areas. Beginning on July 1, 2001, additions to these standards required hospitals to develop a systematic approach to error reduction and to design patient care processes with safety in mind. For CQI initiatives, TJC recommends using things such as flow charts, Pareto charts, run charts or line graphs, control charts, and histograms to display data. We call these "tools" or "instruments," because they help depict the measurements and track the problems and improvements. After the data have been collected, these tools help visualize results of performance improvement understood by most nurses. Other valuable tools are discussed later.

What Are Patient Safety Goals?

A primary driving force for CQI activities is TJC's National Patient Safety Goals (NPSG). In 2001, TJC began instituting annual patient safety goals intended to improve the quality of health care. The hospital national patient safety goals are summarized in Box 22.1 (The Joint Commission, 2016c).

TJC's Board of Commissioners approved the first NPSGs in July 2002. TJC established these goals to help accredited organizations address specific areas of concern regarding patient safety. Each goal includes brief, evidence-based recommendations. Evidence-based means the goals are based on real-world research and/or expert opinions. Each year, the goals and associated recommendations are reevaluated; most are continued and others may be replaced because of emerging new priorities or evidence from research studies. New goals and recommendations are announced in July and become

---

BOX 22.1   THE 2017 JOINT COMMISSION HOSPITAL NATIONAL PATIENT SAFETY GOALS

Goal 1: Use at least two ways to identify patients, such as using the patients' names and dates of birth. Make sure that the correct patient receives the correct blood during a blood transfusion.

Goal 2: Improve the effectiveness of communication among caregivers. Get important test results to the right staff person on time.

Goal 3: Use medications safely. Before a procedure, label medicines that are not labeled, for example, medicines in syringes, cups, and basins. Do this in the area where medicines and supplies are set up. Take extra care with patients who take medicines to thin their blood. Record and pass along correct information about a patient's medicines. Find out what medicines the patient is taking. Compare those medicines to new medicines given to the patient. Make sure the patient knows which medicines to take when he or she is at home. Tell the patient it is important to bring an updated list of medicines every time he or she visits a provider.

Goal 4: Use alarms safely. Make improvements to ensure that alarms on medical equipment are heard and responded to on time.

Goal 5: Prevent infection. Use the Centers for Disease Control and Prevention (CDC) hand hygiene guidelines or the current World Health Organization (WHO) hand hygiene guidelines. Set and use the goals for improving hand cleaning. Implement evidence-based practices to prevent health care–associated infections (HAIs) and infections caused by multidrug-resistant organisms that are difficult to treat.

Goal 6: Identify patient safety risks. Find out which patients are most likely to try to commit suicide.

Goal 7: Prevent mistakes in surgery. Make sure that the correct surgery is done on the correct patient and at the correct place on the patient's body. Mark the correct place on the patient's body where the surgery is to be done. Pause before the surgery to make sure that a mistake is not being made.

Universal Protocol for Eliminating Wrong Site, Wrong Procedure, Wrong Person Surgery™
The Universal Protocol applies to all surgical and nonsurgical invasive procedures. For more information on the Universal Protocol, visit The Joint Commission website: http://www.jointcommission.org/standards_information/up.aspx.

From https://www.jointcommission.org/hap_2017/npsgs/.
For more information on the National Patient Safety Goals, visit The Joint Commission website: www.jointcommission.org/PatientSafety/NationalPatientSafetyGoals/.

effective on January 1 of the following year (TJC, 2016c); for more information on the NPSGs for specific organizations, one can access TJC's website.

MONITORING THE QUALITY OF HEALTH CARE

It is important for nurses to know how to design and conduct simple quality improvement projects to improve processes within their nursing units. Nurses need to know the basics of collecting and analyzing data and what to do with the results. They must be able to educate other nurses about performance improvement as well.

What Is Quality Improvement?

QI refers to the process or activities that are used to measure, monitor, evaluate, and control services, which will lead to measurable improvement to health care consumers. It includes reports that must be generated to track progress. Incidence reports are sometimes referred to as QI reports or variance reports. These help guide the hospital risk management (RM) department and QI department to make system improvements (Box 22.2).

How Do We Monitor Quality?

As stated earlier, someone must monitor quality care compliance to continuously maintain and improve standards of practice. The QI department is typically the department that receives data, analyzes trends, and recommends actions to facilitate improvement in the organization. However, there should also be a CQI Council as a primary decision-making nursing team, as well as *quality circles* (QCs) that function along service lines, collaborating to improve care for a group of patient types.

Examples of service lines include surgical units, medical units, neurologic units, rehabilitation units, and outpatient units. These teams of nurses and other staff review specific problems or indicators each month to determine whether quality care is being delivered. The goal is to keep patients safe by encouraging everyone to practice according to established standards. Each service line provides an annual quality plan for the following year, based on recent problem areas or hot topics identified. Because it is impossible to track everything that nurses consider important to quality care, QCs use various methods to prioritize or target their reviews. They establish unit-specific *quality indicators* for tracking problems on the nursing unit using measurable questions that provide data for trending improvements.

What Is an Indicator and a Metric?

A *quality indicator* is an item of concern that has arisen because of a nursing practice problem. It is often an RM as well. For example, a quality team may have identified a problem with securing urethral catheters properly. This seems to be a recurrent issue. Perhaps several patients had urethral catheters that were inadvertently pulled out. After some investigation and collecting baseline data, the problem was identified as having to do with not securing the catheters properly. Thus the team will collect data for a specific time and will track the nurses' practices. They would count the number of urethral catheters not secured correctly and divide that by the total number of urethral catheters during a specific time frame to obtain the average rate of compliance. The metric or measure is the actual rate of urethral catheters that are secured properly (Table 22.1). The correct practice would be clarified with all nurses according to an established policy. Later, when most of the nurses were securing urethral catheters correctly, there may not be a need to monitor this particular practice any longer. In essence, the indicator is the problem, and the metric is the measurement of that problem.

BOX 22.2 COMMON QUALITY TERMS

Audit: A formal periodic check on quality measures to verify correctness of actions.

DMAIC: A Six Sigma process for improving existing processes that fall below institutional goals or national norms. DMAIC stands for *define, measure, analyze, improve, control.*

Key indicators: Selected data based on TJC mandates or on specific problem areas that may show the need for more extensive data collection or remedial action to resolve an identified problem (e.g., fall rates, medication error rates).

Key performance indicators (KPI): Reflect the things that the team wants to change. These are a part of the DMAIC and RCC process. Typical KPIs are time, costs, distance, numbers of incidents, or items.

Metric: A measurement to determine the rate of compliance or noncompliance with an indicator.

Monitor: Similar to auditing; checking or verifying that an established practice has been retained.

Operational definitions: A statement detailing the thing or event using specific identifiable and measurable wording with written inclusion and exclusion criteria.

Outcome or core measures: Measures that the public consumer considers important for choosing one hospital instead of another.

Pareto principle: 80% of the problems are caused by 20% of sources, people, or things. If you can fix the 20%, you can fix the system.

Patient safety goals: Annual goals established by TJC that highlight problematic areas in health care and describe evidence- and expert-based solutions to these problems. Goals are derived primarily from informal recommendations made in TJC's safety newsletter, *Sentinel Event Alert.*

Performance improvement: A plan and documentation method to demonstrate the procedures that have been used in the past and those that will be implemented for changes in the quality of services based on this previously collected data.

Plan–do–study–act (PDSA): Contained within an RCC for planning, doing, studying, and performing actions intended to drive and maintain change.

Quality assurance: Activities that are used to monitor, evaluate, and control services to provide some measure of quality to consumers.

Quality indicators: Data that indicate whether high-quality care is being maintained. Items of concern that have arisen because of a nursing practice problem (e.g., Foley catheter securing).

Quality measures: Tools used to measure health care functions, outcomes, patients overall health care experience, and organizational systems associated with providing quality health care.

Rapid cycle changes (RCCs): A strategy for process improvement as a part of DMAIC where changes are tried for very short time frames (3 to 7 days).

Six Sigma: A measurement standard in product variation that began in the 1920s when Walter Shewhart showed that three sigma from the mean is the point where a process requires correction. No fewer than 3.4 errors per million opportunities.

Stakeholders: Key people who will be affected by change and who can either positively or negatively influence the improvement.

Total quality management (TQM): A management style where the goal is producing quality services for the customer and where the customer defines what *quality* means.

A unit-based QI nurse is usually assigned the responsibility to audit charts or to verify a procedure by direct observation to determine compliance with a specific nursing practice. The results are compiled and sent to the QI department. After nurses are re-educated about the correct practice, the same indicator is tracked for several months to see whether there has been an improvement. This is done until noncompliance reaches pre-established criteria (e.g., below 5%) and/or compliance is 95%.

Indicators are sometimes selected based on an RM issue. For example, a patient may have suffered an injury because a catheter was not secured correctly. The critical thinking exercise

TABLE 22.1 INDICATOR AND METRIC DESCRIPTORS

INDICATOR	METRIC DESCRIPTORS
Admission documentation	Metric 1—Rate of patient's identified learning needs not documented within 24 hours of admission.
	Metric 2—Rate of skin assessment (Braden scale) not documented within 24 hours of admission.
	Metric 3—Rate of patient's identified spiritual needs not documented within 24 hours of admission.
Foley securing	Metric 1—Rate of Foley catheters not secured in place according to the procedure described in Potter and Perry textbook.
IV tube labeling	Metric 1—Rate of continuous flow IV tubing that has not been labeled with the date and time it needs to be changed.
	Metric 2—Rate of intermittent flow tubing (IVPB) has not been labeled with the date and time it needs to be changed.
Skin care	Metric 1—Rate of high-risk patients, as defined by the Braden scale (<17), who have pressure ulcers within 2 to 4 days of admission.
	Metric 2—Rate of those patients with pressure ulcers who are:
	Stage 1
	Stage 2
	Stage 3
	Stage 4
	Unstageable
	Suspected deep tissue injury
TORAV/VORAV Telephone or verbal orders	Metric 1—Rate of telephoned physician's orders that did not contain read-back verification by using "TORAV" *(telephone order read-back and verified)* documentation with signature of person taking the order on the first two charts of each odd-numbered day.

(Critical Thinking Box 22.1) can help you discover another example of how important chart auditing can be.

Table 22.1 shows some examples of metrics. Metric descriptors contain more detailed information about what is to be measured and what is not measured. For example, if bedside nurses

? CRITICAL THINKING BOX 22.1

An audit review committee composed of the quality coordinator, three nurses, two case managers, a physical therapist, and a pharmacist were charged with the task of reviewing the care for patients undergoing total hip replacement surgeries. The patients' care did not seem to conform to the expected length of stay (LOS) as established by Medicare DRG reimbursement charts. As committee members reviewed the chart and discussed the care of all 20 patients, they noted that Mr. Garcia had been ready for discharge at 10:00 AM on Tuesday, but the case manager for that nursing unit was not able to place him in a rehabilitation unit until 48 hours later. Many of the other 19 charts depicted similar scenarios. As a result, the hospital was not reimbursed for the entire LOS, at a loss of approximately $4000 per incident.

1. Who is responsible for the error?
2. What do you think should be done in this situation?
3. What steps can be taken to prevent this situation from occurring in the future?

were measuring the rate of IV tubing labeled according to policy, they would further define what type of IV tubing is used. Further exploration would determine whether data should include only primary IV lines or both primary and piggyback lines. Most likely, the metrics would include both, but it is always best to be specific about what is to be counted. TJC surveyors typically look at these details.

Of primary importance, metrics and key indicators are developed after baseline data have been collected and careful consideration has been given to how things really exist before any actions toward improvement are implemented. Improvement should not be based on hearsay or what someone *thinks* the problems are. When collecting baseline data, the QI nurse does not tell anyone what indicator is being measured. In this way, the true patterns of clinical practice can be discovered. Otherwise, the results will not be as accurate or would be skewed.

The results of the data are analyzed on a monthly or quarterly basis by the QI department. They are tracked and trended with graphic displays, such as run charts or graphs or bar graphs. Written committee reports are prepared to explain the graphs and to keep a record of the findings. Based on the results over time, new processes may need to be developed or more education done. The QI department personnel generally develop the final reports for major hospital committees, for the Chief Nursing Officer, and for other Councils. Such reports are usually reviewed at each TJC visit. Thus we see that the contributions of each bedside nurse and the unit QI nurse are quite valuable in TJC survey process. TJC often commends hospitals based on their QI efforts.

What Are Core Measure Sets?

TJC mandates that organizations continuously track certain core measures to monitor quality care. Currently, there are 13 core measure sets. Each core measure includes certain performance measures that health care institutions track for reporting. Some of these include advance directives, autopsy rates, leaving against medical advice (AMA) and elopement rates, blood product use rates, blood transfusion reaction rates, conscious sedation complication rates, fall rates, medication error rates, mortality rates, pain management effectiveness, tobacco treatment rates, influenza vaccine administration rates, restraint use, perinatal care, rates of deep vein thrombosis, and surgical site infection rates. Simply put, these remain a part of TJC accreditation standards. Core measure sets are selected based on TJC problem areas that tend to recur. These may show the need for more extensive data collection or remedial action to resolve an identified problem. Regardless of whether there is improvement, TJC core measures must be continually tracked.

What Is Performance Improvement?

Performance improvement (PI) is synonymous with QI, and the terms are used interchangeably. Today, *improvement science* is the term often used, because the process has become very data driven. PI is a plan and documentation method that demonstrates what the standard procedures will be for nurses and others within the hospital. It includes changes that have been implemented based on previous data collection. PI is similar to the nursing process (assess, diagnose, plan, implement, and evaluate). Often QI nurses are called on to conduct small data collection processes and provide reports. Critical Thinking Box 22.2 provides a sample scenario so you can try out these skills.

? CRITICAL THINKING BOX 22.2

Metrics and Indicators

Your nursing unit has experienced a problem with the IV tubing not being labeled to show when it needs to be changed. You are the QI (quality improvement) nurse who must collect data for a process improvement project. The nurse manager has asked you to determine baseline data for a month and report your findings to her.

1. How would you go about doing this?
2. What would be the indicators?
3. What would be the metrics?
4. How would you present the results tabulated for a month to the stakeholders (or managers)?

After the RM and QI departments assess performance within the hospital system regarding the patient care services rendered, a diagnosis of sorts is made that demonstrates where standards are not being met. We often use the Pareto principle by looking for the 20% of sources that caused 80% of the problems. Planning involves fixing the 20% that contributed to the problem. Implementation occurs as new strategies are put into place to resolve the problems or errors. Evaluation takes place as data are collected through time, demonstrating compliance or noncompliance with the new technique. If noncompliant, in-service education may be conducted to emphasize the problem areas, and the measurement process continues.

The United States Pharmacopeial Convention (USP) has played a major role in collecting and trending medication error rates related to patient deaths. This organization has existed since 1820 to promote quality standards for medication use. In 1991, the USP began more intense investigation on prevention of medication errors. With the increased use of herbal and dietary supplements by consumers, the USP has contributed to ongoing efforts in setting standards for dietary supplements. This organization has been instrumental in focusing on problems with both the product and the system where medications and dietary supplements are prescribed, dispensed, administered, and used (United States Pharmacopeial Convention, 2016a).

One important quality initiative started by the USP and now licensed to Quantros is the MED-MARX® study, in which hospitals can enter their medication error data in an effort to help other hospitals understand why errors occur (United States Pharmacopeial Convention, 2016b). MEDMARX reports help hospital QI departments and nurses avoid similar errors in the future.

What Are the Barriers to Quality Improvement?

One of the primary barriers to implementing effective QI programs is cost. The cost of providing high-quality services within the health care organization has increased greatly during the past few decades. This is because of decreased payments from health insurance companies, including Medicare and Medicaid, as well as the increased costs of doing business. Health care organizations continue to look for ways to cut expenses by reducing the high cost of supplies or by reducing staff. However, with the continuing shortage of qualified registered nurses, reducing the number of nurses is neither advisable nor acceptable, especially when we think about the errors that can occur as a result. Nevertheless, improving quality can help offset many of the internal costs of care. When quality is high, liability costs are typically low, and vice versa. Liability risks are often reduced as quality initiatives prevent problems from happening. Soon, the organization begins to reap the rewards of "fire prevention" rather than constant "firefighting." After the hospital organization realizes that the cost of a lawsuit for each death or disability related to a medication error far outweighs the cost of nurses, then quality becomes critical. Other barriers to QI are nurses' loyalty to old practices and failure to recognize that changes are needed and based on evidence.

Nurses are often unaware of the need to change or are unwilling to change their practice from the way they have always done things. Many practicing nurses remain resistant to change, because it seems threatening and because it requires effort, retraining, and restructuring of habits. However, if we always do things the same old way, we will always receive the same results, which might not be good.

Many nurses have learned about how evidence-based practice (EBP) can help them in evaluating current practice. By looking into research studies about hospital issues and using EBP, nurses can make process changes that are tested in practice. This new knowledge provides the confidence nurses need when telling patients, physicians, and other nurses why they used specific practices. In addition, it is important to remain a lifelong learner of new information, especially because there is always uncertainty in decision making.

WHAT ARE SOME OTHER AGENCIES INFLUENCING PATIENT SAFETY?

The National Patient Safety Foundation (NPSF) is a nonprofit organization that for years has demonstrated a commitment to patient safety in health care by providing resources for both health care providers and consumers. Part of their mission is to promote understanding among caregivers and consumers. The NPSF holds an annual conference where patient safety knowledge is shared and where patient safety research results are presented. The organization also funds research to improve safety and quality care (National Patient Safety Foundation, 2016).

The Institute for Healthcare Improvement (IHI) is another nonprofit organization that is highly involved in patient safety initiatives. Founded in 1991, the IHI works to advance quality improvements and conducts seminars and conferences on patient safety topics. Their website has free open school courses in quality, and anyone can take these mini-courses. They are also involved in helping organizations implement patient safety ideas. They offer learning modules in their "open school," where continuing education units or credits are offered (Institute for Healthcare Improvement, 2016).

The Quality and Safety Education for Nurses Institute (QSEN) site has been developed to help prepare future nurses who will be needed in their health care environments to improve patient safety. The idea is to teach student nurses how always to be thinking about how to improve care for patients. It began in 2005 when the American Association of Colleges of Nursing (AACN) emphasized the importance of QI system thinking in nursing education. They took the stance that nurses today need to begin their nursing careers with knowledge about how to create and continuously improve systems of care.

Funded by the Robert Wood Johnson foundation, the QSEN project group came up with six competencies for teaching quality improvement (Table 22.2). The six core competencies include patient-centered care, teamwork and collaboration, evidence-based practice, quality improvement, safety, and informatics. Within each category are specifics about knowledge, skills, and attitudes (commonly referred to as KSAs).

In 2012, the QSEN project transitioned into the Case Western Reserve University QSEN Institute. A textbook has been published entitled *Quality and Safety in Nursing: A Competency Approach to Improving Outcomes* that is designed to have a lasting impact on nursing education. Continued focus of the institute's important work will be on educating faculty in graduate programs to teach quality and safety competencies (Quality and Safety Education for Nurses, 2016).

The Institute of Medicine (IOM) was established in 1970 as a nonprofit organization whose goal is to supply unbiased health care information so health care providers could make informed health decisions by providing reliable research evidence. This organization is responsible for several patient safety publications, including *To Err Is Human: Building a Safer Healthcare System; Keeping Patients Safe: Transforming the Work Environment of Nurses; Crossing the Quality Chasm: A New Health System for the 21st Century;* and *The Future of Nursing: Leading Change, Advancing Health* (Institute of Medicine [IOM],

TABLE 22.2   QSEN CORE NURSING COMPETENCIES
Obtained from: http://qsen.org/competencies/   • Patient-Centered Care   • Teamwork and Collaboration   • Evidence-Based Practice   • Quality Improvement   • Safety   • Informatics

2016). In *The Future of Nursing report,* the IOM stresses the importance of nursing to the health care of the nation to ensure quality care. The report identifies the barriers that impede nurses from practicing effectively. In conclusion, the report identifies eight recommendations that will reduce barriers to the nation's improved health care system (Table 22.3). For each recommendation, the research team identifies actions for educators, legislators, administrators, and nurses to ensure that these important changes happen. Most states have established "action coalitions" to ensure that these steps are initiated.

It is important to note that the report identifies nurses as key figures in promoting needed changes to support health, prevent illness, and care for patients with diverse and complex health care needs. Based on current research related to nursing care outcomes, the report stresses that a successful and safe health care system rests on advances in the education and autonomy of nurses.

The rationale for supporting the value of nurses is that they have specific strengths in such areas as care coordination, health promotion, and quality improvement. Nurses can fill new and expanded roles in a redesigned health care system. This will require that nurses be allowed to practice in accordance with their professional training, and they will need higher levels of education, which will better prepare them to deliver patient-centered, equitable, safe, high-quality health care services. They must be able to engage with physicians and other health care professionals to improve care and assume leadership roles in the redesign of the health care system. In this new system, primary care and disease prevention are the drivers of the system. Payment is based on value, not quantity of services performed, which should slow the increasing costs of health care (IOM, 2011).

The IOM recommendations are available at the IOM site as well as an abbreviated version of the entire report (http://iom.nationalacademies.org/).

Change is vital, improvement the logical form of change.

James Cash Penney

QUALITY IMPROVEMENT METHODS

There are several methods used with quality improvement. Whatever approach is used, the values of the institution will be evident in the quality plan. For example, if an organization places emphasis on worker injury prevention, their CQI program will include this idea. Leadership personnel must be genuinely committed to CQI, or it will not work. They must empower nurses and other employees to help plan and implement the needed strategies for change. Data must be collected systematically—not sporadically or on a whim. Blaming previous personnel for making mistakes does nothing to improve things. The work involves examining system issues with a proactive approach rather than always being reactive. This means anticipating risks and preventing them.

TABLE 22.3 IOM RECOMMENDATIONS FOR THE FUTURE OF NURSING

- Remove scope of practice barriers.
- Expand opportunities for nurses to lead and diffuse collaborative improvement efforts.
- Implement nurse residency programs.
- Increase the proportion of nurses with a baccalaureate degree to 80 percent by 2020.
- Double the number of nurses with a doctorate by 2020.
- Ensure that nurses engage in lifelong learning.
- Prepare and enable nurses to lead change to advance health.
- Build an infrastructure for the collection and analysis of interprofessional health care workforce data.

Obtained from: http://iom.nationalacademies.org/Reports/2010/The-Future-of-Nursing-Leading-Change-Advancing -Health/Recommendations.aspx.

Many organizations use quality teams, working groups, or quality circles (QCs) to conduct much of the data collection and improvement techniques. These groups need to have a sense of collaboration and appreciation for the value and ideas each person brings to the table. They must be committed to being a part of the solution, not a part of the problem.

Some problems we typically encounter in hospitals are delays in room assignments, delays in medication delivery, delays in treatments or other care, and internal system delays (e.g., dietary, linen). All of these time delays ultimately cost us more. Yet efficient people may not even realize these time traps are occurring, because they are so accustomed to developing and using "work-arounds" to eliminate them (Pape, 2006). Work-arounds are a safety threat, because working around something means getting around the problem instead of solving it. This can leave patients vulnerable to medication errors. An example of a work-around is the habit of borrowing medications from another patient in the interest of saving time. This type of practice is dangerous and does nothing to solve the system problem. Perhaps the pharmacy technician missed placing the medication in the patient's drawer or put it in the wrong one.

Other people simply ignore these time traps or delays in getting their work done. Instead, they just put in their 8 or 12 hours and go home, hoping perhaps tomorrow will be better. This is also not a productive way to solve problems on the nursing unit.

> Everyone wins when nurses join others who are willing to make things work well. Thus, it is critical to know about current CQI methods.

TOOLS AND PROCESSES FOR CONTINUOUS QUALITY IMPROVEMENT

Tools for CQI include forms, methods, and analytic techniques that assist in understanding a problem. Quality tools are more specific, because they include tools applied to solving organizational or unit-specific problems. This discussion does not include all the tools that can be used for CQI, but it provides an overview of the more up-to-date tools used today (Fig. 22.4).

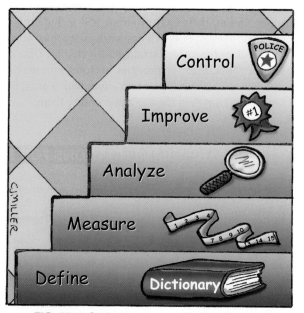

FIG. 22.4 Stair steps to quality health care.

What Is Six Sigma?

Six Sigma (SS) quality improvement methods are the newest wave of change initiatives for CQI. As with any new wave (e.g., root cause analysis; pain as the fifth vital sign), TJC will most likely be inclined toward recommending SS methods in the future for accreditation purposes. If this is the case, CQI employees will need SS education to understand and use the information to benefit the institution.

SS is a measurement standard that began in the 1920s, when Walter Shewhart showed that three sigma from the mean is the point where errors start to occur. Shewhart was one of Edward Deming's teachers and is responsible for the PDSA cycle of process improvement. Credit for coining the term "Six Sigma" goes to Bill Smith of Motorola. SS uses statistics to improve the efficiency of business processes. The primary goal of SS is to increase profits and reduce problems by improving standard operating procedures, reducing errors, and decreasing misuse of the system.

SS methodology is used with improvement science and involves reducing variation in practice through the application of DMAIC (define, measure, analyze, improve, control). In other words, after a protocol is found to be effective, everyone is trained to do it the same way. The SS DMAIC process is used primarily for improving existing processes that do not meet institutional goals or national norms. DMAIC can save companies thousands of dollars per project. SS means having no more than 3.4 defects per million opportunities, or 99.99966% accuracy. The idea is to focus on the voice of the customer (VOC), whether internal or external, and to reduce risks associated with high-volume, high-risk, problem-prone areas of practice. Internal customers are nursing staff that we work with and personnel from other departments. External customers include patients and visitors. This means that even the bedside nurse has a voice as an internal customer of the system. From the time DMAIC is adopted, nursing administrators must be supportive and trained in rapid cycle changes (RCCs) as a part of process improvement.

They must provide both financial and human resources and allow sufficient time for project teams to work. Then they need to be supportive of the efforts put forth. The entire organization must be behind the effort and be enthusiastic about change. Nurses and other health care providers need to have education on the DMAIC and RCC processes, as well. If the organizational culture is too resistant to change, it will be difficult. Often a cultural change is needed before the process will be successful. Every organization tends to have a certain culture by which it operates. When an organization is dealing with DMAIC, the culture should be one that rewards innovative ideas and is not resistant to change.

When referring to *data-driven methods,* we mean looking at real results that have been measured using numbers (calculations). The bottom line is that we know that we are not perfect, but we can strive to perform up to this 99.99966% goal.

Let's put this goal into perspective. If you take a million blood pressure readings, there should be no fewer than 3.4 that were incorrect.

Another important point is that most processes function more effectively if they are kept within a certain range of error. The intent is to control peaks and valleys in performance (those things that are way off target). In this instance, a flat line is a good thing, as long as it is near the 100% mark of compliance.

TABLE 22.4 **DMAIC**	
DMAIC IS PRONOUNCED *DUH-MAY-ICK* AND INCLUDES:	
DEFINE	Define the issue, possible causes, and goals.
MEASURE	Measure the existing system with metrics.
ANALYZE	Analyze the gap between the existing system and goal.
IMPROVE	Improve the system with creative strategies.
CONTROL	Control and sustain the improvement.

The DMAIC process (Table 22.4) provides more reliability and validity than other QI models and has become a national trend in QI strategies. Many companies will only do business with those who are using DMAIC.

In September 2002, the Robert Wood Johnson Foundation (RWJF) started the Urgent Matters organization, which launched improvement programs in selected hospitals as a way to reduce emergency department crowding. Changes were made in multiple hospital systems and were effective at improving patient safety as well as improving hospital throughput (Robert Wood Johnson Foundation, 2010).

Rapid cycle tests of change are part of DMAIC. Recent use of the DMAIC model was found helpful in improving medication administration and reducing medication errors for several hospitals. As a result of a medication administration checklist, nurses' focus was improved and there was less variation in practice. Signs with the words "Do Not Disturb during Medication Administration" reminded other people of the process. The protocol checklists and signs remained as reminders to reduce distractions and were simple, inexpensive tools to keep patients safe. Nurses also liked them because they could get their work done more quickly (Pape et al., 2005; Pape, 2013).

In another QI project, an operating room team improved patient outcomes from postoperative hypothermia by using the DMAIC model. Because of the DMAIC team approach and the use of real data, patients' temperatures showed improvement in the postanesthesia care unit (PACU) because they warmed patients in the preoperative holding area before surgery (Bitner et al., 2007). (See Research for Best Practice Box 22.1.)

HOW DO WE USE DMAIC?

The DMAIC flow diagram (Fig. 22.5) provides an overview of the DMAIC process. The framework shows how the process flows from start to finish and on to the next project. However, depending on the project, the steps may not always follow the path directed by the arrows. Depending on the situation, teams may need to change direction at times.

Sometimes the process may need to stop at the measure phase and go back to the design phase to develop formats for measuring. For example, the team may want to do some brainstorming or conduct RCCs to develop the best data collection form before moving on. Other times the form that was developed did not work, and the team might make a different one to use for data collection. Now we see that the PDSA cycle also fits well with DMAIC (Fig. 22.6). The PDSA is a way to examine change by developing a strategy to test the change (Plan), complete a test of the plan (Do), review the results (Study), and determine modifications that may be needed (Act).

PDSA is used to plan and conduct RCCs. However, there is no "one size fits all" for organizations using DMAIC. Nevertheless, the organization needs to standardize the DMAIC process somewhat so that everyone understands his or her roles and functions during each step. As indicated, the PDSA cycle is contained within the RCC. Thus each project will be done slightly differently. The main focus

RESEARCH FOR BEST PRACTICE BOX 22.1

Nurse–Physician Rounding

Practice Issue

One of the most important steps for reducing error and improving efficiencies is in improving nurse–physician relationships. This quality improvement study considered the impact of nurse–physician rounding on making improvements to their practice and patient care (Burns, 2011).

The study showed that using nurse–physician rounds in this 350-bed hospital did improve communication and efficiencies. The researchers began with a desire to improve patient satisfaction by having their medical needs met. Studies have shown that patients value collaborative communication at the bedside and active participation in their care.

For this pilot project, the team used behavior modification, specific communication techniques, and scripting to help with the process improvement project. Before implementation of the rounding project, an outline of expected behaviors and communication tips was given to all nurses on the unit. Staff members offered feedback on implementation at weekly meetings. The team piloted the project on one unit for 4 weeks. Nurse assignments were faxed to the hospitalist office at 6:00 AM each day so they would be aware of which nurse to contact when they arrived on the unit. Nurse managers and hospitalist managers were visible and available to guide the process.

In the early stages, nurses felt that hospitalists did not value nursing time, and compliance with rounding was low (25% to 30% compliance). However, as the weeks progressed, fewer reminders were needed from nursing leaders about the importance of the project, and rounding increased to 67% compliance. The patients seemed to enjoy the verification by the nurse of what the hospitalist said while at the bedside. The nurses enjoyed knowing firsthand what the medical plan of treatment would be. By the end of the pilot study, patient satisfaction scores showed an increase in physician communication with the patient, and overall teamwork went from 0 percentile to the 100th percentile ranking.

Implications for Nursing Practice

- Nurse–physician relationships can improve through collaborative care.
- Of importance are frequent input and communication in planning and implementation of such a project.
- Support from management is critical to the success of physician/care provider–nurse rounding. The nurse manager needs significant coaching and intervention.
- Physician/care provider support is also critical to the success of the rounding process.
- Daily communication between physicians and nurses will promote the success of the process.
- A standardized rounding tool or checklist can assist patients, nurses, and physicians in communicating effectively (Johnson & Conner, 2014).
- Collaborative rounds between physicians and nurses can improve patient satisfaction scores.

Considering This Information

What would you do to promote collaborating with physicians or other health care providers?

Reference

Burns, K. (2011). Nurse-physician rounds: A collaborative approach to improving communication, efficiencies, and perception of care. *MEDSURG Nursing: The Journal of Adult Health, 20*(4), 194–199.

Johnson, B. T., & Conner, B. T. (2014). What works: Physician and nurse rounding improves patient satisfaction. *American Nurse Today, 9*(12). Retrieved from http://www.americannursetoday.com/nurse-physician-rounding-patient-satisfaction/.

is to keep on track with the goal in mind and to use real data, not guesswork or gossip, to direct decisions. As they say, if you do not measure it, you cannot fix it.

Through an initiative called *Transforming Care at the Bedside* (TCAB), the IHI and the RWJF used RCCs on medical/surgical units. Bedside nurses were involved in making needed changes that improved patient care. The result was the development of many tools and innovative care practices (Rutherford et al., 2004).

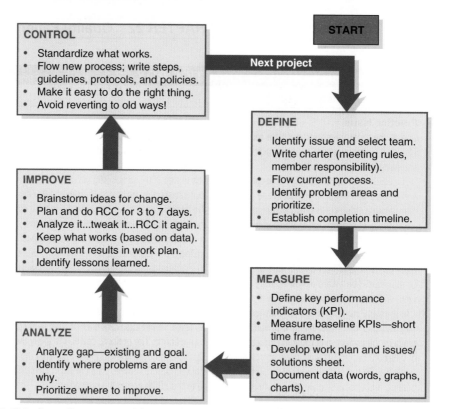

FIG. 22.5 This flow diagram provides an overview of the define–measure–analyze–improve–control (DMAIC) process using rapid cycle changes (RCCs). The framework depicts the flow from the starting point of Define through Control to the next project. However, depending on the project, the process may not always follow the path directed by the arrows. Depending on the situation, teams may need to change direction at times.

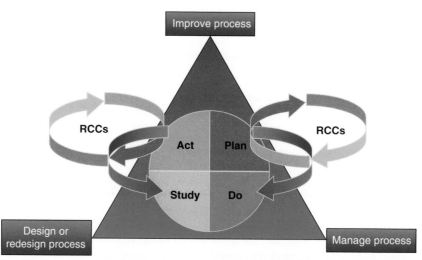

FIG. 22.6 The Six Sigma engine depicts the parts of DMAIC to (1) improve processes, (2) design or redesign processes, and (3) manage processes. The diagram here, designed by Dr. Tess Pape, depicts how the PDSA and RCCs tie into DMAIC. The most powerful difference between Six Sigma's DMAIC and other improvement methods is the precision used in finding and keeping solutions to problems. The plan–do–study–act (PDSA) cycle also fits well with DMAIC (define–measure–analyze–improve–control). PDSA is used to plan and conduct rapid cycle tests (RCCs) of change. There is no "one size fits all" for organizations using DMAIC to move toward Six Sigma.

The Define Phase

In the define phase, a charter is developed as a written document of the work the team will accomplish. A charter is usually developed and agreed on among the team members as to what they see as the problem and where they want to go. First, they identify the business case, main goals, team leaders, and team responsibilities or roles. The business case is a statement about why it is important to consider resolving the problem in terms of cost, injury, or standards.

When team members are chosen, it is important to include only those who want to be a part of the solution and not a part of the problem. This is no place for "whiners" or complainers. Then set team rules (attendance, absence, how decisions are made). During meetings, ask that only one conversation go on at a time (no sidebars). Determine what the limits are on resources (financial, personal, time), and plan to discuss those.

Allow brainstorming during meetings. *Brainstorming* is a process by which a group of people thinks about, talks about, and lists many solutions to the problem. Some ideas may sound crazy at first, but group members should not ridicule them. The oddest ideas can often be changed into very useful ones. Although this may cause some delays in meeting goals, it is a valuable part of the process. That is how great innovative ideas start. During meetings, identify who the stakeholders are and how they will be affected. Stakeholders are key people who will be affected by change and those who can either influence or derail the improvement. Consider how to sell ideas to the stakeholders. Also, identify support resources and supportive people. Who will provide the money and/or support the recommended changes?

Next, write the problem statement and goal statement. The problem statement will be similar to the business case. Write down the cost of doing nothing differently (firefighting) versus the cost of improving. These costs can be in dollar amounts or lost time, injury, errors, or dissatisfaction, for example. Set the goal in terms of how much saving is planned—10%? 25%? By what date?

Example: Problem Statement—The number of patients waiting to be seen by an MD in the emergency department (ED) is excessive, and patients are dissatisfied. Controls are needed so that there is a limited number of minutes between bed placement and MD arrival to bedside. Patients need to be cared for efficiently so that they can get through the system in a timely manner, thus making room for more patients who are waiting in the waiting room. The hospital needs to contain costs and improve patient satisfaction.

Example: Goal Statement—There will be a 25% decrease in amount of time patients must wait in the ED before being seen by a physician.

In the example, the team would "flow out," or make a diagram of the processes (Fig. 22.7), that take place within the problem or the unit. When flow diagramming, use large sheets of paper or write on a dry erase board. If a board is used, someone should still take notes or obtain images and record the flow process on paper so that it can be kept as a record. Flow the current "as is" process. At this point, the team needs to know how things are actually happening, not how they are supposed to happen.

Ask lots of questions, such as why things happen at each step. Identify problem areas for improvements. Think "outside the box" and slay "sacred cows"! This means being willing to be innovative and objective in thinking of possible solutions.

At the start of each team meeting, review the agenda or plan for the meeting. Ask for any additions to the agenda, listen to each person's past assignment results, and review the overall progress that individuals have made. It is important to allow time for discussion and brainstorming. At the end of the meeting, review what major points have been presented, and set assignments for the next meeting.

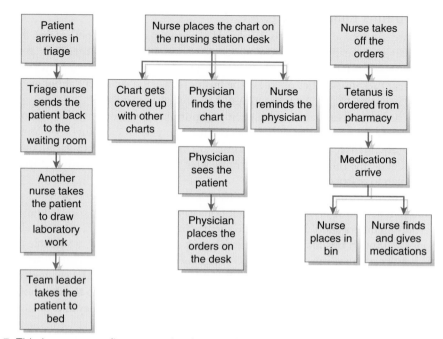

FIG. 22.7 This is a process flow example about patient wait time. There are inputs, processes, and outputs in a typical flow diagram.

Develop a work plan using an Excel spreadsheet used for tracking plans. This keeps the team focused and is used to track brainstorming sessions. Fig. 22.8 provides another flow process example with a medication delivery process diagrammed systematically as a group.

The Measure Phase

Everyone within the team needs to agree on what is to be measured. These are called *key performance indicators* (KPIs). KPIs should reflect the things that the team sees as problem areas. Typical KPIs are time, costs, distance, numbers of incidents, or items. It is best to use whole numbers (with decimals) and measurable facts. Never use what someone *thinks* is a problem. Measure the problem first. It is also important to identify who will be responsible for data collection, retrieval, and analysis. Ultimately, if the team fails to document everything, things will fall apart quickly.

Identify what specifically will be measured to determine improvements and what will not be measured. Operational definitions for the KPIs detail the thing or event using specific wording with written inclusion and exclusion criteria. These are similar to metric descriptors discussed earlier. They define in detail what is to be measured. These definitions tell the team what is not going to be measured. This helps get everyone in agreement on what is identifiable and measurable.

For example: KPI #1—The number of near-miss medication incidents on the nursing unit because of wrong medications found in the automated dispensing machine. We are including only those kept in the automated dispensing machine and are excluding any kept in other areas.

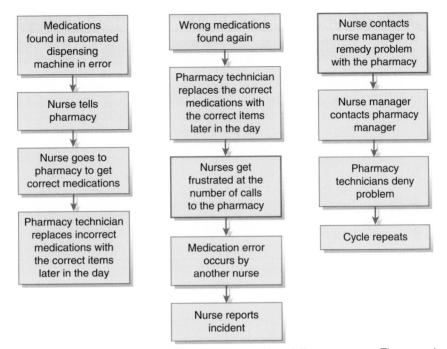

FIG. 22.8 This is a process flow example about a medication delivery process. There are inputs, processes, and outputs in a typical flow diagram.

Begin by measuring baseline numbers. That is, start with what exists currently before any changes are made. In other words, do not meddle with things until you know how bad the problem is. Do not tell anyone what is being investigated or measured. Otherwise, it could skew the measures, and you will not see any true changes when you do RCCs. Baseline measures can be retrospective if data have already been collected, or you can go forward for a couple of weeks to find out what the real data show. Find out what the actual losses are in time, errors, or dollars.

1. Get all the facts about the numbers of errors first. Record them in the work plan.
2. Measure and track the issue throughout a defined period of time based on what would be a realistic time frame to obtain a sample of what is occurring. This may need to be done for 2 to 4 weeks or longer.
3. Document data in words, graphs, pie charts, and bar charts.

The Analyze Phase

The analyze phase is usually a short phase, but it can be longer depending on the issue. Analyze the baseline data collected. Be objective in identifying where the real problems exist. These may be indicated by peaks in the graphs related to the number of incidences over a 2- to 4-week period and may relate to problems with processes. What could the underlying causes of the peaks in the graph be?

1. Identify the *gaps* between the current performance and the goal. Identify how far you need to come to get to the goal.
2. When looking at the data to identify possible sources of variation, avoid blaming people or blaming past ways of doing things.
3. Look at the current process flow diagram again and determine where to begin making a change.
4. Move quickly to the next phase to improve.

TABLE 22.5	**THE PDSA CYCLE WITHIN THE RCC**
PLAN	State the goal of the RCC cycle. Make predictions about what will be expected to happen. Who will be responsible, at what time, and what place? When will it occur? Where will it take place first?
	What are we trying to accomplish?
	How will we know when we get there? Roughly, how far do we expect to come (percentage, minutes)? Use only data that are reflective of the KPIs. For example, you would not measure the time it takes to do something if you are looking at the number of incidences.
	What change can we feasibly make that will result in improvement? Be realistic about what can be changed.
	How long should it take? How many days should you run the RCC to see a result? Keep it as short as possible ... 7 to 10 days.
DO	First, carry out the RCC on one or two nursing units for 3 to 7 days. If it needs tweaking, make a small change, and RCC again for 3 to 7 days or longer, depending on the issue. Then move to another nursing unit.
STUDY	Compare the resulting data to your predictions, to baseline, and contrast it to previous time frames. For example: What was the improvement in time compared with last week?
ACT	Act on what was discovered after the initial RCC. What are the new changes the team can make based on results? What might the next cycle be? Go on to do another RCC to improve the process further.

The Improve Phase

The improve phase is a good place to determine whether measures reflect the true problems. The problem statement and goal statement may need to be revised based on the findings. The data collected may have shown that no real problem exists or that the problem involves other issues.

Now use the PDSA cycle (Table 22.5) to plan and implement some RCCs. The idea is to think of creative ways to improve things. Brainstorm ideas for the RCCs that you might try based on a problem process step within the flow diagram and the baseline metrics. Brainstorming is the process where all team members spontaneously contribute and gather ideas without excluding any idea given. It is usually performed rapidly with all ideas considered and recorded. Be clear about what the target is and play off of each other's suggestions.

The group may consider using a fair voting method or writing out RCC ideas, so all ideas can be obtained without the factors that can influence unbiased sharing. The collective ideas can then be reviewed by the group leader and presented to the group.

1. Ask yourself: Can a step in the process be eliminated? Simplifying steps and deleting steps in a process can often eliminate big defects.
2. Can a new method be tried?
3. Next, conduct the RCC using the PDSA cycle (see Table 22.5) for 3 to 7 days. Include staff education before starting the RCC so that everyone understands what is expected.
4. Conduct the RCC and study the results. Document everything in the work plan.
5. Analyze the data with percentage calculations for improvements over baseline for the previous week.
6. Document all brainstorming sessions.

Use data to determine whether there were improvements or a lack of improvement. What percentage of improvement was there this week compared with last week? Compared with the baseline measure? How many minutes, difference is there? Make decisions based on fact, not assumptions. Small improvements still mean improvement, and they help determine whether you are on the right track or not.

Small changes may need to be made in the process that was tried, so tweak it, and test it again with a change in the RCC over 3 to 7 days. Compare percentages again (against baseline or the previous week) and determine whether there was any improvement.

Market the solutions to the people whose cooperation is needed. If frontline people have been involved at the outset, this part is easier. Prepare for possible objections to the implementation of the change, and plan to overcome them.

The Control Phase

Now you are ready to establish controls to keep things going in the right direction. Controlling and sustaining the improvement is not easy and requires the development, documentation, and implementation of an ongoing monitoring plan.

1. Standardize the steps in the new process and detail new flow diagrams. Write standard operating procedures, protocols, steps, guidelines, or policies so that it will be easier for people to do the right thing and more difficult for them to do the wrong thing.
2. Educate everyone about the new practice. Distribute the information in a systematic manner so that everyone in the organization has an equal chance of being informed. Educate new employees in correct procedures, and be an example for them to follow.
3. Keep people informed of any changes.
4. Prevent reversion back to old ways or breaks in the "critical links" in the process by developing a process to monitor that changes have stuck and gains are sustained. Keep the process on its new course, and maintain the new practices you worked so hard to develop. Backsliding can occur easily, because people tend to return to old habits. Change can be difficult when faced with an unfamiliar or new situation.
5. Continue to measure KPIs routinely to see whether solutions are still working. If slipping occurs, reinforce the new change or do more RCCs.

Box 22.3 provides a simplified example of DMAIC used successfully in one emergency center. Many of the important details have been left out because of limited space. However, the basic process can be seen. Now see what you can do with the DMAIC process on a small scale using the scenario in Critical Thinking Box 22.3.

BOX 22.3 EXAMPLE OF DMAIC IN THE EMERGENCY CENTER

Problem statement: A physician does not see Emergency Department patients in a timely manner.

Define

The team *Defined* the cause of the problem as having to do with where the charts are placed.

Goal—Get the charts to the physicians sooner.

Business case—Cost of doing nothing different = Unhappy patients, possible patient complications, lack of bed space, and bottlenecks in throughput.

Measure

Key performance indicator (KPI) #1 = Time between patient bed placement and being seen by physician.

The team *Measured* the actual average baseline data (KPI #1) during a period of 2 weeks. Baseline = 90 minutes (15 minutes).

Target = Patients should be seen within 30 minutes of bed placement (a 50% improvement) within a month.

continued

BOX 22.3   **EXAMPLE OF DMAIC IN THE EMERGENCY CENTER—cont'd**

Analyze

The team *Analyzed* the gap between existing situation and goal of 30 minutes (gap is 60 minutes). The gap also depended on which physician was on duty.

Can something be done about which physician was on duty? Not really.

The team brainstormed for other ideas. Can something be done about where charts are placed? Yes.

Improve

The team *Improved* by doing RCCs.

KPI #1 = Time of patient bed placement to seen by MD.

RCC #1: For the next 5 days, the team members who were involved placed charts in a separate bin and measured KPI #1.

Result = The physician saw patients on time 34% of the time. So they tweaked the plan and did more RCCs.

RCC #2: For the next 5 days they placed charts on separate bedside table (the deck) and set up a log book of times that charts were placed and picked up.

Still measured KPI #1 = Time of patient bed placement to time seen by physician and added another KPI.

KPI #2 = Time between charts placed on deck and picked up from deck.

Result = Physician saw patients on time 20% of the time.

The team again brainstormed, tweaked the plan, and did more RCCs.

Next 5 days, one physician was assigned as deck officer to oversee the process.

Result = physician saw patients on time 99% of the time within 30 minutes.

Control

The team *Controlled* and sustained the improvement by establishing a standard practice.

They wrote a protocol and announced the new practice

The protocol was always to place charts on deck and to assign a deck officer to monitor timeliness of chart retrieval.

The Department Director monitored effectiveness of the protocol and watched for slippage into old ways.

❓ CRITICAL THINKING BOX 22.3

A retrospective review of several charts showed that documentation for 40% of PRN medications was lacking a previous assessment of pain. About 50% of the charts did not have documentation that the pain was evaluated according to policy within 30 to 45 minutes after the PRN medication was administered. You have been asked to lead a team to resolve the problems that mostly occurred on your nursing unit.

1. What standard of practice has been violated?
2. How would you go about conducting your problem resolution using the DMAIC approach for process improvement?
3. Who would you include on your team?
4. Who will develop the work plan and issue solutions sheet?
5. When will meetings be held? What are the ground rules?
6. What is the business case?
7. What are the goals and targets?
8. What are the KPIs?
9. What RCC can be performed?
10. Imagine that you have some excellent RCC results. What will you do to control the improvement?

> Practice improves results with time, and it can be a lot of fun.

HEALTH CARE PROVIDER CREDENTIALING FOR QUALITY IMPROVEMENT

Some larger health care organizations require that an individual obtain a certification in health care quality within a certain period after the hire date. Persons can become a *Certified Professional in Healthcare Quality* (CPHQ) after taking a certification test to determine their knowledge of quality management, quality improvement, case/care/disease/utilization management, and risk management at all employment levels and in all health care settings.

Although there is no longer a minimum education requirement, those who test should have worked in quality management for a minimum of 2 years and should review testing requirements before investing money into taking the examination. Approximately 75% of those who apply to test actually achieve certification.

CONCLUSION

Quality is about fire prevention, not firefighting, and accountability for one's actions is critical in nursing. We must provide quality care that is cost-effective and meets the health needs of our patients. We do not have the luxury to give a patient all the time we would like or to use any equipment and supplies we want. That is why it is important to find safe solutions that save time and money. Nurses must be accountable to both the quality of care and the economics of providing that care. In quality improvement, the organization must first consider the voice of the customer, whether internal or external. The "squeaky wheel" issues are sometimes where organizations start implementing improvements. However, action should be taken first on those matters that are associated with high-volume, high-risk, problem-prone practices and where errors frequently occur. Proven methods for quality improvement should be emphasized in all health care settings.

DMAIC is one method for improving quality, and it should be taught as a standard process so that everyone in the organization understands the roles and functions during each step. PDSA is used to plan and conduct rapid cycle tests of change. Certainly each organization must evaluate using DMAIC to move toward Six Sigma. The future of quality and patient safety is promising, as more and more health care providers and organizations are committed to investing time, education, and resources for safety changes. Improvement is everyone's business, as cost savings are realized with improved processes and reduced liability. Increasingly, nurses are required to know about quality improvement processes as soon as they begin their careers. See the end of this chapter for relevant websites and online resources that will serve as great resources for you while in nursing school and in your professional practice—so be sure to check them out! The future of health care will demand more vigilance as the Affordable Care Act takes the nursing profession in new directions.

> Change is inevitable! It is the one thing you can always count on. Things will never be the same as they once were. So if you want to prevent other people from making changes for you, you have to get involved in the process. Rather than resist change, embrace it and make it yours! He who fails to invent change is at the mercy of those who will! Regardless of what is going on around you, remember that as a nurse you have a responsibility to provide care in a way that is research based and follows best care practices. It means nurses need to monitor the health care delivery processes and evaluate outcomes to ensure quality of care.

🌐 RELEVANT WEBSITES AND ONLINE RESOURCES

Agency for Healthcare Research and Quality (AHRQ) (2015)
Innovation exchange. Retrieved from http://www.innovations.ahrq.gov/.

Agency for Healthcare Research and Quality (AHRQ) (n.d.)
Innovation exchange—checklists with medication vest or sash reduce distractions during medication administration. Retrieved from http://www.ahrq.gov/health-care-information/topics/topic-innovations-exchange.html.

Agency for Healthcare Research and Quality (AHRQ) (n.d.)
AHRQ's mistake-proofing the design of health care processes. Retrieved from http://archive.ahrq.gov/professionals/quality-patient-safety/patient-safety-resources/resources/mistakeproof/index.html.

Agency for Healthcare Research and Quality (AHRQ) (2016)
AHRQ's patient safety network. Retrieved from http://www.psnet.ahrq.gov/.

Agency for Healthcare Research and Quality (AHRQ) (2016)
AHRQ's patient safety network glossary. Retrieved from http://www.psnet.ahrq.gov/glossary.aspx.

American Nurses Association (ANA) (2013)
ANA National Database of Nursing Quality Indicators (NDNQI). Retrieved from http://www.nursingworld.org/MainMenuCategories/ANAMarketplace/ANAPeriodicals/OJIN/TableofContents/Volume122007/No3Sept07/NursingQualityIndicators.html.

Centers for Medicare & Medicaid Services (CMS) (n.d.)
Retrieved from http://www.cms.gov.

HCAHPS (n.d.)
Hospital care quality information from the consumer perspective. Retrieved from http://www.hcahpsonline.org/home.aspx.

Institute of Medicine (2016)
Retrieved from http://iom.nationalacademies.org/.

Institute for Healthcare Improvement (IHI) (2016)
Retrieved from http://www.IHI.org.

Institute for Healthcare Improvement (IHI) (2016)
Transforming care at the bedside. Retrieved from http://www.ihi.org/offerings/Initiatives/PastStrategicInitiatives/TCAB/Pages/Materials.aspx.

IHI Open School's online course The Fairness Algorithm YouTube Video
Retrieved from http://www.youtube.com/watch?v=8le7vYPUwaM.

Institute for Safe Medication Practices (ISMP) (2016)
Retrieved from http://www.ismp.org/.

Joint Commission Center for Transforming Healthcare (2016)
Safety culture. Retrieved from http://www.centerfortransforminghealthcare.org/projects/detail.aspx?Project=6.

Little K (2009)
Creating run charts. Retrieved from http://www.youtube.com/watch?v=03-8vtwCW9c.

National Patient Safety Foundation (NPSF) (2016)
Retrieved from http://www.npsf.org/.

🌐 **RELEVANT WEBSITES AND ONLINE RESOURCES—cont'd**

Quality and Safety Education for Nurses (QSEN) (2016)
Retrieved from http://qsen.org/.

The Joint Commission (TJC) (2016)
Retrieved from http://www.jointcommission.org/.

The Joint Commission (TJC) (2016)
National patient safety goals. http://www.jointcommission.org/standards_information/npsgs.aspx.

School of Medicine and Health Sciences; George Washington University. Urgent matters (2016)
Retrieved from http://urgentmatters.org/.

World Health Organization (WHO) (2016)
Retrieved from http://www.who.int/en/.

BIBLIOGRAPHY

Bitner, J., et al. (2007). A team approach to the prevention of unplanned postoperative hypothermia. *AORN Journal, 85,* 921–929.

Centers for Medicare & Medicaid Services. (2015a). *2015 Reporting—ACO measures narrative.* Retrieved from https://www.cms.gov/Medicare/Medicare-Fee-for-Service-Payment/sharedsavingsprogram/Downloads/ACO-NarrativeMeasures-Specs.pdf.

Centers for Medicare & Medicaid Services. (2015b). *Hospital compare.* Retrieved from https://www.cms.gov/medicare/quality-initiatives-patient-assessment-instruments/hospitalqualityinits/hospitalcompare.html.

Centers for Medicare & Medicaid Services. (2016a). *Quality measures, reporting, and performance standards.* Retrieved from https://www.cms.gov/Medicare/Medicare-Fee-for-Service-Payment/sharedsavingsprogram/Quality-Measures-Standards.html.

Ehsani, S. R., Cheraghi, M. A., Nejati, A., Salari, A., Esmaeilpoor, A. H., & Nejad, E. M. (2013). Medication errors of nurses in the emergency department. *Journal of Medical Ethics and History of Medicine, 6*(11).

HCAHPS. (2014). *HCAHPS: Patients' perspectives of care survey.* Retrieved from https://www.cms.gov/Medicare/Quality-Initiatives-Patient-Assessment-instruments/HospitalQualityInits/HospitalHCAHPS.html.

Institute for Healthcare Improvement. (2016). *History.* Retrieved from http://www.ihi.org/about/pages/history.aspx.

Institute of Medicine. (2016). *About the IOM.* Retrieved from http://iom.nationalacademies.org/About-IOM.aspx.

Institute of Medicine. (2011). *The future of nursing: Leading change, advancing health.* Committee on the Robert Wood Johnson Foundation initiative on the future of nursing, at the Institute of Medicine. National Academy of Sciences, 1–620.

Institute of Medicine. (2001). *Crossing the quality chasm: A new health system for the 21st century.* Retrieved from http://iom.nationalacademies.org/hmd/Reports/2001/Crossing-the-Quality-Chasm-A-New-Health-System-for-the-21st-Century.aspx.

National Patient Safety Foundation. (2016). *About us.* Retrieved from http://www.npsf.org/?page=aboutus.

Pape, T. M. (2013). The effect of a five-part intervention to decrease omitted medications. *Nursing Forum, 48,* 211–222. http://dx.doi.org/10.1111/nuf.12025.

Pape, T. M. (2006). *Workaround error, AHRQ WebM&M cases and commentaries.* Retrieved from https://psnet.ahrq.gov/webmm/case/118.

Pape, T. M., et al. (2005). Innovative approaches to reducing nurses' distractions during medication administration. *Journal of Continuing Education in Nursing, 36*, 33–39.

Pape, T. M. (2003, April). Applying airline safety practices to medication administration. *MEDSURG Nursing: Journal of Adult Health, 12*, 77–94.

Quality and Safety Education for Nurses. (2016). *Quality and safety education for nurses (QSEN) Institute.* Retrieved from http://qsen.org/.

Robert Wood Johnson Foundation (RWJF). (2010). *RWJF program empowers nurses to improve patient care.* Retrieved from http://www.rwjf.org/en/library/articles-and-news/2010/07/rwjf-program-empowers-nurses-to-improve-patient-care.html.

Rutherford, P., Lee, B., & Greiner, A. (2004). Transforming care at the bedside. IHI Innovation Series white paper. Boston: Institute for Healthcare Improvement. Retrieved from http://www.ihi.org/resources/Pages/IHIWhitePapers/TransformingCareattheBedsideWhitePaper.aspx.

The Joint Commission. (2016a). *Sentinel event alert.* Retrieved from http://www.jointcommission.org/topics/hai_sentinel_event.aspx.

The Joint Commission. (2016b). *Core measure sets.* Retrieved from http://www.jointcommission.org/core_measure_sets.aspx.

The Joint Commission. (2016c). *2017 National Patient Safety Goals.* Retrieved from http://www.jointcommission.org/standards_information/npsgs.aspx.

U.S. Department of Health and Human Services. (2016). *Healthy People 2020.* Retrieved from http://www.healthypeople.gov/.

U.S. Department of Health and Human Services. (2015). *Medication errors.* Retrieved from https://psnet.ahrq.gov/primers/primer/23/medication-errors.

United States Pharmacopeia Convention. (2016a). *About the United States Pharmacopeial Convention.* Retrieved from http://www.usp.org/about-usp.

United States Pharmacopeia. (2016b). *MEDMARX® data reports.* Retrieved from http://www.usp.org/search/site/medmarx.

23

Nursing Informatics

Cheryl D. Parker, PhD, MSN, RN-BC, FHIMSS

ⓔ http://evolve.elsevier.com/Zerwekh/nsgtoday/.

If we cannot name it [nursing practice], we cannot control it, finance it, research it, teach it, or put it into public policy.
Norma M. Lang, PhD, RN, FAAN, FRCN

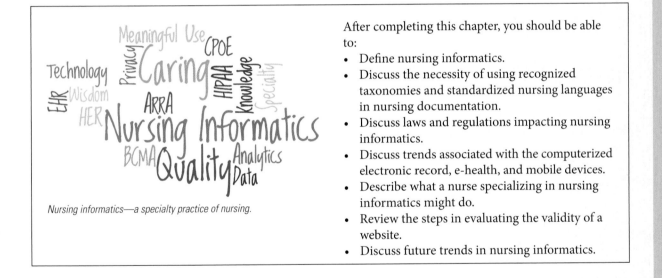

Nursing informatics—a specialty practice of nursing.

After completing this chapter, you should be able to:

- Define nursing informatics.
- Discuss the necessity of using recognized taxonomies and standardized nursing languages in nursing documentation.
- Discuss laws and regulations impacting nursing informatics.
- Discuss trends associated with the computerized electronic record, e-health, and mobile devices.
- Describe what a nurse specializing in nursing informatics might do.
- Review the steps in evaluating the validity of a website.
- Discuss future trends in nursing informatics.

At the crossroads of technology and patient care stand the nurses who have chosen nursing informatics (NI) as their specialty. Nursing informatics is a well-established specialty within nursing, which today has evolved to be an integral part of health care delivery and a differentiating factor in the selection, implementation, and evaluation of health IT that supports safe, high quality, patient-centric care.
Healthcare Information Management Systems Society (HIMSS) Position Paper: Transforming Nursing Practice through Technology & Informatics, June 17, 2011

Computer technology is pervasive today. Everywhere we turn technology is in evidence. The neighborhood grocery store has automated scanners and checkout lines. Your bank has automated tellers, check scanners, wire transfers, and online services. The school and local libraries have automated catalogs, interlibrary lending, and online books. From our homes and smartphones, we can access the world through the Internet, researching any question, texting and e-mailing, watching streaming videos, and purchasing just about anything. You can complete an advanced degree without ever stepping foot on a campus with a faculty and fellow students who can be literally half a world away. A litany of computerized marvels could fill volumes.

Technology has impacted our culture in multiple ways. When answering machines were first introduced, many people considered their use to be quite rude. Now, just the opposite is true—it is rude if your voice mailbox is full. Sending handwritten invitations with an RSVP has been replaced with online invites with automatic tracking of accepts.

The explosion of new technology since the early 1980s that makes all this possible is truly phenomenal. What is even more incredible, and perhaps a bit frightening to some, is that this seems just to be the beginning. The time has come when the thoughts, communications, creations, manuscripts, learning material, and financial assets of the civilized world will exist primarily in electronic form. If the lights went out, civilization as we know it would cease to exist, as most of modern society depends on the electrical and information infrastructure.

Health care is not immune. Some of the most complex automated systems, and certainly some of the most complex requirements for these systems, can be found in the health care environment. Systems to serve the diverse needs of the health care industry—from the administration and financial departments to the many clinical disciplines—need to be implemented and integrated across the continuum of care within modern health care organizations. As a result, the demand for health care professionals who are knowledgeable in the application of this technology is growing rapidly.

Even with technology all around us, some users do not always feel comfortable with it, especially in the patient care environment where everything may be new to us. Health care technology is sometimes confusing, intimidating, and—in large part because it changes so rapidly—downright bewildering to some. Even so, there are some relative constants that make the field less confusing and easier to manage. The goal of this chapter is not to make you a computer guru or even an entry-level informatics nurse. As Hovenga, Kidd, Garde, and Cossio (2010) pointed out so aptly:

> You don't need to be a computer genius to use a computer effectively in your professional life. You just need to understand the basic concepts. It's like driving a car; you don't need to know exactly how the engine works but you do need to learn how to drive the machine, to identify when something is wrong and to understand the road rules so that you minimize the risk of getting into trouble. (p. 14)

The goal of this chapter is to explore how nursing and health care are embracing, harnessing, and using technology to increase the quality of patient care in all health care settings.

Always remember that technology is only a tool to help us care for our patients. It should never replace our critical thinking and nursing judgment!

NURSING INFORMATICS

Nursing Informatics: Why Do I Care?

In the back of your mind you may be thinking, "So why do I care about nursing informatics and technology? I'm still learning to take care of patients." Well, in today's world, technology and patient care are completely interwoven. From the electronic medical record, to the devices you will use to monitor and care for your patients, to the accumulation of data that will allow you to provide care most

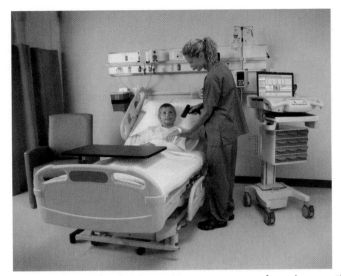

FIG. 23.1 Nurses are finding that technology supports many areas of nursing practice. (Courtesy Rubbermaid Healthcare, Huntersville, NC.)

effectively, technology and informatics are a part of our daily nursing practice whether we realize it or not. Look at Fig. 23.1 and see how many technology-enabled items you can pick out. And who knows? Maybe someday you will decide that nursing informatics is the specialty for you.

What Is Nursing Informatics?

In 1994, the American Nurses Association (ANA) recognized the field of nursing informatics. In 2015, the ANA updated the definition of nursing informatics (NI) as "the specialty that integrates nursing science with multiple information management and analytical sciences to identify, define, manage, and communicate data, information, knowledge, and wisdom in nursing practice" (ANA, 2015, p. 1).

The ANA further identified two distinct roles in nursing informatics: the informatics nurse (IN) and the informatics nurse specialist (INS). The informatics nurse has experience in nursing informatics but does not have an advanced degree in the specialty. The informatics nurse specialist has graduate-level education in informatics or a related field (ANA, 2015). Nurses in both IN and INS roles "support nurses, consumers, patients, the interprofessional healthcare team, and other stakeholders in their decision-making in all roles and settings to achieve desired outcomes. This support is accomplished through the use of information structures, information processes, and information technology" (ANA, 2015, p. 2).

With the advent of both specialty and integrated clinical information systems (CIS), the longitudinal electronic health record (EHR) has become the ultimate goal of health care organizations and is now supported by federal mandate. The EHR will reflect a record of patients' health care throughout their lives. Although this realization of 100% integrated patient data in one longitudinal electronic record is becoming more technologically feasible, few organizations have actually reached this goal. There are still outstanding issues regarding how to handle outside information that comes into a facility; for example, old systems may not be able to interface with new ones, corrupt data may be received from old systems, and resources may be unavailable to enter all the data from old paper charts. Although solutions are being developed to solve some of these problems, it will take time to reach the ultimate goal.

Information is power. The extensive clinical background of the IN/INS is invaluable to the success of the implementation of the hardware and software applications needed to transform health care. Nurses have a unique understanding of workflow, the hospital and clinical environment, and the specific procedures that are necessary for effective health care information infrastructure. Moreover, the IN/INS is critical to the translation of standard information into practical models that can be applied to improve the health care work environment (Delany, 2004).

The 2009 Healthcare Information Management Systems Society (HIMSS) Informatics Nurse Impact Survey asked organizational leaders to provide input on the roles and impact of informatics nurses in their organizations. Organizations responding included hospital or health systems (75%), vendor or consulting firms (11%), and other organizations such as home health, ambulatory care facilities, and academic or government facilities. Nearly all respondents noted that informatics nurses play a significant role in user education. Informatics nurses are also widely involved in workflow analysis, patient safety, compliance with policies and regulations, quality outcomes, system implementation, user support, workflow analysis, and gaining buy-in from end users (HIMSS, 2015). In short, the focus of nursing informatics is to improve patient care with health care technology that encourages clinicians to make more accurate and timely decisions.

So how does one become an expert in this unique field of nursing? What does a nurse specializing in nursing informatics do on a daily basis? And how does informatics impact the work of a clinical nurse?

Experience and Education

In the past, many nurses in informatics roles did not have formal education beyond their nursing preparation. They were "recruited" by their employers to help build and implement an electronic medical record application. These nurses learned as they went along, and advanced degrees were not required. However, this is no longer true. According to the 2011 HIMSS Nursing Informatics Workforce Survey, "Fifteen percent have received on-the-job training and more than half of the 2011 respondents reported having a postgraduate degree (56 percent), which includes Masters in Nursing or other field/specialty and PhD in Nursing or other field/specialty."

Informatics nurses who want to hold leadership roles in nursing informatics will need graduate-level preparation. A student who held a leadership role in NI and was enrolled in a nursing informatics master's program once said that she thought she knew all about nursing informatics, but she learned that she only knew about it at her own organizational level. Her graduate-school education had broadened her perspectives and introduced her to new concepts and ways of thinking (C. Parker, 2011, personal communication).

Role of the IN/INS

The IN/INS must have a basic knowledge of how computers and networks work as well as an understanding of system analysis, design principles, and information management. It is important for the IN/INS to converse with both the clinical staff and the technology staff regarding hardware, software, communications, data representation, and security. An IN/INS will be comfortable with software and hardware implementation, training, testing, presenting, and facilitating knowledge (Critical Thinking Box 23.1).

? CRITICAL THINKING BOX 23.1

What has been your experience and exposure to the use of technology in the hospital? Your school? At home? Think of ways to become more familiar with the use of computers and other technology.

During the publication of this textbook, the majority of IN/INSs are working with EMR/EHR development and implementations. Typical job responsibilities consist of (1) product evaluation; (2) system implementation, including preparing users, training, and providing support; (3) system development and quality initiatives, including system evaluations/problem solving and quality improvement/patient safety; and (4) other duties as assigned (HIMSS 2011 Nursing Informatics Workforce Survey, 2015).

But not all nurses in IN/INS roles work on implementation of the EMR/EHR. Some work for health care product vendors in both the hardware and software areas. They help to inform the next generation of existing products, and they work with engineers/design teams to create new products, always bringing the patient care viewpoint and the needs of the end user to the design process. Others work for consulting firms and specialize in workflow improvement using technology, whereas still others work for government, third-party payers, and educational institutions (HIMSS Nursing Informatics Workforce Survey, 2015). The variety is seemingly endless.

The Certification Process

In 1994, the American Nursing Credentialing Center (ANCC) provided a method for nurses to become certified in this specialty. The baccalaureate degree is the minimum requirement needed to take the certification exam. Nurses can obtain RN-BC certification in informatics nursing through the ANCC.

PROFESSIONAL PRACTICE, TRENDS, AND ISSUES

What Are Regulatory and Accreditation Requirements?

Although there are many regulatory and governmental agencies instituting health care policy, the Health Insurance Portability and Accountability Act (HIPAA) and The Joint Commission (TJC) impact the daily work of every clinician and organization. The nurse must have a clear understanding both of HIPAA regulations and of TJC requirements to be able to provide safe nursing care.

Privacy and Confidentiality

Every health care organization has a responsibility to itself, to its patients, and to the community at large to have good control of its information systems. Because the internal workings of health care rely on accurate and current data and information, personal data about employees and patients must be kept safe and confidential. A corporate security plan is important to an organization.

Maintaining confidentiality implies a trust of the individuals who handle that data and information. These health care workers ensure the privacy of this information and use it only for the purpose for which it was disclosed.

Security policies must be explicit and well defined. Confidentiality agreements should be reviewed and signed when starting employment and yearly thereafter. Breaches of security, confidentiality, or privacy should be addressed and resolved quickly, and the offender should be charged accordingly. Every lapse should be treated openly and made an example for others to note. The informatics nurse may be involved in the investigation process and the writing of the policies and procedures.

HIPAA

In 1996, the HIPAA was signed into law. The law defines standards that were developed to ensure that health care organizations collect the right data in a common format so that the data can be shared, as well as protect the privacy and security of patient data (Simpson, 2001). The major impact from this regulatory legislation is in these areas:

- Health information privacy law

- Data security standards
- Electronic transaction standards

Among many requirements, health care entities must adopt written privacy policies and procedures that define how they intend to abide by the highly complex regulations and how they will protect individually identifiable health information. Each health care organization must ensure that all staff members who have access to patient information have an understanding of the consequences of noncompliance (Gale Group, 2001).

In 1998, it was proposed that all health plans, health plan providers, and health care clearinghouses that maintain or transmit health information electronically be required to establish and maintain responsible and appropriate safeguards to ensure the integrity and confidentiality of the information. Although this seems logical, it is a very difficult and time-consuming task when using automated systems that did not previously meet these requirements (Critical Thinking Box 23.2).

? CRITICAL THINKING BOX 23.2

How have your clinical facility and/or school made changes to accommodate the Health Insurance Portability and Accountability Act (HIPAA) requirements?

The year 2013 brought another wave of "sweeping change" to the HIPAA Privacy, Security, Enforcement and Breach Notification Rules according to Leon Rodriguez, director of the HHS Office for Civil Rights. HHS Secretary Kathleen Sebelius stated, "The new rule will help protect patient privacy and safeguard patients' health information in an ever expanding digital age." According to the January 17, 2013, press release issued by the U.S. Department of Health and Human Services:

The changes in the final rulemaking provide the public with increased protection and control of personal health information. The HIPAA Privacy and Security Rules have focused on health care providers, health plans and other entities that process health insurance claims. The changes announced today expand many of the requirements to business associates of these entities that receive protected health information, such as contractors and subcontractors. Some of the largest breaches reported to HHS have involved business associates. Penalties are increased for noncompliance based on the level of negligence, with a maximum penalty of $1.5 million per violation. The changes also strengthen the Health Information Technology for Economic and Clinical Health (HITECH) Breach Notification requirements by clarifying when breaches of unsecured health information must be reported to HHS.

Individual rights are expanded in important ways. Patients can ask for a copy of their electronic medical record in an electronic form. When individuals pay by cash they can instruct their provider not to share information about their treatment with their health plan. The final omnibus rule sets new limits on how information is used and disclosed for marketing and fundraising purposes and prohibits the sale of an individual's health information without their permission.

The final rule also reduces burden by streamlining individuals' ability to authorize the use of their health information for research purposes. The rule makes it easier for parents and others to give permission to share proof of a child's immunization with a school and gives covered entities and business associates up to one year after the 180-day compliance date to modify contracts to comply with the rule. (U.S. Department of Health & Human Services, 2013a)

Violation of HIPAA standards is no laughing matter. Violations of health information privacy can lead to termination of employment and even indictment and prison time. In 2010, a former researcher at the UCLA School of Medicine was sentenced to 4 months in federal prison and was fined $2000 for violations of the HIPAA privacy rule. He accessed 323 confidential patient records, including celebrities Drew Barrymore, Arnold Schwarzenegger, Tom Hanks, and Leonardo DiCaprio, without a valid reason or authorization but without profiting from it through the sale or use of the information (Dimick, 2010). If a data breach affects more than 500 individuals, Section 13402 (e) (4) of the HITECH Act requires that the secretary of the U.S. Department of Health and Human Services post notification of the covered entity on the HHS website found at http://www.hhs.gov/hipaa/for-professionals/breach-notification/index.html.

HIPAA and the Use of Mobile Computing Devices

Knox and Smith (2007) encourage everyone to think about patient privacy and HIPAA compliance in the clinical area, especially because of the growing use of laptops, tablet PCs, and cell/smartphones that take pictures and record videos (Critical Thinking Box 23.3). According to a research study by Ponemon Institute (2014) on patient privacy and data security, top threats to patient records are the Affordable Care Act, criminal attacks, employee negligence regarding unsecured mobile devices (smartphones, laptops, and tablets), and third parties.

> **? CRITICAL THINKING BOX 23.3**
>
> Do you know your clinical facility's policies on cell phone/smartphone use in patient care areas? How about picture taking, Internet use, Internet access policy, information security access, and user-ID/password agreement?

> You can violate an organization's HIPAA policies and not even realize it!

The influx of new mobile computing technology, such as tablet computers or smartphones, is creating new implications for protection of privacy and security. How to protect confidential information is something that we learn at the beginning of our nursing careers; however, protecting that same information on a mobile device may not be so easily understood. The following is a list of some simple precautions to take to help secure patient information that may be stored on a mobile device. These recommendations should be followed as standard practice.

- Keep careful physical control of the device at all times.
- Use a password or other user authentication and a time-out to reactivate the authentication.
- Install and enable encryption.
- Install and activate remote wiping and/or remote disabling.
- Disable and do not install or use file-sharing applications.
- Disable the infrared ports and Wi-Fi except when they are actually being used.
- Do not send infrared or Wi-Fi transmissions in public locations.
- Keep your security software up-to-date.
- Research mobile applications (apps) before downloading.
- Use adequate security to send or receive health information using public Wi-Fi networks.
- Delete all stored health information before discarding or reusing the mobile device (Pancoast et al., 2003, p. 611; U.S. Department of Health & Human Services, 2013b).

With the use of new technologies there is potential to improve patient safety and outcome, as well as to reduce potential injury; however, at the same time there is an increased risk for exposing confidential patient information. A cautionary approach along with assuming the responsibility for safeguarding the confidentiality of information should be used if you download patient information into a mobile device.

The Joint Commission

TJC wrote the information management (IM) standards in the mid-1990s. The 10 standards outline the need for information management regulation (Clark, 2004). Since that time, information management has been woven throughout the various standards and the National Patient Safety Goals. An example of this is noted in Standard IM.02.01.03 of the revised requirements for the Laboratory Accreditation Program, where the lab must have a "written policy addressing the integrity of health information against loss, damage, unauthorized alteration, unintentional change, and accidental destruction" (The Joint Commission, 2012, p. 1).

TJC sends out a team of experts for a review of every health care organization that wishes to be certified. This team inspects and reviews a variety of areas within each organization. The IN/INS may be called on to lead the effort for preparing for a TJC visit and for maintaining ongoing compliance (Critical Thinking Box 23.4).

？ CRITICAL THINKING BOX 23.4

Have you had the opportunity to be in clinical during a visit by The Joint Commission? If so, what did you observe? How was the staff prepared for the visit?

Models and Theories

Nomenclature, Classification, and Taxonomy

The quote from Dr. Lang at the beginning of the chapter has never been truer. Traditionally, nurses documented care using personal preference, unit standards, or facility policy. Standardized nursing languages, sometimes called nomenclatures, offer a recognized, systematic classification and consistent method of describing nursing practice. Nomenclatures act as descriptors or labels; classifications are group or class entities; and taxonomy is the study of the classifications.

In 1995, the ANA approved the establishment of the Nursing Information and Data Set Evaluation Center (NIDSEC) to review, evaluate against defined criteria, and recognize information systems from developers and manufacturers who support documentation of nursing care within automated nursing information systems (NISs) or within computer-based patient record systems (CPR). They recognized the following 12 nursing practice classification systems (ANA, 2012). Note that the Patient Care Data Set (PCDS) was retired in 2003.

1. North American Nursing Diagnosis Association International (NANDA) Nursing Diagnoses, Definitions, and Classification
2. Nursing Interventions Classification System (NIC)
3. Nursing Outcomes Classification System (NOC)
4. Nursing Management Minimum Data Set (NMMDS)
5. Clinical Care Classification (CCC) (formerly Home Health Care Classification [HHCC])
6. Omaha System
7. Perioperative Nursing Dataset (PNDS)
8. SNOMED CT
9. Nursing Minimum Data Set (NMDS)
10. International Classification of Nursing Practice (ICNP)
11. ABC codes
12. Logical Observation Identifier Names and Codes (LOINC)

If the unique nomenclature of these classification systems is used consistently, gathered data elements can be captured, stored, and manipulated accurately in the electronic medical record. Without a common language, data cannot be aggregated into useful language (Simpson, 2000). The need for consistency causes problems for software vendors as they attempt to produce unique and robust software packages that still use the recognized labels and groupings of nursing practice elements. So what happens?

Currently, each software vendor uses a unique, possibly patented naming convention for their specific functionality and then must "explain and define" these names and labels in their literature or presentations by relating them back to recognized nursing practice or data elements. This causes confusion to the user community.

Learning about and working with standardized nursing languages will ensure nursing contributions are an integral part of any electronic medical record. Understanding those contributions through research and teaching will help to define further the scope of nursing practice. Until complete standardization occurs, nurses must be prepared to use different classification systems at different facilities or even with systems from different vendors within a single facility (Critical Thinking Box 23.5).

? CRITICAL THINKING BOX 23.5

What has been your experience or exposure to these different standard nursing languages? What does your clinical agency use?

Theories

Although there multiple theories that are applicable to nursing informatics practice, the three most common are

- General Systems Theory—This theory organizes interdependent parts working together to produce a product that none used alone could produce. Key elements are input, process, output, control, and feedback.
- Rogers' Diffusion of Innovation Theory—A 5-step process of an individual's decision to adopt an innovation includes knowledge, persuasion, decision, implementation, and confirmation (Rogers, 2003).
- Change Theory—Kurt Lewin's change theory is discussed in Chapter 10.

CLINICAL INFORMATION SYSTEMS

Every day, nurses encounter technology, and this technology is changing the ways that health care is delivered in the hospital, physician's office, or the patient's home. Clinical information systems (CISs) have replaced pencil and paper charting. Florence Nightingale expressed a desire for medical records that were standardized, organized, and legible, and these goals are equally valid today.

In attempting to arrive at the truth, I have applied everywhere for information, but in scarcely an instance have I been able to obtain hospital records fit for any comparison.
Florence Nightingale (Notes on a Hospital, 1873)

A 2001 Institute of Medicine (IOM) report, *Crossing the Quality Chasm: A New Health System for the 21st Century*, identified the development and application of CISs as essential for health care to be able to leverage state-of-the-art technology to deliver the highest quality, lowest cost patient care.

The e-World Is Coming ... Wait, It's Here

Although most "e-words" come from the commerce or business sector, the term is generally understood, despite its lack of precise definition, because of the dynamic environment of the Internet. E-health has come to characterize not only a technical development but also a state of mind, a way of thinking that focuses on improvement of health care via information and communication technology.

The World Health Organization (WHO) provides the following definition: "eHealth is the cost-effective and secure use of information and communications technologies for health and health-related fields" (WHO, 2016). WHO (2016) goes on to define mHealth as "a component of eHealth, and involves the provision of health services and information via mobile technologies, such as mobile phones, tablet computers and Personal Digital Assistants (PDAs)." However, despite its appearance in 2000, by 2015 there is no single consensus definition nor is it included in MeSH taxonomy (https://www.nlm.nih.gov/mesh/MBrowser.html).

Eysenbach (2001) feels that it stands not only for "electronic" but implies a lot of other *e*'s, which he feels represent what e-health is all about (Box 23.1). He states that it should also be **e**asy to use, **e**ntertaining, **e**xciting, and most of all, it should **e**xist (Critical Thinking Box 23.6)!

BOX 23.1   THE 10 E'S IN "E-HEALTH"

1. **Efficiency** leading to decreasing costs by avoiding duplicate or unnecessary diagnostic or therapeutic interventions, through enhanced communication possibilities among health care establishments, and through patient involvement.
2. **Enhancing quality of care** by allowing comparisons among different providers, involving consumers as additional power for quality assurance, and directing patient streams to the best quality providers.
3. **Evidence-based** intervention effectiveness and efficiency should not be assumed but proven by rigorous scientific evaluation.
4. **Empowerment** of consumers and patients by making the knowledge bases of medicine and personal electronic records accessible to consumers over the Internet; e-health opens new avenues for patient-centered medicine and enables evidence-based patient choice.
5. **Encouragement** of a new relationship between the patient and health professional, toward a true partnership where decisions are made in a shared manner.
6. **Education** of physicians and health care providers through online sources (continuing education) and consumers (health education, tailored preventive information for consumers).
7. **Enabling** information exchange and communication in a standardized way among health care establishments.
8. **Extending** the scope of health care beyond its conventional boundaries.
9. **Ethics** e-health involves new forms of patient–physician interaction and poses new challenges and threats to ethical issues such as online professional practice, informed consent, privacy, and equity issues.
10. **Equity** to make health care more equitable is one of the promises of e-health, but at the same time there is a considerable threat that e-health may deepen the gap between the "haves" and "have nots," deepening the "digital divide".

Adapted from Eysenbach, G. (2001). What is e-health? *J Med Internet Res, 3*(2). Retrieved from www.jmir.org/2001/2/e20/.

? CRITICAL THINKING BOX 23.6

A June 2009 survey from the Pew Internet & American Life Project estimates that 61% of American adults surf the Web for health information. How have you (or your family) used the Internet for your own health or medical care? What about your patients? How will you help them use the Internet to better their understanding of their health?

Electronic Medical Record and Electronic Health Record

There is still some debate about whether an electronic health record (EHR) and an electronic medical record (EMR) are the same or different. HealthIT.gov defines EMR as "a digital version of the paper charts.... An EMR contains the medical and treatment history of the patients in that office, clinic or hospital" (HealthIT.gov, 2015, para 1).

They go on to describe an EHR as all that and more. EHRs focus on the total health of the patient—going beyond standard clinical data collected in a single event such as a provider's visit or hospitalization. They provide a broader view on a patient's care. EHRs are designed to reach out beyond the health organization that originally collects and compiles the information. They are built to share information with other health care providers so they contain information from all the clinicians involved in the patient's care (HealthIT.gov, 2015, para 2).

Figs. 23.2 and 23.3 illustrate screenshots from a patient's EMR.

For example, a patient is seen in a primary care provider (PCP) office for complaints of indigestion. The PCP completes a history and physical, does an ECG and basic lab studies. All data are in the computer at the office comprising one EMR for that patient. The patient is sent home with instructions. Later that evening, the patient feels worse and goes to the emergency department (ED). Using standalone EMRs, the following would occur: because it is after hours, the data in the patient's EMR at the PCP office are not available. A new EMR is begun. The next day the PCP would have no idea that the patient was seen in the ED.

Using an integrated EHR, the ED would be able to access the information from the PCP's system, and the next day the PCP would be notified that the patient was seen in ED and would have access to all the data collected during the ED visit.

Advantages of the EHR are listed in Box 23.2. This patient-centric approach to documentation of care is becoming the new standard of care.

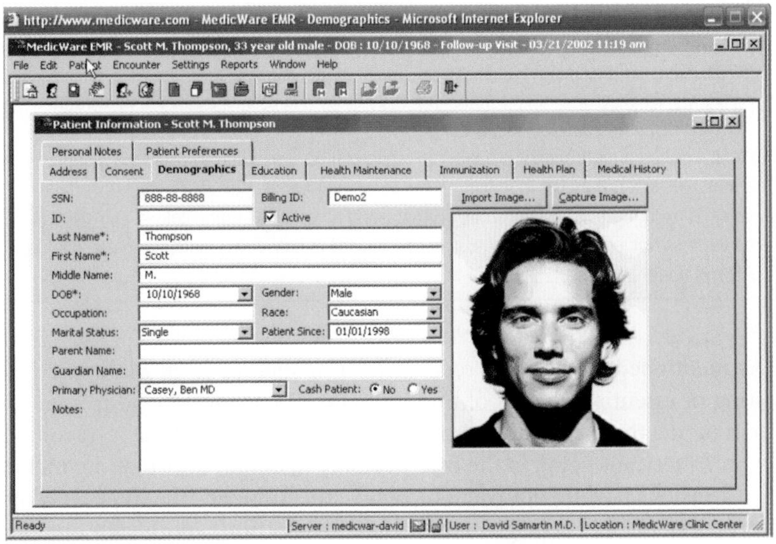

FIG. 23.2 Patient information screen. (Courtesy Medicware, Irwindale, CA.)

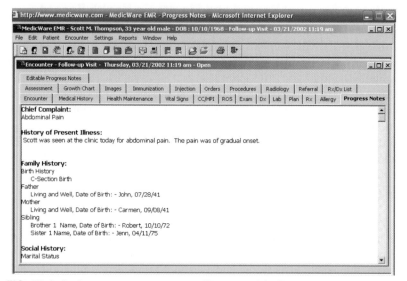

FIG. 23.3 Patient encounter screen. (Courtesy Medicware, Irwindale, CA.)

BOX 23.2 ADVANTAGES OF ELECTRONIC HEALTH RECORDS

- Simultaneous, remote access to patient from many locations
- Legibility of record—no handwriting
- Safer data—backup and disaster recovery system, so less prone to data loss
- Patient data confidentiality—authorized use can be restricted and monitored automatically
- Flexible data layout—can recall data in any order (chronologically or in reverse chronological order)
- Integration with other information resources
- Incorporation of electronic data—can automatically capture physiological data from bedside monitors, laboratory analyzers, and imaging devices
- Continuous data processing—check and filter the data for errors, summarize and interpret data, and issue alerts and/or reminders
- Assisted search—can search free-text or structured data to find a specific data value or to determine whether a particular item has been recorded previously
- Greater range of data output modalities—data can be presented to users via computer-generated voice, two-way pagers, e-mail, and smartphones
- Tailored paper output—data can be printed using a variety of fonts, colors, and sizes to help focus the clinician's attention on the most important data; images can be included to help see a more complete "picture" of the patient's condition
- Always up-to-date

As mentioned in the IOM report, *Key Capabilities of an Electronic Health Record System* (2003), a listing of essential features of the EHR (Box 23.3) must be addressed for our outdated health care system model to take advantage of the potential benefits of the "e-revolution." With an estimated 100 million Americans going to the Internet daily to obtain information, including health information, to make decisions it is imperative to recognize the influence the Internet can have on making changes to improve patient self-management, patient satisfaction, and health outcomes (Forkner-Dunn, 2003). With federal initiatives pushing the adoption of EHRs throughout all health care institutions by the year 2014, how nursing is practiced will be significantly changed. Nursing students need to know how to interact with informatics tools and systems to ensure safe and quality care. "In addition, there is

BOX 23.3 **EIGHT CORE FUNCTIONS OF THE ELECTRONIC HEALTH RECORD**

A committee of the Institute of Medicine of the National Academies has identified a set of eight core care delivery functions that electronic health record (EHR) systems should be capable of performing to promote greater safety, quality, and efficiency in health care delivery.

These eight core functions are:

- Health information and data
- Result management
- Order management
- Decision support
- Electronic communication and connectivity
- Patient support
- Administrative processes and reporting
- Reporting and population health

Data from Institute of Medicine. (2003). Key capabilities of an electronic health record system, *Data Standards for Patient Safety*. Retrieved from www.iom.edu/Reports/2003/Key-Capabilities-of-an-Electronic-Health-Record-System.aspx.

a growing consumer movement wanting to interact with health care professionals through personal health records and various electronic communication devices" (NLN, 2008, p. 1).

Nursing informatics leaders are reporting that we are starting to see more and more nurses who have never documented in a paper record.

Personal Health Record

There is movement toward inclusion of data collected by the patient into the EHR. This is called the personal health record (PHR) and "is an electronic record of an individual's health information by which the individual controls access to the information and may have the ability to manage, track, and participate in his or her own health care" (HHS.gov, n.d.). Personal health records are available from several sources. A health provider may provide them as an extension of an EMR. Insurance providers may have PHRs for their clients. Online services such as WebMD and Microsoft Health Vault are also available. These data could include family history, real-time blood glucose readings, or exercise information sent directly from glucometer to the personal health record. Then, with permission of the patient, these data elements could be uploaded into the patient's PCP's EMR. Sounds good? Well, yes and no. The concepts of a PHR raise some interesting questions concerning data ownership, how to move data from one EMR to another, the rights of the patient to withhold data from a health care provider, and what happens if an online PHR provider ceases operation, such as when Google Health terminated services as of January 1, 2013. The coming few years will bring many changes in the concepts of a PHR. What the successful PHR model will be has yet to be determined.

Technology Changing Workflow for the Better—Medication Fulfillment

Another IOM study, *Preventing Medication Errors* (2006), recommends greater use of information technologies in prescribing and dispensing medications (medication fulfillment), such as point-of-care reference information (handheld devices). Having detailed information about a medication at your fingertips addresses the issue of trying to keep up with all of the relevant information needed for the nurse to administer, and the physician or health care provider to prescribe, a medication safely (Fig. 23.4).

FIG. 23.4 Accessing patient information at point of care. (Courtesy PatientSafe Solutions, San Diego, CA.)

CPOE and Clinical Decision Support

Computerized provider order entry (CPOE) completely changes the workflow for writing orders. CPOE is a technology-enabled process that allows providers such as physicians, nurse practitioners, and pharmacists to enter patient care orders directly into a computer system that transmits these orders directly to the receiving department (pharmacy, radiology, dietary, etc.) without intervening steps such as RN review for clarity and completeness. The true benefits of CPOE come with implementing clinical decision support systems (CDSSs) at the same time (Dixon & Zafar, 2009). With this combination, research has begun to confirm benefits such as "averting problems with handwriting, similar drug names, drug interactions, and specification errors; integration with electronic medical records, decision support systems, and adverse drug event reporting systems; faster transmission to the pharmacy; and potential economic savings" (AHRQ, 2012).

Technology-Enabled Medication Administration

At the current time, technology-enabled medication administration is primarily based on bar-coding technology combined with an electronic medication administration record (eMAR) and technology-controlled medication dispensing equipment in both pharmacy and nursing units. The combination of bar-coded medication administration (BCMA) with an eMAR has been shown to reduce substantially medication administration and transcription errors along with potential drug-related adverse events (Poon et al., 2010). The process of scanning a patient's identification band as one method of patient confirmation, as well as each medication, so that the five rights are verified electronically may take a few more moments, but the rewards for both the patient and nurse are worthwhile. Taking the steps to protect our patients is also protecting our license to practice as an RN or LVN/LPN.

e-Prescribing

In addition, electronic prescriptions (e-prescriptions) can reduce many of the mistakes that occur with handwritten prescriptions. The e-prescription software guarantees that all necessary information is completed legibly. In addition, the software program correlates the patient's prescription with his or her medical history. This allows for automatic checking of drug allergies, drug–drug interactions, and overly high doses. According to *Preventing Medication Errors*, "In addition, once an e-prescription is in the system, it will follow the patient from the hospital to the doctor's office or from the nursing home to the pharmacy, avoiding many of the 'hand-off errors' common today. In light of all this, the committee recommends that by 2010 all prescribers and pharmacies will be using e-prescriptions" (IOM, 2006, p. 3). Unfortunately, despite statistically significant reductions in errors, including complete elimination of legibility errors, e-prescribing did not meet the IOM recommendations by 2010 (Kaushal et al., 2010).

But progress is being made. Medicare Part D requires drug plans that are participating in the new prescription benefit to support electronic prescribing. In a brief prepared by the Office of the National Coordinator for Health Information Technology, Hufstader, Swain, and Furukawa (2012) reported that in December 2008, 7% of physicians in the United States were e-prescribing using an EHR; by June 2012, almost half (48%) of physicians were e-prescribing using an EHR on the Surescripts network. Surescripts is an e-prescription network utilized by approximately 95% of all community pharmacies in the United States routing prescriptions, excluding closed systems such as Kaiser Permanente (Surescripts, 2016).

The American Hospital Association strongly supports the use of technology to protect and improve the quality of care in the hospital. Research data support the proposition that the computerized physician order system (CPOE), computerized decision support systems and bar-code medication administration (BCMA), and electronic medication administration record (eMAR) for medication administration can limit errors and improve care (AHA, 2006).

What Is Meaningful Use?

In 2009, the *American Recovery and Reinvestment Act* (ARRA) and the Centers for Medicare and Medicaid Services (CMS) released a proposed rule on Medicare and Medicaid payment incentives for "meaningful users" of EHRs by hospitals and physicians with financial incentives in the first few years and penalties thereafter. Federal initiatives such as ARRA are pushing the adoption of EHRs throughout all health care institutions by the year 2014, which is an initiative that will dramatically change how nursing is practiced (CMS, 2012a,b,c).

The goal of meaningful use is to promote the spread of electronic health records to improve health care in the United States by complete and accurate information, better access to information, and empowerment of patients to participate more actively in their health. There are three stages described in Table 23.1.

Barriers Still Remain

Despite this new law, there still remain major barriers to the full integration of health information technology. These barriers include

- Lack of standardization across care areas—that is, the need for laboratory data and pharmacy systems to be integrated with the patient's EHR, and the emergency department systems need to share data with the inpatient systems.
- Funding—information technology is costly, and often the major costs are borne by hospitals rather than shared by other providers, payers, and employers.
- Privacy laws—a single set of privacy laws is needed to simplify the task of communicating across facilities, agencies, and local, state, and federal governments.
- Lack of a uniform approach (number) to match patients to their record—a single authentication number is needed to reduce safety risks and to provide a uniform access to a patient's data (AHA, 2006).

TABLE 23.1 STAGES OF MEANINGFUL USE		
STAGE 1 2011-2012 DATA CAPTURE AND SHARING	STAGE 2 2014 ADVANCE CLINICAL PROCESSES	STAGE 3 2016 IMPROVED OUTCOMES
Meaningful Use Criteria Focus	**Meaningful Use Criteria Focus**	**Meaningful Use Criteria Focus**
Electronically capturing health information in a standardized format	More rigorous health information exchange (HIE)	Improving quality, safety, and efficiency, leading to improved health outcomes
Using that information to track key clinical conditions	Increased requirements for e-prescribing and incorporating lab results	Decision support for national high-priority conditions
Communicating that information for care coordination processes	Electronic transmission of patient-care summaries across multiple settings	Patient access to self-management tools
Initiating the reporting of clinical quality measures and public health information	More patient-controlled data	Access to comprehensive patient data through patient-centered HIE
Using information to engage patients and their families in their care		Improving population health

Reprinted from HealthIT.gov. (2016). *How to attain meaningful use?* Retrieved from https://www.healthit.gov/providers-professionals/how-attain-meaningful-use.

TRENDS

When the first edition of this textbook was published in the early 1990s, the section on computer technology was new and innovative. It was the cutting edge of technology that sent many nurse educators, students, and practicing nurses scrambling to make sense of how the computer might affect them. The explosion of knowledge and technology has visibly changed our mindset on the use of computer technology to the extent that computer literacy is integrated within nursing education. Being faced with devices, equipment, computer sensors, "smart" body parts, and EHRs that involve technological skills, information technology impacts the way that nursing is practiced and delivered. In the 2016 NCLEX-RN® Detailed Test Plan, the subcategory of Information Technology is a content section under the category of Management of Patient Care, which is part of the patient need category of Safe and Effective Care Environment (National Council of State Boards of Nursing, 2016) (Box 23.4).

As Forkner-Dunn (2003) so cleverly states, "time to byte the bullet ... the e-health train has not only left the station but is rapidly moving down the track carrying tens of millions of e-patients and many possibilities for transforming patient self-management, improving health outcomes, and enhancing [health provider] patient relationships" (p. 8). Although there are numerous trend areas, using the Internet to communicate and to provide patient self-care, evaluating Internet resources, and using mobile computing devices are certainly in the forefront.

USING THE INTERNET: THE NEXT GENERATION OF HEALTH CARE DELIVERY

Undoubtedly, the Internet has transformed our ability to locate health information and to connect via e-mail and social networking such as Facebook, Twitter, or Pinterest with other individuals who have similar interests. Websites such as PatientsLikeMe.com allow people with chronic

> **BOX 23.4 NCSBN DETAILED TEST PLAN FOR NCLEX-RN®
> EXAMINATION**
>
> The following is an excerpt from the *2016 Detailed Test Plan for the NCLEX-RN®* regarding the content area of Information Technology on the NCLEX-RN® exam:
>
> **Information Technology**
> - Receive and/or transcribe health care provider orders*
> - Apply knowledge of facility regulations when accessing client records
> - Access data for client through online databases and journals
> - Enter computer documentation accurately, completely, and in a timely manner
> - Utilize valid resources to enhance the care provided to a client (e.g., evidence-based research, information technology, policies, and procedures)*
>
> **Confidentiality/Information Security**
> - Assess staff member and client understanding of confidentiality requirements
> - Maintain client confidentiality and privacy*
> - Intervene appropriately when confidentiality has been breached by staff members

*Activity Statements used in the 2014 RN Practice Analysis.
Data from National Council State Board of Nursing. (2016). *NCLEX-RN® Detailed Test Plan Candidate Version.*
Retrieved from https://www.ncsbn.org/2016_RN_Test_Plan_Candidate.pdf.

illnesses to share their feelings, disease progression, and responses to treatments with others in similar situations.

The federal government recognizes the importance of having access and quality information and has established a series of goals in the *Healthy People 2020 Topics and Objectives* (U.S. Department of Health & Human Services, 2016). According to Forkner-Dunn (2003), Internet-based patient self-care is the "next generation of health care delivery" (p. 1). Health information on the Internet can dramatically improve patients' abilities to manage their own health care conveniently. Of course, not all web-based information is accurate, which raises concerns about the quality of information individuals are using and the impact this information has on the overall health of an individual.

> Internet users must still proceed with caution when seeking health care information online, because there is a plethora of incomplete and inaccurate information that can be dangerous.

As nurses, we need to understand better how consumers find health information on the Internet, how to evaluate the quality of information retrieved, and how to help our patients to evaluate critically and manage information (ANA, 2011; Greenberg et al., 2004).

A 2001 study by RAND for the California Healthcare Foundation showed that the information on health websites is often incomplete or out of date and highly commercialized. This might be of little concern if consumers routinely consulted health care professionals about the information. However, the Pew Internet and American Life Project (Pew) found that 69% of consumers did not discuss the information they found online with a doctor or nurse, and considering that most health information on the Internet is written in a style that is above the ninth-grade reading level, many individuals come away from the source of information confused, especially the underserved populations who need the information the most.

The U.S. National Library of Medicine and National Institutes of Health provide an excellent website on Evaluating Health Information at http://www.nlm.nih.gov/medlineplus/evaluatinghealthinformation.html, including some in Spanish.

> Imagine having access to your complete EHR no matter where you are in the world and being able to download portions of whatever documentation you need to a CD-ROM or removable drive (thumb drive).

To meet the requirements of Meaningful Use Stage 2, health care providers will need to more actively engage patients in their health care process. The requirements will necessitate that hospitals and providers supply patients with "the capability to electronically view, download, and transmit relevant information from their provider's electronic health records. This could include lab test results, a list of current medications, and hospital discharge instructions" (McGraw, 2012). Meaningful Use Stage 3 will focus on promoting health information exchange and focusing on improved outcomes (Millard, 2015).

A study by Hill-Kayser and colleagues (2009) described how patients who had survived breast cancer were willing to use and were satisfied with the information provided in a web-based survivorship care plan called Oncolink. Oncolink was described as "a cancer information website based at the University of Pennsylvania that averages 3.9 million page views and more than 385,000 unique visits per month (para 3). It was interesting to note that only 12.6% of the respondents reported receiving cancer survivorship information before visiting Oncolink. In 2015, Oncolink is still a major source of credible information that is helpful to patients and families.

Electronic Communication

Practically everyone is familiar with e-mail. Your instructor may require you to complete assignments and submit your work via e-mail attachment instead of submitting a hard copy. You probably send e-mail to family and friends on a daily basis. Although more than 78% of people in the United States now use the Internet and e-mail daily (and many access health information), few physicians communicate with their patients through e-mail (Ye et al., 2010; Internet World Stats, 2013). Considering the popularity of e-mail and despite its potential for rapid, asynchronous, documentable communication to improve both the quality and efficiency of health services delivery, the use of e-mail communication has not been widely adopted by many physicians. There are several reasons for this, ranging from HIPAA concerns to billing issues.

But e-mail is rapidly being supplemented or even replaced by texting, Twitter, Instagram, and other forms of social media. Classes are moving online and may be 100% asynchronous or may be combined with video conferencing. Many of you may complete your next degree without ever stepping into a traditional classroom.

Telemedicine, Telehealth, and Health Monitoring

If you were asked how long telecommunication has been used in U.S. health care, would you select (a) the Civil War, (b) WWI, (c) WWII, or (d) Korean War? The answer is (a) the Civil War. Okay, it was a bit of trick question since telecommunication in those days was the telegraph. But in the 1900s, physicians were one of the first professions to adopt the telephone in their practice (Zundel, 1996).

Today, the use of telecommunication technologies to provide health care is expanding at a phenomenal rate. Surprisingly, it's not just the under-30 population who is embracing this technology. Long labeled as technology-adverse, the senior population is proving just the opposite, especially since telemedicine visits via two-video reduces the burden of travel to a provider's office.

School nurses are using technology linking primary care providers and mental health professionals directly to both urban and rural settings, providing care without having to take children out of school or parents from work. Using technology to monitor chronic conditions such as Type 1 diabetes has shown to be effective in both the pediatric and adult populations.

Telemedicine has also expanded in the emergency and acute-care setting. Telestroke, telepsychiatry, and teledermatology programs are bringing needed expertise to underserved areas. Imagine you are a new ICU nurse, and rather than being on your own, you have a team of experienced ICU nurses who may be hundreds of miles away yet can see and hear everything you do. If you are tied up with one patient, they can monitor the other for you or help you assess a complex patient situation.

Health-related applications for smartphones are appearing everywhere. People are monitoring their heart rates, sleep patterns, and blood glucose readings. There are attachments for smartphones that can diagnose an ear infection or take a diagnostic quality 12-lead electrocardiogram (ECG). In development now are devices for checking pulmonary edema and contact lenses that monitor glucose levels or intraocular pressure to help manage diabetes and glaucoma. New applications are even helping to diagnose a person's mental state by evaluating vocal inflections, facial expressions, vital signs, galvanic skin responses, and even the frequency and content of electronic communications.

Big Data

Another concept you may hear and wonder about is "big data." The following is a simplistic explanation but provides an idea of what big data is. Think about all the data we collect on a single patient during a 4-day hospital stay. Now add all the data we collect on all the patients in that hospital during that same 4 days. Now to that all the data we collect on all the patients in all the hospitals in the United States during those 4 days—that is a lot of data (i.e., Big Data!), too much to do anything with using traditional data management. So people working in informatics have developed and continue to develop ways of using the massive amounts of data to look for patterns and trends that may help us identify early warning signs, predisposing factors, and other patterns to improve health and health care.

DATA ACCESS AT THE POINT OF CARE

Point-of-care (POC) documentation has surfaced as a need in health care because of the interruption in workflow created by electronic documentation. Thirty years ago, patients' flow sheet documentation was kept on a clipboard at the bedside. The nurse walked into a room, collected vital data, wrote it on the flow sheet, and went on to the next patient. While this was an excellent workflow for the clinical nurse, it made aggregating data across patient visits or patient aggregates a monumental task. Picture the emergency department (ED) nurse, with an unconscious patient, who is confronted with a stack of paper records that have been rolled to the ED in a wheelchair by a medical records person—trying to put together a concise, cohesive picture of the patient's history was next to impossible.

Computers in the Nurses' Station

Enter electronic clinical documentation. This made it easier to review patient data from previous visits and to do research across patient populations, and it completely changed the workflow of the clinician at the bedside. We went from collecting data on multiple patients until we finally had time to sit down in front of a computer to enter the data into the patient's chart. We then attempted to regurgitate all the data we had either scribbled on a piece of paper or, worse yet, tried to commit it to memory. And even worse than that, we had multiple person-to-person conversations, telephone calls, and alerts between gathering data and documentation, all of which interfered with our recall of the details of care that was given to a patient in the previous hours.

Research has shown that point-of-care documentation reduces data latency and data errors (Gearing et al., 2006; Parker & Baldwin, 2008; Wager et al., 2010). A variety of point-of-care devices are now available to return documentation back to the point of care and to help us handle the vast amount of data that we receive every day.

Mobility in the Clinical World

To free clinicians from computers at the nurses' station, computers were put on carts—first desktops, then laptops. The next generation of workstations on wheels added medication storage to improve workflow. While tablet computers have been "the thing" for providers since the introduction of the iPad in 2010, there has not been widespread adoption by nurses at the bedside. Mobile application development has focused on the providers, and nurses have been reluctant to give up a keyboard and large monitor because of the design of the clinical applications they use. Expect this trend to change in the next 5 years as software applications continue to evolve (see Fig. 23.5).

FIG. 23.5 Smartphone communication application using text messaging. (Courtesy PatientSafe Solutions, San Diego, CA.)

Smartphones

Just as personal digital assistants, aka personal data assistants (PDAs), and mobile phones merged to become the smartphone, now smartphones and tablet computers are rapidly merging. By the time you read this chapter, the differences between the two devices will be almost imperceptible if they not have vanished altogether—in fact, some of you may not have ever heard the term PDA (Critical Thinking Box 23.7).

? CRITICAL THINKING BOX 23.7

Do you have a smartphone? If so, how do you use it? If not, do you anticipate purchasing one in the near future? Do you find nurses in the hospital or clinic setting using smartphones on a regular basis? What programs do they or you use?

Smartphones can run applications that can perform cardiac monitoring, monitor blood glucose levels, blood pressure, diet, and activity, as well as allowing users to check for drug interactions, calculate dosages, analyze lab results, schedule procedures, order prescriptions, and automate other clinical tasks, thus reducing the probability of errors and increasing patient safety (Abrahamsen, 2003), but smartphones can also be used for multiple modes of communication. We just have to be careful not to violate HIPAA when using our personal phones! Check Chapter 19 for tips on effectively using social media and other virtual environments in both your profession and personal life.

Applications are now being developed to aid in managing the constant influx of information using multiple modes of communication such as text messaging, voice messages and calls, and alarms (Figs. 23.6 and 23.7). However, because of their limited memory and scaled-down operating systems, it is still impossible to access the entire scope of the patient's electronic record on a smartphone.

Using Data to Improve Care at the Bedside

Companies are now taking data and using it to help the bedside nurse care for patients. For example, gathering real-time patient satisfaction scores and combining them with clinical documentation give clinicians a different view of the care process and how the patient might perceive it (see Fig. 23.8).

EVALUATING INTERNET RESOURCES

What Do I Need to Know to Evaluate an Internet Resource?

In her classic article, McGonigle (2002) suggests a five-step plan to evaluate websites (Box 23.5).

> Remember that anybody can publish anything on the Web. Make sure you critically evaluate the source of the information.

It is important to encourage patients to focus their Internet searching endeavors to well-known and reputable sites. For example, the U.S. Surgeon General's Family History Initiative is a great place to start with promoting the importance of a well-documented family health history. In addition to the Office of the Surgeon General, other U.S. Department of Health and Human

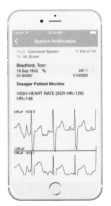

FIG. 23.6 Smartphone communication application text messaging templates. (Courtesy Voalté, Sarasota, FL.)

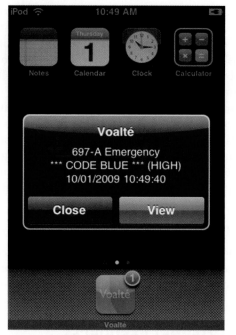

FIG. 23.7 Smartphone communication application alarm. (Courtesy Voalté, Sarasota, FL.)

Activity for 4th Floor - 411 - Bailey

▼ **Patient**

Joan Sharon Bailey	LeadIt Goal Score	Care team		Hospital Visit Indicares	
Age: 12 years (6/14/2002)		Physicians:	Attending - **Magee**	Patient Request Rate:	**0.73** / hr
	At Goal		Admitting - **Magee**	Interaction Wait Time:	**122** secs
		Caregivers:	**Howard Bailey**	Critical Request Rate:	**0.61** / hr
			Ruby Mendoza	Interruption Rate:	**2.12** / hr

▼ **IndiCare® and Activity** (Previous 24 hours)

Patient Request Rate	Patient Interaction Wait Time	Critical Request Rate	Interruption Rate
0.83 / hr ⓘ	**85.63** secs ⓘ	**0.25** / hr ⓘ	**1.79** / hr

411 | 18:00 19:00 20:00 21:00 22:00 23:00 0:00 1:00 2:00 3:00 4:00 5:00 6:00 7:00 8:00 9:00 10:00 11:00 12:00 13:00 14:00 15:00 16:00 17:00

- Normal   ☐ Water OT   ☐ Pain OT   ☐ Toilet Asst OT   ☒ Toilet OT   ✶ Shower OT   ★ Staff Assist   ☆ Admit   ◁ Transfer Out
- Normal OT   ○ Pain   • Toilet Asst   ▲ Toilet   ✦ Shower   ✪ Bed Exit   ✿ Code Blue   ▷ Transfer In   ☐ Discharge
- Water

Inpatient Survey   **Disqualify Patient**

Patient Response

25% ▼

Has a caregiver been in to check on you every hour?
○ Yes ○ No

Responses : 4
Goal : 78%

＋ Notes

86% ▲

Has our staff responded to your requests in a timely manner?
○ Yes ○ No

Responses : 7
Goal : 76%

＋ Notes

100% ▲

Have we done an excellent job in managing your pain?
○ Yes ○ No

Responses : 5
Goal : 82%

＋ Notes

Save Answers

FIG. 23.8 Leadit-patient-activity. (From sphere3consulting.com)

BOX 23.5 HOW TO EVALUATE WEBSITES

Step 1: Authority
Who is/are the author(s)? Describe each author's authority or expertise. Are professional qualifications listed? How can you contact the author(s)? Who is the site's sponsor? What does the URL tell you? What type of domain does it come from (.gov, .mil, .edu, .org)? Is the site copyright protected?

Step 2: Timeliness and Continuity
When were the site materials created? When did it become active on the Web? When was it last updated/revised? Are the links up-to-date? Are the links functional? When were data gathered? What version/edition is it?

Step 3: Purpose
Who is the targeted audience? What is the purpose? Are the goals/aims/objectives clearly stated? Does the website present facts or opinion? Does the website offer an area for consumers and another one for health care professionals?

Step 4: Content: Accuracy and Objectivity
Does the information provided meet the purpose? Who is accountable for accuracy? Are the cited sources verifiable? What is the value of the content of this site related to your topical needs? How complete and accurate are the content information and links? Is the site biased? Does it contain advertisements?

Step 5: Structure, Design, and Access
What is the appearance of the site? Does the site load quickly? Do multimedia, graphics, and art used on the page serve a purpose, or are they just decorative or fun? Is there an element of creativity? Is there appropriate interactivity? Is the navigation intuitive? Are there icons? Is it a secured site? Is an index with links available?

McGonigle, D. (2002). How to evaluate websites. *Online Journal of Issues in Nursing, 6*(2).

Medical Library Association. (2016). *Find good health information.* Retrieved from http://mlanet.org/resources/userguide.html.

U.S. National Library of Medicine. (2015). *MedlinePlus guide to healthy web surfing.* Retrieved from https://www.nlm.nih.gov/medlineplus/healthywebsurfing.html.

Services (USDHHS) agencies involved in this project include the National Human Genome Research Institute (NHGRI), the Centers for Disease Control and Prevention (CDC), the Agency for Healthcare Research and Quality (AHRQ), and the Health Resources and Services Administration (HRSA). A downloadable free tool entitled "My Family Health Portrait" is available at http://www.genome.gov/27527640. This tool helps patients organize their family trees and identify common diseases that may run in their families. After completing the required information, the tool will create and print out a graphic representation of the patient's family generations and the health disorders that may have moved from one generation to the next. This is a powerful tool for predicting illnesses (USDHHS, 2004) and can be brought by the patient to a health care provider appointment.

The CARS Checklist

Acronyms are always helpful for remembering important key features. The CARS checklist (Credibility, Accuracy, Reasonableness, Support), developed by Harris in 1997 and updated in 2007, is designed to help evaluate a website. Although few sources will meet the majority of the criteria, the checklist will help in separating the high-quality information from the poor quality information.

✓ **Credibility**—an authoritative source, includes author's credentials, evidence of quality control such as peer review.

✓ Accuracy—a source that is correct today (not yesterday); comprehensive.

✓ Reasonableness—look at the information for fairness, objectivity, moderateness, consistency, and worldview.

✓ Support—a source that provides convincing evidence for the claims made; a source that you can triangulate (find at least two other sources that support it).

Harris (2007) notes that you will also need a little "café" advice to live with the information you obtained from your Internet search.

- Challenge the information and demand accountability.
- Adapt and require more credibility and evidence for stronger claims—it is okay to be skeptical of the information.
- File new information in your mind rather than immediately believing or disbelieving it.
- Evaluate and reevaluate regularly. Recognize the dynamic, fluid nature of information.

NURSING INFORMATICS AND YOU

Do you see now how your practice will involve informatics on a daily basis? From electronic documentation, to using technology-laden equipment such as smart IV pumps and beds, barcode medication administration, and a variety of POC diagnostics equipment, to communication tools such as smartphones and use of clinical decision support systems, technology will touch every part of your patient care (Research for Best Practice Box 23.1).

In addition, you may become part of the implementation team for a new software application as a super user. Super users are individuals who have been through additional training for a software application and who are responsible for helping others on their unit. You may be a subject-matter expert (SME) at some point in your career and help design the data input screens of an application.

Basic computing and information literacy skills are rapidly becoming required for all nurses, whether working directly with patients in any environment, teaching, or any of the other varied positions held by nurses today.

Informatics Competencies for the Practicing Nurse

A grassroots effort known as TIGER (Technology Informatics Guiding Educational Reform) Initiative "is focused on using informatics tools, principles, theories and practices to enable nurses to make healthcare safer, more effective, efficient, patient-centered, timely and equitable (TIGER, 2013, para 1). Based on an extensive literature review, the TIGER Informatics Competency Collaborative (TICC) developed the *TIGER Nursing Informatics Competencies Model* that includes basic computer competencies, information literacy, and information management (Gugerty & Delaney, 2009). This is an outstanding self-assessment tool to determine if you have gaps in your skill set.

Basic Computer Competencies

There seems to be a lack of consensus regarding what skills are needed to demonstrate basic computer competence (Elder & Koehn, 2009). Rather than develop another set of skills, the TICC basic competency recommendations are based on the European Computer Driving License (ECDL) Foundation's syllabus, which can be found at www.ecdl.org/programmes/index.jsp?p=102&n=2227.

The basic skills include

- Concepts of information and communication technology

Use of Technology Improves Safety of Medication Administration

Practice Issue

Approximately 1.5 million Americans are injured each year because of medication errors. Medication errors in the inpatient setting cost the health system well over $3.5 billion per year. Leape and colleagues (1995) broke medication errors into five phases: 39% of errors occurred during the prescribing phase, 12% during transcription, 11% during dispensing, and 38% during administration. It is the nurse at the patient's side who is the last link in the chain of medication administration. In a 300-bed community hospital, use of bar-code technology reduced medication errors by 80%. The Veteran's Administration in eastern Kansas prevented 549,000 medication errors between 1995 and 2001. At Medical University of South Carolina, a retrospective review of high-alert medication system triggers showed that 17% of scanned medications triggered an error alert. Of that, 55% were for high-alert medications including insulin, hydromorphone, potassium chloride, and morphine (Miller, Fortier, and Garrison, 2011).

Most nurses have heard of the case of the newborn twins of actor Dennis Quaid and his wife Kimberly receiving 10,000 units of heparin instead of 10 units. Although not all adverse drug events (ADEs) are preventable, using bar-code technologies can prevent those that are the result of a breakdown in the Five Rights of Medication Administration. But the technology only works when nurses use it. In a study by Koppel and colleagues (2008), nurses were found to use a work-around instead of using bar-code medication administration (BCMA) in more than 10% of the medications delivered. Five years later Rack, Dudjak, and Wolf (2012) found that more than half of nurses surveyed indicated that they used a work-around rather than the BCMA. They concluded that understanding why work-arounds occur and taking steps to prevent them will help achieve the goal of making the use of BCMA technology easier than developing a work-around. Bowers and colleagues (2015) found that the implementation of the BCMA increased the use of the workstation on wheels at the bedside and the use of the MAR at the point of care, which helped ensure that current orders were being implemented.

Implications for Nursing Practice

Don't use a work-around as a quick-fix solution to a bigger problem. If technology is hampering your work, tell your manager. Don't try to save time by bypassing the BCMA process.

Many of the medication errors were made unknowingly by nurses—BCMA can help ensure that the Five Rights are followed every time.

Considering This Information

Have you used BCMA yet? Has anyone taught you a work-around? Why would you want to bypass a BCMA alert and when?

References

Bowers, A. M, Goda, K., Bene, Victoria, et al. (2015). Impact of bar-code medication administration on medication administration best practices. *CIN: Computers, Informatics, Nursing, 33*(11), 502–508. doi: 10.1097/CIN.0000000000000198.

Coyle, G. A., & Heinen, M. (2005). Evolution of BCMA within the Department of Veterans Affairs: Bar code medication administration. *Nursing Administration Quarterly, 29*, 32–38.

Foote, S. O., & Coleman, J. R. (2008). Success story: Medication administration—the implementation process of bar-coding for medication administration to enhance medication safety. *Nursing Economic$, 26*, 207–210.

Gooder, V. (June 2011). Nurses' perceptions of a (BCMA) bar-coded medication administration system: A case-control study. *Online Journal of Nursing Informatics (OJNI), 15*(2). Retrieved from http://ojni.org/issues/?p=703.

Kelly, K., Harrington, L., Matos, P., et al. (2016). Creating a culture of safety around bar-code medication administration: An evidence-based evaluation framework. *Journal of Nursing Administration, 46*(1), 30–37. doi: 10.1097/NNA.0000000000000290.

Koppel R., Wetterneck T., Telles J. L., et al. (2008). Workarounds to barcode medication administration systems: Their occurrences, causes, and threats to patient safety. *Journal of American Medical Informatics Association, 15*, 408–423.

Institute of Medicine. (IOM). (2006). Medication errors injure 1.5 million people and cost billions of dollars annually. Retrieved from www.nationalacademies.org/onpinews/newsitem.aspx?RecordID=11623.

Leape, L. L., Bates, D. W., Cullen, D. J., et al. (1995). Systems analysis of adverse drug events. *JAMA, 274*, 35–43.

Miller, D. F., Fortier, C. R., & Garrison K. L. (2011). Bar code medication administration technology: Characterization of high-alert medication triggers and clinician workarounds. *Annals of Pharmacotherapy.* 45(2), 162–168. doi: 10.1345/aph.1P262.

Rack, L., Dudjak, L., & Wolf, G. (2012). Study of nurse workarounds in a hospital using bar code medication administration system. *Journal of Nursing Care Quality, 27*(3), 232–239. doi: 10.1097/NCQ.0b013e318240a854.

Rivish, V., & Mondeda, M. (2010). Medication administration pre and post BCMA at the VA Medical Center. *Online Journal of Nursing Informatics (OJNI), 14*(1), 1–21. Retrieved from http:ojni.org/14_1/Rivish.pdf.

Sakowski, J., Newman, J. M., & Dozier, K. (2008). Severity of medication administration errors detected by a bar-code medication administration system. *AJHP: Official Journal of the American Society of Health-System Pharmacists, 65*, 1661–1666.

- Using the computer and managing files
- Word processing
- Spreadsheets
- Using databases
- Presentation
- Web browsing and communication

Information Literacy

The second competency identified by the TIGER initiative is information literacy. The Association of College and Research Libraries (2010, para 1) defined information literacy as "the set of skills needed to find, retrieve, analyze, and use information." After a systematic literature review, Hart (2008) concluded that nurses in the United States are not prepared for evidence-based practice because of the lack of competency in information literacy skills. The TIGER recommendation is that all practicing nurses and graduating nursing students will have the ability to

- Determine the nature and extent of the information needed
- Access needed information effectively and efficiently
- Evaluate information and its sources critically and incorporate selected information into his or her knowledge base and value system
- Individually, or as a member of a group, use information effectively to accomplish a specific purpose
- Evaluate outcomes of the use of information (Gugerty & Delaney, 2009, p. 5)

CONCLUSION

Nursing informatics is a specialty grounded in the present while planning for the future. Informatics nurses face many challenges in their daily activities, because they are in a position to wear many hats and bear many responsibilities. The next challenge after EHR implementation will be using the data in a meaningful way—to improve patient care and lower costs. Computing devices and applications will continue to evolve and improve point-of-care access. Touch screens and voice input are already beginning to have an impact. Change is the only constant. At the end of this chapter are relevant websites and online resources on the concepts that have been presented.

The challenge will be for informatics nurses and informatics nurse specialists to assume leadership roles in informatics, while the nurse educator, manager, and practicing nurse prepare to embrace the generalized applications of working within a computerized environment. No longer will it be sufficient to turn on a computer and complete a simple task. A nurse will need to be able to use technology in all the forms found in health care organizations, access information, as well as access and use data and evaluate the content of the information provided to the patient population. Wishing will not make technology go away, so savvy nurses will focus on the benefits that technology brings to patient care, learn the skills they need, and embrace the future with all the changes it will bring.

RELEVANT WEBSITES AND ONLINE RESOURCES

American Health Information Management Association (AHIMA) (2015)
Website on PHRs. Retrieved from http://www.myphr.com/StartaPHR/what_is_a_phr.aspx.

American Medical Informatics Association (AMIA) (2013)
AMIA NI Working Group. Retrieved from http://www.amia.org/programs/working-groups/nursing-informatics.

American Nursing Informatics Association (ANIA) (2015)
Retrieved from https://www.ania.org/.

Centers for Medicare & Medicaid Services (CMS) (2013)
Medicare and Medicaid Electronic Health Records (EHR) Incentive Programs. Retrieved from http://www.cms.gov/Regulations-and-Guidance/Legislation/EHRIncentivePrograms/index.html?redirect=/ehrincentiveprograms/.

HealthIT.gov (n.d.)
Health Information Privacy, Security, and Your EHR. Retrieved from http://www.healthit.gov/providers-professionals/ehr-privacy-security.

What Is Meaningful Use? (2015)
Retrieved from http://www.healthit.gov/policy-researchers-implementers/meaningful-use.

Your Mobile Device and Health Information Privacy and Security (2014)
Retrieved from http://www.healthit.gov/providers-professionals/your-mobile-device-and-health-information-privacy-and-security.

HIMSS

Nursing informatics **(2013a)**
Retrieved from http://www.himss.org/ASP/topics_nursingInformatics.asp.

Meaningful Use OneSource **(2013b)**
Retrieved from http://www.himss.org/ASP/topics_meaningfuluse.asp.

Impact of the Informatics Nurse Survey Final Report **(2015)**
Retrieved from http://www.himss.org/files/FileDownloads/2015%20Impact%20of%20the%20Informatics%20Nurse%20Survey%20Full%20Report.pdf.

Medicare.gov (2016)
Personal Health Records (PHRs). Retrieved from https://www.medicare.gov/manage-your-health/.

Microsoft (2016)
Microsoft Health Vault. Retrieved from http://www.microsoft.com/en-us/healthvault/.
U.S. Department of Health & Human Services (HHS) (2016). *Health Information Privacy.* Retrieved from http://www.hhs.gov/ocr/privacy/.

WebMD (2016)
WebMD Personal Health Record. Retrieved from http://www.webmd.com/phr.

BIBLIOGRAPHY

Abrahamsen, C. (2003). Patient safety: Take the informatics challenge. *Nursing Management, 34,* 48–51.

Agency for Healthcare Research and Quality (AHRQ). (2012). *Computerized provider order entry.* Retrieved from http://psnet.ahrq.gov/primer.aspx?primerID=6.

American Hospital Association. (2006). *Protecting and improving care for patients and communities health information technology.* Retrieved from http://www.aha.org/content/00-10/Iss-Paper-Health-IT-06.pdf.

American Nurses Association. (2015). *ANA scope and standards of nursing informatics practice* (2nd ed.). Washington, DC: ANA.

American Nurses Association. (2011). *Fact sheet: Navigating the world of social media.* Retrieved from http://www.nursingworld.org/FunctionalMenuCategories/AboutANA/Social-Media/Social-Networking-Principles-Toolkit/Fact-Sheet-Navigating-the-World-of-Social-Media.pdf.

American Nurses Association. (2012). *ANA recognized terminologies that support nursing practice.* Retrieved from http://nursingworld.org/npii/terminologies.htm.

Association of College and Research Libraries. (2010). *Introduction to information literacy.* Retrieved from www.ala.org/ala/mgrps/divs/acrl/issues/infolit/overview/intro/index.cfm.

Clark, J. (2004). *Information management: The compliance guide to JCAHO standards* (4th ed.). Danvers, MA: HCPro Inc.

CMS.gov. (2012a). *Meaningful use.* Retrieved from http://www.cms.gov/Regulations-and-Guidance/Legislation/EHRIncentivePrograms/Stage_2.html.

CMS.gov. (2012b). *EHR incentive program.* Retrieved from http://www.cms.gov/Regulations-and-Guidance/Legislation/EHRIncentivePrograms/Downloads/Dec_EHRIncentivePrograms_PaymentandRegistration_Report.pdf.

CMS.gov. (2012c). *Stage 2.* Retrieved from http://www.cms.gov/Regulations-and-Guidance/Legislation/EHRIncentivePrograms/Meaningful_Use.html.

Delany, C. (2004). IN/INSCTF activities: Response to the President's information technology advisory committee. *CIN: Computers, Informatics, Nursing, 22*(299), 302–305.

Dimick, C. (2010). Californian sentenced to prison for HIPAA violation. *Journal of AHIMA.* Retrieved from http://journal.ahima.org/2010/04/29/californian-sentenced-to-prison-for-hipaa-violation/.

Dixon, B. E., & Zafar, A. (2009). *Inpatient computerized provider order entry: Findings from the AHRQ Health IT Portfolio. (Prepared by the AHRQ National Resource Center for Health IT).* Rockville, MD: AHRQ Publication No. 09-0031-EF Agency for Healthcare Research and Quality.

Elder, B. L., & Koehn, M. L. (2009). Assessment tool for nursing student computer competencies. *Nursing Education Perspectives, 30,* 148–152 (2009).

Eysenbach, G. (2001). What is e-health? *Journal of Medical Internet Research, 3*(2). Retrieved from www.jmir.org/2001/2/e20/.

Forkner-Dunn, J. (2003). Internet-based patient self-care: The next generation of health care delivery. *Journal of Medical Internet Research, 5*(e8).

Gale Group. (2001). HIPAA privacy rule takes effect. *Healthcare Financial Manage, 55,* 9.

Garrett, P., & Seidman, J. (2011). *EMR vs EHR—What is the difference?* Retrieved from http://www.healthit.gov/buzz-blog/electronic-health-and-medical-records/emr-vs-ehr-difference/.

Gearing, P., Olney, C. M., Davis, K., et al. (2006). Enhancing patient safety through electronic medical record documentation of vital signs. *Journal of Healthcare Information Management, 20,* 40–45.

Greenberg, L., D'Andrea, G., & Lorence, D. (2004). Setting the public agenda for online health search: A white paper and action agenda. *Journal of Medical Internet Research, 6*(2). Retrieved from www.jmir.org/2004/2/e18/.

Gugerty, B., & Delaney, C. (2009). *TIGER informatics competencies collaborative (TICC) final report.* Retrieved from http://tigercompetencies.pbworks.com/f/TICC_Final.pdf.

Harris, R. (2007). *Evaluating Internet research sources.* Retrieved from http://www.niu.edu/facdev/programs/handouts/evaluate.htm.

Hart, M. D. (2008). Informatics competency and development within the US nursing population workforce: A systematic literature review. *CIN: Computers, Informatics, Nursing, 26*, 320–329.

HealthIT.gov. (2014). *Your mobile device and health information privacy and security.* Retrieved from http://www.healthit.gov/providers-professionals/your-mobile-device-and-health-information-privacy-and-security.

HealthIT.gov. (2015). *What are the differences between electronic medical records, electronic health records, and personal health records?* Retrieved from http://www.healthit.gov/providers-professionals/faqs/what-are-differences-between-electronic-medical-records-electronic.

HHS.gov. (n.d.). *Personal health records (PHRs) and the HIPAA privacy rule.* Retrieved from http://www.hhs.gov/sites/default/files/ocr/privacy/hipaa/understanding/special/healthit/phrs.pdf.

Hill-Kayser, C., Vachani, C., Hampshire, M., Jacobs, L., & Metz, J. (2009). An Internet tool for creation of cancer survivorship care plans for survivors and health care providers: Design, implementation, use and user satisfaction. *Journal of Medical Internet Research, 11*(3). Retrieved from http://www.jmir.org/2009/3/e39/.

HIMSS Informatics Nurse Impact Study. (2015). *Final report.* Retrieved from http://www.himss.org/ni-impact-survey.

HIMSS. (2015). *Nursing Informatics Workforce Survey.* Retrieved from http://www.himss.org/content/files/2011 HIMSSNursingInformaticsWorkforceSurvey.pdf.

Hovenga, E. J., Kidd, M. R., Garde, S., & Hullin Lucay Cossio, C. (2010). Health informatics: An introduction. *Studies in Health Technology and Informatics, 151*, 9–15.

Hufstader, M., Swain, M., & Furukawa, M. F. (2012). *State variation in e-prescribing trends in the United States.* ONC Data Brief, no. 4. Washington, DC: Office of the National Coordinator for Health Information Technology.

Institute of Medicine: Committee on Quality of Health Care in America. (2001). *Crossing the quality chasm: A new health system for the 21st century.* Washington, DC: National Academies Press.

Institute of Medicine. (2003). *Key capabilities of an electronic health record system. Data standards for patient safety.* Retrieved from http://iom.nationalacademies.org/Reports/2003/Key-Capabilities-of-an-Electronic-Health-Record-System.aspx.

Institute of Medicine. (2006). *Preventing medication errors: Report brief.* Retrieved from https://iom.nationalacademies.org/~/media/Files/Report%20Files/2006/Preventing-Medication-Errors-Quality-Chasm-Series/medicationerrorsnew.pdf.

Internet World Stats. (2013). *Internet usage and population statistics for North America.* Retrieved from http://www.internetworldstats.com/stats14.htm#north.

Kaushal, R., Kern, L. M., Barron, Y., Quaresimo, J., & Abramson, E. L. (2010). Electronic prescribing improves medication safety in community-based office practices. *Journal of General Internal Medicine, 25*(6), 530–536.

Knox, C., & Smith, A. (2007). Handhelds and HIPAA. *Nursing Management, 38*(6), 38–40.

McGonigle, D. (2002). How to evaluate websites. *Online Journal of Nursing Informatics, 6*(2). Retrieved from http://ojni.org/602/web_site_evaluation.htm.

McGraw, D. (2012). *Meeting patient engagement objectives of meaningful use stage 2: Credentialing patients. HealthITBuzz.* Retrieved from http://www.healthit.gov/buzz-blog/meaningful-use/patient-engagement-objectives-meaningful-stage-2/.

Millard, M. (2015). *CMS lays out vision for Stage 3 meaningful use. Healthcare IT News.* Retrieved from http://www.healthcareitnews.com/news/cms-lays-out-vision-stage-3-meaningful-use.

National Council of State Boards of Nursing. (2016). *NCLEX-RN® Detailed Test Plan Candidate Version.* Retrieved from https://www.ncsbn.org/2016_RN_Test_Plan_Candidate.pdf.

National League for Nursing. (2008). *NLN Board of Governors urges better preparation of nursing workforce to practice in 21st-century, technology-rich health care environment.* Retrieved from http://www.nln.org/newsroom/news-releases/news-release/2008/05/29/nln-issues-call-for-faculty-development-and-curricular-initiatives-in-informatics-193.

Pancoast, P. E., Patrick, T. B., & Mitchell, J. A. (2003). Physician PDA use and the HIPAA privacy rule. *Journal of the American Medical Informatics Association, 10*, 611.

Parker, C. D., & Baldwin, K. (2008). Mobile device improves documentation workflow and nurse satisfaction. *CARING Newsletter, 23*(2), 14–18.

Ponemon Institute. (2014). *Third annual benchmark study on patient privacy & data security sponsored by ID experts*. Retrieved from http://www.ponemon.org/blog/fourth-annual-benchmark-study-on-patient-privacy-and-data-security.

Poon, E. G., Keohane, C. A., Yoon, C. S., et al. (2010). Effect of bar-code technology on the safety of medication administration. *New England Journal of Medicine, 362*(18), 1698–1707.

RAND Corporation. (2001). *Proceed with caution: a report on the quality of health information on the Internet*. San Francisco, CA. Sponsored by the California Health Care Foundation. Retrieved from http://www.chcf.org/~/media/MEDIA%20LIBRARY%20Files/PDF/PDF%20P/PDF%20ProceedWithCautionCompleteStudy.pdf.

Rogers, E. M. (2003). *Diffusion of innovation* (5th ed.). New York: Free Press.

Simpson, R. (2000). A systems view of information technology. *Nursing Administration Quarterly, 24*(4), 80.

Simpson, R. (2001). Size up the big three. *Nursing Management, 34*(3), 12–14.

Surescripts. (2016). *Pharmacies connected to Surescripts*. Retrieved from http://surescripts.com/network-connections/mns/connected-pharmacies.

The Joint Commission. (2012). *New and revised requirements for the laboratory accreditation program*. Retrieved from http://www.jointcommission.org/assets/1/18/Prepub_LAB_v21.pdf; http://www.jointcommission.org/patients%E2%80%99_access_to_test_reportschanges_to_clia_regulations_and_hipaa_privacy_rule/.

TIGER. (2013). *The TIGER collaborative teams—phase II activities*. Retrieved from http://www.tigersummit.com/9_Collaboratives. html.

U.S. Department of Health and Human Services. (2004). *U.S. Surgeon General's family history initiative*. Retrieved from www.hhs.gov/familyhistory/.

U.S. Department of Health and Human Services. (2013a). *New rule protects patient privacy, secures health information*. Retrieved from http://www.hhs.gov/news/press/2013pres/01/20130117b.html.

U.S. Department of Health and Human Services. (2013b). *How can you protect and secure health information when using a mobile device?* Retrieved from http://www.healthit.gov/providers-professionals/how-can-you-protect-and-secure-health-information-when-using-mobile-device.

U.S. Department of Health and Human Services. (2016). *Healthy People 2020*. Retrieved from http://healthypeople.gov/2020/topicsobjectives2020/overview.aspx?topicid=18.

Wager, K. A., Schaffner, M. J., Foulois, B., et al. (2010). Comparison of the quality and timeliness of vital signs data during a multi-phase EHR implementation. *Computers, Informatics, Nursing, 38*(4), 205–212.

World Health Organization (WHO). (2016). *Key definitions*. Retrieved from http://www.who.int/tb/areas-of-work/digital-health/definitions/en/.

Ye, J., Rust, G., Fry-Johnson, Y., & Strothers, H. (2010). E-mail in patient-provider communication: A systematic review. *Patient Education and Counseling, 80*, 266–272.

Zundel, K. M. (1996). Telemedicine: History, applications, and impact on librarianship. *Bulletin of the Medical Library Association, 84*(1), 71–79.

24

Using Evidence-Based Practice and Nursing Research

Peter G. Melenovich, PhD, RN, CNE*

ⓔ http://evolve.elsevier.com/Zerwekh/nsgtoday/.

The new challenge is for nurses to use research methods that can clearly explicate the essential nature, meanings and components of nursing so that nurse clinicians can use this knowledge in a deliberate and meaningful way.
Madeline Leininger

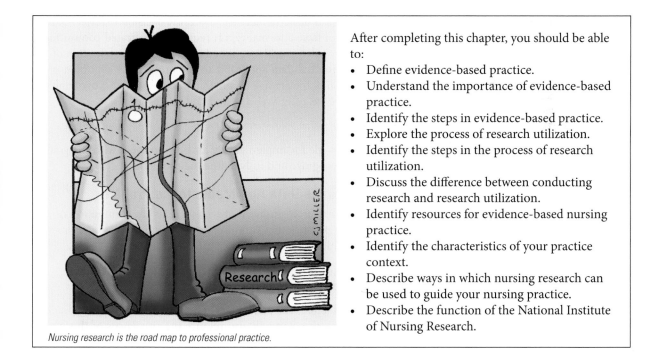

Nursing research is the road map to professional practice.

After completing this chapter, you should be able to:

- Define evidence-based practice.
- Understand the importance of evidence-based practice.
- Identify the steps in evidence-based practice.
- Explore the process of research utilization.
- Identify the steps in the process of research utilization.
- Discuss the difference between conducting research and research utilization.
- Identify resources for evidence-based nursing practice.
- Identify the characteristics of your practice context.
- Describe ways in which nursing research can be used to guide your nursing practice.
- Describe the function of the National Institute of Nursing Research.

* We would like to acknowledge **Mary Mackenburg-Mohn, RN, PhD, CNP,** for her past contributions to this chapter.

WHAT IS EVIDENCE-BASED PRACTICE?

Evidence-based practice (EBP) "is a problem solving approach to clinical practice that integrates: a systematic search for and critical appraisal of the most relevant evidence to answer a burning clinical question, one's own clinical expertise, and patient preferences and values" (**Melnyk & Fineout-Overholt, 2005, p. 6**). Historically health care and more specifically, nursing care, was based on tradition. In other words, we simply replicated what had been previously done in nursing, without question to the support of evidence for what we were doing or the impact on patient outcomes. As nursing has evolved and the expectation for continually improving patient outcomes has come to the forefront, a greater emphasis has been placed on implementing nursing care that is supported through the use of the best research available. Evidence-based practice incorporates many additional sources of data that may contribute to improved nursing care.

Evidence-based practice goes beyond nursing research in considering other sources of documentation that may improve nursing care. Research published by other disciplines is included (e.g., medical research and social research), as well as nonresearch data that may contribute to practice (e.g., financial data and clinical experts). This is prudent at a time when the complexity of health problems is increasing, and the discovery of new data is more rapid than ever before (Research for Best Practice Box 24.1).

The U.S. Department of Health and Human Services has established evidence-based practice centers and clinical practice guidelines that are available through the Internet. These resources include the most current information on completed evidence reports and practice guidelines as well as those that are in progress (see http://www.ahrq.gov/research/findings/evidence-based-reports/overview/index.html and http://www.ahrq.gov/professionals/clinicians-providers/guidelines-recommendations/index.html). However, not all aspects of practice have been evaluated to date. Therefore, the decision to implement an evidence-based practice protocol that does not have a formal report requires a dedicated commitment on the part of all those involved. The steps in applying evidence-based practice include definition of the problem; identifying, reviewing, and evaluating the data applicable to the problem; designing a practice change based on the data; and implementing the change in nursing practice, while recognizing the nurse's experience and patient preferences (see Relevant Websites and Online Resources).

Step 1: Define the Problem

As nursing professionals who will be responsible for implementing an EBP protocol with the goal of improving patient outcomes, we must first recognize and fully define the problem.

Step 2: Identify, Review, and Evaluate the Data Applicable to the Problem

Nurses must be able to locate and evaluate research studies that will serve as the foundation of any potential EBP protocol. The specific nursing practice that will be changed, in addition to the practice context, will determine the types of data included for review.

Step 3: Design a Practice Change Based on the Data While Incorporating the Clinical Expertise of the Nurse and Patient Preferences

Prepare a *written plan* for the new nursing practice. The plan needs to be consistent with your practice context to be effective. For maximum benefit, the plan will also require the consensus of those who will implement it.

Step 4: Implement the Change in Nursing Practice

Move the new plan into nursing practice on a *defined schedule*. Staff in-services may be required so that those involved can fully understand the change. Monitor and evaluate the implementation process.

🔍 RESEARCH FOR BEST PRACTICE BOX 24.1

Wound Care

Practice Issue

The increased acuity of patient needs, combined with advances in wound care, have the potential to create frustrating situations for the new graduate nurse. It is essential for the new graduate to prevent pressure ulcers and provide wound care that reflects current best practice measures and the newest advances in technology.

Implications for Nursing Practice

1. Approximately 2.5 million pressure ulcers occur each year in the United States, adding an estimated burden of more than $11 billion in expenditures, with reported estimated costs of between $500 and $150,000 per individual pressure ulcer (AHRQ, 2014; NPUAP, 2014).
2. Approximately 60,000 patients die annually from complications of pressure ulcers (AHRQ, 2012; Salcido et al., 2012).
3. Wound care has emerged as a specialty practice for RNs (Wound Ostomy Continence Nursing Certification Board, 2016).
4. Wound care needs and procedures can vary significantly across practice settings (Bolton & Baine, 2012).
5. New graduate RNs are more competent in patient care and less competent in clinical reasoning, recognizing limits, and seeking help.
6. New graduate RNs are more likely to use written information, care guidelines, and agency-specific policies to guide their practice.
7. New graduate RNs are more competent with using technology to seek answers and specific information related to current patient care practices.

Considering This Information

What can you do to keep up-to-date on wound care treatments?

References

Agency for Healthcare Research and Quality (AHRQ). (2014). *Are we ready for this change?* Retrieved from http://www.ahrq.gov/professionals/systems/hospital/pressureulcertoolkit/putool1.html.

Bolton, L. L., & Baine, W. B. (2012). Using science to advance wound care practice: Lessons from the literature. *Ostomy Wound Management, 58*(9), 16–31.

Salcido, R., Lorenzo, C., & Popescu, A. (2012). *Pressure ulcers and wound care.* Retrieved from http://emedicine.medscape.com/article/319284-overview.

National Pressure Ulcer Advisory Panel (NPUAP). (2014). *European Pressure Ulcer Advisory Panel and Pan Pacific Pressure Injury Alliance. Prevention and treatment of pressure ulcers: Clinical practice guideline.* Emily Haesler (Ed.) Osborne Park, Western Australia: Cambridge Media. Retrieved from http://www.npuap.org/resources/educational-and-clinical-resources/prevention-and-treatment-of-pressure-ulcers-clinical-practice-guideline/.

Wound Ostomy Continence Nursing Certification Board. (2016). *About WOCNCB.* Retrieved from https://www.wocncb.org/about-us.

Moreover, as noted by Melnyk and Fineout-Overholt (2005), EBP must recognize the great experience that nurses bring to the practice setting and patient input and preferences if successful implementation is to be realized (Fig. 24.1).

Now let's consider using the evidence-based practice process in a hypothetical situation.

Mario works in an intensive care unit in which many of the patients require mechanical ventilation. At a recent staff meeting, Mario and his co-workers learned that their unit's rate of ventilator-associated pneumonia (VAP) was greater than rates in many other hospitals. Concerned by this, Mario volunteered to work on this project. He began with a review of the literature. Using a nursing literature database, Mario was able to find a number of research studies conducted in the past few years that examined the same issue. Additionally, he found that multiple professional organizations had issued evidence-based guidelines to reduce the occurrence of ventilator-associated pneumonia. After reading these articles, Mario drafted a

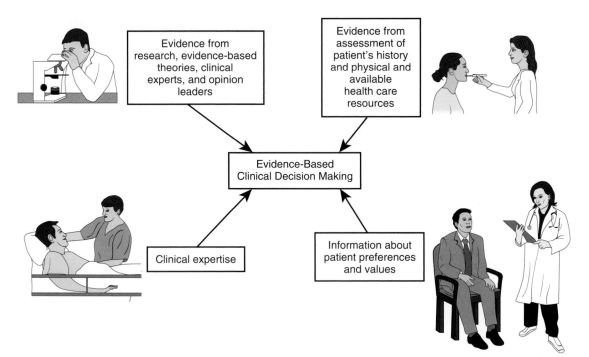

FIG. 24.1 Model of evidence-based clinical decision making. Reprinted with permission from Potter, P. A., Perry, A. G., Stockert, P. A., Hall, A. M., & Ostendorf, W. R. (2017). Fundamentals of nursing (9th ed.). St. Louis: Elsevier, p. 53.

set of clinical practice guidelines based on these articles that reflected the unique needs of his unit and its patient population. Mario then presented his guidelines to the nursing staff and provided short educational in-service sessions on their application. The staff agreed to adhere to these new practice guidelines for a period of 3 months. At the end of that time, they would compare their incidence of VAP using the new clinical guidelines with the incidence of VAP using the old clinical guidelines.

At the end of the 3-month period, Mario and his co-workers were pleased to find a significant decrease in the occurrence of VAP among their patients. Working with nursing administration, Mario's proposed clinical practice guidelines became the new standard of care on his unit.

THE NEED FOR NURSING PRACTICE BASED ON RESEARCH

In the recent past, there has been a continuing increase in costs associated with the delivery and receipt of health care in the United States. At the same time, there has been more and more scrutiny of how those health care dollars are spent. The decision of which health care treatments receive funding from health care insurance is now based primarily on documentation of favorable patient outcomes. In addition, patients want to know that the dollars they spend on health care will help them to get well and feel better—they want to purchase something that works for them. Nurses must be able to demonstrate that the nursing care they provide is cost-effective and improves the health of patients. As we continue to move to a health care setting that recognizes the importance of patient care that utilizes the most current and appropriate evidence, we must understand how research utilization will assist us in meeting the goal of improving patient outcomes through EBP.

WHAT IS NURSING RESEARCH UTILIZATION?

The ability to transfer research into clinical practice is essential for ensuring quality in nursing. The process of research utilization involves transferring research findings to clinical nursing practice. In the process of research utilization, the emphasis is on using *existing* data (findings or evidence) from previous nursing research studies to evaluate a current nursing practice. A major component of the process is reviewing completed nursing research studies that have been published in the literature. In contrast, conducting new research involves the collection of *new* data to answer a specific clinical practice question. Nursing research utilization is a step-by-step process incorporating critical thinking and decision making to ensure that a change in practice has a sound basis in nursing science.

What Are the Steps for Nursing Research Utilization?
Step 1: Preutilization
The first step in the application of nursing research to nursing practice is the recognition that some aspect of nursing practice could be done in a safer, more efficient, more beneficial, or simply a different way. This begins an exploratory phase in which nursing colleagues in the practice setting are consulted regarding their opinions about the need to find a new approach for some aspect of nursing practice. An early question should be: "Is the current practice research based?" When current practice is research based, the next question should be "Is the research on which the practice is based current?" (e.g., the specific details of taking temperatures with mercury thermometers became outdated when digital thermometers were used exclusively in practice).

A second phase of Step 1 is consensus building, which is used to identify the specific practice to be changed. In this phase, the incorporation of the principles of change theory will increase the possibility of success. (See Chapter 10 for information about the challenges of change.) In any practice setting in which there are several nurses, a change will be more acceptable if those affected are included in the decisions related to the change. Clear communication and teamwork are essential elements of this process. Group consensus is crucial for the successful application of research findings.

The third and final phase of Step 1 delineates the aspect of nursing practice that will be changed into a concise statement of the *practice problem*. This statement will answer the question, "In our current nursing practice, what do we want to change, improve, or make more efficient?" The narrower and more specific the statement of the practice problem, the easier your task will be in Step 2.

Step 2: Assessing
The second step in research utilization is the identification and critical evaluation of published research that is related to the practice problem you have identified (Fig. 24.2). Nursing literature is searched to identify those studies that address your practice problem. Although some studies may have explored the exact practice problem that you are examining, it is likely that most research will have approached the problem from a different point of view. Your task will be to analyze and critically evaluate the research reports to determine which findings are adaptable to your practice problem and context.

While reviewing the literature for research reports that have examined your practice problem, it is essential that the research reports you are reviewing are peer-reviewed to ensure credibility. Peer-reviewed or refereed research studies are different from popular sources and non–peer-reviewed research reports, in that the research manuscript is submitted to a scholarly journal where it is

FIG. 24.2 Nine out of ten nurses recommend....

reviewed by a panel of experts (peer reviewers or referees) in that respective field or area of study. An editorial board that is not expert in the content area under study typically reviews non–peer-reviewed reports (e.g., editorials, newsletters, opinion statements). Additionally, peer-reviewed articles have a designated manuscript format, which includes an abstract, research problem/objective, methodology, data collection, discussion, conclusion, and references; whereas non–peer-reviewed or popular/trade journals do not ascribe to a specific formatting style (NCSU Libraries, 2014). So, you might be asking yourself, "What does the peer-review process involve and what are my chances of publishing a research report in a peer-reviewed journal?" North Carolina State University (NCSU) offers an overview of the peer-review process via an online video available at http://www.lib.ncsu.edu/tutorials/peerreview/.

Organizing and summarizing the adaptable findings into an outline format will provide you with your primary working document for the remainder of the use plan (Box 24.1). Box 24.2 contains suggestions for reading a nursing research article.

The use of the Internet and electronic databases has made a thorough search of the current literature easier. However, the enormous volume of materials now available also increases the complexity of a review of literature. For example, the keywords used in a search can either return no articles or hundreds of articles. When you are conducting an electronic search, a valuable technique is to begin searching within the most recent year and then move back one year at a time until an adequate research base is identified. Limiting your searches to the use of nursing-oriented database and peer-reviewed journals may also help you find pertinent literature. The Cumulative Index to Nursing and Allied Health Literature (CINAHL) is an excellent place to start your search. In addition, you may wish to limit your search to journal articles only; otherwise the online database may return reports from magazine articles and newspapers. Listed at the end of this chapter are Relevant Websites and Online Resources to use in locating and reviewing peer-reviewed journals as well as online evidence-based practice resources.

There are times, however, when an electronic search is not adequate. Keep in mind that many of the classic research studies were published before electronic formats were widely used, and these classic studies may not be available online. Also, there may be valuable studies that are available in hard copy

---

BOX 24.1 ANALYZING A RESEARCH ARTICLE FOR POTENTIAL USE OF FINDINGS IN NURSING PRACTICE

1a. The Purpose of the study is:

1b. The importance of this study to nursing practice is:

2. The Research Question/Hypothesis is:

(If the question/hypothesis is not stated, it could be):

3a. The Independent Variable(s) is/are:

3b. The Dependent Variable(s) is/are:

(If there are no independent and dependent variables, the Research Variable[s] is/are):

3c. Definition(s) of the variable(s) of interest to me is/are:

4. The Conceptual Model/Theoretical Framework linked with this study is:

5a. The content areas in the Review of Related Literature are:

5b. The review does/does not evaluate both supporting and nonsupporting studies:

6a. The Research Design used for the study is:

6b. The design is/is not appropriate for the research question:

6c. The control(s) used in this study is/are:

6d. The Study Setting is:

7a. The Target Population is:

7b. The Sampling Method is:

7c. The Sampling Method is/is not appropriate for the design:

7d. The criteria for participants are:

7e. The sample included _____ participants.

7f. The sample is/is not representative of the population:

8a. The Study Instrument(s) is/are:

8b. Instrument validity and reliability information is presented and is of adequate levels for confidence in using the results:

9a. The Data Collection Method(s) is/are:

9b. The Data Collection Method(s) is/are (is not/are not) appropriate for this study:

10. Steps were taken to protect the Rights of Human Subjects:

11a. The Data Analysis Procedure(s) is/are:

11b. The Data Analysis Procedure(s) is/are appropriate for the level of data collected and the research question/hypothesis:

11c. The Research Question/Hypothesis is/is not supported:

12. The author(s) major Conclusions and/or Implications for Nursing Practice are:

BOX 24.2 HOW TO READ A NURSING RESEARCH ARTICLE

A research article should answer the following:

What?

Read the problem statement, purpose, research question, and results/findings. | Is the content of the article related to my question?

Why?

Read the problem statement or the review of literature. | Why was the research done?

When?

Do more recent findings provide a better answer? | When was the study done? Is it classic, current, or outdated?

Read the date of publication.

Continued

BOX 24.2   HOW TO READ A NURSING RESEARCH ARTICLE—cont'd

How?

Read the method and design sections. | What research method was used? Is it a quantitative, qualitative, or mixed-methods approach?

Who?

Read the method section. | Who were the subjects? What was the sample?

Where?

Read the method section. | In what setting was the research done?

So What?

Read the findings and discussion. | Are the findings helpful to my problem and me?

Do Not: | Do not automatically accept what you read; critically evaluate the content. You can only evaluate what is written and reported; do not assume anything about what is not written.

What to Do When

When the statistical procedures are beyond your level of understanding:

- Read the results section, being alert for specific phrases that will tell you the answer to the research question. For example, "the hypothesis was not supported."
- Look at the tables; tables should be understandable without the narrative.
- Assume that the appropriate statistical analysis was performed correctly and that the researcher has interpreted the results correctly.
- Have someone who understands the statistics read the article and ask his or her opinion, or get a consultant.

---

only. Because of these limitations of electronic sources, you may need to make a trip to the stacks in the library if you are looking for historical research. See Box 24.3 for hints on conducting a literature search.

Step 3: Planning

Planning for research utilization is accomplished in three phases. The first phase involves determining the new approach, or *innovation*, that will be used on the basis of the findings from the review of the literature. Previous research findings will be used to design the innovation in the context of your practice setting (e.g., intensive care unit, ambulatory care, home care). The expected *practice outcomes* should also be determined based on the literature and may need to be adjusted according to the characteristics of your particular practice.

Phase two of planning is the establishment of a systematic method for implementing the new approach. A *specific plan* should be established and followed so that the new approach is applied appropriately. Policies and procedures for implementation may need to be written. This phase may include staff training for the new approach.

The third phase of planning involves establishing a *method for evaluating* the practice outcomes, or effects, of the new approach. The outcomes are usually some specific improvements in patient care. Ideally, your evaluation will indicate both the quality and the quantity of the change in the outcome.

Step 4: Implementing

This step involves the implementation or application of the new approach, along with the collection of the evaluation data. By following the specific plan that you established in Step 3, the new approach will

---

BOX 24.3 HINTS FOR CONDUCTING A LITERATURE SEARCH

1. Do some narrowing before you go to online databases. Think about some key terms or alternative terms for your problem. Be prepared to narrow or expand your search, depending on what you find.
2. Plan to spend time conducting your literature search, but do not waste valuable time. Query the online database "help" menu to assist you with getting started.
3. Begin by identifying the major professional nursing journals that publish nursing research. Determine if those journals are available in the database, and start your literature review with those. If your problem is in a specialty area, review specialty journals.
4. If you find an article related to your problem, look at that author's reference list for other current articles and journals.
5. Read the abstract of the article first; this will give you a quick overview of the article to determine if it is relevant to your topic under study.
6. Know the limitations of the databases where you do your search.
7. Carefully appraise information obtained from the Internet that is not part of an established online database, such as Journals@Ovid; EBSCOhost; ProQuest; Thomson Gale PowerSearch.

---

be introduced into practice. It is important that you begin collecting your evaluation data at the same time so that you can clearly determine the effect of the new approach.

Step 5: Evaluating

Step 5 involves the evaluation of the implementation (Step 4) to determine whether the new approach improved practice outcomes. Whether or not you will continue using the new approach in the practice setting may also be determined based on new technology, economic considerations, or changes in staffing. If there is no change in outcomes, you may want to return to the previous practice. Or, the evaluation phase may lead to another research utilization project; for example, if the practice problem is significant and the practice outcomes were not improved, another new approach may be tried.

Research Utilization: What Is It *Not?*

Research utilization does *not* entail simply taking the findings of a single research study and using those findings in nursing practice. Research studies are replicated to rule out chance findings and to validate previous studies. Similar studies with different populations are conducted to determine the applicability of findings to different groups of people. For these reasons, research utilization encompasses the findings of many studies to develop the new approach that will be put into practice.

Data are collected in the process of research utilization. However, research utilization is not the collection of data to answer a research question, as is the case when conducting research. The data collected in research utilization are needed for evaluation to determine whether there is some advantage to the new approach in the practice setting. The data collected must be carefully considered in light of your specific setting.

Research utilization should not be confused with a review of nursing practice. Practice review involves a quality control/risk management process to evaluate the appropriate use of resources related to a specific treatment. As with research utilization, practice review use does not entail the use of nursing research findings during the process of evaluation.

When you review the nursing research literature for research utilization, as mentioned previously, there is no assurance that you will find studies that are directly applicable to your practice situation. Your specific question may not have been the topic of previous research studies. In this case, you may have to either adapt the findings from the literature, conduct your own research, or both.

RESEARCH UTILIZATION COMPARED WITH NURSING RESEARCH AND THE CONDUCT OF RESEARCH

How Is the Use of Research in Practice Different from Conducting Research?

As illustrated in Table 24.1, the major steps involved in both conducting and utilizing research are the same. Both are problem-solving processes involving critical thinking. For example, a clinical practice problem may provide the impetus to conduct and use research. However, there are differences. Conducting research taps into the "ways of knowing," whereas using research taps into the "ways of doing."

TABLE 24.1   COMPARISON OF PROCESSES

An Overview of the Nursing Process, Conducting Research, and Research Utilization

NURSING PROCESS	CONDUCTING RESEARCH	RESEARCH UTILIZATION
Preprocess	**Preplanning**	**Peruse**
Establish a nurse–patient relationship	Identify the need for a research study	Identify a practice problem that needs a new approach
Scan the literature	Determine feasibility	
	Obtain consensus	
Assessing	**Assessing**	**Assessing**
Gather data	Identify the problem	Identify and critically evaluate published research related to your practice problem
	State research purpose	
	Begin to formulate the research question	Identify the findings that are adaptable to your problem and your context
	Review the literature	
Planning	**Planning**	**Planning**
Diagnose	Identify and define the variables	Determine the new approach and the desired outcomes
Set goals	Select a conceptual or theoretical model	
		Establish a systematic method for implementing the new approach
Prioritize	Select research design	
Determine nursing interventions	Finalize research question	Establish a method for evaluating the outcomes of the new approach
	Plan data analysis	
Formulate care plan	Write research proposal	
Negotiate a site for data collection		
Complete human subjects review		
Implementing	**Implementing**	**Implementing**
Initiate the plan	Prepare questionnaires	Begin using the new approach
Train data collectors	Collect data about the outcomes of the new approach	
Obtain subject sample		
Collect the data		
Prepare data for analysis		
Evaluating	**Evaluating**	**Evaluation of the implementation**
Determine the patient response	Analyze the data	Determine whether the practice changes improved the patient outcomes
	Organize the data	
Answer the research question	Decide whether to continue using the new approach	
Interpret the results		
Report the findings		
Plan next project		

When we conduct research, whether in the clinical setting or the laboratory, the primary activity undertaken is the systematic collection of new data. Following specific steps called the protocol, we gather information that will answer a specific research question. For many nursing studies, the *research question* arises from a situation in nursing practice that needs an answer. A research question is often stimulated by a nurse's involvement with patient care delivery. Lusardi (2012) adds that experiences at the bedside propel nurses to implement change within their nursing practice. After a clinical issue or problem has been identified and a review of the literature has been conducted, the next step is to develop a research question that will address the clinical issue. Lusardi (2012) recommends using the PICOT format, where P represents the population of interest, I represents the intervention of interest, C represents the comparison of interest, O represents the outcome of interest, and T represents the time frame. The T element may or may not be applicable (Fig. 24.3).

The *utilization of research* involves the systematic process of integrating the findings of completed nursing research studies into clinical nursing practice.

Research utilization also entails reviewing research that has already been completed to develop a new approach to nursing practice. In reviewing research studies, pay particular attention to the type of research methodology employed—quantitative, qualitative, or mixed methods (Table 24.2). All three processes—research utilization, nursing research, and the nursing process—have the same five major steps. However, the specific tasks for each process are different.

FIG. 24.3 Developing a research question using the PICOT format.

TABLE 24.2   COMPARISON OF QUANTITATIVE, QUALITATIVE, AND MIXED-METHODS RESEARCH DESIGNS

RESEARCH DESIGNS	QUANTITATIVE RESEARCH	QUALITATIVE RESEARCH	MIXED-METHODS RESEARCH
Philosophical paradigm	• Examination of a cause-and-effect relationship • Deductive approach	• Acquire understanding of phenomena by observing behaviors, reactions, statements of study participants • Inductive approach	• Involves aspects of quantitative and qualitative philosophical frameworks. Blending of both deductive and inductive approaches
Purpose of study	• Study focuses on supporting or refuting the null hypothesis • The research variables are discussed and examined in detail to determine if a relationship or causality exists	• Study typically focuses on central concept or aspect for further exploration	• Provides rationale for why both quantitative and qualitative methods are warranted in the study
Research question	• Closed-ended questions • Questions ask, "What differences exist," "What is the effect," "What is the relationship … ?" • Null hypothesis is either supported or refuted based on study findings	• Open-ended questions • Questions ask, "How" or "Why"? • Broad questions that seek to explore perceptions, beliefs, attitudes of a particular phenomenon of interest	• May include both closed-ended and open-ended questions
Data collection	• Follows specific sequence • Similar to scientific method; numeric data collected through questionnaires, surveys, established instruments • Large sample size	• Data collected through observing, interviewing, audio/video recording • Small sample size • Study participants are typically selected by researcher	• Dependent on the type of mixed-method design employed
Data analysis	• Statistical analysis; numeric data reported • Data analyzed is unbiased and objective	• Researcher interprets data by developing themes based on participants' views and observations • Data analyzed is subjective in nature; may include words, artifacts, images, anecdotal statements	• Dependent on the type of mixed-method design employed

What Is the Relationship Between Nursing Theory and Research Utilization?

Nursing theory used as the theoretic framework of a research study is essential for the continued development of nursing theories; new research findings will support theory or will suggest the modification of theory. In contrast, when a specific nursing theory is used as the framework for nursing practice, the focus is on the intervention. The intervention that is designed in the planning phase of research utilization must be consistent with the theory. For example, if Orem's theory of self-care requisites were used for nursing practice, a successful intervention would be one that emphasizes self-care rather than care received from others. There is a close relationship between nursing research and research utilization because of the focus of both on nursing practice.

DEFINING YOUR PRACTICE CONTEXT

Your practice context will determine to what degree you can apply the findings from nursing research to your practice problem. A *practice context* entails a blending of all those factors and systems that contribute to the delivery of nursing care. This blend includes the health, social, and cultural characteristics of the patient population served: the type of practice setting, the economic resources of the setting, the type of health care delivery system, the existing policies and procedures, the staffing pattern, and the administrative structure. Each factor or system can be either enabling or inhibiting, but it is the practice context as a whole that is evaluated to determine the applicability of nursing research findings.

What Are the Health, Social, and Cultural Characteristics of the Patient Population Being Served?

To begin defining your practice context, you will need to identify any characteristics that are specific to the group of people who will be receiving nursing care. Is there some particular health characteristic that should be considered? For example, if you teach prenatal classes, the health characteristic will be pregnancy. Are there some particular social and cultural characteristics that need to be considered? If your prenatal classes are for pregnant teenagers who are single, then social characteristics require special consideration. Be as thorough and as specific as possible in identifying these characteristics.

What Are the Health Care Delivery Characteristics of Your Setting?

As you continue to define your practice context, specify the type of practice setting, the economic constraints of the setting, the type of health care delivery system, the existing policies and procedures, the staffing patterns, and the administrative structures. In other words, include all the characteristics of the care setting that will either contribute to or inhibit the process of applying research findings. If your practice setting were in a hospital where there is a limit to the length of stay for a particular surgery, then a new approach that would increase that length of stay would not be an appropriate one for implementation. Furthermore, when implementing a new approach in practice, care must be taken to preserve or improve the current health care delivery standards.

What Are the Motivators and Barriers for Incorporating Nursing Research Into Your Practice?

Identify your bridges (motivators) and roadblocks (barriers) in the practice setting (Critical Thinking Box 24.1). The more individuals in the practice setting from whom you can attain consensus on the new approach to practice, the easier it will be to implement. Those who understand the need for

> **? CRITICAL THINKING BOX 24.1**
>
> Think about…
> - What are the barriers that might inhibit your use of research findings?
> - Are these findings applicable to your practice setting?
> - How would you go about minimizing the barriers?

making a change in practice will be more likely to support the change. (See Chapter 10 for information on change theory.) Those who feel they had a part in the decision making surrounding the new approach are also more likely to promote it. In both instances, these colleagues become motivators for the implementation of innovation and change.

As with any change process that involves a group of people, it is very likely that some individuals in the practice setting will be resistant to the new approach. Those who are resistant may present barriers that prevent the full implementation of the new process. They may complain about a lack of time to learn the new approach, for example, in an effort to avoid being a part of what they do not support. These colleagues, as well as budgetary and personnel constraints, are examples of barriers.

In addition, the research literature may present barriers to implementing a new approach. For example, if there are only a few research studies reported in the nursing literature that are related to your practice problem, then the lack of replication of the findings may prevent you from developing a research-based approach for your particular practice problem. Another barrier is the time lag from the completion of a research project until the project report is published. This time lag, which may be a few years, may make the research findings obsolete. For example, research related to glass oral thermometers would be obsolete, because your practice setting now uses electronic ear thermometers. When reviewing the literature, try to limit your search criteria to studies published within the previous 5 years, unless it is a classic study that will substantiate the need for conducting research on your practice problem.

THE NATIONAL INSTITUTE OF NURSING RESEARCH

What Is Its Function?

The National Institute of Nursing Research (NINR) is a branch of the National Institutes of Health (NIH), which is under the jurisdiction of the U.S. Department of Health and Human Services. Each institute within the NIH focuses on a specific area of health care research; the NINR is a major source of federal funding for nursing research. The NINR also supports education in research methods, research career development, and excellence in nursing science.

Other functions of the NINR are to establish a National Nursing Research Agenda. This agenda is composed of priority topics for nursing research and may be related to a national health need, or they may be in an area that requires research for the development of nursing science. Many nurses have received funding to support clinical and basic research on health and illness across the life span. Funded research includes health promotion and disease prevention, quality-of-life issues, health disparities, and end-of-life care.

The NINR also has a role in President Obama's American Recovery and Reinvestment Act of 2009. The act was created to assist with the economic recovery of the United States and includes measures to modernize the national infrastructure including health care. For more information, visit the NINR website (http://www.ninr.nih.gov/).

THE AGENCY FOR HEALTHCARE RESEARCH AND QUALITY

What Is Its Function?

As part of the Omnibus Budget Reconciliation Act of 1989, the Agency for Health Care Policy and Research (later renamed the Agency for Healthcare Research and Quality [AHRQ]) was established to enhance the quality and effectiveness of health care services. The AHRQ conducts and supports general health services research, develops clinical practice guidelines, and disseminates research findings and guidelines to health care providers, policymakers, and the public. As mentioned previously, one arm of the AHRQ supports the Evidence-based Practice Centers Program (AHRQ, 2015), which develops reports about interventions that are based on published scientific studies related to health care. For more information about AHRQ, visit their website (www.ahrq.gov/).

CONCLUSION

Nursing has a growing body of evidence on which we can support our practice. Moreover, research utilization is a key component of effectively implementing evidence-based practice protocols aimed at improving patient outcomes. Whether you are a new graduate or an experienced nurse, there are ample opportunities for you to apply research in your area of clinical practice. When areas of practice need to be changed, it is important to have valid information and data to support the need for change. Check out your hospital resources, establish networking and colleague support, and participate in EBP in your setting.

⊕ RELEVANT WEBSITES AND ONLINE RESOURCES

American Speech-Language Hearing Association (2016)
Evidence-based practice tutorials and resources. Retrieved from http://www.asha.org/Research/EBP/Evidence-Based-Practice-Tutorials-and-Resources/.

California State University, Chico (2011)
What is a scholarly article? Retrieved from https://www.csuchico.edu/lins/handouts/scholarly.pdf.

Duke University Medical Center Library & Archives (2016)
Resources for EBP. Retrieved from http://guides.mclibrary.duke.edu/nursing/ebp.

Evidence-based nursing (2013)
Retrieved from http://nursingplanet.com/research/evidence_based_nursing.html.

Evidence-based practice in the health sciences tutorials (2013)
Retrieved from http://ebp.lib.uic.edu.

HealthLeaders Media (2016)
Evidence-based practice and nursing research: Avoiding confusion. Retrieved from http://www.healthleadersmedia.com/page-1/NRS-245879/EvidenceBased-Practice-and-Nursing-Research-Avoiding-Confusion.

Indiana Center for Evidence-Based Nursing Practice (2016)
Retrieved from http://ebnp.org.

Continued

⊕ RELEVANT WEBSITES AND ONLINE RESOURCES—cont'd

International Council of Nurses Evidence-Based Practice Resource (2012)
Retrieved from http://www.nursingworld.org/Research-Toolkit/ICN-Evidence-Based-Practice-Resource.

North Carolina State University (2013)
Anatomy of a scholarly article. Retrieved from http://www.lib.ncsu.edu/tutorials/scholarly-articles/.

North Carolina State University (2013)
Peer review in five minutes. Retrieved from http://www.lib.ncsu.edu/tutorials/pr/.

North Carolina State University (2013)
Scholarly vs. popular materials guide. Retrieved from http://www.lib.ncsu.edu/guides/spmaterials/

University of North Carolina (2015)
Evidence-based nursing introduction. Retrieved from http://guides.lib.unc.edu/c.php?g=8362&p=43029.

BIBLIOGRAPHY

Agency for Healthcare Research and Quality (AHRQ). (2014). *Clinical guidelines and recommendations.* Retrieved from http://www.ahrq.gov/professionals/clinicians-providers/guidelines-recommendations/index.html.

Agency for Healthcare Research and Quality (AHRQ). (2015). *Evidence-based practice centers (EPC) program overview.* Retrieved from http://www.ahrq.gov/research/findings/evidence-based-reports/overview/index.html.

Driever, M. J. (2002). Are evidence-based practice and best practice the same? *Western Journal of Nursing Research, 24,* 591–597.

Lusardi, P. (2012). So you want to change practice: Recognizing practice issues and channeling those ideas. *Critical Care Nurse, 32*(2), 55–64. http://dx.doi.org/10.4037/ccn2012899.

Melnyk, B. M., & Fineout-Overholt, E. (2005). *Evidence-based practice in nursing & healthcare. A guide to best practice.* Philadelphia: Lippincott Williams & Wilkins.

NCSU Libraries. (2014). *Peer review in 3 minutes.* Retrieved from http://www.lib.ncsu.edu/tutorials/peerreview/.

Newhouse, R., et al. (2005). Evidence-based practice: A practical approach to implementation. *Journal of Nursing Administration, 1,* 35–40.

Potter, P. A., Perry, A. G., Stockert, P. A., & Hall, A. M. (2017). *Fundamentals of nursing* (9th ed.). St. Louis, MO: Elsevier.

Spector, N. (2007). *Evidence-based health care in nursing regulation: National Council State Boards of Nursing.* Retrieved from www.ncsbn.org/Evidence_based_HC_Nsg_Regulation_updated_5_07_with_name.pdf.

25

Workplace Issues

Susan Ahrens, PhD, RN

ⓔ http://evolve.elsevier.com/Zerwekh/nsgtoday/.

Fear is the father of courage and the mother of safety.
Henry H. Tweedy

The safety of the people is the supreme law. (Salus populi suprema lex.)
Cicero (106–143 BC)

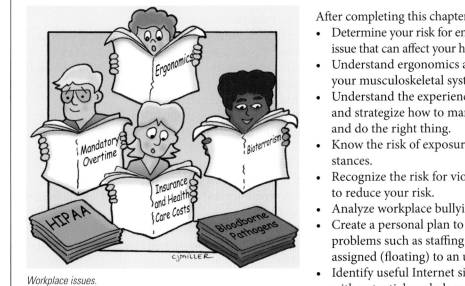

Workplace issues.

After completing this chapter, you should be able to:
- Determine your risk for encountering a workplace issue that can affect your health or well-being.
- Understand ergonomics and ways to safeguard your musculoskeletal system.
- Understand the experience of making an error and strategize how to manage your experience and do the right thing.
- Know the risk of exposure to hazardous substances.
- Recognize the risk for violence at work and how to reduce your risk.
- Analyze workplace bullying and harassment.
- Create a personal plan to handle workplace problems such as staffing shortages and being assigned (floating) to an unfamiliar workplace.
- Identify useful Internet sites to keep up-to-date with potential workplace issues (e.g., OSHA, CDC, ANA).

A hospital, nursing center, clinic, or physician's office can be a potential hazard to your future health and well-being. *This is especially true if you are not informed.* Many nurses are aware of the risk of exposure to infection, but they are not aware of other hazards that exist in health care organizations. Nurses in a health care organization have an increased risk for injury, toxic chemicals, bioterrorism, and violence. How well a health care organization plans and protects workers from occupational hazards is a measure of how safe you can expect to be and what safety measures you need to take as you work. This chapter addresses workplace issues that could potentially affect your health and well-being and addresses what you need to do to avoid injury, occupational exposure, and illness.

QUESTIONS TO ASK WHEN STARTING A NEW POSITION

As a nurse, when you are preparing to start a new position, ask your new employer to answer the following questions to enable you to evaluate the impact workplace issues will have on your health and well-being:

- Is the hospital latex-free? If not, what latex will I be exposed to?
- Inquire about availability of patient safety equipment such as lifts, transfer boards, and gate belts. How much will I be lifting, pulling, and tugging? Does the hospital use lift teams?
- Ask to see a common patient room. Think about moving around in the room, and ask how much moving of furniture, stretchers, or equipment you will be doing. Will I be using a computer? Is it wall mounted so that I need to stand to type, or will there be a desk to sit at when I need to type?
- What is the nursing injury rate for the unit I will be working on?
- Is there worker's compensation in the benefits for the organization? Would I be able to return to work in a light-duty capacity if I am injured? For how long? What are the rules of the state?
- Does the organization have an antiviolence program? How does the organization address bullying behaviors and other hostile work situations such as sexual harassment?
- Is the organization needleless? If not, what is my exposure risk?
- What is the organization's policy for exposure to infectious agents? Does it include testing, medication, counseling, and follow-up? What is the process for this? (This information can often be found in the employee handbook.)
- What is the organization's tuberculosis (TB) prevention plan? Does the plan adhere to Occupational Safety and Health Administration (OSHA) regulations? How often will I be tested?
- Does the organization have an influenza prevention plan? Does it follow the Centers for Disease Control and Prevention (CDC) guidelines?
- Is there a plan for handling potentially toxic or infectious substances such as blood, chemoprophylaxis, and suction canisters? What is my potential exposure? Will I receive training in correct handling? Will annual refreshers be offered?
- Where will I park? Is the area well lit? Is it patrolled? Have there been any serious events in the past 6 months?
- Does the organization provide vaccinations for infections I might be exposed to, such as influenza, chickenpox, and hepatitis B?
- Does the hospital have a surveillance plan for multidrug resistant organisms (MRSA, VRE)? Does it follow current CDC guidelines?
- How often will I be expected to work "off shift" (shifts other than what I normally work), on-call, or mandatory overtime?
- How often will I need to work on a unit other than my assigned unit? How will I be oriented?

ERGONOMIC HAZARDS FOR HEALTH CARE WORKERS

According to the American Nurses Association (ANA), safe patient handling and mobility have become a major safety concern among health care workers (ANA, 2016b), and nurses are considered to be in a profession that puts them at risk for serious musculoskeletal injuries. The most common problems tend to be back and shoulder injuries. Unfortunately, these types of injuries are the most debilitating. Imagine if you cannot raise your arms or reach for things without severe pain. What if you needed help to dress yourself because you lost flexibility in your shoulder joint? What would happen if every step you took resulted in pain in your back and down your leg? What if sitting or lying down did not relieve your distress? These are potential health-related problems of nurses that can be minimized by following safety standards and protocols.

Back Injury

So, what is your risk? That is somewhat unclear, because studies investigating work-related injuries in nursing are sporadic. One study reported that 90% of nurses complain of back pain (Kyung Ja & Sung-Hyun, 2011). In addition, nurses in one study reported changing jobs because of a back, shoulder, or neck injury (Trinkoff et al., 2003). Although this is an older reference, the problem is potentially more serious today because patients are becoming sicker and heavier, and there is more equipment for nurses to work around (including computers and workstations). These factors increase the risk of injury. Back-related injuries reduce the already short supply of nurses, and because there are fewer nurses, the risk for back-related and other musculoskeletal injuries increases. It becomes a vicious cycle.

Why are these injuries so common in nursing? It is simply the nature of the work that nurses do. Lifting, transferring, repositioning, and reaching are the actions that are associated with work-related injuries. Often the configuration of the patient's room and the placement of furniture, monitors, blood pressure cuffs, thermometers, and other hanging devices contribute to injury, because nurses are required to reach and stretch in nonergonomic positions to perform tasks.

In the past, it was believed that good body mechanics with proper lifting techniques could prevent back and shoulder injuries. However, according to the ANA (2016b), the idea that there is a safe way to lift or turn a physically dependent patient manually is no longer valid. Many of the situations in which nurses are injured involve sudden, quick changes in position with human beings. Therefore, proper body mechanics are not enough to safeguard against injury, because the nurse cannot adjust in a way that fully protects the back. *Teaching nurses to use proper body mechanics to lift and turn patients does not result in fewer injuries* (ANA, 2016a). Because of the dangers associated with manual patient handling, the current recommendations by the ANA include eliminating manual lifting and using assistive patient-handling devices for lifting, transferring, and turning patients (ANA, 2016a).

It is important that nurses take good care of their backs, even when they are young, flexible, and strong, because aging contributes to the risk for a career-ending injury. Also, as people age, there is a loss of flexibility and increased musculoskeletal instability. Repetitive stress on the structures of the spine, shoulders, and hips can cause small repeated muscle and tendon damage that could manifest in serious debilitating injury. Consider what happened to Sandy.

Sandy was a strong, flexible, and healthy person. She could lift patients in bed, turn them, bathe them, and ambulate them without help. Very seldom did she ask for help. She could stand, walk briskly, and work for 16 hours without a break. And go back the next day. She was proud of her abilities and the fact that she was everything to her patient. She was the one every nurse on the unit loved to work with because of her independence and willingness to help others.

Today at age 50, things are much different. She sits in an office all day wishing for her bedside job. She had to change jobs because she could no longer work at the bedside. Her shoulders, knees, back, and hips all are damaged from chronic stress from the lifting, straining, and reaching she had done during her career.

The ANA has sponsored a program called "Handle with Care" to raise awareness, promote the use of ergonomic equipment and assistive devices, and encourage health care organizations to invest in a safe patient-handling program. In addition, by reducing work-related injuries to nurses, safe patient-handling programs can reduce some of the hidden costs of health care organizations and improve patient care (ANA, 2016b).

> Prompted by ANA's Handle with Care Campaign®, which began in 2003, eleven states have enacted "safe patient handling" legislation California, Illinois, Maryland, Minnesota, Missouri, New Jersey, New York, Ohio, Rhode Island, Texas, and Washington, with a resolution from Hawaii (ANA, 2016a, para 1).

What can the nurse do to reduce the risk of serious back injury? First, be aware of the potential risk by assessing each patient's dependency needs and abilities when deciding what assistive devices to use. Do not move, lift, or turn a dependent person without an appropriate assistive device or help (Fig. 25.1). Next, know what assistive devices are available to you, and learn how to use them properly. If your organization does not have devices readily available, become an advocate for a safe patient-handling program. It is also important to keep yourself fit, and do not ever "tough it out" when you suffer an injury. Make sure you report your injury according to policy, and follow the advice of your health care provider so that your body can properly heal. For more information on ways to promote safe patient handling and prevent work-related injuries, see the following websites: www.nursingworld.org/handlewithcare. At the ANA site, http://www.rnaction.org/site/PageNavigator/nstat__take_action_sph_113.html, you can join the team to fight for legislation to enact laws protecting nurses from harm (ANA, 2016b). Finally, it has been suggested that nurses consider developing a practice for "warming up" and stretching before they start their workday. This is to be followed up by stretching again at the end of a day. Another strategy to maintain a limber, flexible body core is to enroll in a yoga or Pilates program.

Ergonomic Workstations

Many of today's jobs are performed at a computer work area, often in a "shared" area. This is the case in a hospital setting, where nurses, physicians, and ancillary caregivers frequently use the workstation 24 hours a day. There may be dozens of workers trying to use the same computer workstation almost constantly. Change, variation, and adjustment to fit an individual worker are basic to the well-being of each worker. Workstations should accommodate users of many different heights, weights, and individual needs. Computer vendors must keep in mind that the "typical" nurse is in his or her mid-40s, and letter size and font as well as proper lighting and the avoidance of shadows are vitally important to aid in viewing computer screens.

The successful ergonomic design of an office workstation depends on several interrelated parts, including the task, the posture, and the work activities. The three activities alone can be difficult to handle, but these activities must also interact properly with existing furniture, equipment, and the environment. The combination of the aforementioned makes the picture more complicated. Important parts of the workstation are the chair, the desk, and the placement of the computer (CPU), keyboard, and monitor.

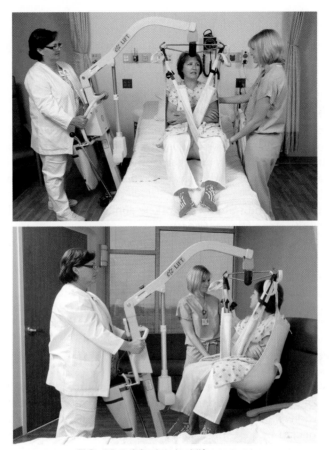

FIG. 25.1 Mechanical lift system.

The chair should be padded appropriately, easily adjustable, and have strong lumbar support. Usually, wheels allow easy movement, and armrests may or may not be used because they sometimes cause more problems, depending on the individual needs of the user. Therefore, armrests should be fully adjustable to accommodate the user.

The desk must be wide and deep enough to accommodate the computer's monitor, keyboard, and mouse, with ample space around the machine to write, use the phone conveniently, and perform all other desktop activities. Keep the area clear of clutter and crowding.

Ideally, the placement of the monitor, keyboard, and mouse would be adjustable for every worker, but because this is rarely possible, the monitor height should be approximately 18 to 22 inches above the desk surface, causing most users to view the screen with slightly lowered eyes. The keyboard should be placed directly in front of the user and the mouse on the user's dominant-hand side of the machine. Some nursing stations designate certain machines as left-handed mouse machines so that the mouse will not need to be switched numerous times during a shift. Be sure to use a mouse pad to ensure traction, lessening the frustration and continual long movements of the mouse (Critical Thinking Box 25.1). Some individuals wearing glasses need "computer lenses" to make reading the monitor easier and also to screen out blue light, which is associated with a higher incidence of cataracts and macular degeneration (Wood, 2014).

> ? CRITICAL THINKING BOX 25.1
>
> What is your workplace environment like? What lift equipment do you have? Have ergonomics been considered? How could you make it better?

Repetitive Motion Disorders

Poor workplace design is often the major source for repetitive motion disorders (RMDs) or cumulative trauma disorders (CTDs). RMDs have been associated with users who work for long periods at poorly constructed or poorly arranged workstations.

Ergonomic design of work tasks can reduce or remove some of the risks. Other solutions may include

- Information and training to workers about body positions that eliminate the opportunity for repetitive stress injuries to occur
- Frequent switching between standing and sitting positions, reducing net stress on any specific muscle or skeletal group
- Routine stretching of the shoulders, neck, arms, hands, and fingers

> Having a good understanding of ergonomic principles can help prevent injuries.

WORKPLACE VIOLENCE: A GROWING CONCERN IN HEALTH CARE

Witnessing the aftermath of a violent attack on a nurse colleague is a powerful realization that the potential for being harmed by another person at work is very real. As a nurse, you are at risk for harm from co-workers, patients, and families. No matter what the occupation, workplace violence is an ongoing concern in the United States. The nature of health care workers' jobs puts them at risk for workplace violence, which can result in injury or death (Foley & Rauser, 2012).

Workplace violence is defined by the United States Department of Labor as "an action (verbal, written, or physical aggression) which is intended to control or cause, or is capable of causing, death or serious bodily injury to oneself or others, or damage to property. Workplace violence includes abusive behavior toward authority, intimidating or harassing behavior, and threats" (n.d.). Nurses often fail to report acts of violence because of a lack of understanding or a belief that "nothing can be changed" (McNamara, 2010). Failure to report risks escalation of the situation until physical violence occurs. In some cases, nurses have never encountered a hostile person before, and they do not understand how to recognize and de-escalate the situation. In other situations, a nurse can have a history of violence and the experience can bring forth images and memories, called post-traumatic stress disorder (PTSD). Anyone who has experienced violence is at risk for experiencing this phenomenon wherein the individual can experience intense emotions such as anxiety, depression, anger, and flash-backs (re-experiencing the initial event) in response to verbal or physical violence.

Recently, a nurse in a large urban hospital was working with a young man who had been hospitalized with chest pain. He had denied any drug use; however, it was found that he habitually used cocaine and also consumed large amounts of alcohol on a regular basis. Once the physician discharged him, the patient grew increasingly agitated waiting for the paperwork for his discharge. He wanted to leave the facility to resume his drug-related behaviors.

The nurse had been working on the unit less than a year after graduation and did not recognize the patient's increasing agitation. He used the call light to repeatedly summon the nurse to the room asking when he could leave. When she entered the room in response to his fifth call and told him it would be another 30 minutes before she could complete the paperwork for his discharge, he attacked her. Before she was able to summon help, she was assaulted and was seriously injured, requiring surgical repair of lacerations and a head injury. The nurse recovered fully from a physical standpoint but suffered severe post-traumatic stress disorder and was not able to return to her chosen profession. A huge emotional toll was also seen in the rest of the nurses on staff, who were fearful of a similar event happening to them.

In response to incidents such as this, along with other events occurring in the local industry, the hospital administration developed a crisis intervention program. This program taught nurses and other hospital staff how to recognize signs of escalating anger that could result in a violent attack and strategies to de-escalate the situation. Nurses were also taught how to protect themselves during an attack; for example, keeping the door between you and the patient for easy escape. The nurse in the above situation had walked over to the window and the patient was able to barricade the door, which kept her from escaping. Knowing how to recognize an escalating situation and how to defend against an attacker helped these nurses believe they could manage future situations that put them at risk for harm.

Additionally, the hospital instituted a "code white" program. A code white stood for a potentially violent situation, which anyone could initiate if *any* person became loud or abusive, made threats, or started throwing objects. A code white ensured that resources were available to help de-escalate the situation and that no nurse or any other staff member would be alone with someone who was acting out. Trained volunteers and other staff from the hospital, including security staff, responded to a code white, which would be announced over the hospital's PA system. It was stressed to nursing staff members that any time they felt unsafe, a code white should be called. The code could be implemented by using the phone system or by pushing a strategically placed alarm button. After instituting the program, there were no further incidents in which nurses were harmed over the ensuing years.

So what do you need to do when you start your first job? First, be familiar with your organization's policies regarding workplace violence. Next, consider taking a crisis intervention course to become familiar with the signs of escalating violence, such as pacing, using foul language, raising one's fist, or using threats. Learn strategies to de-escalate anger. Finally, do not ever try to handle a potentially violent person on your own. Use whatever procedures your organization has put in place to defuse situations; for example, call security or call a code white (Fig. 25.2).

Lateral Violence (Bullying) and Other Forms of Workplace Harassment

As a nurse and individual, it is easy to recognize overt violence. Most hospitals have procedures and policies to handle violent events. Less common is recognition and action related to *horizontal or lateral violence*, which is often called *bullying* in the workplace; however, these terms are different. Lateral violence refers to violence directed to an individual by another individual who is considered a colleague or equal in terms of job scope, whereas bullying is defined by Kirchner (2009) as "the purposeful exertion of power that is perceived by the victim as physically or emotionally threatening" (p. 177). Most of us believe that the backyard bullies of our childhood will disappear in adulthood. Unfortunately, recent evidence has proven otherwise. Our bullies of childhood tend to grow into the bullies of our adulthood. Consider what happened to Judy:

Judy was excited to start work in the critical care department. She was pleased that the manager had selected her to start there, because she understood the criteria for working in that department as a new graduate were very strict. She had chosen a preceptor from the nurses she knew.

FIG. 25.2 Workplace safety is important.

Soon, she found herself to be totally stressed out by work. Always an optimistic, carefree person, she was now nervous and had an onset of migraine headaches. She was not sleeping or eating normally. Her family was very concerned.

At the request of her family, Judy went to see a counselor at the Employee Assistance Program. The counselor helped her identify that other nurses on the unit were bullying her by targeting her and isolating her by their responses to the things she did or said. For example, during shift report, if she asked a question, the nurses at the report table would put down their pens and glare at her or roll their eyes. If she asked for help lifting a patient, everyone would ignore her. The nurse who was the center of the bullying would yell at her in front of everyone for minor transgressions (if she dropped a pill or forgot to write her blood glucose readings on the report board). If Judy made a mistake, everyone would know about it, and the story of the event would grow as it was passed on to others. Judy often overheard these comments and was often angry. The anxiety caused by knowing she would be treated this way every day was impairing Judy's ability to grow and develop as a new nurse. It was also having a negative effect on her patient care and on her health.

Judy needed to understand better what was happening to her so that she could recognize the signs if she was ever the victim of bullying again. She also needed to develop a plan to manage her current situation. She found a website called the Workplace Bullying Institute (www.bullyinstitute.org) that provides a wide array of helpful information and assistance, including coaching and current legislation. With the help of her counselor, Judy developed an action plan to address her situation. After time off to contemplate her work life, and after she realized the bullying behavior would not be addressed at her current place of employment, Judy found another job in a local hospital and started a new position.

At her new place of employment, Judy found a wonderful mentor and was soon growing as a nurse. Her physical health improved, and with help from her counselor and coach, she was once again a mentally healthy person. Judy had learned from her experience and was determined never to allow a bully to have this level of impact on her again.

You may hear after starting your first position that "nurses eat their young." Mild forms of hazing activity are common in many professions and can usually be overcome by those who are victims of

---

BOX 25.1   SIGNS OF BEING BULLIED

Experiences Outside Work
- You feel like throwing up the night before the start of your work week
- Your frustrated family demands that you stop obsessing about work at home
- Your doctor asks what could be causing your skyrocketing blood pressure and recent health problems and tells you to change jobs
- You feel too ashamed of being controlled by another person at work to tell your spouse or partner
- All your paid time off is used for "mental health breaks" from the misery
- Days off are spent exhausted and lifeless; your desire to do anything is gone
- Your favorite activities and fun with family are no longer appealing or enjoyable
- You begin to believe that you provoked the workplace cruelty

Experiences At Work
- You attempt the obviously impossible task of doing a new job without training or time to learn new skills, but that work is never good enough for the boss
- Surprise meetings are called by your boss with no results other than further humiliation
- Everything your tormenter does to you is arbitrary and capricious, working a personal agenda that undermines the employer's legitimate business interests
- Others at work have been told to stop working, talking, or socializing with you
- You are constantly feeling agitated and anxious, experiencing a sense of doom, waiting for bad things to happen
- No matter what you do, you are never left alone to do your job without interference
- People feel justified screaming or yelling at you in front of others, but you are punished if you scream back
- HR tells you that your harassment isn't illegal, that you have to "work it out between yourselves"
- You finally, firmly confront your tormentor to stop the abusive conduct and you are accused of harassment
- You are shocked when accused of incompetence, despite a history of objective excellence, typically by someone who cannot do your job
- Everyone—co-workers, senior bosses, HR—agrees (in person and orally) that your tormentor is a jerk, but there is nothing they will do about it (and later, when you ask for their support, they deny having agreed with you)
- Your request to transfer to an open position under another boss is mysteriously denied

From Workplace Bullying Institute (http://www.workplacebullying.org/individuals/problem/early-signs/).

---

these behaviors. New nurses may feel the need to prove that they can be counted on to provide safe care for their patients. They may find that their work ethic and skills are being "tested" by other nurses. This type of activity usually lasts for the first weeks of a new position and gradually improves as a new nurse becomes integrated into the work life of the unit.

Lateral violence, on the other hand, goes beyond this initial struggle and has serious physical and psychological consequences for the victim as well as negative patient safety outcomes, which has been documented in the research literature (Blair, 2013; McNamara, 2010). In nursing practice, Kirchner (2009) defined lateral violence as a type of workplace abuse that occurs between individuals who are on the same level or equal in terms of their job responsibilities (i.e., nurse to nurse). Bullying is not a single event—it occurs over time.

Lateral violence can occur in any workplace setting. Health care environments are particularly situated to foster bullies, because they are hierarchical in nature and tend to involve a great deal of change. In addition, the underlying culture of health care has tended to foster the idea that there are certain rites of passage that must be endured by all new staff. Many of our health care organizations are fear driven and feel pressured to raise productivity standards higher and higher to improve profits. According to the Workplace Bullying Institute (2015), these factors can create a culture that fosters bullying. A manager, supervisor, physician, or co-worker can be a potential bully. The signs that you may be experiencing bullying are identified by individuals who had been targets at the workplace (Box 25.1).

For most nurses, the idea that another person would deliberately target them for lateral violence and bullying is difficult to comprehend. We often have a naïve belief that bullying is a part of childhood but not a part of adulthood. As a result, the person being bullied can experience a multitude of psychological and physical reactions. Most often, the target of lateral violence believes that the bullying is his or her fault. In the hypothetical situation described, Judy, as a new nurse, believed that she was not doing a good job, and as the bullying continued, she even decided that she should find another profession in which to work. Her migraine headaches were a direct result of the bullying she was receiving. Fortunately for Judy, she found someone to help her to see that she was not the problem, and she made the decision to move on to another environment.

Research has indicated that many psychological and physical effects can result from lateral violence. Lateral violence and bullying create anxiety, fear, and anger in most adults. As lateral violence is unrelenting and often severe in nature, the victimized individual has a heightened stimulation of the sympathetic nervous system. As a result, if you are the target of a bully, you can develop psychological and physical symptoms including vomiting, anxiety disorders, chest pain, and abdominal pain. Depending on the bullying situation, you can also develop the signs and symptoms of post-traumatic stress disorder (Matthiesen & Einarsen, 2004).

Because most of us are totally unprepared to deal with a bully in the workplace, it can be difficult to determine what actions to take to address it. The Workplace Bullying Institute website (http://www.workplacebullying.org/individuals/solutions/wbi-action-plan/) has an excellent plan to follow. Drs. Namie and Namie (2003) suggest that you take the following three steps if you are the target of a bully:

1. *Name it.* Say, "I am being bullied!" "I have a bully at work!" "Jackie is a backyard bully." Other ways to validate it for your own sense of self is to say, "I did not ask for this! Jackie targeted me to bully." This type of self-talk will help validate your experience.

2. *Seek respite.* From their work, Drs. Ruth and Gary Namie believe that if you are being bullied, you need to take time off from work to "BullyProof" yourself. During your time off from work, you need to accomplish five things: (a) check your mental health, (b) check your physical health, (c) research state and federal legal options, (d) gather data regarding the economic impact the bully has had on your unit, and finally, (e) start a job search for a new position, because this will give you more options as you address your current work situation.

3. *Expose the bully.* Most people who are being bullied are not willing to expose the bully. However, for your mental and physical health, you need to consider giving your employer an opportunity to address the situation (Workplace Bullying Institute, 2015).

Consider the following:

Mary determined that a colleague at work was bullying her and that the situation had become intolerable. She came to this realization after a series of painful situations where she had been shunned and deliberately avoided by her colleagues on several occasions. She was concerned, because these situations were growing increasingly severe, causing her to experience stress-related health problems, and putting the patients at risk. Mary was worried that continued unsafe situations might risk her ability to practice nursing. She was preoccupied at work and found herself nearly making a serious medication error. Finally, in desperation, she took a week of vacation to reflect on her options. She searched for another position and found one in another department at the same organization.

Before officially accepting her new position, Mary went to her manager to discuss the problems she was experiencing. She shared with her manager documents and evidence of things that had happened to her and asked the manager what actions she was willing to take to improve the situation.

The manager was not willing to acknowledge the issue or help Mary. As a result, Mary turned in her resignation the next day. Mary started her new job, which was actually a promotion, and she was successful in making the transition. She did not lose any of her seniority or benefits and still worked near her home and family. Mary's health improved, and she was glad she had taken action to improve her work situation.

Often organizations do not understand the tremendous costs in turnover, worker's compensation, absenteeism, and decreased productivity incurred by allowing a culture of bullying to continue. When you expose the bully, make the business case that the bullying individual is simply too expensive for the organization to continue to have working. In other words, do not go into a huge discussion about *your* experience. Rather, point out the recent turnover, sick calls, worker's compensation, and decreased productivity that the bully has cost the organization. Give your employer this opportunity to correct the situation. If the employer does not take positive action to correct the situation, then you may need to consider finding another job.

Given the devastating impact that workplace violence and bullying have on nurses and patient outcomes, the American Nurses Association issued a position statement indicating that the nursing profession has initiated a zero-tolerance policy for workplace violence and bullying and charged all nurses and health care professionals to implement measures for creating a culture of respect (ANA, 2015). The major strategy at the time is to take care of yourself first by protecting your health and well-being.

OTHER WORKPLACE ISSUES

Needlestick and Sharps Safety

In addition to the workplace issues already identified, latex allergy, severe acute respiratory syndrome (SARS), human immunodeficiency virus (HIV), tuberculosis exposure, and needlestick injuries are issues that can affect your health if you are not aware of how to prevent exposure and injury (Box 25.2). The Occupational Safety and Health Administration (OSHA) has established guidelines that organizations must follow to protect workers. The Needlestick Safety and Prevention Act (P.L. 106-430), which became law on November 6, 2000, provides important protections for health care workers regarding needlestick injuries. Advocating for workplace safety, the ANA was instrumental in having this piece of federal legislation passed. This act amends the Blood-Borne Pathogen Standard (administered by OSHA) to require the use of safer devices to protect from sharps injuries. It also requires that employers solicit the input of nonmanagerial employees who are responsible for direct patient care regarding the identification, evaluation, and selection of effective engineering and work-practice controls (Fig. 25.3).

In addition, the act requires employers to maintain a sharps injury log to document, at a minimum, the type and brand of device involved in each incident, the department or work area in which the exposure occurred, and an explanation of how the incident happened. The information is to be recorded and maintained in a way that protects the confidentiality of injured employees. The log serves as an important data source to help determine the relative effectiveness and safety of currently used devices and to guide the development of future products. You need to be familiar with these requirements, as well as any additional guidelines that have been established by your local or state health departments. In some states, the guidelines established by health departments are more strict than those established by OSHA. Today every organization that uses needles or sharp devices should have policies covering needlestick and sharps exposures/injuries to protect and treat their employees.

BOX 25.2 NEEDLESTICK AND SHARPS-RELATED INJURIES

- Needlestick and sharps-related injuries expose all health care workers to potential bloodborne pathogens (hepatitis B virus [HBV], hepatitis C virus [HCV], and human immunodeficiency virus [HIV]).[1]
- It is estimated that 385,000 needlestick injuries occur in hospitals annually.[2]
- The majority of needlestick injuries occur in surgical settings such as the operating room and at the patient's bedside.[3]
- The Food and Drug Administration (FDA), Centers for Disease Control and Prevention (CDC), National Institute for Occupational Safety and Health (NIOSH), and the Occupational Safety and Health Administration (OSHA) issued a statement in 2012 encouraging all health care workers in surgical settings to use only blunt-tip suture needles when suturing muscle and fascia.[1]
- All sharps and needlestick injuries must be recorded by the employer as required under OSHA's Recordkeeping Standard.[3]

Data from:
[1]Centers for Disease Control [CDC]. (2012). *FDA, NIOSH, & OSHA Joint safety documentation: Blunt-tip surgical suture needles reduce needlestick injuries and the risk of subsequent bloodborne pathogen transmission to surgical personnel.* Retrieved from http://www.cdc.gov/niosh/topics/bbp/pdfs/Blunt-tip_Suture_Needles_Safety.pdf.
[2]Centers for Disease Control [CDC]. (2013). *Sharps injuries.* Retrieved from http://www.cdc.gov/niosh/stopsticks/sharpsinjuries.html.
[3]Occupational Safety and Health Administration [OSHA]. (2016). *Healthcare wide hazards: Needlestick/sharps injuries.* Retrieved from https://www.osha.gov/SLTC/etools/hospital/hazards/sharps/sharps.html.

FIG. 25.3 Nurses must be aware of potential threats to their health.

Handling Staffing Shortages

The shortage of experienced nurses has created many challenges and changes in the health care environments in which we work. Many of these changes are just beginning. We will see many more in the years to come as the supply does not meet the demand and the need for nursing grows. As a nurse, you need to understand these issues, how to find the best place to work, and how to cope with situations such as high nurse-to-patient ratios and mandatory overtime.

An organization (hospital, clinic, nursing center) that provides an environment that is conducive to good nursing care is the best place to be. It does not need to be the newest and most technologically advanced hospital in a large city. For instance:

One of the most spectacular places to practice nursing may be a modest nurse-managed clinic that meets the needs of indigent people in a rural county. The salaries may not be as competitive, and the clinic will always need something, but the environment is great in that it allows nurses to care for patients and make a difference in the lives of the people they serve.

Finding a good place to work can be challenging and requires a solid evaluation of the potential work environment. For years, many health care organizations have ignored the needs of nursing (Duclos-Miller, 2002). To attract nurses, many health care organizations use incentives rather than making substantial changes to the environment for nursing (workloads, autonomy). Of course, the lure of higher salaries, benefits, sign-on bonuses, and tuition repayment programs can be highly appealing for new nurses; however, these incentives can distract new nurses from investigating other issues that will have a greater effect on long-term job satisfaction. As a new nurse looking for a position, it may be challenging to find the best fit for you. Fortunately, there are research-based criteria that can help you determine whether an organization provides a good environment for nursing.

In the early 1980s, the American Academy of Nursing (AAN) commissioned a study to determine what characteristics of hospitals attracted nurses. It was interesting to learn that things such as nursing autonomy, low nurse–patient ratios, and collaborative relationships with physicians were some of the draws. From this work, Magnet hospitals were identified that embodied these essential characteristics that promoted nursing. Today, in our current nursing shortage, hospitals actively seek Magnet status to attract nurses. In addition, Magnet hospitals are known to have better patient outcomes. The American Nurses Credentialing Center (ANCC) is responsible for judging whether hospitals achieve this status. A hospital awarded a Magnet Recognition Program would be a good place to work for most nurses (Critical Thinking Box 25.2).

In today's world, no matter where you work, you may need to cope with a situation in which the number of patients under your care and their needs for nursing may be greater than what you are able to provide. What should you do?

First, it is important to understand the chain of command for your organization. In other words, to whom should you report your concerns, and what are your next steps if you are not satisfied with the response you receive from that person? For example, perhaps the supervisor is the person to go to, and if that does not resolve the situation, according to the chain of command, you contact your manager, then the director for the department, then the chief nursing officer. Next, remain calm and use your great assessment skills to determine the exact nature of your situation. Here are some things to consider:

- How many patients do you have? What is going on with each of them? What nursing tasks do you need to accomplish? What are your priorities (safety issues)? What tasks would be "nice to do if you are able and have the time?"
- What are your resources? Do you have someone to whom you can delegate tasks? What support do you have from patients' families (e.g., to help watch a confused patient)?

? CRITICAL THINKING BOX 25.2

To find out more about the characteristics of the Magnet model, see www.nursingworld.org/ancc/magnet/. Determine whether your clinical practice site has a Magnet Recognition Program.

- Are you aware of a nurse colleague who might be able to come and help (e.g., someone who was not considered by those who worked on staffing the unit)? What about someone who works on another similar unit who might be willing to pick up time?
- Is there anyone who can help out for a few hours to cover the gap and make sure there are no safety issues?
- Is there any other way to deliver care? For example, working together as a team to take care of patients can be a more efficient way to function for a particular shift, even though it is not ideal and can result in fragmented care.
- What are your hospital's policies for high-census or high–patient-load situations? For example, can you decrease the frequency of assessment from every 4 hours to every 6 to free up some time?
- Consider how sick your patients are. Is there anyone who might be discharged to lighten the load?

Gather your facts and present your concerns to the next person in authority—a charge nurse or a supervisor. Do not threaten to leave or make rash statements; just present your facts. Ask for whatever assistance is available. Tell this person what your concerns are and what you can and/or cannot accomplish in your shift based on the high patient load. Use a concise, clear outline of the situation and what you need from that individual.

Document Your Concerns

If the support you receive is not appropriate, then you need to calmly tell your charge nurse or supervisor that you are going to report your concerns to the next person in charge. Again, do not threaten. If the situation is continuous rather than intermittent, use the notes you have documented to figure out the pattern of what is happening.

> Remember that difficult situations tend to be in the forefront of your mind, whereas reality might be different. This is human nature.

Consider the following example:

Some nurses told their nurse manager that they were always getting patients from surgery who did not meet criteria to be discharged from the recovery room. The examples that they gave were very disturbing to the new manager, so she asked them to keep a log of patients who were unstable when they reached the unit. In the next month, instead of a large number of patients coming back from the recovery room unstable, they found only two. In both situations, the patients became hypotensive and required a significant amount of care to stabilize their condition. What the staff and the manager realized after looking at the data was that those two situations were so stressful that they "forgot" the 50 patients who came back without a problem. The other important thing that happened was a solution was found to prevent the hypotensive events. The nursing staff worked with the surgical providers and made certain that patients received adequate fluids in the recovery room. During the following months, the nurses had no further events. Improved patient care was the result of the careful and diligent documentation and the nursing staff's willingness to work toward finding a solution. This is why documentation of events is so important.

If your notes tell you that poor staffing occurs more often than not, and you are not able to get your patient care done, then you need to work with your manager to determine the reasons. Is your unit understaffed for the needs of your patients? Does your unit have many vacancies? Does your unit have a lot of sick calls? Are assignments being done correctly? Are nurses performing frequent non-nursing functions such as phlebotomy, running errands, or transcribing orders? Does your unit need someone to help with nonessential nursing duties such as bathing or feeding patients? Many organizations involve staff nurses to help to solve these problems. Volunteer to work with a group to make changes. If your organization or unit is not willing to work with you to make the workload easier, then you may need to consider a job change. Working together as a team and being able to solve staffing issues with creative solutions is the goal of any discussions with leadership. Consider this unit's experience:

Nurses on the telemetry unit on the 7 AM to 7 PM shift were exhausted. They had a large unit of patients with a high acuity. Their patients were generally elderly, had heart failure, and many had multiple chronic health problems. The unit had been approved for an additional RN position, but it had been vacant for over a year as there was a serious nursing shortage in their area. Everyone felt deflated, and people were beginning to feel that the situation was never going to improve. They enjoyed the challenges of the unit, but they were tired. The manager held a staff meeting seeking solutions to their staffing difficulties.

After intense discussions with few solutions, one of the nurses stated, "Most of the time, I just need someone to help me with morning care and making sure my patients get turned and fed before their meals get cold!" The other nurses on the unit agreed with her comments. After discussions, a solution to their short staffing was found.

The manager was able to hire a nursing student to help on the unit for 6 hours in the morning by assisting with hygiene care, turning, feeding, and ambulating patients. The relief of having this help accomplished what they needed, and the morale on the unit significantly improved. As an added bonus, the nursing student soon graduated and decided to stay on the unit because of her positive experience. She started out as a new RN, and her orientation was shortened because of the time she had spent on the unit before her graduation. Everyone won—the patients, the staff, and the health care facility.

Mandatory Overtime

Unfortunately, mandatory overtime is another way that hospitals deal with poor staffing. Mandatory overtime creates a loss of control for the nurse regarding the ability to schedule nonwork activities, including essential family functions. Mandatory overtime may also put safe patient care at risk because of nurse fatigue and subsequent loss of the ability to concentrate, critically think, and thus make good judgments. Although many other professional groups have worked to decrease the incidence of mandatory overtime in cases where fatigue can jeopardize the public's safety, 67% of nurses reported that they worked some sort of mandatory or unplanned overtime per month (Bosek, 2001). Mandating overtime is a major concern of our professional associations (e.g., American Nurses Association; American Association of Critical Care Nurses).

Although it is our professional duty to ensure that nursing services are continued until the patient's care is transferred to another nurse, our duty to ensure that patients receive safe treatment may be in conflict if mandatory overtime results in fatigue and the possibility of a serious error occurring. According to Duclos-Miller (2002), all nurses need to recognize that by accepting a nursing position, we have made a commitment to the organization to provide nursing care at specified intervals. After we accept responsibility for a patient assignment, we have that responsibility either until our services are no longer needed or until we transfer the responsibility to someone else. Does this mean we need to work beyond our capacity?

Many states have enacted legislation prohibiting mandatory overtime. Is your state one of them? You can go to the ANA website to find out whether your state has mandatory overtime legislation.

Legislation opposing mandatory overtime is a priority of the ANA. Legislating overtime of nurses may not be the only answer. Health care organizations must be able to provide care to their patients, and legislation will not be sufficient to alleviate the workloads imposed if there are not enough nurses to take care of patients.

In addition to the previous discussion related to developing a good work environment for nursing, creative solutions can be developed by management and nursing staff to handle shortages without resorting to mandatory overtime. Some ideas include the following:

- Develop an on-call system that provides one or two extra nurses per shift.
- Develop policies that limit mandatory overtime and ensure rotation among all staff.
- Provide incentives to encourage part-time nursing staff to pick up extra time.
- Develop creative shifts for high-activity, high-volume times (e.g., perhaps a special 11 AM to 2 PM shift to provide staff for admissions and transfers and to reduce the workload for the rest of the staff).
- Develop processes to identify shortages with enough time to arrange coverage.
- Reward nurses who do put forth extra effort for the organization. For example, one hospital provides a bonus of $100 for every 100 hours of on-call time (in which an individual agrees to be available to come in if needed).
- Improve the workplace environment in ways that are advocated by the American Association of Critical Care Nurses, and institute recommendations from the "Healthy Work Environment" campaign and by the American Nurses Credentialing Center Magnet program. These recommendations have proven that better environments draw nurses and can alleviate shortage situations.

What should you do if you are mandated to stay over your scheduled shift because of a staffing shortage? First, you should be familiar with your organization's policy regarding mandatory overtime *before* this happens. If the policy is unacceptable to your life circumstances, you probably should not be working in the facility. If you find yourself in a situation in which you believe you are too fatigued to stay over your shift, you need to follow the chain of command in asking for assistance with your situation. Again, you need to assess your situation and provide the charge nurse, supervisor, or manager with the facts of your situation. You need to document your concerns and follow up as needed after the event. If you believe your organization policy regarding mandatory overtime can be improved or eliminated, work with your manager and others to change it.

Most causes of medical errors relate to system problems:
1. Communication problems
2. Inadequate information flow
3. Human problems
4. Patient-related issues
5. Organizational transfer of knowledge
6. Staffing patterns/work flow
7. Technical failures
8. Inadequate policies and procedures (AHRQ, 2003)

Assigned to a Unit That Is Unfamiliar (Floating)—What Do I Do Now?

One interesting phenomenon about health care is that it has a cyclic nature to some extent. What this means is that during certain times of the year, there may be fewer or greater numbers of patients needing any one service at any given time. Thus sometimes on a particular unit you may have more and sometimes fewer patients. It would be great to have a break when your patient volumes are lower; however, it does not work this way in most situations, because there are always units that need help. No one would want patients to suffer from lack of care when there is a nurse available on a unit that has fewer patients. For both economic and logistical reasons (e.g., another unit is very busy), nurses who are less busy are often instructed to work on a unit that is not their "home unit." The question becomes "What will I do if this happens?" Consider the following situation and imagine what you might do.

Denise was finished with her orientation and had been working on her own for approximately 6 months. She had been told about the floating policy on her unit—how everyone took turns if help was needed on another unit. The unit had been very busy since she had started working, so she did not often think of the issue of floating until this evening. When she came to work, the unit was very quiet, and she was told to report to the surgical unit. Since Denise normally worked on a medical unit, she was naturally anxious about this assignment. The nurses on her unit were sympathetic, but they reminded her of the unit's policy and that it was her turn to go to another unit (float).

When Denise arrived on the surgical unit, she was given an assignment of five patients with a variety of surgical problems (gallbladder to colon resection). Most of her patients had tubes, dressings, and a variety of comorbidities such as diabetes and hypertension that complicated their recovery. Two hours into her shift, she was completely overwhelmed. The nurses she was working with were very kind, but they were also busy, and Denise did not want to bother them with ongoing questions about the location of items and the policies for dressing changes and management of nasogastric tubes. Denise managed to get through the night without any mishaps; however, she was charting until 5 AM (she was supposed to be off duty at 3 AM).

Denise continued to be angry and upset about the floating for many days. She was hostile toward the charge nurse, supervisor, fellow nurses, and even her manager for making her do this. Since her unit did not become busy right away, she worried about having to float again. She felt she could handle it occasionally, but not repeatedly. She began to think about leaving. Denise's manager, Joyce, approached her after several days and asked to discuss the situation. Joyce said she had some thoughts and ideas that might help. Denise reluctantly sat down with Joyce to hear her ideas.

Issues surrounding floating are some of the most concerning and intensely felt by nurses, managers, and administrators. Some journal articles and nursing newsletters recommend that nurses agree to float and always take an assignment. Other sources advise nurses to agree to go but to only do basic nursing care and not to take an assignment. The ethical issue involved in floating is that if you are not on your assigned unit, there will be a disproportionately high number of patients to nurses, which would increase errors, or there is the risk of having a less skilled nurse on a unit, which can also lead to problems. Studies have not demonstrated that the risk of a less skilled nurse has contributed to patient harm, whereas studies of nursing workload have indicated that the greater the workload, the greater the risk for harm to patients (Kane-Urrabazo, 2006).

Data are available that support the more patients a nurse has, the more likely that an error will occur (Kane-Urrabazo, 2006); however, there are no data that tell us how many—if any—patients experience adverse outcomes by floating nurses. Although many nurses passionately believe that if they go to another unit the likelihood of an error occurring is very high, there are no data to support this contention.

Therefore, some argue that it is unethical for a nurse to refuse an assignment if it is reasonable. Refusing an assignment to float could result in harm to a patient because of unreasonable workloads on the other unit. On the other hand, the organization owes its nurses, and patients, an orientation session on all the units to which they may be assigned. This notion is based on the ideas of distributive justice (Kane-Urrabazo, 2006). Many states, such as Iowa and Texas, have written guidelines or position statements on floating, as have many nursing organizations such as the American Association of Colleges of Nursing (AACN) and the American Organization of Nurse Executives (AONE). Regulatory agencies such as The Joint Commission (TJC) have stated that leaders in organizations must define the qualifications and competencies necessary to provide patient care. Hospitals need to have floating policies and plans to orient staff to units where they may be assigned. Again, what should conscientious nurses do to ensure the safety of their patients and to protect their ability to practice?

As Denise met with her manager, the manager first thanked her for floating and not making a big deal about it at the time. Her manager acknowledged that floating was very unsettling, and she asked Denise what would have made the change in assignment better. Denise told her manager that she was glad to have been able to help on the other unit, because it was very busy, and she did not know what they would have done had she not been there. However, Denise felt it would have been better if she had been given orientation to that unit and to surgical patients before being asked to float there. She added that it would have helped to know where supplies were located and to know what patient care standards were used to help them recover from surgery.

As a result of Denise's conversation with the manager, an orientation program was developed to help nurses who were floating to other unfamiliar units. To make this successful, the hospital was divided into "pods" of similar units. Nurses would only float within their pod. A support system was built into floating situations by assigning a manager or supervisor "buddy" to check on the floating nurse periodically throughout the shift to see whether there were any issues or problems. A debriefing session was held with each nurse who floated to determine ways to make the experience better.

Several months later, Denise was pulled to help another unit. Although she did not like being off her normal unit, she tolerated the experience much better than she did the first time. She made sure she had a resource person to help her with problems and questions. She was able to leave at her normal time. Overall, she felt good about helping out another unit.

If you are assigned to float, don't panic! Remain professional in all of your actions! It might be helpful to remember first that you are going to help another unit that does not have enough staff to care for their patients. If nothing else, focus on the patients and what you would want for someone you love if he or she were a patient on the busier unit.

Then, think of the other unit, and consider what types of patients are on the unit. When you arrive, ask for any overflow patients who might have needs similar to patients on your normal unit (e.g., any overflow medical patients if you have a medical background). Ask for a quick tour of the unit and the unit standards of care (e.g., how to manage care of the postoperative mastectomy patient). Ask to be assigned to patients who are less complex, because you will be learning as you go along. Ask for help as you need it. Ask whether a nursing assistant can be assigned with you.

If you arrive at the assigned unit and things do not go well, report the experience to your supervisor as soon as possible. Document your conversations. Try to enjoy your patients and appreciate what you have learned during your shift. If it is available to you, use the Internet to investigate unfamiliar patient-care issues. Remember, regardless of your experience, you are doing what is best for the patient.

Making a Mistake—What Do I Do Now?

Every year, thousands of medication errors are made in hospitals (Institute of Medicine [IOM], 1999). In addition to medication errors, other errors compound to contribute to many serious effects on patients every year, including death. The IOM was chartered in 1970 as the advisor for the U.S. health care system regarding the quality of care (www.iom.edu). In 2003, Congress mandated that the IOM perform a comprehensive study regarding drug safety and recommendations for a system-wide change. The landmark 1999 IOM report on errors in health care stated that 44,000 to 98,000 people die every year from errors (IOM, 1999).

Karen was a cautious person and a very cautious nurse. As a new nurse, she was constantly worried that she would make a mistake! Every day, throughout her orientation, she would breathe a sigh of relief at the end of her shift that she had not made a mistake. In fact, a year went by without any event. One very busy day as she charted her last medications for the day, she had the awful realization that she had given an intravenous medication to the wrong patient! She went into the room hoping that somehow the medication (an intravenous piggyback) had not gone through the pump. Unfortunately, the patient had received a dose of medication that she was not ordered to receive!

Karen quickly checked the patient's allergies; then she went about assessing the patient for any untoward effects. Fortunately, the patient did not have any problems at this point. Through checking, Karen determined that the medication did not have any interaction with any other drug the patient was receiving. The medication was rather benign (Pepcid), and a case could be made that the patient would benefit from the medication, even though it was not ordered.

Karen had to decide what to do. She thought of herself as the "perfect" new graduate. She had not made a mistake in the year since she had been out of school. What would happen to her image with her colleagues? What about her manager, who had just last week praised Karen for her "careful attention to detail." Now she thought, "Could I be fired?"

Fortunately for Karen, her patient did not suffer adverse effects from the medication; however, the fact that a very cautious nurse made such an error demonstrates a gap in medication safety. What might have contributed to this event? The only way that this event can contribute to the understanding of what happened is if Karen reports it. Karen did not necessarily realize this, because she was thinking mainly of the implications for the patient and for her practice of nursing.

To meet regulatory agency standards, hospitals must have a process for reporting and analyzing errors. Karen remembered that she was shown the process for reporting medication and other errors or events (including injury to herself). She also remembered that there was a policy for how to do this and how to document the event. She went to the policy manual online and looked it up.

As she read the policy, Karen learned that she needed to complete the online report for medication error, which included all aspects of what happened. The form also asked her to report her feelings regarding the event, because her hospital was trying to understand what it was like to experience an event and what kept nurses from reporting. She learned from reading the policy that the leadership of the hospital appreciated her taking time to complete the form and report the event. She also learned that unless she was deliberately harming the patient, she would not receive disciplinary action; however, her peers would review the event to determine what she could have done to prevent it.

Another step in the process was for Karen to notify the charge nurse, supervisor (or her manager), and the physician. Just what she did not want to do! However, being the cautious and conscientious nurse she was, Karen followed through on completing these steps of the process. To her surprise, the physician, charge nurse, and supervisor were all professional and kind to her when she notified them of the event.

Karen's manager thoroughly discussed the medication error with her the following day. Karen was glad she had taken notes and had thought through what had happened, because this enabled her to provide her manager with a lot of detail about what had happened. Her manager was very matter of fact about the situation and did not berate or otherwise demean Karen in any way. She also suggested (strongly) that Karen see a counselor at the employee assistance program, because she assumed that Karen would have a lot of feelings about what had happened, and these feelings could potentially affect her self-confidence. Karen followed through on this advice as well. She was glad that she did, because she eventually realized that event though her medication error did not have an adverse event on the patient, it had indeed shaken her confidence and was affecting her ability to care for her patients (Research for Best Practice Box 25.1).

CONCLUSION

As you stand at the door, your new license in hand, the greatest human adventure awaits you. Nursing is one of the most difficult and most awesome professions that exist. As a nurse, you have the opportunity to be part of and witness the most intimate moments in the lives of individuals and families. You have the ability to change people and be changed forever.

Nurses in the hospital need to become more involved in the design, management, and environment of their units. Too often, nurses yield their responsibility and power to the nurse manager and lose out on this opportunity. Nurses need to speak up in nonemotional (but passionate) voices to correct situations that put them and their patients at risk. There are solutions to mandatory overtime, floating, work-related injuries, and workplace violence. At the end of this chapter is a list of relevant websites and online resources related to current workplace issues. We need to be at the forefront of developing demonstration projects and research on ways to improve the work and healing environment. With all the wonderful critical thinking and problem-solving skills nurses have, together we can make a difference.

In the meantime …. However grand the profession, it is not without risk, and workplace issues exist that require your vigilance. Make sure that you wash your hands often, stay current about workplace issues, maintain standard precautions, ask for what you need to be safe, take care of your back, and most of all, work hard, but not too much!

🔍 RESEARCH FOR BEST PRACTICE BOX 25.1
Medication and Practice Errors

Practice Issue

As the care of patients becomes more complex, the delivery of medications also becomes more complex. Today, nurses are frequently faced with interruptions during the delivery of medications. Adding to interruptions, other factors such as inadequate communication, medication storage, and failing to follow the six rights of medication administration (right patient, medication, dose, route, time, documentation) can contribute to medication errors (ISMP, 2010). The problem is that, at a time when the reporting of all errors is extremely important, not all are reported (Ulanimo et al., 2006). Nurses fear retribution or disciplinary action, despite the fact that most organizations do not punish nurses in any way for errors that occur (unless they are committed deliberately).

Implications for Nursing Practice

- Nurses need to be aware of potential errors by examining the complexity of their work flow and reporting near misses.
- Nurses need to follow standards of care and avoid shortcuts to care (i.e., have a second nurse verify all high-alert medications prior to giving to your patient)
- During the delivery of medications, nurses must take steps to avoid interruptions (e.g., don't page a physician, don't start a procedure, don't start a conversation with another person, don't answer the phone unless it is absolutely necessary).
- Nurses need to know their hospital policy and procedure for handling and reporting errors.
- Nurses need to read back and verify for accuracy all incoming telephone orders.

🔍 RESEARCH FOR BEST PRACTICE BOX 25.1—cont'd

Medication and Practice Errors

- If a nurse is involved in an error, that nurse should seriously consider counseling to manage the strong feelings that result from making a mistake in a nurse–patient relationship. Nurses often experience post-traumatic stress disorder following an event in which an error is made.
- Nurses should be actively involved in finding solutions to prevent errors in the future. This might include using barcode-assisted medication technologies in conjunction with an electronic medication administration record (eMAR) (Seibert et al., 2014).

Considering This Information
Knowing that you could be involved in an error someday, how can you prepare yourself to prevent this from happening and to be able to handle an error if it does happen?

References
Lilley, L., Collins, S. R., & Snyder, J. S. (2016). *Pharmacology and the nursing process* (8th ed.). St. Louis, MO: Elsevier.
Institute for Safe Medication Practices. (2016). *Targeted medication safety best practices to hospitals.* Retrieved from https://www.ismp.org/Tools/BestPractices/Default.aspx.
Institute for Safe Medication Practices. (2010). *ISMP medication safety alert! Nurse advise-ERR [Newsletter].* Retrieved from http://www.ismp.org/Newsletters/nursing/default.asp.
Institute of Medicine. (1999). *To err is human: Building a safer health system.* Washington, DC: National Academies Press. Retrieved from http://iom.nationalacademies.org/reports/1999/to-err-is-human-building-a-safer-health-system.aspx.
Seibert, H. H., Maddox, R. R., Flynn, E. A., & Williams, C. K. (2014). Effect of barcode technology with electronic medication administration record on medication accuracy rates. *American Journal of Health-System Pharmacy, 71*(3), 209–218. doi: 10.2146/ajhp130332.
Ulanimo, V., O'Leary, C., & Connolly, P. (2006). Nurses' perceptions of causes of medication errors and barriers to reporting. *Journal of Nursing Care Quality, 12,* 28–33.
Wood, G. W. (2014). Light and eye damage. *American Optometric Association.* Retrieved from www.aoa.org/light-and-eye-damage.

🌐 RELEVANT WEBSITES AND ONLINE RESOURCES

American Association of Colleges of Nursing (2016)
Retrieved from www.aacn.nche.edu.

American Association of Critical Care Nurses Healthy Work Environment (2016)
Retrieved from www.aacn.org/wd/hwe/content/hwehome.pcms?menu=hwe.

American Nurses Association (2016)
Retrieved from www.nursingworld.org.

American Nurses Association (2016)
Safe Patient Handling. Retrieved from http://nursingworld.org/MainMenuCategories/Policy-Advocacy/State/Legislative-Agenda-Reports/State-SafePatientHandling.

American Nurses Association (2016)
Incivility, Bullying, and Workplace Violence. Retrieved from http://nursingworld.org/MainMenuCategories/WorkplaceSafety/Healthy-Nurse/bullyingworkplaceviolence.

American Nurses Credentialing Center Magnet Status Certification (2015)
Retrieved from www.nursecredentialing.org/Magnet.aspx.

Continued

RELEVANT WEBSITES AND ONLINE RESOURCES—cont'd

American Organization of Nurse Executives (2016)
Retrieved from www.aone.org.

Institute of Medicine (2016)
Retrieved from http://iom.nationalacademies.org/.

Occupational Health and Safety Administration (n.d.)
Retrieved from www.osha.gov.

The Joint Commission (2016)
Retrieved from www.jointcommission.org.

United States Department of Labor (n.d.)
Retrieved from www.dol.gov.

BIBLIOGRAPHY

AHRQ's Patient Safety Initiative. (2003). *Building foundations, reducing risk. Interim Report to the Senate Committee on Appropriations.* AHRQ Publication No. 04–RG005. Rockville, MD: Agency for Healthcare Research and Quality.

American Nurses Association. (2015). *ANA sets "zero tolerance" policy for workplace violence, bullying.* Retrieved from http://nursingworld.org/MainMenuCategories/WorkplaceSafety/Healthy-Nurse/bullyingworkplaceviolence/ANA-Sets-Zero-Tolerance-Policy-for-Workplace-Violence-Bullying.html.

American Nurses Association. (2016a). *Safe patient handling and mobility (SPHM).* Retrieved from http://nursingworld.org/MainMenuCategories/Policy-Advocacy/State/Legislative-Agenda-Reports/State-SafePatientHandling.

American Nurses Association. (2016b). *Safe patient handling and movement.* Retrieved from http://www.rnaction.org/site/PageNavigator/nstat__take_action_sph_113.html.

Blair, P. L. (2013). Lateral violence in nursing. *Journal of Emergency Nursing, 39*(5), e75–e78. http://dx.doi.org/10.1016/j.jen.2011.12.006.

Bosek, M. (2001). Mandatory overtime: Professional duty, harm, and justice. *JONA's Healthcare Law, Ethics, Regulation, 3,* 99–102.

Duclos-Miller, P. (2002). Mandatory overtime: Is it really necessary? *Connecticut Nurse News,* March-May 2002.

Foley, M., & Rauser, E. (2012). Evaluating progress in reducing workplace violence: Trends in Washington state workers' compensation claims rates, 1997–2007. *Work, 42,* 67–81.

Institute of Medicine. (1999). *To err is human: Building a safer health system.* Washington, DC: National Academies Press. Retrieved from http://iom.nationalacademies.org/reports/1999/to-err-is-human-building-a-safer-health-system.aspx.

Institute of Medicine. (n.d.). *Identifying and preventing medication errors.* Retrieved from http://iom.nationalacademies.org/activities/quality/medicationerrors.aspx.

Kane-Urrabazo, C. (2006). Management's role in shaping organizational culture. *Journal of Nursing Management, 14,* 188–194.

Kirchner, B. (2009). Safety: Addressing inappropriate behavior in the perioperative workplace. *AORN Journal, 90*(2), 177–180. http://dx.doi.org/10.1016/j.aorn.2009.07.003.

Kyung Ja, J., & Sung-Hyun, C. (2011). Low back pain and work-related factors among nurses in intensive care units. *Journal of Clinical Nursing, 20*(3/4), 479–487. http://dx.doi.org/10.1111/j.1365-2702.2010.03210.x.

McNamara, S. (2010). Workplace violence and its effect on patient safety. *AORN Journal, 92*(6), 677–682. http://dx.doi.org/10.1016/j.aorn.2010.07.012.

Matthiesen, S. B., & Einarsen, S. (2004). Psychiatric distress and symptoms of PTSD among victims of bullying at work. *British Journal of Guidance and Counseling, 32,* 335–356.

Namie, G., & Namie, R. (2003). *The bully at work: What you can do to stop the hurt and reclaim your dignity on the job.* Naperville, IL: Sourcebooks.

Owen, B. D. (1989). The magnitude of low-back problem in nursing. *Western Journal of Nursing Research, 11,* 234–242.

Trinkoff, A. M., Lipscomb, J. A., Geiger-Brown, J., Storr, C. L., & Brady, B. A. (2003). Perceived physical demands and reported musculoskeletal problems in registered nurses. *American Journal of Preventive Medicine, 24*(3), 270–275.

Ulanimo, V., O'Leary, C., & Connolly, P. (2006). Nurses' perceptions of causes of medication errors and barriers to reporting. *Journal of Nursing Care Quality, 12,* 28–33.

United States Department of Labor. (n.d.). *DOL workplace violence programs—appendices.* Retrieved from http://www.dol.gov/oasam/hrc/policies/dol-workplace-violence-program-appendices.htm.

Wood, G. W. (2014). Light and eye damage. *American Optometric Association.* Retrieved from www.aoa.org/light-and-eye-damage.

Workplace Bullying Institute. (2015). *The WBI 3-step target action plan.* Retrieved from http://www.workplacebullying.org/individuals/solutions/wbi-action-plan/.

Emergency Preparedness

Tyler Zerwekh, DrPH, REHS, and JoAnn Zerwekh, EdD, RN

ⓔ http://evolve.elsevier.com/Zerwekh/nsgtoday/.

Community health centers do a great deal with limited resources. They provide critical medical care services to many who would otherwise have no other place to go or would end up in an emergency room.
Jan Schakowsky, United States Congresswoman, Illinois, 2006

We are prepared.

After completing this chapter, you should be able to:

- Identify various public health threats to which the medical community is susceptible.
- Identify regulatory initiatives undertaken to prevent and respond to future emergencies.
- Discuss the variety of diseases/agents that are likely to be involved in a biological, chemical, or radiological terrorism attack in addition to the clinical and community health consequences of each.
- Discuss the importance of personal protective equipment (PPE) and when to implement its use.
- Identify approaches to enhance personal and family preparedness for emergencies.

Terrorism alarms millions of people every year. It is a violent and deadly form of intimidation with the intent to debilitate governmental function and create a climate of hysteria. Terrorists take advantage of people's panic to achieve their goals. To the terrorist, an event that results in mass fatalities, disruption, and over-consumption of vital resources is a profitable outcome. Since the events of September 11, 2001, and subsequent anthrax mail attacks, terrorism on U.S. soil is a reality. Preparation for responding to acts of terrorism and other disasters, both natural and technological, has increased immensely, both in the community and on health care fronts. Community health nurses and clinical nurses have been assigned new responsibilities and roles in the wake of massive federal, state, and local efforts to prepare for public health emergencies. This chapter highlights the various public health threats to which the medical community is susceptible, regulatory initiatives undertaken to prevent future emergencies, and recent public health preparedness efforts bestowed to the nursing profession as the shift to an all-hazards clinical response is integrated throughout the medical and nursing community.

WHAT IS PUBLIC HEALTH PREPAREDNESS?

Public health preparedness, as it relates to the nurse, can be divided into two major categories: (1) clinical preparedness and (2) community-based approaches. The clinical aspects of public health preparedness will focus on agent identification and education for various threats, administrative and regulatory efforts to increase preparedness, and epidemiologic clues that may indicate a public health event has occurred.

The basis for public health preparedness is focused on the concept of preparing for chemical, biological, radiological, nuclear, and explosive threats—or CBRNE events. The term *CBRNE* originates from previous military and emergency response organizations such as the U.S. Marine Corps, the U.S. Army, and the Canadian Military Services (U.S. Army, 2016). Although not covered in detail in this chapter (because emphasis will be placed on individual radioactive isotopes and "dirty bombs"), additional information about nuclear weapons and preparedness can be found at the Nuclear Regulatory Commission website (www.nrc.org). The first section of this chapter focuses primarily on chemical, biological, and radiological events as they relate to the preparedness and response measures necessary for the licensed nurse to provide efficient and expedient care.

CLINICAL PREPAREDNESS

What Are Biological Agents?

Given the importance of responding rapidly to a bioterrorism-related outbreak, nurses need to be able to recognize the major syndromes associated with high-risk agents. Anthrax, botulism, plague, and smallpox are considered the four top agents for potential bioterrorism, because plague and smallpox can be spread person-to-person, and botulism and anthrax can be disseminated to a population via airborne release (they are not spread person-to-person). Table 26.1 discusses the etiology, signs/symptoms, transmission, and isolation/prevention of these agents. For more information on diagnostic and medical management of biological agents, visit the Centers for Disease Control and Prevention's website on bioterrorism agents (www.bt.cdc.gov/bioterrorism).

What Are Chemical Agents?

The use of chemical weapons poses an array of problems for the clinical nurse, including contamination, decontamination, and personal protection within the health care facility. Chemical agents can be divided into major classifications based on the makeup of the chemical agent and its clinical presentation. The following section focuses on the primary chemical agents most likely to be used in a terrorist event, along with their symptoms, diagnosis, and treatment options.

Of all the chemical agents of concern for the registered nurse, whether in the clinical or public health sector, nerve agents present the greatest challenge in providing expedient recognition, treatment, and response to a public health event. The nerve agents, also known as *organophosphate esters*, are the most severe, most incapacitating, and most likely to be implemented of all chemical agents (Wetter et al., 2001). Sarin, soman, tabun, and VX gases are the major chemicals in this

TABLE 26.1	BIOTERRORISM AGENTS			
DISEASE/ AGENT	DESCRIPTION PATHOLOGY	SIGNS AND SYMPTOMS	TRANSMISSION	CLINICAL MANAGEMENT
Anthrax B. anthracis	*Pulmonary:* Bacterial spores Toxins cause hemorrhage and obstruction of alveoli in lungs. *Cutaneous:* Spore enters skin through existing cuts or abrasions in 1-7 days after contact. *Gastrointestinal:* Ingestion of contaminated, under-cooked meat Causes inflammatory lesions in the ileum or cecum	*Pulmonary:* Flu-like Respiratory failure Hemodynamic collapse Usually fatal *Cutaneous:* Local skin—head, forearms, hands Localized itching followed by a papular lesion that turns vesicular and develops a black eschar in 2 to 6 days Responds well to antibiotics *Gastrointestinal:* Abdominal pain, nausea, vomiting, fever within 3-5 days Bloody diarrhea, emesis Usually fatal	Anthrax is a durable spore that lives in the soil; transmission by inhalation of the spore, contact with the spore, and the ingestion of contaminated food No person-to-person contact	Vaccine is available. (This vaccine is not traditionally given to health care workers; has limited availability.) Standard isolation precautions Ciprofloxacin—treatment of choice Postexposure antibiotic prophylaxis for 60 days, if vaccine not available; otherwise 30 days
Botulism Clostridium botulinum	A spore-forming anaerobe found in the soil that produces a lethal neurotoxin Neurologic symptoms occur 12-36 hours after foodborne botulism and 24-72 hours after aerosol exposure.	No fever Drooping eyelids, weakened jaw clench, difficulty swallowing or speaking Blurred vision and double vision Arm paralysis followed by respiratory and leg paralysis Respiratory depression Recovery may take months	Ingestion of toxin-contaminated food; the toxin can be made into an aerosol and inhaled (manmade) Improperly canned foods Contaminated wound No person-to-person contact	Antitoxin available with investigational vaccines being studied Standard precautions Careful clean-up of contaminated food Toxin can be inactivated by heating food or beverage to 212°F (100°C) for at least 10 minutes. Interdisciplinary planning for nutrition, respiratory and neurologic support, and rehabilitation during long recovery period

Agent	Description	Signs and Symptoms	Transmission	Treatment/Precautions
Plague *Yersinia pestis*	Bacteria found in rodents and fleas. Types: *Bubonic*. • Most common • Occurs 2-8 days after bite • 50% fatality if not treated. *Pneumonic* • Occurs 1-3 days after inhalation of organism • Survival unlikely if not treated within 18 hour of symptom onset. *Septicemic* (most deadly)	*Bubonic.* Fever, chills, painful lymphadenopathy (bubo—usually in inguinal, axillary, or cervical lymph nodes). *Pneumonic:* • Fever, cough, chest pain • *Bloody sputum* • Sputum can be thick and very purulent or watery with gram-negative rods • Bronchopneumonia and respiratory failure	Direct person-to-person spread. Flea bites. In a bioterrorist event, most likely to be aerosolized	There is no proven vaccine for the pneumonic plague, which is the most likely version in a bioterrorist event, although vaccines are under development. Antibiotics only effective if administered immediately (streptomycin or gentamicin). Droplet isolation precautions and contact precautions until decontamination is complete, when gross contamination is suspected and when incising and draining bubos. Respiratory support
Smallpox *Variola major* virus	Vaccine created in late 1700s. Routine vaccination ceased in the United States with eradication of smallpox in 1979.	Prodrome of fever, myalgia. Lesions progress from macules to papules, to pustular vesicles. *Vesicles on the distal limbs (hands, feet) as opposed to truncated vesicles with chickenpox*	Incubation period 10-17 days. Highly contagious. Direct person-to-person, air droplets and handling contaminated material	Standard, contact, and airborne/droplet precautions (negative pressure room with HEPA filtration) for containment. One case is a public health emergency due to the high communicability. No known cure. Vaccine available and should be given within 2-3 days of exposure. Vaccinia immune globulin (VIG) available
Tularemia *Francisella tularensis*	Bacterial infectious disease of animals. Mortality 35% without treatment	Sudden onset of high fever, sore throat, headache, swollen lymph nodes. Skin ulcer from tick bites. Progresses to pneumonia, pleural effusion with weight loss	Incubation period 1-21 days. No person-to-person spread. Spread by rabbits and ticks. Ingestion of contaminated water, aerosols, or agricultural dusts	Standard precautions. Gentamicin treatment of choice. Vaccine under development
Viral hemorrhagic fevers Marburg virus Ebola virus Lassa fever	Carried by rodents and mosquitos. Virus can be aerosolized	Fever, conjunctivitis, headache, malaise, prostration, nausea, vomiting. Hemorrhage of tissues and organs. Hypotension. Organ failure	Direct person-to-person spread by bodily fluids. Marburg: 5-10 day incubation. Ebola: 2-21 day incubation. Lassa fever: 1-3 weeks' incubation	No vaccine or drug therapy available; however, ribavirin effective in some cases. Isolation for containment. Use standard, contact, and droplet precautions, including PPE. Supportive treatment and care

group that inhibit acetylcholinesterase. These agents are liquid at room temperature, but in vapor form they penetrate the cornea, dermis, and respiratory tract. VX gas presents a unique threat because of its markedly greater toxicity and lower volatility, which translates into greater concern for secondary contamination among stricken patients. The effects of these agents are the result of unopposed action of acetylcholine at muscarinic and nicotinic receptors. Initial effects are related to the muscarinic effects, including rhinorrhea, salivation, miosis, and headache. With severe poisoning, nicotinic effects can be observed. The muscarinic and nicotinic effects are manifested by bronchospasm, vomiting, incontinence, muscle fasciculation, convulsions, respiratory failure, and death (Wetter et al., 2001). The antidotes for nerve agent poisoning include atropine at fairly high doses—several milligrams to hundreds of milligrams in some cases—and pralidoxime (2-PAM), up to 8 mg.

The choking, or pulmonary, chemical agents are similar to the blister agents; however, in the choking agents the mechanism of action takes place primarily in the respiratory system. The agents of note in this category are chlorine gas and phosgene (Wetter et al., 2001).

In chlorine gas, the majority of exposures occur by inhalation and lead to symptoms of ocular, nasal, and respiratory irritation. Common signs and symptoms of exposure can include eye redness and lacrimation, nose and throat irritation, cough, and suffocation. For cutaneous exposures, burning and blistering of the dermal layer are possible. Currently, there is no available biological marker for chlorine exposure (CDC, 2016a).

Another choking chemical agent, phosgene gas, has often been described as smelling like freshly cut grass. The majority of exposures to phosgene occur by inhalation. Phosgene exposure has clinical presentation/symptom patterns similar to those of chlorine gas (CDC, 2016a). See Critical Thinking Box 26.1.

? CRITICAL THINKING BOX 26.1

What personal protective equipment is available to you at your clinical facility? How does your facility handle exposure to hazardous or toxic material (e.g., blood, bacteria, radioactive)?
Does the use of personal protective equipment (PPE) change with the type of threat presenting at a health care facility (chemical vs. biological vs. radiological)?

What Are Radiological/Radioactive Agents?

The clinical or emergency department (ED) nurse is aware of another concept, which is the potential for patients entering the hospital exposed with radiation. The concept of dirty bombs is relatively new to the field of emergency preparedness, coming to prominence after the 9/11 World Trade Center attacks. A dirty bomb is a radiological dispersal device (RDD) that combines an explosive such as dynamite with a radioactive material. In the field, the explosion itself would be of greater concern in terms of damage to property and human life; however, the concern in the hospital ED would be the arrival of patients contaminated with radioactive material. The extent of local contamination would depend on a number of factors, including the size of the explosive, the amount and type of radioactive material used, the means of dispersal, and weather conditions. Those closest to the RDD would be the most likely to sustain injuries caused by the explosion. As radioactive material spreads, it becomes less concentrated and less harmful (U.S. Nuclear Regulatory Commission, 2014). Acute radiation syndrome (ARS) is an acute illness caused by irradiation of the entire body (or most of the body) by a high dose of penetrating radiation in a very short period (usually a matter of minutes). The major cause of this syndrome is depletion of immature parenchymal stem cells in specific tissues (CDC, 2016a). See Table 26.2 for a listing of syndromes associated with ARS. An excellent website to learn more about

TABLE 26.2 ACUTE RADIATION SYNDROMES

SYNDROME	DOSE*	PRODROMAL STAGE	LATENT STAGE	MANIFEST ILLNESS STAGE	RECOVERY
Hematopoietic (bone marrow)	Above 0.7 Gy (above 70 rads) *(mild symptoms may occur as low as 0.3 Gy or 30 rads)*	Symptoms are anorexia, nausea, and vomiting. Onset occurs 1 hour to 2 days after exposure. Stage lasts for minutes to days.	Stem cells in bone marrow are dying, although patient may appear and feel well. Stage lasts 1 to 6 wks.	Symptoms are anorexia, fever, and malaise. Drop in all blood cell counts occurs for several weeks. Primary cause of death is infection and hemorrhage. Survival decreases with increasing dose. Most deaths occur within a few months after exposure.	In most cases, bone marrow cells will begin to repopulate the marrow. Full recovery is probable for a large percentage of individuals; recovery process may last from a few weeks up to 2 yr after exposure. Death may occur in some individuals at 1.2 Gy (120 rads). The LD50/60† is about 2.5 to 5 Gy (250 to 500 rads).
Gastrointestinal (GI)	Above 10 Gy (above 1000 rads) *(some symptoms may occur at as low as 6 Gy or 600 rads)*	Symptoms are anorexia, severe nausea, vomiting, cramps, and diarrhea. Onset occurs within a few hours after exposure. Stage lasts about 2 days.	Stem cells in bone marrow and cells lining GI tract are dying, although patient may appear and feel well. Stage lasts less than 1 wk.	Symptoms are malaise, anorexia, severe diarrhea, fever, dehydration, and electrolyte imbalance. Death is caused by infection, dehydration, and electrolyte imbalance. Death occurs within 2 weeks of exposure.	The LD100‡ is about 10 Gy (1000 rads).
Cardiovascular (CV)/central nervous system (CNS)	Above 50 Gy (5000 rads) *(some symptoms may occur at as low as 20 Gy or 2000 rads)*	Symptoms are extreme nervousness and confusion; severe nausea, vomiting, and watery diarrhea; loss of consciousness; and burning sensations of the skin. Onset occurs within minutes of exposure. Stage lasts for minutes to hours.	Patient may return to partial functionality. Stage may last for hours but often is less.	Symptoms are return of watery diarrhea, convulsions, and coma. Onset occurs 5 to 6 hours after exposure. Death occurs within 3 days of exposure.	No recovery is expected.

*The absorbed doses quoted here are "gamma equivalent" values. Neutrons or protons generally produce the same effects as gamma, beta, or x-rays but at lower doses. If the patient has been exposed to neutrons or protons, consult radiation experts on how to interpret the dose.
†The LD50/60 is the dose necessary to kill 50% of the exposed population in 60 days.
‡The LD100 is the dose necessary to kill 100% of the exposed population.
From Centers for Disease Control and Prevention. (2016). *CDC emergency preparedness and response.* Retrieved from www.cdc.gov/nceh/radiation/factsheets/ars.doc

radiation syndromes and radioactive agents can be found at https://emergency.cdc.gov/radiation/arsp hysicianfactsheet.asp. Also see Critical Thinking Box 26.2.

> **[?] CRITICAL THINKING BOX 26.2**
>
> What is your organization's policy for managing CBRNE events? Who is the designated safety officer? Where is a copy of the organization safety plan and emergency situation's response plan?

What Is a Pandemic?

In April 2009, public health and medical professionals around the country experienced the first wave of an influenza pandemic on U.S. soil in more than 40 years. Not since the Hong Kong pandemic flu strains of 1968 to 1969 had the medical and scientific community seen such a rapid and expansive surge of H1N1 influenza cases both in the United States and worldwide (CDC, 2016c).

A traditional influenza pandemic can be distinguished from regular seasonal flu epidemics in two major facets: (1) widespread, worldwide cases of the same strain and (2) a novel strain of influenza virus unexpected or previously unidentified in the human population (CDC, 2016c). Typical influenza pandemics often work in waves, which are periods of 6 to 8 weeks between spikes in case totals that can be attributed to primary public health prevention (vaccination), a mutation in virus strain, or a new host susceptibility.

The World Health Organization (WHO) has developed a global pandemic influenza preparedness plan that categorizes various events of a pandemic into different phases (Fig. 26.1). Each phase requires both the clinical and public health nurse to execute specific preparedness and responsive measures to mitigate the influenza pandemic threat.

For nurses, pandemic influenza planning and response presents a unique and novel approach to clinical and evidence-based practice. It can be expected during pandemic influenza operations that in the onset of mass vaccinations in the general population, the availability of influenza vaccine will be limited as vaccine manufacturers rush to create and fill vaccine orders. When this occurs, federal health authorities, such as the CDC and Department of Health and Human Services (DHHS), recommend prioritizing population groups to receive the initial limited supplies of influenza vaccine. These priority groups are identified based on individual medical fragility (i.e., immunosuppression) and susceptibility to the pandemic influenza virus. The astute nurse must be aware of the variability of influenza virus from season to season and must consider priority options when vaccinating selected populations based on these factors. The Centers for Disease Control and Prevention Influenza website is an excellent source to locate current influenza vaccine priority groups as well as useful information regarding clinical identification and medical screening (www.cdc.gov/flu/).

The critical component for the community and public health nurse is the careful medical screening and identification of these priority groups to receive the pandemic influenza vaccine. The nurse must be cognizant of different criteria that make the recipient eligible or deferred for a pandemic influenza vaccine. Many times the deferral list for pandemic influenza vaccination is similar to the same deferral groups for seasonal influenza. Some of the maladies and conditions that could defer pandemic influenza vaccination include (1) severe allergy to eggs or egg products, (2) life-threatening allergic reaction to a previous influenza vaccination dose, (3) Guillain-Barré syndrome, and (4) sick or ill or symptoms of illness at the time of vaccination (CDC, 2015c).

What Is Personal Protective Equipment in Disaster Response?

In discussing the previously mentioned CBRNE agents, the nurse must be prepared to manage and treat patients affected by any of these agents. It is important to understand that the first line of defense

WHO Pandemic Influenza Phases (2009)	
Phase	**Description**
Phase 1	No animal influenza virus circulating among animals have been reported to cause infection in humans.
Phase 2	An animal influenza virus circulating in domesticated or wild animals is known to have caused infection in humans and is therefore considered a specific potential pandemic threat.
Phase 3	An animal or human-animal influenza reassortant virus has caused sporadic cases or small clusters of disease in people but has not resulted in human-to-human transmission sufficient to sustain community-level outbreaks.
Phase 4	Human-to-human transmission of an animal or human-animal influenza reassortant virus able to sustain community-level outbreaks has been verified.
Phase 5	The same identified virus has cuased sustained community-level outbreaks in two or more countries in one WHO region.
Phase 6	In addition to the criteria defined in Phase 5, the same virus has caused sustained community-level outbreaks in at least one other country in another WHO region.
Post Peak Period	Levels of pandemic influenza in most countries with adequate surveillance have dropped below peak levels.
Post Pandemic Period	Levels of influenza activity have returned to the levels seen for seasonal influenza in most countries with adequate surveillance.

FIG. 26.1 World Health Organization pandemic phases. (Adapted from WHO *Pandemic phase descriptions and main actions by phase.* World Health Organization. (2009). Retrieved from http://ww w.who.int/influenza/resources/documents/pandemic_phase_descriptions_and_actions.pdf.)

in clinical care for disaster medicine is personal protective equipment (PPE). PPE provides a barrier and protective layer against exposure to the various agents implicated in an event. Different levels of PPE are necessary for different agents. To understand the correct level of PPE needed in clinical response, it is important to identify the different levels of PPE.

Level D is primarily a work uniform and is used for nuisance contamination only. It requires only coveralls and safety shoes/boots. Other PPE is based on the situation (types of gloves, etc.). It should not be worn on any site where respiratory or skin hazards exist. Level C protection should be selected when the type of airborne substance is known, concentration measured, criteria for using air-purifying respirators met, and skin and eye exposure is unlikely. Level B protection should be selected when the highest level of respiratory protection is needed but a lesser level of skin and eye protection is necessary. Level B protection is the minimum level recommended on initial site entries until the hazards have been further identified and defined by monitoring, sampling, and other reliable methods of analysis, and equipment corresponding with those findings has been placed into use. Level A protection should be worn when the highest level of respiratory, skin, eye, and mucous membrane protection is needed. Occasionally, there will be instances where PPE levels will need to be upgraded to a higher level (level D to A) and/or downgraded to a lower level (Level A to D). The reasons for these changes can include suspicion of presence of increased dermal and airborne hazards or hazard analysis information that has confirmed a lower risk threat. *It is imperative to state that only safety officers and/or incident commanders can make the determination and decision to increase or decrease PPE levels.* Fig. 26.2 demonstrates common PPE equipment and practices at the different levels. After the proper PPE is chosen and donned, specific instructions for maintenance, sanitization, replacement, and care must be considered. These specific instructions should be listed in the facility's all-hazards plan or can be found at the Centers for Disease Control and Prevention Emergency Response Resources website: http://www.cdc.gov/niosh/topics/emres/ppe.html.

What Is Disaster Nursing?

As witnessed by the 2005 Hurricane Katrina and Indonesian tsunami events, natural disasters are a reminder of the critical role that emergency and public health nurses play in disaster response.

Disaster nursing integrates a wide range of nursing-specific knowledge and practices that facilitate the promotion of health while minimizing health hazards and peripheral life-damaging factors. Disaster nursing can be further subdivided into two major components: (1) implementation of the public health levels of prevention and (2) emergency triage and response.

In community health nursing, the role of the nurse in disaster response is to effectively promote the three levels of public health prevention. In *primary public health prevention* during disasters, the community health nurse must emphasize the components and principles of preparedness in both the nondisaster stage (before disaster occurs) and in the predisaster stage (disaster is pending). According to Nies and McEwen (2015), "preventive actions during the nondisaster stage include assessing communities to determine potential disaster hazards; developing disaster plans at local, state, and federal levels; conducting drills to test the plan; training volunteers and health care providers; and providing educational programs of all kinds" (p. 561). Community health nurses will be required to maintain strong physical and mental health dispositions during a disaster to provide a concerted response to their patients. This includes knowledge of the disaster plans of the community and the facility, inclusive of staff and patients. Nurses also need to educate their patients in the awareness and implementation of disaster kits and family emergency response plans in anticipation of a potential natural disaster. In the next stage—*secondary public health prevention*—the disaster has occurred and the nurse must emphasize the components and principles of response with a focus on preventing further injury or destruction. The response stage is one of the most important aspects of natural disasters, because it requires efficient execution of nursing practice while maintaining professionalism and mental support to the afflicted community and patients, with safety being considered before search and rescue. As the scale of disaster increases, the role and responsibilities of the nurse increase proportionately (Nies & McEwen, 2015).

The last stage of *public health prevention—tertiary*—focuses on recovery and integrates the community health nurse's operations after the disaster has occurred to restore the community to its previous level of functioning and its residents to their maximum functioning (Nies & McEwen, 2015). In the recovery stage, the nurse is confronted with unexpected or sudden loss of key personnel and patients in addition to the management of mental health issues in individuals related to the disaster. In addition to preventing a recurrence or minimizing the effects of future disasters, the nurse will be involved with debriefing meetings to identify problems with the disaster plan and make revisions.

To protect:	Level D	Level C	Level B	Level A
Skin (dermal)	**Inner barrier:** Street clothes **Outer barrier:** Coveralls, scrubs or other protection	**Inner barrier:** Environmental temperature dependent Street clothes/scrubs to insulated coveralls **Outer barrier:** Hooded chemical-resistant clothing		**Inner barrier:** Totally encapsulating chemical-protective suit **Outer barrier:** Disposable protective suit (if warranted)
Skin—specifically hands	Disposable gloves Cut-resistant gloves, if warranted	Disposable, chemical-resistant inner and outer gloves Cut-resistant gloves, if warranted		Chemical-resistant outer gloves over encapsulating suit Cut-resistant gloves, if warranted
Respiratory		Air purifying respirator (APR) • Full mask for unknown hazards and some zoonoses • Half-mask for non-zoonotic	Self-contained breathing apparatus (SCBA)	
Eyes		Goggles, face shield		(SCBA)
Footwear	Boots or shoes appropriate to perform duties	Chemical-resistant steel toe boots		Chemical-resistant steel toe boots over encapsulating suit

Level D:
Known hazard
No risk of skin contamination
No risk of inhalation
No risk of hazardous material contact

Level A:
Unknown hazard
Skin contamination imminent
Respiratory exposure imminent
Eye exposure imminent

FIG. 26.2 Equipment to provide protection based on personal protective equipment level. (Adapted from http://www.epa.gov/emergency-response/personal-protective-equipment.)

What Are the Levels of Disasters?

During small natural disasters, also known as Level I disasters, the community health nurse works in cooperation with local emergency medical systems and the community to provide medical support. Examples of Level I disasters include auto accidents and house fires. Level II disasters require the community health nurse to respond in a greater capacity using larger casualty practices in coordination with regional response agencies (such as state health and emergency management agencies). Examples of Level II disasters include train derailments, building collapses, and tornadoes. Level III disasters exhaust the most resources (including both the physical and mental resources of the community health nurse). Level III disasters consume local, state, and federal resources to the fullest extent and require an extended response time by the community health nurse that can last weeks and even months. Examples of Level III disasters include earthquakes, tsunamis, and hurricanes.

WHAT IS TRIAGE?

The core concept that ED nurses face is *triage*. Triage is a system of sorting patients according to medical need when resources are unavailable for all persons to be treated. For example, a patient presenting to the ED with chest pain will take priority in receiving intervention over a patient coming in with nausea and diarrhea. Remember ABCs when triaging patients! Although the genesis of triage has been documented in hospitals back to the mid-twentieth century, the concept was brought to wide attention by the California emergency medical services in response to earthquakes in the 1990s. In disaster triage, a mass casualty incident causes a surge of patients in the ED requiring emergency assessment. In addition, disaster patients' needs are usually categorized by the placement of printed triage cards/ tags. Fig. 26.3 depicts a sample triage card. The START (Simple Triage and Rapid Treatment) system is the most common type of disaster triage used by ED personnel (Box 26.1). In non-disaster instances, the Emergency Severity Index (ESI) is another type of triage system used by ED personnel routinely to assist in prioritizing which patients should be seen first. The ESI is a five-level triage system that considers the incoming patient's illness severity and expected health care facility resources that will be needed to treat and stabilize the patient (Bucher, 2014, p. 1675). Both triage systems can be used by trained ED personnel but are not to supersede or instruct medical techniques.

Another concept of triage used at the scene of a disaster is that of advanced triage, where colors replace the common terminology. The standard colors used in advance triage have been paired with the START terminology. All advanced triage concepts are similar and can be applied to START concepts.

The primary contributing factor to triage in the ED is availability of hospital resources. For example, the triage leader must consider bed availability issues for optimal use of resources to provide safe care to all patients. The overall goals of triage, in this system, are to determine whether a patient is appropriate for a given level of care and to ensure that hospital resources are used effectively.

PUBLIC HEALTH PREPAREDNESS AND ADMINISTRATIVE EFFORTS

Nurses who work in health care facilities have been subjected to an increasing number of standards and regulations invoked on their facility by federal and state legislation aimed to prepare and respond to public health emergency events. Among those federal acts that have been ratified since the September 11, 2001, terrorist attacks, the most important outcomes have been the implementation of the Office of the Assistant Secretary for Preparedness and Response (ASPR), the Hospital Incident Command System (HICS), and the National Incident Management System (NIMS).

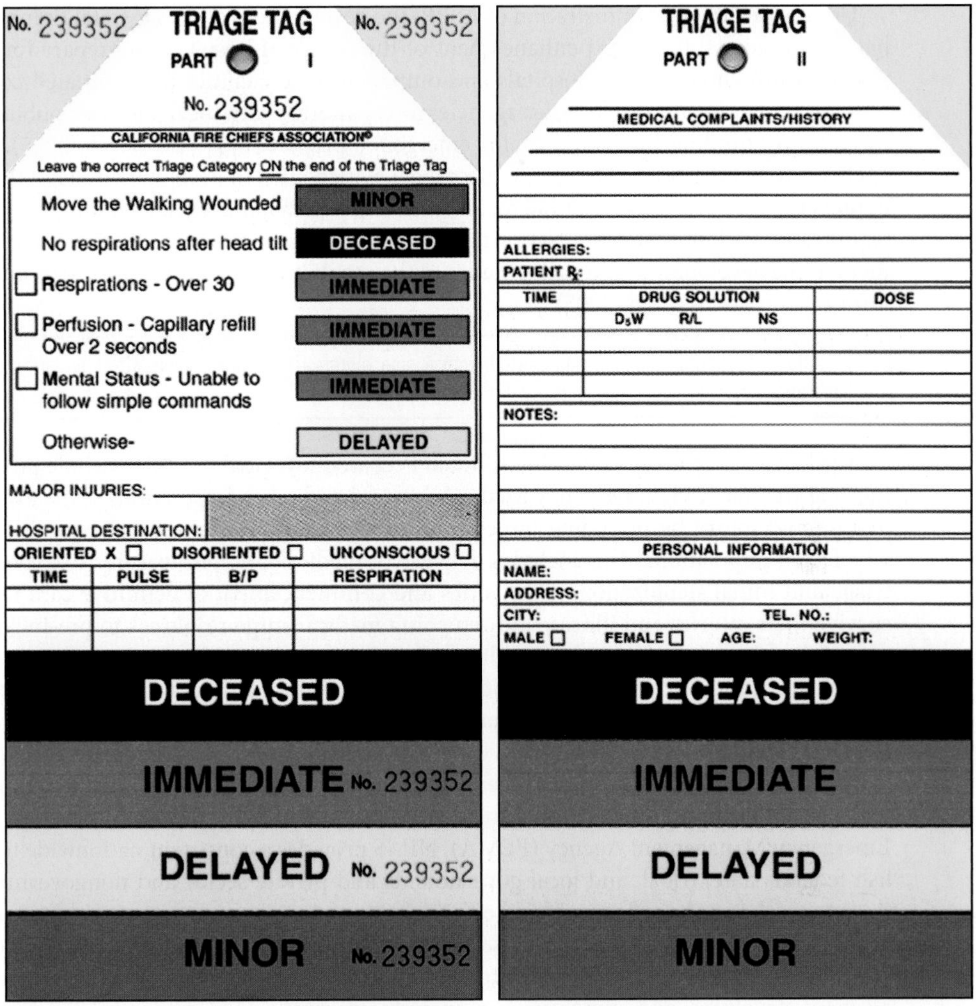

FIG. 26.3 An example of a triage tag.

BOX 26.1 THE START SYSTEM OF TRIAGE

The START system divides injured personnel into four separate groups:

- Deceased (Black)—Injured persons who are beyond the scope of medical assistance. Persons are tagged "Deceased" only if they are not breathing and attempts to resuscitate have been unsuccessful.
- Immediate (Red)—Injured persons who can be assisted or their health aided by advanced medical care immediately or within 1 hour of onset.
- Delayed (Yellow)—Injured persons who can be assisted after "Immediate" persons are medically cared for first. "Delayed" persons are medically stable but require medical assistance.
- Minor (Green)—Injured persons who can be assisted after "Immediate" and "Delayed" persons have been attended to medically. Persons tagged "Minor" will not need medical care for at least several hours and can usually walk with assistance (usually consisting of bandages and first aid).

Under the federal administration of ASPR, the development of the Hospital Preparedness Program has witnessed a shift toward enhancement of the ability of hospitals to prepare for and respond to public health emergencies. Hospitals and outpatient care facilities have initiated coordination with EMS and other health care partner agencies to collaborate with local and state public health agencies in receiving funding for public health emergency preparedness (USDHHS, 2005). This funding is applied toward the National Preparedness Goal, which aims to develop and maintain the capabilities to prevent, protect against, respond to, and recover from major events, including Incidents of National Significance. Additionally, the National Preparedness Goal will assist entities at all levels of government in the development and maintenance of the capabilities to identify, prioritize, and protect critical infrastructure (USDHHS, 2005).

> The National Preparedness Goal has shifted from a sole bioterrorism preparedness effort to *all-hazards preparedness* collaboration.

The key areas of focus under the National Preparedness Goal for 2015 include providing lifesaving medical treatment via Emergency Medical Services and related operations while avoiding additional disease and injury by providing targeted public health, medical, and behavioral health support to all affected populations. This includes delivery of medical countermeasures to exposed populations, triage and initial stabilization of casualties and commencement of definitive care for those likely to survive their injuries and illness, and returning medical surge resources to pre-incident levels while identifying the recovery process. Additionally, all hospitals and health care facilities must incorporate NIMS, education and preparedness training, and evaluations for corrective actions (based on preparedness training) to reach all capabilities established under the Hospital Preparedness Program (USDHHS, 2015).

As mentioned earlier, hospitals receiving ASPR and other federal preparedness funds must comply with the application of the National Incident Management System (NIMS) developed by the Federal Emergency Management Agency (FEMA). NIMS provides a consistent nationwide template to establish federal, state, tribal, and local governments and private sector and nongovernmental organizations to work together effectively and efficiently to prepare for, prevent, respond to, and recover from domestic incidents, regardless of cause, size, or complexity, including acts of catastrophic terrorism. NIMS benefits include a unified approach to incident management; standard command and management structures; and emphasis on preparedness, mutual aid, and resource management (FEMA, 2015a).

> Hospitals and health care facilities were required by The Joint Commission to be NIMS compliant by the end of calendar year 2007, to confirm successful training of hospital staff under NIMS, and to implement the HICS emergency response command structure during hospital emergency responses. The health care agency's Emergency Management Plan should indicate specific responses to the types of disasters likely to be encountered by the organization. The organization needs to identify the potential emergencies that could occur in the defined service territory and how the disaster might affect the ability to continue to provide care and treatment to individuals (The Joint Commission, 2013).

One component of NIMS is for hospitals and health care facilities to execute HICS during hospital emergencies. HICS is a comprehensive incident management system intended for use in both emergent and non-emergent situations. It provides hospitals of all sizes with tools needed to advance their emergency preparedness and response capability—individually and as members of the broader response community. HICS is designed to be implemented for all routine or planned hospital events, regardless of size or type; this helps establish a clear chain of command and standardizes response processes. This standardized response allows entities from different organizations to be integrated under one common structure that can address response issues and delegate responsibilities (California Emergency Medical Services Authority, 2014). Additional information regarding HICS can be found online at http://www.emsa.ca.gov/disaster_medical_services_division_hospital_incident_command_system_resources.

COMMUNITY HEALTH NURSE ISSUES AND PUBLIC HEALTH PREPAREDNESS

Epidemiological Aspects

The epidemiological response to a terrorist event plays a pivotal role in public health, both related and unrelated to biological terrorism. Epidemiologists and infection control nurses must recognize and act on rapid determination that an unusual event has occurred. These nurses must be able to perform surveillance for additional case identification and tracking, and they must prevent the spread of disease through the implementation of effective intervention methods. This component of emergency response, when executed correctly and expeditiously, can significantly reduce morbidity and mortality in exposed populations (Zerwekh & Waring, 2005).

A critical component of an effective epidemiological response to an emergency—both in the health care facility and in the community—is the acute identification and recognition of epidemiological clues that could signal a biological event. Early recognition of these clues can be achieved through surveillance (passive and active) and monitoring of patients presenting to health care facilities (Zerwekh & Waring, 2005). Two major clues that a biological terrorism event has occurred are a clear differential diagnosis and the formation of an epidemiological curve. Additional epidemiological indicators of a biological event are listed in Box 26.2.

BOX 26.2 EPIDEMIOLOGICAL CLUES THAT COULD SIGNAL A BIOLOGICAL EVENT

- Large numbers of ill persons with a similar clinical presentation, disease, or syndrome
- An increase in unexplained diseases or deaths
- Unusual illness in a population
- Higher morbidity and mortality in association with a common disease or syndrome or failure of such patients to respond to regular therapy
- Single case of disease caused by an uncommon agent, such as smallpox, Machupo hemorrhagic fever, pulmonary anthrax, glanders
- Several unusual or unexplained diseases coexisting in the same patient without any other explanation
- Disease with an unusual geographic, temporal, or seasonal distribution—for instance, influenza in the summer or Ebola hemorrhagic fever in the United States
- Similar disease among persons who attended the same public event or gathering
- Illness that is unusual or atypical for a given population or age group
- Unusual or atypical disease presentation
- Unusual, atypical, unidentifiable, or antiquated strain of an agent
- Unusual antibiotic resistance pattern
- Endemic disease with a sudden, unexplained increase in incidence
- Atypical disease transmission through aerosols, food, or water, which suggests deliberate sabotage
- Many ill persons who seek treatment at about the same time

It is possible that none of the listed clues will occur during a given bioterrorism event. However, the presence of one or more indicators on the list should alert infection control nurses, ED nurses, or community health nurses of such an event.

Another practice in both the health care facility and public health realms at the forefront of biological terrorism early detection is the concept of *syndromic surveillance*. Syndromic surveillance applies health-related data, such as trends in patient symptomatology or disease presentation that precedes clinical diagnosis, and can indicate a substantial probability of an outbreak that would warrant further investigation and public health response (Zerwekh & Waring, 2005). For example, investigation of ICD-10 codes, chief complaint, similar signs and symptoms exhibited by patients in the ED, and frequency of antibiotic/prophylactic therapy prescribed can all be applied and integrated into a successful syndromic surveillance network. In the public health setting, monitoring inventory of over-the-counter medications (e.g., cough/cold medicines) and identification of excessive absenteeism of students at a school or employees in the workplace setting are other trends surveyed to detect the possibility of an outbreak or bioterrorism event before clinical diagnosis has been made. Different frameworks (such as the Outbreak Management System) are currently being developed to determine the most efficient approach to a successful syndromic surveillance network. The key concepts of a successful syndromic surveillance program are timeliness of reporting data, validity and quality of data, and system experience (Zerwekh & Waring, 2005).

The epidemiological response plays a pivotal role in public health emergencies. The implementation of surveillance, case identification and tracking, and early intervention methods can significantly reduce morbidity and mortality in exposed populations.

What Is the Strategic National Stockpile?

The CDC Strategic National Stockpile (SNS) program stores large quantities of medicine and medical supplies to protect the citizens of the United States during a public health emergency, including (but not limited to) a terrorist attack, pandemic outbreak, or natural disaster such as an earthquake or hurricane (CDC, 2015b). This national inventory of antibiotics, chemical antidotes, antitoxins, airway maintenance supplies, and other medical equipment will support and refresh existing community resources being implemented during a public health emergency. The SNS "push-pack," once requested, will be delivered to any state or U.S. territory within 12 hours of request. Federal authorities have ensured enough medicine and equipment to supply multiple communities for an extended period during an event. In such an event, public health nurses can expect to be enlisted to assist in the evaluation and delivery of medications and equipment to every person in the affected community (CDC, 2015b).

What Is a CHEMPACK?

The Strategic National Stockpile CHEMPACK is a federal program designed to supplement the medical response in the event of a chemical nerve agent release. The scope of this program is specifically targeted for nerve agents classified as organophosphates (nerve agents), such as sarin and VX gases. The CHEMPACK containers, delivered to each of the 50 states and stored in geographically strategic locales, possess both EMS and hospital caches. Both caches contain such chemical antidotes as MARK-1 kits (intramuscular autoinjectors of atropine and pralidoxime [2-PAM]), atropine injectors, PAM kits, diazepam, and sterile water.

The public health nurse must be aware of the possibility of medication administration during a chemical weapon event and must be refreshed on the proper dosage and clinical practice applications.

What Is ESAR-VHP?

The Emergency System for Advance Registration of Volunteer Health Professionals (ESAR-VHP) is a federally funded program through ASPR that forms a national system that allows efficient use of volunteer health professionals in emergencies by providing verifiable, up-to-date information regarding the volunteer's identity and credentials to hospitals or other medical facilities in need of the volunteer's services. Each state's ESAR-VHP system is built to standards that will allow quick and easy exchange of health professionals with other states, thereby maximizing the size of the population able to receive services during a public health or presidentially declared emergency (Critical Thinking Box 26.3).

?   CRITICAL THINKING BOX 26.3

How do you register for ESAR-VHP in your state? What organization is responsible for coordinating the process? Who should register?

Medical Reserve Corps

The Medical Reserve Corps (MRC), initiated by the U.S. Office of the Surgeon General, is another resource developed to help communities in planning for and responding to a public health or medical emergency (MRC, 2016). Community-based MRC units function as a mechanism to organize and use volunteers who want to donate their time and expertise to prepare for and respond to emergencies on a local scale. MRC volunteers supplement existing emergency and public health resources by including medical and public health professionals such as physicians, nurses, pharmacists, dentists, veterinarians, and epidemiologists. The primary objectives of MRC units are to improve health literacy, increase disease prevention, eliminate health disparities, and most important, improve public health preparedness (MRC, 2016).

Public health nurses need to be aware of the presence of MRC units and are encouraged to enlist in the MRC at their local jurisdiction. During times of medical emergencies, it is likely that public health nurses will be working alongside MRC units in a collaborative effort to minimize morbidity and mortality while maximizing the public health and medical response.

Disaster Medical Assistance Teams

Disaster Medical Assistance Teams (DMATs) are yet another public health preparedness and response resource with which a community health nurse might interact during a medical emergency. These teams, supported through the National Disaster Medical System, are deployable units divided by geographic region (USDHHS, 2015). The units are composed of teams of various clinical health specialties that include (but may not be limited to) communications, logistics, maintenance, and security. These teams are locally based but can be deployed federally on request. The responsibilities of DMAT teams include triage of victims at a disaster site, medical care at the site, and staging of locations outside the disaster site for transportation of patients to alternative health care facilities. DMAT teams also serve as care centers for evacuation areas, where they can set up mobile medical care facilities for injured and traumatized persons evacuating a declared disaster area.

WHAT DO I NEED TO KNOW ABOUT COMMUNITY PREPAREDNESS ISSUES?

The community health nurse has a responsibility not only in promoting public health and preventing disease but also in delivering primary prevention methodologies related to disaster and emergency preparedness. For the community health nurse, the three critical components of preparedness include mental health preparedness, individual preparedness, and family preparedness. The National Response Framework (USDHS, 2015b), which aligns federal coordination structures, capabilities, and resources into a unified local and community response, is presented in Fig. 26.4. The community health nurse must also be cognizant of emerging trends and issues as they relate to disaster preparedness and response.

WHAT DO I NEED TO KNOW ABOUT DISASTER MENTAL HEALTH?

Any type of public health or medical disaster can cause a range of psychological reactions, from acute moderate symptoms to chronic severe stress-related psychological disorders. Traumatic medical emergencies can induce an array of personal stress responses, ranging from horror, helplessness, and anger to more progressive and severe reactions such as depression, substance abuse, and disconnection from

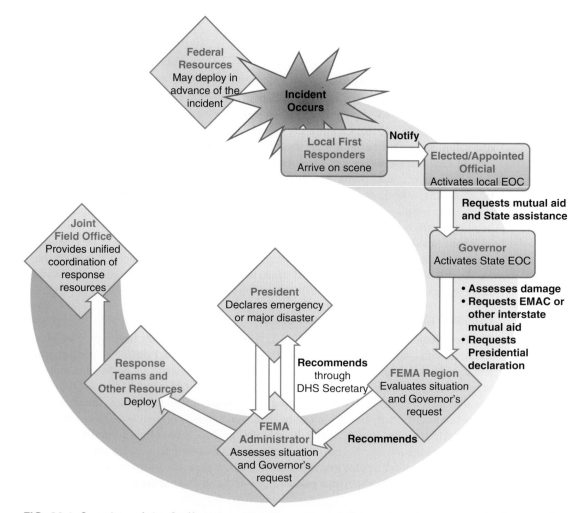

FIG. 26.4 Overview of the Stafford Act support to states, tribal, and local governments that are affected by a major disaster or emergency. (From U.S. Department of Homeland Security: *National response framework.* Retrieved from www.fema.gov/pdf/emergency/nrf/nrf-stafford.pdf.)

society. Traumatic events affect those who witness the event, as well as survivors, rescue workers, and friends and relatives of victims. Although the prevalence of immediate emotional reactions is well documented, the community health nurse must focus and be aware of the development of psychological reactions that persist from days to years after the public health event (CDC, 2016a).

The first practice a nurse should implement is the cognizance and awareness of the onset of psychological reactions in persons suffering from disaster mental health symptoms. When confronted with a patient suffering from such symptoms (Table 26.3), the nurse must identify concrete needs and attempt to assist—for instance, a person may ask, "How do I know if my friend is alive?" or "Are my parents OK?" or "How is my pet doing?" These concrete needs may be critical in identifying early symptom development of mental health problems.

The following guidelines have been recommended for nurses who are responding to patients after a public health emergency or disaster (CDC, 2016a):

- Provide attention to patients' experience and compassion and sympathy for their emotions.
- Empathize with patients and their emotions and experiences.
- Encourage patient discussion of their experience; positive and negative.
- Speak to patients in nonmedical terms—be their friend, their confidant.
- Reinforce their emotions and reactions; these reactions are natural and tacit.

After the community health nurse has identified psychological reactions, it is imperative to help the patient address the associated symptom progression. The following may assist the patient in coping with the emotional stressors (CDC, 2016a):

- Suggest methodologies for relaxation.
- Encourage discussion of the situation or event using a calm and compassionate approach.
- Reinforce sources of support, including, but not limited to, family and friends.
- Encourage a patient's communication of emotions to supportive networks.
- Advocate for a return to normal routine.
- Encourage the patient to defuse day-to-day potential stress-building conflicts that might otherwise catalyze psychological stress onset.

As the medical emergency or disaster continues, the nurse's role is essential in identifying patients whose symptoms could progress to long-term mental afflictions. The following are key exposure

TABLE 26.3 COMMON RESPONSES TO A TRAUMATIC EVENT

COGNITIVE	EMOTIONAL	PHYSICAL	BEHAVIORAL
Poor concentration	Shock	Nausea	Suspicion
Confusion	Numbness	Lightheadedness	Irritability
Disorientation	Feeling overwhelmed	Dizziness	Arguments with friends and
Indecisiveness	Depression	Gastrointestinal problems	loved ones
Shortened attention span	Feeling lost	Rapid heart rate	Withdrawal
Memory loss	Fear of harm to self and/or	Tremors	Excessive silence
Unwanted memories	loved ones	Headaches	Inappropriate humor
Difficulty making decisions	Feeling nothing	Grinding of teeth	Increased/decreased eating
	Feeling abandoned	Fatigue	Change in sexual desire or
	Uncertainty of feelings	Poor sleep	functioning
	Volatile emotions	Pain	Increased smoking
		Hyperarousal	Increased substance use or
		Jumpiness	abuse

From Centers for Disease Control and Prevention (2016). *CDC emergency preparedness and response.* Retrieved from www.cdc.gov/nceh/radiation/factsheets/ars.doc.

factors in determining the potential for long-term psychological manifestations as a result of a disaster (CDC, 2016a):

- Proximity to the event. Persons geographically closer to the event may be inclined to a greater psychological response.
- Previous psychological stability and history of past traumatic events. Patients who have experienced previous traumatic events or were experiencing psychological disorders before the event are predisposed to increased psychological reactions after the event.
- Importance and depth of the event. Patients who lose a friend or immediate family member may be inclined to greater psychological reaction development.

The nurse must be cognizant of continued progression of psychological reactions. Certain symptoms can assist the nurse in recognizing the development and onset of long-lasting psychological reactions, including the development of post-traumatic stress disorder. When such symptoms are identified, the community health nurse is recommended to do the following (CDC, 2016a):

- Refer patients for follow-up with a mental health professional (specifically trained in traumatic events, if possible) to seek additional counseling and guidance.
- Provide follow-up and guidance as needed.

Individual and Family Preparedness Issues

In regular practice, the public health nurse must be cognizant of the concept of community and family emergency preparedness. Whether in mitigation of a previous event or in everyday practice, the promotion of community/family preparedness to the population is critical in minimizing morbidity and mortality and alleviating personal confusion and anxieties during a public health event. Special emphasis toward the promotion of family/community preparedness is encouraged each year during the month of September, which has been designated as National Preparedness Month (USDHS, 2015c).

Community preparedness can be further subclassified under efforts initiated at home, work, and school. Preparedness efforts undertaken at the home should focus on creating a disaster preparedness kit, establishing family emergency communication and evacuation plans, and recognizing potential disasters in the family's community. A family disaster preparedness kit should include enough essential supplies for each family member to last a minimum of 3 consecutive days; it is important for the family to revisit the preparedness kit every 6 months to replace expired supplies (USDHS, 2015a) (Box 26.3 and Critical Thinking Box 26.4). Fig. 26.5 provides common equipment included in a family preparedness kit.

BOX 26.3 RECOMMENDED DISASTER PREPAREDNESS KIT

Recommended Items to Include in a Basic Emergency Supply Kit

- Water
  - One gallon of water per person per day, for drinking and sanitation
  - Children, nursing mothers, and sick people may need more water
  - If you live in a warm-weather climate, more water may be necessary
  - Store water tightly in clean plastic containers such as soft drink bottles
  - Keep at least a 3-day supply of water per person
- Food—at least a 3-day supply of nonperishable food
- Battery-powered or hand-crank radio and an NOAA weather radio with tone alert and extra batteries for both
- Flashlight and extra batteries
- First-aid kit
- Whistle to signal for help
- Dust mask, to help filter contaminated air, and plastic sheeting and duct tape to shelter-in-place
- Moist towelettes, garbage bags, and plastic ties for personal sanitation

BOX 26.3 RECOMMENDED DISASTER PREPAREDNESS KIT—cont'd

- Wrench or pliers to turn off utilities
- Manual can opener for food (if kit contains canned food)
- Local maps
- Cell phone with chargers, inverter, or solar charger

Additional Items to Consider Adding to an Emergency Supply Kit

- Prescription medications and glasses
- Infant formula and diapers
- Pet food and extra water for your pet
- Important family documents such as copies of insurance policies, identification, and bank account records in a waterproof, portable container
- Cash or traveler's checks and change
- Emergency reference material such as a first-aid book or information from www.ready.gov
- Sleeping bag or warm blanket for each person; consider additional bedding if you live in a cold-weather climate
- Complete change of clothing including a long-sleeved shirt, long pants, and sturdy shoes; consider additional clothing if you live in a cold-weather climate
- Household chlorine bleach and medicine dropper (A solution of 9 parts water to 1 part bleach can be used as a disinfectant. Or in an emergency, you can treat water by adding 16 drops of household liquid bleach per gallon of water. Do not use scented or "color-safe" bleaches or bleaches with added cleaners.)
- Fire extinguisher
- Matches in a waterproof container
- Feminine supplies and personal hygiene items
- Mess kits, paper cups, paper plates, plastic utensils, paper towels
- Paper and pencil
- Books, games, puzzles, or other activities for children

Courtesy Department of Homeland Security (www.ready.gov).

CRITICAL THINKING BOX 26.4

What plans have you and your family made regarding disaster preparedness?

The development of a family communications and evacuation plan will help prepare family members to share responsibilities and work together as a team during a public health event. The public health nurse should recommend that family members discuss the types of probable disasters in their community and consider how members might respond to each scenario. Evacuation routes should include primary and secondary meeting places—it is recommended that the primary place be somewhere in the immediate vicinity around the house and that the secondary site be at a location away from the home in case family members are unable to return to the neighborhood (USDHS, 2015a). It is important that each family member know the phone number and address of the secondary site. Families should also nominate an out-of-area family friend who can serve as an emergency contact should the scale of disaster overwhelm local communication resources and local telephone calls become more difficult to make. This contact will serve as the information hub for family members not only if they are separated but also for event update information. It is important to encourage family members to practice their communication and evacuation plans regularly.

FIG. 26.5 Disaster preparedness kit.

Emerging Trends and Issues in Emergency Preparedness

The clinical and community health nursing field must be cognizant that environmental health professionals play extremely important roles in all-hazard emergency preparedness, response, recovery, and mitigation. For nurses to understand how disasters impact the environment is essential to effectively assessing, diagnosing, and treating a patient while providing heightened preventive measures to the community before, during, and after an emergency or disaster.

Carrying out the traditional functions of environmental health, such as safeguarding drinking water supplies, controlling disease-causing vectors, conducting food safety inspections, and ensuring safe and healthy building environments, may be challenging after emergency and disaster events. Clinicians must be able to anticipate, recognize, and respond to many issues. They need access to guidance, information, and resources that will assist them in preparing for, responding to, and recovering from the adverse impacts of emergencies and disasters.

During particular natural disaster emergencies, vectors and their associated diseases move to the forefront of environmental health responses. An excess of standing water, trash/rubbish accumulation, and the potential for wildlife interaction increase the opportunity for vector-borne diseases in humans. The most common of these diseases are directly related to the event that occurred: West Nile virus or other vector-borne diseases from mosquitoes and standing water, leptospirosis and typhus fever from rat harborage around trash/rubbish, and rabies, shigellosis, and other zoonoses from potential interaction and contact with wildlife displaced in the environment because of the emergency. It is important to identify the hazard and to link possible diseases related to the event. For instance, the 2011 Joplin, Missouri, tornado event created much trash/rubbish throughout the neighborhood, and this accumulation of trash served as a shelter and harborage point for rodent activity. The nurse must be astute to the environment affected and the potential hazards related to the event.

Disasters also have an impact on the food safety in an affected jurisdiction. The clinician needs to be aware of the major food-borne illnesses and circumstances that can initiate food-borne outbreaks related to an emergency event. The first concern is for persons being sheltered during an event. As shelters provide food during the person's stay, it is critical to know that food must be properly stored, prepared, cooked, and held at proper temperature during serving times. Likewise, food-service establishments and food retailers can often be impacted by events that may cause the facility to lose power for an extended period and/or be directly affected by the event. A thorough case history during workup can assist the nurse in determining a differential diagnosis. For example, many grocery stores and restaurants were flooded by the 2012 Superstorm Sandy, causing them to lose power for days. These events compromise the integrity of the food by losing safe storage temperatures or coming into direct contact with contaminated and flooded waters. Common diseases from ingestion of these tainted food products include salmonellosis, shigellosis, *E. coli* H7:O157, and noroviruses.

The last major concept of environmental health in disaster response is the notion of pollution control. This general topic has some subsets that the nurse must be aware of: hazardous materials, air/water pollution, and the building environment. Each of these subsets has unique conditions associated with it during a disaster, and the nurse must be mindful of the potential disease processes associated with each. Hazardous materials arise out of physical infrastructure destruction. The most common of these hazardous materials include household hazardous materials (bleach, ammonia, etc.), and diesel fuel/petrol products. These hazards can cause inhalational, ingestion, and dermal irritations, as well as other health issues when exposed to the human body. The nurse needs to be aware of previous exposure history when assessing the patient and be mindful of potential hazardous material exposure.

Air and water quality pollution issues have a substantial presence in the environment during emergencies. Particulate matter and other air toxics can be released from damaged infrastructure and can cause irritations and infections to those exposed to the air without proper personal protective equipment. This was never more evident than during the response to the 2001 World Trade Center attacks, when many citizens and emergency responders suffered respiratory conditions caused by the direct exposure to the particulates and dust in the environment. Water pollution issues also carry a threat to human health, primarily because of exposure from the biological, chemical, and physical hazards within the contaminated water. Salmonellosis, hepatitis, chemical fertilizers, and diesel are some of the more common pathogens seen in contaminated water. These concerns are greatly exacerbated during flood events.

Finally, the nurse must be aware of ailments caused from the building environment. Buildings can be compromised during an emergency, whether it is taking on water from flooding, electrical hazards from electrical lines, or chemical hazards present from the physical destruction of the facility. The nurse needs to be educated on common mold exposures and treatment protocols for the exposed patient. Emergency room nurses may encounter patients who have been burned or electrocuted from the building infrastructure and must use correct burn/electrocution treatment protocols. And last, as discussed previously, there is a risk present in dermal, ingestion, and inhalational exposure to chemicals released in the building environment after a disaster. Additional information, treatment protocols, and resources regarding the clinical and community health response to environmental health related disasters can be obtained at the Centers for Disease Control and Prevention's website at http://www.cdc.gov/nceh/. See box at the end of this chapter for more relevant websites and online resources.

Another emerging clinical and public health threat nurses must be cognizant of is the alarming increase in school and public venue shootings, also known as "active shooters." An active shooter is an individual actively engaged in killing or attempting to kill people in a populated area, and recent active shooter incidents have underscored the need for a coordinated response by public health, medical, clinical, and law enforcement professionals to save lives. Between the Sandy Hook Elementary School shooting on December 14, 2012, and June 30, 2015, there were

122 school shootings resulting in 34 total deaths and over 94 injured. On a larger scale, there have been another 160 active shooter events outside of schools from the years 2000 to 2013 resulting in 486 deaths and 557 wounded. There are several agencies, in addition to health and medical, that will be involved in an active shooter incident. These agencies will vary from jurisdiction to jurisdiction but generally fall into one of the following categories: law enforcement, EMS, fire, emergency management, and public works. Health care facility nurses need to be cognizant that removal of patients' clothing should be kept to a minimum, if possible. Wounds and/or trauma to the patient, gunpowder particles on the clothing or other unique presentations can have considerable investigative value as evidence and should not be modified. Doffing of patient clothing should be done in a manner that will minimize the loss of physical evidence. If the clothing is bloody, do not allow blood and debris from one area or garment to contaminate another area or garment. Do not roll garments up in a ball. Never put wet or bloody garments in plastic bags. Carefully place garments in paper bags (one item per bag), seal, date, and initial. Label the bags with the patient's tracking tag. Handle clothing as little and carefully as possible. Pertinent items that could be considered evidence but need to stay with the patient, such as health aids, should be documented by the nurse and then notification submitted to law enforcement. All of this is best accomplished in discussions of these issues prior to an event and during review and updating of emergency protocols. The clinical and community health nurse must be aware of the risk present in active shooter events, which further underscores the need for appropriate and repeated training within the ICS and triage systems described previously (FBI, 2013).

The 2010 Institute of Medicine Report

Another issue in nursing emergency preparedness focuses around the 2010 Institute of Medicine report titled *The Future of Nursing: Leading Change, Advancing Health*. In relation to emergency preparedness, the Emergency Nurses Association announced the endorsement of the IOM report, and the organization aims to integrate recommendations and practices in emergency care related to emergency preparedness events. Specifically, the initiatives focus around enhancement of education and training, partnerships with physicians and other health care providers, and improving workforce planning.

There are several opportunities in which the clinical and community health nurse can engage to enhance educational and training processes. Nurses can become certified in Basic and Advanced Disaster Life Support trainings aimed to develop a commonality of approach and language in the health care community, which improves the care and coordination of response in weapons of mass destruction (WMD) disasters and public health emergencies. These courses review "all-hazards" topics, including natural and accidental manmade events, traumatic and explosive events, nuclear and radiological events, biological events, and chemical events. The courses also discuss information on the health care professionals' role in the public health and incident management systems, community mental health, and special needs of underserved and vulnerable populations. Another opportunity for higher levels of training and education are opportunities provided by the United States Department of Homeland Security's Center for Domestic Preparedness (CDP). This federal agency clearinghouse is the primary resource for hands-on training, education, and exercises for first responders, including clinical and community health nurses. The trainings are grouped into classes in a classroom and then hands-on educational and training experience covering many topics including emergency care, mass casualty incidents, health care leadership, pandemics, and incident command, to name a few. Additional information and a listing of classes can be found at the CDP website: https://cdp.dhs.gov/training/resident/.

Enhancing partnerships with physicians and other health care providers can be accomplished through novel local best practices being implemented throughout the health care arena. For instance, hospitals, EMS, and public health have begun to employ a practice known as "Triage Tuesday," where every patient delivered to the emergency room by an ambulance is triaged based on their actual symptom presentation. The patient is turned over to the hospital staff, and the emergency room must work the patient based on his or her triage tag. This practice not only increases familiarity with triage tags and with understanding the prioritization of triage skills, but it also bridges the gap between communication and collaboration among hospitals, EMS, and public health.

Last, nurses can enhance the last IOM recommendation of improving workforce planning by becoming active in membership in the groups listed previously (DMAT, DMORT, ESAR-VHP, Medical Reserve Corps). These response groups assist in standardizing planning, response, and recovery activities as they relate to emergency preparedness and response. Another option for increasing workforce planning also centers on adding HICS and ICS courses for nurses to increase their experience. The higher level courses refine the focus of planning and responding to disaster events where nurses will be used.

CONCLUSION

Whether in the clinical or the community environment, the role of the nurse in relation to emergency preparedness continues to expand and develop as local, state, and national preparedness efforts are executed. The nurse must continue to be aware and informed of evolving threats such as biological, chemical, or radioactive terrorism while maintaining up-to-date training and knowledge of effective responses to public health disasters. The initiatives and programs mentioned in this chapter will ultimately aid nurses in comprehensive and efficient preparation, response, recovery, and mitigation to any public health emergency with which they may be confronted throughout their professional nursing tenure.

⊕ RELEVANT WEBSITES AND ONLINE RESOURCES

Centers for Disease Control and Prevention (2016)
Retrieved from http://www.cdc.gov/.

Hospital Incident Command System (HICS) (2016)
Retrieved from www.emsa.ca.gov/hics/hics.asp.

United States Department of Homeland Security's Center for Domestic Preparedness (CDP) (2016)
Retrieved from http://cdp.dhs.gov/resident/index.htm.

BIBLIOGRAPHY

Bucher, L. (2017). Nursing management: Emergency, terrorism, and disaster nursing. In S. L. Lewis, L. Bucher, M. Heitkemper, M. M. Harding, J. Kwong, & D. Roberts (Eds.), *Medical-surgical nursing: Assessment and management of clinical problems* (10th ed.) (pp. 1628–1648). St. Louis, MO: Elsevier.

California Emergency Medical Services Authority. (2014). *HICS overview.* State of California. Retrieved from http://www.emsa.ca.gov/disaster_medical_services_division_hospital_incident_command_system_resources.

Centers for Disease Control. (2015a). *Persons who should not be vaccinated.* Retrieved from http://www.cdc.gov/flu/protect/whoshouldvax.htm#flu-shot.

Centers for Disease Control. (2015b). *Strategic National Stockpile (SNS).* Retrieved from http://www.cdc.gov/phpr/stockpile/stockpile.htm.

Centers for Disease Control. (2016a). *CDC emergency preparedness and response.* Retrieved from http://emergency.cdc.gov/. or www.cdc.gov/nceh/radiation/factsheets/ars.doc.

Centers for Disease Control. (2016b). *National Center for Environmental Health.* Retrieved from http://www.cdc.gov/nceh/.

Centers for Disease Control. (2016c). *Seasonal flu.* Retrieved from http://www.cdc.gov/flu/index.htm and http://www.cdc.gov/flu/pandemic-resources/.

Center for Domestic Preparedness. (2016). *Resident training.* Retrieved from https://cdp.dhs.gov/training/resident/.

Federal Bureau of Investigation. (2013). *Active shooter incidents.* Retrieved from https://www.fbi.gov/about-us/office-of-partner-engagement/active-shooter-incidents.

Federal Emergency Management Agency. (2015a). *The National Incident Management System (NIMS).* Retrieved from http://www.fema.gov/national-incident-management-system.

Federal Emergency Management Agency. (2015b). *The 2015 National Preparedness Goal.* Retrieved from https://www.fema.gov/media-library/assets/documents/25959.

Healthcare and Public Health Sector Coordinating Council. (2015). *Active shooter planning and response in a healthcare setting.* Retrieved from https://www.fbi.gov/about-us/office-of-partner-engagement/active-shooter-incidents/active-shooter-planning-and-response-in-a-healthcare-setting.

Medical Reserve Corps (MRC). (2016). Retrieved from www.medicalreservecorps.gov/HomePage.

Nies, M. A., & McEwen, M. (2015). *Community/Public health nursing* (6th ed.). St. Louis, MO: Elsevier.

The Joint Commission. (2013). *Emergency management standards. Hospital and critical access hospital accreditation programs.* Oakbrook Terrace, IL: The Joint Commission. Retrieved from http://www.jointcommission.org/emergency_management.aspx.

U.S. Army Medical Research Institute of Chemical Defense. (2016). Retrieved from http://ccc.apgea.army.mil/.

U.S. Department of Health and Human Services. (USDHHS) (2005). *Hospital preparedness program.* Public Law 109–417.

U.S. Department of Health and Human Services. (USDHHS) (2015). *Disaster Medical Assistance Teams (DMAT).* Retrieved from http://www.phe.gov/Preparedness/responders/ndms/teams/Pages/dmat.aspx.

U.S. Department of Homeland Security (USDHS). (2015a). *Basic disaster supplies kit.* Retrieved from http://www.ready.gov/kit.

U.S. Department of Homeland Security (USDHS). (2015b). *National response framework.* Retrieved from http://www.fema.gov/national-response-framework.

U.S. Department of Homeland Security (USDHS). (2015c). *Ready 2015-national preparedness month.* Retrieved from http://www.ready.gov/ready2015.

U.S. Nuclear Regulatory Commission. (2014). *Fact sheets on dirty bombs.* Retrieved from www.nrc.gov/reading-rm/doc-collections/fact-sheets/dirty-bombs.html.

Wetter, D. C., Daniell, W. D., & Treser, C. D. (2001). Hospital preparedness for victims of chemical or biological terrorism. *American Journal of Public Health, 91,* 710–716.

Zerwekh, J. T., & Waring, S. C. (2005). The epidemiology of bioterrorism. In R. Pilch & R. Zilinskas (Eds.), *The encyclopedia of bioterrorism.* New York: Wiley and Sons.

INDEX

Note: Page numbers followed by *f* indicate figure, by *t* table, and by *b* box.